Helmut Rempel

Map Folio No. 4

Canada's Special Resource Lands:

A National Perspective of Selected Land Uses

by

Wendy Simpson-Lewis

Jennifer E. Moore

Nancy J. Pocock

M. C. Taylor

Hedley Swan

with the assistance of

Ruth McKechnie

James Lenning

Lands Directorate
Environment Canada

Ottawa
1979

Typesetting: Howarth & Smith Limited
Information Graphics

Page Make-up: The Studio (A division of Shelrac Holding Ltd.).

Lithography and Printing: Pierre Des Marais Inc.

Cover photos by NFB – PHOTOTHEQUE – ONF.

Duncan Bancroft
C. Bruun
Ted Grant
George Hunter
Mia and Klaus
Michael Milne
John Parr Telfer

Canadian Wildlife Service.

R. D. Muir

©Minister of Supply and Services Canada 1979

Available in Canada through

Authorized Bookstore Agents
and other bookstores

or by mail from

Canadian Government Publishing Centre
Supply and Services Canada
Hull, Quebec, Canada K1A 0S9

| Catalogue No. En 73-2/4 | Canada: $12.00 |
| ISBN 0-660-10190-4 | Other countries: $14.40 |

Price subject to change without notice.

Abstract

The management of land in a country as large and diverse as Canada is a particularly complex challenge. The allocation of the land resource among any number of different uses requires a background of baseline data sufficient to permit informed decisions by both government decision-makers and individual citizens. This publication was initiated to provide a national perspective on land areas that warrant special consideration in land use issues. The purpose of this map folio is to locate, describe, and, where possible, map, Canada's prime resource lands for six selected uses: agriculture, recreation, wildlife, forestry, urban growth, and energy development.

The research involves the examination of a variety of parameters, each of which offers a possible definition of important land. The parameters include soil and climatic, economic, social, and aesthetic measures as well as the factors of uniqueness and change. The results are presented in an inventory of maps, illustrations, and texts that identify prime land for each land use. In some instances, areas are identified by only one parameter; in other cases, locations are defined as important by more than one parameter and for more than one land use.

A wide variety of background information relating to six major land uses at the national scale is presented within the covers of this publication. In addition to being a general reference document, it should serve as a stepping stone for more detailed research.

Résumé

La gestion d'un territoire étendu et varié comme le Canada représente une tâche particulièrement complexe. L'affectation judicieuse des ressources du sol par les gouvernements et les citoyens exige des données de base suffisantes qui permettent de prendre des décisions en toute connaissance de cause. La présente publication vise à donner une vue d'ensemble des régions où il convient d'examiner tout particulièrement les questions d'utilisation du sol. Les principales terres du Canada au chapitre de l'agriculture, des loisirs, de la faune, de la foresterie, de la croissance urbaine et de la mise en valeur de l'énergie y sont indiquées, décrites et, quand c'est possible, cartographiées.

Les recherches on porté sur divers paramètres, qui se présentaient comme autant de définitions possibles de ce que l'on considère comme un sol important. Ces paramètres comportaient des évaluations pédologiques et climatiques, économiques, sociales, esthétiques, ainsi que des facteurs de singularité et de changement. Les résultats sont présentés dans un répertoire de cartes, d'illustrations et de textes, où l'on indique quelles parties du territoire conviennent davantage à chacune de ces utilisations. Dans certains cas, ces régions sont définies seulement par un paramètre, dans d'autres, par plusieurs et pour plus d'une utilisation.

La publication renferme une grande quantité d'informations de base sur les six principales utilisations du sol à l'échelle nationale. Outre qu'il s'agit d'un document général de référence, il pourrait servir de point de départ pour une recherche plus approfondie.

Acknowledgements

The authors would like to acknowledge the co-operation and assistance of many individuals and agencies in the preparation of this publication.

Two principal research assistants, Ruth McKechnie and Jim Lenning, made a valuable contribution to the compilation, analysis, and presentation of data, and performed other miscellaneous and sometimes tedious tasks with good humour. Of necessity, the cartographic responsibilities were shared by three separate agencies: the Cartographic Unit of the Lands Directorate in Environment Canada, the Cartographic Unit of the Land Resource Research Institute in the Canada Department of Agriculture, and Fox Photography Ltd. To these drafting staffs, our sincere appreciation. In the preparation of any publication that contains the equivalent of 500 pages of text, the task of typing is onerous. Carole Aubin, Liette Paquette, Christine Lapointe, Marg Poulin, Mary Lou Miles, and Diane Schlitter have shown patience above and beyond the call of duty. Our editor, Jane Buckley, deserves recognition for the expertise she contributed to this report. Lastly, the staff of Environment Canada's library were extremely helpful, co-operative, and understanding of the rather unorthodox research involved in this project.

A research project at the national scale is impossible without the assistance and co-operation of both federal and provincial government departments across Canada. The advice and information provided by all such agencies, especially by the various services within Environment Canada, are gratefully acknowledged. Finally, to the many individuals who provided data, photographs, constructive comments, or other assistance, our sincere appreciation.

Introduction

Canada has the second largest land area of any country in the world. Despite this apparent bounty, the quality of land is variable and only limited areas possess the special characteristics necessary to permit specific uses. Some parts of Canada, because of unique physical capabilities or productive value, may be considered to be special resource lands. Others are critical because of their uniqueness or scarcity. Canadians rely upon the land resource as the basis for all activities. An appreciation of the location and extent of these prime resource lands, their capabilities and problems, is valuable not only to government and industry decision-makers but also to individuals concerned with the proper use and management of Canada's resources.

This reference material is intended as a basic information document for those interested in land matters from a national perspective. It contains background data on six important resource sectors: agriculture, recreation, wildlife, forestry, urban lands, and energy development. Agriculture, forestry, and wildlife are three of the most extensive uses of land in Canada, and are dependent, to a great extent, upon the inherent qualities of the physical environment. Recreation too, depends very heavily upon the physical attributes of the land, such as shorelines, slopes, or scenic areas. The last two sectors, urban areas and energy development, were selected because of their immediate and over-riding importance to Canadians. The urban centres are expanding physically, and at the same time, they are exerting increasing social and economic influence over large areas of urban fringe, rural areas, and hinterland. The current significance of the energy situation and the increasing impact on land of energy production, transportation, distribution, and storage, also warrant attention.

The land resource is the basis for our economy and our society. The quality and availability of the land resource, particularly of the more productive areas, influence everything we do. Where and how and what we do is largely dependent on the amenity and productivity of the land resource, not only in our own neighbourhood, but also in other parts of Canada. In turn, each of us influences the use of resources through individual decisions. Every day, we make choices that affect land use. The size of our families is important. A decision to move from one city to another has land use repercussions. Plans to take a camping holiday across Canada are relevant. Our desire to have two cars, a single-family home, a summer cottage, or to heat our homes with oil, gas, electricity, or wood is important. Even deciding what Canadian or foreign food products to buy for dinner is part of the equation.

If prime agricultural or forest lands or essential wildlife areas are to be preserved, that is our decision. If outdoor recreation resources and urban areas are to be not only maintained, but enhanced, that too is our concern. We influence the level of energy demand which in turn will affect our activities. Each of us has important choices to make, and the sum of these individual decisions determines how land in Canada is used.

R.J. McCormack
Director General
Lands Directorate

Le Canada est le deuxième pays du monde en superficie. Cet avantage est cependant trompeur, car la qualité du sol est variable et les régions qui offrent des possibilités de mise en valeur à des fins précises sont limitées. Par leurs propriétés physiques uniques ou leur valeur productive, certaines parties du pays ont une vocation particulière. D'autres sont d'une importance vitale étant donné leur singularité ou leur rareté. Toutes les activités des Canadiens sont en réalité subordonnées à la disponibilité des ressources du sol. Lorsqu'on fait l'inventaire des sols les plus riches en ressources, qu'on en évalue l'étendue, les capacités et les inconvénients, ce ne sont pas uniquement les décideurs de l'industrie et du gouvernement qui en profitent, mais aussi tous ceux qui tiennent à coeur la mise en valeur et la gestion des ressources du Canada.

Cet ouvrage de référence de base s'adresse à tous ceux qui s'intéressent à la gestion du territoire à l'échelle nationale. Il renferme des données de base sur six importants secteurs: l'agriculture, les loisirs, la faune, la foresterie, le sol urbain et la mise en valeur de l'énergie. L'agriculture, la foresterie et la faune occupent la plus grande part du territoire, et dépendent, dans une large mesure, des qualités inhérentes du milieu physique. Les loisirs aussi sont très fortement conditionnés par l'aspect physique des lieux. Qu'on pense aux plages, aux pentes, à la beauté des sites. Quant aux deux autres secteurs, le sol urbain et l'énergie, ils ont été choisis à cause de leur importance actuelle et prédominante aux yeux des Canadiens. Enfin, les centres urbains s'étendent de plus en plus et exercent, du même coup, une pression sociale et économique croissante sur de vastes secteurs de la banlieue, de la zone rurale et de l'arrière-pays. Les conséquences actuelles de la situation énergétique et les répercussions croissantes sur le territoire de la production d'énergie, de son transport, de sa distribution et de son stockage sont aussi des questions qui méritent d'être examinées.

Le sol est une ressource sur laquelle se fondent notre économie et notre société. Sa qualité et son accessibilité, en particulier dans les régions les plus productives, influent sur toutes nos entreprises dont la nature même, le lieu d'accomplissement, et la façon de procéder, tiennent largement à la valeur et à la productivité des terres, non seulement dans notre propre voisinage mais aussi dans d'autres parties du Canada. D'un autre côté, nous contribuons par nos décisions individuelles à orienter l'exploitation des ressources. Tous les jours, nous faisons des choix dont le territoire se ressent: la taille de notre famille, par exemple, la décision de nous installer dans une autre ville, de faire du camping au Canada, de vouloir posséder deux autos, une maison unifamiliale, un chalet d'été, ou chauffer la maison au mazout, au gaz, à l'électricité ou au bois; même le fait de choisir entre des aliments canadiens ou importés pour le dîner a son importance.

Si les terres agricoles de première valeur, les terrains forestiers ou les territoires vitaux pour la faune doivent êtres protégés, cela dépend de nous. Si les loisirs en plein air et les régions urbaines doivent non seulement se maintenir mais aussi s'accroître et s'améliorer, cela nous concerne aussi. Notre mode de vie influe également sur la consommation de l'énergie qui modifie à son tour nos activités. Chacun de nous a des choix importants à faire, et c'est la somme de ces décisions individuelles qui déterminera de quelle façon les ressources du sol sont utilisés au Canada.

R.J. McCormack
Directeur général
des terres

Metric Conversions

Length

1 cm (centimetre)	=	0.393701 inch
1 km (kilometre)	=	0.621371 mile
1 m (metre)	=	3.28084 feet
1 m (metre)	=	1.09361 yards

Area

1 cm² (square centimetre)	=	0.155000 square inch
1 ha (hectare)	=	2.47105 acres
1 km² (square kilometre)	=	0.386102 square mile
1 m² (square metre)	=	10.7639 square feet
1 m² (square metre)	=	1.19599 square yards

Volume or Capacity

1 L (litre)	=	0.219975 (imperial gallon)
1 L (litre)	=	0.264178 gallon (U.S.)
1 m³ (cubic metre)	=	35.3147 cubic feet
1 m³ (cubic metre)	=	1.30795 cubic yards
1 m³ (stacked), (stacked cubic metre)	=	0.275896 cord (of 128 stacked ft³)
1 hl (hectolitre)	=	2.74969 bu (UK) bushels (British)
1 m³ (cubic metre)	=	0.0008107 acft acre-feet
1 m³ (cubic metre)	=	6.2893 b (barrels)

Mass or Weight

1 g (gram)	=	0.0352740 ounce (avoirdupois)
1 kg (kilogram)	=	2.20462 pounds (avoirdupois)
1 t (tonne)	=	1.10231 short tons (of 2000 lb)
1 t (tonne)	=	0.98421 long tons
1 Ut (Uranium tonne)	=	1.2999 U_3O_8 short tons

Ratios

1 kg/m³ (kilogram per cubic metre)	=	0.0624280 pound per cubic foot
1 km/L (kilometre per litre)	=	2.82481 miles per gallon
1 m²/ha (square metre per hectare)	=	4.35600 square feet per acre
1 m³/ha (cubic metre per hectare)	=	14.2913 cubic feet per acre
1 m³ (stacked)/ha, (stacked cubic metre per hectare)	=	0.111651 cord per acre
1 t/ha (tonne per hectare)	=	0.446090 ton (of 2000 lb) per acre
1 hl/ha (hectolitre per hectare)	=	1.11276 bu (UK)/ac bushels (British) per acre

Energy

1 j (joule)	=	0.00095 Btu (British Thermal Units)

Sources: Amiran, D.H.K., and Schick, A.P. eds. 1961. Geographical Conversion Tables. International Geographical Union. Zürich, Switzerland.

Canadian Standards Association. 1976. Canadian Metric Practice Guide. Toronto.

Metric Commission Canada. 1978. How to Write S1. Ottawa.

Moore, W.C. 1977. Metric Forestry Workbook. Metric Program, Forest Management Institute, Canadian Forestry Service, Fisheries and Environment Canada. Ottawa.

Table of Contents

	Page
Agriculture	1
Introduction	3
Physical factors	3
Economic considerations	18
Factors of change	35
Uniqueness	51
Outdoor Recreation	67
Introduction	69
Physical factors	70
Present land use	81
Tourism	96
Conflicts and issues	98
Wildlife	105
Introduction	107
Wildlife classifications	107
Economic and social considerations	121
Land use issues and factors affecting change	132
Forestry	153
Introduction	156
Forest descriptions and classifications	156
Economic considerations	164
Ecological forest land uses	168
Factors affecting forests	179
Urban Development	189
Evolution of the Canadian settlement pattern	191
Physical characteristics associated with urban land	194
Areas of demand for urban land	196
Changes in urban land use	199
Factors affecting change	204
Land, environmental quality, and the quality of life	206
Energy Development	211
Introduction	213
Physical criteria	213
Economic, environmental, and social considerations	218
Factors affecting change	222
Present land use issues	223
Renewable energy	226
The future	230

Agriculture

National Photography Collection.
Public Archives Canada.
C-42633

Contents

	Page
Introduction	3
Physical Factors	3
Physiography	3
The Canada Land Inventory	3
Climate	8
Temperature	8
Precipitation	11
Frost-free period	12
Growing degree-days above 5°C	13
Bright sunshine	15
An Agroclimatic Resource Index	15
Economic Considerations	18
Improved farmland compared with agricultural sales	19
Agricultural sales	20
Capital investment	23
Total capital value	23
Capital value of land and buildings	25
Major areas of agricultural production	26
Areas of livestock and poultry production	26
Wheat areas	28
Specialty field crop areas	28
Tree fruit and small fruit areas	30
Vegetable areas	31
Economic risk	33
Natural phenomena	33
Man-made influences	34
Factors of Change	35
Urban pressures	35
Urban growth	35
Location of cities	38
Changes in agriculture	41
Changes in farmland	42
Changes in farm characteristics	45
Climatic change	48
Historical context	48
Agricultural repercussions	50
Uniqueness	51
A case study: the Niagara fruit belt	51
Acknowledgements	56
Bibliography	56
Appendix I	59
Appendix II	64

Tables

	Page
1. Costs for correcting limitations on potential farmland, 1975	5
2. CLI classification of soils with capability for agriculture, by province	8
3. Agroclimatic Resource Index and hay yields, by province	16
4. Net changes in total farmland, by province, 1956 to 1976	18
5. Net changes in improved farmland, by province, 1956 to 1976	19
6. Percentage of total farmland, by province and Agroclimatic Resource Index, 1971	19
7. Net change in total farmland, by province and Agroclimatic Resource Index, 1961 to 1971	20
8. Canada's urban and rural population, 1871 to 1976	36
9. Occupation structure of the labour force, 1881	37
10. Occupation structure of the labour force, 1921	37
11. Occupation structure of the labour force, 1951	38
12. Percentage distribution of employment within regions, by industry, 1977	38
13. Average family income for metropolitan and non-metropolitan areas, by region, 1975	38
14. Personal income per person as a percentage of the Canadian average, by province, 1926 to 1976	39
15. Agricultural capability of land within an 80-km radius of 23 Census Metropolitan Areas	39
16. Area of total farmland, by province, 1921 to 1976	41
17. Area of improved farmland, by province, 1921 to 1976	42
18. Number of census-farms, by province, 1921 to 1976	47
19. Average census-farm size, by province, 1921 to 1976	47
20. Farm population, by province, 1931 to 1976	48
21. Total capital value of census-farms, by province, 1921 to 1976	49
22. Percentage of total capital value, by sector, for Canada, 1921 to 1976	49
23. Average capital value per ha of farmland and per farm, by sector and province, 1976	50
24. Selected Niagara fruit areas, 1951, 1971, and 1977	54

Figures

	Page
1. Net changes in improved farmland and total farmland, by province, in ha and ACRH	21
2. Percentage of Canada's improved farmland, by province, 1971	22
3. Percentage of Canada's agricultural sales, by province, 1970	22
4. Percentage of Canada's capital value of land and buildings, by province, 1976	24
5. Percentage of Canada's capital value of machinery and equipment, by province, 1976	24
6. Percentage of Canada's capital value of livestock and poultry, by province, 1976	24
7. Percentage of Canada's wheat sales, by province, 1970	29
8. Percentage of Canada's wheat area, by province, 1976	29
9. Percentage of Canada's specialty field crop sales, by province, 1970	30
10. Percentage of Canada's specialty field crop area, by province, 1976	30
11. Percentage of Canada's fruit sales, by province, 1970	31
12. Percentage of Canada's fruit area, by province, 1976	31
13. Percentage of Canada's vegetable sales, by province, 1970	32
14. Percentage of Canada's vegetable area, by province, 1976	32
15. Population pyramids for Canada, 1976	37
16. Areas in agricultural land resource classes, rated by soil and climate	46

Maps

	Page
1. Soil capability for agriculture: Québec, New Brunswick, Prince Edward Island, Nova Scotia, Newfoundland	6
2. Soil capability for agriculture: Ontario	7
3. Soil capability for agriculture: British Columbia, Alberta, Saskatchewan, Manitoba	10
4. January mean temperature	13
5. July mean temperature	14
6. Average annual precipitation	15
7. Growing degree-days	16
8. Agroclimatic resource areas	17
9. Percentage of Canada's improved farmland, by census division, 1971	22
10. Percentage of Canada's agricultural sales, by census division, 1970	23
11. Value of agricultural sales of census-farms, 1970	24
12. Total capital value of census-farms, 1976	25
13. Capital value of land and buildings as a percentage of total capital value, 1976	26
14. Percentage of Canada's capital value of livestock and poultry, by census division, 1976	27
15. Major wheat areas, 1976	28
16. Major specialty field crop areas, 1976	29
17. Major fruit areas, 1976	31
18. Major vegetable areas, 1976	32
19. Improved farmland as a percentage of total land area, 1951	44
20. Improved farmland as a percentage of total land area, 1976	45
21. Effect of 1°C cooling on barley limit	51
22. Effect of 1°C cooling on wheat limit	52
23. Tender fruit soil of Niagara fruit belt	53
24. Tender fruit climate of southwestern Ontario	53
25. Degree of urbanization in Niagara fruit belt, 1934	53
26. Degree of urbanization in Niagara fruit belt, 1954	53
27. Degree of urbanization in Niagara fruit belt, 1975	54
28. Change in orchard area as a percentage of township block area, 1954 to 1975	54
29. Census of agriculture census divisions, 1971	64
30. Census of agriculture census divisions, 1976	65

Introduction

What makes some land of critical importance for agriculture and other land worthless? Is it the inherent physical characteristics of the soil? Is it a benevolent combination of climatic elements such as moisture, heat, and sunlight? Do certain soil and climatic conditions, joined in a unique combination, constitute special agricultural land? Can economic measures, such as level of capital investment or value of agricultural sales, indicate valuable agricultural areas? Does a geographic concentration of an important crop indicate special farmland? Are locations, that are under intense pressure to undergo land use change, of particular concern? Should significance be attached to areas experiencing net losses of farmland? Is the dynamic rural-urban fringe a critical area? Are the frontiers and risks, created for agriculture by climatic change, important? The answer to all the above questions is "yes".

This chapter focuses on some of the many parameters that can be used to identify and describe special resource lands for agriculture. They include physical, climatic, economic, and social factors. To consider any one of these to the exclusion of all others would be useless, for the setting in which Canadian agriculture exists includes all of these influences and more. Research and experience have shown that agriculture fares poorly when decisions on the use of land are based solely on economics. However, it is equally serious to disregard economic factors in favour of climatic, social, or physical criteria, as each has a rôle to play. How they relate is still a mystery, and how to evaluate their significance remains a challenge.

Physical Factors

It is largely the intrinsic properties of our physical environment which shape the nature of agriculture in Canada. Length of growing season, availability of precipitation, permafrost, soil fertility, slope, and a host of other characteristics may impose limitations which cannot be overcome economically. On the other hand, such factors may combine to produce conditions which, under good management, are favourable to high yields of a variety of crops. While it is true that almost any crop could be cultivated anywhere in Canada given unlimited capital and energy, these inputs are themselves very limited. It is, therefore, important to consider carefully the basic land resource, its limitations, and its potential.

In any given climatic zone, land quality is a delicate balance between many aspects of the soil. However, a resource has little value until it has a use. In its original forested and waterlogged condition, the land in Essex County in Ontario gave little hint of future promise to early pioneers. In this century, however, drained and under wise management, it is among the most productive and versatile crop land in Canada. Here, in such a benign climate for crop growth, there can be little doubt about the cost effectiveness of land drainage.

The same is not true elsewhere. Unfortunately on 95 per cent of Canada's land, climatic factors severely limit production. Since versatility, that is the range of crops that can be successfully grown, is restricted, the feasibility of overcoming soil problems economically depends upon matching crops of sufficient market value to land that is both sensitive and responsive to their specific requirements. This has always been the challenge of farming.

An examination of a broad national overview of the landscape, soil, and climate provides the basic understanding and guide to the first measures of prime agricultural land — physical criteria.

Physiography

The degree of control exercised by the landscape and the soil is best illustrated from examples at the "frontiers of exploitation", where attempts have been made to push outward the margins of certain land uses against the resistance of the natural environment.

In the Maritime marshlands, for example, soils have been reclaimed from the Bay of Fundy by diking. Hampered by fragmentation of individual holdings, drainage of these soils is difficult and in very few areas has anything close to their full potential been realized. By and large, the combined effects of a cool, moist climate and poor soil structure have tipped the balance, and have thwarted the kind of development that happened in Essex County, Ontario.

Corn is an example of a crop pushed beyond its limits, for various reasons, on to unsuitable land. As the mainstay of a number of farming systems in many areas of Ontario, its range has been extended on to steep slopes and easily erodible soils. The resulting damage has impaired both land and water resources. Such areas have great value for farming, but only under continuous cover crops. On gentler slopes, special methods of erosion control are practical and theoretically acceptable as an extra input cost for corn production. But eastwards through Québec and into the Maritimes, corn is restricted to a narrowing range of soils, as yields fall, fertilizer and other inputs rise, and drainage costs become a burden. In these circumstances, only the simplest soil conservation measures can be afforded, thus increasing the chances of land deterioration.

What has actually happened with corn, and to some extent with potatoes, is that large areas of land inherently unsuitable for these crops, along with adjacent water bodies, have been seriously damaged. Losses, through erosion, of expensive, energy-intensive applied fertilizer are a straight dollar loss to present farmers, but the main detriment is to future occupants and users who will inherit a partially "mined" or depreciated resource. This is a case of overloading the land resource through failure to adapt to soil and physiographic limitations. Similar overloading of the soil resource in the drier Prairies might well produce a new dust bowl, if soil management fails to acknowledge real soil limitations including the historic depletion of organic matter and the need for more conservation.

This is not to say that the real advantages and potential of a soil should not be exploited to the full. Rather, the physical properties should be fully appreciated and carefully assessed, as part of any land use planning and management. A detailed description of soils and landscapes in Canada is included in Agriculture – Appendix I. It provides a basic background of information related to the physical criteria which determine, to a considerable degree, those lands best suited for agriculture.

For a number of reasons, these inherent physical characteristics may be considered the most important of criteria in identifying special agricultural land. They are direct indicators of the soil's natural fertility and express, in a general way, the soil's capability for sustaining certain yields for a variety of crops. An excess or deficiency of any variable will indicate the need for increased inputs of supplemental resources such as energy, water, or fertilizer. Generally speaking, physical measures lend themselves more easily to quantification than do political, social, or other factors which influence agriculture. The physical characteristics of soil and landscape are relatively more permanent than the social, economic, or political factors with which they interact. Consequently, an evaluation of land, or any designation of prime farmland, based on physical parameters is likely to remain valid over a longer period of time, which is an important consideration in land use planning and management. Scientific advances in plant breeding can, however, lead to expansion of crops into marginal or frontier areas or to increased yields in existing crop areas.

The Canada Land Inventory

"Qualitative evaluations are a reconnaissance type of survey, producing information for broad scale land use planning purposes, and based largely on the intrinsic characteristics of the land. Qualitative evaluations are essentially concerned with determining the suitability of the land for different uses, e.g. agriculture versus recreation; cropping versus grazing and the suitability of land for different types of agricultural crops. Most land classification schemes are based on qualitative evaluations, it is this type of classification scheme that the planner would be mainly dependent on in designating prime lands".

(Holesgrove, 1976*a*).

A qualitative evaluation of land capability is a reasonably precise method of delineating valuable agricultural lands according to selected physical criteria. Such classifications of land capability exist in many countries including Canada, the United States, and the United Kingdom. The Canada Land Inventory's classification of soil capability for agriculture, begun in the early 1960s, is one of the earliest systems. It is the first method used in this report to define special resource lands for agriculture.

The Canada Land Inventory (CLI) is a comprehensive survey of land capability and use for various purposes. The classification system for agriculture was developed for application in the agricultural and adjoining forest fringes across Canada by the National (now Canada) Soil Survey Committee in co-operation with the federal and provincial Agricultural Rehabilitation and Development Act (ARDA) administrations. The inventory covers approximately one-third of Canada and encompasses all the significant land areas capable of sustained agricultural activities. Although the agricultural capability of areas outside the present CLI boundaries is generally limited by climatic or physiographic factors, small pockets of arable land do exist in river valleys, deltas, and other locations. However, such enclaves are too small to map at small scales, and, while these soils are important locally, they do not affect the national totals.

Assumptions upon which the classification system is based:

1) The CLI is an interpretive classification based on the combined effects of characteristics of climate and soil, on limitations in use of the soils for agriculture, and on their general productive capacity for common field crops.
2) Good soil management practices under a largely mechanized system are assumed.
3) The many kinds of soils within any one capability class are similar with respect to the degree of intensity of restrictions, but not necessarily to the type of limitations or hazards.
4) Land which requires improvements such as clearing, that can be made economically by the farmer, is classed according to its limitations to use after the improvements have been made.
5) Distance to market, road conditions, locations, size of farms, characteristics of land ownership and cultural patterns, and the skill or resources of individual operators are not criteria for capability groupings.
6) Capability groupings are subject to change as new information becomes available or as major reclamation or other works are completed.

The following description of the CLI system of soil capability classification for agriculture was modified from Environment Canada (1972). In this classification system, mineral soils are grouped into seven classes, with various subclasses, according to their potential and limitations for agricultural use as determined by climate and soil characteristics. The class indicates the general suitability of the land for agricultural use. The first three classes are considered capable of sustained production of commonly cultivated crops, the fourth is marginal for arable culture, the fifth is capable of use only for permanent pasture and hay, the sixth is capable of use only for wild pasture, while the seventh class is for soils and land types considered incapable of use for arable culture or permanent pasture. The classification system, at the 1:250,000 and 1:1,000,000 scales, identifies but does not rate organic soils because of insufficient data. Soil areas in all classes may be suitable for wildlife, forestry, recreation, or other uses.

Capability Classes

Class 1 –Soils in this class have no significant limitations for crops;
–These deep soils are level or have very gentle slopes, are well to imperfectly drained and have a good water-holding capacity;
–They are easily maintained in good tilth and productivity, and damage from erosion is slight;
–They are moderately high to high in productivity for a wide range of field crops adapted to the region.

Class 2 –Soils in this class have moderate limitations that restrict the range of crops or require moderate conservation practices;
–These deep soils have a good water-holding capacity, can be managed with little difficulty and are moderately high to high in productivity for a fairly wide range of field crops;
–The moderate limitations of these soils may be any one of a number of factors including mildly adverse regional climate, moderate effects of erosion, poor soil structure or slow permeability, low fertility correctable with limited application of fertilizer and lime, gentle to moderate slopes, or occasional overflow or wetness.

Class 3 –Soils in this class have moderately severe limitations that restrict the range of crops or require special conservation practices;
–Under good management these soils are fair to moderately high in productivity for a fairly wide range of field crops adapted to the region;
–Conservation practices are more difficult to apply and maintain;
–Limitations are a combination of two of those factors described under class 2, or one of the following: moderate climatic limitations; moderately severe effects of erosion; intractable soil mass or very slow permeability; low fertility; moderate to strong slopes; frequent overflow or poor drainage resulting in occasional crop dam-

age; low water-holding capacity or slow in release of water; stoniness sufficiently severe to seriously handicap cultivation and necessitating some clearing; restricted rooting zone; or moderate salinity.

Class 4 —Soils in this class have severe limitations that restrict the range of crops, or require special conservation practices, or both;
—Such soils are suitable for only a few crops, or the yield for a range of crops is low, or the risk of crop failure is high;
—Limitations include the adverse effects of a combination of two or more of those described in classes 2 and 3, or one of the following: moderately severe climate; very low water-holding capacity; low fertility difficult or unfeasible to correct; strong slopes; severe past erosion; very intractable mass of soil or extremely slow permeability; frequent overflow with severe effects on crops; severe salinity causing some crop failures; extreme stoniness requiring considerable clearing to permit annual cultivation; and very restricted rooting zone, but more than 30 cm of soil over bedrock; or an impermeable layer;
—Limitations may seriously affect timing and ease of tillage, planting, harvesting, and maintenance of conservation practices;
—Soils have low to medium productivity for a narrow range of crops but may have higher productivity for a specially adapted crop.

Class 5 —Soils in this class have very severe limitations that restrict their capability to produce perennial forage crops, and improvement practices are feasible;
—Soils have such serious soil, climatic, or other limitations that they are not capable of use for sustained production of annual field crops;
—These soils may be improved by the use of farm machinery for the production of native or tame species of perennial forage plants;
—Limitations include the adverse effects of one or more of the following: severe climate; low water-holding capacity; severe past erosion; steep slopes; very poor drainage; very frequent overflow; severe salinity permitting only salt tolerant forage crops to grow; and stoniness or shallowness to bedrock that make annual cultivation impractical;
—Some soils can be used for cultivated field crops provided unusually intensive management is used;
—Cultivated field crops may be grown in class 5 areas where adverse climate is the main limitation, but crop failures occur under average conditions;
—Some of the soils in this class are also adapted to special crops such as blueberries, orchard crops, or the like, requiring soil conditions unlike those needed by the common crops.

Class 6 —Soils in this class are capable only of producing perennial forage crops, and improvement practices are not feasible;
—Soils have some natural sustained grazing capacity for farm animals but have such serious soil, climatic, or other limitations as to make impractical the application of improvement practices that can be carried out in class 5;
—Soils may be placed in this class because their physical nature prevents improvement through the use of farm machinery, or the soils are not responsive to improvement practices, or because of a short grazing season, or because stock watering facilities are inadequate;
—Limitations include the adverse effects of one or more of the following: very severe climate; very low water-holding capacity; very steep slopes; very severely eroded land with gullies too numerous and too deep for working with machinery; severely saline land producing only edible, salt-tolerant, native plants; very frequent overflow allowing less than 10 weeks effective grazing; water on the surface of the soil for most of the year; and stoniness or shallowness to bedrock that makes any cultivation impractical.

Class 7 —Soils in this class have no capability for arable culture or permanent pasture;
—The soils or lands in class 7 have limitations so severe that they are not capable of use for arable culture or permanent pasture;
—All classified areas (except organic soils) not included in classes 1 to 6 are placed in this class.

Capability Subclasses

Subclasses are divisions within classes that have the same kind of limitations for agricultural use. Thirteen different kinds of limitations are recognized at the subclass level. A brief discussion of these subclasses and their letter designation on maps follows:

This photo illustrates soils rated in CLI classes 2, 3, 4, 5, and 7. The class 2 area has a moderate limitation because of occasional damaging overflow; the class 3 areas are affected by topographic and fertility limitations; and the class 4 and 5 lands are downgraded from class 3 because of steepness of slope. The class 7 area is considered to be of no use for agriculture because of steepness of slopes and generally rough topography.

Adverse climate (C):
—This subclass denotes a significant adverse climate for crop production, as compared to the "median" climate which is defined as one with sufficiently high growing-season temperatures to bring field crops to maturity, and with sufficient precipitation to permit crops to be grown each year on the same land without a serious risk of partial or total crop failures.

Undesirable soil structure and/or low permeability (D):
—This subclass is used for soils difficult to till, or which absorb water very slowly, or in which the depth of rooting zone is restricted by conditions other than a high water table or consolidated bedrock.

Erosion (E):
—Subclass E includes soils where damage from erosion is a limitation to agricultural use. Damage is assessed on the loss of productivity and on the difficulties in farming land with gullies.

Low fertility (F):
—This subclass is made up of soils having low fertility that either is correctable with careful management in the use of fertilizers and soil amendments, or is difficult to correct in a feasible way. The limitation may be due to lack of available plant nutrients, high acidity or alkalinity, low exchange capability, high levels of carbonates, or presence of toxic compounds.

Inundation by streams or lakes (I):
—This subclass includes soils subjected to inundation causing crop damage or restricting agricultural use.

Moisture limitation (M):
—This subclass consists of soils where crops are adversely affected by droughtiness owing to inherent soil characteristics. They are usually soils with low water-holding capacity.

Salinity (N):
—This subclass includes soils with enough soluble salts to adversely affect crop growth or restrict the range of crops that may be grown. Such soils are not placed higher than class 3.

Stoniness (P):
—This subclass is made up of soils sufficiently stony to significantly hinder tillage, planting, and harvesting operations. Stony soils are usually less productive than comparable non-stony soils.

Consolidated bedrock (R):
—This subclass includes soils where the presence of bedrock near the surface restricts their agricultural use. Consolidated bedrock at depths greater than about one m from the surface is not considered as a limitation, except on irrigated lands where a greater depth of soil is desirable.

Adverse soil characteristics (S):
—On the 1:250,000 scale capability maps, this subclass will be used in place of subclasses, D, F, M, and N either individually or collectively. On larger scale maps, it may be used in a collective sense for two or more of these subclasses.

Topography (T):
—This subclass is made up of soils where topography is a limitation. Both the percentage of slope and the pattern or frequency of slopes in different directions are important factors in increasing the cost of farming over that of smooth land, in decreasing the uniformity of growth and maturity of crops, and in increasing the hazard of water erosion.

Excess water (W):
—Subclass W is made up of soils where excess water, other than that brought about by inundation, is a limitation to their use for agriculture. Excess water may result from inadequate soil drainage, a high water table, seepage, or runoff from surrounding areas.

Cumulative minor adverse characteristics (X):
—This subclass is made up of soils having a moderate limitation caused by the cumulative effect of two or more adverse characteristics which singly are not serious enough to affect the class rating.

Correction of the different limitations on farmland involves various amounts of money, equipment, energy, and time. Certain limitations require corrective measures on an on-going basis, while others involve high initial expenditures and minimum maintenance costs. Estimates for ameliorating selected limitations have been documented in Table 1.

TABLE 1.

Costs for correcting limitations on potential farmland, 1975

Limitation	Cost/ha	Explanation
	(dollars)	
Soil infertility	89 to 160	For corn and small grains for lime and fertilizer/ha
	370	For potatoes/ha
Excessive stoniness	740	Initially and yearly maintenance
Forested (for tree and brush removal)	750 to 1,000	Plus fertilizer costs
Poor soil structure		
Tiles	740+	Plus maintenance
Subsurface tillage	40 to 70 per annum	
Excess soil moisture		
Tractor subsoiling	40 to 80 per annum	
Mole drainage (limited application)	80 to 100 every 7 years	
Erosion control		
Cropping changes	?	$ difference in crop returns
Diversion ditches	250 per annum	
Flooding	1,000	Initially for flood control
Deficient moisture supply Irrigation	74 per annum average	

Source: R. Halstead (cited by Geno and Geno, 1976).

The Canada Land Inventory classification is a generalized inventory of agricultural soil resources rather than an index to the most profitable use of land. Caution should be exercised in comparing land classes from one province to another, as differences do exist. Therefore, class 1 soils in Ontario are not necessarily equivalent to class 1 soils in Saskatchewan, especially in terms of potential productivity for a specific crop. Climatic differences affect crop yield and these factors are not fully considered in the CLI.

For the purposes of this report, prime agricultural land is defined by classes 1, 2, and 3 of the Canada Land Inventory soil classification for agriculture. Three regional maps emphasize the limited extent of Canada's prime agricultural land and illustrate its spatial distribution.

Summary of Soil Capability. In the Atlantic Provinces (Map 1), both climatic and geomorphic conditions tend to discourage agriculture in many locations. As a by-product of the cool humid climate, the most prevalent limitation is low fertility. The correction of this problem is expensive. In many areas, poor soil structure is a dilemma. Compact subsoil layers resist water and root penetration so the land is better suited for forage crops than cereal crops, unless the condition is ameliorated. Excessive soil moisture and undesirable relief hinder seeding and harvesting activities, as well as restrict the use of machinery. Slopes are particularly susceptible to erosion. In spite of these limitations, areas of reasonable agricultural potential do exist. Crops including vegetables, particularly potatoes and corn, fruit, forage and small grains, and specialty products such as blueberries are successfully grown.

On the Island of Newfoundland, there is no soil of CLI class 1 or 2 capability for agriculture. In fact, only 0.05 per cent of the Island's total land area is categorized as class 3 capability and 0.58 per cent as class 4. These 68,000 ha occur in small pockets on the extreme southwest tip of the Island, around Deer Lake, on the north shore of Gander Lake, and the Avalon Peninsula. Nevertheless, these soils are of great strategic importance in the province. Greater self-sufficiency in vegetables and other agricultural products is important in light of the high cost of imports. Most of the Island, approximately 67 per cent, is either class 7 or organic soils, of which the latter hold some promise for future agriculture given more attention and proper management. The remaining soils are in classes 5 to 6. Agriculture is hampered by the climate, excessive soil moisture, and shallow stony soils, which result in a low potential for farming.

In Nova Scotia, as in the other Atlantic Provinces, there is no soil of class 1 potential. The 166,259 ha of class 2 land occur along the northern coastal plain between Amherst and Antigonish, in the Annapolis–Cornwallis Valley, and near Truro, but virtually all such soils suffer from low natural fertility. Approximately one-fifth of the province's land falls into class 3 capability for agriculture. These soils are distributed in the lowlands of Cape Breton Island, along the west coast north of Yarmouth, in the Annapolis–Cornwallis Valley, and along the shores of Northumberland Strait, Minas Basin, and Bay of Fundy. Soils in classes 2 and 3 support grains, corn, hay, fruit, and tobacco crops. These soils are affected by a wide range of conditions including undesirable soil structure, low permeability, stoniness, adverse relief, and excessive moisture. The rough uplands of Nova Scotia place severe limitations on farming, and 67 per cent of the province is categorized as having no capability for agriculture. The Maritimes also have significant quantities of class 2 and 3 soils in woodland.

New Brunswick's best farmland consists of 160,792 ha of class 2 soil. These soils represent only two per cent of the total land area and almost all occur in the Saint John, Restigouche, and Tobique River valleys. Class 3 soils account for 16 per cent of the province's land area and are located mainly in river valleys and lowland areas of the eastern half of the province. Potatoes, grains, and hay are common crops, particularly in the upper Saint John River valley. Undesirable soil structure, low permeability, slope steepness, and salinity influence the agricultural use of the land. The capability of all soils in New Brunswick is reduced by low fertility. In Nova Scotia as well as in New Brunswick, class 3 D land (with undesirable soil structure and/or low permeability limitations) is the great agricultural resource. Such soil could be raised economically to the class 2 level of productivity by soil improvement. The resultant increased grain production would reduce dependency on western feed grains.

In Prince Edward Island, a substantial 46 per cent of the land is rated as having class 2 capability. These soils are found in the vicinity of Summerside and Charlottetown as well as on the higher ground in the eastern part of the province. Another 25 per cent of the land is designated as class 3 and these soils are found in irregular patches across the province. Wheat, oats for grain, barley, mixed grains, hay, and potatoes are common crops, but low soil fertility and excessive moisture remain problems.

In the province of Québec, about 95 per cent of the land area is either incapable of supporting any agriculture (class 7) or not classified for agricultural purposes. Attention is, therefore, focused on those limited areas in southern Québec where agriculture is feasible (see Map 1). In this vast province of more than 135 million ha, only 19,533 ha, or 0.01 per cent of land, are rated as class 1 soil. This valuable resource is located in the vicinity of Montréal and Valleyfield, precisely where urban consumption of land is highest. Other prime areas for agriculture include 909,671 ha of class 2 soils and 1,281,043 ha of class 3 land. Most of these favoured soils are restricted to the St. Lawrence Lowlands. This part of Québec is known for its specialty and cash crops such as fruits, vegetables, and nursery products. However, dairy products, poultry and eggs, and livestock account for a large percentage of agricultural sales, about 83 per cent in 1971 for example. Difficulties that confront farmers include low natural fertility, excessive soil moisture, stoniness, rough topography, and undesirable soil structure. In addition to urban areas, rural low-density housing in both Québec and Ontario is threatening the unique lands of good soil and climate, which are truly irreplaceable.

In terms of high-capability soil for agriculture, Ontario is richly endowed (Map 2). This single province contains 51.4 per cent of the entire country's class 1 land. With the exception of scattered areas of class 1 soil in eastern Ontario, the vast measure of prime land lies in southern Ontario, contained by the edge of the Canadian Shield. Here, over two million ha of land have favourable climatic and geomorphic conditions. Here too, encroachment by rural residential development, recreation facilities, transportation needs, and urban growth is greatest.

Nonetheless, this area is of prime importance to Canadian agriculture with its contribution of vegetables, fruits, tobacco, grains and oil seeds, greenhouse and nursery products, as well as livestock. The 2,217,771 ha of class 2 land are found mainly in southwestern Ontario and the Niagara area, with pockets in eastern Ontario. The soft fruit areas of southwestern Ontario are unique outside California due to soil conditions and a lake-modified climate. To a large extent, the 2,909,460 ha of class 3 soils occur in the far eastern corner of the province, in the northern Clay Belt and near Lake of the Woods. In these areas, the agricultural emphasis is more on livestock, dairying, and grains. The most common limitations to agricultural productivity are excessive wetness, undesirable soil structure, and cold temperatures. With the exception of class 4 to 6 soils in river valleys, shorelines, and clay belts, the Canadian Shield is largely class 7 land. Patches of class 4 to 6 soils also occur near Lake of the Woods, in eastern Ontario, along the Shield edge, and scattered across the province.

There is no question but that the three Prairie Provinces comprise the largest single expanse of viable agricultural land in Canada (Map 3). These western provinces are renowned for their wheat, mixed grains, and beef enterprises. Each province has a slightly different resource base. Manitoba has only 162,508 ha of class 1 soil, located mainly around Portage la Prairie. Two and one-half million ha of both class 2 and 3 soils occupy the southwest and south-central quadrants of the province. Limitations to these soils include adverse relief of the stony ridges, and excessive or deficient soil moisture. Soils of classes 4 to 6 surround Lake Winnipeg and Lake Manitoba, but these soils have more severe problems posed by low fertility, rough topography, and stoniness. Manitoba Interlake has a high-class climate, equivalent to productive areas of the western Prairies. Soil problems of class 4 land can be ameliorated to some extent in this area.

Saskatchewan, with nearly one million ha, has more class 1 land than the other Prairie Provinces. Most of this high-capability land is located southeast of Prince Albert but relatively large areas are also found near Yorkton, Kamsack, and along the Qu'Appelle River east of Regina. Saskatchewan also possesses large quantities of class 2 and 3 soils, with 5,873,285 and 9,420,057 ha respectively. These relatively high-capability soils run in irregular bands from Lloydminster in the west through Saskatoon, Moose Jaw, and Prince Albert to the Manitoba border. Here, elements limiting agriculture reflect the different soil and climatic conditions. Deficient soil moisture and droughtiness or aridity as a result of climate are major restrictions. In Saskatchewan as well as Alberta, salinity is a serious and expanding problem. Farming practices must change in order to control it. Soils rated in classes 4 to 6 are found extensively in the south-central and southwest margins of the province and in the vicinity of Prince Albert National Park. In Saskatchewan, wheat, mixed grains, flax, and oil seeds are widely cultivated.

Source: Generalized from the 1:1,000,000 Canada Land Inventory *Soil Capability for Agriculture* maps for *Atlantic Provinces* (1974) and *Québec* (1974), published by the Lands Directorate, Environment Canada.

MAP 1

NFB – PHOTOTHEQUE – ONF – Photo by W. Vollmann.

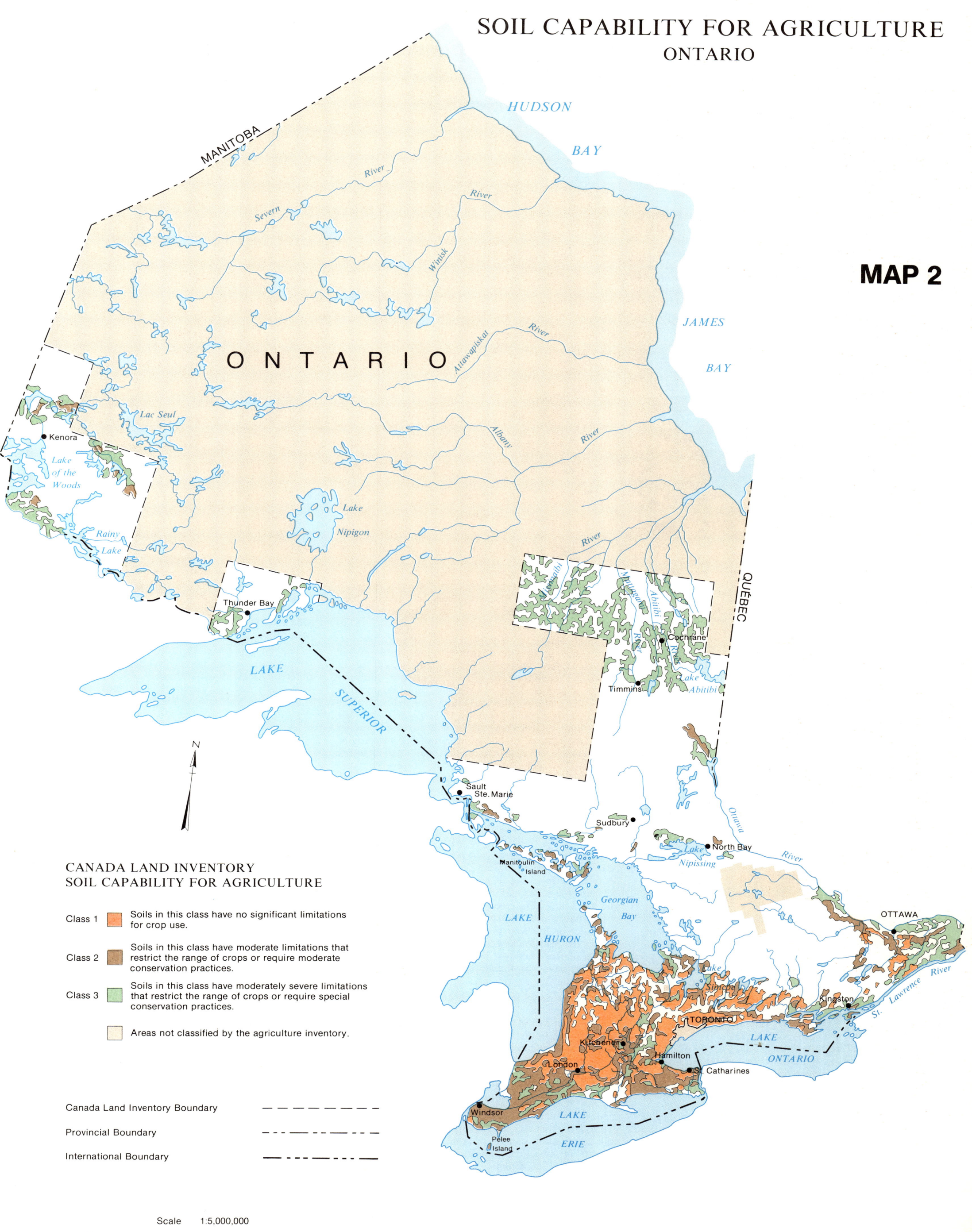

In Alberta, considerable quantities of class 1 agricultural land exist in the proximity of urban areas including Edmonton, Calgary, Lethbridge, and Medicine Hat. Alberta also possesses substantial amounts of class 2 and 3 soils, 3,838,965 and 6,110,044 ha respectively. These high-capability soils are found in the Peace River area and in a broad crescent shape which surrounds the class 1 areas. The most prevalent restrictions on these soils include aridity as a result of climate and deficient soil moisture. In the Peace River district, the soils have structural limitations, low fertility, and are subject to more severe climatic constraints.

In British Columbia, the quantity of high-capability agricultural land is strictly limited (see Map 3). Statistics concerning class 1 to 3 land indicate that only 1,467,414 ha of prime agricultural land may exist in the province. These high-capability soils, which constitute only 1.5 per cent of the province's land area, are largely confined to river valleys and deltas. Limitations to agriculture in other locations include adverse topography and climate. However, there is considerable untapped pasture potential (class 4) in the north-central area.

NFB – PHOTOTHEQUE – ONF – Photo by Duncan Bancroft.

The fertile alluvial material of the Fraser River delta produces fruits, vegetables, horticultural crops, and dairy products for the Vancouver and Victoria markets. Because of the limited amount of high-capability land in British Columbia, this area has special significance for agriculture.

In a country which encompasses 922,130,123 ha of land, it is difficult to understand that land is a finite and extremely valuable resource. Surely there is no shortage of good agricultural land? Analysis of CLI data reveals some startling statistics (Table 2):

1) 86 per cent of Canada's land either has no capability for agriculture or has not been classified for agricultural use. This includes areas within the CLI boundaries which are unclassified, such as urban areas, military reserves, and parks, as well as organic soils, for which there is insufficient data.

2) Of Canada's land area, approximately two per cent, or 18,363,430 ha, are marginal for agricultural use (class 6) and are suitable only for rough grazing.

3) This leaves 105,186,512 ha, or 11 per cent, which can support agricultural production (classes 1 to 5).

4) Of this 105,186,512 ha, only 45,993,529 ha, or five per cent of Canada's land, are free from severe physical limitations according to the CLI, and are capable of supporting crop production (classes 1 to 3). Alberta, Saskatchewan and Manitoba account for 32,161,884 ha of class 1 to 3 soils, representing 70 per cent of the country's total potential cropland. If Ontario's 7,284,007 ha are added, these four provinces account for nearly 86 per cent of Canada's prime (high-capability) soil.

5) Only 0.5 per cent of Canada's land area, or 4,195,047 ha, falls into CLI class 1, soil which has no significant limitations for agriculture and has the highest productivity for a wide range of crops. Over 50 per cent of Canada's class 1 agricultural land is in southern Ontario.

This brief summary of the CLI evaluation of the physical resource base should be sufficient to underscore the fact that a very limited portion of Canada's land can be classified as prime agricultural land. A more detailed description of soil and landscapes across Canada can be found at the end of this chapter (see Appendix I). But soil capability is only the first of several criteria which can be used to identify special agricultural areas.

TABLE 2.

CLI classification of soils with capability for agriculture, by province

Province	1	2	3	CLI class* 4	5	6	7	Total land area
				(ha)				
Newfoundland	0	0	5,504	62,000	387,622	2,889,315	3,739,104	37,049,799
Prince Edward Island	0	261,352	141,524	49,777	76,034	0	27,673	565,673
Nova Scotia	0	166,259	982,457	424,255	82,186	14,321	3,510,690	5,284,281
New Brunswick	0	160,792	1,152,089	2,033,061	1,700,878	11,549	1,839,090	7,209,488
Québec	19,533	909,671	1,281,043	2,585,269	1,659,434	10,671	20,765,333	135,683,931
Ontario	2,156,776	2,217,771	2,909,460	2,625,809	1,915,501	1,140,252	11,221,143	89,122,581
Manitoba	162,508	2,530,258	2,440,485	2,391,269	2,237,832	2,085,319	1,034,231	54,851,419
Saskatchewan	999,727	5,873,285	9,420,057	3,782,988	8,522,735	2,920,046	35,578	57,028,899
Alberta	786,555	3,838,965	6,110,044	9,285,201	11,100,971	3,934,057	4,191,630	64,441,190
British Columbia	69,948	397,688	999,778	2,131,867	6,138,294	5,357,900	14,900,573	93,056,135
Yukon and Northwest Territories	–	–	–	–	–	–	–	377,836,727
CANADA	4,195,047	16,356,041	25,442,441	25,371,496	33,821,487	18,363,430	61,265,045	922,130,123

* These preliminary figures were prepared by computerized inventory and will differ from other CLI estimates prepared by manual procedures. The Yukon and Northwest Territories are not covered by the CLI.

Sources: British Columbia Environment and Land Use Committee Secretariat, 1976. Agriculture Land Capability in British Columbia.
Environment Canada, 1976c. Land Capability for Agriculture: A Preliminary Report.
Canada Land Inventory. Soil Capability for Agriculture. Miscellaneous maps.

Climate

Agriculture and climate are intimately related. Past climates have shaped agricultural soils and the present climate determines the types and varieties of crops the soils may produce. In that sense, climate is a resource and the boundaries it imposes on cultivation can be delineated. This is of particular interest in Canada where agriculture is practised close to its northern economic limit.

Climate serves the biological needs of crops by providing the appropriate quantity, cycling, and mix of light, heat, and moisture. Since plant growth is restricted to specific ranges of air temperature, and may be terminated by frost or excessive heat, temperature can thus be used in the evaluation and delineation of areas that are suitable for cultivation. Accumulated values of temperatures above the growth threshold provide a good estimate of plant maturity, and the mapping of their seasonal values provides additional planning information. These cumulative heat units, however, vary in quality and in their influence on plant processes, depending on whether they were accumulated in particularly warm or cool periods. Seaside locations may have a mild climate and accumulate good seasonal heat unit totals, but prolonged spells without hot weather slows down the maturation of most crops.

An adequate length of growing season, and sufficient heat to meet physiological needs are other requisites. Maps of the frost-free season and of the growing season delineate the zones that meet the needs of specific crops, and allow spatial intercomparisons in the consideration of alternative uses. In using such data, allowance must be made for the way that topography and vegetation control temperature and the occurrence of frost. The existence of frost hollows, soil type, forest clearings, or lakes may have a profound, but local, effect.

The factor of scale is of particular importance in the regions considered marginal for agriculture, because of the way in which climate is controlled by topography. Large departures in temperature and precipitation can occur over short distances, and within an area otherwise considered unsuitable for agriculture it may be possible to delineate zones that are acceptable because of their particular exposure, soil type, or other characteristics. These more reliable lands offer special opportunites in all areas in which agriculture can be practised.

Mean-value maps provide a first look at climatic capability. If general criteria are met for an area, then specific information can be examined to assess potential hazards or additional opportunities. Of fundamental importance is the climatic variability that imposes risks and opportunities that are not apparent in the mean value. Variability is usually greatest in the more arid areas, and minimal near the oceans. Variability may manifest itself as periods of drought, or of excessive rains or snows, that delay or stop field work and damage soils or crops. Other manifestations are extremely cold winters that may damage fruit trees, the unusual tracking of hurricanms inland, and shortened summers. The frequency of occurrence of all such hazards can be determined by statistical methods. Apart from the problem of climatic variability, attention should be given to hazards such as hail, untimely heat and cold, and exessive humidity.

The following text includes detailed description of temperature, precipitation, growing degree-days, and other physical, climatic characteristics, each of which serves as a national, reconnaissance-level evaluation of specific environmental variables.

Temperature

The dominant flow of weather systems across the huge land mass of North America is from west to east. Despite their maritime location, the Atlantic Provinces together with Québec have a modified continental climate. In spite of the influence of modifying features such as the Atlantic Ocean, distinctive differences do exist within this region as a result of the interaction of physiographic and climatic phenomena.

Winter. The Island of Newfoundland, while affected by the continental air, is always influenced by the Labrador Current. The southern and southeastern coasts have moderate January mean temperatures ranging between –6 and –3°C (Map 4). Interior locations experience cooler temperatures of –9 to –7°C, while to the north in the Long Peninsula, the January mean temperature drops to –11°C. In comparison, Labrador has a much more severe winter with January mean temperatures between –12 and –18°C along the coast, and below –23°C inland.

Winter in the Maritime Provinces is characterized by changeable weather, frequently severe storms, and variable temperatures. Such activity results from low-pressure systems skirting the southern fringe of, or crossing, the region every two or three days as they move eastward off the continent, and are replaced by large high-pressure areas of cold, dry, polar air. The January mean temperature ranges from –16°C in northern inland locations of New Brunswick through –10°C in Fredericton to –7°C in Saint John, along the Bay of Fundy, and in Prince Edward Island. However, the ocean's moderating influence is felt more strongly in Nova Scotia where the January mean temperature is generally above –7°C, and rises to –6°C in Cape Breton, –4°C at Halifax, and –3°C along the west coast.

The complexity of Québec's physiography and its geographic location are reflected in its varied climatic conditions. In the southwest, the lower Ottawa Valley and the Montréal area have moderate winters, but the highlands of the Canadian Shield and the northern regions experience longer and much more severe winters. The January mean temperature, in the southwest, reaches –11°C in the Eastern Townships and rises to –9°C near Montréal, due largely to the urban effect. Although situated to the north, the climate on the coastal margins of the Gaspé is modified by the maritime influence and the January mean temperature reading is –12°C. On the North Shore but inland, the –18°C isotherm in January passes north of Lac St-Jean and runs parallel to the shore before swinging northward. Finally, the northern extremity of the province, as well as the heart of the interior, endures January mean temperatures between –23 and –26°C.

The cold snowy winters in northern Ontario are characteristic of its cool continental climate, and reflect the area's latitude and the frequent invasion by cold Arctic air. The –18°C isotherm for January undulates across northern Ontario, joining Lake of the Woods in the west, Lake Nipigon, and Lake Abitibi on the Ontario-Québec boundary. To the north, January mean temperatures may be as low as –26°C. To the south, where temperatures are moderated, cities such as Sudbury and North Bay experience a January mean temperature of –12°C. The influence of the Great Lakes is evident in January mean temperatures of –14, –9, and –8°C recorded for Thunder Bay, Sault Ste. Marie, and Manitoulin Island respectively.

Latitude, together with the moderating influence of the Great Lakes and frequent incursions of warm air from the south, ensure that southern Ontario has a much milder winter than northern Ontario. Lakes Erie and Ontario, together with the St. Lawrence River, lie on one of the continent's major storm tracks. The regular west to east procession of high- and low-pressure systems during the year ensures that prolonged periods of warm or cold weather are infrequent. As air masses proceed over the region every two to five days, there is a considerable variation in day-to-day weather. January mean temperatures of –4°C are characteristic around Sarnia, London, Welland, and Hamilton, while a few favoured locations including Windsor and St. Catharines have a January mean temperature of –3°C. Winter temperatures along the north shore of Lake Erie and along the Niagara Peninsula are sufficiently moderate that the risk of winter kill, an important consideration in the cultivation of tree fruits and small fruits, is reduced. The January mean temperature at Toronto is near –5°C, reflecting its urban setting and the moderating influence of an ice-free Lake Ontario. However, to the north and east, the winters are considerably colder with January means of –12°C in Algonquin Park and the Ottawa Valley.

The southern portions of Manitoba, Saskatchewan, and Alberta have a truly continental climate. The Prairies are subject to a number of influences which result in long cold winters and short warm summers, with a measure of unpredictable and radical weather changes. The Prairies, with a vastly more uniform topography, exhibit more uniform January mean temperatures than central and eastern Canada. The western mountains, running north and south, form a barrier to the moderating influence of the Pacific Ocean. At the same time, the absence of a substantial east to west ridge across such a wide expanse of open land leaves the Prairies open to invasion by extremely cold polar air. January mean temperatures drop from above –9°C at Lethbridge to well below –23°C in northern Manitoba. The general southwest to northeast gradient of winter isotherms occurs for many reasons: the juxtaposition of the mild Pacific Ocean and the ice-covered Hudson Bay, the higher elevation of southwestern Alberta, and the general southward and eastward movement of invading cold Arctic air.

Prairie winters are usually long and intensely cold. They are noted for two special features. First, winter blizzards can bring bitterly cold temperatures and blinding snow driven by howling winds. For example, February 1978 began with a week-long blizzard bombarding southern Saskatchewan with the longest-lasting Prairie storm since 1947. Peak wind gusts registered 98 km/h and the city of Regina, as well as nearby rural communities, were totally isolated by huge snowdrifts. Some homes were buried with snow up to the roof-line. In some instances, cattle starved. Surprisingly, only a trace of new snow was recorded at Regina during the week. In some cases, cold snaps are prolonged, as in the 1955-1956 winter when Edmonton temperatures stayed below freezing for 84 days, and in 1969 when temperatures remained below –18°C for 26 days, under the steady flow of Arctic air.

The second special feature is the chinook which comes, as if in compensation, to areas of the western Prairies, especially southern Alberta, several times each winter. Occasionally, as cold Arctic air moves eastward it is replaced, from the west, by warm dry air which has lost its moisture in its passage over successive mountain ranges and which has become warmer during its descent. Under such conditions, skies clear, temperatures rise dramatically in a few hours, and the snow cover often melts. During an average winter, chinook winds may occur as often as one day in three in the southwestern Prairies. Its effect on depleting the snow cover is important for cattle grazing. However, because it removes moisture by evaporation, it robs spring crops of valuable soil moisture, and the strong winds can then cause severe erosion. In general, however, winters are long and cold.

In British Columbia,(the physiography and contrasting air masses produce great variation in climate. The islands, together with a thin coastal strip, experience mild winters, cool summers, and a small seasonal temperature range under the dominating influence of humid mild air from the westerlies blowing off the Pacific. Sheltered from the Arctic air by the Coastal Mountains, and buffeted by the prevailing westerlies blowing over the warm Pacific waters, the coastal area of British Columbia enjoys the mildest winters in Canada. Generally, winters have small temperature variations. The western coast of Vancouver Island has a January mean temperature of an enviable 4°C, while inhabitants from Vancouver to Prince Rupert enjoy a comparable reading of 2°C. Inland, and somewhat isolated from the Pacific's moderating influence, the interior of British Columbia experiences more of a continental climate with seasonal contrasts increasing in an eastward direction. Winter temperatures in British Columbia are a study in contrast, characteristic of such a complex mountainous region. Here, winter conditions depend more on altitude and physiography than on latitude. January mean temperatures range from –7°C in many southern river valleys to –12°C in the higher areas. Cut off from the moderating nature of the Pacific, the northern interior experiences a more continental climate with long cold winters. The Peace River area registers a January mean temperature of only –15°C, quite a contrast to Victoria's 2°C.

North of latitude 60°, the Yukon and Northwest Territories experience long winters characterized by limited light and bitter cold. In the beautiful but rugged topography of the Yukon, winter temperatures are subject to wide variation, depending on whether the dominant air mass originated over the north Pacific or Beaufort Sea. The mean daily temperatures in January range from –15°C at Whitehorse to –29°C in the Territory's northern area. Proceeding eastward, the Mackenzie Basin in the Northwest Territories has January mean temperatures around –29°C, while the barrens experience mean daily temperatures of –29 to –34°C. In the far northern corner of Canada, January mean readings range from –21°C in Hudson Strait to –37°C in the extreme northern latitudes.

Summer. Certain July temperature values are commonly used as indicators of probable agricultural success. The 5°C reading, for example, is the threshold for much horticultural growth. The 10°C July isotherm generally coincides with the northern limit for agriculture. Most of Canada's farmland lies between the 16 and 23°C July isotherms. Generally speaking, wheat is grown on the warm side of the 15°C July isotherm. The 21°C July isotherm has traditionally been viewed as the northern limit for grain corn and soybean production, although recent advances in earlier maturing crops have altered this boundary somewhat.

Consequently, the accompanying map of July mean temperatures (Map 5) illustrates a series of critical limits for agriculture, including the general boundaries for farming, as well as particular limits for specific crops such as wheat, grain corn, and soybeans. Of particular interest is the 20°C July isotherm, as it delineates those areas where horticulture is practised most successfully in Canada.

In spring and early summer, the Newfoundland coastline and large sections of the Continental Shelf are often shrouded in fog. Westward incursions of the moist air from the Gulf Stream into areas of coastal ice create massive fogs over the cold waters of the Continental Shelf for up to 100 days a year. The summer season is somewhat brief and cool because of the cold waters that surround Newfoundland. In coastal areas, the July mean temperature hovers around 13°C but inland the readings may climb over 16°C. In the coastal fringes of Labrador as well, the Labrador Current prevents the July mean temperature from rising above 10°C during the relatively cool summer, but in the interior it may be three to six degrees warmer.

The arrival of spring in the Maritimes is signalled by dramatic changes in weather systems. As summer approaches, storms become less frequent and warmer humid air masses dominate the region. With few exceptions, July is the year's warmest month. Summer temperatures also reflect the maritime influence. The entire Atlantic Coast of Nova Scotia has a July mean temperature near 17°C, while the inland and Bay of Fundy area readings reach 18°C. The southern coast of New Brunswick, particularly near Saint John, is also influenced by the moist humid winds off the Bay of Fundy and, thus, the July mean temperature is around 18°C. Further inland, and also in Prince Edward Island, the continental influence is more pronounced and July readings reach 19°C.

In the St. Lawrence Valley of Québec, summer comes quickly after a short spring. In the vicinity of the junction of the St. Lawrence and Ottawa rivers, long pleasant summers prevail with July mean temperatures near 21°C. Downstream, the readings fall to 19°C near Québec City and 16 to 18°C in the Gaspé. On the North Shore, however, summer readings decrease rapidly from 16°C along the shore, to 13°C on the Laurentian Plateau, and to 7°C in the far northern areas.

Northern Ontario experiences moderately warm but short summers and, in combination with the long bitter winters, these factors discourage agricultural practices in many areas. The July mean temperature rises from 14°C in the northern reaches of the province, to 19°C in Sudbury and North Bay. Again the influence of Lake Superior is seen in the relatively cool July means of 16°C immediately north of the lake and in the vicinity of Thunder Bay.

Similarly, in southern Ontario the range in July mean temperatures is only six degrees. In spite of moderating winds blowing off the Great Lakes, all areas enjoy a mean of 18°C or above. The extreme southwest, between Windsor and Chatham, has the province's highest July mean temperatures of 22 to 23°C. The readings decline slightly to 21°C at Sarnia, around the southern end of Lake Huron and toward the west end of Lake Ontario. The popular vacation areas of Georgian Bay, Muskoka, and Haliburton reach pleasant July mean temperatures of 18 or 19°C. From Lake Simcoe, along the north shores of both Lake Ontario and the St. Lawrence River to the Ottawa River, centres such as Oshawa, Peterborough, Kingston, Cornwall, and Ottawa all experience a uniform July mean reading of 20°C. Occasionally during the summer, portions of southern Ontario are overcome by unusually hot air from the central interior of the United States, when high humidity and temperatures combine to produce oppressive "muggy" conditions.

The Prairies have short but warm summers, marked by a high daily range of temperature. The seasonal temperature range is also considerable. Again, because of the lack of major topographical control, this region is susceptible to very warm air masses from the southwestern United States. The highest temperature recorded at any weather station in Canada, 45°C, occurred at Yellow Grass and Midale in Saskatchewan on July 5th, 1937. Throughout Alberta, Saskatchewan, and Manitoba, the July temperature gradient is shallow. The 19°C July isotherm encompasses the southeastern corner of Alberta, swings north of Saskatoon, moves south of the Regina area, and then divides Manitoba passing through the north end of Lake Manitoba.

Mid-summer conditions throughout British Columbia are somewhat more stable. Summers along the Pacific Coast are marked by cool to warm sunny weather as sea breezes serve as a refreshing and moderating influence. July mean temperatures rarely exceed 15°C along the coastline, with the exception of the Vancouver area, and the temperatures decrease with elevation. Proceeding inland across the mountain ranges, temperature variability and continentality increase. Summer days are hot and dry in the interior valleys, particularly in the Okanagan and lower Thompson valleys where July mean temperatures exceed 20°C. Diurnal temperature ranges here are among the greatest in Canada, with some valleys experiencing hotter weather than the Prairies.

In Canada's north, spring is very late and summer sees dramatic changes as long hours of sunlight promote rapid growth where suitable soils exist. In the face of the modified angle of the sun, daily temperatures rise rapidly. July mean temperatures in the Yukon increase from 7°C on the Beaufort Sea to 16°C in some inland loca-

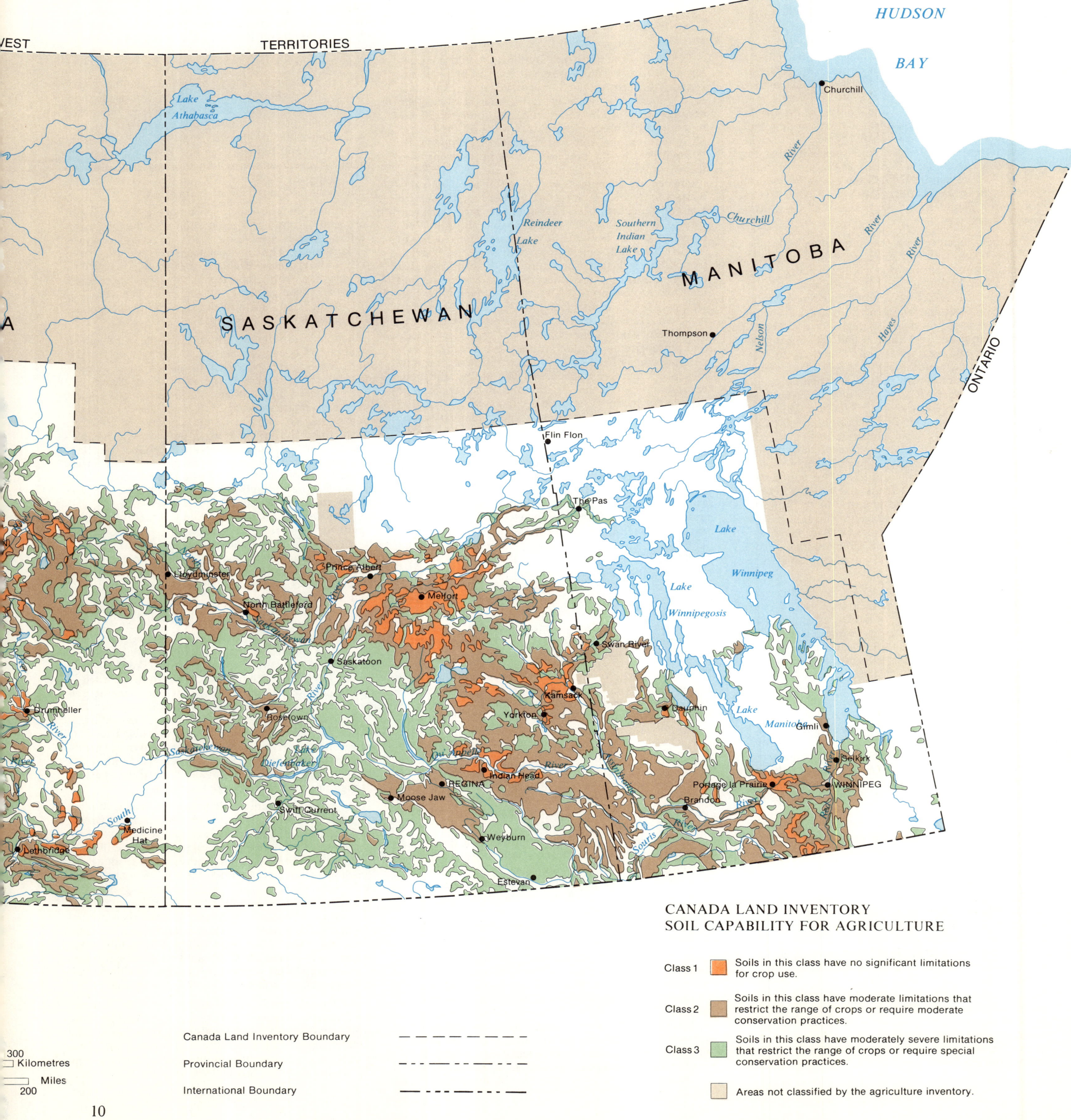

SOIL CAPABILITY F

BRITISH COLUMBIA
ALBERTA
SASKATCHEWAN
MANITOBA

DATA NOT AVAILABLE

Source: Generalized from the 1:1,000,000 Canada Land Inventory *Soil Capability for Agriculture* maps for *Alberta* (1976), *Saskatchewan* (1976) and *Manitoba* (1974), published by the Lands Directorate, Environment Canada.

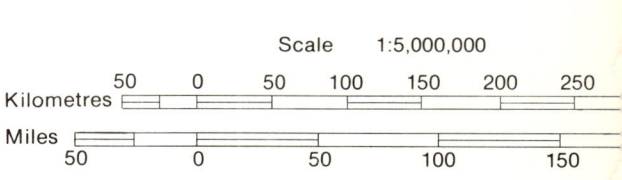

Scale 1:5,000,000

MAP 3

NFB – PHOTOTHEQUE – ONF – Photo by Pierre Gaudard.

tions. Likewise, in the Mackenzie Basin mean daily temperatures for July vary from 7°C along the Beaufort Sea to 16°C along the Mackenzie River, while in the barrens readings are usually in the 10 to 13°C range. As a result of the influence of ice-filled polar waters, the Arctic Archipelago has July mean temperatures between 4 and 7°C.

Precipitation

While temperature limits the broad distribution of crops, it is precipitation and in particular the soil moisture balance that subject agriculture to more localized controls. The balance of precipitation that is left in the soil after percolation and evaporation is that available for growth. The amount of precipitation required for successful agriculture varies with the plant type, soils, and the climate itself. Alfalfa requires about 635 mm over five months whereas hard wheat needs about 460 mm over three and one-half months. Where precipitation is deficient, irrigation may be practicable and soil moisture deficiencies indicate the irrigation demand. Irrigation has generally been profitable in prairie areas where the annual precipitation is less than 330 mm. Precipitation may fall as rain or snow. Rainfall quickly runs off or infiltrates into the soil. Snowfall accumulates until there is a melting opportunity and, accordingly, it assumes additional importance in land management. Generally, lands cannot be worked until they have dried following the spring melt, and if that is delayed the growing season is shortened.

Although the Atlantic Region of Canada is characterized by a generally moist climate, there is considerable variation in average annual precipitation. Precipitation is ample in the growing season: it is spread relatively evenly throughout the year, with a slight emphasis in fall and winter for the more maritime locations and a slight summer maximum for areas more under the continental influence. In Newfoundland, the yearly precipitation varies gradually from a high of more than 1,400 mm in the southeast to less than 900 mm in the Long Peninsula of the northwest. Labrador shares a precipitation pattern with Québec's North Shore as totals decrease from 1,000 mm on the shore to 500 mm in the far north.

Along the south and east coasts of Nova Scotia, average annual precipitation is heavy, exceeding 1,400 mm, and surpassing 1,500 mm on the highlands of Cape Breton. Inland, the total yearly precipitation decreases to 1,150 mm. The Saint John and Bay of Fundy areas in New Brunswick receive 1,150 mm on the average, again with a slight maximum in fall and early winter months. On the other hand, the interior of the province, as well as Prince Edward Island, experience lighter annual precipitation of 900 to 1,000 mm with a slight summer maximum typical of a more continental type of climate.

In Québec, average annual precipitation is heaviest in the Eastern Townships, middle St. Lawrence, and the rugged North Shore areas. The Eastern Townships receive 950 to 1,100 mm and Québec City 1,050 mm, both with a modest summer maximum. Ample precipitation makes tile drainage essential on many farms. In the remainder of the province, factors of elevation and topography greatly influence precipitation characteristics. The central interior may expect 1,000 mm annually, but totals decline to about 400 mm in the north around Ungava Bay.

Snowfall is relatively light on the Atlantic Coast of Nova Scotia where less than 150 cm may fall. Snowfall dominates the winter scene although some winter precipitation occurs in the form of devastating freezing rain. Inland, yearly snowfall increases to over 230 cm. In New Brunswick, average annual snowfall increases from 200 cm on the Bay of Fundy to over 300 cm in the interior. In Prince Edward Island, long-term records indicate an average yearly snowfall of 290 cm at Charlottetown. In Newfoundland, snowfall totals fluctuate widely from less than 200 cm in certain southern coastal sites to over 400 cm at Corner Brook. Snow covers the ground for six to eight months in Labrador, and snowfall is usually quite heavy. Totals vary from 355 cm at Goose Bay to over 500 cm in the southeast corner making it one of the heaviest snowfall areas in Canada. Snowfall is abundant everywhere in Québec and lumbering, tourism, and winter sports are lucrative industries. The Ottawa and St. Lawrence valleys receive 200 to 280 cm annually. In contrast, where moisture-laden air is forced to rise over the steep slopes of the highlands along the North Shore, annual snowfall exceeds 300 cm and reaches 400 cm in some locations.

With the exception of some inland areas, spring and summer are slightly drier than the other seasons. This is fortunate insofar as many soils are close to capacity in their moisture content from the heavier fall and winter precipitation. In a few drier areas, moisture deficiencies are not uncommon in late summer. For example, some locations in Nova Scotia, along the Northumberland Strait in New Brunswick, and Prince Edward Island, as well as in the vicinity of Montréal, do experience water deficiencies. However, they average less than 50 mm per year and agricultural activities are, for the most part, not seriously affected. Generally speaking, excessive wetness in other areas of Canada's eastern region is a much more serious problem for agriculture and often causes delays in planting and harvesting.

The changeable weather which is typical of the Atlantic Region also influences the land capability for, and success of, farming. Although violent storms can occur at any time of the year, they tend to be more frequent and severe in winter. In the fall, southern and eastern portions of the Maritimes and Newfoundland may experience tropical storms spawned in the Carribean. Extremely heavy rains and strong winds may result. Even the critical time of spring planting and early growing season may be marked by gales and driving rain which can cause serious soil erosion, particularly on sloping land or areas as yet without a crop.

In the north and central Shield areas of Ontario, the average annual precipitation increases from 550 mm in the west to 800 mm in the east. Throughout northern areas, winter snowfall varies between 150 and 250 cm. Thus there is a pronounced summer maximum of precipitation with ample rainfall during the growing season. Nowhere is water deficiency above 60 mm and most districts have water deficits at or near zero. Unfortunately, wet weather at harvest time in the Clay Belt proves troublesome to farmers.

Southern Ontario has precipitation that is fairly evenly distributed throughout the year. The average annual precipitation varies from less than 750 mm near Windsor and Renfrew to more than 950 mm near Parry Sound and London. Zones of heavy precipitation occur on the west-facing highland slopes in the lee of the Great Lakes, and along the St. Lawrence. Ontario's snowbelt is found to the east of Georgian Bay and Lake Huron, where 200 to 300 cm of snow per year encourage recreation activities. Winter precipitation in the peninsula of southwestern Ontario can occur as either rain or snow when daytime temperatures hover around freezing. The area around London is well known for its frequent snow bursts. London, to the lee of Lake Huron, experienced several heavy snowfalls in December of 1977. In particular, 57 cm of snow (more than the normal monthly total of 47 cm) was recorded on December 7th. In the three-day period of December 7th to 9th, 101 cm of snow fell. Winds of up to 100 km/h caused severe drifting and isolated this city of 250 thousand people. Freezing rain and ice storms can be equally devastating.

The southern portion of the province is more humid than its northern counterpart, especially during the summer when warm moist air masses dominate. Long periods of excessive dryness or wetness are infrequent owing to the frequency of storms passing through. Summer thunderstorms are common throughout southern Ontario, and are particularly frequent (averaging about five or six thunderstorm days per month in summer) in the London–Sarnia–Windsor triangle. Occasionally hail storms and, infrequently, tornados cause severe local damage to property and crops.

Average annual water deficiencies of 100 to 150 mm occur in the Niagara Peninsula and in the Lake St. Clair area, although less marked moisture deficiencies are common in many parts of southern Ontario in late summer and early fall. Cereal crops, hay, and pasture are susceptible to early-summer drought; both corn and pasture may be adversely affected by late-summer drought. In such circumstances, areas with light-textured soils are most seriously affected, and some irrigation is employed on the sandy soils north of Lake Erie and in the market gardens of Kent and Essex counties.

In the centre of the continental land mass, the Prairies have a true continental climate. The prevailing westerly winds have sacrificed most of their moisture in their passage over successive mountain ranges. Consequently, the Prairie Region is one of the driest in Canada. Total yearly precipitation averages 355 mm at Medicine Hat, 430 mm in Edmonton, 400 mm near Regina, and reaches 610 mm near Lake of the Woods. In contrast to the west coast, the Prairie winter is the driest season with most of the precipitation falling as snow. Snowfall averages 75 to 125 cm in the period from October to April. As mentioned earlier, the notorious Prairie blizzards bring extremely cold temperatures and high winds which whip the snow around. In contrast, during a chinook in southern Alberta, the ground may be free of snow, and winter grazing of some livestock in certain areas may be possible. Maximum precipitation occurs during the summer, when hot weather produces convectional activity. Cyclonic storms are less vigorous in summer, but thunderstorms average about 15 hours per summer month. During June, July, and August, hailstorms occasionally pose a threat to crops and livestock. The region between Edmonton and Calgary experiences more hailstorms than other areas, averaging five days per month during June and July. When annual precipitation is light, as it is here, snowcover and early summer rains are vital to agriculture. In fact, two-thirds to three-quarters of the annual precipitation occurs during the growing season, most in early summer, and the dry fall favours harvesting. It is not surprising that in most agricultural areas, a significant water deficiency exists in late summer. Moisture availability is one of the most critical factors in determining agricultural activities, particularly with respect to the northern limits of wheat, hay, and pasture in northern Alberta and Saskatchewan. The highest water deficiency in the Prairies exists on the Alberta–Saskatchewan boundary north of Medicine Hat where the average annual deficiency exceeds 250 mm. In the event that two or more unusually dry years occur in succession, the crop yields are significantly lessened and the danger of severe soil erosion is increased.

NFB – PHOTOTHEQUE – ONF – Photo by C. Lund.

The success of wheat and other grain crops on the Prairies is determined largely by precipitation. Adequate rainfall at the appropriate times contributes to high yields, but insufficient precipitation will affect both quantity and quality of yields.

The highest annual precipitation recorded in Canada is 4,450 mm which occurred near Ocean Falls, British Columbia, but many coastal areas receive an average of 2,500 to 3,250 mm annually. The Pacific Coast experiences a winter maximum of precipitation, characteristic of the maritime climate. Here, winter conditions are determined by the almost unbroken succession of low-pressure systems with warm moist air which must pass over the Coastal Mountains. To residents of this part of Canada, winter months are overcast and drizzly day-after-day from October to March. Umbrellas are essential in this area, which endures the cloudiest, wettest, winter season in Canada. On average, at the Vancouver airport, there are 23 rainy days in December. In most lowland areas, where winter temperatures generally remain above freezing, most of the annual precipitation falls as rain. However, on the high elevations of the coastal ranges the great accumulation of snowfall has encouraged winter recreation in accessible areas. By contrast, the leeward mountain slopes and coastal valleys receive considerably less annual precipitation. While still maintaining a winter maximum of precipitation, locations such as Victoria on the leeward side of Vancouver Island record less than 750 mm of precipitation per year, a marked contrast to the 3,800 mm recorded in other parts of the Island. However, these precipitation statistics for the west coast are very misleading because the pronounced winter maximum levels overshadow the long, dry, sunny summer season. The amount of moisture available during the growing season is low. For example, the Vancouver area normally receives only 250 mm of rain between May and September. A moisture deficiency is most acute in July and August when this same location receives less than

75 mm of precipitation. The average annual water deficiency, though less severe than in the interior valleys, still varies between 100 and 200 mm in Vancouver and Victoria.

The dry, semi-arid, southern interior valleys of British Columbia are a striking contrast to the lush forests and heavy rains of the Pacific Coast. Located only 300 to 500 km east of the coast, southern sections of the Okanagan and Thompson valleys have virtually semi-desert vegetation. The interior valleys represent one of the driest climates in Canada, receiving less than 280 mm of precipitation annually. Precipitation is distributed relatively evenly throughout the year. During the winter months snowfall totals 75 to 125 cm in the valleys and 200 to 380 cm on higher slopes. Summer precipitation, limited as it is, occurs mostly during intense afternoon thunderstorms. The warm summers with relatively low humidity are favourable to fruit production, but irrigation from mountain streams is necessary to supplement the meager rainfall during the growing season (100 to 150 mm near Kamloops, Lillooet, and Lake Okanagan). The northern areas of the province exhibit precipitation characteristics not too dissimilar to the southern interior and the northern Prairies. Precipitation ranges from 350 to 1,000 mm in the central region to less than 500 mm further north. Summer and fall are the wettest seasons.

In the Yukon, the average annual precipitation of 225 to 500 mm is distributed relatively evenly throughout the year, with a slight emphasis during July and August. Snowfall averages between 100 and 200 cm, with the larger amount occurring on the west-facing slopes of the Mackenzie Mountains and the Liard Valley. Moving inland, the Mackenzie Basin, as most other parts of the Northwest Territories, experiences light average annual precipitation. The average moisture deficiency, 200 to 400 mm annually, is a deterrent to agricultural activities which might otherwise be made possible in some areas by climatic and soil conditions. In the barrens, annual precipitation decreases from south to north ranging from 300 to 175 mm. Snowfall accounts for half of the total precipitation in this area of longer, colder winters. Average annual precipitation decreases from a maximum of 375 mm in southern Baffin Island to less than 75 mm at Eureka on Ellesmere Island. As winters become more dominant in the far north, snowfall accounts for 70 per cent of yearly precipitation.

Frost-Free Period

The mean number of days between the last occurrence of frost in spring and the first occurrence of frost in fall is taken as the frost-free period. Spring and fall frosts and the number of frost-free days are of vital concern in agriculture for classifying areas suitable for certain crops and in deciding planting schedules. The interval is particularly useful in deciding where it is safe to grow tender crops such as tomatoes, corn, beans, and blossomed fruits.

> "Although plant damage frequently occurs when air temperature drops to 0°C, many plants can withstand lower temperatures. The ability of a plant to withstand freezing temperatures varies not only with the type of plant but also with the previous weather, the duration of freezing and the rate of temperature change. Usually when the measured screen temperature ranges between –1.7 to 0°C, damage occurs to tender crops such as beans, tomatoes, corn and cucumbers. At temperatures of –3.9 to –2.2°C potatoes, sugar beets, celery and onions are damaged. Damage to annuals, even to hardy plants such as cabbages and turnips, is usually severe when temperatures drop to -4.4°C or less." (Brown *et al.*, 1968).

With field crops in particular, the occurrence of the first (particularly an early) killing fall frost is more serious than the last spring frost. Factors such as latitude, geographic location, local topography, soil type, drainage, clearing size, elevation, general weather systems, continental, maritime, and lacustrine factors all influence the incidence of frost, and thereby the land capability. Local controls such as topography, land use, and close proximity to water bodies are especially important. Because of this, marked contrasts in the length of the frost-free season over short distances are evident in all parts of the country. Frost-free statistics may differ considerably from year to year, and this variability must be considered in planning many farming operations.

It should be noted that the growing season is not identical to the frost-free period. The growth of grass is slow when daily minimum temperatures fall below 0°C and at that time maximum temperatures would usually be about 11°C and the mean temperature about 5°C. Thus the dates in spring and fall, corresponding to a mean temperature of 5°C, are often used as the start and end of the growing season (Chapman and Brown, 1966). The growing season begins three to five weeks earlier, and ends three to six weeks later than the average frost-free period. Simply stated, it is the period which favours plant growth.

Within the eastern region, there is a wide variety in the length and time of the frost-free season. In the inland areas of Newfoundland, the difference in the period between frosts may be less than 90 days. The ocean's moderating effect in coastal areas of Nova Scotia, New Brunswick, and Prince Edward Island results in a frost-free period of 120 to 130 days between late May and early October. A few small pockets in the Annapolis Valley have up to 140 days without frost while Yarmouth has up to 160 days, longer than any other location along the Atlantic Coast. The higher upland elevations of Nova Scotia's inland experience a much briefer frost-free season of less than 100 days. The situation is much the same in New Brunswick, where the duration of the frost-free season ranges from 130 days along the Bay of Fundy to less than 90 days in the northern interior.

In northern Québec and Labrador, the serious problems posed by a short frost-free period of 40 to 80 days are further compounded by the widespread presence of permafrost. To the south, along the North Shore, Sept-Iles has a more moderate but still restrictive climate for agriculture. With mean spring and fall frost dates of June 10th and September 5th, the 85-day frost-free period and resultant growing season are brief. The Lac St-Jean and Saguenay River area experiences a frost-free period of 100 to 110 days which is slightly longer than other geographical locations to the south.

In the Gaspé, some fortunate shoreline sites may have up to 130 frost-free days, and the city of Gaspé experiences a frost-free season between June 5th and September 15th. The inland areas of the peninsula have a considerably shorter frost-free season of 90 days. Along the United States border in the Eastern Townships, the mean spring and fall frost dates are around May 31st and September 15th leaving a frost-free period of just over 100 days. Parts of the Ottawa and St. Lawrence valleys have the longest growing season in Québec. Montréal experiences a mean spring frost date in mid-May, while the mean fall frost date is delayed to the end of September. Therefore, Montréal and vicinity have the distinct advantage of the province's longest growing season and a 150-day frost-free period for agriculture. This is evident in the variety of specialized cash crops including vegetables, tree fruits, small fruits, tobacco, and greenhouse/nursery products that are cultivated for the large Montréal market.

NFB – PHOTOTHEQUE – ONF – Photo by Ben Low.

Around Montréal, the long growing season and frost-free period are two factors that permit farmers to cultivate a large selection of vegetables for the urban market.

Ontario's central and northern areas experience short frost-free periods which seriously restrict agriculture. In the far north, frost is experienced until late June. Proceeding southward, the last spring frost occurs generally around June 10th in the Timmins and Cochrane area, June 5th near New Liskeard, and May 31st in the Sault Ste. Marie–Sudbury–North Bay locations. The mean fall frost date in northern Ontario varies from late August in the far north, to September 25th at Sault Ste. Marie. In the Northern Clay Belt, the average first fall frost date is the first week of September on high ground, and earlier on low peat areas. On the average, frost is a hazard to grain crops in any area where the first fall frost occurs prior to September 10th. In general, the northern Ontario region has a frost-free period from less than 50 days to a maximum of 120 days near Sault Ste. Marie. Agricultural activities are largely dictated by this critical frost-free period, which, in northern Ontario particularly, is subject to wide local variation. In the Northern Clay Belt, many crops such as field corn will not mature so the emphasis is on early maturing crops such as potatoes, barley, and silage.

In southern Ontario, late spring and early fall frosts are suppressed by the moderating influence of the Great Lakes. This provides an immense advantage and a certain security to specialty fruit and vegetable farmers along the lakes. The near-freezing waters of the Great Lakes in early spring hold back the start of the growing season along the shoreline, until the danger from a late killing frost is over. This is an advantage to agriculture because the retarding of early growth protects crops, particularly orchards, from late spring frosts. The seven- to ten-day delay to the start of the growing season is often a needed measure of protection to southern Ontario agriculture. However, these relatively cool waters continue to reduce the number of growing degree-days until August when the accumulated difference between shoreline and more inland locations is at a maximum. In other words, although the moderating influence of the Great Lakes results in a longer growing season and frost-free period, the total heat available for crop growth is less along the lake perimeters.

In the extreme southwestern corner of the province, the mean spring frost date varies from April 30th around Pelee Island to about May 12th in areas west of the Niagara Escarpment, while the mean fall frost date is delayed until mid-October. Thus, this region with an average frost-free period of 140 to 180 days is one of Canada's finest agricultural areas. To the north and east, the mean spring frost date is advanced to mid-May along the shores of Lake Ontario and the St. Lawrence River, and to early June in Algonquin Park. Similarly, the average date of the first fall frost is moved forward to late September or early October in eastern Ontario, and to mid-September in Algonquin Park. Thus, compared to the long frost-free period of 180 days near Pelee Island, the Sarnia, Chatham, Welland, and Toronto areas average 150 to 160 days. The season is 140 days along the St. Lawrence, 125 days along the southern edge of the Shield, and 100 days or less in Algonquin Park. In areas where the frost-free period is longest, in Kent and Essex counties, along Lake Erie, and in the Niagara fruit belt, farmers make use of the longer growing season for cash crops, tree fruit and tender fruit production, and early vegetable gardening. In many locations, two crops may be harvested. In the central and eastern portions of the province, where the growing season is shorter and crops are more susceptible to risk of frost damage, mixed farming, beef, and livestock, as well as dairying, are more important than cash crops.

In the Prairies, southwestern Alberta has the longest frost-free period, 125 days near Medicine Hat. The frost-free season varies between 70 and 110 days throughout the southern sections of Saskatchewan and Manitoba. Moving north, west, or east from the Lethbridge–Medicine Hat area, the mean spring frost date is delayed from late May to mid-June, while the mean fall frost date advances from mid-September to late August. In these agricultural areas, locations experiencing a mean fall frost date after September 1st have a moderate hazard for cereal grains while croplands with fall frost before August 25th are vulnerable to a serious frost hazard. In fact, the greatest proportion of the grain growing area of the Prairies averages an 80- to 120-day frost-free period, which is barely adequate for some grain crops to reach maturity. However, improvements in strains of hardy wheat mean that frost is not assessed as a serious threat in areas with a frost-free period of 90 days or longer.

JANUARY MEAN TEMPERATURE (°C)
MAP 4

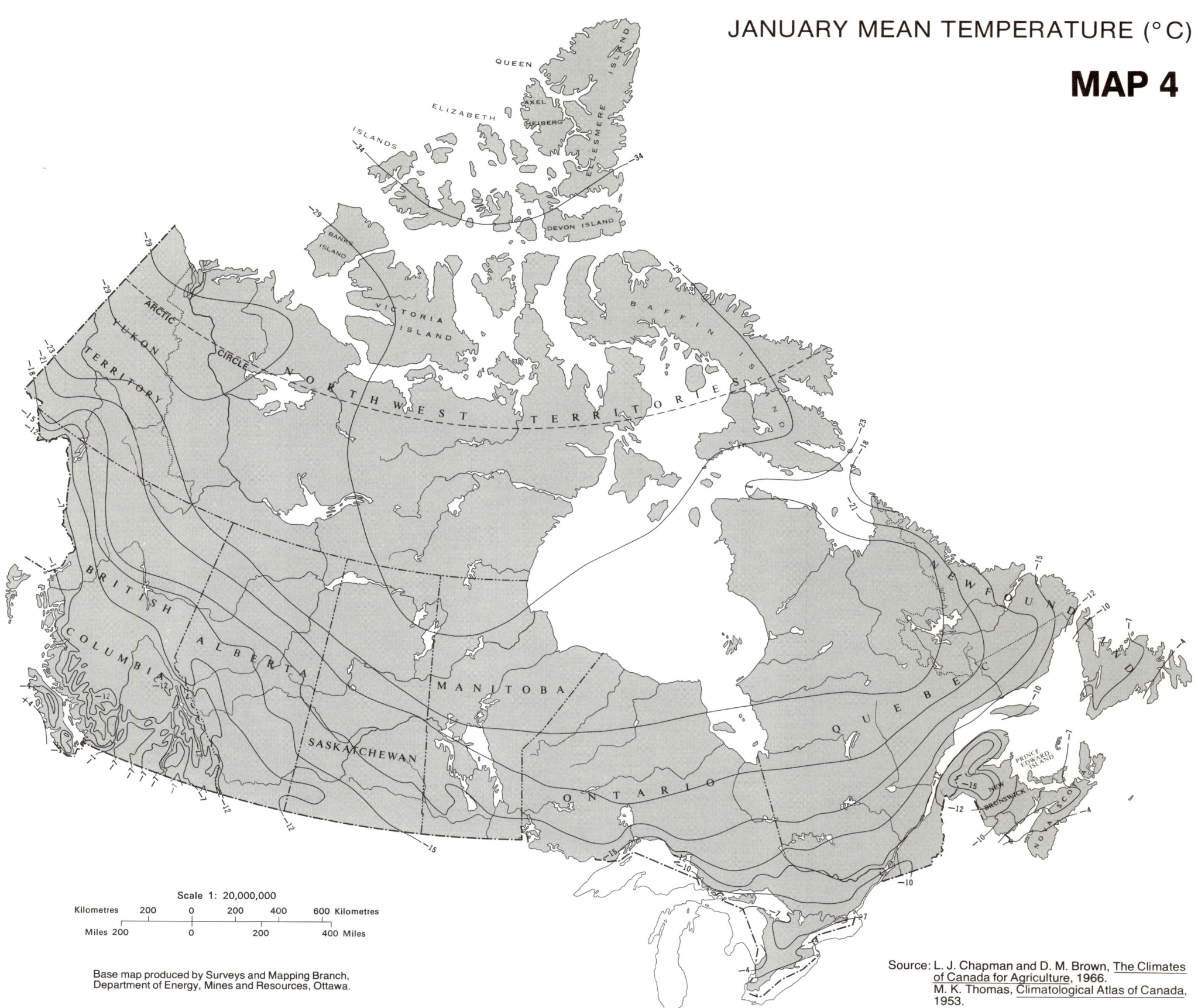

Base map produced by Surveys and Mapping Branch, Department of Energy, Mines and Resources, Ottawa.

Source: L. J. Chapman and D. M. Brown, The Climates of Canada for Agriculture, 1966.
M. K. Thomas, Climatological Atlas of Canada, 1953.

Not surprisingly, Canada's longest frost-free period, 240 days, occurs on the southern tip of Vancouver Island. The Pacific Coast generally averages 180 to 200 frost-free days depending on the extent of the maritime influence. For example, Victoria gets an early spring start with the mean spring frost usually occurring around April 1st, while the mean fall frost is not expected until December 1st. The wide variation in the duration of the frost-free period in the interior is due in large part to local factors including elevation, terrain, slope, air drainage, susceptibility to cold air masses, and influence of nearby water bodies. Throughout the southeast part of the province, the frost-free period ranges from 60 days in areas of higher elevation to 140 days in certain protected valleys. In the lower Fraser and Okanagan valleys, where frost damage to fruit and vegetable crops is a critical concern and where protective measures such as smudge pots are not an uncommon sight, the frost-free period is 180 and 140 days respectively. To the north, the length of the frost-free time tapers off rapidly to between 50 and 70 days in the interior, and frost can occur in mid-summer.

In the Yukon, the frost-free period varies considerably but reaches a maximum of 85 days at Watson Lake. Eastward to the Mackenzie Basin where the mean monthly temperatures are below freezing from October to April, the frost-free season varies from 50 to 100 days, depending on local geography. The barrens experience long cold winters with mean monthly temperatures below 0°C for eight or nine months. Frost is possible during any month and the frost-free season is confined to a period of 40 to 60 days. Across much of the Arctic Archipelago, there is no appreciable period free from frost.

Growing Degree-days above 5°C

Growing degree-days is a cumulative measure of the duration and warmth of the growing season. Most grasses, crops, and ornamental plants in Canada exhibit little if any growth when the daily minimum temperature drops below 0°C and the mean daily reading falls to 5°C. Those dates in spring and fall correspond to a mean daily temperature of 5°C, and generally indicate the beginning and end of the growing season. As such dates occur earlier in the spring and later in the fall than the average date of the last spring and first fall frosts, the growing season is slightly longer than the frost-free period. For agricultural purposes, the mean annual number of degree-days above 5°C takes into account both duration and warmth of the growing season and, therefore, as an index, reflects the total amount of heat available for plant growth. The number of degree-days above 5°C is accumulated between the dates of occurrence of 5°C in both the spring and fall. The growing degree-day measure has been widely used in the food processing industry to schedule plantings so that harvests do not occur within too brief a period for processing at the factories. The concept has also been used to delimit areas suitable for particular crop types, and as a means of predicting the hatching dates of various insects.

The wide range of values found within the Atlantic Provinces and Québec is illustrated clearly on Map 7. Locations such as the Annapolis Valley, the southeastern edge of Nova Scotia, portions of the Saint John River valley, and Prince Edward Island, which register 2,750 to 3,000 degree-days, are particularly favoured. Once again, however, it is the Ottawa and St. Lawrence valleys which possess the most advantageous growing season conditions. The highest degree-day values in Québec occur in the vicinity of Montréal where the index exceeds 3,250. The 3,000 degree-day line stretches down the Ottawa Valley from Pembroke, along the Shield edge, and as far along the St. Lawrence River as Québec City before it turns southward to divide the Eastern Townships. In these more favoured locations, silage corn, and to a more limited extent early hardy corn hybrids, are important crops. With the exception of the Lac St-Jean area which is encircled by the 2,000 and 2,250 degree-day lines, the index readings decrease rapidly to 1,500 in both the inland areas of Gaspé and in the rocky Shield area of central Québec. In the northern portions of Québec and Labrador there are less than 1,000 degree-days recorded.

In Ontario, the 2,000 degree-day isoline runs south of both Lake Nipigon and White River, and through Kapuskasing and Cochrane. The 2,500 degree-day isoline extends up the Ottawa Valley into the New Liskeard Clay Belt, while major northern cities, such as Sault Ste. Marie and Sudbury, lie near the 2,750 degree-day line. The 3,000 degree-day isoline appears to separate less advantageous areas from the more prosperous. This

JULY MEAN TEMPERATURE (°C)
MAP 5

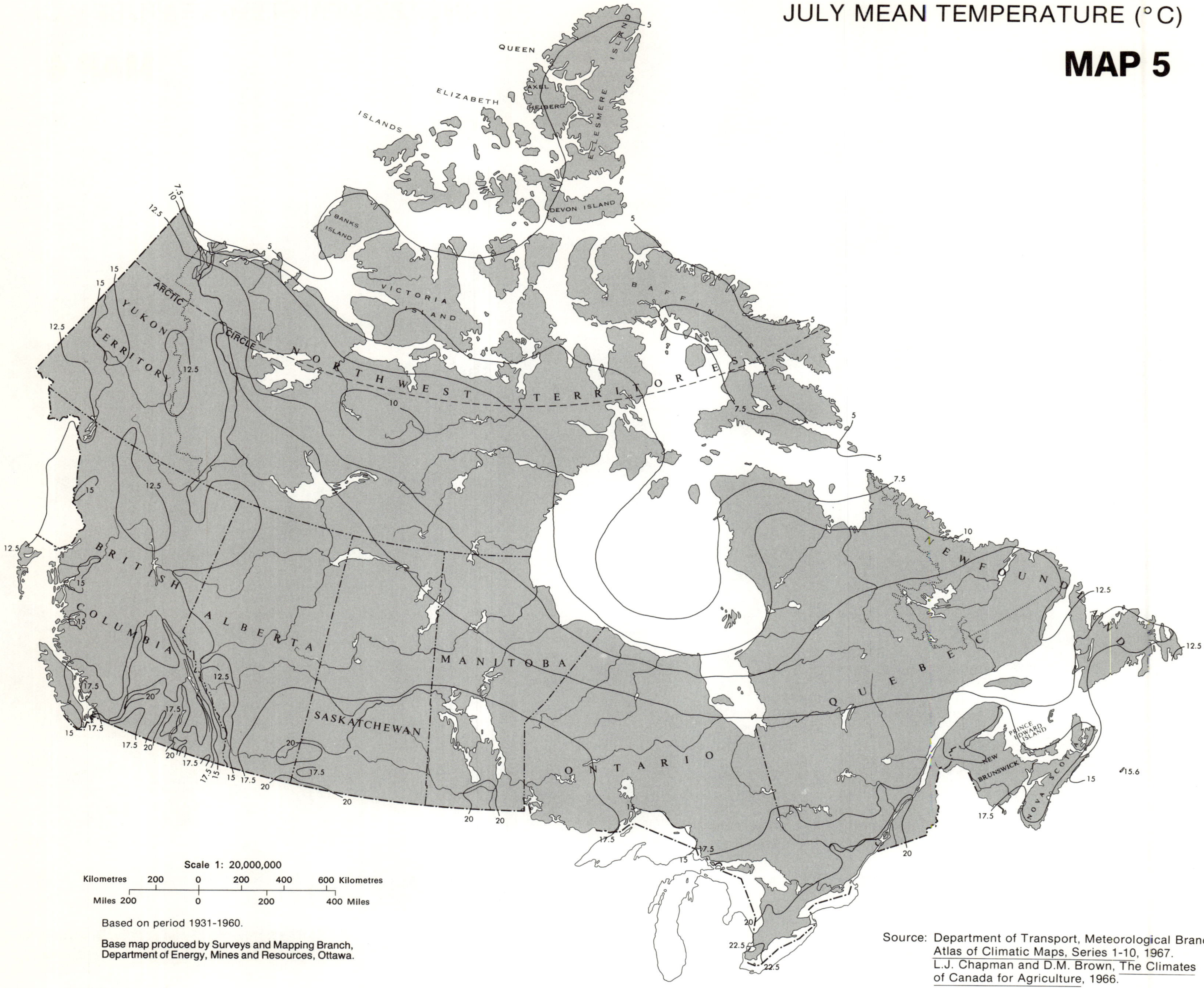

Scale 1: 20,000,000

Based on period 1931-1960.

Base map produced by Surveys and Mapping Branch, Department of Energy, Mines and Resources, Ottawa.

Source: Department of Transport, Meteorological Branch, Atlas of Climatic Maps, Series 1-10, 1967.
L.J. Chapman and D.M. Brown, The Climates of Canada for Agriculture, 1966.

3,000 degree-day limit is marked by an isoline which extends from Parry Sound on Georgian Bay, loops down along part of the southern edge of the Canadian Shield, and then swings north to Pembroke on the Ottawa River. The climatic conditions for agriculture improve southward as the 3,500 degree-day isoline links Goderich on Lake Huron, to the London area, then skirts the north shore of Lake Ontario, extending along the St. Lawrence toward Cornwall. As a general rule, silage corn is an important crop for livestock in locations with fewer than 3,500 degree-days while corn, soybeans, and tobacco are important crops where degree-days exceed the 3,500 value. Although the Niagara fruit belt registers fewer than 4,000 degree-days, the mild winter temperatures give the area a major advantage for tender fruit crops by protecting them from killing temperatures. Once again, it is obvious why the southwestern Ontario region is able to support a wide range of specialized crops. The 4,000 degree-day boundary generally indicates the northern extent of agricultural areas devoted to specialized production of grain corn, sugar beets, soybeans, and other cash crops. Pelee Island records the highest value in Canada, with average annual readings of 4,450 degree-days.

Across the Prairies, the values drop from a maximum of 3,000 degree-days south of Winnipeg to fewer than 1,000 near Hudson Bay. Grain, corn, and sugar beets are cultivated only in the warmest areas, and cereal grains are best confined to areas with more than 2,000 degree-days. North of that limit, agricultural activities are usually restricted to cultivation of hardier mixed grains, rapeseed, and fodder crops. For example, the Peace River area registers just over 2,000 degree-days but warmth is condensed into a short frost-free period

Photo by Agriculture Canada.

Diversified agricultural production is the nature of farms established on the arable soils of the Peace River district.

varying from 60 to 100 days. However, the longer days offer some compensation. The plan is to cultivate rapidly maturing and frost-resistant grain or forage crops which will take advantage of the long summer days and which will still survive the late spring and early fall frosts. Wheat, rapeseed, rye, oats, and alfalfa are grown in the Peace River area.

In western Canada, only a few locations can approach the high degree-day levels of southern Ontario. Limited sites in the southern Okanagan Valley register 4,000 degree-days. Generally, the Okanagan, Fraser, and Thompson River valleys receive 3,000 to 3,500 degree-days. Unlike Ontario, where the 4,000 degree-day isoline has particular relevance for specialty and cash crops, this level seems to have no special significance for fruit crops in British Columbia. Vancouver and Victoria record 3,500 and 3,000 degree-days respectively. Once again, the pattern of mountains and river valleys is reflected in the degree-day data in the interior of British Columbia. Readings generally vary from 1,500 to 3,500 degree-days depending on elevation and topography.

In Canada's north, the central area of the Yukon together with the central and southern portions of the Mackenzie Basin receives more than 1,500 degree-days, the highest levels north of 60° latitude. While the northern section of the Yukon and the eastern margin of the Mackenzie Basin record between 1,000 and 1,500 degree-days, the remainder of the barrens and high Arctic regions register fewer than 1,000 degree-days in their much abbreviated growing season.

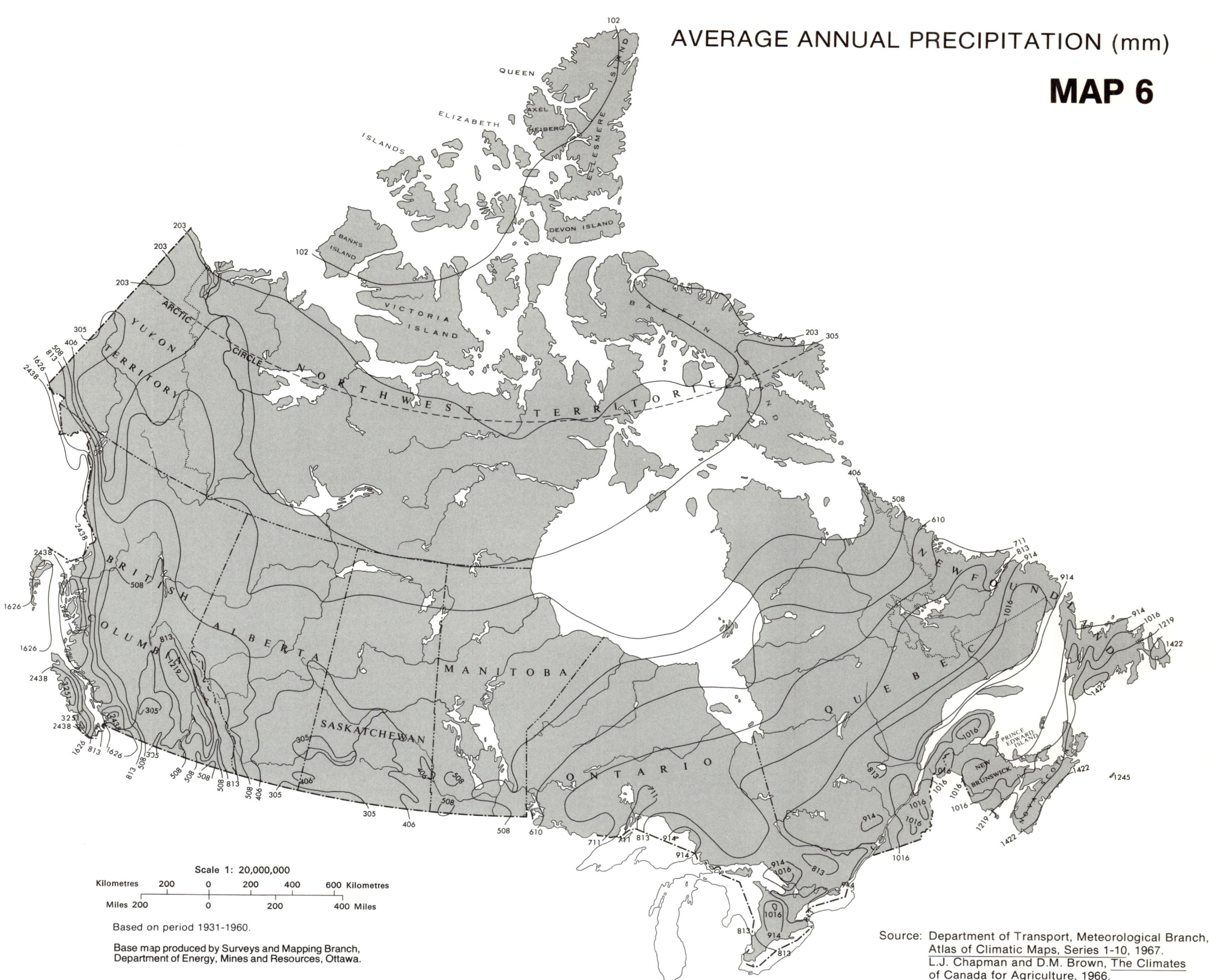

AVERAGE ANNUAL PRECIPITATION (mm)

MAP 6

Scale 1: 20,000,000

Based on period 1931-1960.

Base map produced by Surveys and Mapping Branch, Department of Energy, Mines and Resources, Ottawa.

Source: Department of Transport, Meteorological Branch, *Atlas of Climatic Maps, Series 1-10*, 1967.
L.J. Chapman and D.M. Brown, *The Climates of Canada for Agriculture*, 1966.

Bright Sunshine

The light factor or photoperiod becomes important in the north, where certain crops capable of continuous growth through the long summer day mature early enough to escape killing frosts in late August and September.

The coasts of Newfoundland, with their frequent blanket of fog, receive only 1,400 hours of bright sunshine annually. New Brunswick, Nova Scotia, Prince Edward Island, and portions of Québec receive 1,600 hours of sun in coastal areas, and 1,800 hours further inland. In northern Québec, the amount of sunshine is less than 1,400 hours. In northern Ontario, mean annual sunshine ranges from 1,500 hours in the James Bay region to 2,000 hours near Lake of the Woods. In southern Ontario, totals vary between 1,800 and 2,000 hours, with long periods of bright sun during the growing season. The Prairies are known for their high clear summer skies. Average yearly sunshine of up to 2,400 hours qualifies the south-central Prairies as the sunniest part of Canada. Mean annual total hours of bright sunshine decrease rapidly through British Columbia. While interior locations may receive 1,800 hours yearly, parts of the Pacific Coast receive less than 1,400 hours. In the north, the annual number of bright sunshine hours varies from 2,000 at Fort Smith to 1,400 at Frobisher Bay.

An Agroclimatic Resource Index

One problem that arises in studying the land's potential for agriculture is that comparison of the resource base in different locations is very difficult. One of the more neglected factors has been climate. It was to this problem that Williams (1975) of Agriculture Canada addressed himself, and, in the process of investigating a qualitative approach to evaluation of certain climatic parameters, he devised an Agroclimatic Resource Index (ACRI). He reasoned that from an agroclimatic standpoint, the length of the frost-free period, a temperature yardstick, was of prime importance. The frost-free season is the average number of days between the average dates of the last spring and first fall frosts, based on the occurrence of 0°C or lower in a Stevenson screen (thermometer shelter). The longer the frost-free period, the more valuable is an area for agricultural production, particularly of temperature-sensitive crops. Hence, this measure became the basic element in formulating ACRI.

The following description of ACRI methodology and research findings is based on Williams' original paper (1975). A map is available at the scale of 1:5,000,000 which shows the normal frost-free season across Canada (Canada Department of Agriculture, 1976). When the number of frost-free days at any point on this map was divided by 60 (the shortest duration for which there was an isoline on the frost-free map), a convenient index was produced. Adjustments were then made to the index to account for two other important types of climatic restrictions on agriculture. In regions with a significant shortage of moisture such as in the drier parts of the Prairies and some interior valleys of British Columbia, the index was modified downward, by applying Sly's data on moisture index (Canada Department of Agriculture, 1976), to reflect the degree of moisture limitation. On the other hand, some coastal locations have a different climatic shortcoming. In spite of a long frost-free season, summer heat may be inadequate for crops requiring a long growing season to fully mature. Therefore, utilizing growing degree-day information, the agroclimatic index was again altered downward to reflect the lack of sufficient summer heat in coastal areas. The resultant agroclimatic index, ACRI, has values which vary from 1.0 in the north or agricultural frontier areas to 3.0 in the south near Windsor, Ontario. Map 8 illustrates the ACRI values of different locations in Canada.

The practical utility of ACRI depends on its success in reflecting the variation in possibilities for agricultural production. However, evaluating the extent of agreement between ACRI values and actual land productivity or crop yield is more complicated than it may first appear. For example, a specific crop may mature in one location with 80 days remaining before the first fall frost, but in a second location the same crop may mature with only 20 days left before the first frost. Yield statistics for that crop in two locations may not be conspicuously different, but the potential for agriculture certainly varies.

However, for purpose of comparison, hay is one crop

15

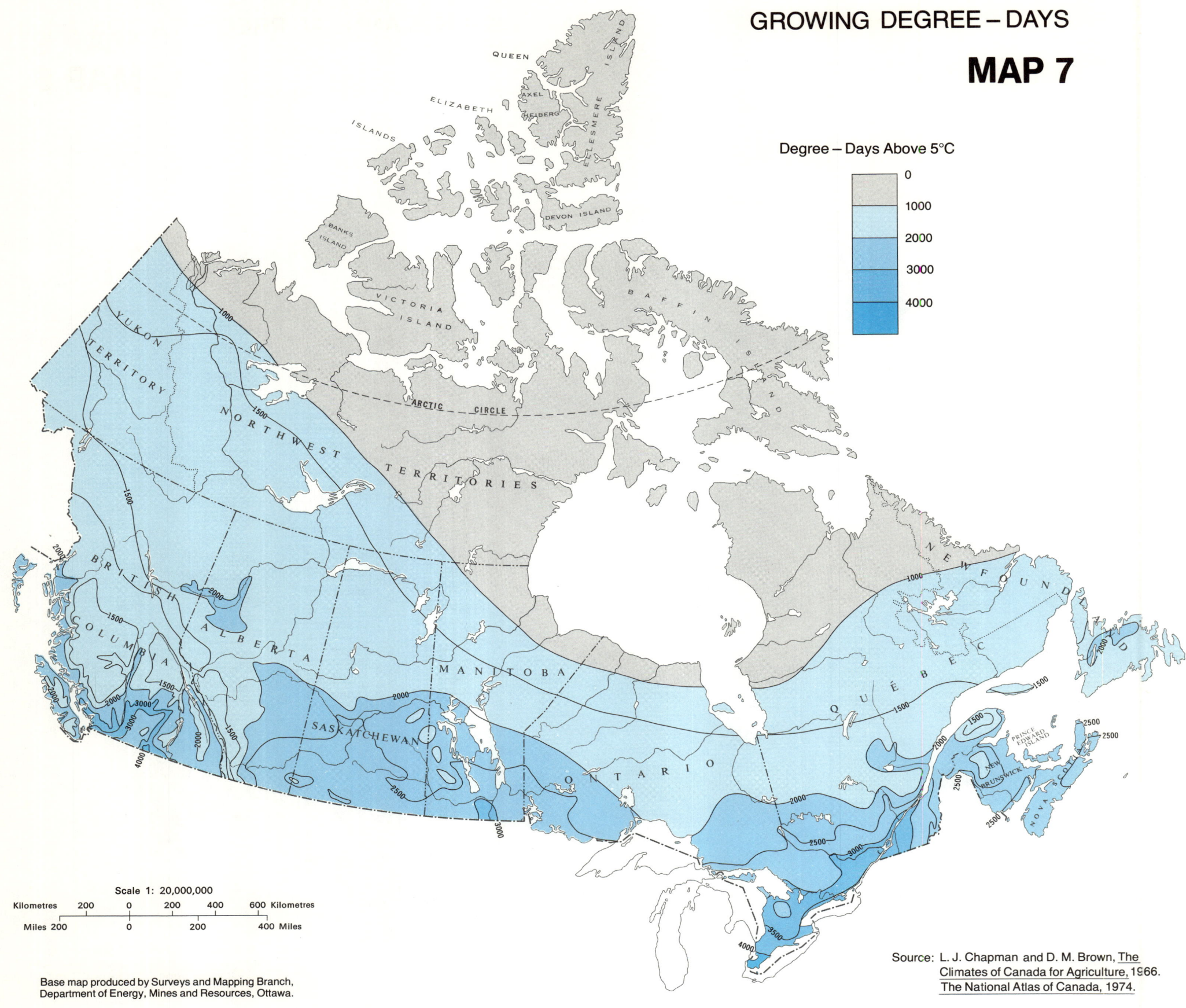

which avoids this difficulty. Hay continues to grow throughout the season and, where weather/climate factors permit, may be harvested several times during the growing season. As a forage crop it is cultivated across Canada and is of almost universal interest and importance to farmers. Table 3 indicates the degree of conformity between ACRI values and hay yields. In the first column is the generalized provincial ACRI value. The second column reflects the ratio of the provincial ACRI to the ACRI value of 3 for Kent and Essex counties in southern Ontario—the highest readings in Canada. The third column is the provincial hay yield per ha as expressed as a decimal fraction of the Kent–Essex hay yields. As can be seen, the relative hay yields and ACRI values are quite similar for most provinces except British Columbia. Had ACRI been based solely on the frost-free period, without the downward adjustment for degree-days, the degree of correlation in British Columbia would have been higher. Perhaps the long frost-free season here is particularly important for this crop, or other factors may complicate the hay/climate relationship.

Williams also compared production of a number of field crops in Essex County with that in two Prairie census divisions, and his analyses provided further confirmation that the potential for agricultural production and the agroclimatic resources, as indicated by ACRI values, were roughly proportional. In general, a location with an ACRI value of 3.0 should be considered twice as valuable, from the agroclimatic standpoint, as an area with an ACRI assessment of 1.5.

TABLE 3.

Agroclimatic resource index and hay yields, by province

Province	ACRI value	$\frac{ACRI}{3}$	Hay yield 1969 to 1973 as ratio to that of Kent-Essex counties
Ontario	2.44	.81	.80
Québec	2.00	.67	.61
Prince Edward Island	1.82	.61	.60
Manitoba	1.81	.60	.57
Nova Scotia	1.74	.58	.60
New Brunswick	1.70	.57	.59
Alberta	1.50	.50	.53
Saskatchewan	1.44	.48	.47
British Columbia	1.35	.45	.83
Newfoundland	1.21	.40	
Yukon and Northwest Territories	1.00	.33	
Kent-Essex counties	3.00	1.00	1.00

Source: Williams, 1975. _An Agroclimatic Resource Index for Canada and Its Use in Describing Agricultural Land Losses._

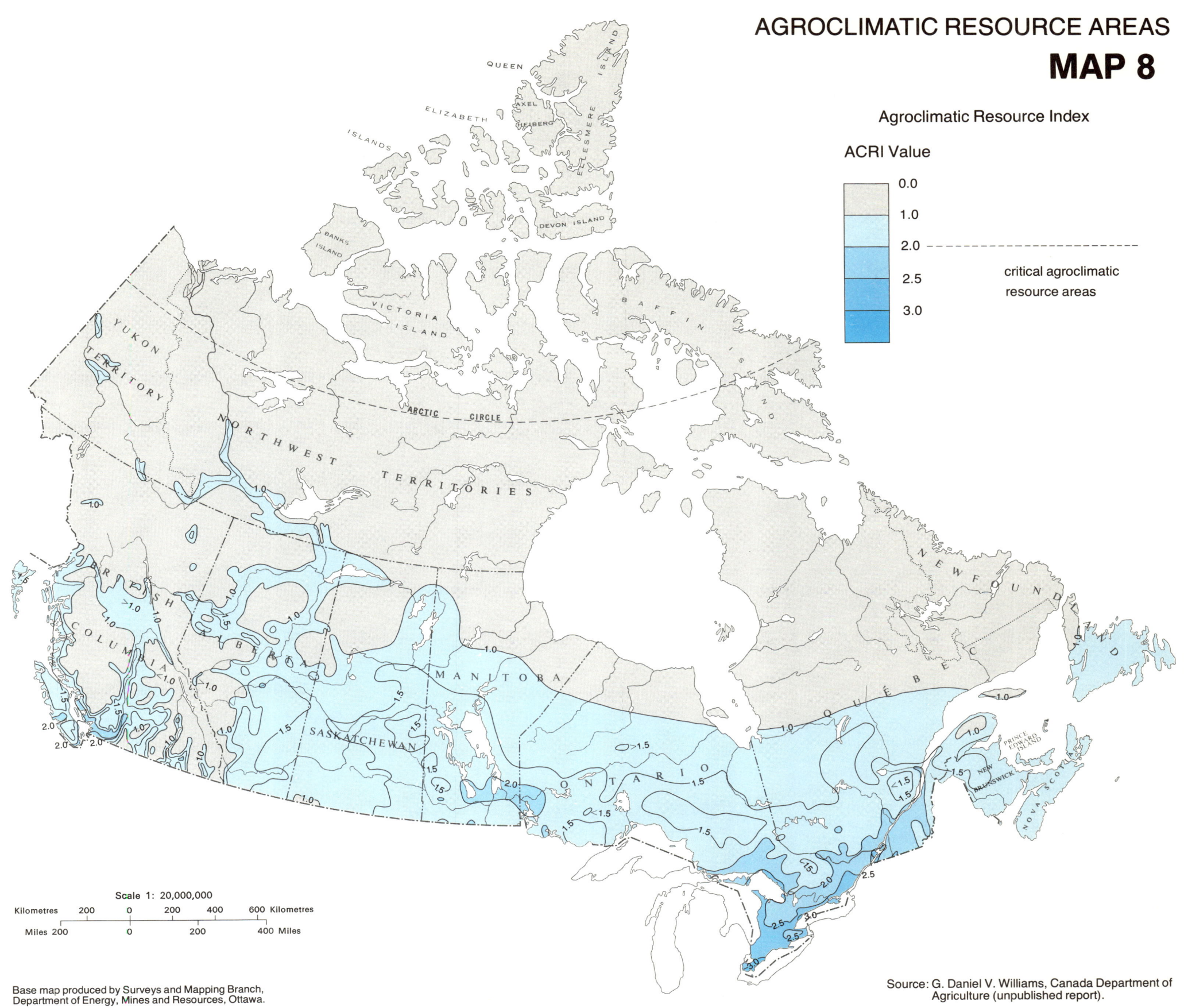

AGROCLIMATIC RESOURCE AREAS
MAP 8

Agroclimatic Resource Index

Source: G. Daniel V. Williams, Canada Department of Agriculture (unpublished report).

Base map produced by Surveys and Mapping Branch, Department of Energy, Mines and Resources, Ottawa.

ACRI then permits comparison of areas which lose or gain farmland. First as a general picture, compare the provincial ACRI levels with the change in total farmland and improved farmland areas in 1956, 1966, and 1976 in Table 4 and Table 5. In 1976, Ontario and Québec had 15 per cent of Canada's total farmland (16 per cent of Canada's improved farmland), but about 22 per cent of the farmland resource when agroclimatic factors are considered. From 1966 to 1976, gains in total farmland were experienced mainly in Alberta and British Columbia which have ACRI values of 1.50 and 1.35 respectively, while considerable farmland was lost in Ontario and Québec, the only two provinces with provincial ACRI values of at least 2.00. As can be seen in the accompanying tables, of those provinces experiencing net losses of farmland and improved farmland between 1966 and 1976, Ontario and Québec accounted for the greatest proportion by far, 77.5 per cent of total farmland loss and 89.6 per cent of improved farmland loss.

The unbalanced distribution of agroclimatic resources is further illustrated by Table 6 based on 1971 census division data in relation to ACRI values. Less than 15 per cent of Canada's total farmland was located in areas where ACRI values equalled or exceeded 2.0, while 38 per cent of total farmland possessed agroclimatic resources which were less than half the ACRI value of Kent and Essex counties. This is particularly evident in Saskatchewan. It has over one-third of Canadian farmland but the ACRI value is less than 2.0 for all Saskatchewan's farmland, and values less than 1.5 predominate. In 1971, census divisions that had the climatically most-favoured five per cent of Canadian farmland, with ACRI values of 2.5 or greater, also contained 42 per cent of Canada's urban population. Consequently, these lands continue to be under the most pressure from other land uses including urban development and transportation.

From 1961 to 1971, there was a net loss of 2.74 million ha of total farmland with ACRI values of 1.5 or greater, and a net gain of 1.58 million ha with poorer agroclimatic resources (Table 7). In effect, the loss of agroclimatic land resources was much greater than the 1.16 million ha net loss would suggest. Only Ontario and Québec have any farmland with an ACRI value of 2.5 or greater. Between 1961 and 1971, these two provinces had a net loss of nearly 300 thousand ha of such agricultural land. Historical comparisons at the more detailed level of census divisions are often difficult, and occasionally impossible, because of boundary changes between census periods. In the period from 1961 to 1971, this is the situation in British Columbia where drastic boundary alterations preclude any meaningful comparison at that level. However, census divisions in the nine remaining provinces were studied. As a result of boundary changes in individual census divisions, several of the units had to be aggregated to ensure valid area comparisons. Of the resulting 205 single or grouped census divisions, only 36 had net gains in total farmland between 1961 and 1971. Of these 36 divisions, only two had ACRI values of 2.0 or greater.

To further illustrate the need to consider agroclimatic resources in analysing farmland losses, the term "Agroclimatic Resource Hectare", or ACRH, was coined. This is the product of the ACRI value and the number of ha of farmland. ACRH was calculated for selected census divisions for purposes of comparison. Here is an example. Between 1961 and 1971, in Alberta Census Division No. 13, total farmland increased by 76,704 ha. During this same period, total farmland in York and Peel census divisions in Ontario decreased by 23,134 and 17,945 ha respectively. From a strictly statistical point of view, it would appear that the one Alberta census division's gain of 76,704 would more than compensate for the two Ontario divisions' loss of 41,079 ha. But, the 2.5 ACRI value of land in York and Peel is more than twice the value of 1.2 in Alberta's Census Division No. 13. The relative gain in agricultural land resources in this latter division, taking the climate into account was ACRH = 1.2 x 76,704 = 92,045. The relative loss in York and Peel was ACRH = 2.5 x 41,079 = 102,698. Thus, the agroclimatic land resource loss in the two census divisions in Ontario was greater than the gain in Alberta's Census Division No. 13. Figure 1 summarizes the net changes in improved farmland and total

17

TABLE 4.

Net changes in total farmland, by province, 1956 to 1976

Province	ACRI value	Area of total farmland			Net changes in total farmland			
		1956	1966	1976*	1956 to 1966 change	1956 to 1966 ACRH change	1966 to 1976 change	1966 to 1976 ACRH change
		(ha)	(ha)	(ha)	(ha)	(ACRI x ha)	(ha)	(ACRI x ha)
Yukon and Northwest Territories	1.00	1,812	1,727	1,879	− 85	− 85	+ 152	+ 152
British Columbia	1.35	1,836,885	2,141,798	2,449,613	+ 304,913	+ 411,633	+ 307,815	+ 415,550
Alberta	1.50	18,604,219	19,823,370	20,206,174	+1,219,151	+1,828,727	+ 382,804	+ 574,206
Saskatchewan	1.44	25,412,723	26,471,169	26,512,476	+1,058,446	+1,524,162	+ 41,307	+ 59,482
Manitoba	1.81	7,257,006	7,723,221	7,699,925	+ 466,215	+ 843,849	− 23,296	− 42,166
Ontario	2.44	8,045,293	7,214,200	6,261,928	− 831,093	−2,027,867	− 952,272	−2,323,544
Québec	2.00	6,438,829	5,214,992	4,009,087	−1,223,837	−2,447,674	−1,205,905	−2,411,810
New Brunswick	1.70	1,206,592	733,193	466,796	− 473,399	− 804,778	− 266,397	− 452,875
Nova Scotia	1.74	1,123,302	749,462	493,310	− 373,840	− 650,482	− 256,152	− 445,704
Prince Edward Island	1.82	431,193	375,148	295,850	− 56,045	− 102,002	− 79,298	− 144,322
Newfoundland	1.21	29,063	20,038	32,399	− 9,025	− 10,920	+ 12,361	+ 14,957
CANADA		70,386,917	70,468,318	68,429,437	+ 81,401	−1,435,437	−2,038,881	−4,756,074

* Figures for 1976 include total farmland for all agricultural holdings. Therefore, total farmland totals given here will differ from those found in other tables which include data for census-farms only.

Sources: Williams, 1975. <u>An Agroclimatic Resource Index for Canada and Its Use in Describing Agricultural Land Losses</u>.
Statistics Canada, 1977*e*. <u>Census-farms by Size, Area and Use of Land</u>. Catalogue 96-854.

farmland, by province, in ha and ACRH for the periods 1956 to 1966 and 1966 to 1976.

Once again, concern should focus not only on the quantity of land undergoing change but also, and most importantly, the quality of farmland being lost or gained. Undeniably, the best agricultural lands from an agroclimatic viewpoint are located in southern Canada, surrounding large urban areas. Even if climatic conditions remain as favourable as they have been in recent decades, the permanent loss of such land cannot be balanced by gains in northern regions. If climatic cooling occurs, the result will be a contraction of the agricultural frontier in northern Canada. Areas of marginal climatic capability for agriculture will most surely be lost first. Land in the Great Lakes region, St. Lawrence Lowlands, and lower Fraser Valley will likely continue to be the best, agroclimatically speaking. The importance of considering this factor, and retaining this prime resource, will become more crucial in the future.

Some time in the future, Canada may have a need to use as much land as possible for agricultural production. As the population grows, the need for food will increase, but the amount available for import may decrease as the overall world requirements increase. Any climatic deterioration would intensify such problems. At the same time, for economic, trade, or humanitarian reasons, Canada might wish to increase its food exports. If farmland, particularly the best farmland, is not protected now, it will be much more difficult to meet such future challenges. The land with an ACRI value greater than 2.0, and especially that with an ACRI value of at least 2.5, is under the most pressure for diversion to direct urban or indirect urban uses, and its loss will have the greatest impact, since the relative productive capacity can be assumed to be proportional to ACRI. It would be almost impossible to return farmland to agricultural use once it has been used for urban development. Farmland with ACRI values greater than 2.0 may therefore be considered as critical land. Appropriate policies and practices are needed to manage these special resource lands wisely.

In the foregoing portion of this chapter, the elements of soil capability and climate have been used to identify the most favourable areas for agriculture. Although these physical criteria are important, there are other parameters that may also be helpful in delineating special agricultural areas. In the following section, economic considerations are discussed.

Photo by Agriculture Canada.
The high quality of the soil and climatic conditions in southwestern Ontario is evident in the bountiful yields of vegetables. This 81-ha radish crop is located on the Point Pelee Marsh near Leamington.

Economic Considerations

"Economic criteria such as income/revenue/profit per acre and so on reflect such factors as the demand for agricultural products, supply of competitive products, demand and supply of other inputs (e.g. fertiliser) and locational factors. Economic criteria can be a valuable supplementary aid to identifying prime land, but should not be solely relied on". (Holesgrove, 1976*b*)

The first step in this study's approach to describing special land for agriculture was the collection and presentation of data which involved identifying those physical characteristics which determine land quality. These environmental factors included soil type and fertility, slope, temperature, and moisture conditions, among others. The Canada Land Inventory and Agroclimatic Resource Index were examples of qualitative evaluation or interpretation of such data. To this point, prime agricultural land has been defined strictly by physical parameters. However, it is essential to realize that other factors come into play which may mean that "prime" land is not necessarily land of the highest physical capability. For example, land of only moderate agricultural capability may assume greater importance or value for certain farm uses because of its proximity to a large market. Land closer to large urban markets is important for high-value, perishable goods such as fruits, vegetables, and certain greenhouse products. In addition, such locations are favoured for those goods whose low value per unit often precludes expensive transportation.

In other words, economic considerations such as distance to market, transportation costs, land supply, product demand, and competition for land form part of an economic evaluation and are significant in delineating valuable agricultural land. Any data relating to farm income, agricultural sales, agricultural capital investment, or land prices, when examined in relation to the land unit, can provide another perspective of land's importance. While most economic criteria fluctuate more than certain physical characteristics, they represent another approach to the challenge of identifying and describing the best land for agriculture.

Much of the data that is so important to a national perspective on agriculture is derived from the Census of Agriculture conducted every five years by Statistics Canada. It is one of the best sources of information that permits comparison of aspects of farming from coast to coast. The census questionnaire tends to reflect the then-current interests of data users and agricultural specialists. However, the nature and extent of the census questionnaire varies from the more extensive decennial census (1961 and 1971) to the less detailed quinquennial

TABLE 5.

Net changes in improved farmland, by province, 1956 to 1976

Province	ACRI value	Area of improved farmland			Net changes in improved farmland			
		1956	1966	1976*	1956 to 1966 change	1956 to 1966 ACRH change	1966 to 1976 change	1966 to 1976 ACRH change
		(ha)	(ha)	(ha)	(ha)	(ACRI x ha)	(ha)	(ACRI x ha)
Yukon and Northwest Territories	1.00	288	251	606	− 37	− 37	+ 355	+ 355
British Columbia	1.35	472,185	653,743	773,477	+ 181,058	+ 244,428	+ 120,234	+ 162,316
Alberta	1.50	9,610,052	11,038,699	11,858,597	+1,428,647	+2,142,971	+ 819,898	+1,229,847
Saskatchewan	1.44	16,392,778	18,401,214	18,929,645	+2,008,436	+2,892,148	+ 528,431	+ 760,941
Manitoba	1.81	4,635,346	5,036,923	5,216,916	+ 401,577	+ 726,854	+ 179,993	+ 325,787
Ontario	2.44	5,087,952	4,858,142	4,479,763	− 229,810	− 560,736	− 378,379	− 923,245
Québec	2.00	3,492,494	3,087,596	2,396,884	− 404,898	− 809,796	− 690,712	−1,381,424
New Brunswick	1.70	384,987	258,461	188,725	− 126,526	− 215,094	− 69,736	− 118,551
Nova Scotia	1.74	254,910	196,627	168,682	− 58,283	− 101,412	− 27,945	− 48,624
Prince Edward Island	1.82	261,231	230,598	203,790	− 30,633	− 55,752	− 26,808	− 48,791
Newfoundland	1.21	9,807	8,323	11,139	− 1,484	− 1,796	+ 2,816	+ 3,407
CANADA		40,602,030	43,770,077	44,228,224	+3,168,047	+4,261,778	+ 458,147	− 37,982

* Figures for 1976 include improved farmland for all agricultural holdings. Therefore, improved farmland totals given here will differ from those found in other tables which include data for census-farms only.

Sources: Williams, 1975. *An Agroclimatic Resource Index for Canada and Its Use in Describing Agricultural Land Losses.*
Statistics Canada, 1977e. *Census-farms by size, Area and Use of Land.* Catalogue 96-854.

TABLE 6.

Percentage of total farmland, by province and Agroclimatic Resource Index, 1971

ACRI value	Atlantic Provinces	Québec	Ontario	Manitoba	Saskatchewan	Alberta	British Columbia	ACRI total	Urban population 1971
	(per cent)								
>3.0	0	0	0.5	0	0	0	0	0.5	1.9
2.5-2.9	0	0.2	4.0	0	0	0	0	4.2	39.7
2.0-2.4	0	3.8	4.1	1.8	0	0	0.2	9.8	24.9
1.5-1.9	2.0	2.2	0.8	9.4	14.6	17.3	1.1	47.4	27.2
1.0-1.4	0	0.2	0	0	23.8	11.9	2.1	38.1	6.2
<1.0	0	0	0	0	0	0	0	0	0.1
Total	2.0	6.4	9.4	11.2	38.4	29.2	3.4	100.0	100.0

Source: Williams, 1977. *Personal communication.*

census (1966 and 1976), for both historical and economic reasons. This is particularly relevant to the economic approach to identifying special farmland, for many questions relating to specific income, expenditure, and sales were not included in the most recent, 1976, Census of Agriculture. For this reason, more use has been made of the 1971 census material than would otherwise be the case.

What value is there in this older data? Agriculture experts consulted felt that the overall patterns indicated by data from the early 1970s would not differ significantly from the situation in the late 1970s. Changes in agricultural land use occur relatively slowly in many areas, and changes in farm type or operations are not taken without serious consideration. Government programs and subsidies tend to discourage rapid and drastic changes in farm operations. In many cases, generations of families have operated the same farm, and, in rural Canada particularly, agriculture, lifestyle, and occupation are closely tied to each other as well as to the land resource base. Furthermore, the national overview is based on census divisions rather than on the finer census subdivisions or enumeration areas, and changes are likely to be slower in appearing at this more general level.

Improved Farmland Compared with Agricultural Sales

Two basic indicators of agricultural activity are the area of improved farmland and the value of agricultural sales. When such information is mapped at the census division level, not only are the two patterns distinctive but also the contrast is particularly interesting. In Figure 2 and Map 9, the Prairies have the largest share of Canada's improved farmland. Saskatchewan alone accounted for 43 per cent of this country's improved farmland in 1971 and 1976. When combined with Alberta and Manitoba, these three provinces accounted for over 81 per cent of the country's improved farmland in 1971 and 82 per cent in 1976. Ontario and Québec lag far behind with ten and six per cent respectively in 1971, and ten and five per cent in 1976. How different this is from Figure 3 and Map 10 which illustrate Canadian agricultural sales, where Ontario is responsible for nearly one-third of all Canadian agricultural sales. Alberta, Saskatchewan, and Québec follow with 20, 17, and 13 per cent respectively.

The Atlantic Provinces account for little more than one per cent of improved farmland but slightly less than four per cent of agricultural sales. The reasons for this difference in the Atlantic Provinces' share of improved farmland and agricultural sales are explained later in this section.

In Québec, the significantly smaller size of census divisions is one reason why the census units in this province, particularly around Montréal, do not appear to contribute more substantially to the total Canadian improved farmland or value of sales at the census division level. However, the patterns of farm type, crop specialities, capital investment, and other aspects of agriculture described later, will provide a better picture of farming in Québec. The smaller census divisions in Québec and the considerably larger divisions in the Prairies have their origins in different historic settlement patterns. In Figures 2 and 3, Québec accounts for less than six per cent of total improved farmland and nearly 13 per cent of agricultural sales.

Photo by Agriculture Canada.

Vegetables, such as this carrot crop, grown on the fertile soils of the Holland Marsh north of Toronto, make a significant contribution to the specialty and cash crop sales in the province of Ontario.

TABLE 7.

Net change in total farmland, by province and Agroclimatic Resource Index, 1961 to 1971

ACRI value	Atlantic Provinces	Québec	Ontario	Manitoba	Saskatchewan	Alberta	British Columbia	ACRI total
				(thousands of ha)				
>3.0	0	0	− 10	0	0	0	0	− 10
2.5–2.9	0	− 34	− 254	0	0	0	0	− 288
2.0–2.4	0	− 710	− 607	+ 136	0	0	− 49	−1,230
1.5–1.9	−788	− 551	− 187	+ 203	+ 194	+ 57	−137	−1,209
1.0–1.4	+ 3	− 71	0	0	+ 66	+ 865	+720	+1,583
Total	−785	−1,366	−1,058	+ 339	+ 260	+ 922	+534	−1,155

Source: Williams, 1977. *Personal communication.*

Ontario's contribution to Canadian agricultural sales is concentrated in the southwestern portion of the province for several reasons. The versatility of the land resource base permits a wide range of products to be grown. Moreover, the existence of large urban markets in Toronto, Hamilton, and London, among other cities, dictates that some versatile land must be used for high-value crops. Specialty and cash crops, including greenhouse and nursery products, soybeans, corn, peas, beans, and carrots among other vegetables, as well as apples, tender fruits, tomatoes, and other fruits, are the high-value perishable goods that help account for Ontario's large share of Canadian agricultural sales. For example, according to the 1971 Census of Agriculture, in Norfolk census division,[1] more than half the census farms cultivated tobacco, and approximately 74 per cent of agricultural sales were accounted for by tobacco and potatoes. In Toronto census division, sales of greenhouse and nursery products accounted for 79 per cent of all agricultural sales. Dairy products are also high value, and in Perth census division, the sale of cattle, pigs, poultry, and dairy and egg products accounted for 92 per cent of all the agricultural sales.

To find large areas of improved land throughout the Prairie Provinces is understandable. The land and climate are well suited to grain cultivation and such crops require large areas in order to be economically viable.

NFB – PHOTOTHEQUE – ONF – Photo by C. Lund.
The patchwork of cultivated fields stretches to the horizon.

The land was relatively easy and inexpensive to clear, insofar as grass cover rather than forest was predominant in the southern Prairies during settlement and the land was reasonably level and free of rocks. The census divisions themselves are also large and this too affects the picture to some extent. But, in comparison with many other agricultural areas of the country, Prairie farmers often cultivate crops whose value per unit is considerably lower. This is especially true where wheat and other grain crops dominate. Such crops require large land tracts but the dollar return per unit is significantly lower. While one ha of wheat in Saskatchewan may yield $180, the same area under tree fruits and small fruits in southern Ontario might produce sales of $2,700. Only where exceptionally large wheat and grain areas exist within reasonably large census divisions in the Prairies, do these census divisions rate as contributing a more significant share to Canadian agricultural sales. That is not to depreciate the contribution that wheat as a crop makes to the Canadian economic scene. Rather, it reflects the relatively low value per ha of that agricultural activity.

In southern Manitoba, where wheat sales are added to income from cattle, pigs, dairy products, and small grains, the contribution to national farm sales is much more significant. In central Alberta, generally it is the very high sales of cattle, combined with oilseeds, wheat, and other grains that explain the high contribution to Canadian sales. In Census Division No. 2 in south-central Alberta, cattle and wheat rank first and second in value of sales. However, in 1970, this unit also accounted for 75 per cent of the province's irrigated land. Consequently, 77 per cent of the province's vegetables and 87 per cent of its sugar beet crop were grown here in 1971. The high value of these crops, when combined with exceptional levels of cattle sales and high sales of wheat, means that this census division accounted for 2.95 per cent of all Canadian agricultural sales in 1970, an amount exceeding that of any other census division in Canada.

In British Columbia, the relatively high value of sales compared to the small area of improved farmland in the Greater Vancouver, Fraser–Cheam and Central Fraser Valley results from the high-value nature of the agricultural activities near areas of population concentration. Approximately 73 per cent of the province's vegetable sales, 80 per cent of the high-value hen and chicken business, 66 per cent of dairy and egg sales, as well as 64 per cent of greenhouse and nursery product sales were accounted for in these three census divisions in 1970.

Agricultural Sales

The value of agricultural sales per unit of land is one rough economic measure of the return for effort in agriculture. Looking at the value of agricultural sales per improved farmland unit (ha or acre), presented on Map 11, one of the most striking features may be the high values in parts of Newfoundland. What can be the explanation for this anomaly? The very small amount of improved farmland in Newfoundland, as compared with other provinces, distorts the national picture. It should be noted that although these lands have high value of sales per ha, their impact is at the local or provincial level, rather than at the national level. In 1971 and 1976, Newfoundland accounted for only 0.02 per cent of Canada's improved farmland although its total land area is four per cent of Canada. Yet its share of Canadian sales in 1970 was 0.20 per cent, small yet remarkable considering its minute share of improved farmland. Why? First of all, the scarcity of good farmland and the resultant scarcity of fresh farm produce harvested in the province mean that the farmers can demand and receive high prices for their goods. Milk prices in Newfoundland tend to be 15 per cent higher than in Nova Scotia for example. Secondly, the few farms have relatively few ha of improved land. Naturally, the types of goods produced are high value in order to provide the farmers with some reasonable return for their efforts and relatively high expenses. Poultry production is a high-value business and both fresh dairy and egg products command high prices in an essentially captive or isolated market. The cost of transporting fresh produce is high so locally grown, hardy vegetables such as potatoes, cabbage, and carrots bring good economic returns. Furthermore, exports of soil-related products are restricted for reasons of crop disease. In summary, the low number of farms and farmers, the scarcity of good farmland, the captive or isolated market, and the nature of high-value goods produced serve to explain Newfoundland's rather unique situation.

To some extent, the same arguments hold true for parts of Nova Scotia, particularly in Cape Breton. However, the fruit orchards, vegetable, and dairy areas surrounding Halifax are also significant with regard to sales per land unit. Likewise in New Brunswick, the St. John census division stands out with its urban market, limited quantity of improved farmland, and specialty crop orientation (56 per cent of agriculture sales in 1970 accrued to greenhouse and nursery products). The specialty potato areas along the Saint John River are easily identified on the accompanying maps, especially Victoria census division in the northwest where, in 1970, 90 per cent of all agricultural sales resulted from the potato crop. This area contains some of the province's best farmland, and if the climate were not so cold, more varied crops could be grown.

In Québec, one question arises: Why is the highest value of sales per ha in Québec census division and not in the vicinity of Montréal? In the first instance, there is a significant concentration of poultry farms in Québec census division and this type of farm enterprise has a high economic return. This area supplies not only Québec City but also the Montréal market with dairy products, vegetables, and poultry. Although the census divisions of Rouville and Deux Montagnes near Montréal are tree fruit and small fruit areas, there is not as much fruit production near Montréal compared with Toronto, Niagara, or Vancouver and consequently the level of sales per ha is lowered by the cultivation of lower value crops. In general, the cultivation of lower value crops around Montréal is reflected by the map. Down the St. Lawrence River a short distance, Joliette census division has nearly one-half of the province's tobacco area, and is an example of an area that specializes in a relatively high-value crop. The census divisions with moderate dollar returns per ha surrounding Montréal are largely dairy and fresh produce suppliers for the urban centres.

In general, the value of sales per ha decreases with distance from the major urban areas. This phenomenon is reflected in the changes in farm type from the urban fringe to the furthest edge of the hinterland. Again, the highest value and generally perishable crops are closest to the urban markets. In southern Ontario, there is a distinct series of bands or rings radiating outward from Toronto. In Toronto census division, 80 per cent of all agricultural sales accrued from greenhouse and nursery

Photo by Agriculture Canada.
Greenhouse operations are capital-intensive enterprises whose high-value crops include nursery and horticultural products destined for urban markets.

---

[1]. A reference map with the names of all census divisions is included in Appendix II to this chapter. Specific census division names will permit readers to locate specific units, but are not necessary to appreciate the general patterns presented by the maps.

FIGURE 1.

NET CHANGES IN IMPROVED FARMLAND BY PROVINCE
IN HA AND ACRH

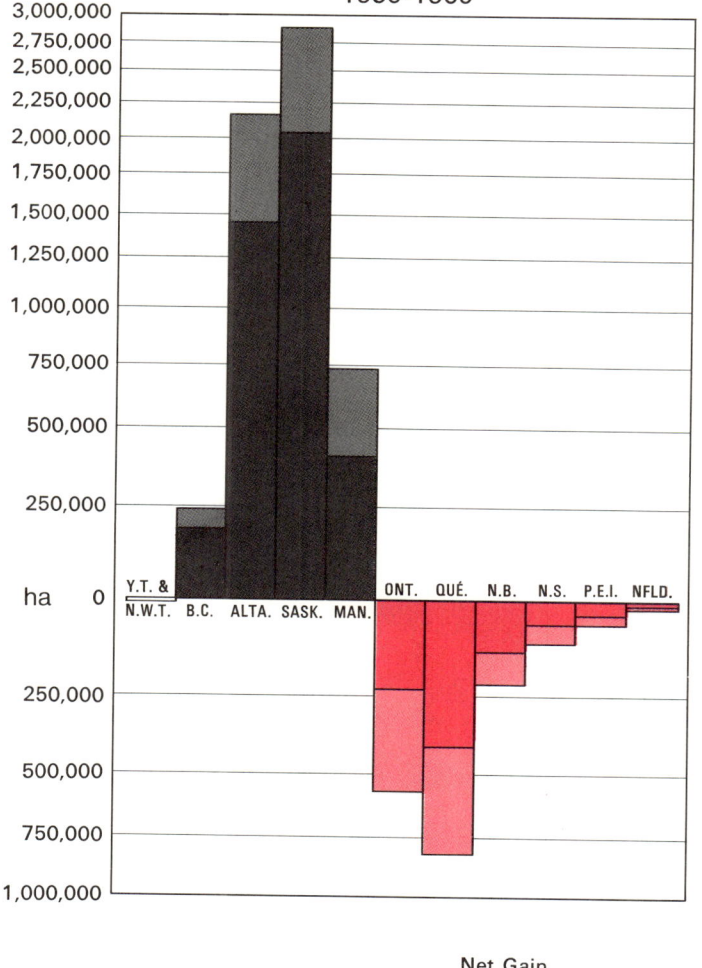

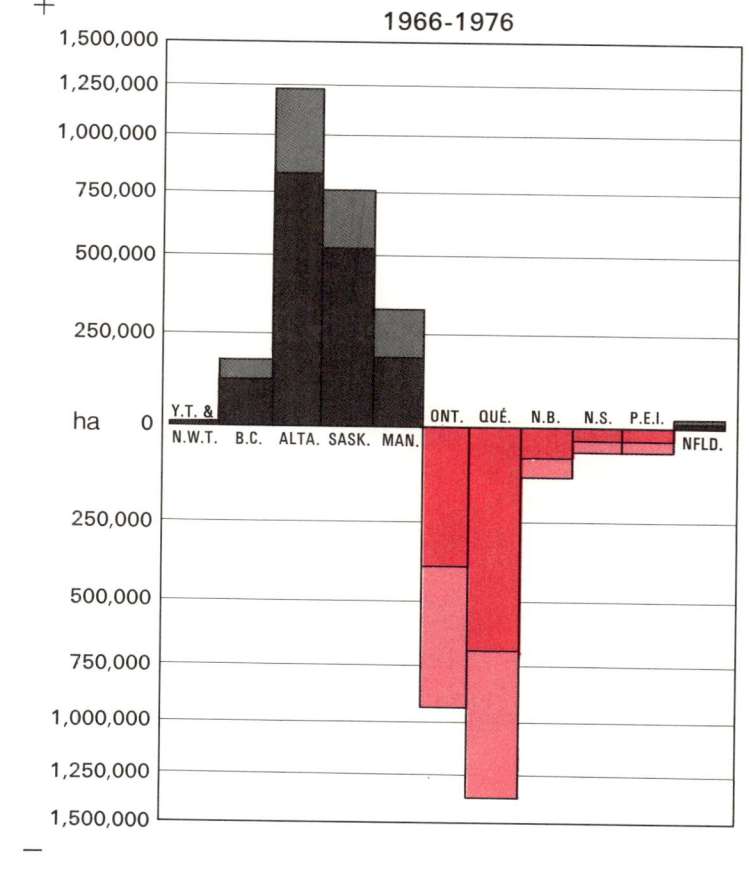

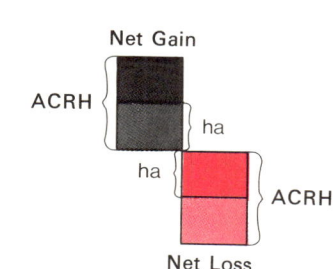

NET CHANGES IN TOTAL FARMLAND BY PROVINCE
IN HA AND ACRH

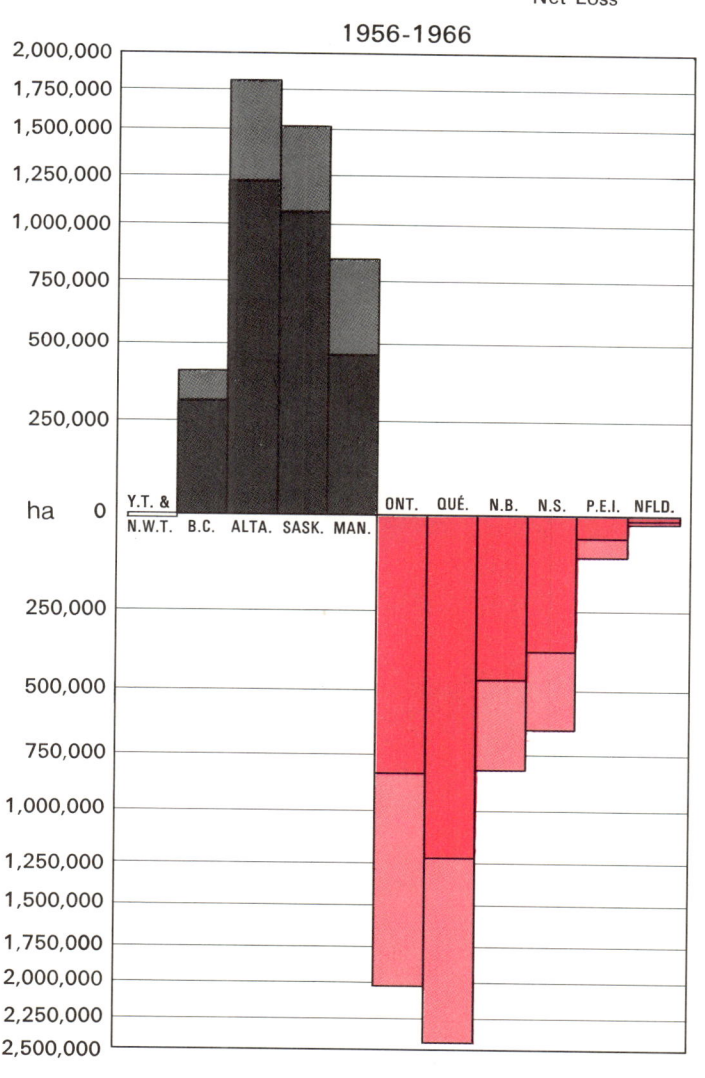

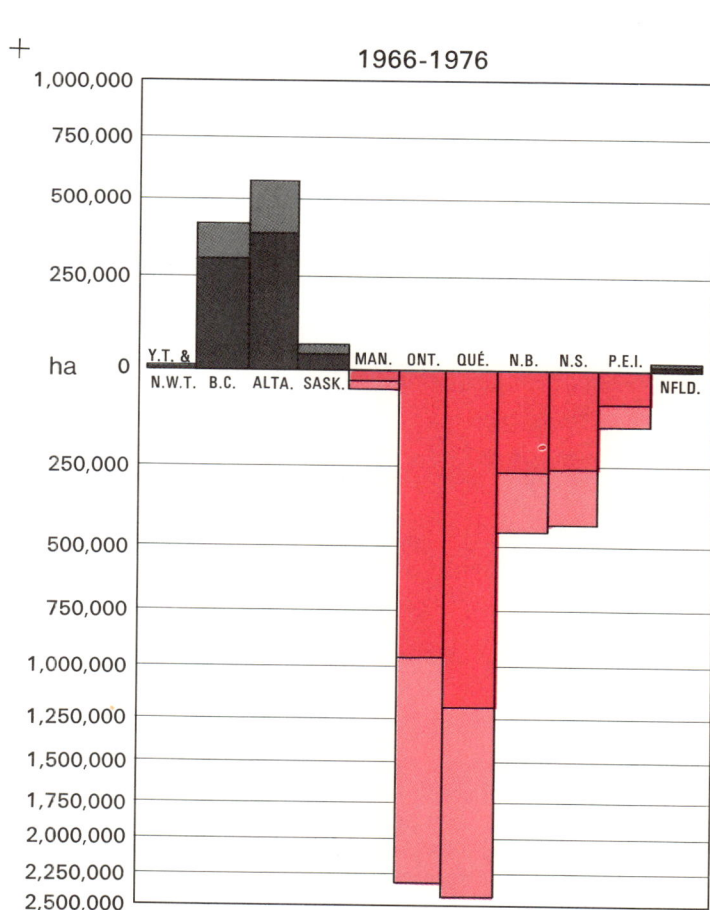

PERCENTAGE OF CANADA'S IMPROVED FARMLAND BY CENSUS DIVISION, 1971

MAP 9

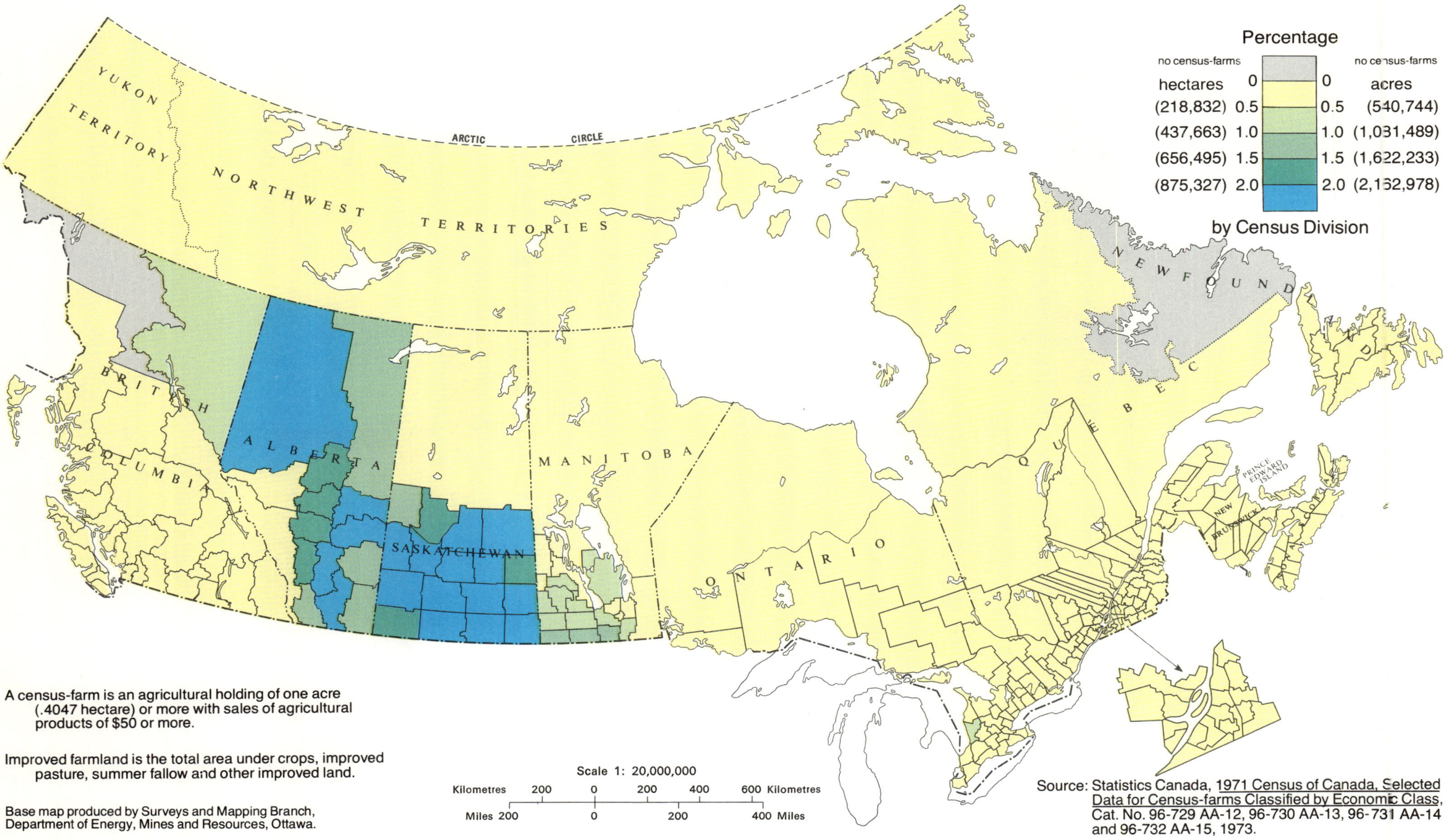

Percentage
no census-farms
hectares 0
(218,832) 0.5
(437,663) 1.0
(656,495) 1.5
(875,327) 2.0
no census-farms
0 acres
0.5 (540,744)
1.0 (1,031,489)
1.5 (1,622,233)
2.0 (2,162,978)
by Census Division
YUKON TERRITORY
NORTHWEST TERRITORIES
ARCTIC CIRCLE
NEWFOUNDLAND
BRITISH COLUMBIA
ALBERTA
SASKATCHEWAN
MANITOBA
ONTARIO
QUEBEC
PRINCE EDWARD ISLAND
NEW BRUNSWICK
NOVA SCOTIA
A census-farm is an agricultural holding of one acre (.4047 hectare) or more with sales of agricultural products of $50 or more.
Improved farmland is the total area under crops, improved pasture, summer fallow and other improved land.
Base map produced by Surveys and Mapping Branch, Department of Energy, Mines and Resources, Ottawa.
Scale 1: 20,000,000
Kilometres 200 0 200 400 600 Kilometres
Miles 200 0 200 400 Miles
Source: Statistics Canada, 1971 Census of Canada, Selected Data for Census-farms Classified by Economic Class, Cat. No. 96-729 AA-12, 96-730 AA-13, 96-731 AA-14 and 96-732 AA-15, 1973.

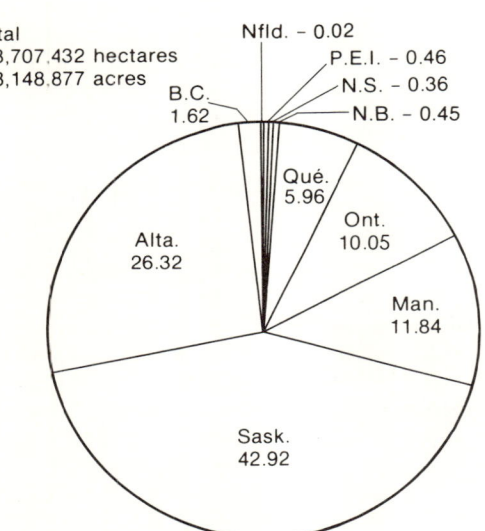

FIGURE 2.

Percentage of Canada's improved farmland, by province, 1971

Total
43,707,432 hectares
108,148,877 acres
Nfld. - 0.02
P.E.I. - 0.46
N.S. - 0.36
N.B. - 0.45
B.C.
1.62
Qué.
5.96
Ont.
10.05
Man.
11.84
Sask.
42.92
Alta.
26.32

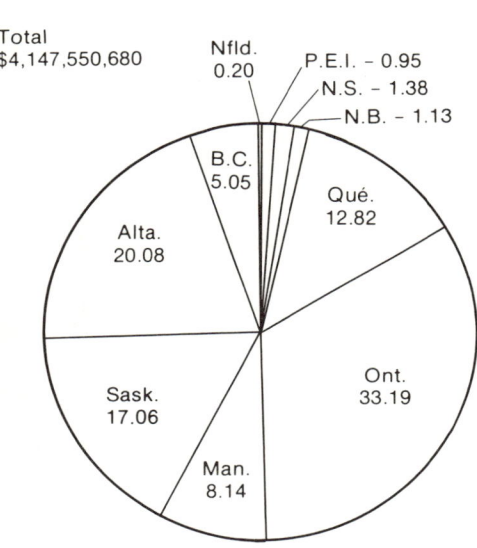

FIGURE 3.

Percentage of Canada's agricultural sales, by province, 1970

Total
$4,147,550,680
Nfld.
0.20
P.E.I. - 0.95
N.S. - 1.38
N.B. - 1.13
B.C.
5.05
Qué.
12.82
Ont.
33.19
Man.
8.14
Sask.
17.06
Alta.
20.08

Source: Statistics Canada, 1973*a*. Canada. Catalogue 96-701 Vol: IV-Part 1.

products in 1970, although their share of improved farmland area was only one per cent. The crops with not only high value but also high yield per ha, are fruits and berries, vegetables, and greenhouse or nursery products. Farms specializing in these crops are clustered around the "Golden Horseshoe" along the western end of Lake Ontario and in southwestern Ontario. With direct urban or urban-related uses competing for the land, only the highest value farm activities are feasible. For instance, the census division of Niagara accounted for 51 per cent of the province's total tree fruit and small fruit sales in 1970 and contained 78 per cent of the province's small fruit (berries and grapes) area in 1971 (79 per cent in 1976). Immediately to the west, Haldimand–Norfolk census divisions along Lake Erie, in 1971 contained 47 per cent of Ontario's, and 40 per cent of Canada's, tobacco area (48 and 42 per cent respectively in 1976). Moving outward from these high-value specialty crop areas, the decline of value of sales per ha reflects a change in farm type. Fresh vegetables destined for the urban market are replaced by vegetables for canning and processing and by more hardy vegetables better able to withstand travel. So too, the dairy or poultry farms come into prominence as the producers try to stay within the 80- to 95-km milk shed of major cities. Although newer handling methods give some flexibility to this boundary, the pattern is unlikely to change drastically as these farms are well established, operate under quota systems, and involve substantial investment in buildings and equipment. Unless new requirements are forthcoming from the urban market, the dairy farms will continue to exist within easy transportation distance of the market. Moving still further outward, livestock and grain and forage crops become dominant in areas such as Bruce and Huron census divisions along Lake Huron. These two units had the highest values of cattle sales in the province (34 and 32 million dollars respectively) in 1970. In Ontario, the limits imposed on agriculture by the Canadian Shield are quite evident (see Map 11). The Shield edge clearly marks the transition from specialty to mixed-purpose farms, and reflects other characteristics which result from such a change in farm operations.

The value of sales per land unit is uniformly low across the three Prairie Provinces, due largely to two factors: the low value of sales per ha, and the relatively low yields of grains per ha. For example, wheat sales, at a general price of $2.75 per bushel and 70 bushels per ha, can in no way compare to fruit or vegetable sales in southern Ontario or in the Montréal area on a unit land basis. However, the specific types of spring wheat grown in Saskatchewan are well matched to the climate and soil characteristics of the province, just as the higher value crops of fruits and vegetables are well suited to the St. Lawrence Lowlands' physical, climatic, and market conditions.

In British Columbia, the pattern of value of sales per ha reflects the province's distribution of population and good farmland. The highest values are, not unexpectedly, in the Greater Vancouver census division, where fresh fruits, vegetables, greenhouse products, livestock, and dairy and egg products for the large market are most important. Immediately to the east, the Central Fraser Valley census division is a specialty area which, in 1970, accounted for 57 per cent of provincial sales accruing from hens and chickens. Here too, dairy, egg, fruit, and vegetable products are also important. These two census units account for the largest share of British

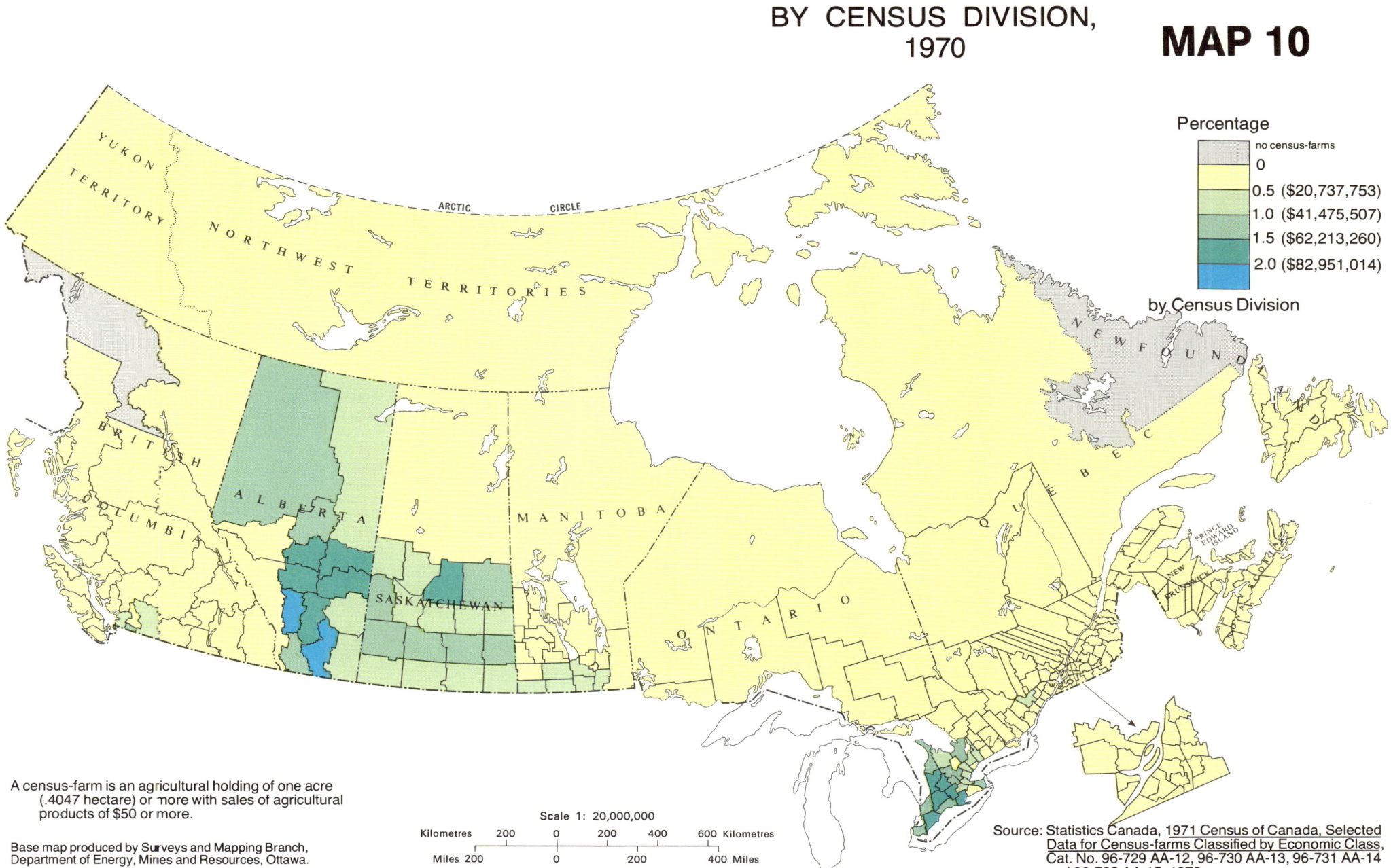

Columbia's cultivated small fruit areas (58 per cent in 1971, but only 53 per cent in 1976). Berries, such as strawberries, raspberries, and cranberries, have exceptionally high yields per ha and high sales per unit. In south-central British Columbia, the Central Okanagan and Okanagan–Similkameen census divisions account for the largest share of the province's tree fruit and small fruit sales, with the emphasis on apples, peaches, pears, cherries, plums, prunes, and apricots. On Vancouver Island, poultry, dairy, egg, greenhouse, and nursery enterprises are reflected in the relatively high economic return per unit of land. The moderately high levels of agricultural sales per improved farmland unit also reflect the scarcity, isolation, and high cost of high-capability farmland in British Columbia.

Capital Investment

"It seems to me nowadays that there's getting to be so much money required to run a farm, keep it up with implements and stock and all such things like that, and the value of your land, that you're getting so much money invested before you can farm, then why farm?" (Anderson, 1977)[2].

Total Capital Value

Total capital value in agriculture comprises the reported value of three major investment areas: land and buildings; machinery and equipment; and livestock and poultry inventories (Figures 4, 5, and 6). The figures re-

[2] Excerpts from Remembering the Farm by Allan Anderson are reprinted by permission of The Macmillan Company of Canada Limited.

ported by census-farm operators in 1976 were estimates of the market value, not the original, replacement, or assessed value. This measure of investment in agriculture

Total capital investment reflects the intensity of land use. The level of investment is directly related to a number of factors including type and value of crops, land capability, strength and stability of market conditions, and proximity to large markets. Areas of higher investment highlight the locations perceived to present higher, more stable, or more reliable income potential. Here, people are willing to make more substantial investment because of expected higher return for their efforts.

Similarity between the configuration of total capital value (Map 12) and value of agricultural sales (see Map 11) suggests that different crops and farm types reflect differing intensities of land use, and that different farm activities necessitate varying levels of capital investment. For example, in Nova Scotia, higher levels of investment, as compared with New Brunswick, reflect both a stronger livestock industry necessitating higher is related to the land unit (ha or acre) as opposed to the farm itself for several reasons. The focus of this report is the land resource base and not the farm organization. Drastic variation in farm size across Canada is a response to soil and climatic conditions, historical development and settlement, market opportunities, economic pressures, crop types, and other factors. Only in a restricted geographical region, where farm type and size were more uniform, would capital investment on a per farm basis be meaningful. For the purpose of this study, comparison on a per ha basis is a more accurate way of assessing the levels of capital investment in agriculture.

investment in cattle stock and buildings, and a prosperous fruit industry in the Annapolis Valley. In New Brunswick, lower investment levels may result from predominantly mixed farming, and the generally lower values of land and buildings. Where mixed farms are further from market and are located on generally lower quality land, as they are in many cases in New Brunswick, capital investment must be contained within the expected economic return, which tends to be lower.

These same factors exist in Québec where proximity to large urban markets, better quality of land, increased competition for available land, type of specialty and cash crops, plus livestock and dairying enterprises, all combine to necessitate higher capital investment in any or all the sections of land/buildings, machinery/equipment, or livestock/poultry inventories. The area of investment within the three categories of total capital value varies with the above factors. Across Québec in general, the land and buildings capital sector is usually the largest but the proportion varies considerably. For example, in Île-de-Montréal and Île-Jésus which comprise Montréal, investment averages $6,177 to $9,884 per ha, and 86 per cent of total capital value is in land and buildings, 13 per cent in machinery and equipment, and one per cent in livestock and poultry. This percentage breakdown is due largely to the fierce competition from urban uses for the limited high-quality farmland, and the high-value, high-intensity nature of the specialty and fresh fruit and vegetable crops. On the other hand, in the Eastern Township census division of Beauce, where dairying is most common, the level of investment is lower, $1,235 to $2,471 per ha, and the percentage of investment among the three categories is 58, 22, and 20 per cent respectively. Further from the mar-

VALUE OF AGRICULTURAL SALES OF CENSUS-FARMS 1970

MAP 11

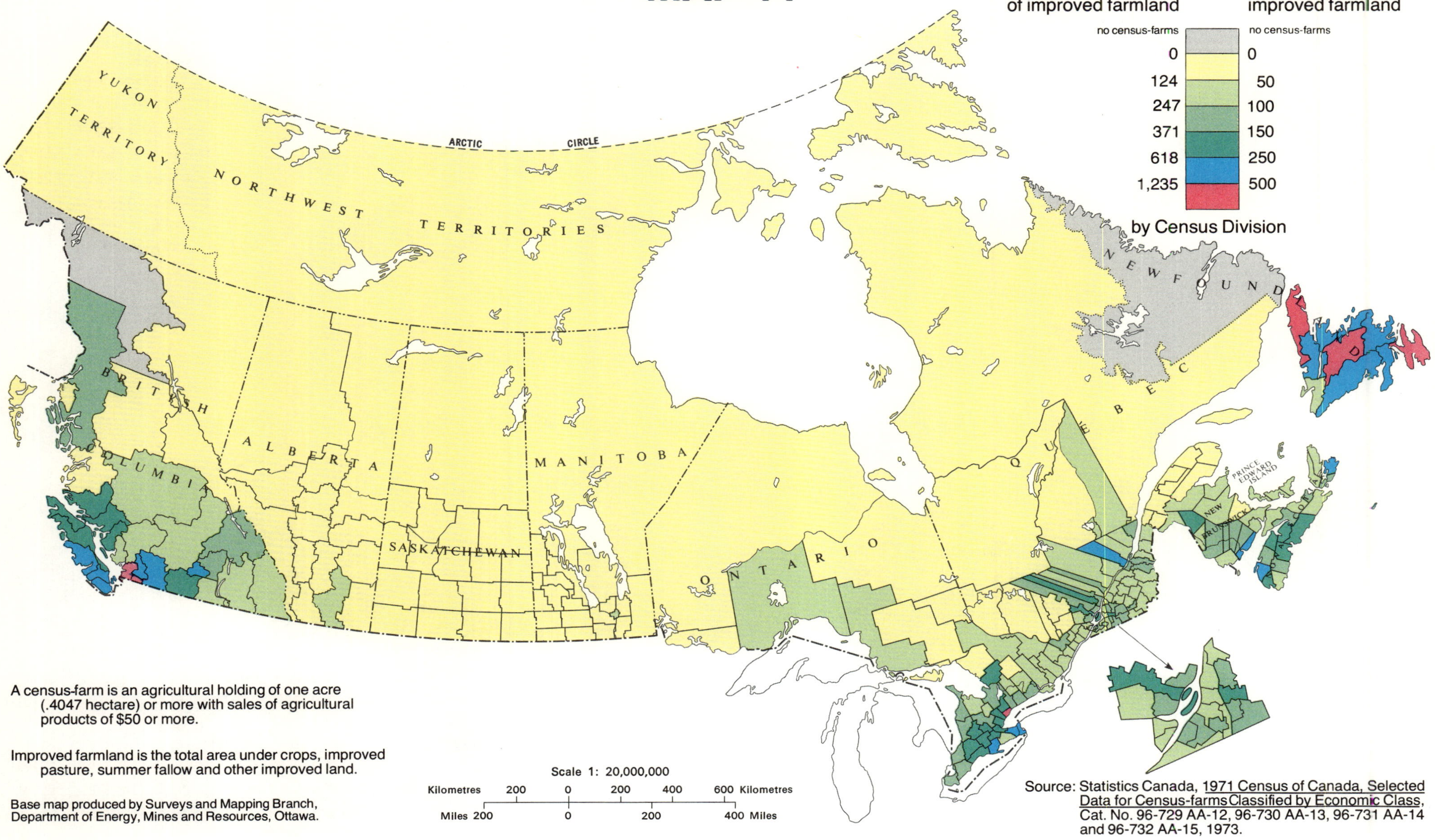

Dollars per hectare of improved farmland / Dollars per acre of improved farmland

- no census-farms / no census-farms
- 0 / 0
- 124 / 50
- 247 / 100
- 371 / 150
- 618 / 250
- 1,235 / 500

by Census Division

A census-farm is an agricultural holding of one acre (.4047 hectare) or more with sales of agricultural products of $50 or more.

Improved farmland is the total area under crops, improved pasture, summer fallow and other improved land.

Base map produced by Surveys and Mapping Branch, Department of Energy, Mines and Resources, Ottawa.

Scale 1: 20,000,000

Source: Statistics Canada, 1971 Census of Canada, Selected Data for Census-farms Classified by Economic Class, Cat. No. 96-729 AA-12, 96-730 AA-13, 96-731 AA-14 and 96-732 AA-15, 1973.

FIGURE 4.
Percentage of Canada's capital value of land and buildings, by province, 1976

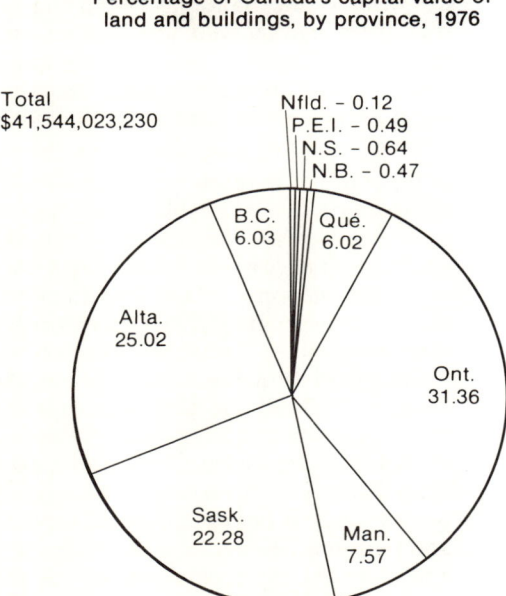

Total $41,544,023,230

- Nfld. – 0.12
- P.E.I. – 0.49
- N.S. – 0.64
- N.B. – 0.47
- B.C. 6.03
- Qué. 6.02
- Alta. 25.02
- Ont. 31.36
- Sask. 22.28
- Man. 7.57

FIGURE 5.
Percentage of Canada's capital value of machinery and equipment, by province, 1976

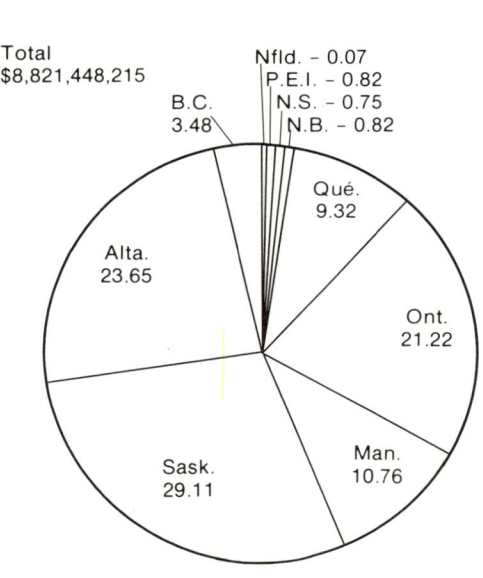

Total $8,821,448,215

- Nfld. – 0.07
- P.E.I. – 0.82
- N.S. – 0.75
- N.B. – 0.82
- B.C. 3.48
- Qué. 9.32
- Alta. 23.65
- Ont. 21.22
- Sask. 29.11
- Man. 10.76

FIGURE 6.
Percentage of Canada's capital value of livestock and poultry, by province, 1976

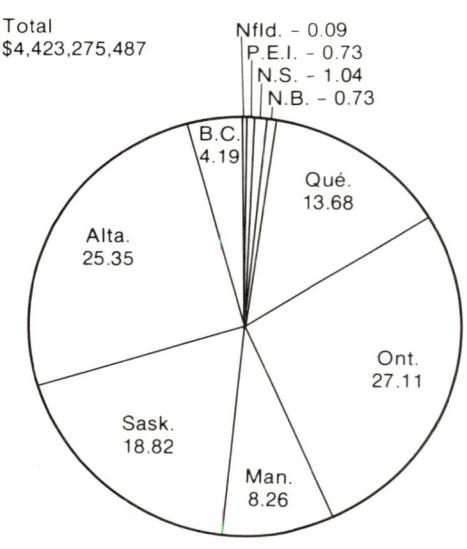

Total $4,423,275,487

- Nfld. – 0.09
- P.E.I. – 0.73
- N.S. – 1.04
- N.B. – 0.73
- B.C. 4.19
- Qué. 13.68
- Alta. 25.35
- Ont. 27.11
- Sask. 18.82
- Man. 8.26

Source: Statistics Canada, 1978a. Canada. Catalogue 96-800.

ket along the north shore of the Gaspé, where farms experience generally poorer climatic and soil conditions, and where agricultural sales per ha are considerably lower, total capital value is less than $1,235 per ha. In the census division of Matapédia, where mixed livestock is the most common enterprise, the proportion of investment in the three major areas is 50, 30, and 20 per cent respectively. The lower land investment is a function of the lower capability of the soil, less intensive competition for land, longer distance from market, less intensive use, and other factors.

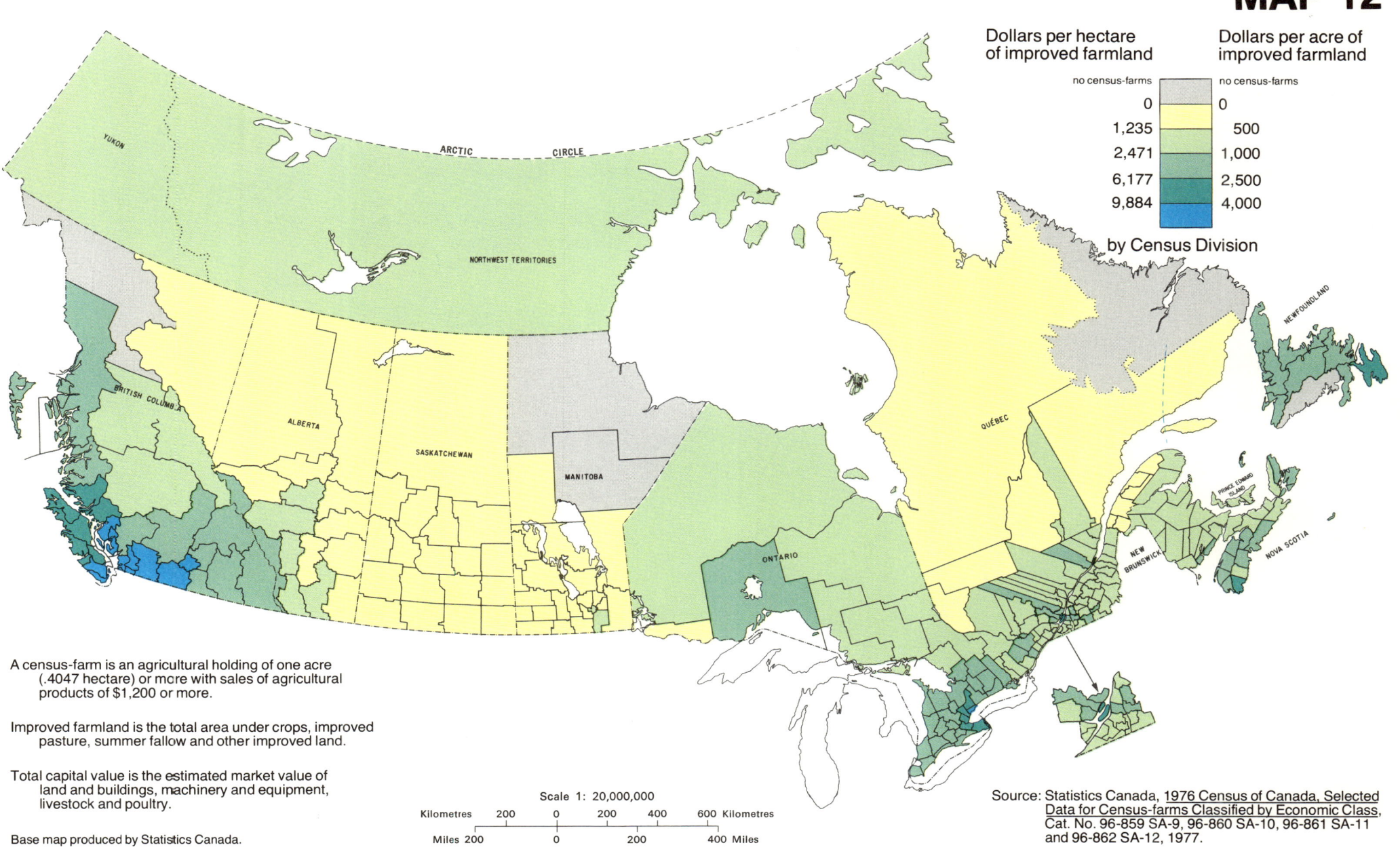

TOTAL CAPITAL VALUE OF CENSUS-FARMS 1976
MAP 12

A census-farm is an agricultural holding of one acre (.4047 hectare) or more with sales of agricultural products of $1,200 or more.

Improved farmland is the total area under crops, improved pasture, summer fallow and other improved land.

Total capital value is the estimated market value of land and buildings, machinery and equipment, livestock and poultry.

Base map produced by Statistics Canada.

Scale 1: 20,000,000

Source: Statistics Canada, 1976 Census of Canada, Selected Data for Census-farms Classified by Economic Class, Cat. No. 96-859 SA-9, 96-860 SA-10, 96-861 SA-11 and 96-862 SA-12, 1977.

In Ontario, the configuration is a familiar one. Around Toronto, land is of high capability for urban uses as well as for agriculture. Consequently, the competition for land is fierce and the cost of land is extremely high. The value of greenhouse and nursery products, fresh fruit, and vegetables is high, but then the intensity of land use and crop yield per ha are both high. Total capital value is $17,378 per ha, with 95 per cent accounted for by land and building values. Moving outward from Toronto, the next highest level of capital value, $6,177 to $9,884, coincides with the area around the western end of Lake Ontario. The orchard, fresh fruit, and vegetable areas are intensively farmed and land is relatively expensive as urban expansion is concentrated here. The next level of investment, $2,471 to $6,177 per ha, reflects a general change in farm type, increased distance to major urban centres, expectations of slightly lower economic return, and other factors. Livestock and dairy operations, special grain crops for animal feed, and poultry businesses are the most common activities. Once again, the boundary of the Canadian Shield marks another transition not only in farm type, to mixed livestock and forage crop production, but also in intensity of land use, and level of economic investment.

Throughout much of the Prairies, the level of investment is generally below $1,235 per ha, as the result of farm size and type. In Saskatchewan in 1976, for example, census-farms averaged 271 ha of improved farmland compared to Ontario's 56-ha average. Although total capital value per farm is high, expenditures are spread over larger areas, as on wheat farms, thus reducing the per unit investment. Capital value of land and buildings averages about 73 per cent of total capital value. In Alberta, the pattern is much the same until the farm type and land use intensity change. For example, the sugar beet areas developed on irrigated land in Census Division No. 2, in the extreme south-central part of the province, necessitate slightly higher expenditures for irrigation equipment.

In British Columbia, the pattern of investment levels reflects the familiar factors of limited quantity of high-quality farmland, distance to market, competition for land near urban areas, and varying types of farm operations. Land and building investment tends to be high, in some cases due to the high price of land near Vancouver, and, in other cases, to the expensive type of buildings required for the poultry business found in the Fraser Valley area. The range of total capital values throughout British Columbia exceeds that of any other province.

Capital Value of Land and Buildings

"I'd have no trouble selling the farm; I could sell it next week if I wanted to, but I'll bet it goes to a city man instead of to a farmer. At least the city man could pay more for it. At one time, with the river running through here, this would be called one of the poorer farms, too much waste land. But now it's possibly worth more than a really productive farm. A farm like mine today, it would be no trouble at all getting anywheres from eighty to a hundred thousand dollars for it. And there's the problem, for any young chap to buy a farm, and try to make a living out of it farming, he'd die of a broken heart before he'd ever get it paid for." (Anderson, 1977).

In discussing special lands for agriculture, it is natural to take a closer look at the land and buildings component of total capital value. Unfortunately the value of land, as separate from buildings, is not available from Statistics Canada's Census of Agriculture. In studying the proportion of total capital value constituted by land and buildings in 1976 by census division, the pattern is not surprising (Map 13). In the vicinity of many urban areas from St. John's to Victoria, the value of land is usually higher because of competition from residential, industrial, recreation, transportation, or other urban-oriented uses. In fact, the configuration of census divisions where 80 per cent or more of the total capital value is in land and buildings delineates many of the major urbanized areas of Canada.

In the Atlantic Provinces, the pattern is largely the result of factors which have been described earlier. The relative scarcity of good farmland, competition for that land from other uses, proximity to urban areas, and type of farm operations all play a rôle. Near St. John's (Census Division No. 1) for example, competition for good land is extreme and nearness to the urban market is important. The majority of farms are dairy operations which also entail a relatively high expenditure for buildings. Consequently, 86 per cent of the total capital value is associated with the land and buildings component, with only seven per cent in each of machinery/equipment and livestock/poultry inventories. On the other hand, in the census division of Victoria in northwestern New Brunswick, the situation is different. Here, farms are almost totally involved with potatoes, and the larger urban markets are further from the agricultural area. As a result, the investment distribution of total capital value is quite different with a far greater emphasis on the machinery required on such potato specialty farms. The distribution among the land/buildings, machinery/equipment, and livestock/poultry sectors is 62, 34, and 4 per cent respectively.

In Québec, the more marginal or subsistance farming areas are evident (see Map 13). In the census division of Matapédia in central Gaspé, the farms are usually involved in sheep, swine, or beef cattle operations. The distribution of total capital value among the three components is: 50 per cent in land and buildings, 30 per cent in machinery and equipment, and 20 per cent in livestock and poultry inventory. This census division had the lowest proportion, 50 per cent, of total capital value devoted to land and buildings of any unit with census-farms in Canada in 1976. Its geographic location, the overall economic situation, and the physical environment contribute to this circumstance.

These same factors, when appearing in a quite different context, distinguish the urban belt through Québec and Ontario. The pattern is particularly pronounced in the Windsor–Québec axis where Québec City, Montréal, Ottawa–Hull, Toronto, Hamilton, and other urban centres along this axis are clearly indicated. This is the case, particularly in the Toronto and Montréal areas, where more intensive farming, high-value crops, and adjacent markets produce an economic return that allows

CAPITAL VALUE OF LAND AND BUILDINGS AS A PERCENTAGE OF TOTAL CAPITAL VALUE 1976
MAP 13

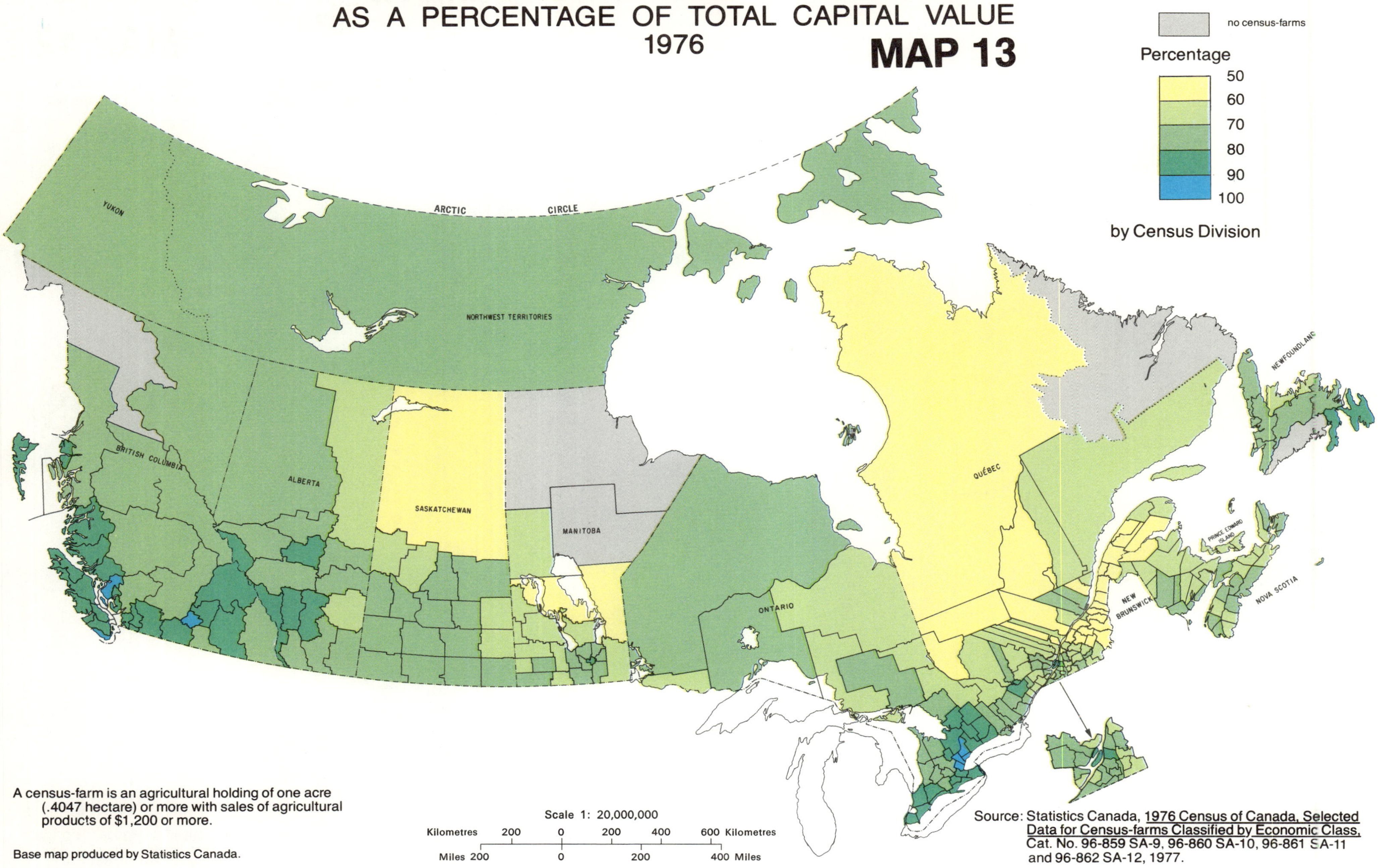

no census-farms

Percentage
- 50
- 60
- 70
- 80
- 90
- 100

by Census Division

A census-farm is an agricultural holding of one acre (.4047 hectare) or more with sales of agricultural products of $1,200 or more.

Base map produced by Statistics Canada.

Scale 1: 20,000,000

Source: Statistics Canada, 1976 Census of Canada, Selected Data for Census-farms Classified by Economic Class, Cat. No. 96-859 SA-9, 96-860 SA-10, 96-861 SA-11 and 96-862 SA-12, 1977.

---

farmers to bear higher capital investment in land. Such investment in land is certainly substantial in many urban areas of the axis. In Ottawa–Hull, the proportion of total capital value invested in land and buildings is 81 per cent, but this figure rises to 86 per cent in Montréal and to a staggering 95 per cent in Toronto. The influence of the cities on land markets and prices in their surrounding area decreases with distance, as seen around Montréal. Nonetheless, what better illustration of intense competition for the high-quality land in or near large urban centres?

Moving westward to the Prairies, the higher proportion of capital value in the machinery/equipment and livestock/poultry sectors is a reflection of the wheat, grain, and beef farms which dominate many areas. However, the Winnipeg area presents a pattern similar to that of the Windsor–Québec axis, with the land and buildings proportion of total capital value generally decreasing with the distance from the city. Many residents of Winnipeg have hobby or horse farms, recreational properties, or small, intensively farmed market gardens around the city. The high capability of the soil for agriculture in this area is a significant factor in determining this pattern.

Presently, the proportion of total capital value accounted for by the machinery and livestock inventory components is higher in the wheat areas of Saskatchewan and cattle country of Alberta, while land and building expenses are relatively less in the Prairies than in central Canada.

With regard to Saskatchewan and parts of Alberta, one note should be made. It was stated earlier that land was less scarce here than in the Windsor–Québec axis for example, and that land and building capital value investment was lower than in many other parts of Canada. However, during the 1970s there has been pressure to expand farmland northward. The Prairies represent one of the last large frontiers or reserves for farming on the North American continent. In recent years, land values have been bid up by land investors or speculators, in some cases from the United States, and consequently, land prices have escalated. What effects such rises in land prices will have on farmers involved with the production of relatively low value per unit crops such as wheat, remain to be seen.

In British Columbia, the scarcity and distribution of good quality farmland, the presence of high-value, intensive agricultural activities such as horticulture, the high building expenses associated with poultry and dairy enterprises common to the Fraser Valley, and the high value of orchard land in the Okanagan all help to explain the pattern. In addition, people's desire to own a piece of land, especially scenic, coastal, or mountain landscape within commuting distance of Vancouver or Victoria, has served to increase the price of land.

Major Areas of Agricultural Production

Areas of Livestock and Poultry Production

Ideally, 1975 sales figures for specific crops from the 1976 Census of Agriculture would be an excellent way of highlighting Canada's most valuable lands for each crop or activity. Unfortunately, the 1976 quinquennial census did not incorporate questions regarding exact value of sales for specific crops. Consequently, for the

---

Photo by Agriculture Canada.

In the Windsor-Québec axis, investment in the land and buildings sector of total capital value is substantially higher than in other areas of Québec and Ontario. Not only are the farm buildings expensive, but also agriculture must compete with other uses for the land resource base.

Photo by Agriculture Canada.

This scene shows combines, worth nearly one-quarter million dollars, custom-cutting flax near Brandon, Manitoba. Considerable capital can be invested in machinery and equipment on large grain farms, and consequently many operations are contracted out to custom-cutters.

PERCENTAGE OF CANADA'S CAPITAL VALUE OF LIVESTOCK AND POULTRY BY CENSUS DIVISION 1976

MAP 14

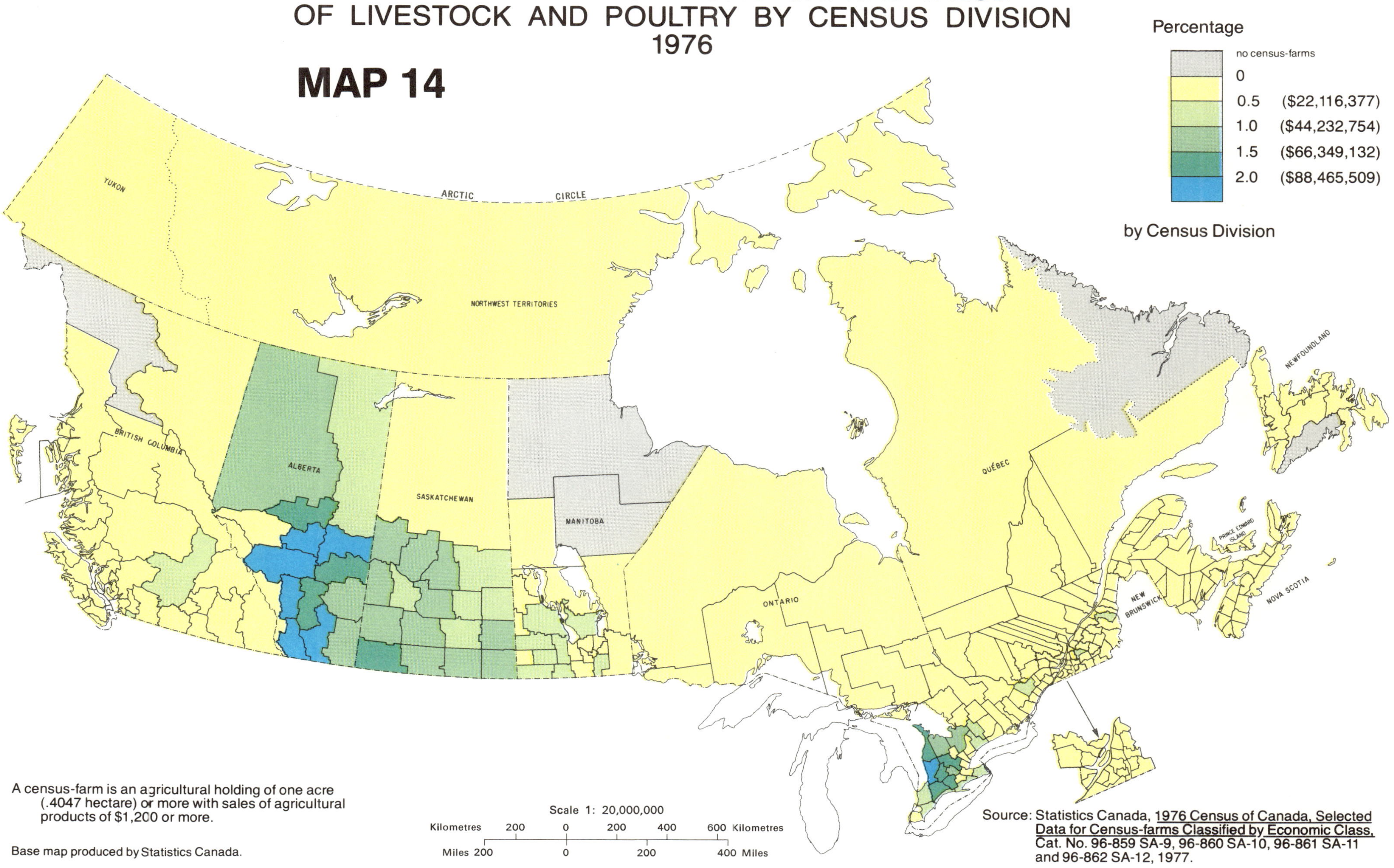

Percentage
- no census-farms
- 0
- 0.5 ($22,116,377)
- 1.0 ($44,232,754)
- 1.5 ($66,349,132)
- 2.0 ($88,465,509)

by Census Division

A census-farm is an agricultural holding of one acre (.4047 hectare) or more with sales of agricultural products of $1,200 or more.

Base map produced by Statistics Canada.

Scale 1: 20,000,000

Source: Statistics Canada, 1976 Census of Canada, Selected Data for Census-farms Classified by Economic Class, Cat. No. 96-859 SA-9, 96-860 SA-10, 96-861 SA-11 and 96-862 SA-12, 1977.

purposes of this study, the focus has been shifted from those census divisions with significant sales, to those with marked concentration of crop area. Thus, crop area data for 1976 have been employed in order to identify those particular locations which possess significant areas of specific crops important to Canadian agriculture.

In reviewing the agricultural sales statistics for 1970, it was seen that a large proportion, approximately 65 per cent, of all agricultural sales related to livestock and poultry, including beef and dairy cattle and their numerous products, swine, poultry, poultry products, and sheep. The livestock and poultry business is examined here with a view to identifying those regions which contribute most significantly to agriculture at the national level. The 1976 capital values of livestock and poultry for Canada's 258 census divisions were utilized to help identify the major areas of livestock and poultry production.

The total capital value of livestock and poultry in Canada, in 1976, was an astounding $4,423,275,487. While cattle are a common scene on most Canadian farms (69 per cent of all census-farms reported cattle in 1976) the distribution of commercial livestock and poultry operations, as indicated by levels of capital investment, is shown on Map 14. Two major concentrations exist in southwestern Ontario and southern Alberta. In Ontario, Huron census division on Lake Huron and its five neighbouring units accounted for nearly one-half billion dollars in capital value of livestock and poultry, of which 78 per cent related to cattle alone. This area is a major supplier of beef for Ontario, but swine, poultry, and dairy products are also significant. These census divisions are also, not coincidentally, large producers of

corn, feed grains, and forage crops which help support the livestock industry. Not far away, the meat packing industry is located in the Toronto and Kitchener–Waterloo areas. In the immediate vicinity of most urban centres in eastern and central Canada, most notably Montréal and Toronto, capital values of livestock are low. This supports earlier statements that the areas adjacent to urban centres are most frequently utilized for higher value, higher yield crops such as fruits and vegetables. This is most evident in the "Golden Horseshoe" along the western shore of Lake Ontario where capital values of livestock and poultry are as low as in areas of northern Ontario.

Both southern and central Alberta have the criteria required for large-scale beef production; the availability of appropriate land, the natural shelter provided by the topography, the large tracts of land to support grazing, and the availability of feed grains. Here, the emphasis on cattle, specifically beef, is much more pronounced than in Ontario. The six census divisions with the greatest livestock investment accounted for $655,722,129 of capital value of livestock and poultry in 1976, of which 91 per cent related specifically to cattle. Expansion of the meat packing industry in Calgary and Edmonton, during the last ten years, has considerably reduced the costly eastward shipment of meat on the hoof.

Toward the Alberta–Saskatchewan boundary, although livestock remains an important commodity, wheat, other grains, and oilseeds enter the picture. This combination of wheat, grains, and livestock is common throughout much of Saskatchewan and parts of Manitoba. This is one agricultural area that has seen changes in farm type, mainly in response to fluctuations in wheat prices. If wheat prices drop significantly, some farmers

Photo by Agriculture Canada.

Feedlot facilities, such as this one near Raymond, illustrate the nature and scale of some beef operations in Alberta.

respond by moving into livestock production, particularly beef. Replacement or feeder cattle are readily available from Alberta, and beef operations tend to be feed lot rather than range oriented. This is because wheat farms occupy large areas, because land is not fenced to the same extent as in other regions of Canada, because the cost of fencing is prohibitive, and because feed grain is available.

27

MAP 15

MAJOR WHEAT AREAS 1976

Census division areas as a percentage of total Canadian area

hectares			acres
no census-farms, or census-farms without wheat crop	0	0	no census-farms, or census-farms without wheat crop
(56,118)	0.5	0.5	(138,672)
(112,237)	1.0	1.0	(277,344)
(336,711)	3.0	3.0	(832,031)
(561,185)	5.0	5.0	(1,386,718)

by Census Division

Wheat crop includes winter, durum and spring wheat.

A census-farm is an agricultural holding of one acre (.4047 hectare) or more with sales of agricultural products of $1,200 or more.

Base map produced by Statistics Canada.

Scale 1: 20,000,000

Source: Statistics Canada, 1976 Census of Canada, Crops on Census-farms, Cat. No. 96-851 SA-1, 1977.

Although southern Alberta and southwestern Ontario appear to have the largest share of the livestock and poultry operations in Canada, it is equally significant that all of the 253 census divisions, which reported census-farms in 1976, also reported livestock operations. This emphasizes that this farm activity is able to adapt to the various physical, climatic, economic, social, and political environments found across the country. Whether it be at a subsistance or large-scale commercial level, the livestock aspect of farming is a definitive characteristic of Canadian agriculture. No other single farm activity is found as widely throughout Canada.

Wheat Areas

When asked to name Canada's major agricultural crop or major farm export commodity, many Canadians would likely answer "wheat". Indeed, in 1970, wheat ranked third in value of agricultural sales behind cattle and dairy products. Wheat has unique status as the single, most valuable, cultivated farm crop in Canada, and in the late 1970s, continues to play a major rôle in Canada's balance of trade. If Alberta and Ontario are Canada's meat and livestock product suppliers, then Saskatchewan is undeniably the "breadbasket". Although most areas of the country cultivate some wheat, there is a very definite concentration of wheat production and sales (Map 15 and Figures 7 and 8).

In southern Saskatchewan, and to a lesser extent in southeastern Alberta and southwestern Manitoba, both soil type and climatic conditions are suited to the production of coarse grains, oilseed, and fibre crops as well as the world-renowned hard spring wheat. The vast land mass offers large land parcels, which are, to a great ex-

Photo by Agriculture Canada.
Endless fields of wheat are characteristic of the farm landscape in Canada's "breadbasket". These particular fields are located between Biggar and Harris, Saskatchewan.

tent, unfragmented by physical obstacles, political boundaries, or small lot divisions. Of the approximately 11,224,000 ha of wheat grown in Canada in 1976, nearly two-thirds were cultivated in Saskatchewan alone. When Alberta and Manitoba's contributions are added, the three Prairie Provinces accounted for 97 per cent of the country's wheat area. The extent to which the southern Prairies predominate is seen in another statistic. All census divisions which contained more than 0.5 per cent (56,118 ha) of Canada's total wheat area in 1976 were found in Alberta, Saskatchewan, or Manitoba. Together these 39 units accounted for 95 per cent of Canada's wheat land.

Specialty Field Crop Areas

The specialty field crops include tobacco, sugar beets, and potatoes, plus other miscellaneous and unclassified crops. Unlike wheat, crops such as tobacco and sugar beets require more specialized growing conditions. Hence, the areas which will support such crops are more restricted. Map 16 highlights the census divisions which have significant shares of specialty field crop areas (see also Figures 9 and 10).

Tobacco requires light sandy soil for optimum cultivation, and only 39,744 ha of tobacco were cultivated in Canada in 1976. Forty-two per cent of Canada's total tobacco area was found in one Ontario census division, Haldimand–Norfolk on the north shore of Lake Erie. If its immediate neighbours Elgin, Brant, Oxford, and Middlesex are added, together they account for 80 per cent of Canada's tobacco-growing area. This is not to say that these census divisions do not participate in other farm operations or even gain the largest share of agricultural sales from other crops. What it does mean is that these few units have almost a monopoly of this crop in Canada and, for this specific crop, these areas must be considered as important. Others areas which cultivate tobacco, but to a considerably lesser extent, include Kings and Queens census divisions in Prince Edward Island (the eastern and western of the province's

MAP 16 MAJOR SPECIALTY FIELD CROP AREAS 1976

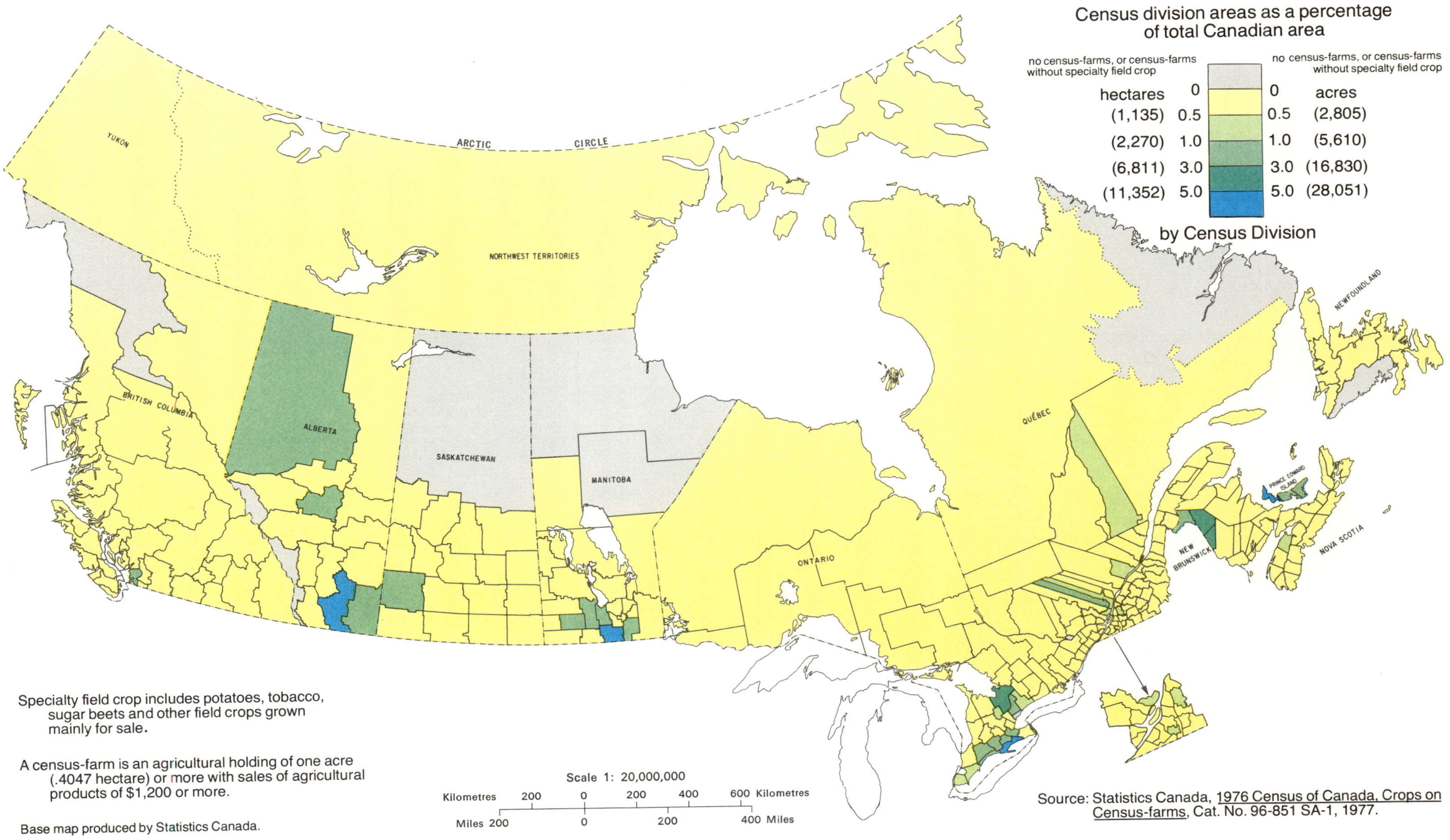

Census division areas as a percentage
of total Canadian area
no census-farms, or census-farms without specialty field crop
hectares 0 — 0 acres
(1,135) 0.5 — 0.5 (2,805)
(2,270) 1.0 — 1.0 (5,610)
(6,811) 3.0 — 3.0 (16,830)
(11,352) 5.0 — 5.0 (28,051)
by Census Division
YUKON
ARCTIC CIRCLE
NORTHWEST TERRITORIES
BRITISH COLUMBIA
ALBERTA
SASKATCHEWAN
MANITOBA
ONTARIO
QUÉBEC
NEWFOUNDLAND
PRINCE EDWARD ISLAND
NEW BRUNSWICK
NOVA SCOTIA
Scale 1: 20,000,000
Kilometres 200 0 200 400 600 Kilometres
Miles 200 0 200 400 Miles

Specialty field crop includes potatoes, tobacco, sugar beets and other field crops grown mainly for sale.

A census-farm is an agricultural holding of one acre (.4047 hectare) or more with sales of agricultural products of $1,200 or more.

Base map produced by Statistics Canada.

Source: Statistics Canada, 1976 Census of Canada, Crops on Census-farms, Cat. No. 96-851 SA-1, 1977.

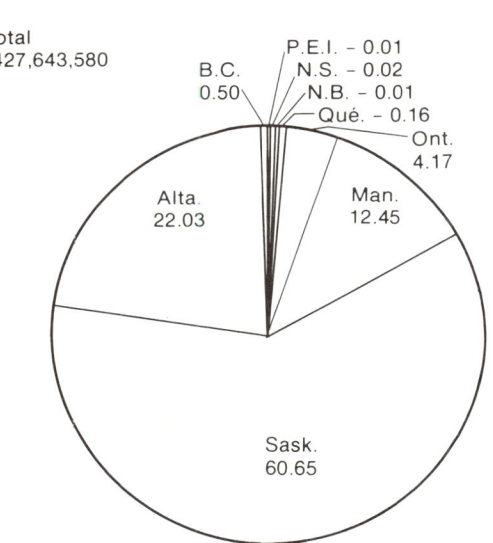

FIGURE 7.

Percentage of Canada's wheat sales, by province, 1970

Total
$427,643,580
B.C.
0.50
P.E.I. - 0.01
N.S. - 0.02
N.B. - 0.01
Qué. - 0.16
Ont.
4.17
Alta.
22.03
Man.
12.45
Sask.
60.65

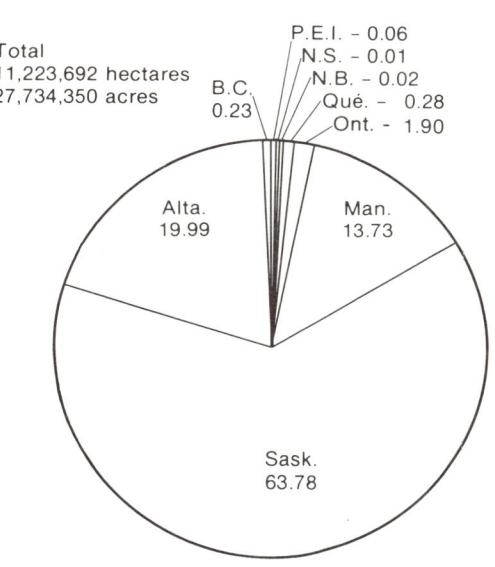

FIGURE 8.

Percentage of Canada's wheat area, by province, 1976

Total
11,223,692 hectares
27,734,350 acres
B.C.
0.23
P.E.I. - 0.06
N.S. - 0.01
N.B. - 0.02
Qué. - 0.28
Ont. - 1.90
Alta.
19.99
Man.
13.73
Sask.
63.78

Source: Statistics Canada, 1973*a*. Canada. Catalogue 96-701 Vol: IV-Part 1.
Statistics Canada, 1977*d*. Crops on Census-farms. Catalogue 96-851.

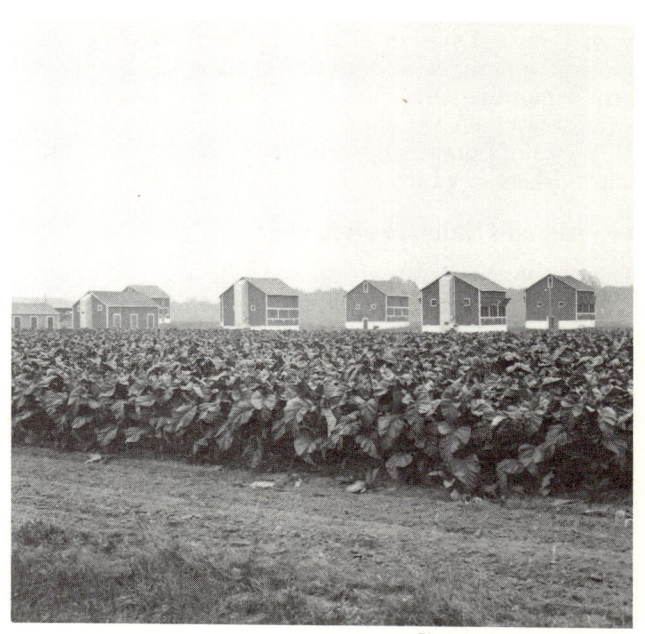

Photo by Agriculture Canada.

Of all field crops, tobacco has one of the highest values. The fields and kilns of this farm near Delhi, Ontario are at the centre of an area that accounts for 80 per cent of tobacco land in Canada.

three census divisions), as well as the Berthier–Joliette area on the North Shore of the St. Lawrence River, just downstream from Montréal.

Sugar beets grown for sugar are another specialized and concentrated crop. In 1976, Canadian census-farms grew only 33,846 ha, and over 70 per cent of this crop area was found in only two census divisions. In southern Alberta, Census Division No. 2 (on the Canada–United States border) accounted for 43 per cent of Canada's sugar beet area. As mentioned earlier, this area possesses extensive irrigation facilities which provide the high moisture conditions necessary for sugar beets. In Manitoba, Census Division No. 3 (south of Winnipeg and also on the international border) accounted for 9,250 ha or 27 per cent of the country's sugar beet area. The increased precipitation, irrigation operations, and silty soils associated with the Red River valley are well suited to growing sugar beets. Other areas which cultivate this specialty crop to any significant degree are Alberta's Census Division No. 1 in the extreme southeastern corner of the province, Manitoba's Census Divisions No. 2 and 9 southeast and west of Winnipeg, and Québec's St-Hyacinthe–Bagot area east of Montréal.

Potatoes require a cooler climate and slightly acidic soil, and will grow in more areas than the two previous specialty field crops. Parts of the Maritimes are ideally suited to the production of this important crop. Prince County, the middle census division in Prince Edward Island, has more land (13,209 ha) in potatoes than any other division in Canada. The potato crop of all three units is one of the reasons that the Island is known as the garden province. This basic crop is also the reason that Kings County in Nova Scotia stands out among other census divisons. However, perhaps more than any

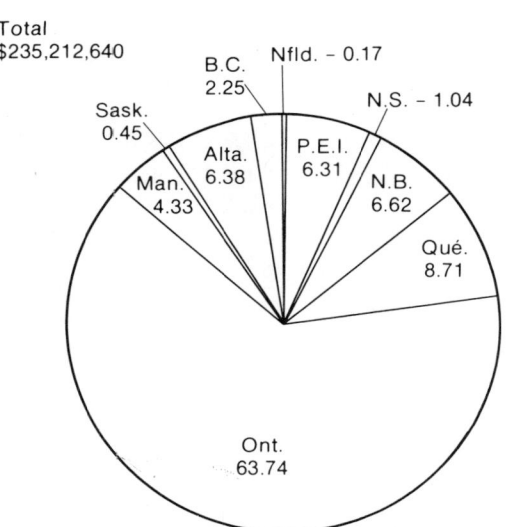

FIGURE 9.
Percentage of Canada's specialty field crop sales, by province, 1970

Total $235,212,640
Nfld. - 0.17
B.C. 2.25
N.S. - 1.04
Sask. 0.45
Alta. 6.38
P.E.I. 6.31
Man. 4.33
N.B. 6.62
Qué. 8.71
Ont. 63.74

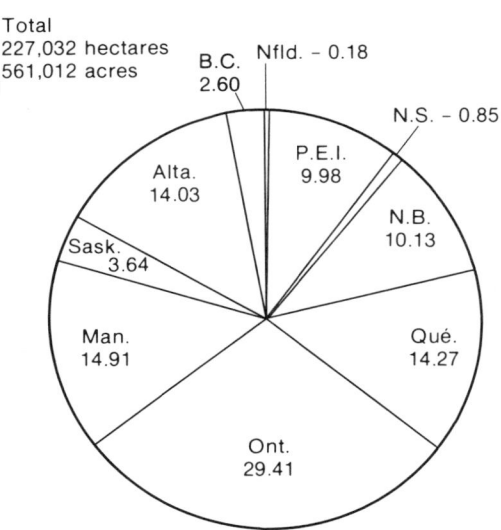

FIGURE 10.
Percentage of Canada's specialty field crop area, by province, 1976

Total 227,032 hectares 561,012 acres
Nfld. - 0.18
B.C. 2.60
N.S. - 0.85
P.E.I. 9.98
Alta. 14.03
N.B. 10.13
Sask. 3.64
Man. 14.91
Qué. 14.27
Ont. 29.41

Source: Statistics Canada, 1973a. *Canada.* Catalogue 96-701 Vol: IV-Part 1.
Statistics Canada, 1977d. *Crops on Census-farms.* Catalogue 96-851.

Photo by Agriculture Canada.
Although potatoes are grown in many locations across Canada, certain areas of the Maritimes are ideally suited to this crop. These extensive fields, not far from Grand Falls New Brunswick, confirm the province's reputation as a major producer of this vegetable.

other area in Canada, it is New Brunswick that is known as potato country. The province accounted for one-fifth of the country's potato area, and three units in the northwestern corner, Victoria, Carleton, and Madawaska, accounted for 96 per cent of the province's 22,308 ha of potato fields. As in Prince Edward Island, the potatoes serve many needs; the fresh food table market, the seed potato market, and the frozen food and processing needs of large manufacturers. Potatoes are grown widely throughout Québec, and five census divisions, not mentioned earlier under tobacco or sugar beets, stand out: Chicoutimi in central Québec, Portneuf and Montmorency No. 2 near Québec City, and Napierville and L'Assomption in the vicinity of Montréal. In Ontario, Simcoe and Dufferin census divisions, which lie between Georgian Bay and Toronto, and Essex County in the extreme southwest tip of the province, have sizable areas in potato fields. In Manitoba, Census Division No. 3, the sugar beet centre, along with Nos. 7 and 8 to its immediate northwest are important potato regions. In Alberta, the other sugar beet capital Census Division No. 2 in the south, as well as the Peace River area of Census Division No. 15 in the northwest, also grow large quantities of potatoes as a standard crop. In British Columbia, one small area is notable, namely the Greater Vancouver–Richmond area which contains a sizable area of potatoes, grown mainly for the fresh vegetable markets in Vancouver and Victoria.

Tree Fruit and Small Fruit Areas

The distinctive nature of the climatic and soil conditions required for most fruit production, or the stimuli and methods required to alleviate any shortcomings in other areas, through irrigation for example, mean that few areas are successful. The accompanying map of tree fruit and small fruit areas (Map 17) underscores the limited land base which meets the rather stringent growing requirements for many fruit crops. Every Canadian should easily be able to identify Canada's three major fruit areas: the Annapolis Valley, the Niagara Peninsula, and the Okanagan Valley. Four census divisions, Kings in Nova Scotia, Niagara in Ontario, and Central Okanagan and Okanagan–Similkameen in British Columbia, when combined, account for approximately 45 per cent of tree fruit and small fruit areas in Canada. In addition, Québec has 17 per cent of the total fruit area. The extent of the concentration of this agricultural operation is highlighted by Figures 11 and 12, as well as by Map 17. Of the 258 census divisions, only 36 possess 370 ha or more of fruit lands, equivalent to 0.5 per cent of the country's total area. Furthermore, these 36 census units accounted for 86 per cent of the land devoted to these specialized crops in 1976.

Throughout the Atlantic Provinces, the low-bush or wild blueberry thrives on the acidic soils found in many areas. The blueberry crop is important commercially, particularly in areas of Newfoundland, Nova Scotia, and New Brunswick. In Nova Scotia, however, there is a distinction to be made between the tree fruit and small fruit areas. The Annapolis Valley (Kings and Annapolis census divisions along the Bay of Fundy) supports a variety of tree fruit production, but the emphasis is clearly on apples. In Kings census division, in 1971,

Photo by Agriculture Canada.
A major centre for cultivation of sugar beets is found in southern Alberta. The type of extensive irrigation equipment required to overcome moisture deficiency is illustrated on a sugar beet farm near Taber.

93 per cent of all tree fruit land was in apple orchards. On the other hand, the emphasis in other fruit-growing areas of the province is on small fruits, especially berries. In areas such as Cumberland, Pictou, and Colchester, the blueberry is king. In southwestern New Brunswick, apples and strawberries are both important commercial crops.

Blueberries are an important crop throughout much of Québec, but the major fruit areas lie in the more favourable soils and climate of the St. Lawrence Lowlands. In the Deux-Montagnes, Huntingdon, Missisquoi, and Rouville census divisions, which lie to the west, south, and east of Montréal, apple orchards dominate the landscape, with strawberries and raspberries occupying less land. Pressures exerted by urban expansion, together with increasing production costs, have reduced orchard areas around Montréal during the last few years.

In Ontario, the edge of the Canadian Shield effectively delineates the limit of large-scale commercial orchards. Along the shore of Lake Ontario between Kingston and Hamilton, and along southern Georgian Bay, apples, sour cherries, and to a lesser extent pears and peaches, are the predominant fruit crops. Near Hamilton on the extreme western tip of Lake Ontario, the fruit industry's orientation changes. Here, the benefits of unparalleled climatic conditions, principally a long frost-free season and reduced risk of frost damage, become apparent, particularly in the Niagara area where tender fruits are grown. In terms of the relative value of crops in 1978, the descending order might be: grapes, peaches, pears, sour cherries, sweet cherries, plums, prunes, and apricots. The degree to which this tender fruit belt dominates Canada's fruit industry is indicated by 1971 census data, the last census for which individual fruit data are available. The census division of Niagara alone accounted for 81 per cent of Canada's grape-growing area, 59 per cent of peach area, 55 per cent of sour cherry area, and more than one-third of the country's pear, plum/prune, and sweet cherry areas. In southwestern Ontario, the emphasis is on apples, strawberries, and pears, but the extreme southwestern corner with its moderate climate and good soil sees peaches assume more significance, along with apples and pears. Southwestern Ontario is the reserve area for fruit trees and grapes, but lacks the same degree of security from frost damage found in the Niagara Peninsula.

In the west, only a few small pockets of fruit cultivation exist on the Prairies, and apples, cherries, prunes and plums, or berries are the most common crops. Only the well-known Okanagan and lower Fraser valleys of British Columbia have fostered large fruit-growing regions. The Okanagan is justifiably famous for its apples, peaches, pears, sweet cherries, and grapes. The combined census divisions of Central Okanagan and Okanagan–Similkameen accounted for 14 per cent of Canada's tree fruit and small fruit area in 1976. In 1971, these two units accounted for 45 per cent of Canada's sweet cherry area, 28 per cent of pears, 73 per cent of apricots, 19 per cent of apples, and 14 per cent of peaches. One distinction should be made between the Okanagan, and Niagara or Annapolis fruit areas. The Okanagan has developed only through the construction of extensive irrigation systems, without which the natural semi-arid conditions could not support a fruit industry. Lastly, in the lower Fraser Valley, the emphasis is on small fruit production. Here, strawberries, raspberries, cranberries, and high-bush cultivated blueberries are important commercial crops for markets in Vancouver and Victoria.

Photo by Agriculture Canada.
Orchards near Kelowna testify to the status of the Okanagan Valley as one of Canada's three special fruit-production areas.

MAP 17

MAJOR FRUIT AREAS 1976

Fruit crop includes small fruits grown mainly for sale, and tree fruits on farms having 25 or more fruit trees.

A census-farm is an agricultural holding of one acre (.4047 hectare) or more with sales of agricultural products of $1,200 or more.

Base map produced by Statistics Canada.

Source: Statistics Canada, 1976 Census of Canada, Crops on Census-farms, Cat. No. 96-851 SA-1, 1977.

In spite of other differences, the major fruit-growing areas of Canada share at least one thing in common. All are continuing to feel great pressures for land use change from the expansion of nearby urban centres. Whether it is a desire for a vacation home on the shore of scenic Lake Okanagan, or the desirability of industrial or residential location in the Niagara Peninsula or Annapolis Valley, the specialized fruit lands of Canada, with their unique soils and climates, face stiff competition. Because of the marked concentration of the fruit lands, any change in their land use means significant change to Canada's fruit industry as a whole, and thus, these areas are indeed special agricultural resource lands.

Vegetable Areas

The first impression gained from the accompanying map of vegetable areas in Canada (Map 18) might be that, while most of the country does grow small quantities of vegetables, relatively few census divisions account for most of the produce. The delta area of British Columbia's Lower Mainland, the marshland areas south of Montréal, as well as central and southwestern Ontario have become the dominant vegetable-producing locations in Canada (Figures 13 and 14). The appropriate soils, favourable climate, and nearby urban markets have stimulated the transition from other types of farm activities to these more specialized crops. This category of vegetables excludes potatoes (found under specialty field crops) and includes only those vegetables grown mainly for sale.

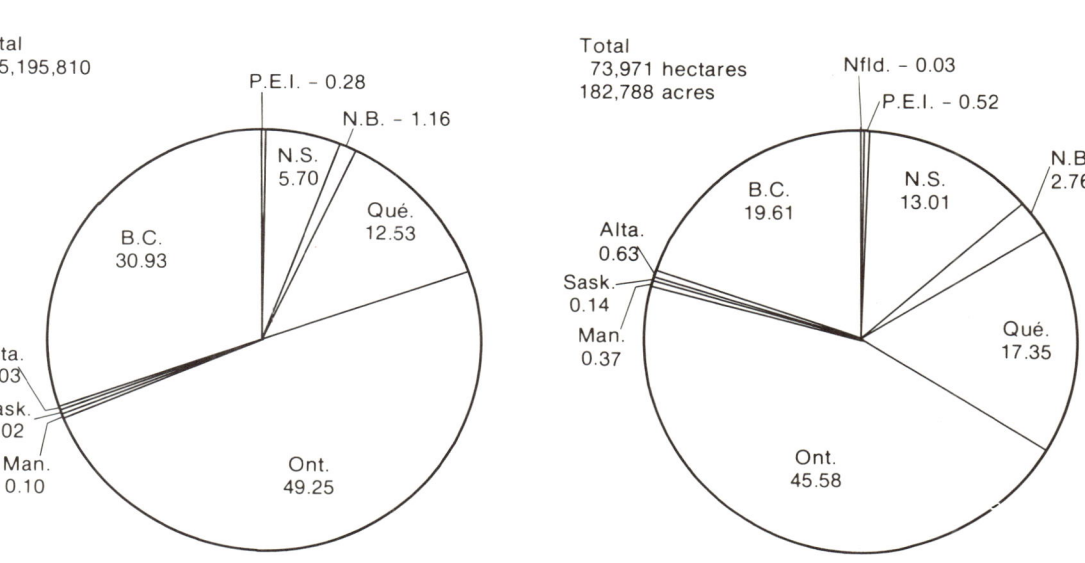

FIGURE 11. Percentage of Canada's fruit sales, by province, 1970

FIGURE 12. Percentage of Canada's fruit area, by province, 1976

Source: Statistics Canada, 1973a. Canada. Catalogue 96-701 Vol: IV-Part 1.
Statistics Canada, 1977d. Crops on Census-farms. Catalogue 96-851.

MAP 18

MAJOR VEGETABLE AREAS 1976

Census division areas as a percentage of total Canadian area

hectares		acres
	no census-farms, or census-farms without vegetable crop (grey)	
0	0	0
(566) 0.5		0.5 (1,399)
(1,132) 1.0		1.0 (2,797)
(3,396) 3.0		3.0 (8,392)
(5,660) 5.0		5.0 (13,987)

by Census Division

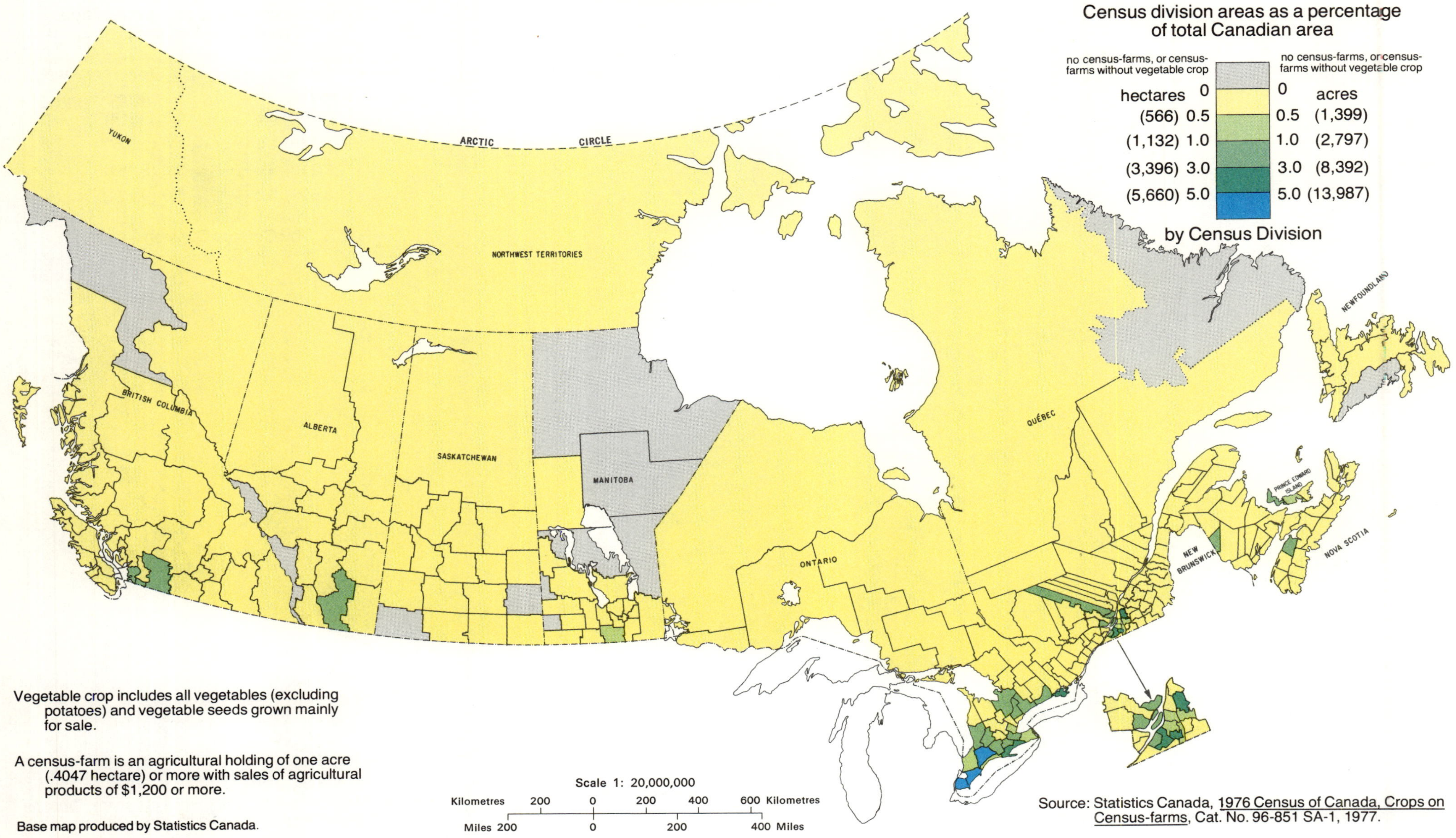

Vegetable crop includes all vegetables (excluding potatoes) and vegetable seeds grown mainly for sale.

A census-farm is an agricultural holding of one acre (.4047 hectare) or more with sales of agricultural products of $1,200 or more.

Base map produced by Statistics Canada.

Scale 1: 20,000,000

Source: Statistics Canada, 1976 Census of Canada, Crops on Census-farms, Cat. No. 96-851 SA-1, 1977.

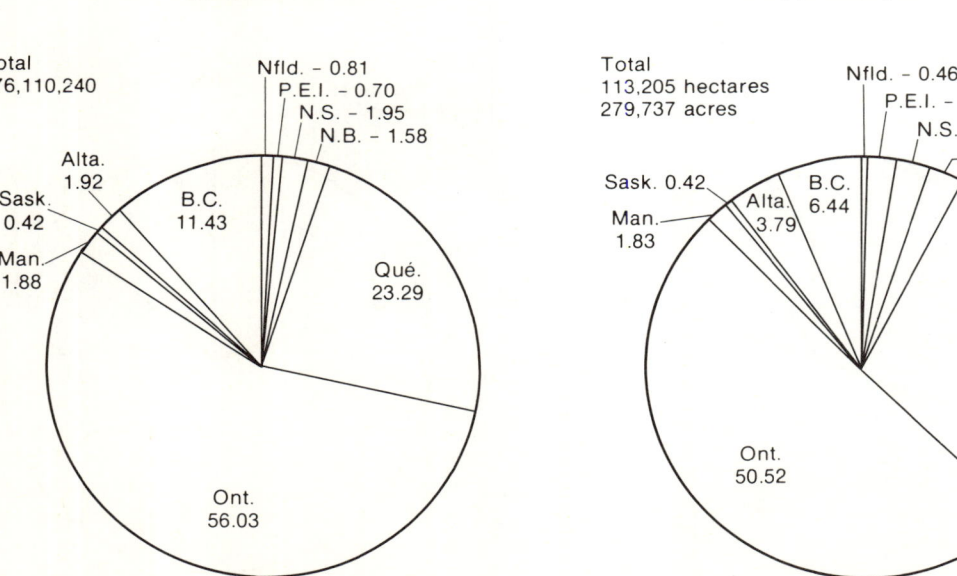

FIGURE 13.
Percentage of Canada's vegetable sales, by province, 1970

Total $76,110,240

- Nfld. – 0.81
- P.E.I. – 0.70
- N.S. – 1.95
- N.B. – 1.58
- Qué. 23.29
- Ont. 56.03
- B.C. 11.43
- Alta. 1.92
- Sask. 0.42
- Man. 1.88

FIGURE 14.
Percentage of Canada's vegetable area, by province, 1976

Total 113,205 hectares 279,737 acres

- Nfld. – 0.46
- P.E.I. – 2.05
- N.S. – 2.59
- N.B. – 2.49
- Qué. 29.41
- Ont. 50.52
- B.C. 6.44
- Alta. 3.79
- Sask. 0.42
- Man. 1.83

Source: Statistics Canada, 1973a. Canada. Catalogue 96-701 Vol: IV-Part 1.
Statistics Canada, 1977d. Crops on Census-farms. Catalogue 96-851.

In the Atlantic Provinces, soils are less fertile and climatic conditions less favourable than in many other vegetable-growing areas. Fewer varieties of crops are grown here, and the contribution to Canada's vegetable crop, aside from the potato, is limited to three specific areas. The census divisions that stand out in Prince Edward Island, Nova Scotia, and New Brunswick all grow green peas, beans, carrots, and rutabagas as their major vegetables.

Although a wide variety of vegetables are cultivated across the province of Québec, the undisputed centre is Montréal and its vicinity. The large urban population and the processing industries provide ready markets. In the marshland of the Napierville–Sherrington region, carrots, onions, and lettuce are the specialties. In the Châteauguay and St-Hyacinthe area, the emphasis changes to sweet corn, beans, and green peas. In Montréal, as well as its immediate surroundings, sweet corn, green peas, beans, cauliflower, and cabbage are predominant. As in southern Ontario, the prospect of early seeding and harvest permitted by the favourable soil and climatic conditions found in the St. Lawrence Lowlands play a significant rôle in determining the pattern of vegetable crops.

In 1976, Ontario accounted for just over 50 per cent of the vegetable area in Canada. It is in southern and southwestern Ontario where the factors of versatile soils, advantageous climate, and proximity of large urban markets are found in a most favourable combination. The Holland Marsh, in Simcoe and York census divisions north of Toronto, has soils which are ideally suited to the production of carrots, onions, celery, and lettuce. Here, more than one-half of the census divi-

Photo by Agriculture Canada.

The Holland Marsh is one main reason why Ontario accounts for more than half of Canada's vegetable-growing area. A drive past the flat, rich land of the marsh reveals endless rows of fresh vegetables, including one of the specialty crops, celery.

sions' vegetable area is in carrots and onions alone. Cabbage, broccoli, and lettuce are commonly grown in lakeshore areas in south-central Ontario. Southwestern Ontario is the country's centre for vegetables grown specifically for processing. Tomatoes, sweet corn, green peas, and cut beans grown here are contracted for canning and freezing, to a considerable extent, to major processors who have located adjacent to these production areas. Essex and Kent census divisions, in the extreme southwest corner of Ontario, specialize in tomatoes, sweet corn, and green peas for both the fresh and processing markets. In 1971, Essex County with 3,541 ha, and Kent County with 2,734 ha, each accounted for a larger area of tomatoes than the rest of Canada combined. In the heart of southwestern Ontario, Middlesex is a specialty area for sweet corn and green peas. In 1971, the 4,485 ha of sweet corn grown in this census division exceeded the crop seeded by British Columbia, Alberta, Saskatchewan, Manitoba, New Brunswick, Nova Scotia, Prince Edward Island, and Newfoundland combined. Immediately north of Middlesex in Huron and Perth census divisions, where soil and climate conditions are slightly less favourable, the main vegetable crop is rutabagas. Toward the western end of Lake Ontario, cut beans are more important. The edge of the Canadian Shield is clearly visible on the accompanying map (*see* Map 18), and its influence on the success of various agricultural activities is worth emphasizing.

The Prairie Region is not a major vegetable region for many of the reasons already described under physical factors. In Manitoba, only Census Division No. 3 contributed more than one-half of one per cent of the country's total vegetable area in 1976. Here, carrots, onions, sweet corn, peas, and cut beans are grown for the Winnipeg table market or for processing. In southern Alberta, Census Division No. 2 with its considerable irrigation facilities, accounted for three-quarters of the province's vegetable area in 1976. Here, corn for canning or freezing, together with green peas and carrots, is most common.

In British Columbia, only the delta lands of the lower Fraser Valley close to Vancouver and Victoria are suitable for large-scale commercial vegetable production. In the Greater Vancouver census division, although green pea and bean crops occupy more land, cauliflower, cabbage, and celery destined for the urban markets are concentrated here. Immediately to the east, in Central Fraser Valley, broccoli is important to the extent that this single census division accounted for nearly one-half of the broccoli area in Canada in 1971. In this same location, sweet corn and green peas are also important. Further up the river valley in the Fraser-Cheam census division, peas, sweet corn, cut beans, and broccoli dominate. Together, these three census units accounted for three-quarters of the province's vegetable area in 1976, and this monopoly is likely to continue.

Economic Risk

"I started in '28 and I farmed for fourteen years and never got a crop. It started in with the dust storms, about three or four years dust storms; then it started in with the grasshoppers; then after the grasshoppers were through, it started in with the rust. We went through all those years without anything, on a $14.40 cheque from the government to keep four of us for the month. We was hailed out two years in a row, never had a chance at all of getting ahead. We stuck it out, because the times would break if we stuck it out long enough, but it went fourteen years and it never did break." (Anderson, 1977).

Farmers are risk-takers. No sooner was the first field broken to plant seed, than insects and plant diseases competed for the produce. In early times, there was little defence against such pestilence. Today, although some chemical pesticides may pose certain hazards, they have dramatically reduced the risks, crop losses, and financial gambles which face Canadian farmers. The same control is not exercised over climatic hazards. When compared with similar phenomena around the globe, the droughts, floods, and other natural events that confront Canadians are often less devastating. Nevertheless, in the past they have been sufficiently damaging to destroy entire crops and drive people from the land. These phenomena continue to influence the success and failure of Canadian agriculture to a very large degree.

Superimposed over the physical setting, however, is a pervasive web of man-made economic influences able to substantially alter land use patterns. Historically, significant areas of land have been cleared for agricultural use, only to revert to tree and native crops or grass cover as economic influences dictated. In recent decades, however, a new dimension has been added. Within the urban fringe areas, the pressures and competition for prime land for housing, industrial development, and recreational purposes have become more intense. Here, in spite of soil of high capability for agriculture, the factor of economics, politics, and the land market may determine that other "higher" uses will prevail. These influences have the power to remove farmland from its traditional resource base and to shift it to areas which impose greater costs and risks. These social, economic, and political elements provide increasing risks to agricultural production.

Natural Phenomena

"In Canada, about 2,800 species of insects, 250 weed species, 500 plant diseases and 50 species of nematodes or worms are potential pests." (Today's Generation, 1973).

"Millions, billions, trillions, Yes, I remember grasshoppers. They would stop the trains. No traction. What a country!

.... They would black out the sky and when they passed, nothing would be left. I've seen an ordinary kitchen broom leaning up against the side of a granary where we were crushing oats and when the hoppers were finished, all that was left of that broom was the handle and you couldn't tell it had been a handle because it was so chewed up except for the metal band which kept the bristles held together. Grasshoppers didn't eat machinery, but by God, I've seen them eat the leather off the seat of a John Deere tractor." (Broadfoot, 1973)[3].

It has been stated that Canada loses 40 per cent of its annual potato crop, 31 per cent of the oat crop, and 18 per cent of the wheat crop to disease, insects, and weeds. (Today's Generation, 1973). Scab fungi, corn

[3.] Excerpts from Ten Lost Years (Doubleday Canada Ltd.) are reprinted by permission of the author, Barry Broadfoot.

borers, root maggots, and cutworms are common pests in field crops. The last two have become particularly successful at resisting chemical pesticides and they continue to plague vegetable crops at considerable expense to farmers. Livestock too suffer from diseases and pests ranging in size from blackflies to grizzly bears (Gurba, 1977). Poultry enterprises face the threat of virulent diseases which are particularly contagious in enclosed indoor facilities. Livestock raised outdoors are attractive to biting insects. Grazing is interrupted and cattle spend energy and lose weight running around pastures trying to escape flies. It is estimated that loss of production, in terms of milk or meat, may be up to 15 per cent of the estimated gains. Warble flies are a particular nuisance and, although data concerning losses from such pests are difficult to measure, Alberta meat packing plants estimated, in 1976, that six or more warble grubs would reduce the value of a beef carcass by 18 cents per kg for a loss of $44.00 on each 250-kg carcass. This represented a loss of two million dollars in Alberta alone (Gurba, 1977). Pests are particularly serious in the only available new land for livestock in northern Canada. Both insects and carnivorous animals including mosquitos, blackflies, horse flies, coyotes, wolves, and grizzly bears thrive in northern areas. Livestock production as well as human settlement is restricted by the ability to control or cope with such pests.

In addition to pests which damage crops annually, other insects and diseases occur sporadically. Grasshoppers, aphids, Bertha armyworms, rusts, and blights explode periodically and cause excessive damage and crop loss. In the history of Canadian agriculture, each of these pests has, at some time, been responsible for crop failures of national significance. In the 1920s, grasshoppers invaded the fields around Medicine Hat and Lethbridge in Alberta, and the only plant to survive was the thistle. The insects even stripped bark from fence posts (Today's Generation, 1973). Potatoes are susceptible to the Colorado potato beetle and late blight. The blight is particularly serious in areas such as the Maritimes where the potato crop is of major economic importance, but all areas are susceptible. The Irish potato famine, caused by the blight, was a contributing factor in the deaths of nearly one million people in 1845. Although it is unlikely that the blight and famine could be repeated at such a scale, crop loss in parts of Canada can reach 40 per cent. The nemesis of wheat is wheat rust, a disease that destroyed nearly the entire wheat crop in 1916.

Photo by Agriculture Canada.

Apple scab is the scourge of part-time and full-time orchardists alike.

How are these pests controlled? The strategy is to document their annual and periodic behavior with the aim of predicting outbreaks. In Saskatchewan for example, data have established that grasshopper damage is a function of crop conditions, weather, and numbers of grasshoppers which tend to have a predictable time pattern of major outbreaks. Regions where this insect has continuously caused economic losses have been identified and the probability of crop damage in various districts can be calculated. The cold winter weather in Canada also serves to control insect pests. In countries with warmer climates, insects proliferate at a much higher rate all year round. Crop protection measures also include monitoring of insects and pests. Infrared aerial photography can be used to identify potato late blight, field bean blight, and infestations of corn leaf aphids. A monitoring system has also been developed for the control of cereal and leaf rusts. Farmers can beat the rust spores by making timely shifts in growing resistant crop varieties. Increased accuracy of disease forecasting through modelling can reduce the need for fungicides and pesticides. In some instances, new strains of resistant grains can be developed in response to particularly serious and persistent losses to specific diseases. In 1937 and 1953, wheat breeders made available the new rust resistant varieties, Coronation and Selkirk, with the result that crop losses from rust have been reduced to less than ten per cent. The rôle of pesticides in ensuring higher crop yields is also important. Before 1900, bunt and smut disease reduced Canada's oat crop to two-thirds of its possible yield. In the 1970s, chemically treated seed reduces losses to less than two per cent.

Of the 200 economically important weed species, one of the most serious is wild oats. Infestations occur on over 16 million ha of the Prairies and annual losses caused by wild oats across Canada have been estimated between $250 and $854 million. In 1976, a weed survey in Saskatchewan concluded that 76 per cent of fields contained wild oats, and established the cost of this weed to farmers at $311 million that year (Saidak, 1977). This loss is reduced by the application of various herbicides.

In addition to various disease and insect pests which impose economic losses on agricultural activities, climatic variability and specific climatic phenomena also present risks and impose costs.

"Although both gradual trends and shorter-term variability have a potential impact on agriculture, coping with variability is the tougher challenge. A gradual change to, say, a cooler regime might be accommodated in affected regions by an orderly shift from corn to cereal production or from cereals to forage. Plant breeders could concentrate on producing varieties that yield well in shorter growing seasons. However, the task of finding varieties that produce well through a kaleidoscope of wet, dry, warm and cool seasons, or of planning successful farming strategies in such highly variable periods is much more formidable." (Gillespie, 1977).

Canadian agriculture is especially vulnerable to climatic change and variability. The climate for agriculture is generally less favourable as compared to other major food producing areas of the world. When combined with an overall inability to predict seasonal or annual conditions, it leaves much of Canadian agriculture susceptible to economic losses from climatic factors. The more northerly farm areas are particularly vulnerable to climatic change. For example, the Peace River area may experience crop failure following minor variation in climatological factors. However, this area also represents one of the most significant reserves for agriculture in Canada. Given the climatic fluctuations of the 1970s, and an inability to foretell the future, such areas may have a rather tenuous status as agricultural reserves. In other parts of Canada, major economic impact on Prairie cereal production, or corn production in Ontario, would likely occur only with more substantial temperature or moisture variations. However, lest complacency set in, a recent study suggested that even with today's technology, a return of the weather experienced between 1933 and 1936 would reduce current annual wheat production in Canada to only two-thirds of the 1970s yields (Gillespie, 1977).

Aside from climatic variability, which is a concept that is often difficult to understand, specific climatic phenomena represent another economic risk. Drought, freezing rain, high winds, hail, flooding, and unseasonable frosts are some of the events which can result in immediate and visible crop damage. A few examples will serve as illustrations. With very few exceptions, most of Canada's farming areas are subject to hail storms. The greatest impact, however, is felt by the cereal crops on the Prairies and by broad-leaved plants such as the corn crop in southern Ontario. The high winds that often accompany a hail storm produce a double impact. Either some of the crop may be beaten down with minor losses at harvest time, or the crop may be totally destroyed. Such hail storms tend to be summer phenomena over the Prairies, which does not allow time for replanting. While hail storms are more common in certain areas such as southern Manitoba and south of Montréal, the storms are generally unpredictable and uncontrollable. No preventive measures are available and the only protection to the farmer is crop insurance.

The risk posed by seasonal drought varies across Canada. It is less severe in maritime locations and more prevalent in the continental areas such as the Prairies. While the 1978 growing season with its shortage of precipitation showed that repercussions in eastern Canada can be serious, drought is principally a western Prairie phenomenon. Here the annual rainfall is limited, and much of the land is not, and can not be, irrigated. A 15 to 20 per cent crop loss on an annual basis is not unusual. The consequences of insufficient moisture include limited germination, reduced plant growth, and poor yield. It is a periodic event whose impact may be reduced by farming practices which limit the amount of soil moisture lost to wind and sun. Trash farming leaves a cover of stubble to help retain soil moisture and the ground is cultivated without turning the sod over or exposing moist soil to drying agents. Shelter belts and wind breaks serve to reduce the drying and erosive effects of wind. They aid in building up the moisture supply by creating snow drifts and accumulating snow cover during winter, which is so important in the open Prairie fields. Cultivation patterns now consist of strips with tree belts between, rather than the former landscape which was totally cultivated.

Lastly, untimely frost can affect a wide spectrum of crops across Canada. The most severe impacts include those felt by cereal, vegetable, and fruit crops. In the case of fruit trees, not only may the year's crop be lost but damage to the tree may be so serious that the tree itself is lost. Untimely frost can offset all the other benefits of a location, including soil, moisture, and market conditions. Another consideration is the fact that freezing can cause damage at many times of the year. Taking the peach crop as an example, rootstock may be seriously damaged during winter temperatures of –5°C and the trees may be killed at –13°C. Mean winter temperatures in such areas of tender fruit should therefore ideally not drop below –3.9°C. In spring and early summer, when trees are in flower at the early pink stage, damage occurs from –5 to –3°C according to the length of exposure. At the delicate period when fruit is set, serious injury occurs at –1°C. Hard, ripe fruit can be seriously damaged at a temperature of –1.4°C. Although the freezing temperatures causing injury to peaches vary from those affecting other fruits and vegetables, all can be injured or destroyed by inopportune freezing (Dubé, 1978). Other than simply living with the risk of frost, preventive measures include development and selection of earlier maturing and hardy crops, development of hardy rootstocks, improved frost-warning systems, and increased air circulation through use of fires, smudge pots, and helicopters at a time of frost danger.

Man-made Influences

In addition to the natural hazards of flood, frost, disease, and insects, there are economic risks or costs that result from man-made sources. The economic viability of agricultural activities is affected by farm productivity, capital investment requirements, operating expenses, wholesale and retail prices, consumer demands, supply and availability of products, and competition from non-Canadian suppliers. At the national and international levels, fluctuating currencies and their changing relationships with each other, market speculation in commodities and currencies, political forces and situations, trade balances, tariff policies, consumption patterns of agricultural products, transportation policies, labour costs, and labour productivity, plus many other factors too numerous to list, all have an impact on Canadian agriculture and, hence, on land use patterns.

Photo by Agriculture Canada.

Snow and ice can be particularly damaging to fruit trees. Not only can the damage reduce the current year's crops, but it can also destroy the tree itself.

Many of these same influences are also present at a much smaller scale. In particular, the rural-urban fringe holds opportunities for both economic gain as well as risk for those engaged in agriculture. The nearer a location is to an urban centre, the more valuable land becomes for residential, industrial, recreation, transportation, or other purposes. As urbanization moves closer, land values rise and only the most intensive, modernized agricultural practices will pay, assuming the land will support such use. In such areas, land speculation, parcel fragmentation, land prices, and land use conflicts are all tied together. Speculation reflects the general attitude that land is more an economic commodity rather than an ecological resource. As some farmers sell their land for personal reasons or to obtain their retirement money, uncertainty haunts the remaining farmers. Fragmentation of agricultural holdings results in some reduction in the scale of rural land uses and reduces future land use options for farmers.

While the consequences of urban expansion into largely rural areas are not entirely negative, some of the most serious concerns are described:

1) Rapid intrusion of urban-oriented uses into rural areas frequently creates an atmosphere of uncertainty. Many agricultural enterprises require long-term investment which will be undertaken only if a reasonable economic return is anticipated. If there is no certainty that the land will remain in agriculture, then it is less likely that the investments or improvements will be made. This has direct repercussions on farm income (Rodd and Van Vuuren, 1975).

2) A substantial portion of the cost of installing new or expanded services required by exurbanites moving into rural areas is borne by the taxpayers of the established rural communities and farm areas. Expanded facilities are often not needed or desired by the farm population. Society at large feels it is entitled to some common level of services regardless of location. The provision of these facilities translates into an increased tax burden for the original rural inhabitants (Russwurm, 1974).

3) Urban intrusion into farm areas may also include snowmobiling or hunting on agricultural property. Damage to crops or injury to livestock is common. Losses due to theft, vandalism, dogs, and other nuisances is a serious problem, particularly in orchard areas.

4) Agricultural parcels may suffer from weed infestation from neighbouring non-farm properties. These can result in increased production costs or yields of lower quality.

5) Increased demand for and consumption of groundwater by residential or industrial uses in farm areas may result in overdraining the soils. Irrigation may then be required, or farmers may be forced to change crops to deep-rooted plantings.

6) Rural road networks or highways are often widened to facilitate the increased volume of traffic generated by non-farm population or recreationists. Frequently, field shapes are altered to permit highway improvements and this often reduces the efficiency of mechanized equipment for seeding, fertilizing, or harvesting, or may impede use of certain vehicles. The actual loss of land to road widening is the most serious factor. The loss of, or damage to, the crop during actual construction is also a concern. For the farmer involved in livestock, the removal and rebuilding of fences may prevent the use of land for grazing of beef and dairy cattle. Serious inconvenience and expense may be incurred if farmers are required to relocate herds on other land. In dry summers, alternative pastures may not be available, thus requiring the purchase of expensive feed. Furthermore, the removal of trees which acted as wind breaks may inconvenience farm operators. High salt levels, resulting from road salting, are of concern to greenhouse operators and to farmers utilizing contaminated irrigation water as crop damage can result.

7) Although gas emissions from automobiles are not yet a major problem, abnormal amounts of gasoline additives have been found in crops along major highways (Goettel, 1969).

8) Chemical pollution or pollution fallout from industrial plants does not always result in dramatic results which can be observed immediately. Changes can occur slowly, and the contamination of beef or dairy cattle or crops may go unnoticed for long periods. Lead poisoning from paint companies and metal refineries is one example. There are several cases in Canada where farmers have encountered lengthy delays, as investigators attempted to establish the source of pollution, before any financial compensation was forthcoming.

9) Urban sewage effluent contains phosphorous and nitrogen. When higher water temperatures are combined with the added nutrients, a rich environment for aquatic growth is created. When this water is used for irrigation, the additional growth of weeds can clog ditches, ponds, and reservoirs. Such water is a rich medium for algae growth and certain algae are toxic to livestock. Thus, some water impounded for stock watering may be impaired. Pathogenic agents in urban sewage include viruses and parasites and consequently may pose a threat to truck garden irrigation. Through time, agricultural groundwater may be contaminated by urban or urban-related land uses such as industry, fuel storage, and waste disposal. Groundwater used for washing milking equipment and for human consumption must be of high quality, and contamination from urban related sources may threaten this resource (Goettel, 1969).

10) Insect spraying programs in the vicinity of cities or recreational sites concern dairy and meat producers because of the non-specific, long-term pesticides often used to control insects. Milk production is particularly susceptible to chemical sprays and farmers may suffer financial losses if milk is contaminated.

11) Specialty suppliers of agricultural machinery, fertilizers, and other products often leave rural areas when the decline in numbers of farmers becomes significant. In addition to the loss of possible off-farm employment, farmers lose the advice and assistance of local suppliers and must deal with urban-based suppliers. Longer times required for repair work during seeding or harvesting is often equivalent to money lost.

Over time, the relative importance of these natural and man-made hazards has changed. In terms of historical and present-day priorities, as measured by dollar losses, the most significant hazards have been (i) drought, (ii) diseases, (iii) insects, and (iv) excessive rain. However, the significant hazards of the present day are (i) excessive rain followed by (ii) drought, (iii) rodent and bird damage, and (iv) frost damage.

The development of disease and insect controls, as well as better cultivation practices, has been responsible for much of the change in order and magnitude of losses. Unfortunately, the impacts attributable to temporary or permanent loss of productive land, or lower quality and smaller yields brought about by social, economic, or political decisions, land use conflicts, land conversion, or pollution, have not been measured. While the sale, conversion, and loss of farmland may represent an economic gain to an individual or company in the short-term, it may be a greater economic and aesthetic loss to society in the long-term. It is possible that such losses warrant placing man-made influences at the top of the list of hazards.

These natural and man-made risks are difficult to describe and yet they too figure in the delineation of special lands. Little research concerning the economic losses related to each hazard has been done at a national scale. Even less has been accomplished in mapping areas of high, low, or average economic risk. Nevertheless, anyone associated with agriculture will testify that no farm activity and no geographical area is free from the vagaries of nature and man.

> "We could look out on our fields and see them burning up in June, when in other years that was the time for good rains. Where were the rains? Where did all those billions of grasshoppers come from? And the rust.
>
> It seemed every year you'd read that someone at some university had invented a wheat that would resist rust, but somebody was inventing a bigger and stronger rust. Musta been." (Broadfoot, 1973).

The preceding section focused on some of the economic characteristics useful in identifying critical farmland. Locations that account for significant amounts of agricultural sales, areas that involve high capital investment, or regions that possess sizable areas of selected crops, may be interpreted as constituting special agricultural land resources. But there are additional factors to consider. One of these, the rôle of change, is discussed in the following section.

Factors of Change

> "With the older way of farming with the teams, there was less rushing, hurrying, and we weren't trying to do as much; we were getting along with a smaller acreage and we could get along with fewer cows and make a living much easier, I think, than we can today. And if I was young today, I doubt very much whether I'd be looking to a farm or not. It's such a change from the old way of doing things that it's just almost unthinkable for me for to carry on the way it's going now." (Anderson, 1977).

What are the changes?

Where are they occurring?

Why are they happening?

What are the consequences?

Changes in agriculture are not isolated, but are part of a continuum that has its origin in land settlement patterns of centuries past and its future in today's public opinions and political decisions. Transformations that are now occurring in agriculture can only be appreciated and evaluated within the context of past trends and future goals. But, the types of changes in society as well as in agriculture are so numerous and their relationships so complex, that a complete overview is impossible. Instead, a few examples are presented:

1) Urban pressures represent a major source of change. What social and economic factors have contributed to changing rural-urban relationships? Where are the pressures and repercussions on agriculture most significant? Why have they occurred?

2) The Canadian land resource base is shifting. Agricultural land is being lost in eastern and central Canada, in marginal areas and in urban areas, while it is being gained in the Prairies and the northern frontier. What is the significance of changes in these geographical patterns? What changes are taking place in the agriculture industry and to those people involved in farming?

3) What about climatic change? Relatively minor climatic fluctuations and events in the past have had drastic effects on Canadian agriculture. What is happening now, and why? Where are changes likely to occur and what are the possible consequences?

[3] Excerpts from Ten Lost Years (Doubleday Canada Ltd.) are reprinted by permission of the author, Barry Broadfoot.

The issues of urban pressures, shifting agricultural land base, changes in the industry itself, and climatic fluctuations are only a few of the ongoing changes. Nonetheless, they can serve as examples of how physical, economic, social, or political influences can affect land use activities such as agriculture. Perhaps one of the most important questions is: Where are the changes occurring? These areas represent another type of special land–dynamic areas where land uses may be converted, pressures are more intense, problems are being attacked if not resolved, and the very characteristics of agriculture have changed or will be forced to change in response to a complexity of influences.

Urban Pressures

Where are the changes in agricultural land occurring and why?

Only 0.5 per cent of Canada's land has no significant limitations for agriculture. Not surprisingly, the qualities that delineate good soil for farming also identify those same soils as high capability for other uses including urban settlement and growth. Generally speaking, prime farmland and urban development occur in many of the same locations—a trend started early in Canadian history. During native, French, and English waves of exploration, settlements clustered along rivers, the sole networks for transportation and communication. The river valleys, deltas, and lowlands were also favoured for agriculture, and it was the socially and economically-stable resource base provided by agriculture that allowed the early settlements to survive the changing functions of fur trading, lumbering, merchandising, and finance, through which many of the towns evolved.

As a result, much prime farmland is now adjacent to major urban centres and transportation routes. For purposes of easy access to large markets and quality of transportation facilities, this proximity is beneficial.

NFB – PHOTOTHEQUE – ONF – Photo by George Hunter.

As urban centres reach outward, the urban fringe expands at the expense of other land uses. Frequently, the land is converted from productive agriculture into idle land, before being transformed into direct urban or urban-related uses such as expressways, factory sites, and parking lots.

However, the very urban market which creates the demand for farm produce affects the farmland's ability to meet this demand. At first glance, this may seem surprising in light of the fact the Canadian cities themselves occupy less than two per cent of the country's total land area. But, there are two reasons, among many others, why cities have in the past, and will in the future, continue to influence land uses throughout the country.

Urban Growth

> "The farm was on the northern outskirts of Quebec City, well within the present-day city boundaries. I think it was considered a large farm, perhaps two hundred acres, about that size anyway. It was a very pretty location and I think they did all sorts of mixed farming. . . . Today the farm is completely gone. It is now a playground for an orphanage, I believe. The river is gone, although it was a natural drainage river; they put pipe in and it is all levelled over, all the huge beautiful elm trees have vanished of course. The house is gone, and the last time I was down you couldn't really tell where it had been—it's just gone, gone, disappeared." (Anderson, 1977).

Canada became a highly urbanized nation in a relatively short period of time. In 1867, Canada was a rural, agricultural country of three and one-half million people, of whom only 18 per cent were urban dwellers. By 1900, one-third of Canadians lived in cities, and this proportion increased to one-half in the early 1920s. In 1976, this figure increased to 75.5 per cent and it is anticipated that, by 2001, 90 per cent or more of the total population will be urban. Since World War II, Canada's rate of urban growth exceeded that of any other western industrialized nation. In the period 1871 to 1976, although total population increased six-fold, the urban component grew by a factor of 24 (Table 8).

were born outside of Canada. However, the immigrants' choice of certain provincial destinations is clearly shown in the fact that only three per cent of the urban population in Newfoundland were foreign-born, but 25 per cent of urban Ontario residents were foreign-born, in 1971 (Hill, 1976a). Between 1961 and 1977, 55 per cent of immigrants who arrived were between 15 and 34 years of age, while only 35 per cent of Canada's population were in the same age bracket in 1976.

The specific demographic characteristics of immigrants, combined with their occupations, skills, lifestyles, and preferences for urban or rural settings have had both short- and long-term effects on land use in

TABLE 8.

Canada's urban and rural population, 1871 to 1976

Year	Urban population	Percentage of total population		Rural population
1976	17,366,965	75.5	24.5	5,625,635
1971	16,410,785	76.1	23.9	5,157,525
1966	14,726,759	73.6	26.4	5,288,121
1961	12,700,390	69.6	30.4	5,537,857
1956	10,714,855	66.6	33.4	5,365,936
1951	8,628,253	61.6	38.4	5,381,176
1941	6,252,416	54.3	45.7	5,254,239
1931	5,572,058	53.7	46.3	4,804,728
1921	4,352,122	49.5	50.5	4,435,827
1911	3,272,947	45.5	54.5	3,933,696
1901	2,014,222	37.6	62.4	3,357,093
1891	1,537,098	31.8	68.2	3,296,141
1881	1,109,507	25.7	74.3	3,215,303
1871	722,343	19.6	80.4	2,966,914

Sources: Dominion Bureau of Statistics, 1963b. Population: Rural and Urban Distribution. Catalogue 92-536.
Urquhart and Buckley, 1965. Historical Statistics of Canada.

Historically, the dominant economic activities helped determine the rate of urbanization at the provincial levels. In British Columbia, Ontario, and Québec, the major rôles in manufacturing, finance, trade, and services meant that the urban-rural balance in these provinces tipped in favour of urban residents between 1901 and 1921. On the other hand, in provinces where the population was committed largely to primary resource activities such as farming and fishing, urbanization was delayed. In several of the Atlantic and Prairie Provinces, the urban population did not overtake the rural population until the mid-1900s. As recently as 1976, Prince Edward Island still had a predominantly rural population (63 per cent of total population). Today, in the natural evolution of the urbanization process, it is the nature, extent, and rate of urban growth that is the prime factor influencing land use both within the city boundary and in the hinterland. This dramatic urbanization of the country occurred for a variety of reasons.

Immigration. Canada's growth rate has always been influenced to a great degree by the nature and rate of immigration. Seeking new opportunities, freedom from religious or political forces, or hoping to take advantage of expanding resource frontiers, immigrants came in numbers sufficient to help shape Canada's development. By virtue of ethnic differences including age structure, fertility, marital status, and sex ratios, foreign-born residents have had considerable impact on the nature of urban growth and rural development (Hill, 1976a). The distribution of immigrants in rural/urban terms has been of government interest for many decades. At the turn of the century, immigration policy was aimed specifically at discouraging immigration to urban areas in order to avoid congestion, unemployment, and cultural problems. In fact, only farmers, farm workers, and domestics were encouraged to immigrate to Canada, in an effort to accelerate settlement and development of agriculture in the Prairies. By 1921, in spite of such government policy, only in the agricultural provinces of Alberta and Saskatchewan were foreign-born Canadians less urbanized than Canadian-born citizens. Since 1941, foreign-born citizens have been more highly urbanized than Canadian-born citizens in every province. Preference for urban living is much more pronounced among the immigrant population and there is a marked tendency to choose the largest metropolitan centres. Of urban residents in 1971 (the last year for which statistics are available), 18.5 per cent were foreign-born, while only 7.7 per cent of non-urban citizens

Canada. From their significant rôle in opening the Prairies for agriculture in the early 1900s to increasing the demand for private and public goods, services, jobs, and housing in urban centres in the mid-1900s, foreign-born Canadians will continue to play a large part in determining land use patterns.

Migration Within Canada. The ability of cities to attract Canadians from other parts of the country has always been strong but it has played a key rôle in attracting rural residents. The migration of rural dwellers to urban centres has occurred for a variety of economic, social, and political reasons. At various times during the past decades, there have been periods of excessive supply of agricultural produce, due in part to improved technology and farm management practices as well as increased productivity. These improvements have come at considerable expense, and consequently production costs for the farmer have risen dramatically. At the same time, excessive supply has played a part in lowering the prices that farmers receive for their goods at various times. As a result, many farmers were unable to maintain a profit and were forced to sell or abandon their land at a time when land was cheap. A series of disastrous growing seasons which combined into the dust bowl and depression times of the 1920s and 1930s, the two World Wars which required wartime effort, and a growing emphasis on cities with regard to planning, policy development, financing, and politics hastened a decline in the relative importance of rural areas.

This departure of significant numbers of farmers reduced the demand and basis of operation for local agricultural suppliers and processors such as machinery dealers, mill operators, and meat processors. Many small-scale businesses were not able to continue competing successfully with larger urban-based companies. As local farm-related services went out of business or moved out of the area, the decline of many rural communities was accelerated. Centralization of farm-supply and service businesses in urban areas increased and, consequently, local non-farm employment opportunities for the rural labour force declined. The family labourer and hired hand, replaced by more efficient machinery or unemployed as farms went under, were compelled to join other rural residents and migrate to the cities in search of jobs. This loss of rural residents, particularly the younger workers and their families, left a heavier financial and tax burden on fewer rural people. As growing cities attracted a greater share of money for expansion of facilities and services, rural areas re-

Photo by Agriculture Canada.

Many rural farm residents have abandoned the risky and unsettled business of farming in favour of jobs in cities and towns. Such jobs often offer higher pay and greater security.

ceived less attention—part of the overall decline in the fortunes of many parts of rural Canada.

The differences among the demographic profiles of the urban, rural farm, and rural non-farm populations are evident in Figure 15. Because of the continuing concentration of large numbers of people in urban areas, immigration patterns oriented to urban areas, and the concentration of job opportunities, as well as government, health, education, housing, and other facilities in cities, the urban pyramid has exhibited large and consistent increases in all age categories above 15 years. In the urban population, females outnumber males in all age categories between 20 and 90+ years, reflecting the concentration of traditional job opportunities for women in cities and the exodus of women from rural to urban areas. The rural farm pyramid indicates more men than women in all categories except 35 to 39 and 80 or over. In agricultural areas, it is more common for men to remain working on farms while many women seek non-farm work in towns and cities. The distinct contraction in the middle of this pyramid results from the significant numbers of people of labour-force age, particularly between 20 and 35 years of age, who have left rural farm areas in search of jobs or urban lifestyles. The loss of young people is also apparent in the 0- to 4-year age group which has shrunk considerably during the last 15 years. The rural non-farm pyramid illustrates almost equal numbers of males and females, largely a result of the movement of young families to rural non-farm residences.

FIGURE 15.

Population pyramids for Canada, 1976

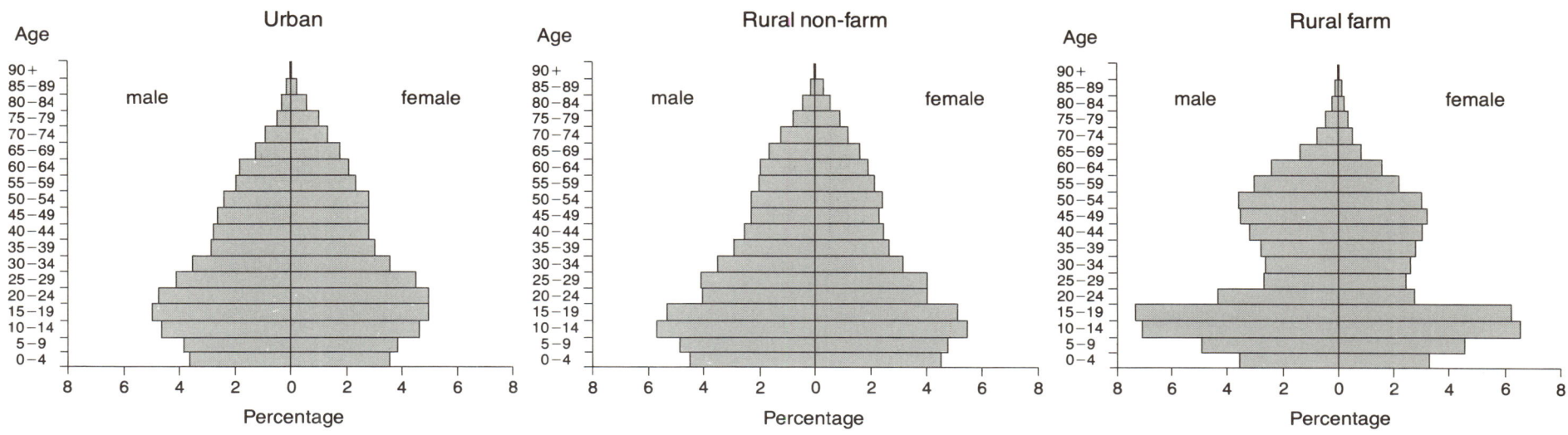

Source: Statistics Canada, 1978b. Population: Demographic Characteristics, Five-Year Age Groups. Catalogue 92-823.

Patterns of Change in the Labour Force. Accompanying any dramatic geographical movement of population is a change in the structure of the labour force including both employed and unemployed people. The rural to urban migration of workers is directly related to the most significant shift in Canada's occupational structure, the change in emphasis from the primary sector (agriculture, forestry, fishing, mining, and trapping) to the tertiary sector (retail and wholesale trade, service activities, and transportation) and to the secondary sector (manufacturing and construction). The extent to which the movement from primary to tertiary activities has occurred is evident in Tables 9, 10, 11, and 12. In 1977, primary activities accounted for only seven per cent of the employed labour force, as compared with 51 per cent in 1881. It is important to note that the shift among sectors did not occur equally in all areas of Canada. For reasons of markets, accessibility, location of resources, and historical development, the Prairie Provinces retain a larger portion of the employed labour force in agricultural activities, while Ontario and Québec increase their concentration of processing, manufacturing, and construction. The employment data indicate the nature of changes in the urban and rural structures of the national economy. Occupation types, employment levels and opportunities, job diversity, and income are all related to a wide range of socio-economic characteristics, which in turn influence the use of land for various purposes. For example, the construction of a major car-assembly plant near London, Ontario, or the closing of a mine site in Nova Scotia, and the resulting shifts of the labour force, have obvious repercussions.

Income. Income and employment opportunities vary between regions and provinces. As a general rule for industrialized and developing countries, the highest average incomes occur in the larger cities. In Canada, certain resource or frontier cities such as Labrador City are the exception. Generally speaking, however, the relationships between income level and city size reflect occupational structure variation; income levels are associated with the dominant economic function and urban hierarchy (Bennett, 1976). While in absolute numbers most low-income families live in urban areas, the proportion of families with low incomes is higher in rural areas and in Atlantic Canada (Table 13). Seasonal characteristics of income are also relevant. In certain regions of the country, particularly in the Atlantic Provinces, the advent of winter signals the end to much outdoor-oriented employment such as fishing and tourism. Ontario and British Columbia have been the most heavily urbanized provinces since 1881, and personal incomes in these two provinces continue to be the highest (Table 14). Income levels and population numbers are directly related to demand for goods and services. The use of land for housing, recreation, and industrial or service-oriented businesses is thereby affected.

Age Structure of Cities. The age structure of any city or area is an important determinant of urban population growth and consequently influences present and future demands for goods and services including land. Age structure and family income levels are related to demands for various land uses, particularly for housing and recreation. The younger, more mobile sectors of population (15 to 35 years) have migrated to some extent in response to higher income levels and higher number of jobs available in larger urban centres as compared with rural areas and smaller urban places (*see* Figure 15). People in this age range in 1978, the product of the "baby boom", are over-represented in the larger and higher income cities. As mentioned before, immigrants tend to be young and to locate in the larger metropolitan centres, thus contributing further to the demand for goods and services.

TABLE 9.

Occupation structure of the labour force, 1881

Occupation category	Canada	British Columbia	Prairies	Ontario	Québec	Atlantic
Primary	51.3	44.4	65.2	49.4	49.5	56.8
Manufacturing	24.3	27.8	16.4	26.8	25.1	18.2
Construction	4.5	5.5	5.1	4.8	4.4	4.2
Transportation	2.9	5.5	1.4	2.2	2.6	4.9
Trade	5.3	5.5	4.1	5.1	5.3	5.6
Service	11.6	11.1	7.6	11.5	13.0	9.1
Total	100.0	100.0	100.0	100.0	100.0	100.0

Source: Li, 1976. Canadian Urban Trends.

Tables 9, 10, 11, and 12 were reproduced by permission of Copp Clark Publishing Limited and the Minister of Supply and Services Canada.

TABLE 10.

Occupation structure of the labour force, 1921

Occupation category	Canada	British Columbia	Prairies	Ontario	Québec	Atlantic
Primary	36.6	29.4	55.2	28.2	30.9	43.4
Manufacturing	20.8	19.3	7.1	26.4	26.9	17.4
Construction	5.8	8.0	3.2	6.7	6.5	5.4
Transportation	7.8	11.2	7.2	8.1	7.1	7.7
Trade	9.4	11.2	8.3	10.7	9.9	8.2
Service	19.2	20.8	19.3	19.9	17.9	16.9
Total	100.0	100.0	100.0	100.0	100.0	100.0

Source: Li, 1976. Canadian Urban Trends.

TABLE 11.

Occupation structure of the labour force, 1951

Occupation category	Canada	British Columbia	Prairies	Ontario	Québec	Atlantic
Primary	19.8	13.7	37.3	13.1	17.2	27.1
Manufacturing	25.1	24.0	13.6	29.8	29.4	20.1
Construction	6.2	6.8	4.8	6.4	6.8	5.9
Transportation	9.5	11.9	8.8	9.4	9.3	10.9
Trade	10.1	11.9	10.1	10.7	9.3	9.3
Service	28.2	31.7	25.1	30.6	27.9	26.1
Total	100.0	100.0	100.0	100.0	100.0	100.0

Source: Li, 1976. Canadian Urban Trends.

TABLE 12.

Percentage distribution of employment within regions, by industry, 1977

Industry category	Canada	British Columbia	Prairies	Ontario	Québec	Atlantic
Primary	7.3	6.1	16.8	4.9	4.8	7.8
Manufacturing	19.6	16.3	9.2	24.5	22.6	13.3
Construction	6.6	7.6	7.8	6.1	5.8	7.3
Transportation	8.5	10.2	9.1	7.4	8.2	11.3
Trade	17.4	18.5	18.1	16.6	17.3	18.4
Service	40.6	41.4	38.9	40.5	41.3	41.9
Total	100.0	100.0	100.0	100.0	100.0	100.0

Source: Statistics Canada, 1977c. The Labour Force. Catalogue 71-001.

TABLE 13.

Average family income for metropolitan and non-metropolitan areas, by region, 1975

Type of area	Canada	British Columbia	Prairies	Ontario	Québec	Atlantic
			(dollars)			
Metropolitan areas	17,607	18,703	17,572	18,484	16,202	15,234
Non-metropolitan areas						
non-metropolitan cities	15,662	15,306	17,036	16,773	15,777	13,829
small urban areas	14,511	17,057	14,262	15,197	13,950	12,056
rural areas	13,434	14,516	13,417	15,769	12,324	10,984

Source: Statistics Canada, 1977b. Family Incomes. Catalogue 13-208.

Age, size, and type of housing units, especially single-family dwellings, fluctuate with age structure and population growth rate. A higher proportion of young couples with children will most definitely create a greater demand for single-unit homes, schools, and recreation facilities. On the other hand, the need for apartments or other multiple-unit dwellings will increase with the ratio of single, older, or retired people. Obviously, as cities experience different numbers of people in different stages of the life cycle, the demands for housing change. The requirements of a city such as Victoria with a significant number of retired people will differ considerably from the housing requirements of a new resource town like Labrador City or a major metropolitan centre such as Montréal. Generally, cities with higher growth rates tend to have higher median house values compared with slower growth centres. Such rapid growth pushes house prices up as demand outpaces supply and where housing units tend to be newer. The average value of single detached, owner-occupied, non-farm dwellings in Canada rose by 73 per cent between 1961 and 1971, while median rent increased by 69 per cent (Hill, 1976b). House values tend to rise more sharply than average annual family income, meaning that housing constitutes a larger financial burden for people in larger urban centres. This may result in an increased exodus to city or urban-fringe suburbs where land and housing costs are lower. The growth of large suburban communities, such as Delta, Surrey, or North Vancouver around Vancouver; Mississauga and Scarborough near Toronto; or Dollard-des-Ormeaux, in the Montréal urban community, are part of this phenomenon.

Desire To Own a Piece of Land. There has often been, on the part of Canadians, a desire to own a piece of land. Land, and therefore housing, has traditionally been cheaper in the urban fringe. Hence, the exodus from downtown to suburbs. The discrepancy between city and fringe land costs was particularly great in the early stages of suburban growth. In the development process, land, air, and space were perceived as free or public goods. Consequently, suburbs reflected a relatively lavish use of land as a cheap resource. Home owners wanted large backyards, two-car garages, and gardens. Today, increased land costs are a major component of high house prices, but the desire for land and space, engendered generations ago, is still with Canadians.

A factory closing in a small, one-industry town in rural Canada, the beginning of pipeline construction in the north, or the opening of a university in an urban centre may drastically change the age structure of the associated communities. Immigration and internal migration patterns, income, age, education, occupation, lifestyle preferences, employment levels, job diversity, and other social, economic, and demographic interactions are complex to say the least. Each has a specific rôle to play but when combined they influence the demand for land for residential, recreational, commercial, industrial, transportation, and other uses.

The combined result of the influences described above, is increasing urbanization, particularly in the Lower Mainland of British Columbia (Skoda, 1975; and Gibson, 1976) and in the corridor between Windsor and Québec City (Simpson-Lewis, 1974; and Yeates, 1975). The continued demographic and physical growth of metropolitan areas has direct repercussions on all other land uses. Some of the most serious impacts relate to agriculture.

Location of Cities

The second reason why cities will continue to influence land uses, particularly agriculture, is that most Canadian cities are located on or near prime agricultural land, and considerable urban expansion takes place on high-capability farmland in many instances. To examine this situation more closely, analysis and programming of Canada Land Inventory data through the Canada Geographic Information System was initiated and some interesting information was generated (Manning and McCuaig, 1977; and Neimanis, 1978). The purpose of the research was to determine the quantity and quality of soil within an 80-km radius of 23 Census Metropolitan Areas (CMAs) (Table 15).

Several rather startling results from this analysis serve to highlight the fact that certain areas in southern Canada with the greatest urban pressures are also in the context of the largest areas of prime agricultural soil. Nearly 57 per cent of Canada's class 1 soil for agriculture is located within the 80-km radius of 23 CMAs with a combined population of 12,798,825 in 1976. The areas contained by this perimeter also include 29 and 20 per cent of class 2 and 3 soils respectively. Southern Ontario has almost a monopoly on prime agricultural land. Consider that nearly one-quarter of Canada's class 1 land for agriculture is within an 80-km radius of Kitchener alone. It is estimated that from the top of the CN Tower in Toronto, a person can see 37 per cent of Canada's class 1 soil for agriculture within a 161-km radius.

In a study of 71 urban areas, the quantity and quality of land converted to direct urban use between 1966 and 1971 was documented (Gierman, 1977). Of all rural land converted to urban uses, 63 per cent was rated in the three highest capability classes for agriculture, and more than 18 per cent was evaluated as class 1 land representing soil with no limitations for agriculture. In Ontario, 79 per cent of rural land converted to urban uses was prime farmland (classes 1 to 3). In Manitoba and Prince Edward Island, 91 and 99 per cent of land which underwent this type of land use change was prime agricultural land. Of all rural land transformed to urban land, 76 per cent was farmland (54 per cent improved land and 22 per cent unimproved land).

TABLE 14.

Personal income* per person as a percentage of the Canadian average, by province, 1926 to 1976

Province	1926	1929	1933	1939	1946	1950	1961	1963	1967	1971	1973	1976
(percentage of Canadian average)
Newfoundland						51	60	58	61	64	65	68
Prince Edward Island	57	59	51	53	58	56	62	63	62	63	69	69
Nova Scotia	67	71	77	76	86	74	77	74	77	78	78	79
New Brunswick	64	65	66	65	75	69	68	66	69	73	73	75
Québec	85	92	94	88	82	85	88	87	91	89	90	93
Ontario	114	122	129	124	115	121	118	117	116	117	114	109
Manitoba	109	98	93	90	103	100	97	97	95	94	96	94
Saskatchewan	102	67	47	77	97	87	78	107	81	80	89	100
Alberta	113	92	74	87	108	103	102	100	99	99	102	104
British Columbia	121	128	132	125	114	123	116	114	111	109	108	109

*Includes all transfer payments and imputed net income of farmers.

Sources: Bennett, 1976. *Canadian Urban Trends*. Reproduced by permission of Copp Clark Publishing Limited and the Minister of Supply and Services Canada.
Statistics Canada. 1977a. *National Income and Expenditure Accounts 1962-1976*. Catalogue 13-201.

TABLE 15.

Agricultural capability of land within an 80-km radius of 23 Census Metropolitan Areas

Census Metropolitan Area	Class 1	Class 2	Class 3	Class 4	Class 5	Class 6	Class 7	Unclassified	Organic soils	Total*
				(ha)						
Calgary	200,724	321,942	473,051	140,173	355,238	243,979	236,760	28,225	9,879	2,009,971
Chicoutimi-Jonquière	0	42,831	44,348	77,457	27,089	0	1,473,254	2,079	74,137	1,741,195
Edmonton	288,641	482,582	489,118	278,091	142,413	140,165	7,799	18,529	97,903	1,945,241
Halifax	0	27,210	268,984	75,482	13,796	4,517	616,928	48	14,283	1,021,248
Hamilton	427,300	416,410	226,438	77,358	71,058	47,102	6,404	67,272	39,639	1,378,981
Kitchener	934,578	408,155	282,486	74,641	80,755	52,777	10,949	30,343	85,163	1,959,847
London	644,436	523,731	208,650	77,073	63,201	21,258	9,310	8,332	30,121	1,586,112
Montréal	20,448	530,199	307,171	335,431	77,398	247	329,485	46,431	70,382	1,717,192
Oshawa	452,576	135,882	99,947	143,921	28,088	90,211	1,395	45,877	88,401	1,086,298
Ottawa-Hull	89,641	244,840	307,121	214,270	91,301	167,316	645,787	8,098	130,931	1,899,305
Québec	0	47,925	160,880	409,667	169,576	0	959,651	7,300	111,210	1,866,209
Regina	66,368	706,925	663,583	133,326	358,283	67,510	4,100	11,640	0	2,011,735
Saint John	0	14,966	102,958	208,696	232,474	7,070	420,075	109,689	4,072	1,100,000
St. Catharines-Niagara	138,577	233,896	105,557	16,497	4,726	10,026	3,600	59,373	5,565	577,817
St. John's	0	0	902	12,304	49,307	114,717	268,428	1,774	90,314	537,746
Saskatoon	15,828	265,796	812,484	373,211	321,312	191,261	843	4,870	0	1,985,605
Sudbury	0	10,465	44,086	34,514	70,367	43,224	1,479,195	1,393	28,730	1,711,974
Thunder Bay	0	8,735	78,564	70,394	138,898	30,839	531,488	2,570	28,374	889,862
Toronto	492,052	271,486	179,789	90,691	55,819	80,198	14,602	68,656	68,735	1,322,028
Vancouver	1,634	15,323	33,971	50,189	63,126	12,153	217,082	576,618	16,846	986,941
Victoria	760	12,353	23,095	17,201	36,606	16,116	38,251	234,994	2,003	381,379
Windsor	21,401	300,742	52,234	0	1,206	887	12,129	6,025	2,295	396,919
Winnipeg	48,293	582,305	582,561	266,432	189,858	79,031	25,365	15,384	153,876	1,943,105
Total within 80-km radius**	2,356,891	4,637,554	4,986,123	2,962,348	2,486,018	1,281,424	7,293,894	1,159,364	1,021,355	28,184,971
Canadian total***	4,146,157	16,193,836	25,131,059	24,895,981	34,059,020	15,742,928	58,524,819	72,133,814	16,780,359	
Percentage of Canadian total within 80-km radius of 23 CMAs	56.84	28.63	19.84	11.89	7.29	8.13	12.46	1.60		

* Totals do not add up to the theoretical area of a circle with an 80-km radius due to water bodies, areas outside CLI coverage, and international boundaries.
** Total excludes any double counting due to overlapping of circles.
*** Canadian total includes only areas within CLI boundaries; includes B.C. data using unimproved rating; includes areas of Newfoundland within a 161-km radius of St. John's; and excludes the Yukon and Northwest Territories.

Sources: Manning and McCuaig, 1977. *Agricultural Land and Urban Centres*.
Neimanis, 1979. *Canada's Cities and Their Surrounding Land Resource*.

Other studies have shown that urban growth continues to take place on the most favoured climatic areas for agriculture (Williams, 1973). For example, in examining urban growth by census divisions for the 1961 to 1966 period, it was found that those census divisions with the warmest five per cent of farmland had nearly half of the Canadian urban population growth. The areas of concentrated urban population growth also are favourably located with respect to moisture resources. At least one-third of Canadian farmland has an average annual water deficiency of over 127 mm. Twelve of the thirteen metropolitan centres with populations greater than 190,000, in 1966, were in areas where water deficiencies were 127 mm or less (Williams, 1973) and this situation is even more pronounced today.

Although most Canadian urban centres are located on or near high-capability farmland, it should be noted that the cities themselves occupy relatively little land. In 1976, 76 per cent of Canadians were urbanites and urban areas occupied between one and two per cent of Canada's land area. The consumption of land for direct urban uses is comparatively small. But, concern also centres around the much larger quantities of land required for indirect or urban-related uses such as transportation, industrial development, and recreation. How do these land requirements affect rural land uses?

The horizontal expansion of many cities has been stimulated with each improved transportation mode from the horse-cart to the subway. As more improved modes of transportation were introduced to the urban system, their effect was not necessarily to reduce the travel time for all commuters but rather to increase the size of city population as more commuters, located further from the core, utilized the system. It was the door-to-door convenience of the car which was perhaps the greatest factor in expanding the commutershed.

> "It has great advantages for much personal use. It saves time. It enables a man to live where he wishes in relation to his place of work, or to his children's schooling. It takes everything from door to door—the shopping parcels, the baggage, the golf clubs, everything. It vastly widens the range of visits, hospitality and friends. It has become the vital prime-mover for vacations ... It tows a trailer, a caravan, a boat. It does all this and much more." (Hodson, 1972).

The widespread use of the automobile, the prevalence of two-car families in many areas, the increased convenience of urban transportation, and the willingness to commute between home and work, contributed to the constant pressure for urban expansion. In effect, some of the locational constraints which had earlier resulted in high-density development were reduced and consequently the size, shape, and density of cities changed.

Although some vacant land does exit within city limits, it tends to have a high scarcity value, but, the numbers of people desiring to own their own home has never been greater. Consequently, urban growth often migrates outward, down the price gradient, to the rural-urban fringe, where a greater quantity of less expensive land is available for housing developments. Combined with an unprecedented number of young, mobile, first-time home buyers who often move from downtown apartments to suburban townhouses or single-family units, the result is the development of suburbs which rely on the automobile for their lifeline to the downtown area.

Consider too, how many large shopping malls are located in suburban areas which cater to automobile-oriented consumers. The original purchase price of land here was significantly lower than in more central locations and vast parking space is a major component of modern, all-encompassing shopping centres. For this same reason, many industrial and service companies choose to locate on urban outskirts, where land costs are lower, yet the large urban market is relatively close at hand. In fact, industrial parks are common to many Canadian suburban areas where they take advantage of the labour force residing in the same area.

Consider the proportion of land that is devoted to transportation. Roads and streets, downtown parking lots, garages and services centres, driveways, bus stations, and other facilities all utilize land. A survey revealed that land use consumption for urban passenger transportation and access varies according to city size and sector. Generally speaking, about 40 per cent of land within cities is devoted to road transportation and access (Lea, 1975). However, other urban transport media also utilize urban or rural land. Commuter trains, subways, and other vehicles with their attendant facilities, together with freight facilities including rail, stockyards, and port facilities, all place demands on land.

NFB – PHOTOTHEQUE – Photo by George Hunter.

Large suburban shopping centres are convenient for nearby residents, but such malls consist of low-structured buildings and large paved parking lots. Such a design was made possible by the lower cost of land here in the suburbs, as compared with more central downtown locations. Such suburban land was probably converted from agriculture to direct urban use through a series of land use changes and owners, over time.

NFB – PHOTOTHEQUE – ONF – Photo by George Hunter.

Railway marshalling yards, such as this one near Winnipeg, are large users of land adjacent to cities. Large tracts of land are also required by other forms of transportation such as airports. Frequently, such land has high capability for agriculture or other uses.

Airports too may have sizeable land requirements, usually in the rural areas surrounding major urban centres. For example, the Toronto II, or Pickering Airport, site was to occupy 7,285 ha of land, rated largely as class 1 for agriculture. The accompanying community development would have removed more prime land from agriculture. The operation of runways, hangars, terminals, and parking lots at airports prohibits many farming activities. Furthermore, as a hub of transportation, airports tend to attract commercial and industrial activities, so that frequently, complexes develop around airports. As the process advances, there is additional pressure on remaining agricultural holdings to give way to urban-related land uses.

Leisure and recreation opportunities desired by the largely urban Canadian population place demands on land resources. Some demands are met by designated areas within urban centres while others are fulfilled by isolated wilderness areas. However, much of the land required for outdoor recreation is found in the intermediate countryside. From extensive campgrounds to highway picnic sites to skidoo trails, outdoor recreational activities require varying quantities of land with specific characteristics. While some people are willing to commute greater distances for special wilderness opportunities, the majority of campers, cottagers, or skiers desire appropriate sites within a few hours drive of their urban homes. With an increasing emphasis on health and physical fitness, a continuing desire to get away from urban environments, the continuing speculation in land as an investment and hedge against inflation, flexible and shorter work weeks, and increased pressure "to see Canada first", demands on rural land for recreational purposes can only escalate, largely at the expense of rural land uses, specifically agriculture.

Finally, there are a number of miscellaneous urban-related land uses which locate in the rural areas surrounding cities. These uses develop where land is cheaper, and where zoning and pollution restrictions may be less stringent. Car graveyards, scrap yards, dumps, racetracks, gravel pits, and quarries are activities whose land requirements are difficult to measure but whose impact on rural areas has been documented (Black and Stewart, 1976).

All the trends described above have contributed in some way to the creation of a dynamic rural-urban fringe around many urban centres. It is the consequence of a large number of interrelated factors, not of any single influence, and that is what makes land-related issues so difficult to understand and resolve. This area of changing land uses, conflicts, and problems, itself represents an area of concern for agriculture. Here, social, economic, and demographic, as well as land use changes occur rapidly. Once committed to urban or urban-related land uses, farmland seldom returns to agriculture. Land formerly farmed but now under low-density residential development or industrial park simply becomes a part of the rather amorphous urban pressure system.

Changes in Agriculture

"Farming has changed. You've got a few great big farms now. You know they're farming... well, I don't say they're farming, they're soil miners. They roar in with huge machines and rip up acres and throw down acres of fertilizer and weed killers and plants and up they sprout, and they tear them all off again. Haven't got the old farmer's feel for the land, you know, the land for their sons. They're developing the land... they're using the land right now to pay off the huge loans they probably got from the bank or somebody else. And it's a different way of doing business.

It wasn't farm 'business' when you had time to talk to your cows and you had a mixture of things. If the pea crop was bad, well, you had corn; if the corn was bad, you had pigs. If the pigs were bad, you had chickens; if the chickens were bad... well, you don't put all your eggs in one basket. But now it's mass, large crops, large and it's roar, roar, rush, rush, don't think of anything but get it in, get it out, get the money in, the money out back to your bank, pay off your loan to get more money to borrow more money to... you know it't a big rat race.

And you've got all these people coming in diluting the old farms, the old alliances, the honest web of families and friends and neighbours and self-help. And this is being diluted all the time, and not only by people coming in who are living here just for the weekend. You know, they can sell their house in Toronto and take half the money and buy a place in Prince Edward County, live here, and some of them commute back and forth until they can afford to find something here and set up an antique business or something." (Anderson, 1977).

Changes in agriculture occur in response to a variety of internal and external forces. Monetary factors such as fluctuating prices at the farm gate, rapidly rising production and operation expenses, variable but low farm incomes, and shortage of funds are of prime concern. Marketing systems for farm products, the relatively slow growth in Canadian food demands, increasing self-sufficiency of other countries, and loss of some foreign markets each requires attention and consideration. Increasing technological development, commodity surpluses, regional disparities, management problems, trade agreements, political forces, land use conflicts, and the general decline in power and influence exercised by farm areas are but a few of the numerous factors which cause changes in agriculture.

In recent years, a growing concern has focused on changes in the agricultural land base itself. The conversion of land in general, and the quantity and quality of farmland lost to direct urban and urban-related uses, have attracted particular attention. A number of landmark studies have documented land conversion (Bogue, 1956; Crerar, 1962; Gertler and Hind-Smith, 1962; Clawson, 1971; Girt et al., 1972; and Gierman, 1977). Attention has also centred on the problems encountered in the dynamic urban fringe where urban and agricultural land uses meet (Krueger and Bryfogle, 1971; Rodd, 1972; Punter, 1974; and Russwurm, 1974). The market mechanisms involved in land development or conversion have been examined (Bryant, 1965; Martin 1974, 1975a and 1975b; and Spurr, 1976). Other research efforts have concentrated on areas seen to have unique capabilities for agriculture, such as the Niagara fruit belt (Krueger, 1976 and 1978) or areas with superior agroclimatic resources (Williams, 1973; and Williams, Pocock and Russwurm, 1978). Reviews of specific land use planning problems, as in the case of the B.C. Land Commission Act, (Rawson, 1976), or reviews of Canadian policy in general (Gray, 1976) are another contribution. The interests and concerns of farm operators themselves (Canadian Federation of Agriculture, 1974), professional groups (Soil Conservation Society of America, Ontario Chapter, 1976) or individual professionals (Pearson, 1973a and 1973b) emphasize the need for proper management of foodlands. The task of providing a summary of land and people-related concerns associated with agriculture has been approached by many (Geno and Geno, 1976; and Beaubien and Tabacnik, 1977). Such research is possible through the extensive work done on evaluation and classification of land for agriculture (Leahey, 1946; Hoffman, 1970 and 1971; Nowland, 1975a and 1975b; and Shields and Ferguson, 1975), to name only a few.

Land uses, as well as the factors which determine land use patterns, represent extremely complex subject areas involving perceptions, historical development, socio-economics, geography, and peoples' expectations, all within a political decision-making context. As in any other areas involving such varied interests, there is some lack of agreement concerning the seriousness of agriculturally-related land use issues and the trends evident over the last few decades. Nevertheless, the abandonment of marginal farmland, fluctuating prices at the farm gate or retail level, shifting of land uses from less intensive to more intensive, declining soil quality, rising production costs, the cost/price squeeze, demographic changes, selling of prime farmland for urban or recreational purposes, eroding of unique soil resource areas, or climatic changes and their possible ramifications, all relate back to the land base for agriculture. Therefore, the first example of change in agriculture is an overview of net changes in farmland area at the provincial and census division levels, over the last few decades.

TABLE 16.

Area of total farmland, by province, 1921 to 1976

Province	1921	1931	1941	1951	1956	1961	1966	1971	1976
					(ha)				
Newfoundland				34,416	29,063	22,081	20,038	25,376	29,423
Prince Edward Island	492,311	482,079	473,041	443,270	431,193	388,576	375,148	313,493	278,050
Nova Scotia	1,911,621	1,741,032	1,544,597	1,284,393	1,123,302	902,641	749,462	537,796	400,249
New Brunswick	1,727,891	1,680,151	1,604,275	1,404,404	1,206,592	890,208	733,193	541,947	402,328
Québec	6,983,913	7,002,995	7,309,920	6,793,458	6,438,829	5,746,130	5,214,992	4,371,212	3,654,134
Ontario	9,157,916	9,243,711	9,060,416	8,450,158	8,045,293	7,518,722	7,214,200	6,460,249	5,966,816
Manitoba	5,915,032	6,123,793	6,835,918	7,175,490	7,257,006	7,353,379	7,723,221	7,692,642	7,610,995
Saskatchewan	17,816,070	22,531,049	24,266,187	24,955,095	25,412,723	26,068,960	26,471,169	26,328,517	26,432,628
Alberta	11,854,899	15,774,177	17,514,321	17,992,813	18,604,219	19,113,436	19,823,370	20,035,194	20,039,981
British Columbia	1,157,682	1,433,262	1,632,386	1,903,010	1,836,885	1,823,802	2,141,798	2,356,662	2,351,802
Yukon and Northwest Territories	656	2,103	1,125	175	1,812	3,476	1,727	1,800	1,796
CANADA	57,017,991	66,014,352	70,242,186	70,436,682	70,386,917	69,831,411	70,468,318	68,664,888	67,168,202

Sources: Dominion Bureau of Statistics, 1947. Agriculture-Canada. Vol. VIII, Parts I and II.
———, 1953. Agriculture-Canada. Vol. VI, Part I.
———, 1957. Agriculture-Canada. Vol. II, Bulletin 2-11.
———, 1963a. Agriculture-Canada. Catalogue 96-530.
———, 1968. Agriculture-Canada. Catalogue 96-601.
Statistics Canada, 1973a. Agriculture-Canada. Catalogue 96-701.
———, 1977e. Census-farms by Size, Area and Use of Land. Catalogue 96-854.

TABLE 17.

Area of improved farmland, by province, 1921 to 1976

Province	1921	1931	1941	1951	1956	1961	1966	1971	1976
					(ha)				
Newfoundland				11,729	9,807	8,278	8,323	7,749	9,755
Prince Edward Island	310,534	309,908	298,426	234,353	261,231	234,547	230,598	199,975	194,147
Nova Scotia	401,651	341,823	328,779	267,901	254,910	201,347	196,627	156,223	147,853
New Brunswick	553,639	538,345	499,979	407,281	384,987	297,093	258,461	197,243	171,344
Québec	3,668,464	3,639,936	3,667,663	3,573,083	3,492,494	3,182,632	3,087,596	2,610,312	2,245,347
Ontario	5,329,640	5,371,577	5,408,152	5,136,958	5,087,952	4,869,724	4,858,142	4,396,904	4,333,292
Manitoba	3,261,001	3,448,825	3,977,867	4,355,305	4,635,346	4,841,828	5,036,923	5,181,774	5,181,499
Saskatchewan	10,132,636	13,577,275	14,398,141	15,705,100	16,392,778	17,449,779	18,401,214	18,788,799	18,895,957
Alberta	4,762,527	7,182,825	8,144,677	9,013,092	9,610,052	10,234,267	11,038,699	11,517,895	11,790,925
British Columbia	220,345	285,296	361,431	464,505	472,185	527,431	653,243	710,348	736,237
Yukon and Northwest Territories	192	460	425	32	288	440	251	629	576
CANADA	28,640,629	34,696,270	37,085,540	39,196,339	40,602,030	41,847,366	43,770,077	43,767,851	43,707,432

Sources: Dominion Bureau of Statistics, 1947. Agriculture-Canada. Vol. VIII, Parts I and II.
—————, 1953. Agriculture-Canada. Vol. VI, Part I.
—————, 1957. Agriculture-Canada. Vol. II, Bulletin 2-11.
—————, 1963a. Agriculture-Canada. Catalogue 96-530.
—————, 1968. Agriculture-Canada. Catalogue 96-601.
Statistics Canada, 1973a. Agriculture-Canada. Catalogue 96-701.
—————, 1977e. Census-farms by Size, Area and Use of Land. Catalogue 96-854.

Changes in Farmland

Changes in Area of Farmland. At the national level, the area of total farmland, which includes improved and unimproved land, has experienced only modest fluctuations between 1921 and 1976 (Table 16). This basically static picture hides two important trends. Firstly, it conceals changes within its two components of improved and unimproved land. In 1921, total farmland area was divided evenly between improved and unimproved land (Table 17). In 1976, 65 per cent of Canada's total farmland was improved with a reserve of unimproved land of only 35 per cent. But, the differences among provinces are more dramatic. In Newfoundland and British Columbia, where less land is in the higher CLI capabilities, only 33 and 31 per cent of farmland was improved. On the other hand, in Ontario, which possesses over half of Canada's class 1 soil for agriculture, the proportion of improved land was at its highest, 73 per cent. It appears that the reserve of unimproved land is diminishing and that the capability of such land may be such as to limit it to certain uses.

Secondly, the relatively uniform amount of total farmland at the national level obscures the vastly different historical trends among the provinces. For example, from 1921 to 1976 quantities of both total and improved farmland declined steadily in all three Maritime Provinces. In Québec, by 1976, the area of farmland had decreased by 50 per cent since 1941, and improved farmland declined steadily between 1921 and 1976, amounting to a loss of nearly 40 per cent. In Ontario, the area of total farmland has shrunk steadily and without exception since 1931, to the state that total farmland has been reduced by nearly one-fifth. More disturbing is the accompanying, but more rapid, 20 per cent diminution in improved farmland since 1941.

The gains in farmland, which have until recently balanced the losses in eastern and central Canada, have occurred in the west. Manitoba's farmland increased by 31 per cent between 1921 and 1966, but since that time there has been a slight decline. Here too, improved farmland increased by nearly 60 per cent from 1921 to 1971 after which a very slight loss was experienced. In Saskatchewan, gains in total farmland reached nearly 50 per cent between 1921 and 1966, but since then a levelling off and slight loss have occurred. The gain in improved farmland, between 1921 and 1976, has been an impressive 86 per cent but the increase between 1971 and 1976 was the smallest in 55 years. In Alberta, total farmland grew by 69 per cent although the rate of increase slowed considerably after 1966. Improved farmland increased dramatically by 148 per cent in the past 55 years but again the increase was least between 1971 and 1976. In Canada's most western province, total farmland doubled between 1921 and 1976, but suffered a slight loss after 1971. Improved farmland expanded consistently between 1921 and 1976.

However, looking more closely at the national figures, total farmland entered a static period in 1941, followed by a steady decline between 1966 and 1976. Improved farmland too experienced a net decrease between 1971 and 1976. While these losses are slight and may in part be accounted for by changing definitions, they nonetheless reveal that the pendulum may be starting to swing in the other direction. For the first time, the consistent increase in improved farmland has been reversed. This serves to highlight the fact that the large gains in the west, which have previously offset losses in the east and central regions, may be at an end. In Saskatchewan, for example, the gain in improved farmland, between 1971 and 1976, was less than 0.6 per cent. In some western provinces the rate of increase has dropped drastically, and in others it has been transformed into net losses. Should this trend be evident in the 1981 Census, Canada may be in the midst of a serious period of net decline in farmland.

Maps 19 and 20 illustrate the percentage of total land area occupied by improved farmland for census divisions in 1951 and 1976. Unfortunately, many drastic changes in census division boundaries occurred during the 25-year period and, until computer techniques are able to accommodate boundary alterations which affect thousands of farm records over prolonged periods such as 25 years, direct comparison of data is difficult if not impossible. Therefore, net loss or gain of improved farmland by census divisions cannot be shown on one map. Only a calculation such as the percentage of total land area occupied by improved farmland at two time periods is possible. This approach has disadvantages particularly where existing farmland occupies a small proportion, for example less than ten per cent, of total land area. This is the case in many marginal agricultural areas of Canada. Here, a large loss of improved farmland would not necessarily result in a category change in the percentage of total land occupied by improved farmland between 1951 and 1976.

The purpose of the maps (see Maps 19 and 20) is not so much to provide a specific value or percentage for each census unit but rather to indicate general trends across Canada. They do indicate, however, where appreciable losses or gains have occurred.

In Newfoundland, serious physiographic and climatic limitations restrict agriculture and explain why only 0.02 per cent of the province's total land area was occupied by improved farmland in both 1951 and 1976. The

A 16996-79 Original photo supplied by the Surveys and Mapping Branch, Department of Energy, Mines and Resources.

This 1960 photo illustrates a former rural agricultural area in the process of land use conversion as a result of increasing urban pressure from Toronto. Much of the farmland has gone out of production as new suburban residential development has expanded to Highway 401, which runs east-west. The drive-in theatre (fan-shape near the right edge of the photo) and many of the non-farm buildings were present before 1949 and were the first indications of urban intrusion into the rural area.

A 23665-48 Original photo supplied by the Surveys and Mapping Branch, Department of Energy, Mines and Resources.

By 1974, the area has become totally urban. The Don Valley Parkway, running north-south, now intersects Highway 401. Virtually all farmland has been converted to either residential land uses, particularly high-rise apartments, or commercial areas, now surrounding the drive-in theatre. It is estimated that approximately 92 per cent of the land in this area changed use between 1949 and 1974.

loss of improved farmland at the provincial level was 17 per cent during this 25-year period. Although this represents less than two thousand ha it is significant in an area with such a limited agricultural resource base. On the maps, the loss of farmland is not reflected in a change in the proportion of total land area because the percentage was already in the lowest category, zero to one per cent.

In Canada's garden province of Prince Edward Island, improved farmland area fell from 261,353 ha to 194,154 ha, a loss of 26 per cent. The percentage of land area occupied by improved farmland declined from 46 to 34 per cent between 1951 and 1976. All three census divisions experienced significant net losses of improved farmland, between 22 and 35 per cent, in this 25-year period.

Consistent with the pattern throughout the Atlantic Provinces during this 25-year period, Nova Scotia experienced a net loss of improved farmland of approximately 120 thousand ha. This represents an overall decline of 45 per cent. The percentage of land area covered by improved farmland at the provincial level fell from five per cent to less than three per cent. Net loss of improved farmland was consistent as all census divisions exhibited declines. In relative terms, the decrease was most severe in the marginal farm areas of Cape Breton and the southwest coast, where many census divisions lost more than 80 per cent of their 1951 improved farmland. However, in terms of area, even the more economically viable farm areas lost appreciable amounts of improved land. Kings census division in the area of the Annapolis Valley lost 7,700 ha, or 20 per cent, of its improved farmland.

In New Brunswick, 58 per cent of the province's improved farmland was lost between 1951 and 1976. A reduction of 235,431 ha is significant in Atlantic Canada. All census divisions lost improved farmland and some losses were extreme. For example, the St. John census division forfeited 87 per cent of its improved farmland, and such a loss must have an impact on the supply of fresh produce to the Saint John market. Other areas, especially along the eastern coast, lost up to 80 per cent of their improved land. These significant declines are not readily apparent on Maps 19 and 20 as many of these census divisions already had such small portions (less than ten per cent) of land in improved farmland in 1951.

In the period 1951 to 1976, Québec experienced a serious decline in improved farmland amounting to 37 per cent, or 1,327,656 ha. Much of the province is not conducive to agriculture and improved farmland accounted for only 2.6 and 1.7 per cent of total land area in 1951 and 1976. Of the 74 census divisions in 1976, only one registered a net gain in improved farmland and this was in part due to boundary changes. In marginal farming areas where physiographic, climatic, and economic conditions tend to discourage agriculture, small farms have been consolidated and some of the poorer land retired. For example, in Gaspé-Est and Îles-de-la-Madeleine, 92 and 97 per cent of improved farmland was lost between 1951 and 1976. In such marginal locations, improved agriculture already constituted a small proportion, often less than ten per cent, of total land area in 1951, and thus even significant declines in farmland are hidden within the lowest categories on Maps 19 and 20.

On the other hand, large losses of improved farmland also occurred in regions with more viable farming activities. In the Eastern Townships census divisions of Beauce and Compton, a combined loss of improved farmland exceeded 100 thousand ha and represented a decline of 50 per cent in improved farmland. Of concern too are the substantial losses in Québec's best agricultural areas. In the census divisions constituting the city of Montréal, three-quarters of all improved farmland disappeared between 1951 and 1976. These special gardening areas came under increasing pressure from urban uses and high land values reflected the strong competition for "developable" land. The serious decreases in improved farmland, particularly in the vicinity of Montréal, are reflected in the declining proportion of total land area occupied by improved farmland, illustrated on Maps 19 and 20.

In Ontario, as in Québec, much of the northern portion of the province does not support large areas of improved agriculture. The edge of the Canadian Shield marks a transition in agriculture. North of the Shield edge, consistent and heavy losses of improved agricultural land have occurred between 1951 and 1976. Here, less favourable climatic, soil, and economic conditions may result in marginal or unprofitable situations for farmers. Much of the loss of improved farmland resulted from farmers' failure to successfully battle the cost/price squeeze and from increased demand for recreational land within driving distance of the large urban centres to the south. For example, the increased popularity of cottage areas in Haliburton and Muskoka census divisons may have contributed to the declines in improved farmland of 81 and 63 per cent respectively.

MAP 19

IMPROVED FARMLAND AS A PERCENTAGE OF TOTAL LAND AREA
1951

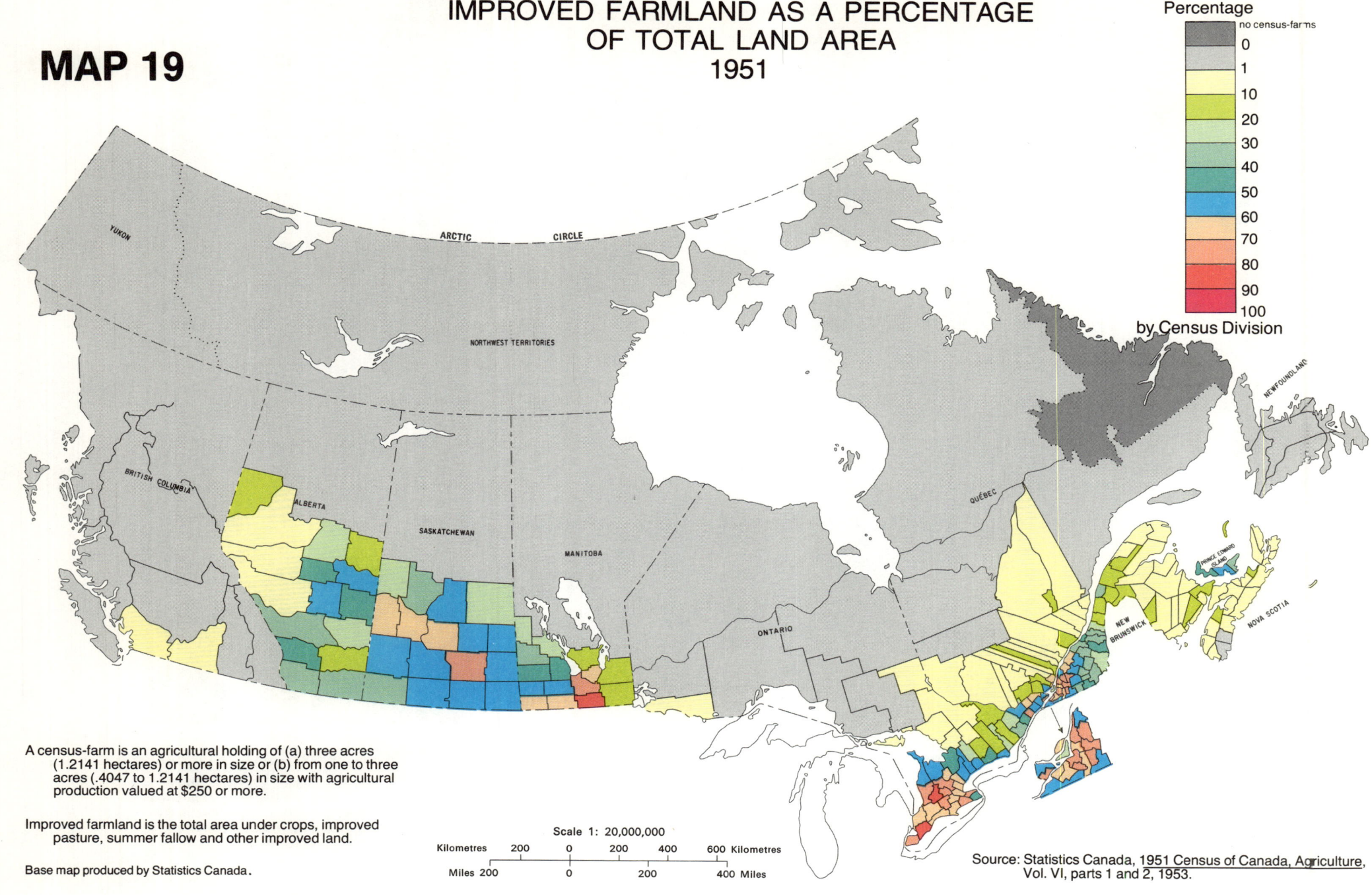

A census-farm is an agricultural holding of (a) three acres (1.2141 hectares) or more in size or (b) from one to three acres (.4047 to 1.2141 hectares) in size with agricultural production valued at $250 or more.

Improved farmland is the total area under crops, improved pasture, summer fallow and other improved land.

Base map produced by Statistics Canada.

Scale 1: 20,000,000

Source: Statistics Canada, 1951 Census of Canada, Agriculture, Vol. VI, parts 1 and 2, 1953.

In general, the eastern corner of the province experienced a steady loss of improved farmland largely as a result of less favourable growing conditions, distance from major markets, and urban pressures in the Ottawa area. The Ottawa–Carleton census division experienced a net loss of over 27,400 ha, representing more than one-fifth of all improved farmland. However, the most notable losses occurred in the "Golden Horseshoe" between Toronto and Niagara Falls–St. Catharines, a region well suited to the cultivation of a wide variety of fruits, vegetables, and other cash crops. Here, high land values reflect the strong competition for land among agricultural, residential, industrial, recreational, and transportation uses. In this area, one-third of the 451,199 ha of improved farmland have rapidly been converted to other uses in only 25 years. Overall, the province lost 803,512 ha of improved farmland representing a decline of one-sixth of the province's active improved agricultural resource base. The changes in the presence of agriculture in the Ontario landscape, especially around Toronto, are seen in the declining proportion of total land area occupied by improved agriculture.

Only upon reaching Manitoba, is the trend in improved farmland reversed. Between 1951 and 1976, the province had a net gain of 826,379 ha, an increase of 19 per cent. Such gains were not consistent across the province, but occurred mainly to the south and west of Winnipeg. Here, as throughout the west, direct comparison of 1951 and 1976 data is difficult because of significant boundary changes. It should be noted that in 1976, Census Division No. 3 in the extreme south of the province had the greatest proportion of its land area, 91 per cent, occupied by improved farmland. This situation reflects the dramatic physical differences in the resource base that exist here as compared with other locations across Canada.

In Saskatchewan, all census divisions except the largest unit in the far north experienced sizable net gains in improved farmland. This is reflected in the increased proportion of total land occupied by this land use, between 1951 and 1976, shown on Maps 19 and 20. In total, a net gain of 3,191,529 ha represented a 20-per cent increase at the provincial level. The important status held by agriculture in Saskatchewan is witnessed by the fact that, in 1976, one-third of the province's land area was under improved agricultural use.

In Alberta and British Columbia, particularly radical boundary changes of census divisions make historical comparisons impossible. However, at the provincial level Alberta had a net increase of improved farmland of 2,778,253 ha, an increase of 31 per cent in 25 years. The percentage of total land area occupied by improved farmland rose from 14 to 18 per cent during this period. In British Columbia, the area of improved farmland increased by 59 per cent, or 271,758 ha. Nevertheless, this farming activity accounted for a minuscule share, 0.8 per cent, of the province's total land area.

Across Canada, between 1951 and 1976, the greatest losses occurred in areas with soils of the highest capability for agriculture. The loss of one ha in southern Ontario is compensated for by one ha in Saskatchewan only as far as numbers are concerned. With regard to soil capability, productivity, or diversity, the substitute is not neccessarily equal (Figure 16). In a study of grain crops, productivity relationships between soil capability classes were established (Hoffman, 1971). With class 1 equalling 1.0, indices of 0.8, 0.64, and 0.49 were obtained for soils of classes 2, 3, and 4 respectively. Therefore,

"... reported farmland losses in the East have a significant impact on Canadian production potential since it is usually the best land agroclimatically that is removed from farming. For each hectare lost in southern Ontario and Québec, many more hectares must be developed elsewhere for equivalent yield. Losses of farmland use in the favourable areas cannot continue or the present ability to satisfy Canadian needs will diminish. There is no point in replacing land which can grow fruit, vegetables and corn with land suitable only for barley or hay. Careful thought must precede any plans for irreversible developments." (Geno and Geno, 1976).

Soil Quality. This may be an appropriate point to interject that, in addition to locational changes of agricultural activities, there are physical changes occurring to the land itself. One particular set of physical problems is having profound effects in Saskatchewan (Rennie, 1978). A combination of decline in soil productivity, wastage of nitrogen, and increase in soil salinity is having serious repercussions on soil quality. Difficulties arise from the fact that more nutrients are removed from the soil than are replaced. This has developed because of the common practice of summer fallow, and at pres-

44

MAP 20

IMPROVED FARMLAND AS A PERCENTAGE OF TOTAL LAND AREA
1976

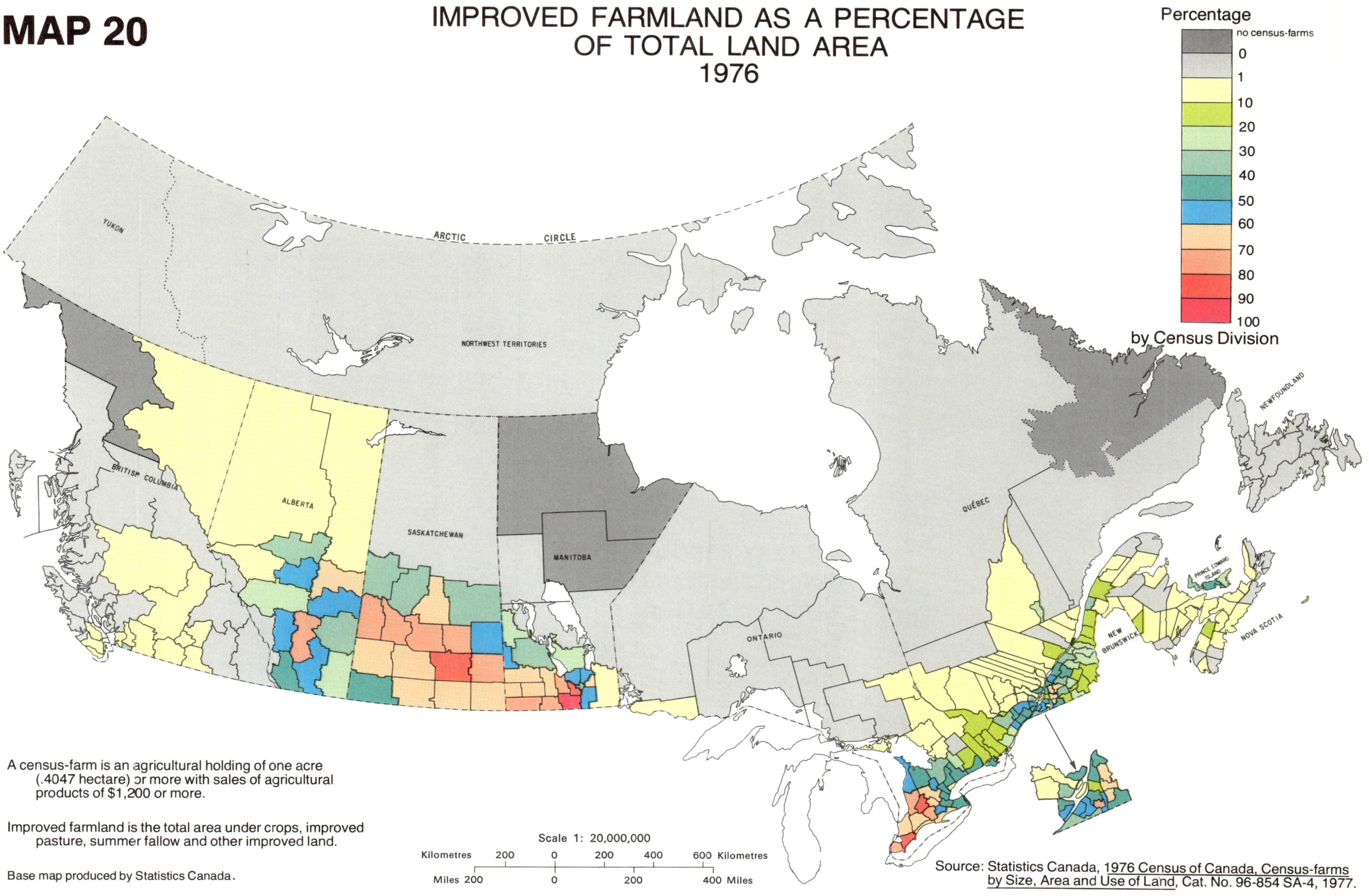

A census-farm is an agricultural holding of one acre (.4047 hectare) or more with sales of agricultural products of $1,200 or more.

Improved farmland is the total area under crops, improved pasture, summer fallow and other improved land.

Base map produced by Statistics Canada.

Scale 1: 20,000,000

Source: Statistics Canada, 1976 Census of Canada, Census-farms by Size, Area and Use of Land, Cat. No. 96-854 SA-4, 1977.

---

ent, 40 per cent of the province's crop land is left fallow every year. With the drop in organic matter, soil structure deteriorates, as does the soil's ability to hold water. This leads to increased runoff. As a result, the soil tends to crust or bake and it becomes much more susceptible to wind and water erosion. Such trends, when combined with climatic conditions similar to those of the 1930s, could lead to dust bowl conditions.

Of the many related problems, it appears that the increasing quantity of land affected by salinity is perhaps the most serious. It has been estimated that during the past 20 years, more than 1,200,000 ha, or seven per cent, of Saskatchewan's total crop land, have been infiltrated by salts. On some of the affected areas, wheat production has dropped by 50 per cent, while other areas are salt-crusted and completely bare. Although the majority of affected land is still farmed, productivity is markedly reduced. One of the major reasons for concern is that the salinity problem is most severe on the province's richest soils. It is affecting the area which has traditionally counterbalanced the loss of farmland in other parts of Canada. It is a problem that is becoming more acute every year.

Changes in Farm Characteristics

"I really believe that the day of the small farmer is pretty nearly over, that is, the fellow that will still stick right on the farm and make his living entirely off the farm. I think it's too bad when I see so many of the neighbours have to take a job in a factory so that they can meet the payments. It's really not right when a property is worth a lot of money that you can't make a living off of it." (Anderson, 1977).

Strongly saline soils are of little or no use for agriculture. In the area identified as class 5, salt tolerant forage crops can be established and maintained. However, the area marked as class 7 contains an excessive salt concentration that prevents the growth of useful vegetation. Unfortunately, saline soils are rapidly becoming an acute problem on the Prairies.

Number of Census-farms. In addition to changes in the resource base for agriculture, changes also occur in farm structure, agricultural operations, and farm population in response to both internal and external pressures. One response to economic, social, and other pressures is the decline in number of farms (Table 18). The number of census-farms in Canada reached a maximum in 1941, when 732,832 farms were recorded. Since that time, there has been a steady decline in the number of census-farms, but the rate of decline has accelerated. The percentage reductions in farms in the 1941 to 1951, 1951 to 1961, and 1961 to 1971 periods were 15, 23, and 24 per cent respectively. The accompanying table illustrates that the loss of farms is not spatially consistent across Canada, with the Atlantic Provinces and Québec experiencing the greatest declines.

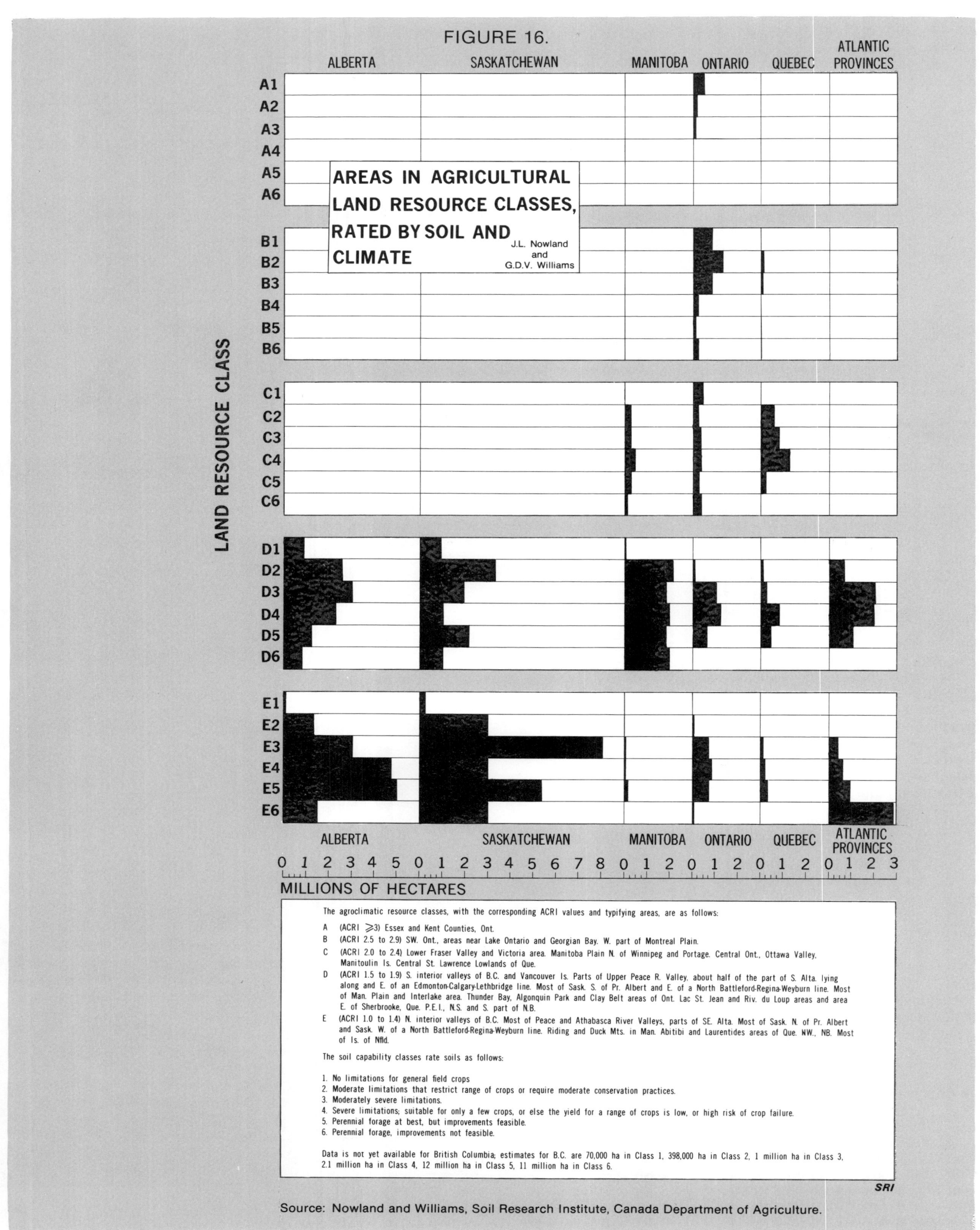

FIGURE 16. AREAS IN AGRICULTURAL LAND RESOURCE CLASSES, RATED BY SOIL AND CLIMATE. J.L. Nowland and G.D.V. Williams.

Source: Nowland and Williams, Soil Research Institute, Canada Department of Agriculture.

TABLE 18.

Number of census-farms, by province, 1921 to 1976

Province	1921	1931	1941	1951	1956	1961	1966	1971	1976
Newfoundland				3,626	2,387	1,752	1,709	1,042	398
Prince Edward Island	13,701	12,865	12,230	10,137	9,432	7,335	6,357	4,543	3,054
Nova Scotia	47,432	39,444	32,977	23,515	21,075	12,518	9,621	6,008	3,441
New Brunswick	36,655	34,025	31,889	26,431	22,116	11,786	8,706	5,485	3,244
Québec	137,619	135,957	154,669	134,336	122,617	95,777	80,294	61,257	43,097
Ontario	198,053	192,174	178,204	149,920	140,602	121,333	109,887	94,722	76,983
Manitoba	53,252	54,199	58,024	52,383	49,201	43,306	39,747	34,981	29,963
Saskatchewan	119,451	136,472	138,713	112,018	103,391	93,924	85,686	76,970	69,578
Alberta	82,954	97,408	99,732	84,315	79,424	73,212	69,411	62,702	57,310
British Columbia	21,973	26,079	26,394	26,406	24,748	19,934	19,085	18,400	13,033
Yukon and Northwest Territories		10	41	26	4	22	26	19	18	17
CANADA	711,090	728,623	732,832	623,091	575,015	480,903	430,522	366,128	300,118

Sources: Dominion Bureau of Statistics, 1947. *Agriculture-Canada*. Vol. VIII, Parts I and II.
————, 1953. *Agriculture-Canada*. Vol. VI, Part I.
————, 1957. *Agriculture-Canada*. Vol. II, Bulletin 2-11.
————, 1963a. *Agriculture-Canada*. Catalogue 96-530.
————, 1968. *Agriculture-Canada*. Catalogue 96-601.
Statistics Canada, 1973a. *Agriculture-Canada*. Catalogue 96-701.
————, 1977f. Number and Area of Census-farms by Census Divisions. Catalogue 96-857.

TABLE 19.

Average census-farm size, by province 1921 to 1976

Province	1921	1931	1941	1951	1956	1961	1966	1971	1976
					(ha)				
Newfoundland				9	12	13	12	24	74
Prince Edward Island	36	38	39	44	46	53	59	69	91
Nova Scotia	40	44	47	55	53	72	78	89	116
New Brunswick	47	49	50	53	55	76	84	99	124
Québec	51	51	47	51	53	60	65	71	85
Ontario	46	48	51	56	57	62	66	68	78
Manitoba	111	113	118	137	147	170	194	220	254
Saskatchewan	149	165	175	223	246	278	309	342	380
Alberta	143	162	176	213	234	261	286	320	350
British Columbia	53	55	62	72	74	91	112	128	180
Yukon and Northwest Territories	66	51	43	44	82	134	91	100	106
CANADA	80	91	96	113	122	145	163	187	224

Sources: Dominion Bureau of Statistics, 1947. *Agriculture-Canada*. Vol. VIII, Parts I and II.
————, 1953. *Agriculture-Canada*. Vol. VI, Part I.
————, 1957. *Agriculture-Canada*. Vol. II, Bulletin 2-11.
————, 1963a. *Agriculture-Canada*. Catalogue 96-530.
————, 1968. *Agriculture-Canada*. Catalogue 96-601.
Statistics Canada, 1973a. *Agriculture-Canada*. Catalogue 96-701.
————, 1977e. Census-farms by Size, Area and Use of Land. Catalogue 96-854.

Farm Size. The 55-year period, between 1921 and 1976, saw a marked change in the average size of the farm (Table 19). Total land area, including improved and unimproved land, increased from 80 to 224 ha per farm during this period, which also saw changes in many socio-economic aspects of agriculture. A number of factors including mechanization of many farm activities, increased efficiency of mechanical innovations, larger land tracts, the necessity of spreading rising production costs over larger farm parcels, consolidation of farms as smaller-scale farms left agriculture, development of joint or corportate farms, and the establishment of agribusiness played a part in this trend. The rôles that farm operation and crop type play in relation to farm size are clear, particularly in the grain and livestock farms of the Prairies.

Farm Population. In the course of urbanization in Canada, particularly since World War II, not only has the majority of population become urban (76 per cent in 1976) but, within the rural sector, farm population has become the minority. In 1976, rural farm population accounted for only four per cent of Canada's total population, and 18 per cent of the rural population. Between 1931 and 1976, farm population fell from 3,289,140 to 1,056,571, a decline of 68 per cent in 45 years (Table 20). However, the trend has accelerated to such an extent that the decrease in farm population, between 1971 and 1976, was 29 per cent, the sharpest decline in the 45-year period. Obviously, the numbers of new entrants into agriculture do not fully compensate for those leaving. The net loss of farm population is largely the result of out-migration of young people unable to find suitable employment opportunities in rural farm areas, retirement of farmers and their families, and farmers who abandon the farm for a variety of economic, social, or personal reasons. When combined with pressures for farm consolidation, rising capital funds required to enter farming, and other changes occurring in rural Canada, this trend in farm population is not surprising. Such declining farm population, however, has serious implications for the future strength, vitality, and viability of rural communities.

Age of Farmers. One particular demographic characteristic that is cause for concern is the average age of farmers, often used as an indicator of the continuing or future vitality of farming in any given area. In 1976, 31 per cent of farm operators were over 54 years of age, whereas only ten per cent of Canada's entire labour force was older than 54. It is interesting that nearly ten per cent of all farm operators were 65 or older, but that less than two per cent of the total labour force falls into this age category. Increasing capital commitment necessary to enter farming often prolongs the period before a new entrant can afford to begin farming, or it places a severe financial burden on young people. Employment and economic pressures tend to affect young or prospective farmers more seriously than the well-established farm operator. The loss of young farmers, farm labourers, and their families has serious implications for the future stability and security of rural areas. Furthermore, as older farmers retire, the distinct possibility of a dramatic change in farm ownership in the next 10 to 20 years leaves many unanswered questions. But a, resurgence of young farmers, between 1971 and 1976, is reason for hope. In 1921, 26 per cent of all farmers were under 34 years of age. In 1971, this proportion had dropped to a low of 15 per cent, but in 1976 it rose to 19 per cent, due in part to improved farm employment conditions through assistance provided by government and agricultural organizations.

The association of older farm operators with more marginal farm areas is a generalization that is nevertheless true in many parts of Canada. A less favourable land resource base, fewer opportunities, reduced chance to incorporate modern mechanical or other innovations, distance to markets, and the risk of smaller economic return tend to discourage young, prospective farmers. In general, such younger people tend to locate on better quality soils and in more advanced agricultural areas. However, the high cost of high-quality farmland is another predicament.

Total Capital Value. Total capital value includes investment in three categories; land and buildings, machinery and equipment, and livestock and poultry. The trend in total capital value, between 1921 and 1976, is one of decline throughout the period of the Depression and World War II, and one of increase since the war (Table 21). The rise in investment was particularly rapid between 1971 and 1976 when contributing factors included escalating land prices and production costs, inflation, generally good grain crops, and improved markets.

47

TABLE 20.

Farm population, by province, 1931 to 1976

Province	1931	1941	1951	Farm population 1956	1961	1966	1971	1976
Newfoundland			19,975	13,055	11,090	9,236	5,156	1,452
Prince Edward Island	55,478	51,067	46,855	43,296	34,753	31,041	21,338	12,279
Nova Scotia	177,690	143,709	115,414	98,944	58,020	46,283	26,977	12,479
New Brunswick	180,214	163,706	149,916	128,978	63,334	52,042	27,453	12,184
Québec	777,017	838,861	792,756	765,459	585,485	507,869	334,579	198,195
Ontario	800,960	704,420	702,778	683,148	524,490	498,025	391,713	286,415
Manitoba	256,305	249,599	219,233	206,729	172,946	161,662	131,202	101,904
Saskatchewan	564,012	514,677	399,473	362,231	305,740	281,089	233,792	193,068
Alberta	375,097	383,964	345,222	332,191	287,814	281,583	237,924	190,785
British Columbia	102,367	102,446	120,292	112,668	84,655	91,443	79,353	47,791
Yukon and Northwest Territories	74	42	82	56	73	92	78	19
CANADA	3,289,140	3,152,449	2,911,996	2,746,755	2,128,400	1,960,365	1,489,565	1,056,571

Sources: Dominion Bureau of Statistics, 1947. Agriculture-Canada. Vol. VIII, Parts I and II.
______________, 1953. Agriculture-Canada. Vol. VI, Part I.
______________, 1957. Agriculture-Canada. Vol. II, Bulletin 2-11.
______________, 1963*a*. Agriculture-Canada. Catalogue 96-530.
______________, 1968. Agriculture-Canada. Catalogue 96-601.
Statistics Canada, 1973*a*. Agriculture-Canada. Catalogue 96-701.
______________, 1978. Agriculture-Canada. Catalogue 96-800.

During this 55-year period, there were noticeable shifts among the relative shares of total capital value held by the three categories (Table 22). For example, in the 1920s through the 1940s, machinery and equipment accounted for less than 15 per cent of total farm investment. Not only was there a lack of cash flow during these hard times, there was also not a wide selection of equipment, and farm machinery manufacturing was secondary to other concerns. However, after World War II, as farm machinery manufacturing expanded and more farming operations became mechanized, more substantial investment in equipment, which offered labour-saving and efficiency benefits reached a peak. Since 1951, this component has not maintained its share of capital investment. Likewise, fluctuation in livestock and poultry investment reflects the close tie between this type of investment and prices received for livestock products, quantity of supply or numbers of livestock, production costs, and production efficiency. Lastly, the proportion of tota capital value accounted for by land and buildings has increased significantly since 1951. The fact that in 1976, land and building investment accounted for more than three-quarters of the total capital value, indicates, among other things, a premium placed on good agricultural land.

Table 23 illustrates that average capital investment per ha and per farm varies from one province to another. Furthermore, the division between the three sectors of investment also varies across the country. The high price of land in southern Ontario and the lower Fraser Valley of British Columbia is associated with more intensive land use. On the other hand, the higher level of investment in machinery on Prairie farms generally reflects the more extensive nature of agricultural land use activities. Different levels of investment in livestock and poultry, as well as buildings, correspond to the various types of livestock operations across Canada. Poultry, dairy, and hog productions are concentrated in central and eastern Canada. These types of livestock operations require excellent environmental control and a high degree of automation which result in relatively high levels of expense. Beef production has a major centre in Alberta, and housing for beef cattle is often limited to relatively inexpensive shelters or wind breaks. Table 23 also indicates that capital investment per farm and per ha relates to farm size and type of operation, which change across the country.

> "This big machinery, big farms, and big operations, this means that the small man has not a chance in the wide world to ever get into business himself. If he does, he's either got to go head and ears into debt so far that he can make an awful lot of money one year, or he goes broke. Way back years ago, people would have one, two horses, a couple of cows, a couple of sheep, and a sow and a few hens, and that would be the full stock they'd have to start off on a farm. And you could go and work out for a couple of years, and you could own it. But now you couldn't start, if you worked out for twenty years, you couldn't earn enough to start farming." (Anderson, 1977).

Climatic Change

"Everybody talks about the weather,
but nobody does anything about it."

(Warner, 1897)

Historical Context

As the expression goes, more and more people have been complaining about the weather, but, during the 1970s, complaints about the climate have been justified. This decade has already suffered an abnormal frequency and combination of droughts, floods, frosts, and storms. Abnormal in the sense that people perceive this number of events as outside the range of normal climate, as dictated by the somewhat vague parameter of recent memory. Within the context of a longer time frame however, these occurrences are not unusual. In the past, changes in climate, particularly temperature, have produced drastic alterations in activities on earth. As a result of climatic variation, civilizations have prospered or perished, massive human migrations have ensued, species of flora and fauna have become extinct, and the very structure of the earth has been transformed.

In the proper historical context then, recent climatic events are not as abnormal as they may seem. Nonetheless, virtually every activity on earth is vulnerable to the impact of climatic permutation. Human settlement patterns, transportation, recreation, agriculture, energy consumption, and health are all affected by even slight changes in climate. Certain activities become either possible or impossible. Productivity or degree of success increases or decreases. It is simply a question of adjustment to the magnitude of change. But what causes climatic change? In the long-term, these alterations are not fully understood, let alone susceptible to any control. The reasons for modification of climate in the short-term are much better discerned. They may result from natural or man-made activities. For example, a change in the earth's radiation balance may be due to volcanic eruptions which spew volcanic dust into the atmosphere. On the other hand, increasing levels of carbon dioxide and particulate matter in the atmosphere may result from the combustion of fossil fuels for home heating, transportation, industrial and manufacturing purposes, energy production, and other activities. Regardless of the reasons for the recent series of climatic incidents, they have become the subject of intensive investigation. Are they unrelated, chance events or are they part of a developing sequence of substantial climatic changes? Even within the scientific community, some questions remain unanswered. The following overview of climatic change and variability is based on World Meteorological Organization material which has been reproduced, with slight modification (World Meteorological Organization, 1976*a* and 1976*b*).

Past climate

- During the past two million years or so, there has been a long sequence of alternations between glacial and interglacial epochs of climate, in which the glacial epochs have tended to recur at approximately 100,000-year intervals. For about the past 8,000 years, the Earth has been in a comparatively warm interglacial phase of this ice-age sequence.
- Since the recovery of the Earth from the last glacial stage, about 8,000 to 10,000 years ago, the global climate has fluctuated within much narrower limits. In part the post-glacial climate changes have involved expansions and retreats of polar ice and mountain glaciations, at intervals of aproximately 2,000 to 3,000 years, in what is described as a "neo-glacial cycle". The "Little Ice Age", a period of temperatures 1 or 2°C lower than today and stormy conditions in the North Atlantic, lasting from about 1550 to 1850 A.D., was a part of the neo-glacial cycle.
- Since the time of the Little Ice Age, and up to 1950, the world generally warmed about 1°C, but the rate of warming has been irregular and it is not certain whether the Little Ice Age has yet run its full course. This warming was especially pronounced during the first half of the 20th century, with temperatures rising most rapidly (several degrees C in 50 years) in the Atlantic sector of the Arctic.
- Since then, the climatic trends characteristic of the first half of the 20th century appear, generally speaking, to have reversed direction at least in the northern hemisphere. Temperatures have fallen especially in the Arctic and the Atlantic Sub-Arctic (by several degrees C in some areas) where the extent of sea ice has again been increasing. The atmospheric circulation of the northern hemisphere appears to have reverted to a pattern resembling that of the last part of the 19th century, with a tendency towards greater variability of weather conditions in many areas. These changes may have begun to falter, if not actually to reverse yet again, in the last few years.
- As a general conclusion, knowledge of past climates suggests that the interglacial warmth of the past 8,000 years or so will eventually change to a colder, more glacial regime. The onset of that change may be a number of millennia or centuries away, conceivably it may already have begun. It seems likely that this transition will be sufficiently gradual so that in the next 100 to 200 years it would be almost imperceptible amid the ubiquitous variability of climate. There is however a very small yet finite probability that a much more rapid cooling of climate will occur in the same time period. On the other hand, it must be recognized that such assessments would be invalid if, as now considered probable, the addition of carbon dioxide to the atmosphere, and other effects of human activities during the next 200 years, contribute to a general warming of global climate.

Physical causes of climatic fluctuations

- Present understanding of the causes of climatic fluctuations is rudimentary. A great many physical mechanisms have been proposed, and the relative importance of these causes differs with the time scale being considered. Climatic fluctuations and variability may arise in part from sources within the atmosphere/ocean/land system. Many potential mechanisms exist to produce internal variability of the system, on a wide range of time scales. These follow directly from the feedback from any one part of the system to another, together with the widely disparate reaction times of the different parts.
- Climatic fluctuations may also arise in part from influences originating outside the climatic system. Well-known examples are possible variations of the radiant energy output of the sun, variations of the quantity of particles in the upper atmosphere originating from volcanic eruptions, and the accumulation of carbon dioxide in the atmosphere from fossil fuel combustion.
- One illustration of the kind of interaction that probably contributes significant variability to the climatic system is that between snow cover, reflection of solar radiation, and air temperature. If a small decrease of temperature occurs which favours the development of a snow cover, the greater reflection of solar radiation from the snow will locally reduce solar heating of the Earth's surface and atmosphere. The reduced heating will then lower air temperature still further, preserving the snow and perhaps favouring additional snowfall over a wider area. A similar, but opposite, chain of events is involved if the starting point is a small increase of temperature. The end effect is both to amplify small climatic disturbances, and to prolong them.

TABLE 21.

Total capital value of census-farms, by province, 1921 to 1976

Province	1921	1931	1941	1951	1961	1966	1971	1976
				(dollars)				
Newfoundland				19,656,779	23,937,400	30,353,400	31,469,600	58,116,717
Prince Edward Island	58,977,962	58,332,029	46,695,077	87,153,205	96,296,500	128,620,700	161,894,300	307,202,239
Nova Scotia	136,841,573	105,877,410	88,363,861	152,464,945	145,588,800	163,785,100	206,085,000	376,837,096
New Brunswick	127,567,675	103,530,618	80,795,359	157,778,559	145,363,000	150,778,900	173,212,000	302,906,099
Québec	1,085,234,333	877,273,510	739,746,962	1,399,363,121	1,624,879,600	1,883,869,700	2,200,283,600	3,928,217,554
Ontario	1,688,908,794	1,397,665,762	1,189,600,261	2,547,969,618	3,741,596,000	4,884,129,600	6,897,524,200	16,101,601,960
Manitoba	637,388,045	388,142,128	339,178,276	916,786,792	1,154,087,600	1,757,369,100	2,055,618,800	4,458,598,388
Saskatchewan	1,650,069,196	1,272,662,978	896,013,231	1,991,773,250	2,864,359,300	4,911,436,500	5,492,078,800	12,655,391,274
Alberta	968,437,018	869,431,858	711,020,196	1,789,616,297	2,717,496,800	4,215,619,600	5,242,097,400	13,602,705,745
British Columbia	201,384,913	174,837,175	150,062,927	408,265,668	657,166,300	949,110,000	1,606,924,400	2,996,212,762
Yukon and Northwest Territories	48,147	127,459	85,440	48,138	450,400	248,000	668,900	957,098
CANADA	6,554,857,656	5,247,880,927	4,241,561,590	9,470,876,372	13,171,221,700	19,075,320,600	24,067,857,000	54,788,746,932

Sources: Dominion Bureau of Statistics, 1947. *Agriculture-Canada*. Vol. VIII, Parts I and II.
_____, 1953. *Agriculture-Canada*. Vol. VI, Part I.
_____, 1957 *Agriculture-Canada*. Vol. II, Bulletin 2-11.
_____, 1963a. *Agriculture-Canada*. Catalogue 96-530.
_____, 1968. *Agriculture-Canada*. Catalogue 96-601.
Statistics Canada, 1973a. *Agriculture-Canada*. Catalogue 96-701.
_____, 1977f. *Number and Area of Census-farms by Census Divisions*. Catalogue 96-857.

TABLE 22.

Percentage of total capital value, by sector, for Canada, 1921 to 1976

	Total capital value sector		
Year	Land and buildings	Machinery and equipment	Livestock and poultry
	(per cent)		
1921	77.1	10.1	12.8
1931	77.2	12.4	10.4
1941	71.4	14.1	14.5
1951	58.4	20.4	21.2
1961	65.5	19.5	15.0
1966	69.1	18.6	12.3
1971	70.4	16.2	13.4
1976	75.8	16.1	8.1

Sources: Statistics Canada, 1973a. *Agriculture-Canada*. Catalogue 96-701.
_____, 1978. *Agriculture-Canada*. Catalogue 96-800.

Effects of man's activities on climate

— Many scientists have suggested that man's activities may be responsible in various ways for changes of climate occurring now or in the future. On a local scale, as in urban areas, human effects on climate are a demonstrable reality. The relative warmth of large cities, known as the "urban heat island effect", is a well documented example. The burning of oil and coal increases the amount of carbon dioxide in the atmosphere, and this could produce a long-term warming and, as a consequence, large-scale changes in rainfall distribution. If most known reserves of such fuels are consumed in the next century or two, as it now seems they may be, atmospheric carbon dioxide concentrations would be likely to increase several fold above present levels. The best information now available indicates that such a large carbon dioxide increase would result in a very significant warming of global climate, by several degrees and that, because of the slow pace of removal mechanisms, this warming would persist for many centuries after the fossil fuel reserves have been substantially depleted. Further climatic effects, as yet difficult to foresee in specific detail, would also be likely.

— The release of chemicals (for example, chlorofluoromethanes) and the increase in the dust content in the atmosphere, as a result of man's activities, if not checked, might also alter the climate. Direct thermal emissions from urban and industrial areas have already affected climate on a local scale and could have wider effects if these emissions were to increase. However, it is impossible at this time to give an accurate assessment of the magnitude of such changes.

— There is as yet insufficient evidence to conclusively indicate whether or not human activity affects climatic variability on larger geographical scales. Human effects are, nevertheless, to be recognized as of potentially great importance in altering the natural evolution of large-scale climate over the next century or two.

Impact of climatic variability on man's activities

— The recent occurrences in certain regions of climatic extremes persisting for a few weeks, months, or even years, such as shifts in the monsoon belt, excessive rain, droughts, and high or low temperatures, have led to speculation that a major climatic change is occurring on a global scale. While such a global change could occur from natural causes, the trend towards such a change is likely to be gradual, and would be almost imperceptible. This is because the fluctuations over shorter periods of time are likely to be so much larger as to obscure these long-term trends. It is these shorter-term climate changes, which may be due to natural or man-made causes, that now require urgent attention and further studies. The natural shorter-term variability of climate is becoming of increasing importance as the result of growing pressures on limited natural resources. It is this variability which has been high-lighted by the disastrous droughts and weather extremes in many parts of the world which have caused so much human suffering, political instability and have adversely affected economic development.

— The biosphere and many human activities such as land use, agriculture, and energy consumption, are sensitive to weather and climate, the degree of sensitivity varying in different climatic zones of the globe. This sensitivity is growing in importance in many parts of the world as population pressure and demands are rapidly increasing. Present ecosystems and many of the complex, interdependent systems developed by modern man are fairly well adapted to the climatic conditions that prevailed in the past, and are therefore quite sensitive to changes in climate. For example, the present systems used for food and fibre production are predicated on average climatic conditions and even a modest change in climate would have serious social and economic repercussions. A cooling of the Earth by as little as 1°C could result in a shorter growing season and a shift of the boundary of major wheat production regions, and decrease fish catch and timber production in middle and higher latitudes; in lower latitudes, however, such a change could be beneficial. Similarly, warmer global temperature could result in improved production in some latitudes and reduced yield in others. Various studies have also shown that even in the absence of a dramatic climatic shift, these systems could still be significantly affected by the occurrence of climatic variability greater than experienced in the past.

TABLE 23.

Average capital value per ha of farmland and per farm, by sector and province, 1976

Province	Number of census-farms	Average farm size	\multicolumn{4}{c	}{Average capital value per ha of farmland}	\multicolumn{4}{c	}{Average capital value per farm}
			Total	Land and buildings	Machinery and equipment	Livestock and poultry	Total	Land and buildings	Machinery and equipment	Livestock and poultry
		(ha)	\multicolumn{4}{c	}{(dollars)}	\multicolumn{4}{c	}{(dollars)}
Newfoundland	398	74	1,975	1,639	196	140	146,022	121,198	14,464	10,360
Prince Edward Island	3,054	91	1,105	728	261	116	100,590	66,300	23,734	10,556
Nova Scotia	3,441	116	942	662	164	115	109,514	77,005	19,112	13,397
New Brunswick	3,244	124	753	492	181	80	93,374	60,982	22,409	9,984
Québec	43,097	85	1,075	685	225	166	91,148	58,042	19,068	14,038
Ontario	76,983	78	2,699	2,184	314	201	209,158	169,270	24,312	15,576
Manitoba	29,963	254	586	413	125	48	148,803	104,933	31,680	12,191
Saskatchewan	69,578	380	479	350	97	31	181,888	133,014	36,911	11,963
Alberta	57,310	350	679	519	104	56	237,353	181,373	36,418	19,562
British Columbia	13,033	180	1,274	1,065	130	79	229,894	192,127	23,527	14,240
Yukon and Northwest Territories	17	106	533	377	129	27	56,300	39,802	13,627	2,871
CANADA	300,118	224	816	619	131	66	182,557	138,426	29,393	14,738

Source: Statistics Canada, 1978. *Agriculture Canada.* Catalogue 96-800.

Agricultural Repercussions

"... in January, 1931, and that was the year we got no snow and we lived in this old shack and our neighbor across the road summer fallowed, yes, in January, and we got half his field in our house. It blew, it blew steady, day after day, and the only time it stopped was after dark.... That was a crazy year. The whole weather was upside down. Nothing mattered.

... in mid-January, I was in the old Galt Hospital in Lethbridge and there was a tree outside my window that was budding out. It should have been twenty below outside. It was so unusual. We didn't get no snow until sometime in March and that wind just blew and blew and blew and it just took the topsoil away. Miles high, so it seemed, into the sky. They were really chinook winds. Southwest winds. Blew soil right into Ontario." (Broadfoot, 1973).

What does all this mean to Canada and to Canadian agriculture specifically? Consider how the 1975 killing frost in Brazil affected the Brazilian coffee crop. In Canada, certainly an economic repercussion was felt. At the individual's level, each cup of coffee cost more. Consider the unexpected failure of the Peruvian anchovy fishery in the early 1970s. With the sudden disappearance of this source of protein, the demand for, and price of, soybeans rose dramatically. With rising demand and prices, agricultural activities were altered and considerable land in suitable areas such as southwestern Ontario was diverted to soybean production—a land use pattern repercussion.

If, as suggested as one possibility, we return to a time of more unstable climatic conditions, agricultural potential and productivity will change. A seemingly insignificant decrease in average annual temperature would be accompanied by a reduction in the growing season, thereby eliminating the cultivation of certain crops in specific locations. A minor decline in precipitation would increase the areas requiring irrigation and might remove some of the more arid lands from cultivation altogether. In contrast, a slight increase in precipitation might well increase the agricultural potential of the southern Prairies, but would likely pose more serious problems over a more extensive area. In already wet regions, such as New Brunswick and other coastal locations, activities such as ploughing, seeding, crop drying, and harvesting could be hampered. Extra wetness would adversely affect the production costs/gross income relationship, and some land would be abandoned. In addition, climatic fluctuations are a major factor in determining the increased incidence or decline of insects, pests, and diseases. Temperature, precipitation, humidity, wind, and other weather phenomena all play a rôle in advancing or discouraging invasions of pests or diseases, which in the past, have plagued agriculture. Ultimately, any agricultural adjustments made in response to climate variability would likely necessitate immediate and possibly extensive implementation of technical innovations, which commits large amounts of energy and capital, both finite resources in their own right. In brief, a return of the climatic conditions of earlier decades would have significant repercussions on our utilization of other scarce resources. A return to the good old days of romantic and sentimental reflection might in fact be a return to the dust bowl days or to Noah's Ark.

Fur traders' journals and settlers' diaries from the Prairies and the Red River settlement, reveal the anguish caused by climatic fluctuations and their impact on agriculture (McKay and Allsopp, 1977):

1819: "In many places grasshoppers were 3″ deep and could be shovelled with a spade. Even the leaves and bark were stripped from trees."

1836: "On the 7th of June we had a heavy fall of snow, and on the following day the ice was the thickness of a penny piece on the water; but still nothing serious happened to damp our hopes still the 19th of August when the severity of the frost blasted our fairest prospects by destroying the crops."
Alexander Ross — The River Settlement

1868: "The crop of 1868 was a complete failure - even seeds having to be imported (due to drought and grasshoppers)."
The Nor-Wester — February 12, 1869.

The variability of climatic conditions is illustrated by the crop outlook the following year:

1869: August 24 "Never before have the crops looked better than they have this summer. In many instances the wheat is 6 feet in height."
The Nor-Wester — August 24, 1869.

Whatever the direction, it will differ from our recent experiences of the 1950s and 1960s when Canadian crop yields from cultivation of much of the arable land were high. Factors including scientific and technical advance of agricultural practices, the introduction of special hybrid crops, together with unusually favourable weather over a long period, combined to produce a consistently high level of productivity. The hybrids developed from 1930s to the 1960s and the very productive crops now cultivated across Canada are based on the 1930 to 1960 climate which many have come to expect. But, it seems that recent high-yield crops are even more vulnerable to climatic changes than the older varieties. A return to genetic diversity appears to be one response to the threat of climatic change and variability.

In spite of scientific advances and technical innovations, man's economic and social activities continue to be very much dependent on climate. Agricultural activities are particularly susceptible to climate variations. Agricultural potential in Canada is severely restricted by temperature, moisture, and other climatic variables. It is clear, however, that the best agroclimatic resource areas are located in those very sites where urban expansion air, water and land pollution, and recreation requirements are absorbing, degrading, or consuming agricultural land. Moreover, a shift toward a cooler climate would remove more northern farmland from production, thus placing a greater urgency on preserving the prime agroclimatic resources of southern Canada.

A Scenario. The possible impact of climatic fluctuations on crops can be illustrated, for the purpose of land use evaluation and planning, by using crop–climate models. In particular, the impact of a cooler temperature regime on two crops, barley and wheat, was investigated by Williams and Oakes at Agriculture Canada. The following description of this methodology was modified from Williams and Oakes (1978). Using relief maps and calculations based on daily maximum and minimum temperature normals and photoperiod data, climatic resources for barley and wheat were mapped for Canada at a scale of 1:5,000,000. In computing the climatic resources that would be available under a cooler climatic regime, 1°C was subtracted from the temperature normals for every month. This lowered the estimated climatic resource level for locations in several important ways. It made the assumed planting date later and the estimated first fall frost earlier, and because of lower summer temperatures, it lengthened the time required for a crop to mature. In other words, less heat would be available over a shorter period.

As a complement to the climatic data, soil-geomorphic limits were abstracted from the Soils of Canada map (Canada Department of Agriculture, 1972), also at a scale of 1:5,000,000. Land composed predominantly of one or more of the following: rocky, stony, permafrost, organic soil, or steeply dissected to mountainous terrain was considered outside the soil limits. Attention can then be focused on those areas that are within the soil–geomorphic limits when the effects of possible climatic fluctuations are examined. The impact of a 1°C climatic cooling on the maturing of barley and wheat is seen on the accompanying maps (Maps 21 and 22). The ripening limits based on the 1941 to 1970 climate and on the 1°C cooler climate are illustrated.

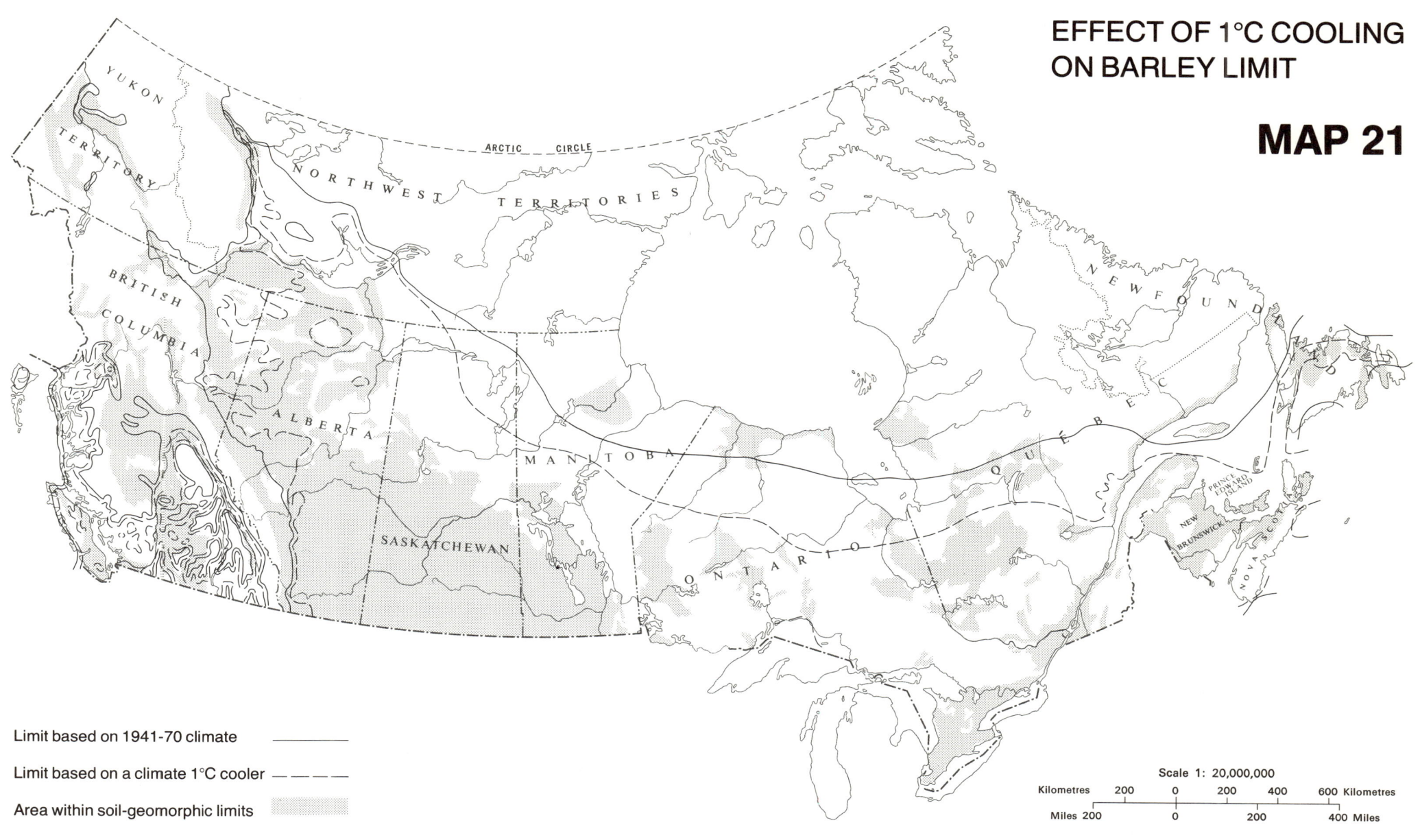

EFFECT OF 1°C COOLING ON BARLEY LIMIT

MAP 21

Limit based on 1941-70 climate ———
Limit based on a climate 1°C cooler – – –
Area within soil-geomorphic limits ▒▒▒

Scale 1: 20,000,000

Barley is the quickest maturing cereal, and the calculations were based on an early variety, so the climatic limits shown for this crop with temperatures 1°C cooler provide a useful indication of the possible outer limits for cereal production under such a cooler climatic regime. As can be seen, the reduction of the barley maturing zone would be minimal because much of the shift of the frontier would be over land that is unsuitable for cultivation from a soil–geomorphic standpoint. This is clearly the case in Manitoba and Saskatchewan where the southward relocation of the frontier would occur over the Canadian Shield.

On the other hand, wheat is a later-maturing cereal crop, and the southward shift of the ripening limit under the influence of a cooler climate is reason for considerably more concern. To begin with, the boundary of the wheat maturing zone is much further south than the barley limit. Any southward shrinking of the wheat maturing zone would occur principally in areas where soil–geomorphic conditions are conducive to cereal crop production. This is particularly evident in Alberta and Saskatchewan, Canada's breadbasket provinces. From analysis of these maps, it was estimated that a 1°C cooling would reduce Canada's potential crop land by one-seventh for barley and one-third for wheat.

In addition, although reduced heat stress in summer could be beneficial in some instances, the cooler climate would generally have an adverse effect on the maturation not only of wheat and barley, but also of most other crops, particularly in areas close to their northern limits. In southern Canada, conditions would become slightly less attractive for the cultivation of certain crops. Although it is unlikely that a 1°C cooling would drastically affect the tender fruit industry in the Niagara area, it would increase the risk of crop damage due to frost, it would shorten the growing season slightly, and it would reduce the heat available during that season. More severe climatic changes, such as significantly lower winter temperatures, could destroy the industry. It is important to realize that many of the specialty crops grown in southern Canada, particularly tender fruits, cannot be relocated because of unique climatic requirements. The processes and consequences of continuing to divert such specialty lands to urban or other uses have been explored for many years. In northern areas of the country, where many agricultural activities already have a rather tenuous existence under severe climatic constraints, it is inevitable that the production of certain crops, for example wheat, could be eliminated during a period of climatic cooling. It is the margin of safety and the severity of repercussion that are significant.

In one sense then, not only prime climatic or agroclimatic resource areas, but also marginal or frontier areas, may be viewed as critical. At the present time, these fringe areas represent spaces of expansion and promise for agriculture. In these areas, competition from other land uses including urban growth and recreation is less severe than in the more densely populated regions in the south. Technical innovations, progress in farm management practices, and advances in plant breeding for northern areas have acted as catalysts in furthering agriculture, particularly in the fringe areas. Such improvements continue to permit expansion of crop areas as well as better yields. However, in the event of disadvantageous climatic fluctuations, these marginal areas will be seriously affected, and could be lost to Canadian agriculture entirely.

Having presented a scenario of a cooler climate, it is important to remember that it is only one of a number of possibilities, each with its own dynamic consequences. There remains some uncertainty as to the probable direction and magnitude of future climatic change and variability. Many meteorologists feel that increased levels of carbon dioxide in the atmosphere may well produce the greenhouse effect and, thus, a warming trend. Such a course of events could open up frontier land to agriculture. However, climate is much too complex to fit neatly into any one scenario. Trends are difficult to detect because they are usually gradual and are often masked by large year-to-year fluctuations. Also, the probable impact may be complicated by the fact that different trends may be occurring during different times of the year. For example, summers might become cooler and wetter while winters might become milder.

Given this, while the answers may lie outside the reaches of this study, the following questions remain: What effects would climatic variability have on the country's agricultural production? As a nation which exports farm produce, what would happen to the degree of agricultural self-sufficiency and trade balance? If Canada is affected by climatic cooling, what would be the global impact of such an event? What influence does climatic change have on potential for other crops, crop yields, diseases, and insects? In the face of more variable climatic conditions which could bring a prolonged cool period, how does one evaluate the continuing loss of some of Canada's most favoured agroclimatic areas? Is it a wise practice to divert Canada's prime agricultural land to urban, recreation, transportation, and other uses? Can Canadian agricultural policies and practices, which were developed during an extended period of generally favourable climate, cope with the repercussions of climatic change? The agricultural potential of resource land is directly related to the characteristics of its climate, and much remains to be learned.

In this section, the factors of change have been discussed. By examining changes in the agricultural resource base and in soil quality, farm characteristics, and climatic conditions, other methods of defining critical lands have been introduced. In the next section, the concept of uniqueness is presented.

Uniqueness

A Case Study: The Niagara Fruit Belt

"It is scarcity, or the threat of scarcity, that is focussing critical attention on the land resource." (Canadian Federation of Agriculture, 1974).

Some of the major concerns brought to the attention of the public within the last decade have dealt with the preservation and protection of scenic landscapes as well as historical and archeological sites. Canadians have been encouraged to recognize the value of preserving endangered species, and the need to select appropriate pipeline routes so as not to interfere with migratory routes. It follows, therefore, that Canadians should recognize the necessity of preserving for agriculture those farmlands which are unique and scarce in Canada. In one definition, unique farmland has been described as land

"... that is scarce and used for the production of specific (or speciality) food or fibre crops. It has the unique combination of soil quality, location, growing season, and moisture supply needed to produce sustained high-quality or high yields of a specific (or speciality) crop when treated

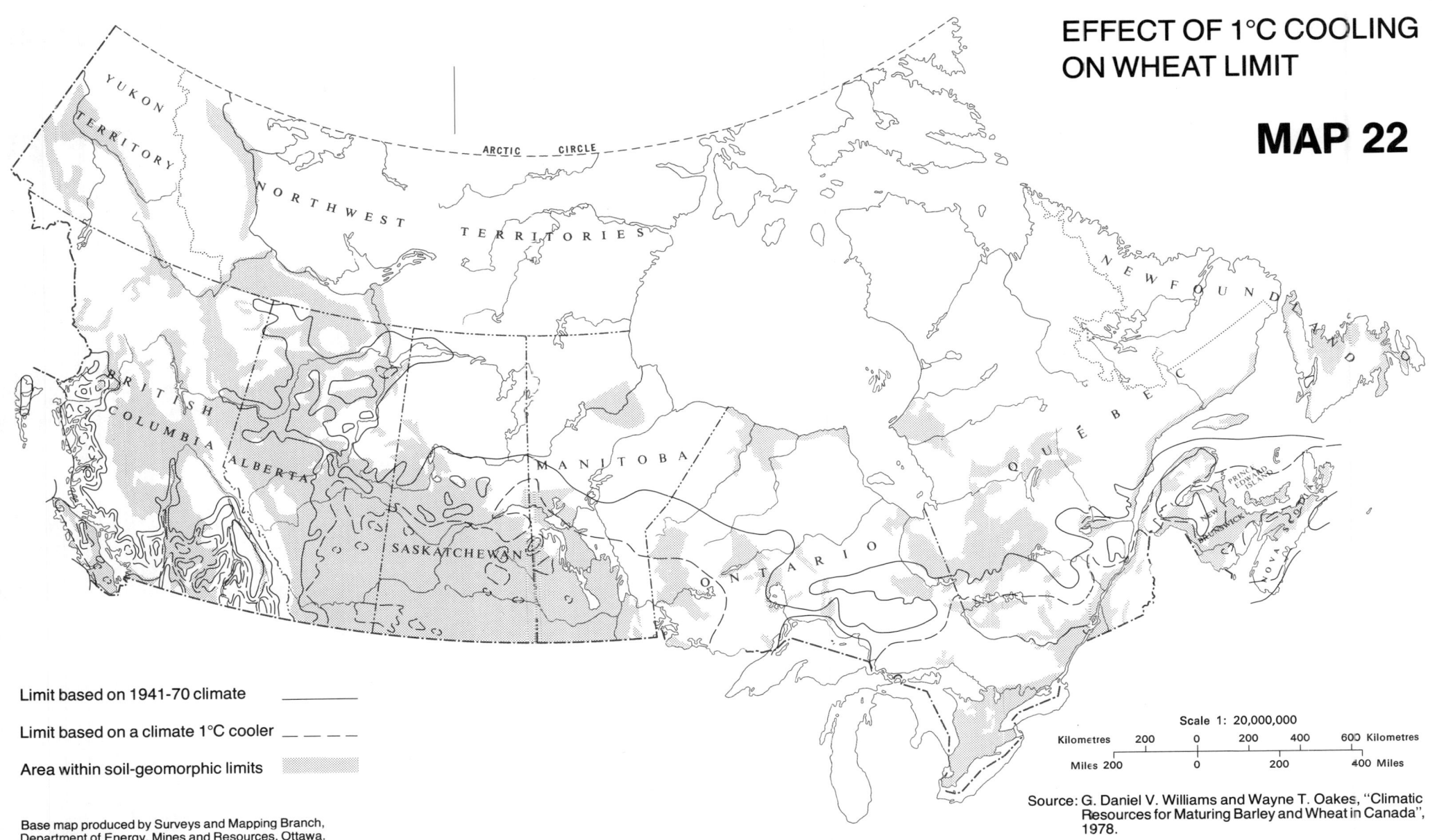

EFFECT OF 1°C COOLING ON WHEAT LIMIT

MAP 22

Limit based on 1941-70 climate ──────
Limit based on a climate 1°C cooler ─ ─ ─ ─
Area within soil-geomorphic limits

Base map produced by Surveys and Mapping Branch, Department of Energy, Mines and Resources, Ottawa.

Scale 1: 20,000,000

Source: G. Daniel V. Williams and Wayne T. Oakes, "Climatic Resources for Maturing Barley and Wheat in Canada", 1978.

---

and managed according to modern farming methods." (United States Department of Agriculture, 1975).

The Niagara fruit belt of Ontario is a unique region within Canada, if not North America. Nevertheless, since the mid 1950s the area devoted to the production of tender fruit crops has been steadily declining, due largely to the continuous pressures of urban expansion. Now, more than 20 years later, the lack of positive action directed towards preserving the Niagara fruit belt, leads one to question the importance Canadians place on threatened and unique agricultural resources.

Located on the south shore of Lake Ontario, the Niagara fruit belt occupies the narrow lakeshore plain below the Niagara Escarpment. It extends eastward from Hamilton to the Niagara River and projects south at one point into the Fonthill kame moraine. The width of the plain is approximately eight to ten km near St. Catharines, broadening towards the Niagara River and narrowing in the west near Grimsby, before continuing to Hamilton. At the foot of the escarpment (elevation 122 m) the plain gently slopes towards the low cliffs of the Lake Ontario shoreline where the elevation is about 82 m. (*See* Map 23)[4].

According to the Canada Land Inventory soil capability for agriculture, the soils are mainly class 1 and class 2. Moving from the shoreline of the lake to the foot of the escarpment, the soils change from sand underlain by glacial till to a silty-clay loam. The deep, well-drained, light-textured soils are good for cultivation of tender fruit crops of peaches and sweet cherries but other fruit crops (apples, sour cherries, pears, prunes, and plums) grow well on well-drained clays. The term "tender fruit" refers to the least hardy tree fruits: peaches, sweet cherries, and apricots. However, this term is sometimes expanded, for use in a more general context, to include more hardy fruit crops such as pears and sour cherries. However, it is not the presence of the favourable soils alone which accounts for the success of the tender fruit crops. An ameliorating effect on temperature due to the adjacent water bodies, combined with the frost-shelter created by the escarpment, a mean annual precipitation of approximately 700 mm, a frost-free period of 169 days, and the warm temperatures experienced over the long growing season, all contribute to an ideal situation for growing tender fruits.

[4]. Maps 23, 25, 26, 27, and 28 are reproduced from The Canadian Geographer, Vol. XXII, No. 3. 1978.

(*See* Map 24). A study by the Ontario Department of Agriculture (Mercier and Chapman, 1955) cited by Jackson (1977) revealed that:

> "... the survey has failed to show another section in southern Ontario with as many advantages as that belt of land directly below the Niagara Escarpment between Queenston and Hamilton" (Mercier and Chapman, 1955).

Extensive fruit production does occur in other regions of southern Ontario, the southwest area of Québec, the lower Saint John River valley, and the Annapolis Valley. However, due to the less favourable climate and soil conditions, the main concentration is directed towards the cultivation of apples, not tender fruits. There are two other areas in Canada with the necessary conditions for tender fruit orchards, the Kent–Essex area of southwestern Ontario and the southern Okanagan Valley of British Columbia. Although these two areas have the appropriate soils and climate, a number of limiting factors prevent a shift to these areas as alternate sources (other than importation) of tender fruits. The Kent–Essex area, a belt of land located along the northern shore of Lake Erie, has twice the probability of experiencing low winter and spring temperatures which result in frost damage to peach blossoms and buds. Although some peaches are grown in this region, the reliability of supply in the long run is poorer. Nevertheless, these conditions have nourished a profitable vegetable industry in the Kent–Essex area, which supplies fresh fruits and vegetables to markets and processors along the entire Windsor–Québec axis. It seems unlikely that these farmers would change from the reliability of these cash crops to undertake the more hazardous and intricate business of tender fruit production. The Okanagan Valley of British Columbia is the only other area capable of producing the tender fruit crops now being grown in the Niagara fruit belt. Here again, however, the climate is less favourable for tender fruit production. In addition to frequent spring frost damage, low winter temperatures cause serious tree and crop losses on an average of once in seven years (Krueger, 1976). The limited amount of available and suitable land, due to widely varying topography and soil conditions, is another constraint in the Okanagan Valley. Even if the Okanagan could supply the eastern markets, the problems of the high cost of transport and the spoilage of tender fruit during transit would remain.

Within Canada, the Niagara fruit belt is superior to any other orchard area, producing a major share of the nation's peaches, grapes, as well as cherries (sweet and sour), pears, plums, apples, and small fruits. A noted geographer and authority on the Niagara fruitlands has stated that investigations show that Niagara has the best natural environment for peaches and other tender fruits in all of Canada. It is better than all of the United States except California, where irrigation is required and where urbanization is also a major threat to fruit growing. Niagara has less chance of frost damage to peaches than Georgia, which is dubbed the peach state of the United States (Krueger, 1977).

In the Niagara Peninsula, agriculture is beset by many problems including imperfectly drained soils, fluctuating prices for produce, competition from foreign produce, lack of capital, low net income per farm, inefficient part-time farmers, and urban encroachment. However, a cursory examination of the situation that has developed in the Niagara fruit belt leaves little doubt that urbanization is the most significant factor in the decline of this limited land resource. Recently published research has confirmed that since 1965 the pace of urban growth has accelerated, and the sprawl pattern has remained unchanged (Krueger, 1976 and 1978).

The Niagara area not only possesses the unique qualities needed for the production of tender fruit crops, but it is also situated within an area highly attractive to industrial and urban development. The attractions include abundant water supply for industrial uses as well as for transportation, well-developed highway and railroad systems, and a productive agricultural industry. The present patterns of urban development represent the infrastructure of a rapidly expanding urban belt or conurbation, extending from Oshawa to Hamilton and east along Lake Ontario to the Niagara River. This trend has led to extensive turnover of tender fruit soils to urban expansion (*see* Maps 25, 26, and 27).

Between the years 1931 and 1951, urban expansion was slowly reaching into areas that were predominantly utilized by orchards and vineyards. Nevertheless, the area of fruitlands increased by approximately 6,880 ha despite the urban intrusion. This trend did not continue. By 1951, increases in fruitland began to stabilize, showing an increase of only 130 ha during the period 1954 to 1958. This gain did not offset the loss of 263 ha of orchard nor did it compensate for the 4,047 ha which became non-productive due to urban side effects such as

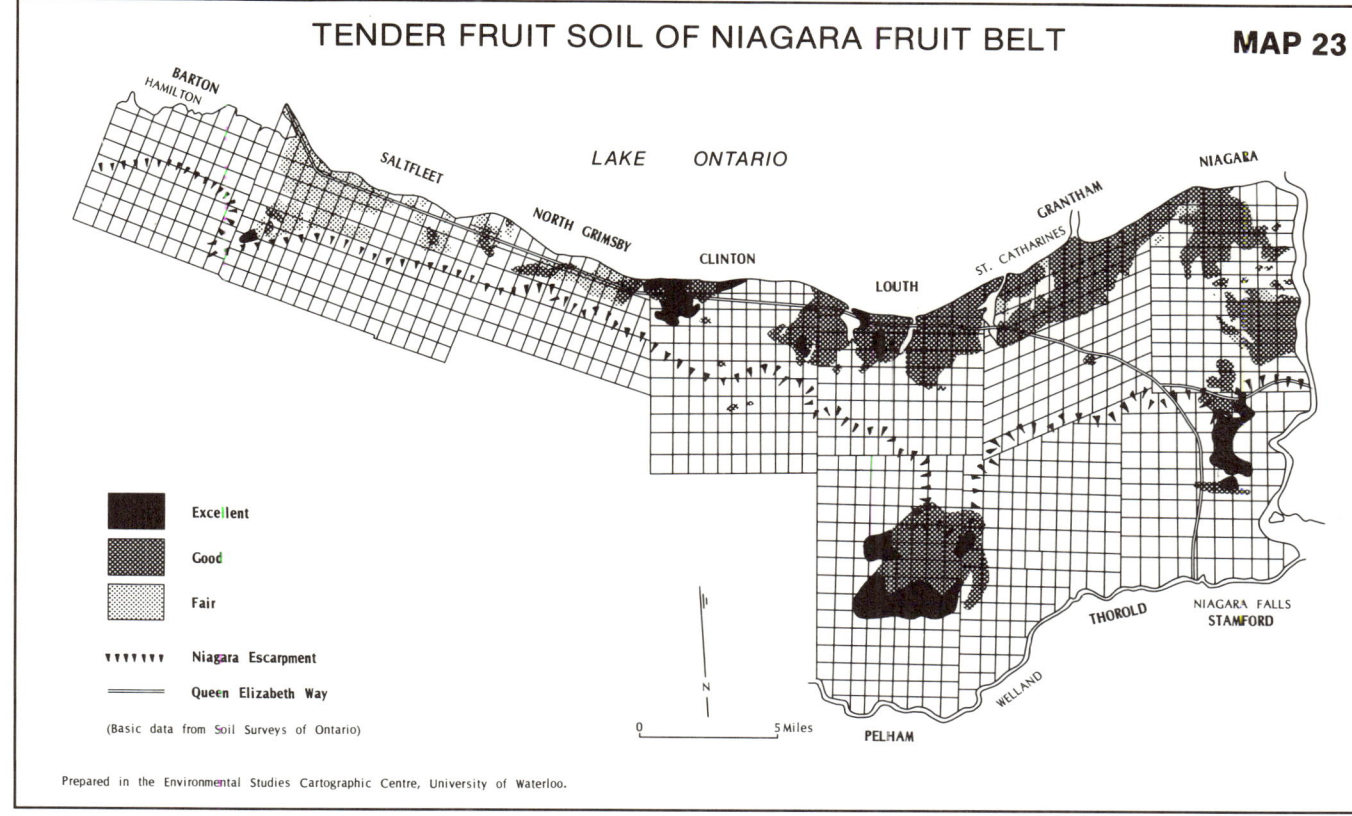

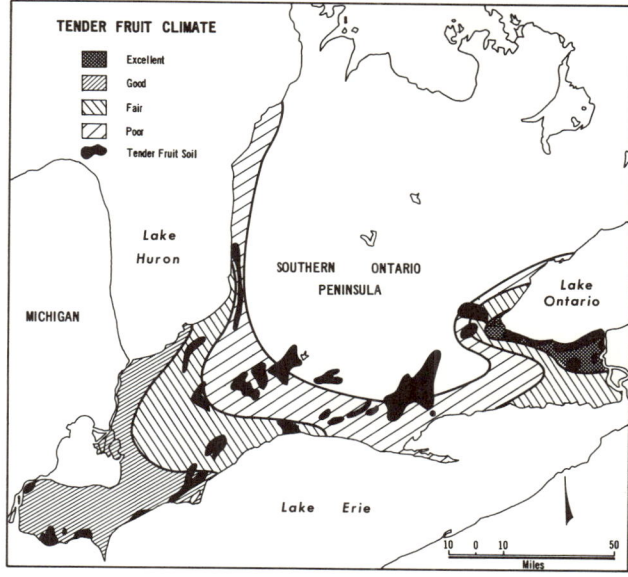

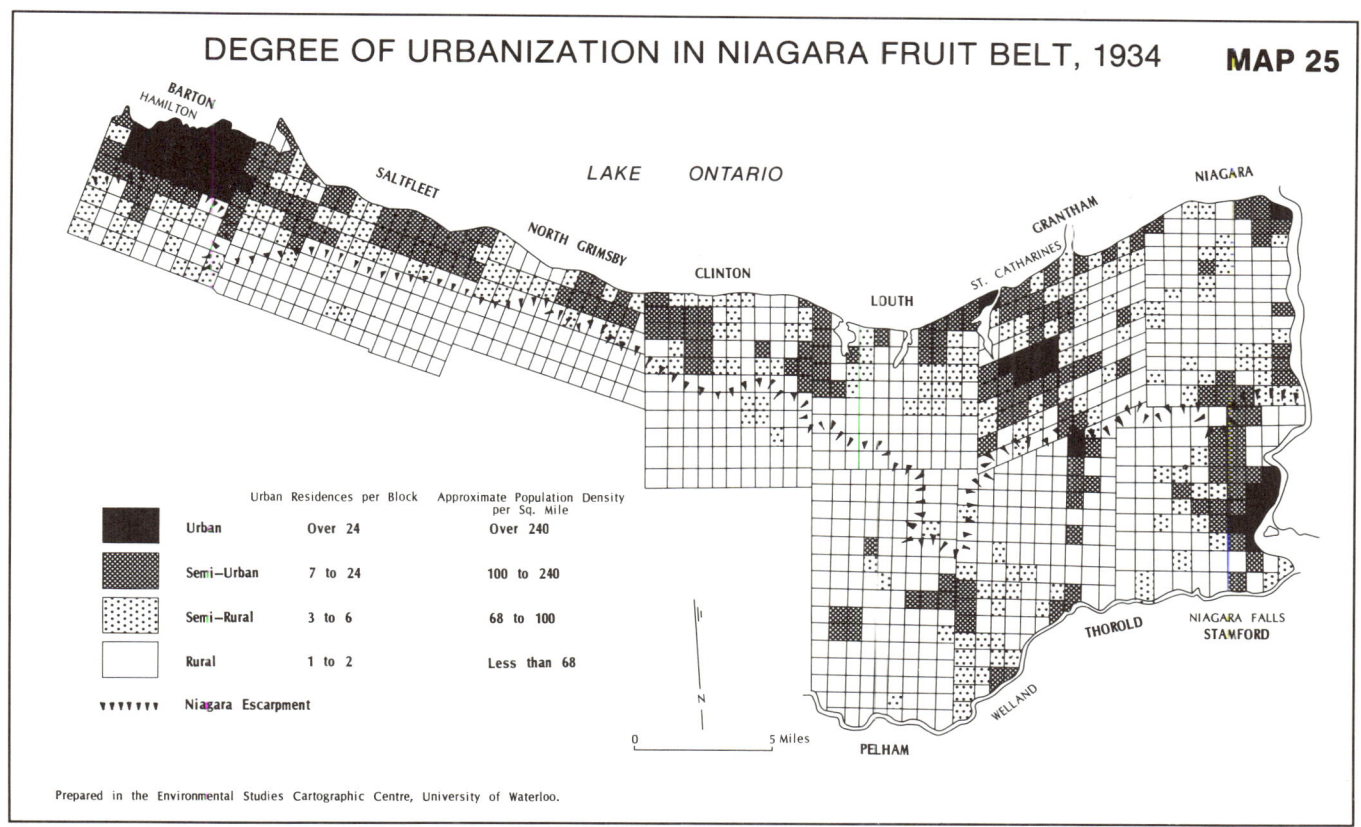

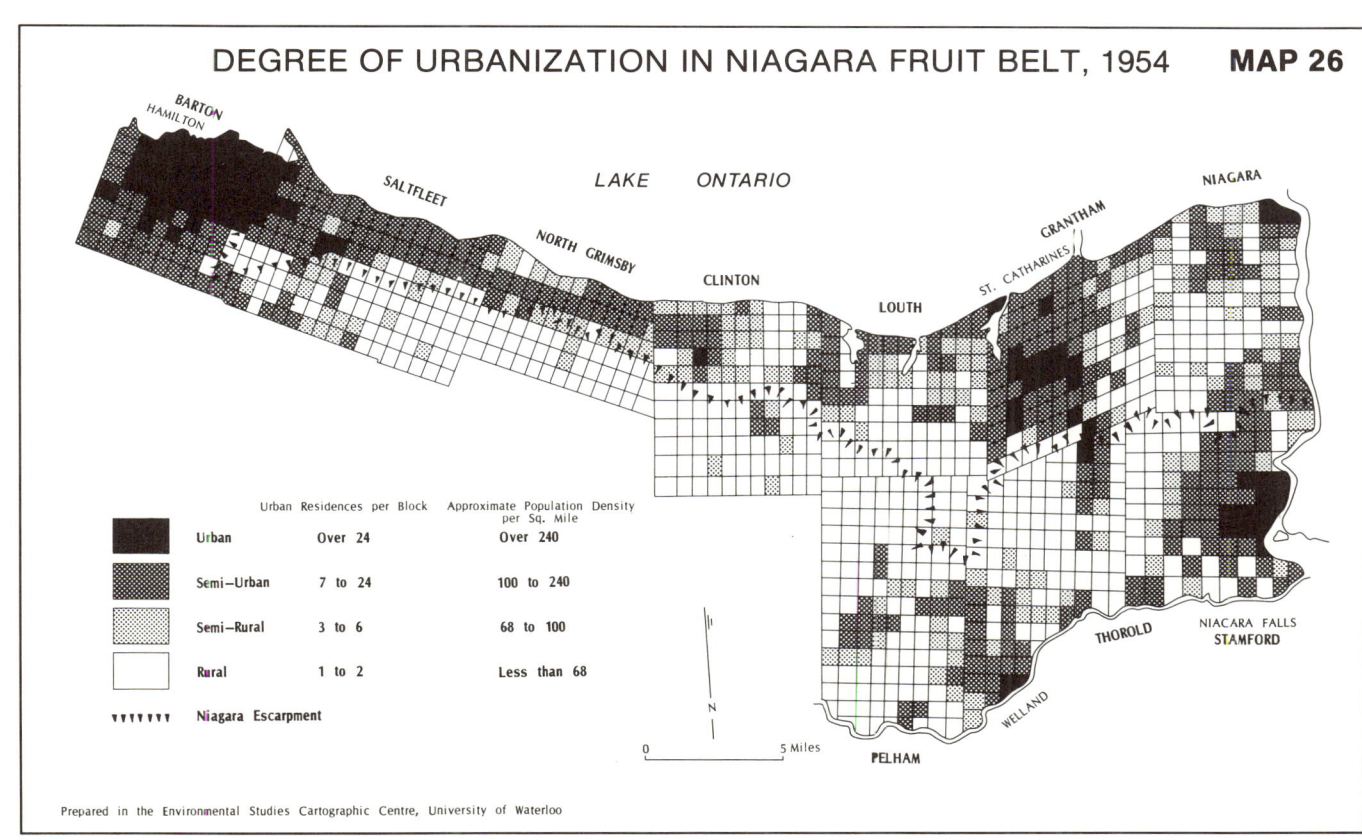

The small blocks on Maps 23, 25, 26, 27, and 28 are township concession blocks, usually bounded by roads.

land speculation. The significant problems involved the loss of irreplaceable tender fruit soils. Table 24 indicates the recent rapid decline in land devoted to peaches and to all tree fruits (see also Map 28). The only increases in area were made by vineyards with an increase of 1,926 ha over the 26-year period, 1951 to 1977. This is partly the result of the fact that grapes do not require tender fruit soils and they are planted extensively on heavier clay soils.

Unfortunately, it is quite clear that urbanization has more ramifications than just land losses. The following side effects are some of the additional problems faced within the Niagara fruit belt:

1) Large tracts of fruitland lie idle in the path of urban expansion, awaiting development.

2) The subdivision of farms into smaller units brings about a loss of fruit production, since more than one-half of all small farms are operated on a part-time basis. This also means loss of productivity per ha and often constitutes a source of disease, weed, and insect infestation for larger orchards.

3) As urban expansion approaches and uncertainty as to the future increases, there is a reluctance to plant new orchards which require five years to mature.

4) The influx of non-farm residents brings about a heavier demand on municipal services. Because new residential developments do not pay sufficient taxes to cover the costs of these additional or extended services, an increased tax burden is placed on agricultural land.

5) Speculation brings about soaring land prices, and on expensive land many agricultural uses can not pay their way.

6) Lack of confidence in the future of the industry prevents many growers from undertaking any long-term investment needed to ensure continued high production.

7) The grower is virtually caught in a cost/price squeeze, due to unstable prices, competition from foreign imports, and rising expenses. It was discovered by Reeds (1969) that approximately 60 per cent of all full-time orchardists had negative returns to family labour meaning a net income less than interest charges on farm capital (Krueger, 1977). The end result, in many cases, is that growers sell their land to developers at the high prices brought about by speculation.

In 1963, it was recognized that action was needed and should involve all levels of government. Only in that way could the problem be approached from a number of directions: increased protection from unfair imports, examination of marketing and tax policies, legislation involving the preservation of agricultural land, and strictly enforced policies on rural land severances. In an Ontario Department of Economics and Development report (1963) it was revealed that, "should the rate of conversion as it prevailed in recent years be accelerated, we can expect that within a few decades, the 'tender' fruit areas will have disappeared from the Niagara scene. It is not necessary, however, for the events expressed by this pessimistic view of the future of the Fruit Belt to run their course." (Jackson, 1977a).

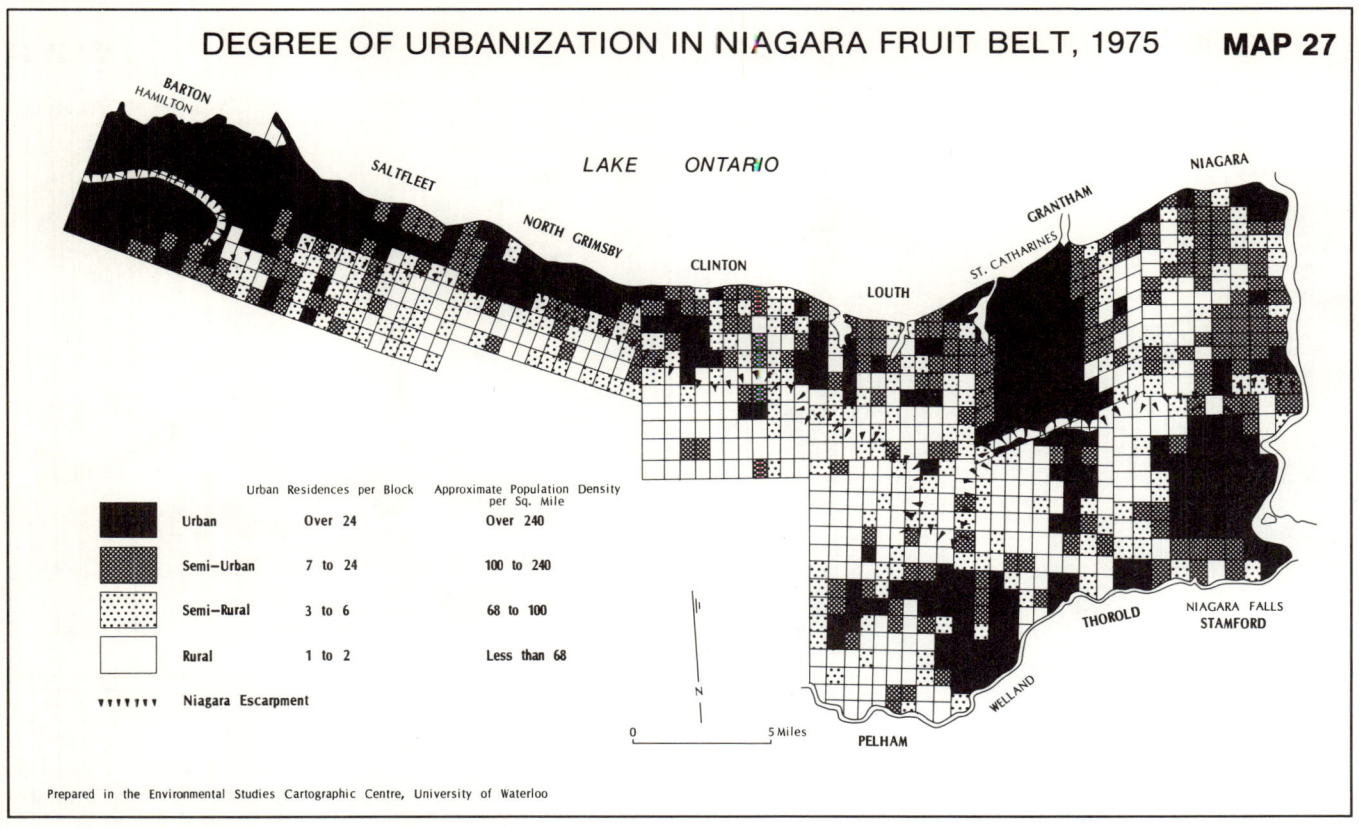

TABLE 24.

Selected Niagara fruit areas, 1951, 1971, and 1977

Fruit crop	Area 1951	Area 1971	Area 1977	Percentage change 1951 to 1971	Percentage change 1971 to 1977	Percentage change 1951 to 1977
	(ha)			(per cent)		
Peaches	5,707	3,764	2,772	-34	-26	-51
All tree fruits	13,185	10,079	6,502	-24	-35	-51
Grapes	8,257	8,858	10,183	+ 7	+15	+23
All fruit crops	22,232	19,442	16,906	-13	-13	-24

Sources: Dominion Bureau of Statistics, 1953. *Agriculture-Canada.* Vol. VI, Part II. Statistics Canada, 1973b. *Agriculture-Ontario.* Catalogue 96-707. Ontario Ministry of Agriculture and Food, 1977a. *Fruit and Vegetable Annual Summary.*

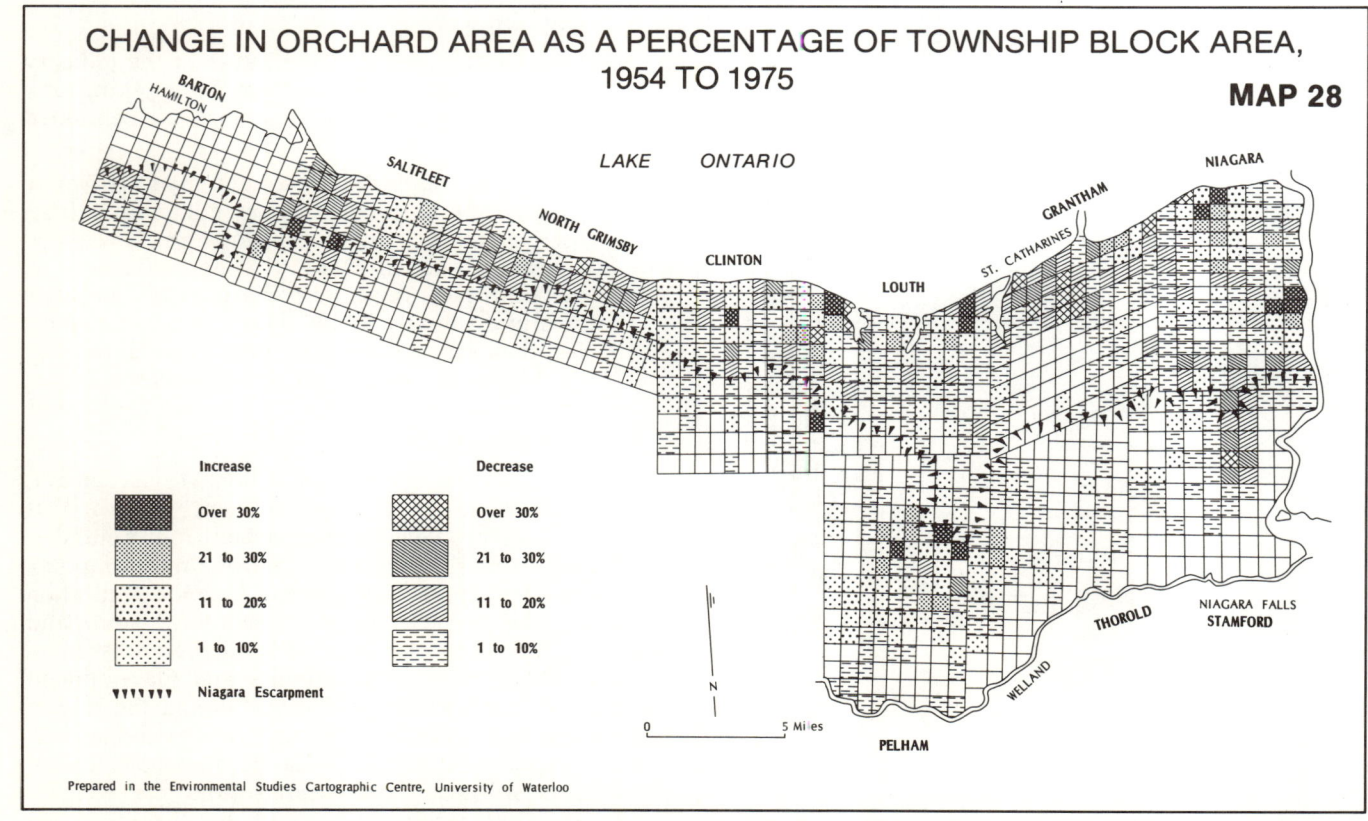

The problem, however, is a very complex one, beginning with the establishment of control over urban development, and followed by organized planning in order to establish a regional land use program that would continue over a long period of time. Thus, rather than just protecting existing orchards and processing industries, a goal of preserving the unique soils of the Niagara fruit belt as a renewable agricultural resource was established. The problems of the Niagara Region were then documented in the Mayo Commission report, established in 1965 to review the governmental structure of several counties within the Niagara Peninsula. Results of this commission suggested that any regional planning within the Niagara Peninsula required the development of a regional government. In 1969, the Ontario legislature passed Bill 174 which constituted the Regional Municipality of Niagara. The next step involved the preparation of a series of research and analysis reports by authorized consultants, to establish a set of alternate development concepts to be presented to the Regional Planning and Development Committee by 1973. After being reviewed and revised, the resulting document, Regional Niagara Policy Plan (Regional Municipality of Niagara, 1973), stated as its first goal "... to protect the agricultural industry and its land resources in recognition of its contribution not only to the economy of the Region and the nation, but as a worthwhile lifestyle and an important component in the overall character of the Region" (Jackson, 1977a).

To obtain this goal, it was declared that all urban development would be encouraged south of the Niagara Escarpment in order to preserve the tender fruit lands for agricultural purposes. The plan was approved and adopted in 1973 by the Planning and Development Committee and Regional Council. However, the plan was incomplete as far as defining the existing urban areas or the future extent of urban growth in relation to agricultural land. This problem required more research and preparation by all parties concerned, and was finally submitted to the provincial government in 1974.

Meanwhile, since the announcement by the Mayo Commission in 1965, urban encroachment on tender fruit soils continued unchecked. Decreases in farm occupancy, rising land values, and commitments regarding actual and planned municipal services increased the complexity of the situation at the expense of the very agricultural land to be preserved. Nevertheless, the revised Regional Plan submitted in 1974 had adopted a set of urban boundaries based on the premise that, by 1991, the Niagara Region would require sufficient urban land to accommodate an additional population over and above the expected increase. This meant that the three counties containing tender fruit soils would forfeit even more of their tender fruit soil to urban expansion. The new additions were obviously contrary to the original plan of maintaining the unique soils of the area in agricultural use. Under the circumstances, the Province rejected the plan in 1975 on the basis that about 2,104 ha of fruitland, representing approximately ten per cent of the total tender fruitlands in the province, were designated for urban purposes (Jackson, 1977a).

The Planning and Development Committee revised the rejected plan under the title of Review of the Regional Urban Areas Boundaries. New estimates were compiled based on a smaller population increase between 1976 and 1996. Planning staff proposed major reductions in the urban area boundaries in 1976. It was suggested that a reduction of 2,800 to 3,200 ha in the urban area boundaries would still permit revised projected growth over the life of the Plan. Despite the decrease in projected population and extension of the time period, a breakdown of the lands allocated for urban uses indicated that 1,036 ha of tender fruit soil, 832 ha of good grape-growing land, and 1,973 ha of good general agricultural land would be lost. In essence, more land had been set aside to accommodate a smaller population increase than originally estimated. In other words, land designated for urban uses was still greater than the projected needs. The ensuing debate involved the conservationists, civic groups, individual citizens, and professional experts on one side, and the municipalities and building and development groups on the other. The developers expressed fears over problems arising from urban lands already purchased, areas of land already serviced or capable of being serviced, restraints on owners and developers of certain lands, and the need to adopt a 'laissez-faire' concept of land development. The result was a stalemate between those who favoured preservation of a natural resource and those who favoured the proposed extension of urban boundaries. The latter argument was summarized in the Regional Municipality of Niagara's report (1976) stating that "... proposed changes to urban boundaries are seen as a threat to their dreams of selling their property for development purposes and for a good financial return" (Jackson, 1977a). In June 1976, a report by the Planning and Development Department was considered on the premise that the urban boundary revisions be accepted by the majority of local municipalities of the Region. The municipal emphasis on urban expansion was accepted by the majority of committee members who agreed to adopt the urban boundaries suggested in the previous report, with additional reductions to rural land for urban purposes and areas of future consideration to be given an urban classification. The same arguments to extend the urban boundaries were presented at the Regional Council meeting held in August of 1976. Regional Council rejected the planning staff proposals and reduced the urban area boundaries by approximately 200 to 240 ha. However, the submission of the revised plan was not accepted by the province in February of 1977. The urban boundaries proposed by the Regional Council were reduced by about 1,200 ha by an official Cabinet decision and included assurance of direct participation by the Provincial government concerning the maintenance of a future land base for agriculture. The Cabinet decision reduced the area allocated for urban development on land north of the Niagara Escarpment by 1,214 ha, based on short-term requirements of future urban land needs over 15 years. However, this still designated more land for urban development than the Niagara Regional studies indicated were required. Regional Council accepted the decision but the municipalities and developers referred the issue to the Ontario Municipal Board. In October 1978, both those supporting a reduction in the urban area boundaries (including the Preservation of Agricultural Lands Society (PALS), local farmers, and conservationists) as well as those advocating an enlargement of the urban area (including municipal officials and land developers) were in the process of contesting the Cabinet decision before the Ontario Municipal Board.

There are numerous social, political, and economic factors involved in the continuing decline of the Niagara fruit belt. The failure of the Regional Municipality to maintain the existence of one of its major resources is clear. Nevertheless, other problems included the complexity involving the agricultural industry, production and markets, farm income fluctuations, lack of farm labour, and the classification of farm enterprises as small-scale, part-time, resident or non-resident holdings. There is little sense of urgency on the part of many citizens, concerning the loss of a little farm land in a country the size of Canada. Over the years, there has been little commitment by any level of government to preserve the fruitlands. At the federal level, there is a lack of protection from cheaper imports. Citing the Ontario Federation of Agriculture:

"The market for canned peaches has been lost – not for lack of land, but because of tariff and trade rules. In 20 years, imports have risen from less than 20 per cent to more than 82 per cent of the Canadian market. Two-thirds of farm imports are commodities that can be produced in Canada. Add to this the fact that well over 70 per cent of Canada's pack of fruits and vegetables is being processed by U.S.-owned plants and it is apparent why the fruit processing industry is no longer 'Canadian'. Nor is it geared to the needs of Canadian farmers." (Clement and Janzen, 1978).

Protection of the fruit growing and fruit processing industries is seen by some as inadequate. The province has passed much responsibility for land use policies to local and regional governments and has no clear policy of farmland protection. The Green Paper on Planning for Agriculture: Food Land Guidelines (Ontario Ministry of Agriculture and Food, 1977b) is a discussion paper, and municipal and regional governments are not compelled to adopt the principles contained within it. Municipal governments are interested in development as a means of increasing assessment, and this often conflicts with preservation of agricultural lands.

It is clear that there is a reluctance on the part of many citizens to accept any controls over land values and land ownership which affect their right to consider land as a saleable commodity. The representation of Regional Councils generally overlooks the public interests and favours the local interests seeking expansion in order to increase urban and industrial growth. The lack of provincial or regional plans permits the indiscriminate expansion of service facilities, and allows some municipalities to maintain an urban expansion attitude. There are numerous causes associated with the relative failure of halting the loss of tender fruit soils, however, the last to be mentioned here is probably the most important.

The intervention and commitments established by the provincial government serve to indicate that many problems exist concerning the status of certain unique or scarce lands within Canada. Accompanying the decision of the provincial government to roll back the Niagara urban area boundaries, was the publication of a Green Paper on Planning for Agriculture: Food Land Guidelines. The purpose of this paper was to aid in the identification of agricultural resource lands, to locate high priority agricultural lands, and to designate agricultural lands as well as to develop agricultural policy provisions to supplement municipal plans. The only problem is whether or not these guidelines will be authorized by law and then put into action.

The conflict of agricultural land use versus urban or other land uses is by no means restricted to the Niagara fruit belt. This situation is occurring in many other areas of Canada, resulting in the loss of unique agricultural land at a disturbing rate. The production of food is a more economic and consistent undertaking when the conditions involve high-quality land and a favourable climate. Similar economic factors are true of urban development when undertaken on the same high-quality land. However, the additional costs accrued by construction on lower quality land is a one-time expense, while the additional costs of producing food on land of lower capability becomes an annual expense. Only five per cent of Canada's total land area is improved agricultural land. Only one-half of one per cent has class 1 or 2 capability for agriculture and only a very small fraction of that can produce specialty crops. In the case of unique or scarce agricultural lands producing specialized or specialty crops, these losses are of greater impact. In the future, to what extent will these losses diminish Canada's self-sufficiency and increase her dependence on foreign sources?

In relation to resource protection, there is a need for national and provincial land use policies. Should provincial governments exercise their power to place land in reserve for specific uses or to protect future options as British Columbia did under the B.C. Land Commission? Could such policies dictate that high-capability land for food production (classes 1, 2, and 3) be preserved with initial preferences given to agriculture where conflicts may arise? What steps could the federal government take to strengthen the viability of Canadian food production and processing industries? Should resources be seen only from the viewpoint of the current owners? This appears to be the dichotomy facing Canadians, whether to pursue short-term objectives which tend to benefit individuals, or long-term goals which serve society.

The Niagara fruit belt is a good example of a scarce land resource. It is an example known to any student of geography, land use planning, or resource management. Exhaustive research has documented the uniqueness and demise of this special Canadian agricultural resource during the last few decades. A regional government is in place and it has as part of its mandate the rational planning of land uses and specifically the protection of the best fruitlands. Yet this unique physical asset faces continued erosion from social, economic, and political influences. If this very special resource land in Niagara is not preserved, what prospects face other prime agricultural lands in Canada?

Conclusion

The purpose of this chapter has been to identify special resource lands for agriculture, at the national scale. Soil capability and climatic data provided an overview of areas most favourable to farming activities. Another approach highlighted economic factors including value of agricultural sales, level of capital investment, concentration of crop areas, and economic risk. Still another consideration is the location, nature, and rate of change. In addition to the marginal or frontier areas, the major arena for change appears to be the rural-urban fringe. A multitude of demographic, social, and economic trends means that pressures exerted by expanding urban centres are greatest on the prime farmland that adjoins most cities. Changes in farm characteristics such as number of farms, farm size, farm population, capital investment, and area of farmland are barometers of agriculture's future in Canada. The possible impact of climatic change was illustrated by a scenario of a cooler temperature regime. The areas subsequently removed from agriculture represent a different definition of critical land. Scarcity or uniqueness of land, and the pressures exerted on such areas, were the last elements used to help identify special land for agriculture.

Although it is difficult to present detailed information at the national scale, the maps and text of this chapter have illustrated areas that have special agricultural importance based on various parameters. However, it is necessary to go beyond this stage and ask questions. Is there any consistency among the critical areas identified by these various factors? Do the areas of superior climatic conditions coincide with areas of high capital investment? Do the locations with the highest soil capability also have the largest net losses of farmland? Are the areas under greatest pressures for urbanization the same areas that supply urban centres with high-value agricultural products?

Furthermore, it must be recognized that agriculture is only one of a number of land uses that compete for the same resource base. In the following chapters, special lands for recreation, wildlife, forestry, urban development, and energy will be examined. This will serve to underline the fact that the management of land for a variety of purposes is a complex challenge involving every Canadian.

Acknowledgements

The author would like to acknowledge several individuals and agencies whose assistance and advice were given generously and received with appreciation.

Dr. W. Baier
  Head, Agrometeorology Section
  Land Resource Research Institute
  Canada Department of Agriculture

K.M. Hunter
  Food Production and Marketing Branch
  Canada Department of Agriculture

Prof. Ralph R. Krueger
  Department of Geography
  Faculty of Environmental Studies
  University of Waterloo

G.A. McKay
  Director, Climatological Applications Branch
  Atmospheric Environment Service
  Environment Canada

D.W. Phillips
  Developmental Climatologist
  Climatological Services Division
  Atmospheric Environment Service
  Environment Canada

Drs. J.A. Shields, K. Valentine,
    and C. Tarnocai, Mr. J.L. Nowland,
  Soil Correlators
  Land Resource Research Institute
  Canada Department of Agriculture

R.A. Treidl
  Agricultural and Forest Meteorologist
  Applications and Impact Division
  Atmospheric Environment Service
  Environment Canada

G.D.V. Williams
  Agrometeorology Section
  Land Resource Research Institute
  Canada Department of Agriculture

Data Processing and User Services Section
  Census of Agriculture Division
  Statistics Canada

Bibliography

Agricultural Economics Research Council of Canada. 1973. Agriculture and the Energy Question. Ottawa.

Agricultural Institute of Canada. 1960. Agricultural Institute Review: A Look at Canadian Soils. Vol. 15, No. 2. March-April 1960. Ottawa.

_____. 1973. Agrologist. Vol. 2/4. July/August 1973. Agricultural Institute of Canada. Ottawa.

_____. 1975. Agrologist. Special Report: Land Use in Canada – Farm Land: Canada's Threatened Natural Resource. Vol. 4/4. Autumn 1975. Ottawa.

Alberta Land Use Forum. Alberta Land Use Forum Public Hearings into Land Use. Technical Reports 1-12 and Summary Reports 1-12A. Edmonton.

Alonso, William. 1964. Location and Land Use. Harvard University Press. Cambridge.

American Institute of Planners. 1975. Journal of the American Institute of Planners. Agriculture and Urbanization. Vol. 41, No. 6. November 1975. Washington, D.C.

Anderson, Allan. 1977. Remembering The Farm. Macmillan of Canada. Toronto.

Appleton, Peter L. 1973. The Canadian Agriculture and Food System. Agricultural Economics Research Council of Canada. Ottawa.

Archer, Paula. 1976. Urbanization on Agricultural Land: Trends and Implications for National Housing Policies. A Background Paper for CMHC Discussion and Use. Central Mortgage and Housing Corporation. Ottawa.

Arcus, Peter L. 1974. "New Directions in Land Use Control in British Columbia." Canadian Journal of Agricultural Economics. Vol. 22, No. 1. February 1974. Ottawa.

Baxter, David. 1974. "The British Columbia Land Commission Act: A Review." Presented at a conference on The Management of Land for Urban Development sponsored by the Canadian Council on Urban and Regional Research held April 5-6, 1974. Ottawa.

Beaubien, Charles, Rivers, Patricia, and Lash, Timothy. 1975. Population, Technology and Land Use. Study on Population and Technology. Science Council of Canada. Ottawa.

_____, and Tabacnik, Ruth. 1977. People and Agricultural Land. Perceptions 4, Study on Population, Technology and Resources. Science Council of Canada. Ottawa.

Beltzner, Klaus. ed. 1976. Living with Climatic Change. Proceedings of the Toronto Conference Workshop held Nov. 17-22, 1975. Science Council of Canada. Ottawa.

Bennett, David. 1976. "Income." Canadian Urban Trends. National Perspective Volume 1. Edited by D. Michael Ray. Ministry of State for Urban Affairs. Copp Clark Limited. Toronto.

Black, William A., and Stewart, Douglas. 1976. Land Pollution in the National Capital Region. Occasional Paper No. 5. Lands Directorate, Environment Canada. Ottawa.

Bogue, Donald J. 1956. Metropolitan Growth and the Conversion of Land to Non-agricultural Uses. Scripps Foundation Studies in Population Distribution, No. 11. Scripps Foundation. Oxford, Ohio.

Bostock, H.S. 1970. Physiographic Regions of Canada. Map 1254A. Geological Survey of Canada, Surveys and Mapping Branch, Department of Energy, Mines and Resources. Ottawa.

Boughner, C.C., and Thomas, Morley K. 1959. The Climate of Canada. Meteorological Branch, Air Services, Department of Transport. Queen's Printer. Ottawa.

Bourne, L.S., and Doucet, M.J. 1970. Dimensions of Metropolitan Physical Growth: Land Use Change: Metropolitan Toronto. Research Report No. 38. Centre for Urban and Community Studies, University of Toronto. Toronto.

British Columbia Environment and Land Use Committee Secretariat. 1976. Agriculture Land Capability in British Columbia. Prepared for the British Columbia Department of Agriculture and the Canada Department of Regional Economic Expansion. Victoria.

Broadfoot, Barry. 1973. Ten Lost Years 1929-1939: Memories of Canadians Who Survived the Depression. Doubleday Canada Ltd. Toronto.

Brown, D.M., McKay, G.A., and Chapman, L.J. 1968. The Climate of Southern Ontario. Climatological Studies No. 5. Department of Transport. Queen's Printer. Ottawa.

Bryant, G.W.R. 1965. "Land Speculation: Its Effects and Control." Plan Canada. Vol. V, No. 3. Canadian Institute of Planners. Ottawa.

_____. 1976. Farm-generated Determinants of Land Use Changes in the Rural-Urban Fringe in Canada, 1961-1975. Prepared for the Lands Directorate, Environment Canada. Ottawa.

Bryson, Reid A. 1975. "The Lessons of Climatic History." Environmental Conservation. Vol. 2, No. 3. Autumn 1975. Lausanne, Switzerland.

Bureau of Municipal Research. 1977. Food for the Cities: Disappearing Farmland and Provincial Land Policy. Proceedings of a conference held March 30-31, 1977 in Toronto. Toronto.

Canada Committee on Agrometeorology. 1977. Climatic Variability in Relation to Agricultural Productivity and Practices. Theme papers prepared for the 1977 CCA Meeting held January 11-12, 1977 in Winnipeg, Manitoba. Research Branch, Canada Department of Agriculture. Ottawa.

Canada Department of Agriculture. 1972. Soils of Canada. Map. Soil Research Institute, Research Branch. Ottawa.

_____. 1976. Agroclimatic Atlas. Agrometeorology Research and Service Section, Chemistry and Biology Research Institute, Research Branch. Ottawa.

Canada Department of Agriculture Committee on Land Use. 1975. Agricultural Land Use in Canada. Ottawa.

Canadian Federation of Agriculture. 1974. Working Paper on Land Use Policy. October-December 1974. Ottawa.

Canada Land Inventory. Soil Capability for Agriculture. Maps at 1:1,000,000. Atlantic Provinces (1974), Québec (1974), Manitoba (1974), Ontario (1975) Saskatchewan (1976), and Alberta (1976). Lands Directorate, Environment Canada. Ottawa.

Chapman, L.J., and Brown, D.M. 1966. The Climates of Canada for Agriculture. Canada Land Inventory Report No. 3. ARDA, Department of Forestry and Rural Development. Queen's Printer. Ottawa.

Chudleigh, E.L. 1972. Alternatives for the Ontario Tender Fruit Industry. Ontario Ministry of Agriculture and Food. Toronto.

Clawson, Marion. 1971. Suburban Land Conversion in the United States. Johns Hopkins Press. Baltimore.

Clayton, J.S., et al. 1977. Soils of Canada. Volume 1. Soil Report. Research Branch, Canada Department of Agriculture. Ottawa.

Clement, Wallace, and Janzen, Anna. 1978. "Just Peachy: The Demise of Tender Fruit Farmers." This Magazine. Vol. 12, No. 2. Toronto.

Collins, Richard C. 1976. "Agricultural Land Preservation in a Land Use Planning Perspective." Journal of Soil and Water Conservation. Vol. 31, No. 5. September-October 1976. Ankeny, Iowa.

Country Guide. 1975. "Farm Land: The Race to Protect this Threatened National Resource." January 1975. Public Press Ltd. Winnipeg.

Crerar, A.D. 1962. "The Loss of Farmland in the Growth of the Metropolitan Regions of Canada." Resources for Tomorrow. Supplementary Volume. Queen's Printer. Ottawa.

Cutler, Maurice. 1975. "Foreign Demand for Our Land and Resources." Canadian Geographical Journal. Vol. 90, No. 4. April 1975. Royal Canadian Geographical Society. Ottawa.

_____. 1975. "Are We Alienating Too Much Recreational Land and Too Much of Our Best Agricultural Land?" Canadian Geographical Journal. Vol. 90, No. 5. May 1975. Royal Canadian Geographical Society. Ottawa.

Department of Energy, Mines and Resources. 1974. The National Atlas of Canada. Surveys and Mapping Branch. The Macmillan Company of Canada Limited. Ottawa.

Department of Geography, University of Western Ontario. 1976. Ontario Geography. No. 10. London.

Department of Transport. 1967. Atlas of Climatic Maps, Series 1-10. Meteorological Branch. Ottawa.

Dideriksen, Raymond I., and Sampson, R. Neil. 1976. "Important Farmlands: A National View." Journal of Soil and Water Conservation. Vol. 31, No. 5. September-October 1976. Ankeny, Iowa.

Dominion Bureau of Statistics. 1947. Agriculture–Canada. Vol. VIII, Parts I and II. Ottawa.

_____. 1953. Agriculture–Canada. Vol. VI, Parts I and II. Ottawa.

_____. 1957. Agriculture–Canada. Vol. II, Bulletin 2-11. Ottawa.

_____. 1963a. Agriculture–Canada. Catalogue 96-530. Ottawa.

_____. 1963b. Population: Rural and Urban Distribution. Catalogue 92-536. Ottawa.

_____. 1968. Agriculture–Canada. Catalogue 96-601. Ottawa.

Dorling, M.J., and Barichello, R.R. 1975. "Trends in Rural and Urban Land Uses in Canada." Canadian Journal of Agricultural Economics–Agricultural Land Use in Canada. Proceedings of the 1975 Workshop of the Canadian Agricultural Economics Society held March 19-21, 1975 in Banff, Alberta.

Dubé, P.A. 1978. Unpublished material.

Environment Canada. 1972. Soil Capability Classification for Agriculture. Canada Land Inventory Report No. 2. Lands Directorate, Ottawa.

_____. 1973a. Canadian Normals Temperature 1941-1970. Volume 1. Atmospheric Environment Service. Downsview.

_____. 1973b. Canadian Normals Precipitation 1941-1970. Volume 2. Atmospheric Environment Service. Downsview.

_____. 1976c. Land Capability for Agriculture: A Preliminary Report. Canada Land Inventory Report. Lands Directorate. Ottawa.

Federal Task Force on Agriculture. 1969. Canadian Agriculture in the Seventies. Report of the Task Force prepared for the Canada Department of Agriculture. Queen's Printer. Ottawa.

Gardner, B. Delworth. 1977. "The Economics of Agricultural Land Preservation." American Journal of Agricultural Economics. Vol. 59, No. 5. Proceedings of the Annual Meeting of the Agricultural Economics Association held July 31-August 3, 1977 in San Diego.

Gardner, James S. 1976. "Natural Hazards of Climatic Origin in Canada." Canada's Natural Environment. Edited by G.R. McBoyle and E. Sommerville. Methuen. Toronto.

Geno, Barbara J., and Geno, Larry M. 1976. Food Production in the Canadian Environment. Perceptions 3, Study on Population, Technology and Resources. Science Council of Canada. Ottawa.

Gentilcore, Louis. ed. 1972. Studies in Canadian Geography: Ontario. University of Toronto Press. Toronto.

Gertler, L.O. ed. 1968a. Planning the Canadian Environment. Harvest House. Montréal.

_____. 1968b. The Niagara Escarpment Study: The Fruit Belt Report. Ontario Department of Treasury and Economics. Toronto.

_____, and Hind-Smith, Joan. 1962. "The Impact of Urban Growth on Agricultural Land: A Pilot Study." Resources for Tomorrow. Supplementary Volume. Queen's Printer. Ottawa.

Gibson, Edward M. 1976. The Urbanization of the Strait of Georgia Region. Geographical Paper No. 57. Lands Directorate, Environment Canada. Ottawa.

Gibson, James A. 1977. "On the Allocation of Prime Agricultural Land." Journal of Soil and Water Conservation. Vol. 32, No. 6. November-December 1977. Ankeny, Iowa.

Gierman, David M. 1976. Rural Land Use Changes in the Ottawa–Hull Urban Region. Occasional Paper No. 9. Lands Directorate, Environment Canada. Ottawa.

__________. 1977. Rural to Urban Land Conversion. Occasional Paper No. 16. Lands Directorate, Fisheries and Environment Canada. Ottawa.

Gillespie, Terry J. 1977. "Climatic Variability." Agrologist. Vol. 6/3, Summer 1977. Agricultural Institute of Canada. Ottawa.

Girt, John L., *et al.* 1972. Planning for Agriculture in Southern Ontario. ARDA Report No. 7. Prepared by The Centre for Resources Development, University of Guelph for the Ontario Ministry of Agriculture and Food. Guelph.

Godson, W.L. 1975. "Is the Earth Getting Hotter or Colder?" Canadian Geographical Journal. Vol. 90, No. 5. May 1975. Royal Canadian Geographical Society. Ottawa.

Goettel, A.W., *et al.* 1969. "Agriculture as a Recipient of Pollution." AIC Review. Vol. 24/3. Agricultural Institute of Canada. Ottawa.

Gray, Edward C. 1976. A Preliminary Paper on Canadian Agricultural Land-Use Policy. Reference Paper No. 3. Commissioned by the Food Prices Review Board. Ottawa.

Grenier, Fernand. ed. 1972. Études sur la géographie du Canada: Québec. University of Toronto Press. Toronto.

Gurba, Joseph B. 1977. "Livestock Pest Control." Agrologist. Vol. 6/3, Summer 1977. Agricultural Institute of Canada. Ottawa.

Halstead, R.L., and Dumanski, J. eds. 1977. Land Evaluation and Systematic Data Collection. Proceedings of Workshops held March 22-24, 1977 in Ottawa and February 10-11, 1977 in Saskatoon.

Hare, F. Kenneth, and Thomas, Morley K. 1974. Climate Canada. Wiley Publishers of Canada Limited. Toronto.

Hill, Frederick I. 1976*a*. "Ethnicity and the Cultural Mosaic." Canadian Urban Trends. National Perspective Volume 1. Edited by D. Michael Ray. Ministry of State for Urban Affairs. Copp Clark Limited. Toronto.

__________. 1976*b*. "Housing and Household Characteristics." Canadian Urban Trends. National Perspective Volume 1. Edited by D. Michael Ray. Ministry of State for Urban Affairs. Copp Clark Limited. Toronto.

__________. 1976*c*. "Age Structure and the Family Life Cycle." Canadian Urban Trends. National Perspective Volume 1. Edited by D. Michael Ray. Ministry of State for Urban Affairs. Copp Clark Limited. Toronto.

Hodson, H.V. 1972. The Diseconomics of Growth. Ballantine Books. New York.

Hoffman, Douglas W. 1970. Land Use Capability for Agriculture. Canada Land Inventory, ARDA Branch, Department of Regional Economic Expansion and Ontario Department of Agriculture and Food. Toronto.

__________. 1971. The Assessment of Soil Productivity for Agriculture. ARDA Report No. 4. Toronto.

Holesgrove, Rod. 1976*a*. Critical Environmental Areas: Protection of Prime Agricultural Land from Urban Development. Prepared for the Organization for Economic Co-operation and Development. Paris.

__________. 1976*b*. Definition of Critical Environmental Areas. Prepared for the Organization for Economic Co-operation and Development. Paris.

Holland, Stuart S. 1964. Landforms of British Columbia: A Physiographic Outline. Bulletin No. 48. British Columbia Department of Mines and Petroleum Resources. Victoria.

Howard, John F. 1972. The Impact of Urbanization on the Prime Agricultural Lands of Southern Ontario. M.A. Paper, Department of Geography, University of Waterloo. Waterloo.

Hoyt, P.B., Rice, W.A., and Hennig, A.M.F. 1978. "Utilization of Northern Canadian Soils for Agriculture." Symposium Session Papers. Volume 3. Proceedings of the 11th International Congress of Soil Science held June 19-27, 1978 in Edmonton, Alberta.

International Federation of Institutes for Advanced Study. 1974. The Impact on Man of Climatic Change. Report of the IFIAS Workshop held May 6-10, 1974 at The Meteorological Institute. University of Bonn. Germany.

Irving, Robert M. ed. 1978. Readings in Canadian Geography. Third Edition. Holt, Rinehart and Winston of Canada, Limited. Toronto.

Jackson, John N. 1977*a*. "The Niagara Fruit Belt: A Resource in Jeopardy." Contact. Vol. 9, No. 2. Journal of Urban and Environmental Affairs. Faculty of Environmental Studies, University of Waterloo. Waterloo.

__________. 1977*b*. Land Use Planning in the Niagara Region: Values in Conflict. Niagara Region Study Review Commission. Thorold.

Krueger, Ralph R. 1959. Changing Land-Use Patterns in the Niagara Fruit Belt. Transactions of the Royal Canadian Institute. Vol. XXXII, Part 2, No. 67.

__________. 1972. "The Geography of the Orchard Industry of Canada." Readings in Canadian Geography. Revised Edition. Edited by Robert M. Irving. Holt, Rinehart and Winston of Canada, Limited. Toronto.

__________. 1976. "Monitoring the Land-Use Controversy in the Niagara Fruit Belt: 1931-1977." G.I.R.M.S. Geographical Inter-University Resource Management Seminars. Vol. 7. Department of Geography, Wilfred Laurier University. Waterloo.

__________. 1977. "The Preservation of Agricultural Land in Canada" and "The Destruction of a Unique Renewable Resource: The Case of the Niagara Fruit Belt." Managing Canada's Renewable Resources. Edited by Ralph R. Krueger and B. Mitchell. Methuen. Toronto.

__________. 1978. "Urbanization of the Niagara Fruit Belt." The Canadian Geographer. Vol. XXII, No. 2. Canadian Association of Geographers. Montréal.

__________. *et al.* eds. 1970. Regional and Resource Planning in Canada. Revised Edition. Holt, Rinehart and Winston of Canada, Limited. Toronto.

__________. and Bryfogle, R. Charles. eds. 1971. Urban Problems: A Canadian Reader. Holt, Rinehart and Winston of Canada, Limited. Toronto.

Land Use Task Force. 1975. H.W. Thiessen, Chairman. Land Use Issues Facing Canadians. A discussion paper for The Canadian Council of Resource and Environment Ministers. Edmonton.

Lea, N.D. & Associates Ltd. 1975. Land Use Consumption by Urban Passenger Transportation. Report prepared for the Ministry of State for Urban Affairs. Ottawa. (unpublished).

Leahey, A. 1946. "The Agricultural Soil Resources of Canada." Agricultural Institute Review. Vol. I. Agricultural Institute of Canada. Ottawa.

Li, Shiu-Yeu. 1976. "Labour Force Statistics and a Functional Classification of Canadian Cities." Canadian Urban Trends. National Perspective Volume 1. Edited by D. Michael Ray. Ministry of State for Urban Affairs. Copp Clark Limited. Toronto.

MacNeill, J.W. 1971. Environmental Management. Constitutional Study prepared for the Government of Canada. Queen's Printer. Ottawa.

Macpherson, Alan G. ed. 1972. Studies in Canadian Geography: The Atlantic Provinces. University of Toronto Press. Toronto.

Mandelker, Daniel R. 1975. "Critical Area Controls: A New Dimension in American Land Development Regulation." Journal of the American Institute of Planners. Vol. 41, No. 1. January 1975. Washington, D.C.

Manitoba Environmental Council. 1977. William Bell, Chairman. Rural Land Use Conflicts: Some Solutions. Winnipeg.

Manning, Edward W., and McCuaig, James D. 1977. Agricultural Land and Urban Centres. Canada Land Inventory Report No. 11. Lands Directorate, Environment Canada. Ottawa.

Martin, Larry R.G. 1974. Problems and Policies Associated with High Land Costs on the Urban Fringe. Draft paper prepared for a conference on The Management of Land for Urban Development sponsored by the Canadian Council on Urban and Regional Research. Ottawa.

__________. 1975*a*. A Comparative Urban Fringe Study Methodology. Occasional Paper No. 6. Lands Directorate, Environment Canada. Ottawa.

__________. 1975*b*. Land Use Dynamics on the Toronto Urban Fringe. Map Folio No. 3. Lands Directorate, Environment Canada. Ottawa.

Mayo, H.B. 1966. Niagara Region Local Government Review: Report of the Commission. Ontario Department of Municipal Affairs. Toronto.

McKay, G.A. 1976. "Climatic Resources and Economic Activity in Canada." Canada's Natural Environment. Edited by G.R. McBoyle and E. Sommerville. Methuen. Toronto.

__________, and Allsopp, T. 1977. "Climate and Climatic Variability." Climatic Variability in Relation to Agricultural Productivity and Practices. Theme papers prepared for the 1977 CCA Meetings held January 11-12, 1977 in Winnipeg, Manitoba. Canada Committee on Agrometeorology and Research Branch, Canada Department of Agriculture. Ottawa.

McKeen, Colin D., Madsen, Harold F., and Burrage, Robert H. 1977. "Pest Management." Agrologist. Vol. 6/3, Summer 1977. Agricultural Institute of Canada. Ottawa.

Mercier, R.G., and Chapman, L.J. 1955. Peach Climate in Ontario. Report of the Horticultural Experiment Station and Products Library, Vineland, Ontario. Department of Agriculture. Toronto.

Minister of State for Urban Affairs. 1976. Human Settlement in Canada. Ottawa.

National Academy of Sciences and National Academy of Engineering. 1972. Urban Growth and Land Development: The Land Conversion Process. Report of the Land Use Subcommittee of the Advisory Committee to the Department of Housing and Urban Development. Washington, D.C.

Neimanis, V.P. 1979. Canada's Cities and Their Surrounding Land Resource. Canada Land Inventory Report No. 15. Lands Directorate, Environment Canada. Ottawa.

Nelson, J.B., and Nicolson, D.N. 1960. Ontario's Shrinking Farm Lands. Farm Economics Branch, Ontario Department of Agriculture. Toronto.

Nelson, J.G., Scace, R.C., and Kouri, R. eds. 1974. Canadian Public Land Use in Perspective. Proceedings of a Symposium sponsored by the Social Science Research Council of Canada held October 25-27, 1973 in Ottawa.

Nowland, John L. 1975*a*. The Agricultural Productivity of Soils of the Atlantic Provinces. Monograph No. 12. Research Branch, Canada Department of Agriculture. Ottawa.

__________. 1975*b*. The Agricultural Productivity of Soils of Ontario and Québec. Monograph No. 13. Research Branch, Canada Department of Agriculture. Ottawa.

Ontario Agricultural College, University of Guelph. 1972. Notes on Agriculture – Rural Development: People, Resources, and Communities in a Changing Society. Vol. VIII, No. 2. June 1972. Guelph.

__________. 1974*a*. Notes on Agriculture – Physical Resources in Rural Development. Vol. X, No. 2. April 1974. Guelph.

__________. 1974*b*. Agriculture in the Whirlpool of Change. Centennial Symposium held October 17-18, 1974. Bryant Press Limited. Toronto.

__________. 1975. Ontario Soils: Physical, Chemical and Biological Properties and Soil Management Practices. Publication 492. Prepared for the Ontario Ministry of Agriculture and Food. Guelph.

Ontario Agricultural College and Office of Continuing Education, University of Guelph. 1974. Proceedings: Priorities in Rural Development. Proceedings of a Workshop held April 15-17, 1974 at the University of Guelph. Guelph.

Ontario Department of Economics and Development. 1963. Economic Survey of the Niagara Region. Special Research and Surveys Branch. Toronto.

Ontario Institute of Agrologists. 1975. Foodland – Preservation or Starvation. July 23, 1975. Toronto.

Ontario Ministry of Agriculture and Food. 1977*a*. Fruit and Vegetable Annual Summary. Toronto.

__________. 1977*b*. Green Paper on Planning for Agriculture: Food Land Guidelines. Toronto.

Organization for Economic Co-operation and Development. 1975. Working Party No. 1 of the Committee for Agriculture (Agricultural Policies) Land Use: General Report. AGR/WPI (75)4. Paris.

Pearson, G.G. 1975. "Preservation of Agricultural Land: Rationale and Legislation – The B.C. Experience." Canadian Journal of Agricultural Economics – Agricultural Land Use in Canada. Proceedings of the 1975 Workshop of the Canadian Agricultural Economics Society held March 19-21, 1975 in Banff, Alberta.

Pearson, Norman. 1973*a*. Agriculture and Land Planning. Paper given at Plant Research Institute, Research Branch, Canada Department of Agriculture. January 12, 1973. Ottawa.

__________. 1973*b*. "Preserving Good Farmland." Agrologist. Vol. 2/4, July/August 1973. Agricultural Institute of Canada. Ottawa.

Prince Edward Island. 1973. Report of the Royal Commission on Land Ownership and Land Use. Royal Commission on Land Ownership and Land Use. Queen's Printer. Charlottetown.

Punter, J.V. 1974. The Impact of Exurban Development on Land and Landscape in the Toronto Centred Region (1954-1971). A report prepared for Central Mortgage and Housing Corporation. Ottawa.

Putnam, Donald F., and Kerr, Donald P. 1964. A Regional Geography of Canada. J.M. Dent & Sons (Canada) Limited. Toronto.

__________, and Putnam, Robert G. 1970. Canada: A Regional Analysis. J.M. Dent & Sons (Canada) Limited. Toronto.

Raup, Philip M. 1976. "What is Prime Land?" Journal of Soil and Water Conservation. Vol. 31, No. 5. September-October 1976. Ankeny, Iowa.

Rawson, Mary. 1976. Ill Fares the Land: Land-Use Management at the Urban/Rural/Resource Edges: The British Columbia Land Commission. Urban Prospects. Ministry of State for Urban Affairs and The Macmillan Company of Canada Limited. Ottawa.

Ray, D. Michael., *et al.* eds. 1976. Canadian Urban Trends. National Perspective Volume 1. Ministry of State for Urban Affairs. Copp Clark Publishing. Toronto.

Reeds, L. 1969. Niagara Region Agricultural Research Report. Ontario Department of Treasury and Economics. Toronto.

Regional Municipality of Niagara. 1973. Regional Niagara Policy Plan. St. Catharines.

_____. 1976. Summary of Information on the Review of Urban Area Boundaries. St. Catharines.

Rennie, Donald. 1978. "Prairie land seen in danger as soil quality falls swiftly." The Globe and Mail. July 11, 1978. Toronto.

Robinson, J. Lewis. ed. 1972. Studies in Canadian Geography: British Columbia. University of Toronto Press. Toronto.

Rodd, R. Stephen. 1972. "Urban Field of Influence on Agricultural Land-Use Patterns." Notes on Agriculture. Vol. VIII, No. 2. July 1972. Ontario Agricultural College, University of Guelph. Guelph.

_____, and Van Vuuren, Willem. 1975. "A New Methodology in Countryside Planning." Canadian Journal of Agricultural Economics–Agricultural Land Use in Canada. Proceedings of the 1975 Workshop of the Canadian Agricultural Economics Society held March 19-21, 1975 in Banff, Alberta.

Rowe, J.S. 1972. Forest Regions of Canada. Publication No. 1300. Canadian Forestry Service, Department of the Environment. Ottawa.

Russwurm, Lorne H. 1967. "Expanding Urbanization and Selected Agricultural Elements: Case Study, Southwestern Ontario Area, 1941-1961." Land Economics. Vol. 43. February 1967. Madison.

_____. 1974. The Urban Fringe in Canada: Problems, Research Needs, Policy Implications. Discussion Paper B. 74.4. Ministry of State for Urban Affairs. Ottawa.

Saidak, Walter J. 1977. "Weed Science Research." Agrologist. Vol. 6/3, Summer 1977. Agricultural Institute of Canada. Ottawa.

Sargent, Frederic O. 1976. Rural Environmental Planning. University of Vermont. Vervana, Vermont.

Schmid, A. Allan. 1968. Converting Land from Rural to Urban Uses. Resources for the Future, Inc. Johns Hopkins Press. Baltimore.

Schmude, Keith O. 1977. "A Perspective on Prime Farmland." Journal of Soil and Water Conservation. Vol. 32, No. 5. September-October 1977. Ankeny, Iowa.

Science Council of Canada. 1976. Population, Technology and Resources. Report No. 25. Maracle Press. Oshawa.

Shields, Jack A., and Ferguson, Wilfred Samuel. 1975. "Land Resources, Production Possibilities and Limitations for Crop Production in the Prairie Provinces." Reprinted from Symposium on Oilseed and Pulse Crops in Western Canada. Western Cooperative Fertilizer Ltd. Calgary.

_____, and Nowland, John L. 1975. "Additional Land for Crop Production: Canada." Reprinted from the Proceedings of the 30th Annual Meeting of the Soil Conservation Society of America, (Land Use: Food and Living) held August 10-13, 1975 in San Antonio, Texas.

Simmons, James, and Simmons, Robert. 1969. Urban Canada. The Copp Clark Publishing Company. Toronto.

Simpson-Lewis, Wendy L. 1974. The Windsor-Québec Axis. Map. Ministry of State for Urban Affairs and Lands Directorate, Environment Canada. Ottawa.

Skoda, Louis. 1975. Georgia Strait Urban Region. Map. The Ministry of State for Urban Affairs and Lands Directorate, Environment Canada. Ottawa.

Sly, W.K., and Coligado, M.C. 1974. "Agroclimatic Maps for Canada – Derived Data: Moisture and Critical Temperatures Near Freezing." Technical Bulletin 81. Agrometeorology Research and Service, Chemistry and Biology Research Institute, Agriculture Canada. Ottawa.

Smith, P.J. ed. 1972. Studies in Canadian Geography: The Prairie Provinces. University of Toronto Press. Toronto.

Smithsonian Institute, Center for Natural Areas and Office of International and Environmental Programs. 1974. Planning Considerations for Statewide Inventories of Critical Environmental Areas: A Reference Guide. Report Three. Prepared for the U.S. Army Corps of Engineers. Washington, D.C.

Soil Conservation Society of America. 1974. Land Use: Persuasion or Regulation?. Proceedings of the 29th Annual Meeting held August 11-14, 1974 in Syracuse.

Soil Conservation Society of America, Ontario Chapter. 1976. Crisis in the Countryside. Proceedings of the Summer and Fall Meetings, November 1976. Thornhill.

Special Committee on Farm Income in Ontario. 1969. Everett Biggs, Chairman. The Challenge of Abundance. Report of the Special Committee. Ontario Department of Agriculture and Food. Toronto.

Spurr, Peter. 1976. Land and Urban Development: A Preliminary Study. James Lorimer & Company. Toronto.

Statistics Canada. 1973a. Agriculture–Canada. Catalogue 96-701. Ottawa.

_____. 1973b. Agriculture–Ontario. Catalogue 96-707. Ottawa.

_____. 1973c. Selected Data for Census-farms classified by Economic Class: Atlantic Provinces. Catalogue 96-729 AA-12. Ottawa.

_____. 1973d. Selected Data for Census-farms classified by Economic Class: Québec. Catalogue 96-730 AA-13. Ottawa.

_____. 1973e. Selected Data for Census-farms classified by Economic Class: Ontario. Catalogue 96-731 AA-14. Ottawa.

_____. 1973f. Selected Data for Census-farms classified by Economic Class: Western Provinces. Catalogue 96-732 AA-15. Ottawa.

_____. 1977a. National Income and Expenditure Accounts 1962-1976. Catalogue 13-201. Ottawa.

_____. 1977b. Family Incomes. Catalogue 13-208. Ottawa.

_____. 1977c. The Labour Force. Catalogue 71-001. Ottawa.

_____. 1977d. Crops on Census-farms. Catalogue 96-851. Ottawa.

_____. 1977e. Census-farms by Size, Area and Use of Land. Catalogue 96-854. Ottawa.

_____. 1977f. Number and Area of Census-farms by Census Divisions. Catalogue 96-857. Ottawa.

_____. 1977g. Selected Data for Census-farms classified by Economic Class: Atlantic Provinces. Catalogue 96-859 SA-9. Ottawa.

_____. 1977h. Selected Data for Census-farms classified by Economic Class: Québec. Catalogue 96-860 SA-10. Ottawa.

_____. 1977i. Selected Data for Census-farms classified by Economic Class: Ontario. Catalogue 96-861 SA-11. Ottawa.

_____. 1977j. Selected Data for Census-farms classified by Economic Class: Western Provinces. Catalogue 96-862 SA-12. Ottawa.

_____. 1978. Agriculture–Canada. Catalogue 96-800. Ottawa.

Stone, Leroy O. 1967. Urban Development in Canada: An Introduction to the Demographic Aspects. Dominion Bureau of Statistics. Queen's Printer. Ottawa.

Swart, Mel. 1976. "New boundaries fail to preserve prime fruitland." The Globe and Mail. August 23, 1976. Toronto.

_____. 1978. "The battle for Niagara fruitland." The Globe and Mail. October 12, 1978. Toronto.

Tarnocai, C. 1978. "Distribution of Soils in Northern Canada and Parameters Affecting Their Utilization." Symposium Session Papers. Volume 3. Proceedings of the 11th International Congress of Soil Science held June 19-27, 1978 in Edmonton, Alberta.

Task Force on the Orientation of Canadian Agriculture. 1977. Orientation of Canadian Agriculture: A Task Force Report. Vol. I Part A "A Review of the Canadian Agriculture and Food Complex – the System," Vol. I Part B "A Review of the Canadian Agriculture and Food Complex – the Commodities," Vol. II "Domestic Policies and External Factors which have Influenced the Development of Canadian Agriculture," and Vol. III "Economic and Social Factors Related to Agriculture and Food." Agriculture Canada. Ottawa.

Taylor, Griffith. 1947. Canada: A Study of Cool Continental Environments and Their Effect on British and French Settlement. Methuen & Co. Ltd. London.

The Institute of Ecology (TIE) and the Charles F. Kettering Foundation. 1976. Impact of Climatic Fluctuation on Major North American Food Crops. Washington, D.C. and Dayton, Ohio.

Thomas, Morley K. 1953. Climatological Atlas of Canada. A joint publication of the Division of Building Research, National Research Council and the Meteorological Division, Department of Transport. Ottawa.

_____. 1961. A Bibliography of Canadian Climate 1763-1957. Division of Building Research, National Research Council and the Meteorological Branch, Department of Transport. Queen's Printer. Ottawa.

_____. 1973. A Bibliography of Canadian Climate 1958-1971. Division of Building Research, National Research Council and the Meteorological Branch, Department of Transport. Queen's Printer. Ottawa.

_____. 1974. "Canada's Climates Are Changing More Rapidly." Canadian Geographical Journal. Vol. 88, No. 5. May 1974. Royal Canadian Geographical Society. Ottawa.

Today's Generation. 1973. "We have to get pests before they get us." Vol. XXXIII, No. 7. March 1973. Canadian High News Ltd. Toronto.

Treidl, R.A. 1977. "Climatic Fluctuations and Their Impact on Canadian Agriculture and Forestry." Climatic Variability in Relation to Agricultural Productivity and Practices. Theme papers prepared for the 1977 CCA Meetings held January 11-12, 1977 in Winnipeg, Manitoba. Canada Committee on Agrometeorology and the Research Branch, Canada Department of Agriculture.

Tremblay, Marc-Adélard, and Anderson, Walton J. eds. 1966. Rural Canada In Transition: A Multidimensional Study of the Impact of Technology and Urbanization on Traditional Society. Agricultural Economics Research Council of Canada. Ottawa.

Troughton, Michael J. 1976. Landholding in a Rural-Urban Fringe Environment: The Case of London, Ontario. Occasional Paper No. 11. Lands Directorate, Environment Canada. Ottawa.

_____. Nelson, J. Gordon, and Brown Si. eds. 1975. The Countryside in Ontario. Proceedings of the Countryside in Ontario Conference held April 19-20, 1974 at the University of Western Ontario. London.

United States Department of Agriculture. 1975. Perspectives on Prime Lands. Background papers for a Seminar on the Retention of Prime Lands held July 16-17, 1975 in Washington, D.C.

Urquhart, M.C., and Buckley, K.A.H. eds. 1965. Historical Statistics of Canada. Macmillan Company of Canada Limited. Toronto.

Valentine, Keith W.G., et al. eds. 1978. The Soil Landscapes of British Columbia. Resources Analysis Branch, Ministry of the Environment. Victoria.

Warkentin, John. ed. 1968. Canada – A Geographical Interpretation. Prepared under the auspices of the Canadian Association of Geographers. Methuen. Toronto.

Warner, Charles Dudley. 1897. The Hartford Courant. Editorial. August 24, 1897.

Wibberley, G.P. 1959. Agriculture and Urban Growth: A Study of the Competition for Urban Land. Michael Joseph Ltd. London.

Williams, G. Daniel V. 1973. "Urban Expansion and the Canadian Agroclimatic Resource Problem." Greenhouse-Garden-Grass. Vol. 12, No. 1. Spring 1973.

_____. 1975. An Agroclimatic Resource Index for Canada and Its Use in Describing Agricultural Land Losses. Agriculture Canada report prepared for the Science Council of Canada. Ottawa. (unpublished).

_____. 1977. Personal communication.

_____. 1978. Personal communication.

_____. and Oakes, Wayne T. 1978. "Climatic Resources for Maturing Barley and Wheat in Canada." Essays on Meteorology and Climatology in Honour of Richmond W. Longley. Department of Geography, University of Alberta. Edmonton.

_____. Pocock, Nancy J., and Russwurm, Lorne H. 1978. "The Spatial Association of Agroclimatic Resources and Urban Population in Canada." Readings in Canadian Geography. Third Edition. Edited by Robert M. Irving. Holt, Rinehart and Winston of Canada, Limited. Toronto.

Wonders, William C. ed. 1972. Studies in Canadian Geography: The North. University of Toronto Press. Toronto.

World Meteorological Organization. 1976a. Technical Report by the WMO Executive Committee Panel of Experts on Climatic Change. June, 1976. Geneva.

_____. 1976b. "WMO Statement on Climatic Change." WMO Bulletin. Vol. XXV, No. 3. July 1976. Geneva.

Yeates, Maurice. 1975. Main Street: Windsor to Quebec City. Macmillan Company of Canada Limited in association with the Ministry of State for Urban Affairs and Information Canada. Toronto and Ottawa.

Appendix I

Physiography of Canada

The Atlantic Provinces

The Atlantic Region is dominated by the complex landscape of the Appalachian Mountains which, unlike Canada's Cordillera, are old and worn. The highlands, uplands, mountains, and plateaux of New Brunswick, Nova Scotia, and Newfoundland, are composed of quartzites, granites, gneisses, and other hard, crystalline rocks. Rough terrain, scarred by glacial features, and poor soils have done little to foster much settlement. It is the broad, lowland areas with their underlying sedimentary rocks of sandstones, shales, and limestone which accommodate the greater proportion of the population and most of the agricultural activities.

Given the physiographic, climatic, and vegetative characteristics of the Atlantic Provinces, it is not surprising that the dominant soils of the area are Podzols, although large areas of Brunisols, Luvisols, Gleysols, and Organic soils also occur. The high precipitation and low evaporation have deeply weathered the soils, and a leached layer is typical of most of the soils. Those soils that evolved from glacial scouring of the highlands and uplands, and deposition of thin glacial drift, are shallow, leached, stony, and relatively infertile. With a few exceptions, it is the lowland soils which have developed from thicker till blankets, and fluvial or marine deposits which have significant potential for agriculture. These support the fruit and vegetable crops, dairy and beef production, and cash crop businesses, so essential to the Atlantic Region.

Natural forest cover consists of varying proportions of coniferous and deciduous species, except where bare rock precludes plant growth. The Great Lakes–St. Lawrence forest of northern New Brunswick is a mixture of boreal forest species (white and red spruce, balsam fir, jack pine, and birch) and other forest types (hemlock, birch, maple, white and red pine). True boreal cover is found throughout much of Newfoundland and the extreme north of New Brunswick. In better-drained locations, balsam fir, white spruce, aspen, and birch dominate but black spruce and tamarack are common in poorly drained areas. In much of Labrador and on the northern tip of the Island, where wind exposure, thin soils, and unfavourable climate prevail, the forest–tundra transition of stunted boreal species such as tamarack, black spruce, and white spruce alternates with tundra barrens. In southern and central Newfoundland, are the sparsely forested, heath-and-moss barrens. Here, stunted, open patches of black spruce and balsam fir are interspersed with moss-and-heath barrens, lakes, and rock outcrops. It is the Acadian forest, however, that dominates a significant area of the Atlantic Provinces including southern New Brunswick, Prince Edward Island, and Nova Scotia. Related to the Great Lakes–St. Lawrence forest it is characterized by yellow birch, maple, balsam fir, and red spruce. Once again, black spruce bogs occupy some of the rocky, damp, rugged areas of the uplands.

Newfoundland. The extensive plateaux of the Island of Newfoundland form the northeast corner of the Appalachian Region. Much of the Island's land surface is exposed bedrock or rock outcrops with a very thin, stony soil developed from glacial till which has little or no agricultural value. The rugged Newfoundland Highlands of the west coast rise steeply from a narrow coastal plain to over 800 m and then slope down toward the southeast. The surface of this tilted peneplain is undulating, and is either dotted by boreal forest species or is generally barren. The marked southwest–northeast orientation of the highlands, is repeated in many other physiographic features including moraines, rivers, bays, and peninsulas.

The Atlantic Uplands reflect differential erosion of the hard and soft rocks of a peneplain 180 to 300 m above sea level. The undulating terrain contains both bedrock protrusions and depressions in which peat bogs have developed, the latter especially in the south-central region. Where wetness, slope, and stoniness are not severe, some morainic and glaciofluvial gravels along valleys can be of use for agriculture. Some of the peat deposits throughout the Island are potential areas for hay and vegetable crops, once proper water control is achieved. However, most of the land remains characterized by the coarse, shallow, discontinuous, bouldery, leached, and relatively infertile glacial debris with its boreal cover, and as such holds little promise for agriculture.

Only isolated areas, such as the Newfoundland Central Lowland, the Codroy Valley of the west coast, the small river valleys, and portions of the Avalon Peninsula (where the St. John's market is a stimulus) hold moderate potential for agriculture. Some of these locations, such as the coastal fringe of St. George's Bay have produced good vegetable and hay crops once the land has been cleared, and the blueberries produced on certain barrens, especially the Avalon Peninsula, are a valuable crop. Other small valleys and coves such as the Exploits, Gander, and Codroy valleys, and the Deer Lake–lower Humber River lowland in western Newfoundland contain thicker soils developed from glaciofluvial material and alluvium. Where there is a more level landscape, these soils, which are coarse but less stony and more accessible, provide reasonable opportunity for the cultivation of limited crops.

The vast land area of Labrador is dominated by a series of mountains, highlands, and plateaux. Virtually all of northern Labrador is rough rockland. Although the southern portion does possess some areas of soil, these are characterized by excessive stoniness and rock outcrops. These physical features together with extreme climatic conditions render Labrador largely unsuitable for agriculture.

Nova Scotia. Although Nova Scotia is noted for its picturesque coastline, rocky offshore islands, and rolling lowlands, the province is dominated by the often rugged Nova Scotia Highlands, part of the Appalachian system. The thin, bouldery till, rocky outcrops, and relatively wet, cold climate render this area inhospitable to agriculture and comparable to parts of the barren plateaux of Newfoundland.

The plateaux of the Cobequid Mountains and Antigonish Highlands seldom exceed 300 m in elevation. The discontinuous soil in the Cobequid Mountains is shallow, coarse-textured, stony, acidic, and has low inherent fertility. However, blueberries are a successful enterprise in some areas. In the Antigonish and Cape Breton highlands, while fertility, erosion, topography, and stony soils derived from tills severely limit the land for agriculture, it has good capability for both coniferous species (white pine, red pine, and white spruce) and deciduous species (maple, birch, and beech) characteristic of the Acadian forest.

The Atlantic or Southern Uplands of Nova Scotia extend from Yarmouth on the southwest coast to Canso in the northeast. Because of strong glacial scouring, the granite and quartzite bedrock yield a thin, bouldery till with numerous rock outcrops. Peat bogs occupy the more poorly drained depressions which dot the upland. Although the landscape is fairly well drained, the region is stony and rugged and has little or no capability for agriculture. Only uplands underlain by slate offer a possibility of productive farming. The less resistant slate has resulted in medium loams characterized by extensive drumlin fields in Yarmouth, Queens, and Lunenburg counties. Where these deeper soils are not too stony, cultivation of grains and hay is possible, and Christmas tree production is of local importance. The lower-lying areas of sandy loam between the drumlins are poorly drained, the soils are thinner and interrupted by rock outcrops and bouldery materials, and therefore are of little use for agriculture.

The Nova Scotia Highlands are contrasted by a band of lowlands along portions of the province's coasts. These till lowlands, underlain by sedimentary rocks such as sandstones, shales, and mudstones, have a gently undulating to rolling surface less than 150 m in height. Where they are well drained, the less stony and deeper sand loams to clay loams are valuable for field crops. However, over level terrain or in depressions where drainage is poor, peat bogs and pockets of organic soils have developed.

Many of the province's major valleys have valuable local deposits of relatively fertile fluvial soils. The Annapolis–Cornwallis Valley, for example, is renowned for its farm produce. The soils are highly valued for the cultivation of fruits and vegetables as well as grains. The narrow coastal fringes and tidal marshland also have a high potential for agriculture. Reddish-brown, fine-textured silt and silty clay loams have been deposited along the shores of Cobequid and Chignecto bays. Once reclaimed, these soils are highly productive for agriculture, but only where regional drainage schemes are not frustrated by intense fragmentation of holdings.

New Brunswick. The highlands and uplands of New Brunswick, also part of the Appalachians, are formed from a dissected rugged peneplain underlain by a variety of resistant igneous and metamorphic rocks. Areas underlain by granites are characterized by shallow, stony, sandy loams. Regions of slates and argillites have produced well-drained but stony loams over hilly topography while areas underlain by quartzites have yielded more gravelly, sandy loams with fewer stones and reasonable drainage. The Podzols formed on these rocks share certain characteristics which render them largely unsuitable for agriculture.

In New Brunswick, the Maritime Plain is an area of generally low relief, under 180 m, that occupies the eastern and parts of the central and southwestern portions of the province. The topography varies from an undulating surface dissected by river valleys, to horizontal poorly drained surfaces where extensive swamps and peat deposits are found. Underlain by gray, brown, or reddish sandstones and shales, the soil texture varies from sandy loam to clay loam. Where they are well-drained, these more stone-free Podzols are capable of sustained yields of potatoes, hay, and field crops. In the narrow coastal fringe of the lowland, postglacial marine sediments vary from coarse beach sands and gravels to finer silts and clays which are more favourable for agriculture.

The main river valleys of the province contain extensive glaciofluvial deposits and alluvium. In many locations, the low plateau areas which flank the main rivers such as the Saint John and Tobique are covered by a relatively thick deposit of ablation till which, although acidic and low in fertility, is relatively stone-free. These finer-textured soils are able to sustain certain crops and support the hay and potato crops of New Brunswick. These relatively productive soils, however, represent only a small proportion of the total land area and their capability varies with local differences in surface texture, drainage, and other factors.

As in Nova Scotia, some areas bordering on the Bay of Fundy contain tidal marshlands with marine and fluviomarine deposits. Because they lie below the level of high tide, these silts and clays must be protected by dikes before their high capability for agriculture can be utilized.

Prince Edward Island. Prince Edward Island's gently rolling surface is part of the Maritime Plain. It lies generally under 50 m above sea level and is occasionally broken by hills rising to 150 m. The mineral soils are developed from glacial till or marine and lacustrine sediments and are underlain by sedimentary rocks. The greatest part of the Island is covered by the distinctive red to reddish-brown soils evolved from glacial till which ranges from well-drained sandy loam to more poorly drained clay loam. Many of the soils are susceptible to erosion, most are infertile and acidic, but the gentle slopes support healthy yields of potatoes and forage crops with dairying. The clay loams, where well drained, provide an excellent agricultural base but occupy a very small proportion of the Island.

Québec

Canada's largest province includes an interesting variety of landscapes which are part of three major physiographic regions: the Canadian Shield, the Appalachian Region, and the St. Lawrence Lowlands.

The dominant physiographic region is the vast Canadian Shield of Precambrian gneisses and granites. The Laurentians rise abruptly and spectacularly from the St. Lawrence Valley but the northwest margin is a much more gradual decline toward James and Hudson bays. In the extreme north, the area is characterized by a treeless tundra populated by lichens, mosses, grasses, or stunted shrubs. Underlain by continuous or discontinuous permafrost, subject to bitter and harsh winters, buffeted by high winds, and plagued by poor drainage, this area has no potential whatsoever for agriculture.

To the south, soil development is hindered, drainage is poor, and the coniferous cover of the boreal forest produces a highly acidic humus. Because of the short, cool summers, both evaporation and decomposition of organic material is limited. As a result, excessive moisture in the coarse soil permits severe leaching. These factors combined with a slightly less severe yet still inadequate growing season hold no promise for farming activities.

The southern plateau area directly north of the Laurentians possesses a thin mantle of coarse soils over the Precambrian bedrock. However, certain soils do offer limited potential. Over waterlaid clays, a more viable soil layer has developed and where drainage problems have been ameliorated, as in the Lac St-Jean area and in part of the Clay Belt, agriculture is possible.

The most southern portion of the Shield is the Laurentian Highlands. This region represents a transition in climate, vegetation, and soil from the generally inhospitable and rugged northern and interior region to the more fertile lowlands. Although in some valleys alluvial deposits are conducive to farming, the relatively cool, short summers and rough surface limit the potential for agriculture.

The second major physiographic unit in Québec, the Appalachians, extends through the southeastern Eastern Townships and forms the Gaspé Peninsula. Starting at the Québec–New Brunswick border, the Chaleur Uplands spread into the southern part of Gaspé. Next, the Notre-Dame, also known as the Shickshock Mountains in the east, run roughly parallel to the Chaleur Uplands and the St. Lawrence. Rising to heights of 1,200 m, this relatively flat, boreal-forested plateau is dissected by rivers cutting into its margins. In the Gaspé, pockets of grazing and limited crop cultivation occur in coastal regions where the slopes are not too severe and where local climatic conditions are favourable. To the southwest in the Eastern Townships, uplands alternate with the Sutton Mountains and Megantic Hills whose folded, resistant summits vary between 600 and 1,200 m in height. It is in the levelled terraces and river valleys, where soil and climatic factors offer fewer restrictions, that livestock and mixed crops are common on the Podzolic, Luvisolic, and Brunisolic soils.

Finally, the third physiographic unit comprises the Central and East St. Lawrence lowlands, including Anticosti Island and a significant area of the southern corner of Québec. The triangular shape of the lowland begins in a narrow belt downstream from Québec City and expands southwestward along the St. Lawrence to the Ontario and New York borders. The level to undulating landscape covers the gently sloped limestone, dolomite, shale, and sandstone beneath. The Monteregian Hills, of which Mount Royal on the Île-de-Montréal is best known, are volcanic remnants which rise to 300 m from the plain. Their surfaces, if not totally covered by the mixed species of the Great Lakes–St. Lawrence forest, are used for parkland, housing, and orchards.

Generally speaking, most of the farmland is found on the wide, flat-bottomed, clay valleys of the Montréal Plain. Soil and climatic conditions are such that this arable land is among the most productive in Canada. The moderately high fertility of the Brunisolic and Gleysolic soils is complemented by the warmer summers and longer growing season. Livestock and dairying, as well as mixed farming, predominate. In addition, the deep soils which developed over sand, silt, and clays deposited in low-lying areas are ideally suited to intensive horticulture when these soils have been properly drained.

Québec vegetation. In the extreme north, the harsh physical and climatic environment permits only the existence of the treeless tundra with lichens, mosses, and shrubs. Where conditions are slightly less severe, the forest–tundra transition zone is typified by barrens and stunted species of both black and white spruce as well as tamarack. Throughout central Québec, a patchwork of open woodland, barrens, and muskeg exists over the upland and lowland areas. Black spruce and tamarack are dominant but where better-drained soils exist, balsam fir and white spruce appear. To the south, the predominant forest is a mixture of balsam fir, both black and white spruce, white birch, and trembling aspen, with the large areas of wet, organic soils covered by the usual black spruce–tamarack combination also found in the Clay Belt.

Southern Québec, including the Eastern Townships, Lac St-Jean area, and most of the Gaspé, is dominated by the Great Lakes–St. Lawrence forest. The proportions of hardwoods, softwoods, conifers, and broadleaf trees vary with soil type and depth as well as drainage. The characteristic sugar maple, beech, yellow birch, red maple, and eastern hemlock are common on deeper soils and well-drained slopes. On shallow soils and rocky ridges, the boreal species of balsam fir and white spruce are more frequent while cedar, black spruce, and tamarack occupy wet, poorly drained areas.

Ontario

The central and largest portion of Ontario is covered by the Canadian Shield which is bounded on the north by the Hudson Bay Lowland and on the south by the St. Lawrence Lowlands. The horizontal sedimentary strata of the northern lowland slopes very gradually northeastward and eastward toward Hudson and James bays. Due to the presence of continuous or discontinous permafrost and poor drainage, the landscape consists of tundra and areas of muskeg and organic material in the far north.

Shallow soils, over igneous and metamorphic rocks, and generally moderate relief characterize the Canadian Shield in Ontario. The Severn and Abitibi uplands, rise gradually from the Hudson Bay Lowland and cover much of the Shield. These Precambrian uplands between 275 and 375 m are covered by a thin layer of drift and numerous bogs. Further south, in a belt extending east–west just north of Lake Superior, an acidic, largely unproductive soil supports coniferous forest, As in the regions described above, neither the physical nor climatic factors are sufficient to permit significant agricultural activities. The best land for farming and forestry in northern Ontario is found on the deeper till and lacustrine deposits of the large Clay Belt around Cochrane and in a smaller pocket near Lake Timiskaming.

Further south, as in Québec, a transition zone occurs. In parts of the central and far west corner of Ontario, more moderate climatic conditions, mixed forest cover, and better drainage have fostered the development of more fertile Luvisolic (formerly Gray Brown Podzolic) soils. However, this southern fringe of the Shield is utilized more for its forestry and recreation potential.

In southern Ontario, the St. Lawrence Lowlands are divided into two sections by the Precambrian rock of the Frontenac Axis. In eastern Ontario, the Central St. Lawrence Lowland, bounded by the axis together with the Ottawa and St. Lawrence rivers, consists of the same southwestward sloping sandstones, shales, and limestones as its counterpart in Québec. Some of the rolling till plains are less fertile and many areas of the clay plains are poorly drained. Improvements in drainage and other soil management practices have not been as widely adopted in eastern Ontario compared with southwestern Ontario. Today, as in the past, dairying is the dominant farm type.

South-central and southwestern Ontario constitute the West St. Lawrence Lowland and present a diversity of physiographic features, soil characteristics, and vegetation cover. This lowland is divided by southern Ontario's most striking landform, the Niagara Escarpment, a sinuous 600-km cuesta of dolomite extending north from Niagara Falls through the Bruce Peninsula to Manitoulin Island. Its mixed-forested crest rises between 75 and 300 m above the surrounding lowland. In this portion of the province are numerous glacial and postglacial features. Moraines, drumlins, spillways, eskers, and plains were created by a pushing, gouging, melting ice front as it advanced and retreated. The hummocky, rolling terrain and lighter-textured soils associated with till plains, drumlins, and esker landscape of western Ontario contrast with the flat relief and heavier-textured sediments of the extensive clay plains found near Toronto, along the north shore of Lake Ontario, and in the extreme southwest of the province.

Soil characteristics, together with surficial terrain, landform, and local climatic factors determine, to a considerable degree, the type and size of farm operation and the productivity in terms of yield. The climatic and soil advantages of this area make it perhaps the most productive arable land in the country. The highly fertile Luvisolic soils are conducive to cultivation of a variety of crops. The lighter-textured soils also support tree fruits and other fruits while heavier soils are well suited for beef and dairy operations and common field crops. However, considerable effort has been extended to areas which have certain disadvantages. The sand plain of Norfolk County was an agriculturally-depressed area before profitable tobacco farming was introduced and proper soil management practices were initiated to overcome moisture deficiency and relatively low soil fertility. In other sites, the poor natural drainage of some clay plains has been improved, resulting in highly profitable cultivation of cash crops, especially around Toronto and in extreme southwest. In drumlin fields, where there exists a combination of poorly and well-drained land, the upper slopes are often used as pasture or kept in woodlot. Without proper conservation measures, the areas of more variable relief such as drumlins and moraines near Peterborough may present difficulties that tend to discourage agriculture.

Ontario vegetation. In northern Ontario, the nature of the boreal forest is dictated by climatic and soil conditions. In the extreme north, permafrost, exposure to winds, and a cool growing season have produced a forest–tundra transition zone, where tundra barrens alternate with patches of stunted spruce, tamarack, alder, and willow shrub. In the Hudson Bay Lowland where flat topography, poor drainage, and permafrost are prevalent, there exists a subarctic open woodland of black spruce and tamarack interspersed with large areas of muskeg. On the northern areas of the Canadian Shield, a mixture of black spruce and jack pine dominates the irregular terrain and thin soil of the uplands, while a combination of black spruce and tamarack is more common on the poorly drained lowlands. Where soil texture, drainage, and climate are more favourable, white spruce, balsam fir, trembling aspen, and balsam poplar are found. In central Ontario, the dominant boreal species are gradually interspersed with trees of the Great Lakes–St. Lawrence forest, characterized by spruce, balsam fir, white birch, and trembling aspen.

Between the boreal forest to the north and the deciduous forest to the south, a mixed forest of pine, eastern hemlock, and yellow birch predominates. This Great Lakes–St. Lawrence forest varies with topography, soil, and climate. Along Georgian Bay where the Shield is covered by a thin layer of glacial till, the forest is more boreal in nature with balsam fir and white spruce most common. In the rock outcrop areas around Sudbury and North Bay, trembling aspen, white birch, and jack pine dominate. Most common in the south are mixed stands of sugar maple, beech, basswood, yellow birch, and red maple from the deciduous forest, and the pine and hemlock species which are characteristic of the Great Lakes–St. Lawrence forest.

Lastly, the deciduous forest occupies the southern portion of the Ontario peninsula. In this area, a favourable climate, and more generous glacial deposits have allowed beech, maple, oak, and basswood to prosper. However, these same favourable conditions have also encouraged agricultural, recreational, and urban land uses to prosper. As a result, the natural forest cover, for the most part, is confined to farm woodlots.

The Prairie Provinces

Together, the three Prairie Provinces of Manitoba, Saskatchewan, and Alberta include several physiographic regions including the Hudson Bay Lowland, Canadian Shield, Interior Plains as well as the Rocky Mountain Foothills and Southern Rocky Mountains of the Cordillera. The Hudson Bay Lowland occupies a small area in the northeast corner of Manitoba. Here, only raised gravel beaches break the otherwise monotonous landscape of flat, muskeg plains dotted with shallow lakes. The Canadian Shield is further represented by the Severn and Kazan uplands which constitute the northern portions of Manitoba and Saskatchewan. Metamorphic rocks have been eroded to a generally low relief which varies between 150 and 600 m. Bogs, lakes, and muskeg areas have resulted from glacial advance and retreat over the rough terrain and the interruption of previous drainage. The shallow deposits of stony, sandy till are generally quite inhospitable to agriculture.

To most Canadians, however, the Prairies are exemplified by the Interior Plains whose wide, expansive landscape includes nearly level lacustrine clay deposits, gently undulating and hummocky till plains, as well as rough hummocky morainic uplands. This broad area of sedimentary bedrock has been sculpted by ice and water into three distinctive levels or steppes. Elevation is highest in the most western level and consequently drainage is mainly eastward. The First Prairie Steppe, or the Manitoba Lowlands, lies between the Shield and the Manitoba Escarpment. Its lower areas are occupied by large fresh-water lakes including Lakes Winnipeg, Manitoba, and Winnipegosis. Deposited by postglacial Lake Agassiz, fertile black soils have developed from waterlaid clays and silts, particularly in the southern part of the basin. The Red River valley is one such richly endowed area. Winnipeg, at an elevation of 240 m, is at the heart of this nearly level, former lake bed. On the other hand, in the Interlake area between Lakes Winnipeg and Manitoba, the lacustrine clay deposits are much shallower, and stony till or rock outcrops break through the surface.

The divide between the First and Second Prairie steppes is a resistant layer of sedimentary rock overlain by glacial debris. Interrupted by rivers, this barrier now consists of east-facing hills collectively known as the Manitoba Escarpment. The average elevation is approximately 300 m but individual hills vary between 210 and 425 m. The crest of this escarpment is marked by stony, medium-textured morainic deposits and lakes. As such, Riding, Pembina, Turtle, and Duck mountains have importance for recreation and several are designated as provincial or National parks.

The Second Prairie Steppe is much larger than the Manitoba Lowlands. Often called the Saskatchewan Plain, this area is composed primarily of gently undulating and hummocky till plains which are frequently broken by many small, undrained, low-lying areas known as sloughs. Here too, are the familiar clay plains which are the product of postglacial lake basins. The clay deposits include the Souris Basin as well as the Regina, Rosetown, Saskatoon, and Melfort plains. Regina is situated on this Second Prairie Steppe at an elevation of approximately 575 m. A number of isolated upland areas of varying size rise above the surrounding plain. The extremities of these uplands are usually very hummocky or dissected and elevations rise abruptly 400 m above the plain. Moose Mountain, Touchwood Hills, Allan Hills, and Duck Mountain Uplands are a few of these uplands.

To the west, the Missouri Coteau separates the Second and Third Prairie steppes. Running from south-central Saskatchewan into northeastern Alberta, this upland is accompanied by ridged and hummocky moraines which rise 60 to 150 m above the Saskatchewan Plain. Such morainic deposits are best suited to grazing.

The Third Prairie Steppe or Alberta High Plain rises gradually from 760 m at the Missouri Coteau to 1,079 m at Calgary and eventually to nearly 1,220 m where it reaches the foothills. This steppe contains noticeably more varied relief as it has been cut deeply by the Saskatchewan River system. A variety of uplands standing perhaps 100 m or more above the general plain elevation include Wood Mountain and Milk River Ridge in southern Alberta, and the Caribou Mountains in the north. Best known, however, is the dissected plateau of the Cypress Hills which rise to 1,385 m or nearly 500 m above the surrounding plain.

Lastly, in the Prairies, the picturesque foothills and Southern Rocky Mountains of the Cordilleran Region demarcate the southern half of the Alberta–British Columbia boundary. The highly folded sedimentary rock of the young mountain system is an impressive complement to the Prairies.

Vegetation and Soils. The Hudson Bay Lowland and Canadian Shield that occupy northern Manitoba as well as the northeast corner of Saskatchewan are characterized by subarctic vegetation underlain by continuous or discontinuous permafrost. As a transition between subarctic and boreal forest, it is associated with sparse or badly stunted black spruce, white spruce, balsam fir, aspen, poplar, and white birch which occur in open stands. Organic soils have developed in the low-lying, poorly drained, peat-filled areas. The mineral soils that developed under such physical conditions are termed Eutric Brunisols and tend to be shallow, sandy to stony, and relatively infertile. Under adverse climatic conditions, and frequently plagued by inadequate drainage, most soils in these regions have little potential for agriculture.

To the west and south, the remainder of the Canadian Shield is covered by boreal forest. Here, a combination of spruce, aspen, white birch, balsam fir, larch, and jack pine occur. The Brunisolic soils that have evolved are generally sandy, acidic, leached, often stony, and have low natural fertility. For these reasons, no significant areas of Brunisols in the Prairie Region have been utilized for agriculture.

To the south, where the edge of the Shield gives way to the Great Plains, both vegetation and soil characteristics change. Mixed forest with a high deciduous element replaces the true boreal forest with its coniferous emphasis. To a considerable degree, the mixed wood belt coincides with the zone of Gray Luvisols which covers the northern half of Alberta, Saskatchewan, and Manitoba. The Gray Luvisols (formerly termed Gray Wooded soils) have a grayish layer near the surface as a result of downward leaching of clay, giving rise to an underlying layer with a clay accumulation. The value of this soil type for agriculture depends largely on the absence of adverse limitations due to topography, stoniness, or low moisture-holding capacity.

In Alberta, Gray Luvisols cover about one-half of the province and a variety of physiographic settings. For example, this soil type predominates on the lacustrine basins. Here, medium- to fine-textured, waterlaid sediments on level to undulating landscapes are most common. Much of the agricultural activity on this soil type in this province occurs on such basins, as in the Peace River district. On the other hand, the till plains varying from fine to coarse texture are characterized by hummocky to rolling terrain. Agriculture has developed to a much lesser extent on the till plains. Whether on lacustrine basins or till plains, principal crops are coarse grains, legumes, rapeseed, and to a lesser extent, wheat. This choice of crops reflects the shorter growing season characteristic of Gray Luvisol areas. Production of livestock has been increasing, especially where more hilly terrain discourages field cultivation.

In Saskatchewan, this same soil group covers the northern portions of the province. In the northeast, on lowland areas under 460 m elevation, the undulating and hummocky plains of glacial till are occasionally blanketed by nearly level lacustrine or alluvial sediments. These soils which are mainly medium and coarse textured, are interspersed among larger areas of organic soils (peat bogs). On upland areas above 460 m, medium-textured glacial tills dominate the undulating to hummocky terrain; sandy fluvial soils are also common. Wheat, coarse grains, and forage crops are common. Problems of a short frost-free period, deficient soil nutrients, and surface crusting may occur on cultivated land. An alternative land use is livestock grazing.

In Manitoba, Gray Luvisols have developed under the mixed forest of the Manitoba Lowlands north of Winnipeg in the Interlake area. This is one major agricultural land reserve that does not have frost hazard for field crops common to the Prairie Region. The great amount of limestone in the parent material has resulted in a shallow soil profile. These shallow profiles coupled with stoniness and frequently poor drainage of the medium- to fine-textured lacustrine deposits on lowland areas, result in lower potential for agriculture and thus livestock production and pasturing are most common. The upland areas of the Manitoba Escarpment, Duck, Riding, and Porcupine mountains, are covered by medium-textured glacial till which in turn is overlain in places with lacustrine or fluvial deposits. However, the generally rough, hummocky topography, small lakes and peat-filled depressions, combined with low soil fertility and erosion, restrict agriculture to mixed farming with an emphasis on grain.

In the grasslands to the south, the relationship between climatic influences, such as precipitation and temperature on one hand, and vegetation and soils on the other, becomes very apparent. The similarity between vegetation and soil patterns is well documented. Although this part of the Prairie Region accounts for only one-third of the area of the three provinces, its importance for agriculture is well known.

The three distinctive crescents of parkland, and mixed-grass and short-grass prairie vegetation correspond to the zones of Black, Dark Brown, and Brown Chernozemic soils. The outer crescent of parkland skirts the Alberta–British Columbia boundary at the 49th parallel, passing northward through Calgary to Edmonton and then sloping southeastward to southern Manitoba. The transitional vegetation is characterized by open areas of tall grasses interspersed with occasional aspen or poplar groves. Under favourable moisture conditions, ranging from 400 to 500 mm annually with a moisture deficiency between 75 and 125 mm, a Black Chernozemic soil has developed. With its high content of organic matter, deep profile, and rich dark colour, this soil is regarded as one of the more fertile in Canada. Because of favourable climatic and soil conditions, grain yields, particularly those of wheat, are higher and more reliable than in other grassland areas. Such excellent conditions have encouraged a diverse agricultural economy where livestock and dairy products often account for a greater share of farm incomes than do grains.

To the south, under slightly drier conditions, 350 to 400 mm of precipitation annually and a higher moisture deficit of 150 to 225 mm, mixed-prairie grasses predominate. In river valleys and surrounding sloughs, small groves of poplar, willows, and shrubs are found. Here in the zone of Dark Brown soils, the reduction of available moisture accounts for a reduced humus content. Soils have relatively high natural fertility, good moisture-holding capacity (when not sandy), and resistance to erosion, making them highly productive for many agricultural uses. The Regina Plains, for example, are covered by waterlaid, well-drained, stone-free clay and silt deposits. The level topography facilitates mechanized farming and these Dark Brown Chernozemic soils are some of the best of Saskatchewan wheat lands, contributing substantially to the "breadbasket" reputation of the Prairies.

The third crescent of prairie vegetation lies to the south and covers southeastern Alberta and southwestern Saskatchewan, both areas occurring on the Third Prairie Steppe. The vegetation cover of short grass is sparse, reflecting the reduced amount of moisture available which in turn results in lower levels of organic matter characteristic of the Brown Soil Zone. This represents the driest area of the treeless Prairie, where less than 350 mm of precipitation falls annually. The longest frost-free period, 110 days, and high temperatures in early spring, make this moisture less effective than in the mixed-grass crescent where cooler spring temperatures delay the snow melt.

Solonetzic soils are also prevalent in the Brown Soil Zone. These soils are characterized by their poorly structured, hard, compact subsoils and high salt content which adversely affect crop growth. Although Solonetzic soils occur within all the major soil zones, their adverse effects on crop production are most pronounced in the Brown Soil Zone where the surface soil is deficient in organic matter and plant nutrients. Native areas of these soils are characterized by scattered shallow pits or "burn-outs", where the surface soil has been eroded, exposing the white-capped "tough" structured subsoil.

As in all soil zones, cultivation results in rapid depletion of the organic matter and deterioration of the soil structure. This becomes particularly critical in the Brown Soil Zone, often resulting in severe erosion by wind or water. In years of abnormally abundant precipitation, bountiful wheat crops can be produced, but the uncertainty of summer rains on the Prairies makes wheat a risky venture which may aggravate other unwise soil management practices and result in wind erosion. Not surprisingly, this semi-arid region has witnessed several large-scale irrigation projects in attempts to overcome the significant moisture deficiency which exceeds 200 mm. Under dryland farming, clay loam and finer-textured soils are considered suitable for sustained field crop production, whereas loam-textured soils are marginal. Sandy, stony, and hilly soils are best left in grass.

British Columbia.

The diversity of Canada's geographic character is nowhere more striking than in British Columbia, where the two major physiographic regions are the Interior Plains and the Cordillera. Each region contains a variety of physical subdivisions. The soils of British Columbia are as varied as the landscape, climate, and vegetation. Complexity of geological parent material, adverse topography and climate, and restrictive drainage mean that agricultural land is limited. In fact, it is estimated that over 90 per cent of the province is too high, too steep, or too rocky for farming or close settlement (Putnam and Putnam, 1970).

The Interior Plains are represented, in the northeast of the province, by the Alberta Plateau and its subdivisions, the Fort Nelson and Peace River lowlands. The Alberta Plateau is a flat to gently rolling upland with elevations for the most part between 900 and 1,200 m. It is thickly wooded in the south and west, but there is open muskeg in the east and north. The Liard and Peace River systems drain the upland and the Fort Nelson and Peace River lowlands which lie below 370 m elevation. These lowlands are marked by fine-textured lacustrine materials and glacial drift with drumlins. Much of the land in the Peace River Lowland has been cleared, and the level to gently rolling landscape and lacustrine deposits have good potential for agriculture. Surface soils in this area are generally fine to medium textured. The principal types of soils are Gray Luvisols, Black Chernozemic, and Solonetzic. Cereals, such as wheat, oats, and barley, as well as hay, are cultivated. Mixed farming, featuring livestock production, is also common. In the Fort Nelson Lowland, however, soil drainage is restricted and a muskeg–lake pattern dots the land.

The Cordilleran Region occupies 90 per cent of the province and supplies the more spectacular features. Three major subdivisions, namely the Eastern, Interior, and Western systems, cover the complex arrangement of physiographic units.

The Eastern System is composed of the Rocky Mountain Foothills and the Rocky Mountains. The foothills form a continuous belt from the 49th parallel to the Liard River and flank the eastern margin of the Rocky Mountains. The three sets of ranges that collectively comprise the Rocky Mountains form a 1,370-km chain of strongly folded and faulted sedimentary rocks. Some peaks exceed 3,000 m. The mountain ranges have a varied and complex array of soils depending on aspect, moisture supply, and temperature conditions. A succession of soils may include Gray Luvisols, Ferro-Humic Podzols, and Dystric Brunisols up a forested slope, followed by Sombric Brunisols, Humic Regosols, and probably Cryosols through the alpine meadows to the snowfields. In the river valleys and on the more gentle lower valley slopes Gray Luvisols, Eutric Brunisols, Gleysols, and Regosols are found. Unfortunately, the soils of arable quality are isolated and too remote for any large-scale practical use. The Rocky Mountains provide spectacular alpine scenery for tourism and have some importance for mining.

The Eastern System is separated from the Interior System by the Rocky Mountain Trench, a deep, 1,450-km long valley which runs from the 49th parallel almost to the Liard River. This spectacular trench, whose width varies between three and sixteen km, contains the headwaters of many major rivers, including the Columbia, Fraser, and Kootenay. The slopes of the trench exhibit the variety of soils consistent with a diversity of climate, elevation, and vegetation. On the valley floor, much of the recent alluvial deposits are poorly drained while terraces are coarse textured and frequently excessively drained. In the southern portion of the trench, soils suffer from stoniness, insufficient natural water supply, and the high cost of clearing, while in the north, a shorter growing season and remoteness restrict their use.

The Interior System includes a wide variety of plains, basins, highlands, plateaux, and mountains, which can be grouped into the Southern, Central, and Northern plateaux, each with a mountain area.

The Southern Plateau and Mountain Area includes most of the central and southern interior of the province and is composed of the Columbia Mountains and the Interior Plateau. The Cariboo, Monashee, Selkirk, and Purcell ranges of the Columbia system vary in altitude and peak configuration due partly to differences in glaciation, bedrock type, and erosion history. Many of the rugged peaks exceed 3,000 m. In the Columbia Mountains, opportunities for farming are confined to river valleys. The most common soils are Humo-Ferric Podzols, Gray Luvisols, and Dystric Brunisols, depending mainly on elevation. Small-scale mixed farms have developed in response to the relative isolation of patches of arable land. Where demand from a market exists and terrain permits, dairying, beef production, and poultry are emphasized. Elsewhere, general farming and livestock ranching are more common.

The Interior Plateau is an area of basins, plateaux, and highlands approximately 380 km in width and 900 km in length, encircled by mountains. This region of low to moderate relief is drained almost entirely by the Fraser River system. The Nechako, Fraser, and Thompson plateaux are also part of the Interior Plateau. These units, at elevations between 1,200 and 1,800 m, have flat to gently rolling terrain along with many glacial features. For agriculture, the most significant features are the glaciolacustrine silts, which are particularly evident in the Okanagan, Thompson, and North Thompson valleys of the Thompson Plateau. A significant share of arable soil is found in the Okanagan and Thompson valleys where Brown, Dark Brown, and Black Chernozemic soils are most common on the lower slopes. Under irrigation, these soils yield excellent fruit and vegetable crops. The Interior Plateau complex also includes the Quesnel, Shuswap, and Okanagan highlands which for the most part are of moderate relief with peaks ranging between 2,000 and 2,800 m. The Fraser Basin, a gently rolling area lying generally below 950 m, has a relatively thick covering of drift, and glacial features are common. Lakes and organic meadows dot the landscape in the numerous enclosed depressions. The Nechako and Fraser basins contain mainly fine-textured Gray Luvisols and forage crops occupy the main areas of cultivated land. Further north, agriculture is severely restricted by climate.

The northern and central parts of the Interior System are the complex and much glaciated Central Plateau and Mountain Area (comprising the Stikine Plateau, the Skeena Mountains, and Nass Basin, as well as the Hazelton, Cassiar, and Omineca mountains) and the Northern Plateau and Mountain Area (Yukon Plateau and Liard Plain). Throughout this area, vertical zonation of soils occurs. Alpine tundra vegetation and rock exposures occupy higher mountain slopes and Podzolic and Brunisolic soils occur on lower slopes, supporting forest vegetation. Only in a few river valleys, such as the Nass, Skeena, and Stikine, are small amounts of agriculturally valuable soils found.

The Western System of the province includes three major subdivisions, the Coast Mountain Area, the Coastal Trough, and the Outer Mountain Area. The ranges that make up the Coast Mountains constitute an unbroken 1,500-km chain that extends along the Pacific Coast from the Fraser River to the Yukon–British Columbia border. The northern section is composed of the Boundary Ranges with a large proportion of ice-covered area and several peaks exceeding 3,000 m. The Kitimat Ranges of the central section have few glaciers, more round and uniform summits, and peaks which generally do not exceed 2,400 m. To the south, the Pacific Ranges contain the highest peaks of the Coast Mountains, including Mount Waddington at 4,016 m.

Lastly, the Cascade Mountains occupy a small part of southern British Columbia. Peaks are usually below 2,400 m and again the topography indicates intense alpine glaciation. With the exception of a few river valleys, this region of forested slopes, alpine meadows, and ice fields is almost completely unsuitable for agriculture. Lumbering, mining, recreation, and watershed management activities far overshadow the limited agricultural land use. Under conditions of heavy precipitation (with much snow) and a dense forest cover, a variety of soils developed, but all are generally subjected to leaching and suffer from acidity. The soils are dominantly Humo-Ferric or Ferro-Humic Podzols and support dense cover of western red cedar, western hemlock, and Douglas-fir.

The second major subdivision is the Coastal Trough, a broad depression partly submerged by water. Its width varies between 16 and 160 km and it is divided by a natural constriction into two sections. The northern portion is known as the Hecate Depression and for the most part is submerged beneath the Queen Charlotte Strait, Queen Charlotte Sound, and Hecate Strait. The areas above sea-level include the Queen Charlotte, Nahwitti, and Hecate lowlands. The southern portion, the Georgia Depression, is also partly submerged beneath the Strait of Georgia and Puget Sound. Two important above-water areas are the Georgia and Nanaimo lowlands, and here the majority of the province's population is wedged between the Coast and Insular mountains. The latter extends 280 km along the east coast of Vancouver Island, is generally below 600 m, and possesses a relatively deep layer of glacial and glaciofluvial materials. It is the Georgia and Nanaimo lowlands, however, that possess the greatest potential for agriculture. Much of the province's most valuable land, and some of Canada's most productive soils, are among those found in the flood plains and deltas of this coastal lowland. Although the alluvial material requires diking or draining, these soils are highly productive in agricultural use. With the market of the Vancouver and Victoria urban areas, production of small fruits, vegetables, ornamental and horticultural crops, as well as dairying and forage crops are important activities. Of concern to agriculturalists are the effects of intensive farming on soil fertility, the high costs of diking and draining, as well as the housing, industrial, and recreational pressures exerted on this land.

The third and last sector of the Western System is the Outer Mountain Area, which comprises the St. Elias Mountains in the north, and Insular Mountains of the Queen Charlotte Islands and Vancouver Island to the south. The former rise abruptly from the water to 4,500 m height in some cases, and constitute some of the most rugged topography in Canada. The Insular Mountains form the backbone of the island chain and their moderate maximum relief of 1,100 m on the Queen Charlotte Islands belies their rugged character. On Vancouver Island, summits exceed 2,100 m in the central part of the island. The Outer Mountains allow for little opportunity for agriculture. The climate is limiting, many slopes are highly unstable, and there is a dense coniferous forest. The soils are mainly Podzolic with very thick organic surface layers. Some limited areas near Alberni are considered arable.

Vegetation. As befitting an area of complex physiographic and climatic patterns, the distribution and nature of the vegetative cover is equally varied. Temperature and precipitation are the two main controlling elements. In the drier areas of the southern interior valleys, where low precipitation and high evapotranspiration rates limit tree growth, a natural grassland exists. In certain valleys, where annual precipitation is less than 300 mm and where such limited moisture is less effective due to humidity or wind conditions, only drought-resistant bunch-grasses, cactus, and sagebrush survive the arid conditions. In the Peace River country of northeastern British Columbia, the vegetation is largely a forest of trembling aspen. On some of the Peace River valley's south-facing slopes, a Prairie parkland of grassland and aspen groves occurs.

The Columbia forest (Rowe, 1972) occupies the upper valleys of the Fraser and Thompson rivers, a significant portion of the Kootenay River valley, and the Quesnel Lake area. This coniferous forest is similar to the coast forest but with fewer species. The characteristic species of western hemlock and western red cedar reflect the greater amounts of moisture available. Depending on elevation and precipitation, Douglas-fir, western larch, western white pine, and Engelmann spruce are associated species.

The montane forest of the central Interior Plateau and several southern mountain valleys evolved in response to the dry climate. Here, the average annual precipitation of between 300 and 750 mm determines that only the more drought-resistant evergreens thrive. This is particularly true in the very dry valleys of the south where ponderosa pine dominates. In many locations, the forest is open and interspersed with grass. At higher elevations in the south, and in more northern locations where more moisture is available, Douglas-fir, lodgepole pine, trembling aspen, Engelmann spruce, and white spruce prevail.

The Pacific Coast forest, as most other forests in British Columbia, is dominated by large conifers, especially western red cedar and western hemlock. Douglas-fir thrives in the southern parts of the mainland and Vancouver Island while to the north, Sitka spruce is abundant, especially on the immediate coast. The volume of wood contained in these stands represents an extremely valuable resource.

The subalpine portions of the Cordillera and parts of the Interior Plateau are dominated up to the treeline by a coniferous forest, whose prevailing species include Engelmann spruce, alpine fir, and lodgepole pine. However, depending on location, both black and white spruce as well as trembling aspen from the boreal forest, Douglas-fir from the montane forest, or western hemlock and western red cedar from the Columbia and coast forests, may intrude. While such forests are less lush than the coast forest because of low temperatures and reduced precipitation, they are not without commercial value. Lastly, superimposed here, as in all mountainous areas, is an alpine zone. Above the treeline, upper slopes may be ice-covered, bare rock, or may support an alpine meadow cover.

The boreal forest makes an appearance in the north and northeast parts of the province. The characteristic species include both black and white spruce, alpine fir, tamarack, trembling aspen, and lodgepole pine, the latter two occur particularly in previously burnt areas. Depending on conditions, certain broadleaf species such as white birch and balsam poplar are not uncommon especially in river valleys. To the north where less favourable soils and a cool, dry climate prevail, the ratio of black spruce and tamarack to other species increases.

The Territories

The Yukon and Northwest Territories account for more than one-third of Canada's land area. Two major but vastly different physiographic regions dominate this large expanse. Firstly, the Canadian Shield occupies the central and western mainland of the Northwest Territories, as well as the eastern portion of Baffin Island. Here, the old Precambrian crystalline rocks have been eroded into the familiar undulating terrain composed of rolling hills, valleys, and lakes.

Secondly, the younger Borderlands, represented by five physiographic regions, dominate the remainder of the Territories. The Great Slave and Great Bear lakes area of the Northwest Territories is part of the Interior Plains. This region is composed of plateaux, plains, and hills which increase in elevation from north to south. Among the most notable features is Canada's longest river, the Mackenzie, which winds much of its 4,240-km course through this region. Secondly, the Cordilleran Region constitutes a small portion of the western Northwest Territories but completely dominates the Yukon. The Eastern, Interior, and Western Systems of the Cordillera, described in the physiography of British Columbia, present physiographic features which vary from cirques in the mountains' highest reaches to drumlin fields and outwash plains on valley floors. The unglaciated northwest section of the Yukon presents spectacular scenery including the Ogilvie Mountains. Next, a more gentle and rolling terrain of low mountains and hills characterizes the Arctic Lowlands Region. The Arctic Coastal Plains Region is a narrow strip, ranging in width between 50 and 100 km, along the western Arctic Coast. The Mackenzie Delta with its complex pattern of lakes, channels, and low-lying areas is part of this region and has particular significance for wildlife. Lastly, the Innuitian Region has a varied and more rugged topography than surrounding areas.

Vegetation. In northern Canada, three major vegetation regions predominate; the arctic, subarctic, and boreal. First, the arctic region is divided into three subdivisions. The high arctic vegetation region is characterized by sparse cover and large areas without any vegetation. Only on wet sites, is there continuous plant cover. Moving southward into the mid-arctic vegetation region, sedges and grasses are found where water is available throughout the summer. Stunted willows are found in damp depressions and on south-facing slopes. The low arctic includes the northern portions of the mainland and here plant cover is continuous. Depending on soil and moisture conditions, shrubs, mosses, or lichens are most common.

The boundary between the arctic and subarctic vegetation regions is delineated by the treeline which winds southeastward from the Mackenzie Delta area to the Northwest Territories–Manitoba boundary near Hudson Bay. The types of plants or trees that occur are determined by the same factors which influence the position of the treeline: winter drought, winter winds, summer temperatures, availability of moisture, depth of snow cover, and permafrost. In the subarctic region, an association of lichens and trees is common. Lichens form a thick blanket of ground cover and tree species vary with soil and moisture conditions. More moderate physical and climatic conditions permit growth of black spruce, white spruce, and jack pine while tamarack is more common on wet soils. Alders, willows, and other shrubs are also present.

The boreal forest dominates the southern Yukon and southwestern Northwest Territories. Here, conditions permit a more dense, closed forest with black and white spruce, tamarack, balsam fir, and lodgepole pine as the dominant species. In addition, jack pine as well as the occasional deciduous species such as birch, aspen, or balsam poplar are found.

Soils. In the arctic and subarctic regions, soil development has been inhibited and Cryosols are by far the most widespread soils. Their lack of development results from a variety of interrelated factors which include: nature of the parent material; short season of biological activity; presence of permafrost; limited vegetation cover; and slope. These soils are often associated with patterned ground such as polygons, circles, and stripes.

In the forested areas of the Cordillera and Interior Plains regions, two soil types, Cryosols and Brunisols, dominate. Variations in soil type result from the variation in topography, climate, slope, and altitude. In the mountains and high plateaux, soils are generally shallow and coarse textured while the most arable soils are found in the Interior Plateaux.

The portion of the Canadian Shield below the treeline possesses more moderate climatic and physical conditions which have permitted more advanced vegetative cover and hence slightly more developed, albeit generally coarse, soils with low fertility. Along the Northwest Territories–Alberta border, in areas covered with fine-textured mineral deposits and where organic matter from more varied forest cover occurs, areas of Gray Luvisols have developed.

Northern Agriculture. The north is not a signficant factor in the national perspective of agriculture. Nevertheless, to disregard the Yukon and Northwest Territories would be a mistake. The reasons for the limited agricultural development reflect the environmental constraints. As a general rule, temperature and precipitation decrease with northern latitudes. One of the most significant handicaps to agriculture is the lower temperatures of soil and air. To some extent, however, the longer summer days promote rapid growth and partially compensate for the relatively short frost-free season. Although decreasing precipitation is also a restriction on agriculture, the reduced quantity is somewhat offset by the fact that most of the precipitation occurs during the summer. The success of forage crops or livestock grazing is also affected by the climatic extremes which are often characteristic of northern Canada. Widely varying frost-free periods and fluctuations in degree-day values add a large measure of uncertainty to northern agriculture (Hoyt *et al.*, 1978).

Nevertheless, with proper management and use of hybrids developed specifically for the north, cultivation of hardy, cool season vegetables and forage crops, as well as livestock grazing, are possible. In fact, at one time a dairy herd was maintained at Aklavik (Taylor, 1947). Within the Yukon, wheat, oats, and forage crops can be cultivated but with varying degrees of success. With appropriate shelter and supplements to locally grown feeds, swine and poultry can be raised. In the Northwest Territories, the Slave, Liard, and Mackenzie river valleys and grass meadows hold the greatest potential for agriculture. Where the land is forested, as along the Liard River, the considerable cost of clearing is a handicap, and presently agriculture is limited to garden plots.

In addition to climatic and other physical limitations which discourage agriculture, there are two other factors which are important. The relatively low population is scattered across the north and does not represent a sufficiently large or centralized market to stimulate large-scale farming. Secondly, the high cost and variable nature of transportation affects the cost of moving equipment and supplies as well as the economic feasibility of transporting produce to the small, local, and scattered markets.

APPENDIX II

CENSUS OF AGRICULTURE CENSUS DIVISIONS
1971
MAP 29

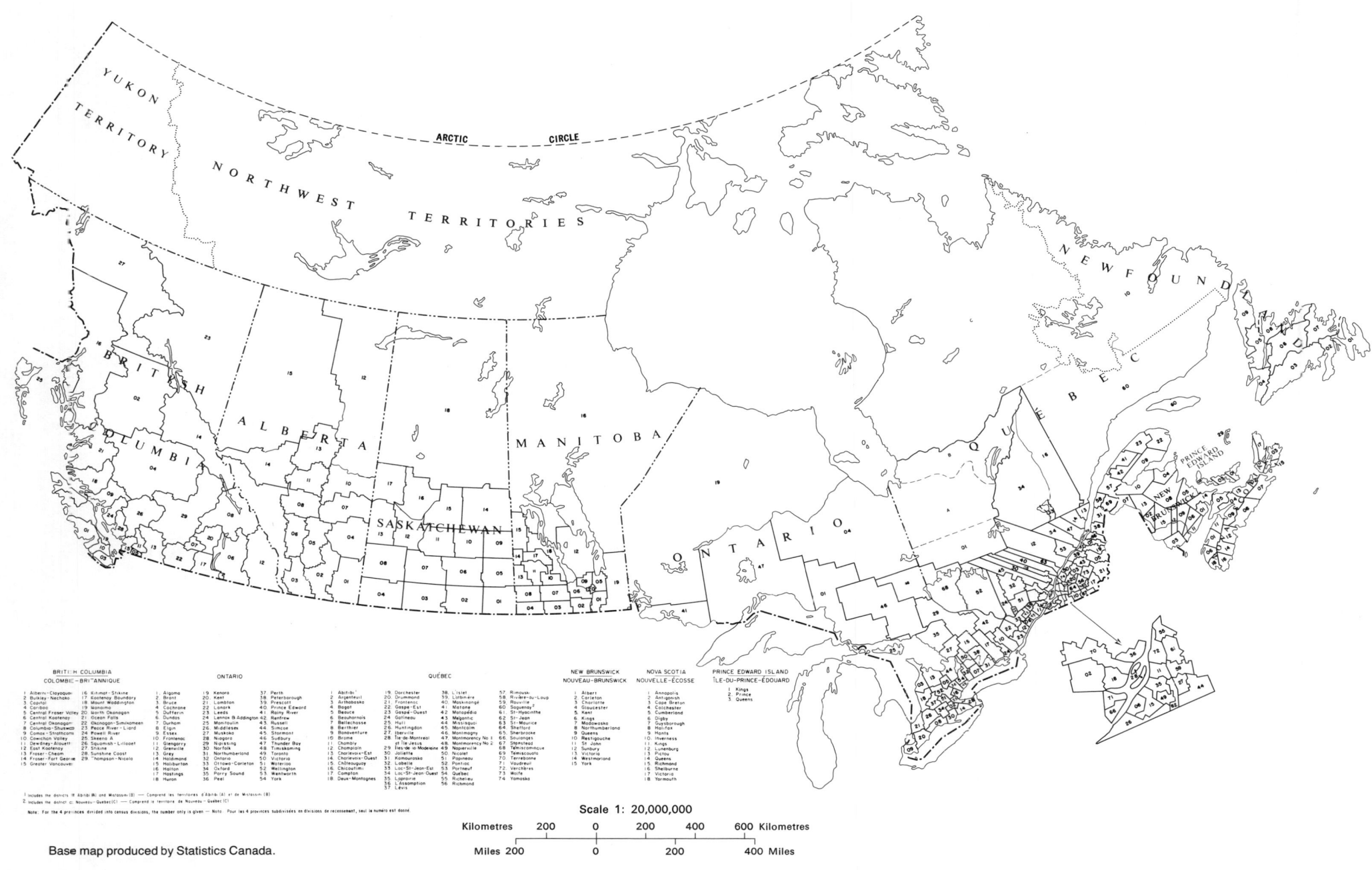

CENSUS OF AGRICULTURE CENSUS DIVISIONS
1976

MAP 30

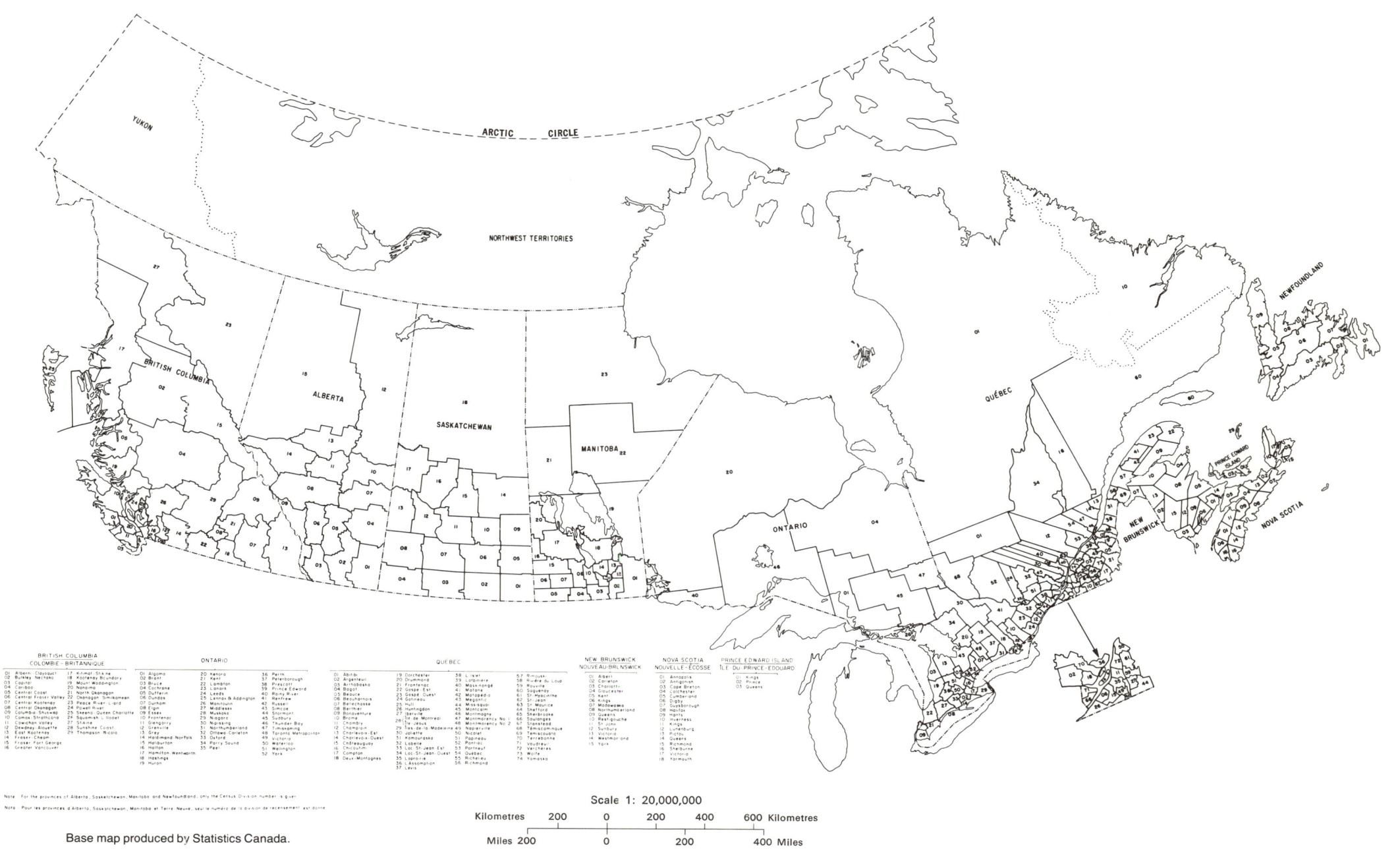

Outdoor Recreation

National Photography Collection.
Public Archives Canada.
C-37686

Contents

	Page
Introduction	69
Physical factors	70
Climate	70
Landscape evaluation for outdoor recreation	73
Natural areas of Canadian significance	75
Wild rivers as critical areas	76
Northern Land Use Information Series	77
The Canada Land Inventory: capability for outdoor recreation	77
Present land use	81
Factors affecting present land use	81
Quantitative terms	81
Qualitative factors	81
Private sector	84
Cottage lands in the private sector	85
Commercial sector	87
Commercial accommodation in the hinterlands	88
Public sector	89
Parks	92
Present land use and future planning	96
Tourism	96
Tourist flows	96
Accommodation and revenue	97
Employment	98
Summary	98
Conflicts and issues	98
Carrying capacity	98
Land use conflicts	99
Social and economic demands	99
Acknowledgements	103
Bibliography	103

Tables

	Page
1. Participation rates in selected outdoor activities, by region, 1976	69
2. Percentage change in the participation rates in selected outdoor activities, by region, 1972 to 1976	69
3. Variation in participation rates for selected activities, by age, sex, and socio-economic level, 1972	69
4. Climatic criteria for designation of a suitable day, by activity or activity grouping	72
5. Land area, by capability class and province	79
6. Shoreline length, by capability class and province	79
7. Inventoried shoreline, by class, for those areas within 40, 80, 121, and 161 km of the centre of Census Metropolitan Areas	80
8. Summary of methods using physical criteria to identify important outdoor recreation lands	79
9. Provincial and territorial area, by tenure, 1973	81
10. Area classification, by province or territory, 1973	84
11. Households owning one or more vacation homes, by province and Census Metropolitan Area, June 1971	85
12. Distribution of households owning one or more vacation homes, by urban and rural class and province, 1971	87
13. Participation rates in four commercial recreation activities associated with urban areas, by province, for persons 14 years and over, 1971	88
14. Number of locations for travellers' accommodation, by province, territory, and type of establishment, 1972 and 1975	88
15. Percentage change in the number of establishments for travellers' accommodation, by province, territory, and establishment type 1972 to 1975	89
16. Open space for recreation in Montréal, Toronto, and Vancouver, 1971	92
17. Park classification system for National and provincial parks, 1976	92
18. Population, area, and park area, by province and territory, 1976	94
19. Visitation at National Parks, by region, 1975/76 and 1976/77	94
20. Visitation at provincial parks, 1974 and 1975	94
21. Campground use at National and provincial parks, by province, 1974/75 and 1975	95
22. Recreation use in the Lake of the Woods Planning Area by the private, commercial, and public sectors	97
23. Tourist arrivals world-wide and Canada, 1968 to 1975	98
24. Receipts from non-resident travellers in Canada, and total current account receipts for all countries, 1970 to 1976	99
25. Payments by travellers resident in Canada, and total current account payments for all countries, 1970 to 1976	99
26. Average duration of stay by United States' visitors in Canada, by province or territory of main destination, 1974 and 1975	99
27. Accommodation, by type for major accommodation groups, by province or territory, 1975	101
28. Comparison of provinces according to the number of United States' visitors and the number of commercial accommodation establishments, 1975	101
29. Employed in selected tourist services compared to total employed, by province, 1977	102

Figures

	Page
1. Schematic representation of recreation seasonal patterns at any typical location	70
2. Timelines for tourism and recreation seasons at Edmonton, Regina, and Winnipeg	72
3. Number of park visits per km^2 of National and provincial parks, by province	95
4. Changes in visitation at National Parks, by region, 1950–51 to 1976–77	96
5. Changes in visitation at Ontario provincial parks, 1960 to 1976	96
6. Number of Canadian residents returning to Canada, 1972 to 1976	98
7. Balance of payments on travel account, quarterly, 1970 to 1978	99
8. Number of visits by United States' residents, by province and territory of main destination, 1974 and 1975	100

Maps

	Page
1. Summer and winter recreational periods	70
2. Duration of the winter season in days (Prairie Provinces)	71
3. Duration of high summer in days (Prairie Provinces)	71
4. Number of days suitable for skiing during winter (Prairie Provinces)	71
5. Number of days suitable for passive activities during high summer (Prairie Provinces)	71
6. Climatic suitability for all winter outdoor recreational activities (Prairie Provinces)	71
7. Climatic suitability for all complete summer outdoor recreational activities (Prairie Provinces)	71
8. Index of Canada's landscape attractivity for outdoor recreation	74
9. Natural areas of Canadian significance	75
10. Wild rivers surveyed	76
11. Land Use Information Series	78
12. Land capability for outdoor recreation: Québec, New Brunswick, Prince Edward Island, Nova Scotia, Newfoundland	82
13. Land capability for outdoor recreation: Ontario	83
14. Land capability for outdoor recreation: British Columbia, Alberta, Saskatchewan, Manitoba	86
15. Outdoor recreation opportunity	90
16. Major parks in Canada	91
17. Percentage of households owning vacation homes	93

Introduction

Outdoor recreation includes all those activities which help to restore and refresh people out-of-doors, and in which they engage voluntarily during leisure time for their personal satisfaction. One element essential for outdoor recreation is the use of land, and it is possible to relate the various activities to particular types of land. However, before establishing this relationship, it is necessary to consider which activities can be included as outdoor recreation, and which characteristics of the land are important for satisfying the requirements for these activities.

Many activities can be considered as outdoor recreation. They range from the popular pursuits of driving for pleasure, swimming, and picnicking to very specialized activities such as mountain climbing and whitewater canoeing. Many activities are individualistic and the land used, such as a favourite swimming hole, a special site in a local park, or a major wilderness area, may be considered to be essential by an individual for enjoyment of outdoor recreation. Thus, for the entire population we can relate their participation rates for a number of activities to the particular lands suitable for the activities, and these resources then represent, for the general public, essential lands.

To determine the level of demand for land and associated facilities for recreation, studies have been done throughout Canada and the United States to identify the activities and the number of people who participate in each. It is necessary to recognize the variation in participation rates in different regions and in different activities in order to determine the importance of land for recreation (Table 1).

The changes in the participation rates are another important variation for consideration in evaluating the demands for land across Canada. The regional differences and the changes over time in the participation in outdoor activities influence the types, locations, and extent of land that is, and will be important for outdoor recreation (Table 2).

A complexity of factors affects participation rates in outdoor recreation. The demand for outdoor recreation is constantly being altered by the economic and social changes which occur in Canada and which influence the Canadian lifestyle. For example, increases in the world price of petroleum have affected, to varying degrees, the individual's economic status which, in turn, affects the types of recreation available to that person. Gasoline price increases have influenced to some extent the travel patterns of all North Americans. Perhaps the decrease in the participation rate in pleasure driving can be directly related to the increased cost of gasoline. Increasing costs of participation in some activities may also have led to the substitution of less-expensive activities. For example, greater increases in participation have occurred in cross-country skiing as compared to alpine skiing.

Social changes also influence the types of activities in which people participate. In recent years in Canada, considerable effort has been directed at improvement in people's health by encouraging more active participation in outdoor recreation. Notable changes in some of the more participatory activities have taken place. Cross-country skiing, hiking, and jogging have become very popular within a short period of time.

The individual's personal characteristics directly affect the demand for outdoor recreation. Variables in age, sex, health, education, profession, income, ancestry, family size, type of residence, and size of community among other factors influence the types of recreation in which an individual participates (Table 3). From Parks Canada surveys of the participation rate in selected activities according to age, sex, and socio-economic level, it is possible to ascertain which groups are creating particular demands for recreation, and equally important, which groups are not creating demands. The participation rates determined by the national surveys give an indication of the types of recreation desired by Canadians.

The types of land that are essential for providing opportunities for these activities can be determined by relating observed patterns of land use for recreation in different landscapes to the various characteristics of the land. In order to develop methods by which to define lands essential for outdoor recreation in Canada, this report will consider first the physical aspects of the land. These range from very general criteria, such as national climatic variations, to the more specific criteria used in the Canada Land Inventory classification for outdoor recreation. In the second section, present land use is re-

TABLE 1.

Participation rates in selected outdoor activities, by region*, 1976

Activity	Canada	Atlantic	Québec	Ontario	Prairie	Western
(percentage of population 18 years and over)						
Driving for pleasure	66	66	69	68	67	60
Picnicking	57	53	53	58	66	59
Walking or hiking	54	44	62	54	48	54
Swimming	42	41	39	50	40	37
Tent camping	19	17	18	17	19	24
Trailer camping	12	13	9	13	19	12
Canoeing	14	11	15	17	14	12
Cross-country skiing	10	3	22	8	7	6
(percentage of population 14 years and over)						
Tennis	13					
Golf	11	Data not gathered by region			
Alpine skiing	7	(for alpine and cross-country)			

* Regions correspond to administrative regions of Parks Canada.

Sources: Parks Canada, 1977a. *Longitudinal Data on the Participation of Canadians in Outdoor Recreation Activities, 1967-1976.*
Ministry of State for Fitness and Amateur Sport, 1977. *Highlights of the 1976 Fitness and Sport Survey.*

TABLE 2.

Percentage change in the participation rates in selected outdoor activities by region*, 1972 to 1976

Activity	Canada	Atlantic	Québec	Ontario	Prairie	Western
(percentage of population 18 years and over)						
Driving for pleasure	1	0	2	3	-1	-1
Picnicking	2	3	4	1	2	1
Walking or hiking	9	17	10	10	9	7
Swimming	70	-	-	-	-	-
Tent camping	1	6	1	-3	4	0
Trailer camping	5	11	5	8	14	-4
Canoeing	10	65	8	12	21	4
Cross-country skiing	53	33	57	60	53	36
(percentage of population 14 years and over)						
Tennis	197					
Golf	74					
Alpine skiing	153	(for alpine and cross-country)			

* Regions correspond to administrative regions of Parks Canada.

Sources: Parks Canada, 1977a. *Longitudinal Data on the Participation of Canadians in Outdoor Recreation Activities, 1967-1976.*
Ministry of State for Fitness and Amateur Sport, 1977. *Highlights of the 1976 Fitness and Sport Survey.*

TABLE 3.

Variation in participation rates for selected activities, by age, sex, and socio-economic level, 1972

Activity	Age groups (years)			Sex		Socio-economic level				
	30-39	40-49	50+	Male	Female	Upper	Upper-middle	Middle	Lower-middle	Lower
(percentage of population over 10 years of age)										
Picnicking	62	55	36	52	55	59	58	58	50	44
Canoeing	11	6	3	12	8	15	11	9	8	7
Tent camping	21	16	4	22	16	17	20	20	20	18
Hunting	12	11	5	19	3	9	13	11	11	11

Source: Parks Canada, 1973. *Trends in Participation in Outdoor Recreation Activities.*

lated to other factors used in the delineation of prime lands. With an uneven distribution of quality resources for recreation and an equally uneven but different distribution of the user populations, some regions in the country are more important than others for the provision of opportunities for recreation. In the third section, factors related to economic and social conditions are also used to identify localities where land for recreation is essential: for example, in some areas, people are dependent on the attractiveness of resources to tourists for the generation of jobs, income, and the continuation of a particular lifestyle. Finally, the identification of essential lands by various methods leads to discussions of problems and issues in land use.

Physical Factors

Canada's varied physiographic and climatic characteristics provide a multitude of conditions that both Canadians and visitors from other countries consider highly attractive for outdoor recreation. The beaches

NFB PHOTOTHEQUE – ONF – Photo by Duncan Cameron.
Fine summer weather and excellent beaches attract large numbers of Canadian and foreign visitors to Prince Edward Island.

NFB PHOTOTHEQUE – ONF – Photo by Patrick Morrow.
Different seasons and landscapes offer opportunities for other types of outdoor recreation. In British Columbia, Mount Robson provides a challenge to mountaineers.

and pleasant summer weather in Prince Edward Island, and the mountains and snow in Alberta and British Columbia, attract many people. Other physical conditions may be conducive to more specialized activities, for example exploring caves for recreation attracts only a small portion of the population. In this section, several methods are used to define and classify important recreation lands using climatic and physiographic criteria.

Climate

The opportunity to participate in most outdoor activities and the satisfaction that is gained is highly dependent on daily changes in the weather. Rainy days have ruined many camping trips or days at the beach. Even more important than daily changes in the weather are the climatic variations. Land in Canada extends from Middle Island (41°41′) in Lake Erie to the northern tip of Ellesmere Island. Altitude varies from Mount Logan at 4,862 m to sea level along 71,261 km of coastline, so there are many climatic conditions that both encourage and limit outdoor activities.

Climatic information can be used to classify areas for recreation in several ways. The simplest method is illustrated in Map 1. More refined methods are used to determine the suitability of both specific locations and broad areas for outdoor recreation and tourism. The Meteorological Applications Branch of the Atmospheric Environment Service of Environment Canada has done important research in various parts of Canada on the application of meteorological information for development of outdoor recreation and tourism. Part of the research involved the development of methodologies in classification and comparison of the suitability of cities and regions for general outdoor recreation and selected popular activities. A recent publication describes and applies these methods to the Prairie Provinces (Masterton et al., 1976).

Particular types of outdoor activities can be related to the marked seasonal variations in climate which occur in Canada. In Figure 1, the schematic representation of seasonal patterns in recreation is adaptable to any location. In Figure 2, the criteria used to differentiate seasons in the schematic representation are applied to the three provincial capitals of the Prairies. From this it is possible to compare the cities as to their suitability for various types of activities. For example, Regina has 11 more days of complete summer than Edmonton and 19 more days of high summer i.e. that period when activities on beaches are most enjoyable. Such differences can greatly influence the patterns of recreation in an area and thus the demands on particular lands.

This approach can be expanded so that each community can be evaluated, and, from these data, it is possible to extrapolate and identify the suitability of areas for outdoor recreation at various times of the year. The classification of areas by their appropriateness for a variety of outdoor recreation and its application to the Prairie Region is a significant and unique method with which to define lands most suitable for recreation. The method is made up of three stages: definition of activity groups; development of the concept of suitable days for activities and selection of criteria; and the calculation and analysis of suitable days for activities.

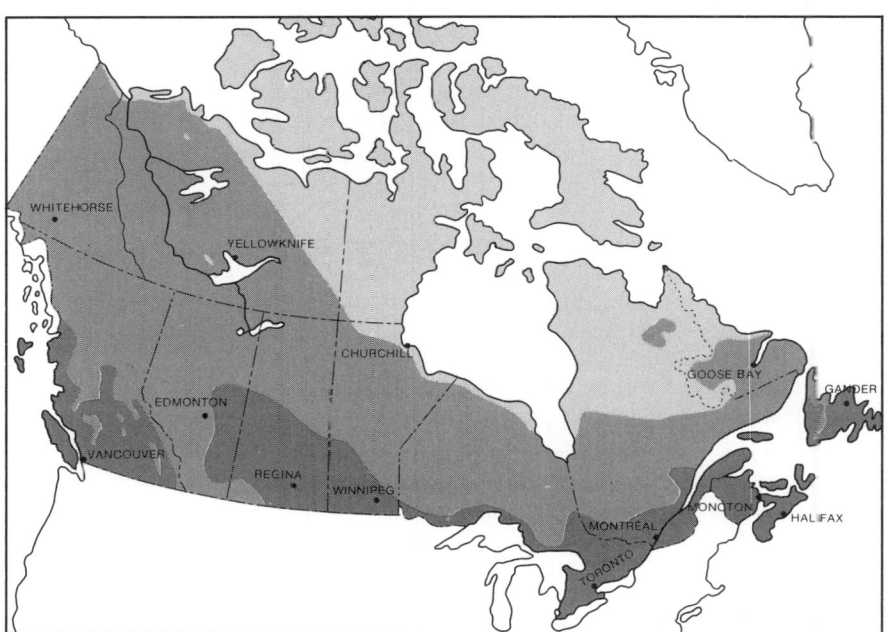

Source: Statistics Canada, 1975b. Canada 1976.

MAP 1
SUMMER AND WINTER RECREATIONAL PERIODS

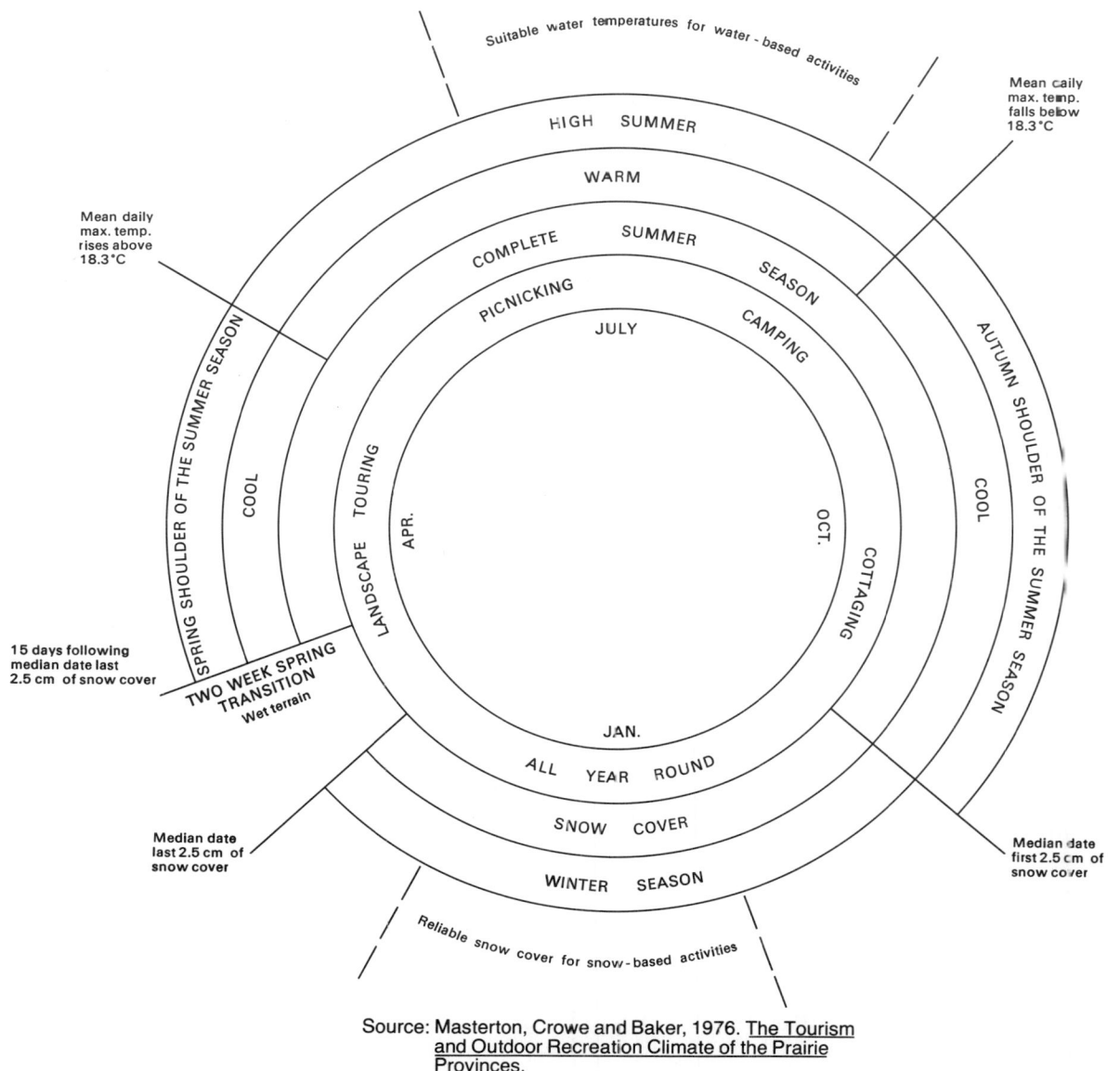

FIGURE 1. Schematic representation of recreation seasonal patterns at any typical location

Source: Masterton, Crowe and Baker, 1976. The Tourism and Outdoor Recreation Climate of the Prairie Provinces.

Recreational Activity Groupings

"The multiplicity of outdoor leisure-time activities currently enjoyed by North Americans can be grouped conveniently into six, broad climate-related categories as follows:

Year-round Pursuits
– landscape touring

Winter Pursuits
– skiing
– snowmobiling

Summer Pursuits
– passive activities
– vigorous activities
– beaching activities

Driving for pleasure and landscape touring, while most popular during summer season, also take place during winter when climatic and road conditions permit. Among the climatic determinants of satisfaction, visibility is of prime importance. Temperature conditions are less consequential because of the insulation and heating system of the automobile.

Downhill and cross-country skiing, snowshoeing, snowmobiling, tobogganing, ice fishing and skating are all winter activities requiring a suitable snow and/or ice base, reasonable visibility, and temperatures which never become too severe. In this study, winter climatic quality is evaluated in relation to skiing and snowmobiling, with the only significant difference between the requirements for the two being the lower threshold temperature allowed for snowmobiling. The pattern revealed by this analysis is considered a reasonable indication of quality conditions for the two activities.

The many forms of recreation enjoyed during warm summer weather have been classified into three general categories.

Passive activities require little participant energy expenditure. Unseasonable cool weather may detract from the enjoyment of such activities as reading and relaxing out-of-doors and leisurely gardening, walking and picnicking. The occurrence of precipitation may inhibit or markedly reduce the enjoyment of these activities.

Vigorous activities demand more participant energy expenditure and include sports such as football, volleyball, bicycling and soccer. High temperature in combination with high humidity is a major limiting factor. The occurrence of precipitation is a hindrance that may be virtually inhibiting on occasion.

Beaching activities, particularly when sun exposure is a primary objective as in sunbathing, require a high degree of warmth to be enjoyable. Swimming and other water-based activities displaying strong water temperature correlations are discussed subsequently. (*See* Table 4).

The Concept of Suitable Activity Day

Criteria for specific outdoor activities must be qualified if spatial and temporal analysis is to be achieved. Admittedly, there is a considerable degree of subjectivity in this process. The concept of a suitable day for various activities or activity groupings forms the basis for quality evaluation (Crowe *et al.*, 1973; and Gates, 1975). The climatic conditions considered necessary for the designation of any day as suitable for particular activities are as follows:

Conditions must have been fulfilled simultaneously for at least five hours (not necessarily consecutive) between 10:00 a.m. and 6:00 p.m., local standard time.

If the conditions were met, the assumption is made that the majority of actual or prospective participants in a particular activity or activity grouping would consider the weather satisfactory. It is important to note that conditions may have exceeded the minimum requirements. In effect, some days may have been more suitable than others. In general, the greater the number of suitable days, the stronger the climatic potential for a given activity or activity grouping. (*See* Maps 2 to 7 *inclusive*).

Calculation and Analysis of Suitable Activity Days

A computer program was prepared to calculate the mean frequency of suitable days for landscape touring, passive activities, beaching activities, skiing, and snowmobiling from the hourly weather data for 60 stations by ten-day intervals within each month. The results were treated and mapped by two distinct procedures.

Initially, frequencies for suitable days by ten-day intervals for the various activities and activity groupings were converted to percentages on the basis of the total number of possible days. For example, the print-out from this program for Medicine Hat, Alberta, shows that of the 200 days occurring in the second third of July between 1953 and 1972, inclusive, satisfactory conditions for passive activities were present 169 days, or 85 per cent of the time. (*See in* Figure 2 *further examples of this step*). On the average, therefore, eight or nine of the middle ten days of July (11th to the 20th) were climatically suitable for this activity grouping. The actual number of suitable days varied from year to year, there being as few as five in 1962, and as many as ten in 1959, 1960, 1964 and 1969.

Secondly, the number of suitable days accumulated during the summer and winter seasons for each of the related activities or activity groupings were determined for the stations and the results mapped. On the basis of the range of values displayed, three quality classes were distinguished, and this provided the data base for seasonal quality discussion." (*See* Maps 6 and 7). (Masterton *et al.*, 1976).

FIGURE 2. Timelines for tourism and recreation seasons at Edmonton, Regina and Winnipeg

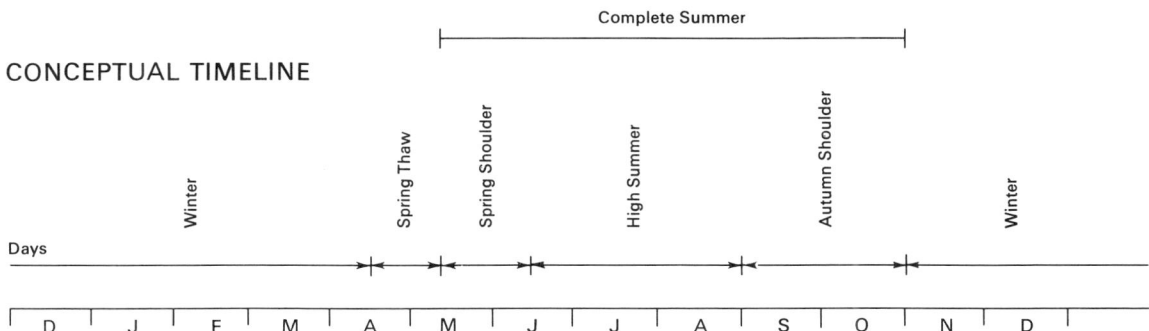
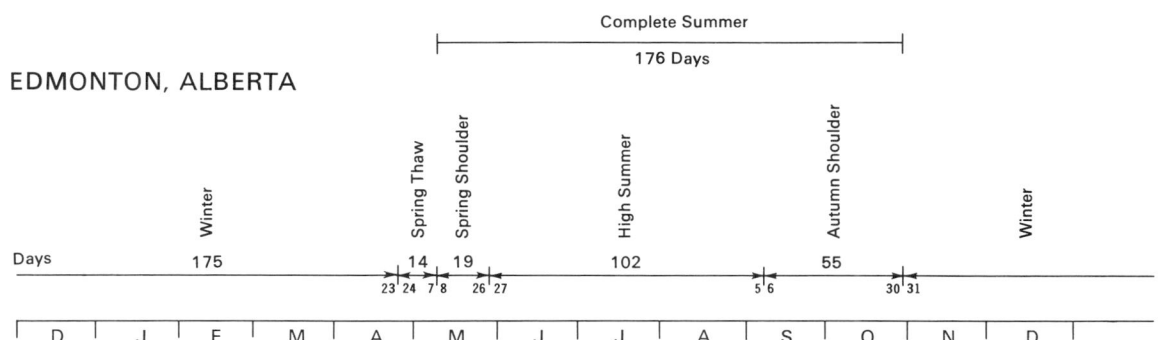
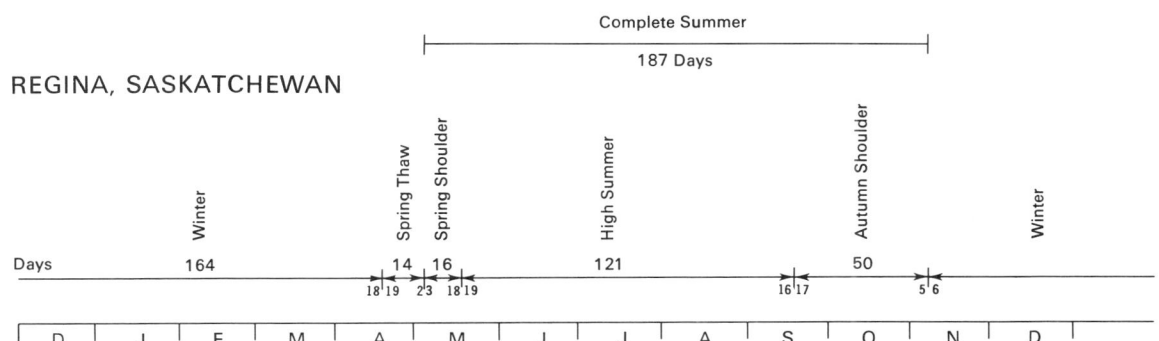
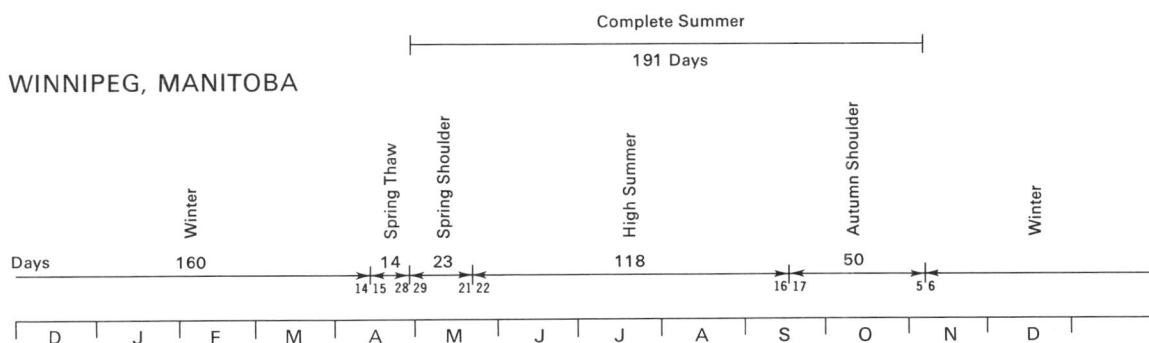

Source: Masterton, Crowe and Baker, 1976. *The Tourism and Outdoor Recreation Climate of the Prairie Provinces.*

TABLE 4.

Climatic criteria for designation of a suitable day, by activity or activity grouping

Activity	Temperature (°C)	Visibility (km)	Cloud cover (tenths)	Wind Speed (km/h)	Snow cover (cm)	Precipitation
Landscape touring	-24.4 to 31.7	> 4.8	N/A	< 41.6	N/A	nil
Skiing	> -14.1	> 0.8	N/A	< 25.6	> 2.5	nil or light
Snowmobiling	> -21.2	> 0.8	N/A	< 25.6	> 2.5	nil or light
Passive activities	> 12.2	> 3.2	< 8	< 33.6	N/A	nil
Vigorous activities	12.2 to 31.7	> 3.2	< 8	< 33.6	N/A	nil
Beaching activities	> 17.8	> 1.6	< 8	< 25.6	N/A	nil

N/A means not applicable.

Source: Masterton, *et. al.*, 1976. *The Tourism and Outdoor Recreation Climate of the Prairie Provinces.*

MAP 2

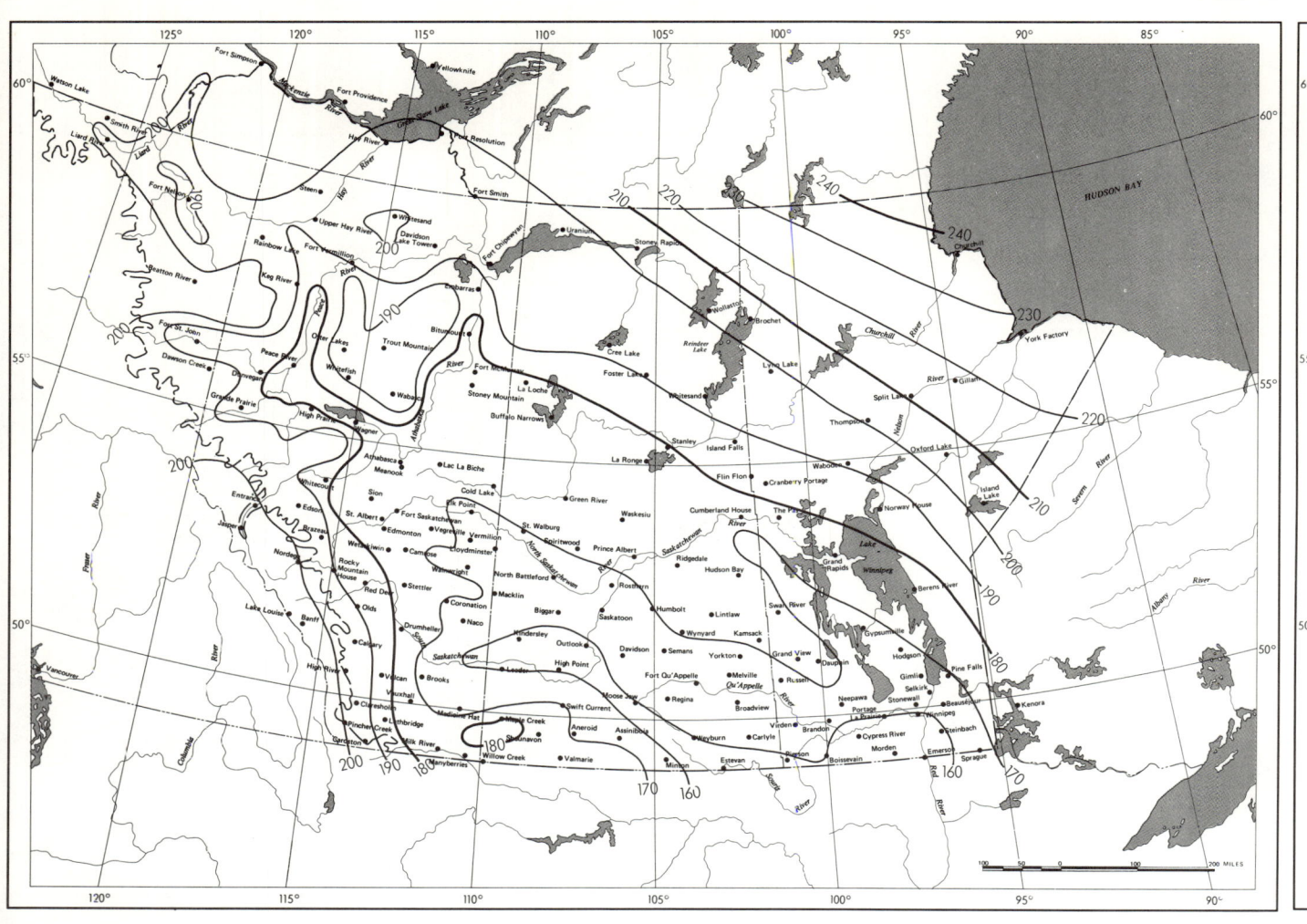
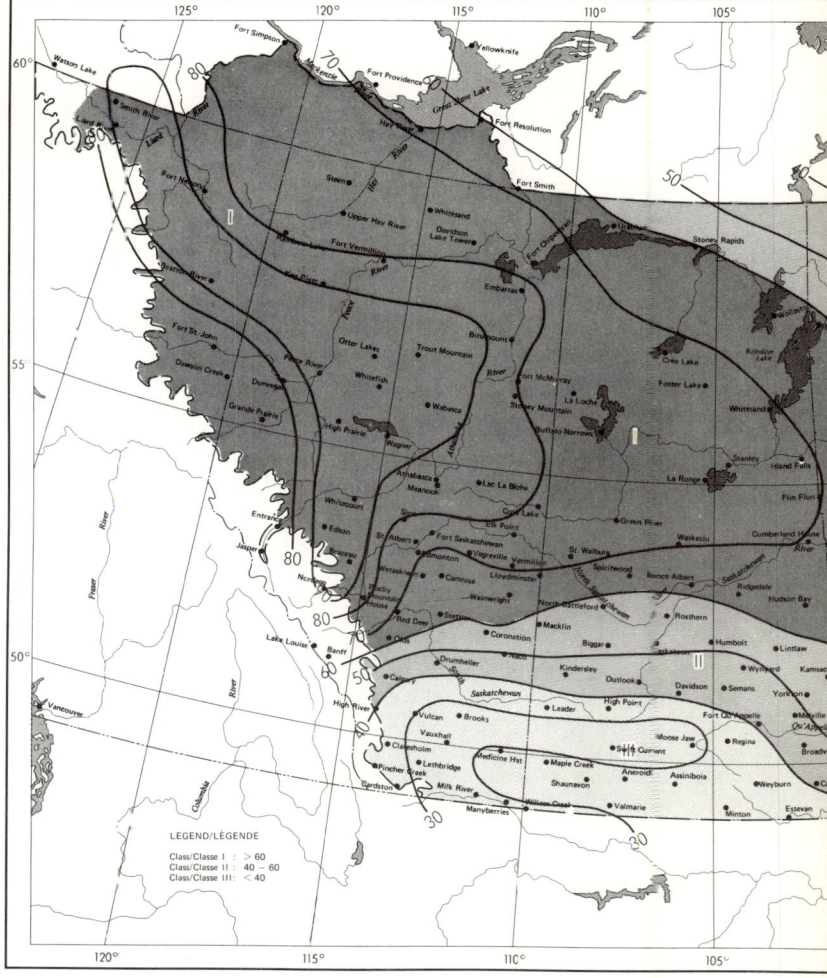

Duration of the winter season in days

Number of days suitable for skiing dur

MAP 3

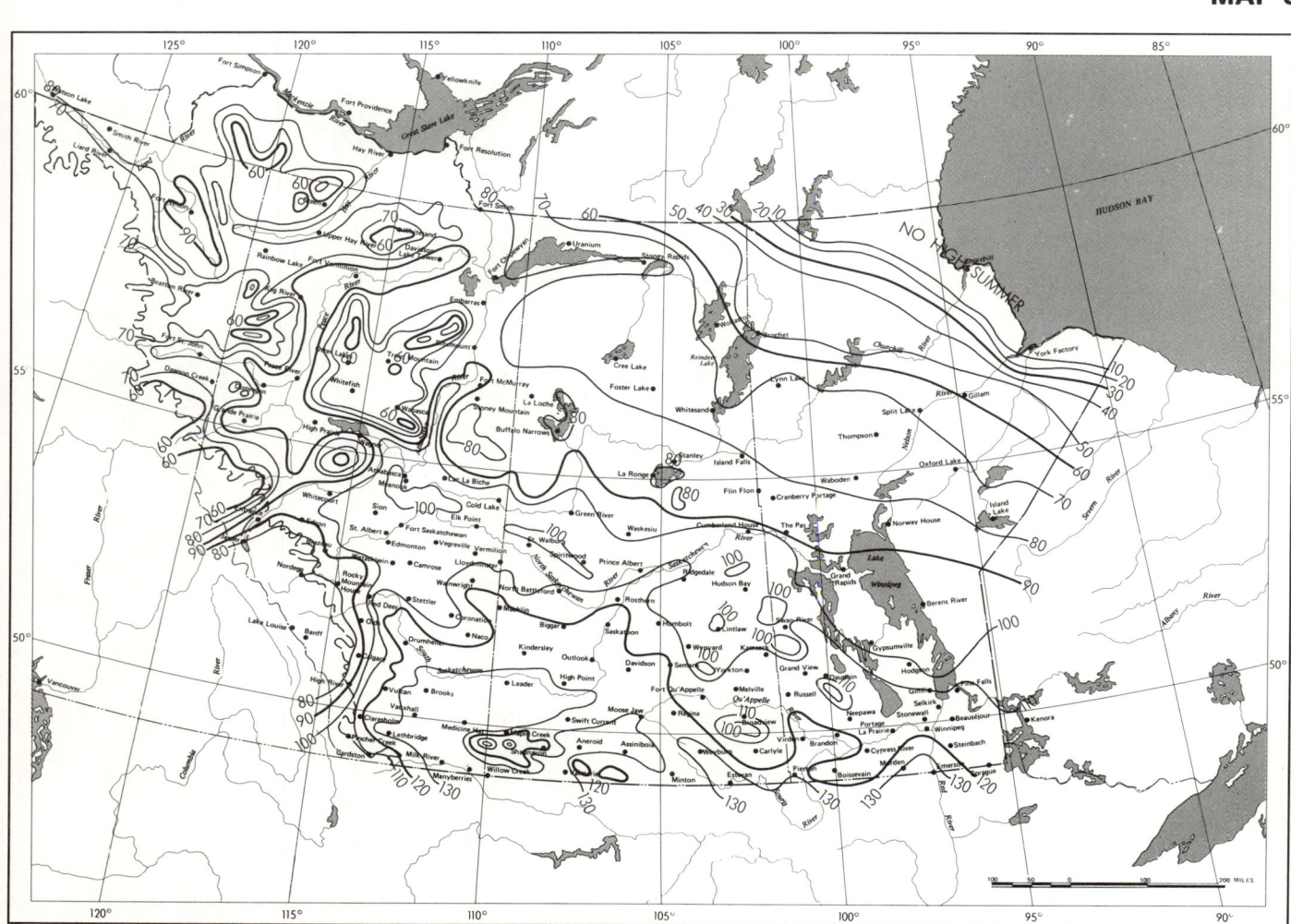
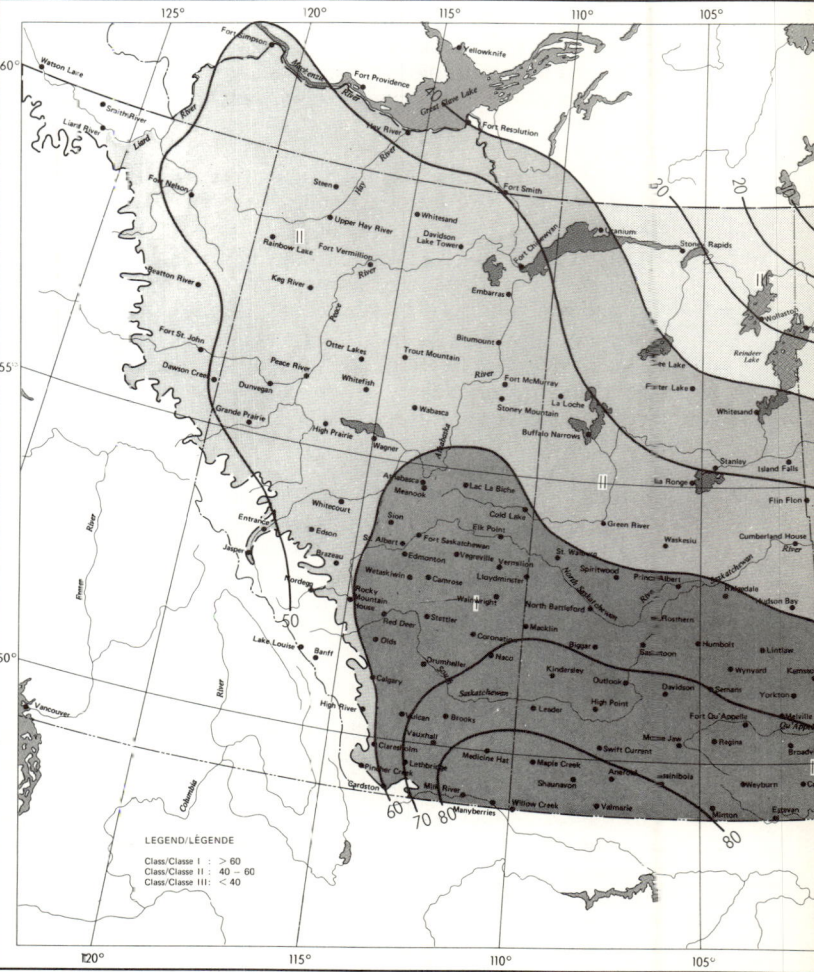

Duration of high summer in days

Number of days suitable for passive activities du

The above maps have been selected from the following publication: Masterton, J.M., Crowe, R.B., and Baker, W.M., 1976.
The Tourism and Outdoor Recreation Climate of the Prairie Provinces. Meteorological Applications Branch, Environment Canada. Toronto.

MAP 4

MAP 6

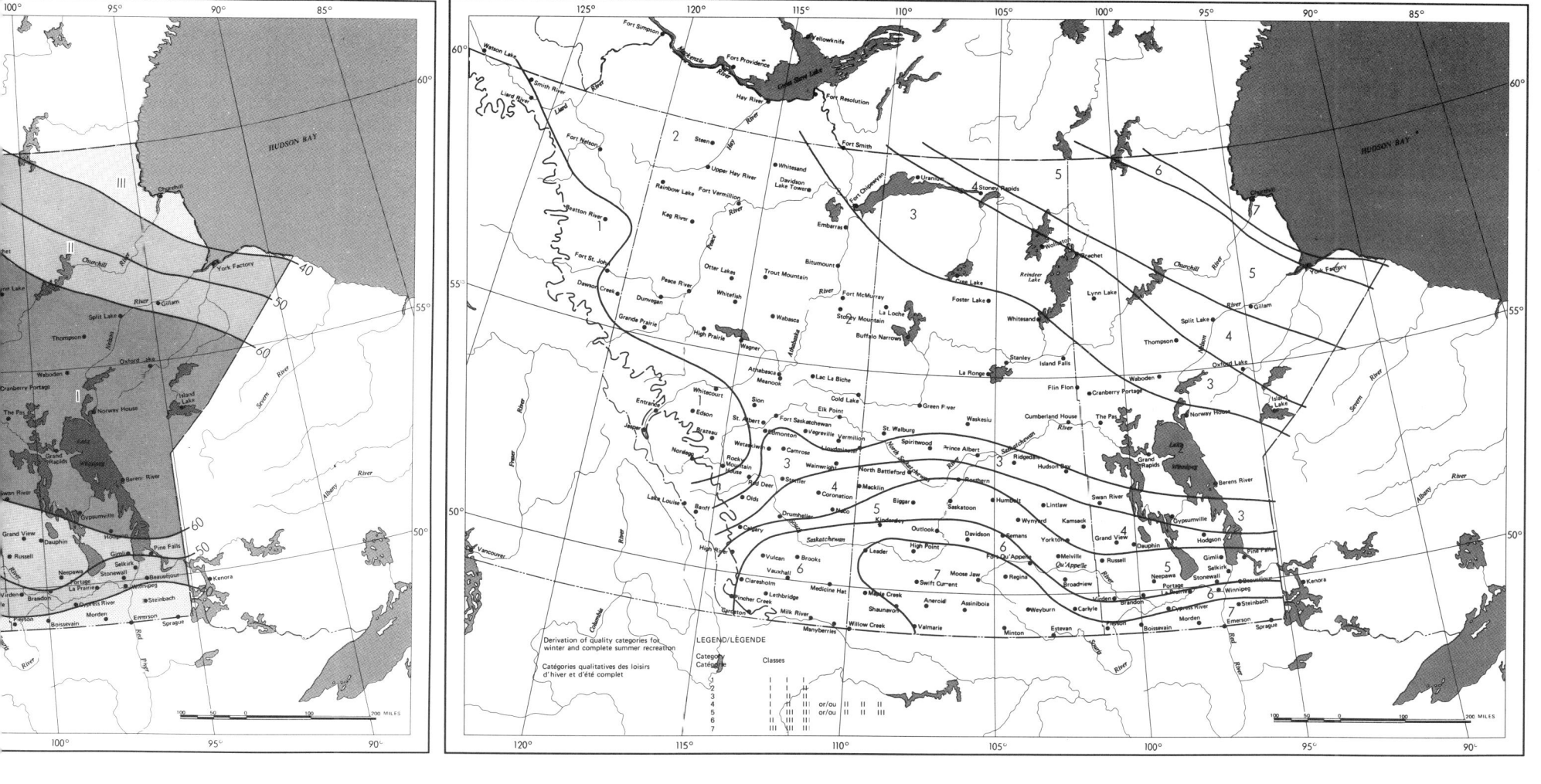

Climatic suitability for all winter outdoor recreational activities

MAP 5

MAP 7

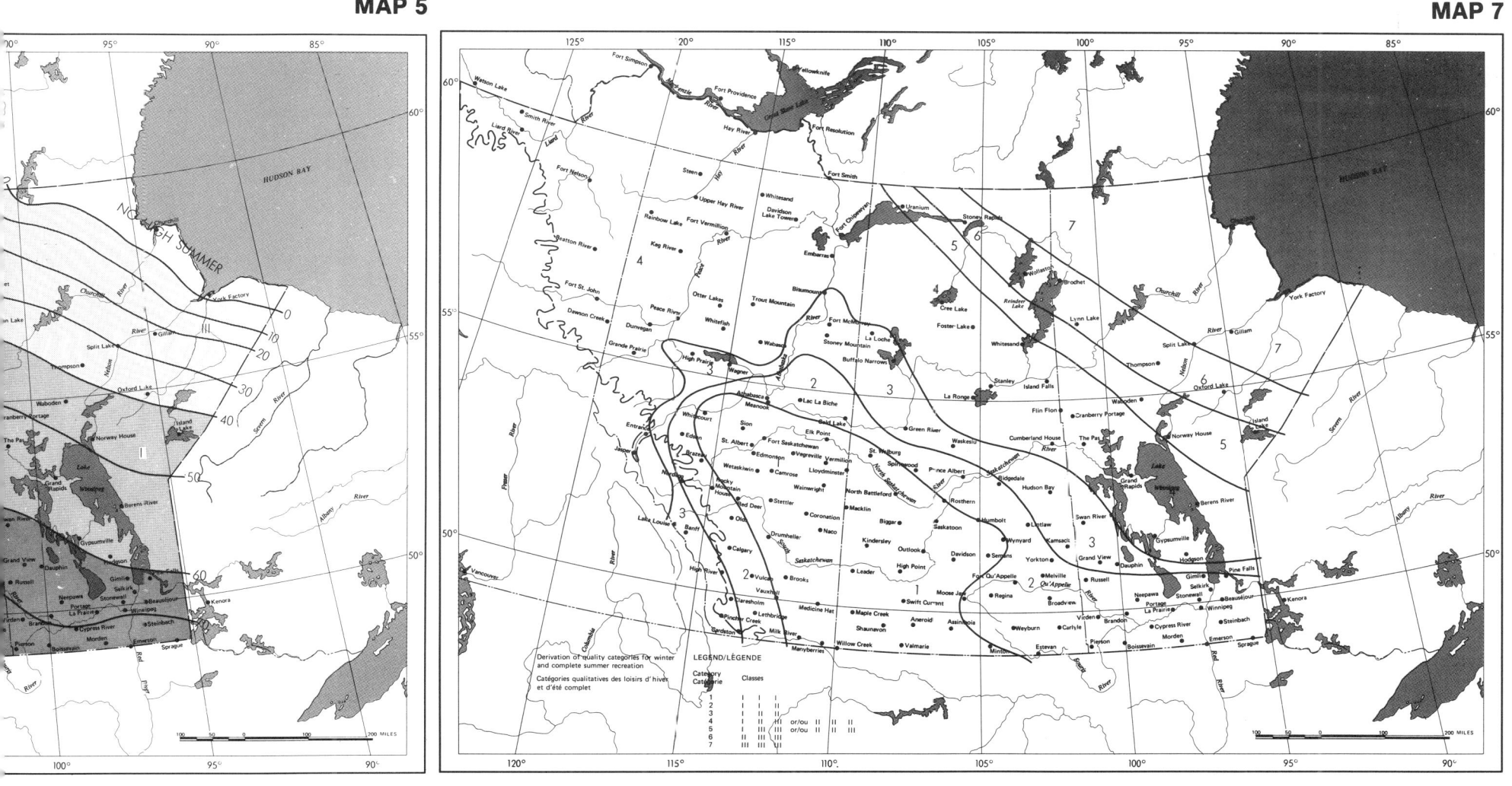

Climatic suitability for all complete summer outdoor recreational activities

MAP 2-7

Canadian Government Office of Tourism photo.

MAP 8

Photo by H.A. Roberts.

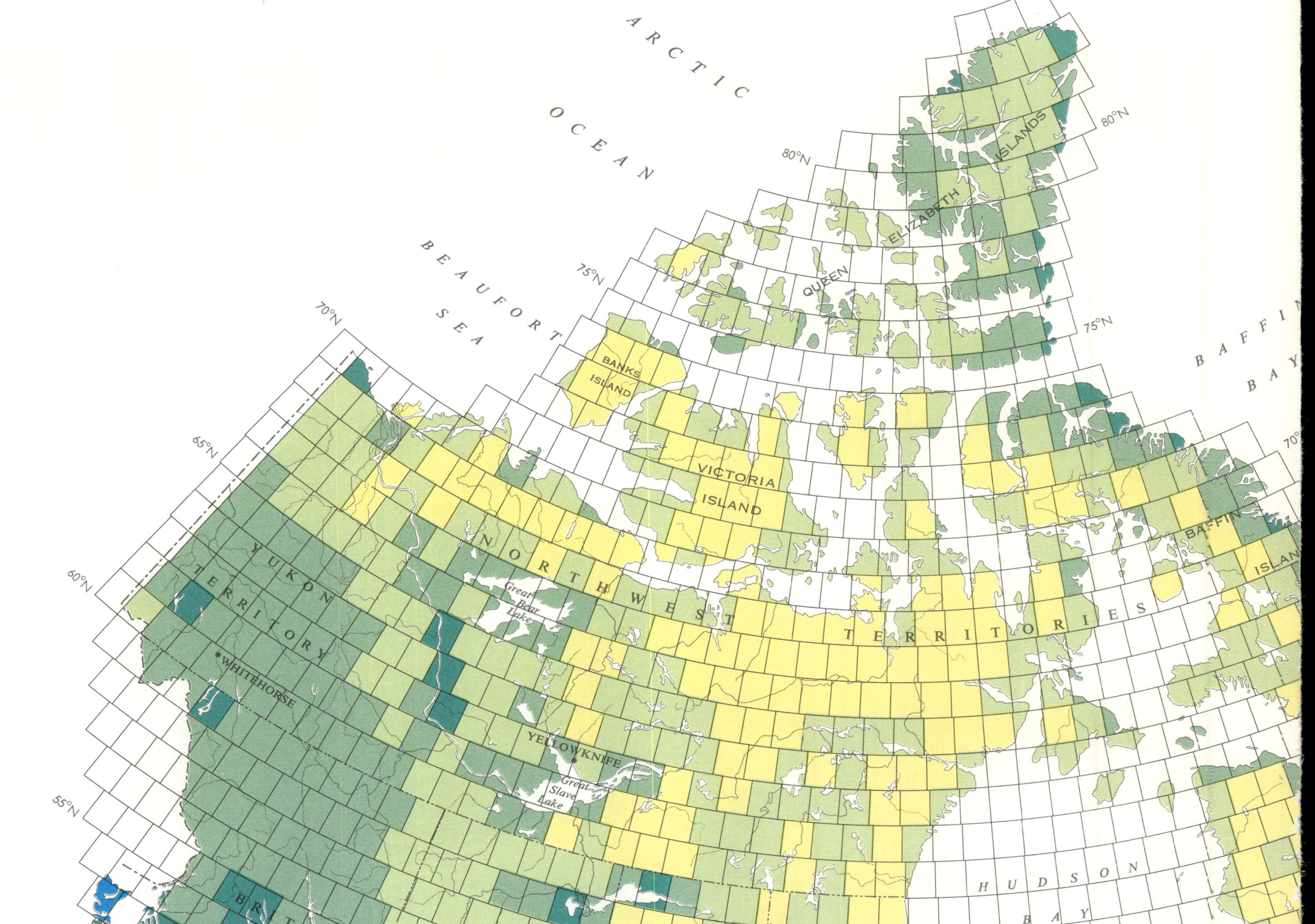

Scale 1: 15,000,000

Kilometres 100 0 200 400 600 Kilometres

Miles 100 0 100 200 300 400 Miles

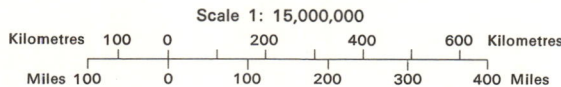

Base map and grid produced by Surveys and Mapping Branch, Department of Energy, Mines and Resources, Ottawa.

INDEX OF CANADA'S LANDSCAPE ATTRACTIVITY FOR OUTDOOR RECREATION

LEGEND

Total Rank for Each Grid Unit	Landscape Attractivity
3-6	low attraction
7-8	
9-10	moderate attraction
11-12	
13-15	high attraction

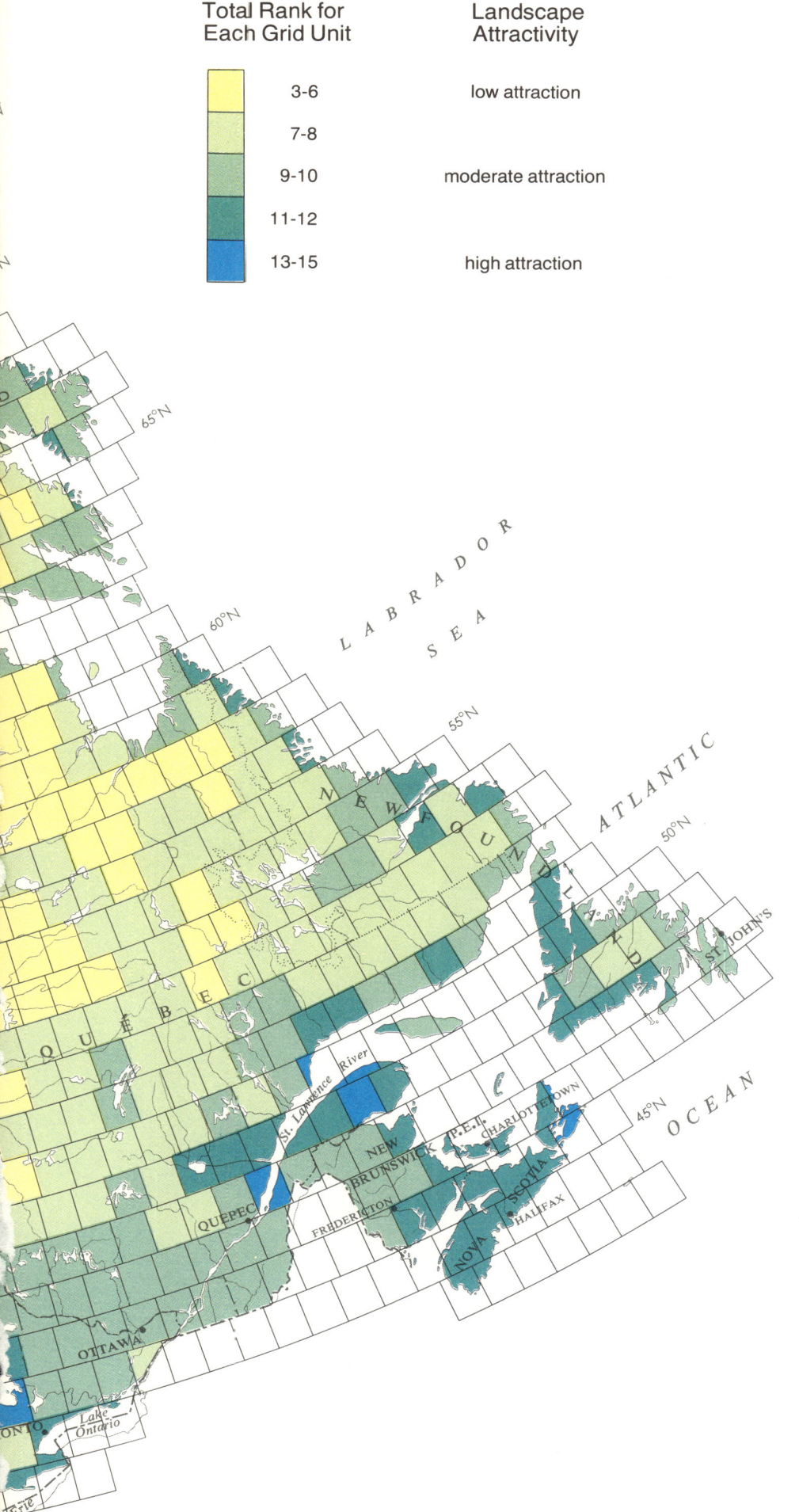

METHODOLOGY

COMPONENTS	CRITERIA		RANK
RELATIVE TOPOGRAPHIC RELIEF	RELIEF CLASSES:	less than 92 metres	1
		92-305 metres	2
		306-610 metres	3
		611-1067 metres	4
		greater than 1067 metres	5
VEGETATION REGIONS	FORMATION TYPES:	GENERAL CHARACTERISTICS:	
	Areas with almost no vegetation	Glaciers and permanent snowfields.	1
	Tundra	Lichen, sedges, shrubs.	
	Bogs/Organic Terrain	Moss and sedge, strings of needle-leaf trees.	
	Tundra-Open Woodland and Open Woodland	Lichen, shrubs, patches of needle-leaf trees. Lichen, scattered needleleaf trees.	
	Forest-Boreal	Needleleaf trees, some shrub and barren patches.	2
	Parkland	Broadleaf and needleleaf trees with patches of grassland.	3
	Grassland	Low, medium and tall grass.	
	Forest-Boreal	Needleleaf and boreal broadleaf, some southern broadleaf and western coniferous trees.	4
	- Pacific Coastal and Interior 'Wet Belt'	Needleleaf trees.	
	- Subalpine	Needleleaf trees often with an open distribution.	
	Forest		5
	- Plateau-Montane	Needleleaf, boreal broadleaf trees, some grassland.	
	- Southeastern Mixed	Needleleaf and broadleaf trees.	
	- Southern Broadleaf	Broadleaf trees.	
PRESENCE OF WATER	FRESH WATER: Area of Water as a percentage of grid units 10,000 square kilometres in area	Trace - 4%	1
		5 - 11%	2
		12 - 18%	3
		19 - 30%	4
		31 - 99%	5
	SALT WATER: Units with salt water area were increased in rank according to the percentage of area per unit. (Measurements are approximate).	Less than 5% — no increase	
		5 - 10% — plus 1 rank	
		11 - 15% — plus 2 ranks	
		16 - 25% — plus 3 ranks	
		greater than 25% — plus 4 ranks	

Sources: Relative relief data are derived from preliminary compilation by the Surveys and Mapping Branch, Department of Energy, Mines and Resources, Ottawa.

Vegetation regions and presence of water data are taken from The National Atlas of Canada produced by the Department of Energy, Mines and Resources, Ottawa, 1974.

This method, as applied to the three Prairie Provinces, is illustrated using a number of maps. Maps 2 and 3 indicate the duration of the winter and high summer seasons; Maps 4 and 5 are used as examples of the results obtained from mapping suitability days for different recreation activities, in these cases skiing and passive summer activities; and, Maps 6 and 7 indicate the climatic suitability for all winter and all complete summer recreation activities.

Problems develop, however, if this same method with the identical criteria is extended to all of Canada. The subjective nature of the criteria becomes questionable and unreliable when the method is applied across regions with different climatic conditions. For example, the minimum acceptable temperature for passive activities in the Yukon may be significantly lower than in southern Ontario. However, since it defines and classifies areas of different attractiveness for recreation, this method is one with which to define the most suitable areas for outdoor recreation within climatic regions.

Landscape Evaluation for Outdoor Recreation

In addition to the variety of climatic conditions in Canada, outdoor activities are also influenced by biophysical elements of the landscape. The patterns of rock, soil, water, and vegetation are combined in many attractive ways. The appeal that these various landscapes have for outdoor recreation is, however, difficult to evaluate.

In a wide range of activities, each has different requirements for resources. For example, landscapes which are suitable habitats for deer or moose, and which are thus attractive to hunters, would not necessarily appeal most to hikers or cross-country skiers. An additional problem in the measurement of a landscape's attractiveness arises from the variety of backgrounds and experiences of the viewers who may perceive attractiveness differently. Someone who has experienced only a limited variety of landscape types may be more impressed by a new landscape than one who has travelled widely. Thus, any method used to assess landscapes for recreation will be subjective and open to exceptions.

In the many studies which have been done to classify and rank landscapes for various activities[1], certain common premises exist. For example, landscapes which are rare in their combination of components are perceived to be more attractive than those that are common to many regions. For the most part, however, past studies have indicated that it is the variety in the components of a landscape which chiefly determine its attractiveness for recreation.

For a national perspective on lands considered essential for outdoor recreation, a methodology for the evaluation of attractiveness of landscape has been developed and applied to all of Canada. Its basic premise is that landscapes in which there is a variety of topography, vegetation, and water, are attractive for the general appreciation of landscape such as might occur when driving for pleasure. These three physical components of landscape were chosen as a basis for an index of attractivity. The components, the classes and the assigned ranking for each class are indicated in the evaluation methodology presented on Map 8. The process for the selection of the components, the classes and ranks was subjective, and any changes would result in a significantly different pattern on the map. In this classification, accessibility was not evaluated. The present and past land uses, which provide the cultural component in many landscapes and are often an attractive aspect, were also not considered. Once the criteria were established, the ranking for each component was assigned to a grid unit of 10,000 km². For each grid unit there are three scores, and their total represents the index. The range in the index is 3 to 15. Again an arbitrary division in this range was made in order to produce five classes, each of which was colour coded for each grid unit as seen on Map 8. The pattern suggests that major shorelines and mountainous areas are the most attractive. This method does not identify some attractive features such as glaciers, as, for example, is shown by the lower class in the south-western grid unit of the Yukon Territory, which includes parts of Kluane National Park. The insensitivity of this approach is such that it will not identify many of the special, rare, or uniquely attractive areas in Canada. These must be identified at a more detailed level, or by other methods. This approach does, however, represent one method of evaluating at the national scale, the varied landscapes of Canada as to their attractiveness for general outdoor recreation activities.

[1] A recent publication (Arthur and Boster, 1976) gives an annotated bibliography of the major methods used in the United States. In Canada, studies by Jurand (1972), Coomber (1971), and Parks Canada (1976a) are relevant.

Photo by K.G. Taylor.

Landscapes which possess a variety of topography, vegetation, and water are regarded as most attractive for general outdoor recreation activities. This alpine meadow near Lake O'Hara in British Columbia provides a picturesque setting for wilderness camping.

Canadian Government Office of Tourism photo.

Natural Areas of Canadian Significance

Another method identifies important resource lands for recreation using more-selective criteria. Some natural areas are considered either unique or particularly representative of various regions in Canada. Although such areas are not necessarily useful for a large variety of recreation activities, they are generally spectacular or very special natural areas which are attractive to the public, and represent a significant, although often fragile, resource for some outdoor activities.

An inventory program by Parks Canada for the identification of these areas has continued for a number of years. Its objective is to ensure that areas which adequately represent each of a number of "natural regions" in Canada are preserved. By identifying these significant areas it is hoped that the natural heritage will be protected either within the National Parks System or by other federal, provincial, or territorial agencies, private organizations or individuals, for the lasting benefit, education, and enjoyment of Canadians.

The method used to define these natural areas differs from those methods described previously. The park planning program uses 39 terrestrial "natural regions" that cover all of Canada, in order to select representative, unique, or natural areas. To identify sites within each region, the following criteria are considered:

"*Representativeness* – one of the 'best' sample areas representing the characteristic features of a natural region or natural history theme; or

Uniqueness – an area that encompasses features that are unique, rare, or 'one-of-a-kind' to distinguish them significantly from other parts of the natural region; and

Naturalness – the area must be either in a relatively natural state or, if modified by man, capable of a high degree of restoration to natural conditions." (Parks Canada, 1976*b*)

This method is very selective in the classification of areas, for only the most significant areas are identified (Map 9). Some of the better-known areas already identified include: Sable Island (Nova Scotia), the Torngat Mountains (Labrador), Long Point (Ontario), the headwaters of the Bloodvein River in Ontario and Manitoba, the Athabasca Sand Dunes (Saskatchewan), the Cypress Hills (Saskatchewan and Alberta), the Firth River/British Mountains (Yukon), and the Pingos of the Tuktoyaktuk Peninsula (Northwest Territories). No spatial definitions are applied to the sites, that is, no boundaries are given. Several of the special sites defined in this way may also be identified by the other classification systems described here.

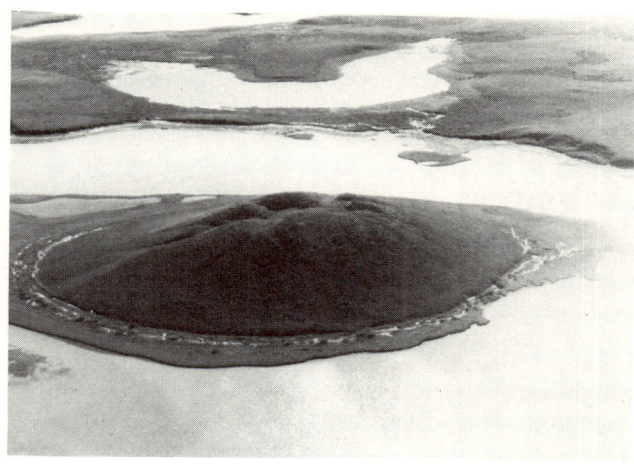

Photo by K.G. Taylor.

The pingos of the Tuktoyaktuk Peninsula are one example of the natural areas identified by Parks Canada for protection.

MAP 9
NATURAL AREAS OF CANADIAN SIGNIFICANCE

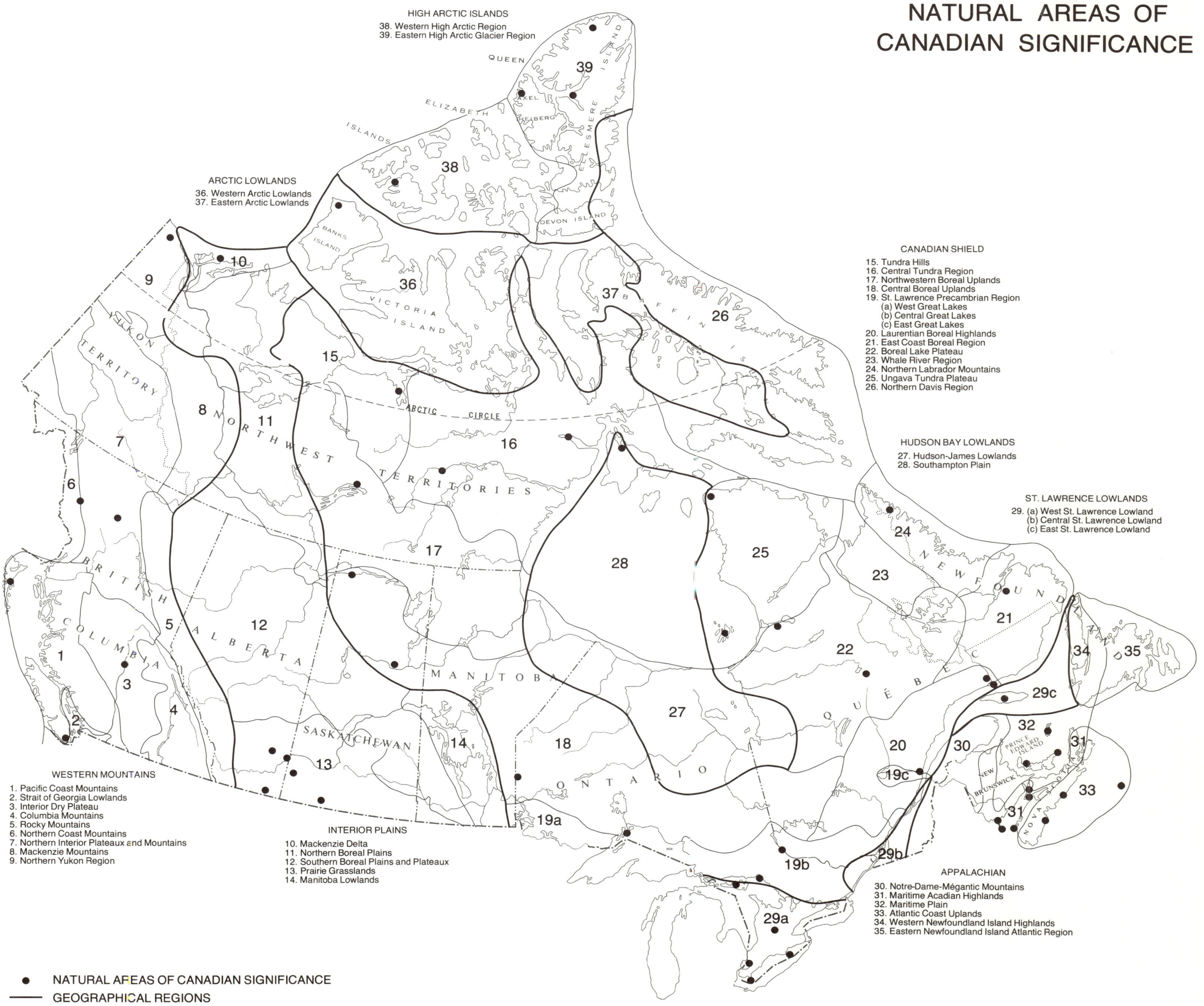
HIGH ARCTIC ISLANDS
38. Western High Arctic Region
39. Eastern High Arctic Glacier Region
ARCTIC LOWLANDS
36. Western Arctic Lowlands
37. Eastern Arctic Lowlands
CANADIAN SHIELD
15. Tundra Hills
16. Central Tundra Region
17. Northwestern Boreal Uplands
18. Central Boreal Uplands
19. St. Lawrence Precambrian Region
(a) West Great Lakes
(b) Central Great Lakes
(c) East Great Lakes
20. Laurentian Boreal Highlands
21. East Coast Boreal Region
22. Boreal Lake Plateau
23. Whale River Region
24. Northern Labrador Mountains
25. Ungava Tundra Plateau
26. Northern Davis Region
HUDSON BAY LOWLANDS
27. Hudson-James Lowlands
28. Southampton Plain
ST. LAWRENCE LOWLANDS
29. (a) West St. Lawrence Lowland
(b) Central St. Lawrence Lowland
(c) East St. Lawrence Lowland
WESTERN MOUNTAINS
1. Pacific Coast Mountains
2. Strait of Georgia Lowlands
3. Interior Dry Plateau
4. Columbia Mountains
5. Rocky Mountains
6. Northern Coast Mountains
7. Northern Interior Plateaux and Mountains
8. Mackenzie Mountains
9. Northern Yukon Region
INTERIOR PLAINS
10. Mackenzie Delta
11. Northern Boreal Plains
12. Southern Boreal Plains and Plateaux
13. Prairie Grasslands
14. Manitoba Lowlands
APPALACHIAN
30. Notre-Dame-Mégantic Mountains
31. Maritime Acadian Highlands
32. Maritime Plain
33. Atlantic Coast Uplands
34. Western Newfoundland Island Highlands
35. Eastern Newfoundland Island Atlantic Region
QUEEN ELIZABETH ISLANDS
AXEL HEIBERG
ELLESMERE ISLAND
DEVON ISLAND
BANKS ISLAND
VICTORIA ISLAND
BAFFIN IS
ARCTIC CIRCLE
YUKON TERRITORY
NORTHWEST TERRITORIES
BRITISH COLUMBIA
ALBERTA
SASKATCHEWAN
MANITOBA
ONTARIO
QUÉBEC
NEWFOUNDLAND
PRINCE EDWARD ISLAND
NEW BRUNSWICK
NOVA

- ● NATURAL AREAS OF CANADIAN SIGNIFICANCE
- ━ GEOGRAPHICAL REGIONS
- ─ NATIONAL PARKS NATURAL REGIONS

Scale 1: 20,000,000

Kilometres 200 0 200 400 600 Kilometres

Miles 200 0 200 400 Miles

Base map produced by Surveys and Mapping Branch, Department of Energy, Mines and Resources, Ottawa.

Source: Parks Canada, 1976*b*.

Wild Rivers as Critical Areas

"Wild rivers are a priceless part of our natural heritage. These waterways, untouched by the march of man's technological progress, are the arteries of our land, and one of the main elements in its growth to nationhood". (Parks Canada, 1976*a*)

Wild rivers are significant natural features providing opportunities for recreation, but they have characteristics which are highly susceptible to the effects of other resource demands. The methods described previously may have defined portions of Canada's wild rivers, as many of them are situated within natural areas of significance to Canada. However, due to their linear extent through various landscapes, most will have escaped recognition.

In the Wild River Survey conducted between 1971 and 1973, the scenic resources of the major wild rivers in Canada were identified and evaluated by Parks Canada. This program involved the selection of rivers with representative bio-physical elements. The major drainage basins were defined and, from each, at least one river was selected for study to ensure that the biological distinctions, which exist among the basins would be represented. To meet the need that physiographic variations be represented, additional rivers found in each of the major physiographic regions of Canada were selected. These regions are compatible with the "natural regions" defined in other Parks Canada system planning programs. From the large number of rivers that were identified, 67 were chosen to be inventoried (Map 10).

In addition to the inventory of the rivers, an evaluation of the scenic resources was also completed. The method used is similar to the technique described in the evaluation of landscapes, although the criteria are more inclusive and are directed at that particular type of landscape associated with wild rivers. The results show that river landscapes with the most scenic appeal have a mixture of topography, diverse and luxurious vegetation, and the presence of waterfalls and rapids.

Wild rivers are directly associated with activities of both white-water and still-water canoeing and wilderness adventure. Their importance, however, seems to extend beyond the actual activity. They represent a type of landscape and resource that non-participants also appreciate. Their past use as exploration and trade routes gives them historical importance. A more intangible benefit provided by these rivers is the knowledge that there exist in Canada, places that are still wild and open to the challenges of future generations.

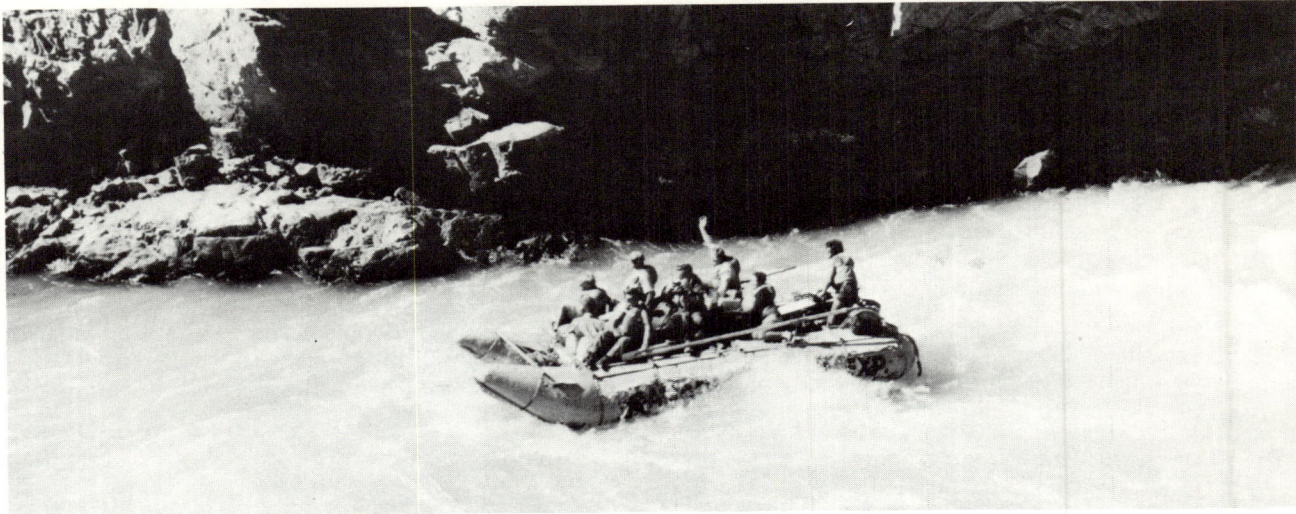

NFB PHOTOTHEQUE – ONF – Photo by George Hunter.

Wild rivers, such as the Chilcotin in British Columbia, offer a variety of canoe and wilderness adventures. Here, rafters are shown shooting the rapids in Farewell Canyon.

MAP 10
WILD RIVERS SURVEYED*

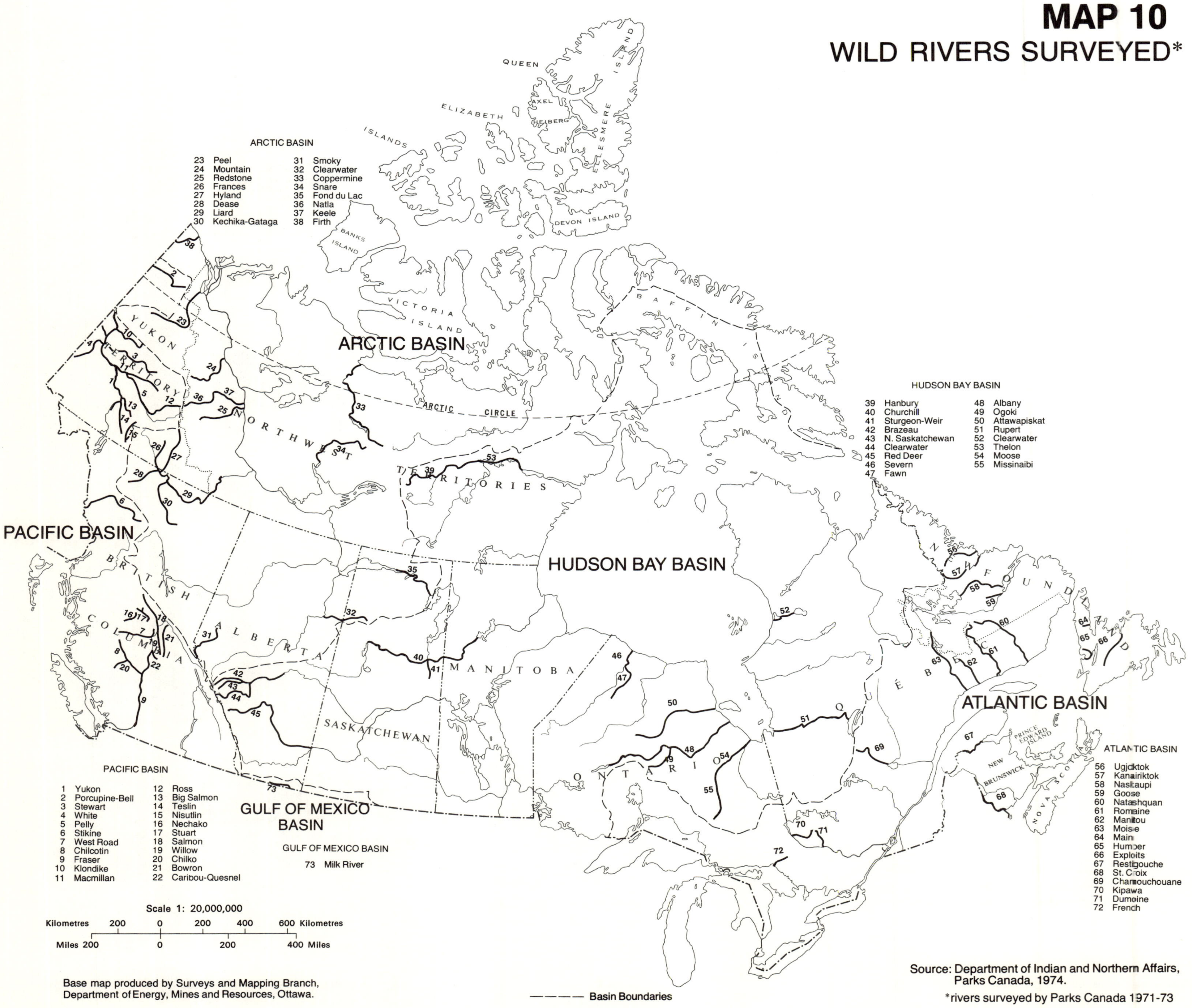
ARCTIC BASIN
23 Peel
24 Mountain
25 Redstone
26 Frances
27 Hyland
28 Dease
29 Liard
30 Kechika-Gataga
31 Smoky
32 Clearwater
33 Coppermine
34 Snare
35 Fond du Lac
36 Natla
37 Keele
38 Firth
HUDSON BAY BASIN
39 Hanbury
40 Churchill
41 Sturgeon-Weir
42 Brazeau
43 N. Saskatchewan
44 Clearwater
45 Red Deer
46 Severn
47 Fawn
48 Albany
49 Ogoki
50 Attawapiskat
51 Rupert
52 Clearwater
53 Thelon
54 Moose
55 Missinaibi
PACIFIC BASIN
1 Yukon
2 Porcupine-Bell
3 Stewart
4 White
5 Pelly
6 Stikine
7 West Road
8 Chilcotin
9 Fraser
10 Klondike
11 Macmillan
12 Ross
13 Big Salmon
14 Teslin
15 Nisutlin
16 Nechako
17 Stuart
18 Salmon
19 Willow
20 Chilko
21 Bowron
22 Caribou-Quesnel
GULF OF MEXICO BASIN
73 Milk River
ATLANTIC BASIN
56 Ugjoktok
57 Kanairiktok
58 Naskaupi
59 Goose
60 Natashquan
61 Romaine
62 Manitou
63 Moisie
64 Main
65 Humber
66 Exploits
67 Restigouche
68 St. Croix
69 Chamouchouane
70 Kipawa
71 Dumoine
72 French
QUEEN ELIZABETH ISLANDS
AXEL HEIBERG
ELLESMERE ISLAND
DEVON ISLAND
BANKS ISLAND
VICTORIA ISLAND
BAFFIN ISLAND
ARCTIC BASIN
ARCTIC CIRCLE
YUKON TERRITORY
NORTHWEST TERRITORIES
PACIFIC BASIN
BRITISH COLUMBIA
ALBERTA
SASKATCHEWAN
MANITOBA
ONTARIO
QUÉBEC
NEWFOUNDLAND
HUDSON BAY BASIN
ATLANTIC BASIN
GULF OF MEXICO BASIN
NEW BRUNSWICK
NOVA SCOTIA
PRINCE EDWARD ISLAND
Scale 1: 20,000,000
Kilometres 200 0 200 400 600 Kilometres
Miles 200 0 200 400 Miles
Base map produced by Surveys and Mapping Branch, Department of Energy, Mines and Resources, Ottawa.
Basin Boundaries
Source: Department of Indian and Northern Affairs, Parks Canada, 1974.
*rivers surveyed by Parks Canada 1971-73

Northern Land Use Information Series

The evaluation and identification of recreation resources has been carried out in various parts of Canada to provide basic information for land use planning and resource management. Environment Canada has produced an information series in map form for the Arctic Land Use Research Program of the Department of Indian and Northern Affairs. This series of maps is being prepared for all of the Yukon Territory and a major part of the Northwest Territories. Its purpose is to provide, at a reconnaissance level, an information base that can be of assistance in regional land use planning and in the management of the resources. The information on each map sheet (N.T.S. 1:250,000) includes wildlife populations, fisheries, land use, socio-economic and cultural data, and a variety of information on the resources for recreation in the region.

The information on recreation appears in two forms: a recreation-terrain evaluation as an assessment of the general landscape aesthetics; and a site identification and classification of areas and points of high potential for recreation and tourism.

In the method of landscape evaluation described previously, the three components of landscape used were landform, water, and natural vegetation. In this evaluation of recreation terrain, however, the criteria for each component selected, although similar, were more complex and each was weighted in such a manner that the landform component was considered more important than water, and the water component more important than the vegetation element.

The method used to classify particular areas or points for recreation capability is based on that used in the outdoor recreation sector of the Canada Land Inventory (CLI). In this northern region of Canada, however, only sites of high capability are identified. The definitions established for the CLI are also interpreted more broadly for these northern areas, but the premises are the same. Sites are selected and rated either in relation to their ability to attract and sustain intensive use, or on their national significance or uniqueness.

Map 11 illustrates the methods used. The program identifies a broad range of important resources for recreation in Canada. Its reconnaissance nature provides both the broad recreation-terrain analysis plus a more detailed inventory and classification of particular sites for parts of northern Canada.

The Canada Land Inventory: Capability for Outdoor Recreation

Another method of evaluating the importance of land for outdoor recreation was developed for the Canada Land Inventory program. The full CLI program consisted of the mapping and assessment of 2.5 million ha in the southern areas of Canada for agriculture, forestry, recreation, and wildlife capability as well as present land use. In addition to the inventory, a computerized system for storage and manipulation of data was also developed — the Canada Geographic Information System, CGIS. The classification and assumptions used for the determination of capability for recreation have been published and are summarized here.

Summary of Land Capability Classification for Outdoor Recreation

"Seven classes of land are differentiated on the basis of the intensity of outdoor recreational use, or the quantity of outdoor recreation which may be generated and sustained per unit area of land per annum under perfect market conditions.

'Quantity' may be measured by visitor days, a visitor day being any reasonable portion of a 24 hour period during which an individual person uses a unit of land for recreation.

'Perfect market conditions' implies uniform demand and accessibility for all areas, which means that location relative to population centres and to present access do not affect the classification.

'Intensive and dispersed activities' are recognized. 'Intensive activities' are those in which relatively large numbers of people may be accommodated per unit area, while 'dispersed activities' are those which normally require a relatively larger area per person.

Important factors affecting the classification are:
- The purpose of the inventory is to provide a reliable assessment of the quality, quantity and distribution of the natural recreation resources within settled parts of Canada.
- The inventory is essentially of a reconnaissance nature, based on interpretation of aerial photographs, field checks, and available records. The finished maps should be interpreted accordingly.
- The inventory classification is designed in accordance with present popular preferences in non-urban outdoor recreation. Urban areas (generally over 1,000 population with permanent urban character), as well as some non-urban industrial areas, are not classified.
- Land is ranked according to natural capability under existing conditions, whether in natural or modified state. But no assumptions are made concerning its capability if it is given further major artificial modifications.
- Sound recreation land management and development practices are assumed for all areas in practical relation to the natural capability of each area.
- Water bodies are not directly classified. Their recreational values accrue to the adjoining shoreland or land unit.
- Opportunities for recreation afforded by the presence in an area of wildlife and sports fish are indicated in instances where reliable information was available. But the ranking does not reflect the biological productivity of the area; wildlife capability is indicated in a companion series of maps.

Classes

1 – LANDS IN THIS CLASS HAVE VERY HIGH CAPABILITY FOR OUTDOOR RECREATION

Class 1 lands have natural capability to engender and sustain very high annual use based on one or more recreational activities of an intensive nature.

Class 1 land units should be able to generate and sustain a level of use comparable to that evident at an outstanding and large bathing beach or a nationally known ski slope.

2 – LANDS IN THIS CLASS HAVE A HIGH CAPABILITY FOR OUTDOOR RECREATION

Class 2 lands have natural capability to engender and sustain high annual use based on one or more recreational activities of an intensive nature.

3 – LANDS IN THIS CLASS HAVE A MODERATELY HIGH CAPABILITY FOR OUTDOOR RECREATION

Class 3 lands have natural capability to engender and sustain moderately high annual use based usually on intensive or moderately intensive activities.

4 – LANDS IN THIS CLASS HAVE MODERATE CAPABILITY FOR OUTDOOR RECREATION

Class 4 lands have natural capability to engender and sustain moderate annual use based usually on dispersed activities.

5 – LANDS IN THIS CLASS HAVE MODERATELY LOW CAPABILITY FOR OUTDOOR RECREATION

Class 5 lands have natural capability to engender and sustain a moderately low total annual use based on dispersed activities.

6 – LANDS IN THIS CLASS HAVE LOW CAPABILITY FOR OUTDOOR RECREATION

Class 6 lands lack the natural quality and significant features to rate higher, but have the natural capability to engender and sustain low annual use based on dispersed activities.

7 – LANDS IN THIS CLASS HAVE VERY LOW CAPABILITY FOR OUTDOOR RECREATION

Class 7 lands have practically no capability for any popular types of recreation activity, but there may be some capability for very specialized activities with recreation aspects, or they may simply provide open space.

Some of the most outstanding seascape viewing points in eastern Canada are found along the northeast part of the Cabot Trail in Cape Breton Highlands National Park, Nova Scotia. With ample space for development and access, this class 2 area has a natural capability to sustain high total annual use based on intensive activities.

Subclasses

Subclasses indicate the kinds of features which provide opportunity for recreation. They are, therefore, positive aspects of land and do not indicate limitations to use. Features may be omitted from a unit, either because of the imposed three-feature limit, or because their presence was unknown or unconfirmed.

The subclasses are:

A – land providing access to water affording opportunity for angling or viewing of sports fish;

B – shoreland capable of supporting family beach activities. In high class units this includes family bathing. In classes 4 and 5, the activities may preclude bathing due to water temperature or other limitations;

C – land fronting on and providing direct access to waterways with significant capability for canoe tripping;

D – shoreland with deeper inshore water suitable for swimming, or boat mooring or launching;

E – land with vegetation possessing recreational value;

F – waterfall or rapids;

G – significant glacier view or similar experience;

H – historic or pre-historic site;

J – area offering particular opportunities for gathering and collecting items of popular interest;

K – shoreland or upland suited to organized camping. This subclass is usually associated with other features;

L – interesting landform features other than rock formations;

M – frequent small water bodies, or continuous streams occurring in upland areas;

N – land (usually shoreland) suited to family or other recreation lodging use;

O – upland which affords an opportunity for viewing of upland wildlife;

P – areas exhibiting cultural landscape patterns of agricultural, industrial or social interest;

Q – areas exhibiting variety, in topography or land and water relationships, which enhances opportunities for general outdoor recreation such as hiking and nature study or for aesthetic appreciation of the area;

R – interesting rock formations;

S – a combination of slopes, snow conditions and climate providing downhill skiing opportunities;

T – thermal springs;

U – shoreland fronting water accommodating yachting or deep water boat tripping;

V – a vantage point or area which offers a superior view relative to the class of unit(s) which contain it, or a corridor or other area which provides frequent viewing opportunities;

W – land affording opportunity for viewing of wetland wildlife;

X – miscellaneous features with recreational capability;

Y – shoreland providing access to water suitable for popular forms of family boating;

Z – areas exhibiting major, permanent, non-urban man-made structures of recreational interest." (Environment Canada, 1978).

NFB PHOTOTHEQUE – ONF – Photo by Michel Pellerin.

A scenic waterfall on La Chute aux Rats in Québec illustrates one type of feature included in the CLI subclasses.

77

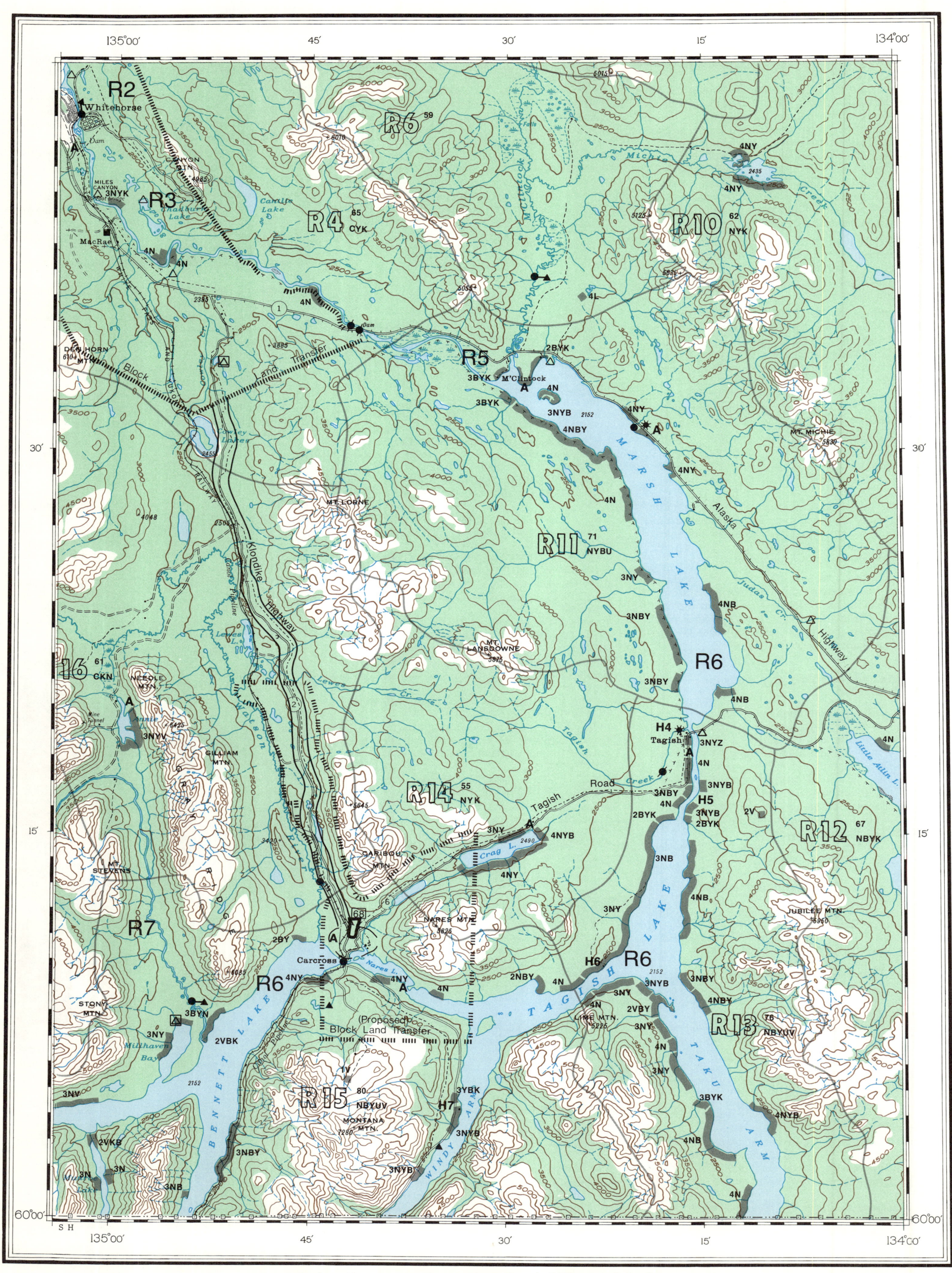

Scale: 1/250,000 or Approximately 4 Miles to 1 Inch

LAND USE INFORMATION SERIES
WHITEHORSE
YUKON TERRITORY

Base map produced from reproduction material provided by the Surveys and Mapping Branch, Department of Energy, Mines and Resources, with minor modifications by the Department of the Environment.

Map produced by the Lands Directorate, Environmental Management Service, Department of the Environment, 1973.

RECREATION - TOURISM

Source: Lands Directorate, Department of the Environment.

A. RECREATION - TERRAIN EVALUATION

The recreation-terrain evaluation prepared for this map set is an assessment of the natural recreation capability of regions and sites in a selected area of the Yukon, based on the distribution of landforms, water, and natural vegetation. Sites and regional boundaries were located by interpretation of 1:250,000 topographic maps and aerial photographs. Regional evaluation is based on the assessment of selected landscape features that together comprise a maximum of 105 points, as outlined in the accompanying table "Regional Recreation - Terrain Evaluation". Specific regional capabilities are indicated by letter symbols. The more outstanding sites for outdoor recreation are evaluated in accordance with Canada Land Inventory Capability Classes 1 to 4. In this Yukon map set, however, a limited number of subclasses indicating the recreational capabilities of sites are used. A maximum of three subclasses is assigned to each site. Regions with high values can be considered scenic or attractive from the point of view of recreational interest. However, regions with relatively low ratings may contain attractive sites. Regions and sites that have high ratings should be recognized as having high capability for outdoor recreation, and should receive commensurate attention in planning and development.

EXPLANATION OF SYMBOLS

Regional Symbol:
- unit number — **R1** — total value **75**
- regional boundary — **CAL** — recreational capabilities of regions (when applicable)

Site Symbol:
- site location — ■ or ▬ — site class **2FR**
- recreational capabilities of sites (arranged in descending order of importance)

SITE CLASSES
- Class 1 Very high capability for outdoor recreation
- Class 2 High capability for outdoor recreation
- Class 3 Moderately high capability for outdoor recreation
- Class 4 Moderate capability for outdoor recreation

RECREATIONAL CAPABILITIES OF REGIONS AND SITES

- **A** Alpine Activities (climbing, skiing, etc.)
- **B** Family Beach Activities
- **C** Canoeing
- **F** Rapids/Falls
- **G** Glacier Viewing
- **J** Gathering/Collecting
- **K** Camping
- **L** Landform Features (unconsolidated materials)
- **N** Cottaging
- **R** Geological Interest
- **T** Thermal Springs
- **U** Cabin Cruising/Yachting
- **V** Viewing (Classes 1 & 2 only)
- **Y** Family Boating
- **Z** Man-made Features

REGIONAL RECREATION-TERRAIN EVALUATION
of large units delimited on this map

		Landform components			Water components				Vegetation	Other factors	
Region or unit number	Relief	Slope variety	Geology	Water surface	Distinctive water forms	Shoreline configuration	Shoreline characteristics	Natural vegetation	Extrinsic view	Total Value
Maximum Value											
	15	15	10	10	10	5	10	25	5	105
Values of Regions											
*1	11	10	4	3	4	2	7	22	1	64
*2	10	10	5	2	3	2	7	21	1	61
*3	9	8	4	4	3	2	7	22	1	60
4	9	9	5	4	6	2	6	22	2	65
*5	9	9	4	9	3	3	8	21	1	67
6	9	9	6	2	3	2	4	22	2	59
*7	11	11	7	3	3	3	5	22	1	66
*8	9	11	7	2	3	1	2	21	1	57
*9	9	11	4	5	4	2	7	21	1	64
10	8	10	5	3	5	3	6	22	0	62
11	10	8	6	8	6	3	7	22	1	71
12	7	10	5	7	5	3	7	22	1	67
13	9	11	6	10	4	3	7	24	2	76
14	8	8	3	4	4	1	5	20	2	55
15	13	11	6	9	5	3	9	24	0	80
16	10	9	6	3	4	2	5	21	1	61
*17	10	12	6	2	4	1	4	21	1	61
*18	11	13	8	6	5	2	7	22	1	75
*19	9	10	6	4	6	2	5	17	1	60
*20	10	11	5	2	3	2	5	20	1	59

B. OUTDOOR RECREATION POTENTIAL

The area covered by this map sheet has potential for a wide variety of recreational activities; however, glacier viewing is limited to the small Rothwell Glacier in the Takhini - Primrose lakes region. One of the significant landform features evaluated as a site is the landslide on the Wheaton River. The kame deltas and terraces prevalent throughout the Mt. Granger and Mt. Arkell regions have not been indicated on the map. The lower half of the Takhini River valley was damaged by an extensive forest fire in the mid-1950s and some potential sites along the river have not been indicated because of present forest cover limitations. The valley is currently being reforested by natural regeneration. The variable turbidity of Primrose, Takhini, and Rose lakes may limit some water-oriented recreational activities. The cold waters of the large Tagish - Bennett lakes system limit the capability of these lakes for beach activities. Marsh Lake, which has warmer waters, has a higher recreational capability. These lakes have the highest potential for yachting and cruising in the Yukon. Viewing is outstanding throughout the area covered by this map sheet; however, only the most obvious viewing sites are indicated.

C. AREAS, ROUTES, POINTS OR FACILITIES OF RECREATION INTEREST

Sources: Tourism and Information Branch of the Department of Tourism, Conservation and Information Services, Government of the Yukon Territory (1); National and Historic Parks Branch, Department of Indian and Northern Affairs (2); Yukon Lands and Forest Service, Water, Forests, and Land Division of the Northern Economic Development Branch, Department of Indian and Northern Affairs (3); local residents (4).

SYMBOLS
(Not all symbols occur on every map)

- **R1** Area, route or point of recreation interest
- ✷ Location of sports fishing camp
- △ Campground, roadside park or picnic site
- △ Proposed campground

COMMENTS

*R1   Lake Laberge is fished by sportsmen for lake trout, grayling, pike, and inconnu (1).

R2   There are numerous trails through the wooded areas near Whitehorse. An extensive network of trails just east of the city is especially popular for cross-country skiing and snowmobiling. A commercial ski hill is operated on the eastern slope of Haeckel Hill (1,4).

R3   Chadburn Lake is used by residents of Whitehorse for fishing and canoeing (1).

*R4   Jackson, Fish, and Alligator lakes are known locally for sports fishing for grayling and lake trout. The trails to the lakes are used for snowmobiling in winter (1).

R5   In summer the Yukon River provides a popular boating route from Marsh Lake to Dawson. Except for a dam at Whitehorse, the river is free-flowing and has no major obstructions. The river is of historical interest as part of the main access route to the Klondike; for many years it served as the principal transportation link between Whitehorse and Dawson. Many relics of this era along the river enhance the interest of the trip. The river provides excellent scenic viewing, camping sites, and sports fishing.

R6   The Carcross - Tagish region is considered to be an important recreational area. The extensive water bodies of Marsh, Tagish, and Bennett lakes provide good boating, and beaches are located near Carcross and on the north shore of Tagish Lake. There are many summer cottages along the north shore of Tagish Lake, and a number on the northern and eastern shores of Marsh Lake. Sports fishing for grayling, lake trout, and pike is excellent in the lakes. The scenery is spectacular, and camping, hiking, and climbing are popular activities. The region is easily accessible and is well used, particularly by residents of Whitehorse.

R7   A cross-country ski trail runs southward from Annie Lake along the Wheaton River and across West Arm to the White Pass and Yukon railway (1).

*Not applicable to this sheet

REFERENCE

- Road, hard surface, all weather, 2 lanes
- Road, loose surface graded and drained 2 lanes
- Other roads .... poor condition
- Trail
- Railway (narrow gauge) .... Station or stop
- Abandoned railway grade
- Telephone or telegraph line .... along road
- Building
- School .... S•
- Post Office .... P•
- Provincial boundary and monument
- Height in feet above mean sea-level 8055
- Glacier
- Intermittent stream
- Marsh or swamp
- Sand or gravel
- Contours (interval 500 feet) 5000
- Contours (position approximate) 5000
- Wooded areas
- Landing ground
- Power transmission line

Surveyed, 1944 and compiled, 1947 by the Topographical Survey.
Base map first Published 1949.

Approximate magnetic declination, 31°30' East.

MAP 11

Photo by J. Ritchie Mickelson.

This scenic view of a glacier and the Takkakaw Falls in British Columbia is rated as class 2 by the CLI classification.

Canadian Government Office of Tourism photo.

The Fortress of Louisbourg on Cape Breton Island is rated as a class 1 historic site. Its attractive site and nation-wide significance are enhanced by its very high capability to engender intensive use.

The badland and hoodoo features found in Dinosaur Provincial Park, north of Brooks, Alberta, are rated as having class 2 capability for outdoor recreation. The area is widely known for its abundant dinosaur fossils and interesting rock formations.

TABLE 5.

Land area, by capability class and province

Province	1	2	3	4	5	6	7	Unclassified land within CLI area	Provincial totals
					(ha)				
Newfoundland	6,083	74,035	518,381	876,359	3,568,969	4,764,818	273,312	82,585	10,164,542
Prince Edward Island	10,811	6,952	50,698	56,577	111,885	278,772	41,022	5,121	561,838
Nova Scotia	639	11,103	63,389	315,924	1,135,313	3,158,395	429,886	176,756	5,291,405
New Brunswick	930	23,962	112,624	34,004	2,587,164	3,368,522	538,907	159,089	7,138,202
Québec	38,248	245,005	1,474,800	2,384,394	7,101,426	16,792,329	571,407	86,935	28,694,624
Ontario	41,004	123,890	1,248,974	3,841,605	5,485,047	15,582,556	932,022	272,659	27,527,757
Manitoba	2,294	19,890	156,756	960,679	3,331,637	10,619,122	2,824,189	2,716,788	21,631,355
Saskatchewan	7,269	15,687	242,024	1,165,193	9,042,761	24,341,366	1,548,782	633,857	36,966,939
Alberta	5,344	27,663	126,807	2,771,534	22,426,927	19,461,612	1,056,645	2,175,934	48,052,466
British Columbia	18,612	161,339	1,028,429	4,731,590	13,944,559	36,269,084	3,286,814	574,074	60,014,501
CANADA	131,234	709,526	5,022,962	17,450,859	68,735,688	134,636,576	12,502,986	6,883,798	246,073,629
					(percentage)				
Per cent of total area	.05	.29	2.04	7.09	27.93	54.71	5.08	2.30	100.00

Source: Taylor, 1978. Land Capability for Recreation: Summary Report.

TABLE 6.

Shoreline length, by capability class and province

Province	1	2	3	4	5	6	7	Unclassified shoreline within CLI area	Provincial totals
					(km)				
Newfoundland	90	887	5,422	11,218	19,668	25,542	2,700	890	66,417
Prince Edward Island	313	178	812	382	430	244	116	49	2,524
Nova Scotia	32	265	1,140	5,467	7,417	7,428	1,489	800	24,038
New Brunswick	24	149	1,673	3,911	2,576	1,494	937	246	11,010
Québec	258	2,220	24,649	36,547	27,237	17,780	831	559	110,081
Ontario	333	1,896	22,371	63,671	30,792	12,128	479	991	132,661
Manitoba	54	484	3,293	10,250	17,190	9,863	4,903	14,217	60,254
Saskatchewan	81	210	3,708	9,131	14,799	10,059	1,054	1,262	40,304
Alberta	76	220	1,518	13,912	24,694	6,377	527	1,624	48,948
British Columbia	347	1,782	10,698	26,055	26,927	6,843	1,956	867	75,475
CANADA	1,608	8,291	75,284	180,544	171,730	97,758	14,992	21,505	571,712
					(percentage)				
Per cent of total shoreline	.28	1.45	13.17	31.58	30.04	17.10	2.62	3.76	100.00

Source: Taylor, 1978. Land Capability for Recreation: Summary Report.

TABLE 8.

Summary of methods using physical criteria to identify important outdoor recreation lands

	General outdoor recreation activities	Specific outdoor recreation activities
Major land areas - comprehensive	1. Climatic evaluation 2. Landscape evaluation 3. Recreation/terrain evaluation (Northern Land Use Information Series)	1. Canada Land Inventory
Specific or selected sites or areas	1. Natural areas of Canadian significance	1. N.L.U.I.S. - site identification and classification 2. Wild River Studies

Within the CLI area, land classified into classes 1 to 3 is considered as critical for outdoor recreation. Its distribution across Canada (Maps 12 to 14) is very uneven. The selected results derived from the Canada Geographic Information System are presented in a number of formats, and indicate that the total land area of high capability represents only 2.38 per cent or approximately 5.8 million ha of the area inventoried (Table 5). In terms of shoreline length, there are 85,000 km of high-capability shoreline (Table 6). This may seem considerable, but it represents only 15 per cent of the total shoreline inventoried. Another important finding relates to the amount of high capability shoreline within easy access of Canada's major population centres. Within 161 km of all Census Metropolitan Areas, 17.25 per cent of all shoreline was classified as having high capability, however, the variation among these centres was very high. Ottawa-Hull, for example, has over 150 km of class 1 shoreline within 161 km, whereas Saint John and Chicoutimi-Jonquière have no class 1 shoreline within this radius (Table 7).

From this detailed information, we can identify specific sites that are essential for outdoor recreation and also identify to which population centres the sites may be most important.

The methods for identifying lands for outdoor recreation by means of physical criteria are classified into four groups (Table 8). Each method defines portions of Canada which, under selected criteria, can be considered to be prime areas for outdoor recreation. There is little to be gained from the combination of the methods in an attempt to cover "all" possibilities. The criteria selected for definition of the areas are often very subjective and may vary from area to area.

The following sections will deal with other methods for defining important recreation lands. These methods are not independent of the physical methods applied. Usage, for example, is highly related to the attractiveness of the site. However, factors of access, costs, and the occurrence of a facility are also involved.

TABLE 7.

Inventoried shoreline, by class, for those areas within 40, 80, 121, and 161 km of the centre of Census Metropolitan Areas

Census Metropolitan Area	Radii*	1	2	3	4	5	6	7	8**	Census Metropolitan Area	Radii*	1	2	3	4	5	6	7	8**
					(km)										(km)				
St. John's	40	–	14	15	129	156	597	26	83	Thunder Bay+	40	–	38	183	514	120	68	3	68
	80	–	34	84	438	1,421	2,890	146	175		80	0	47	590	1,517	545	132	3	68
	121	8	59	378	1,259	3,028	4,388	415	264		121	–	47	656	1,752	582	150	3	69
	161	10	93	610	1,790	3,948	6,596	536	645	Toronto	40	–	–	9	10	8	7	–	106
Halifax	40	–	8	140	535	618	745	116	151		80	–	28	79	212	234	22	–	234
	80	–	19	297	1,156	1,605	2,140	206	169		121	45	93	370	779	949	88	–	359
	121	–	29	433	2,002	2,842	3,392	507	190		161	85	251	1,353	3,045	2,267	522	34	403
	161	–	134	621	2,881	4,425	4,792	1,025	551	Windsor	40	–	44	24	32	16	15	16	53
Saint John	40	–	24	132	380	314	314	47	79		80	25	228	145	133	104	16	16	69
	80	–	41	265	804	1,192	839	178	105		121	38	234	180	174	134	16	16	83
	121	–	44	515	1,883	2,268	1,941	458	305		161	67	238	186	203	172	17	16	83
	161	–	58	848	3,637	4,069	3,409	1,116	494	Winnipeg	40	–	4	22	169	113	1	–	114
Chicoutimi-Jonquière	40	–	14	168	247	551	487	45	16		80	–	39	641	539	341	55	31	116
	80	–	29	561	1,134	2,199	2,653	95	32		121	14	112	1,177	1,113	947	237	69	121
	121	–	48	1,057	2,186	4,021	5,497	219	16		161	19	197	1,930	3,023	2,779	1,025	249	124
	161	–	74	2,509	3,841	6,417	7,950	286	72	Regina	40	–	–	–	0	25	21	–	–
Montréal	40	5	22	287	279	181	25	39	148		80	4	19	203	72	61	96	–	–
	80	7	77	824	857	525	73	62	203		121	5	19	285	283	624	351	–	1
	121	12	253	1,785	2,060	1,596	439	88	228		161	5	33	365	434	1,310	1,157	–	2
	161	51	510	3,427	4,004	3,206	1,014	158	292	Saskatoon	40	–	1	9	26	390	291	–	31
Québec	40	–	26	87	218	227	198	6	67		80	–	6	10	227	1,063	714	–	31
	80	2	50	519	923	999	564	33	98		121	–	12	69	658	2,118	1,278	–	32
	121	14	123	1,355	2,358	2,362	1,536	89	158		161	9	14	188	1,440	3,543	1,757	–	43
	161	25	219	2,670	4,334	4,331	2,775	142	185	Calgary	40	–	–	–	156	163	21	–	90
Hamilton	40	–	–	3	37	194	6	–	100		80	–	1	10	596	452	74	–	90
	80	4	47	54	196	554	38	3	271		121	4	59	132	1,090	829	180	–	219
	121	33	114	111	317	721	53	3	327		161	5	77	310	2,048	1,888	578	2	391
	161	75	148	251	690	1,054	127	3	368	Edmonton	40	–	4	10	400	203	13	–	21
Kitchener	40	–	2	1	12	197	19	–	62		80	10	14	176	1,239	912	147	–	89
	80	–	2	7	101	463	38	3	178		121	10	14	265	2,398	2,766	904	18	90
	121	53	104	122	363	865	91	3	222		161	13	43	383	3,687	6,312	1,684	20	100
	161	110	192	432	939	1,144	159	3	285	Vancouver	40	–	192	101	264	199	4	2	232
London	40	2	–	5	10	105	7	–	10		80	60	370	913	1,146	674	34	64	291
	80	37	10	30	94	291	17	3	26		121	69	456	1,558	2,351	1,369	139	108	418
	121	63	215	171	287	723	30	3	143		161	99	521	2,036	3,421	2,452	254	108	483
	161	72	328	254	496	892	80	3	234	Victoria	40	13	41	232	215	62	6	–	92
Ottawa-Hull	40	9	15	127	408	182	79	44	89		80	33	240	508	486	185	35	–	124
	80	22	126	725	1,716	1,530	315	64	108		121	40	368	826	1,010	478	52	–	378
	121	80	471	3,076	4,716	3,683	1,151	91	147		161	84	460	1,494	2,280	1,416	88	64	410
	161	157	806	5,628	8,063	6,246	2,049	130	314	Totals++	40	36	487	1,757	5,553	4,680	3,296	369	1,722
St. Catharines-Niagara	40	2	24	34	117	121	4	1	70		80	228	1,534	8,011	21,102	18,763	12,046	946	2,760
	80	2	30	45	166	270	7	1	236		121	534	3,401	18,779	42,949	40,442	24,393	2,180	4,130
	121	22	106	95	266	556	47	3	290		161	987	5,049	33,979	72,199	69,925	39,973	3,997	6,002
	161	36	149	236	617	871	71	3	341	Shoreline length by class as a percentage of total shoreline for areas within 161 km of CMA centres.					(%)				
Sudbury	40	5	14	164	1,395	535	370	24	40										
	80	8	77	1,325	7,350	3,143	1,147	38	47										
	121	24	221	4,181	13,599	6,981	2,433	72	70			.43	2.18	14.64	31.11	30.13	17.22	1.72	2.59
	161	47	457	7,692	19,601	10,601	3,719	96	113										

* The 40, 80, 121, and 161-km radii correspond to 25, 50, 75, and 100-mile radii.

** Unclassified lands may include lands committed to intensive urban use lying within municipalities of over 1,000 population, such as military reserves and National Parks.

Source: Taylor, 1978. Land Capability for Recreation: Summary Report.

+ Thunder Bay is situated such that some of the area beyond the 40-km radius is outside the CLI area. No coverage at all is available beyond the 121-km radius.

++ These totals do not consider the existence of overlaps between CMAs for example, the overlaps in area coverage amongst Toronto, Hamilton, Kitchener, St. Catharines, London, and Windsor.

Present Land Use

Areas presently used for outdoor recreation can also be considered as necessary in meeting the recreation needs of Canadians. The major problem with this approach is that much of Canada would be defined as important to some degree. Most areas are used for some activity whether it is the backyard of a city home for gardening, the country roads for driving for pleasure, or the vast undeveloped areas of northern Canada that may be used by a few wilderness adventurers each year.

NFB PHOTOTHEQUE – ONF – Photo by Paul Baich.

An area such as the Marian River in the Northwest Territories may generate relatively little use but may offer an individual a unique recreation opportunity.

It is essential, therefore, to use some kind of indicator to represent the degree of importance for each area. The most obvious index would be the amount of recreation use that takes place in any defined area. The greater the amount of use per unit area, the greater the importance of the area for that particular use. This simple relationship would put many areas at a disadvantage due to the type of activity for which the site or area is suitable or is being used. For example, a picnic site along a major tourist route may receive considerable use throughout the season. This would indicate that the area is important for picnicking, yet it may be only one of many such sites or potential sites in the locality. On the other hand, a wilderness area such as a wild river may have very little use based on a per unit area and, as such, it would not be considered essential even though the river itself might be considered to be of national significance for wilderness canoeing. The index of importance must, therefore, be related to both the amount and the type of recreation use.

Factors Affecting Present Land Use

Attractiveness. The physical attractiveness of an area for various activities is a key factor in determining the type and amount of use. Elements of the physical landscape have already been addressed, but many cultural elements can be equally attractive. Also the type, quantity and quality of facilities are important factors that influence the use of an area for recreation. Areas that provide a variety of facilities for different types of recreation attract more use than single-purpose areas.

Canadian Government Office of Tourism photo.

Only minutes away from Vancouver, Grouse Mountain is an attractive site accessible to a large urban population.

Accessibility. This is often considered to be the most important factor which influences the patterns and levels of recreation use. Distance, as a simple measure of access, has both time and financial implications. As the distance increases, the time for travel increases; this limits the amount of time available for on-site recreation and may reduce the attractiveness of the site. The trip itself may have some benefits and thus the negative aspect of distance may be reduced. Greater distances involve increases in travel and other related costs, and as the total costs of the activity increase, so the level of use for recreation in areas distant from demands will tend to decrease. The reverse, for both time and cost, is also true. As the costs or relative costs in time and/or dollars required to reach a site decrease, its level of use may increase. This seems to be the case for air travel to Europe and other holiday centres abroad.

Quantitative Terms

The inter-relationships of all these factors, the physical attractiveness, the attractiveness of the facility, and the accessibility of the area, to the levels of recreation use are not clear. Although no single comprehensive model for predicting use has been formulated, considerable research has been done to develop methods to describe and predict, in quantitative terms, recreation use for particular activities or for selected types of sites.

One method that has been developed is the calculation of the "Outdoor Recreation Opportunity Quotient". Map 15 and the accompanying text illustrate how areas with varying opportunity for recreation are defined. The results delineate areas that have higher and lower opportunity for park-type recreation. Areas with a relatively low opportunity quotient cannot, at this time, be classed as lands essential for recreation. For example, much of the area to the south and east of Windsor has a low opportunity quotient, but it cannot be assumed that all this land is important for recreation activities. Within these areas, however, lands presently used for recreation and those sites with high capability for recreation can be considered to be important in meeting present and future recreation demands, and, as such, are important for outdoor recreation.

Although this concept has not been applied to all of Canada, a pattern for a national opportunity quotient can be suggested. By comparing the areas of population concentration in Canada and the United States with the locations of major park areas (*see* Map 16), it is suggested that the opportunity quotient would be lowest in the southern portions of Ontario (*compare* Map 15), where there are major population concentrations and few large parks, and that it would be highest in the areas of western Canada where there are significant numbers of large parks and lower concentrations of population. The east and west coasts and much of the northern portions of the provinces as well as the territories might have a moderate opportunity quotient due to the limited numbers of parks and fewer people. It must be remembered, however, that this pattern of recreation opportunity is only hypothesized, and is related only to park-type recreation opportunities. Other patterns of recreation opportunity for different types of areas, such as skiing sites, may be entirely different.

Qualitative Factors

Qualitative factors, such as land ownership, also influence the amount of recreation. The private, commercial, and public sectors control varying proportions of land for many uses, one of which is recreation.

National land tenure data, as they relate to outdoor recreation are presented in Table 9. They show that federal and provincial land areas designated as parks account for about five per cent of the total area of Canada with Crown lands, under both federal and provincial authority, making up 84 per cent. The remaining 11 per cent is held privately or held by public agencies such as municipalities and regional authorities for various uses which include parks and conservation areas. Also included in the private tenure class are those lands held by the commercial sector for recreation/tourist facilities.

It is difficult to isolate the amount of land in the Crown and private land tenure classes that is used for outdoor recreation, since many activities do not demand the exclusive use of the land. For example, on Crown lands, activities may include forestry, mining, and trapping, plus a multitude of recreation activities (hunting, fishing, camping, and canoeing). Much of the privately owned land also serves multiple purposes. Agricultural lands may provide opportunities for snowmobiling, hunting, hiking, and general landscape viewing.

The management of land also affects the type, amount, and the quality of the recreation. Each sector provides a proportion of the total recreation supply, and there are also overlaps amongst the sectors. For example, the commercial sector provides most of the downhill skiing facilities, but some are operated by the public sector in parks.

TABLE 9.

Provincial and territorial area, by tenure, 1973

Tenure class	Newfoundland	Prince Edward Island	Nova Scotia	New Brunswick	Québec	Ontario	Manitoba	Saskatchewan	Alberta	British Columbia	Yukon and Northwest Territories	CANADA
					(km^2)							
Federal Crown land	435	13	179	1,572	873	1,256	259	5,801	3,095	894	3,854,135	3,868,512
Provincial Crown land	383,718	396	15,829	31,318	1,230,885	897,721	491,150	384,145	330,712	850,765	3,641	4,620,280
National Parks	2,339	18	1,331	433	1,142	1,922	2,976	3,874	53,588	4,690	57,701	130,014
Provincial parks	277	13	54	215	194,235	41,859	8,767	4,809	6,104	34,571	–	290,904
Private land	17,719	5,216	38,093	39,893	113,433	125,748	146,888	253,223	267,638	57,608	246	1,065,705
Total area	404,488	5,656	55,486	73,431	1,540,568	1,068,506	650,040	651,852	661,137	948,528	3,915,723	9,975,415
Fresh water area	34,030	–	2,649	1,344	183,876	177,375	101,585	81,625	16,795	18,066	137,764	755,109

Source: Statistics Canada, 1973a. Canada Year Book 1973.

Source: Generalized from the 1:1,000,000 Canada Land Inventory *Land Capability for Outdoor Recreation* maps for *Atlantic Provinces* (1973) and *Québec* (1977), published by the Lands Directorate, Environment Canada.

MAP 12

Canadian Government Office of Tourism photo.

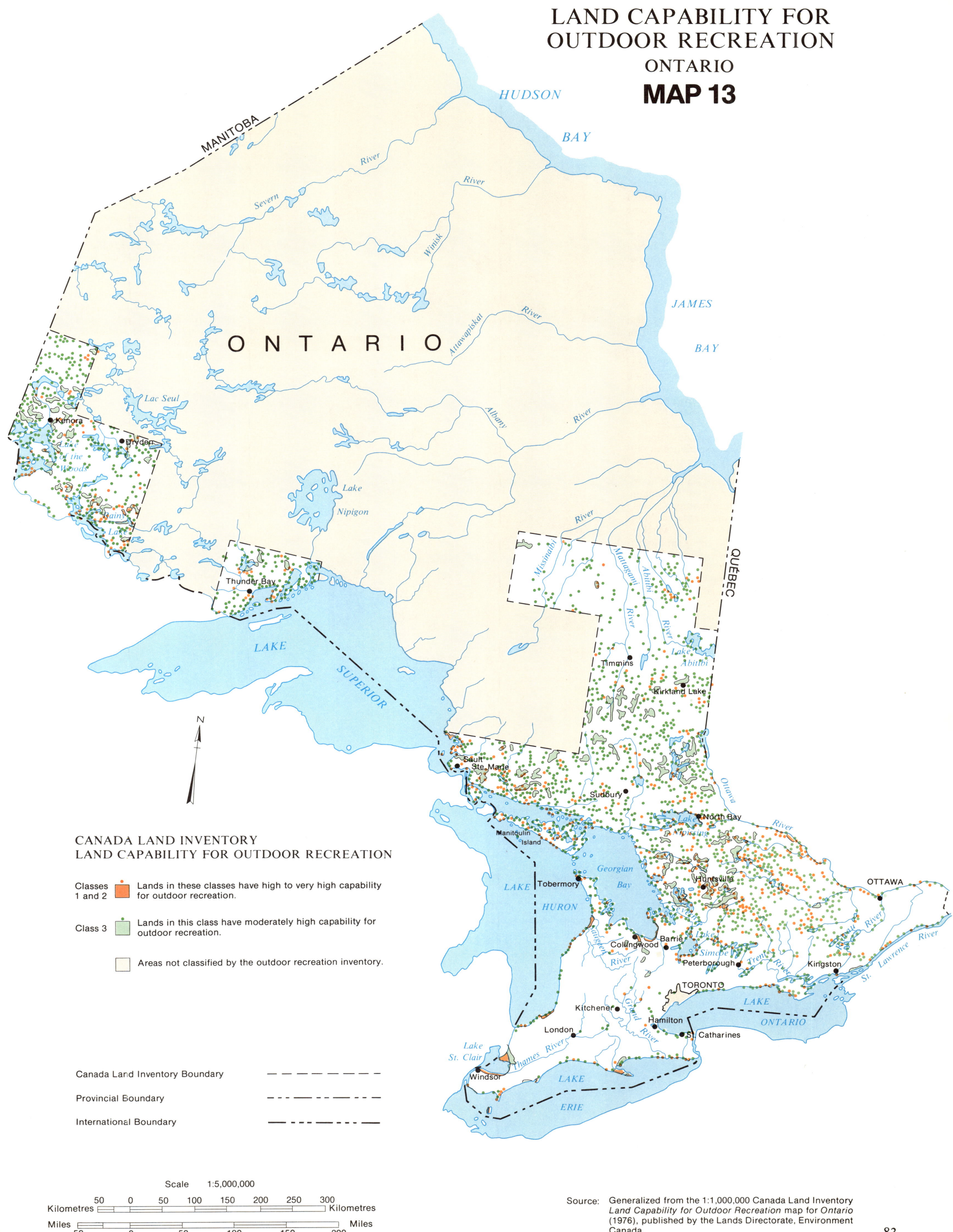

Land tenure can also restrict, through regulations or cost of the facility and access, the amount and type of use made of the resources. Land held in private ownership is often restricted to limited use by the owner, family, and friends. This can reduce public access to shoreline and to lands for hunting, fishing, snowmobiling, or other activites. Commercial ownership can restrict the level of use by means of admission charges. Some users cannot, or are not, willing to pay the costs of using commercial facilities such as campgrounds, skiing facilities, and tourist resorts.

Finally, the public sector, which includes all levels of government, can restrict or regulate use in the same manner as the other two sectors by denying or restricting access to public lands, regulating seasons for camping, fishing, or hunting, charging admission for use of facilities, or by locating facilities in areas that are not readily accessible.

Private Sector

The range of activities that occur on privately held lands vary according to their location in urban, rural, or hinterland areas.

Urban Areas. In the urban areas, privately held lands used for recreation are primarily backyards or common areas, depending on the type of housing. Activities in these areas include backyard picnics, barbecues, gardening, swimming, and various other types of household-oriented activities. Since a majority of leisure time is spent in and about the house, these activities provide an important proportion of the total experience in outdoor recreation.

The space available for these types of outdoor activities is becoming a problem as the density of housing increases. Much new housing is built in multiple-housing units, which reduces the private space available. Many multiple-unit developments lack the space in which to barbecue or throw a ball, without infringing on the personal space of others. People may substitute indoor leisure activities for outdoor recreation, or they may use public and commercial sector areas for recreation. While the ramifications of this potential change are unknown, perhaps some are evidenced by increased demands for municipalities to provide facilities and open spaces within the urban areas. For example, planning legislation in many provinces demands that as part of any land development, a certain proportion be dedicated for open space.

Private space for outdoor recreation is at a premium in many urban residential developments. As a result, demands placed on public and commercial facilities are increasing.

Photo by Agriculture Canada.

A pleasant afternoon drive through the rural countryside offers many urban dwellers a change from the city environment. Agricultural land use patterns, country landscapes, and farm buildings, found in the rural fringe around many cities, constitute an important recreation resource.

Rural Areas. In the rural areas, outdoor recreation on private land is more evident. In the agricultural areas, driving for pleasure, hunting, snowmobiling, and other extensive-type activities are common. Although neither the amount of recreation nor the amount of land used is generally known, it varies from region to region depending on factors such as the type of agriculture, the mixture of agriculture and forest land, land ownership patterns, and the availability of other facilities for recreation. Agricultural land (Table 10) makes up only a small proportion of the total area of Canada, but much of it is found in proximity to the major population centres and is thus accessible to people. For this reason, agricultural areas are of great significance in supplying land for outdoor recreation.

Changes are taking place, however, which could influence the amount of recreation that will be permitted to take place in agricultural areas. Increased numbers of recreationists, such as hunters, snowmobilers, and hikers, have caused damage in farming areas, with the result that either lands are posted to keep people out altogether or formal arrangements have to be made between the land owners and the recreationist. Another factor limiting recreation by the general public in agricultural areas is that hobby farms, second homes, and chalets are taking up more of the attractive landscapes. This type of land use, although recreation oriented, is often much more restrictive to public recreation than is full-time farming.

Hinterlands. The region beyond the rural areas is generally Crown land. Within the Crown lands are many privately held properties used for various purposes often based on the use of local natural resources. Recreation properties are some of the most evident. Private cottages and commercial resorts are bases for many activities such as fishing and hunting.

It is also these enclaves of private land in a predominantly public area that generate various types of conflicts: environmental, private versus public recreation use, and resource-user conflicts. The use of land for cottages illustrates the amount, distribution, and change in land use that is occurring in the private sector, particularly within the hinterland region.

TABLE 10.

Area classification, by province or territory, 1973

Classification	Newfoundland	Prince Edward Island	Nova Scotia	New Brunswick	Québec	Ontario	Manitoba	Saskatchewan	Alberta	British Columbia	Yukon and Northwest Territories	CANADA
(thousands of ha and percentage of total provincial area)											
Forest land	12,749	251	4,444	6,311	69,606	43,223	13,548	12,821	27,657	54,491	77,947	323,045
	31.6	44.3	80.1	86.2	45.2	40.8	20.8	19.7	41.8	57.5	19.9	32.4
Wildland	23,567	nil	nil	251	56,662	37,162	32,470	17,904	17,151	35,860	298,077	519,104
	58.5			3.4	36.8	35.0	49.9	27.5	25.9	37.8	76.1	52.1
Agriculture	6	312	316	468	3,686	5,204	8,528	26,426	19,070	1,526	1,800	67,344
	0.0	55.0	5.7	6.4	2.4	4.9	13.1	40.5	28.8	1.6	0.5	6.8
Other, urban, etc.	83	2	453	108	824	2,887	106	877	560	298	nil	6,199
	.2	0.4	8.2	1.5	0.5	2.7	0.2	1.3	0.8	0.3		0.6
Total land area	36,405	565	5,213	7,138	130,778	88,476	54,653	58,028	64,438	92,175	377,824	915,693
Water	3,961	2	334	180	23,291	17,688	10,357	7,163	1,679	2,573	13,778	81,006
	9.8	0.4	6.0	2.5	15.1	16.7	15.9	11.0	2.5	2.7	3.5	8.1
TOTAL	40,366	567	5,547	7,318	154,069	106,164	65,010	65,191	66,117	94,748	391,602	996,699

Source: Statistics Canada, 1977a. *Canadian Forestry Statistics 1975.* Catalogue 25-202.

Cottage Lands in the Private Sector

Amount and Location. The use of land for cottages or for vacation homes provides an important proportion of the opportunities for outdoor recreation available to Canadians. Although comprehensive data on the numbers of cottages in Canada are not available at the national level, data relating to numbers and distribution of households owning vacation homes[2], are available from the 1971 Census of Canada (Baker, 1973). Although the location of the vacation home was not determined, the data can be used to determine ownership patterns, regional variations, and some other socio-economic relationships (Table 11).

Of the 6,030,805 households in Canada in 1971, 395,190 or 6.5 per cent owned one or more vacation homes, and of those households, 381,700 indicated that they owned only one vacation home. Although it is known that not all the vacation homes are located in Canada, the percentage found in other countries has been suggested to be less than two per cent (Ontario Department of Tourism and Information, 1968).

In Canada, much of the land used for cottages or vacation homes is owned by non-Canadians. In many regions, there are numerous American owners. For example, in the Lake of the Woods area of northwestern Ontario, of approximately 2,800 cottages on the lake, 1,000 are owned by non-Canadians (Ontario Ministry of Natural Resources, 1977a).

From the census information, neither the location of the vacation home, nor the type of home (such as chalet, cottage, or hunting camp) was identified. Previous research has shown, however, that most use of cottages by Canadians takes place within 320 km of the permanent residence and is associated with shoreline areas (Ontario Department of Tourism and Information, 1968; Baker, 1973; Jaakson *et al.*, 1975; Ontario Ministry of Natural Resources, 1973a; and Alberta Land Use Forum, 1974b). Thus, if it is assumed that the majority of the vacations homes owned by Canadians are located in Canada, it is possible to relate, with some degree of reliability, the location of vacation homes to that of the household owning them.

The range of the percentages of households owning one or more vacation homes in each census division has been divided into five classes and mapped according to class (Map 17). The resulting pattern shows that in many parts of central Canada, for example Québec and Ontario, the percentage levels are consistently higher than those in the western provinces, and in most cases, higher than those in the Maritime Provinces. The Maritimes, however, have more census divisions with percentages above the Canadian average of 6.5 per cent than the western provinces.

Some factors affecting this distribution may be socio-economic in nature, such as income or whether the permanent household is urban or rural (Table 12). Perhaps accessibility to areas attractive for vacation homes most affects the ownership pattern. Historically, vacation homes have been oriented to the shorelines and coasts of Canada, where there was availability, access, and attraction to what must have seemed like a limitless resource. The present pattern of households owning vacation homes is strongly associated with the lakes and rivers of the Canadian Shield. The lower level of ownership in the coastal areas may be related to other factors, including physical limitations of the shoreline for construction, or of the water temperature or quality for common activities associated with cottage life. The Prairie Region is affected to a greater degree by the lack of suitable shorelines (*see* Table 6).

---

[2]The definition used by Statistics Canada is applicable for this discussion. A vacation home is defined as a home owned by a member of the household and used only for vacation or recreational purposes on a seasonal basis. Hunting cabins, ski chalets, and summer cottages are examples, as are any other dwellings used mainly for recreation purposes. Trailers, cabin cruisers, houseboats, and such are not included in the definition (Statistics Canada, 1973b).

TABLE 11.

Households owning one or more vacation homes, by province and Census Metropolitan Area, June 1971

Province and Census Metropolitan Areas	All households	Households owning one or more vacation homes	Percentage of households owning one or more vacation homes
			(per cent)
CANADA	6,030,810	395,190	6.6
All CMAs	3,488,785	248,380	7.1
Newfoundland	110,185	5,220	4.7
St. John's	29,640	2,585	8.7
Prince Edward Island	27,790	1,395	5.0
Nova Scotia	206,920	13,975	6.8
Halifax	59,510	4,655	7.8
New Brunswick	157,240	12,180	7.7
Saint John	28,640	2,765	9.7
Québec	1,603,680	138,050	8.6
Chicoutimi-Jonquière	29,700	3,925	13.2
Montréal	805,435	68,320	8.5
Hull	37,840	4,020	10.6
Québec	127,240	10,305	8.1
Ontario	2,225,210	159,650	7.2
Hamilton	146,255	6,945	4.7
Kitchener	66,570	3,815	5.7
London	87,160	4,460	5.1
Ottawa	132,180	12,965	9.8
St. Catharines-Niagara	88,885	2,980	3.4
Sudbury	39,415	4,940	12.5
Thunder Bay	32,250	3,170	9.8
Toronto	773,825	70,230	9.1
Windsor	74,090	2,060	2.8
Manitoba	287,915	16,540	5.7
Winnipeg	166,220	12,600	7.6
Saskatchewan	267,615	13,220	4.9
Regina	42,580	2,980	7.0
Saskatoon	38,615	1,900	4.9
Alberta	464,240	13,340	2.9
Calgary	121,100	3,120	2.6
Edmonton	144,510	6,395	4.4
British Columbia	667,325	21,235	3.2
Vancouver	345,870	11,420	3.3
Victoria	66,255	1,825	2.8

Source: Statistics Canada, 1973b. *Housing: Household Facilities.* Catalogue 93-737.

Photo by V. Mann.

Attractive shoreline areas of the Canadian Shield, such as the Muskoka lakes in Ontario, have had summer homes as part of the landscape since before the turn of the century.

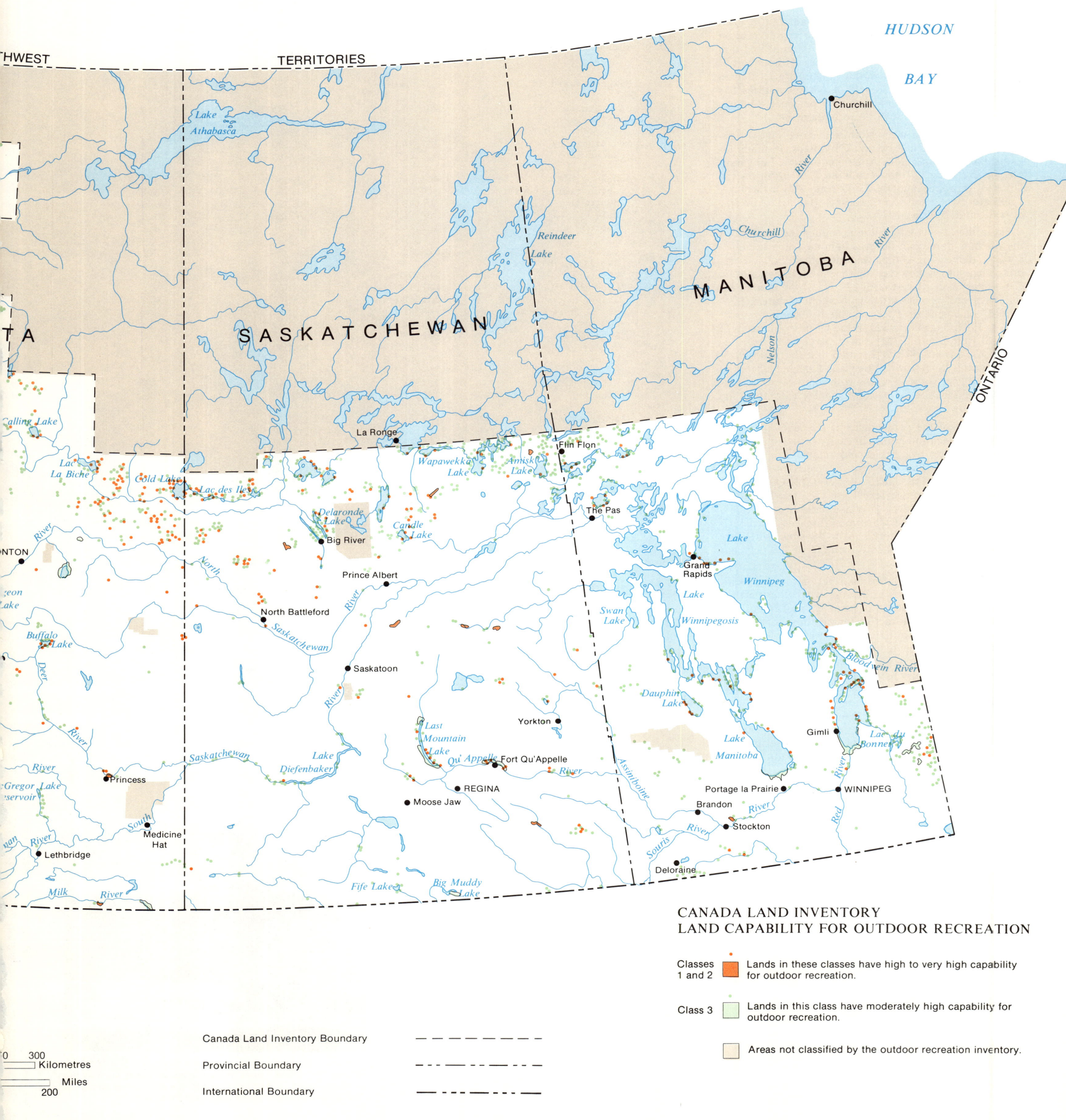

LAND CAPABILITY

BRITISH COLUMBIA
ALBERTA
SASKATCHEWAN
MANITOBA

DATA NOT AVAILABLE

Source: Generalized from the 1:1,000,000 Canada Land Inventory *Land Capability for Outdoor Recreation* maps for *Alberta* (1975), *Saskatchewan* (1976) and *Manitoba* (1974), published by the Lands Directorate, Environment Canada.

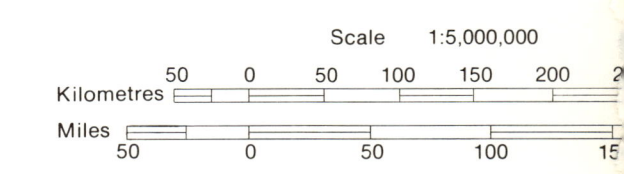

Scale 1:5,000,000

MAP 14

Canadian Government Office of Tourism photo.

TABLE 12.

Distribution of households owning one or more vacation homes, by urban and rural class and province, 1971

Province and Territory	Total households	Urban total	Urban population groups (>100,000)	(10,000-99,999)	(<10,000)	Rural total	Rural groups (Non-farm)	Farm
	(percentage of Canadian total)	(percentage of provincial total)	(percentage of urban total)			(percentage of provincial total)	(percentage of rural total)	
Newfoundland	5,220 / 1.3	4,475 / 85.7	0 / –	2,985 / 66.7	1,490 / 33.3	745 / 14.3	725 / 97.3	20 / 2.7
Prince Edward Island	1,395 / .4	990 / 71.0	0 / –	925 / 93.4	60 / 6.1	410 / 29.0	330 / 80.5	80 / 19.5
Nova Scotia	13,785 / 3.5	10,580 / 75.7	4,210 / 39.8	3,160 / 29.9	3,205 / 30.1	3,210 / 24.3	3,025 / 94.2	185 / 5.8
New Brunswick	12,180 / 3.1	9,515 / 78.1	0 / –	7,140 / 75.0	2,380 / 25.0	2,665 / 21.9	2,485 / 93.2	180 / 6.8
Québec	138,050 / 34.9	122,115 / 88.5	81,545 / 66.8	24,485 / 20.0	16,080 / 13.2	15,935 / 11.6	13,665 / 85.8	2,270 / 14.2
Ontario	159,650 / 40.4	143,285 / 89.7	98,030 / 68.4	30,700 / 21.4	14,565 / 10.2	16,360 / 10.3	14,130 / 86.4	2,230 / 13.6
Manitoba	16,540 / 4.2	15,020 / 90.8	12,410 / 82.6	1,415 / 9.4	1,200 / 8.0	1,520 / 9.2	1,205 / 79.3	315 / 20.7
Saskatchewan	13,220 / 3.3	9,485 / 71.7	4,950 / 52.2	2,310 / 24.4	2,225 / 23.5	3,735 / 28.5	2,250 / 60.2	1,485 / 39.8
Alberta	13,340 / 3.4	11,860 / 88.9	9,205 / 77.6	880 / 7.4	1,775 / 15.0	1,490 / 11.1	860 / 57.7	625 / 42.3
British Columbia	21,235 / 5.4	17,770 / 83.7	11,705 / 65.9	3,990 / 22.5	2,085 / 11.7	3,465 / 16.3	3,015 / 87.0	450 / 13.0
Yukon and Northwest Territories	565 / 0.1	405 / 71.7	0 / –	245 / 60.5	160 / 39.5	160 / 28.3	160 / 100.0	0 / –
CANADA	395,190	345,500 / 87.4	222,055 / 64.3	78,220 / 22.6	45,225 / 13.1	49,690 / 12.7	41,860 / 84.0	7,830 / 16.0

For purposes of confidentiality, all last or "unit" digits in this table (including totals) are randomly rounded (either up or down) to "0" or "5". Since totals are independently rounded, they do not necessarily equal the sum of individual rounded figures.

Source: Statistics Canada, 1973b. Housing: Household Facilities. Catalogue 93-737.

Canadian Government Office of Tourism photo.

Golf courses, such as this one in Lunenburg, Nova Scotia, are for the most part a commercial facility in urban areas. They can occupy significant amounts of land and provide recreation opportunity for many people.

Change. Since before the turn of the century, areas such as the Muskoka lakes in Ontario, the Eastern Townships of Québec, the Lake of the Woods area, the Pembina Valley in Manitoba, St. Andrew's in New Brunswick, and other vacation spots in the Maritimes have had summer homes as a dominant feature in the landscape. As areas have become accessible either by train, boat, or highway, the development of vacation homes seems to have followed rapidly. Periods of growth have often corresponded to the affluent times and to times of rapid change, particularly after the First and Second World Wars. Although data are only available for selected areas, the general trend is for cottages to be continually growing in number with concentration in some areas and expansion into new areas. This growth indicates that cottage land will continue to provide significant recreation opportunities. However, the increasing rate of ownership of vacation homes (seven per cent per year from 1971 to 1974) will seriously affect land use in various regions (Statistics Canada, 1976b). As the supply of suitable lakeshore decreases, the cost of owning vacation property will increase, property further from the centres of demand will be developed, and other types of vacation homes, such as upland chalets, may be sought. Another result of this increased demand may be the substitution of cottage recreation by other types of activities, such as international holiday travel or mobile homes.

Critical Lands. Lands for cottages will continue to be in greatest demand in the lake, river, and coastal areas of Canada. With the annual increase in the growth of this activity at seven per cent, the supply of suitable land will decrease. Competition from other recreation users, such as public parks and commercial operations, will also affect the supply of suitable areas. Greater pressures will be exerted on existing cottage areas to intensify, and on other types of areas, such as the scenic uplands, to develop as estate areas. Demands in areas further from the major population centres will increase, but the majority of people will continue to want land that is readily accessible. Thus, important lands for cottages will continue to be located within the 320-km radius, or within a three- to four-hour drive of the major cities of Canada.

Commercial Sector

The commercial sector provides important facilities for recreation, but, at the national level, they are considerably less significant in total than those components provided by the private and public sectors. Only in certain localities or regions, such as resort areas, does the commercial sector provide a more significant proportion of the total supply for all recreation. However, it can provide opportunities for certain types of recreation that neither the private nor public sectors supply. The types of facilities vary greatly, but generally they are intensive in nature, that is, the facility will operate with a large amount of use per unit area. Golf courses, tennis courts, ski hills, campgrounds, and other specialized facilities are often characterized by relatively intensive use and high capital investment. They are usually operated commercially as they are beyond the capability of most individuals to own. They can not always be operated by the public sector as they are too specialized and would be in direct competition with commercial operations. The types of facilities developed by the commercial sector vary according to the location of demands, and, to a somewhat lesser degree, the location of the physical resource base.

Urban Areas. Commercial recreation in urban areas is most often associated with indoor facilities. However, outdoor facilities, such as tennis courts and golf courses, can occupy important land areas within the urban areas and provide opportunities for many people. Data on the actual amount of use are not available for activities associated with the commercial sector, but, by considering the participation rates in these types of activities, it is possible to see considerable variations from province to province (Table 13). Golf, for example, although not exclusively operated by the commercial sector and not always found solely in urban areas, represents, for the most part, a commercial facility in urban areas. The level of participation in this activity varies considerably from province to province, from rates of 1.6 per cent in Newfoundland to 10.5 per cent in Alberta. The importance of these facilities in the total recreation supply is quite variable.

Rural Areas. In the rural fringe of the urban areas, golf courses are still highly visible but other developments such as ski hills, riding stables, swimming beaches, and campgrounds are associated with the more physically attractive elements of the landscape, and provide other types of opportunities. Their importance in supplying recreation opportunity is difficult to estimate. If not provided by the commercial sector, the public sector sometimes provides equivalent facilities, or, more often, the activity simply does not take place in that region. In the rural areas, the commercial operator needs lands suitable for, and capable of, attracting and sustaining intensive use for recreation. He must compete with both private and public sectors for this land. Often, however, only the second best areas are available at a reasonable price, and this is a decided disadvantage if there is any competition from the public sector in supplying facilities.

Canadian Government Office of Tourism photo.

In the rural fringe of many urban areas, ski hills become a highly-visible element of the landscape. Some excellent ski slopes are found in the Laurentians north of Montréal within easy access of a large urban population.

Hinterlands. In the hinterlands, the commercial sector relies almost exclusively on the quality and quantity of the natural resources to attract its clientele. The physical attractiveness of the area, the opportunity for a successful fishing or hunting trip, and free access to the public lands and waters for various activities are the resource base on which many operations depend. Without these, existing resorts would be severely restricted in the types of opportunities they could provide. This dependence on natural resources is a major problem for the commercial sector in the hinterlands. As demand for the same resources increases, whether from forestry, mining, trapping, commercial fishing enterprises, or from the public or private sectors, commercial development will be very susceptible to decreases in availability of the resources on which it depends. Under such pressures, the commercial sector diversifies where possible, but many older resorts and businesses are not in a financial or locational position that allows them to provide for other activities. Resorts in remote locations can not always compete for recreationists who are attracted to resorts with more amenities. Resorts built to accommodate a particular type of guest, such as hunters and fishermen, are not necessarily suitable or attractive for family vacations. The site locations of some resorts do not necessarily attract customers with other more-varied interests.

For these reasons, it is important to much of the present commercial sector that the land and resources in the hinterlands remain attractive to their customers. It is equally important that developers of any additional commercial facilities take into account that pressures on the natural resource base will increase, and that any new development must be able to attract and satisfy a more diversified type of recreationist.

TABLE 13.

Participation rates in four commercial recreation activities associated with urban areas, by province, for persons 14 years and over, 1971

Province	Activities			
	Golf	Tennis	Curling	Bowling
	(per cent of population participating)			
Newfoundland	1.6	2.6	2.1	5.4
Prince Edward Island	5.7	2.4	3.4	9.5
Nova Scotia	5.0	2.9	3.0	12.0
New Brunswick	4.3	2.6	2.5	10.6
Québec	5.4	4.4	1.3	11.2
Ontario	9.1	5.6	3.5	13.5
Manitoba	8.1	3.8	11.8	10.3
Saskatchewan	6.7	2.4	14.5	8.2
Alberta	10.5	6.0	12.4	4.1
British Columbia	8.8	7.2	4.1	11.8
CANADA	7.5	5.0	4.4	11.8

Source: Statistics Canada, 1976b. *Travel, Tourism and Outdoor Recreation: A Statistical Digest 1974 and 1975.* Catalogue 66-202.

Canadian Government Office of Tourism photo.

Remote hunting or fishing camps in the hinterland cater to a relatively small and specialized group of recreationists. Many of these commercially operated enterprises rely heavily on free access to large quantities of high-quality land and water resources.

Commercial Accommodation in the Hinterlands

Amount and Location. To illustrate the extent and variation of recreation in the commercial sector and its implications for land use, the aspect of commercial accommodation will be considered. Commercial accommodation has been classified into six groups of travellers' accommodation by Statistics Canada. These are: hotels, motels, tourist homes, tourist courts and cabins, tent and trailer campgrounds, and outfitters. Table 14 lists the provincial distribution in the number of locations for each group. The last three groups are primarily associated with hinterland areas, although there are exceptions. The amount of use generated by these establishments is dependent on factors of capacity, season of operation, and variation in occupancy. However, this type of information, which would provide a better base for comparing the importance of this sector with others, is not available at the national level.

The provincial variations in the figures, some of which are related to the distribution of suitable resources, some to the accessibility to Crown land, and some to their location relative to markets, give an indication of the relative importance of recreation in the commercial sector in each province. They also give an indication of the potential amount of demand for land in the various provinces. In Ontario, Québec, British Columbia, and Saskatchewan, for example, the competition for resources by outfitters is generally high, and is particularly high in some regions of these provinces. This competition also exists in other provinces, such as New Brunswick, where a smaller number of resorts or outfitters may be fully utilizing the accessible natural resources at the present time.

Thus, in each province, the importance of land for commercial accommodation depends on both the number of competitors and the potential capacity and availability of the resources. Tied to this there is other competition for the land and the resources by forestry, mining, commercial fishing, and other activities.

Change. As available data do not locate the various types of commercial accommodation in each province, it is difficult to delineate the changes that have taken place. However, it is possible to describe the general trend (Table 15). The total number of establishments for travellers' accommodation has decreased in most provinces. Tourist courts and cabins have decreased in all provinces except for Prince Edward Island. Only the tent and trailer group increased in all provinces. Nationally, the increase was about 23 per cent between 1972 and 1975, or just over seven per cent per annum over the three-year period. Generally, accommodation in the commercial sector experienced a period of very little growth except in Newfoundland, New Brunswick, and the Northwest Territories where some growth has occurred. Even here, the growth was only in the number of hotels, motels, and tent and trailer campgrounds.

TABLE 14.

Number of locations for travellers' accommodation, by province, territory, and type of establishment, 1972 and 1975

Province and Territory	Hotels		Motels		Tourist homes		Tourist courts cabins		Tent and trailer campgrounds		Outfitters		Total establishments	
	1972	1975	1972	1975	1972	1975	1972	1975	1972	1975	1972	1975	1972	1975
Newfoundland	71	81	20	37	28	27	24	18	39	45	23	44	205	252
Prince Edward Island	17	23	60	59	122	108	86	88	56	57	1	1	342	336
Nova Scotia	90	97	158	163	78	55	78	71	140	172	3	2	547	560
New Brunswick	67	72	170	171	22	21	64	60	72	124	40	45	435	493
Québec	1,917	1,681	734	736	215	148	135	99	555	676	396	426	3,952	3,766
Ontario	1,260	1,170	1,505	1,436	48	25	2,144	1,729	916	1,555	1,022	1,006	6,895	6,521
Manitoba	267	261	121	113	–	–	61	50	70	107	52	65	580	596
Saskatchewan	444	390	157	153	1	1	64	51	71	88	71	108	808	791
Alberta	441	467	325	326	–	–	62	53	106	120	10	14	944	980
British Columbia	502	534	845	842	1	–	352	307	446	477	206	190	2,352	2,350
Yukon	39	39	25	19	–	–	5	4	34	52	6	1	109	115
Northwest Territories	15	19	8	11	–	–	2	1	11	18	13	35	49	84
CANADA	5,139	4,834	4,128	4,006	515	385	3,007	2,531	2,516	3,091	1,843	1,973	17,218	16,844

Source: Statistics Canada, 1976b. *Travel, Tourism and Outdoor Recreation: A Statistical Digest 1974 and 1975.* Catalogue 66-202.
_____, 1977f. *Traveller Accommodation Statistics, 1975.* Catalogue 63-204.

TABLE 15.

Percentage change in the number of establishments for travellers' accommodation, by province, territory, and establishment type, 1972 to 1975

Province and Territory	Type of establishment						
	Hotel	Motel	Tourist homes	Tourist courts and cabins	Tent and trailer campgrounds	Outfitters	All establishments
	(percentage change in numbers)						
Newfoundland	14.08	85.00	-3.57	-25.00	15.38	91.30	-22.93
Prince Edward Island	35.29	-1.67	-11.48	2.33	1.79	0.0	-1.75
Nova Scotia	7.78	3.16	-29.49	-8.97	22.86	-33.33	2.38
New Brunswick	7.46	0.59	-4.55	-6.25	72.22	12.50	13.33
Québec	-12.31	0.27	-31.16	-26.67	21.80	7.58	-4.71
Ontario	-7.14	-4.58	-47.91	-19.36	26.09	-1.57	-5.42
Manitoba	-5.43	-6.61	—	-18.03	52.86	25.00	2.76
Saskatchewan	-12.16	-2.55	0.0	-20.31	23.94	52.11	-2.10
Alberta	5.90	.31	—	-14.52	13.21	40.00	3.81
British Columbia	6.37	-.36	100.00	-12.78	6.95	-7.77	-0.09
Yukon	0.0	-24.00	—	-20.00	52.94	-83.33	5.50
Northwest Territories	26.67	37.50	—	-50.00	63.64	169.23	71.43
CANADA	-5.94	-1.50	-25.24	-17.74	22.85	5.10	-2.17

Sources: Statistics Canada, 1977f. Traveller Accommodation Statistics, 1975. Catalogue 63-204.
          _____, 1978d. Travel, Tourism and Outdoor Recreation: A Statistical Digest 1975 and 1976. Catalogue 66-202.

NFB PHOTOTHEQUE – ONF – Photo by Crombie McNeill.

With increasing emphasis on physical fitness, many urban residents take advantage of existing green spaces. Here joggers enjoy exercising along the Driveway in Ottawa.

Of the three accommodation groups associated primarily with the hinterland region, there have been significant increases only in the tent and trailer campground group (23 per cent increase in the period from 1972 to 1975). This is comparable to changes occurring in the private sector in which cottage lands have increased at about seven per cent per annum over a similar period. The slow growth rates and the actual decreases in the number of establishments in some groups suggest that there may be problems in the commercial sector as a whole. The reasons for the slow growth in accommodation are probably related to broader economic problems which include increases in labour, capital, and land costs, relatively high transportation and accommodation costs in Canada, and other economic problems, at the national and international levels, facing the entire tourism industry. Increasing demand for land and recreation resources may also be affecting particular areas but it is difficult to isolate these from the other problems. It is suggested, however, that if the growth in the number of establishments could be accurately located within Canada much of it would be found in areas of unused resource potential such as in the Yukon and Northwest Territories. The new facilities are, in effect, being developed to meet new recreation demands such as those for camper and mobile home type of recreation.

Critical Lands. The importance of the land and resource base for commercial accommodation will be difficult to determine even with additional data. As demands for land increase, whether for recreation, agriculture, forestry, urban growth or other purposes, the importance of the land is also going to increase. In areas where demands overlap, as have those for recreation, it will become more crucial to maintain the rôle that each sector plays in providing opportunities for recreation. It appears from the available data, that the commercial sector, in many areas, may be reaching a point at which the demands for land and resource resources by the other sectors are coming into conflict, or significant changes are taking place in the types of demands for recreation. The evaluation of the importance of the land and resources for this sector can be accomplished only if all other demands on, and uses of the resources were known.

Public Sector

Public lands used for outdoor recreation can be divided into areas designated for recreation and open spaces where recreation is generally permitted.

Urban Areas. Within the urban context, lands designated for outdoor recreation offer a wide range of opportunities for active recreation such as baseball, swimming, bicycling, and the more passive activities of walking and picnicking. Many parks are designed for specialized activities to the exclusion of others. Other urban public lands may function primarily as flood control areas or as transportation and transmission corridors, but they also provide spaces for recreation. Together these two types of areas can provide significant opportunities for recreation and an aesthetically pleasing environment for living. The amount of use made of any particular park or open space will be affected by accessibility, types of facilities, and socio-economic factors of the users. In the urban areas, the amount of land classified as either parks or open space has not been determined at the national scale for several reasons. There are problems of definition in the terminology. Also, the need for this type of information at the national scale has not existed, and the rapid changes that occur in land use make the upkeep of data difficult.

NFB PHOTOTHEQUE – ONF – Photo by Crombie McNeill.

For many urban residents, especially those without cars, neighbourhood parks and open spaces provide many opportunities for outdoor activities. Most urban green spaces are used year-round. Tobogganing is a favourite winter sport of many youngsters.

As an example of the amount and variation of open space that is available in urban areas, the three largest metropolitan centres, Montréal, Toronto, and Vancouver are used for illustration (Table 16). In 1971, the proportions of open space to the total area varied greatly between Toronto and the other two urban areas. Part of this difference may be related to the size of each urban area; Toronto is more than twice the physical size of Montréal, and 25 per cent larger than Vancouver. Figures for the amount of open space per 1,000 population have been used to evaluate the adequacy of recreation opportunity, and these suggest that opportunities for recreation are higher in Vancouver than in the other two cities, and that Montréal is, by comparison, lacking open space for recreation.

Such evaluations could be erroneous if, for example, the majority of open space in one city were not accessible or designed for recreation, or a disproportionate amount of its open space was related to one type of recreation. Thus, comparisons using this type of data can only be made using particular types of recreation. The question of how much recreation opportunity is adequate faces all levels of the public sector and has yet to be resolved.

Rural Areas. In the urban fringe and rural regions of the provinces, public lands make up only a small percentage of the total area. They can be classified into those areas designated specifically for recreation, and those managed for multiple uses which may include forestry, wildlife and waterfowl production or protection, and environmental management of flood-susceptible or erosion-prone areas. The extent of these multiple-use areas varies provincially, as some provinces are more involved in intensive resource management than others. This involvement appears to occur in rural areas where the majority of the land is in private ownership, and where there are relatively high concentrations of people with environmental and land management problems. These may include the control of land in hazard lands or the management of marginal agricultural lands.

The assessment of the importance of land held by the public sector in the rural areas is hampered by the lack of data about land ownership, method of management, and types of recreation for which the land is used. Information on lands designated for recreation use such as parks, conservation, and wildlife areas is available but must be obtained from many sources. The largest problem is determining the importance of recreation in the undesignated, multiple-use lands. With increases in population and changes in participation, areas such as public forests, which may not have been significant for recreation in the past, are becoming more important. To determine the importance of any particular area it is necessary to relate the area and the many activities to the entire recreation supply. There is a recognized need to supply recreation opportunities in those areas close to the urban centres in Canada. Accessibility is becoming an increasingly important factor in locating opportunities for recreation. As travel costs continue to rise and urban centres continue to grow, the lands held by the public sector in these areas will be in greater demand and will increase in significance.

Hinterlands. In the hinterland areas of Canada, Crown land accounts for 85 per cent of the total land held in the public sector. Some areas are designated specifically for recreation, generally as parks. Other areas, for example wildlife and waterfowl sanctuaries, are designated for preservation objectives rather than directly for recreation. The majority of these lands are accessible to the public and are managed as multiple-use areas, but their importance in providing recreation opportunity is generally unknown. The types of use include hunting and fishing, but the large areas involved and their general inaccessibility from major centres of population, mean that the majority of this public land will not be used for recreation.

RECREATION OPPORTUNITY

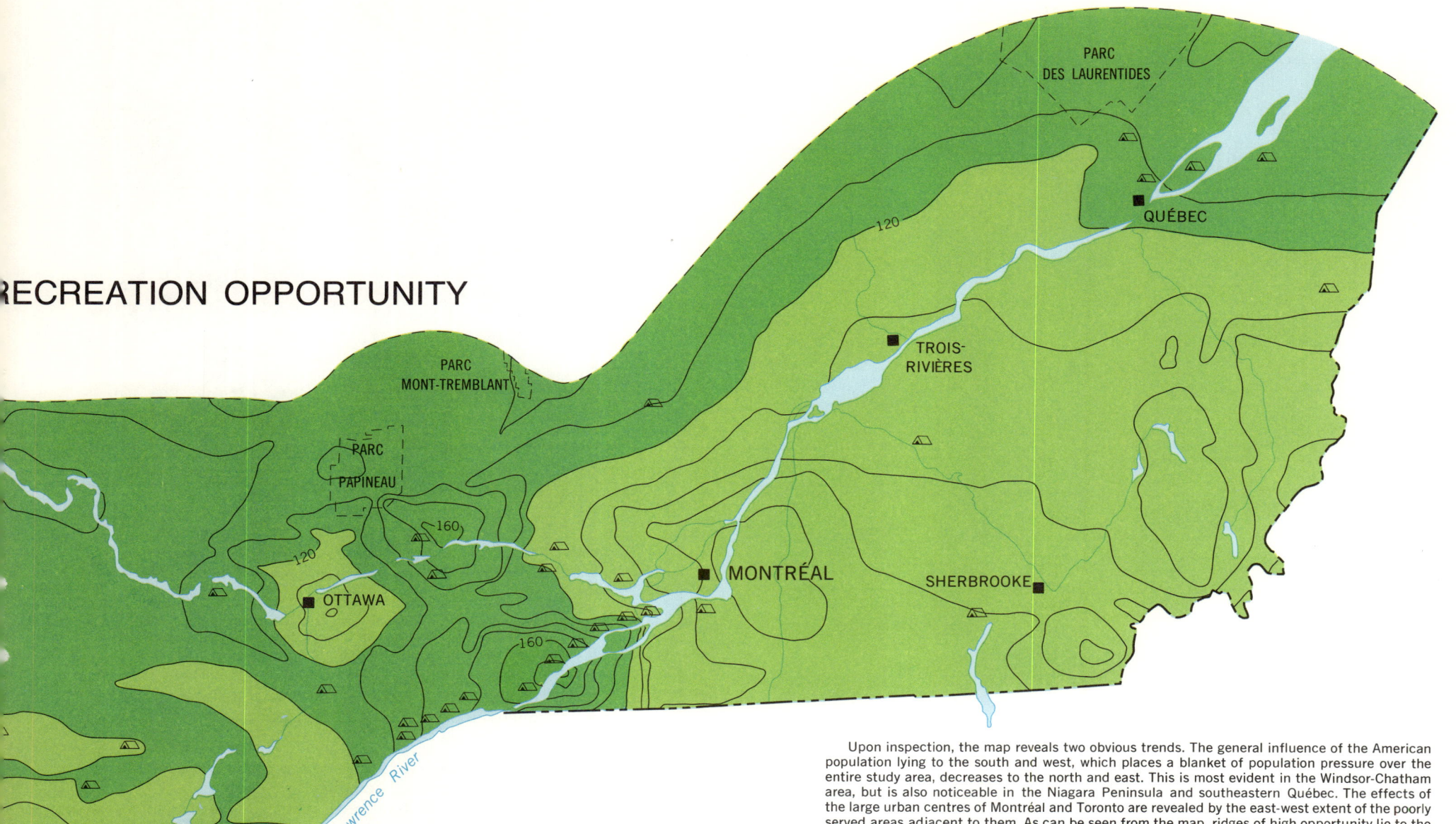

metropolitan areas have
es. The accompanying
ous areas. The mapping
uities throughout the
ty adjacent to Toronto

ortunity to engage in
al or provincial govern-
e termed the 'Outdoor
ie supply of recreation
is defined as being the

ary pressure one would
ould feel less pressure
ting the total pressure
wns in Canada drops off
population 10,000) and
uld be:

This figure is referred to as the population potential. This equation can be modified to incorporate the population potential exerted by all population centres within a certain distance.[2] The population potential at any point is:

$$pp = \frac{P_1}{D_1} + \frac{P_2}{D_2} + \frac{P_3}{D_3} \ldots$$

where P_1, P_2, P_3 ... are the populations of the population centres and D_1, D_2, D_3 ... are their respective distances from this point. Because of the additional pressure put on Canadian recreational resources by visitors from the United States, the American influence was considered as a special factor. State populations, allocated to the centroids of the states, were added to the right hand side of the equation as if they were Canadian population centres.

Calculation of the demand measure is followed by a determination of a supply measure termed the supply potential. The method employed is similar to that of finding the population potential. The supply of opportunity attributable to an individual recreation site is also assumed to decrease with distance. The simplest way of weighting the recreation sites, comparable to the weighting of population centres by their population, is to utilize the actual land area of each recreation site. There is a point to be considered with regard to using site area as a weight. The relationship between area and opportunity may not increase in direct proportion, in people's perception. In this case, instead of using the actual site area, the natural logarithm of area is utilized as a weight. This decision was reached after considering a law of psychology, Fechner's Law, which states that the human response to a stimulus does not increase linearly but rather logarithmically. What this means in terms of recreation areas is that people are generally unable to perceive the difference in area between two parks with only a proportionally small size difference. In using the natural logarithm, adjustment is made for this. In the case of two parks, one ten times the area of the other, the larger will be perceived as 3.3 times bigger, according to Fechner's Law. Similarly, if the ratio of the areas is 2.5:1, the perceived ratio is about 1.92:1. The practical effect of using Fechner's Law is that more weight is given to the smaller parks, and less to the larger. The supply potential at any point is expressed as:

$$SP = \frac{\ln S_1}{D_1} + \frac{\ln S_2}{D_2} + \frac{\ln S_3}{D_3} \ldots$$

where $\ln S_1$, $\ln S_2$, $\ln S_3$ are the natural logarithms of the physical areas of the recreation sites and D_1, D_2, D_3 ... are their respective distances[2] from this point.

The measures of supply potential (SP) and population potential (PP), once calculated, can be combined to express accessibility. In general, where the supply potential is high and the population is low, there is a high degree of accessibility to recreation sites. This accessibility is defined in terms of an opportunity ratio calculated for each point by the equation:

$$OR = \frac{SP}{PP}$$

The opportunity ratio is converted into an Opportunity Quotient through adjustment so that the average is given the value of 100, the rest ranging above and below this figure. It is this Opportunity Quotient which is contoured on the above map. It can be seen, for example, that residents of Québec City have approximately 1.71 times as much recreation opportunity, as defined here, as the residents of Toronto (120/70), while those of Ottawa have 1.57 times as much recreation opportunity (110/70).

Upon inspection, the map reveals two obvious trends. The general influence of the American population lying to the south and west, which places a blanket of population pressure over the entire study area, decreases to the north and east. This is most evident in the Windsor-Chatham area, but is also noticeable in the Niagara Peninsula and southeastern Québec. The effects of the large urban centres of Montréal and Toronto are revealed by the east-west extent of the poorly served areas adjacent to them. As can be seen from the map, ridges of high opportunity lie to the northwest of Kitchener-Waterloo, to the north of Peterborough and Kingston, and generally to the north of the study area. These are broken by areas of lower opportunity appearing in the area between Kingston and Ottawa, and around Kingston itself. The high values of the Algonquin Park site reflect the relative abundance of recreation land and the comparative lack of population in that area, while in the Muskoka-Haliburton region, the pressure of the cities to the immediate south holds down the quotient, although it is considerably above that of the Lake Ontario shore area. Similarly, the area of relatively high opportunity in the northern region of the Québec portion on the map, reflects the potential for recreation that is available, especially to residents of Ottawa-Hull, Montréal, Trois-Rivières, and Québec City, as provided by such parks as Mont-Tremblant, Papineau, and Laurentides.

The measurement of intangible concepts, such as recreation opportunity, is exceedingly complex and plagued by both theoretical and practical problems. Many of the questions and assumptions inherent in the gravitational approach employed here are being dealt with in present research projects which have yet to be reported. It is believed, however, that the foregoing methodology presents a reasonably accurate portrayal of recreation opportunity in the Windsor-Québec study area.

Today, all types of pressure are exerted on the urban dweller. Crowding, crime, pollution, traffic congestion and innumerable other frustrations are associated with urbanization. People are looking to the country for fresh air, open space and recreation opportunity. However, recreation activities such as camping, hiking, biking, downhill and cross-country skiing and snowmobiling require land, and recreation frequently faces competition from other uses for this resource. The demand for recreational land is increasing dramatically, and competition among users of existing recreation areas is such that certain sites suffer from the same crowding and pollution problems the vacationers seek to escape. At the present time there does not appear to be sufficient recreational land to satisfy the particular needs of over 10,000,000 urban dwellers in the Windsor-Québec axis. Recently, however, several interesting techniques of partially resolving this situation have been suggested. Ontario has proposed a multi-purpose parkway belt system designed to provide open space and recreation opportunity for urban residents and to reserve certain land for future use, in addition to preventing uncontrolled urban sprawl and linking communities via service corridors. Preservation of at least portions of unique features such as the Niagara Escarpment is essential for recreation as well as other purposes. What other decisions must be made, and what action taken, to ensure the quantity and variety of recreational land resources necessary to meet future requirements?

1 The recreation sites considered in this study were those recorded during the 1969 Canada Outdoor Recreation Demand Study (CORDS) Facility Inventory. They include National and Provincial Parks, picnic areas and recreation preserves, but do not include areas administered by local governments or conservation authorities.
Gatineau Park is under the jurisdiction of the National Capital Commission and is not included in this study.

2 The distance cut-off for this study was arbitrarily set at 500 miles. This means, in effect, that we are dealing with the opportunity to recreate at sites within a 1 day drive from the origin of the recreators.

Data Source

Canada, Department of Indian and Northern Affairs, 1969 Canada Outdoor Recreation Demand Study Facility Inventory, unpublished data.

Special acknowledgement is made to Dr. J.H. Ross and his assistants of the Outdoor Recreation-Open Space Division, Lands Directorate, for the preparation of this map and contribution to the text.

Source: Simpson-Lewis, Wendy, 1974. The Windsor-Québec Axis.

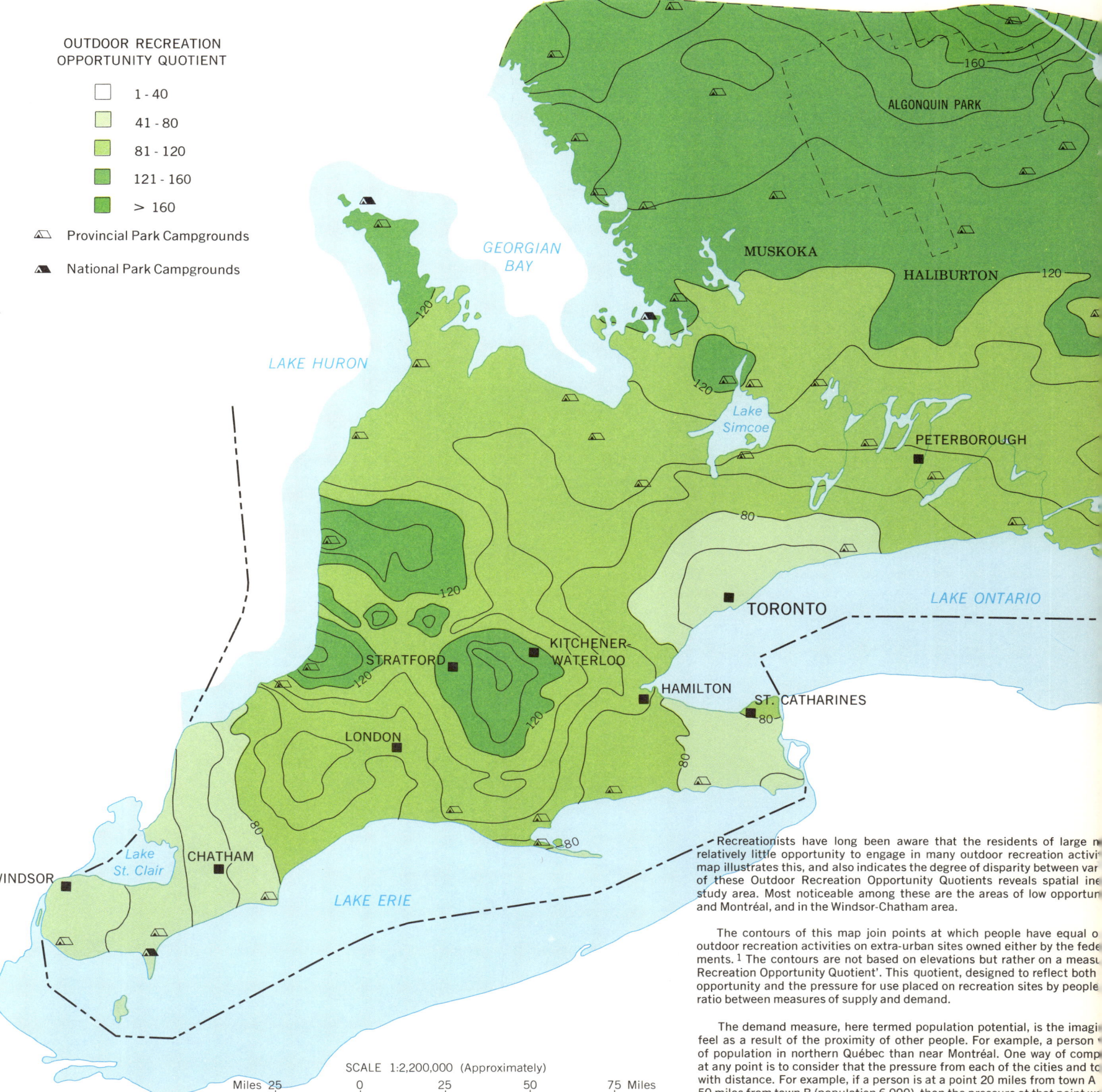

OUTDOOR R

Recreationists have long been aware that the residents of large m
relatively little opportunity to engage in many outdoor recreation activi
map illustrates this, and also indicates the degree of disparity between var
of these Outdoor Recreation Opportunity Quotients reveals spatial ine
study area. Most noticeable among these are the areas of low opportun
and Montréal, and in the Windsor-Chatham area.

The contours of this map join points at which people have equal o
outdoor recreation activities on extra-urban sites owned either by the fede
ments.[1] The contours are not based on elevations but rather on a measu
Recreation Opportunity Quotient'. This quotient, designed to reflect both
opportunity and the pressure for use placed on recreation sites by people
ratio between measures of supply and demand.

The demand measure, here termed population potential, is the imagi
feel as a result of the proximity of other people. For example, a person
of population in northern Québec than near Montréal. One way of comp
at any point is to consider that the pressure from each of the cities and to
with distance. For example, if a person is at a point 20 miles from town A
50 miles from town B (population 6,000), then the pressure at that point wo

$$pp = \frac{10{,}000 \text{ people}}{20 \text{ miles}} + \frac{6{,}000 \text{ people}}{50 \text{ miles}} = 620 \text{ people/miles}$$

MAP 15

Canadian Government Office of Tourism photo.

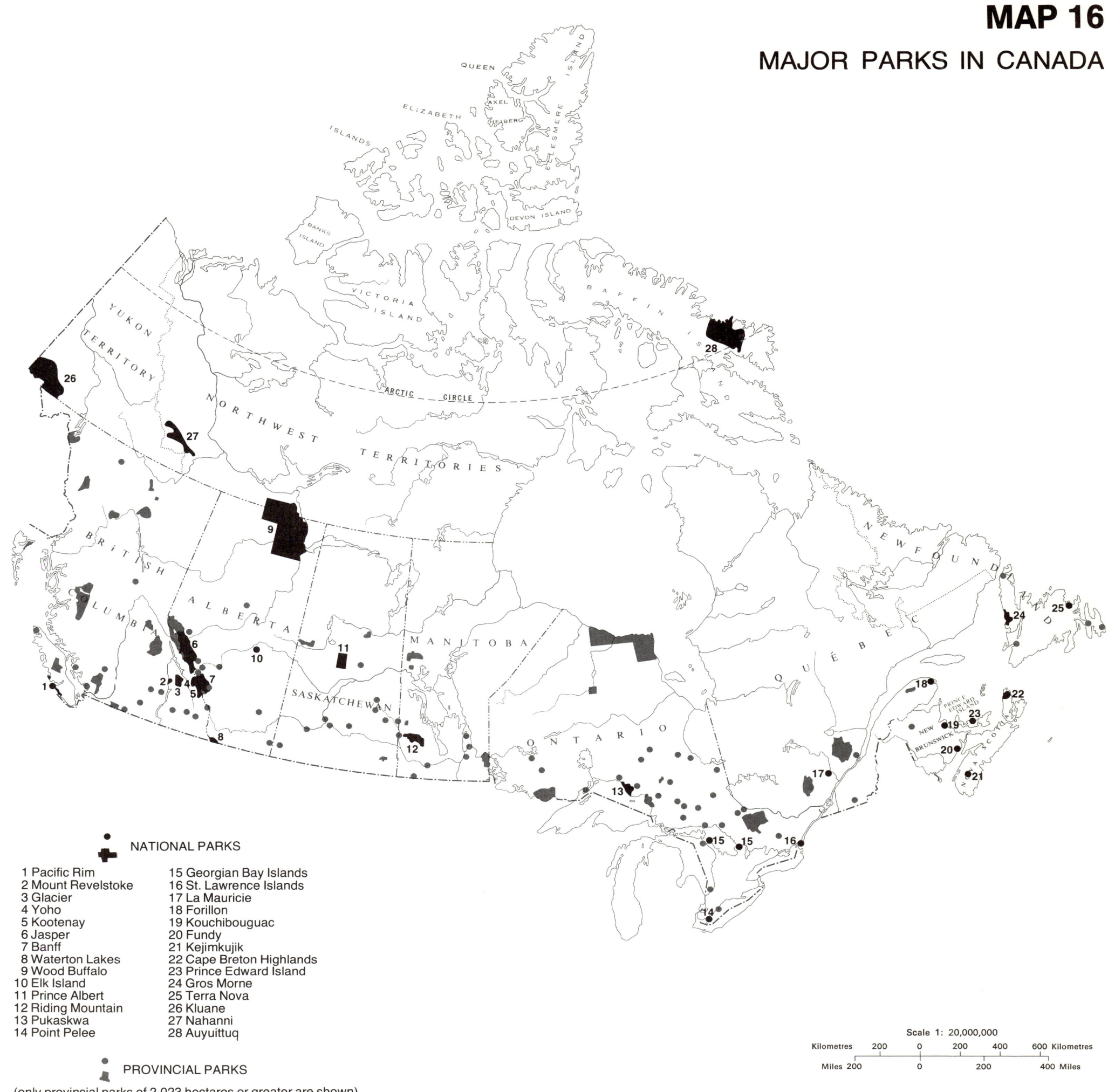

TABLE 16.

Open space for recreation* in Montreal, Toronto, and Vancouver, 1971

	Montréal+	Toronto++	Vancouver
Open space** (ha)	3,400	7,689	5,628
Proportion of open space to total area (per cent)	4.1	12.3	4.5
Open space per 1,000 population (ha)	1.5	3.7	5.5

* Recreation includes all individual or group activities.

** Open space includes all public open space and golf courses, but excludes cemetaries.

+ Includes Île-de-Montréal, Île-Jésus, Longueuil, and St-Bruno-de-Montarville.

++ Metropolitan Toronto only.

Source: Ministry of State for Urban Affairs, 1974. *Urban Open Space Study for Canadian Communities.*

In areas along transportation routes, there are higher levels of use than in the less accessible areas. There are also higher levels of use in specific locations which offer particular attractions, such as wild rivers, known fishing lakes, or areas that produce large concentrations of game for hunting and viewing.

In Canada, the economic base of many small communities is dependent on the use of mineral and forest resources in the hinterlands. The importance of public areas to these local residents is considerable. As the communities are small, the variety of public facilities for recreation is less than that supplied by larger communities. As a result, the Crown lands, particularly in the immediate environs of the community, become the prime recreation area for local people.

The level of importance of Crown lands relates more to the type of activities than to the location, and is dependent on natural resources not usually available in the urban or rural regions. The amount of use has not been studied at the national or even the provincial level, but problems that have developed with the use of Crown lands by recreationists have come to the attention of many provinces, states, and other countries (Hendee *et al.*, 1976; Masse, 1975; and Ontario Ministry of Natural Resources, 1975). The problems include over-utilization of a resource, such as game or fish, maintenance and control problems (garbage, fires, damage to equipment of other resource users), and competition between the public and commercial sectors.

In the hinterland areas of Canada, the most significant public lands designated for recreation are the provincial and National parks. Some provinces have also, in a somewhat less formal manner, designated small sites for bathing, picnicking, boat launching, and primitive camping. These do not generally provide the range of facilities or attractions found in the formal parks but do offer a less-contrived recreation environment.

Parks

The provincial and National parks of Canada are located not only in the hinterland region, but also are now located or being located in the rural and urban fringes to meet the demand for recreation. They have often been selected to protect or manage a particular attraction, such as a special beach, a special land or water feature, or a vegetation type. The data available for provincial and National parks indicate the importance of public parks and how it has changed.

Amount and Location. National and provincial parks serve two prime purposes: they provide a natural environment for many recreation activities; and they preserve natural and historical resources for present and future generations. The amount and type of park land held by the federal and provincial governments is shown in Table 17. As of June 1976, there were 1,880 parks of various classes encompassing 33,255,860 ha.

Their distribution by province shows that there are major variations in the number, type, and size of parks (Map 16).

—The majority of park areas (total of National and provincial) is classed as wilderness, 89.2 per cent.

—The largest proportion of the National Park area is classed as wilderness, 99.3 per cent.

—The largest share of the National Park area is located in Alberta, 40.9 per cent of the total, with the Yukon and Northwest Territories together accounting for another 44.7 per cent.

Photo by K.G. Taylor

Alberta, together with the Yukon and Northwest Territories, accounts for 85 per cent of Canada's National Parks area. The salt flats near the Alberta-Northwest Territories border are one of the interesting features of Wood Buffalo National Park.

—The provinces supply 60.9 per cent of the total designated park area in Canada.

—The provision of areas for historical, ethnological, and archaeological interpretation is dominated by the National Park system which provides 83.4 per cent of the total area in that class.

—Provincial and territorial parks number 1,706, the majority of which are classed as parkway/highway areas, followed by specialized recreation areas.

—The park area per person varies from 0.033 ha per person in Prince Edward Island to 100.9 ha per person in the Yukon. Generally, the range is between a low of 0.1 in the Maritimes to a high of 3.25 in Alberta. The large wilderness parks skew this distribution considerably. (*Derived from* Tables 17 and 20).

TABLE 17.
Park classification system for National and provincial parks, 1976

Province and Territory	Wilderness areas National	Wilderness areas Provincial	Historical, ethnological and archaeological National	Historical, ethnological and archaeological Provincial	Unique areas National	Unique areas Provincial	Natural environment recreation areas National	Natural environment recreation areas Provincial	Specialized outdoor recreation areas National	Specialized outdoor recreation areas Provincial	Parkway, highway parks National	Parkway, highway parks Provincial	Total designated park area National	Total designated park area Provincial	Park and recreational reserves National	Park and recreational reserves Provincial
						(ha)										
Newfoundland	233,907	722,462	8,802	–	–	902	–	15,827	–	3,026	–	14	242,709	742,231	–	34,067
Prince Edward Island	–	–	91	81	–	539	1,813	736	–	504	–	136	1,904	1,996	–	1,345
Nova Scotia	133,206	–	5,380	64	–	–	–	1,888	–	2,376	–	132	138,586	4,460	–	6,597
New Brunswick	43,124	–	260	–	–	454	–	21,072	–	980	–	126	43,384	22,632	–	–
Québec	78,427	8,053,000	251	120	–	829,920	35,613	15,540	–	5,790	–	140	114,291	8,904,510	–	4,034,656
Ontario	187,778	3,020,290	550	–	1,554	1,533	1,839	940,451	–	4,146	–	405	191,721	3,966,825	–	511,684
Manitoba	297,596	–	105	10	–	34,328	–	854,850	–	1,243	–	1,072	297,701	880,503	–	3,558
Saskatchewan	387,470	–	1,778	2,561	–	34,108	–	477,774	–	12,837	–	790	389,248	528,070	–	4,988
Alberta	5,301,044	560,899	219	–	–	34,639	19,425	55,848	–	5,750	–	102	5,320,688	657,238	–	30,200
British Columbia	430,310	4,401,677	48	644	–	3,027	13,986	135,170	–	7,674	–	129	444,344	4,548,321	–	–
Yukon	2,201,538	–	20	–	–	–	–	–	–	–	–	2,092	2,201,558	2,092	–	979,558
Northwest Territories	3,607,932	–	–	–	–	11	–	2,198	–	676	–	31	3,607,932	2,916	740,753	6,850
CANADA	2,902,332	16,758,328	17,504	3,480	1,554	928,461	72,676	2,521,354	–	45,002	–	5,169	12,994,066	20,261,794	740,753	–

– means nil

Source: Federal-Provincial Parks Conference, 1976. *Park Classification System, National and Provincial Parks.*

MAP 17

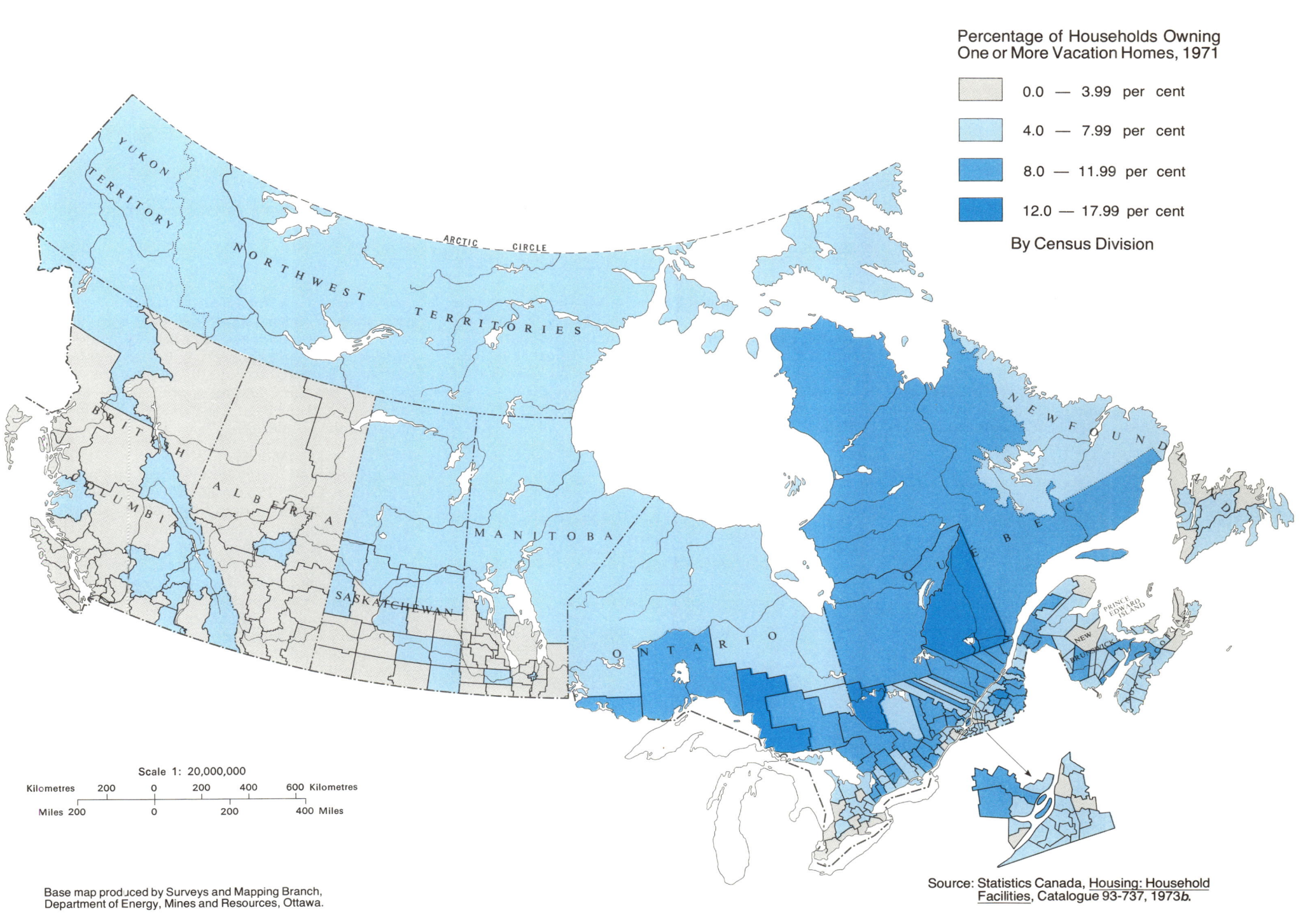

PERCENTAGE OF HOUSEHOLDS OWNING VACATION HOMES

Percentage of Households Owning One or More Vacation Homes, 1971

- 0.0 — 3.99 per cent
- 4.0 — 7.99 per cent
- 8.0 — 11.99 per cent
- 12.0 — 17.99 per cent

By Census Division

Base map produced by Surveys and Mapping Branch, Department of Energy, Mines and Resources, Ottawa.

Source: Statistics Canada, Housing: Household Facilities, Catalogue 93-737, 1973b.

TABLE 18.

Population, area, and park area, by province and territory, 1976

Province and Territory	Population 1976	Area land and water	Population density	Provincial parks Number	Area	National Parks Number	Area	Totals Number	Area	Population/ park area
		(km²)	(population/km²)		(ha)		(ha)		(ha)	(ha)
Newfoundland	557,725	404,363	1.37	74	742,231	9	242,709	83	984,940	1.77
Prince Edward Island	118,229	5,654	20.91	41	1,996	3	1,904	44	3,900	.03
Nova Scotia	828,571	55,469	14.93	91	4,460	12	138,586	103	143,046	.17
New Brunswick	677,250	73,409	9.22	61	22,632	7	43,384	68	66,016	.10
Québec	6,234,445	1,540,093	4.04	16	8,904,510	20	114,291	36	9,018,801	1.45
Ontario	8,264,465	1,068,175	7.73	389	3,966,825	19	191,721	408	4,158,546	.5
Manitoba	1,021,056	649,839	1.57	149	880,503	7	297,701	156	1,178,204	1.15
Saskatchewan	921,323	651,651	1.41	457	528,070	5	389,248	462	917,318	1.00
Alberta	1,838,037	660,933	2.78	62	657,238	6	5,320,688	67	5,977,926	3.25
British Columbia	2,466,608	948,234	2.60	283	4,548,321	10	444,344	293	4,992,665	2.02
Yukon	21,836	536,120	.04	60	2,092	4	2,201,558	64	2,203,650	100.92
Northwest Territories	42,609	378,393	.01	23	2,916	2	3,607,932	25	3,610,848	84.74
CANADA	22,992,604	9,972,334	2.30	1,760	20,261,794	104	12,994,066	1,810	33,255,860	100.4

Sources: Statistics Canada, 1974b. *Canada Year Book, 1974.*
           , 1977c. *Population: Geographic Distributions: Federal Electoral Districts.* Catalogue 92-801.
Federal-Provincial Parks Conference, 1976. *Park Classification System, National and Provincial Parks.*

From the data presented in Tables 17 and 18, the variation in the number and size of parks among the provinces is quite significant. If the number of parks occurring in each province is used as an indicator of importance in the provision of recreation opportunities, then Saskatchewan, Ontario, and British Columbia provide the most important recreation areas in Canada. On the other hand, if size is used as a measure of importance, then the National Parks in Alberta are by far the most important. However, number and size alone are not the only measures appropriate in assessing the importance of park areas. Many factors influence the designation of land for parks including the purpose for which the parks system was created. For example, National Parks are created to protect large areas of Canadian significance, but are not necessarily chosen or designated to provide for intensive recreation use. Many park areas of much smaller size have been created to serve single recreation activities such as picnicking. The importance of parks in meeting the needs of people for recreation is related to both the number and the size of the park, but the importance can only be assessed in terms of whether or not the parks are meeting the demands of the people.

Park Use. The amount of use, in terms of visitor-days and campground use at National and provincial parks, is shown in Tables 19 and 20. Several problems arise in gathering statistics relating to park use, particularly in terms of definition. Only the visitor-day data are consistent among all the parks and, therefore, adequately indicate the variations that occur from province to province. Comparisons are complicated due to differences in the types of parks in the two systems, the types of facilities, and the differences in the costs of using the parks. For example, at that time there were no entrance fees for National Parks in the Atlantic and Québec regions and this alone may have encouraged more use in those regions.

TABLE 19.

Visitation at National Parks, by region, 1975/76 and 1976/77

Region and park	National Parks visitations April 1, 1976 to March 31, 1977	National Parks Campground use: 1975/76	1976/77	change
	(numbers of vehicles)	(number of party-nights)*		(percentage)
ATLANTIC	1,785,589	167,394	170,437	1.8
Cape Breton Highland	366,677	38,850	35,481	- 8.7
Fundy	237,677	37,676	32,200	-14.5
Gros Morne	26,338	3,425	5,581	62.9
Kejimkujik	50,986	19,454	20,417	5.0
Kouchibouguac	35,316	5,004	5,766	15.2
Prince Edward Island	403,839	42,752	42,985	0.5
Terra Nova	664,870	20,233	28,007	38.4
QUÉBEC	300,691	14,334	17,428	21.6
Auyuittuq**	504	***	34	
Forillon	199,473	9,166	10,968	19.7
La Maurice	100,714	5,168	6,426	24.3
ONTARIO	141,694	12,318	9,559	-22.4
Georgian Bay Island	N.A.	9,124	8,147	-10.7
Point Pelee	132,045	(no facility)		
St. Lawrence Island	9,649	2,194	1,412	-35.6
PRAIRIE	439,629	50,323	59,066	17.4
Prince Albert	59,408	15,209	17,584	15.6
Riding Mountain	380,221	34,166	40,758	19.3
Wood Buffalo	N.A.	948	724	-23.6
WESTERN	5,149,398	429,684	427,665	- 0.5
Banff	2,218,583	190,310	196,679	3.3
Elk Island	107,521	(no facility)		
Glacier	439,420	13,660	15,178	11.1
Jasper	706,794	119,929	121,157	1.0
Kootenay	433,471	33,433	31,967	- 4.4
Mount Revelstoke	472,208	(no facility)		
Pacific Rim	177,118	12,799	15,238	19.1
Waterton Lakes	154,368	25,351	28,917	14.0
Yoho	439,915	34,202	18,529	-45.8
TOTALS	7,817,001	674,053	684,155	1.5

* A unit of measure defined as one night of campground use by one group of people occupying a campsite.

** The unit of measure for this park is persons not vehicles.

*** This park was not in existence at that time.

N.A. means data not available.

Source: Parks Canada, 1977b. *Park-Use Statistics, 1976-77.*

TABLE 20.

Visitation at provincial parks, 1974 and 1975

Province	Visitor-days* 1974	1975
	(thousands)	
Newfoundland	2,250	2,710
Prince Edward Island	846	N.A.
Nova Scotia	N.A.	N.A.
New Brunswick	3,810	3,633
Québec	3,932	5,458
Ontario	11,032	11,140
Manitoba	3,569	4,077
Saskatchewan	2,905	3,155
Alberta	5,241	5,331
British Columbia	10,746	9,857
CANADA	44,331	45,361

* Total number of persons visiting each day including campers. (Campers count as a visitor-day per night of stay).

N.A. means data not available.

Source: Statistics Canada, 1978d. *Travel, Tourism and Outdoor Recreation: A Statistical Digest 1975 and 1976.* Catalogue 66-202.

If we assume that the amount of use as indicated by visitor-days does represent an index of importance, then the National Parks in the Western Region are the relatively more important, followed by those in Atlantic, Prairie, Québec, and Ontario regions (see Table 19). The number of visitor-days in provincial parks, in 1974, varied considerably across Canada. Comparison of visitation data with data relating to park size (Figure 3) does not reveal any particular relationship. Québec, with nearly 9 million ha of parks, had only 3.4 million visitor-days in 1973, whereas New Brunswick, with less than 23 thousand ha of parks, had over 3.8 million visitor-days. The relationship between numbers of visitors and park type could be better demonstrated, but data to establish this relationship are not generally available from provincial park statistics for aggregation to the national level.

The amount of campground use also indicates the importance of the parks, and two figures, party-nights and camper nights, are used to describe this amount. In the National Parks, campground use is counted in party-nights, which is defined as the occupation of one campground site for one over-night stay by a person or group of persons. In the provincial parks, campground use is counted in terms of camper nights, which is the total number of campers multiplied by the number of nights they stayed. To compare these two figures, a conversion must first be made. Provincial data from Ontario and Manitoba indicate the average party size for camping to be approximately 2.5 people. This has been used to convert National Park campground use in party-nights to camper nights (Table 21). Provincial parks consistently have greater amounts of camper nights than the National Parks, except in New Brunswick and Nova Scotia. This is a function of facilities and of park purpose. Provincial parks include a wider range of park types than the National Parks of which most are designed to preserve the national heritage rather than to provide recreation facilities. Thus, for camping, the provincial parks are more important.

It is much more difficult to establish the relative importance of areas which are little used for recreation. In these cases, it is appropriate to use other criteria, such as uniqueness or physical representativeness of an area, as described in the section on physical factors. Therefore, to establish the significance of a park, its use cannot be the sole criterion.

Change. The amount of use in park areas in Canada has increased dramatically in the last 25 years. In the National Parks, the number of visits has increased from 1.8 million in the 1950/1951 season to 16.7 million in the 1976/1977 season (Parks Canada, 1977a) (Figure 4). The changes in use have fluctuated more in the last ten years, during which time there have been some yearly declines in the amount of use. The increases in use during this ten-year period may have been as a result of the creation of new facilities rather than in the increases in use of the existing facilities. For example, between 1973/1974, when the first National Parks were opened in the Québec Region, and 1976/1977, an additional 600,000 visitors were added to the total. This represents only four per cent of the total use across Canada but, combined with use at additional new facilities in Newfoundland, Nova Scotia, and New Brunswick, the results suggest that most increases are a result of more parks rather than a much greater use of the existing parks.

Canadian Government Office of Tourism photo.

Provincial parks, such as Killarney Provincial Park near Sudbury, play an important rôle in meeting demands for camping facilities.

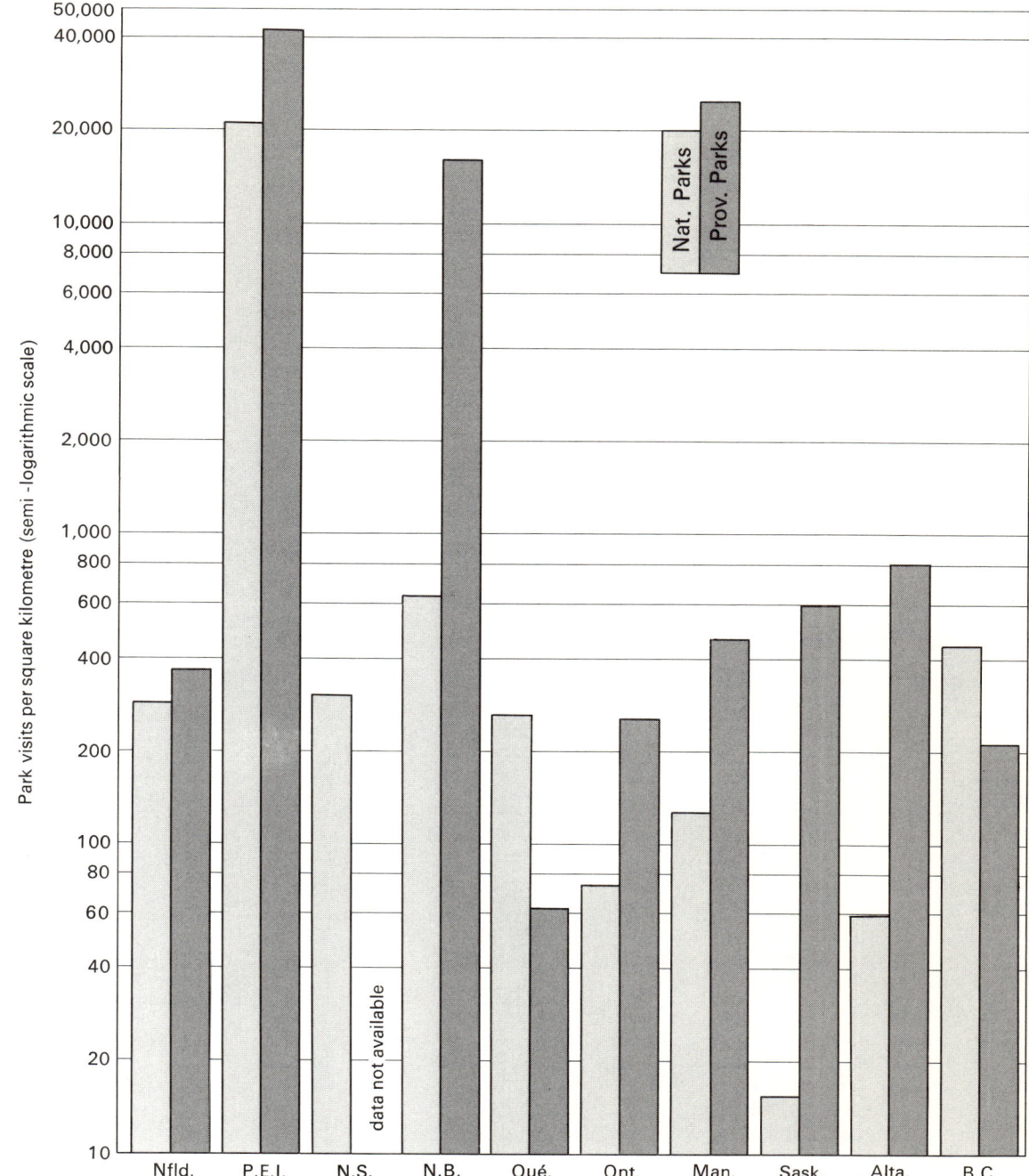

FIGURE 3. Number of park visits[1] per km² of National and provincial parks, by province

(1) Data-National Parks visitation 1976-77.
Provincial parks visitation 1975. (Prince Edward Island-1974).

Source: Statistics Canada, 1978d. Travel, Tourism and Outdoor Recreation: A Statistical Digest 1975 and 1976, Catalogue 66-202.

TABLE 21.

Campground use at National and provincial parks, by province, 1974/75 and 1975

Province	National Parks 1974/75 Party-nights	Camper nights*	Provincial parks 1975 Camper nights	Total Camper nights
Newfoundland	24,000	60,000	418,000	478,000
Prince Edward Island	43,000	107,500	197,000	304,500
Nova Scotia	58,000	145,000	63,000	208,000
New Brunswick	43,000	107,500	339,000	446,500
Québec	14,000	35,000	1,032,000	1,067,000
Ontario	11,000	27,500	3,979,000	4,006,500
Manitoba	28,000	70,000	1,099,000	1,169,000
Saskatchewan	22,000	55,000	1,117,000	1,172,000
Alberta	340,000	850,000	791,000	1,641,000
British Columbia	93,000	232,500	2,793,000	3,025,500
TOTAL	676,000	1,690,000	11,828,000	13,517,000

* Party-nights are converted to camper nights at 2.5 campers per party.

Source: Statistics Canada, 1978d. Travel, Tourism and Outdoor Recreation: A Statistical Digest 1975 and 1976. Catalogue 66-202.

In the provincial parks, similar trends have also occurred. Statistics on park use in Ontario (Figure 5) have shown similar increases in use from 1960 to 1976, (approximately 89 per cent over the 16-year period). In addition to the general increase in use, a pattern of variability in the levels of use is also evident, with major decreases in visitation occurring particularly since 1971. The reasons for these extensive changes in the last few years can only be surmised to be associated with broad economic factors, substitution of use of provincial park facilities by commercial park facilities, and any number of other substitutions or preference changes in participation in recreation.

Critical Lands. From the data on changes in park use, it is evident that parks have in the past played an increasingly important rôle in providing recreation opportunity. In recent years, major variations in the rates of visitation at both National and provincial parks, perhaps indicate that some basic changes are occurring in the demands for the existing facilities. Participation in camping has continued to grow, as have the number of tent and trailer accommodations provided by the commercial sector. While park areas are not necessarily becoming less important, it appears that a greater emphasis or degree of importance will be placed on similar types of facilities provided by the commercial sector.

Present Land Use and Future Planning

Land presently used for outdoor recreation in Canada is not clearly defined in all provinces, but in all sectors there are two basic divisions; areas designated primarily for recreation and recreation-oriented activities, and those undesignated areas which allow recreation. Designated lands include, in the private sector, hobby farms and cottage land; in the commercial sector, campgrounds and golf courses; and, in the public sector, parks at all levels. The undesignated recreation areas include in the private sector, backyards, farms, and woodlots; in the commercial sector, hotels and motels which often double as both business travel accommodation, and direct recreation accommodation; and, in the public sector, open spaces in urban areas, hazard lands, conservation lands, and multiple-use Crown lands. The amount of land and facilities available for recreation has not been determined nationally and is known only for smaller regions. Also, the amounts of recreation use taking place is unknown, so it is difficult to establish the relative importance of the various types of lands for recreation use.

The Lake of the Woods Planning Area in northwestern Ontario illustrates the relative importance of the land utilized by the three sectors for recreation. Here, the three sectors have been dealt with in comparable terms using factors of land use and recreation use (Table 22). The present pattern of use indicates that the land held by the private sector has been the most important in providing recreation. The questions to be asked now, however, relate to what the future rôle of the three sectors should be. With comparable information on the amount of use generated from the various recreation lands in the three sectors, future allocations and developments by the three sectors can influence the rôle and importance that each will play in the future generation of recreation use.

At a larger scale, regionally, provincially, or nationally, it would be advantageous to have compatible and comprehensive data on present land use with which to evaluate the importance of each sector over broader areas. This would enable decisions to be made with a better understanding of how changes in the amount of recreation land and its use in one sector affect the other sectors.

Parks Canada photo.

Tent and trailer accommodations in provincial and National parks, including this location in Fundy National Park in New Brunswick, are important in meeting recreation demands. In the future, however, increased significance will be placed on similar facilities provided by the commercial sector.

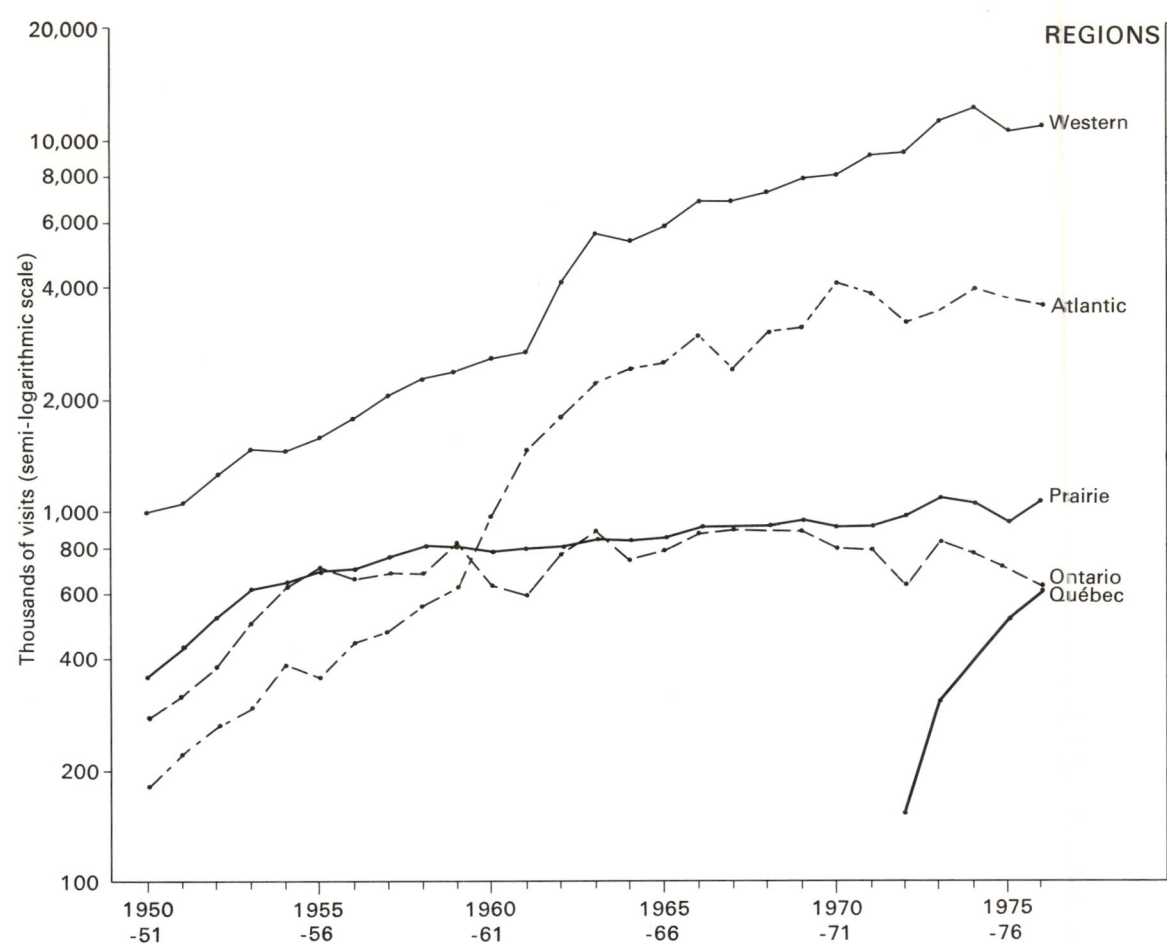

FIGURE 4. Changes in visitation at National Parks, by region, 1950-51 to 1976-77

Source: Parks Canada, 1977b. Park—Use Statistics, 1976-1977.

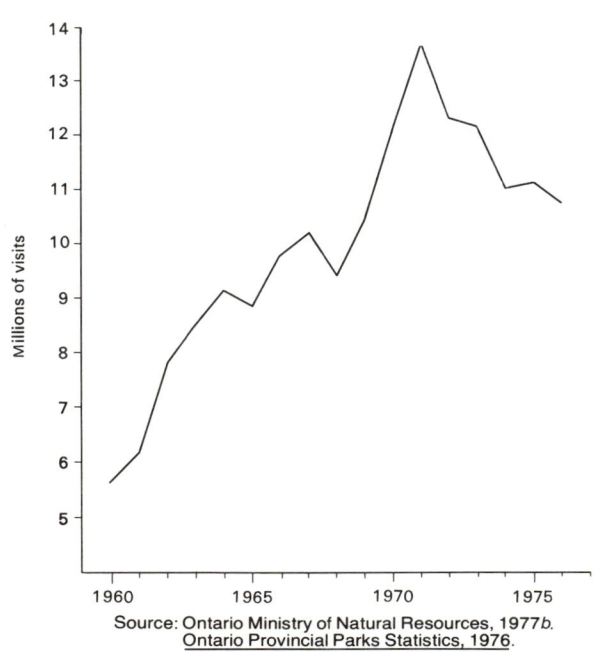

FIGURE 5. Changes in visitation at Ontario provincial parks, 1960 to 1976

Source: Ontario Ministry of Natural Resources, 1977b. Ontario Provincial Parks Statistics, 1976.

Tourism

In the definitions of significant lands for outdoor recreation based on physical factors and present land use, the importance of the land is related only to the actual users. In another perspective, the land, with its physical capabilities, present land use, and facilities, can be considered as a resource from which economic gains can be derived through tourism. Land used for outdoor recreation by tourists provides economic returns to the public and commercial sectors, and affects the private sector in various ways. The importance of tourism in any area is measured by the number of dollars generated, the amount of employment created, and the costs of providing services. The economic importance of tourism must be measured in relation to other activities. Tourism and the lands related to it may provide only a small proportion of the total employment in some areas, whereas in others it may be much more significant.

To examine the importance of tourism across Canada, three measures will be considered: the numbers of non-resident and resident visitors in Canada; the amount, type, and distribution of accommodation; as well as the amount and distribution of employment and revenue gained. As described previously, the relative importance of land for recreation changes with participation rates, with the costs of travel, and with other factors. Changes in tourist activities also influence the degree of importance of the recreation resources. A study of the benefits of tourism compared to the costs required to support it raises questions related to the allocation of land, to the social and environmental impacts of tourism, and to other conflicts.

Tourist Flows

International tourism has grown considerably in the last three decades, for the same general reasons that growth has occurred in most recreation activities: increases in leisure time, disposable income, and accessibility. In international tourism, Canada has received a considerable proportion of the tourist arrivals, primarily because of its location next to the United States. However, in Canada in the last ten years, the percentage of world-wide tourist arrivals has decreased (Table 23), largely as result of fewer arrivals from the United States. Through the years, the reasons for this change include shortages and high costs of gasoline, generally poor weather conditions in summer, higher costs of travel accommodation and service in Canada, plus other economic factors.

The economics of tourism in Canada are also influenced by the fact that more Canadians are travelling outside Canada (Figure 6). The net result of the decrease in the number of non-resident tourists arriving in Canada and the increase in the number of Canadians travelling outside Canada, is a continuing decrease in the balance of payments on travel (Figure 7). Since receipts from travel in Canada by non-residents accounted for 4.2 per cent of the total current account in 1976, and payments by Canadian residents for travel abroad are 6.1 per cent of total current accounts, it is evident that tourism both in Canada and abroad is of major economic importance (Tables 24 and 25), and that the deficit in this area is a serious problem for Canadians.

The importance of non-resident travellers to the various regions of Canada varies significantly. Considering only the number of visitors from the United States staying one or more nights, Ontario, Québec, and British Columbia have recorded the largest numbers (Figure 8). The inequality between the provinces is related to the same factors that influence all land use for recreation: accessibility, attractiveness, and economic conditions.

TABLE 22. Recreation use in the Lake of the Woods Planning Area by the private, commercial, and public sectors

PRIVATE SECTOR

Cottage use

Residence of owner	Cottages	Average number of user days per cottage per Year	User days
Ontario	1,323	300	396,900
Manitoba	2,018	350	706,300
United States and other	1,599	220	276,760
Total	4,599		1,379,960

Other private recreation

In this area, much of the land is Crown land. Other recreation occurring on private lands, such as farms, is assumed to be small. Local use generated from marinas and public access points is considered in other sectors.

COMMERCIAL SECTOR

Commercial accommodation

Accommodation type	Number of locations	Capacity	Occupancy rate	User days*
			(per cent)	
Housekeeping and American Plan	54	2,639	62	163,618
American Plan	44	1,496	49	73,304
Housekeeping, trailer court and camping	115	6,176	67	413,797
Total	213	10,311		650,714

Outpost camps

Number of units	Capacity	Occupancy rate	User days**
		(per cent)	
22	110	25	3,850

Marinas***

Number of rented slips	Season	Boats used	Average number in boat	User days
		(per cent)		
636	70 weekdays	10	3	
	30 weekend days	90		

Calculation: (630 x 70 x 0.1 x 3)+(636 x 30 x .9 x 3) = 64,872

Total   719,436

PUBLIC SECTOR

	Camper days	Visitor-days	User days
Provincial parks	85,675	151,903	237,578

Crown land use

Recreation use generated from Crown land sites such as water access points, roadside areas, etc. was projected from a 1972 survey of Crown land recreation use.   149,311

Total   386,889

SUMMARY OF RECREATION USER DAYS

	User days	Percentage of total
Private Sector	1,379,960	55.5
Commercial Sector	719,436	28.9
Public Sector	386,889	15.6
TOTAL	2,486,285	

* Based on 100-day season.
** Based on 140-day season.
*** Use generated by marina slip rentals to local non-cottager boaters in the planning area.

Source: Ontario Ministry of Natural Resources, 1977a. *Lake of the Woods General Land Use Plan*.

The number and duration of trips taken by Canadians within Canada also reflects the importance of tourism for each province. Ontario has recorded the largest number of trips (including trips by Ontario residents within their province) followed by Québec, British Columbia, and Alberta. In addition to the number of trips taken, the duration of the trip also relates to the affect that tourism has on an area. The longer the stay, generally the larger are the expenditures in that area. Trips in British Columbia have the longest average at 14.1 nights, with Québec receiving only 10.3 (Canadian Government Office of Tourism, 1977c). Table 26 indicates the average duration of stay by United States' visitors in Canada. These differences of a few nights are economically significant for the provinces when they are multiplied by the number of visits and subsequently by the expenditures per visit.

Not only is the number of visitors from the United States declining, but also the same is true of Canadians as tourists in Canada. In 1976, only 62 per cent of vacation trips taken by Canadians were solely within Canada. This has dropped from a high of 71 per cent in both 1971 and 1972, which indicates that outside destinations are becoming more attractive than destinations in Canada. These changes are affecting all regions to different degrees. Lower tourist levels depress the building trades, lower employment opportunities, and decrease provincial tax revenues.

Accommodation and Revenue

The importance of tourism in any province is related to the revenue and employment that it generates, and one of the most important facilities for this is the provision of accommodation. In 1971, of the employment related to travel, tourism, and recreation, 54.4 per cent was attributed to businesses in the accommodation and food services (Statistics Canada, 1978d). Other major employment and income aspects related to tourism include the provision of amusement and recreation services.

In the previous section dealing with land used by the commercial sector, the distribution and amount of accommodation were described (*see* Tables 14 and 15). In Table 27, additional data include the number of rooms, cabins, and tent and trailer sites for each of the major accommodation groups, and the total receipts gained from each group. Ontario, Québec, and British Columbia dominate in the amounts of accommodation and the receipts generated.

To establish the relative importance of tourism for each province, one simple measure relates the amount of accommodation available by type (room, cabin, or tent and trailer site) to the number of visits of one or more nights by United States' visitors. This relates demand, as represented by the number of visits, to supply[3] (Table 28). The results show that Ontario again has the most visitors per location, followed by Alberta and Manitoba with the next largest number of visits per location. Saskatchewan and the Atlantic Provinces have considerably lower values. This variation may be explained by factors such as the length of season for tourist activities, the type of attractions for visitors in the regions, and the relative importance of business travel in the province.

[3] Some of the supply to accommodate visitors is provided in the homes of friends and relatives, and in private cottages. The number of visitors to any province does not include other Canadians or other foreign visitors and, thus, the number of United States' visitors represents only part of the demand.

TABLE 23.

Tourist arrivals* world-wide and Canada, 1968 to 1975

Year	Tourist arrivals world-wide Total arrivals	Annual change	Tourist arrivals in Canada World-wide arrivals in Canada Total arrivals	Annual change	Arrivals from United States Total arrivals	Annual change	Tourist arrivals in Canada as percentage of world-wide total
	(thousands)	(per cent)	(thousands)	(per cent)	(thousands)	(per cent)	(per cent)
1968	141,000		11,573		11,211		8.2
		7.1		5.7		5.0	
1969	151,000		12,232		11,769		8.1
		11.9		10.6		10.4	
1970	169,000		13,530		12,994		8.0
		7.1		4.9		5.0	
1971	181,000		14,188		13,645		7.8
		10.5		-2.7		-4.2	
1972	200,000		13,812		13,067		6.9
		7.5		4.6		3.5	
1973	215,000		14,453		13,523		6.7
		-2.8		-4.5		-5.8	
1974	209,000		13,803		12,735		6.6
		1.9		-1.0		-1.9	
1975	213,000		13,663		12,499		6.4

* Tourist arrivals - those staying one or more nights.

Sources: Statistics Canada, 1976b. *Travel, Tourism and Outdoor Recreation: A Statistical Digest 1974 and 1975*. Catalogue 66-202.
_____, 1978d. *Travel, Tourism and Outdoor Recreation: A Statistical Digest 1975 and 1976*. Catalogue 66-202.

FIGURE 6. Number of Canadian residents[1] returning to Canada, 1972 to 1976

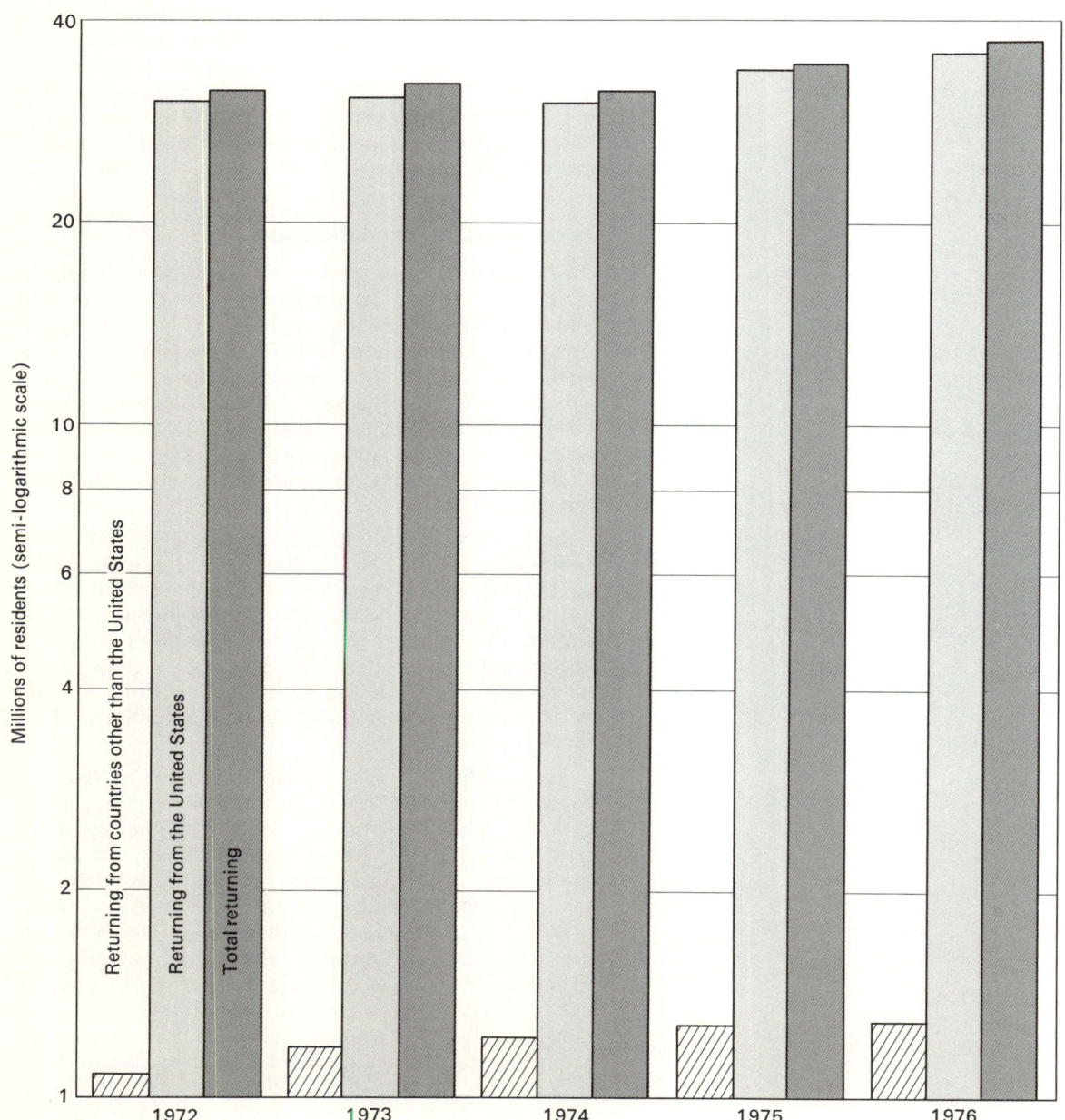

(1) Data represent the number of re-entries by Canadians (any Canadian may re-enter Canada more than once during the same year).

Source: Statistics Canada, 1978d. Travel, Tourism and Outdoor Recreation: A Statistical Digest 1975 and 1976, Catalogue 66-202.

Employment

Perhaps the most relevant measure of the importance of tourism for an area is the amount of employment that it generates. Because tourism involves many types of employment including direct service in the provision of accommodation, food, amusement, and recreation services, and, indirectly, in transportation and the construction of facilities, it is difficult to describe completely the ramifications that tourism has on employment. However, by considering one aspect, the relative significance of this activity in the provinces can be illustrated.

The total number of Canadians employed in 1977 was approximately 9.8 million, of which about 28 per cent were classified in the sector of community, business, and personal service (Table 29), in which tourism-oriented services are classed. One sector that can be identified specifically with tourism represents those involved in providing travellers with accommodation and food. Other sectors, that are associated with tourism, yet not considered as part of the employment total here, are those involved in the amusement and recreation services. Typical services provided in this sector would include employment in the operation of motion picture theatres and bowling alleys. By comparing the proportion of those involved only in the accommodation and food services to the employment in the community, business and personal service, it is possible to determine which provinces have the greater proportions of the service sector involved in tourism-oriented facilities.

British Columbia, Prince Edward Island, and the Yukon and Northwest Territories have high proportions of employment in the service sector associated with the provision of accommodation and food services. This pattern differs from that produced from numbers of accommodation units or flows of tourists, and indicates more clearly the direct effect that tourism has on the resident population.

Summary

Data on the amount and variety of tourism are continually growing, thus providing more opportunities for analysis. The importance of this industry in some provinces and regions can be defined in more detail. Data needed to establish the significance of tourism will be: the number of tourists, the amount of accommodation and other facilities; the amount of revenue generated by this sector; and the extent of employment that is provided by tourism in the area.

Conflicts and Issues

Outdoor activities are varied and the amount of recreation that takes place in any area is subject to many factors involving physical, economic, and personal variables. Lands important to meet the demands of Canadians for direct recreation and for deriving a livelihood from tourism, are equally varied. The methods described here illustrate a few approaches that can be used to identify lands that are significant for some outdoor recreation activities.

In defining these lands, several conflicts and issues which relate directly to the problems of acquisition and management of recreation lands have been recognized. Questions regarding the use of recreation land have been posed by people in many parts of Canada. The attractiveness of a resource must be related to its capacity to physically sustain use, but what is the capacity of the resource? Who is to use the resource? Will it be privately owned or operated by the public through government? What is the area to be used for? Is there a conflict with other resource users? What are the social and economic implications of tourism in an area? These questions and others relate to the significance of various lands for outdoor recreation.

Carrying Capacity

The physical capacity of the land to attract and sustain outdoor recreation varies greatly for different areas and for different activities. This has been illustrated by the various methodologies, particularly by the Canada Land Inventory, which use physical criteria to define important recreation lands. A major problem in providing for recreation, whether in a wilderness park or at a day-use bathing beach, is to determine how much use can be maintained in the area before the physical attributes of the site are destroyed, or before the area becomes too crowded for the particular activity and, hence, unattractive.

FIGURE 7. Balance of payments on travel account, quarterly, 1970 to 1978

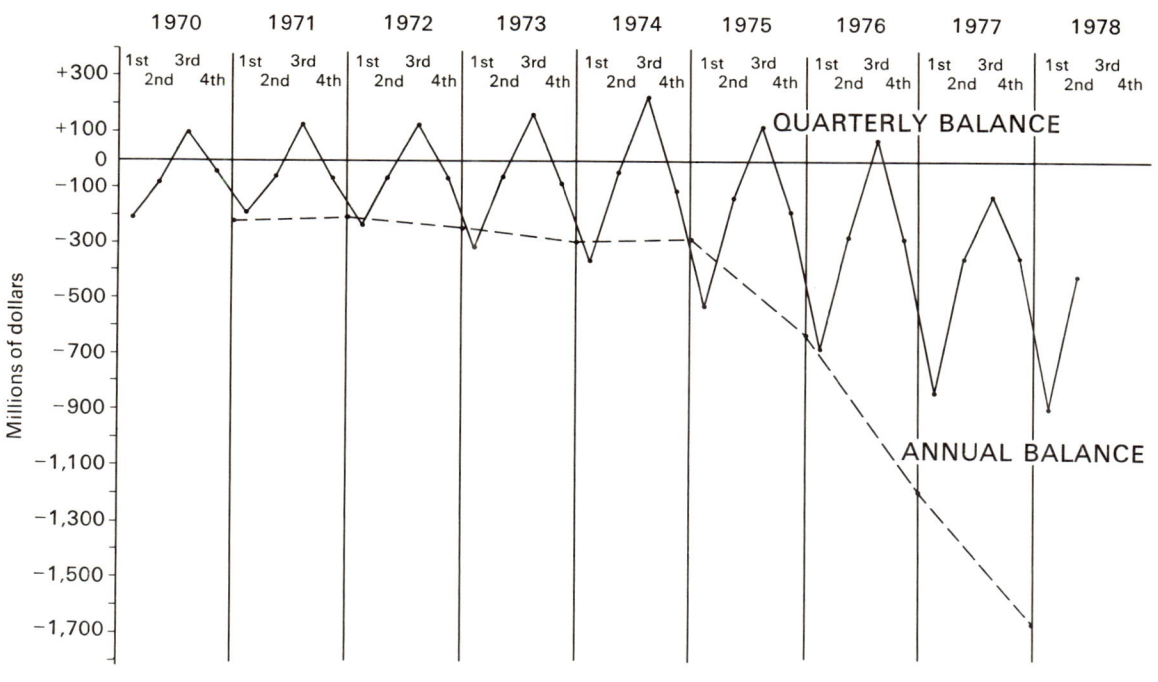

Source: Statistics Canada, 1978c. Travel between Canada and Other Countries: January-June 1978, Catalogue 66-001.

TABLE 26.

Average duration of stay by United States visitors in Canada, by province or territory of main destination, 1974 and 1975

Province or Territory of main destination	Average duration of stay in Canada 1974	1975
	(number of nights)	
Atlantic	6.5	5.7
Québec	4.2	3.9
Ontario	4.3	4.0
Manitoba	3.7	3.5
Saskatchewan	5.4	4.6
Alberta	3.9	5.4
British Columbia	4.0	4.2
Yukon and Northwest Territories	3.4	3.5
Touring	19.7	11.5

Source: Statistics Canada, 1978d. Travel, Tourism and Outdoor Recreation: A Statistical Digest 1975 and 1976. Catalogue 66-202.

TABLE 24.

Receipts from non-resident travellers in Canada, and total current account receipts for all countries, 1970 to 1976

Receipts	1970	1971	1972	1973	1974	1975	1976
	(millions of dollars)						
Travel receipts	1,206	1,246	1,230	1,446	1,694	1,815	1,930
Current account receipts	21,511	23,146	25,514	31,725	40,259	41,430	46,609
	(per cent)						
Travel receipts as a percentage of current account receipts	5.6	5.4	4.8	4.6	4.2	4.4	4.2

Source: Statistics Canada, 1978d. Travel, Tourism and Outdoor Recreation: A Statistical Digest 1975 and 1976. Catalogue 66-202.

TABLE 25.

Payments by travellers resident in Canada, and total current account payments for all countries, 1970 to 1976

Payments	1970	1971	1972	1973	1974	1975	1976
	(millions of dollars)						
Travel payments	1,422	1,448	1,464	1,742	1,978	2,542	3,123
Current account payments	20,840	22,840	26,169	31,707	41,751	46,395	50,938
	(per cent)						
Travel payments as a percentage of current account payments	6.8	6.3	5.6	5.5	4.7	5.5	6.1

Source: Statistics Canada, 1978d. Travel, Tourism and Outdoor Recreation: A Statistical Digest 1975 and 1976. Catalogue 66-202.

With demands for more and varied opportunities for recreation coupled with demands for land from all other sectors, the limited resources have to be used effectively. Areas with the capacity to support intensive use should be utilized in appropriate ways to meet demands and, similarly, areas of low carrying capacity, such as sensitive biological areas, must also be managed to maintain their attraction. Land managed beyond its capacity to support use will, in the long run, reduce the supply by effectively destroying that resource and placing added pressure on the remaining land resources.

Land Use Conflicts

The demand for land for outdoor recreation is just one of many demands for the land resource. In some cases, depending on the activity, recreation can function in accord with other land uses. Multiple use of land for forestry, agriculture, mining, trapping, and recreation is desirable as it maximizes the use of the resource. Some activities do, however, require areas to be set aside exclusively and specifically for recreation. In these areas, conflicts in the allocation and designation of the land often arise. Wilderness preservation usually restricts other activities such as forestry, mining, and trapping. Bathing conflicts with other shoreline activities, such as sand and gravel removal and industrial development. The problem is to determine which use is more important. This can only be established in relationship to the needs and wants that people have for the resources. When one land use is favoured over another, the remaining resources become more vital in meeting the other demands of people.

In the allocation of recreation resources, a special case develops when determining to which sector, private, commercial, or public, the recreation resource will be allocated. Each sector provides a particular range of facilities to meet the recreation demands. If the recreation resource is allocated without regard to other needs, one sector could have insufficient land suitable to meet particular requirements. Thus, the solution to land use conflicts and the allocation of the recreation resources are also going to affect greatly the future supply and type of recreation opportunity available.

Social and Economic Demands

Outdoor recreation has become an important part of the Canadian lifestyle. The opportunity to participate in diverse activities is a benefit for which Canadians have been willing to pay in the form of taxes, lost opportunities by using land exclusively for outdoor recreation, and in a number of other costs. These values have evolved over many years and will probably continue to develop as population grows and as people gain more leisure time and disposable income. Other major social factors that will tend to increase the demands for outdoor recreation will be a greater awareness of the quality of the environment and an increased consciousness of the benefits of, and need for, physical fitness. Both the recognition of the need for the preservation of unique and representative environments for Canadians, and the need for maintaining high standards in the quality of the environment lead to conflicts in land use. Areas of national and regional importance are being set aside essentially for preservation and heritage objectives, but at the same time, these areas are providing for outdoor recreation. This leads to the designation of areas for exclusive use for one activity and this can negatively affect other demands for the resource.

The attitude towards the use of land, as the result of increased environmental standards and public awareness of environmental problems, may be the most significant factor that affects the supply of land for outdoor recreation. As the quality of the environment becomes a more important social and economic goal, the standards for all developments become more stringent. This includes standards for the use of recreation lands. In some provinces, the standards of water quality have risen to such a level that some recreation developments are being rejected even though their direct effects on water quality have never been determined. Densities of cottage lands surrounding lakes are now lower in new developments, for both environmental and aesthetic reasons. Use of wilderness areas is being limited to maintain the environmental quality according to both the physical carrying capacity and social standards of crowding. These standards have developed in response to increased levels of use, to many cases of environmental degradation, and to changing values. It is suggested that in the future, the area of land required for outdoor recreation will continue to increase and that the standards for development and maintenance of recreation facilities and land will become more strict and limiting. In addition, the values that Canadians associate with the environment will become a more integral part of the total value system. Thus, the land resource for all uses including recreation will become more vital.

In addition to an increased social awareness of land resources for outdoor recreation, there will be a demand on the resources to produce more economic returns. Tourism in Canada has been suffering a decline in both the amount of in-Canada tourism and the number of non-resident tourists. This trend is of national economic significance and there will be programs to reverse this flow of dollars out of Canada. Promotion of in-Canada

Canadian Government Office of Tourism photo.

The provision of accommodation and food services accounts for a sizable portion of income and employment generated through tourism. Lodges, such as this one in Banff National Park, provide employment opportunities for area residents and generate revenue.

Parks Canada photo.

Parks Canada photo by Dalton Muir.

Allowing too many people to utilize a park, thereby pushing the land past its capability to sustain use, is one way of destroying a resource. In addition, the inappropriate behaviour of only a few individuals can also cause the deterioration of a recreation resource. Here in Pacific Rim National Park and Banff National Park, people have discarded articles which are incompatible with the maintenance of an attractive recreation setting.

tourism will put additional pressure on the resources. This does not assume the resource base can not handle the pressure, but it does suggest that it will become more difficult to develop recreation resources with the ever increasing demands for land and stricter environmental standards.

Conflicts, between objectives to provide recreation opportunities for local resident populations and to utilize the same resource base for tourism, have developed in various parts of Canada and will increase in the future. In the more attractive areas of Canada, there are often two basic demands. Both local residents and tourists desire the use of recreation resources. However, the increased pressures generated by tourist operations may preclude the use of the resource by the local people, or the quality of the resource may deteriorate in the opinion of the local resident.

A further problem that occurs between residents and non-residents is associated with land ownership. Land ownership by non-residents has a variety of effects on the resident population and local administration. Some of these are inflated land prices, limitations on public access to the recreation resources, and conflicts with other land use objectives such as agricultural production. In addition, increased demands for services, such as police protection and highway maintenance, can result in additional expenditures which may or may not be recouped in taxes or other local economic gains. Local governments also come under pressure from non-residents when their demands are not in accord with those of local residents. Notwithstanding the negative impacts, positive effects include additional jobs, increase of revenue in the area and the addition of facilities and services which could not be supported by the local population alone and which can be vital to the area's economy.

In summary, there are a number of conflicts and issues related to the social and economic aspects of outdoor recreation that will put demands on the land resources. Proper land management will become more essential if the land resource is to meet the needs and desires of all Canadians.

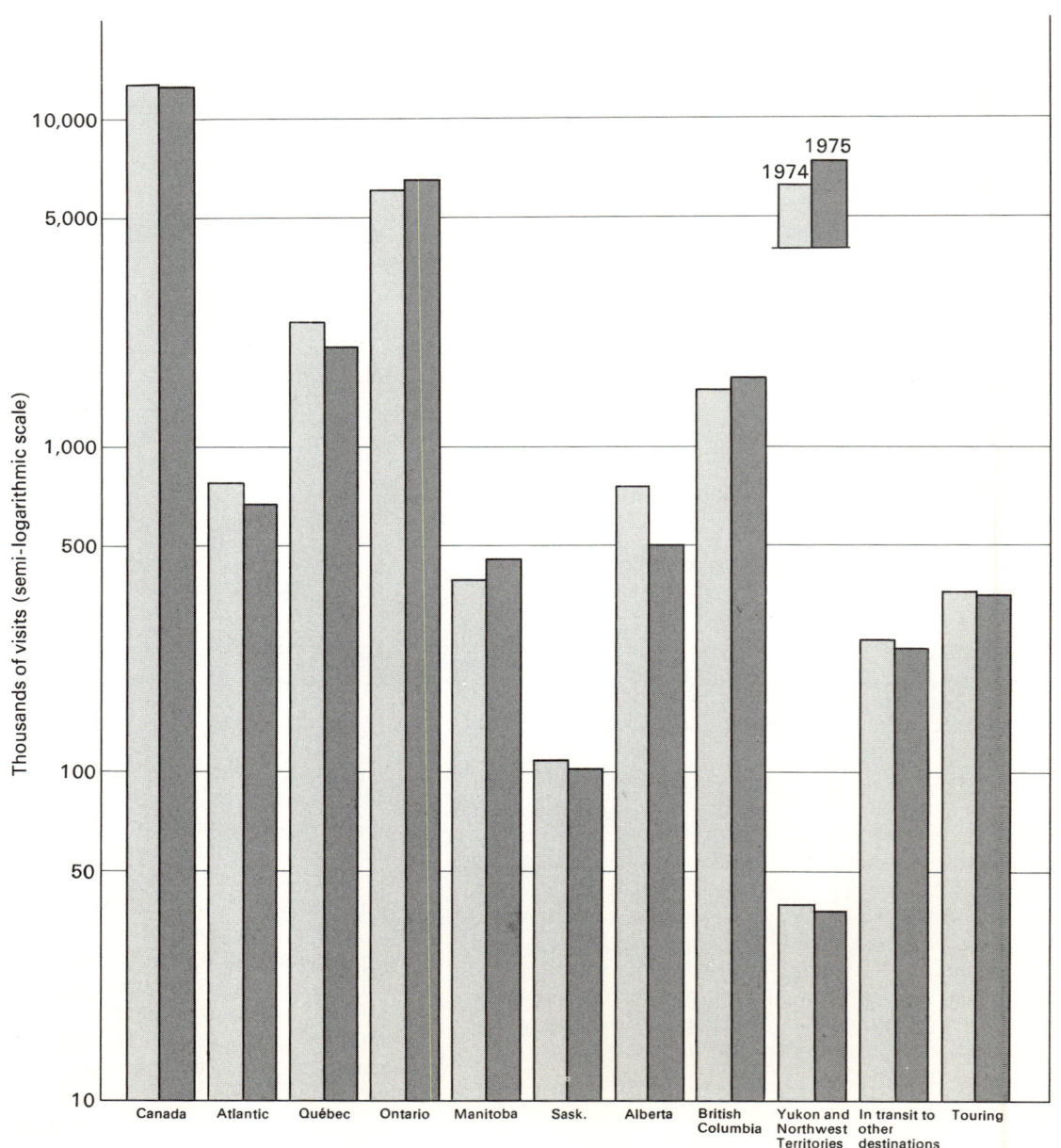

FIGURE 8. Number of visits[1] by United States' residents, by province and territory of main destination, 1974 and 1975

(1) a stay in Canada of one or more nights.

Source: Statistics Canada, 1978d. Travel, Tourism and Outdoor Recreation: A Statistical Digest 1975 and 1976, Catalogue 66-202.

TABLE 27.

Accommodation, by type for major accommodation groups, by province or territory, 1975

Major accommodation group	Accommodation type	Newfoundland	Prince Edward Island	Nova Scotia	New Brunswick	Québec	Ontario	Manitoba	Saskatchewan	Alberta	British Columbia	Yukon and Northwest Territories
						(number)						
Hotels	Locations	81	23	97	72	1,681	1,170	261	390	467	534	58
	Rooms	2,658	917	5,464	3,411	52,537	57,733	8,555	10,415	20,333	28,475	1,822
	Cabins	N.A.	N.A.	N.A.	N.A.	N.A.	N.A.	N.A.	N.A.	N.A.	N.A.	N.A.
	Tent or trailer sites	N.A.	N.A.	N.A.	N.A.	N.A.	N.A.	N.A.	N.A.	N.A.	N.A.	N.A.
Motels	Locations	37	59	163	71	736	1,436	113	153	326	842	30
	Rooms	447	1,068	3,332	3,210	13,359	23,674	1,852	3,467	7,838	15,937	496
	Cabins	75	102	221	236	425	1,165	78	33	213	689	–
	Tent or trailer sites	N.A.	N.A.	N.A.	N.A.	N.A.	N.A.	N.A.	N.A.	N.A.	N.A.	N.A.
Tourist homes	Locations	27	108	55	21	148	25	–	1	–	–	–
	Rooms	164	408	237	94	1,465	219	–	8	–	–	–
	Cabins	2	3	6	1	–	12	–	–	–	–	–
	Tent or trailers sites	–	1	2	–	–	16	–	–	–	–	–
Tourist courts and cabins	Locations	18	88	71	60	99	1,729	50	51	53	307	5
	Rooms	9	54	51	63	134	473	49	41	11	130	5
	Cabins	162	704	577	477	933	13,257	545	504	828	2,703	43
	Tent or trailers sites	15	53	33	24	–	4,574	213	216	660	2,229	–
Tent and trailer campgrounds	Locations	45	57	172	124	676	1,155	107	88	120	477	18
	Rooms or cabins	12	15	132	55	132	55	463	1,650	69	48	129
	Tent or trailer sites	3,116	5,403	13,639	10,151	68,976	115,635	10,760	8,029	22,853	30,634	338
Outfitters	Locations	44	1	2	45	426	1,006	65	108	14	190	35
	Rooms	26	–	–	28	315	587	46	74	31	142	77
	Cabins	86	5	10	143	2,804	7,540	490	809	84	1,351	156
	Tent or trailer sites	5	–	–	–	1,160	4,001	304	626	143	2,032	2
TOTALS	Locations	252	336	560	393	3,766	6,521	596	791	980	2,350	146
	Rooms	3,304	2,447	9,084	6,806	67,810	82,686	11,098	14,005	9,913	44,684	2,400
	Cabins	337	829	946	912	4,625	23,624	1,182	1,394	1,254	5,408	199
	Tent or trailer sites	3,136	5,457	13,674	10,175	70,136	124,226	11,277	8,871	23,656	34,895	340

N.A. means data not available.
– means no data.

Source: Statistics Canada, 1977f. Traveller Accommodation Statistics, 1975. Catalogue 63-204.

TABLE 28.

Comparison of provinces according to the number of Unites States' visitors and the number of commercial accommodation establishments, 1975

Ranking by number of United States' visitors		Ranking by number of accommodation locations*		Ranking by number of United States' visits per accommodation location		Ranking by expenditures in Canada		Ranking by average spending per visit	
(thousands of visitors)		(number)		(number)		(millions of dollars)		(dollars)	
Ontario	6,495	Ontario	6,521	Ontario	996	Ontario	474	Alberta	120.60
Québec	2,012	Québec	3,766	Alberta	782	Québec	219	Québec	108.80
British Columbia	1,628	British Columbia	2,350	Manitoba	758	British Columbia	154	Yukon and Northwest Territories	105.30
Atlantic Provinces	661	Atlantic Provinces	1,641	British Columbia	642	Atlantic Provinces	69	Atlantic Provinces	104.40
Alberta	514	Alberta	980	Québec	534	Alberta	62	Saskatchewan	95.20
Manitoba	452	Saskatchewan	791	Yukon and Northwest Territories	368	Manitoba	39	British Columbia	94.60
Saskatchewan	105	Manitoba	596	Atlantic Provinces	214	Saskatchewan	10	Ontario	73.00
Yukon and Northwest Territories	38	Yukon and Northwest Territories	199	Saskatchewan	133	Yukon and Northwest Territories	4	Manitoba	61.90

*Refer to Table 14.

Source: Statistics Canada, 1978d. Travel, Tourism and Outdoor Recreation: A Statistical Digest 1975 and 1976. Catalogue 66-202.

Photo by Robert Cooper, The Canadian Press.

A serious deterioration in water quality, often the result of overuse or resource conflicts, effectively reduces the recreation resource base. This is particularly critical near urban centres where pollution may deprive residents of valuable recreation sites and may also pose health hazards.

TABLE 29.

Employed in selected tourist services compared to total employed, by province, 1977

Province	All industries Total labour force	Community, business, and personal service Labour force	Percentage of all industries	Accommodation and food services Labour force	Percentage of community, business, and personal service
	(thousands)	(thousands)	(per cent)	(thousands)	(per cent)
Newfoundland	161	48	30	7	15
Prince Edward Island	45	13	29	N.A.	N.A.
Nova Scotia	298	87	29	14	16
New Brunswick	232	65	28	10	15
Québec	2,504	714	29	111	16
Ontario	3,762	1,036	28	177	17
Manitoba	433	121	28	20	16
Saskatchewan	402	102	25	17	17
Alberta	853	233	27	41	18
British Columbia	1,065	303	28	61	20
CANADA	9,754	2,720	28	460	17

N.A. means data not available.

Source: Statistics Canada, 1978e. Labour Force Survey Division.

Canadian Government Office of Tourism photo.

Acknowledgements

The author would like to acknowledge several individuals and agencies for their co-operation and advice in the preparation of this chapter.

R.B. Crowe
Atmospheric Environment Service
Environment Canada

Gerry Lee
Chief, Federal Land Services Division
Lands Directorate
Environment Canada

Dr. J.H. Ross
Alberta Department of Recreation, Parks and Wildlife

Canadian Government Office of Tourism
National Geographical Mapping Division
Department of Energy, Mines and Resources

Bibliography

Alberta Land Use Forum. 1974*a*. Recreation and Miscellaneous Land Uses. Technical Report No. 3. Lands Division, Alberta Lands and Forests. Edmonton.

———. 1974*b*. Use of Our Lakes and Lakeshore Lands. Technical Report No. 12. The Technical Committee on Lakes and Lake Shoreland. Edmonton.

Alberta Municipal Affairs. 1977. Cottage Owner Survey – Island Lake and Baptiste Lake. Regional Planning Section. Edmonton.

American Society of Planning Officials. 1976. Subdividing Rural America–Impacts of Recreational Lot and Second Home Development. Council on Environmental Quality. Department of Housing and Urban Development and the Appalachian Regional Commission. Washington.

Arthur, L.M., and Boster, R.S. 1976. Measuring Scenic Beauty: A Selected Annotated Bibliography. General Technical Report 25. USDA Forest Service. Fort Collins, Colorado.

Baker, W.M. 1964. ARDA Program in Relation to Recreation and Tourism. ARDA Project No. 14017. Ottawa.

———. 1966. Tourist and Outdoor Recreation Patterns and Prospects in the Qu'Appelle Valley and on Last Mountain Lake. ARDA. Ottawa.

———. 1973. The Nature and Extent of Vacation Home Data Sources and Research in Canada. Statistics Canada. Ottawa.

Beaubien, Charles, and Tabacnik, Ruth. 1977. People and Agricultural Land. Perceptions 4, Science Council of Canada. Ottawa.

Bregha, Francis J. 1977. Canadian Recreation Development Social Dimensions. Occasional Paper No. 15. Lands Directorate, Fisheries and Environment Canada. Ottawa.

Bloomfield, Janice, and Harrison, Peter. 1976. The Shorezone: An Annotated Bibliography. Occasional Paper No. 12. Lands Directorate, Environment Canada. Ottawa.

Campbell, Colin K. 1967*a*. An Analysis of Summer Cottage Shoreland Use in the Georgia Lowland Region of British Columbia. Canada Land Inventory, Department of Forestry and Rural Development. Vancouver.

———. 1967*b*. Analysis of Shoreland Use and Capability for Cottaging in the Georgia Lowland of British Columbia. ARDA Project No. 16014. Ottawa.

Canada Land Inventory. Land Capability for Outdoor Recreation. Maps at 1:1,000,000. Atlantic Provinces (1973), Manitoba (1974), Alberta (1975), Saskatchewan (1976), Ontario (1976), and Québec (1976). Lands Directorate, Environment Canada. Ottawa.

Canada–Ontario–Rideau–Trent–Severn Study Committee. 1971. The Rideau Trent Severn: Yesterday Today Tomorrow. Toronto.

———. 1973*a*. The Kingston – Quinte Area: Yesterday Today Tomorrow. Toronto.

———. 1973*b*. The Simcoe Couchiching Area: Yesterday Today Tomorrow. Toronto.

Canadian Council on Rural Development. 1975. Economic Significance of Tourism and Outdoor Recreation for Rural Development. Ottawa.

Canadian Facts Co. Ltd. 1967, 1968, and 1970. Vacation Travel by Canadians 1967, 1968, 1970. Canadian Government Travel Bureau. Toronto.

Canadian Government Office of Tourism. 1974. Tourism: Its Magnitude and Significance. Research Bulletin No. 2. A Study of the Factors Involved in Measuring the Impact on Canada of International and Domestic Travel. Ottawa.

———. 1977*a*. Tourism: Situation Reports No. 1 to No. 5. Ottawa.

———. 1977*b*. Travel Intentions of Canadians in 1977. Marketing Research, Research Division. Ottawa.

———. 1977*c*. Vacation Travel by Canadians in 1976, Volume 1: Analysis. Ottawa.

Clawson, Marion, and Knetsch, J. 1966. Economics of Outdoor Recreation. Baltimore, Maryland.

Coomber, N. 1971. Techniques for the Evaluation of Environmental Intangibles. Department of the Environment. Ottawa.

Crowe, R.B. 1970. A Climatic Classification of the Northwest Territories for Recreation and Tourism. 5 Volumes (Limited Publication). Meteorological Service, Canada Department of Transport. Toronto.

———, McKay, G.A., and Baker, W.M. 1973. The Tourist and Outdoor Recreation Climate of Ontario. Volume One: Objectives and Definitions of Seasons. Meteorological Applications Branch, Environment Canada. Toronto.

———. 1977. The Tourist and Outdoor Recreation Climate of Ontario. Volumes One, Two, and Three. Atmospheric Environment Service, Fisheries and Environment Canada. Toronto.

Cutler, Maurice. 1975. "Are We Alienating Too Much Recreational Land and Too Much of Our Best Agricultural Land?" Canadian Geographical Journal. Vol. 90, No. 5. May 1975. Royal Canadian Geographical Society. Ottawa.

D'Amore, L.T., and Associates Ltd. 1976. Tourism in Canada–1986. Canadian Government Office of Tourism. Montréal.

Department of Energy, Mines and Resources. 1974. The National Atlas of Canada. Surveys and Mapping Branch. The Macmillan Company of Canada Limited. Ottawa.

Department of Indian and Northern Affairs and Department of the Environment. 1973. Land Use Information Series Map Sheet 105 D – Whitehorse. Ottawa.

Department of Regional Economic Expansion. 1970. Land Capability Classification for Outdoor Recreation. Canada Land Inventory Report No. 6. Queen's Printer. Ottawa.

Environment Canada. 1973. Canada Geographic Information System – Overview. Lands Directorate. Ottawa.

———. 1978. The Canada Land Inventory: Objectives, Scope and Organization. Canada Land Inventory Report No. 1. (reprinted). Lands Directorate. Ottawa.

Federal–Provincial Parks Conference. 1976. Park Classification System, National and Provincial Parks. Conference held October 18-22, 1976 in Regina, Saskatchewan. Parks Canada, Department of Indian and Northern Affairs. Ottawa.

Gates, A.D. 1975. The Tourism and Outdoor Recreation Climate of the Maritime Provinces. Meteorological Applications Branch, Environment Canada. Toronto.

Graham, W.W. 1967. Cottage Development in Rural Areas. ARDA Project No. 15039. Ottawa.

Gunn, Clare A. 1976. "Tourism – Recreation – Conservation Synergism." Contact. Vol. 8, No. 4. Journal of Urban and Environmental Affairs. Faculty of Environmental Studies, University of Waterloo. Waterloo.

Harrison, Peter. 1977. Recreational Aspects of Shorezone Development. A Conceptual Discussion of Management and Provision. Occasional Paper No. 13. Lands Directorate, Environment Canada. Ottawa.

Hendee, J.C., Hogans, M.L., and Koch, R.W. 1976. Dispersed Recreation on Three Forest Road Systems in Washington and Oregon: First Year Data. Research Note PNW-280. USDA Forest Service. Portland, Oregon.

Jaakson, R., Buzynski, M., and Botting, D. 1975. Carrying Capacity and Lake Recreation Planning. Department of Urban and Regional Planning. University of Toronto. Tornnto.

Juurand, Priidu. 1972. Wild River Survey 1971 Quantitative Comparison of River Landscapes. National and Historic Parks Branch, Parks Canada. Ottawa.

Lewington, Ann. 1970. The Effect of Transportation Facilities on the Development of Recreation – A Case Study of the Winnipeg River. B.A. Thesis. Department of Geography, University of Western Ontario. London.

Litton, R. Burton. 1968. Forest Landscape Description and Inventories. Research Paper DSW-49. USDA Forest Service. Berkeley, California.

———. 1971. An Aesthetic Overview of the Role of Water in the Landscape. National Water Commission. Berkeley, California.

Manitoba Department of Tourism, Recreation, and Cultural Affairs. 1976. Manitoba Park Statistics, 1975. Winnipeg.

Masse, William. 1975. A Preliminary Overview on the Impact of Outdoor Recreational Activity in Northwestern British Columbia: The Stewart–Cassiar Area. Environment Canada. Vancouver.

Masterton, J.M., Crowe, R.B., and Baker, W.M. 1976. The Tourism and Outdoor Recreation Climate of the Prairie Provinces. Meteorological Applications Branch, Environment Canada. Toronto.

Ministry of State for Fitness and Amateur Sport. 1977. Highlights of the 1976 Fitness and Sport Survey. Fitness and Amateur Sport Branch. Ottawa.

Ministry of State for Urban Affairs. 1974. Urban Open Space Study for Canadian Communities. Ottawa.

Murtha, Peter A., and Greco, M.E. 1975. Appraisal of Forest Aesthetic Values: An Annotated Bibliography. FMR-X-79. Forest Management Institute. Ottawa.

Nelson, J.G., and Scace, R.C. 1968. The Canadian National Parks: Today and Tomorrow. The National and Provincial Parks Association. Calgary.

Ontario Department of Tourism and Information. 1968. Analysis of Ontario Cottage Survey, 1968. Travel Research Report No. 55. Travel Research Branch. Toronto.

Ontario Ministry of Natural Resources. 1973*a*. Estimation of the Number of Cottages in Southern Ontario by County. Policy Research Branch. Toronto.

———. 1973*b*. Lake Temagami Plan for Land Use and Recreation Development. Toronto.

———. 1975. Northwestern Ontario Cottage Study, 1972. Land Use Co-ordination Branch. Toronto.

———. 1976. Lower Great Lakes Day Use Recreation Access Study (Draft). Land Use Co-ordination Branch. Toronto.

———. 1977*a*. Lake of the Woods General Land Use Plan. Toronto.

———. 1977*b*. Ontario Provincial Parks Statistics 1976. Parks Management Branch. Toronto.

Parks Canada. 1973. Trends in Participation in Outdoor Recreation Activities. CORD Study, Technical Note 22. National and Historic Parks Branch. Ottawa.

———. 1974. A National Wild Rivers System Proposal. Planning Division, National Parks Branch. Ottawa.

———. 1976*a*. Wild Rivers: Quebec North Shore. Department of Supply and Services. Ottawa.

———. 1976*b*. Natural Areas of Canadian Significance: A Preliminary Study. Planning Division, National Parks Branch. Ottawa.

———. 1977*a*. Longitudinal Data on the Participation of Canadians in Outdoor Recreation Activities 1967–1976. Socio-Economic Research Division, Program Coordination Branch. Ottawa.

———. 1977*b*. Park-Use Statistics, 1976–77. Socio-Economic Research Division, Program Coordination Branch. Ottawa.

Project Planning Associates Ltd. 1970. Recreation Community Development in the Canadian Shield Portion of Southern Ontario. ARDA Project No. 25068. District of Muskoka, Town of Bala.

———. 1973. Urban Open Space in Canada: The Federal Role. Ministry of State for Urban Affairs. Ottawa.

Ragatz, R.L. 1974. Recreational Properties in Appalachia: An Analysis of the Markets for Privately Owned Recreational Lots and Leisure Homes. Appalachian Regional Commission. Eugene, Oregon.

Redpath, D. Kenneth. 1975. Recreation Residential Developments: A Review and Summary of Relevant Material. Occasional Paper No. 4. Lands Directorate, Environment Canada. Ottawa.

Ross, J.H. 1973. A Measure of Site Attraction. Occasional Paper No. 2. Lands Directorate, Environment Canada. Ottawa.

Rousseau, S. 1973. Trends in Participation in Outdoor Recreation Activities. CORD Study, Technical Note 22. National and Historic Parks Branch, Parks Canada. Ottawa.

Sargent, F.O. 1967. Scenery Classification. Vermont Resources Research Center. Burlington, Vermont.

Saskatchewan Department of Tourism and Renewable Resources. 1976. Proceedings of 15th Federal–Provincial Parks Conference, Parks Today & Tomorrow, A Challenge, held October 18-22, 1976 in Regina, Saskatchewan.

Simpson-Lewis, Wendy. 1974. The Windsor-Québec Axis. Map. Ministry of State for Urban Affairs and Environment Canada. Ottawa.

Smith, V. Kerry, and Krutilla, John V. 1974. "A Simulation Model For the Management of Low Density Recreational Areas." Journal of Environmental Economics and Management. Vol. 1, No. 3. New York.

Stankey, G.H., and Lime, D.W. 1973. Recreational Carrying Capacity: An Annotated Bibliography. General Technical Report IWT-3. USDA Forest Service. Ogden, Utah.

Statistics Canada. 1973*a*. Canada Year Book 1973. Ottawa.

———. 1973*b*. Housing: Household Facilities. Catalogue 93-737. Vol. II, Part 4. Ottawa.

———. 1974*a*. Accommodation, Food and Recreational Services Employment Earnings and Hours of Work, 1972. Catalogue 72-602. Annual/Various. Ottawa.

_____. 1974*b*. Canada Year Book 1974. Ottawa.

_____. 1975*a*. Households: Income of Household Heads Showing Dwelling Characteristics. Catalogue 93-711. Vol. II, Part 1. Ottawa.

_____. 1975*b*. Canada 1976. Ottawa.

_____. 1976*a*. Service Trades Business Location Statistics. Catalogue 97-742. Vol. IX. Ottawa.

_____. 1976*b*. Travel, Tourism and Outdoor Recreation: A Statistical Digest 1974 and 1975. Catalogue 66-202. Annual. Ottawa.

_____. 1977*a*. Canadian Forestry Statistics 1975. Catalogue 25-202. Annual. Ottawa.

_____. 1977*b*. Construction in Canada, 1975–1977. Catalogue 64-201. Annual. Ottawa.

_____. 1977*c*. Population: Geographic Distributions: Federal Electoral Districts. Catalogue 92-801. Ottawa.

_____. 1977*d*. Travel Between Canada and Other Countries: July–September 1977. Catalogue 66-001. Quarterly. Ottawa.

_____. 1977*e*. Travel Between Canada and Other Countries 1975. Catalogue 66-201. Annual. Ottawa.

_____. 1977*f*. Traveller Accommodation Statistics, 1975. Catalogue 63-204. Annual. Ottawa.

_____. 1978*a*. Household Facilities and Equipment: May 1977. Catalogue 64-202. Annual. Ottawa.

_____. 1978*b*. Quarterly Estimates of the Canadian Balance of International Payments. Third Quarter 1977. Catalogue 67-001. Quarterly. Ottawa.

_____. 1978*c*. Travel Between Canada and Other Countries: January–June 1978. Catalogue 66-001. Quarterly. Ottawa.

_____. 1978*d*. Travel, Tourism and Outdoor Recreation: A Statistical Digest 1975 and 1976. Catalogue 66-202. Annual. Ottawa.

_____. 1978*e*. Labour Force Survey Division. (unpublished material).

Taylor, M. Craig. 1978. Land Capability for Recreation: Summary Report. Canada Land Inventory Report No. 14. Lands Directorate, Environment Canada. Ottawa.

United States Department of Agriculture. 1970. Economic Impact of Second-Home Communities. A Case Study of Lake Layonka, Da. Economic Research Service. Washington, D.C.

_____. 1977. Proceedings: River Recreation Management and Research Symposium. January 24-27, 1977. Forest Service. St. Paul, Minnesota.

United States Department of the Interior. 1967. Northern New England Vacation Home Study – 1966. Bureau of Outdoor Recreation. Washington, D.C.

Wolfe, R.I. 1956. Recreational Land Use in Ontario. Ph.D. Dissertation. University of Toronto. Toronto.

_____. 1962. "The Summer Resorts of Ontario in the Nineteenth Century." Ontario History. Vol. LIV, No. 3. Toronto.

_____. 1965. "About Cottages and Cottagers." Landscape. Autumn 1965. Berkeley, California.

Contents

	Page
Introduction	107
Physical Classifications	107
Supply of land for wildlife	107
Canada Land Inventory	109
Methodology	109
Identification of high capability areas for ungulates	110
Identification of high capability areas for waterfowl	116
Sensitive areas for migratory birds in coastal eastern Canada	120
Northern Land Use Information Series	120
International Biological Programme	121
Economic and social considerations	121
Activities related to wildlife	121
Fur trapping	125
Recreational hunting	126
Other activities	128
Lands allocated for wildlife	129
Provincial wildlife lands	129
Federal wildlife lands	132
National and provincial parks	132
Land use issues and factors affecting change	132
Indicators of change	132
Rare, threatened and endangered species	132
Superabundant species	133
Issues and conflicts	133
Acknowledgements	136
Bibliography	136
Appendix I	138
Appendix II	144
Appendix III	145

Tables

		Page
1.	Number of species of mammals and birds in Canada	107
2.	Some values of wildlife	107
3.	CLI areas of high capability for wildlife: ungulates	110
4.	CLI areas of high capability for wildlife: waterfowl	110
5.	Some essential migratory bird staging grounds in northern and western Canada	120
6.	Fur trapping by number of trapped pelts	126
7.	Value of raw fur production	128
8.	Number issued and revenue from hunting licenses, by province or territory of sale	129
9.	Game harvest by species, by province and territory	130
10.	National and provincial parks and reserves essential for wildlife habitat, by province and territory, 1976	130
11.	Classification of land tenure, 1973	133

Figures

		Page
1.	Land use by region, 1973	107
2.	Fur production in Canada	125
3.	Percentage value of raw fur production, by region, 1975-76	125
4.	Percentage value of number of pelts produced, by region, 1975-76	125

Maps

		Page
1.	Land capability for wildlife–ungulates: Québec, New Brunswick, Prince Edward Island, Nova Scotia, Newfoundland	111
2.	Land capability for wildlife–ungulates: Ontario	113
3.	Land capability for wildlife–ungulates: British Columbia, Alberta, Saskatchewan, Manitoba	114
4.	Land capability for wildlife–waterfowl: Québec, New Brunsick, Prince Edward Island, Nova Scotia, Newfoundland	115
5.	Land capability for wildlife–waterfowl: Ontario	117
6.	Land capability for wildlife–waterfowl: British Columbia, Alberta, Saskatchewan, Manitoba	119
7.	Sensitive areas for migratory birds in coastal eastern Canada	122
8.	Land Use Information Series – Franklin Bay	123
9.	Northern Land Use Information Series – synthesis of critical areas	124
10.	IBP proposed ecological sites	127
11.	Wildlife protected lands	131
12.	Rare, threatened and endangered mammals	134
13.	Rare, threatened and endangered birds	135
14.	Major vegetation regions	138
15.	Major physiographic regions	139
16.	Average annual precipitation	140
17.	January mean temperature	141
18.	July mean temperature	142
19.	Mean depth of maximum snow cover	143

Introduction

All of Canada's surface area may be considered as wildlife land and capable of maintaining a variety of species groups such as insects, reptiles, amphibians, birds, fish, and mammals. Each group contributes to the ecological diversity of the country, but, because of the paucity of scientific research into the life cycles of many species and the land-oriented nature of this study, the definition of wildlife includes only non-domesticated mammals and birds.

There are 198 species of mammals and 550 species of birds (Table 1), that are known to spend at least some

TABLE 1.

Number of species of mammals and birds in Canada

Order	Selected Species	Number of Species
Mammals		
Rodentia	squirrel, chipmunk, marmot, beaver, mice	68
Carnivora	fox, bear, racoon, fisher, lynx, bobcat	38
Cetacea	whale, dolphin, porpoise	34
Insectivora	shrew, mole	20
Chiroptera	bat	17
Artiodactyla	deer, moose, caribou, sheep	12
Lagomorpha	pika, hare, rabbit	8
Marsupialia	opossum	1
Total		198
Birds		
	migratory and non-migratory	550

Source: Van Zyll de Jong, C.G., and Ouellet, W. 1978. Museum of Natural Sciences, Ottawa. Personal communication.

stages of their life cycle in Canada. The use of land by these species is a function of several factors, of which the most important are the availability of habitat and the adaptability of species to changing environmental conditions. The interaction of vegetation, topography, and climate to supply adequate food, water and shelter for the seasonal and other life cycle requirements of wildlife, represents the physical capability of the land to provide habitat. In addition, the density and the diversity of species composition supported by land is related to the preferences and adaptability of wildlife or, the range of habitat conditions which is essential for survival, growth, and reproduction. Some species[1], for example the Whooping Crane, prairie dog, Kirtland's Warbler, and wood bison, depend on very specialized habitat conditions while others, such as the Herring Gull, beaver, and white-tailed deer, are more flexible in satisfying their needs and can adjust to moderate changes in habitat. The increasing use of land for agriculture, mineral and energy production, urbanization, recreation, and forestry has affected the ability of land to provide habitat. Activities such as dredging, drainage of wetlands, forest clear-cutting, flooding for hydroelectric sites, land clearing for transportation networks, and urban settlements are a few examples of land uses that transform original habitat conditions and, consequently, imply a change in both the density and diversity of wildlife composition. Species that are adaptable will adjust and perhaps increase their numbers, sometimes to the point of becoming nuisance or pest species. Conversely, those species with more specialized habitat needs may be forced to abandon an area where the alternative use has so modified the original physical environment that the basic survival, growth, and reproduction requirements are not met. Thus, any assessment of the suitability of land to provide wildlife habitat has two dimensions:

(i) the inherent physical characteristics of the land, and

(ii) the effect of land conversion on the productivity of the land for wildlife use.

The identification of special lands using only these physical criteria assumes perfect knowledge of wildlife habits and preferences. However, as stated, an understanding of all the ecological relationships is not definitive and any evaluation must be prefaced by the acknowledgement of such information gaps. Because of this, a second approach, relating directly to the values attached to the use of wildlife and indirectly to the land resource as the provider of habitat, is necessary to supplement the assessment of lands critical for wildlife.

Some of the major values of wildlife are listed in Table 2, but no attempt will be made to attack in detail the thorny problem of wildlife valuation. Elsewhere, Cocheba and Langford (1978), Hammack and Brown (1974), Clawson and Knetch (1966), and others have discussed the problems of wildlife as an example of a resource which does not operate solely within the confines of the market place. For example, although activities such as trapping and recreational hunting may be quantified in dollar values, the majority of uses (see Table 2) are of a much more intangible nature. Since resource allocation questions are usually answered by assessing dollar values, wildlife has often been undervalued and frequently considered as a residual use. Thus, large commercial projects, such as the expansion of agriculture in the Prairie Provinces, commercial forest activities in British Columbia, and the enormous energy development projects including James Bay and the Fernie Basin, have resulted in the conversion of land at the expense of losing or changing wildlife habitat.

Issues also arise among wildlife users themselves. One such issue concerns various waterfowl species which rest or stage on the Prairie Sloughs. They are both an attraction to local duck hunters and a menace to nearby grain farmers whose fields provide a delectable forage. Similarly, in the north, ungulates including moose and caribou are required as a source of food and clothing by the Inuit and as recreational game to hunters from the south.

To summarize, the labelling of lands critical for wildlife from the perception of wildlife itself provides an intricate pattern of values which are not mutually exclusive and which are fraught with the inevitable issues which develop from the pressures for use. As with the physical assessment of these lands, the evaluation from the users' viewpoint for defining unique, sensitive, or scarce habitat lands is also plagued by incomplete data. Nevertheless, by identifying the various users of wildlife and discussing some of the issues and factors affecting change in uses, an approach is made towards a definitive description of special lands for wildlife.

Physical Classifications

Although ecological complexities and diversities of wildlife ecology pose inherent difficulties in any classification of the land surface, there is a need to identify lands important as wildlife habitats for a range of indicator species. With few exceptions, for example the Canada Land Inventory which is limited to two species groups, ungulates and waterfowl, most existing inventories of wildlife have been confined to regional or site-specific studies and hence do not portray a national supply of land essential for wildlife. Therefore, as a general approach towards assessing the land productivity to support wildlife habitat, the major natural vegetation associations and the land environments altered by man are considered for selected ungulates, aquatic and terrestrial furbearers, waterfowl, and other migratory and non-migratory bird species. This national descriptive assessment establishes a framework within which the more detailed classifications, such as the Canada Land Inventory, may be evaluated. Two regional studies, one in northern Canada and the other in eastern Canada, also are included. The identification of ecological reserves through the International Biological Programme is sited as another type of national inventory which identifies lands critical for wildlife. Combined, these descriptions of the physical parameters determine the suitability of Canada's land area to meet wildlife demands, and also portray the dynamic or changing aspects of the land surface which sets the background for the ensuing discussions of land essential for wildlife.

The Supply of Land for Wildlife

Canada's land resource is a composite interaction of climate, physiography, and natural vegetation regions (Appendix I), transformed in some areas by agriculture, urban, forestry, and other land uses (Figure 1). Although vegetation provides the medium for food supply and the habitat in which wildlife perform their life functions, topography, climate, and soils may affect individually and cumulatively the distribution and composition

TABLE 2.

Some values of wildlife

Economic value	Recreational value	Social value	Biological value	Scientific value
food	game hunting	aesthetic quality	scavengers for vermin	experimental subjects
clothing	bird watching	vicarious experience	indicators of environmental quality	development of new drugs
	nature study		pollinators and disseminators of plant seeds	
	photography		carriers of disease and parasites	

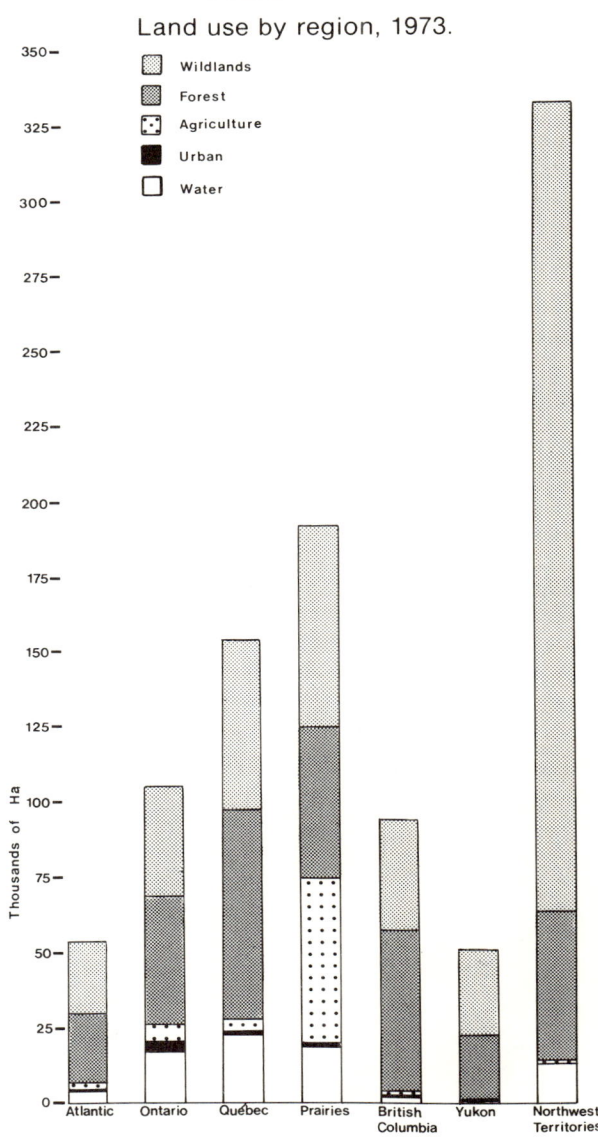

FIGURE 1.

Land use by region, 1973.

- Wildlands
- Forest
- Agriculture
- Urban
- Water

Source: Statistics Canada. 1977b. Perspective Canada II, A Compendium of Social Statistics.

of wildlife. Mountains can form physical and climatic barriers to species dispersion. For example, mule deer, mountain sheep, and mountain goats are natives of the Rocky Mountains while coyotes and Prairie Chickens occupy the adjacent Alberta Plain. In addition, altitude, exposure, and mountain slope result in vertically-differentiated zones of vegetation, each with a seasonal distribution of wildlife. Similarly, precipitation and tempera-

---

[1] The capitalization of names of mammal and bird species, adopts the systems used by the Canadian Wildlife Service and the National Museum of Natural Sciences.
   Birds. All specific names are capitalized (eg. Common Goldeneye), except for species whose full name is not indicated (eg. merganser, geese, ducks).
   Mammals. All mammal names are in lower-case (eg. moose) except for species with proper names (eg. Roosevelt elk).

ture regimes and factors such as wind, are important wildlife location determinants (see Appendix I). For example, snow depth and consistency may act negatively to impede movement of some ungulates and, at the same time, provide winter shelter and burrows for other furbearers such as martens. Precipitation is an essential element in the annual productivity of the Prairie Sloughs, the major breeding area for North American waterfowl. Exposure to wind, particularly in coastal areas and in the northern tundra, stunts vegetation growth and thus indirectly affects species composition. Lastly, soil fertility is considered the fundamental element in determining the quality, size, and abundance of any species of wildlife within an occupied range, and, combined with climate and topography, determines the major natural vegetation regions. Also reflected in vegetation are environmental conditions induced by disease and fire, and changes resulting from alternative land uses.

The Atlantic Provinces. Newfoundland (including Labrador), Prince Edward Island, Nova Scotia, and New Brunswick represent a 539,103 km² composite of coniferous mixed hardwood and tundra natural vegetation associations providing habitat to a variety of ungulate furbearer and bird species. Isolated farm and urban habitat are also available. In addition, the extensive coastal features and offshore islands, which annually attract millions of seabirds and shorebirds, combine to enhance the plethora of habitat niches yielding the diversity in the Atlantic Region. Covering the upland and lowland extensions of the upwarped eastern rim of the Canadian Shield in Labrador and the ancient fold mountains of the Appalachians in the remaining provinces, the forest and wildland areas which account for 76 per cent (see Figure 1) of the provinces' vegetation, provide habitat for white-tailed deer, moose, and caribou, the predominant ungulates, and other furbearers and aquatic furbearers.

Québec. Covering 1.5 million km² and ranging from the 46°N to the 63°N latitude, it is not surprising that Québec's vegetated surface varies from windswept tundra barrens in the north, through transition to boreal forest in the mid-section, to a mixture of hardwood, softwood, conifers, and broadleaf trees in the Great Lakes–St. Lawrence forest in the south. Precipitation ranges between 406 mm in the north to 1,016 mm in Gaspé. Similarly, January mean temperatures vary between –25 and –10°C and July mean temperatures between 7.5 and 17.5°C, both in a north-south gradient. Snow depth ranges from 76 to 152 cm and, in the deeper concentrations, affects ungulate mobility. Caribou, moose, and deer are the ungulates that dominate the province from north to south, although both caribou and moose are found in the boreal areas of the Shickshock Mountains with elevation reaching 1,219 m at Mont Jacques-Cartier. Throughout the forested areas, furbearers and aquatic furbearers seek the diversity of the rivers, bogs, and marshes which occur throughout. Waterfowl, shorebirds, and seabirds use the wetlands and rugged coastlines along the north and south shores of the St. Lawrence River.

Ontario. The Hudson Bay–James Bay Lowland, the Canadian Shield, and the St. Lawrence–Great Lakes Lowland provide three distinctive physiographic regions for wildlife habitat in Ontario. Of these regions, the volcanic, sedimentary, and granitic rocks of the Precambrian Canadian Shield dominates most of the province's 1,068,587 km². Oriented in a northwest to southeast direction, the Shield terrain is stony and rolling to hilly with the northern portion lying within the scattered and discontinuous permafrost zone. Soils of the shield are primarily podzolic, organic or rockland and support the boreal forest and its northern and southern transition areas. Mean January temperatures are from –20°C in the north to –10°C near Lake Huron. Mean July temperatures range from 12.5°C in the north and climb to about 17.5°C in the south. Average annual precipitation varies from about 711 to 1,010 mm. In the south, the Shield supports excellent deer, furbearer, and aquatic furbearer habitat. The more northern portions are dominated by moose and some caribou.

In the north, the Hudson Bay Lowland is a flat, poorly-drained, coastal plain underlain by paleozoic sedimentary bedrock. The meandering rivers, with their low-lying alluvial banks, provide suitable conditions for some boreal forest growth. Away from the river basins, muskeg is the dominant vegetation of the terrain. Climate is a limiting growth factor. Waterfowl and shorebird habitat is extensive on the coastal lowlands.

The lowlands of southern Ontario were covered by the deciduous forest in the southwest, and also the transitional mixed-deciduous Great Lakes forest. However, the productive humic gleysol and gray-brown luvisol soils, complimented by the moderating influence of the Great Lakes on the continental climate, have resulted in less than ten per cent of the original forest vegetation remaining (Putman 1970). Mean annual precipitation varies from 813 to 1,016 mm, the greater amount occurring in the lee of the Great Lakes where snowfall is heavy. Mean January temperatures vary from –5 to –10°C and mean July temperatures vary from 20 to 22.5°C. Limestone plains, shallow and excessively stony, flank the shield in eastern and central Ontario and continue along the Niagara Escarpment in the Bruce Peninsula and on Manitoulin Island. Till plains of western and central Ontario provide gently undulating to strongly rolling relief with drumlin field, moraine, and esker formations. Bogs and marshes occupy old lagoons along former shorelines and parts of spillways or depressional areas in moraine system. In the agriculturally dominant areas, woodchuck, cottontail, jackrabbit, ground squirrel, raccoon, meadow vole, coyote, skunk, porcupine, robin and blackbird thrive. White-tailed deer have pushed their habitat frontiers north, as the southern treed areas disappeared. The wetlands of the Great Lakes shorelines and the Ottawa and St. Lawrence valleys support essential waterfowl habitat, especially during annual migrations.

NFB – PHOTOTHEQUE – ONF – Photo by Ed Caeser

A Red fox, whose habitat ranges throughout the boreal and mixed, coniferous-deciduous forests, is seen here chasing a snowshoe hare.

NFB – PHOTOTHEQUE – ONF – Photo by Ed Caeser.

Pine marten, denizens of climax coniferous forest, are shown here in Alberta. A species whose population has been severely depleted by trapping and loss of habitat, the pine marten has retreated to isolated locations in the northern parts of most provinces.

The Prairie Provinces. Comprising 1,978,721 km², the Prairie Provinces descend from the Rocky Mountains at the British Columbia-Alberta boundary, through the Interior Plains and on to the Canadian Shield at the northeastern limit. Accompanying these physiographic regions are vegetative areas of alpine and subalpine forest, boreal forest, parkland, and grassland. Within these varied ecosystems, habitat for ungulates, furbearers, waterfowl, and other migratory bird species is available, although in decreasing quality and quantity.

The eastern Rocky Mountains, created by intense folding and faulting, are characterized by cirques, serrate ridges, horned peaks, hanging and U-shaped valleys. Here too, diverse topographical features affect the precipitation and temperature regimes. Average annual precipitation varies between 508 and 1,219 mm, the westerly slopes receiving more than the easterly slopes and valleys. Mean January temperatures range between –10 and –5°C and mean July temperatures range between 12.5 and 17.5°C. In the lower altitudes, Engelmann spruce is the dominant subalpine forest species. Areas having a history of past fires or disturbances are typified by lodgepole pine. Alpine fir, whitebark pine, limber pine, and alpine larch are common in the higher altitudes. Although lithosols and podzols are the most common soil types in the uplands where drainage is poor, in the lower dryer valleys the brown wooded brunisols predominate. Mule deer, white-tailed deer, elk, moose, and localized populations of bighorn sheep and mountain goat are endemic to the Rockies. The white-tailed deer have become increasingly numerous in the drainage basins of the front ranges, in valleys, and on south-facing slopes where aspen and poplar stands provide the required browse. Mule deer winter at higher elevations, thus ranging further west on the eastern Rockies since preference is for relatively open terrain. Moose populations fluctuate depending on the availability of willow browse. Open wetlands in valley bottoms and on muskeg flats also provide preferred moose habitat. Elk seek grassland as the core of their summer and winter grazing range. These species are most common in the southern portion of the front ranges, but the Clearwater, Red Deer and North Saskatchewan rivers also provide excellent quality winter range. Black bears are numerous throughout the eastern Rockies. Grizzly bears require true wilderness and large territory for survival and are confined to the more remote areas.

Eastward, the foothills provide the transition between mountains and plains. The southern Saskatchewan and Alberta plains are characterized by undulating to rolling till plains, interspersed by areas of hummocky moraine and areas of lacustrine and outwash deposits. The semi-arid short and mixed-grass prairie of southeastern Alberta and southwestern Saskatchewan overlay the fertile brown and dark brown chernozemic soils. These grasslands once provided range for bison, but with the conversion of the land for agricultural uses, only captive herds can be found. Another grazer, the pronghorn antelope, has evolved to live symbiotically with ranchers and farmers. These fleet-of-foot mammals feed on sagebrush, forbes and occasionally, grass. Small furbearers, such as Richardson's ground squirrel (the prairie gopher), prairie dog, cottontail rabbits, and the snowshoe hare and waterfowl are also inhabitants of the grasslands. Semi-circling the southern grasslands is a distinctive crescent of transitional vegetation where precipitation is slightly higher (between 400 to 500 mm) than in the southern region. This aspen parkland is the prime duck producing habitat, characterized by potholes and permanent-water filled depressions interspersed with tall grass and aspen or poplar groves. Several upland

Photo by the Canadian Wildlife Service

Richardson's ground squirrel, more commonly known as the Prairie "gopher" is an example of an indicator species in the grasslands. Their abundant numbers are perceived to be a nuisance by farmers.

108

areas such as the Viking and Beaverhill moraines, the Neutral and Sand Hills, and the Cypress Hills at the Alberta-Saskatchewan boundary support populations of antelope, elk, Sharp-tailed Grouse, mule and white-tailed deer.

North of the aspen parkland, the boreal forest dominates in the less populated portions of each province. Moose occupy the wetter areas, caribou and an increasing number of deer roam the northern forests of black and white spruce, balsam fir, aspen, poplar, larch, jack pine, and white birch. In the northeast, a transition between subarctic and boreal forest, the stunted black spruce and white spruce growth grades into an open woodland interspersed by low-lying, poorly drained, peat-filled depressions. The Hudson Bay Lowland occupying Manitoba's northeast support, essential staging habitats for migrating birds during the large annual migrations.

British Columbia. The 948,600 km² of rugged mountains, deeply dissected plateaus, interior plains, and coastal lowlands in British Columbia combine to create the most diverse physical environment in all of Canada. This variety of landscape provides habitat for more wildlife than any of the other provinces or territories.

The Pacific Coast area including the Fraser, Georgia, Nahwitti, Hecate, Queen Charlotte and the Nanaimo lowlands, a narrow band of coastal flats extending from Vancouver to the southern edge of the Alaska panhandle, are a striking contrast to the surrounding Coast and Insular mountains. The protected location of these lowlands gives them less precipitation and warmer temperatures than the more elevated climate. The maritime climate and the humic gleysol and dystric brunisol soils are ideal for agriculture, urbanization, and wildlife land uses. Although coastal forest is the natural vegetation in these lowlands, much of it has been removed for agricultural use and also to satisfy the growth of the Vancouver and Victoria urban regions. Here too, the extensive tidal mud flats of Boundary Bay and the estuarine marshes of the Fraser Delta foreshore provide the largest waterfowl wintering area in coastal British Columbia. Most of the numerous deltas or protected inlets along the mainland and island coasts, offer good winter feeding grounds to ducks, geese, swans, loons, and grebes. Shorebirds arrive during spring and fall migration, to feed in the intertidal zone before continuing to nesting sites further north. Of these shorebirds, the most numerous are Arctic Loon, Sooty Shearwater, Northern Phalarope, Black Brant, Surf and White-winged Scoter, Bonaparte Gull, and Black-legged Kittiwake. Seabirds nest primarily on the cliffs of the northwest and southeast portions of the Queen Charlotte Islands, Scott Islands, Solander Island, Clayoquot and Barkley Sounds of western Vancouver Island, Mandarte Island and Mitlenatch Island in the Strait of Georgia. On these islands, dense colonies of murres, puffins, murrelets, cormorants, auklets, petrels and Glaucous-winged Gulls concentrate during the breeding season from May to August. The Pacific Coast populations of Bald Eagle and Peregrine Falcon, both birds of prey, locate near the major seabird colonies. River otter, mink, and raccoon hunt along the seashore and live on the intertidal life.

Paralleling the coastline are the massive Coast Mountains, with peaks reaching to 3,658 m. This mountain system extends westward to include the moderately rugged Queen Charlotte Islands and Vancouver Island ranges. These ranges form a barrier to Pacific and Arctic maritime air masses which, on ascending, lose their moisture on the west-facing slopes. As a result, annual precipitation varies from over 3,251 mm on the coast to less than 305 mm in the interior. The abundance of rainfall combined with moderate temperatures and acidic podzols, have produced in the lower altitudes, a dense coniferous coastal forest of Douglas-fir, western hemlock, and western red cedar. On the Queen Charlotte Islands and the northern coastal area, the Sitka spruce replaces the Douglas-fir as a major tree species. Deciduous forests are found only in commercially clear-cut or burned out areas. The dense canopy of climax coast forest does not provide good deer or moose habitat because there is little accessible browse. However, recently burned and commercially forested areas provide adequate browse for the larger ungulates. Small furbearers, for example marten, fisher, and ermine are common in climax coniferous forests. In higher, drier, and cooler altitudes and in the glacially-enlarged valleys, western red cedar and Sitka spruce comprise the alpine forest. Approaching the treeline, between 1,219 and 1,524 m, the forest canopy is increasingly interspersed with alpine meadows. Above this limit, vegetation is limited to alpine sedges and shrubs and to glaciers and permanent snowfields. Most wildlife species cannot survive above an elevation of 2,591 m. In the upper vegetation zones, mountain sheep and mountain goats are the dominant species. Mountain sheep prefer the drier leeward slopes where snowfall is less than 1,524 cm. The interior plateaus, supporting montane forest and including the Fraser, Thompson, and Kootenay rivers, provide grazing and forage habitat particularly for wintering ungulates and some waterfowl.

Canadian Wildlife Service – Photo by R.A. Edwards

One of the few remaining flocks of Trumpeter Swans is shown on Lonesome Lake in central British Columbia. Shallow lakes, with aquatic food plants, are preferred by these relatively sedentary waterfowl.

The Territories. More than one-third of Canada's land surface lies in the mountains, plateaus, lowlands, and plains of the Yukon and Northwest Territories. This vast and varied landscape is most often typified by the extreme climate, which accounts for the low biological productivity of the region and contributes to the recognition of the fragility and sensitivity of arctic ecosystems. Continuous and discontinuous permafrost occurs throughout, and affects the amount of water and type of soil available for plant growth. The dominant tundra vegetation occurs in a variety of forms on the Arctic Islands, the extensive barrens of the Northwest Territories, and the alpine meadows of the Yukon Cordillera. In protected areas, particularly along river valleys, where soil and climatic conditions are more favourable, sparse and stunted stands of birch, willow, spruce, and tamarack occupy the woodland transition, which develops into boreal forest in the southwest. Only the hardiest of wildlife species seek habitat in the north. The characteristic terrestrial mammals of the tundra include caribou, polar bear, grizzly bear, muskox, arctic fox, wolf, wolverine, ground squirrel, arctic hare, and lemming. The alpine areas of the Yukon also support mountain sheep and mountain goat. In addition, moose, wood bison, red fox, muskrat, and beaver, all at their northern range limit, find shelter in the boreal and adjacent riverine habitats. Most bird species use the northern habitat seasonally for nesting and breeding during the short summer. Many species of ducks, geese, swans, shorebirds, seabirds, and songbirds return annually to reproduce on the rugged coastal cliffs, gravel ridges, grassy hummocks, or dispersed wetlands found throughout the region. Several species including the Raven, Snowy Owl, Gyrfalcon, Willow and Rock Ptarmigan, auk, Black Guillemot, Thick-billed Murre, and, the Dovekie dwell year-round on the tundra, and as the true indigenous species, are individually adapted to endure the rigors of the northern environment.

NFB – PHOTOTHEQUE – ONF – Photo by Scott Miller and Dave Hiscocks

Muskoxen, one of the few mammals which seeks habitat in the northern Archipelago, are seen on the tundra of Blacktop Ridge, Ellesmere Island, Northwest Territories.

Canada Land Inventory

Methodology

The land capability classification for the wildlife sector of the Canada Land Inventory (CLI) was developed to examine and describe the ability of land to produce and support wildlife. For the settled portions of Canada, the analysis considered constraints on wildlife populations imposed by climate, fertility, topography, and habitat interspersion. Because of the great diversity of wildlife species, their different environmental requirements, their mobility, and other behavioural attributes, a single inventory could not effectively represent the capability of land to produce or support all species of wildlife. For this reason, the CLI capability classification was restricted to two groups of species: waterfowl and ungulates. These were chosen because they have wide national distribution and a broad appeal to the public.

The original CLI wildlife capability classification is rated in a 7-class system, ranging from lands having the highest capability (class 1) to those with the lowest capability (class 7). Each capability class is an expression of the combined environmental factors that control the numbers of ungulates or waterfowl that can be produced and supported on a unit of land. Only class 1 lands have no significant limitations to the production of waterfowl or ungulates. The remaining six classes all have varying limiting factors or capability subclasses which affect the quality and/or quantity of the habitat for ungulates and waterfowl. These limitations or capability subclasses may be grouped into two categories: those limitations relating to climate (for example: aridity, snow depth, exposure or aspect) and those limitations relating to the characteristics of the land (for example: soil fertility, soil moisture, landform, or inundation) (*see* Appendix II).

Inherent in the classification system is the assumption that no consideration is given to present land use including the concepts of location, access, ownership, and distance from cities. In all cases, capability ratings are based on the optimum vegetational stage (successional stage) that can be maintained with good wildlife management practices. Although the land capability for waterfowl and ungulates has been rated in seven classes, their differing needs for survival and reproduction have necessitated the creation of special classes for each group. These classes include winter ranges for ungulates and waterfowl, and migration stops for waterfowl. In addition, the ungulate classification evaluates caribou, deer, elk, mountain goat, moose and/or sheep as representative indicator species within the boundary areas.

For the purpose of evaluating critical lands for wildlife, the original CLI methodology has been modified so

NFB – PHOTOTHEQUE – ONF – Photo by Ted Grant

Rocky Mountain (bighorn) sheep are found in habitats of higher elevations; between the treeline and alpine meadows.

that only the areas with higher capability for waterfowl and ungulates are considered. The accompanying regional maps for waterfowl and ungulates, at a scale of 1:5,000,000, are generalized adaptations of the original CLI published maps which have appeared at scales of 1:250,000 and 1:1,000,000. Based on the original seven-class system, only the generalized classes 1, 2, and 3 are identified as essential for the production of waterfowl and ungulates. This abbreviated classification, initially developed for maps in the CLI 1:1,000,000 scale series, has been selected for use in this map compilation (see Appendix II). When assessing high-capability areas, the rationale used in modifying the original classification system for the generalized version centred on priorizing migration and wintering areas for waterfowl, and winter ranges for ungulates. In this respect, migration and wintering areas are viewed as the most pervasive element in assuring species survival.

Approximately 26 per cent of Canada's potential lands for wildlife have been analyzed by the CLI. Although this coverage does not include all the productive habitat for waterfowl and ungulates, particularly in northern Canada, it does survey the high-density breeding areas of waterfowl in the Prairie Sloughs, the important resting areas for waterfowl along the Atlantic, St. Lawrence and Pacific coasts and significant areas of winter and summer range habitat for the various ungulate species. Tables 3 and 4 and Maps 1 to 6, indicate the size and location of these high-capability lands for waterfowl and ungulates. As suggested, more than 70 per cent of the high-capability waterfowl lands, primarily used for nesting and breeding, are in Saskatchewan and Alberta. Similarly, the ungulate assessment concludes that British Columbia, Alberta, Saskatchewan, and Québec provide three-quarters of the lands with high capability for ungulate wintering and reproduction.

Identification of High Capability Lands for Ungulates

The Atlantic Provinces. More than 12 million ha in the Atlantic Provinces have been classified as lands with high capability for use by ungulates. Traversing the upland and lowland extensions of the Appalachian Region, the stands of coniferous, mixed coniferous-deciduous and tundra transition forest provide good quality, habitat for moose, deer, and some caribou, the ungulate indicator species for the region.

The location of class 1 lands, is determined primarily by a combination of factors such as the availability of accessible browse and protective cover and climatic limitations, for example snow depth which may impede ungulate mobility. On insular Newfoundland, the prime caribou and moose wintering areas occurs in the south coast between Channel Port-aux-Basques and St. Alban's, in isolated pockets on the Burin Peninsula, east of St. George's Bay in the Serpentine Range, and parallel to the headwaters of the Gander River. Included within these areas are the barren windswept uplands, where the caribou food plants of lichens and sedges are found. At lower altitudes in the areas of scrub forest, moose browse on the wind-pruned spruce and fir. Similarly, the Atlantic Uplands of the Atlantic Coast of Nova Scotia and Cape Breton Island, the Nova Scotia Highlands north of the Bras d'or Lakes, and along the north shore of the Minas Basin are characterized by a modified barrens and mixed forest complex. Moose range occurs at higher altitudes where balsam fir, white and black spruce alternate with peat bogs. Of all the class 1 lands in Nova Scotia, the area within the Cobequid Mountains surrounding the Minas Basin supports the most valuable wintering grounds for moose. Deer wintering ranges predominate in the lower areas and in river valleys where scattered stands of maples, birches, aspen, and some beech mix with the conifers. Scattered throughout the New Brunswick Highlands, the Chaleur Uplands, and the Maritime Plain are 1,207,803 ha of winter range essential for deer and moose. Northern New Brunswick, within the Chaleur Uplands and the New Brunswick Highlands have elevations rising to 610 m. Cutting through the terrain in deep narrow valleys are rivers such as the Restigouche, Nepisiguit, and their tributaries which flow into the Bay of Chaleur at Bathurst, and the Tobique River which drains into the Saint John River. Together, these rivers and their associated vegetation of mixed Acadian coniferous and deciduous trees provide sections of protected winter habitat for both moose and deer. In addition, the less precipitous highlands further to the south, paralleling the Bay of Fundy coast, support winter habitat. The Maritime Plain provides generally flat to occasionally undulating terrain and narrow shallow streams, as exemplified by the Richibucto and Kouchibouguac rivers and part of the Southwest Miramichi River. Moose and deer seek protective cover in winter among the fir, pine, maple, and hemlock species, which grow among these river basins.

Approximately 3.8 million ha of the Atlantic Region have been designated as class 2 land. The majority of these lands are on the Island of Newfoundland, where there are more than 2.6 million ha of moose and caribou habitat. The extensive areas of sparsely forested, heath and moss barrens in the south and central uplands of the island (including the Burin Peninsula, areas around St. John's on the Avalon Peninsula, and the summits of the Long Range which forms the backbone of the northern peninsula), provide good quality habitat for caribou. Comparable moose habitat is limited to the lower coniferous-forested slopes and river valleys where the common class limitations of exposure, shallow soils, and climate are less severe. In addition, the flat to gently rolling plain of the Newfoundland Lowland, (encompassing Red Indian Lake in the west, and the Exploits River which drains from it through Gander in the east), with typical boreal conifers of balsam fir, black and white spruce, is desirable primarily as moose habitat and also, to a lesser extent, for caribou. Similarly, the coastal plain surrounding St. George's Bay provides sections of prime moose habitat within the coniferous stands. Nova Scotia's 235,643 ha of high-capability moose and deer habitat are found in the highlands near Antigonish, the Cobequid Mountains northeast of the Minas Basin, and between Kentville and Digby in the Annapolis Lowland. The rolling to hilly Cobequid Mountains, with their mixed hardwood and coniferous forested areas interspersed with poorly-drained bogs and rock barren, supplies the best moose habitat in the province. Conversely, the white and red pine and trembling aspen, (the original vegetation of the Annapolis Valley) and the transition to upland area, (having both coniferous and mixed hardwood), support the most favourable habitat for white-tailed deer. Fertility, landform and soil moisture are the most frequent limitations. The well-drained upper slopes of the Chaleur Uplands and the New Brunswick Highlands are endowed with a growth of tolerant hardwoods, sugar maple, beech and yellow birch. On the lower, steeper and more poorly-drained slopes, the hardwoods and the conifers of balsam fir, red spruce, white pine and hemlock are common. Combined, these areas provide most of New Brunswick's 867,285 ha of high-capability habitat for moose and deer. Although low fertility, soil com-

TABLE 3.

CLI areas of high capability for wildlife: Ungulates

Province and territory	Total CLI coverage area	High capability areas*			
		Class 1	Class 2	Class 3	Total Classes 1,2,3
	(ha)				
Newfoundland	10,485,346	504,680	2,698,123	3,531,061	6,733,864
Prince Edward Island**	-	-	-	-	-
Nova Scotia	5,303,583	148,766	235,643	1,307,550	1,691,959
New Brunswick	7,127,438	575,521	867,285	2,569,073	4,001,879
Québec	26,005,253	1,207,803	11,854,045	4,948,122	18,009,970
Ontario	27,004,587	0	4,217,024	2,853,813	7,070,837
Manitoba	18,886,078	764,204	2,850,350	4,591,281	8,205,835
Saskatchewan	35,503,785	428,532	2,956,864	13,395,901	16,781,297
Alberta	45,476,426	3,671,453	5,204,164	10,220,002	19,095,619
British Columbia	55,933,636	2,870,295	5,652,262	7,731,968	16,254,527
Yukon Territory**	-	-	-	-	-
Northwest Territories**	-	-	-	-	-
Canada	231,726,132	10,171,254	36,535,760	51,148,771	97,855,785

* Classification is based on the generalize 1:1,000,000 CLI methodology (see Appendix II)
** Prince Edward Island, Yukon and Northwest Territories were not assessed.

Source: Canada Land Data Systems, 1977.

TABLE 4.

CLI areas of high capability for wildlife: Waterfowl

Province and Territory	Total CLI coverage area	High capability areas*			
		Class 1	Class 2	Class 3	Total Classes 1,2,3
	(ha)				
Newfoundland**	-	-	-	-	-
Prince Edward Island	895,885	127,899	1,981	173	130,053
Nova Scotia	7,255,690	318,494	1,418	14,118	334,030
New Brunswick	7,865,099	260,691	8,545	28,032	297,268
Québec	29,031,582	667,925	6,407	28,098	702,430
Ontario	31,986,165	1,176,493	4,449	82,627	1,263,569
Manitoba	23,532,347	625,499	508,600	869,742	2,003,841
Saskatchewan	36,842,855	771,574	3,194,162	4,886,871	8,852,607
Alberta	46,466,717	264,261	2,539,295	2,139,821	4,943,377
British Columbia	62,702,537	461,176	52,235	131,691	645,102
Yukon Territory**	-	-	-	-	-
Northwest Territories**	-	-	-	-	-
Canada	246,578,877	4,674,012	6,317,092	8,181,173	19,172,277

* Classification is based on generalized 1:1,000,000 CLI methodology (see Appendix II)
** Newfoundland, Yukon and Northwest Territories were not assessed.

Source: Canada Land Data Systems, 1977.

paction, and excessive moisture are the typical class limitations, they do not impede the high-capability production potential in the areas that parallel the Saint John River between St. Stephen and Fredericton, and in the area west of Moncton. Most areas are rated for both moose and deer. Within the Maritime Plain, two pockets of prime ungulate habitat are located north of the Southwest Miramichi River. In addition, 7,407,684 ha of class 3 ungulate habitat have been defined in the three inventoried Atlantic Provinces. These areas are similar to those described in class 2 but with more significant limitations affecting the vegetation. Excessive snow depth, exposure, soil fertility, soil moisture, soil depth, and landform are the dominant limitations relating to the production of ungulates.

Québec. Moose, deer, and some caribou are the indicator species for ungulates in Québec. In the boreal forest and the coniferous-deciduous mixed areas, moose are most common. Deer (predominantly white-tailed) thrive in the deciduous open stands and caribou are rated in the few areas above treeline and in the forest-tundra transition zone of the irregular, rugged plateaux of the Gaspé. Of the 26,005,253 ha classified in Québec, more than 18 million ha are considered to be high-capability lands for the indicator species.

River valleys and lakes, with their associated aquatic plants, accessible browse including maple, yew, honeysuckle, mountain ash, hazel, and adjacent forest stands, provide the winter habitats essential for species survival. In western Québec, the tributaries of the Ottawa River including the Coulonge, Noire, l'Avale, Lièvre, and Rouge rivers, have scattered pockets of class 1 habitat in their drainage basins. Lying within the Laurentian Highlands, these rivers traverse the boreal and mixed forest regions and the vegetation supports white-tailed deer, and, in the more northern areas, moose. Moisture, infertility, poor distribution of landforms, and snow accumulation are the common lower class limitations in the areas away from the river valleys. In the Eastern Townships, prime wintering areas are found dispersed among the Megantic and Sutton hills near Sherbrooke. Lying within the southwestern boundary of the Appalachian Region, moose winter habitat is supplied in the isolated boreal areas, and white-tailed deer winter yards are in the more numerous maple, birch, pine, spruce, and hemlock vegetated areas. The lower slopes of the Shickshock Mountains in Gaspé, dominated by balsam fir, black and white spruce, satisfy moose winter range requirements. The area adjacent to the Cascapedia River, cutting through the upland plateau and emptying into the Bay of Chaleur, support mixed associations of pine, maple, birch, and some red spruce, and is a prime wintering area for white-tailed deer. Snow depth is the main limiting factor for the area. Similar wintering grounds are found at the mouths and in the river valleys of the majority of the rivers flowing northward and emptying into the St. Lawrence River.

Approximately 11.8 million ha of the high-capability ungulate lands have been designated as class 2. In the Abitibi Upland, including part of the clay belt north of Lake Temiskaming, prime moose habitat is supported by black spruce in the gently rising uplands, and in the lowlands by tamarack, spruce-cedar swamps, sedge fens, and heath bogs. Further to the east surrounding Val d'Or, there is less contiguous habitat for moose because soil moisture and adverse topography impose class limitations. To the south and east, the Laurentian Highlands scattered with both mixed hardwood and coniferous forests, traverse the remaining classified area north of the St. Lawrence River. Moose prefer the more northern areas dominated by the coniferous, spruce, fir, and tamarack interspersed by the many lakes and bogs which are a prominant characteristic of the Canadian Shield. Prime deer habitat is located in the mixed forests, particularily along the boundary with the St. Lawrence Lowland. Excessive or deficient soil moisture, low fertility, adverse topography, and shallow soil depth are common class limitations. Eastwards, stretching from the southeast corner of Québec through to the Gaspé, areas of upland and lowland habitat, comprised by both boreal and mixed forests, provide an expanse of high-capability contiguous habitat for moose, deer, and caribou. Deer dominate the upland slopes of the Megantic and Sutton hills where maple, birch, spruce, pine, and hemlock supply shelter and browse. Lowland depressions with stands of cedar, tamarack, and black spruce, and hardwood swamps of black ash, provide some moose habitat. Further to the east, the deeply-dissected rolling terrain increases in elevation to 1,200 m at the summits of the Notre Dame Mountains near Gaspé. The valleys are typified by balsam fir, white spruce, ash, elm, and aspen and are important as deer habitat. The summits of the plateaux in the northwest of the peninsula, above 830 m, support alpine tundra vegetation including sheep-laurel and reindeer moss, suitable as caribou habitat. In this area, habitat is restricted by class limitations of soil mositure, infertility, and rockiness. Class 3 lands with slight limitations for ungulate production include almost 5 million ha. The larger concentrations of class 3 lands are in the area north of Val d'Or, in the highlands to the east and west of the Saguenay River where caribou occupy some sections of open forest and tundra transition, the uplands north of Sherbrooke, and the exposed areas of the Gaspé, which are influenced by adverse climate.

Ontario. The ungulates inventory, covering about 30 per cent of the total land area in Ontario, surveys the high capability areas lying within the extensive sections of boreal and boreal–transition forests of the Canadian Shield in the central, northern, and western areas. Also included is the southern populated area of the St. Lawrence Lowland with its original hardwood forests. Moose and white-tailed deer are the rated indicator species. Deer occupy the southern hardwood and mixed hardwood vegetation associations, and moose range in the boreal and transition forests in the north.

Although more than 7 million ha of high-capability class 2 and 3 ungulate lands have been classified in the province, no essential class 1 wintering grounds have been identified. In southern parts, where there are small amounts of snowfall, for example between 20 and 30 cm in the area around Lake Erie, the white-tailed deer do not form large winter concentrations. Therefore, essential class 1 lands have not been mapped. However, in response to present land use and lack of original forest vegetation, these ungulates may actually gather and seek shelter in the few remaining protected areas which have not been cleared for agriculture production or other uses. In the CLI, because the land has been rated according to its capability in terms of original natural vegetation and not present land uses, anomalies such as this exist in certain areas within the national boundaries. Excessive soil moisture, fertility, and soil depth are the dominant class limitations for the class 2 and 3 ungulate habitats and account for the sparse distribution. There are high-capability moose production lands in the area north of Timmins where aspen, white spruce, balsam fir, and some white birch grow on the moist, deep, fertile clays. Browse is also provided by the submergent and emergent vegetation in the bog and aquatic sites. Similar class 2 and 3 moose habitat areas are found on the lands surrounding Lake Abitibi and Lake Temiskaming. Here too, the combination of aquatic browse plants, important for summer diet, and the adjacent mixed stands of conifers and some deciduous areas, satisfy shelter and other food requirements for year-round habitation. Pockets of high-capability lands for moose and deer are identified in the area south of Lake of the Woods and around Dryden. The Lake of the Woods area lies within the northwestern section of the Great Lakes–St. Lawrence forest and can be described generally as a transition area with both coniferous and deciduous trees, grasses, and herbs. Deer prefer the regenerating areas on the clay plain. In addition, to the west of Thunder Bay, similar essential habitats for deer have been described on the fertile clay soils supporting characteristic white spruce, balsam, and trembling aspen. Adjacent bogs and some lake shorelines provide summer and winter browse. Contrasting the isolated locations of prime ungulate habitat in the Canadian Shield, are the extensive production habitats of the St. Lawrence Lowland with its hardwood and mixed forests. In the southwest, the marginal pattern of the sand and clay till limestone plain produces a mosaic of flat to rolling and undulating terrain which was originally covered by the deciduous species including maple, beech, black walnut, hickory, and oak. Hence, this area has been rated as class 2 lands for white-tailed deer. The central and northern sections of the lowland, stretching from Manitoulin Island to Tobermory on the Bruce Peninsula, through Peterborough and Kingston, and continuing in the southeastern triangle bounded by the Ottawa River and the St. Lawrence River, are dominated by essential lands primarily for white-tailed deer and some moose. Here too, the glacial deposition features include the undulating to rolling relief, underlie the mixed forest. This area is limited by excessive or insufficient soil moisture, low soil fertility, and soil depth.

The Prairie Provinces. A total of 44,082,751 ha of high capability ungulate habitat has been identified in the three Prairie Provinces. Decreasing in elevation from the subalpine forests on the Alberta foothills to the poorly-drained peatlands and boreal forest of Manitoba's northeast, a diversity of wildlife habitats have been located for the indicator species in each province.

Moose, white-tailed and mule deer, elk, and woodland caribou, the ungulates in Manitoba, are supported by 8,205,835 ha of essential habitat. Boreal forest, aspen parkland, and grassland traverse the Canadian Shield and Interior Plains. Most of the 764,204 ha of prime wintering habitat lies within the Saskatchewan Plain between the Manitoba–Saskatchewan boundary and the Manitoba Escarpment. Pockets of class 1 habitat have been identified within the mixed wood section of the boreal forest. Moose, white-tailed and mule deer, and elk are provided essential winter forage and protective cover by the variety of boreal and broadleafed trees found in the uplands and lowlands south of Swan River and near Riding Mountain National Park. In addition, the Manitoba Lowlands, north of the Interlake area, have been designated as high-capability lands for ungulates. Much of the Interlake area and the area west of Lake Manitoba, with its overlying scrub vegetation offers little high-quality ungulate habitat.

Canada hand Inventory – Photo by H.D. Goulden

This open woodland in an upland area of Manitoba provides high-capability habitat for moose, deer, and elk.

More than 13 million ha of the high-capability ungulate habitat in Saskatchewan, have been designated as class 3. Paralleling the southern boundary of the parkland and grassland transition which bisects the province from northwest to southeast, most class 3 habitats lie within the aspen groves of the parkland and, further north, within the mixed woods of the boreal forest. Elk and white-tailed deer are the indicator species in the parkland, and deer, moose, and woodland caribou dominate the more northern boreal forest. In the southwest, the Cypress Hills and, to a lesser extent, the Great Sand Hills, create their own micro-climate and support islands of high-quality tree, shrub, and grass habitat for white-tailed and mule deer, antelope, and some elk. Isolated pockets of class 1 habitat for wintering ungulates are distributed along the riverine and upland habitats throughout the province. In the southwest, the protected Frenchman River and Notukeu Creek valleys support antelope winter range. Nearby, the unique Cypress Hills, sloping westwards to reach an elevation of 1,466 m represents one of the few Prairie landforms unaltered by pleistocene glaciation. On the higher north facing slopes, lodgepole pine, spruce, jack pine, and tamarack intersperse with aspen poplar, provide a sharp contrast to the surrounding arid Prairie, and support white-tailed and mule deer, and antelope. Further north in the area of the Great Sand Hills, the growth of aspen poplar, buckbush, willow, rose and sagebrush, satisfy the needs of wintering deer and antelope. In addition, the well-defined shrub and tree cover in the aspen grove and mixed-grass transition area of Last Mountain Lake and along the Qu'Appelle River valley supports wintering white-tailed deer. Finally, the Moose Mountains in the southeast near Moosomin, an end moraine characterized by hills and numerous kettle-filled shallow lakes and bisected by Pipestone Creek, support high-capability wintering habitat for moose, white-tailed deer, and elk. Class 2 ungulate habitat includes 2,956,864 ha which are interspersed throughout the expansive class 3 habitat areas. In general, the class limitations including lack of landform diversity, climate, aridity, poor fertility, and soil moisture deficits, are not as prevalent as they are in class 3 areas. Of particular importance as class 2 habitat are: the Saskatchewan Delta near Cumberland House, the area surrounding the Pasquia Hills east of Melfort, between Last Mountain Lake and the Qu'Appelle River and along the North Saskatchewan River valley.

Of the 45,476,426 ha included in the Alberta CLI, 3,671,453 ha have been identified as class 1 wintering habitats, 5,204,164 as class 2, and more than 10 million

Source: Generalized from the 1:1,000,000 Canada Land Inventory *Land Capability for Wildlife-Ungulates* maps for *Atlantic Provinces* (1977) and *Québec* (1976), published by the Lands Directorate, Environment Canada.

MAP 1

Photo by Ministry of Industry and Tourism, Ontario.

MAP 3

Photo by the Alberta Public Affairs Bureau.

LAND CAPABILITY

BRITISH COLUMBIA
ALBERTA
SASKATCHEWAN
MANITOBA

Source: Generalized from the 1:1,000,000 Canada Land Inventory *Land Capability for Wildlife-Ungulates* maps for *British Columbia-North* (1976), *British Columbia-South* (1976), *Alberta* (1976), *Saskatchewan* (1974) and *Manitoba* (1976), published by the Lands Directorate, Environment Canada.

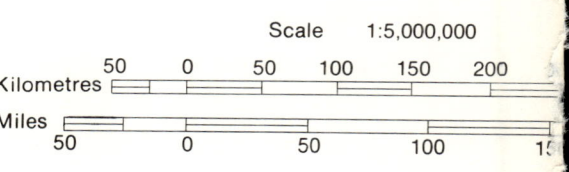

Scale 1:5,000,000

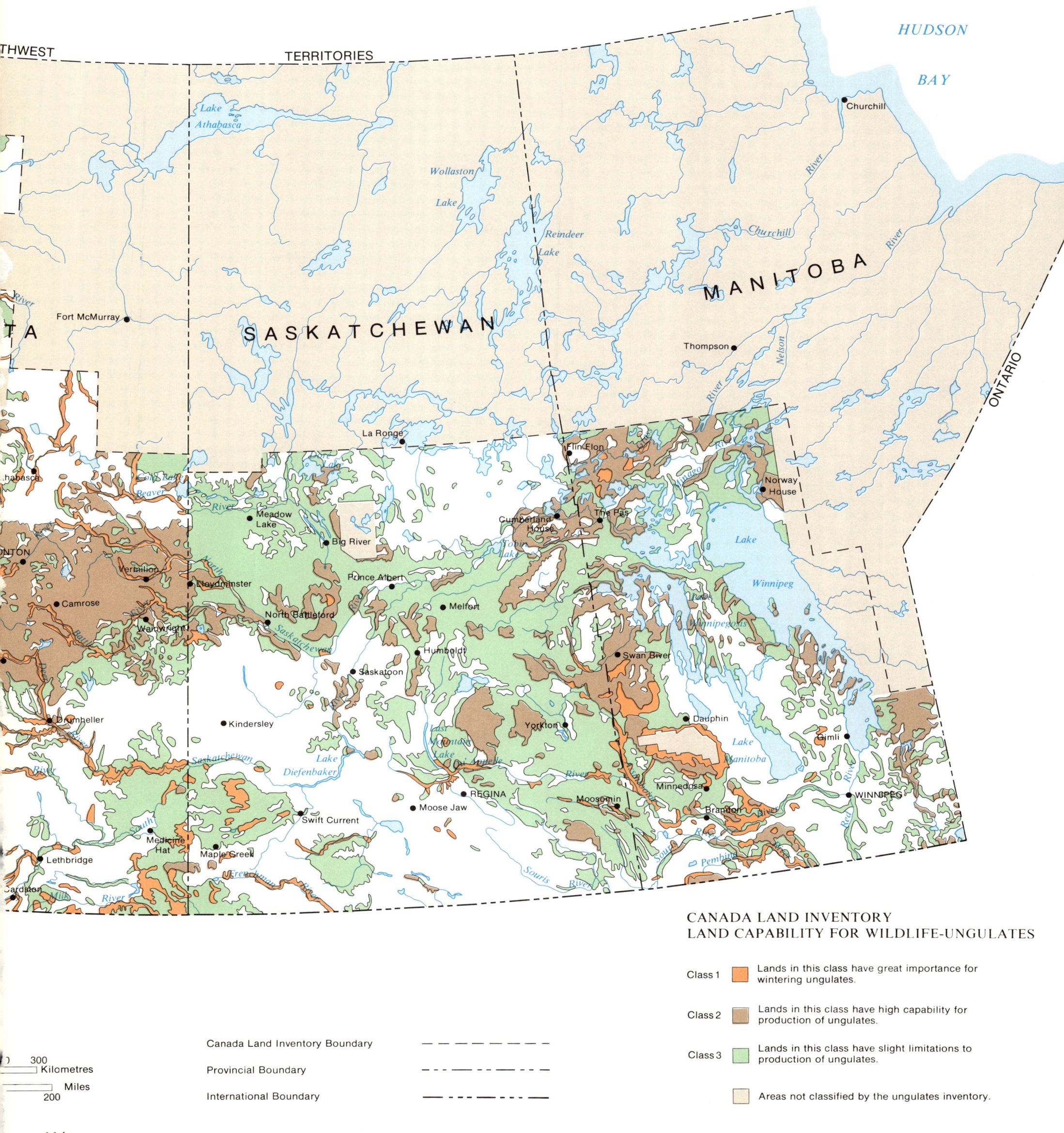

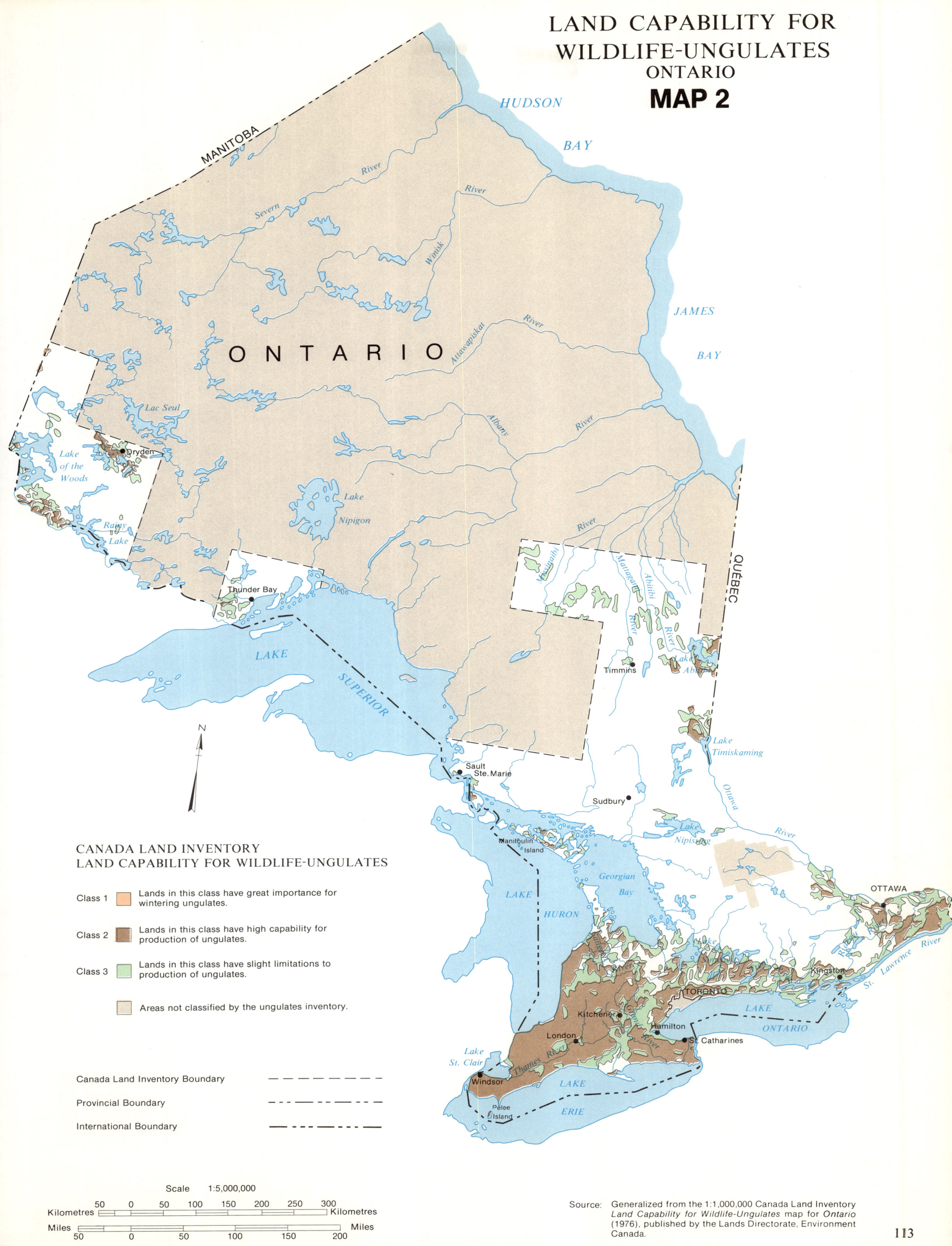

MAP 4

Photo by the Canadian Wildlife Service.

Source: Generalized from the 1:1,000,000 Canada Land Inventory *Land Capability for Wildlife-Waterfowl* maps for *Atlantic Provinces* (1976) and *Québec* (1976), published by the Lands Directorate, Environment Canada.

ha of class 3 habitats. These habitats have slight limitations including soil fertility, adverse topography, climate, aridity and soil moisture. Alberta's terrain rises in steps from the arid southwestern mixed-grass Prairie and the southwest-northeast arc of the aspen grove parkland on the Alberta Plain, through the more northern mixed wood boreal forest of the Alberta Plateau, to the subalpine and alpine forests of the eastern Cordillera in the Rocky Mountains. This diversity of landscape supports prime ungulate habitat for antelope, mule and white-tailed deer, moose, elk, mountain sheep, and mountain goat. Class 1 lands are scattered across the province, in a finger like pattern paralleling the major river valleys draining from the Rocky Mountains. In the northern part of the inventory area, the Peace River valley, bisecting the undulating to gently rolling Peace River Lowland, supports wintering populations of moose, elk, white-tailed and mule deer. Traversing the western boundary of the province, the broad incised river valleys of the foothills, lying within the transition area between the boreal and subalpine forests, provide a varied, protected shelter for moose, elk, mule and white-tailed deer. To the east, the meandering river valleys of the Alberta Plain include the Athabasca, North and South Saskatchewan, Battle, and Red Deer rivers. All have tree-covered banks which provide the essential winter browse and cover for deer, elk, and some moose in the parklands, and deer, elk and antelope in the more southern grasslands.

Class 2 and 3 habitat areas, are equally dispersed throughout the province. In the north, fanning out from the Peace River valley, high-capability habitat for moose and deer are identified in the mixed wood portion of the boreal forest. Also included are the poorly-drained areas where black spruce, tamarack, Labrador tea and other sedges, grasses, and mosses dominate. The drier more southern reaches of the Peace River area, which are important for white-tailed deer and antelope are predominately parkland with wooded bluffs and low shrub cover. Adjacent to the National parks of the Rocky Mountains are areas of class 3 habitat, primarily for moose, elk, and white-tailed deer. Portions of the subalpine forest (alpine fir, whitebark pine, limber pine, larch, Engelmann spruce, and lodgepole pine) and the lower transitional foothills section have been classified as essential ranges. To the south, the drier montane forest supports a similar mountain habitat but, in addition, some Prairie bunch grasses and forbes have invaded the river valleys. Further to the east, the sub-arid short-grass Prairie surrounding Medicine Hat provides forage primarily for antelope and some deer. In this region, many areas are too dry to provide high-capability ungulate habitat. Tree shelter, usually clusters of trembling aspen, willow, and poplar, is found only along the river valleys. North of Medicine Hat, the Alberta section of the Middle Sand Hills supports growth of roses, cinquefoil, and snowberries, a valuable browse for mule deer and antelope. In addition, antelope range on the sage-brush, blue, gama, and spear grasses.

British Columbia. Elk, mule, white-tailed and black-tailed deer, moose, mountain caribou, mountain sheep, and mountain goat are the indicator species which find protected food and shelter in the variety of vegetation in the mountains, plateaux, valleys, coastal lowlands, and northeastern plains of British Columbia. In total, 30 per cent of the 55,933,636 ha surveyed, have been identified as high-capability lands.

Photo by the Canadian Wildlife Service

Mule deer, one of the indicator species for the ungulates assessment of the Canada Land Inventory, prefer the boreal, subalpine, and alpine habitats found in Alberta and British Columbia.

Classes 1 and 2 lands support the essential summer and winter ranges of the indicator species. Throughout the Cordillera, these habitats are found in the river valleys, the bottomlands, and at lower elevations on the mountain slopes. In the southeast, within the Columbia and portions of montane forests, the Rocky Mountain Trench provides winter range for deer, elk, and moose. Douglas-fir, lodgepole pine, larch, trembling aspen, and browse species of willow, red-osier dogwood, black cottonwood, Douglas maple and sedge meadows grow along the Columbia River drainage basin in the southern part of the trench. To the west, the valleys of Kootenay, Slocan, and the Arrow lakes have been rated class 2 for deer and elk. Dominated by the Columbia forest, these habitats range below the 1,219 m elevation. Within the Interior Plateau, characterized by the montane forest and parkland, class 1 and 2 areas appear in the bottomlands of the upper Fraser, the Chilcotin, the Nechako rivers and their respective drainage basins. These valleys support important wintering areas for moose and mule deer. Here, Douglas-fir and western red cedar, with an understory of Douglas maple, trembling aspen and red-osier dogwood, intersperse with the associated grasslands of bluebunch, wheatgrass, shrubs and forbs. Similarly, the Peace River and its tributaries on the northeastern Alberta Plateau provide critical wintering habitats for moose and deer. Throughout the winter, moose congregate in the trembling aspen, birch and willow found in river valleys. Mule deer, impeded by snow depth, seek the south and west-facing breaks of river valleys where wind and sun action keeps the ground relatively snow free. The Pacific Coast forest which dominates the Vancouver Island and Eastern System mountains, supports essential habitat for deer, elk, moose, and some caribou. Although wintering ranges are severely limited by deep snow and steep or rocky terrain, the low-lying bottomlands and slopes of coastal fjords provide some protective cover that satisfies wintering ungulate needs. The majority of class 3 habitat lands lie in the higher elevations of the Cordillera, which are characterized by subalpine and alpine forests. Engelmann and white spruce, Douglas and alpine fir with some palatable browse species of willow, scrub birch, and trembling aspen eventually give way to shrubby thickets and grassy meadows at elevations above 2,134 m. Only mountain goats use the highest rock crags. Mountain sheep, mountain goat, mountain caribou, mule deer, Vancouver Island black-tailed deer, and Roosevelt elk use the high treed and meadow slopes for summer range. In the province's northwest, extensive areas of class 3 habitats for deer and moose have been identified in the mixed wood section of the boreal forest.

Identification of High Capability Lands for Waterfowl

The Atlantic Provinces. Extensive and, in some places, deeply-indented coastlines characterized by tidal lagoons, mud flats, and saltwater marshes, attract thousands of waterfowl to the Atlantic Provinces during annual migrations. Several inland freshwater marshes also support valuable waterfowl breeding habitats. In total, 761,351 ha of high-capability habitat for waterfowl have been classified as essential in Nova Scotia, New Brunswick, and Prince Edward Island.

More than 707,084 ha of class 1 migrating and wintering habitat has been identified in the Atlantic Region. Brant and Canada Geese, and migrating ducks use the sheltered waters of the large bays of Prince Edward Island as resting and feeding grounds. The Atlantic Coast of Nova Scotia, with its many harbours and estuaries, supplies migration habitat for waterfowl including Canada Geese, Black Duck, eider, scoter, scaup, and merganser. Also important are the low coastal wetlands of the Maritime Plain including the saltwater marshes and riverine estuaries of the Northumberland Strait which are used extensively during migration by Brant and Canada Geese, Common Goldeneye, Greater and Lesser Scaup. Further to the east, the salt marshes and mud flats of Chignecto Bay and the Minas Basin, supporting the salt-tolerant plant species, provide few production sites for waterfowl, but are excellent stopover areas for migrating geese and ducks. Also, the shores surrounding Digby in the Annapolis Valley are capable of supporting waterfowl during spring and fall migration. In New Brunswick, prime habitats used during annual migrations are located in the lowland salt and freshwater marshes along the Northumberland Strait and along the wetlands of the lower Saint John River and the Bay of Fundy coast. The tidal lagoons of the Northumberland Strait attract migrating Canada Geese, Black Duck, Greater Scaup, Oldsquaw, Green-winged Teal, merganser, scoter, and eider. Similarly, the Saint John River and the Bay of Fundy area, including Grand Manan Island, are used extensively during migration by brant and Canada Geese, Greater and Lesser Scaup, goldeneye, and sea ducks.

Combined class 2 and 3 lands identify 54,267 ha of high-capability areas for waterfowl production. With the exception of the coastal sites and Prince Edward Island, the majority of the rivers and lakes in the Atlantic Region are of little value as good quality production habitat. Generally, the wetlands associated with lakes are limited by water depth and infertility. However, there are several significant production sites which should be identified because of their importance to Black Duck, Blue and Green-winged Teal, goldeneye, Wood Duck and merganser. These include the wetlands along the floodplains of the Musquodoboit River which is east of Halifax, isolated ponds and lakes in Cape Breton Island, and the riverine marshes along the border between Nova Scotia and New Brunswick. Also, the lowlands of the Maritime Plain, and along the lower Saint John River, support some high-capability wetlands. Here, flooding is a limiting factor but it is also important in replenishing riverine fertility.

Québec. The shorelines of the Ottawa River, the St. Lawrence River, Lac St-Jean, and Îles-de-la-Madeleine provide the prime waterfowl capability areas in Québec. Of the 702,430 ha of high-capability waterfowl habitat, approximately 90 per cent are designated as class 1. The extensive tidal mud flats of the St. Lawrence River support waterfowl during their spring and fall migrations. Greater Snow Geese use the essential migration habitat in the area between Québec City and Cap Tourmente. Habitat is also supplied to many diving and dabbling ducks which stop during the northern and southern treks. Eastward, the marshes near Baie Comeau support migrating eider ducks and some nesting sites for Black Duck, Green-winged Teal, merganser, and goldeneye. The shallow sandy barrier beach ponds and the submergent and emergent plants on the north shore of Lac St-Jean are used extensively by migrating waterfowl. In addition, the marshes associated with the lowlands of the St. Lawrence River near Montréal and along the southern section of the Richelieu River, provide similar migration stopover sites. In the interior upland of the province, few marshes have high capability for supporting waterfowl. Adverse topography and inundation or excessive fluctuation of water levels are the common class limitations. Most rivers, with their steep banks and swift currents, are unsuitable for waterfowl production. However, the fertile alluvial deposits of estuaries such as along the Restigouche River emptying into Chaleur Bay, and areas near Gaspé have a higher potential for waterfowl production. In the western portion of the province, the Ottawa River valley and Lake Temiskaming supply another expanse of prime migration habitat. Some Pintail, Green and Blue-winged Teal, Black Duck, Shoveler and goldeneye nest in the area. Migration habitat is also available on the tidal lagoons of Îles-de-la-Madeleine. Black Duck, Green-winged Teal, Canada Geese, and scoter gather to rest during spring and fall migration. Here too, the main limiting factors are fertility and topography. The topography and vast amounts of sand on the island complex, combine to produce narrow intermittent wetlands with low-quality vegetation.

Canada Land Inventory – Photo by G. Arsenault

The tidal marshes at Cap Tourmente in Québec, provide high-capability feeding and resting habitat for Greater Snow Geese during spring and autumn migrations.

Ontario. The variety of wetlands surrounding the Great Lakes, the St. Clair marshes, the Ottawa and St. Lawrence River valleys, the Trent-Severn River, and the isolated fertile marshes within the northern portions of the province near Lake of the Woods, Thunder Bay, and Lake Abitibi, combine to provide 1,176,493 ha of class 1 habitat for waterfowl. With the exception of sev-

eral pockets of class 2 and 3 high-capability production areas in the uplands of Ontario, the major function of the province's wetlands is to satisfy the essential seasonal migrating stopover requirements. The valuable littoral areas of Lake Erie and Lake Ontario support the annual migrations of species such as Mallard, Black Duck, Blue and Green-winged Teal, Wood Duck, Pintail, Canvasback, Bufflehead, Lesser and Greater Scaup, widgeon, and goldeneye. Whistling Swan and Canada Geese also seek the shorelines and marshes of Lake Erie. The productive marshes of Lake St. Clair provide the food and cover requirements for the many migrating species including dabbling ducks. Some Blue-winged Teal nest along the shorelines. In addition, prime resting habitat in southwestern Ontario is found along the banks of the Grand and the Niagara rivers. Several of the morainic areas near Kitchener supply high-quality production habitat for breeding Blue-winged Teal, Wood, and Black Duck. The vegetation in these permanently wet depressions and marshes, consisting of sedges, rushes, cattails, burreeds, and pondweeds, are also used by the less common nesting species of Gadwall, American Widgeon, shoveler, Ring-necked Duck, Redhead and Ruddy Duck. Elsewhere in southern Ontario, the main limitation to productive nesting hatitat, is the lack of permanent marshes. Further to the east in the central St. Lawrence Lowland, the shores of the lower Ottawa, the Rideau, and the St. Lawrence rivers are all utilized as prime migration route stopover sites. To a lesser extent, nesting habitat is provided for some Black Duck, Mallard, Green and Blue-winged Teal and merganser. In addition, Canada Geese seek the marshes of the eastern St. Lawrence River. The area between Lake Simcoe, Peterborough, and Kingston, paralleling the region between the Canadian Shield and the St. Lawrence Lowland, supports pockets of resting habitat for the annual migrations. Only the shallower lakes and bog ponds provide suitable resting and some nesting habitat with useful submergent and emergent edge plants for the variety of Pintail, Bufflehead, Redhead, Canvasback, scaup, widgeon, teal, and scoter, and Canada Geese which utilize the area. As with most sections of the Canadian Shield, the common waterfowl production limitations are related to topography, the extensive areas of exposed bedrock, the lack of vegetative edge on the deep and steep-sided lakes, and the rapid flow rates of streams and rivers. Although these limitations predominate, there are several important habitat areas in the more northern sectors of the province. Surrounding Lake Nipissing, and the adjacent fertile lands, the marshes associated with the shallow bays, beaver ponds, bogs and meandering streams, support nesting Black Duck, Mallard, Ring-necked Duck, Green and Blue-winged Teal, Wood Duck, and merganser. Ducks and geese are also supported by the shorelines of Lake Nipissing, Lake Temiskaming, and along the North Channel of Lake Huron including Georgian Bay, during the spring and fall migration. In the northeastern part, the significant migration habitats are located around Lake Abitibi and along the Abitibi River within the poorly-drained clay belt. Pondweeds, water and yellow-pond lilies, sedges, rushes, bulrushes, cattails, and wild rice support the local waterfowl populations.

The Prairie Provinces. Of the many vegetation types associated with the Canadian Shield, the Interior Plains, and the eastern Cordillera in the Prairie Provinces, the grassland and transition aspen parkland belt covering a southern semi-circle arcing from southeastern Alberta to southwestern Manitoba, provides most of the 15,799,825 ha of high-capability waterfowl production habitat. Essential nesting cover is supported by the unique Prairie Sloughs, the water-filled swale and kettle potholes dispersed throughout the expansive moraine and till plains. In addition, the northern boreal forest areas particularly in Manitoba, along the banks of the North and South Saskatchewan rivers, and the smaller lakes, are identified as high-capability migration habitat, used as spring and fall stopover sites.

In Manitoba, the variety of wetlands associated with the Manitoba Interlake area, the Saskatchewan River delta, Dauphin Lake, and other isolated pockets, support 625,499 ha of class 1 waterfowl habitat. Specifically, the shorelines of Lake Winnipegosis and adjacent lakes have extensive beds of pondweeds and are major migration stops for migrating Canada Geese and Whistling Swan. Similar submergent vegetation surrounding Dauphin Lake is used seasonally by populations of ducks and geese including Mallard, Canvasback, Redhead and Lesser Scaup. The high-quality nesting grounds found within the Saskatchewan Plain in the southwestern part of the province include 1,378,342 ha of class 2 and 3. Where the permanent and temporary water areas are evenly dispersed within the mixed-grass Prairie and the aspen parkland, class 2 sites have been identified. These highest capability nesting sites are located around Minnedosa, south of the Assiniboine River along the Manitoba–Saskatchewan boundary, and south of the Souris River traversing the Pembina till plain. Class 3 habitats support similar vegetation as class 2 habitats, but the limitations relating to landform dispersion, reduced marsh edge, and fertility generally denote a poorer dispersion of permanent and temporary water bodies. Small pockets of class 2 and 3 habitat are located in the Saskatchewan Delta area near The Pas. Here species such as Wood and Black Duck nest in the extensive wetlands of the delta.

Almost 50 per cent of the high-capability waterfowl production, staging, and resting habitats of the Prairie Provinces, lies within the southern half of Saskatchewan. These 8,852,607 ha represent the largest single provincial concentration of essential waterfowl habitat. Class 1 habitats encompass the larger lakes including Big Quill Lake, Old Wives Lake and Lake Diefenbaker, the Saskatchewan River west of Saskatoon, and, in the north near Cumberland House, the Saskatchewan Delta. Ross, White-fronted, and Lesser Snow Geese are among the returning migrating birds who seek the western portion of the Saskatchewan River as resting sites while in transit. The wetlands of Last Mountain and Quill lakes are also used as staging habitats by geese and ducks. Important staging habitat for ducks which nest in northern Alberta and the Arctic include the larger water bodies previously mentioned, the larger wetland complexes distributed throughout the grassland and aspen parkland, and, the Saskatchewan Delta, Sisona Lake, and west of Meadow Lake, all within the boreal forest. The uniform interspersion of wetlands and uplands in the pothole region of Saskatchewan is the major reason that more than 7 million ha of class 2 and 3 production habitat have been identified. The combination of aspen and shrub-ringed sloughs with those surrounded by the mixed-grass and the variety of submergent and emergent marsh plants growing in the wet areas, support the varied nesting and food requirements of the many duck species which conduct the vital life-cycle functions in this region. In addition, production habitat is provided for geese in the southwestern grassland and along the South Saskatchewan River and in the aspen parkland of eastern Saskatchewan. Areas of lower capability habitat, such as in much of the short-grass prairie and the northern boreal forest, are inhibited by class limitations including landform dispersion, aridity, soil moisture, and reduced marsh edge.

Of the 4,943,377 ha of essential waterfowl habitat identified in Alberta, only 264,261 ha have been designated as class 1 sites. Pockets of these important staging and resting stopover habitats are scattered throughout the central part of both the grassland and aspen parkland areas, along the southern river valleys, in isolated pockets of the boreal forest, specifically surrounding Hay and Zama lakes and Utikuma Lake. More than 4,679,116 ha of class 2 and 3 habitat have been located primarily within the western extension of the aspen parkland and in some grassland stretching along the Alberta portion of the Alberta Plain. In addition, extensions of parkland habitat near Grande Prairie, the western end of Lesser Slave Lake, and within the Peace River Lowland, support smaller quantities of these high-capability habitat. Much of the western portion of the province is limited by adverse topography and water depth as the Prairie terrain rises in steps towards the foothills.

Canada Land Inventory – Photo by G. Adams

This aspen parkland is an example of class 1 habitat for waterfowl. The interspersion of small temporary ponds with the larger permanent water areas provides ideal conditions for waterfowl production.

British Columbia. Less than one per cent of the inventory area has been identified as essential waterfowl habitat in British Columbia. Dominated by mountainous terrain and deep fast-flowing rivers, common class limitations include; adverse topography, unfavourable climate, excessive water depth and poor marsh edge. Of the 645,102 ha of high capability habitats identified, the majority have been delineated as class 1, wintering or migrating habitat. The tidal flats and bottomlands of the Fraser Delta support migrating ducks, Canada and Snow Geese, brant and Whistling Swan. Similarly, the tidal flats of the coastal lowlands of southeastern Vancouver Island and the Gulf islands attract many species of ducks and geese. Some of the migrating and wintering populations include American Widgeon, Green-winged Teal, Pintail, goldeneye, scaup, scoter, Black Brant, Canada and Snow Geese, and Whistling Swan. In addition, Black Brant seek the gravel beaches of west Vancouver Island as an important migrating habitat. East of the Fraser River near Merritt, within the sub-arid grassland surrounded by montane forest, the numerous shallow alkaline lakes ringed with submergent and emergent aquatic plants, provide the best nesting habitat in the province. Nesting species include Mallard, Pintail, Blue-winged Teal, Ruddy Duck, scaup and goldeneye. To the northwest, the open parkland along the Chilcotin and Fraser river valleys, also support nesting habitat for a variety of ducks and geese. Near Prince Rupert, along the coast near the Skeena River and other estuaries, migrating waterfowl seek stopover habitats. In the southwestern portion of the province, within the Columbia Mountains, only the low-lying Rocky Mountain Trench, and Creston Valley contain the abundance of aquatic vegetation necessary for migrating ducks and geese.

Although the ungulates and waterfowl assessment of the Canada Land Inventory represents the first comprehensive national survey, there are several limiting factors which should be considered in its interpretation. As with all sectors of the CLI each province was responsible for their own landscape classification and hence variations occur particularly along provincial boundaries. One of the problems with land capability analyses is that sometimes present land use and the original capability of the land are quite different. For example, as mentioned in southern Ontario, although the original vegetation cover was deciduous hardwoods much of the forest stand has been removed and hence the rated capability for ungulates varies from the actual land use. However, in the more northern parts of the inventory area present land use and land capability are nearly synonymous. Because of this, Ontario expanded the CLI into an Ontario Land Inventory (OLI) which added another indicator class for determining the degree-of-effort or management techniques required to return a land unit to the level of the assigned capability class. This system is essential in the highly populated southern areas where much of the natural vegetation has been transformed. In addition, the OLI included furbearers and upland birds (beaver, European hare, Sharp-tailed and Ruffed Grouse, Hungarian Partridge, Ring-necked Pheasants, puddle ducks, Wood Ducks and diving ducks).

In summary, there are 19,172,277 ha of critical waterfowl habitats in southern Canada. This represents only seven per cent of the total CLI coverage area. Critical ungulates habitat includes 97,855,787 ha or 42 per cent of the total CLI coverage area (Tables 3 and 4).

CLI has been examined as one national approach towards identifying special lands for ungulates and waterfowl. Consider now two regional methodologies which identify other sensitive areas for wildlife.

Photo by Environment Canada

The submergent and emergent aquatic vegetation of Creston Valley in southwestern British Columbia attracts many species of ducks and geese during spring and fall migrations.

MAP 6

Canada Land Inventory, Photo by G. Watson.

WILDLIFE-WATERFOWL

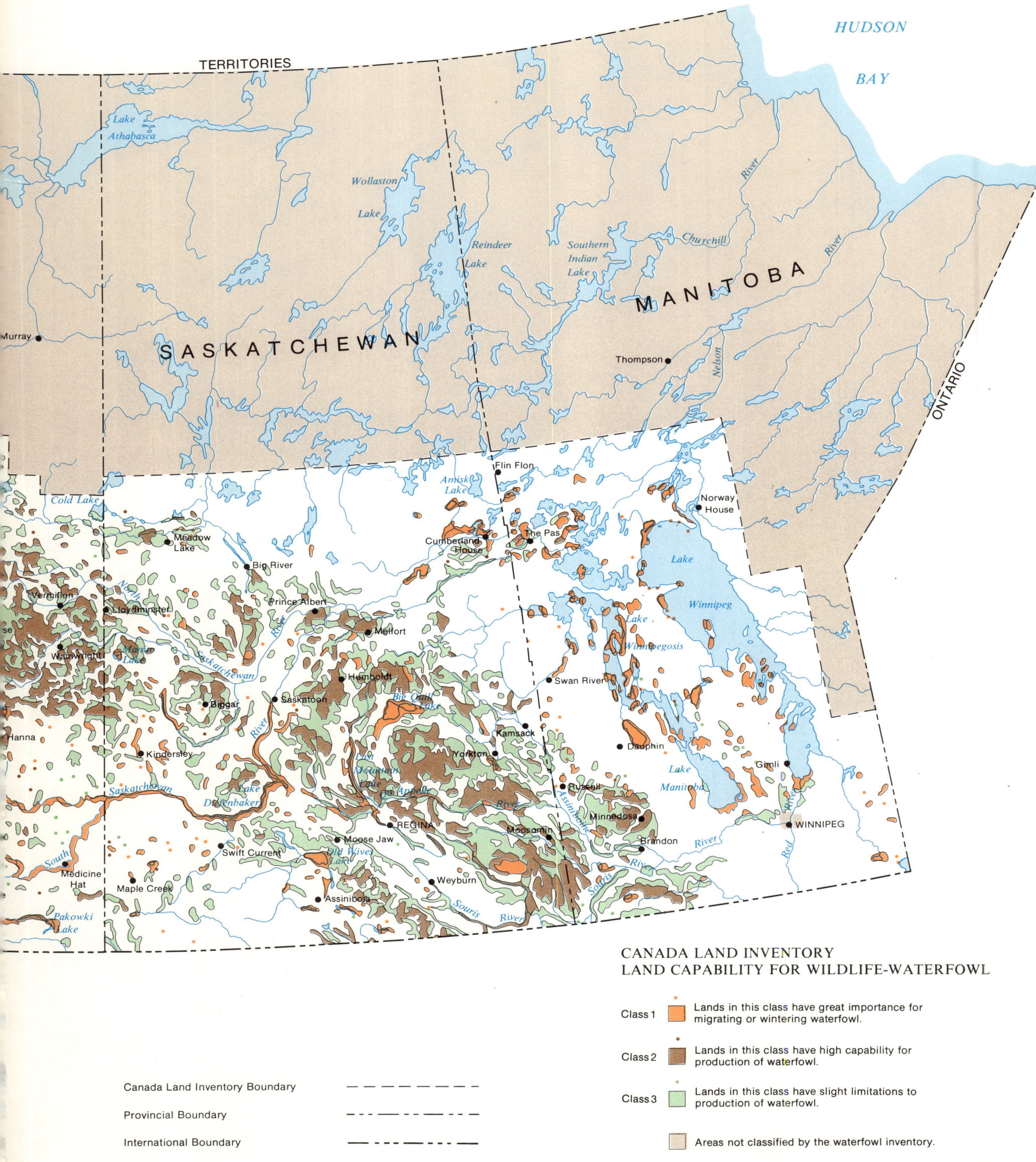

CANADA LAND INVENTORY
LAND CAPABILITY FOR WILDLIFE-WATERFOWL

Class 1 — Lands in this class have great importance for migrating or wintering waterfowl.

Class 2 — Lands in this class have high capability for production of waterfowl.

Class 3 — Lands in this class have slight limitations to production of waterfowl.

Areas not classified by the waterfowl inventory.

Canada Land Inventory Boundary ── ── ──
Provincial Boundary ── · ── · ──
International Boundary ── · · ── · · ──

LAND CAPABILITY FOR

BRITISH COLUMBIA
ALBERTA
SASKATCHEWAN
MANITOBA

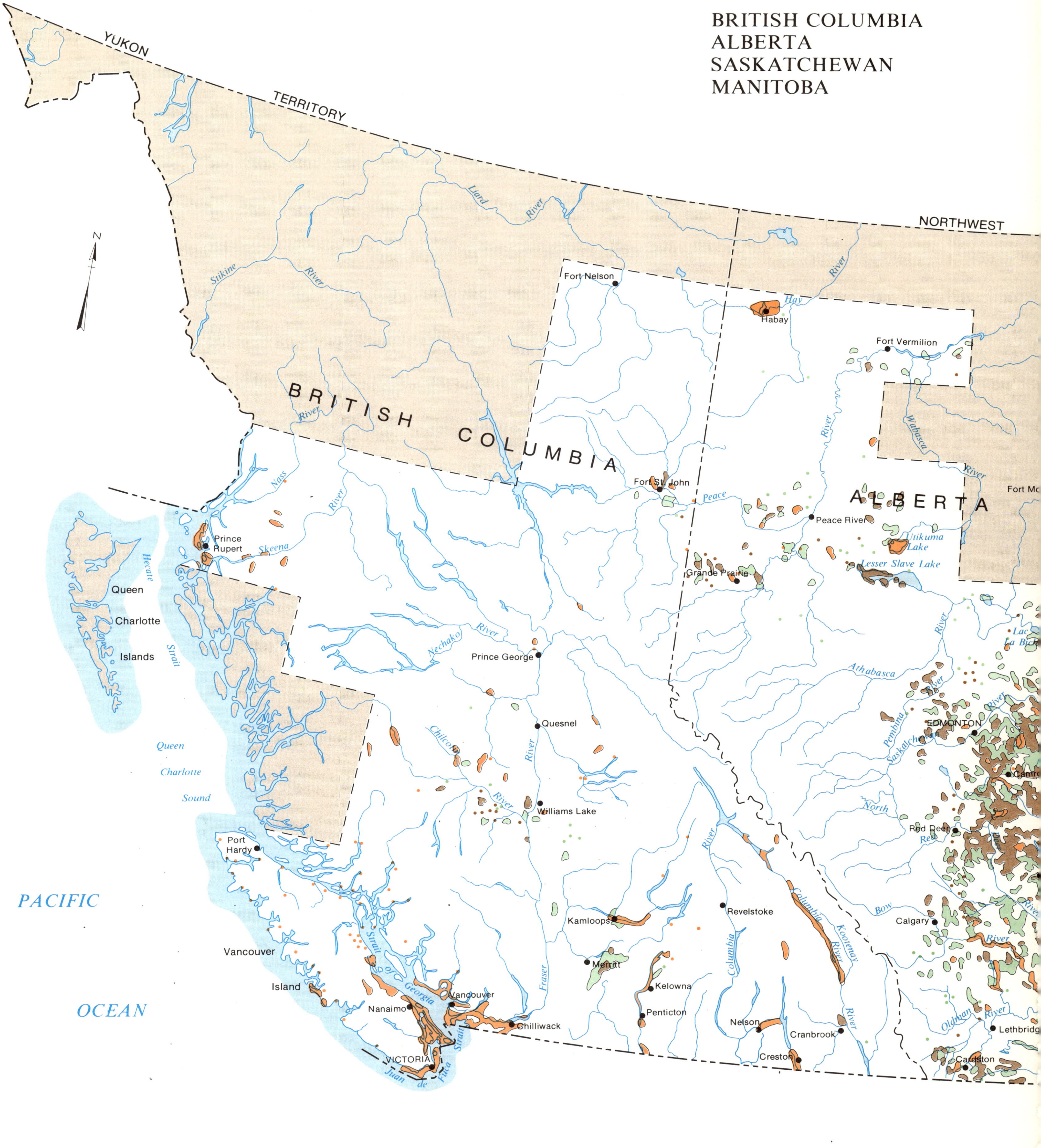

Source: Generalized from the 1:1,000,000 Canada Land Inventory *Land Capability for Wildlife-Waterfowl* maps for *British Columbia-North* (1976), *British Columbia-South* (1975), *Alberta* (1974), *Saskatchewan* (1976) and *Manitoba* (1974), published by the Lands Directorate, Environment Canada.

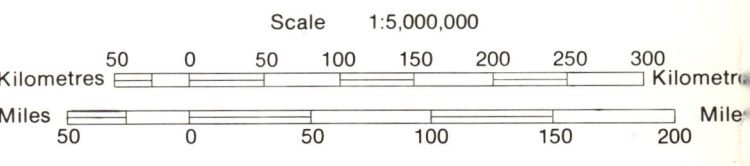

Scale 1:5,000,000

119

Sensitive Areas for Migratory Birds in Coastal Eastern Canada

Map 7 locates the extensive critical and important areas for migratory birds of the sensitive inshore estuaries and marine habitats of Ontario, Québec, and the Atlantic Provinces. Based on known seasonal concentrations of diving and dabbling ducks, geese, swans, shorebirds, and seabirds (including sea ducks), the data should be considered as preliminary and subject to change upon completion of future habitat studies (Carreiro and Tessier, 1976).

The rugged rock cliffs, ledges, and grassy bluffs of Newfoundland's east coast and offshore islands including Funk and Baccalieu islands; the north shore, Anticosti and Bonaventure islands, and Bird Rocks near Îles-de-la-Madeleine in Québec; the coastal uplands, particularly Bird Island near Cape Breton Island in Nova Scotia, and Machias Seal Island off the New Brunswick coast in the Bay of Fundy, accommodate the major year-round and seasonal seabird colonies for Gannet, Razorbill, Black-legged Kittiwake, Atlantic Puffin, cormorant, murre, and auklet. Sea ducks including Common Eider, Oldsquaw and scoter also locate throughout the area. The salt and freshwater tidal marshes and lagoons of the Maritime Plain, extending from the east coast of New Brunswick through to Prince Edward Island, support a variety of shorebirds, ducks, geese, and small concentrations of seabirds. While shorebirds including heron, tern, and plover use the region during summer and fall, some ducks and geese are present in all seasons. Nesting species include Black Duck, Common Goldeneye, Red-breasted Merganser, Green-winged Teal, Atlantic Brant, and Canada Geese. Larger populations of ducks and geese stage in the marshes and tidal flats during the spring and fall migrations. In addition, small numbers of Black Duck, merganser, goldeneye, Oldsquaw, eider, and scoter overwinter in the more protected bays and lagoons of the coastal zone. Inland, the unique wetlands of the lower Saint John River are inundated during spring, summer, and fall, with concentration of breeding, diving, and dabbling ducks, including Black Duck, Common Goldeneye, Wood Duck, Green-winged Teal, Hooded Merganser, Pintail and American Widgeon. Some of the Black Duck, Common Goldeneye, Common Eider, scoter, and Bufflehead winter in the area.

The tidal marshes of the lower St. Lawrence River, the freshwater marshes along its inland reaches, and the expansive shorelines of the lower Great Lakes attract large staging populations of diving, dabbling, and sea ducks, geese, and some swans during the spring and fall migrations, and some nesting waterfowl and shorebird species which remain during the summer months. The most common migrating waterfowl species in the region include Whistling Swan, Blue and Green-winged Teal, Black Duck, Wood Duck, Ruddy Duck, Mallard, Pintail, Redhead, merganser, Canvasback, goldeneye, Bufflehead, scaup, Oldsquaw, scoter, Canada and Lesser Snow Geese, and Atlantic Brant. Some of the more critical staging habitats are, Cap Tourmente east of Québec City, near Cornwall, Prince Edward Point near the Bay of Quinte in Lake Ontario, Long Point and Rondeau marshes of Lake Erie, and the St. Clair marshes of Lake St. Clair between Lake Huron and Lake Erie. Nesting species include Black Duck, Mallard, and Blue-winged Teal which seek the protected submergent and emergent vegetation of the shorelines and the adjacent uplands. Some merganser, scaup, redhead, mallard, Black Duck, Oldsquaw, scoter, and Canada Geese winter along the St. Clair and Niagara rivers and the lakeshore between Hamilton Harbour and Toronto. Shorebirds including tern, Great Blue Heron, and plover concentrate in the tidal flats of the St. Lawrence River. Several gull species are also common throughout.

Photo by James Raffan

A Great Blue Heron, a shorebird widely distributed throughout Canada, is seen in an example of its' natural habitat, near Lake Huron in Ontario.

The surrounding shorelines of James Bay and the coastal islands found within the Hudson Bay and Eastmain lowlands of the Canadian Shield, encompassing tidal sedge and tundra marshes, mudflats and ponds between old beach ridges, support a variety of critical staging and nesting habitats for many migratory birds. Each spring, thousands of ducks, geese, some swans, shorebirds, and seabirds return to this critical staging ground. While most species continue further north, some remain to nest. Pintail, Mallard, Black Duck, Green-winged Teal, and sea ducks including eider, scoter, scaup, and Oldsquaw find suitable nesting locations. A colony of Lesser Snow Geese returns to nest at Cape Henrietta Maria. Breeding shorebirds include plover, sandpiper, Northern Phalarope, Marbled Godwit, Yellowleg and snipe. Gulls are common particularly on the offshore islands and Québec portion of the coastline. Among the staging waterfowl species which seek the nourishment of the marshes and mudflats during the spring and fall migration are Canada and Lesser Snow Geese, Pintail, Black Duck, widgeon, merganser, goldeneye, Green-winged Teal, and Whistling Swan.

It is interesting to note that an almost perfect correlation exists between the sensitive areas identification for coastal eastern migratory birds (Map 7) and the Canada Land Inventory – waterfowl assessment of high-capability areas (Map 2). Although the comparison is limited to waterfowl (ducks, geese, swans) in the Atlantic Provinces (excluding Newfoundland) and southern Ontario and Québec, the positive correlation indicates that for this area, high-capability land and water areas and the critical and important present land use areas, are almost synonymous.

Although staging grounds have not been mapped in western and northern Canada, some wetlands which are considered as essential staging habitats for migrating waterfowl have been identified (Table 5). Except for the Yukon Territory, the remaining essential staging grounds are all indicated as CLI – waterfowl high-capability areas (Map 6).

Northern Land Use Information Series (NLUIS).

As an example of an on-going reconnaissance-level resource map inventory, the NLUIS provides an essential renewable resource information tool for identifying critical and important wildlife habitat areas in the Yukon and Northwest Territories. Based on current research knowledge concerning the life-cycle requirements, migration patterns, and population numbers of major northern wildlife species, important and critical habitat areas have been mapped for the 2,610,793 km² which have been surveyed. In addition to wildlife habitat information, data on hunting and trapping, recreation and tourism, forest resources, soil capability for agriculture, and, urban settlements have been superimposed on the map sheets at a scale of 1:250,000. Used by both government administrators and industrial strategists, this map series is recognized as a valuable baseline source of resource information for present and future northern land use management decisions.

TABLE 5.
Some essential migratory bird staging grounds in northern and western Canada

Area	Species
Yukon Territory	
Mackenzie Delta and North Slope	Whistling Swan, White-fronted Geese, Snow Geese
Old Crow Flats	White-fronted Geese, diving ducks
British Columbia	
Fraser Delta Foreshore	Brant, Snow Geese, ducks, shorebirds
Cariboo Parklands	Diving ducks
Alberta	
Peace-Athabasca Delta	Ross' Geese, Snow Geese, ducks
Hay-Zama Lakes	Snow Geese, ducks
Saskatchewan	
Kindersley	White-fronted Geese, Ross' Geese
Last Mountain Lake	Sandhill Crane, Whooping Crane, ducks
Manitoba	
Waterlen Lakes	Canvasback, Redhead, (also moulting area)
St. Rose, Delta, Netleylibow, Cumberland, The Pas, White Water Lake, Oak Plum Lakes	Ducks, (also breeding and moulting areas)
Oak Hammock marsh	Geese

Source: Cooch, G., 1978. Canadian Wildlife Service, Environment Canada. Personal communication.

For the purpose of identifying critical lands for wildlife, the NLUIS is one of the largest regional analyses which presently covers more than one-third of Canada's northlands. Map 8 illustrates the methodology applied to the wildlife component of the series, and uses a portion of Franklin Bay 97C as an example. The wildlife legend is divided into three sections comprising: an explanation of the symbols which represent the indicator species, the habitat function, and the seasonal use of the map area; some general notes concerning hazards to wildlife in the north; and specific comments relating to the wildlife units indicated on the sample map. As illustrated on Map 8, only the wildlife area symbols preceded by an asterisk are considered to represent critical habitat lands. Some areas such as along the steep banks of the Horton River (*7REns) are noted as critical nesting sites for Golden Eagles and Peregrine Falcons during late spring and early summer, while other areas for example between the Horton and Hornaday river watersheds (*6xty) are evaluated as critical muskox habitat for calving, summer and winter range, and hence are occupied year-round. These essential seasonal and year-round habitat requirements are related to the life-cycle functions of the indicator species which are elaborated in the map's General Notes on Hazards to Wildlife. In-

Photo by Environment Canada

Gannets, a colonial-nesting seabird found along eastern and western rock-ledged coasts, are shown on Bonaventure Island.

cluded as critical are, the spring and early summer denning sites of foxes and wolves, the May-through-June calving areas for barren-ground caribou and their spring and fall migration routes, the spring calving areas and the summer and winter ranges for muskox, the winter and early spring den sites of polar bears, the coastal nesting sites of seabirds during the breeding season, the May-to-September nesting and breeding sites for waterfowl, and the spring and summer ground locations of raptors which are considered a rare and endangered species. In general, these are the time periods when harassment to wildlife and their habitats can be devasting, and hence, other interfering land use activities should be minimized. The identification of all wildlife areas on this map series are preliminary. As wildlife populations and distributions are studied in more detail, it is expected that the boundaries of the critical areas will change accordingly.

Map 9 represents a synthesis of all the critical habitat lands identified in the 162 NLUIS map sheets which had been completed by 1978. The unique Mackenzie Delta and, in the west, the Yukon Coastal Plain support critical seasonal habitats for waterfowl, ungulates, and aquatic furbearers. The shrub, sedge, and meadow tundra of the Yukon Coastal Plain supply fall staging habitats for Canada Geese and spring/summer calving and post-calving grounds for the migrating herds of Porcupine barren-ground caribou. Breeding, staging, and moulting habitats also are provided for a variety of ducks, geese, swans, loons, and shorebirds on the coastal plain and throughout the numerous streams, lakes, and wide flats of the delta and offshore islands. Included are species of King and Common Eider, Oldsquaw, Pacific Black Brant, White-fronted Geese, scoter and scaup. In the tundra sections adjacent to the delta are critical spring calving areas for reindeer.

Inland, along the Alaska–Yukon boundary the numerous lakes of the Old Crow Plains support populations of breeding waterfowl, muskrat, and wintering Porcupine barren-ground caribou. Migration corridors within the Old Crow Range, the Porcupine Plateau, and the British Mountains are also essential for caribou survival. Along the steep eroded banks of the Porcupine River and its tributary, the Bell River, are summer nesting sites for Peregrine Falcon. Rising from the banks of the Bell River, the sedge, grass and shrub-covered lower slopes of the Richardson Mountains are used by barren-ground caribou during the calving and post-calving period. In addition, the steep rocky cliffs of these mountains have several raptor nesting locations.

Photo by the Canadian Wildlife Service

This scene identifies the essential challenge of careful land management in the north. Programs such as the Northern Land Use Information Series, provide a baseline source of resource data which are valuable in minimizing land use conflicts.

Banks Island, the western-most island of the Arctic Archipelago, supports habitat ranges for wintering and calving muskox and Peary caribou, polar bear denning, Peregrine Falcon and Gyrfalcon nesting, and nesting, moulting and staging of waterfowl species including Snow Geese, Black Brant and Common and King Eider. Habitats vary from the sparsely vegetated, dissected uplands in the northeast to the shallow lakes and ponds surrounded by tundra in the southwest.

South of Amundsen Gulf, muskox and Bluenose barren-ground caribou range on the shrub, sedge and lichen-covered tundra of the Anderson and Horton plains. In the winter, the caribou usually retreat to the more protected southern and western woodlands. Bisecting the plains are the steep banked Anderson, Horton, and Hornaday rivers which support spring and summer nesting habitats for Golden Eagle and Peregrine Falcon. Towards the southeast, the hills of the Horton Plain elevate to the Coronation Hills in the northwestern extension of the Canadian Shield. Here too, raptors return to the steep rocky outcrops for nesting. Further east, along the Coronation Gulf and throughout Bathurst Inlet, similar valuable breeding and nesting habitat is provided for raptors, particularly the Peregrine Falcon. In the uplands east of the inlet, the Bathurst barren-ground caribou herd congregates for the calving period. Passing through the southern part of the inlet, this herd annually travels from the woodlands west and south of the Coppermine River to the tundra-covered uplands along the coast. This region is frequented by nesting, moulting, and staging ducks and geese.

The East Arm Hills surrounding the eastern bays of Great Slave Lake, characterized by steep cliffs, cuestas, and canyons, support nesting habitat during late spring and early summer for Peregrine Falcon and Gyrfalcon. Contrasting the rugged eastern portion of Great Slave Lake is the low-lying Great Slave Plain in the west. Stands of black spruce in the permafrost muskeg, and white spruce, white birch, trembling aspen, and tamarack interspersed with lichens, are found throughout the Mackenzie Bison Sanctuary which borders on the lake. Winter range for wood bison and calving grounds for woodland caribou also have been identified. South of Great Slave Lake and bordering the Alberta–Northwest Territories boundary, wood bison habitat and Whooping Crane nesting sites are dispersed throughout the shallow lakes, bogs, and extensive spruce and jack pine sections of Wood Buffalo National Park.

Photo by Environment Canada

Two whooping crane, a species with very specialized habitat requirements, are seen in their nesting grounds in Wood Buffalo National Park.

Between the Mackenzie Plain and the Yukon boundary, the Mackenzie Mountains in the Eastern System of the Cordillera support habitats for woodland caribou, moose, wolf, thinhorn sheep, grizzly bear, and Sandhill Crane. Located within the alpine forest–tundra transition, the variety of essential habitats include salty mineral licks used by ungulates in the low-lying valleys, protected river valleys, treeline and lower vegetated slopes, alpine tundra, and rugged upland cliffs and peaks. Similarly, the mountains, (Selwyn, Pelly, Wernecke, Taiga, Ogilvy, St. Elias) and the Yukon Plateau of the Cordillera bisected by two trenches (Tintina and Shakwak) and numerous river valleys, contain thinhorn and dall sheep winter and lambing ranges, grizzly bear and wolf denning sites, woodland caribou calving grounds, and mountain goat wintering range. In addition, nesting sites for Trumpeter Swan are identified along the banks of the Nisling River.

Having briefly discussed two regional approaches to identify prime wildlife habitats, the next assessment, involves an international project, which describes areas of both national and international significance.

International Biological Programme (IBP)

Under the auspices of the United Nations, Canada, as a participant in the International Biological Programme, has been able to progress towards establishing a nationally representative network of ecological reserves. In order to comply with the overall objective of the program which aimed at identifying and protecting areas of both biological and physiographic importance for present and future scientific and educational uses, both sites in their national state and sites with some degree of alteration or disturbance were included. Although IBP does not yet fully represent the ecological diversity that occurs in Canada (Peterson, 1975), it is nonetheless a valuable assessment of special lands which have been identified using the following criteria.

"*Ecological Zone . . . . Section.* Forest Regions of Canada by J.S. Rowe has been used for the wooded part of the country to geographically designate the forest "region" and "section" within which the IBP area falls. The vegetation within the IBP area may or may not be typical of the section in which it occurs. Areas within the Alpine Tundra, Arctic Tundra and Grassland regions are referred to only as these three major biome types without further elaboration. IBP areas in British Columbia are identified using the biogeoclimatic classification and map of V.J. Krajina . . .

Structural Groups: Major Plant Community Types. F.R. Fosberg's Structural Code is given for each community, followed by important plant species of component strata:

(a) primary structural group (canopy spacing)
 — closed canopy in one or more strata
 — open canopy in all strata (significant amounts of bare substrate comprising up to 50 per cent of area)
 — sparse plant cover (plants scattered, bare substrate dominant, comprising more than 50 per cent of area)

(b) formation class (growth habit and stature of dominant species)
 — forest
 — scrub
 — dwarf scrub
 — tall grass
 — short grass
 — broad-leaf herbs
 — bryoids
 — submerged meadows
 — floating meadows

(c) formation group (deciduous or evergreen)

(d) formation (growth-forms of dominant species with emphasis on leaf types) . . .

Other Environmental Criteria. Additional data used to define sites include:
 — Significant Plant Species
 — Representative Animal Species
 — Special Biological Features
 — Special Physical Features
 — Landscape Description
 — Aquatic Habitats
 — Major Soils
 — Human Impact . . .

Conservation Status. Sites are classified as areas with formal conservation status (i.e. ecological reserves, National Parks, provincial parks, national wildlife areas, bird sanctuaries, game preserves etc.) or as areas with no formal conservation status (i.e. undesignated crown land or privately-held land)." (LaRoi, and Babb, 1975).

By 1975, these criteria had been applied to 1,322 checksheets analyzing each IBP area. These proposed ecological sites cover more than 13 million ha of the national landscape (less than one per cent of the total land surface) and are widely distributed throughout the major vegetation regions (Map 10). The site distribution reflects on the interpretation of the ten regional panels which were assembled to conduct the program. Site sizes vary from small colonial nesting bird locations, such as on the rugged Queen Charlotte Islands coasts, to large northern areas, for example the 5,957 km^2 of boreal forest – tundra transition surrounding Caribou Point northeast of Great Slave Lake. Caribou Point has been identified for its characteristic diverse flora and fauna. Representative wildlife species have been mentioned in most of the IBP areas and although only one of the many criteria used to identify ecological sites, it is nonetheless integral in preserving the diversity of these inventoried ecosystems.

In addition, more than 346,000 km^2 have been identified in the north. These areas, not included in the initial IBP checksheets, identify a variety of sensitive lands in both the Northwest and the Yukon Territories. Seabird, waterfowl, and shorebird breeding habitats on the northern archipelago and coastlines, muskox and caribou calving grounds on the barrens, and mountain habitat, combine to define the extent of the north's special lands. Unique vegetation, important archaeological sites, and points of historic interest also have been included in the program.

Economic and Social Considerations

From the user's viewpoint, the variety of activities relating to wildlife is associated with a diversity of perceptions of special land. The hunter, trapper, bird watcher, scientist, conservationist, preservationist, farmer, and urban dweller value wildlife, and, indirectly the land because of its productivity. Since no single modelling technique exists through which all wildlife activities can be quantified, it remains extremely difficult to assess the economic and social productivity quotients for wildlife. Because of this, decision makers and land use planners have had problems in comparing wildlife with other land use activities, particularly when assessing issues concerning the allocation of the land resource.

Activities Relating to Wildlife

The use of wildlife has been an integral part of the development of Canada. Fur trapping and recreational hunting, historically the major uses of wildlife, have been primary concerns of wildlife managers and in the

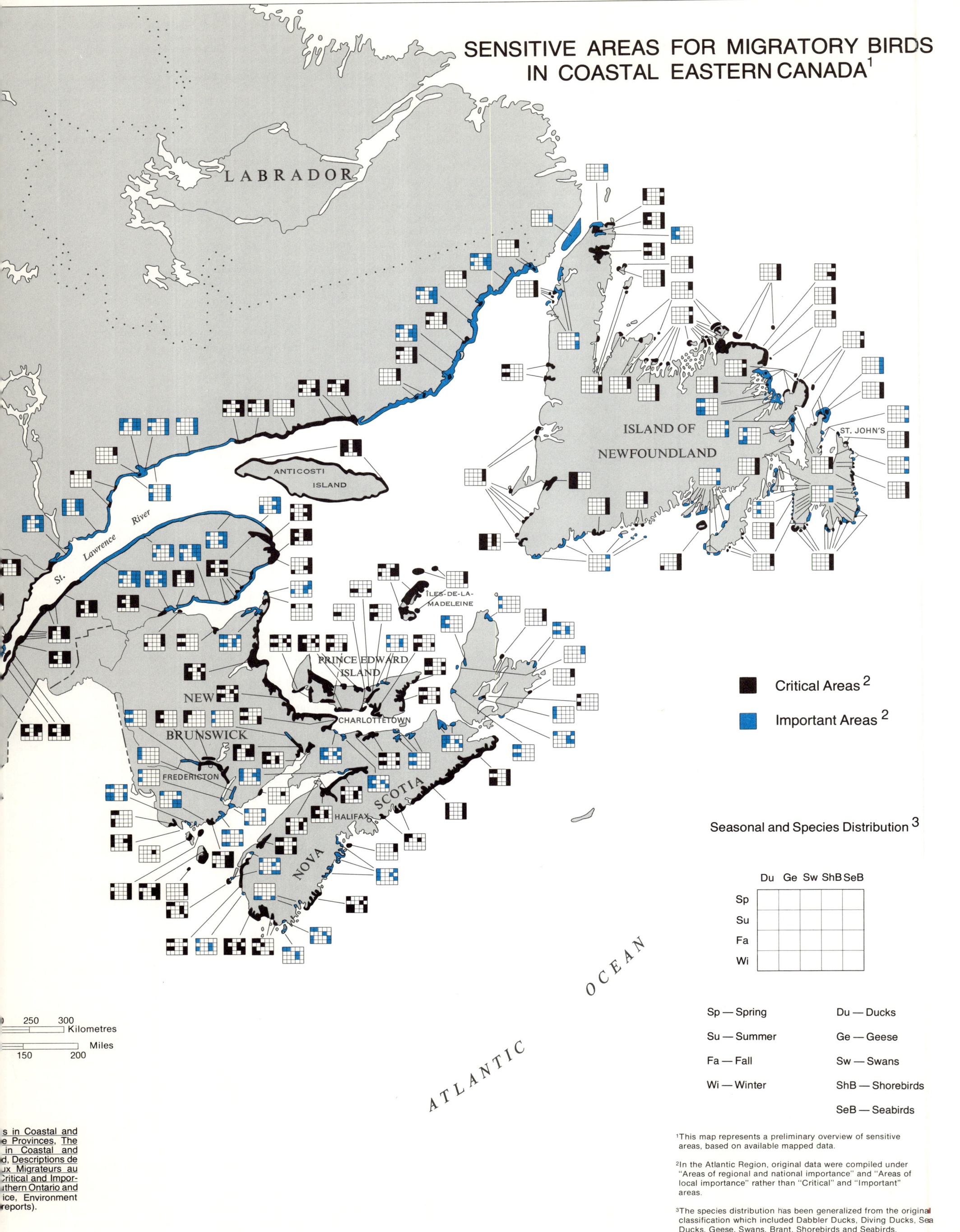

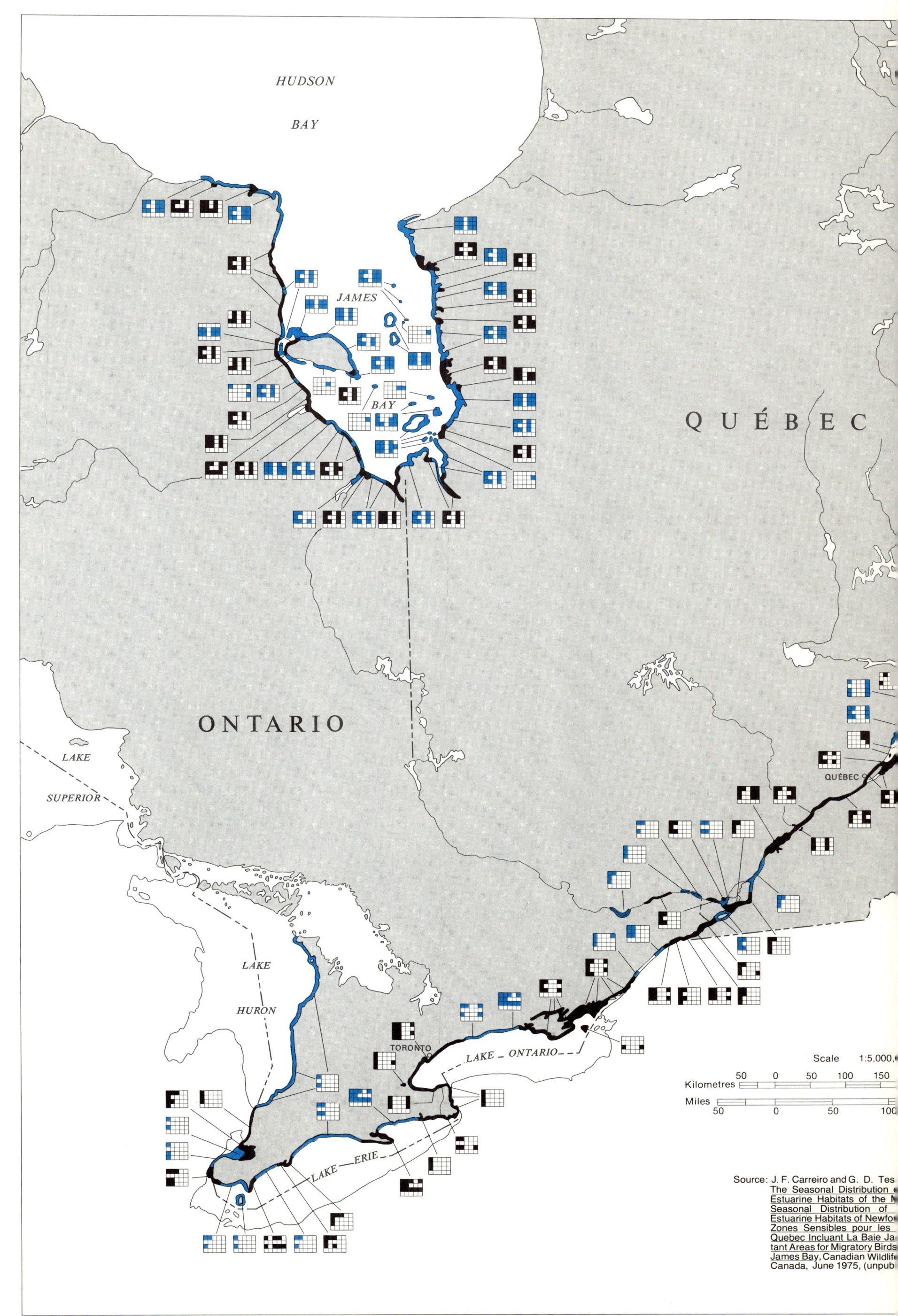

MAP 7

Photo by Environment Canada.

MAP 8

Photo by Ted Johnson.

GENERAL NOTES ON HAZARDS TO WILDLIFE
Source: Canadian Wildlife Service, Department of Fisheries and the Environment.

GENERAL COMMENTS: Disturbance of animals or alteration of wildlife habitat by careless or intensive human activity can cause a significant reduction in animal populations. Harassment by land vehicles and aircraft can be destructive and should be avoided particularly during critical periods in the life cycle of animals. During the winter, animals have a limited energy supply and frequent or severe disturbance may lead to death from exhaustion, starvation, or a reduced resistance to disease and parasites. In spring and early summer, young animals are especially vulnerable and adults are easily disturbed. During these and other critical periods, movement of men and equipment through wildlife zones should be restricted and essential travel should be by the most appropriate route. Aircraft should stay well above ground level and avoid disturbing animals at all times.

ARCTIC FOX: Denning sites are critical to foxes during spring and early summer when young are being raised. Dens should not be destroyed as they may receive use in successive years.

BARREN-GROUND CARIBOU: Calving areas are most critical for barren-ground caribou, and should be avoided during the main calving period (late May through June). On winter range, fires are particularly serious since lichens, the main forage plants, regenerate very slowly. Activities or structures that create barriers or deflect herds along main migration routes may delay animals or prevent them from reaching vital habitat areas.

MARINE MAMMALS — WHALE, SEAL, NARWHAL, OR WALRUS: Oil pollution is probably the most serious threat to marine mammals, affecting them, for example, either by direct contamination or by the destruction of their food supply. Underwater seismic blasts may also be damaging. Harassment of animals in calving areas is undesirable.

MUSKOX: Both winter range and spring calving areas are critical for muskox. Animals must be left undisturbed when they are moving to, and utilizing these areas.

POLAR BEAR: Den sites are critical to bears during the winter for hibernation and the birth of young. Dens should be left undisturbed and continuous activity near denning or seasonal concentration areas should be avoided. Inadequate food storage and disposal of garbage or sewage at camps attract bears, which can lead to unnecessary destruction of these animals. Adequate garbage and sewage disposal and protected kitchens and food caches could help prevent such killings. Contact the Northwest Territories Fish and Wildlife Service or the Canadian Wildlife Service in Yellowknife or Edmonton for specific suggestions.

RARE AND ENDANGERED SPECIES — RAPTORS: Regions critical to rare and endangered species should be avoided in spring and summer. All activities that might alter habitat and threaten the survival of species facing extinction must be strictly controlled. For further information on specific areas, contact the Canadian Wildlife Service in Yellowknife or Edmonton.

SEA BIRDS: Important sea-bird nesting areas should be avoided during the breeding season. Sea birds generally feed within a 30-mile radius of their nesting areas and this zone must be considered a critical part of their habitat. Pollution of feeding areas would be disastrous.

WATERFOWL: Waterfowl habitat should be avoided during breeding and nesting seasons (approximately May 15 to September 1). Molting and staging areas are less critical but harassment of flightless and congregated birds must be avoided. Although waterfowl habitat is not used during the winter, any activity which might cause destruction or alteration of such sites should be avoided or controlled. Oil spills are particularly destructive to waterfowl and their habitat. Alterations of water levels resulting from activities such as dam construction may also adversely affect waterfowl.

WOLF: Wolves are found in most areas of the north. Dens should be avoided during spring and early summer when young are being raised.

WOLVERINE: Wolverine are wide-ranging animals found in most areas of the north. They are attracted to camps where food is stored improperly and waste is accessible. Adequate precautions against bears will also prevent damage from wolverine.

COMMENTS ON WILDLIFE UNITS

4SLty — Ringed seals and, in lesser numbers, bearded seals are found throughout this area. During winter, the adults remain under the ice in bays while most of the younger seals stay at the edge of the fast ice. The ringed seal is the most important in the Inuit economy, supplying meat for men and dogs, and skins for clothing (1).

*6Xty — More than one thousand muskox live in the Horton and Hornaday river watersheds (see also map-sheet 97-D, Brock River); some move into the forest-tundra transition in winter and use the tundra for calving and summer range. Any area occupied by these animals, especially females with calves, must be considered critical. Muskox may move beyond the boundary indicated (1,2).

*7REns — Critical nesting areas for golden eagles and peregrine falcons, rare and endangered species, may be found in the steep banks of the Horton River. These nesting areas must be avoided during late spring and summer, and all nest sites must be left undisturbed (1).

8Bm^S_W — During early winter and late spring, barren-ground caribou of the Bluenose herd migrate through this region, which lies between the forested winter range to the south and the tundra calving area to the north. The spring migration to the calving area is very important and must not be obstructed (1,2).

*9Bns — Thousands of barren-ground caribou of the Bluenose herd calve on the Bathurst Peninsula. This area must be considered critical for this species and should be avoided from mid-May through July. Cows with calves must not be disturbed (1,2).

11 — This wildlife zone consists of hilly, open shrub-tundra with numerous shallow lakes. Several large rivers have deeply incised valleys. Muskox and barren-ground caribou calve throughout much of this region. Many swans, geese, and ducks nest and molt adjacent to the numerous bays and ponds. Arctic foxes and their dens are common throughout this wildlife zone. Falcons and golden eagles may also be found throughout the zone (1).

12 — This wildlife zone encompasses the forest-tundra transition. Vegetation in the tundra region is dominated by grasses sedges and lichens, and in the forested region by sporadic stands of spruce. Many species usually associated with either forest or tundra habitat may be found in this zone, and wolf dens are particularly numerous through this transition (1).

The following wildlife species may be found in suitable habitat, during all or part of the year, in this map-sheet area: barren-ground caribou, colored fox, polar bear, wolf, wolverine and muskox. Swans use some lakes as nesting sites during summer and should not be disturbed (1).

Sources: Canadian Wildlife Service, Department of Fisheries and the Environment — literature review and field surveys from November 1974 to November 1976 (1); Fish and Wildlife Service, Department of Natural and Cultural Affairs, Government of the Northwest Territories, comments and advice (2); local hunters, trappers and other residents of the Northwest Territories, comments (3).

WILDLIFE

Wildlife populations are a vital northern resource. Each species has specific habitat requirements and some species are less adaptable to changes of habitat than others. In this map series, wildlife units represent general habitat areas within which the indicated species are found. The season of use and the habitat function are also shown. It should be emphasized that the maps are not intended to show species distribution in its entirety and that not all habitats are represented by map units. Wildlife zones, indicated on the map by a dashed red line, represent broad generalized regions of wildlife range. These zones may be quite large and may contain a number of habitat types, the distribution of which is controlled by local factors such as topography, vegetation, or recent forest fires. The zones themselves are usually physiographically determined: for example, a lowland area containing numerous ponds, lakes and marshes will constitute a wildlife zone favourable for beaver, moose, mink and muskrat. As the distribution of wildlife may vary within any given zone, it should be noted that the species listed as prevalent in a particular wildlife zone may differ somewhat between map sheets.

Important and critical areas designate habitats that are required for the maintenance or survival of wildlife populations. These include many regions known to be used by large numbers of animals, such as areas of seasonal concentration. Human activities can have serious consequences in these regions and critical areas are particularly susceptible to permanent damage. Dates given are approximate and may vary from year to year as biological or climatic factors change.

Note: All wildlife information in this map series is preliminary. Wildlife distribution and populations in much of the area covered by this map set have not been fully studied by biologists. Some data may therefore be incomplete or fragmentary and many areas which are important to wildlife are not included. Reliable information on fur-bearing mammals is particularly difficult to obtain and unless otherwise indicated, comments on furbearers are of a general nature. As new surveys have been used to obtain data on wildlife for this map set, boundaries designating wildlife units may not match those presented on maps of the adjoining sets. However, data pertaining to the general occurrences of animals should correspond. For further information about the area or specific wildlife species, contact the Canadian Wildlife Service in Yellowknife or Edmonton.

WILDLIFE LEGEND

This legend is derived from the *Arctic Ecology Map Series;* the black asterisks indicate new symbols that have been subsequently added.

EXPLANATION OF SYMBOL

unit number — habitat function e.g. breeding
critical wildlife area — *1Wbs
species e.g. waterfowl — seasonal use e.g. summer

Note: Symbols not associated with boundaries indicate a general occurrence when approximate limits cannot be established. Migration routes indicate very general areas and directions. All sanctuaries are considered critical areas.

CODE	BOUNDARY	SPECIES
AF	———	Arctic fox
AN	———	Area of note*
B	○	Barren-ground caribou
CF	———	Red (colored) fox*
G	△	Grizzly bear
M	⊥⊥	Muskrat
MK	———	Mink*
MS	▲	Moose*
O	———	Otter*
P	———	Polar Bear
RE	▲	Rare or endangered species
S	———	Sea-birds
SL	———	Seal*
T	●	Marten*
V	×	Beaver
W	■	Waterfowl
WF	———	Wolf*
WH	———	Whale*
WL	———	Walrus

CODE	BOUNDARY	SPECIES
WV	———	Wolverine*
X		Muskox
	▬▬▬	Units notable for two or more species.
	– – –	Boundary of a wildlife zone.

HABITAT FUNCTION
b Breeding area
d Denning area
l Staging area
m Migratory route
n Calving or nesting area
r Range
t All habitat functions

SEASONAL UTILIZATION
s Spring or summer
w Fall or winter
y Year-round use

OTHER
⇔ Migration route

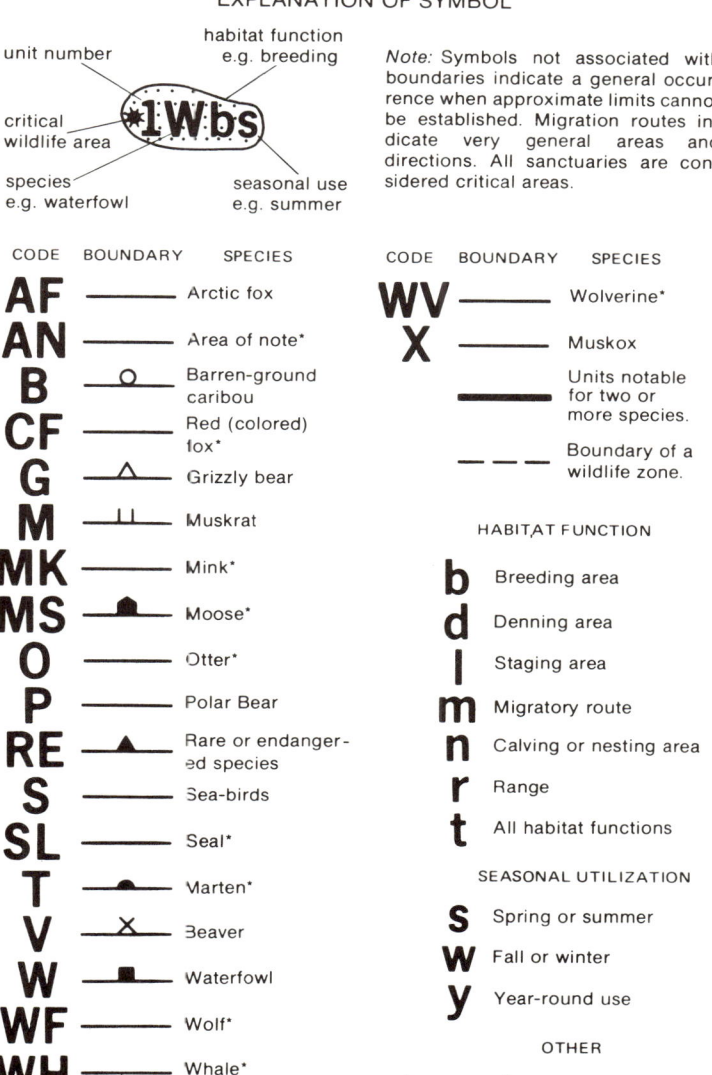

FRANKL
DISTRICT OF M
NORTHWEST T

Scale 1:250,000

Base map produced from reproduction material provided by the Surveys and Mapping Branch, Department of Energy, Mines and Resources, with minor modifications by the Department of Fisheries and the Environment.

Map produced by the Lands Directorate, Environmental Management Service, Department of Fisheries and the Environment, 1977.

LAND USE INFOR

Indian and Northern Affairs   Affaires indiennes et du Nord

MAP 9 NORTHERN LAND USE INFORMATION SERIES-SYNTHESIS OF CRITICAL AREAS

MAMMALS

	species included
Ungulates	woodland caribou, barren-ground caribou, Peary caribou, muskox, reindeer, wood bison, mountain sheep, mountain goat
	major caribou migration routes
Furbearers	arctic fox, red (coloured) fox, polar bear, grizzly bear, wolf
Aquatic Furbearers	muskrat, beaver

BIRDS

	species included
Waterfowl	Trumpeter swan, Ross' goose, Lesser Snow goose, Canada goose, black brant, common and king eider, old squaw, scoter, scaup, other ducks, Thayer's gull
Raptors	peregrine falcon, gyrfalcon, golden and bald eagle, osprey
Cranes	sandhill crane, whooping crane

Scale 1 : 9,500,000

Kilometres 200 100 0 100 200 300 400 Kilometres

Miles 100 0 100 200 Miles

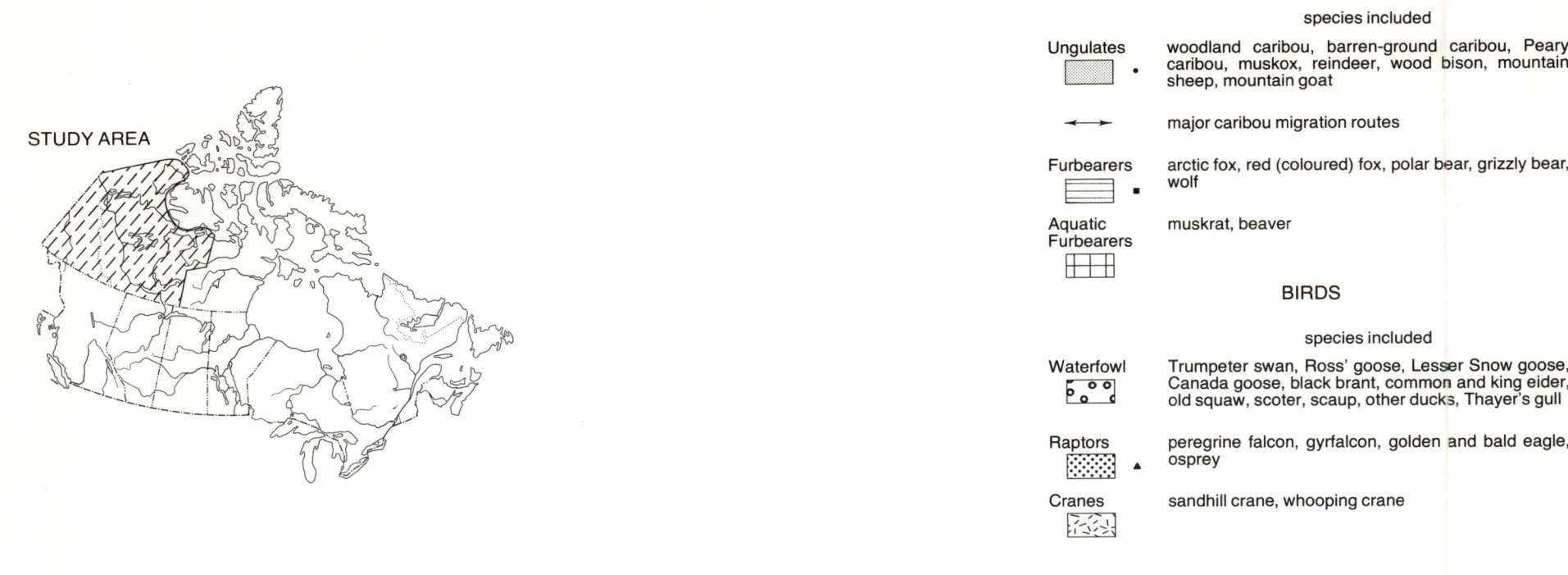

Source: Land Use Information Series, Indian and Northern Affairs, Produced by Lands Directorate, Department of Fisheries and the Environment, 1972–ongoing.

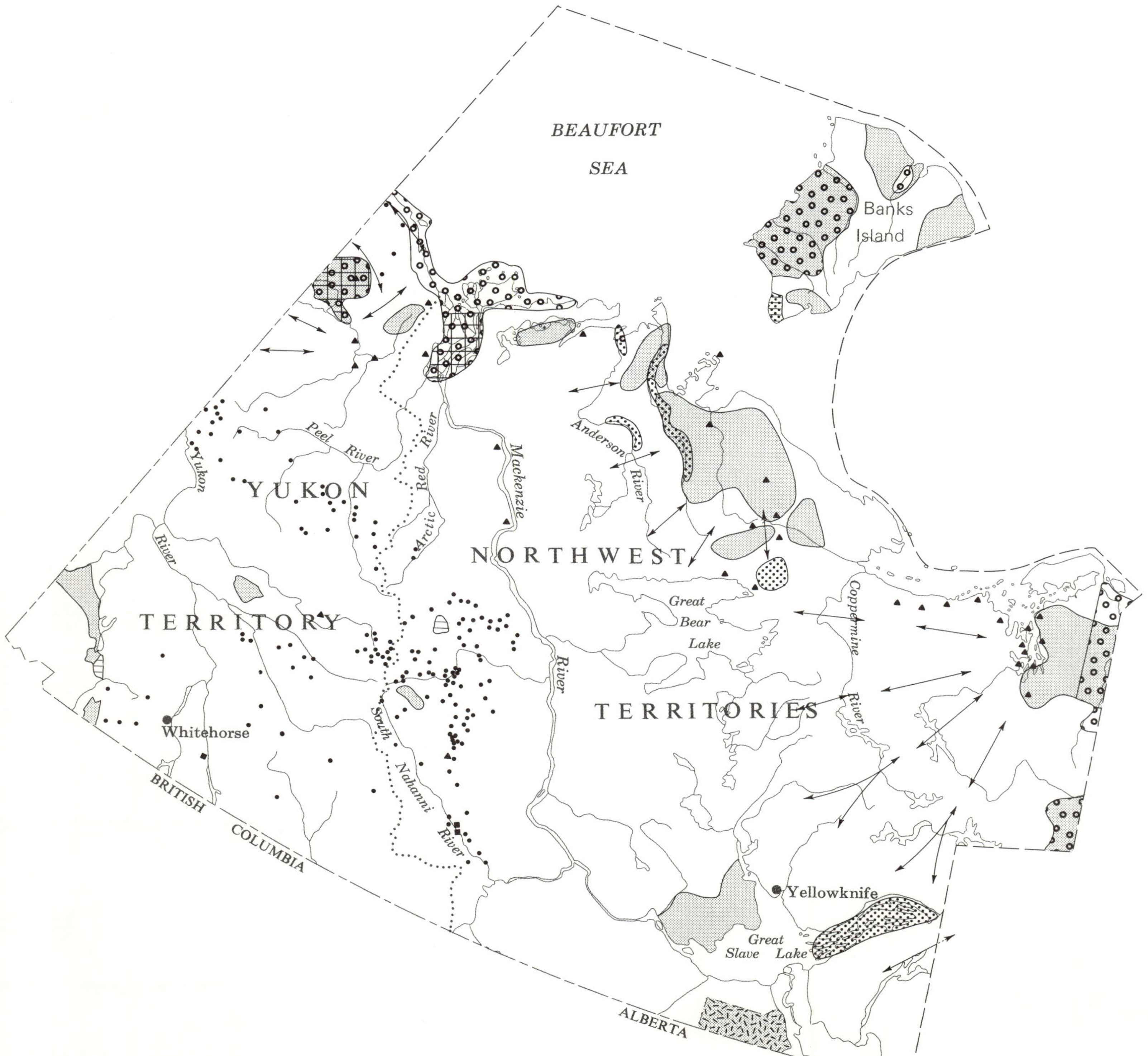

protection of wildlife lands. Harvest surveys, licencing requirements, and quota systems support a national data base which permits a restricted quantification of these activities. The other use activities such as bird watching, hiking, photography, and educational interpretation, although not quantifiable in value-added terms, do represent a significant expenditure on equipment, reading material, and growing memberships in the many conservation-oriented interest groups which are associated with the larger urban centres. These aesthetic demands are receiving more attention from federal and provincial managers, particularly through the designation of National and provincial parks and ecological reserves.

This sector focuses on the past and present use of land to support wildlife activities. In addition, a review of the allocation of wildlife lands depicts the national distribution of lands managed specifically for wildlife use. The discrepancies between the demand for lands for wildlife use and the availability of specially-designated areas will be discussed in the next sector concerning wildlife issues.

Fur Trapping

Wildlife provided the resource base for the initial economic development of Canada. Prior to European settlement in the early 1800s, wildlife supported the only major use of any of the renewable resources. As a food source, beaver, moose, and deer satisfied the palates of the indigenous population in the east, plains bison, beaver and antelope in the west, and barren-ground caribou in the north. Skins were used for clothing, tents, and kayaks and sinews for sewing. Although often use was wasteful, it appears not to have had a significant effect on the depletion of the resource.

The expansion of European settlement during the 18th and 19th centuries, precipitated in part by the demand for furs, has had a large impact on determining the course of exploration and development of the country (Foster, 1978). What started out to be a casual exchange of furs between European fishermen and the eastern Indian tribes, escalated to concentrate on the highly competitive trade of beaver fur to supply the European demand for felt hats. As beaver colonies in the east, along the St. Lawrence River, the Saguenay, St. Maurice and Ottawa rivers were trapped to near extinction, the frontiers were pushed further inland, paralleling the major waterways, towards the west and the north. By the late 18th century, the two rival fur companies (Hudson's Bay and Northwest) had staked out the area west to the Pacific Ocean and north to include all the land encompassing Hudson Bay, the land and rivers dominated by the expansive Canadian Shield supporting the prime beaver habitats. The availability of staple food supplies such as fish, moose, deer, buffalo, corn, and maple sugar for the traders and voyageurs was also a significant factor in the expansion of the fur trade. Also, secondary development associated with the fur trade included settlement growth, clearing of land for agriculture, and boat building. Aided by the technology of the Industrial Revolution, the demand for raw furs in England and France continued to increase through the first part of the 19th century. In 1821, after each company was pushed to the verge of bankruptcy, the Northwest Company and the Hudson's Bay Company merged under the umbrella of the Hudson's Bay Company. Relative prosperity ensued for the next forty years, although the abundance of beaver decreased markedly. At the same time, the lumber trade started to expand in eastern Canada and eventually replaced fur as the staple export.

NFB – PHOTOTHEQUE – ONF – Photo by Marcel Cognac

Historically, the valuable beaver pelt spurred Canada's early economic development. Presently, although still an important furbearer for the fur industry, beaver are also used as an edible meat by northern natives. In addition, as seen here, the beaver is one of Canada's most successful dam builders, flooding forests and sometimes affecting transportation routes.

After the 1821 merger, the first attempts were made to conserve beaver. Trapping was discouraged, particularly for cubs during the summer months. In addition, higher prices for the less valuable furs such as muskrat acted as an impetus for beaver conservation. However by the 1850s with agricultural expansion increasing in the west, available beaver habitat declined further. This was encouraged by the termination of exclusive land rights of the Hudson's Bay in Rupert's Land. Although other furs were produced for domestic and export consumption, the European demand for beaver diminished with silk becoming the desirable substitute for the fashionable hat industry. Beaver populations continued to fluctuate at low levels through the early 20th century. Not until principles of sustained-yield management were invoked did the fur industry lose its reputation as a purely destructive form of resource exploitation. Concepts of controlled seasons, quotas, registered traplines or fur block systems, careful species introduction, and allocation of reserves have contributed to the stabilization of the industry. Specifically, some of the significant events in fur conservation include: the registered trapline system, introduced in British Columbia in 1926 and subsequently adopted by all provinces except Prince Edward Island, Nova Scotia, and New Brunswick; furbearer management reserves inaugurated in 1932 by the protection of 19,425 km² near Rupert's House bordering James Bay; and habitat manipulation, for example a project established in The Pas, Manitoba in 1932, experimented with fluctuating water levels to satisfy muskrat habitat requirements (Bryan, 1973). Quotas for species with naturally small populations such as polar bear and cougar, and those with highly cyclic populations, for example lynx, have been used as an effective management technique.

In 1975, the value of raw fur production was 53.9 million dollars. Of this, 66 per cent was contributed by wildlife trapped pelts and the remaining one-third by ranch-raised pelts, consisting primarily of mink pelts (Figure 2). Ontario is the largest producer of raw furs;

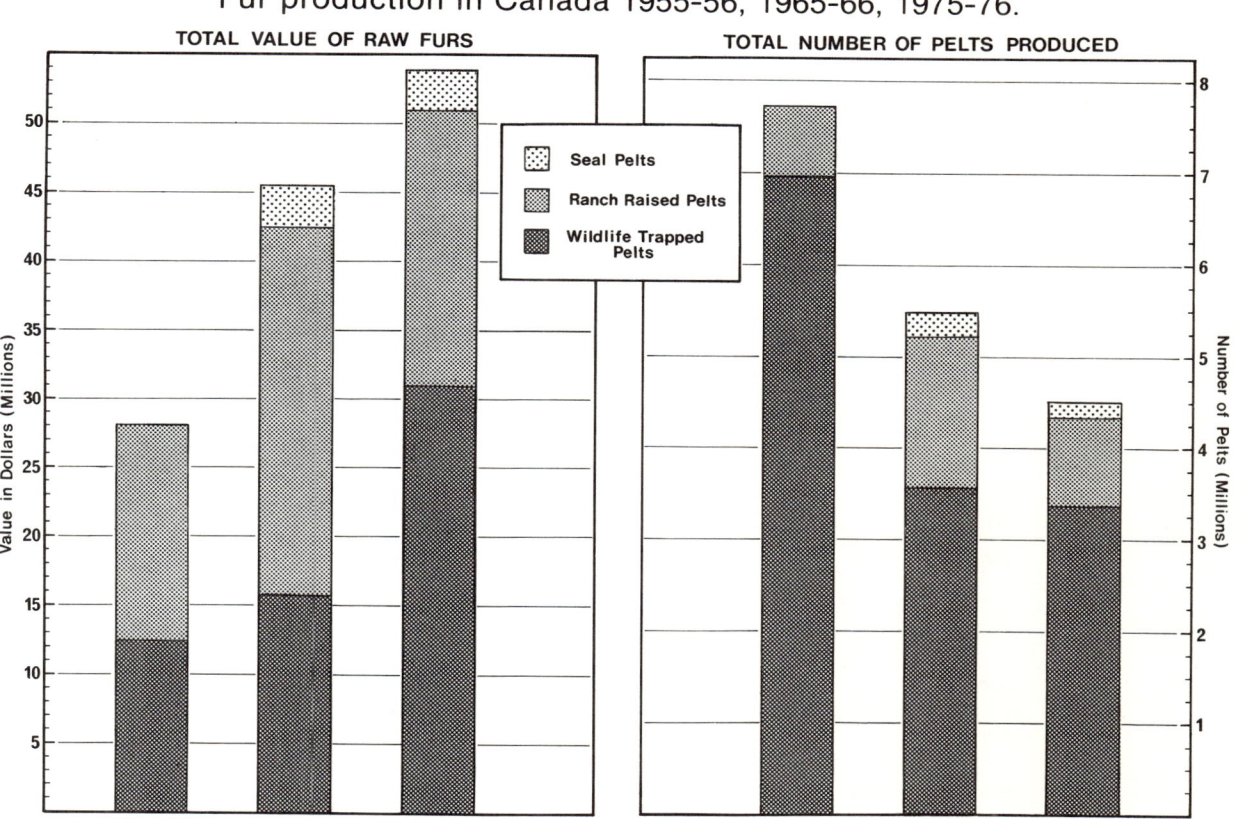

FIGURE 2.
Fur production in Canada 1955-56, 1965-66, 1975-76.

Source: Dominion Bureau of Statistics. 1957. Fur Production Season 1955-56. Memorandum.
———. 1967. Fur Production Season 1965-66. Catalogue 23-207 Annual.
Statistics Canada 1977a. Fur Production Season 1975-76. Catalogue 23-207 Annual.

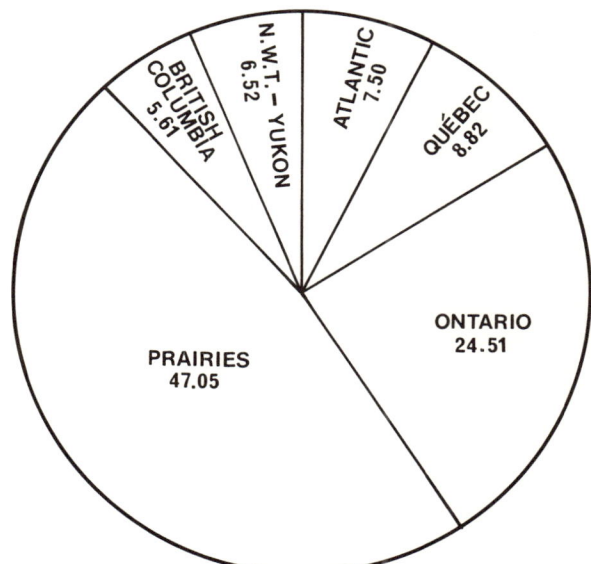

FIGURE 3.
Percentage value of raw fur production, by region 1975-76.

Canadian Total: $53,942,714

FIGURE 4.
Percentage value of number of pelts produced by region 1975-76.

Canadian Total: 4,500,531

Source: Statistics Canada. 1977a. Fur Production Season 1975-76. Catalogue 23-207 Annual.

furs were worth $16.6 million in 1975. Other important fur producing provinces include Alberta, Québec, Manitoba, British Columbia, and Saskatchewan (Figures 3 and 4). Although the relative importance of the fur industry has declined since the 19th century, it still contributes substantially to the national income. Since 1955, the value of the raw fur industry has trebled. At the same time, the number of pelts taken has decreased by 50 per cent (Figure 1). Loss of furbearer habitat, cyclical fluctuations of species, and market demands account for the variability and combine to control trapping activity.

were in northern Ontario. Squirrel pelts amounted to more than 100 thousand in each of the Prairie Provinces. Fur farms produced more than 400 thousand pelts in Ontario and more than 100 thousand in each of British Columbia, Nova Scotia, and Québec. Generally, farms are located near the southern populated sections of the country.

Muskrat, beaver, coyote, lynx, fox, raccoon, and otter were the most valuable trapped fur species in 1975 (Table 7). Fox was the prime pelt in the Atlantic Provinces (except Newfoundland). Beaver pelts were worth more than $2 million in Ontario and $1 million in Québec.

sumed as edible meats. An estimate in Ontario valued the net worth of furbearers for meat consumption in 1976 at $4.2 million (Canadian Trappers Federation, 1976). Similarly, the Report of the Mackenzie Valley Pipeline Inquiry estimated the value of furbearers for human food production in the Western Arctic to be $10.2 million.

In recent years it has generally been accepted that most furbearers are underharvested (Industry, Trade and Commerce, 1977) thus emphasizing the untapped potential of the industry.

Recreational Hunting

The activities relating to subsistence and recreational hunting are also well rooted in the early economic development of Canada. As suggested, hunting linked with trapping in the 17th and 18th centuries was essential as a major provider of food to the voyageurs, traders, and of course, the Indian and Inuit. Although use of wildlife as a primary food source has declined, it still remains important to the native peoples who depend on caribou, seal, some whales, waterfowl, and ptarmigan.

The introduction of firearms during the fur trade era ushered in recreational hunting which has had a significant impact on the changing status of Canadian wildlife populations and reflects a major component of wildlife management programs and priorities today. Eighteenth century viewpoints perceived British North America as having an unlimited, self-perpetuating, and superabundant wildlife resource supported by a vast frontier of a largely unexplored hinterland. Hence, activities such as shooting for sport escalated unchecked through the 19th century. Waterfowl, upland game, and big game were the largest suppliers for the game harvest. In addition, the large colonial seabird nesting colonies along the St. Lawrence River and off the east coast were raided heavily by fishermen for fish bait and as a meat and egg supply to the expanding eastern settlements. Of all the seabird colonies that nested in the coastal regions of Atlantic Canada in the 19th century, the gannets were the most vulnerable. From an estimated 200 thousand gannets in 1830, the population declined to 8 thousand by 1880 and of these it is believed that a mere 3 thousand birds remain on Bonaventure Island (Foster, 1978). In the west, similar events were recorded for buffalo and antelope.

The British North America Act of 1867 made no mention of wildlife but assumed that wildlife, like the other natural resources, would be the responsibility of the individual provinces except for the Northwest Territories. By the 1860s, a variety of closed seasons had been established and several provinces included game legislation on the original statute books. Later, the signing of the Migratory Birds Convention Act in 1917 gave the federal government authority over the harvest of migratory birds. Since then, an increasingly complex matrix of licencing, hunting seasons, and bag limits has affected the hunting of wildlife. At the same time, the establishment of a national network of parks, sanctuaries, and reserves has supported the maintenance of wildlife habitat.

TABLE 6.

Fur trapping+ by number of trapped pelts, 1955-56, 1965-66, 1975-76

Region and year	Major species						
				(number)			
1955-56++	Muskrat	Squirrel	Ermine	Beaver	Rabbit	Other Furbearers	Total
Atlantic	55,938	23,262	10,767	16,374	2	12,547	118,890
Québec	141,511	16,918	22,433	36,302	-	28,685	245,849
Ontario	546,466	-	30,962	113,200	-	95,980	786,608
Prairies	3,386,756	1,066,663	292,818	93,573	117,707	54,165	5,011,682
British Columbia	57,822	201,281	13,126	12,131	-	22,449	306,809
N.W.T. & Yukon	330,238	82,965	9,491	10,456	-	42,515	475,665
CANADA	4,518,731	1,391,089	379,597	282,036	117,709	256,341	6,945,503
1965-66	Muskrat	Squirrel	Beaver	Ermine	Mink	Seal	Other Furbearers	Total
Atlantic	28,622	5,105	17,304	9,261	5,918	153,589	16,294	236,093
Québec	103,835	5,676	53,930	16,132	9,920	24,356	27,296	241,145
Ontario	469,726	9,297	149,408	17,537	26,092	-	61,701	733,761
Prairies	1,003,782	782,568	113,982	120,061	33,340	-	100,126	2,153,859
British Columbia	31,077	62,637	27,300	9,325	5,628	-	10,365	146,332
N.W.T. & Yukon	193,265	24,808	10,711	6,356	4,683	51,197	23,246	314,266
Other+++	-	-	-	-	-	16,797	-	16,797
CANADA	1,830,307	890,091	372,635	178,672	85,581	245,939	239,028	3,842,253
1975-76	Muskrat	Squirrel	Beaver	Raccoon	Weasel	Seal	Other Furbearers	Total
Atlantic	49,547	2,845	6,700	11,034	2,097	94,617	18,386	185,226
Québec	161,208	4,630	46,472	17,866	7,009	7,604	46,858	291,647
Ontario	432,233	5,803	136,680	44,077	3,576	-	59,925	682,294
Prairies	1,236,990	392,244	128,063	5,528	54,608	-	149,602	1,967,035
British Columbia	21,050	27,190	13,693	748	7,308	-	19,974	89,963
N.W.T. & Yukon	200,988	12,795	3,316	-	1,601	34,270	40,185	293,155
Other+++	-	-	-	-	-	-	-	31,200
CANADA	2,102,016	445,507	334,924	79,253	76,199	167,691	334,930	3,540,520

+ Does not include ranch raised wildlife fur species.
++ Seals were not considered in 1955-56.
+++ In some cases it is not possible to sub-divide seal trapping or value by region.

Source: Dominion Bureau of Statistics, 1957 and 1967. Fur Production, Season 1955-56. Memorandum.
_____, 1967. Fur Production, Season 1965-65. Catalogue 23-207.
Statistics Canada, 1977a. Fur Production, Season 1975-76. Catalogue 23-207.

Muskrat, squirrel, beaver, raccoon, and weasel (ermine) are the major land and aquatic furbearers in terms of numbers taken (Table 6). These species, having a national distribution, are a component of the take for the 80 thousand trappers (Canadian Trappers Federation, 1978) in each of the provinces and the territories. Seal, although not a terrestrial furbearer, found off the coasts of the Atlantic Provinces, Québec, British Columbia and the Yukon, has been included so that its relative importance in the fur industry may be compared to the other furbearers (Figure 2). Canada's forest land and adjacent water areas in the northern portion of most provinces, the territories and in the east throughout the Atlantic Provinces support habitats where trapping activities dominate. In 1975, over 100 thousand muskrat pelts were trapped in Québec, Ontario, Manitoba, Saskatchewan, Alberta, and the Northwest Territories. Half the number of beaver trapped in Canada,

Muskrat pelts netted more than $1 million in each of Ontario, Manitoba, Saskatchewan, and Alberta. Lynx was the most valuable furbearer in British Columbia and the Northwest Territories. In terms of unit price, the five species with the highest price per pelt include; polar bear ($474), lynx ($216), grizzly bear ($190), cougar ($165), and wolverine ($153). However, in total, these species accounted for only .4 per cent of the total number of pelts taken in 1975.

The fur production data included are useful for identifying trends in the industry, but as with most sources of wildlife information, data inconsistencies are a significant limiting factor. For example, native harvesting of furbearers, a prime source of northern incomes, is poorly documented and not adequately represented (see Tables 6 and 7). To date, furbearers have been considered primarily for their fur value. Yet in northern communities, beaver, raccoon, muskrat, and lynx are con-

More than 2.5 million hunting permits were issued in 1975. Here, a hunter on Manitoulin Island takes aim, awaiting the arrival of a flock of ducks.

126

MAP 10

NFB – PHOTOTHEQUE – ONF – Photo by George Hunter.

IBP PROPOSED ECOLOGICAL SITES

• Location of IBP — CT Checksheeted Sites

Major Vegetation Regions

- Tundra and Alpine Tundra
- Tundra and Boreal Forest Transition
- Boreal Forest
- Southeastern Mixed Forest Great Lakes— St. Lawrence Forest
- Southeastern Mixed Forest—Acadian Forest
- Deciduous Forest
- Subalpine Forest
- Columbia Forest
- Montane Forest
- Coast Forest
- Parkland (Boreal Forest and Grassland Transition)
- Grassland (Tallgrass and Shortgrass Prairie)

modified after J.S. Rowe

STATUS and SIZE of IBP SITES

	Areas with protected status[1]		Areas with no protected status		TOTAL	
	Number of IBP Sites	Size (hectares)	Number of IBP Sites	Size (hectares)	Number of IBP Sites	Size (hectares)
NEWFOUNDLAND	18	352,160	49	302,006	67	654,166
NOVA SCOTIA	11	9,481	62	12,980	73	22,461
NEW BRUNSWICK	11	726	17	8,150	28	8,876
PRINCE EDWARD ISLAND	3	119	12	3,056	15	3,175
QUÉBEC	—	—	25	52,375	25	52,375
ONTARIO	156	776,727	323	104,848	479	881,575
MANITOBA	34	1,038,985	36	116,872	70	1,155,857
SASKATCHEWAN	24	353,381	76	1,189,150	100	1,542,531
ALBERTA	147	2,511,587	50	111,420	197	2,623,007
BRITISH COLUMBIA	43	116,199	173	499,474	216	615,673
YUKON TERRITORY	2	44,000	10	1,155,389	12	1,199,389
NORTHWEST TERRITORIES	5	967,390	33	1,611,239	38	2,578,629
CANADA	454	6,170,755	866	5,166,959	1,320	11,337,714

NOTE: 1. Areas designated as having "protected status", may include federal and provincial wildlife refuges, national and provincial parks and ecological reserves. Sites with both a "protected" and a "non-protected" portion are considered as "areas with some protected status".

Source: Environment Canada, Canadian Forestry Service, *Canada A Forest Nation*, 1974
G.H. LaRoi and T.A. Babb, *Canadian National Directory of IBP Areas*, 1968-1975.

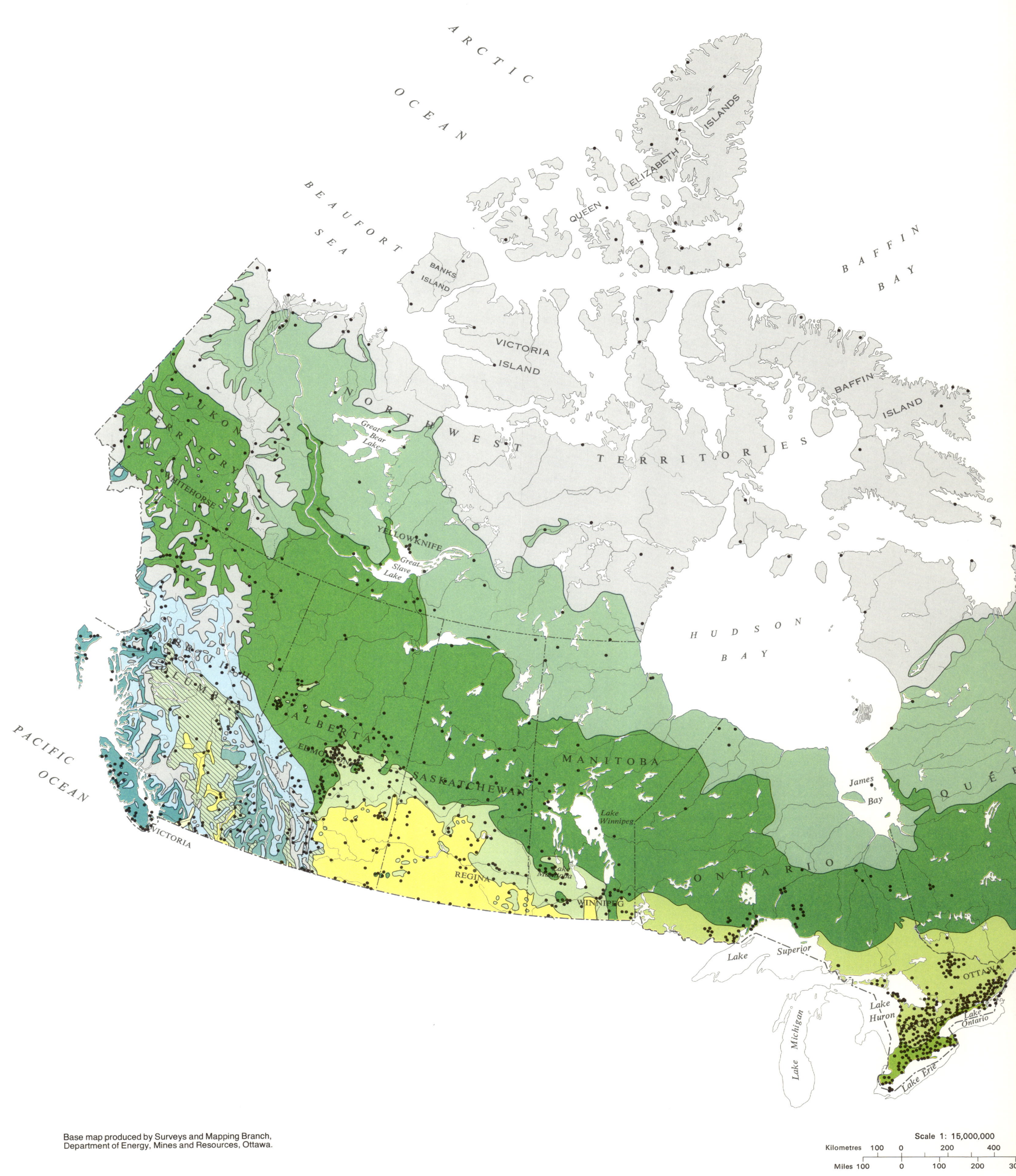

TABLE 7.
Value of raw fur production+, 1955-56, 1965-66, 1975-76

Region and year	Major species						
				(dollars)			
1955-56++	Muskrat	Beaver	Mink	Squirrel	Ermine	Other Furbearers	Total
Atlantic	63,484	258,554	89,540	2,676	8,483	43,844	466,581
Québec	198,115	580,832	180,285	1,692	17,946	182,812	1,161,682
Ontario	595,648	1,386,700	616,240	-	27,866	363,069	2,989,523
Prairies	3,142,627	946,643	960,309	525,289	434,226	199,899	6,208,993
British Columbia	50,305	126,648	214,129	74,474	13,520	93,519	572,595
N.W.T. & Yukon	263,274	112,731	90,393	36,104	10,122	448,711	961,335
CANADA	4,313,453	3,412,108	2,150,896	640,235	512,163	1,331,854	12,360,709
1965-66	Beaver	Muskrat	Mink	Lynx	Marten	Seal	Other Furbearers	Total
Atlantic	252,030	30,788	61,858	3,414	3,342	1,630,842	149,545	2,131,819
Québec	984,222	285,546	173,600	203,289	132,634	192,412	286,362	2,258,165
Ontario	2,285,942	836,112	245,265	55,940	194,097	-	365,836	3,983,192
Prairies	1,664,126	1,741,967	604,246	157,211	23,463	-	1,312,803	5,503,816
British Columbia	423,150	57,492	54,873	76,825	38,955	-	125,247	776,542
N.W.T. & Yukon	129,677	255,484	86,204	47,826	110,817	305,646	281,183	1,216,837
Other+++	-	-	-	-	-	1,009,933	-	1,009,933
CANADA	5,739,147	3,207,389	1,226,046	544,605	503,308	3,138,833	2,520,976	16,880,304
1975-76	Muskrat	Beaver	Fox	Coyote	Lynx	Seal	Other Furbearers	Total
Atlantic	156,133	130,860	369,819	-	66,220	1,497,000	608,972	2,829,004
Québec	507,805	1,092,092	702,840	-	612,370	242,568	1,012,307	4,169,982
Ontario	1,862,924	2,882,581	562,877	96,322	266,951	-	2,304,890	7,976,545
Prairies	4,028,628	2,303,603	1,494,272	2,926,272	842,757	-	2,065,486	13,661,018
British Columbia	93,252	266,329	43,645	121,545	799,681	-	507,619	1,832,071
N.W.T. & Yukon	763,569	47,936	699,729	6,244	257,437	810,486	524,760	3,110,161
Other+++	-	-	-	-	-	589,072	-	589,072
CANADA	7,412,311	6,723,401	3,873,182	3,150,383	2,845,416	3,139,126	7,024,034	34,167,853

+ Does not include ranch raised wildlife fur species.
++ Seals were not considered in 1955-56.
+++ In some cases it is not possible to sub-divide seal trapping or value by region.

Source: Dominion Bureau of Statistics, 1957 and 1967. Fur Production, Season 1955-56. Memorandum.
──────, 1967. Fur Production, Season 1965-66. Catalogue 23-207.
Statistics Canada, 1977a. Fur Production, Season 1975-76. Catalogue 23-207.

In 1975, more than 2.5 million hunting licences were issued, generating a revenue of $18.1 million (Table 8). Included are licences issued to both resident and non-resident hunters by federal, provincial, and territorial wildlife agencies for big game, upland game, small game, and migratory birds. Although the precise definitions vary from province to province, in general, big game consists of moose, deer, (white-tailed, black-tailed, and mule), antelope, caribou, elk, mountain sheep, mountain goat, bison, bear (brown, black, polar, and grizzly) and cougar; small game includes rabbit, hare, squirrel, fox, coyote, wolf, and wolverine; upland birds are dominated by pheasant, grouse, partridge, quail, and ptarmigan; and migratory birds include duck, geese, snipe, woodcock, gallinules, rails, coots, Sandhill Crane, Morning Dove and Band-tailed Pigeon (Dean, 1975). Almost 600 thousand game licences were issued in Ontario in 1975. British Columbia sold more than 400 thousand and Alberta and Québec each issued more than 300 thousand licences. Federal Migratory Game Bird Hunting Permits were sold to more than 139 thousand participants in Ontario, more than 53 thousand in Alberta, and between 43 thousand and 33 thousand in each of Saskatchewan, Manitoba, Québec, and the Yukon (Table 8). Provincial game data sources are impossible to disaggregate further because of the variety of licencing techniques adopted by each province. For example: in New Brunswick, big game licences entitle hunters to hunt small game; in Nova Scotia, deer licences include permits to hunt bears; in Québec, moose licences are combined with caribou; in Ontario, moose licences entitle residents to hunt bears, and non-residents to hunt bears, deer, wolves, and small game; in Manitoba, residents may hunt elk and moose on one licence; in British Columbia and the Yukon, a basic licence permits the holder to hunt big game and game birds. In addition, Manitoba and Alberta require hunters to purchase wildlife certificates, and both Alberta and British Columbia issue special species hunting stamps or big game tag licences (Federal–Provincial Wildlife Conference, 1976).

Most provinces are subdivided into game management zones. Within each zone, the allowable harvest is determined annually for each game species. Estimates for the harvest are based on a variety of field and aerial reconnaissance surveys conducted by the provincial wildlife agencies. Special permits are issued in British Columbia and Alberta for mountain sheep and mountain goat, two species with smaller and more vulnerable populations. In 1975, an estimated 7,673,599 game birds and mammals were taken in Canada (Table 9). Representing the plethora of provincial response techniques, all game data should be regarded as preliminary.

Data on the harvest of migratory birds are much more reliable. In 1966, the Canadian Wildlife Service initiated an obligatory hunting permit system for all hunters of migratory birds and in 1967, a questionnaire survey based on a stratified sample of the hunter population was initiated to determine national harvest and species composition. Since then, statistical manipulation of the computerized data has enabled a reliable estimate of species kill, intensity of kill, participation rates, and species distribution. A recent report summarized the status of migratory game bird hunters and hunting.

Ducks make up most of the migratory bird kill in Canada. In the eight years from 1970 to 1977, the average estimated duck kill by permit holders was 3.7 million. The kill has increased annually with the exception of 1973 and 1977 when poor weather during the hunting season reduced the kill, especially in Saskatchewan and Manitoba. Also, the exceptionally dry weather conditions in the spring of 1977 led to a reduced production of young. Mallards account for more than half the kill in the four western provinces and are the most important species in Ontario. East of Ontario, the Black Duck dominates. National duck and goose kills show that the highest duck kill areas were in southeastern Québec, central Alberta, and southwestern British Columbia in 1969-70 and 1974-75 (averaging between 8 and 13 ducks per km²); and in southern Manitoba and southern and eastern Ontario in 1969-70 but not in 1974-75. Goose kill during 1970-77 averaged 450,000, and was comprised mostly of Canada Geese. Snow Geese are second in importance and are followed by White-fronted Geese, Ross' Geese and Brant. In 1972 and 1974, protracted snow cover in the Arctic breeding grounds caused poor production and resulted in declines in kill. The larger races of Canada Geese breed in lower latitudes and are not as susceptible to the effects of weather. Highest goose kills occurred in Saskatchewan in 1969-70 and 1970-74 (2.9 to 3.7 geese per km² near Kindersley Saskatchewan) and near Lake Manitoba in 1974-75 (2.5 to 3.7 geese per km²). An increased goose kill was also evident in southwestern Saskatchewan and southeastern Alberta in 1974-75. Except for parts of the Prairie Provinces and along the shores of the St. Lawrence River and southern James Bay, the goose kill in both hunting periods was generally small. Woodcock are the most commonly hunted non-waterfowl species of migratory birds. The average annual kill between 1970 and 1977 was 120,000. The largest harvest of woodcock occurs in Ontario, Québec, New Brunswick, Nova Scotia, and Prince Edward Island. Common Snipe represent the next most frequently hunted species and the estimated kill between 1970 and 1977 averaged 99,000. Québec is consistently the province with the greatest snipe kill followed by Newfoundland and Ontario. Coot and Sandhill Crane are the remaining migratory birds, both of which are harvested in very small quantities. (Adapted from Boyd and Finney, 1978).

Other Activities.

Wildlife viewing, hiking, photography and the educational interpretation of wildlife and the ecological environment are each associated with a special land use. Increasing visitation in National and provincial parks (see Recreation, Table 19), the greater availability of nature trails in urban and ex-urban parks, the growing number of school outings at nature centres, and the number of TV programs explaining wildlife interactions with natural habitats, are some of the indicators of expanding activities relating to wildlife. Present membership estimates for the Canadian Nature Federation are 18 thousand and for the Canadian Wildlife Federation are greater than 300 thousand. In addition, the Canadian Conservation Directory lists more than 300 citizen's groups concerned with the values of the natural environment. Included are wildlife associations, nature clubs, pollution fighting organizations, hiking groups, sportsmen's and professional associations, etc. (Mosquin and MacDougall, 1976).

Photo by the Canadian Wildlife Service

With 76 per cent of Canada's population dwelling in urban areas, the need to create habitat for urban-dwelling wildlife is important. A backyard bird feeder, which attracts a variety of song birds, is an example of one technique used by many residents.

TABLE 8.

Number issued and revenue from
hunting licences, by province or territory of sale, 1968-69 and 1975-76

Type of licence issued and province of issue	Number of licences issued		Revenue	
	1968-69	1975-76	1968-69	1975-76
	(thousands)		(thousands of dollars)	
Provincial and Territorial Game Licences*				
Newfoundland	47.3	78	577.1	399
Prince Edward Island	4.1	6	8.6	14
Nova Scotia	89.2	112	341.7	660
New Brunswick	77.0	109	370.2	541
Québec	353.6	423	1,886.4	3,022
Ontario	633.7	596	5,134.1	5,043
Manitoba	103.8	60	570.8	433
Saskatchewan	164.9	145	1,054.8	1,259
Alberta	359.5	213	1,433.0	1,620
British Columbia	426.2	363	1,318.6	3,212
Yukon Territory	3.4	5	47.7	166
Northwest Territories	5.6	–	32.7	–
CANADA	2,268.3	2,110	12,775.7	16,369
Federal Migratory Game Bird Hunting Permits**				
Newfoundland	17.7	30.1	35.4	105
Prince Edward Island	3.7	4.9	7.4	17
Nova Scotia	9.0	14.0	18.0	50
New Brunswick	9.6	12.9	19.2	45
Québec	37.1	63.8	74.2	223
Ontario	139.2	148.7	278.4	520
Manitoba	38.7	42.9	77.4	150
Saskatchewan	43.6	57.8	87.2	202
Alberta	53.6	69.2	107.2	242
British Columbia	33.3	25.9	66.6	91
Yukon Territory	–	.5	–	2
Northwest Territories	–	.7	–	3
CANADA	385.5	471.4	771.0	1,650

* Includes licences to hunt big and small game species.
** Includes licences to hunt ducks, geese and where seasons are open, coots, snipes, woodcock, pigeons, doves and cranes.

Sources: Statistics Canada, 1978. *Travel, Tourism and Outdoor Recreation. A Statistical Digest. 1975 and 1976.* Catalogue 66-202.
_____, 1972b. *Travel, Tourism and Outdoor Recreation. A Statistical Digest 1972.* Catalogue 66-202.

Lands Allocated for Wildlife

More than 567,866 km² (six per cent of the total land area) have been set aside specifically for wildlife use and are maintained by wildlife agencies under the authority of the federal, territorial, and provincial governments (Map 11). The size, purpose, major species, important habitat features and, where possible, the sanction of hunting and trapping activities within each protected area are listed in Appendix III. In addition, there are 405,390 km² of National and provincial parks and park reserves which are essential for the conservation of wildlife habitat (Table 10) (*see* Recreation, Map 16). Although these wildlife lands do not protect all the critical habitats in Canada, they do represent a cross-section of special resource lands allocated for the variety of wildlife uses previously discussed.

Provincial Wildlife Lands

Many provincial wildlife lands are managed primarily for producing a harvestable surplus of big, small, and upland game. Most areas permit controlled hunting and trapping, and maximum sustained-yield strategies are achieved through habitat manipulation techniques such as burning, forest culling, and some species introduction. For example, in New Brunswick, ten Provincial Game Management Areas are managed for moose and deer. Québec has, throughout the boreal, mixed wood forest and in the northern tundra transition, more than 17,575,850 ha of Provincial Reserves which have been set aside for moose, deer, caribou, and fish. Ontario's Provincial Wildlife Areas located primarily within the southern populated portion of the province, are oriented towards multiple use activities including hunting.

Photo by the Canadian Wildlife Service

Wildlife education is an important element in high school curricula. Here, a group of students use the facilities of Wye Marsh, a National Wildlife Area near Hamilton, Ontario.

Waterfowl, upland game (hare, grouse, pheasant) and white-tailed deer are the target species in most of the wetlands, woodlands, and open grass areas. Manitoba has 49 Wildlife Management Areas ranging in size from the 1.7 million ha of Cape Churchill occupying the lowlands bordering Hudson Bay, to the 60 ha of Gerald W. Malaher supporting a mixed forest interspersed by small open meadows. Dominant game species are moose, elk, white-tailed deer, Ruffed and Sharp-tailed Grouse. Pasquia and Porcupine, both Wildlife Management Units in Saskatchewan's southern boreal forest, are the two largest areas in the province for the management of big game. During the past ten years, because of the other designations of areas such as community pastures, provincial forests, and parks, Saskatchewan has re-designated some wildlife lands in an attempt to achieve a more consistent policy for wildlife management. In addition, a Special Wildlife Development Fund, using in part monies obtained from hunting licences, has purchased 12,141 ha of deer habitat[1]. These lands, in the aspen parkland and southern boreal forest, threatened by brush clearing operations have been acquired, and where necessary, forage crops have been planted to provide browse (Rump and Harper, 1977). In Alberta, a similar system was established in 1973, which has improved habitat for moose by stimulating aspen suckering, and for bighorn sheep by range fertilization. These Buck for Wildlife Areas have also improved habitat for upland birds (pheasant and Hungarian Partridge) by planting shelterbelts, and for waterfowl by stabilizing marsh levels. British Columbia's 756,710 ha of upland habitat dispersed throughout the mountains and valleys, have been established for elk, deer, bighorn sheep, mountain goat, and caribou, the major big game species in the province. One management technique used successfully has been prescribed burns on bighorn winter range in the East Kootenays.

Environment Canada – photo by V. Neimanis

Wildlife interpretation is an essential tool of wildlife management, particularly on wildlife lands near urban centres. An observation tower at Port Royal Conservation Authority in southern Ontario, is shown.

Environment Canada – photo by J. McCuaig

Saskatchewan's Last Mountain Lake is an important staging area for ducks, geese, and Sandhill Crane. More than 12 thousand ha at this site have been protected as a provincial Wildlife Management Unit and a federal National Wildlife Area.

Approximately 30 per cent of the 46 million ha of provincial and territorial wildlife protected lands are sanctuaries, preserves or conservation areas and generally do not permit other hunting or trapping activities. More than half of these mammal areas are in the north. Mountain sheep, mountain goat, caribou, grizzly bear, and wolves are the major species protected by the three grame sanctuaries in the Yukon. Of the eight game pre-

[1] Not included in Appendix III.

TABLE 9.

Game harvest by species, by province and territory, 1968 and 1975

Provinces, territories and year	Moose	Deer	Caribou	Elk	Antelope	Mountain sheep	Mountain goat	Bison	Bear**	Cougar	Wolf	Wolverine	Coyote	Rabbit, hare	Grouse***	Pheasant	Ptarmigan	Hungarian partridge	Wood-Cock	Snipe	Ducks	Geese	Sandhill Crane
1968																							
Newfoundland	9,443	-	1,000	-	-	-	-	-	37	-	-	-	-	630,000	-	-	39,000	-	-	-	62,296	4,868	-
Prince Edward Island	-	-	-	-	-	-	-	-	-	-	-	-	-	-	64,590	6,165	-	1,530	6,795	5,385	21,602	6,041	-
Nova Scotia	-	-	-	-	-	-	-	-	-	-	-	-	-	260,615	173,557	-	-	-	15,000	-	75,884	5,501	-
New Brunswick	727	22,642	-	-	-	-	-	-	1,400	-	-	-	-	50,047	-	-	-	-	-	-	64,340	2,351	-
Québec	7,190	8,446	495	-	-	-	-	-	-	-	-	-	-	-	-	-	-	-	-	-	347,891	13,418	-
Ontario	13,500	20,000	-	-	-	-	-	-	-	-	-	-	-	-	-	-	-	-	-	-	804,592	24,432	-
Manitoba	2,830	23,000	30	340	-	-	-	-	-	-	-	-	-	-	185,646	-	5,657	5,737	-	-	296,353	20,063	-
Saskatchewan	6,200	40,500	79	575	2,675	-	-	-	-	-	-	-	-	-	177,550	12,000	-	85,000	-	-	293,537	72,294	-
Alberta	17,318	24,911	-	4,918	955	-	-	-	393	-	-	-	-	-	-	-	-	-	-	-	459,521	59,050	-
British Columbia	25,754	77,396	1,441	2,462	-	682	2,282	-	3,424	16	-	-	-	-	616,032	-	-	-	-	-	374,731	12,987	-
Yukon Territory	894	-	1,317	-	-	243	22	-	253	-	68	128	119	-	9,108	-	1,674	-	-	-	-	-	-
Northwest Territories	1,096	1	16,022	-	-	94	8	70	871	-	-	-	-	-	10,944	-	26,522	-	-	-	-	-	-
CANADA	84,952	216,896	20,384	8,295	3,630	1,300	2,397	70	6,378	16	68	128	119	940,662	1,237,377	18,165	72,853	92,267	21,795	5,385	2,800,747	221,005	-
1975																							
Newfoundland	4,763	-	744	-	-	-	-	-	86	-	-	-	-	1,400,000	-	-	108,000	-	-	-	101,695	8,150	-
Prince Edward Island	-	-	-	-	-	-	-	-	-	-	-	-	-	25,000	12,239	-	-	2,012	694	1,153	28,445	6,354	-
Nova Scotia	-	-	-	-	-	-	-	-	-	-	-	-	-	559,148	108,831	11,220	-	2,415	13,280	11,752	117,994	9,428	-
New Brunswick	1,093	5,554	-	-	-	-	-	-	637	-	-	-	-	-	325,484	-	-	-	17,662	-	59,061	2,988	-
Québec	7,843	2,918	1,432	-	-	-	-	-	454	-	-	-	-	-	-	-	-	-	-	-	467,892	52,221	-
Ontario	11,310	12,570	-	-	-	-	-	-	3,630	-	-	-	-	-	-	-	-	-	-	-	938,302	50,770	-
Manitoba	2,050	-	14	175	-	-	-	-	-	-	-	-	-	-	154,152	-	7,805	10,499	-	-	299,221	152,392	-
Saskatchewan	2,525	22,896	69	328	1,309	-	-	-	327	-	-	-	-	-	93,089	10,398	-	39,239	-	-	807,295	157,144	3,703
Alberta	8,095	11,174	20	1,538	1,083	325	28	-	24	24	-	-	-	-	-	-	-	-	-	-	850,709	120,480	-
British Columbia	14,936	29,028	955	1,171	-	324	1,039	-	2,876	242	-	-	-	-	-	-	-	-	-	-	266,223	12,782	-
Yukon Territory	1,574	-	1,234	-	-	265	25	-	189	-	33	9	-	-	8,456	-	-	-	-	-	5,003	424	-
Northwest Territories	598	1	18,678	-	-	172	12	81	631	-	-	-	-	-	12,926	-	29,094	-	-	-	9,541	1,633	-
CANADA	54,787	84,141	23,146	3,212	2,392	1,086	1,104	81	8,854	266	33	9	-	1,984,148	715,177	21,618	144,899	54,255	31,636	12,905	3,951,381	574,766	3,703

* Big and small game data for moose, deer, caribou, elk, antelope, mountain sheep, mountain goat, bison, bear, cougar wolf, wolverine, coyote, rabbit, grouse, pheasant, ptarmigan, and Hungarian partridge have been collected from each provincial and territorial game branch. Data for ducks, geese, and Sandhill Crane are from the National Harvest Survey conducted annually by the Canadian Wildlife Service, Environment Canada.
** Includes brown, black, polar, and grizzly bear.
*** Includes Ruffed, sharp-tailed, and spruce grouse.

TABLE 10.

National and, provincial parks and reserves essential for wildlife habitat*, by province and territory, 1976

Province and territory	National parks	Provincial parks	Park reserves	Total
		(ha)		
Newfoundland	233,907	739,191	34,067	1,007,165
Prince Edward Island	1,813	1,275	1,345	4,433
Nova Scotia	133,206	1,888	6,597	141,691
New Brunswick	43,124	21,526	-	64,650
Québec	114,040+	8,898,460	4,054,656	3,067,156
Ontario	191,171	3,962,274	511,684	14,665,129
Manitoba	297,596	878,178	3,558	1,179,332
Saskatchewan	387,470	511,882	4,988	904,340
Alberta	5,301,044	651,386	80,200	6,032,630
British Columbia	444,296	4,539,874	-	4,984,170
Yukon Territory	2,201,538	-	979,558	3,181,096
Northwest Territories	3,607,932	2,209	747,603++	4,357,744
CANADA	12,957,137	20,208,143	6,424,256	39,589,536

*Parks essential for wildlife are derived from the Parks Classification System and include:
    Class A - Wilderness Areas (minimum size of 11,620 ha)
    Class C - Unique Natural Areas or Monuments
    Class D - Natural Environment Recreation Areas (minimum size of 202 ha)
    Class G - Park and Recreational Reserves (Land Bank)
\+ Includes Gatineau Park, 35,613 ha.
++ Includes East Arm, Great Slave Lake, N.W.T., 740,753 ha.

Source: Federal-Provincial Parks Conference. 1976. Parks Classification System, National and Provincial Parks.

MAP 11

Photo by James Raffan.

WILDLIFE PROTECTED LANDS

Federal Lands

● <100,000 hectares

■ >100,000 hectares

Provincial and Territorial Lands

▲ <100,000 hectares

■ >100,000 hectares

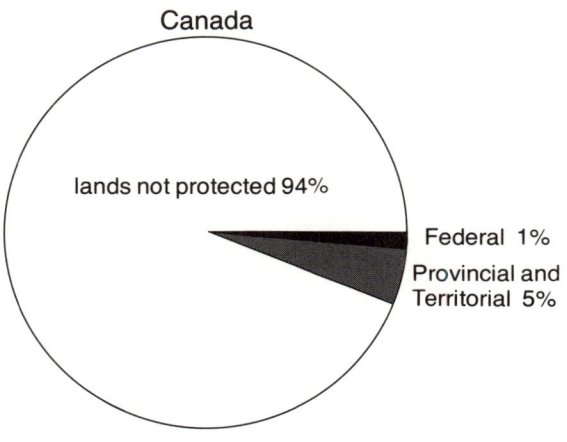

Canada

lands not protected 94%

Federal 1%

Provincial and Territorial 5%

Note: Wildlife Protected Lands are defined as lands whose primary function is the management of wildlife. Included are migratory bird sanctuaries, national wildlife areas, wildlife management areas, game reserves etc. With the exception of Polar Bear, Quetico and Killarney provincial parks in Ontario, no other national or provincial parks have been mapped.

WILDLIFE PROTECTED LANDS

	Total Land Area (hectares)	Federal Wildlife Land[2] (hectares)	Provincial and Territorial Wildlife Land[3] (hectares)	Total – Federal, Provincial and Territorial Wildlife Land (hectares)
Newfoundland	37,047,225	648	171,836	172,484
Prince Edward Island	565,634	588	4,799	5,387
Nova Scotia	5,283,914	4,225	126,019	130,244
New Brunswick	7,208,987	8,467	308,868	317,335
Québec	135,674,501	40,241	17,641,827	17,682,068
Ontario	89,116,387	40,084	2,952,703	2,992,787
Manitoba	54,847,607	63	2,898,221	2,898,284
Saskatchewan	57,024,936	73,662	863,714	937,376
Alberta	64,436,712	17,979	904,249	922,228
British Columbia	93,049,668	1,416	922,977	924,441
Yukon Territory	53,182,561	—	1,101,820	1,101,820
Northwest Territories	324,627,908	10,160,188	18,633,942	28,794,130
CANADA	922,066,040	10,347,609	46,530,975	56,878,584

Source: 1. Statistics Canada, Canada Yearbook, 1974.
2. Canada Gazette, Part II, Vol. 108, No. 18, "Migratory Bird Sanctuary Regulations" and Vol. III, No. 21, "Wildlife Area Regulations".
3. personal communication with wildlife branches in each of the provinces and territories.

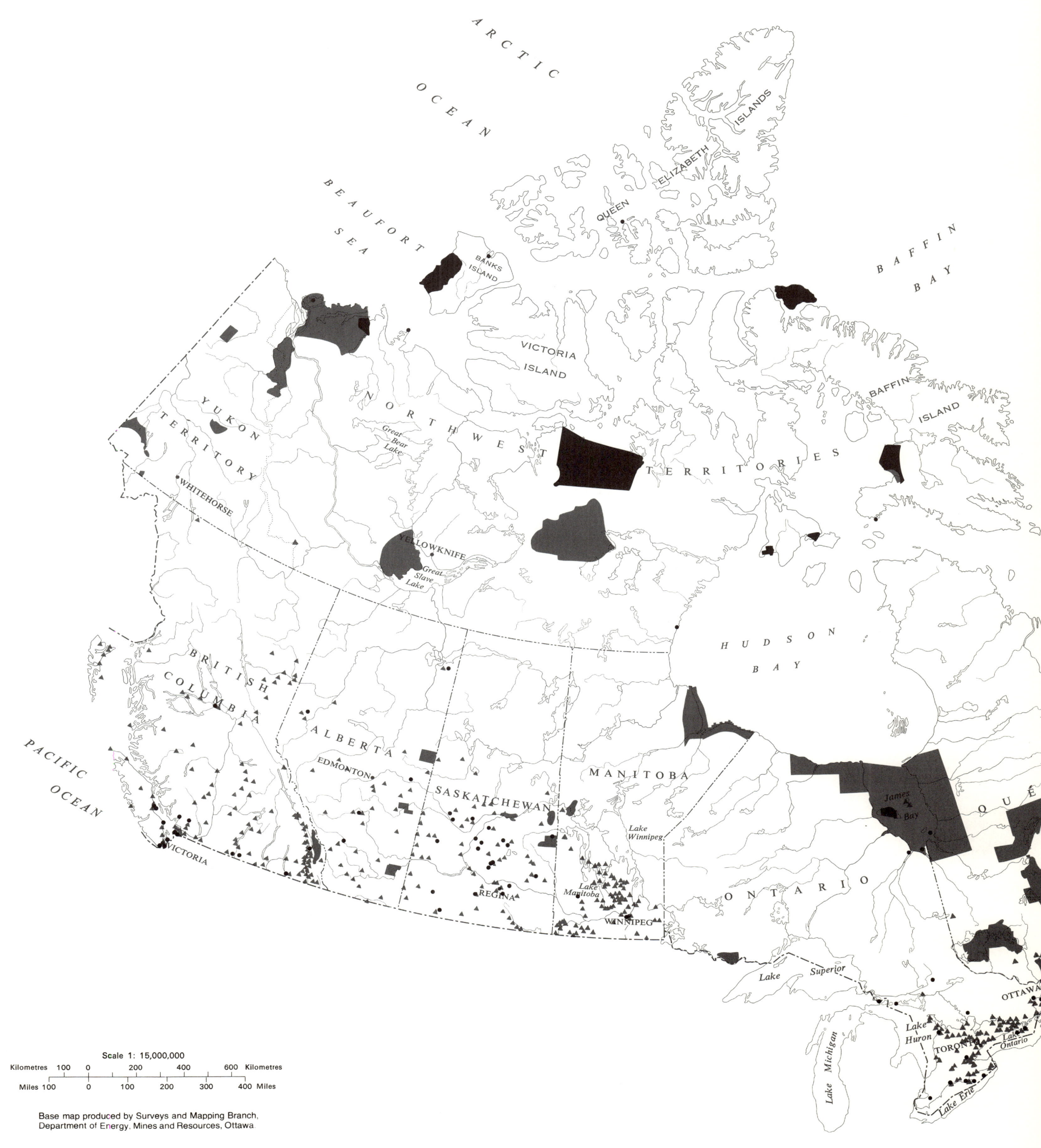

serves and game sanctuaries in the Northwest Territories, muskoxen, wood bison, and reindeer are the three specific species mentioned. In the southern regions, Newfoundland, New Brunswick, and Alberta, each have identified special wildlife lands. The pine marten and woodland caribou are supported by 170,947 ha of habitat on the Island of Newfoundland. Moose, caribou, and deer seek protection in 28,403 ha of New Brunswick's Game Refuges. A variety of boreal, subalpine, aspen parkland, and grassland habitats have been designated as Wildlife Sanctuaries in Alberta for big game and upland furbearers.

In addition, migratory bird habitat also has been protected by the provinces. In the east, seabirds and waterfowl are the primary concern. The rugged coastal islands off the Island of Newfoundland have been established as Conservation Areas and are important particularly during the breeding season for the colonial nesting birds. Hunting is strictly prohibited. Nova Scotia has designated coastal areas for waterfowl feeding, staging, breeding, and some wintering habitat. Québec has conserved 4 *scirpus* tidal marshes as Migratory Bird Areas which are essential for resting waterfowl and an additional six sanctuaries which are used by other migratory birds. Here too, hunting and trapping activities are not permitted. Many of Ontario's Conservation Authorities are aimed at providing wildlife viewing and other recreational opportunities. Shorebirds, waterfowl, grouse, pheasant, and song birds occupy the wetlands and woodlands in southern Ontario. The Bird Refuges primarily in the Interlake region of Manitoba have been set aside for waterfowl use. Nesting ducks use the wetlands in the spring and summer and migratory geese seek spring and fall staging habitat. Most of Saskatchewan's Game Preserves in the mid-grass and shortgrass Prairie and in the aspen parkland are protected for waterfowl use. Also, Wildlife Refuges have been established to protect colonial bird species, including Double-crested Cormorant and White Pelican, Great Blue Heron, and the prairie dog located along the Frenchman River in the southwest. Alberta has ten Migratory Bird Sanctuaries and three Bird Sanctuaries designated for waterfowl staging and production habitat and for other migratory birds such as the Trumpeter Swan. Approximately 68 thousand ha of wetlands are included in British Columbia's Wildlife Management Areas. The types of wetlands vary from estuarine, salt marshes, and intertidal mud flats in the coastal areas to flood plain marshes and lake shorelines with submergent and emergent vegetation. Waterfowl, shorebirds, seabirds, and raptors use the wetlands and adjacent areas for nesting, resting, staging, and for wintering habitat. Other activities such as hunting and trapping are permitted in some areas.

Federal Wildlife Lands

Federally allocated wildlife lands include more than 10.3 million ha, of which 98 per cent are located in the Northwest Territories and the Yukon. Managed by the Canadian Wildlife Service, these Migratory Bird Sanctuaries and National Wildlife Areas supply essential migratory bird habitat, particularly in the northern nesting grounds. In the Arctic Archipelago, Bylot and Banks islands are the largest Migratory Bird Sanctuaries. The coastal rock cliffs and tundra on Bylot Island support the major breeding grounds of Greater Snow Geese and also good habitat for seabirds including murres. Similarly, the tundra plains of Banks Island provides nesting habitat for Snow Geese. The apparently barren landscape of Seymour Island, north of Bathurst Island, supports the only known breeding habitat for the Ivory Gull. On the barrens, the sanctuary on Queen Maud Gulf, providing 6.2 million ha of tundra and lakes, is visited annually by Ross' Goose. The remaining northern sanctuaries occupying a variety of tundra formations, support critical nesting and breeding habitat for Snow and Canada Geese, brant, and Eider Duck. In addition essential habitats for seabirds are found along coastal areas. Since the north represents some unique nesting grounds, protection, although not precluding other land use activities, controls access through a permit system. Although in the north, all sanctuaries are located on federally-owned land, in the provinces, ownership of sanctuaries may be private, institutional, municipal, provincial, or federal. According to the regulations under the Migratory Birds Convention Act, land use controls are permitted only for the regulation of activities that would interfere with the bird populations (Dean, 1975). These regulated constraints sometimes pose management problems. Nevertheless, the Migratory Bird Sanctuaries protect vital nesting and resting habitat along the St. Lawrence River, the Bay of Fundy, coastal Nova Scotia, Newfoundland and New Brunswick, for ducks, geese, seabirds, and shorebirds. In the agriculturally dominated areas of southern Québec and Ontario, sanctuaries provide resting locations for migrating ducks and geese. Saskatchewan has 15 Migratory Bird Sanctuaries, scattered through the short- and mixed-grass Prairie, and the aspen parkland, ranging in size from 32 to 26,063 ha. Trumpeter Swan, geese and ducks are protected by the four sanctuaries in Alberta. All of British Columbia's sanctuaries are located in the Juan de Fuca Straits near Vancouver and Victoria.

With the passing of the Canada Wildlife Act in 1973, the Canadian Wildlife Service became empowered to purchase land for the protection and conservation of wildlife habitat (Dean, 1975). To date, 39 National Wildlife Areas have been acquired covering 33,413 ha. The focus has remained on waterfowl habitat, and lands designated include salt marshes, mud flats, intertidal zones, ponds, freshwater marshes, and estuaries. Habitat manipulation techniques used are diking and planting of lure crops. For example, in Last Mountain Lake Saskatchewan, about 202 ha of lure crops have been planted to attract ducks, geese, and Sandhill Crane away from the surrounding agricultural areas.

National and provincial parks

Although wildlife protection is not the primary reason for the designation of National and provincial parks, the majority of the larger parks are considered to support essential wildlife habitat (Table 10). National parks and most provincial parks are planned so that user activities are regulated. Hence intensive recreation functions and/or extensive conservation areas are maintained within the park boundaries. Wood Buffalo and Elk Island National parks, and Polar Bear provincial park in Ontario are obvious examples of wildlife-oriented parks. In general, the National parks distributed throughout Canada support representative wildlife. In the west, the mountain parks of Alberta, British Columbia, and the Yukon, comprising more than 60 per cent of the area of National parks, are important reserves for mountain goat and sheep, bear, elk, deer, and moose. In the east coast, adjoining parks provide habitat for a variety of shorebirds, seabirds and also for large and small mammals.

Photo by the Canadian Wildlife Service

National Parks are important reserves for wildlife. Here, wood bison are seen grazing in Elk Island National Park.

Recently, Parks Canada has identified 39 terrestrial natural regions which are used as a systematic baseline planning tool for the identification of new parks. These natural regions of Canadian significance have been derived from a physiographic classification of Canada, with an additional subdivision of one class, the Canadian Shield, using Rowe's Forest Regions of Canada (Appendix I), (*see* Recreation, Map 9). Within each natural region, Natural Areas of Canadian Significance (NACs) have been identified using three criteria: representativeness, uniqueness, and naturalness (Parks Canada, 1976). With a few exceptions, wildlife has been mentioned in the majority of NACs identified For example in Labrador, the Mealy and Torngat mountains have included caribou, moose, beaver, and fox as the indicator mammals, in addition to other waterfowl and shorebird species such as Canada Geese, Harlequin Duck, Common Eider, Rough-legged Hawk, Gyrfalcon and Arctic Tern. Unique areas such as Sable Island are also included. Sable Island is the only breeding ground for the Ipswich Sparrow. Other breeding birds include ducks, gulls, terns, Sandpiper and other migrants during the spring and fall. Cypress Hills, represents another special area which supports populations of mammals and birds not found in the surrounding Prairie plains. Val Marie in southern Saskatchewan is interesting for its sample of original prairie vegetation and Prairie fauna. Representative species include the common antelope, Richardon's ground squirrel or gropher, the Prairie Falcon, Ferruginous Hawk, Sage Grouse and the black-tailed prairie dog. In the north, areas including the Fosheim Peninsula on Ellesmere Island, Bathurst Inlet, Banks Island, and Wager Bay provide the sensitive breeding sites to both birds and mammals. In addition, provincial parks support 20.2 million ha of prime wildlife habitat (Table 10). Québec, followed by British Columbia and Ontario, provide 86 per cent of total habitat within provincial parks.

As a result of the International Biological Programme (IBP) discussed in the physical sector, several initiatives have been directed towards protecting the checksheeted IBP sites. The number, size and protected status of the checksheeted IBP sites are indicated on Map 10. Some IBP sites are protected through federal or provincial wildlife and/or park designations. However, in addition, several provinces have used the IBP results as an initiative to implement ecological reserve legislation. British Columbia is the forerunner, having classified 75 areas totalling 80,260 ha as ecological reserves (British Columbia, 1976). New Brunswick and Québec are the remaining provinces which have implemented ecological reserve legislation. Other active provincial interests in an ecological reserve program include: Ontario where a committee within the Parks Branch of the Ministry of Natural Resources has used IBP data as background material for identifying wilderness parks; Alberta which has identified 32,600 ha of Natural Areas; and also Newfoundland, which has an active wildlands committee. In addition, IBP sites in northern Canada are being used to identify unique and sensitive landscapes which require protection.

Land Use Issues and Factors Affecting Change

The physical sector identifies some of Canada's unique, sensitive, and nationally representative wildlife lands. Although not conclusive or adequate for all species of wildlife, it depicts a cross-section of on-going regional and national research. From the user perspective, special lands are described through the variety of activities relating to the use of wildlife. Of all the factors, it is the location of lands managed for wildlife habitat that provides the most appropriate indication of the strengths and weaknesses of wildlife in achieving a share in the land allocation process. Not only is it important to consider wildlife and land use, but it is also necessary to monitor the changing allocation of land to other uses. Since wildlife is a wandering resource, it knows no boundaries, and any change in the use of land will directly or indirectly affect wildlife and its habitat.

Indicators of Change

Given the unsolved mysteries of wildlife ecology, one technique for assessing change is by discussing the known fluctuations in wildlife species composition and diversity. For example, there are species which are considered to be rare, threatened or endangered, and, there are species whose populationr appear to be superabundant.

Rare, Threatened, and Endangered Species

Resulting from a joint federal-provincial initiative, a committee dealing with the status of endangered wildlife in Canada was established in 1977. Five status categories for rare, threatened, endangered, extirpated and extinct were identified and defined:

Rare species. Any indigenous species of fauna or flora that, because of its biological characteristics, or because it occurs at the fringe of its range, or for some other reason, exists in low numbers or in very restricted areas in Canada, but is not a threatened species.

Threatened Species. Any indigenous species of fauna or flora that is likely to become endangered in Canada if the factors affecting its vulnerability do not become reversed.

Endangered Species. Any indigenous species of fauna or flora whose existence in Canada is threatened with immediate extinction through all or a significant portion of its range, owing to the action of man.

Extirpated Species. Any indigenous species of fauna or flora no longer existing in the wild in Canada, but existing elsewhere.

Extinct Species. Any species of fauna or flora formerly indigenous to Canada, but no longer existing anywhere. (Federal–Provincial Wildlife Conference, 1978).

Nineteen species have been identified in the initial review of status reports (Maps 12 and 13). Rare includes Trumpeter Swan, Caspian Tern, Peregrine Falcon–subspecies *pealei*, and black-tailed prairie dog. White Pelican, Peregrine Falcon–subspecies *tundrius*, and Piping Plover are considered to be threatened. Endangered is composed of Peregrine Falcon–subspecies *anatum*, Greater Prairie Chicken, Whooping Crane, Eskimo Curlew, Vancouver Island marmot, sea otter, eastern cougar, and wood bison, and extirpated consists of swift fox and the black-footed ferret. Burrowing Owl, Greater Sandhill Crane, Kirtlands Warbler, Gyrfalcon, Double-crested Cormorant, fisher, and northern kit fox were also listed but not classified, by the committee.

NFB – PHOTOTHEQUE – ONF

The Burrowing Owl, a native of the short-grass Prairie, appears to have suffered a significant reduction in population. Loss of habitat, primarily through the expansion of agricultural production in the southern Prairies and British Columbia, is the main reason for the decline.

As suggested, habitat alteration and human disturbance are the major factors affecting species population depletion. Some species such as: the Piping Plover whose present primary range includes the sand beaches of Sable Island and the Îles-de-la Madeleine and Long Point in Ontario; the Vancouver Island Marmot who seeks the steep talus slopes and alpine and subalpine meadows on the Vancouver Island range; the sea otter whose present range extends off the coasts of Vancouver and the Queen Charlotte islands; and the black-footed ferret, the swift fox and the Greater Prairie Chicken which dwell within the true Prairie grasslands, never had abundant populations in their respective restricted ranges and are now reacting to loss of habitat. Threats are most severe in the agriculturally dominated Prairies or where a variety of recreational or industrial activities impose on these non-gregarious species. Other species such as the Whooping Crane which nest in the boreal wetlands of Wood Buffalo National Park, the Eskimo Curlew a ground nester on the northern tundra, and the wood bison which presently exists within Elk Island National Park and the Mackenzie Bison Sanctuary, are examples of species whose populations were severely depleted by human exploitation during the late part of the 19th century. In addition, the White Pelican and Double-crested Cormorant, both colonial nesting fish-eating birds, not protected by the Migratory Bird Convention Act (1917), are included because of their susceptibility to toxic chemicals, their sensitivity to human disturbance during the nesting season, and threats to their low-lying habitat by flooding and irrigation development. The Peregrine Falcon whose subspecies include *pealei* seek the nesting habitat of the British Columbia coast and Queen Charlotte Islands, *tundrius*, found throughout the Arctic tundra, and *anatum*, characteristic of the taiga have all been affected by reduced reproduction rates. Pesticide residuals in their prey, appear to have caused problems of egg-shell thinning and egg breakage. Falconry has also posed a threat to their populations.

The committee has also identified the Great Grey Owl, pocket gopher, badger, grizzly bear, Ivory Gull, wolverine, Ipswich Sparrow, Prairie Falcon, Grey Fox, Newfoundland pine marten, Queen Charlotte Island weasel, fin-back whale, grey whale, northern elephant seal and the Ferruginous Hawk on the most recent candidate list for which status reports are now being prepared (Federal–Provincial Wildlife Conference, 1978).

Photo by the Canadian Wildlife Service

White pelican, a fish-eating bird is extremely sensitive during the nesting period. Also, the susceptibility of these birds to toxic chemicals, ingested from their prey, appears to have had an impact on the reduction of their population. Five pelicans are shown here with a flock of gulls in a lake in Northern Alberta.

Superabundant Species

Species which are not considered to be habitat specific, usually experience expanding populations as lands such as forests or wildlands are converted to agriculture, urban, or industrial uses. Often superabundant wildlife populations, sometimes including imported or exotic species, are labelled as a nuisance or a pest. For example, in the urban environment, common starlings and house sparrows, imported from Europe, have successfully competed to the disadvantage of Red-headed Woodpeckers, bluebirds, tree and cliff swallows (Dagg, 1974). The abundance of natural predators and the existence of artificial food sources may create localized superabundant populations. Toronto's Centre Island has an estimated three thousand Giant Canada Geese, a population which appears to be tripling every five years. Although visitors to the island park find the wildlife attractive, a serious hazard is posed to the nearby Toronto Island airport. In the rural landscape, agricultural habitat has encouraged the presence of Red-winged Blackbirds, starlings, crows, magpies, skunks, foxes, and groundhogs etc., often to the detriment of agricultural crops and livestock. Gulls are another example of a species which are highly adaptable and have taken advantage of changes in the environment. The east coast Herring Gull population has expanded exponentially during this century, in sharp contrast to other seabird populations. Growth is attributed to increasing food sources such as the offal discarded by the fisheries industry and garbage and sewage disposal from expanding human populations. Other gulls which have experienced a similar trend in Atlantic Canada include Black-legged Kittiwake and Great Black-backed Gull (Brown, *et al.* 1975).

Issues and Conflicts

In addition to assessing wildlife change from a species viewpoint, it is also useful to return to consider the implications of changing land use patterns on wildlife. Issues such as land tenure will be important for future decisions regarding the allocation of wildlife land. Other issues including the loss of wetlands and impacts of forestry operations, agriculture expansion, urban alteration and northern development identify the problems and prospects for wildlife.

Land Tenure. Nearly 90 per cent of Canada's land is owned either by the federal or provincial crown. Almost all of the federal crown lands are in the Northwest and Yukon Territories. With the exception of Prince Edward Island, Nova Scotia and New Brunswick, the remaining provinces control more than 50 per cent of the land. Although private land includes only ten per cent of the owned lands, they are concentrated in the southern populated portions of each province, in the rural agricultural, urban, and industrial areas, where pressures for change are intensifying.

In terms of wildlife management, the majority of protected habitats are within the forested and wilderness lands owned by the crown. In addition, at the federal level, the Canadian Wildlife Service operates some Migratory Bird Sanctuaries on a lease basis. The more recent National Wildlife Area program operates through the purchase of private land. To date more than $10 million has been spent on the acquisition of wetlands, the present program priority. Similarly, several provinces such as Ontario, Saskatchewan, and Alberta have embarked on programs for the purchase of private lands, joint management, or in assisting private management of wildlife lands. Previously-mentioned examples of purchase of private lands include the Wildlife Development Fund administered in Saskatchewan and the 'Bucks for Wildlife' program implemented in Alberta. Ontario's Wildlife Extension Landowner Agreement Areas program is managed under agreements between landowners and the Ministry of Natural Resources. For this program, the landowners receive assistance from the wildlife branch for management of the land. In return the public are allowed access to wildlife resource on the property.

Loss of Wetlands. Although there is presently no accurate statistic measuring the loss of wetland areas in Canada, estimates show that agricultural, industrial, and urban expansion in the southern portion have seriously depleted wetland quantity and quality. Bellrose has reported that almost 1.21 million ha have been drained in the Prairie Provinces. In addition, there have been serious isolated losses such as the .7 million ha of the delta of the Saskatchewan River (Bellrose, 1976). Agriculture statistics relating to improved farmland invariably includes loss of wildlife habitat, either through loss of wetlands and/or loss of woodlands (original vegetation). For example, recent research conducted in the Minnedosa pothole region (aspen parkland) of southwestern Manitoba, a prime nesting area for waterfowl, studied land use change between 1928 and 1974. The study areas covering 10,619 m², was subdivided into three land uses; cultivated/cleared, woodlots/brushland, and wetlands. In 1928, 48 per cent of the study area was cultivated/cleared; 38.8 per cent was woodlot/brushland, and 13.2 per cent was wetland. By 1974 the wetlands had decreased to 5.7 per cent, the woodlots/brushland decreased to 9.6 per cent and the cultivated/cleared lands had expanded to 84.7 per cent (Rakowski *et al.* 1977). In southern Ontario, of the 4,330 ha of prime marshes formely located along the north shore of Lake Ontario, only 1,025 ha remain. Similarly in Ontario, an estimated 50 per cent of the original wetlands have been lost in the area south of Lake Simcoe (Mosquin and Suchal, 1976). In addition, Gierman (1977) documented the change in land use surrounding 71 of Canada's urban areas. Between 1966 and 1971, 48 per cent (41,677 ha) of high-capability ungulate lands, and six per cent (5,417 ha) of high-capability waterfowl lands were converted to urban uses.

Loss of wetlands, land tenure, and the remaining significant issues including; crop depredation (valued at $250 million in 1976), impact of oil spills, future development of the north, and industries which contribute to pesticide contamination, all relate to wildlife and its use of the land. These are some of the issues which will affect the future health of Canada's wildlife resource and ultimately determine the allocation of special wildlife lands.

TABLE 11.
Classification of land tenure by province and by territory, 1973.

Province and territory	Total land and water area	Crown Land Federal	Crown Land Provincial	Private Land
	(square kilometres) (percentage of total provincial and territorial area)			
Newfoundland	404,519	2,774 .7	384,024 94.9	17,721 4.4
Prince Edward Island	5,656	39 .7	409 7.2	5,208 92.1
Nova Scotia	55,490	1,624 2.9	15,884 28.6	37,982 68.5
New Brunswick	73,437	2,173 3.0	31,536 42.9	39,728 54.1
Québec	1,540,687	2,792 .2	1,425,230 92.5	112,665 7.3
Ontario	1,068,587	9,881 .9	939,652 88.0	119,055 11.1
Manitoba	650,090	5,377 .8	499,955 76.9	144,758 22.3
Saskatchewan	651,904	15,364 2.4	388,984 59.7	247,555 37.9
Alberta	661,188	63,289 9.6	336,842 50.9	261,056 39.5
British Columbia	948,601	8,974 1.0	885,404 93.3	54,222 5.7
Yukon and Northwest Territories	3,916,026	3,912,143 99.9	3,642 .09	241 .01
CANADA	9,976,185	4,024,430 40.3	4,911,562 49.2	1,040,191 10.4

Source: Statistics Canada. 1974. *Canada Yearbook*.

RARE, THREATENED and ENDANGERED MAMMALS MAP 12

RARE, THREATENED and ENDANGERED SPECIES, as defined by the Committee on the Status of Endangered Wildlife in Canada (1978) includes:

Rare—Black-tailed Prairie Dog

Endangered—Vancouver Island Marmot, Sea Otter, Eastern Cougar, Wood Bison

Extirpated—Swift Fox, Black-footed Ferret

 Historical Range

 Present Range

Wood Bison

Vancouver Island Marmot

Northern Kit Fox

Sea Otter

Fisher

Black-footed Ferret

Black-tailed Prairie Dog

Eastern Cougar

MAP 13

Canadian Wildlife Service. Photo by R.D. Muir

NED
RDS

SPECIES
us of Endangered

Peregrine

Falcon—subspecies

pecies *anatum*,
Whooping Crane,

assification
Burrowing Owl

ge

Burrowing Owl

Greater Prairie Chicken

Greater Sandhill Crane

Caspian Tern

Piping Plover

Kirtlands Warbler

Eskimo Curlew

Whooping Crane

RARE, THREA
and
ENDANGERED

RARE, THREATENED and ENDAN
as determined by the committee on
Wildlife in Canada (1978) includes:

Rare—Trumpeter Swan, Caspia
Falcon—subspecies *pe*

Threatened—White Pelican, Pe
tundrius, Piping P

Endangered—Peregrine Falcon
Greater Prairie C
Eskimo Curlow

In addition, species not yet included
are Gyrfalcon, Double-crested Corm
and Greater Sandhill Crane.

 Historica

 Present

Peregrine Falcon

Gyrfalcon

Trumpeter Swan

White Pelican

Double-crested Cor

135

Acknowledgements

The author would like to acknowledge the assistance and advice received from the many individuals associated with the provincial, federal, and territorial wildlife branches. Specifically, the compilation of the Wildlife Protected Lands Inventory (see Appendix III) is the result of the cooperation of all these wildlife personnel.

Also, discussions with the headquarters staff of the Canadian Wildlife Service, including Dr. N. Novakowski, Dr. G. Cooch, Mr. P.B. Dean, and Mr. T.J.F. Lash, and their counterparts in the regions, aided in the preparation of this chapter.

Bibliography

Banfield, A.W.F. 1974. The Mammals of Canada. University of Toronto Press. Toronto.

Barto, W.P. 1974. The Agricultural, Forestry, Recreational and Wildlife Opportunity Cost of Pipelines, Hydro Lines and Highways. The Natural Resource Institute, University of Manitoba. Winnipeg.

Bellrose, F.C. 1976. Ducks, Geese and Swans of North America. Stackpole Books. Harrisburg.

Bird, J.B. 1967. The Physiography of Arctic Canada. The Johns Hopkins Press. Baltimore.

Black, J.D. 1968. The Management and Conservation of Biological Resources. F.A. Davis Company. Philadelphia.

Blood, D.A. 1977. Birds and Marine Animals – The Beaufort Sea and the Search for Oil. Department of Fisheries and the Environment. Ottawa.

Boyd, H., and Finney, G.H. eds. 1978. Migratory Game Bird Hunters and Hunting in Canada. Report Series No. 43. Canadian Wildlife Service, Fisheries and Environment Canada. Ottawa.

British Columbia. 1976. Ecological Reserves in British Columbia. Department of Environment. Victoria.

Brown, R.G.B. 1974. Bird Damage to Fruit Crops in the Niagara Peninsula. Report Series No. 27. Canadian Wildlife Service, Environment Canada. Ottawa.

_____, et al. 1975. Atlas of Eastern Canadian Seabirds. Canadian Wildlife Service, Environment Canada. Ottawa.

Bryan, R.K. 1973. Much is Taken, Much Remains; Canadian Issues in Environmental Conservation. Duxbury Press. North Scituate.

Cameron, R.L. 1972. Fish and Wildlife – The Recreational Resource. Department of Recreation and Conservation, Government of British Columbia. Victoria.

Canada Gazette. 1974. "Migratory Bird Sanctuary Regulations". Canada Gazette. Part II, Vol. 108, No. 18. Queen's Printer. Ottawa.

_____. 1977. "Wildlife Area Regulations". Canada Gazette. Part II, Vol. 111, No. 21. Queen's Printer. Ottawa.

Canada Land Data Systems. 1977. Lands Directorate, Environment Canada. Miscellaneous Data. Ottawa.

Canada Land Inventory. Land Capability for Wildlife – Ungulates. Maps at 1:1,000,000. Saskatchewan (1974), Alberta (1976), British Columbia – North (1976), British Columbia – South (1976), Manitoba (1976), Ontario (1976), Québec (1976), Atlantic Provinces (1977). Lands Directorate, Environment Canada. Ottawa.

_____. Land Capability for Wildlife – Waterfowl. Maps at 1:1,000,000. Alberta (1974), Manitoba (1974), British Columbia – South (1975), Atlantic Provinces (1976), British Columbia – North (1976), Québec (1976), Ontario (1977). Lands Directorate, Environment Canada. Ottawa.

Canadian Environment Advisory Council. 1978. Annual Review 1976. Minister of Supply and Services Canada. Ottawa.

Canadian Trappers Federation. 1978. Personal communication. Barrie.

Canadian Wildlife Federation. 1970. Endangered Wildlife in Canada. Canadian Wildlife Federation. Ottawa.

Canadian Wildlife Service. 1969. Saskatoon Wetlands Seminar. Department of Indian Affairs and Northern Development. Ottawa.

_____. 1972. Arctic Ecology Map Series. Critical Wildlife Areas. Descriptive Report. Canadian Wildlife Service, Environment Canada. Ottawa.

_____. 1973. Pesticides and Wildlife. Canadian Wildlife Service, Environment Canada. Ottawa.

Carreiro, J.F., and Tessier, G.D. 1976. Descriptions of Sensitive Areas for Migratory Birds in Newfoundland, The Maritimes, Québec and Ontario. Canadian Wildlife Service, Environment Canada. Ottawa.

Chambers, A.D. 1974. Purcell Range Study: Integrated Resource Management for British Columbia's Purcell Mountains. Prepared by Resource Science Centre, University of British Columbia. Vancouver.

_____. 1976. "An Approach to Multiple Use Problems." Ecological Bulletin. Vol. 21. Stockholm.

Chapman, L.O., and Brown, D.M. 1966. The Climates of Canada for Agriculture. Canada Land Inventory Report No. 3. ARDA. Department of Forestry and Rural Development. Queen's Printer. Ottawa.

Clawson, M., and Knetch, J. 1966. Economics of Outdoor Recreation. Johns Hopkins Press. Baltimore.

Clayton, J.S., et al. 1977. Soils of Canada. Vol. 1. Research Branch, Canada Department of Agriculture. Supply and Services Canada. Ottawa.

Cocheba, D.J., and Langford, W.A. 1978. The Wildlife Valuation Problem: A Critical Review of Economic Approaches. Occasional Paper No. 37. Canadian Wildlife Service, Fisheries and Environment Canada. Ottawa.

Colpitts, L.K. 1974. The Cost and Feasibility of Wildlife Habitat Maintenance on Private Lands in the Minnedosa Pothole Country. The Natural Resource Institute, University of Manitoba. Winnipeg.

Cooch, G. 1978. Canadian Wildlife Service, Environment Canada. Personal communication. Ottawa.

Dagg, A.I. 1974. Canadian Wildlife and Man. McClelland and Stewart. Toronto.

Dean, P.B. 1975. Land Use for Wildlife (draft). A Discussion Draft prepared for the Interdepartmental Committee on National Land Use Policy, by Co-ordinator, Wildlife and Land Use Planning, Canadian Wildlife Service, Fisheries and Environment Canada. Ottawa.

_____. 1976. "Wildlife Needs and Concerns in Urban Areas." Ecological (Biophysical) Land Classification in Urban Areas. Ecological Land Classification Series No. 3. Compiled and edited by E.B. Wiken and G.R. Ironside from Proceedings of a Workshop, Canada Committee on Ecological (Biophysical) Land Classification held November 23-24, 1976 in Toronto. Lands Directorate, Fisheries and Environment Canada. Ottawa.

Deems, E.F., and Pursley, D. 1978. North American Furbearers, Their Management, Research and Harvest Status in 1976. International Association of Fish and Wildlife Agencies in co-operation with the Maryland Department of Natural Resource–Wildlife Administration. College Park.

Department of Transport. 1967. Atlas of Climatic Maps, Series 1-10. Meteorological Branch. Toronto.

Dominion Bureau of Statistics. 1957. Fur Production Season 1955-56. Memorandum. Ottawa.

_____. 1967. Fur Production Season 1965-66. Catalogue 23-207. Annual. Ottawa.

Environment Canada. 1975. Canada Water Year Book. Inland Waters Directorate. Ottawa.

_____. 1978. The Canada Land Inventory: Objectives, Scope and Organization. Canada Land Inventory Report No. 1 (reprinted). Lands Directorate. Ottawa.

Erskine, A.J. 1977. Birds in Boreal Canada. Report Series No. 41. Canadian Wildlife Service, Fisheries and Environment Canada. Ottawa.

_____. 1978. The First Ten Years of the Co-operative Breeding Bird Survey in Canada. Report Series No. 42. Canadian Wildlife Service, Fisheries and Environment Canada. Ottawa.

Federal–Provincial Parks Conference. 1976. Parks Classification System, National and Provincial Parks. Conference held October 18-22, 1976 in Regina, Saskatchewan. Parks Canada, Indian and Northern Affairs. Ottawa.

Federal–Provincial Wildlife Conference. 1974. Transactions. Conference held June 25-27, 1974 in Victoria, British Columbia. Canadian Wildlife Service, Environment Canada. Ottawa.

_____. 1975. Transactions. Conference held July 1-3, 1975 in St. John's, Newfoundland. Canadian Wildlife Service, Environment Canada. Ottawa.

_____. 1976. Transactions. Conference held July 6-8, 1976 in Fredericton, New Brunswick. Canadian Wildlife Service, Environment Canada. Ottawa.

_____. 1977. Transactions. Conference held July 5-7, 1977 in Winnipeg, Manitoba. Canadian Wildlife Service, Fisheries and Environment Canada. Ottawa.

_____. 1978. Transactions. Conference held June 27-30, 1978 in Québec, Québec. Canadian Wildlife Service, Environment Canada. Ottawa.

Fish and Wildlife Division. (no date) Wildlife and the Island. Department of the Environment, Province of Prince Edward Island. Charlottetown.

Foster, J. 1978. Working for Wildlife, The Beginning of Preservation in Canada. University of Toronto Press. Toronto.

Fox, I.K., and Nowlan, J.P. 1978. The Management of Estuarine Resources in Canada. Report No. 6. Canadian Environment Advisory Council. Minister of Supply and Services. Ottawa.

Fyfe, R. 1976. "Bringing Back the Peregrine Falcon." Nature Canada. Vol. 5, No. 2. June 1976. Canadian Nature Federation. Ottawa.

Gierman, D.M. 1977. Rural to Urban Land Conversion. Occasional Paper No. 16. Lands Directorate, Fisheries and Environment Canada. Ottawa.

Gilbertson, M., and Reynolds, L. 1974. A Summary of DDE and PCB Determinations in Canadian Birds 1969 to 1972. Occasional Paper No. 19. Canadian Wildlife Service, Environment Canada. Ottawa.

Godfrey, W.E. 1966. The Birds of Canada. Queen's Printer. Ottawa.

Hammack, J., and Brown, G.M., Jr. 1974. Waterfowl and Wetlands: Towards Bioeconomic Analysis. Resources for the Future, Inc. Johns Hopkins University Press. Baltimore.

Hare, F.K., and Thomas M.K. 1974. Climate Canada. Wiley Publishers of Canada Limited. Toronto.

Hawley, A., and Peden, D.G. 1977. "Canada's Buffalo Renaissance." Canadian Geographical Journal. Vol. 95, No. 2. October/November 1977. Royal Canadian Geographical Society. Ottawa.

Holesgrove, Rod. 1976. Definition of Critical Environmental Areas. Report prepared for Organization for Economic Co-operation and Development. Paris.

Hunt, C. 1976. "The Development and Decline of Northern Conservation Reserves in the Arctic." Contact. Vol. 8, No. 4. November 1976. Journal of Urban and Environmental Affairs, Faculty of Environmental Studies, University of Waterloo. Waterloo.

Industry, Trade and Commerce. 1978. Report on the Status of Canadian Wildlife Used by the Fur Industry, Revised Edition (1977). Industry, Trade and Commerce. Ottawa.

Johnson, B.C. 1976. Second Marsh Oshawa, Biological and Social Values. Canadian Wildlife Service, Environment Canada. Ottawa.

Keith, R.F., and Wright, J.B. 1978. Northern Transitions, Volume II. Proceedings from Second National Workshop on People, Resources and the Environment North of 60°. Canadian Arctic Resources Committee. Edmonton.

Kelsall, J.P., Telfer, E.S., and Wright T.D. 1977. The Effects of Fire on the Ecology of the Boreal Forest with Particular Reference to the Canadian North: a Review and Selected Bibliography. Occasional Paper No. 32. Canadian Wildlife Service, Fisheries and Environment Canada. Ottawa.

Kiel, W.J., Jr., et al. 1972. Waterfowl Habitat Trends in the Aspen Parkland of Manitoba. Report Series No. 18. Canadian Wildlife Service, Environment Canada. Ottawa.

Krajina, V.J., et al. 1974. Ecological Reserves in British Columbia. Canadian Committee for the International Biological Programme, Conservation of Terrestrial Communities Subcommittee (CCIBP-CT) Region 1: British Columbia. Vancouver.

Kuyt, E. 1972. Food Habits of Wolves on Barren Ground Caribou Range. Report Series No. 21. Canadian Wildlife Service, Environment Canada. Ottawa.

_____. 1976. "Whooping Cranes: The Long Road Back." Nature Canada. Vol. 5, No. 2. June 1976. Canadian Nature Federation. Ottawa.

LaRoi, G.H., and Babb, T.A. eds. Canadian National Directory of IBP Areas. 1968-1974. CCIBP/CT, A Contribution of the Conservation of Terrestrial Biological Communities Subcommittee, Canadian Committee for the International Biological Programme. University of Alberta Printing Services. Edmonton.

Maini, J.S., and Carlisle, A. eds. 1974. Conservation in Canada: A Conspectus. Canadian Forestry Service, Environment Canada. Ottawa.

McKeating, G.B., ed. 1974. Nature and Urban Man. Proceedings from Canadian Nature Federation Conference held August 21-27, 1974 at University of Western Ontario, London, Ontario. Canadian Nature Federation. Ottawa.

McLaren, I.A., and Peterson, E.B. 1975. "Ecological Reserves in Canada: The Work of IBP-CT." Nature Canada. Vol. 4, No. 2. April-June 1976. Canadian Nature Federation. Ottawa.

McLean, A. 1976. "Protection of Vegetation in Ecological Reserves in Canada." The Canadian Field-Naturalist. Vol. 90, No. 2. April-June 1976. The Ottawa Field Naturalists' Club. Ottawa.

Miller, F.L., et al. 1977. Peary Caribou and Muskoxen on Western Queen Elizabeth Islands, Northwest Territories, 1972-74. Report Series No. 40. Canadian Wildlife Service, Fisheries and Environment Canada. Ottawa.

Miller, J.B. 1976. Wetland Classification in Western Canada, A Guide to Marshes and Shallow Open Water Wetlands in the Grasslands and Parklands of the Prairie Provinces. Report Series No. 37. Canadian Wildlife Service, Environment Canada. Ottawa.

Milton Freedman Research Limited. 1976. Innuit Land Use and Occupancy Project, Volume Three: Land Use Atlas. Prepared for Department of Indian and Northern Affairs. Ottawa.

Ministère du Tourisme, de la Chasse et de la Pêche. 1975. Workshop on Remote Sensing of Wildlife. Service de la Recherche Biologique, Gouvernement du Québec. Québec.

Mosquin, T., and MacDougall, S. eds. 1976. Canadian Conservation Directory 1975/1976. Canadian Nature Federation. Ottawa.

_____, and Suchal, C. eds. 1976. Canada's Threatened Species and Habitats. Proceedings of the Symposium on Canada's Threatened Species and Habitats held in Ottawa, May 20-24, 1976. Canadian Nature Federation. Ottawa.

Myers, N. 1978. "Disappearing Legacy, The Earth's Vanishing Genetic Heritage." Nature Canada. Vol. 7, No. 4. October-December 1978. Canadian Nature Federation. Ottawa.

Nelson, J.G. 1976. "The Future Role of Conservation Reserves in the Arctic." Contact. Vol. 8, No. 4. November 1976. Journal of Urban and Environmental Affairs, Faculty of Environmental Studies, University of Waterloo. Waterloo.

Nettleship, D.N., and Smith, P.A. eds. 1975. Ecological Sites in Northern Canada. Canadian Committee for the International Biological Programme, Conservation Terrestrial-Panel 9. Ottawa.

Northwest Territories. 1978. Important Areas of Ungulate Distribution. Manuscript maps at a scale of 1:1,000,000. Fish and Wildlife Service. Yellowknife.

Oetting, R.B. 1973. Manitoba's Wildlife Heritage: A Guide for Landowners. Province of Manitoba, Department of Mines, Resources and Environmental Management. Winnipeg.

Parks Canada. 1976. Natural Areas of Canadian Significance. A Preliminary Study. Parks System Planning Division, National Parks Branch, Indian and Northern Affairs. Ottawa.

Pearce, P.S., et al. 1976. Impact on Forest Birds of the 1975 Spruce Budworm Spray Operation in New Brunswick. Progress Notes No. 62. March 1976. Canadian Wildlife Service, Environment Canada. Ottawa.

Perret, N.G. 1969. Land Capability Classification for Wildlife. The Canada Land Inventory Report No. 7. Lands Directorate, Environment Canada. Ottawa.

Peterson, E.B. 1975. Canada's Progress Towards a Nationally Representative System of Ecological Reserves. Paper presented at the Symposium on Ecological Reserves, 13th Pacific Science Congress, held August 1975 in Vancouver, British Columbia. Vancouver.

Peterson, R.L. 1966. The Mammals of Eastern Canada. Oxford University Press. Toronto.

Pimlott, D.H., Kerswill, C.J., and Bider, J.R. 1971. Scientific Activities in Fisheries and Wildlife Resources. Report 15. Background Study for the Science Council of Canada. Ottawa.

Policy, Planning and Research Branch. 1976. Designated Land Areas in Saskatchewan. Saskatchewan, Department of the Environment. Regina.

Rakowski, P., et al. 1977. Present Status of Waterfowl Habitat in the Prime Duck Production Area of Manitoba. Unpublished report. Canadian Wildlife Service, Environment Canada. Winnipeg.

Report of the Mackenzie Valley Pipeline Inquiry. 1977. Mr. Justice Thomas R. Berger, Chairman. Northern Frontier Northern Homeland. Vol. I and II. Supply and Services Canada. Ottawa.

Rogers, R.E. 1976. Biocides and Birds: A Survey of the Effects of Biocides on Birds. A Staff Report, Alberta Environment Conservation Authority. Edmonton.

Rowe, J.S. 1972. Forest Regions of Canada. Publication No. 1300. Canadian Forestry Service, Department of the Environment. Ottawa

Rump, P.C., and Harper, K. 1977. Land Use in Saskatchewan. Policy, Planning and Research Branch, Saskatchewan Department of the Environment. Regina.

Saskatchewan-Nelson Basin Board. 1972. Environmental Considerations. Appendix 7. Study on Water Supply for the Saskatchewan-Nelson Basin, sponsored by Canada, Alberta, Saskatchewan, and Manitoba. Saskatoon.

Shelford, V.E. 1963. The Ecology of North America. University of Illinois Press. Urbana.

Smith, L.C. 1975. "Urban Wildlife – Is It Wanted and Needed." The Canadian Field–Naturalist. Vol. 89, No. 4. October-December 1975. The Ottawa Field-Naturalists' Club. Ottawa.

Smithsonian Institution, Center for Natural Areas and Office of International and Environmental Programs. 1974. Planning Considerations for Statewide Inventories of Critical Environmental Areas: A Reference Guide. Prepared for U.S. Army Corps of Engineers. Smithsonian Institution. Washington.

Sorenson, M.F. 1978. Observations of Mallards in the Parkland of Alberta. Occasional Paper No. 36. Canadian Wildlife Service, Fisheries and Environment Canada. Ottawa.

Statistics Canada. 1972a. Fur Production, Season 1970-71. Catalogue 23-207. Annual. Ottawa.

_____. 1972b. Travel, Tourism and Outdoor Recreation: A Statistical Digest 1972. Catalogue 66-202. Annual. Ottawa.

_____. 1974. Canada Year Book 1974. Published by authority of the Minister of Industry, Trade and Commerce. Information Canada. Ottawa.

_____. 1976. Report on Fur Farms 1975. Catalogue 23-208. Annual. Ottawa.

_____. 1977a. Fur Production, Season 1975-76. Catalogue 23-207. Annual. Ottawa.

_____. 1977b. Perspective Canada II, A Compendium of Social Statistics. Published under the authority of the Minister of Industry, Trade and Commerce. Ottawa.

_____. 1978. Travel, Tourism and Outdoor Recreation: A Statistical Digest 1975 and 1976. Catalogue 66-202. Annual. Ottawa.

Stelfox, J.G. 1976. Range Ecology of Rocky Mountain Bighorn Sheep in Canadian National Parks. Report Series No. 39. Canadian Wildlife Service, Fisheries and Environment Canada. Ottawa.

Stewart, D. 1974. Canadian Endangered Species. Gage Publishing Limited. Toronto.

Sugden, L.G. 1976. Waterfowl Damage to Canadian Grain: Current Problems and Research Needs. Occasional Paper No. 24. Canadian Wildlife Service, Environment Canada. Ottawa.

_____. 1978. Canvasback Habitat Use and Production in Saskatchewan Parklands. Occasional Paper No. 34. Canadian Wildlife Service, Fisheries and Environment Canada. Ottawa.

Tarnocai, C. 1978. "Distribution of Soils in Northern Canada and Parameters Affecting Their Utilization." Symposium Session Papers. Vol. 3. Proceedings of the 11th International Congress of Soil Science held June 19-27, 1978, in Edmonton, Alberta.

Thomas, Morley K. 1953. Climatological Atlas of Canada. A joint publication of the Division of Building Research, National Research Council and the Meteorological Division, Department of Transport. Ottawa.

Thomasson, R.D. (no date) Ontario Land Inventory Methodology Series – Wildlife. Ministry of Natural Resources. Toronto.

Thompson, A.R. Research Ltd. 1974. Land, Law and Wildlife: A Legal Study on Landowner – Wildlife Relationships. (5 Parts) Manuscript Report. Canadian Wildlife Service, Environment Canada. Ottawa.

Van Zyll de Jong, C.G., and Ouellet, W. 1978. Museum of Natural Science. Personal communication. Ottawa.

Vermeer, K. 1970. "Distribution and Size of White Pelicans, *Pelecanus erythrorhynchos*, in Canada." Canadian Journal of Zoology. Vol. 48. 1970. National Research Council of Canada. Ottawa.

_____. 1973. "Great Blue Heron and Double-crested Cormorant Colonies in the Prairie Provinces." The Canadian Field-Naturalist. Vol. 87, No. 4. October-December, 1973. The Ottawa Field-Naturalists' Club. Ottawa.

_____, and Reynolds, L.M. 1970. "Organochlorine Residues in Aquatic Birds, in The Canadian Prairie Provinces." The Canadian Field-Naturalist. Vol. 84. 1970. The Ottawa Field-Naturalists' Club. Ottawa.

_____, and Vermeer, R. 1975. "Oil Threat to Birds on the Canadian West Coast." The Canadian Field-Naturalist. Vol. 89. 1975. The Ottawa Field-Naturalists' Club. Ottawa.

Whitman, W.R. 1976. Impoundments for Waterfowl. Occasional Paper No. 22. Canadian Wildlife Service, Environment Canada. Ottawa.

Appendix I

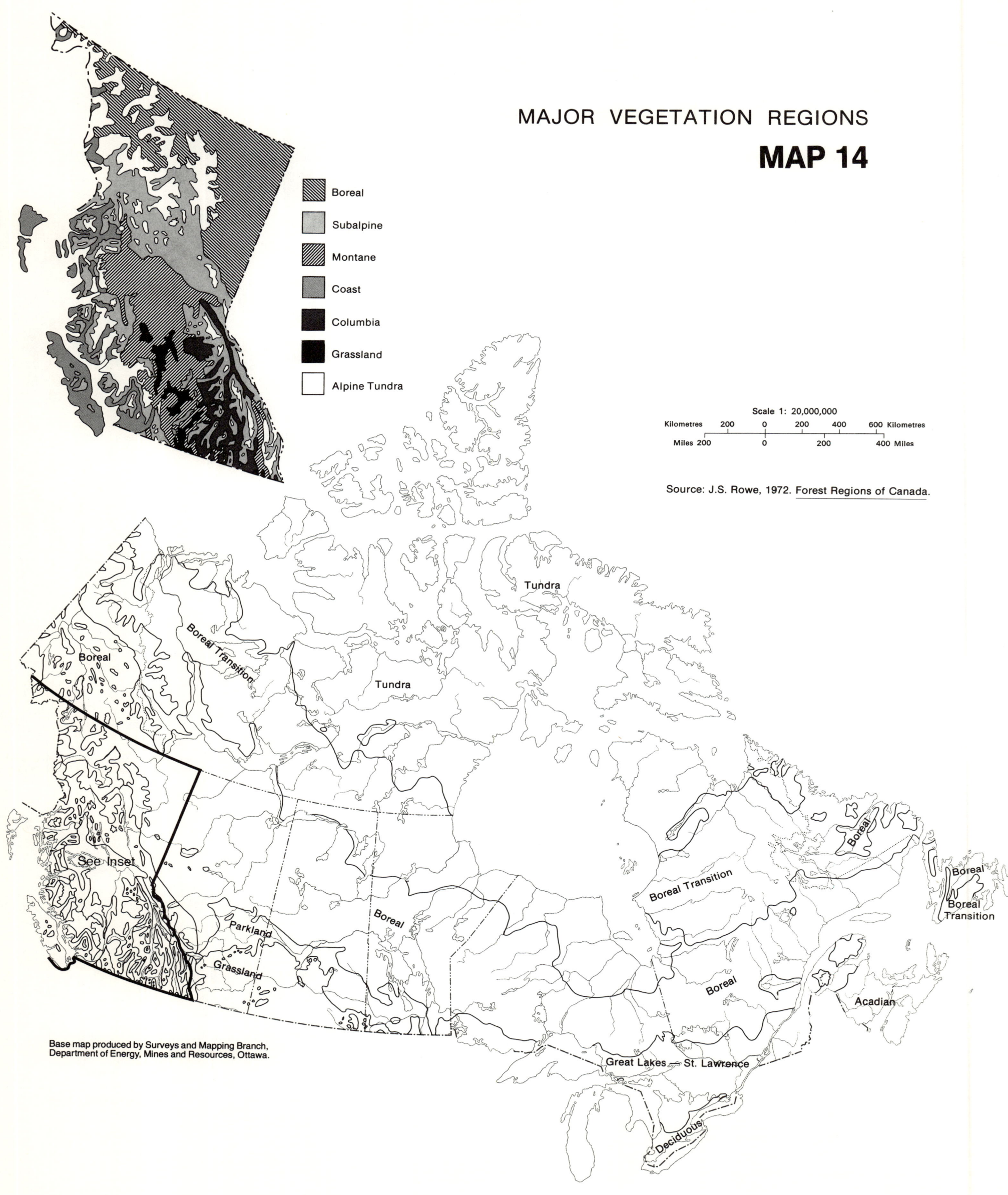

MAJOR PHYSIOGRAPHIC REGIONS

MAP 15

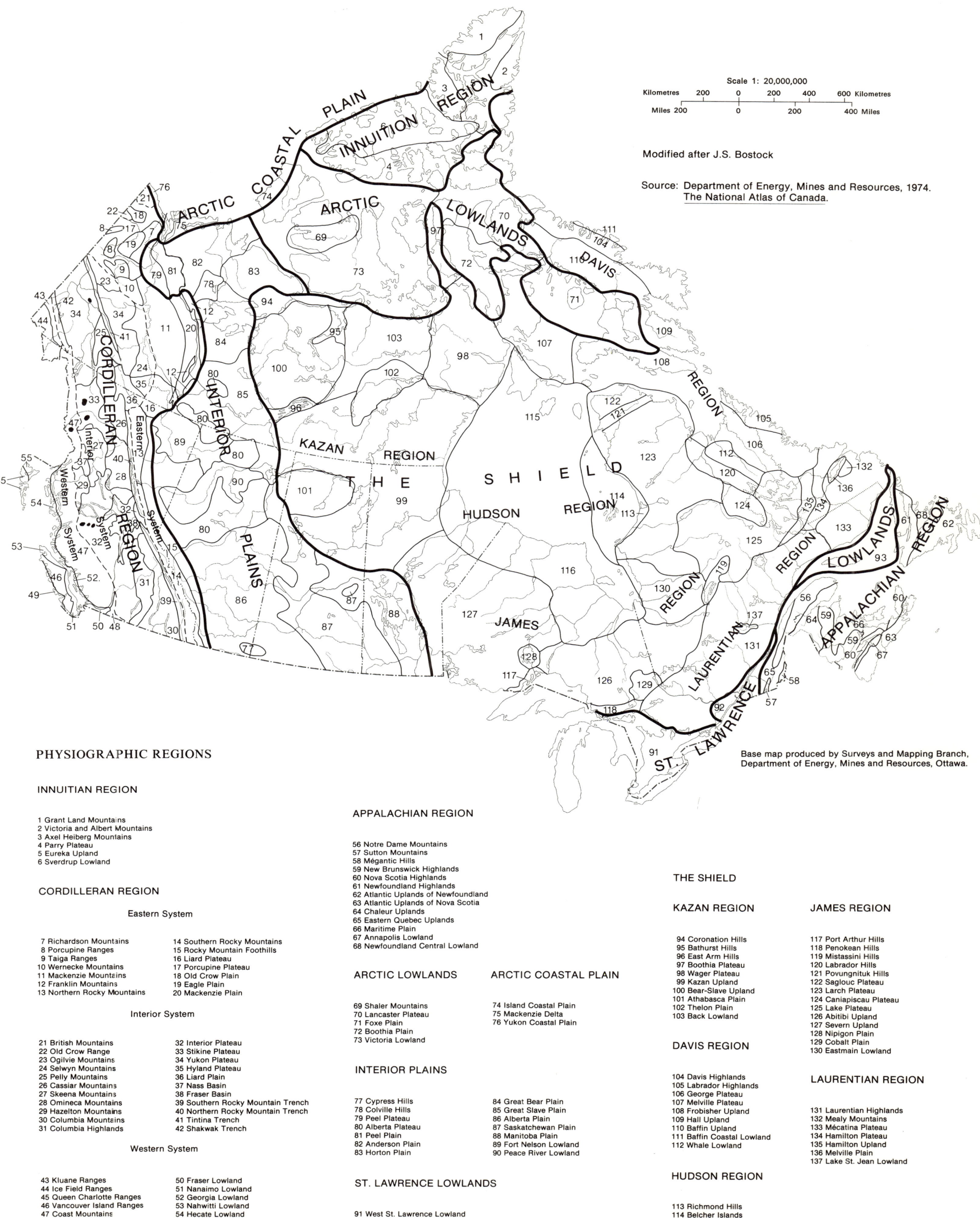

Modified after J.S. Bostock

Source: Department of Energy, Mines and Resources, 1974. The National Atlas of Canada.

Base map produced by Surveys and Mapping Branch, Department of Energy, Mines and Resources, Ottawa.

PHYSIOGRAPHIC REGIONS

INNUITIAN REGION

1 Grant Land Mountains
2 Victoria and Albert Mountains
3 Axel Heiberg Mountains
4 Parry Plateau
5 Eureka Upland
6 Sverdrup Lowland

CORDILLERAN REGION

Eastern System

7 Richardson Mountains
8 Porcupine Ranges
9 Taiga Ranges
10 Wernecke Mountains
11 Mackenzie Mountains
12 Franklin Mountains
13 Northern Rocky Mountains
14 Southern Rocky Mountains
15 Rocky Mountain Foothills
16 Liard Plateau
17 Porcupine Plateau
18 Old Crow Plain
19 Eagle Plain
20 Mackenzie Plain

Interior System

21 British Mountains
22 Old Crow Range
23 Ogilvie Mountains
24 Selwyn Mountains
25 Pelly Mountains
26 Cassiar Mountains
27 Skeena Mountains
28 Omineca Mountains
29 Hazelton Mountains
30 Columbia Mountains
31 Columbia Highlands
32 Interior Plateau
33 Stikine Plateau
34 Yukon Plateau
35 Hyland Plateau
36 Liard Plain
37 Nass Basin
38 Fraser Basin
39 Southern Rocky Mountain Trench
40 Northern Rocky Mountain Trench
41 Tintina Trench
42 Shakwak Trench

Western System

43 Kluane Ranges
44 Ice Field Ranges
45 Queen Charlotte Ranges
46 Vancouver Island Ranges
47 Coast Mountains
48 Cascade Mountains
49 Estevan Coastal Plain
50 Fraser Lowland
51 Nanaimo Lowland
52 Georgia Lowland
53 Nahwitti Lowland
54 Hecate Lowland
55 Queen Charlotte Lowland

APPALACHIAN REGION

56 Notre Dame Mountains
57 Sutton Mountains
58 Mégantic Hills
59 New Brunswick Highlands
60 Nova Scotia Highlands
61 Newfoundland Highlands
62 Atlantic Uplands of Newfoundland
63 Atlantic Uplands of Nova Scotia
64 Chaleur Uplands
65 Eastern Quebec Uplands
66 Maritime Plain
67 Annapolis Lowland
68 Newfoundland Central Lowland

ARCTIC LOWLANDS

69 Shaler Mountains
70 Lancaster Plateau
71 Foxe Plain
72 Boothia Plain
73 Victoria Lowland

INTERIOR PLAINS

77 Cypress Hills
78 Colville Hills
79 Peel Plateau
80 Alberta Plateau
81 Peel Plain
82 Anderson Plain
83 Horton Plain
84 Great Bear Plain
85 Great Slave Plain
86 Alberta Plain
87 Saskatchewan Plain
88 Manitoba Plain
89 Fort Nelson Lowland
90 Peace River Lowland

ST. LAWRENCE LOWLANDS

91 West St. Lawrence Lowland
92 Central St. Lawrence Lowland
93 East St. Lawrence Lowland

ARCTIC COASTAL PLAIN

74 Island Coastal Plain
75 Mackenzie Delta
76 Yukon Coastal Plain

THE SHIELD

KAZAN REGION

94 Coronation Hills
95 Bathurst Hills
96 East Arm Hills
97 Boothia Plateau
98 Wager Plateau
99 Kazan Upland
100 Bear-Slave Upland
101 Athabasca Plain
102 Thelon Plain
103 Back Lowland

DAVIS REGION

104 Davis Highlands
105 Labrador Highlands
106 George Plateau
107 Melville Plateau
108 Frobisher Upland
109 Hall Upland
110 Baffin Upland
111 Baffin Coastal Lowland
112 Whale Lowland

HUDSON REGION

113 Richmond Hills
114 Belcher Islands
115 Southampton Plain
116 Hudson Bay Lowlands

JAMES REGION

117 Port Arthur Hills
118 Penokean Hills
119 Mistassini Hills
120 Labrador Hills
121 Povungnituk Hills
122 Saglouc Plateau
123 Larch Plateau
124 Caniapiscau Plateau
125 Lake Plateau
126 Abitibi Upland
127 Severn Upland
128 Nipigon Plain
129 Cobalt Plain
130 Eastmain Lowland

LAURENTIAN REGION

131 Laurentian Highlands
132 Mealy Mountains
133 Mécatina Plateau
134 Hamilton Plateau
135 Hamilton Upland
136 Melville Plain
137 Lake St. Jean Lowland

139

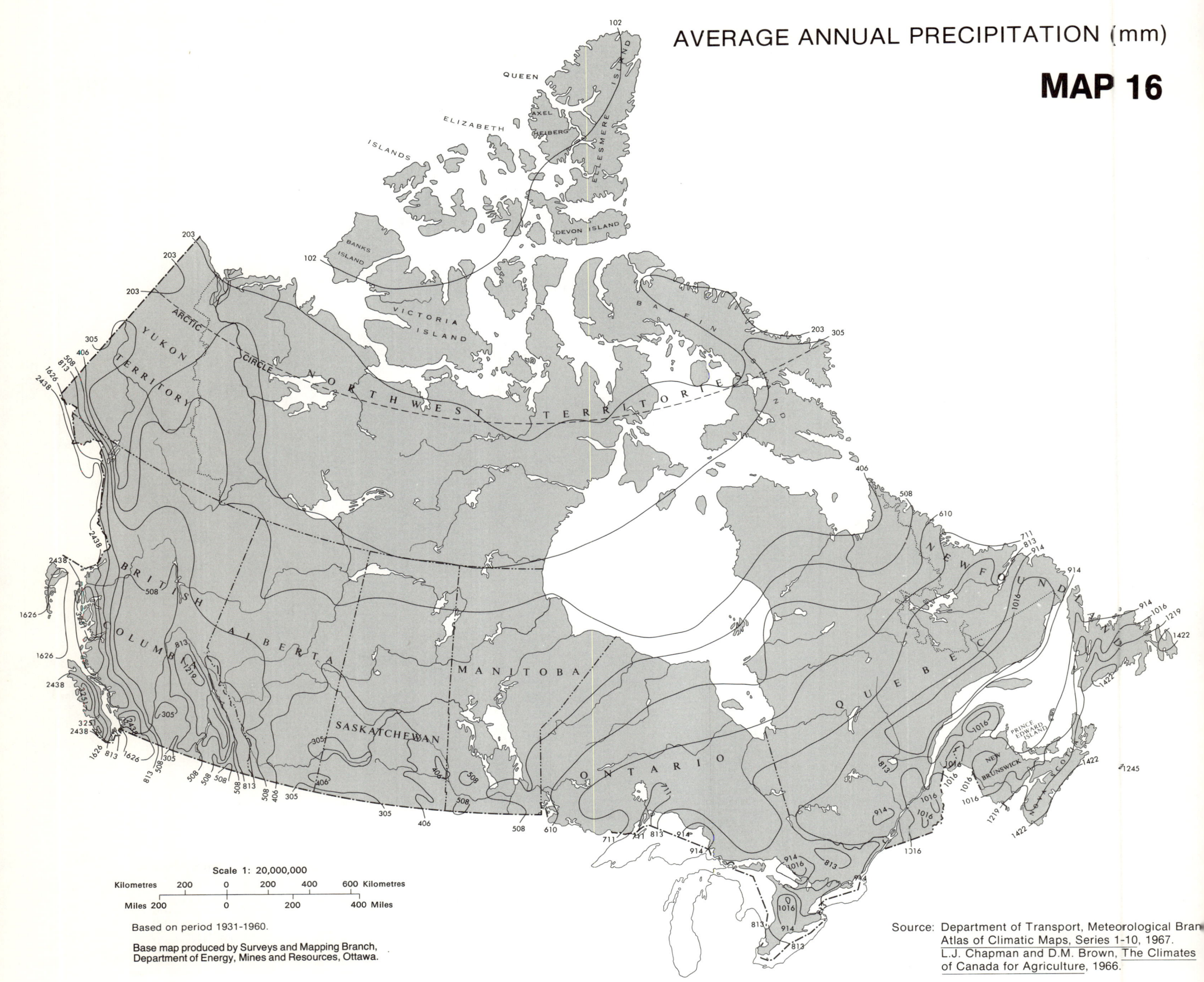

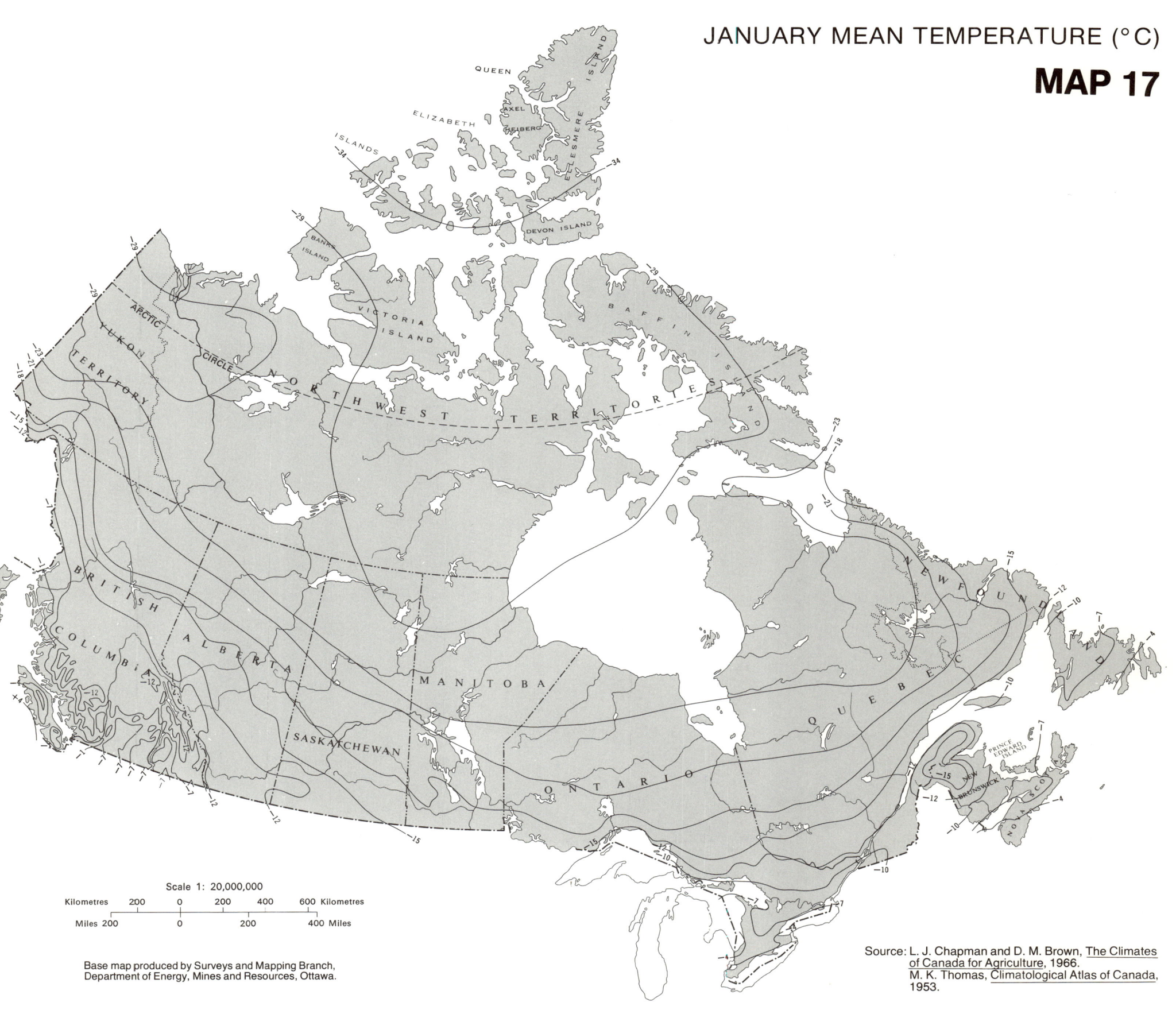

JANUARY MEAN TEMPERATURE (°C)
MAP 17

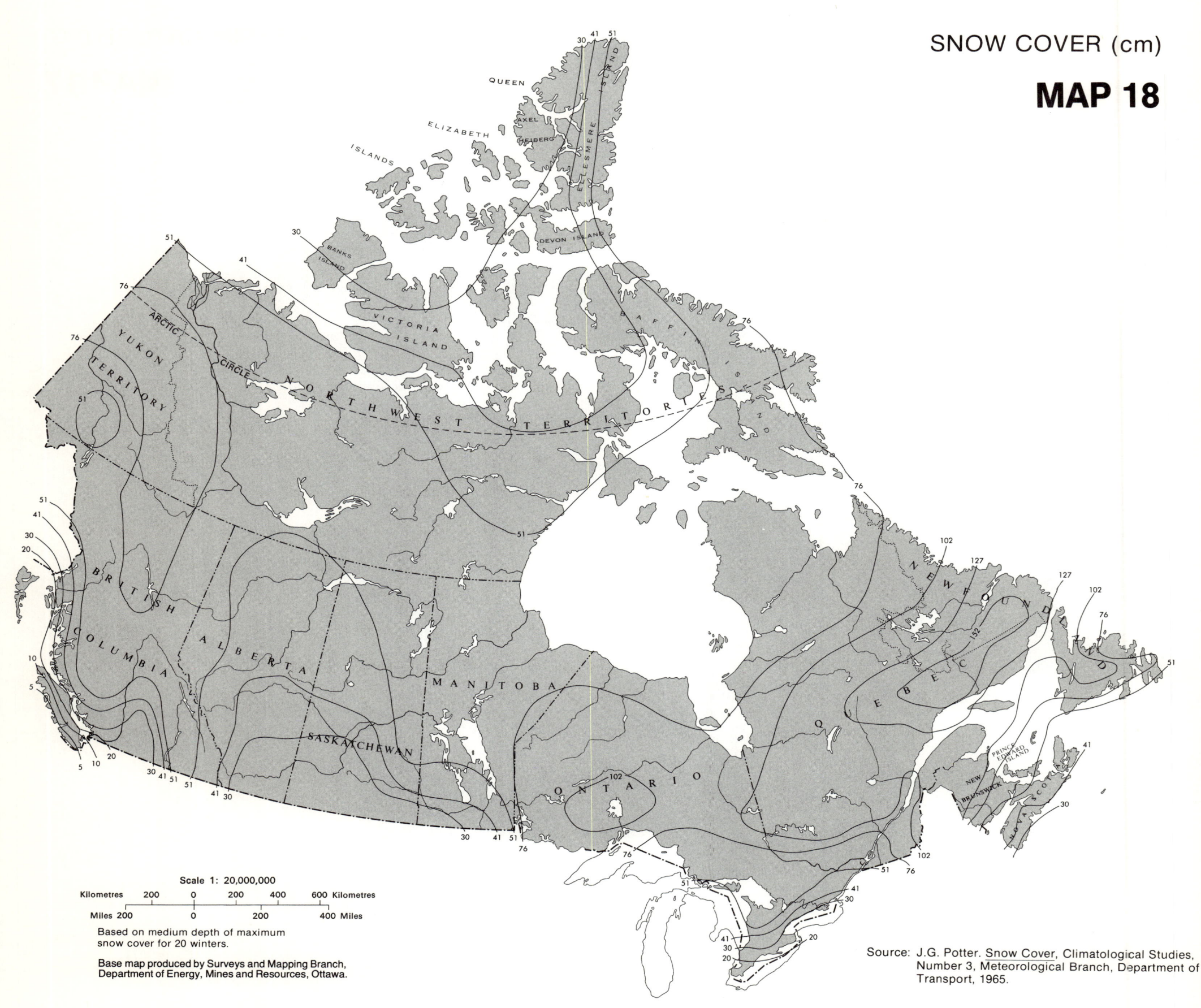

SNOW COVER (cm)
MAP 18

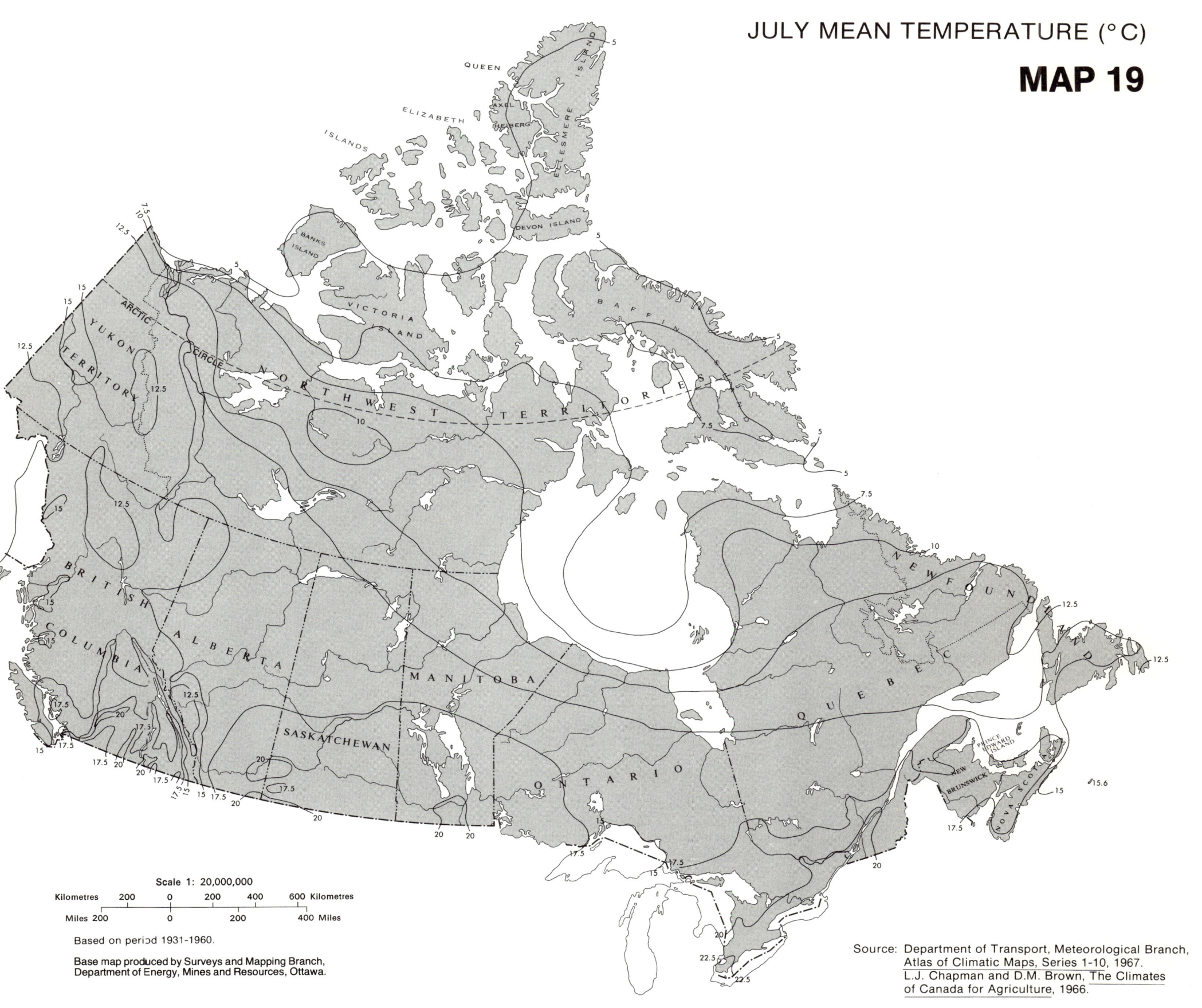

JULY MEAN TEMPERATURE (°C)
MAP 19

Appendix II
CLI – Limitations Affecting the Classification of Ungulates and Waterfowl

Ungulates

In most cases the limitations do not have a direct effect on the animals but they affect the ability of the land to produce suitable food and cover plants. For convenience the subclasses are placed in two main groups: those relating to climate and those relating to inherent characteristics of the land.

Climate. The following subclasses are used to denote significant climatic factors that may affect either the animals or the ability of the land to produce suitable food and cover.

Aridity. The limitation is primarily a climatic factor which restricts the development and growth of suitable food and cover plants. It is closely associated with moisture-holding capacity of soils but is used to denote those areas of minimal precipitation where rainfall is not available for plant growth due to rapid runoff. It is also used to denote droughty areas where very low precipitation and high rate of evaporation and transpiration retard the growth of browse species.

Climate. The limitation is a combination of climatic factors, such as excessive cold or moisture, which reduce the quantity, quality, or availability of food and cover or which affect the production and survival of ungulates. It is used primarily to denote land units with extreme weather conditions, very short growing season or areas where very high rainfall reduces the capability for ungulates.

Snow Depth. The limitation is prolonged periods of snow conditions which reduce the mobility of ungulates and/or the availability of food plants. It is difficult to define the limitation or provide uniform standards for use across Canada because it may be due to one or more of the following factors: depth, texture, size of snow granules, compressibility, density, and uniformity of the snow. Experience and knowledge of snow conditions on the winter ranges will assist the surveyor in arriving at a decision on whether or not snow is a limiting factor to the production or survival of ungulates.

Exposure or Aspect. The limitations are special climatic factors, such as exposure to prevailing winter winds or hot, dry summer winds, that adversely affect the animals and their habitat. In most areas this is a minor limitation but it can be a major limitation to the production of food and cover plants in some coastal areas that are exposed to continuous strong gales.

Land. The following subclasses are used to denote significant characteristics of the land that limit its usefulness for producing suitable food and cover. Some subclasses may also have a slight adverse effect on the animals.

Fertility. The limitation is due to a lack of available nutrients in the soil for optimum growth of food and cover plants. It is applied to units of land where the quality and quantity of cover is affected by the uniform lack of nutrients. Because ungulate production is dependent upon a variety of habitats, the associated ecotones or "edge" pockets of soils low in nutrients within a fertile soil area are not necessarily a limitation. Indicators used to assess fertility include diversity of food and cover plants and agricultural fertility ratings.

Landform. The limitation is a poor distribution or interspersion of landforms necessary for optimum ungulate habitat. It is applied to areas with a moderate amount of topographical relief but which are not irregular enough to provide the desired complex of aspect or "edge" for the ungulate species under consideration. It is applied also to areas which lack essential adjacent escape terrain, cover, or other special habitat requirements.

Inundation. The limitation is excessive water level fluctuation or tidal action that adversely affects the habitat or survival of ungulates. This subclass is used to denote large tidal areas where food and cover production is limited by tides. It is used also for areas such as river bottomlands or areas associated with some hydro-electric developments where water level fluctuations adversely affect the quantity or quality of the food and cover.

Soil Moisture. The limitation is poor soil moisture conditions, either excessive or deficient, which adversely affect the development and growth of vegetation or which limit the mobility of ungulates. In most instances the subclass is used to denote those areas where there is an excess of soil moisture due to poor internal drainage. It can be used also to denote areas of adequate precipitation with porous soils that have poor moisture-holding characteristics.

Adverse Soil Characteristics. The limitation is due to excessive salinity or alkalinity, lack of essential trace elements, or abundance of toxic elements in the soil. Although used sparingly across Canada, the limitation may be of major importance on some ungulate ranges. It is used only where it has been demonstrated that adverse soil characteristics affect the growth or development of optimum vegetation or the health and survival of ungulate species.

Soil Depth. The limitation is due to the restriction of rooting zones by bedrock or other impervious layers. It is generally used to denote large areas of shallow soils or exposed bedrock. Small areas of shallow soils or outcrops are not necessarily a limitation and in fact may enhance the capability of an ungulate range by providing a variety of habitat types and the associated ecotones.

Adverse Topography. The limitation is due to excessive steepness or flatness of the land. It is used primarily to denote areas with such extreme slopes that the development of optimum vegetation is reduced or the use of the area by ungulates is restricted. Where it is used to denote flat landscapes, it is usually associated with other limitations such as poor distribution of landforms.

Waterfowl

The following subclasses are used to denote significant factors that may affect either waterfowl or the ability of land to produce suitable habitat conditions.

Aridity. The limitation is the inherent susceptibility of the land to periodic drought, which results in low water levels or premature drying of marshes and ponds during the breeding season. There is no aridity limitation if a high proportion of the basins, which go dry in late summer, hold water through July in most years.

Free-flowing Water. The limitation is usually due to excess of swiftly-flowing water which inhibits the development of marsh habitat along a watercourse. It may also be due to a lack of flow through low-lying areas which results in habitat of poor quality. It may be due also to a lack of consistent flow in rapidly drained channels or intermittent stream courses.

Climate. The limitation is by adverse climatic factors which inhibit development of favorable habitat and restrict waterfowl production. This limitation is usually associated with high elevations in mountain areas where ponds and water bodies are ice-free for only a short period each year.

Fertility. The limitation is due to a lack of sufficient nutrients in the soil and/or water for optimum growth of vegetation essential to waterfowl production. This limitation is applied to areas such as coarse-textured sands and gravels, exposed tills, highly carbonated soils, leached grey wooded and podzolic soils, or deep peat soils. Indicators used to assess fertility include water quality measurements, abundance and diversity of aquatic vegetation, and agricultural fertility ratings.

Landform. The limitation is a poor distribution or interspersion of natural basins or landforms which inhibit the development of optimum waterfowl habitat. This limitation, while closely associated with both topography and moisture-holding capacity of the soils, is used to designate those areas where a poor distribution and interspersion of small marshes result in reduced waterfowl production.

Inundation. The limiting factor is excessive fluctuation of water level or tidal action which adversely affects the habitat or the nesting success of waterfowl. It is used to indicate the shorelines of lakes which are subject to severe drawdown during the spring and summer, and watercourses where runoff waters are very high during the spring nesting season and leave exposed gravel or mud bars later in the summer. The limitation is also used in areas, such as the shores of the Bay of Fundy, which are adversely affected by tidal waters.

Reduced Marsh Edge. The limitations are topographic or other features that adversely affect the width or development of optimum marsh conditions along the edges of water areas. Marsh edge refers to the zone extending from the normal full stage level to a water depth of one m and is usually marked by the maximum extent of emergent vegetation. Steep gradients, which result in a marsh zone of less than three m in width, are considered a limitation to the capability of the wetland. Shoreline development, the ratio of shoreline length to total area, is also considered on large lakes or marshes. A large marsh with small islands and an irregular shoreline has a higher capability for waterfowl production than does a marsh with a regular shoreline. Both shoreline features are used in considering the limitation due to reduced marsh edge.

Soil Moisture. The limitation is the poor water-holding capacity of certain soils, which adversely affects the formation and permanence of water areas. It refers to the internal drainage patterns of the soil profile and includes coarse-textured and well-drained soils, such as loamy sands, sands, and gravels, that are not influenced by seepage or subsurface moisture. Usually, granular soils fall in this category, but rock outcrops or shallow drift over rock may also be included.

Adverse Soil and Water Characteristics. The limitation is excessive salinity, alkalinity, acidity, lack of essential trace elements, or abundance of toxic elements which limit the development of plant and animal communities essential for waterfowl production. This subclass is used to designate very saline soils, or saline or alkaline lakes, or other areas where it has been demonstrated that these chemical factors are limiting waterfowl production.

Soil Depth. The limitation is the restriction of the rooting zone by bedrock or other impervious layers, which limit the development and growth of suitable plant communities. It applies to landforms such as severely eroded soils, rock outcrops, and areas with a shallow layer of soil over rock. It also applies to the marshes in the Canadian Shield which have rocky shorelines.

Adverse Topography. The limitation is surface relief, slope or gradient, patterns of knolls and depressions, or surface drainage patterns which adversely affect the capability of the land to support waterfowl. Areas with the same severe limitations are level depressionless plains, very steep slopes, or deeply dissected and well-drained moraines and plateaus.

Water Depth. The limitation is deep or shallow waters which limit the development of optimum waterfowl habitat. Usually it is used to indicate large, deep bodies which are mapped separately, but it may be used also to indicate large marshes or lakes which are uniformly shallow and choked with single stands of vegetation, such as cattail. (Adapted from Perret, 1969).

Appendix III

Wildlife Protected Lands Inventory

Newfoundland

Status	Name	Size (Hectares)	Purpose	Major Species	Important Habitat Feature	Activities Hunting/Trapping
Migratory Bird Sanctuary (Federal)	St. Peter's Bay	648	protection of migratory birds	-	-	No / No
Conservation Area (Provincial)	Little Grand Lake	84,179	protection of pine marten population	pine marten	climax boreal forest	Yes / No
	Avalon	86,768	preservation of wildlife habitat (caribou)	caribou	boreal forest and moss-heath barrens	Yes / Yes
	Hare Bay Islands	485	protection of seabird colonies	puffins, Razorbill	rugged coastal offshore islands	No / No
	Gannet Islands	172	protection of seabird colonies	cormorants	rugged coastal offshore islands	No / No
	Cape St. Mary's	65	protection of seabird colonies	Gannet, Black-legged Kittiwake, murres, Razorbill	rugged coastal offshore islands	No / No
	Gull Island	75	protection of seabird colonies	Black-legged Kittiwake, murres, puffins, Razorbill	rugged coastal offshore islands	No / No
	Great Island	58	protection of seabird colonies	Black-legged Kittiwake, murres, puffins, Razorbill	rugged coastal offshore islands	No / No
	Funk Island	27	protection of seabird colonies	Gannet, Black-legged Kittiwake, murres, puffins, Razorbill	rugged coastal offshore islands	No / No
	Green Island	7	protection of seabird colonies	Black-legged Kittiwake, murres, puffins, Razorbill	rugged coastal offshore islands	No / No

Prince Edward Island

Status	Name	Size (Hectares)	Purpose	Major Species	Important Habitat Feature	Activities Hunting/Trapping
Migratory Bird Sanctuary (Federal)	Black Pond	588	protection of migratory birds	Black Duck, Blue and Green-winged Teal, Ringed-neck Duck, Pintail, widgeons	*barachois* pond, fragile sand dunes	No / With special Permit
Wildlife Management Area (Provincial)	Indian River-Kensington	344	waterfowl and muskrat production habitat, Canada geese migration area	Canada Geese and common duck species	impounded salt marsh	No / No
	Orwell Cove	740	migration and waterfowl staging area	Canada Geese and Black Duck	salt marsh	No / Limited
	Moore's	512	education, interpretation, Black Duck wintering area	Black Duck, Canada Geese	fresh water pond-marsh	No / No
Non-designated Protected Wildlife Area (Provincial)	Arsenault's Pond - Tignish	9	fishing, waterfowl and fur production	trout, waterfowl, aquatic furbearers	freshwater pond-marsh habitat	Yes / Yes
	Gordon's Montrose	1	fishing, waterfowl and fur production	trout, waterfowl, aquatic furbearers	freshwater pond-marsh habitat	Yes / Yes
	Leard's Coleman	8	fishing, waterfowl and fur production	trout, waterfowl, aquatic furbearers	freshwater pond-marsh habitat	Yes / Yes
	Wright's Middleton	4	fishing, waterfowl and fur production	trout, waterfowl, aquatic furbearers	freshwater pond-marsh habitat	Yes / Yes
	Cass's Coveland	4	fishing, waterfowl and fur production	trout, waterfowl, aquatic furbearers	freshwater pond-marsh habitat	Yes / Yes
	Warren's Head of Hillsboro	4	fishing, waterfowl and fur production	trout, waterfowl, aquatic furbearers	freshwater pond-marsh habitat	Yes / Yes
	Canavoy	5	fishing, waterfowl and fur production	trout, waterfowl, aquatic furbearers	freshwater pond-marsh habitat	Yes / Yes
	MacLean's (Vernon)	2	fishing, waterfowl and fur production	trout, waterfowl, aquatic furbearers	freshwater pond-marsh habitat	Yes / Yes
	Leard's (Morell)	9	fishing, waterfowl and fur production	trout, waterfowl, aquatic furbearers	freshwater pond-marsh habitat	Yes / Yes
	Pius MacDonald's	36	fishing, waterfowl and fur production	trout, waterfowl, aquatic furbearers	freshwater pond-marsh habitat	Yes / Yes
	Whitlock's Pond	62	fishing, waterfowl and fur production	trout, waterfowl, aquatic furbearers	freshwater pond-marsh habitat	Yes / Yes
	Larkin's Selkirk	68	fishing, waterfowl and fur production	trout, waterfowl, aquatic furbearers	freshwater pond-marsh habitat	Yes / Yes
	Munn's or Dewar's	3	fishing, waterfowl and fur production	trout, waterfowl, aquatic furbearers	freshwater pond-marsh habitat	Yes / Yes
	MacLure's	64	fishing, waterfowl and fur production	trout, waterfowl, aquatic furbearers	freshwater pond-marsh habitat	Yes / Yes
	Hardy's York	8	fishing, waterfowl and fur production	trout, waterfowl, aquatic furbearers	freshwater pond-marsh habitat	Yes / Yes
	Blanchard's Pond- Tignish	4	fishing, waterfowl and fur production	trout, waterfowl, aquatic furbearers	freshwater pond-marsh habitat	Yes / Yes
	Forest Hill	170	fishing, waterfowl and fur production	trout, waterfowl, aquatic furbearers	freshwater pond-marsh habitat	Yes / Yes
	Johnston's River	120	fishing, waterfowl and fur production	trout, waterfowl, aquatic furbearers	freshwater pond-marsh habitat	Yes / Yes
	Dromore #1	12	fishing, waterfowl and fur production	trout, waterfowl, aquatic furbearers	freshwater pond-marsh habitat	Yes / Yes
	Everglades - Martinvale	35	fishing, waterfowl and fur production	trout, waterfowl, aquatic furbearers	freshwater pond-marsh habitat	Yes / Yes
	Clearsprings	4	fishing, waterfowl and fur production	trout, waterfowl, aquatic furbearers	freshwater pond-marsh habitat	Yes / Yes
	Bell's New Glasgow	7	fishing, waterfowl and fur production	trout, waterfowl, aquatic furbearers	freshwater pond-marsh habitat	Yes / Yes
	Pisquid Pond	50	fishing, waterfowl and fur production	trout, waterfowl, aquatic furbearers	freshwater pond-marsh habitat	Yes / Yes
	South Lake	104	migration and wintering area	mergansers, Black Duck	tidal inlet and salt marsh	Yes / Yes
	Murray Islands	96	colonial bird nesting island, migration and wintering area	herons, merganser, goldeneye, gull	series of small islands in Murray Harbor	Yes / -
	McKenna's Marsh	8	colonial bird nesting island, migration and wintering area	herons, mergansers, goldeneye, gull	series of small islands in Murray Harbor	Yes / Yes
	Johnston's - St. Charles	40	colonial bird nesting island, migration and wintering area	herons, mergansers, goldeneye, gull	series of small islands in Murray Harbor	Yes / Yes
	Affleck's Bedeque	16	colonial bird nesting island, migration and wintering area	herons, mergansers, goldeneye, gull	series of small islands in Murray Harbor	Yes / Yes
	Greenwich	618	to conserve sand dunes and *barachois* pond	red fox, small mammals, waterfowl, muskrat	sand dune barrier beach pond	Yes / Yes
	Morell River	222	maintain greenbelt and restrict development	brook trout, atlantic salmon, Black Ducks	a major river system	Yes / Yes
	Nail Pond	640	waterfowl production and migration area	Canada Geese, common ducks	large barrier beach pond	Yes / Yes
	Deroche Pond	770	waterfowl production and migration area	Canada Geese, common ducks, muskrat	large barrier beach pond	Yes / Yes

Nova Scotia

Status	Name	Size (Hectares)	Purpose	Major Species	Important Habitat Feature	Activities Hunting/Trapping
Migratory Bird Sanctuary (Federal)	Big Glace Bay Lake	389	-	protection of migratory birds	-	No / Yes
	Kentville	389	-	protection of migratory birds	-	No / Yes
	Port Joli	1,295	-	protection of migratory birds	-	No / -
	Sable Island	-	-	protection of migratory birds	-	- / -
National Wildlife Area (Federal)	John Lusby	596	managed for waterfowl	Canada Geese, Black Ducks	salt marsh	Yes / Yes
	Wallace Bay	440	managed for waterfowl	Canada Geese, Black Ducks	salt marsh	Yes / Yes
	Amherst Point*	414	managed for waterfowl	Black Ducks, Blue-winged Teal	freshwater marsh, upland forest	No / Yes
	Sand Pond	518	managed for waterfowl	Black Ducks	-	Yes / Yes
	Margaree Island	40	-	Canada Geese, Black Ducks, Brant	salt marsh, vegetated sand dunes	No / No
	Boot Island	144	-	-	-	Yes / -
Waterfowl and Furbearer Management Area (Provincial)	Missaquash	2,446	waterfowl and muskrat production, wild rice research and outdoor recreation	waterfowl, muskrat	-	Yes / Yes
	Maccan	138	waterfowl and muskrat production, wild rice research and outdoor recreation	waterfowl, muskrat	-	Yes / Yes
	Palmer Brook	24	waterfowl and muskrat production	waterfowl, muskrat	-	Yes / Yes
	Beaver Dam Meadow	53	waterfowl production	waterfowl	-	Yes / Yes
	Chebogue River Meadow	61	waterfowl production	waterfowl	-	Yes / Yes
	Middleboro	12	waterfowl and muskrat production	waterfowl, muskrat	-	Yes / Yes
Waterfowl Sanctuary (Provincial)	Melbourne Lake	24	managed for waterfowl	waterfowl	-	No / No
	Martinique Beach	308	waterfowl wintering area	waterfowl	-	No / No
	Debert	269	waterfowl feeding, resting and viewing area	waterfowl	-	No / No
	Hollahan Lake	223	waterfowl resting area	waterfowl	-	No / No
	Saint Andrews	182	managed for waterfowl	waterfowl	-	No / No
Wildlife Management Area (Provincial)	Tobeatic	49,212	integrated resource management	-	-	No / No
	Antigonish Harbour	61	waterfowl feeding and resting area	-	-	No / No
	Manganese Mines	225	managed for nature interpretation	-	-	No / No
Game Sanctuary (Provincial)	Waverly	5,180	managed for outdoor recreation	-	-	No / No
	Liscomb	45,326	managed for outdoor recreation	-	-	No / No
	Chignecto	22,275	integrated resource management	-	-	No / No

* Status under revision

New Brunswick

Status	Name	Size (Hectares)	Purpose	Major Species	Important Habitat Feature	Activities Hunting/Trapping
Migratory Bird Sanctuary (Federal)	Aero Lake	78	protection of migratory birds	–	–	No / Yes
	Grand Manan	78	protection of migratory birds	–	–	No / Yes
	Machias Seal Island	1,036	protection of migratory birds	–	–	No / No
National Wildlife Area (Federal)	Tintamarre	1,538	managed for waterfowl	Black Duck, Blue-winged Teal, Pintail, Canada Geese	production and migration marshes	Yes / Yes
	Portage Island	440	managed for waterfowl	–	–	Yes / Yes
	Shepody	1,811	managed for waterfowl	Black Duck, Canada Geese, shorebirds	tidal marshes, tidal flats, *spartina*	Yes / Yes
	Cape Jourimain	208	managed for waterfowl	–	upland and salt marsh	– / –
	Portobello	3,278	managed for waterfowl	waterfowl, Wood Duck, goldeneyes, big game, furbearers	freshwater marsh, adjacent shrub and floodplain	– / –
Provincial Game Refuge (Provincial)	Kouchibouguac	22,534	–	–	–	No / No
	Utopia	3,108	–	–	–	No / No
	Wilson's Point	52	–	–	–	No / No
	U. of New Brunswick	1,554	–	–	–	No / No
	Odell	155	–	–	–	No / No
Provincial Game Management Area (Provincial)	Mount Carleton	17,354	–	–	–	Yes / Yes
	Bantalor	15,281	–	–	–	Yes / Yes
	Becaguimac	11,137	–	–	–	Yes / Yes
	Burpee	19,685	–	–	–	No / No
	Canaan	22,534	–	–	–	Yes / No
	Kedgwick	82,883	–	–	–	Yes / Yes
	Lepreau River	24,347	–	–	–	Yes / Yes
	Tracadie River	3,885	–	–	–	Yes / Yes
	Plaster Rock- Renous	84,178	–	–	–	Yes / Yes
	Fredericton	181	–	–	–	No / No

Quebec

Status	Name	Size (Hectares)	Purpose	Major Species	Important Habitat Feature	Activities Hunting/Trapping
Migratory Bird Sanctuary (Federal)	Betchouane	130	seabirds production and protection	Ring-billed Gull, Herring Gull	isolated islands	No / No
	Rochers-aux-Oiseaux	855	seabirds production and protection	Gannet	isolated islands	No / No
	Île de Bonaventure	518	protection of gannet	Gannet	isolated islands	No / No
	Baie Bradore	104	seabirds production and protection	puffins	isolated islands	No / No
	Île Carillon	1,010	heron production and protection	Great Blue Heron	isolated islands	No / No
	Île du Corossol	725	seabirds production and protection	Black-legged Kittiwake	isolated islands	No / No
	Île à la Brume	4,144	seabirds production and protection	Ring-billed Gull	isolated islands	No / No
	Île aux Hérons	26	seabirds production and protection	Great Blue Heron	isolated islands	No / No
	Île aux Basques	52	seabirds production, waterfowl habitat	Black Duck, Eider Duck, Herring Gull	isolated islands	No / No
	Mont-St-Hilaire	907	research, education, interpretation	song birds	deciduous forest	No / No
	Philipsburg	518	waterfowl habitat	Wood Duck, Black Duck, Common Goldeneye Blue and Green-winged Teal	beaver pond	No / Yes
	Senneville	570	education, forest conservation	warblers, sparrows, Pileated Woodpecker	original deciduous forest	No / Yes
	St- Augustin	6,864	seabirds production and protection	Herring Gull	isolated islands	No / No
	Îles Sainte-Marie	3,367	seabirds production and protection	murres, Razorbill	isolated islands	No / No
	Watshishu	11,655	seabirds production and protection	terns	isolated islands	No / No
	Île des Loups	3,238	seabirds production and protection	puffins, Razorbill	isolated islands	No / No
National Wildlife Area (Federal)	Îles de la Paix	130	waterfowl habitat	surface feeding ducks: Mallard, Pintail, Black and Wood Duck	isolated islands	Yes / No
	Cap-Tourmente	2,020	stopover for migrating greater snow geese	Snow Geese	*scirpus* marsh	Yes / No
	Dundee/Lac St- François	1,140	staging area for migrating waterfowl	Mallard, Pintail, Gadwall, Black Duck, Redhead	cattail marsh	Yes / Yes
	Îles de Contrecoeur	26	waterfowl habitat	Pintail, Gadwall and Widgeons	isolated islands	Yes / No
	Baie de L'Isle Verte	259	production of black duck, stopover for migrating	Black Duck, Canada Geese (migration)	*spartina* marsh	Yes / Yes
	Îles de la Madeleine	1,983	waterfowl	waterfowl, shorebirds, songbirds	sand dunes, ponds, marshes, barrier beaches	
Migratory Bird Area (Provincial)	Longue Pointe	3,264	waterfowl resting area	surface feeding ducks	*scirpus* marsh	No / No
	Saint-Vallier	389	waterfowl resting area	diving duck: Greater and Lesser Scaup, Black Duck and Canada Geese	*scirpus* tidal marsh	No / No
	Montmagny	1,234	waterfowl resting area	Snow Geese	*scirpus* tidal marsh	No / No
	Cap-Saint-Ignace	155	waterfowl resting area	Snow Geese	*scirpus* tidal marsh	No / No
Sanctuary (Provincial)	Parke	11,914	interpretation and conservation	Gannet	deciduous and mixed forest	No / No
	Pointe Taillon	176	forest conservation	–	boreal forest	No / No
	Duchesnay	8,910	interpretation, forest research and conservation	Greater Snow Geese	deciduous (maple) and mixed forest	No / No
	Grosse-Île	518	quarantine station	–	rocky island	No / No
	Provancher	997	ecological reserve	Black Duck	deciduous and mixed forest	No / No
	Ixworth	606	conservation	–	deciduous and mixed forest	No / No
Reserve (Provincial)	La Vérendrye	1,361,582	conservation and recreation	moose	boreal forest	No / No
	Aiguebelle	25,900	recreation, hunting and fishing	moose	boreal forest	No / No
	Baie-Comeau-Hauterive	388,506	recreation, hunting and fishing	moose	boreal forest	Yes / Yes
	Causapscal	37,814	recreation, hunting and fishing	salmon and moose	deciduous and mixed forest	Yes / No
	Forestville	130,279	recreation, hunting and fishing	moose	boreal forest	Yes / Yes
	Labrieville	27,195	recreation, hunting and fishing	moose	boreal forest	Yes / Yes
	Chute St - Philippe	11,914	recreation, hunting and fishing	moose	boreal forest	Yes / Yes
	Mistassini	2,453,023	recreation, hunting and fishing	moose	boreal forest	Yes / Yes
	Assinica	961,421	recreation, hunting and fishing	moose	boreal forest	Yes / Yes
	Baie-James	6,170,242	hydro project, hunting and fishing	moose and caribou	boreal forest	Yes / Yes
	Baillargeon	2,362	hunting and fishing	moose and deer	mixed forest	Yes / No
	Cap-Chat	12,108	hunting and fishing	moose and deer	deciduous and mixed forest	Yes / No
	Escourt	777	hunting	moose and deer	deciduous and mixed forest	Yes / No
	Chicoutimi	174,051	hunting and fishing	moose	boreal forest	Yes / No
	Paul Sauvé	557	recreation and camping	–	–	No / No
	Chibougamou	1,102,578	hunting and fishing	moose	boreal forest	No / No
	Chic – Chocs	81,845	hunting and fishing	caribou	boreal forest	Yes / Yes
	Haute Mauricie	1,728,331	hunting and fishing	moose and deer	deciduous and mixed forest	Yes / Yes
	Île d'Anticosti	802,911	hunting and fishing	deer	boreal forest	Yes / Yes
	Joliette	48,848	hunting and fishing	deer	mixed forest	Yes / No
	Papineau – Labelle	173,792	hunting and fishing	deer	mixed forest	Yes / No
	Mastigouche	177,158	hunting and fishing	salmon and deer	mixed forest	Yes / No
	St -Maurice	46,873	hunting and fishing	moose and deer	mixed forest	Yes / No
	Rimouski	79,773	hunting and fishing	deer	mixed forest	Yes / No
	Portneuf	77,748	hunting and fishing	moose	mixed forest	Yes / No
	Kipawa	463,616	hunting and fishing	moose	boreal forest	Yes / Yes
	Mont Ste -Anne	6,661	recreation - skiing	–	mixed forest	No / No
	Matane	121,991	hunting and fishing	deer and moose	mixed forest	Yes / No
	Ste -Véronique	5,180	hunting and fishing	–	boreal forest	Yes / No
	Petite Nation	–	hunting and fishing	salmon	–	Yes / No
	Pontiac	74,852	hunting and fishing	deer	mixed forest	Yes / No
	Baldwyn	22,015	hunting and fishing	deer	mixed forest	Yes / No
	Sept-Îles- Port-Cartier	841,761	hunting and fishing	moose	boreal forest	Yes / No

Ontario

Status	Name	Size (Hectares)	Purpose	Major Species	Important Habitat Feature	Activities Hunting/Trapping	
Migratory Bird Sanctuary (Federal)	Beckett Creek	104	protection of migratory birds	–	–	No	
	Chantry Island	78	protection of migratory birds	–	–	No	
	Fielding	1,295	protection of migratory birds	–	–	No	
	Guelph	622	protection of migratory birds	–	–	No	
	Moose River	1,450	protection of migratory birds	–	–	No	
	Pinafore Park	311	protection of migratory birds	–	–	No	
	Rideau	777	protection of migratory birds	–	–	No	
	St. Joseph's Island	233	protection of migratory birds	–	–	No	
	Upper Canada	2,357	protection of migratory birds	–	–	No	
	Young Lake	544	protection of migratory birds	–	–	No	
	Hannah Bay	29,786	protection of migratory birds	–	–	No	
National Wildlife Area (Federal)	Big Creek	751	waterfowl migration stop-over habitat	waterfowl	freshwater marsh	partial	Yes
	Eleanor Island	26	waterfowl habitat	waterfowl	–	No	No
	Mohawk Island	4	gull habitat	gull colony	–	No	No
	Mississippi Lake	233	waterfowl habitat	waterfowl	freshwater marsh	No	No
	Wellers Bay	52	waterfowl habitat	waterfowl	freshwater marsh, sand dunes	Yes	Yes
	St. Clair	259	waterfowl habitat	waterfowl	freshwater marsh	No	Yes
	Long Point	1,012	major migration route	passerines, waterfowl	sand dunes, freshwater marsh	–	–
	Prince Edward Point	190	major migration route	owls, passerines, birds of prey	regenerating uplands	–	–
Provincial Wildlife Area (Provincial)	Aylmer	184	provide habitat, hunting and viewing of waterfowl	captive Canada Geese, breeding flock, Whistling Swans, other waterfowl, songbirds	wetland impoundments, agricultural land	–	–
	Brighton	386	provide habitat and hunting for upland game	Ruffed Grouse, woodcock, cottontails, European hare, some ducks and stocked pheasants	open field, orchards, wooded bottomlands, and beaver ponds	–	–
	Bruce	3,483	provide various recreational activities	Ruffed Grouse, varying hare, woodcock white-tailed deer, some waterfowl, songbirds	escarpment physiography	–	–
	Camden Lake	1,255	provide habitat, hunting and viewing of waterfowl	Mallard, Blue-winged Teal, Black and Wood Ducks, some Ring-necked Ducks, scaup and Pintails, some mink and raccoon, captive flock of Canada Geese		–	–
	Fingal	293	to manage small game and waterfowl	captive flock of Canada Geese, ducks, pheasants, European hare, cottontails	agricultural area, open fields, waterfowl impoundments	–	–
	Gananoque	607	provide upland game and waterfowl habitat, hunting and viewing	Ruffed Grouse, woodcock, pheasants, cottontails, European hare, varying hare, and waterfowl, and many species of songbirds	rock ridges interspersed with farm fields, beaver ponds, wet lowlands, hardwood bush	–	–
	Holland Marsh	526	provide waterfowl habitat, hunting and viewing	Mallard, Black and Wood Ducks and Blue-winged Teal, diving ducks, some Ruffed Grouse and woodcock	wetland, and associated agricultural land	–	–
	Hullett	2,347	provide waterfowl habitat, hunting and viewing	captive flock of Canada Geese, other waterfowl, Ruffed Grouse, European hare, stocked pheasants, wintering hawks, migrating songbirds	proposed large waterfowl impoundment and dam, many farmed fields	–	–
	Kolapore Uplands	486	provide various recreational activities	Ruffed Grouse, woodcock, varying hare, European hare, white-tailed deer	Niagara Escarpment physiography	–	–
	Long Point	708	provide waterfowl hunting and viewing	ducks of many species, geese, Whistling Swans, fly-catchers, vireos, thrushes, warblers and many other songbirds	major wetland area	–	–
	Luther Marsh	1,197	provide habitat and hunting for upland game and waterfowl	waterfowl, small game, white-tailed deer, captive flock of Canada Geese, Black-crowned Night and Great Blue Herons	important wetland for heronries	–	–
	Nonquon	1,133	provide waterfowl and upland game hunting and viewing	waterfowl species, upland game species	river bottomland, proposed impoundments, upland area	–	–
	Point Petre	1,214	provide habitat and hunting for waterfowl and small game, viewing and photography of wildlife	Bufflehead and puddle diving ducks, Sharp-tailed Grouse (introduced), Ruffed Grouse, pheasant, woodcock, hares, squirrels, cottontails, fox coyote, raccoon, white-tailed deer	small impoundments for waterfowl, picturesque limestone ledges and gravel shoreline	–	–
	Puslinch	202	provide small game management	cottontails, Ruffed Grouse, some waterfowl	–	–	–
	Rankin	939	provide wildlife based recreation	waterfowl, Ruffed Grouse, woodcock, varying hare white-tailed deer, captive Canada Geese flock	bottom lands and uplands	–	–
	St. Edmunds	6,799	provide hunting and viewing for upland species	white-tailed deer, Ruffed Grouse, varying hare	wooded and rocky area	–	–
	Scugog Island	182	provide pheasant hunting	pheasant	old fields	–	–
	Tiny Marsh	931	provide hunting and viewing for waterfowl and upland species	diving and dabbling ducks, Ruffed Grouse, woodcock, stocked pheasants	diked impoundment for waterfowl, peripheral upland area	–	–
	Winchester	1,457	provide hunting and viewing for waterfowl and upland species	waterfowl, Ruffed Grouse, woodcock, hares, white-tailed deer, coyotes	important large wetland	–	–
	Wye Marsh	971	provide hunting and viewing for waterfowl and upland species	waterfowl, Ruffed Grouse, woodcock, hares	rolling wooded uplands, open fields, important marsh		–
Conservation Authorities (Provincial)	Rattlesnake Point	231	preservation of natural wilderness	buffalo, elk, upland small game	Niagara Escarpment, cliffs, forest, open space	–	–
	Mountsberg	535	stream augmentation, wildlife management	upland game, waterfowl	large reservoir, rolling land, woodlots, fields	–	–
	Taquanyah	136	wildlife management	upland game	low, level, grassy, mixed bush	–	–
	Luthermarsh	4,072	water management, wildlife area	ducks, other bird species, muskrats, deer	marsh, lake, swamp	–	–
	F.W. Dickson	30	preserve natural area	–	hardwood tamarack, marsh	–	–
	Bannister Wrigley Complex	104	preserve natural area	–	shallow marshy lakes	–	–
	Orangeville Reservoir	331	headwater protection supplementary flow	migrating waterfowl	large reservoir, low marsh, upland rolling area	–	–
	Rattray Marsh	10	protection of natural area	shorebirds, waterfowl	marshy lakeshore	–	–
	Rogers Reservoir	39	reservoir	waterfowl	marsh, reservoir, plain	–	–
	Beaver Meadow	88	management of marshland species, upland game	beaver, waterfowl, other birds	hardwood bush, marsh and agricultural land	–	–
	Little Bluff	26	waterfowl and habitat improvement for upland game	waterfowl, upland game	hardwood bush, marsh, beach, open fields	–	–
	Frank E. Goderich	110	habitat improvement for upland game	upland game	hardwood and coniferous forest	–	–
	Keating	150	propagation of local wildlife species	marshland and upland game	open meadow, bottom woodland, marsh	–	–
	Hoards	54	protection of marshland	waterfowl	marsh	–	–
	Perth	171	waterfowl management	Canada Geese, other waterfowl	open meadow, wetland, marsh forests	–	–
	Mill Pond	437	waterfowl and upland game management	waterfowl, upland small game	variety of terrain from marsh to upland	–	–
	Thurlow	241	waterfowl, habitat improvement	upland game and waterfowl	wetland, marsh, upland forest	–	–
	Rowan Mills	22	provide food and cover for wildlife	jackrabbit, grouse, cottontail, Wood Duck	semi-steep valley walls to floodplain, deciduous forest	–	–
	Bognor Marsh	573	wetland and marsh management	waterfowl, upland game and deer	Niagara Escarpment, upland hardwood, wetlands	–	–
	Wodehouse Marsh	389	wetland management, habitat improvement	waterfowl	fragile marsh, unique bog and wetland	–	–
	Bowmanville Harbour	232	preservation of marshland	waterfowl	marsh	–	–
	Lynde Shores	113	preservation of marshland	waterfowl, shorebirds	low marsh, woods, beach, open land	–	–
	Binbrook	148	wildlife management - recreation	–	reservoir, swamp, wooded area, beach	–	–
	Humberstone Marsh	81	waterfowl habitat	waterfowl	agriculture, woodlot, marsh	–	–
	Willoughby Swamp	221	wildlife management and preservation	small game	hardwood forest	–	–
	Buells Creek	557	waterfowl habitat protection	Canada Geese, other waterfowl	open meadow, upland forest, marsh, pond	–	–
	The Glen	688	habitat improvement	herons, deer, Wood Duck, grouse	escarpment bluff areas, marshes, wetlands, pastures	–	–
	McNab Lake Skinner Marsh	506	wetland management	Wood Duck, herons, shorebirds, furbearers	wetland and marsh	–	–
	Rankin	1,258	provide wildlife based recreation	waterfowl, Ruffed Grouse, woodcock, hare, deer	wetlands, marshes, low forest lands	–	–
	Bannock Burn	2,486	nature viewing	deer	wooded slopes and stream bank	–	–
	Wildwood	837	flood control for waterfowl	ducks and geese	artificial lake, lowlands	–	–
	Fisher	61	improve habitat for upland game	Wood Duck, grouse, cottontails, upland game	gently rolling to steep valley walls, deep ravines, mixed deciduous forests	–	–
	Vittoria	28	improve habitat for upland game	upland game, grouse, pheasant, Wood Duck	steep valley walls, floodplain lands, valley bottom lands, cedar swamp	–	–
	Christie	338	provide recreation, flood control	stocked pheasants	artificial lake, rolling open landscape	–	–
	Valens	243	provide recreation, flood control	waterfowl and other migratory birds	large lake, marsh and open grass areas	–	–
	Glen Major	358	provide forest and wildlife protection	upland small game	rolling, hummocky and wooded	–	–
	Goodwood	125	wildlife area	upland small game, deer	rolling, open and reforested land	–	–
	Oakbank	4	wildlife protection	–	glacial lake	–	–
	Palgrave	229	forest and wildlife preservation	upland small game, deer	rolling, densely wooded	–	–
	Stouffville	43	provide recreation, flood control	–	narrow river valley	–	–
	Heber	229	multi-use management	upland small game	mixed valley woodland, wet woodland, open areas	–	–
	Cranberry Marsh	355	preserve swamp area	waterfowl, shorebirds	marsh, farm fields	–	–
	Buckhorn	410	wilderness preserve and outdoor education centre	typical upland game species	rocky, many lakes, shallow soils	–	–
	Cavan Swamp	841	preserve swamp area and wildlife	waterfowl, furbearers, deer	swamp area with unique flora	–	–
	The Heronry	134	wildlife management	Great Blue Heron (nesting)	wooded	–	–
	Miller Creek	16	wildlife management	waterfowl	marsh	–	–
	Sawer Creek	308	preservation of wetlands for wildlife habitat	waterfowl	swamp, marsh, wooded areas	–	–
	Squirrel Creek	111	recreation, wildlife preservation	upland game	rough bush land, some marsh	–	–
	Osprey Wetlands	142	headwater control and wildlife	waterfowl	low wet areas, marsh headwaters	–	–
	Minesing Swamp	142	wildlife preserve & management area	variety of waterfowl, birds, other animals	swamp	–	–
	Rice Lake	70	recreation, wildlife habitat protection	waterfowl, upland small game	marshy wetlands, rolling uplands	–	–
	Beverly Swamp	502	protect headwaters area, flood control wildlife habitat	waterfowl, grouse, migrating waterfowl, deer	low lying swamp area	–	–

Manitoba

Status	Name	Size (Hectares)	Purpose	Major Species	Important Habitat Feature	Activities Hunting/Trapping
National Wildlife Area (Federal)	Pope Reservoir	31	protect waterfowl habitat	waterfowl	–	No / No
	Rockwood	32	protect waterfowl habitat	waterfowl	–	No / No
Wildlife Management Areas (Provincial)	C. Stuart Stevenson	130	protect wildlife habitat	–	broken fields, aspen bluffs	Yes / –
	Gerald W. Malaher	60	protect wildlife habitat	–	mixed forest, small open meadows	Yes / –
	Grahamdale	1,489	protect wildlife habitat	–	ridges of aspen interspersed with grassy meadows	Yes / –
	Grant's Lake	363	protect wildlife habitat	waterfowl, game birds	marsh	Yes / –
	McCreary	10,555	protect deer and grouse habitat	white-tailed deer, Sharp-tailed Grouse	grassland with aspen, oak and tamarack swamp	Yes / Yes
	Moosehorn	194	protect Canada Geese production habitat	Canada Geese	marsh	Yes / –
	Neelin	65	protect wildlife habitat	–	mature aspen, oak and birch forest	Yes / –
	Ninette	130	protect wildlife habitat	–	mixed aspen and oak forest with open fields	Yes / –
	Basket Lake	7,187	protect wildlife habitat	–	poplar, willow and grassland	Yes / –
	Bernice	65	protect wildlife habitat	–	treeless farm land	Yes / –
	Onanole	453	protect wildlife habitat	–	wooded area	Yes / –
	Pierson	194	protect wintering habitat	deer	aspen bluffs, grassland, willow-fringed area	Yes / –
	Proulx Lake	3,302	protect wildlife habitat	–	poplar, willow and grassy areas	Yes / –
	Rembrandt	1,360	protect Ruffed Grouse habitat	Ruffed Grouse, deer	poplar forest with white spruce, open grass meadow	Yes / –
	Mantagao Lake	50,325	protect ungulate habitat	elk, white-tailed deer, upland game	forest, marsh and muskeg	Yes / Yes
	Narcisse	13,779	protect deer and grouse habitat	white-tailed deer, grouse	grassland with shrub, immature poplar, white spruce	Yes / –
	Oak Hammock Marsh	3,393	protect and restore waterfowl production habitat	waterfowl	marsh and upland	Yes / –
	Peonan Point	2,331	protect deer winter habitat	white-tailed deer	–	Yes / –
	Sandridge	1,878	protect deer habitat	white-tailed deer	–	Yes / –
	Saskeram	93,372	protect wildlife habitat	moose, waterfowl, furbearers	–	Yes / Yes
	Sharpewood	2,266	protect deer habitat	white-tailed deer, grouse	aspen forest with small scattered marshes	Yes / –
	Sleeve Lake	14,958	protect deer and grouse habitat	white-tailed deer, grouse	marsh	Yes / –
	Souris River Bend	1,813	protect deer and grouse habitat	white-tailed deer, Sharp-tailed Grouse	wooded river bank	Yes / –
	Steeprock	2,020	protect furbearer habitat	furbearers	marsh	Yes / –
	Tom Lamb	226,373	protect waterfowl nesting habitat	waterfowl	–	Yes / Yes
	Watson P. Davidson	5,828	protect moose and deer habitat	white-tailed deer, moose	–	Yes / –
	Whitewater Lake	8,988	protect wildlife habitat	waterfowl	–	Yes / –
	Broad Valley	3,691	protect deer and grouse habitat	white-tailed deer, Sharp-tailed Grouse	wetland and upland area	Yes / –
	Broomhill	324	protect and develop grouse habitat	Sharp-tailed Grouse	upland area	Yes / –
	Cape Tatnam	404,052	protect polar bear, geese and caribou habitat	polar bear, geese woodland caribou	fragile coastal and tundra ecosystem	Yes / –
	Clematis	6,890	protect deer and grouse habitat	white-tailed deer, Sharp-tailed Grouse	meadow, marsh, aspen forest, open shrub	Yes / –
	Dog Lake	32,376	protect waterfowl nesting habitat, migration stopover for Canada Geese	waterfowl, Canada Geese, gulls, White Pelicans Double-crested Cormorants	combination of tree covered islands and exposed rocky shoals	Yes / –
	Gypsumville	2,461	protect deer, grouse and waterfowl habitat	white-tailed deer, waterfowl, grouse	aspen forest, shrub cover, black spruce bog	Yes / –
	Harperville	648	protect deer and grouse habitat	white-tailed deer, Ruffed and Sharp-tailed Grouse	wooded, meadow and marsh land	Yes / –
	Hilbre	3,523	protect deer and grouse habitat	white-tailed deer, Ruffed Grouse	marsh and aspen forest	Yes / –
	Inwood	2,720	protect deer and grouse habitat	white-tailed deer, Rugged Grouse	–	Yes / –
	Langruth	1,787	protect deer, grouse and waterfowl habitat	white-tailed deer, Sharp-tailed Grouse, waterfowl	grassland, aspen forest and marsh	Yes / –
	Lauder Sandhills	2,564	protect deer winter habitat	white-tailed deer, upland game birds	open sandhill terrain with wooded areas of aspen	Yes / –
	Lee Lake	6,967	protect waterfowl nesting habitat	waterfowl, Canada Geese	marsh and muskeg	Yes / –
	Little Birch	22,792	protect deer and grouse habitat	white-tailed deer, Sharp-tailed Grouse	–	Yes / –
	Lundar	1,101	protect deer and grouse habitat	white-tailed deer, Sharp-tailed Grouse	Interlake aspen forest	Yes / –
	Upper Assiniboine*	1,014	protect wildlife habitat	white-tailed deer, waterfowl, grouse	–	– / –
	Pembina Valley*	2,020	protect wildlife habitat	white-tailed deer, waterfowl, grouse	–	– / –
	Brandon Hills*	691	protect wildlife habitat	white-tailed deer, waterfowl, grouse	–	– / –
	Turtle Mountain*	130	protect wildlife habitat	white-tailed deer, waterfowl, grouse	–	– / –
	Parkland*	518	protect wildlife habitat	white-tailed deer, waterfowl, grouse	–	– / –
	Tiger Hills*	63	protect wildlife habitat	white-tailed deer, waterfowl, grouse	–	– / –
	Whitemud Watershed*	324	protect wildlife habitat	white-tailed deer, waterfowl, grouse	–	– / –
	Cape Churchill	1,683,552	resource management	polar bear, Snow Geese, Canada Geese, barren-ground caribou	–	– / –
Game Bird Refuges (Provincial)	Big Grass Marsh	16,965	protect waterfowl and grouse habitat	waterfowl, Sharp-tailed Grouse, muskrat	–	No / Yes
	Delta	1,916	protect waterfowl habitat	waterfowl	–	No / –
	Dog Lake Islands	583	protect waterfowl resting and nesting habitat	waterfowl, White Pelicans, Double-crested Cormorants Ring-billed gulls, Canada Geese	–	No / –
	Fort Whyte	932	protect game bird	–	–	No / –
	Grant's Lake	583	nesting and staging habitat for waterfowl	Snow and Blue Geese	–	No / –
	Jackfish Lake	2,383	protect breeding and resting for geese	geese	–	No / Yes
	Lee Lake	1,554	protect local breeding habitat for Canada Geese	Canada Geese	–	No / –
	Lynch Point	259	protect wildlife habitat	waterfowl	–	No / –
	Marshy Point	389	protect game bird habitat	–	–	No / –
	Netley Marsh	1,067	protect staging habitat for waterfowl	waterfowl	–	No / –
	Oak Lake	2,469	protect waterfowl nesting and production habitat	waterfowl	–	No / –
	Pointe du Bois	389	protect Canada Geese breeding habitat	Canada Geese	–	No / –
	Red Deer Point	9,013	protect game bird and moose habitat	moose, white-tailed deer, game birds	–	No / Yes
	Reykjavik	2,590	protect nesting habitat for Greater Canada Geese	Greater Canada Geese	–	No / –
	Rock Lake	1,839	protect waterfowl resting habitat	–	–	No / –
	St. Ambroise	344	protect waterfowl habitat	waterfowl	–	No / –
	Sleeve Lake	3,885	protect waterfowl habitat	waterfowl	–	No / –
	Swan Lake	9,324	protect geese nesting and resting habitat	geese	–	No / –
	West Shoal Lake	11,137	protect waterfowl habitat	Canada and Snow Geese	–	No / –
	Whiteshell	64,493	wildlife protection in a public recreation area	Ruffed Grouse, waterfowl, moose and white-tailed deer	–	No / –
Wildlife Refuges (Provincial)	Bird's Hill	648	protect wildlife habitat	–	–	No / –
	Carman	1,269	protect wildlife habitat	–	–	No / –
	Minnedosa Lake	1,878	protect waterfowl staging and some wildlife habitat	waterfowl	–	No / –
	St. Charles	5,025	protect wildlife habitat	white-tailed deer	–	No / –
	Spruce Woods	8,651	protect wildlife habitat	mule deer	–	No / –
Furbearing Animal Refuges (Provincial)	Red Pine	453	protect red squirrels which aid in reforestation	red squirrel	–	Yes / –
	Turtle Mountain	28,297	protect furbearing animals	weasel, mink, skunk, wolf, fox, deer, muskrat, beaver	–	Yes / –
Goose Refuges (Provincial)	Alfred A. Hole	1,036	protect private goose flock	Canada Geese	–	No / –
	Marshy Point	14,271	protect resting grounds and breeding habitat for Canada Geese	Canada Geese, introduced Giant Canada Geese	–	No/Yes / –
	Oak Lake	16,188	to establish a nesting population of Canada Geese	Canada Geese	–	– / –
Public Shooting Grounds (Provincial)	Big Point	3,393	to provide public hunting and recreation	waterfowl	–	– / –
	Delta	7,770	to provide public hunting	waterfowl	–	No / –
	Marshy Point	6,475	to provide public hunting	waterfowl	–	– / –
	Netley	17,846	to provide public hunting and recreation	waterfowl	–	Yes / –
	Oak Lake	1,269	to provide public hunting and recreation	waterfowl	–	– / –
	Pelican Lake	2,435	to provide public hunting and recreation	waterfowl	–	– / –
	Waterhen	14,440	to provide public hunting and recreation	waterfowl	–	– / –
	Whitewater	1,684	to provide public hunting and recreation	waterfowl	–	– / –

* New areas not included on map.

Saskatchewan

Status	Name	Size (Hectares)	Purpose	Major Species	Important Habitat Feature	Activities Hunting/Trapping	
Migratory Bird Sanctuary (Federal)	Basin and Middle Lakes	8,720	protect waterfowl	waterfowl	aspen grove parkland	–	–
	Duncairn Reservoir	1,560	protect waterfowl	waterfowl	short-grass prairie	–	–
	Indian Head	32	protect migratory birds	–	aspen grove parkland	–	–
	Last Mountain lake	4,792	protect waterfowl	waterfowl, marsh and colonial species	mid-grass prairie	–	–
	Lenore Lake	8,822	protect waterfowl	waterfowl, pelicans and other shorebirds	aspen grove parkland	–	–
	Murray Lake	1,166	protect waterfowl	waterfowl	aspen grove parkland	–	–
	Neely Lake	809	protect waterfowl	waterfowl	southern boreal forest	–	–
	Old Wives Lake	26,063	protect waterfowl	waterfowl and colonial species	short-grass prairie	–	–
	Opuntia Lake	1,396	protect waterfowl	waterfowl	aspen grove parkland	–	–
	Redberry Lake	6,394	protect waterfowl	waterfowl and colonial species	aspen grove parkland	–	–
	Scentgrass Lake	633	protect waterfowl	waterfowl	aspen grove parkland	–	–
	Sutherland	130	protect migratory birds	–	aspen grove parkland	–	–
	Upper Rousay Lake	2,024	protect waterfowl	waterfowl	short-grass prairie	–	–
	Val Marie Reservoir	506	protect waterfowl	waterfowl	mid-grass prairie	–	–
	Wascana Lake	130	protect waterfowl	Canada Geese			
National Wildlife Area (Federal)	Last Mountain Lake	6,064	migration and production habitat, plant lure-crops	waterfowl, Sandhill Crane, upland mammals	freshwater marsh and upland	–	–
	Stalwart	632	migration and production habitat, plant lure-crops	waterfowl, Sandhill Crane, upland mammals	freshwater marsh and upland	–	–
	Tway Lake	97	waterfowl marsh habitat	waterfowl	wetland	–	–
	Bradwell	130	waterfowl marsh habitat	waterfowl	wetland	–	–
	St. Denis	361	waterfowl marsh habitat	waterfowl	wetland	–	–
	Prairie	2,775	–	–	–	–	–
	Webb	426	–	–	–	–	–
Game Preserves (Provincial)	Andrews Lake	1,036	protect waterfowl	waterfowl	short-grass prairie	No	Yes
	Berube Lake	1,554	protect waterfowl	waterfowl	southern boreal forest	No	Yes
	Blaine Lake	365	private buffalo herd	buffalo	aspen grove parkland	No	Yes
	Boggy Creek	842	protect private property	–	mid-grass prairie	No	Yes
	Charron Lake	531	protect waterfowl	waterfowl	aspen grove parkland	No	Yes
	Crystal Beach	7,770	protect deer	deer	mid-grass prairie	No	Yes
	Dafoe	868	protect waterfowl	waterfowl	aspen grove parkland	No	Yes
	Estevan Park	583	protect private property	–	short-grass prairie	No	Yes
	Kendal	723	protect waterfowl	waterfowl	aspen grove parkland	No	Yes
	Little Manitou	85	protect private property	–	mid-grass prairie	No	Yes
	McLaren Lake	883	protect waterfowl	waterfowl	short-grass prairie	No	Yes
	Macklin	453	protect private property	–	mid-grass prairie	No	Yes
	Marsden	777	protect waterfowl	waterfowl	aspen grove parkland	No	Yes
	Melville	1,344	protect upland game birds	upland game birds	aspen grove parkland	No	Yes
	Moose Jaw	648	protect private property	–	mid-grass prairie	No	Yes
	Neely Lake	642	protect waterfowl	waterfowl	southern boreal forest	No	Yes
	Outlook	3,792	protect waterfowl	waterfowl	mid-grass prairie	No	Yes
	Patterson Lake	146	protect waterfowl	waterfowl	southern boreal forest	No	Yes
	Radisson lake	692	protect waterfowl	waterfowl	aspen grove parkland	No	Yes
	St. Peter	1,554	protect deer	deer	aspen grove parkland	No	Yes
	Saltcoats	421	protect waterfowl	waterfowl	aspen grove parkland	No	Yes
	Scentgrass Lake	1,360	protect waterfowl	waterfowl	aspen grove parkland	No	Yes
	Upper Rousay	518	protect waterfowl	waterfowl	aspen grove parkland	No	Yes
	Valeport	259	protect waterfowl	waterfowl	mid-grass prairie	No	Yes
	Wascana	1,133	protect waterfowl	waterfowl	mid-grass prairie	No	Yes
	Willow Bunch	1,322	protect deer	deer	short-grass prairie	No	Yes
	Wood Mountain	3,885	protect pheasant	pheasant	short-grass prairie	No	Yes
Wildlife Refuges (Provincial)	Backes Island	6	protect colonial bird species	Double-crested Cormorants, White Pelicans	southern boreal forest	No	No
	Fairy Island	65	biological research	–	southern boreal forest	No	No
	Fishing Lake	–	preserve natural state, protect wildlife	–	aspen grove parkland	No	No
	Frenchman River	65	protect prairie dog colony	prairie-dog	short-grass prairie	No	No
	Gatehouse Island	4	protect colonial bird species	Double-crested Cormorants, White Pelicans	southern boreal forest	No	No
	Heglund Island	78	protect colonial bird species	Double-crested Cormorants, White Pelicans	short-grass prairie	No	No
	Hidden Valley	130	bird watching	–	mid-grass prairie	No	No
	Horseshoe Lake	57	protect Canada Geese and Great Blue Heron	Canada Geese, Great Blue Heron	aspen grove parkland	No	No
	Ingvald Opseth	65	nature sanctuary	–	aspen grove parkland	No	No
	Isle of Bays	194	protect colonial bird species	Double-crested Cormorants, White Pelicans	short-grass prairie	No	No
	Nisku	1,710	protect Canada Geese breeding project	Double-crested Cormorants, White Pelicans	mid-grass parkland	No	No
	Redberry	34	protect colonial bird species	Double-crested Cormorants, White Pelicans	aspen grove parkland	No	No
	Rock Island	5	protect colonial bird species	Double-crested Cormorants, White Pelicans	southern boreal forest	No	No
	Scheelhaase Island	13	protect colonial bird species	Double-crested Cormorants, White Pelicans	southern boreal forest	No	No
Wildlife Management Units (Provincial)	Antelope	13,812	protect livestock and property	–	mid-grass prairie	Yes	Yes
	Brokenshell No. 1	9,130	protect livestock and property	–	mid-grass prairie	Yes	Yes
	Brokenshell No. 2	3,290	protect livestock and property	–	short-grass prairie	Yes	Yes
	Buckland	6,657	protect private property	–	aspen grove parkland	Yes	Yes
	Cookson	5,478	protect wildlife	–	southern boreal forest	Yes	Yes
	Cypress Hills	18,229	protect wildlife	–	mid-grass prairie	Yes	Yes
	Elbow	12,158	protect livestock and property	–	mid-grass prairie	Yes	Yes
	Estevan – Cambria	2,666	protect livestock and property	–	short-grass prairie	Yes	Yes
	Fort à la Corne	130,543			aspen grove parkland and southern boreal forest	Yes	Yes
	Hearts Hill	6,314	protect livestock and property	–	mid-grass prairie	Yes	Yes
	Last Mountain Lake	8,381	protect waterfowl	waterfowl	mid-grass prairie	Yes	Yes
	Lomond	7,273	protect livestock and property	–	short-grass prairie	Yes	Yes
	Mantario	10,101	protect livestock and property	–	mid-grass prairie	Yes	Yes
	Mariposa	10,670	protect livestock and property	–	mid-grass prairie	Yes	Yes
	Mount Hope	13,031	protect livestock and property	–	aspen grove parkland	Yes	Yes
	Newcombe No. 1	8,029	protect livestock and property	–	short and mid-grass prairie	Yes	Yes
	Newcombe No. 2	9,907	protect livestock and property	–	mid-grass prairie	Yes	Yes
	Pasquia	262,357	manage big game	–	southern boreal forest	Yes	Yes
	Porcupine	280,878	manage big game	–	southern boreal forest	Yes	Yes
	Progress	8,198	protect waterfowl	waterfowl	mid-grass prairie	Yes	Yes

Alberta

Status	Name	Size (Hectares)	Purpose	Major Species	Important Habitat Feature	Activities Hunting/Trapping	
Migratory Bird Sanctuary (Federal)	Inglewood	39	protect migratory birds	waterfowl, nongame migratory birds	island in Bow River	No	No
	Red Deer	130	protect migratory birds	waterfowl, nongame migratory birds	Red Deer River valley	No	No
	Richardson Lake	16,577	protect migratory birds	geese and nongame migratory birds	boreal forest	No	No
	Saskatoon Lake	1,136	protect migratory birds	Trumpeter Swans and waterfowl	aspen parkland transition	No	No
National Wildlife Area (Federal)	Blue Quills Marsh	97	waterfowl habitat	waterfowl, nongame migratory birds	aspen parkland	No	No
Migratory Bird Sanctuary (Provincial)	Birch Lake	2,849	waterfowl staging and production habitat	waterfowl, nongame migratory birds	aspen parkland	No	No
	Henderson Park	130	waterfowl habitat	waterfowl, nongame migratory birds	short-grass prairie	No	No
	Lac La Biche	22,275	waterfowl staging and production habitat	waterfowl, nongame migratory birds	boreal forest	No	No
	Many Islands Lake	3,108	waterfowl staging and production habitat	waterfowl	mid-grass prairie	No	No
	Ministik Lake	4,921	waterfowl staging and production habitat	waterfowl	aspen parkland	No	No
	Miquelon Lake	2,072	waterfowl staging and production habitat	waterfowl	aspen parkland	No	No
	Pakowki Lake	2,072	waterfowl staging and production habitat	waterfowl	short-grass prairie	No	No
	Red Deer	130	protect migratory birds	geese and nongame migratory birds	Red Deer river valley	No	No
	Richardson Lake	16,577	protect migratory birds	geese and nongame migratory birds	boreal forest	No	No
	Saskatoon Lake	1,136	protect migratory birds	Trumpeter Swans, other waterfowl	Peace River parkland	No	No
Wildlife Sanctuaries (Provincial)	Green Valley	4,144	contiguous habitat	ungulates – deer, some moose	Peace River parkland	No	No
	Primrose Lake	486,417	waterfowl and wildlife	White Pelican colony, ungulates	boreal forest	No	No
	Robb	2,072	sheep winter/summer range	bighorn sheep	subalpine forest	No	No
	Sheep River	4,662	sheep winter range	bighorn sheep, grouse	subalpine forest	No	No
	Suffield	256,159	maintain prairie grassland habitat	pronghorn antelope, mule and white-tailed deer	Middle Sand Hills	No	No
	Wainright	58,795	ungulate and upland game bird habitat	mule and white-tailed deer, Sharp-tailed Grouse	aspen parkland – Sand Hills	No	No
	Wapiti River	4,921	ungulate winter range	ungulates, upland furbearers	vegetation – river valley	No	No
	Claresholm	1,554	ungulate habitat	ungulates	mid-grass prairie	No	No
	Cold Lake	2,331	wildlife habitat	moose, otter	boreal forest	No	No
	Sarcee Camp	518	ungulate habitat	ungulates	mid-grass prairie	No	No
Bird Sanctuaries (Provincial)	Blackburn	777	waterfowl production	waterfowl, nongame migratory birds	aspen parkland	Yes	Yes
	Cygnet Lake	259	waterfowl production	waterfowl, nongame migratory birds	aspen parkland	Yes	Yes
	Kirkpatrick Lake	4,921	geese staging and production habitat	geese, nongame migratory birds	mid-grass prairie	Yes	Yes
Buck For Wildlife Areas (Provincial)	Buffalo Lake	228	habitat development project	waterfowl, upland game and nongame migratory birds	aspen parkland	Yes	Yes
	McVinnie Property	65	habitat development project	upland and nongame migratory birds, mammals	mid-grass prairie	Yes	Yes
	Millicent	324	habitat development project	upland game birds, nongame migratory birds	mid-grass prairie	Yes	Yes
	Eagle Lake	8	habitat development and protection	waterfowl, nongame migratory birds	mid-grass prairie	Yes	Yes
	Lychak Property	648	habitat development and protection	upland game birds, nongame migratory birds, waterfowl, mammals	aspen poplar	Yes	Yes
	Shiningbank Range	5,957	habitat development and protection	ungulates	boreal forest	Yes	Yes
	Chet Wayne Property	73	habitat development and protection	upland game birds, nongame migratory birds	mid-grass prairie	Yes	Yes
	Bigelow Reservoir	344	habitat development and protection	upland game birds, waterfowl	aspen parkland	Yes	Yes
	Beaverhill Lake	6,071	habitat development and protection	upland game birds, nongame migratory birds	aspen parkland	Yes	Yes
	Chip Lake	6,475	habitat development	waterfowl, nongame migratory birds	aspen transition zone to spruce	Yes	Yes
	Stirling Lake	220	habitat development and protection	waterfowl, nongame migratory and upland game birds	short-grass prairie	Yes	Yes
	Moose Creek	1,036	habitat improvement	ungulates	boreal forest	Yes	Yes

British Columbia

Status	Name	Size (Hectares)	Purpose	Major Species	Important Habitat Features	Activities Hunting/Trapping	
Migratory Bird Sanctuary (Federal)	Christie Islet	1	protection of migratory birds	-	-	-	-
	Esquimalt Lagoon	-	protection of migratory birds	-	-	-	-
	George C. Reifel	-	protection of migratory birds	waterfowl	-	-	-
	Nechako River	-	protection of migratory birds	-	-	-	-
	Shoal Harbour	-	protection of migratory birds	-	-	-	-
	Vaseaux Lake	-	protection of migratory birds	Canada Geese, swans, ducks	-	-	-
National Wildlife Area (Federal)	Alaksen	271	waterfowl habitat, lure cropping	waterfowl, (wintering)	delta, tidal marsh, foreshore, upland	-	-
	Creston Valley	149	freshwater marsh management	waterfowl	freshwater marsh	-	-
	Marshall/Stevenson	32	migration habitat	waterfowl	saltwater	-	-
	Rosewall Creek	13	migration habitat	waterfowl	estuary	-	-
	Nanoose Bay	-	-	-	-	-	-
	Vaseux-Bighorn	366	winter range - California bighorn sheep	California bighorn, Canada Geese, swans, ducks	freshwater marsh, lake, desert vegetation	-	-
	Wilmer Marsh	471	waterfowl habitat	waterfowl	freshwater marsh	-	-
	Widgeon Valley	125	waterfowl habitat	upland wildlife, ducks, Canada Geese	delta, marsh and upland	-	-
	Qualicum	36	-	-	-	-	-
Wildlife Management Area (Provincial)	Gold Lake	285	-	Roosevelt elk	wet meadow	-	-
	Esquimalt Harbour	19	waterfowl resting habitat	waterfowl and shorebirds	intertidal mud flats	-	-
	Oyster Lagoon	8	waterfowl habitat	waterfowl and shorebirds	estuary	-	-
	Mud Bay/Baynes Sound	2,651	waterfowl habitat	waterfowl, shorebirds,, salmon	intertidal mud flats	-	-
	Scott Islands	1,900	seabird nesting habitat	seabirds, murres, murrelets, guillemots, auklets	rocky offshore islands	-	-
	Tofino-Browning Passage	1,440	waterfowl, migrating and wintering habitat	waterfowl and shorebirds	intertidal mud flats	-	-
	Hardy Bay	141	waterfowl, shorebird habitat	waterfowl, shorebirds, raptors, anadromous fish	estuary	-	-
	Boundary Bay	5,907	intertidal habitat	waterfowl, shorebirds, raptors, marine mammals	intertidal mud flats, salt marsh	-	-
	Duck and Barber Islands	336	waterfowl habitat	waterfowl, raptors	deltaic islands	-	-
	Green River	189	waterfowl habitat	waterfowl	freshwater marsh	-	-
	Ladner Marsh	74	waterfowl habitat	waterfowl	deltaic marsh	-	-
	Pitt Lake	1,478	waterfowl, aquatic bird habitat	waterfowl, Sandhill Cranes, raptors	freshwater marsh and bog	-	-
	Roberts Bank	9,677	intertidal habitat	waterfowl, shorebirds, raptors marine mammals	intertidal mud flats, salt and estuarine marshes	-	-
	Serpentine Fen	76	waterfowl habitat	Canada Geese, ducks, raptors	deltaic marsh, upland	-	-
	Sturgeon Bank	11,432	intertidal habitat	waterfowl, shorebirds, raptors, marine mammals	intertidal mud flats, salt and estuarine marshes	-	-
	Westham Island	-	intertidal habitat	waterfowl, shorebirds, raptors	intertidal mud flats, salt and estuarine marshes	-	-
	Woodward Island	160	waterfowl habitat	waterfowl, raptors	deltaic islands	-	-
	McGillvray Creek	301	riparian wildlife habitat	Wood Duck, Great Blue Heron, waterfowl, black-tailed deer	flood plain marsh, upland	-	-
	Ashnola River	11,443	California bighorn sheep winter habitat	California bighorn sheep	grasslands with southern slope	-	-
	Nkwala	139	upland bird habitat	California Quail, chukar	open range	-	-
	Otter Lake	60	waterfowl habitat	waterfowl	eutrophic lake with submergent vegetation	-	-
	Swan lake	465	waterfowl and upland bird habitat	waterfowl, pheasant	eutrophic lake with submergent vegetation	-	-
	Vaseaux Lake	7	waterfowl habitat	waterfowl	eutrophic lake with submergent vegetation	-	-
	Nahatlach Lake	31	waterfowl habitat	waterfowl	eutrophic lake with submergent vegetation	-	-
	Kamloops Lake/Dewdrop	6,429	wildlife management	mule deer	open range with southern slope	-	-
	Lock Lomond	111	Canada Geese nesting and rearing habitat	Canada Geese	grass upland and island, barrenshore	-	-
	Salmon Arms (Shuswap Lake)	36	waterfowl habitat	waterfowl, Canada Geese	productive mud flats	-	-
	Tunkwa Lake	3	waterfowl nesting and rearing habitat	waterfowl, Canada Geese	forest with grass understory on upland	-	-
	Hemp Creek/Wells Gray Park	432	ungulate migration route, winter range	moose and deer	open range with southern slope	-	-
	Yalakom Creek	11,172	ungulate winter range	mule deer, California bighorn sheep	open range with southern slope	-	-
	Perry River/Rocky Creek	50	ungulate migration route	mountain caribou	climax forest	-	-
	Shorts Creek	1,169	ungulate range	California bighorn sheep	southwest slope, grass/shrub community	-	-
	Alkali Lake	33	waterfowl habitat	waterfowl	eutrophic lake with submergent vegetation	-	-
	Beaverfoot Kootenay	52,339	ungulate range	elk, deer, Rocky Mountain bighorn sheep	southwest slope, grass/shrub and mixed forest	-	-
	Big Sheep Creek	1,765	wildlife habitat	-	access corridor to Big Sheep Creek	-	-
	Blaeberry/Kicking Horse River	14,417	ungulate winter range	white-tailed deer	southwest slope, grass/shrub and mixed forest	-	-
	Bull River	560	ungulate winter range	Rocky Mountainn bighorn sheep, mule deer	southern slope, grass/shrub communities	-	-
	Columbia Lake (east side)	5,584	ungulate winter range	elk, deer, Rocky Mountain bighorn sheep	southwest slope, grass/shrub and mixed forest	-	-
	Columbia River Floodlands	14,569	waterfowl habitat	waterfowl	flood plain of Columbia River-Rocky Mountain Trench	-	-
	Deer Park-Syringa Creek	14,474	ungulate winter range	mule deer, white-tailed deer	southern slope, grass/shrub and mixed forest	-	-
	Canal Flats	205	waterfowl habitat	waterfowl	flood plain marsh, wet meadow communities	-	-
	Elizabeth Lake	85	waterfowl habitat	waterfowl	lake with emergent and submergent vegetation	-	-
	Bummer's Flats	778	waterfowl and ungulate habitat	waterfowl, ungulate, mule deer, elk	flood plain marsh, wet meadows, open forest range	-	-
	Elk River	1,408	ungulate winter range	elk, mule deer, moose	southwest slope, grass/shrub/mixed forest community	-	-
	Kimberly	195	ungulate wintering, upland bird habitat	elk, Sharp-tailed Grouse	climax grassland communities	-	-
	Kootenay Park Boundary	4,400	ungulate winter range	Rocky Mountain bighorn sheep elk, deer	southwest slope, grass/shrub/mixed forest community	-	-
	Kootenay River-Canal Flats	76,876	ungulate winter range	Rocky Mountain bighorn sheep elk, deer	southwest slope, grass/shrub/mixed forest community	-	-
	Larsen Lake	47	waterfowl habitat	waterfowl	lake with emergent and submergent vegetation	-	-
	McGinty Lake	23	waterfowl habitat	waterfowl	lake with emergent and submergent vegetation	-	-
	McMurdo Station	120	ungulate winter range	white-tailed deer	southwest slope, douglas fir	-	-
	Moberly Marsh	665	waterfowl habitat	waterfowl, moose, elk	flood plain marshes and mixed grass/forest	-	-
	Fenwick-Ft. Steele	548	waterfowl habitat	waterfowl	flood plain marshes	-	-
	Reed Lakes	123	waterfowl habitat	waterfowl	lake with emergent and submergent vegetation	-	-
	Saugum Lake and Saugum Creek	46	waterfowl nesting habitat	waterfowl	lake with associated marshes	-	-
	Sheep Mountain	119	ungulate winter range, migration route	Rocky Mountain bighorn sheep	southern slope, grassland community	-	-
	St. Mary's Lake	50	waterfowl habitat	waterfowl	lake with emergent and submergent vegetation	-	-
	Spring Lake	210	waterfowl habitat	waterfowl	lake with emergent and submergent vegetation	-	-
	Wasa Slough	136	waterfowl habitat	waterfowl	extensive freshwater marsh	-	-
	Wolf Creek	160	ungulate habitat	mule and white-tailed deer, elk, bighorn sheep	southern slope, grass/shrub/mixed forest community	-	-
	White River	313,326	ungulate habitat	mule and white-tailed deer, elk bighorn sheep	southern slope, grass/shrub/mixed forest	-	-
	Kettle River	24	ungulate habitat	mule deer	grass/shrub/mixed forest community	-	-
	Fassiferne	1,344	ungulate winter range	elk, mule and white-tailed deer	southern slope, grass/shrub/mixed forest community	-	-
	Wilmer Marsh	355	waterfowl habitat	waterfowl	flood plain marsh	-	-
	Three Sons - Premier Ridge	486	waterfowl habitat and upland ungulate winter range	waterfowl, mule and white-tailed deer, Rocky Mountain bighorn sheep, elk	flood plain marshes, wet meadows, southern slope grass/shrub/mixed forest communities	-	-
	Newgate	314	ungulate winter range	elk, mule and white-tailed deer	grass/shrub/mixed forest communities	-	-
	Grand Forks	7,667	ungulate winter range, waterfowl habitat	mule and white-tailed deer, upland birds, waterfowl	grass/shrub/mixed forest communities	-	-
	Canim Lake	11,139	ungulate winter range	mule deer, moose, upland birds	southern slope, grass/shrub/mixed forest community	-	-
	Goose Island Group	2,272	geese and pelagic birds nesting areas	Canada Geese, pelagic birds	interspersion of bog and rocky upland	-	-
	Konni Lake	506	ungulate winter range, domestic grazing	mule deer, California bighorn sheep	southern slope, grass/shrub/mixed forest community	-	-
	Moffat Creek	728	waterfowl and ungulate habitat	moose, sportfish	grass and willow meadow	-	-
	Puntzi Lake	1,452	waterfowl habitat	waterfowl	freshwater marshes	-	-
	Bella Coola River	2,023	ungulate winter range	moose, mule deer, waterfowl	flood plain	-	-
	Horsefly Bay	143	waterfowl habitat	waterfowl, moose	freshwater marshes and lakeshore	-	-
	Klinaklini River	1,720	ungulate winter range	moose, mule deer	flood plain	-	-
	Junction	4,325	ungulate habitat	California bighorn sheep, mule deer, upland birds	grassland	-	-
	Bearskin Bay	314	waterfowl habitat	Canada Geese, other waterfowl and shorebirds	sheltered estuary	-	-
	Delkatla Slough	665	waterfowl habitat	Canada Geese, Sandhill Cranes, Trumpeter Swans	estuary and extensive salt marsh	-	-
	Khutzeymateen Inlet	302	waterfowl habitat	Trumpeter Swans, Canada Geese ducks	sheltered estuary	-	-
	Watun River	90	waterfowl habitat	waterfowl, raptors, shorebirds	riparian	-	-
	Naden Harbour	1,193	waterfowl habitat	Canada Geese	estuary, intertidal mud flats	-	-
	Nadina River Valley	6,270	ungulate winter habitat	moose	riparian	-	-
	Yakoun River	308	waterfowl habitat	Trumpeter Swans and other waterfowl	riparian, river estuary, intertidal mudflat	-	-
	Haney Lake	118	ungulate habitat	moose, mule deer	southern slope, grass/shrub/mixed forest community	-	-
	Beatton River	3,696	ungulate winter range, Galinaceous birds	white-tailed and mule deer, moose, Sharp-tailed Grouse	open river break, southwest slope	-	-
	Cameron River	86,734	ungulate winter range	moose, mule deer	boreal forest	-	-
	Cecil Lake	-	waterfowl habitat	waterfowl	productive shallow lake	-	-
	East Pine	464	ungulate winter range	mule deer, moose	open river break and boreal forest	-	-
	Hudson-Hope	482	ungulate winter range	mule deer, white-tailed deer	open river breaks	-	-
	Kishatinaw River	34,516	ungulate winter range	moose, deer	open river break and boreal forest	-	-
	Moberly River	3,560	ungulate winter range	moose	flood plain	-	-
	Peace River Breaks	50,242	ungulate range	moose, deer	open river break	-	-
	Sukunka River	34,456	ungulate winter range	elk, deer, moose	flood plain	-	-
	Hominka River	4,766	waterfowl and ungulate habitat	Canada Geese, waterfowl, moose, caribou, wolf, bear	riparian	-	-
	Nechako River	156	waterfowl habitat	Canada Geese	flood plain and river islands	-	-
	Starratt Property	176	waterfowl habitat	waterfowl	marsh and wet meadows	-	-
	Grove Burn	24,173	ungulate and furbearer habitat	moose, lynx, wolverine, bear, wolf, coyote	burned over area of boreal forest in early sucession	-	-
	Ryder Creek	49	watershed and public recreation	black-tailed deer, black bear, beaver, Ruffed Grouse, waterfowl	watershed	-	-
	Buttertubs Slough	22	waterfowl habitat	waterfowl, raptors	marsh and upland grass/shrub community	-	-
	Wigeon Creek	7,934	-	-	watershed	-	-
	Antler's Saddle	106	ungulate winter range	deer	grass/shrub communities	-	-
	Carpenter Lake	28,350	mule deer winter range	mule deer	open forest winter ranges	-	-
	Little Fort	152	waterfowl habitat	Canada Geese	domestic pasture	-	-
	Spallumcheen Forest	3,838	deer wintering range	mule deer	open forest winter ranges	-	-
	Cedar Creek	32	white-tailed deer habitat	white-tailed deer	grass/shrub and mixed forest, winter range	-	-
	Golden	8,568	-	-	interior douglas fir	-	-
	Queens Bay	46	ungulate habitat	mule deer	winter range	-	-
	East of Creston	65	ungulate winter range	white-tailed and mule deer	southern slope, grass/shrub/mixed forest	-	-
	Wigwam Flats	4	ungulate winter range	deer, Rocky Mountain elk and bighorn sheep	grass/shrub/mixed forest	-	-
	Churn Creek	124	ungulate winter range	California bighorn sheep	grassland and mixed forest	-	-
	Horse Lake	218	waterfowl and ungulate habitat	waterfowl, black bear, beaver, mule deer, moose	freshwater marsh	-	-
	Morley Lake	308	waterfowl and ungulate habitat	waterfowl, black bear, beaver, mule deer, moose, otter	shallow marshlands	-	-
	Ootsa Lake	334	ungulate habitat	moose	wet meadow	-	-
	Reef Island	14,550	sea otter habitat	sea otter habitat	hemlock	-	-
	Tako Creek	132	moose winter range	moose	riparian, winter range	-	-
	Lazo Marsh	33	waterfowl habitat	waterfowl, raptors , pheasant	freshwater wetland	-	-
	Somenos Lake	51	waterfowl habitat	waterfowl, raptors	freshwater marsh, wet pasture	-	-

Yukon

Status	Name	Size (Hectares)	Purpose	Major Species	Important Habitat Feature	Activities Hunting/Trapping
Game Sanctuary (Territorial)	Kluane	518,016	to protect dall sheep, mountain caribou, moose, goat, wolf	sheep, mountain caribou	—	No / No
	McArthur	181,306	to protect fannin sheep	fannin sheep, mountain caribou	hot spring, unique vegetation, glacial refugium	No / No
	Fishing Branch River Reserve	402,498	to protect salmon and grizzly bear	grizzly bear, salmon, caribou	open water all year	Yes / No

Northwest Territories

Status	Name	Size (Hectares)	Purpose	Major Species	Important Habitat Feature	Activities Hunting/Trapping
Migratory Bird Sanctuary (Federal)	Akimiski Island	336,710	protection of migratory birds	Canada Geese	tundra, spruce and willow	No / —
	Anderson	108,265	protection of migratory birds	Canada Geese, Brant	estuarine and tundra	No / —
	Banks Island #1	2,051,861	protection of migratory birds	Snow Geese	tundra	No / —
	Banks Island #2	14,245	protection of migratory birds	Snow Geese	tundra	No / —
	Bylot Island	—	protection of migratory birds	Greater Snow Geese, murres, seabirds	coastal rock cliffs and tundra	No / —
	Cape Dorset – Sakkiak Island	3,367	protection of migratory birds	Eider Ducks	island tundra	No / —
	– West Fox Islands	14,245	protection of migratory birds	Eider Ducks	island tundra	No / —
	– South Andrew Gordon Bay	8,288	protection of migratory birds	Eider Ducks	island tundra	No / —
	Cape Parry	148,671	protection of migratory birds	seabirds	coastal rock cliffs	No / —
	Dewey Soper	815,875	protection of migratory birds	Snow Geese, Brant	coastal tundra	No / —
	East Bay	116,554	protection of migratory birds	Snow Geese, Brant	coastal tundra	No / —
	Harry Gibbons	148,930	protection of migratory birds	Snow Geese, Brant	coastal tundra	No / —
	Kendall Island	60,608	protection of migratory birds	Snow Geese	deltaic tundra	No / —
	McConnell River	32,894	protection of migratory birds	Snow Geese, Canada Geese	coastal tundra	No / —
	Queen Maud Gulf	6,277,918	protection of migratory birds	Ross' Geese	tundra and lakes	No / —
	Boatswain	17,872	protection of migratory birds	migrating Canada Geese and Snow Geese	coastal mudflats	No / —
	Hannah Bay	3,885	protection of migratory birds	migrating Canada Geese and Snow Geese	coastal mudflats	No / —
	Seymour Island	—	protection of migratory birds	Ivory Gulls	limestone rock rubble	No / —
Game Preserve (Territorial)	Peel River	621,619	preservation of game	—	—	No / Yes
	James Bay	8,288,256	preservation of game	—	—	No / Yes
	Norah Willis Michener Territorial Park	907	preservation of game	—	—	No / Yes
Game Sanctuary (Territorial)	Thelon	3,885,120	preservation of game	muskoxen	—	No / No
	Twin Island	69,932	preservation of game	—	—	No / No
	Bowmen Bay	69,932	preservation of game	—	—	No / No
	Mackenzie Bison	1,813,056	preservation of game	wood bison	—	Yes / Yes
Reindeer Reserve (Territorial)	Reindeer Reserve	3,885,120	preservation of game	reindeer	—	Yes / Yes

Forestry

National Photography Collection.
Public Archives Canada.
PA-11629

Contents

	Page
Introduction	156
Forest descriptions and classifications	156
The Canada Land Inventory	156
Objectives and criteria	156
Summary of land capability	157
Forest regions of Canada	160
Forest classification of the Maritime Provinces	161
Forest site regions of Ontario	164
Economic considerations	164
An overview	154
Historic growth of the forest industries	165
Contribution of forestry to the Canadian economy	166
Ownership and administration of Canada's forests	166
Timber volumes	166
Canada's forest resource	166
Forest lands	166
Allowable annual cuts	167
Future harvests and the AAC	167
Ecological forest land uses	168
Forest management for water control and supply	168
Ecologically sensitive and unique areas	169
The International Biological Programme	169
Canadian Institute of Forestry's natural areas programme	170
Other systems of identification and reservation of natural areas	170
Habitat provision	172
Urban and aesthetic forests	172
Legislation and policy	172
Urban trees and forests	173
Forestry and agriculture	176
Forest utilization for energy production and conservation	177
Energy from the forests	177
Forestry and recreation	178
Factors affecting forests	179
Hazards	179
Forest fires	179
Forest diseases	181
Insect infestations	181
Forest administration and management	182
Ownership	182
Management	182
Conclusion	184
Acknowledgements	185
Bibliography	185

Tables

	Page
1. Forest zones and ecoregions: Characteristic species, number of site districts, and associated climate	161
2. Land area classification	166
3. Inventoried production forest land area by ownership	166
4. Inventoried production forest land by productive and unproductive classes, by province or territory, 1976	167
5. Timber volume, by species	167
6. Timber volume, by province or territory	167
7. Facilities of the Greater Vancouver Watershed District	169
8. Volume of water sold under the Greater Vancouver Water District program	170
9. Status and size of proposed IBP ecological sites	170
10. Established ecological reserves in British Columbia	171
11. Tree bylaw and related data derived from Ontario Municipal Forestry Survey	173
12. Growth of urban and rural population in Canada, 1951 to 2000	174
13. Heating values of selected woods	177
14. Area of moderate to severe defoliation caused by spruce budworm	182
15. Forest areas sprayed, 1975 to 1978	182

Figures

	Page
1. The hydrologic cycle	168
2. Impact of green space on microclimate	175
3. Screening effect of trees	175
4. Fire weather index block diagram	180

Maps

	Page
1. Land capability for forestry: Québec, New Brunswick, Prince Edward Island, Nova Scotia, Newfoundland	158
2. Land capability for forestry: Ontario	159
3. Land capability for forestry: British Columbia, Alberta, Saskatchewan, Manitoba	162
4. Forest regions of Canada	163
5. Forest classification of the Maritime Provinces	164
6. Forest site regions of Ontario	165
7. Ecotour map	179
8. Forest fire weather zones of Canada	183

Introduction

Forests, the most ubiquitous feature of the Canadian landscape, serve the country's people economically, socially, and ecologically. Considered usually as extensive tracts of land covered with trees and suitable for regular harvesting, the realm of forestry may be extended to a delineation covering minute patches of trees isolated from their natural environment for aesthetic value alone. Forests may be:

Economic or fibre forests in which trees are considered a crop, are economically valuable for their fibre content, and are generally distinct from man's other activities.

Ecological forests in which trees are managed to provide maintenance of sub-elements, are preserved for representation of natural ecosystems, and are reserved and managed for wildlife habitat provision.

Urban and aesthetic forests in which trees provide a general amelioration of the environment for the psychological well-being of urban dwellers.

Agricultural forests in which trees are located in active agricultural areas, provide protection from the elements for humans, domestic animals, and crops by modification of the micro-climate.

Recreational forests in which trees provide the primary landscape scene located in areas where outdoor recreational activities take place.

Such delineation emphasizes the particular uses, values, and benefits of forests to man; the majority of forest areas exhibit traits of more than one category.

Unlike mineral deposits which are a finite resource, forests are renewable by both natural and artificial regeneration; this is the most precious characteristic of the resource for all uses. High succession and climax trees (i.e. hardwoods) have minimal natural regeneration abilities as they need a closed forest system; low succession trees have high natural regeneration abilities and are thus adaptable to an open forest system. In terms of commercial forestry, the lower succession trees are more amenable to resource management and therefore dominate the industry, which runs on a sustained or increasing yield principle. Unlike water which may have uses along the course of its bed, forests are location stable and, therefore, the forest industry must have a firm allocation of land for relatively long periods of time; thus, land tenure becomes a second important characteristic for the fibre resource. Susceptibility to management, fire, and disease is a third important characteristic of the forest.

The importance of the use of forests as a natural protective device for domestic agricultural production is evidenced most strongly in the harsh unprotected lands of the Prairies. The Prairie Farm Rehabilitation Act's Shelterbelt Program serves as an illustration of the contribution of agricultural forests to Canada's resources as a whole.

The ecosystem concept, a concept of totality of all natural and human resources in an area, is well used in defining the attributes of forested land. On one hand, the sub-elements of the system may be managed to supply actual products, such as water. On the other hand, preservation or reservation of forest lands for ecosystem representation is another desirable use. The International Biological Programme and the Canadian Institute of Forestry Natural Area Program cover all of Canada's territory. The National Parks and the majority of provincial parks have their own program for setting aside ecologically significant tracts of land. In addition, a number of other government agencies and private organizations endeavour to preserve parts of Canada's natural heritage.

The importance of urban and aesthetic forest is difficult to assess on the basis of its individual characteristics or as a whole. The basic principles and general contribution will be discussed, but, quantification of its characteristics such as psychological relief and aesthetic enjoyment cannot be assessed on a large-scale basis.

The forestry landscape plays an extremely important rôle in the recreational pursuits of Canadians and visitors to Canada. The trees are taken for granted in the natural landscape pattern, yet it would be difficult to conceive the majority of parks and recreational lands without them. The rôle of forested land for the provision of recreation is fully examined in the Recreation chapter of this report.

Forest Descriptions and Classifications

Forests and their nature may be understood most readily by physical descriptions or classifications which emphasize either primary data or interpretive evaluation depending on the objective of the study. Simple physiographic — climatic classifications define spatial

NFB – PHOTOTHEQUE – ONF – Photo by Chris Lund.

Forests provide a resource base for many uses including commercial forestry, recreation, wildlife habitat, and energy production. Nevertheless, forests are a natural resource that many Canadians take for granted.

limits, species distribution, and growth rates of vegetation on a general level. Rowe's (1959) Forest Regions of Canada, which defined major geographic belts or zones characterized vegetationally by a broad uniformity in physiognomy and in the composition of the dominant tree species, is the best known work using primary descriptive data. Interpretative descriptions include works by Loucks (1962), Hills (1952), Jurdant (1975), and Keser (1970). Loucks' Forest Classification of the Maritime Provinces distinguished ecoregions, "geographic unit(s) within which ecological relationships between species and sites are essentially similar, and within which silvicultural treatments may be expected to obtain comparable results", in those provinces.

Hills described Forest Site Regions as regions "within which specific plant successions occur upon specific landform positions" in the province of Ontario; Jurdant's (1975) Ecological Survey was carried out for defined areas in Québec, and Keser's (1970) Forest Classification for some areas of British Columbia. The difference among Hills', Jurdant's, and Keser's classifications is terminology. The Canada Land Inventory for forestry is a secondary and interpretive classification system, which covers the settled regions of Canada.

These and the multitude of other classifications, including systems used by provincial forest offices for compilation and assessment of their resources, provide an excellent insight into the general and exact physical nature of forests and forest lands. As an illustration of the variety of current physical classification systems, the descriptive approaches developed by the Canada Land Inventory, Rowe, Loucks, and Hills will be discussed briefly. These physical descriptions will provide a starting point for further discussion of important uses and areas of forests.

The Canada Land Inventory

Objectives and Criteria

The forestry sector of the Canada Land Inventory (CLI) has objectives and criteria that are directed toward providing a classification system which rates the "potential (productive) capability of the land under indigenous tree species growing at full stocking and under good management". The system is thus designed to aid in the identification of lands where intensive management practices associated with commercial forestry would be justified. The "best" mineral and organic soils in Canada for commercial tree growth are rated class 1 while soils not expected to yield timber in commercial quantities (i.e. the poorest soils) are rated class 7.

There are three categories defining characteristics of the classification. First, the capability class is an expression of all environmental factors — the environment of subsoil, soil, surface, local and regional climate, as well as the characteristic tree species — as applied to tree growth. Secondly, the capability subclasses, factors which limit tree growth, are important as they can determine or affect management, and may, in some cases, be corrected. Thirdly, the Indicator Species — tree species that can be expected to yield the volume associated with each class — are indigenous species adapted to the region and land.

The classification was designed to ensure systematic and consistent evaluation of land throughout the country. Accordingly, the following criteria and procedures were used in the delineation of the land for presentation in map form.

1) The land surface is separated into homogeneous units on the basis of physical characteristics.

2) Each unit is assigned to a class on the basis of all known or inferred information about the unit, including subsoil, soil profile, depth, moisture, fertility, landform, climate, and vegetation.

3) Except for class 1, the limitations are shown or implied. When the highest class in a region (other than class 1) has no subclass associated with it, regional climate may be assumed to be the limiting factor. Different types of land may have the same capability rating, but for different reasons. The types of limitations are shown in the subclass.

4) Associated with each capability class is a productivity range based on the mean annual increment of the best species or group of species adapted to the site at, or near, rotation age. Productivity ranges are expressed in a gross merchantable cubic-metre volume down to a minimum diameter of ten cm. The productivity ranges are for normal or full-stocked stands. Thinnings, bark, and branch wood are not included.

5) Since only well-stocked stands are measured to indicate the capability class, the implication is that only good management produces such stands.

6) In a capability class, location, access, distance to markets, size of units, ownership, or present state are not considered. Present cover or production are only used as additional information for rating capability.

7) Classification is based on the natural state of the land without improvements such as fertilization, drainage, or other amelioration. Improved forest management may change the productivity range. Also, if the limitations shown in the symbol are altered, there may be class changes. Since the classes are based on relatively permanent features, significant changes can only be brought about by costly and continuing practices.

8) Special crops such as Christmas trees are not considered.

The CLI forestry classification is based on the soil's inherent ability to grow commercial timber. For forestry, class 1, 2, and 3 soils are considered viable for commercial timber operations. The general characteristics of these three classes are as follows:

Class 1 — Lands having no important limitations to the growth of commercial forests.

Soils are deep, permeable, of medium texture, moderately well-drained to imperfectly drained, have good water-holding capacity and are naturally high in fertility. Their topographic position is such that they frequently receive seepage and nutrients from adjacent areas. They are not subject to extremes of temperature or evapotranspiration. Productivity is usually greater than 7.8 m^3/ha per annum. When required, this class may be subdivided on the basis of productivity into: Class 1 (7.8 to 9.1 m^3/ha), Class 1a (9.2 to 10.5 m^3/ha), Class 1b (10.6 to 11.9 m^3/ha), Class 1c (12.0 to 13.3 m^3/ha), Class 1d (13.4 to 14.7 m^3/ha), and by 1.4 m^3/ha classes thereafter, as required.

Class 2 — Lands having slight limitations to the growth of commercial forests.

Soils are deep, well-drained to moderately well-drained, of medium to fine texture and have good water-holding capacity. The most common limitations (all of a relatively slight nature) are: adverse climate, soil moisture deficiency, restricted rooting depth, somewhat low fertility, and the cumulative effects of several minor soil characteristics. Productivity is usually from 6.4 to 7.7 m^3/ha per annum.

Class 3 — Lands having moderate limitations to the growth of commercial forests.

Soils may be deep to somewhat shallow, well-drained to imperfectly drained, of medium to fine texture with moderate to good water-holding capacity. They may be slightly low in fertility or suffer from periodic moisture imbalances. The most common limitations are: adverse climate, restricted rooting depth, moderate deficiency or excess of soil moisture, somewhat low fertility, impeded soil drainage, exposure (in maritime areas) and occasional inundation. Productivity is usually from 5.0 to 6.3 m^3/ha per annum. Classes 4 to 7, on the other hand, have moderately severe to very severe limitations which either seriously impair or totally impede the growth of commercial forests. The soils range from deep soils to shallow bedrock, commonly have deficiency or excess of moisture, excessive stoniness, excessive carbonates, and have productivity ranging from 4.9 to less than .7 m^3/ha per annum.

Capability Subclasses. In addition to general characteristics, information on the specific limitations of the class in a particular area is given for all but class 1. The

Canada Land Inventory photo.
This mature Douglas-fir stand near Victoria is in an area rated as class 1 for forestry

departures from the general characteristics of the region are based on climate, soil moisture, permeability, depth of rooting zone, and other soil factors. These may be summarized as follows:

Climatic Subclasses

A— drought or aridity as a result of climate.

C— a combination of more than one climatic factor, or two or more features of climate that have significance.

H— low temperatures — that is, too cold.

U— exposure.

Soil Moisture Subclasses

M— soil moisture deficiency

W— excess soil moisture

X— a pattern of "M" and "W" too intimately associated to map separately

Z— a pattern of wet organic soils and bedrock too intimately associated to map separately.

Permeability and Depth of Rooting Zone Subclasses

D— physical restriction to rooting caused by dense or consolidated layers, other than bedrock.

R— restriction of rooting zone by bedrock.

Y— intimate pattern of shallowness and compaction, or other restricting layers.

Other Soil Factors Subclasses

E— actively eroding soils

F— low fertility

I— soils periodically inundated by streams or lakes

K— presence of perennially frozen material

L— nutritional problems associated with high levels of carbonates

N— excessive levels of toxic elements, such as soluble salts

P— stoniness which affects forest density or growth

S— a combination of soil factors, none of which affect the class level by themselves, but which cumulatively lower the capability class.

Tree Species Indicators. The species which can be expected to yield the volume associated with each class are also shown. Only indigenous species adapted to the region and land are shown. Examples of these are:

tA	Trembling aspen
bPo	Balsam poplar
tL	Tamarack
jP	Jack pine

On the maps (at 1:250,000 and 1:000,000) printed for the CLI program, areas are delineated and have accompanying symbols consisting of: (A) a capability class from 1 to 7; (B) a maximum of three subclasses; and, (C) a maximum of two indicator species. Because of the small scale of map used in this report, only generalized information on classes 1 to 3, those classes that repre-

tors which affect the size, type, and location of trees and forests within the region. Cool, short growing seasons inhibit tree development and growth. An examination of soil survey data shows that low levels of soil fertility are prevalent throughout the region. Exposure in the coastal zones and areas of high elevation dramatically curtails tree maturity. Areas with coarse soils or steep slopes do experience severe runoff, although precipitation is not a limiting factor in forest development.

Summary of Soil Capability

The Island of Newfoundland has approximately 3.8 million ha of productive forest land within a total area of 37 million ha. Essentially, Newfoundland's capability for commercial forestry is poor, with nearly 80 per cent of the land being of class 6 and class 7 capability (Map 1.). Class 2 is the highest capability land occurring in Newfoundland. However, since the amount is less than 0.1 per cent of the total land, these areas are so small that mapping at large scales is difficult. Class 3 lands account for approximately 2.0 per cent of the total productive forest area, in a narrow band between Victoria Lake and Grand Falls and an area immediately south of Corner Brook. Class 4 lands total approximately 15.0 per cent, and, with the exception of the Bay d'Espoir and Roddickton areas, occur mainly within the west and north central areas of the Island. The typical forest lands of Newfoundland are of class 5 capability. This class accounts for approximately 40.0 per cent of the total productive forest area while the remaining 43.0 per cent consists of class 6 lands.

Prince Edward Island's productive forest has been exploited over the years to the point at which very little forested area of any commercial value remains. Approximately 250 thousand ha of potentially productive forest exists in P.E.I. of which 90.0 per cent is privately owned. The Canada Land Inventory classified the Island as having a moderate to low capability for productive forest growth. The presence of class 5 land is confined to the north and south coastal regions. Approximately 50.0 per cent of Prince Edward Island is class 4 and 40.0 per cent is class 5 capability land. The remaining 10.0 per cent of the land area is a mixture of class 6 and class 7 capabilities.

The productive forest lands of Nova Scotia occupy 4.4 million ha of land covering approximately 84.0 per cent of the entire province. There are virtually no class 1 or class 2 lands in Nova Scotia. Class 3 land is limited in quantity to less than 3 per cent of the land area and is scattered in isolated pockets throughout the province in protected areas. Class 4 capability lands are found on nearly all soil series with the exception of coarse, fine-textured or highly exposed soils. They cover about 40.0 per cent of the province from Yarmouth to St. Georges Bay, in northern Cumberland County, and Cape Breton Island. Class 5 lands account for approximately 50.0 per cent of the land area, and are located in the southwest part of the province, along the southwest shoreline and in the north between Cobequid and Chignecto bays. The remaining 7 to 8 per cent of the land area is a mixture of class 6 and class 7 lands, characterized by shallow soils and wet peat bogs occurring mainly along the southeast shoreline between Halifax and Chedabucto Bay.

The productive forests of New Brunswick cover an area of 5.7 million ha representing approximately 80.0 per cent of the provincial land area. According to the CLI, the land capabilities range from class 3 to class 7 with no land of class 1 capability. Class 2 lands do exist but are too obscure to be mapped at larger scales. The class 3 lands occupy only 1.0 to 2.0 per cent of the total land area, occurring in protected areas of river valleys or well inland from the coast. The larger concentrations of class 3 land appear along the Saint John River between the towns of St-Léonard and Woodstock. Class 4 lands are distributed extensively throughout the province, and cover approximately 56.0 per cent of the total land area. Concentrated heavily in the northwest and southeast parts of the province, class 4 lands dominate the east central regions of New Brunswick, intermingling with other classes in the area. Lands of class 4 capability are subject to conditions that result in compaction and dense subsoil horizons which limit the amount of water and root penetration. Class 5 lands, which cover 40.0 per cent of New Brunswick, are characterized by extremely coarse and fine-textured soils. These lands are very exposed at higher elevations and are very wet

in low-lying areas. Class 5 lands are found in the northeast corner of the province, along the eastern coast, and well into the central regions. A heavy concentration also appears between the Saint John River and the southwest shoreline. Class 6 and 7 lands make up only 1.0 to 2.0 per cent of the total land area and are situated along the coast.

Québec. Of the land classified by the CLI in Québec, only a minute amount is rated as having class 1 capability. The majority of the CLI area is in classes 3 and 4, with class 5 lands interspersed throughout. Class 6 and 7 capability lands occur in small parcels scattered across the northern part of the study area.

In general, it is southwestern Québec which has the highest land capabilities for forestry. Pockets of class 1 capability land are scattered northwest along the Ottawa River, around Hull, in the Montréal area, around Granby, southwest of Thetford Mines, and on the south shore of the St. Lawrence, east of Québec City. Class 2 capability lands dominate the St. Lawrence shoreline southward from Île d'Orléans, to the Ontario border. Class 2 lands occur in many river valleys including the St. Maurice, the Coulonge, the Dumoine, the Coulon, and Rivière du Lièvre. The area surrounding Montréal is predominantly class 2, as are areas near Hull and Mont Laurier. Class 3 and 4 lands cover the area south of the St. Lawrence to the international border, as well as the area north of class 1 and 2 pockets scattered along the shoreline of the St. Lawrence. Class 5 land pockets are scattered throughout the Gaspé area, around Rivière-du-Loup, west of Lac St-Jean, east of Lac Abitibi, and southeast of Chicoutimi. The northwestern corner of the study area has patches of class 5 land, with class 4 lands predominating, while along the northern limit small parcels of class 6 and 7 lands are most common. These occur north of Lac Abitibi, Val-d'Or, Lac St-Jean, and the Manicouagan River. Finally, southeastern Québec has patches of class 6 and 7 lands interspersed with higher capability areas. More detailed quantification of land in each of the CLI classes was not available at the time of writing.

Ontario. Referring to the CLI's Land Capability for Forestry, Ontario has been subdivided into site regions numbered 1 to 7 from north to south. Site regions 2 to 7 are of main concern here since only these regions are within the Canada Land Inventory boundaries.

Of the 75.5 million ha of forest land in Ontario, about 40.0 million ha are considered productive (Map 2). Class 1, high-capability lands for forestry, occur only within site regions 6 and 7 in the area above Lake Erie between London, Long Point Bay and north of Kitchener. The remaining large concentrations are located in central Huron County, west and north of Toronto, and east along the shoreline to Port Hope. Smaller areas are found in the Niagara Peninsula, and in the vicinity of Chatham.

In southern Ontario, class 2 capability land is dominant in site regions 6 and 7 within a line running north of Lake Simcoe and east to Kingston. Smaller isolated areas occur in central parts of Manitoulin and in eastern Ontario south of, and adjacent to, the Ottawa River.

Class 3 lands are located mainly in site regions 5, 6, and 7, with smaller areas in site region 4 near New Liskeard and Lake Temiskaming. There are isolated pockets in southern and eastern Ontario with more extensive concentrations south of Ottawa and east along the St. Lawrence River. Other class 3 lands appear in the vicinity of Algonquin Provincial Park, Belleville, northwest of Toronto to Georgian Bay, and south along the Lake Huron shoreline. Smaller isolations are found in Manitoulin and west of Lake Nipissing.

The majority of class 4 and class 5 lands form an arc which extends from eastern Ontario to the northern limit of the CLI boundary. The width ranges from the eastern provincial border, south to Kingston, and east of Georgian Bay. A break in this trend occurs near Lake Nipising where class 6 land lies from the west to the east border. Class 4 occurs most in the southern reaches while class 5 lands dominate the northern area. Class 6 lands are the major capability in the central portion of the inventory area. This includes the southern part of site region 5. Additional isolated pockets of class 6 land occur east of Georgian Bay to Brockville on the St. Lawrence River. The northern part of the inventory area, site regions 2 and 3, is where the majority of class 7 capability land is located. The only other area of concentration appears along the northern and eastern coasts of Georgian Bay.

157

Source: Generalized from the 1:1,000,000 Canada Land Inventory *Land Capability for Forestry* maps for *Atlantic Provinces* (1975) and *Québec* (1977), published by the Lands Directorate, Environment Canada.

MAP 1

Canadian Government Office of Tourism photo.

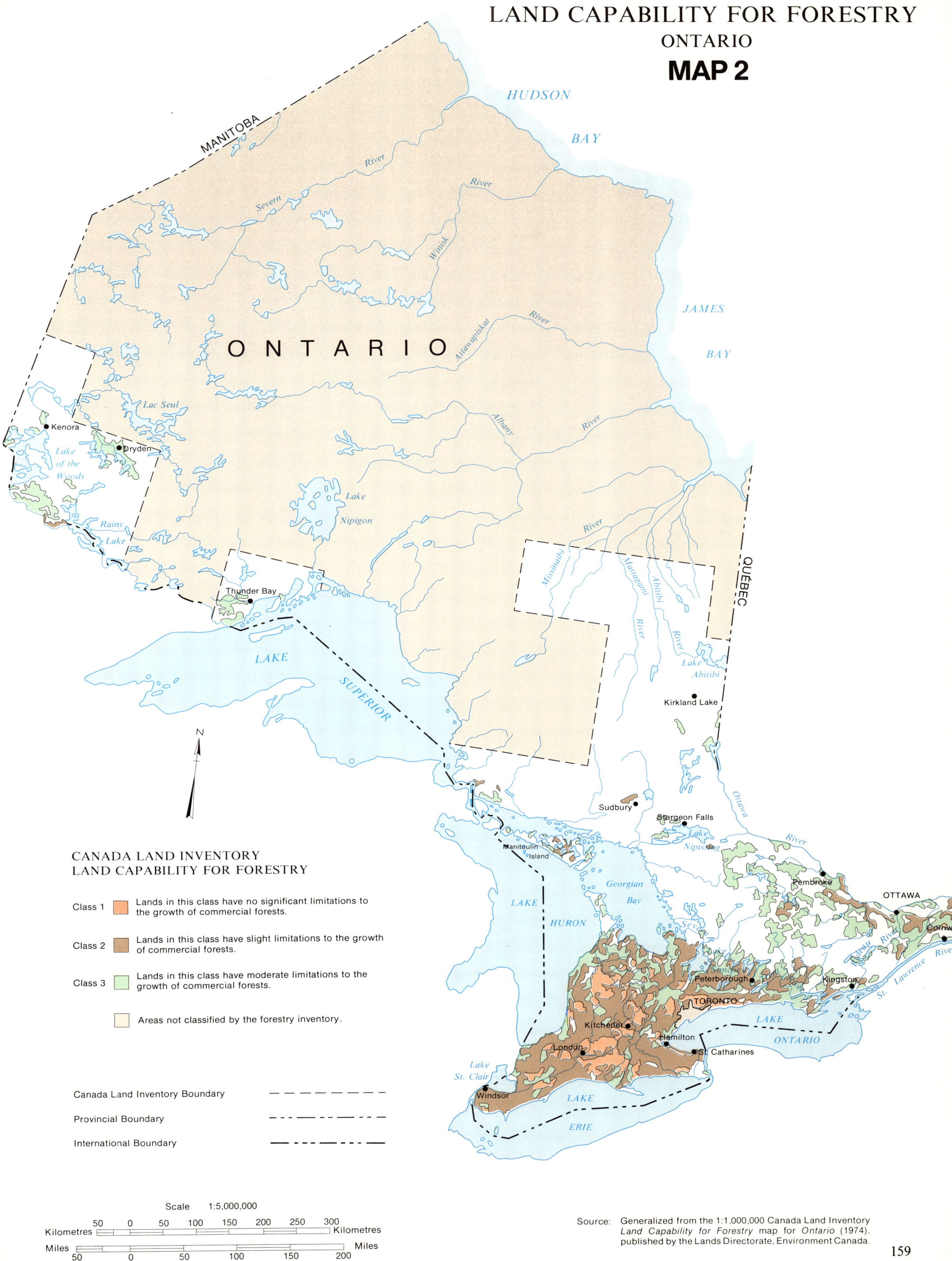

Besides the large area of CLI coverage in southern and central Ontario, there are two other regions covered by the CLI within the province. The first includes Thunder Bay and environs, located on Lake Superior. Here, the land classifications are dominated by class 6 in the north and south with two relatively large areas of class 3 land south and west of the urban centre. A large tract of class 5 land runs through the centre of the inventory, broken up by the presence of class 4 lands. The second area is located in the southeast corner of the province surrounding Lake of the Woods. This area is a mosaic of classes 3 to 7. There are, however, two large areas of class 3 land capability, one in the south and the other in the northeastern section. Class 5 lands dominate the northern and eastern parts of the coverage while the remaining area is a mixture of classes 4 to 7.

Manitoba. There are no soils of class 1 or class 2 forest capability in Manitoba (Map 3). Class 3 capability land occupies the smallest amount of the total land area classified, and is scattered in the mid-western and south-eastern part of the province. Small areas of class 3 land stretch from Powerview near Lake Winnipeg, along the Winnipeg River, through southern Lac du Bonnet, and continue until just south of Pointe du Bois. Several small parcels of class 3 land are found close to the Manitoba–Ontario border. In the west, class 3 areas extend north to south between Lake Winnipegosis and Dauphin, and between Swan River and Roblin. To the north, class 3 land forms a band running along the Saskatchewan River, between Cedar Lake, through the Pas to the Saskatchewan border. Class 4 land capability areas are predominant in the western and central areas of the province, extending from the Saskatchewan border eastward to Lake Winnipegosis, and from Red Deer Lake southward to the northern boundary of Riding Mountain Provincial Park. Class 4 lands occupy the northeastern shoreline of Lake Manitoba, the southwestern shoreline of Lake Winnipeg, and stretch north and south along the Assiniboine and the Red rivers. The southeastern corner of the province has scattered patches of class 4 land as well. Areas of the three lowest capability classes for forestry, classes 5, 6, and 7, occupy the southern part of Manitoba. Class 5 land occurs in the south-central area around Winnipeg, Portage La Prairie, and north of Brandon. Further south, class 5 capability land follows the shoreline of the Pembina and Souris rivers. The southwestern region is dominated by class 6 soils with small isolated pockets of classes 5 and 7. Class 7 capability land dominates the southeastern corner of the study area, and occupies the shoreline area of Lake Winnipeg stretching northward to the CLI boundary. Of the area of the province classified by the CLI, the majority falls into classes 5, 6, and 7, indicating a generally low capability for forestry in Manitoba.

Saskatchewan. In Saskatchewan, less than half of the area covered by the Canada Land Inventory was classified for forestry and of that only one-quarter is productive. The unclassified area of the CLI lies predominantly in the southern part of the province with the exception of the west and east corners. There is a complete absence of land of class 1 capability within the CLI boundary and very little of class 2 or class 3. The only lands displaying these capabilities are located in the northeast section just south of Cumberland Lake and scattered throughout the northern portion of the inventory area. The class 5 lands which dominate the north, are broken by extensive areas of class 4 lands in the vicinity of Prince Albert National Park. Other areas of class 5 appear north of Lake Ballantyne and Lake Amik. Lands with class 6 capability occur sporadically throughout the northern part of the inventory area, however, large expanses do prevail in the northern southwest corner and the extreme southeast section of the province. Class 7 lands are found in abundance in the southwest part of the province and along the Saskatchewan — Manitoba border to the northeast.

Alberta. Less than 50 per cent of the province has been covered by the CLI land capability classification for forestry. The main area is situated in the western half of the province from Edmonton to the foothills, south to the United States border, and north to the 57th parallel. Extensions of this area cover regions east of Edmonton to the Saskatchewan border and north into the Peace River district.

Within the CLI inventory, no area had the capabilities of class 1 or class 2 land. Class 3 land exists in limited quantities, accounting for approximately 1.0 per cent of the total inventory area. These lands appear throughout the central regions of the coverage with major concentrations north and south of Lesser Slave Lake and following the river courses of the Athabasca, Pembina, McLeod, and North Saskatchewan. Class 4 lands dominate the inventoried area with the exception of the Rocky Mountain Foothills. These slopes display distinct regions of class 5 and class 7 lands in two bands running along the Rockies. The upper foothills are class 7 lands with class 5 lands following the river valleys into the lower foothills where they predominate Other class 5 lands occur in the extreme northern portion of the inventoried area, specifically along the Peace River. Class 6 lands are scattered in isolated pockets throughout the inventoried area while other lands of class 7 capability are found mainly in the south, east-central and northern parts of the area.

British Columbia. The CLI 1:1,000,000 maps for land capability for forestry in British Columbia, and the accompanying data, are not available.

Forest Regions of Canada

The standard reference for regional forest descriptions is Rowe's Forest Regions of Canada prepared in 1959 as a revision of Halliday's 1937 Forest Classification of Canada. It delineates eight major regions, geographic belts, or zones characterized vegetationally by a broad uniformity in physiognomy and in the composition of the dominant tree species within Canada. The regions are shown in Map 4. A brief description of each is given below:

Boreal Forest Region. This Region comprises the greater part of the forested area of Canada, forming a continuous belt from Newfoundland and the Labrador coast westward to the Rocky Mountains and northwestward to Alaska. The white and the black spruces are characteristic species; other conifers are tamarack, which is absent only in the far northwest, balsam fir, and jack pine prominent in the eastern and central portions, and alpine fir and lodgepole pine in the extreme western and northwestern parts. Although the forests are primarily coniferous, there is a general mixture of broadleaved trees such as white birch and its varieties, trembling aspen, and balsam poplar; the latter two species playing an important part in the central and southcentral portions, particularly in the zone of transition to the prairie. In turn, the proportion of black spruce and tamarack rises northward, and with increasingly rigorous climatic and soil conditions the closed forest gives way to the subarctic open lichen — woodland which finally merges into tundra. In the east a considerable intermixture of species from the Great Lakes — St. Lawrence forest such as eastern white and red pines, yellow birch, sugar maple, black ash, and eastern white cedar occurs.

Subalpine Forest Region. This is a coniferous forest found on the mountain uplands in western Alberta and in British Columbia. The Region extends northward to the major divide separating the drainage of the Skeena, Nass, and Peace rivers on the south from the Stikine and Liard rivers on the north. The characteristic species are Engelmann spruce, alpine fir, and lodgepole pine. There is a close relationship with the Boreal Forest Region, from which the black and white spruces and trembling aspen intrude. There is also some entry of interior Douglas-fir from the Montane Forest Region, of amabilis fir from the Coast Forest Region, and of western hemlock and western red cedar from the Columbia and Coast Forest Regions. Other occasional species are western larch, whitebark pine, and limber pine and on the more western ranges, yellow cypress and mountain hemlock.

Montane Forest Region. The Montane forest has developed in response to the prevailing dry climate of the central plateau of British Columbia and several southern mountain valleys adjacent to the Alberta boundary. The Region is a northern extension of the typical forest of much of the western mountain system in the United States and comes in contact with the Coast, Columbia, and Subalpine forests. The characteristic tree is the interior or "blue" form of Douglas-fir. It is found throughout but more particularly in the central and southern parts. Lodgepole pine and trembling aspen are generally present, the latter being particularly well represented in the north-central portions. Engelmann spruce and alpine fir from the Subalpine Forest Region, together with western white birch, become important in the northern parts. White spruce is recognized as an important constituent of the exploitable forests. In the southern portion, ponderosa pine is abundant between the continental divide on the east and the Fraser Valley on the west. Extensive prairie communities of bunch-grasses and forbs are found in many of the river valleys.

Coast Forest Region. This is part of the Pacific Coast forest of North America. Essentially coniferous, it consists principally of western red cedar and western hemlock, with Sitka spruce abundant in the north, and with coast Douglas-fir in the south. Amabilis fir and yellow cypress occur widely, and together with mountain hemlock and alpine fir, are common at higher altitudes. Western white pine is found in the southern parts, and western yew is scattered throughout. Broadleaved trees, such as black cottonwood, red alder, and bigleaf maple, have a limited distribution in this Region. Arbutus and Garry oak occur in Canada only on the southeast coast of Vancouver Island and the adjacent islands and mainland; the centres of population of these species lie to the south in the United States.

Columbia Forest Region. A large part of the Kootenay River valley, the upper valleys of the Thompson and Fraser rivers, and the Quesnel Lake area of British Columbia contain a coniferous forest closely resembling that of the Coast Forest Region though less rich in species. Western red cedar and western hemlock are the characteristic trees in this interior "wet belt". Associated are the interior Douglas-fir, which is of general distribution, and in the southern parts, western white pine, western larch, grand fir, and western yew. Engelmann spruce from the Subalpine Forest Region is important in the upper Fraser Valley, and is found to some extent at the higher altitude forest levels in the remainder of the Region. At lower elevations in the west and in parts of the Kootenay Valley, the forest grades into the Montane Forest Region and in a few places, into native grasslands.

Deciduous Forest Region. A small portion of the deciduous forest, widespread in the eastern United States, occurs in southwestern Ontario between lakes Huron, Erie, and Ontario. Here, with the broadleaved trees common to the Great Lakes — St. Lawrence Forest Region, such as sugar maple, beech, white elm, basswood, red ash, white oak, and butternut, are scattered a number of other broadleaved species which have their northern limits in this locality. Among these are the tulip-tree, cucumber-tree, pawpaw, red mulberry, Kentucky coffee-tree, black gum, blue ash, sassafras, mockernut and pignut hickories, and the black and pin oaks. In addition, black walnut, sycamore, and swamp white oak are largely confined to this Region. Conifers are few, and there is only a scattered distribution of eastern white pine, tamarack, eastern red cedar, and eastern hemlock.

Great Lakes—St. Lawrence Forest Region. Along the Great Lakes and the St. Lawrence River valley lies a forest of a very mixed nature, characterized by the eastern white and the red pines, eastern hemlock, and yellow birch. With these are associated certain dominant broadleaved species common to the Deciduous Forest Region, such as sugar maple, red maple, red oak, basswood, and white elm. Other wide-ranging species are the eastern white cedar and large-tooth aspen, and to a lesser extent, beech, white oak, butternut, and white ash. Boreal species, such as the white and the black spruces, balsam fir, jack pine, trembling aspen, balsam poplar, and white birch are intermixed, and in certain central portions as well as in the east, red spruce becomes abundant.

Acadian Forest Region. Over the greater part of the Maritime Provinces there is a forest closely related to the Great Lakes — St. Lawrence Forest Region and, to a lesser extent, to the Boreal Forest Region. Red spruce is a characteristic though not exclusive species, and associated with it are balsam fir, yellow birch, and sugar maple, with some red pine, eastern white pine, and eastern hemlock. Beech was formerly a more important forest constituent than at present, for the beech bark disease has drastically reduced its abundance in Nova Scotia, Prince Edward Island, and southern New Brunswick. White spruce has increased in importance since the turn of the century by its widespread invasion of abandoned farmland. Other species of wide distribution are the black spruce, red oak, white elm, black ash, red maple, white birch, grey birch, trembling aspen, and balsam poplar. Eastern white cedar though present in New Brunswick is extremely rare elsewhere, and jack pine is apparently absent from the upper Saint John Valley and only occasional in the western half of Nova Scotia. (Rowe, 1972).

Each of the eight regions is further subdivided into sections, geographic areas possessing individuality which is expressed relative to other sections in a distinctive patterning of vegetation and of physiography. Only occasionally do subsections occur. The example of the Niagara Section, whose boundaries correspond to the Deciduous Forest Region, is given here:

Niagara Section

The Niagara Section includes the main body of the rather low-lying portion of the Ontario peninsula which is enclosed by lakes Ontario, Erie, and Huron. Here, very favourable climatic and soil conditions have allowed the extension into Canada of many trees, shrubs, and herbs from the deciduous forest to the south.

The forest communities are dominated by broadleaved trees. The characteristic association, common in part to both the Great Lakes — St. Lawrence and the Deciduous Forest regions, consists primarily of beech and sugar maple, together with basswood, red maple, red oak, white oak, and bur oak. Also within this area is found the main distribution in Canada of black walnut, sycamore, swamp white oak, and shagbark hickory, with the more widely distributed butternut, bitternut hickory, rock elm, silver maple, and blue-beech. Other species with a sporadic occurrence as scattered individuals or groups, either on specialized sites or within the characteristic forest types of the Section, are the following: tulip-tree, black cherry, mockernut and pignut hickories, chinquapin oak, pin oak, black oak, black gum, blue ash, cucumber-tree, pawpaw, Kentucky coffee-tree, red mulberry, and sassafras. The chestnut used to be present before the blight removed it from the forests.

The presence of the species just listed, and the predominance of beech within the main association, indicates a close relationship to the forests of the east-central United States. There is, furthermore, a poor representation of needle-leaved species, though eastern hemlock is sometimes scattered through upland forests, eastern white pine occurs locally in small stands on coarse-textured soils (often with an understorey of black and scarlet oaks), eastern red cedar is found on gravelly or rocky sites. Occasional peat bogs may support the boreal relicts, black spruce and tamarack, or eastern white cedar. As most of the land is now closely settled, the natural forest vegetation has been mostly reduced to farm woodlots, hedge-rows, and remnant stands on soils too poor to farm.

The Section is underlain by successive Palaeozoic formations — from west to east, Devonian, Silurian, and Ordovician. These limestones and shales are covered by glacial material of considerable depth, with some clay-and-sand deposits from glacial lakes Iroquois and Algonquin present on the northeast and northwest sides, respectively. The topography is undulating to flat or plain-like. Owing to the influence of favourable climate plus broadleaved vegetation and underlying calcareous bedrock, very fertile soils of the gray brown luvisols and humic gleysols have developed. (Rowe, 1972).

Having briefly presented Rowe's forest classification at the national scale, two regional classifications are cited next.

Forest Classification of the Maritime Provinces

In response to the need for a detailed description of forested lands for use in forest management, Loucks developed a classification for the Maritime Provinces based upon the ecoregion concept (Map 5). An ecoregion is a geographic unit within which relationships between species and site are essentially similar, and within which silvicultural treatments may be expected to produce comparable results; it is recognized by the characteristic species composition and development on the zonal site type. For broad comparison, forest zones (groups of ecoregions with similar dominant species composition) are used; for more detailed descriptions, site districts are used which are subdivisions of the ecoregion based on pattern of relief, drainage, or types of bedrock. Accordingly, Loucks delimits 7 forest zones, 11 ecoregions, and 55 site districts. Table 1 lists the forest zones and ecoregions and lists the characteristic species and associated climate of each. The Spruce Taiga Zone and its ecoregion, which is synonymous with the site district, is given as an example.

Spruce Taiga Zone. Short, dense spruce and fir alternates with shrub barrens and peat bogs on the flat central portion of the Cape Breton Plateau. The vegetation has been termed 'taiga' for its apparent similarity to Taiga described by Hustich (1949) in Québec, and the northern taiga mapped in the Soviet Union. Some features of the landscape suggest that the vegetation pattern is alpine. But there is such a similarity to the non-alpine forests of Québec and Newfoundland that the Cape Breton Island component cannot be singled out. Some distinguishing characteristics are noted in the description of the single Ecoregion representing this zone in the Maritime Provinces.

Cape Breton Plateau Ecoregion (Cape Breton Plateau District)

Consists of the oval tableland forming the Cape Breton Plateau. The essentially stable association on the few deep, well-drained soils is stunted black spruce, white spruce, balsam fir and white birch. Mountain-ash is scattered and balsam fir predominates in a few areas. The shallow soils on the low ridges support an ericaceous shrub cover, while sedge and sphagnum bogs are found on seepage slopes and in depressions.

Sheep laurel, rhodora, Labrador-tea, and Schreber's moss figure most prominently in the lesser vegetation of the forested portions. The shrubs also form a dense cover on the exposed barrens, along with lichens and sphagnum.

Very little of the District is capable of an economic level of wood production, but a few sites are sufficiently sheltered to permit satisfactory height growth of spruce. Stunting from exposure to wind, as well as windthrow and crown breakage, limit the quantity of timber that can be grown on the better sites. Most of the latter are accessible from the Cape Breton Highland District.

Meteorological records from Burgeo, Newfoundland, where a comparable vegetation is reported, give an indication of the climate of the plateau. At Burgeo the mean June, July, August temperature is 12°C; the potential evapotranspiration of 45 cm almost equals the limit beyond which, according to Hare (1950), the climate is too severe for a closed forest.

The District is bounded by the 457-m contour, depending on the local exposure. Other 457-m uplands are found to the south, in the Cape Breton Highlands District, and, if flat with dense stands and uplands barrens, should be included. The soils are shallow sandy loams largely derived from the granite. Azonal soils include the shrub-covered bedrock and the peat bogs. Problems relating to poor drainage, and the presence of peat bogs on slopes create difficulties for logging. (Loucks, 1962).

TABLE 1.

Forest zones and ecoregions: Characteristic species, number of site districts, and associated climate

Zone	Ecoregion	Characteristic species	Number of site districts	Associated climate
Sugar Maple--Ash		sugar maple, beech, white ash		warm, dry
	St. John River	sugar maple, beech, ironwood white ash, butternut, basswood	1	warm, dry
Sugar Maple--Hemlock--Pine		sugar maple, beech, white pine, eastern hemlock, yellow birch		moderately warm, moderately dry
	Restigouche-Bras d'Or	sugar maple, beech, balsam fir, yellow birch, white pine, white spruce	6	moderately cool, moderately dry
	Magaguadavic-Hillsborough	sugar maple, beech, white pine eastern hemlock, balsam fir, red spruce	8	moderately warm, moderately dry
Sugar Maple--Yellow Birch--Fir		sugar maple, yellow birch, balsam fir, beech		cool, moist
	Maritime Uplands	sugar maple, yellow birch, balsam fir, beech, white spruce, red spruce, red maple	11	cool, moist
Red Spruce--Hemlock--Pine		red spruce, balsam fir, eastern hemlock, white pine, red maple		moderately warm, moderately dry
	Clyde River-Halifax	red spruce, white pine, eastern hemlock, red oak, red maple, black spruce, beech	5	warm, dry
	Maritime Lowlands	balsam fir, red spruce, black spruce, eastern hemlock, white pine, red maple, jack pine, white spruce, beech	12	moderately cool, moderately dry
Spruce-Fir Coast		white spruce, balsam fir, white birch		cool, wet
	Fundy Bay	red spruce, balsam fir, white birch white spruce, black spruce, yellow birch, mountain ash	3	cool, wet
	Atlantic Shore	white spruce, balsam fir, black spruce, white birch	2	cool, wet
Fir--Pine--Birch		balsam fir, white birch, white spruce, white pine		cold, moist
	New Brunswick Highlands	balsam fir, white birch, white pine, trembling aspen, white spruce, black spruce, yellow birch, mountain ash	4	cold, moderately dry
	Gaspé-Cape Breton	balsam fir, white birch, white spruce, black spruce	2	cold, wet
Spruce Taiga		black spruce, balsam fir, white spruce		cold, wet
	Cape Breton Plateau	black spruce, balsam fir, white spruce, white birch, mountain ash	1	cold, wet

Source: Loucks, O.L. 1962. *A Forest Classification for the Maritime Provinces.*

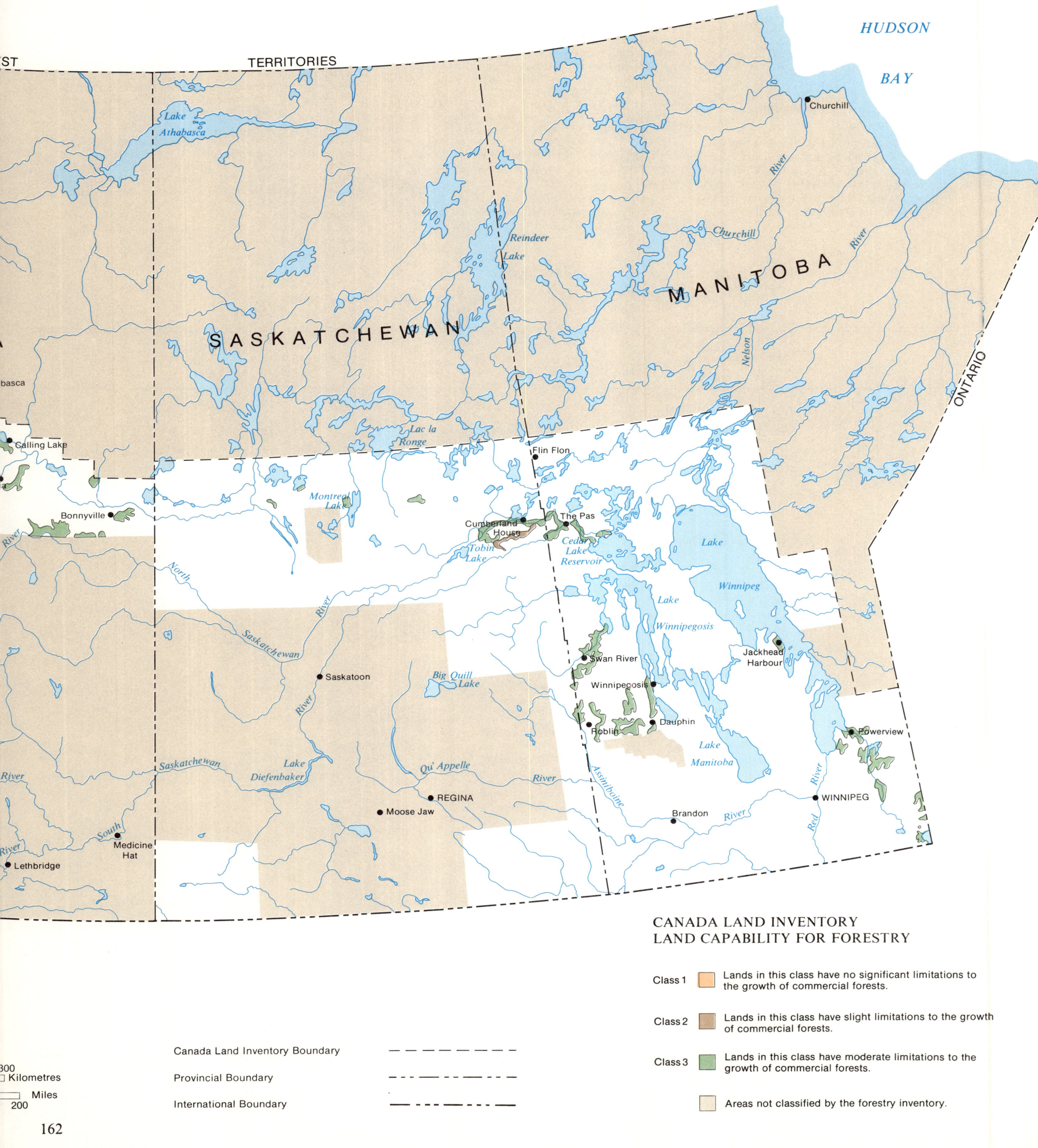

LAND CAPABILIT[Y]

BRITISH COLUMBIA
ALBERTA
SASKATCHEWAN
MANITOBA

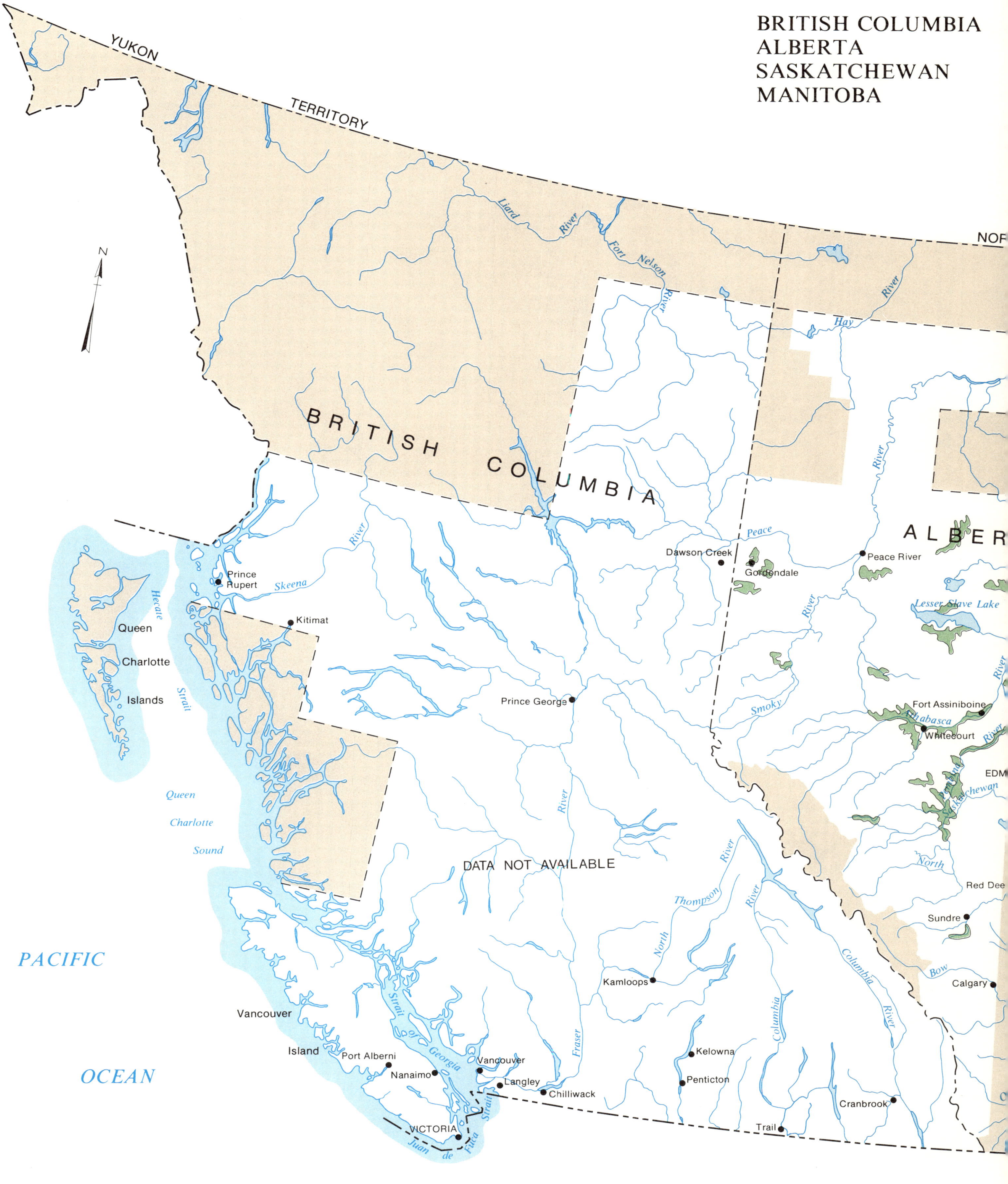

DATA NOT AVAILABLE

Source: Generalized from the 1:1,000,000 Canada Land Inventory *Land Capability for Forestry* maps for *Alberta* (1976), *Saskatchewan* (1976) and *Manitoba* (1978), published by the Lands Directorate, Environment Canada.

Scale 1:5,000,000

MAP 3

NFB – PHOTOTHEQUE – ONF

MAP 4

Photo by J. Ritchie Mickelson.

FOREST REGIONS OF CANADA

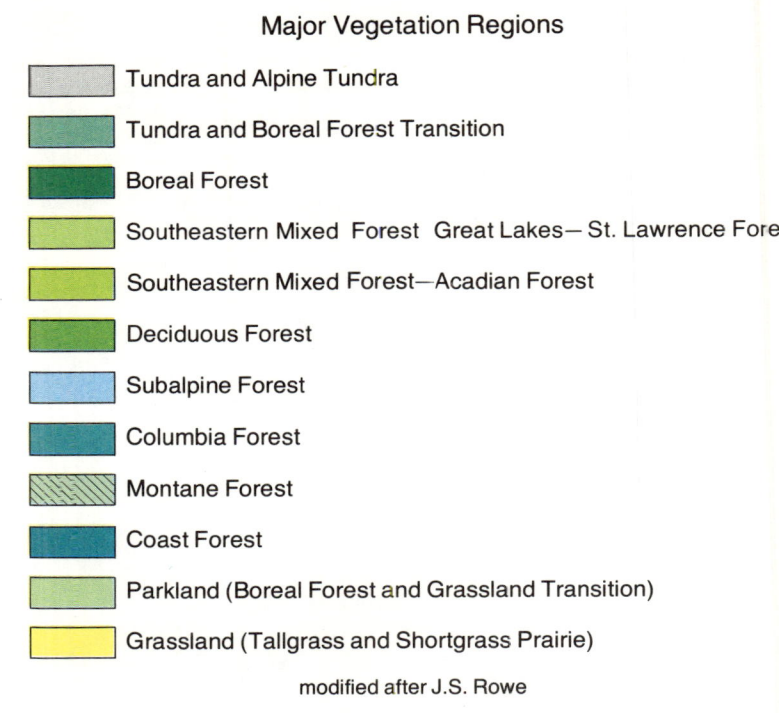

Major Vegetation Regions
- Tundra and Alpine Tundra
- Tundra and Boreal Forest Transition
- Boreal Forest
- Southeastern Mixed Forest Great Lakes— St. Lawrence Forest
- Southeastern Mixed Forest—Acadian Forest
- Deciduous Forest
- Subalpine Forest
- Columbia Forest
- Montane Forest
- Coast Forest
- Parkland (Boreal Forest and Grassland Transition)
- Grassland (Tallgrass and Shortgrass Prairie)

modified after J.S. Rowe

Source: Environment Canada, Canadian Forestry Service, *Canada A Forest Nation*, 1974

Base map produced by Surveys and Mapping Branch, Department of Energy, Mines and Resources, Ottawa.

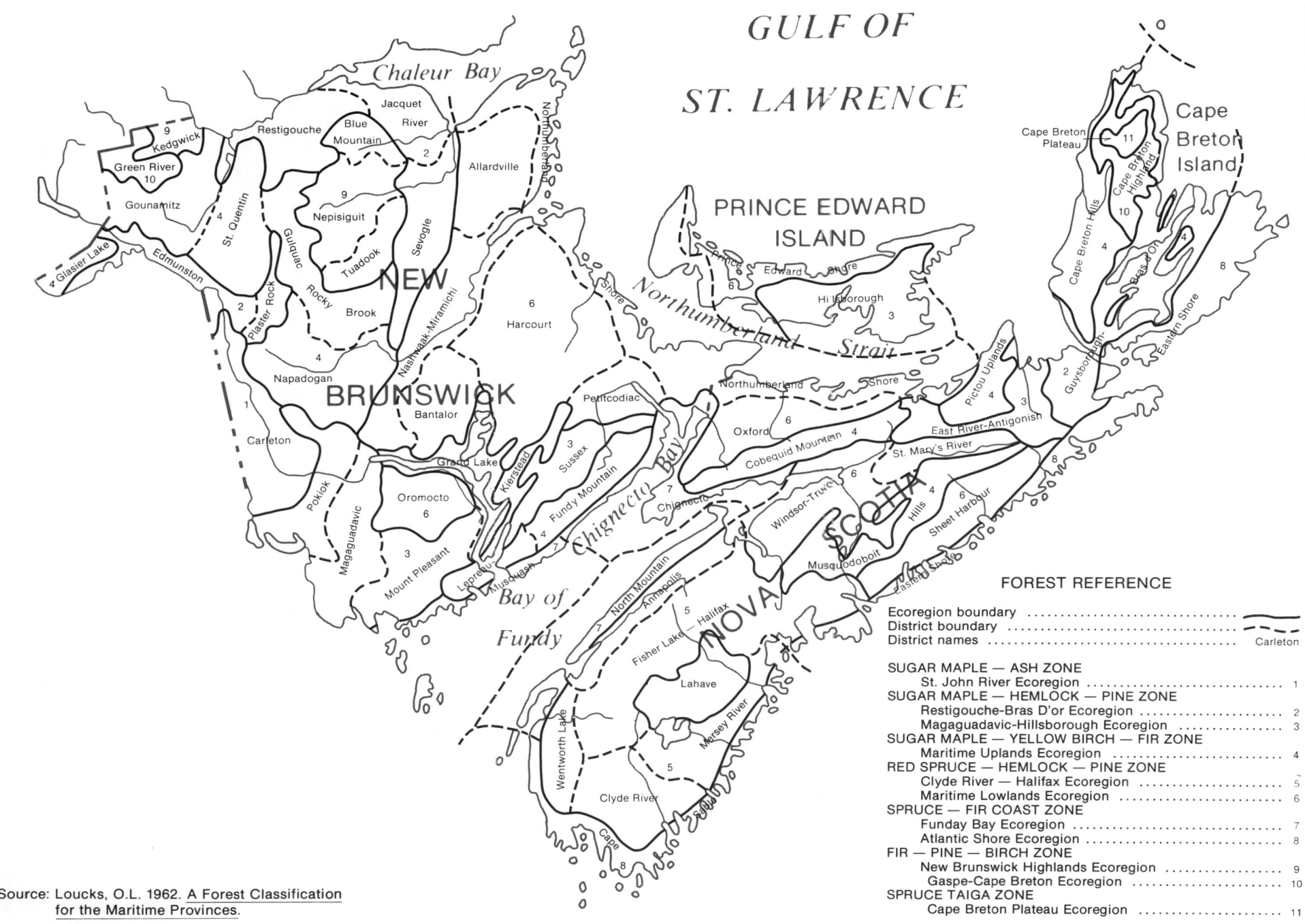

Forest Site Regions of Ontario

In 1950, Angus Hills established the forest site region as a broad integrated pattern of soil sites within which the potential forest production could be compared. Although the pattern of site types reflects the the air temperature and humidity of its macroclimate, the effectiveness of the site region is determined not by meteorological data, but by the response of the succession of natural communities of terrestrial plants growing in normal physiographic habitats. Map 6 shows the location of the regions in Ontario. Within a site region, amplification or reduction of the effect of macroclimate on vegetation successions can occur by a change in either the air temperature gradient or the air moisture gradient, or the soil moisture gradient.

The air temperature gradient may be subdivided into three broad classes:

Normal: the local climate neither amplifies nor attenuates the effect of the macroclimate on vegetation.

Colder than Normal: the local climate is reflected by development of vegetation associated with normal sites of colder, more northerly regions and occurs on landscape features known to diminish the effectiveness of the regional microclimate such as protected depressions which have inadequate air drainage.

Hotter than Normal: the local climate is reflected by development of vegetation associated with normal sites of warmer (more southerly) regions and occurs on landscape features known to amplify the effectiveness of the regional microclimate such as in broad protected valleys with good air drainage or in the gently undulating inner portions of a moderately broken uplands which benefit from a relative mass elevation effect. (Hills, 1952).

Likewise, the air moisture gradient may be subdivided into; normal, wetter than normal, and drier than normal. The final influencing factor, soil moisture, is subdivided into:

Fresh: that is the normal moisture regime for moderately humid belts of the temperature zone.

Drier: although the supply of available moisture limits growth during part of the growing season, the degree of dryness is relative to the region.

Wetter: growth is limited by excessive moisture and restricted aeration during part of the growing season. Wetter refers to moist rather than wet. (Hills, 1952).

The symbol association with each region refers to the thermal zone by number as shown: 1 – coldest, microthermal; 2 – cool, microthermal; 3 – moderate, microthermal; 4 – warm, microthermal; 5 – hottest, microthermal; 6 – coldest, mesothermal; 7 – cool, mesothermal; and to the level of air humidity and location by letter: E – humid eastern Ontario; H – humid western Ontario; S – subhumid western Ontario.

Since the work was completed in the early 1950s, Hills has revised the boundaries of the site regions to reflect the current state of knowledge at the time of each revision. The 13 site regions described here reflect the state of knowledge of the mid-1960s. Further revision of the classification has occurred (Thie and Ironside, 1976).

Economic Considerations

An Overview

The forests of Canada would probably have remained in their native state for a much longer period of time had it not been for the demands of the British market.

The use of Canadian timber began with the supply of masts and square timber to Great Britain in the 17th and 18th centuries for ships and shore structures of the Royal Navy in their battles with the French Republic and Napoléon. Canada provided an alternative source of supply to that coming traditionally from the Baltic countries.

The most important export was white pine which grew up to 600 m in height and up to 2 m at the butt. Straight grained, easily worked, resistant to warp, and free of knots, it was ideal for masts, spars, and trim. The next most important species exported were red pine and spruce that were strong but not as easily worked or as dimensionally stable as white pine.

The story of the timber trade touches on many aspects of history; war and peace, economic policy, and the relation between political action and private interest. In the background there lie such questions as settlement, the building of new communities, and metropolitanism, both in its economic and in its wider human aspect.

No one could study the forest industries without reflecting on nature's productive ability. The forests were there waiting to be used. The animals sheltered gave rise to the fur industry and meeting man's clothing needs. The trees themselves gave rise to another indus-

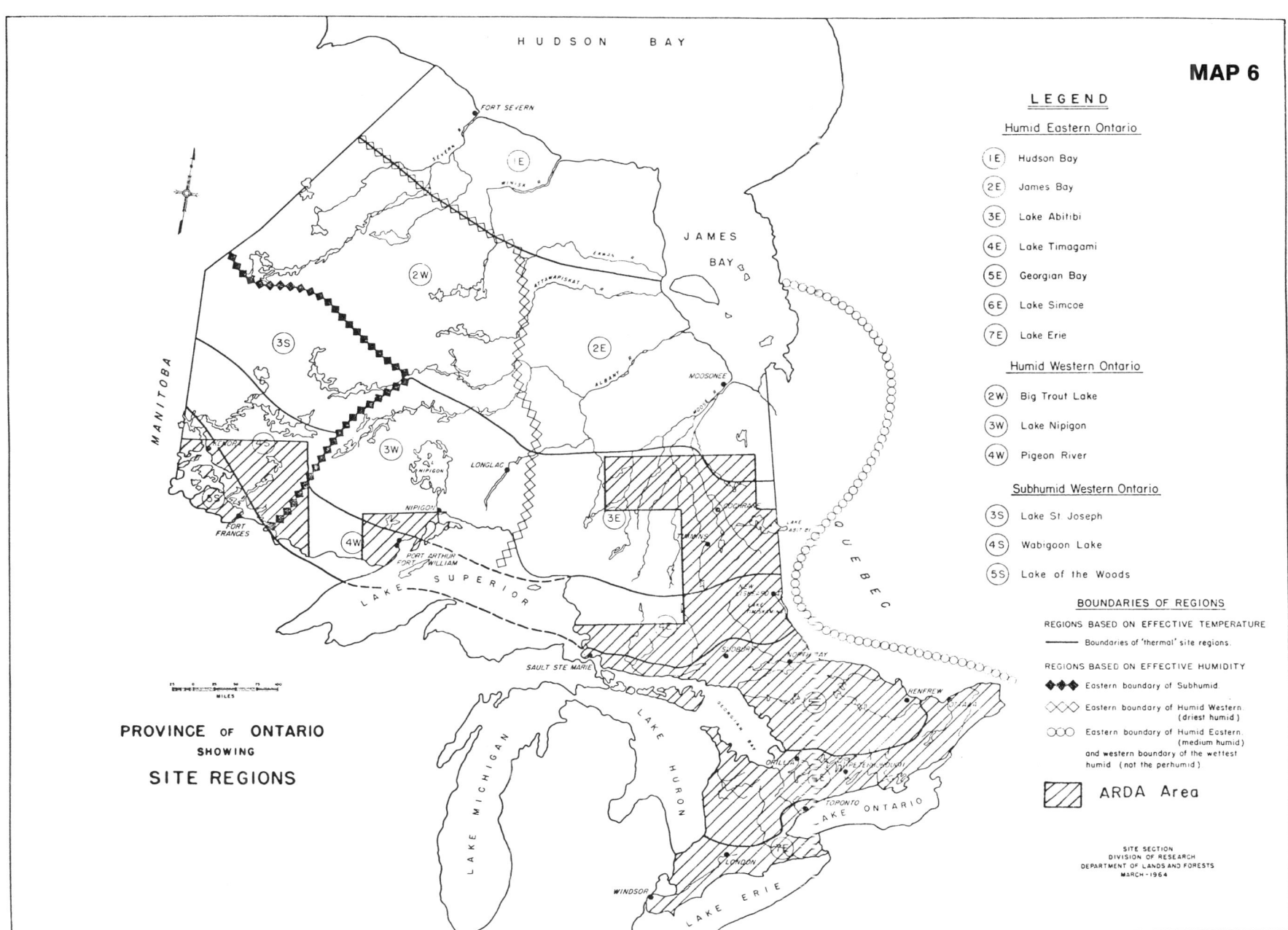

In the period of early exploration and settlement, several tree species were valued for their use in shipbuilding. Centuries later, forests still play a key rôle in transportation, this time in railway construction.

Forest resources have given rise to many industries, including shipbuilding. Canada has earned a reputation for building a variety of boats, from canoes to fishing trawlers, and this is particularly true in the Maritime Provinces.

try. The forest meant work and shelter, and shelter gradually developed into huts, houses, furniture, shops, and ships. For generations, the trees were there for the taking and nowhere was the taking easier or more improvident. A large page in Canada's history was written around this spoilation.

The "Canadian settler" it was said, "cordially hated a tree". The land being practically empty and the forest an enemy, no one thought of fitting it into a way of life. It was to be got rid of, burned or, if some market could be found, sold with maximum speed, profit, and wastefulness. On the other hand, a large proportion of allocations given to settlers seemed to have been taken up not for settlement but for the timber. Where the forest stood on good agricultural land, removal may have been defensible; where it stood on the Canadian Shield or the Appalachian ridges and was taken away, there was left nothing.

Historic Growth of the Forest Industries

Until the 1920s, and after the square-timber trade, lumber was the primary product of the forest industries. The pulp-and-paper industry then began to develop in eastern Canada and expanded rapidly until the outbreak of war. After the war, establishment of new mills was less rapid, but the size of the individual new mills increased and many older ones were modernized and expanded.

Rise of the pulp-and-paper industry coincided with a rapid decline in the number of sawmills and increasing concentration of lumber production in fewer, larger, and more efficient mills. Between 1961 and 1975, for example, the number of sawmills big enough to be reported by Statistics Canada dropped from about 3,500 to 1,400.

In British Columbia, a sawmill and plywood industry based on the large old-growth timber of the west coast dominated the scene until the 1950s. Subsequently, enormous expansion of the pulp-and-paper industry has occurred. Initially, this development took place in the coastal regions, but, since 1960, the expansion of both the solid wood products and pulp industries in the interior of British Columbia has rivalled that of the west coast.

The pulp-and-paper industry in western Canada is relatively new, highly integrated, and increasingly significant. British Columbia produces about two-thirds of Canada's softwood lumber on a large scale and efficiently, but many of the big coastal sawmills and plywood mills are becoming obsolete and unsuited to the second-growth forests of the future. The forest industry in Ontario and Québec traditionally has had a strong pulp-and-paper orientation, although their production of lumber has grown rapidly during the past decade. Québec and Ontario account for about two-thirds of Canada's newsprint production and half of its total wood pulp, other paper, and paperboard. Unfortunately, many of the older mills are small and inefficient. Although small in comparison with those of the three large provinces, the forest industries of the Atlantic and Prairie provinces are major factors in the regional economies.

NFB – PHOTOTHEQUE – ONF – Photo by Bob Brooks.
The establishment and growth of pulp-and-paper industries have significant economic impact, especially in British Columbia, Québec, and Ontario.

NFB – PHOTOTHEQUE – ONF – Photo by George Hunter.
Not only is forestry a major employer, but its contribution to the balance of trade, through exports, is important to all Canadians.

Contribution of Forestry to the Canadian Economy

Estimating the value of Canada's forest resources is impossible because so much of the value is intangible. However, it is possible to be more specific on its economic importance.

The forest resource supports 300 thousand jobs directly and another 400 to 600 thousand indirectly in secondary manufacturing and service industries. The forest products industry is Canada's leading commodity sector in terms of sales, employment, export earnings, and regional dispersion. In regional impact, it ranks first in manufacturing in British Columbia, Québec, and the Atlantic Provinces, second in the combined Prairie Provinces, and fourth in Ontario. It is the economic mainstay of many single-industry towns throughout the country. The sector is unique in that it is based on a substantial renewable resource, which, in addition to providing the raw material for the wood-using industries, confers significant environmental and social benefits to the country as a whole, including the scenic background for a $3-billion outdoor recreation industry.

Value of shipments of forest products fluctuate from year to year, but in 1976 they amounted to $13.1 billion, of which $6.5 billion were exported. The sector's net exports of $5.7 billion were more than five times Canada's trade surplus in energy commodities in 1976, and were considerably higher than the expected deficit in the petroleum account forecast for Canada in 1985. In the first nine months of 1978, the trade in wood and paper products contributed $6.4 billion to Canada's overall $1.6 billion positive trade balance. Iron and steel contributed $0.3 billion; crude petroleum, $1.4 billion; food, $1.0 billion; and transportation equipment, including autos and auto parts, $0.8 billion. Value added by the forest industries totalled $6.3 billion for approximately ten per cent of the total value added in the national economy.

Out of the 141,584,000 m³ of timber harvested in Canada, about 67 per cent is cut for logs, 29 per cent for pulpwood, and 4 per cent for fuelwood and other roundwood such as poles, shakes, and fencing.

More than 80 per cent of the logs are further processed into lumber and specialty products. One-third of the lumber is consumed domestically and two-thirds is exported.

The construction industry uses about half the lumber. Most of it goes into new residential construction and the rest into repairs, alterations, and non-residential construction. The other half of the lumber goes into millwork, furniture, and other industries.

About five per cent of all logs are peeler logs which are used to make veneer and plywood. One-third of this output is exported, while two-thirds is used domestically in the construction industry. A relatively new end-use in this area is particle board.

Ownership and Administration of Canada's Forests

By terms of Confederation, the provinces own almost all forest land and other natural resources within their boundaries as a cornerstone for provincial financing. In areas of old settlements, the provinces initially adopted policies of selling or granting forest land. As a result, some 23 million ha of Canada's forest (seven per cent) are owned privately, mostly in the Maritime Provinces, southeastern Québec and Ontario, and the southern part of Vancouver Island.

The provincial tenure arrangements have a major influence on forest land use in Canada. Tenure is used to allocate rights to use timber or land or both, to regulate exploitation, stimulate economic and social development, influence the amount and form of revenue gained from the forests, and guide forest management operations. The period or term, size, and conditions of tenure are important factors for forest management because these influence the forest industry's investment decisions and the degree to which the Crown has options and flexibility to pursue policy goals.

Details of forest administration and the rôle of private industry in forest management vary considerably from province to province. In recent years, however, the provinces have tended to become increasingly involved in direct management of the resource.

Although the provinces have pre-eminent jurisdiction over Canada's forest resources, the federal government has heavy involvement in many policies and activities critical to their management and use. These include matters such as fiscal management, regional development, industrial efficiency, research and development, tariffs and trade, competition, transportation, environment, and manpower and labour.

Timber Volumes

The supply of roundwood used by the Canadian forest products industry is produced by the logging industry, farmers, and mill operators, from both publicly and privately-owned forest land. Only about 2.5 per cent of roundwood used in Canada is imported, and most of it is valuable hardwoods for shop use. The volume of roundwood which producers are willing to supply to the forest products manufacturing sector depends on roundwood prices, harvesting and transportation costs, and stumpage. Therefore, apart from log prices, the supply of roundwood depends upon the willingness and ability of the logging industry to extract and deliver roundwood to the manufacturing plant, and upon the willingness and ability of the forest land owners to sell standing timber.

Canada's Forest Resource

Forest Lands

About 3,417 thousand km² are classified as forest land (Table 2). Of this, 2,642 thousand km² are owned by provincial governments; 575 thousand km², mostly in the territories and National Parks, are administered by the federal government; and the remaining 199 thousand km² are privately-owned.

Three per cent of the forest land is reserved for non-timber uses and cannot ordinarily be harvested. Of the total reserved forest land, 47 thousand km² are under federal jurisdiction and about 27 thousand km² are owned by provincial governments. The reservation of provincial forest land will probably increase in response to demands for recreational opportunities and environmental protection.

TABLE 2.

Land area classification

Land type	Area
	(thousands of km²)
Land Area	
forest land	3,417*
agricultural land	730
all other land	5,071
Total land area	9,218
Water area	757
Total area	9,975

* Includes non-inventoried forest land in Québec (179,000 km²) and Prince Edward Island (3,000 km²).

Source: Forest Management Institute, Environment Canada. 1979. Miscellaneous unpublished data.

TABLE 3.

Inventoried production forest land area, by ownership

Province or territory	Provincial	Crown Federal	Private	Total
	(thousands of km²)			
Newfoundland	327	*	8	335
Prince Edward Island				NA
Nova Scotia	10	*	30	40
New Brunswick	28	*	36	65
Québec	397	*	37	435
Ontario	515	6	49	570
Manitoba	245	1	5	251
Saskatchewan	121	2	NA	124
Alberta	315	3	NA	318
British Columbia	474	3	5	482
Yukon Territory	–	219	NA	219
Northwest Territories	–	95	NA	95
Total	2,432	329	170	2,934

* less than 500 km².

Figures may not add due to rounding.

Source: Forest Management Institute, Environment Canada. 1979. Miscellaneous unpublished data.

Only 2,934 thousand km² on non-reserved inventoried production forest land are capable of growing commercial timber crops within a reasonable length of time. Of this, the provincial governments control 2,432 thousand km² or 83 per cent of the total (Table 3). It is interesting to note that only 1,984 thousand km² of the 2,934 thousand km² are considered productive (Table 4). All but 100 thousand km² of the total inventoried productive forest land is located in the provinces. The better growing sites in the territories are confined to the main river valleys in the southern Yukon and the southwestern portion of the Northwest Territories.

Timber volumes by species on inventoried, productive, production forest land in provinces as of 1976 are shown in Tables 5 and 6. In addition, it has been estimated that there are just less than 227 million m³ of immature and 57 million m³ of mature timber, mostly spruce, in the Yukon and Northwest Territories. According to the 1976 National Forest Inventory there are 523 million m³ of timber in the Yukon. There are approximately 6 million m³ of timber in Prince Edward Island, mostly on private land.

These aggregate data should not be misconstrued to mean that sizeable volumes for certain species are available throughout Canada. The scattered nature and the condition of the timber within provinces may preclude economical harvesting. Scarcity of timber varies among regions within each province. Interpretation of these aggregate volumes, therefore, can only provide a very broad view of Canadian timber stocks.

TABLE 4.

Inventoried production forest land by productive and unproductive classes, by province or territory, 1976

Province or territory	Forest land		
	Productive	Unproductive	Total
	(thousands of km²)		
Newfoundland	85	250	335
Prince Edward Island			N/A
Nova Scotia	38	2	40
New Brunswick	61	4	65
Québec	373	61	435*
Ontario	430	140	570
Manitoba	132	119	251
Saskatchewan	80	44	124
Alberta	203	115	318
British Columbia	482	–	482
Provincial total	1,884	735	2,620
Yukon Territory	67	152	219
Northwest Territories	33	62	92
CANADA	1,984	949	2,934

* excludes 179,000 km² of forest land not inventoried.

Figures may not add due to rounding.

Source: Forest Management Institute, Environment Canada. 1979. Miscellaneous unpublished data.

TABLE 5.

Timber volume*, by species

Softwood species	Volume	Hardwood species	Volume
	(millions of m³)		(millions of m³)
White pine	179	Poplar	1,434
Ponderosa and red pine	43	Aspen	693
Jack and lodgepole pine	2,701	Black cottonwood	45
Larch	48	Yellow birch	291
Spruce	5,688	White birch	1,031
Hemlock	1,837	Beech	45
Douglas-fir	505	Maple	358
Fir	2,692	Ash	22
Eastern white and western red cedar	1,014	Other hardwoods	92
Yellow cedar	170		
Other softwoods	4		
Total	15,202**	Total	4,079**

* Volume of wood of main stem of trees or stands. It includes the volume of all reported species and maturity classes in all ownerships on inventoried, productive forest land.

** Includes volumes in Newfoundland, Québec, and Ontario for which no species breakdowns are available.

Figures may not add due to rounding.

Source: Forest Management Institute, Environment Canada. 1979. Miscellaneous unpublished data.

Coniferous species account for about 80 per cent of the growing stock. Spruce is the predominant coniferous species and accounts for 38 per cent of coniferous volume and for nearly one-third of the total growing stock. Balsam fir, jack and lodgepole pines comprise the next most abundant species and account for 14 per cent each of the total coniferous growing stock. Hemlock, ponderosa pine and Douglas-fir are also abundant, but occur mainly in British Columbia.

Poplar and aspen are the most abundant hardwood species in Canada and account for one-half of total hardwood volume. Almost one-half of Canada's poplar stocks occur in the Prairie Provinces where it accounts for almost all the hardwood volume in the region. Most of the remaining stocks of poplar occur in Ontario where this species accounts for about one-half of the province's hardwood volume. White birch, maple, yellow birch, and beech are abundant in Ontario, Québec, New Brunswick, and Nova Scotia.

TABLE 6.

Timber volume*, by province or territory

Province or territory	Timber volume		
	Softwoods	Hardwoods	Total
	(millions of m³)		
Newfoundland	573	47	620
Prince Edward Island			N/A
Nova Scotia	151	65	216
New Brunswick	482	185	667
Québec	1,906	856	2,762
Ontario	2,589	1,681	4,270
Manitoba	410	163	573
Saskatchewan	274	185	459
Alberta	939	592	1,531
British Columbia	7,561	205	7,766
Yukon Territory	214	39	253
Northwest Territories	103	61	164
CANADA	15,202	4,079	19,281

* Volume of wood of main stem of trees or stands. It includes the volume of all reported species and maturity classes in all ownerships on inventoried, productive forest land.

Figures may not add due to rounding.

Source: Forest Management Institute, Environment Canada. 1979. Miscellaneous unpublished data.

Allowable Annual Cuts

Provincial governments have placed, or are in the process of placing, most of their non-reserved forest land under sustained-yield management. The intent is to ensure that timber supplies will be available in the future for wood industries, and to stabilize employment in forest-based communities.

Sustained-yield management consists of two concepts: 1) continuity of growth and, 2) continuity of yield or harvests. These are not necessarily synonymous unless a management area supports an array of immature and mature merchantable timber, referred to as a "normal" forest. The forests of Canada which are managed for sustained yield have been so managed for only a short time and are characterized by age-class im-

NFB – PHOTOTHEQUE – ONF – Photo by Ted Grant.

The practice of sustained-yield management is critical not only to the vitality and health of the forestry industry, but also to the country as a whole. Failure to maintain continuity of both growth and harvest will have severe repercussions across many sectors of the economy.

balances far different from those of normal forests. These imbalances have resulted from natural catastrophies such as fire, disease, insect damage, and windstorms as well as from destructive logging practices.

It is the objective of provincial forest services to enforce rates of harvests, referred to as allowable annual cuts (AACs), which will bring about normality in the forests within one rotation. The resulting forests would contain stands ranging from one year to rotation age, and yield continuous regular harvest. To this end, provincial forest lands are divided into management units. A management plan is prepared for each unit that outlines resource inventories, resource uses, protection strategy, access development, crop establishment, and tending schedules, and a cutting budget and schedule equivalent to the AAC. AACs for management units, as well as yields from land not managed on a sustained-yield basis, currently total 215 million m³ of which 176 million m³, or 82 per cent, consist of softwood timber (see Tables 5 and 6).

The total AAC is a good indication of the physical and, to some extent, the economic limit of annual harvest from provincial Crown forest lands. In most provinces, a significant proportion of the northern forests is not currently harvestable primarily because of a lack of transportation facilities to move logs to mills. In other provinces, AACs are conservatively stated to avoid over-allocating timber cutting rights in the event that the AACs may have to be revised downwards in the future.

The current AACs are applicable only for the next five or ten years and are subject to periodic revision. Revisions are made following withdrawals of forest land for non-timber uses, catastrophic timber losses, changes in utilization standards, changes in the AAC calculation procedures, new developments in forest product markets and technology, and improved forest inventory and growth data. Revisions are made in some provinces as a result of silvicultural practices which are expected to improve forest growth rates or reduce the rotation age.

Future Harvests and the AAC

Harvests are expected to reach almost 220 million m³ by the year 2000. Approximately 185 million m³ of this will be softwoods and 35 million m³ will be hardwoods. This level of harvest corresponds to the economically accessible AAC under changing economic conditions. Under current conditions, the economically accessible AAC is about 140 million m³.

It is difficult to determine regionally what the AAC will be by 2000 without knowing what the expected demand and supply of roundwood might be regionally. Similarly, it is difficult to establish in what form and species the wood will be delivered to mills. Wood has consisted largely of sawlogs cut to various sizes depending on forest product and mill requirements.

The sizes and sources of logs have changed over the years as economic conditions, available forests, and forest policies have changed. As Douglas-fir became scarcer, the sawmill industry began to use more hemlock. As spruce became increasingly scarce, pulpmills began to use more jack pine and lodgepole pine. As softwood timber became more scarce, some pulpmills began to use hardwoods. Mixed-wood stands selectively logged for softwood timber remain mixed, but with less softwood than in the original stands. Thus, past forestry practices will make the preferred soft-wood timber more scarce in the future. Forest policy changes in some provinces may help to reverse this trend.

As stands of timber became more remote and costly to harvest and transport, the forest industry began to harvest to closer utilization standards. In some areas in eastern Canada, the industry is beginning to chip whole trees in the woods. As roundwood became more costly, the industry began to reallocate logs from pulpmills to sawmills and residues from sawmill waste burners to pulpmills. This is being facilitated by the integration of pulp-and-paper mills with sawmills in order to achieve the best return from delivered roundwood. Integration has been common in western Canada for several decades, but has been a relatively recent development in eastern Canada.

Data about the area of forest depleted annually are still only approximations. Estimates suggest that although harvests and forest product output have increased during the last decade, the area logged annually has not varied much from 800 thousand ha. It is quite possible that with intensified utilization and silviculture the forest products industry could expand on a reduced forest land base. In fact, it may become attractive to do so, considering the reluctance of the labour force to work in remote locations, the increase in transportation costs relative to intensifying utilization and silviculture in forest near mills, and the fragility and poor growth potential of remote forests.

The current AAC Canada-wide appears to be sufficient to support annual harvests of 220 million m³ by the year 2000. However, there is concern that the AAC may be inadequate to support expanded harvests in some regions, especially Nova Scotia and New Bruns-

167

wick. Programs have been initiated in many provinces to rehabilitate stands which have deteriorated from past utilization practices, and to accelerate restocking on burned and cut-over forest land. It is estimated that about 24 million ha are not satisfactory stocked, and have gone out of production; in 1968, 30 million ha of forest land were reported to be unstocked. It is likely that these statistics over-state the reforestation "backlog" for several reasons. In British Columbia, for example, it was estimated that 60 per cent of the unstocked land covered by old surveys had since regenerated naturally. Furthermore, the statistic in many provinces includes areas of selectively logged stands, sites with poor growth capacity, and northern burned-over forest lands which are left to regenerate naturally. In British Columbia, the B.C. Forest Service found that after adjusting the area of unstocked forest land for these factors, the land requiring reforestation is only 15 per cent of the total inadequately stocked forest land in public sustained yield units.

There is widespread concern that current AACs might have to be reduced as old-growth forests are liquidated and replaced with second-growth forests. It is argued that the forests, of a size which are currently being harvested, take longer to grow than subsequent crops and therefore second-growth forest will yield less volume per ha than the existing virgin forests. In fact, a reduction in current harvests in old-growth forests would delay not only the realization of old-growth timber volumes but also the initiation of new growth.

Besides restocking programs, other silvicultural programs to increase future harvest and to increase current AACs are being followed or planned in various regions. As a result of the way in which AACs are calculated, any increase in the productive area of timber growth in a management unit may result in an immediate increase in the AAC over one rotation. This is referred to as the "allowable cut effect" (ACE). The increased AAC is realized through accelerated depletion of mature timber stocks. The ACE works in reverse as a result of declining timber stocks and growth due to destructive agents. The ACE has been adopted by the B.C. Forest Service and others to encourage intensive silviculture.

The AAC can also be expected to change as a result of changes in forest policy, inventories, and methods of its calculation.

The future AACs on lands in all classes of ownership will depend on changes in owners' goals. In order to cope with changing goals, many provincial governments have struck royal commissions and task forces to investigate evolving problems and to make recommendations for policy changes. Many of the recommendations will affect future AACs on both public and private lands, through changes in tenure arrangements, forestry programs, forest land zoning, forest practices regulations, and financial incentives.

As small private forests change hands, the timber supply from these tracts will probably decline. This may be tempered somewhat, depending on the impact of government incentives designed to encourage private land forest management. Such incentives have been in the form of property tax rebates, loans, and extension services. The possible rôle which stumpage prices for Crown timber have as an incentive or disincentive to private forest owners to grow and sell timber should not be ignored. However, past experience throughout North America indicates that the large, rather than the small, forest owners are more likely to react to such incentives. Small forest land parcels are increasingly being held for purposes other than timber management.

A much more definitive assessment of the adequacy of timber stocks for the future will not be possible until information becomes available to link periodically the forest land base and timber stocks with net forest growth, allowable annual cuts, harvests and other depletions, and silvicultural practices by region.

Ecological Forest Land Uses

The term ecological forests here refers to forests: in which trees are managed to provide maintenance of sub-elements such as soil stabilization and water regime maintenance; that are ecologically sensitive or unique and may provide ecosystem representation; and forests whose natural resources provide wildlife habitat. In addition, the rôle of ecological forests in urban areas, agriculture, energy production and conservation, and recreation will be discussed. It is evident that special forest resource lands exist within each of these uses.

The most commonly managed sub-elements of a forest are soil and water. Large-scale soil stabilization programs, such as in the Norfork County (Ontario) blow sands district, smaller-scale programs along highways and on public recreation lands, and private undertakings connected with severe local soil erosion and landscape design, are carried out. Documentation of these programs is sketchy and statistical information sparse, thus soil stabilization programs will not be elaborated upon. Water regime maintenance and supply programs are carried out widely; their management is usually associated with municipal water supply or large-scale regional maintenance and distribution of water.

Forest Management for Water Control and Supply

General Principles. Unlike static natural resources such as minerals, forests, and to a lesser degree wildlife, water is locationally dynamic so that the first use of the resource may be made at any point along the course of its drainage basin. Water, itself, moves through the hydrologic cycle (Figure 1) from ocean to clouds, overland by wind, earthward by precipitation, and thence back to the ocean by percolation, with evaporation and transpiration providing short circuits. The rate of infiltration (the absorption of water into the ground) and the infiltration capacity, are determined by soil type and compaction. When a soil has been saturated by water and allowed to drain under gravity so that no more water moves downward, the field capacity of the water has been reached. The wilting point, the point at which vegetation cannot extract further water, is a level within the actual field capacity and dependent on soil type and texture. These are major factors of water control to be considered in forest management.

The objective of management for water yield may be to increase, to maintain, or to decease yield. With perceived shortages in the future, water yield increase is the focus of this section. To achieve this, the majority of the water in the watershed area in which it falls should be retained to induce optimum or maximum storage in the soil reservoir; the key to this is a stable soil mantle with organic material on top which permits the water to infiltrate and percolate through the soil rather than to run off in streams as overland flow.

The evapotranspiration and interception components of the hydrological cycle are most subject to influence by man and may be altered by land management practices. First, by removing vegetation and ground litter, the force of rain hitting the soil surfaces decreases the infiltration rate and increases the overland flow. Secondly, if an area is mechanically compacted whether or not intentionally, the infiltration rate is decreased and overland flow increased on the area. The water yield is increased by this practice, however, water quality is lessened proportionately. Thirdly, by clearcutting an area, the potential evapotranspiration rate is minimized, and the water yield is maximized in the first year. However, the annual increase will decrease each year thereafter as cutovers regenerate and new stands are established. Lastly, by minimizing the ratio of border length to cut area, similar effects can be realized as shown in clearcut areas.

All watersheds are amenable to management for control of amount, timing, and quality of water yield. The Greater Vancouver Water District provides an illustration of watershed management at the local scale for the provision of municipal water supplies.

The Greater Vancouver Water District Case Study. The Greater Vancouver Water District manages a total of 58,536 ha of forest land in the three mountainous and mostly uninhabited areas north of Vancouver. By a combination of methods and control of water yield described previously, and with an adequate support system of dams, reservoirs, holding tanks, and mains, the Corporation acquires, supplies, and distributes the water yielded within its bounds to municipal areas which are members of the Greater Vancouver Water District, and to non-members such as the University Endowment Lands and the City of North Vancouver.

The Corporation's facilities include: two major dams, the Cleveland on the Capilano River and the Seymour on the Seymour River, as well as minor ones at Burwell Lake and Palesade Lake; six watershed reserves, one near each dam site, one on Coquitlam Lake and one at Lock Lomond with a total usable capacity of 365,589 million L; 13 service reservoirs with a total capacity of 527 million L; five tanks with a capacity of 8,282,448 L; 12 pumping stations with a total maximum installed capacity of 889,945 L/minute; and, over 322 km of enamel-lined and coated steel pipe of 30 to 230 cm in diameter. Table 7 indicates the relative capacity of each of the individual facilities.

The municipal members and non-members of the Greater Vancouver Watershed area, the area size of each, and the volume of water sold to each for the year 1974 are shown in Table 8. Including waste water, the total water used in 1974 was 249,980,642 L and for the four preceding years, 246,675,708 L (1973), 233,472,644 L (in 1972), 220,028,806 L (in 1971), and 214,093,140 L (in 1970). Assuming the same rate of population growth within the service area and similar weather conditions, the average increase in supply of water in the next five years will be the same as experienced over the last five years.

In addition to this primary function of water supply, other uses of the land are made. The forests are harvested on a sustained-yield management program, and approximately 18,451 ha of productive timberland are managed. There are approximately 1,8000,000 M.B.M. of mature timber with an annual allowable cut of 25,000 M.B.M., and the species harvested include western red cedar, hemlock, balsam, Douglas-fir, spruce, and yellow cedar.

There is a very restricted use of the watershed for other purposes. Some permits are issued to fishermen holding resident anglers licences, however, the fishing is confined to the lower stretch of the Seymour, well downstream of the potable water storage area and the permitees are confined to the immediate vicinity of the river. At infrequent intervals of one to two years, per-

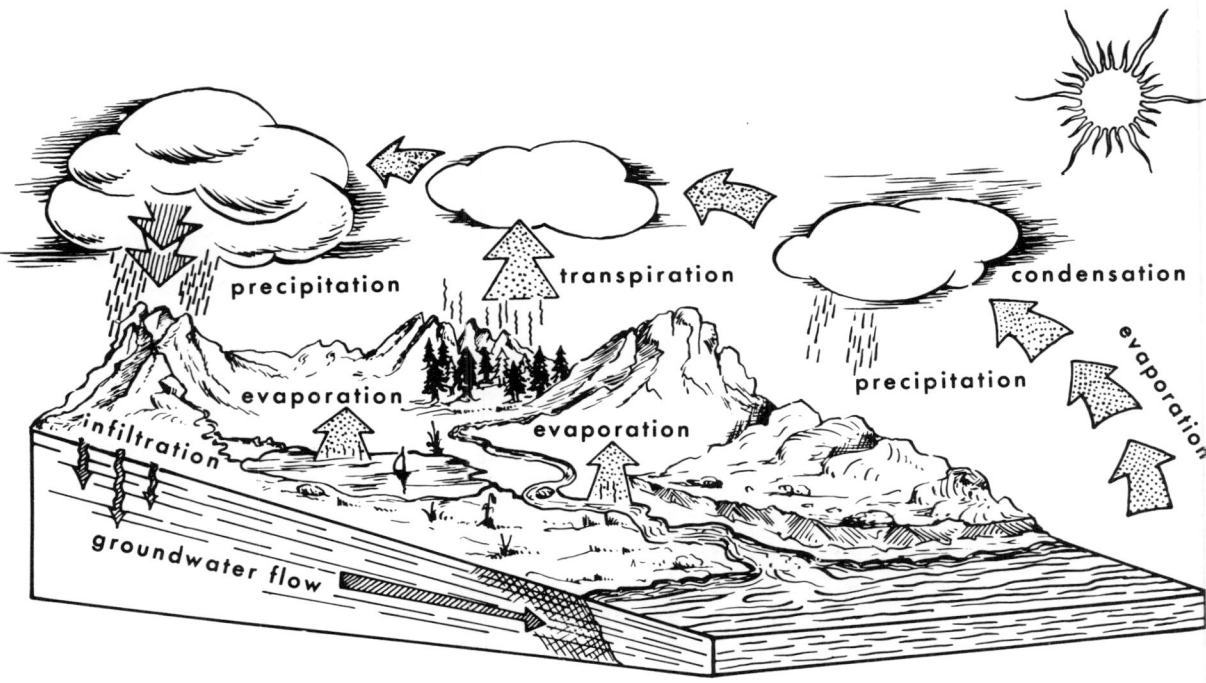

FIGURE 1. The Hydrologic Cycle

Source: Morris, M.V. 1969. Water.

mission is granted to three mountaineering clubs, Varsity Club, B.C. Mountaineering Club, and Alpine Club, for outings for which all members participating must receive health clearance, and the group is supervised by a Water District escort.

Ecologically Sensitive and Unique Areas

The International Biological Programme

Sixty countries, including Canada, are participating in the world-wide research programme, the International Biological Programme, concerned with the biological and physiographic basis of organic production and human welfare. It is divided into seven sections; the Conservation of Terrestrial Biological Communities (IBP/CT) is of eminent concern. Under a reserve system, the preservation of these natural and semi-natural areas for the "future of biology and human welfare" is to provide for:

1) the maintenance of large, heterogeneous gene pools;
2) the perpetuation of samples of the full diversity of the world's plants and animal communities in outdoor laboratories for a wide variety of research;
3) the protection in particular of samples of natural and semi-natural ecosystems for comparison with managed, utilized, and artificial ecosytems;
4) outdoor museums and areas for study, especially in ecology; and
5) education in the understanding and enjoyment of the natural environment and for the intellectual and aesthetic satisfaction of mankind.

The criteria for selection of natural and semi-natural areas is more complex than the "ready-made" criteria for the selection of the Canadian Institute of Forestry's natural areas. The general requirements are given below.

General IBP/CT Requirements

The selection of areas for inclusion in the final CT list of recognized and proposed reserves (Nicholson, 1968) are governed by the following criteria:

1) the areas should, taken together, contain adequate and manageable samples of the entire range of major ecological formations or ecosystems in the world and illustrate the degree of variation within each;
2) the series should include sites which, although they do not qualify for inclusion under the first criteria, support species of plants and animals of outstanding interest or great rarity;
3) the series should include sites which are of scientific interest because of the human management to which they have been subjected, even if this has in some cases led to more or less far-reaching modification of the biota;
4) the series should include sites which are important because they have been the scene of detailed and well-documented research;
5) the series should include sites which contain for example, deposits of peat, lignite or sediment from which information may be obtained about past vegetational and climatic changes, and also sites which are of special palaeontological importance; and
6) the series should include sites which are of special physiographic or geomorphological interest and which represent unusual habitats.

In selecting this series, the following general considerations are also borne in mind:

1) areas should be included whether or not they appear to be under immediate threat. Experience has shown that no reliance can be placed on the survival by good fortune even of very remote areas, and a comprehensive series of the sites which are required for science and education must be selected and preserved if further irreplaceable material is not to be lost;
2) other things being equal, preference should be given to sites that can conveniently be worked by existing or proposed research institutions; to sites that can be supervised and managed effectively; and to sites least likely to be affected by adverse neighbouring development and by air and water pollution;
3) areas must be of adequate size to support viable populations of the species which characterize them and for which they are established;
4) research areas must also be large enough to allow for the increasing amount of land demanded by modern field experimental research, especially since disturbance or damage arising from such research often modifies these areas and hence requires resting or replacement of such sites from time to time; and
5) while consideration of amenities and attractiveness to tourists should not determine the selection of an area for protection for scientific purposes, there are sometimes advantages in locating scientific reserves near to or within larger areas of high landscape value, since it then becomes justifiable to protect a larger and more viable unit.

In Canada, the IBP/CT activities were organized under ten original panels covering the following areas: (1) British Columbia, (2) Alberta, (3) Saskatchewan, (4) Manitoba, (5) Ontario, (6) Québec, (7) Maritimes (New Brunswick, Nova Scotia, Prince Edward Island), (8) Newfoundland and Labrador, (9) Arctic Region (beyond the treeline in the Northwest Territories), and (10) the Subarctic Region (beyond the treeline in the Northwest Territories and Yukon).

The Maritime Panel's definition of "ecological reserve" is generally agreed upon as a flexible definition of such a protected site and explains the importance of the reserves. The definition states:

"*An Ecological Reserve is a legally protected natural area where human influence is kept to a minimum. Change, itself a natural phenomenon, is not interfered with, but is allowed as far as possible to proceed uninterrupted by man. Natural areas are segments of a regional landscape* — samples of environmental systems or ecosystems. They contain examples of characteristic or rare plant and animal communities, or are areas of biological or physiographical importance. Though most natural areas comprise ecosystems with a history of relatively little human disturbance, ecosystems that have been modified by man have value for scientific research. Such areas offer an opportunity to observe developmental processes in the modified ecosystem and to study distinctive habitats, soil conditions and plant associations that result from man's influence. Ecological Reserves are established for scientific research and educational use. They are *not* another type of recreational area. The term 'reserve' is used rather than 'preserve' to emphasize the productive use of these areas for scientific and educational purposes, and to indicate the function these areas perform as natural reservoirs of living material." (McLaren and Peterson, 1975).

TABLE 7.

Facilities of the Greater Vancouver Watershed District, 1978

Watershed reservoirs		Service reservoirs	
Reservoir	Usable capacity	Reservoir	Capacity
	(millions of L)		(millions of L)
Capilano Lake	56,770	Prospect Avenue	4.68
Seymour Lake	25,276	Vancouver Heights	45.91
Coquitlam Lake	241,911	Sasamat	27.28
Palisade Lake	19,502	Little Mountain	140.02
Burwell Lake	15,093	Kersland	79.10
Loch Lomond	7,037	Westburnco No. 1	37.14
		Westburnco No. 2	77.74
		Whalley	35.46
		Burnaby Mountain	13.64
		Haney	5.91
		Clayton	7.27
		Central Park	36.37
		Newton	16.37
Total	365,589	Total	526.89

Tanks		Pumping stations	
Tank	Capacity	Station	Maximum installed capacity
	(L)		(L/minute)
Prospect Avenue	690,548	Cleveland Dam	50,306
Glenmore (2 tanks)	909,200	Sasamat	90,829
Burnaby Mountain	2,364,000	Kersland	119,105
Hellings	4,318,700	Vancouver Heights	159,110
		Burnaby Mountain	41,732
		Maple Ridge	16,820
		Little Mountain	143,963
		North Delta	51,643
		Westburnco	85,238
		Seymour Dam	1,182
		Haney Reservoir	3,637
		Central Park	136,380
Total	8,282,448	Total	889,945

Source: Greater Vancouver Water District, 1979. Personal communication.

TABLE 8.

Volume of water sold under the Greater Vancouver Water District Program

Members and non-members of the district	Areas	Metered sales, 1974
	(km²)	(million L/day)
City of Vancouver	113.2	288.7
District of Burnaby	90.7	77.3
City of New Westminster	14.5	34.4
District of North Vancouver	155.4	39.8
District of West Vancouver	82.9	22.5
Township of Richmond	129.5	54.5
District of Coquitlam and Fraser Mills	143.2	27.5
City of Port Coquitlam	25.1	11.3
District of Pitt Meadows	48.4	2.8
District of Maple Ridge	266.8	10.3
District of Surrey	344.5	43.3
District of Delta	326.3	38.7
City of Port Moody	12.2	16.7
City of North Vancouver	10.9	2.2
University Endowment Lands	13.0	14.4
City of Langley	10.1	–
Totals	1,786.7	684.4

Source: Greater Vancouver Water District. 1975.

TABLE 9.

Status and size of proposed IBP Ecological Sites, 1975

	Areas with protected status*		Areas with no protected status		Total	
	Number of IBP sites	Size	Number of IBP sites	Size	Number of IBP sites	Size
		(ha)		(ha)		(ha)
Newfoundland	18	352,160	49	302,006	67	654,166
Nova Scotia	11	9,481	62	12,980	73	22,461
New Brunswick	11	726	17	8,150	28	8,876
Prince Edward Island	3	119	12	3,056	15	3,175
Québec	–	–	25	52,375	25	52,375
Ontario	156	776,727	323	104,848	479	881,575
Manitoba	34	1,038,985	36	116,872	70	1,155,857
Saskatchewan	24	353,381	76	1,189,150	101	1,542,531
Alberta	147	2,511,587	50	111,420	197	2,623,007
British Columbia	43	116,199	173	499,474	216	615,673
Yukon Territory	2	44,000	10	1,155,389	12	1,199,389
Northwest Territories	5	967,390	33	1,611,239	38	2,578,629
CANADA	454	6,170,755	866	5,166,959	1,320	11,337,714

* Areas designated as having "protected status" may include federal and provincial wildlife refuges, National and provincial parks and ecological reserves. Sites with both a "protected" and a "non-protected" portion are considered as "areas with some protected status".

Source: LaRoi, Babb, and Perley, 1976. Canadian Directory of IBP Areas 1968-1975.

By 1975, about 1,300 IBP sites had been check-listed (see Map 10 in the Wildlife chapter). They range in size from one-half ha in the case of certain special habitats such as island nesting sites for marine waterfowl to over 2,590 km² in some of northern Canada's proposed ecological reserves which are intended to contain both summer and winter ranges of major animal species. With the passage of the provincial Ecological Reserves Act in 1971, British Columbia became the first province to give legal protection status to ecological reserves; Québec followed in 1972, and New Brunswick in 1975. Ontario does not have an ecological reserves act as such, but has protected reserves under legislation that pre-dated the IBP/CT work, mainly through the Provincial Parks Act and the Conservation Authorities Act, and continues to do so. Other provinces have quasi protection status for some of the proposed reserves, mostly under the auspices of National and provincial parks. The distribution and area of these sites are given in Table 9. In addition, since 1975, more areas have been identified for consideration. These areas include 346,000 km² proposed in the north. These locations, not included in the initial IBP checksheets, identify a variety of sensitive lands in both the Yukon and Northwest Territories.

British Columbia has established the greatest number of ecological reserves and has paid the most attention to forest communities. Table 10, gives the general location, size, and the object or community-type of each area preserved. A quick glance will show the emphasis that has been placed on forest communities, with approximately, one-third of the total areas reserved for forest ecosystem representation.

Canadian Institute of Forestry's Natural Areas Programme

Recently the Canadian Institute of Forestry adopted a policy for the selection, protection, and management of natural areas, whereby the Canadian Institute of Forestry encourages the reservation of a number of natural areas representing undisturbed samples of all significant forest and forest-related vegetation in Canada. Weetman (1970) and Weetman and Cayford (1972) define a natural area as "a naturally occurring physical or biological unit where natural conditions are maintained insofar as possible. An area is preserved to exemplify typical or unique vegetation and its associated biotic, edaphic, geologic and acquatic features in as near-natural condition as possible, usually by allowing the ordinary physical and biological processes to operate without human intervention".

The importance of these areas has been set forth in the Canadian Institute of Forestry's Policy for Selection, Protection, and Management of Natural Areas and states that natural areas serve one or more of the following purposes:

1) Science. To provide outdoor laboratories for the study of natural processes in relatively undisturbed ecosystems by biologists, wildlife specialists, soil scientists, microclimatologists, geomorphologists, and others in an environment that is relatively free of human intervention or that, through management practices when necessary, is maintained to preserve particular ecological conditions.

2) Benchmarks. Natural areas provide benchmarks against which land management practices can be gauged.

3) Preservation of gene pool resources. Natural areas will help to maintain the diversity present in natural ecosystems by the preservation of natural communities. They may also aid in conserving rare or endangered plants and animals in their natural habitat.

4) Education. Natural areas will serve as outdoor classrooms for the education of the increasing numbers who consider the primeval landscape a cultural heritage of intrinsic interest.

5) Living museum. Natural areas will preserve representative examples of forest vegetation in a state as nearly natural as possible, closely approximating conditions that existed at the time of settlement. (Weetman and Cayford, 1972).

The criteria for selection of natural areas is basically simple. Rowe delineated 8 major forest regions and 90 sections. The Canadian Institute of Forestry advocates representation in every section, although, as pointed out by Rowe, undisturbed examples of certain forest types are already difficult to find. Ideally, the size of the natural areas should be 120 to 4,050 ha, however, in certain instances this is not possible and areas as small as four ha have been recognized. The highest priority is to be given to reservation of natural areas (1) representing undisturbed examples of the major, commercially important forest types, and (2) protecting rare and endangered species of plants and animals. Since the intent of natural areas is the permanent reservation of land, locations which offer present or future foreseeable conflict, i.e. locations threatened by urbanization, recreational and industrial development, or by highway and reservoir construction, are avoided. To provide long-term protection of the land, ownership is usually the provincial or federal government or universities. In instances where all potential sites for a given forest cover are privately held, agreements between the Canadian Institute of Forestry and the individual land owner may be suitable.

Protection of the natural areas includes guidelines for: identification of the purpose and objectives; enclosure by fencing against domestic livestock and other adverse usage where necessary; publicity for scientific and educational purposes but not for recreational or otherwise infringing uses; physical improvements to be limited to necessary facilities needed to carry out scientific and educational work; fire, insect, and disease control; and mineral and oil entry.

The intent of the program is for scientific and educational purposes. Statistical data and map locations for the areas within the program are not available.

Photo by G. Ironside.

Porter Lake is a typical example of boreal forest vegetation on shallow glacial drift over acidic Precambrian rock. The area contains a long and well-defined esker, is part of the winter range of barren-ground caribou, and is identified as an IBP area.

Other Systems for Identification and Preservation of Natural Areas

Other systems of identification and reservation of natural areas and forest communities exist under both national and provincial legislation in Canada. At the national level, National Parks of the Department of Indian and Northern Affairs have identified 39 terrestrial natural regions in Canada, the locations of which are given in the Recreation chapter of this report. One objective of National Parks in their acquisition of new land areas for National Parks is to acquire at least one park in each of these areas. Since National Parks are established and managed primarily to preserve represent-

TABLE 10.

Established Ecological Reserves in British Columbia

Location	Area (ha)	Object or community-type preserved
Cleland Island, Clayoquot Sound	8	Marine wildlife
East Redonda Island	6,212	Three biogeoclimatic zones with many habitats
Soap Lake, south of Spences Bridge	884	Alkaline lake with Douglas-fir forest
Lasqueti Island	201	Juniper-cactus parkland
East of Nicklen Lake	101	Undisturbed highland lake
Buck Hills Road near Lumby	16	Western larch stand
Trout Creek, near Summerland	75	Ponderosa pine parkland
South of Clayhurst	316	Peace River parklands
Southwest of Tow Hill, Graham Island	514	Sand dunes and peat bog
Rose Spit, Graham Island	170	Coastal dunes of Graham Island
Sartine Island, part of Scott Islands	13	Marine wildlife
Beresford Island, part of Scott Islands	8	Marine wildlife
Triangle Island, part of Scott Islands	85	Sea bird colony
Solander Island, off Cape Cook, Vancouver Island	8	Marine wildlife
Saturna Island	131	Coastal Douglas-fir forest
Saltspring Island	254	Arbutus-Douglas-fir forest
Canoe Islets near Valdes Island	0.6	Marine wildlife
Rose Islets, Trincomali Channel	0.8	Marine wildlife
Mount Sabine north of Canal Flats	8	Sedge meadow
East side of Columbia Lake	32	Calcareous vegetation along a stream and on a meadow
Skagit River	73	Douglas-fir forest, California rhododendrons
Vicinity of Ross Lake	61	Ponderosa pine in coastal Douglas-fir forest
Moore Islands, Whitmore Islands, and McKenney Islands, Hecate Strait	73	Sea bird colony
Baeria Rocks, Barkley Sound	1.2	Sea bird colony
Dewdney Island and Glide Islands, Hecate Strait	3,845	Coastal western hemlock, plant communities, and marine wildlife
Ram Creek, East Kootenays	121	Hotsprings
Southwest of Princeton	32	Ponderosa pine stands
Ambrose Lake, Sechelt Peninsula	228	Coastal bog lake
Three miles northwest of Tranquille	235	Ponderosa pine and sagebrush plant community
Vance Creek-Trinity Valley Road	49	Transition between the Interior Douglas-fir and Interior western hemlock zones
Lew Creek drainage basin near south shore of Trout Lake	815	Three biogeoclimatic zones in one drainage basin
West end of Evans Lake, west of Slocan Lake	185	Yellow cedar stand in Interior subalpine zone
West Osoyoos Lake	4	Semi-arid plant communities
Big White Mountain	951	Subalpine and alpine plant communities
Approximately ten miles south of Williams Lake	30	Saline communities of the Interior Plateau with many insects
Northwest of Carp Lake	583	Long compound esker, well-developed liche (Cryptogamic) communities
Saltspring Island-Mount Maxwell	65	Undisturbed stand of Garry oak
Takla Lake	263	Most northerly known occurrence of Douglas-fir
Sunbeam Creek, north of McBride	511	Engelmann spruce-subalpine fir zone
Kingcome River and Atlatzi River	414	Lodgepole pine in the coastal rain forest
Tacheeda Lakes	526	Sub-boreal zone in the McGregor Plateau
Southwest of Mara Lake	148	Unique bog, rare species of orchids
Near Wap Lake, north of Mabel Lake	1,376	Secondary and climax Interior western hemlock zone
Jeffrey, East Copper and Rankine Islands	121	Marine wildlife, nesting colonies of seabirds

ative and unique natural environments, they are closely allied with the Canadian Institute of Forestry's Natural Areas concept. Thirty-seven of Rowe's 90 forest sections have representation within the National Parks System (National Parks Canada, 1971).

Within each park, five possible classes of park areas have been delineated (Class 1: Strict Preservation Areas; Class 2: Wilderness Areas; Class 3: Natural Environment Areas; Class 4: Outdoor Recreation Areas; and Class 5: Intensive Use Areas). The degree of protection of the natural attributes of an area varies with the class of the area. The purpose of classes 1, 2, and 3 ecological reserves within the parks, are as follows:

Class 1: Strict Preservation Areas
Purpose: to provide strict preservation of those portions which contain fragile, unique or representative examples of flora, fauna or geomorphology and special historical or cultural features. No access is permitted except by small groups led by park staff.

Class 2: Wilderness Areas
Purpose: to preserve the natural environment, to retain its primeval character, as well as its influence on man. The uses applicable to this zone are those which are "extensive" in character and have minimal impact on the landscape. Access is by non-motorized means.

Class 3: Natural Environment Areas
Purpose: to ensure the preservation of those natural areas which, because of their proximity to use areas, cannot be regarded as wilderness in the traditional sense. The uses permitted in this zone are the same as for Class 2. (Falkner and Carruthers, 1974).

The development of the natural regions concept has recently been aided by a recent planning document which identifies 55 natural areas which satisfy the following criteria of Canadian significance:

Representativeness: of the "best" sample areas representing the characteristic features of a natural region or natural history theme; or

Uniqueness: an area that encompasses features that are unique, rare, or "one-of-kind" to distinguish them significantly from other parts of the natural region; and

Naturalness: the area must be either in a relatively natural state or, if modified by man, capable of a high degree of restoration to natural conditions.

It is hoped that negotiations can be made that will give some of these areas protection under the National Parks Act while filling voids in the National Parks System at the same time.

The various provincial parks systems also afford some degree of protection to land areas within their jurisdiction. Ontario's is probably the best known for its preservation of significant ecosystem representations, under the Nature Reserve and Primitive Park categories. Alberta's Provincial Wilderness Areas, Saskatchewan's and Ontario's Wildlife Areas, and Ontario's Conservation Authorities' Reserves, to mention a few, also offer varying degrees of protection for significant natural areas. Private organizations such as the Nature Conservancy of Canada and Ducks Unlimited also reserve natural areas of significance whose attributes, in some cases, may be connected with forest ecosystems. These are described under their major purpose in the Wildlife chapter.

Photo by Agriculture Canada.

Many agencies endeavour to increase awareness and knowledge of forest resources through public education programs. The outdoor classroom provides an excellent opportunity for students to learn more about forest-related activities.

NFB – PHOTOTHEQUE – ONF – Photo by Nelson Marrifield.

The preservation of representative or unique natural environments is one objective of many provincial and federal agencies. The Department of Indian and Northern Affairs ensures that forests of various types remain an important element within the National Parks system.

Habitat Provision

The varied fish and wildlife resources of Canada are prolific, and their habitats are dependent on forest cover. Each species is sensitive to changes in the forest cover whether these changes be by natural processes or human activity. Sudden alteration of forest cover, such as clearing for roads associated with commercial forestry, affects the hydrological regime and water quality of the streams, and has often been detrimental to both commercial fisheries and to sport fish activities.

A number of ungulate species (moose, elk, and caribou) rely seasonally on mature forest cover and are threatened by severe alterations in forest cover. Large furbearing animals such as the grizzly bear and many smaller animals and birds also rely heavily on a dense forest cover. On the other hand, some wildlife populations benefit from forest operations and natural disturbances such as fire. The habitat of species such as deer, moose, and grouse, which prefer a less dense forest cover, are often enhanced by the periodic removal or disturbance of the forest canopy.

The effects of forest disturbance on wildlife cannot be generalized, as the effects depend heavily on the pattern and character of change. A detailed description of the nature and character of habitat requirements for a variety of important waterfowl and ungulate species in Canada is given in the Wildlife chapter, and the effect of change in one or more elements of a habitat on its species user is also detailed.

NFB – PHOTOTHEQUE – ONF – Photo by N. Lightfoot.

Each type of forest cover, regardless of its character, provides shelter, food, and habitat for wildlife.

Urban and Aesthetic Forests

"The battle to save trees and parks is just the same as saving architectural artifacts. It's not just a question of saving houses but of keeping the world fit to live in." (Fitch, 1976).

Aesthetics, sense perception, an appreciation of character, power, and other qualities within a comprehensive idea of beauty, are derived from man's ability to create visual order from the concept of order in nature to stimulate and satisfy pleasurable feelings or emotions. Aesthetics, which form part of the natural attributes, amenities, intrinsic qualities, recreational benefits, and social values for which forest lands are valued, has long been recognized in the natural environment; however, the loss thereof has not been cause for concern until further evidence of physical degradation (chemical or biological change) has occurred. Today, the social value of aesthetics has gained importance, and management of forest lands for aesthetics is being carried out for its sake alone or in conjunction with other purposes on federal, provincial, and municipal levels, with emphasis and needs at the municipal level taking on a unique form.

Legislation and Policy

On a federal level, the duties of the Minister under the Federal Department of Environment Act include the promotion, encouragement, and institution of "practices and conduct leading to the better protection and enhancement of environmental quality", which,

TABLE 10. cont'd

Location	Area (ha)	Object or community-type preserved
Port Chanal, west coast of Graham Island	9,834	Virgin littoral environment, Sitka spruce, mosses and hepatics, falcon rookeries
Headwaters of Sikanni Chief River	2,401	Engelmann spruce at northern extremity of range, subalpine lichens
South of Parker Lake near Fort Nelson	259	Natural bog habitat, preservation of *Sarracenia purpurea* (pitcher plant)
Bowen Island	397	Bedrock associations with Douglas-fir and red cedar, dry subzone of western hemlock
Kingfisher Creek, Hunters Range	1,441	Representative flora of northern Monashee Mountains
Northeast of Cecil Lake	128	Sphagnum bog community with black spruce
Northeast of Little White Mountain	124	Marshy area with many varieties of wild flowers
Southeast of Masset	837	Protection of watershed containing unique species of stickleback
Between Coglistiko and Baezaeko Rivers	1,098	Protection of waterfowl breeding grounds, well-developed aquatic communities.
Nitinat Lake, Vancouver Island	59	Westerly distribution of Douglas-fir
Cardiff Mountain near Konni Lake	65	Outstanding example of columnar basalt lavas
Goosegrass Creek west of McNaughton Lake	2,185	A cross-section of three biogeoclimatic zones which includes a sample of mountain hemlock
Chickens Neck Mountain	680	Climax stands of white spruce and subalpine fir
Twenty-miles west of Lower Post	777	Terrestrial and aquatic communities associated with the boreal black and white spruce zone
Near Bob Quinn Lake	2,046	Coastal western hemlock zone near its northern limit and associated Engelmann spruce -- subalpine fir and alpine tundra
Drywilliam Lake near Fraser Lake	95	To preserve an excellent old growth stand of Douglas-fir
Shuswap River north of Sugar Lake	70	Western red cedar in Interior wetbelt
Alluvial Terrace near Fort Nelson	121	White spruce developing within stands of black cottonwood
On Skeena River near confluence with Exchamsiks River	91	To preserve mature beach cottonwood on alluvial floodplain
In vicinity of Far Mountain, Ilgachuz Range	2,914	Vegetational types of Central Interior Plateau and Coast Mountains
Near Chasm Park	188	Ponderosa pine near its northern limits
Ten Mile Point, Victoria	11	Subtidal marine life
Satellite Channel	343	Subtidal marine life
Gladys Lake, Spatsizi Plateau	33,185	Stone sheep, mountain goats and their environment
Baynes Island, Squamish River	71	Black cottonwood forest on undisturbed island of sedimentary deposits
Mount Tinsdale, near of Barkerville	418	Representative communities of alpine tundra zone and Interior subalpine zone
Blackwater Creek	234	Boreal forest and portion of extensive low moor area
Nechako River	133	Conserve a good stand of tamarack
Torkelsen Lake	182	Low moor with cloudberry
Endowment Lands, U.B.C.	89	Puget Sound Lowlands forest
Clanninick Creek near Kyuquot	37	Alluvial Sitka spruce
	80,260.6	Total

Source: British Columbia Department of Environment, 1976. *Ecological Reserves in British Columbia*.

172

though not specifically stating so, does foster management for aesthetic purposes. The National Parks Policy on forestry states that the forests of the National Parks should be protected and maintained to preserve their natural, recreational, scenic, and other aesthetic values; the actual management of the forest lands "depends upon the most desirable use of the area. A wilderness zone should contain a completely natural forest. An area around a townsite or campground should be managed so as to maintain a forest, a forest that will withstand the necessary visitor use without altering the natural scene appreciably". Permissible forest operations for aesthetics include: the removal of dead, diseased, or infested timber in an area used extensively by park visitors; artificial reforestation of areas where a forest is desirable and natural regeneration is not occurring; and cultural cutting of green timber to develop or maintain healthy recreational forests in, for example, developed areas along scenic drives. The Forestry Research Act enables the Canadian Forestry Service to provide advisory and research assistance to agencies or individuals to encourage better municipal tree management. The nation's railroad carriers have the authority under the Railway Act to manage the trees and forests along specified rights-of-way whether on rural or urban land.

More specific legislation governing the management of forest land for aesthetic purposes may be found at the provincial level. All provinces provide for protection and maintenance of forests in provincial parks legislation for preservation of aesthetic values in much the same way as National Parks. In addition, various other provincial legislation provides for some form of aesthetic management: Nova Scotia's Forest Improvement Act "requires the maintenance, protection, and rehabilitation of the forests ... to improve conditions for wildlife, recreation and scenic values." Prince Edward Island's Recreational Development Act provides for aesthetic management in recreational areas both within the provincial parks and within both protected and unprotected areas outside the provincial parks; Ontario's Wilderness Areas Act provides for "care, preservation, improvement, control and management of wilderness areas having regard to its ... aesthetic values"; although the objective of Ontario's Woodlands Improvement Act does not directly provide for trees for aesthetics, the result of the program does; and, Alberta's Environment Conservation Act, among other purposes, pertains to the management of lands for the preservation of natural resources for their aesthetic value. Other provincial legislation and management schemes also provides for aesthetic management. For example, otherwise merchantable timber may be reserved from forest management areas in Saskatchewan "for the conservation of aesthetic and artistic values including: timber within three hundred feet of the edge of the right-of-way of provincial highways and other designated roads, and timber within three hundred feet of the top of the bank of any lake, river or stream as may be designated". Ontario's Ministry of Natural Resources forest management guidelines contain a section related to aesthetics which include reiteration of good forest practices. For example, "Roads that fulfill the objectives of (a) driver safety, (b) response to site conditions through sensitive alignment, (c) site protection of the right-of-way have greater aesthetic appeal than those that ignore such consideration...." The Trees Act of Ontario protects trees from trespass and illegal cutting on wooded sites of 0.8 ha or more.

Aesthetic and urban forest legislation on the municipal level is well obscured in legislation on other matters. No comprehensive study on the legislation has been done to date, however, partial information for the municipalities of Ontario is available from a survey sponsored by the Association of Municipalities of Ontario and the Ontario Shade Tree Council.

The survey (Andresen, 1976b) sought to establish a profile of municipal tree management and policies in Ontario. The results (Table 11) show that:

- Tree inventories upon which tree management and subsequently tree bylaws are based, were few.
- Most municipalities have tree removal policies which are incorporated within operational programs but only four per cent of municipalities have policies to protect trees.
- Allocation of specific funds for tree planting and maintenance work is closely related to the interest in tree protection.
- The majority of municipalities would be prepared to initiate new tree programs if provincial or federal funds became available.

Despite the seeming paucity of legislation on urban and aesthetic forests, two facts are encouraging. Most of the relevant legislation is recent; it may reasonably be assumed that an increasing proportion of legislation will deal with this topic. The second is a project sponsored by the Canadian Forestry Service and carried out by the Canadian Environmental Law Association and the University of Toronto Urban Forestry Studies Programme. The objectives are to review all relevant legislation applicable to urban tree management in Ontario, to recommend reform of tree legislation to bring older laws into current reality, and to compose a model tree bylaw that can be adapted for local use.

TABLE 11.

Tree Bylaw and Related Data Derived from Ontario Municipal Forestry Survey

Response category	City or borough	Town [1]	Village	Township [2]	Upper tier municipality
Total population	5,179,040	1,161,162	129,189	1,398,451	--
Total number of governments	44	142	121	486	39
Number of governments responding	34	80	56	207	22
Current tree bylaws in force	29.4*	10.0	0.0	2.9	9.1
Other bylaws that apply to trees	47.1	15.0	7.1	16.0	22.7
Public trees inventoried	26.5	2.5	0.0	0.5	13.6
Tree removal policy	76.5	47.5	26.8	19.3	50.0
Tree protection policy	47.1	10.0	1.8	2.9	18.2
Specific funds for tree work	50.0	11.3	1.8	2.9	9.1
New programs of provincial funds available	70.6	68.8	42.9	29.5	45.5
Want tree bylaw and related information	88.2	67.5	39.3	38.2	63.6

[1] Includes separate towns.

[2] Includes improvement districts.

* Following percentages indicated a "yes" response.

Source: Andresen, J.W. 1976b. Urban Forestry in Ontario: Municipal Challenges and Opportunities.

Urban Trees and Forests

The concept of urban forests as natural zones meeting urban society's needs and providing forest products has until recently been a neglected area of concern. The complex problems of establishing and maintaining urban forests and trees must be solved if the urban forest concept is to be accepted as a necessary land use option. Existing situations involving the attitudes and interests towards urban trees and forests have qualified this relatively obscure subject as a critical issue.

Canadians, unlike societies in Europe, have not yet fully realized that urban trees and forests are valuable and essential assets in community life. Due to the extremely high demands placed upon forest reserves in Europe, the importance of the city forests was recognized before the turn of the century. City jurisdictions were established over the majority of the countries forest resources, utilizing them not only for forest products but also maintaining them for the people as a place for enjoying the re-creating powers of nature. This type of multiple use approach to urban forests has kindled, within the European societies, an appreciation and respect for the environment which in Canada is experienced and practised by a small minority of the population. "A need to concentrate our efforts on educating the public to understand that the basic principles of conservation is not hoarding but the wise and planned use of our resources. Man needs nature for rest and recreation as well as for more material items ..." (Brown, 1970).

By the end of the 19th century, the clearing of land and establishment of cultivation in Canada was at a general high point. With the opening of the west and long distance transportation, local agriculture began to decline. Following, was a trend towards urbanization. The population growth during this century has been concentrated in those centres where settlement was firmly established. This trend towards urbanization has shown little evidence of declining in the future, giving rise to questions such as; what problems are involved concerning accommodation and what structural changes are needed? Combined with this increase in urban populations are the attitudes that there is an endless forest resource, as well as apathetic or indifferent emotions concerning the human needs trees and forests fulfill. Canadians in general, place little value on the presence of forest lands close to their cities or the recreational and aesthetic values they offer. "Urban Canadians have limited access to, and (limited) familiarity with, forest practices and their ecological implications .... The proper management of the Canadian forest depends to a high degree on ... an enlightened public.... Urban and amenity forestry is a logical part of the answer to this dilemma from a general forestry, as well as a national, point of view". (Jorgensen, 1974).

"Almost all Canadians will be living in cities by the turn of the century" (Kelly, 1975). The trend of increasing population pressures on the environment is a matter of growing concern regarding the protection and improvement of urban green spaces as well as incorporating long-range plans for future development. Canada has become urbanized more rapidly than any other industrialized nation in the world. These population concentrations are uniquely located within the country and the future trends indicate that increased populations will be required to live in a metropolitan environment.

Urbanization: Problems and Trends. Since the turn of the century there has been a shift concerning rural and urban populations. This shift has resulted in 76 per cent of Canadians living in cities and towns. Of this 76 per cent, 35 per cent live in Toronto, Montréal, and Van-

NFB – PHOTOTHEQUE – ONF – Photo by Kryn Taconis.

Once urban forests are destroyed, it is very difficult to re-establish green spaces in urban centres. Where city parks are maintained or created, as in Saskatoon, urban dwellers have more opportunities to enjoy outdoor recreation activities.

TABLE 12.

Growth of urban and rural population, in Canada, 1951 to 2000

	1951		1966	
	(millions)	(per cent)	(millions)	(per cent)
Urban	8.6	61.6	14.7	73.6
Rural	5.3	38.4	5.3	26.4
Total	13.9	100.0	20.0	100.0

Projections

	1981						2000					
	Low		Medium		High		Low		Medium		High	
	(millions)	(per cent)	(millions)	(per cent)	(millions)	(per cent)	(millions)	(per cent)	(millions)	(per cent)	(millions)	(per cent)
Urban	21.2	85.5	21.7	85.4	23.2	85.6	28.5	94.1	31.8	94.1	39.1	94.0
Rural	3.6	14.5	3.7	14.6	3.9	14.4	1.8	5.9	2.0	5.9	2.5	6.0
Total	24.8	100.0	25.4	100.0	27.1	100.0	30.3	100.0	33.8	100.0	41.6	100.0

Sources: Urquhart and Buckley, 1965. *Historical Statistics of Canada.*
Jorgensen, 1974. *Towards an Urban Forestry Concept.*

couver. This tendency to urbanize has increased since 1961 by "6.5 per cent, averaging more than 4 per cent a year which exceeds the second highest rate of 2.7 per cent in the United States" (Jones and MacArthur, 1976). The projected population increase has been estimated at between 28 and 35 million people by the year 2000, (Conservation Council of Ontario, 1971). Since the majority of Canada's population is located in areas such as southern Ontario, the west coast, and along the St. Lawrence Valley, a question that comes to the forefront is: Will these regions continue to be the focal point of urban settlement? With a continued increase in population, a region such as southern Ontario will eventually develop into a continuous megalopolis extending from Windsor to Québec City.

Taking into consideration that projected urban population figures are based on present trends, the low growth figure for the year 2000 of 28.5 million people also indicates that the present urban centres in Canada would increase in area by 50 per cent (Table 12). A continuation of future predictions has also indicated that two thirds of this projected figure would be assimilated by the nine largest cities in Canada (MacNeill, 1971).

Project Planning Associates undertook an open space study for Canadian communities in 1973 based on an examination of 376 communities of 5,000 population and over. An indication of their findings stated briefly emphasizes vast national differences considering that "the ratio was highest in the Prairies at 4.05 to 13.8 hectares per 1000 inhabitants and ... lowest in Quebec where it is usually 0.8 to 2.0 hectares per 1000". Further evidence of problems that exist, especially in Québec, are stated by Rey-Lescure (1974) concerning the need for Montréal to establish 11,332 ha of land for parks to accommodate 2.8 million people as well as 50,587 ha for the projected 5 million inhabitants of the metropolitan area. These requirements are based on the National Recreational Association Guidelines of recommended desirable acreages per thousand population with respect to urban and regional parks.

The statistics that have been presented in the previous text and tables are quite revealing in the light of present circumstances involving urban trees and forests in Canada. Nevertheless, these figures are subject to change due to continous implementation of political and economic issues as well as changing social awareness. If these changes do not take place and urban populations continue to increase, the present and future qualities necessary for an urban environment will decrease. The answer lies in the undertaking of measures requiring the inclusion of forest lands and green spaces into the urban structure of communities, supported by the establishment of adequate management policies and programs.

What is Urban Forestry? In the near future, Canadians will become more dependent upon trees and forests not only for the different materials they supply but for the aesthetic resources they provide. Are sufficient steps being taken at present to assure Canadians that the full benefits of trees and forests will be available? In order to enjoy a quality environment, it is necessary to develop and maintain trees and forests as essential elements within the framework of society's requirements for adequate recreation, clean air, clean water, and housing. The present and future needs of urban trees and forests are based on an ecological as well as a human approach to the establishment of forest management programs.

Terms such as urban foresty, environmental forestry, landscape forestry, amenity forestry, and regional forestry have all been used in reference to trees and forests within or adjacent to the urban community. What is being described in these terms? Jorgensen (1970) defined the term urban forestry which has become a generally accepted definition relating the scope and goals of this discipline:

"Urban Forestry is a specialized branch of Forestry and has as its objective the cultivation and management of trees and forests for their present and potential contributions to the physiological, sociological and economic well being of urban society. These contributions include the overall ameliorating effect of trees on their environment, as well as their recreational and general amenity value". (Jorgensen, 1970).

The definition emphasizes the need of urban forestry management to involve, not only single tree species, but the entire forest landscape within the scope of urban influences. This approach will hopefully develop a mutual understanding of local landscapes by planners, the public, and urban foresters.

NFB – PHOTOTHEQUE – ONF – Photo by Pierre Gaudard.

Without the breathing space and change of scenery provided by small areas of urban trees, city life can be less enjoyable. It is believed that many urban social problems are related to the growth of the concrete jungle at the expense of more natural pastoral habitat.

Urban forestry is a relatively new field which operates in an area between the horticulturist and large-scale forest operations. The practices of single tree management are of concern to both horticulture and urban forestry, however, the approach taken by each discipline is somewhat different. Horticulture involves extensive cultivation and maintenance techniques, whereas the urban forester practises methods involving minimum continued care and maintenance preserving the natural ecological support systems of tree growth. Both disciplines are necessary facets of tree and forest maintenance.

The problems of land speculation and expanding land developments, involving a multitude of construction projects progressing in unplanned and irregular patterns, exemplify the attitudes towards declining quality of life in urban centres. There seems to be a precedence placed on these activities above and beyond the need for open green spaces and amenity woodlands within these same urban communities. These trends are evidence in the case for adopting and establishing urban forestry programs to protect and preserve all urban trees and forests. Urban forestry "embraces a multimanagerial system" that includes landscape design, municipal watersheds, wildlife habitats, outdoor recreation, tree care in general, the production of wood fibres, forest products and many other services (Andresen, 1975).

Beneficial Aspects and Urban Forest Management. Moving into the last quarter of this century people are experiencing greater pressures on land and its uses than at any other time in history. When considering the management of trees and forests to improve aesthetics, Canadians are selecting just one of many values that trees and forests provide. Trees and forests play a vital rôle in the aesthetics of urban communities. These aesthetic values are difficult to assess, however, within the urban landscape scene. Trees and forests provide a broad and

NFB – PHOTOTHEQUE – ONF – Photo by Raymond Mercier.

Today, many urban youngsters are forced to play in the streets, because of lack of backyards and playgrounds. The simple pleasure of climbing a tree is not available to some children who do not have access to city parks or urban forests.

vital range of values which may go totally unnoticed by the general public as they go about their daily activities. The answer to this problem lies in the fact that within urban forestry there is a dual purpose existing in overall management of trees and forests, with aesthetics as one of the main goals. Within the context of this study, it would be impossible to adequately relate each and every one of the functions that urban trees and forests fulfill in every day urban life. It is necessary, nevertheless, to establish the most beneficial qualities. The environmental services that trees and forests exhibit with respect to the quality of urban life are:

– Aesthetics (landscaping);
– Recreational amenity (active and passive);
– Outdoor education basis;
– Products and by-products (wood, food);
– Local climate regulation (temperature, humidity, wind and shade);
– Water conservation and flood control (maintaining a certain equilibrium of the water table of an area);
– Air quality improvement (pollution and dust control, air filters and "sinks");
– Noise abatement (buffers for traffic, industrial zones);
– Historical importance;
– Wildlife (provide food and shelter);
– Prevention of erosion to hillsides and river banks.

Two benefits of urban forestry are illustrated below. Figure 2 portrays temperature distribution in the vicinity of an urban park in Montréal. The greater evapotranspiration in the park produces a pool of cool air which is advected by the southwest wind into adjacent built-up areas at least four blocks downwind. (Oke, 1977). Figure 3 illustrates the screen effect provided by trees or forests and the reduction of noise levels by absorption, diffusion, and the reduction of wind velocity (Cook and Van Haverbeke, 1971).

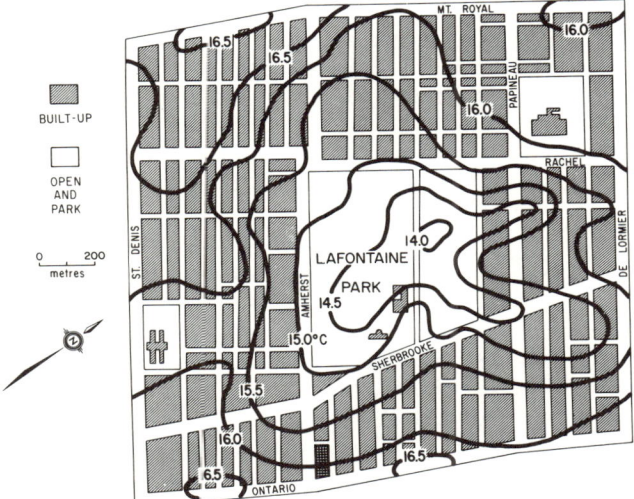

FIGURE 2. Impact of Green Space on Microclimate

Source: Oke, T.R. 1977. "The Significance of the Atmosphere in Planning Human Settlement".

FIGURE 3. Screening Effect of Trees

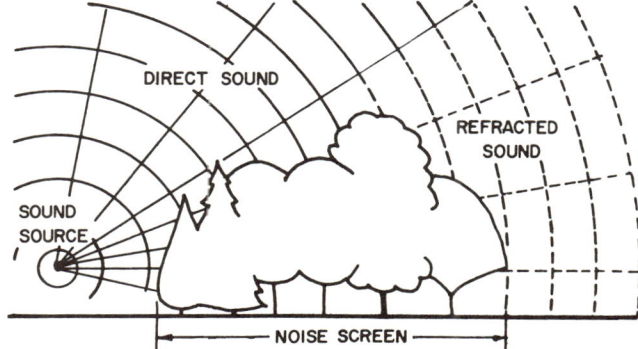

Source: Cook, D.I., and Van Haverbeke, D.F. 1977. "Trees and Shrubs for Noise Abatement".

The incorporation of urban forestry management into an urban community development structure should involve all aspects of the physical, biological, and social environment. Only by the establishment of a well-planned management program can the full benefits of urban trees and forests be achieved. At present, the primary rôle of Canadian forests is to supply goods and services,

nevertheless, the management priorities of urban trees and forests are reversed in terms of importance. When these priorities are established and maintained in the correct order, the results achieved will be multitudinous. In order to assume the complete success of this type of management approach, there is a need to instill within the public an awareness that these areas will only yield their full potential when users understand and appreciate their own impact on these resources.

The initiation of urban forestry management programs at present are all based on certain requirements which form the basis of ecosystem planning. The following fundamentals are generally accepted facets involved in many approaches to planning needs:

– The primary requirement is a policy decision to conserve natural ecosystems and incorporate them into community design.
– Ecological changes inherent in an urban as compared with rural or wild environments must be considered.
– Diversity of species is desirable not only for aesthetics but also for long-term insurance against disease (Dutch elm).
– Specific susceptibility to human impact or wearing must be taken into account.
– Pre-stressing of urban forests and woodlots which are destined to be severely disturbed by development.
– Rehabilitation of seriously disturbed urban forests and woodlots.
– Effective liaison and supervision is essential throughout the planning, development, and developed stages of a new community if the natural ecosystems are to survive and improvement programs are to succeed considering future pressures and alternative use (Horton, 1976).

These are the basics for the establishment of proper management goals within urban forestry. In order to achieve this approach, there is a definite problem which exists and must be overcome. The problem concerns the present attitudes which are centered on the costs of establishing and maintaining urban trees and forests rather than assessing their contributions. The first step is to "develop a better understanding of the interaction between trees and human endeavours" (Jorgensen, 1970). Increased financing, improved land zoning, and future insight are crucial elements in land use planning for the future, plus the co-operation between all levels of government, as well as the direct involvement of citizens.

Instituting Urban Trees and Forests into Community Planning. The implementation of open-space, greenbelt, or urban forestry planning in urban or suburban regions of Canada almost invariably involves forest land. Nevertheless, there is no possible way of discerning the limit of social and political trends that may conceivably affect urban forestry programs in an urbanizing society. Urban forestry must therefore become integrated with broader environmental and natural resources policy considerations. This necessity also involves increased education in urban forestry as well as the organization of forest management and much needed research for the future.

Recognizing the fact that trees, woodlots, and urban forests are essential components of community life, and can be managed to be aesthetically desirable, the next step is to plan for and actually allocate the space to be used by trees whether it is for street, park, greenbelt, suburban woodlots, or urban forest uses. A basic approach would involve first, the determination of the location and amount of land available or that could be set aside for such purposes. Secondly, decisions will determine to what major use or combination of uses such lands will be devoted. The last phase involves the assessment of the potentials for manipulation or adaptation of the vegetation to fulfill these purposes. These basics are the key to the management of trees for the improvement of aesthetics in an urban environment. The final measure of success will be a compromise between effective planning and its implementation, limited by ecological, economic, and social factors. There follow some specific examples of the incorporation of urban trees and forests into community design. While each is somewhat different, there are many similarities.

The metropolitan City of Ottawa, situated at the confluence of the Ottawa and Gatineau rivers, established under the National Capital Act (1958) the National Capital Commission whose mandate was the development, conservation, and improvement of the National Capital Region. From this point on, the Canadian Government began to acquire the 16,674 ha that constitutes most of the city's greenbelt. This 3.6 km crescent-shaped belt enclosed the Ottawa urban area to the south, terminating east and west of the city at the Ottawa River.

NFB – PHOTOTHEQUE – ONF – Photo by Malak.

NFB – PHOTOTHEQUE – ONF – Photo by Crombie McNeill.

Residents of cities where an urban greenbelt is part of the urban environment, are very fortunate. People living in the Ottawa-Hull area enjoy nature and cross-country ski trails, picnic sites, bicycle paths, and other facilities within the greenbelt maintained by the National Capital Commission.

This mandate was later amended at the Constitutional Conference in 1969 to incorporate the City of Hull and surroundings as part of the Canadian Capital Region comprising 4,024 km².

Urban green space within the National Capital Region involves the establishment and maintenance of various types of vegetation which may best be described as "extensive or even wilderness forests, scattered forests between urban developments, rural woodlots adjacent to the urban fringe, bog and wetlands, parklands and finally trees, shrubs and lawns along parkways, city streets and boulevards" (Black, 1977). Within this scenic setting, the facilities that have been developed by the National Capital Commission include allotment gardens, canal skating rinks, toboggan slides, ski trails, boating, riding trails, recreation for the handicapped, nature trails, fishing, bikeways, and natural history interpretation all within an urban forestry setting. The NCC's Interpretation Service was only established within the past three years, and works, not only with the general public, but also with the schools of the region to expand needed knowledge and awareness. "A new awareness of the requirements for an urban environment of exemplary quality came with the NCC; an awareness that was aided by the growing perception of urban residents that greenspace enhances the attractiveness and the desirability of the urban environment.... Against this background the Ottawa greenbelt is conceived as a means for conserving and protecting environmental resources for future generations and viewed as a means for containing and shaping the forms of urban growth" (Black, 1977). But other excellent examples of urban forestry exist in other Canadian cities. Montréal, Pickering, and Winnipeg, for example.

In the late 1940s, 242.8 ha of property at the western end of Île-de-Montréal were set aside for the purpose of demonstrating woodland management techniques. Part of McGill University's Macdonald College, the Morgan Arboretum today has evolved over the past three decades from an unused nature preserve, to a demonstration forest, into a multipurpose urban-forested area offering a number of aesthetic, educational, and recreational pursuits for the people of Montréal. Services include educational and resource awareness benefits, recreational activities such as walking, hiking, snowshoeing, skiing, and nature observations, as well as forest by-products which help management costs and serve as educational tools in urban forest management training. "An appropriate and important role of the urban forest is to assist people in developing an understanding of the complex and dynamic nature of the forest, of its value producing potential, and of its sensitivity to a wide spectrum of influences. The fact that this role can be effectively played has been amply demonstrated by the Morgan Arboretum experience". (Jones and MacArthur, 1977).

The relevance of procedures concerning adequate planning may best be acquired taking as a model the North Pickering Project. This new town, to be developed northeast of Toronto on 10,000 ha divided into three land use regions, was sponsored by the province of Ontario in 1975. The land use zones include a projected urban core of 75,000 population, surrounded by agricultural and peripheral parkway belts. The major priority was the conservation of the natural and historical features encompassing all facets of the physical, biological, and social environment. Since the inception of this project, all the aims put forth have been accomplished.

In Manitoba, the City of Winnipeg has exhibited concern through positive action by instituting controls on urbanization governing quality agricultural land, wildlife habitats (upland and wetland), and land with high outdoor recreational/environmental possibilities. Undertaken in 1971, the implementation of a two-phase program called the Winnipeg Region Study was established. The first phase, involving the compilation of research data has been completed, while phase two, a more lengthy task, was designed to examine the requirements necessary to protect unique areas of the natural and man-made environment. Here, the problems of private ownership have led to the expropriation of certain lands where acquisition by purchase was not feasible. Within phase two, the issues involving the protection of wildlife habitats and the establishment of recreational areas both require a need for the preservation, establishment, and maintenance of urban forests. To fully understand the elements involved, Caldwell (1973), has related the inter-relationships of urban wildlife protection and the protection of urban trees and forests, in one of a number of such studies.

In summary, while urban and aesthetic forests have received attention from some researchers, it is only recently that larger numbers of people have become aware of the special rôle played by trees and forests in urban environments.

Forestry and Agriculture

Shelterbelts

A shelterbelt is a physical barrier of living trees and shrubs of sufficient height, density, extent, and design to present an effective obstacle to wind.

Purpose. The primary purpose of a shelterbelt is to reduce wind velocity in order to control soil erosion and drifting. It is also used to trap snow on fields during winter in order to increase soil moisture, reduce evaporation, and increase air and soil temperatures. Shelterbelts are an important means of protection for crops, gardens, orchards, farm homes, buildings, and livestock. They increase the value of property and are fundamental for aesthetic reasons. They also serve as snowfences to prevent highways from becoming blocked by drifting snow, to provide dividing lines on the farms, and to supply fuel, fencing material, and a habitat for wildlife and birds. They act as stabilizers for soils and as sound barriers.

A shelterbelt creates a microclimate in its immediate vicinity which is less rigorous then the general climate for the area. Planted at right angles to the wind direction, an efficient shelterbelt may reduce wind velocity for a distance of 2H on the windward side and 20H on the leeward side (where H is defined as the effective height of the shelterbelt). Within the protected zone, soil drifting and plant damage are significantly reduced. By affecting the wind movement, the air temperatures within the shelterbelt and its zone of influence are also affected. Seasonally, spring levels may be 3°C warmer, summer levels 2.5°C cooler than in open unprotected fields. Diurnally, air temperatures in the protected zone, which are related to the eddy zone produced by the shelterbelt, can be super-heated in the day and supercooled in the night and thus prove dangerous to plant growth. The relative humidity in the protected zone is higher than in open unprotected ares. Evaporation is influenced by wind velocity, air temperature, relative humidity, distance from wind breaks, shelterbelt permeability and composition. The greater the wind speed, the greater the amount of evaporation; likewise, the higher the temperature and the lower the relative humidity, the greater the capacity of the air to absorb moisture. Thus, the rate of evaporation in the protected zone is lower than in unprotected areas, with the most significant reductions occurring on the leeward side of the shelterbelt.

In addition to creating a microclimate, shelterbelts may have profound influence on the soil medium by affecting its structure, moisture content, and temperature. Shelterbelts may change the soil structure both within the planting and for some distance beyond. Porosity and infiltration capabilities are increased, humus content is augmented, and leaching of soluble salts, carbonate, and sulphate is increased. Shelterbelts influence the soil moisture content by controlling the snow cover during the winter season through direct uptake of moisture from the soil surface. Dense wide shelterbelts cause deep drifts to form within the shelterbelts for a short distance from the leeward margin, leaving most of the leeward areas relatively bare. More open plantings disperse the snow as a thinner and more uniform layer over a much greater distance on the leeward side. In addition to increasing moisture content of the soil, snow cover also provides insulation against frost which in turn affects downward percolation of snow melt. Soil temperatures in areas protected by shelterbelts vary with soil depth, from temperatures prevailing in unprotected areas, with site location, and distance to the shelterbelt plantings. Inside a 9- to 21-m high shelterbelt, soil temperatures at the 2- to 5-cm depths were approximately 2°C colder than for comparable depths outside the planting. At the five-cm depth, temperatures were 2°C colder between shelterbelts and at 10-, 15-, and 20-cm depths approximately 2°C, .8°C, and .5°C warmer respectively than open field temperatures. At the 50-cm depth the soil temperatures leeward at ½H distance from the shelterbelt were 1.7°C colder and at 2H, .5°C warmer in the spring and summer than temperatures at the same depth in open fields, and were 1.7°C to 3°C colder for both locations in the fall and winter.

Design. Before planting, a comprehensive plan should be made, with consideration of the natural features of the farm and natural forest which may occur. The exact location where trees are to be planted must be decided and species selected. Other points to be decided are the number of rows, distance apart of rows, distance apart of plants in a row, and number of plants of each species required. Shelterbelts planted for purely protective purposes that do not involve the growing of crops should be so designed that they will hold the drifting snow within the trees, preferably through the entire width of the belt. However, trees and shrubs planted for protection of fields and crops require fewer rows and less density than those planted for the protection of farmsteads. The ideal direction in which to plant shelterbelts is at right angles to the prevailing winds. Trees should be planted in the same direction the fields are worked giving additional consideration to the north and west sides of the fields to be protected. Field shelterbelts need not be planted closer together than 200 m except where special crops are grown.

Where road protection by field shelterbelt is desired, in addition to protection of fields, the distance from the center of the road to the shelterbelt should be 50 m. Greater protection is obtained by block planting. This method requires farmers to organize themselves into associations and plant trees in a grid pattern covering a large territory. A cumulative effect is thus achieved, giving greater protection and advantages to the area.

The requirements of a good shelterbelt are: protection at ground level, maximum ultimate height of nine m, a narrow crown, rapid growth, and reasonably long life.

An effective type of field shelterbelt is that of the single row barrier of mixed tree species. Close spacing controls the height of the trees to approximately eight to nine m, thus preventing the trees from shading crops and reducing yields.

In western Canada, the most popular species used for shelterbelts is the Caragana (a tree) originally imported from Siberia. The trees should be planted 45 cm apart with every sixth or eighth tree substituted by elm, ash or maple, balsam, poplar, or willow. These trees are long lived and produce root systems which do not extend too far into the fields to compete with the crops for soil moisture.

In Alberta, spacing recommendations have deviated from the earlier mentioned close plantings. Farmers are now encouraged to plant tall growing deciduous trees and evergreens at least two m apart in the row and five to six m between rows. Farmers are advised to plant no more than four rows for a farmstead shelterbelt, and preferably single rows for field and roadside shelterbelts. Mixing of different varieties within rows is not recommended. Inclusion of a row of evergreens in a multiple-row shelterbelt is generally recommended.

There is an advantage in planting low, spreading shrubs on the windward sides of the shelterbelt thereby creating a stronger wind barrier. Wind protection is achieved for a distance of approximately 20 times the height of the trees. As a result of their ability to hold snow and their aesthetic value, white spruce, Scotch pines, and lodgepole pine are planted primarily in farmstead belts.

NFB – PHOTOTHEQUE – ONF – Photo by G. Hunter.

In addition to benefits derived from the planting of shelterbelts with field crops, many farmsteads utilize shelterbelts around farm buildings to provide a barrier to wind, snow, and noise.

Historic Uses. In Canada, shelterbelts were first planted on the dry western Prairies when early settlers discovered a treeless plain. The government recognized the difficulties of establishing trees in the arid region, and in 1901 inaugurated a co-operative tree-planting program. Later, in 1936, under the federal Prairie Farm Rehabilitation Act, farm-sponsored Field Shelterbelt Associations were organized at Lyleton, Manitoba, Conquest and Aneroid in Saskatchewan, and Porter Lake, Alberta. In the west, they were used to break the force of the hot drying winds in summer thereby lowering evaporation and saving moisture.

In eastern Canada, many early home builders built shelterbelts around farm buildings, on lanes, and along highways. Windbreaks are used in Ontario to prevent erosion of the light soils in the tobacco areas, and on the muck soils of onion and garden districts. Highway departments now use them for permanent snow fences. Well-planned plantings of trees on the drainage area increase snow accumulation and thus provide a greater water supply for the storage basin.

Agricultural Uses. Although the precise influence of shelterbelts on the production of horticultural products, vegetables, and fruits can not be determined, increases in production have been noted. For example, Foskett (1955) showed in South Dakota increases up to 287 per cent in weight of butternut squash per hill over lowest yield to windward at various distances from a one-m snow fence placed midway in the plantings. Read (1964) and others reported increased yields within the shelterbelts, as opposed to open fields. The influence of shelter on fruit production has received concerted attention. The benefits include: reduction in mechanical damage to plant growth and fruit, a reduction in percentage of wind-thrown fruits, and increase in fruit quality because of decreased bruising, protection against desiccating winds, more pollination by insects, and higher fruit yields.

Shelterbelts assist field crop production by protecting agricultural areas from soil erosion, controlling snow and increasing soil moisture content for use by a growing crop, and reducing wind damage to plants. Researchers have classified crops on the basis of their differential response to wind protection from shelterbelts. Low-response crops include drought-hardy cereals such as spring wheat, maize, and hardy small grains; moderate- to good-response crops include fodder crops (alfalfa, lupine, clover, grass, hay, and seed wheat grasses), rice and some coarse grains; high-response crops include vegetables, fruits, and tobacco. The low-response group usually shows a significant increase in yield in years of low rainfall, while the moderate- and high-response groups also respond under favourable moisture conditions. The long-term and wide-scale application of shelterbelt protection implies that real benefits have been realized. The flax, oats, alfalfa, and wheat statistics given in a study by Bonnefoy and Bonnefoy (1965) illustrate yield gains for these crops under the climatic conditions of the Prairie Provinces.

Livestock make greater gains, produce more, suffer smaller losses, and make more efficient use of feeds if protection from high summer temperatures and cold winds are provided. It was also found that ranches on open and unprotected areas required 50 per cent more winter feed than ranches having natural protection provided by topography, trees, and brush.

Other Uses. Preliminary studies (Cook and Van Haverbeke, 1971) have indicated that appropriate shelterbelts can reduce noise levels by 50 per cent. These sound barriers can be useful between industrial and residential areas, highway and other areas, and within the same area to separate housing and playgrounds in residential areas. Shelterbelts act as snowtraps, which makes them effective as snow fences to protect roads from snow drifting and to lessen the amounts of snow drifting that occurs on roads.

Farmstead windbreaks shelter farm buildings and reduce heating costs and physical damage by wind. To some extent, they also provide a source of fuel for house heating and wood materials such as posts and poles for farm use.

Shelterbelts can be effectively used for production of water supplies. This use and its mechanics has been well illustrated in previous sections. The Whitemud River Watershed provides an excellent example of shelterbelt plantings being used for soil stabilization. In addition to the aesthetic qualities, shelterbelts provide a feeling of well-being that the proximity of living trees and other plant material gives to people.

Forest Utilization for Energy Production and Conservation

"Energy is the key factor in the achievement of economic growth ... A shortage of energy will eventually be the most important constraint upon man's material development, but if part of the fuel supply within a country is founded on renewable resources, there will be less danger of economic growth being curtailed by a sudden rise in the price of imported fuel or the depletion of an indigenous resource". (Earl, 1975).

The forest provides four types of fuel: wood, charcoal, methanol, and producer gas. Although all are derived from the same organic source, the various fuels differ in both calorific value and physical properties, allowing for flexibility of choice for the consumer. In conditions of forest abundance, wood is often the most practical solid fuel for heating and cooking purposes; charcoal, a smokeless fuel, has gained in popularity especially in urban areas because of its transport advantage over wood, its convenience, and a desire for cleaner air. For certain types of engines requiring a very high-octane fuel, methanol may be ideal; while, for many industrial uses producer gas may be the most practical fuel.

Wood. Energy from wood, the primary forest fuel, is obtained by combustion. Fuelwood can be obtained from any tree either directly or from waste material produced at sawmills and wood-using industries.

Wood is simple to prepare and use, the moisture content being the influencing factor of efficiency. While the gross calorific value of oven-dry wood averages 4.7, conifers usually have a slightly above-average value of approximately 4.8 and may exceed 5.0. The heating values of the wood vary by the species of the tree from which the fuelwood is obtained (Table 13).

Charcoal. The simplest method of upgrading the value of wood as a fuel is to chemically reduce the organic material to charcoal under controlled conditions. While the value of a tonne of oven drywood is 4.7 million bilocalories Kcal, the value of a tonne of charcoal is 7.1 Kcal.

Charcoal, smokeless and almost sulphur-free, may be used: in stoves for home heating, and for grilling and barbecuing; for direct drying in industries such as for maturing and curing hops, tobacco, and other commodities where a special atmosphere is required; for indirect drying purposes in central heating systems; as an internal fuel in lime and cement manufacture; in water purification and sewage works; and in the production of a number of commodities such as cyanide, carbide, pigments for printing and paints, plastics, and rubber.

Statistics on the total production of charcoal in Canada are not obtainable because the majority of producers manufacture charcoal in insufficient quantities to be reported separately. The quantity of charcoal produced by major manufacturers of charcoal, which does not represent the majority of the quantity, is expressed in terms of shipments of own manufacture. The figures do not include the amount of charcoal the company produces and uses itself.

Methanol and Producer Gas. Methanol is produced by distillation of wood.

TABLE 13.

Heating values of selected woods

Species	Density	Heat	Equivalent in heating oil
	(kg/m³)	(j/m³) (millions)	(L)
Hickory	449	8,966	996
Red oak	405	7,999	886
Beech	405	8,145	905
Hard maple	384	8,497	941
Yellow birch	375	7,677	850
Ash	369	6,622	732
Elm	344	7,179	796
Soft maple	313	7,032	777
Tamarack	313	7,032	777
Cherry	319	6,885	764
Spruce	263	5,303	586
Hemlock	263	5,245	582
Aspen	238	5,186	573
Basswood	238	4,981	550
White pine	225	5,010	555

Source: Camden House Publishing, 1977. Harrowsmith.

"In distillation, the wood charge is heated in a closed container so arranged that all gases and liquids evolved pass out through a condenser. The non-condensable gases can be utilized as an energy source and the condensed gas and water-soluble tar collected, (then) they can be decanted and fractionally distilled to give useful chemical products. The by-products have the following uses: gas for burning as fuel; methyl alcohol as an industrial solvent and for possible preparation of methyl esters of fatty acids with glycerine by-products, and for fuel for internal combustion and jet engines; acetic acid for conversion to acetone and also for use in the textile industry; acetone as an industrial solvent; wood oil; creosote for timber preservation; and pitch for road-making when blended with asphalt." (Earl, 1975).

By controlled heating of wood and charcoal, producer gas and water gas may be obtained. Producer gas consists of carbon monoxide and nitrogen produced by burning carbon in a supply of air insufficient to convert it into carbon dioxide. When the gas is used in furnaces, it is burned immediately after production, so that its heat of formation is not wasted. If, however, it is used for internal combustion engines it must be washed before use, and there is then considerable loss of heat. Water gas on the other hand, is a mixture of carbon monoxide and hydrogen (with small quantities of carbon dioxide and nitrogen), made by driving steam or a fine spray of water over incandescent charcoal. The water gas so obtained is either burned, or used as a source of hydrogen (Bosch process), or used for synthesizing methyl alcohol (Earl, 1975).

Statistics on the production of these energy sources in Canada are not available.

Energy From The Forests

The production, distribution, and consumption of energy in the modern world comprise a complex scenario of supply and end-use patterns. Electricity, petroleum products, natural gas, and coal are used in a vast variety of motive power, heating, and lighting applications. During this century, petroleum has become the dominant energy source, supplying some 50 per cent of the world's energy needs or as much as all other sources combined. However, Canada will not be isolated from international oil scarcities and escalating costs. An urgent need for energy conservation and for the development of alternative domestic energy sources is equally obvious. The urgency is underlined by the lead time that is required for technological, economic, and institutional investigations before policy decisions can be made and alternative energy systems can be put in place.

Of major interest to Environment Canada, through its forestry mandate, is the utilization of the forest resource as a perpetually renewable source of energy. By the process of photosynthesis the sun's energy is captured by trees and plants and used to convert cabon and water to wood fibre, bark, leaves, flowers, fruit, and seed. This vegetation, collectively referred to as forest biomass, represents a tremendous storage of chemical energy in a form that can be used as fuel. It has been estimated, as an example, that the present consumption of energy in the United States is about equal to the rate of storage of solar energy in that country's biomass system. In Canada, the annual capture of the sun's energy in this manner far exceeds the energy demand.

The potential for the implementation of biomass-generated energy systems can be conveniently expressed in terms of three levels of conventional energy substitution. The first would achieve energy self-sufficiency in the forest products industry, equivalent to about one and one-quarter per cent of Canada's current primary energy consumption, through the utilization of the mill residues available from existing industry operations. Much of the basic conversion technology needed to accomplish this already exists. The direct combustion of residues in conventional boilers to produce steam (and electricity) is well established commercially, with its application being largely a matter of site-specific economics. Other direct combustion technologies require further development and demonstration, however, as do biomass gasification techniques.

Devices for the conversion of forest biomass to energy can be classified under the broad headings of suspension burners, pile burners (single- and multiple-chamber), fluid-bed burners, and wood gasifiers. Suspension burners involve the combustion of finely divided dry fuel suspended in air; a number of proven systems are available, but all require considerable fuel drying and size preparation. Pile burners employ one or more furnace chambers with controlled air inputs to achieve complete combustion; there is a wide variety of designs, with some units proven and in commercial use and others still experimental. Fluid-bed combustors burn the biomass material in a bed of hot granular inert material such as sand which is kept in motion by a stream of combustion air fed from below; some units are being successfully operated, while others are being developed.

Wood gasification is an old technology which is being revived with a view to providing a transportable gas for conversion to heat by combustion, a gaseous fuel for modified diesel-electric generators, or a chemical feedstock for the synthesis of liquid fuels, such as methanol, or other industrial chemical commodities. Gasifiers are simply reactors in which biomass fuel is burned in the presence of moisture and a deficiency of oxygen, producing and combustible gas. On the continuous commercial scale there are significant material preparation and gas cleaning problems, and to date a reliable, proven system for large-scale use has not been demonstrated under practical North American conditions. Several units are, however, under active development. In particular, there is considerable potential for forest industry applications of gasification for fuel using pulp mill lime kilns or lumber drying kilns, and for power generation using gas turbines or reciprocating engine-coupled generators, with attendant replacement of the fuel oil and natural gas presently being used.

Industrial fuel substitution by direct combustion or gasification of mill residues represents the shortest-term opportunity for forest biomass energy development. By extending the forest industry's woodlands operations to include harvesting of all available biomass (branches, tops, crooked boles, foliage, and unused species not now being removed) the raw material supply would exceed the quantity needed for industry energy self-sufficiency. This would provide the opportunity for supplying energy as heat or power to municipalities and utilities, as well as the development of ancillary wood-based chemical industries on a localized basis. This level of biomass energy implementation is seen as medium-term, with the potential of replacing petroleum-based fuels, natural gas, and petrochemical feedstocks to the extent of an estimated eight per cent of the country's total primary energy consumption. The federal government recently announced a comprehensive program aimed at achieving this potential. It involves research and development, prototype demonstration, and incentives for commercial implementation.

The first element in the government's overall approach to stimulating biomass utilization for energy purposes is a program known as ENFOR, Energy from the Forest, conducted by the Canadian Forestry Service of Environment Canada. ENFOR is a contract program sponsoring research, development, or small- to medium-scale demonstration projects addressing the broad objective of producing and utilizing forest biomass as a source of energy, prepared fuels, or energy-intensive chemicals. In practical terms, data on the availability of the forest resource for energy production are severely lacking. Traditionally, the inventories and production methods have been oriented towards the merchantable timber that is utilized by the forest products industry for the manufacture of lumber, plywood, pulp-and-paper, and related commodities. The measurement, harvesting, and transport of the total biomass available in the forests introduces a new dimension into the conventional forestry operations, and substantial study is needed before the energy production opportunity can be fully exploited on a commercial basis. To address these problems, as well as the complementary subject of efficient conversion of forest biomass material to usable energy forms over the range of industry operations from very large pulp mills to very small sawmills, the ENFOR program was established in the fiscal year 1978/79 and will continue to 1983/84.

Any Canadian organization able to conduct pertinent research, development, or demonstration work may submit an ENFOR proposal. Projects are supported in two general areas: Forest Biomass Production including inventory, forest management (growth and yield, silviculture, and harvesting) and economic, social, and ecological impact; and Forest Biomass Conversion, which includes feedstock preparation, prepared fuels conversion technology, and industrial chemicals conversion technology. The federal government enters into contract agreements with the organizations concerned for the conduct of approved projects, and the contracts are managed by regional Forestry Service research establishments.

Through other programs operated by the Department of Energy, Mines and Resources, there is provision for assisting large-scale prototype demonstrations under federal/provincial energy agreements, and for encouraging general commercial implementation of forest biomass energy technology. In particular, capital cost-sharing assistance is available under EMR's new Forest Industry Renewable Energy (FIRE) program to forest industry firms contemplating the installation of facilities using proven technology for the conversion of forest or mill residues to energy or prepared fuels.

In the long term, for 1990 and beyond, a potential for substitution of up to 25 per cent of current primary energy requirements is foreseen. In addition to the initiatives previously mentioned, this would entail a capability to produce liquid fuels from forest biomass on a large-scale commercial basis. While the present forest industry structure would likely form the organizational basis, this concept would require development in the Canadian context of entirely new forest management and harvesting approaches to supply the necessary quantities of biomass. Intensive management strategies aimed at maximizing forest growth and yield for its biomass content, rather than for the traditional structural wood or fibre content, would emerge. At the present time, the production of methanol for motor fuel (gasoline) blending appears to be the most likely liquid fuels option.

Although these forest biomass energy initiatives are being spurred by the anticipated petroleum price and supply situation, the potential for rational development of the forest industry and complete utilization of the forest resource should not be overlooked as separate and perhaps equally important issues. The opportunity being presented to the industry for development of a more diversified product base is very substantial in terms of job creation and profitability.

Forestry and Recreation

Forest landscape plays an important rôle in the recreational pursuits of Canadians and visitors to Canada. It is difficult to conceive of the forested parks deprived of their cover. Trees are taken for granted in the natural pattern of things, yet without them the prospect is stark and unattractive. Much of the following description has been adapted from Stanton (1976).

Canada ranks fifth in importance in international tourism, preceded by the U.S.A., Italy, Spain, and France. The total spent by international and domestic travellers in 1977 amounted to more than $10 billion. Statistics are too sketchy to permit other than a guess at the proportion of this considerable income which can be associated directly or indirectly with activities in the forested landscape. Nevertheless, it has been suggested that the figure is in the vicinity of $4 billion.

The demand for recreation in Canada is expanding rapidly and all indications suggest that it is not likely to slacken in the foreseeable future. Leisure time is increasing and population is growing and becoming increasingly urbanized. In 1971, 17 companies were identified as being on a four-day work week. A mere six months later, this figure had increased to 60. It has also been estimated that by the year 2000 the total Canadian population will have some 350 billion hours of time at its disposal. It will spend about five per cent of this time working. Forty per cent will be spent in eating, sleeping, and personal maintenance, while the remaining 55 per cent will be free time. A further indicator of the pressures for recreation that can be anticipated is the forecast that population will rise by about 67 per cent by the year 2001 and that 94 per cent of the people will then be located in urban regions.

There are essentially four areas providing forest recreational opportunities in Canada. These are the forest tracts leased to woodland operators, National Parks, provincial parks, and other areas of forest land.

Forests that have been open for logging have not always been available to recreationists; in fact, the early attitude was to keep the public out, primarily on the grounds of vandalism, increased road costs, liability, fire, and safety. Over the years, this situation has changed as the people have come to realize that the land in question is their land and woodland operators have recognized that this is indeed a fact of life and concessions are necessary. The forest industry has opened some 39,000 km of road to the public and some companies are providing camping sites, boat launching ramps, picnic grounds, and other amenities.

The National and provincial parks of Canada together occupy an area of 34.4 million ha and play a major rôle in outdoor recreation. At present, there are 28 National Parks and one National Park Reserve in Canada. The one reserve, along with ten of the parks, was added to the system between 1968 and 1972. This is a measure of the concern felt by Canadian society with respect to the need for more recreational areas. Some of the largest forested parks are from 5,000 to 10,000 km² in extent and are concentrated in the north and west. National Park use is increasing. In 1971, 14 million peo-

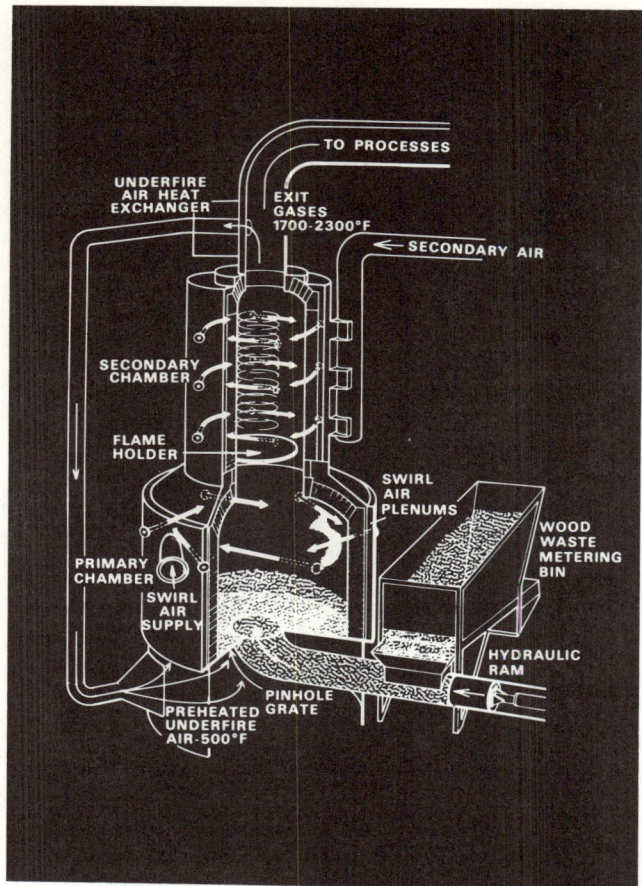

The Lamb Cargate "Wet Cell" prototype installed at the Plateau Saw Mills in British Columbia is an example of advanced Canadian technology in the transformation of wood residues to energy for use in the forest products industry.

Lamb Cargate Industries, New Westminster, B.C.

Photo by R. Overend, N.R.C.

Photo by K.G. Taylor.

Regardless of season, forests provide an attractive setting for outdoor recreation. As increasing numbers of Canadians live in cities, it is important that opportunities for outdoor activities in the rural-urban fringe be maintained.

ple visited the system and, by 1977, this figure had increased to 18.5 million.

The National Parks policy as related to forest land is to maintain scenic and recreational values with a minimum disturbance of the natural features. Fellings for fire and erosion control and for the maintenance of forest health are kept to a minimum and commercial logging is not permitted. Public appreciation of the natural environment is fostered by the provision of exhibits, lectures, leaflets, and nature trails.

Canada has more than 1,800 provincial parks covering some 249,000 km² and many of the larger ones, ranging up to 18,000 km², are at least partly forested. Although the principal objective in these parks is to provide land for recreational use, certain sites are preserved for scientific purposes and commercial logging is permitted in some instances. In 1977, close to 55 million people visited the provincial parks.

Outside of the parks and areas devoted to logging there are still considerable tracts of forest land with excellent recreation potential. However, present access tends to limit the use of the more northern forests to the occasional angler, hunter, or canoeist while some otherwise attractive areas closer to population centres are currently lightly used because of the presence of biting insects.

The forest landscape in the areas described above can encourage or discourage people from enjoying the forest. Just how the forest is enjoyed is important to the development of those facilities needed for recreation. The gentle slopes of montane areas may well lend themselves to hiking trails, while cedar or black spruce lowlands, infested with black flies, may only be enjoyable because they support wildlife that people watch in a passive manner.

The variety and uniqueness of certain forested areas attract many people. Even to the detriment of the forest. Increases in population pressure, and the desire to get away from it all, have attracted many to the semi-wilderness of regional, municipal, or provincial parks. The heavy use, plus in many cases inadequate planning, leads to a rapid deterioration of the recreational forest environment. The improvement of this situation rests in the education of the resource planners and the public using the resource.

NFB – PHOTOTHEQUE – ONF – Photo by Freeman Patterson.
The peace and quiet of a forest contribute to an ideal setting for a picnic.

In many communities, various public awareness groups have developed trails and centres for interpretation of the surrounding environment. The Canadian Forestry Service has developed two centres in Canada that give the public a picture of the meaning of forests and the forest industry in the environment. In doing so, they have also developed areas that become actively recreational. The forest trails at the Petawawa Forest Experiment Station near Chalk River, Ontario and the Kananaskis Forest Experiment Station between Calgary and Banff, Alberta, host over 30,000 visitors per year, not counting the school groups that use each centre as an educational tool. Other groups in eastern Canada use municipal forests and areas for educational purposes such as nature walks or studying the sugar bush operations both old and new.

Recreation in the forest can be divided, as gathered from the above descriptions, into active and passive activities. These activities vary from season to season. The early morning jog in the crisp fall air allows one to be active and passive in enjoying the forested areas. The run is exhilarating to the body, yet the beauty of the red maple leaves, brown oak leaves, or the softness of white pine needles is like music to the soul. The thrust of the ski on the trail, the sharpness of the air, the beauty of the cardinals in the trees and ice-coated buds that glitter

MAP 7
ECOTOUR MAP

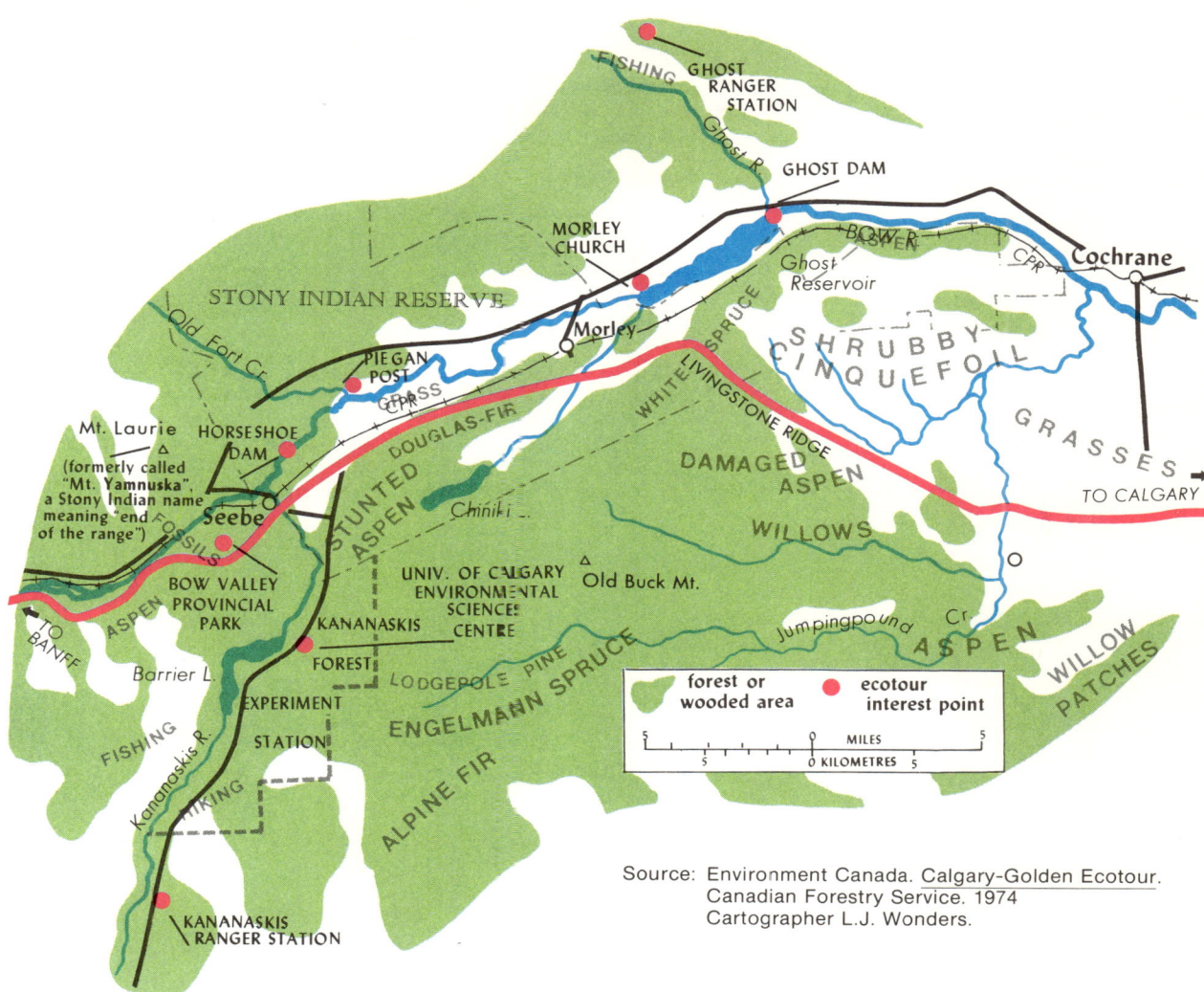

Source: Environment Canada. Calgary–Golden Ecotour.
Canadian Forestry Service. 1974
Cartographer L.J. Wonders.

in the late evening sun, all make the winter forest enjoyable. Carefully driving through the backroads looking for pussy-willows and other harbingers of spring; the first green tuft of larch needles; or the return of the first white-throated sparrow, all add to the quality of life many have come to enjoy in the forests. While the other seasons in the forest give some happiness, certainly it is summer at the cottage, camping, hiking, fishing, or bird watching that brings home the stark realization of what the forests really mean to most people.

The series of Ecotour maps published by the Canadian Forestry Service of Environment Canada is a practical illustration of how the recreational aspects of forestry can be combined with other resources for recreation. These maps were designed to stimulate an interest in landscape ecology along major Canadian highways. Information concerning natural and human history is provided. In any section of an Ecotour, details are presented for specific sites to explain points of ecological or historical interest. Maps and sketches are used to portray the inter-relationships of plants and animals with their environment. In the accompanying example (Map 7), taken from the Calgary–Golden Ecotour, the plunging streams and forest-clad slopes of Alberta's foothills are ideally suited for many uses including wood production, water supply, wildlife habitat, and recreation.

Factors Affecting Forests

All forests may be affected either by the hazards of fire and disease and insect infestations, or by administration and management. Total control of these factors is virtually impossible and in some cases undesirable; however, minimization of the detrimental effects and maximization of the desirable benefits can result in optimal use of the forest resource.

Fires may occur as a result of natural environmental conditions or adverse climatic conditions; they may also be man-made purposely or unintentionally. Disease may be one of a number of varieties: root, stem, foliage, systemic, or miscellaneous including windfall and winter dry; insect infestations are numerous and like diseases may cause damage ranging from the not noticeable loss of a leaf to the complete destruction of all trees and their components in a given area; both diseases and insects may attack either standing trees, cut wood, or finished wood products. Diseases and insects may be introduced to the forest environment either as a natural result of ecosystem development, intentionally by man as a check on another disease or insect, or inadvertently by man such as the introduction of Dutch elm disease

to Canada by packing crates made of wood that were infected with the offending fungus. Administration and management of forest lands are governed by provincial authority over the resource, land tenure, and actual programs carried out on the land; usually this involves some type of manipulation of the number and species of trees in a given forest area for a specific use.

When detailing these factors, it must be remembered that the quantification given is not mutually exclusive and that statistics of loss for a given area may be duplicated according to the number of influences in that area. For example, if there is an area of 40 ha of which 30 ha are infected with spruce budworm and of which 20 ha were lost due to forest fires, the figures would be included in both disease statistics and forest fire statistics. Together the figures report losses for 50 ha even though the area of land is but 40 ha.

Hazards

Forest Fires

Over 75 thousand forest fires sweep over an average of 809,400 ha of forest land in Canada a year destroying in excess of 13 million dollars worth of merchantable timber. No figures exist though to document the damage to soils and wildlife or to water resource or recreation values destroyed by these fires.

In Canada, the susceptibility of an area to forest fire is detailed in the Fire Weather Index, a numerical rating based on meteorological measurements of fire intensity in a standard fuel type (Van Wagner, 1974). Fuels determine the quantity of material potentially available for combustion; topography affects the rate of spread; and, weather determines the characteristics of fire behavior as well as influencing the quantity of fuel which will burn. Figure 4 shows the six components of the index.

The three primary components, whose purposes follow, the Fine Fuel Moisture Code, the Duff Moisture Code, and the Drought Code are sub-indexes that follow from day to day the moisture contents of three classes of forest fuel of different drying rates; the two intermediate components, the Initial Spread Index and the Adjusted Duff Moisture Code, are sub-indexes representing the rate of spread and amount of fuel; the final component is the Fire Weather Index which represents the intensity of the spreading fire as an energy output.

1. *Fine Fuel Moisture Code (FFMC)*, which represents the moisture content of litter and other cured fine fuels in a forest stand, in a layer of dry weight about .24 kg/m²;

179

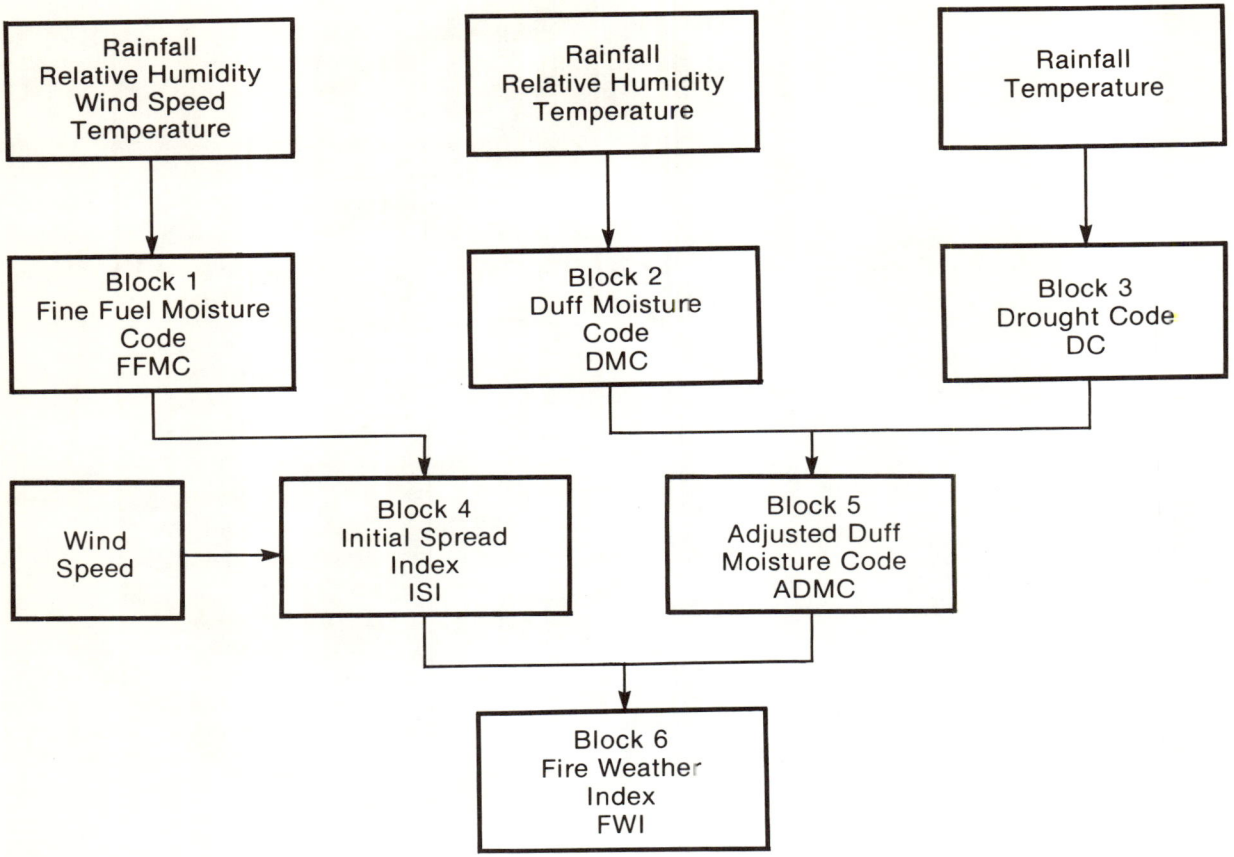

FIGURE 4. Fire Weather Index Block Diagram

Source: Van Wagner, C.E. 1974. Structure of the Canadian Forest Fire Weather Index.

2. *Duff Moisture Code (DMC)*, which represents the moisture content of loosely compacted, decomposing organic matter 5 to 10 cm deep and weighing about $4.9 kg/m^2$ when dry;

3. *Drought Code (DC)*, which represents a deep layer of compact organic matter weighing perhaps $49 kg/m^2$ when dry;

4. *Initial Spread Index (ISI)*, a combination of wind and the FFMC that represents rate of spread alone without the influence of variable quantities of fuel;

5. *Adjusted Duff Moisture Code (ADMC)*, a combination of the DMC and the DC that represents the total fuel available to the spreading fire;

6. *Fire Weather Index (FWI)*, a combination of the ISI and the ADMC that represents the intensity of the spreading fire as energy output rate per unit length of fire front. (Van Wagner, 1974).

On the basis of Fire Weather Index data available, Simard (1973) produced a map which delineates seven forest fire weather zones across Canada (Map 8).

Zone 1, Minimal (Average FWI = 0 to 2)

Only a small portion of the forested area of Canada lies within this zone. It is restricted entirely to coastal regions. Approximately 65 per cent of the FWI observations will be zero. Little or no control efforts are likely to be required for fires occurring on these days. About 34 per cent of the days will require some, if only minimal control efforts. On only 1 per cent of the days will a sufficient effort to control light surface fires be required. Thus, while forest fire control cannot be totally ignored in this zone it will certainly be a relatively minor undertaking.

Zone 2, Very Low (Average FWI = 2 to 4)

Generally, this zone is located immediately inland from Zone 1 along the northern limit of the treeline. The percentage of days on which fires require little or no control effort drops to 40 per cent while the proportion of days requiring only minimal control rises to 50 per cent. On 7 per cent of the days the fire control organization will probably encounter light surface fires. In addition, on 3 per cent of the days surface fires are likely to be of moderate intensity, with an occasional hot surface fire occurring.

Zone 3, Low (Average FWI = 4 to 6)

The major areas of Zone 3 are close to the northern limits of the forested area and in eastern Canada. Every province has some area in this zone. On 35 per cent of the days little or no fire control efforts will be needed while on an additional 45 per cent minimal control efforts will be sufficient. On 15 per cent of the days, light to moderate intensity surface fires are likely to be encountered. The major difference between Zone 2 and 3 is that on 4 per cent of the days in Zone 3 hot surface fires can occur and on about 1 per cent of the days, torching out may be encountered.

Zone 4, Moderate (Average FWI = 6 to 10)

This is the most widely distributed zone in Canada. It is found in every province. The largest areas are in western Canada. Zone 4 can be considered the normal or average forest fire weather zone in Canada. The full range of intensities can be expected to occur with some degree of regularity in this zone. One major difference between Zone 4 and the previous zones is that on only 20 per cent of the days light surface fires are likely to be encountered, while on 17 per cent of the days surface fires will be of moderate to hot intensity. A second major difference between this and previous zones is that on 3 per cent of the days torching out and occasional crown fires can occur. The latter may be potentially uncontrollable during daylight hours (depending on the fuel complex). This latter condition is likely to be reached for brief periods once every few years rather than on one or two days every year.

Zone 5, High (Average FWI = 10 to 14)

This zone is found primarily in western and southern Canada. The percentage of days on which fires will require little or no control efforts drops slightly to 15 per cent while the proportion of days requiring minimal control remains at 40 per cent. The percentage of days with light surface fires drops slightly to 10 per cent while days with moderate and hot surface fires rises to 25 per cent. Torching out may occur on 7 per cent of the days. The major difference between Zone 5 and 4 is that in Zone 5 on 3 per cent of the days, fires will be potentially uncontrollable with occasional conflagrations and fire storms developing. These intensity levels are likely to be reached or at least approached in a majority of fire seasons.

Zone 6, Very High (Average FWI = 14 to 20)

This zone is primarily found in southwestern Canada. While the map indicates that much of the Prairies lies in Zone 6, forest fires are of little consequence in the Prairies due to the lack of surface fuels. The small percentage of days requiring little or no control efforts (5 per cent) precludes such an operational policy inasmuch as fires not contained quickly on such days could become problems as the FWI will quickly climb back to higher values. Minimal control efforts will be needed on 30 per cent of the days. This zone contains the highest percentage of days in the surface fire class — 45 per cent. Of this total, 10 per cent of the days will have light fires, 20 per cent moderate and 15 per cent hot. Torching out may occur on 15 per cent of the days. The percentage of days with potentially uncontrollable fires increases to 5 per cent.

Zone 7, Extreme (Average FWI = 20+)

The significant portions of this zone are limited to two areas in southern British Columbia. Virtually no days are free from a need for some fire control efforts, and only on 25 per cent of the days will a minimum effort be sufficient. The proportion of days with surface fires drops to 30 per cent while days when torching out may occur increases to 20 per cent. The main difference between Zones 6 and 7 is that the percentage of days with potentially uncontrollable fires jumps to 25 per cent in Zone 7. Few, if any fire seasons will not have the latter type of days and they will probably last for extended periods. Forest fire control will be a major or at least very important proportion of the total forestry activity in these regions. It is in this zone that absolute FWI extremes are likely to occur. The highest value recorded between 1957 and 1966 was 153 at Kimberly in southeastern British Columbia." (Simard, 1973).

In futher work, Simard (1975) plotted the average occurrence of fires across Canada. He found that:

"Wildland fire occurrence ranges from a low of zero to a high of an average of 73 fires per $2,590 km^2$ per year. In general, low fire occurrence densities (less than 4 fires per $2,590 km^2$ per year) are found throughout the Territories; the northern half of British Columbia, Alberta, Saskatchewan and Manitoba; the northern two-thirds of Québec and Ontario; most of Newfoundland and all of Labrador. Not surprisingly, these are also regions of relatively low population and road density. In addition, low occurrence densities are found throughout the primarily agricultural regions of Alberta, Saskatchewan, Manitoba, Ontario and Québec. Finally, there are numerous isolated areas of low occurrence scattered throughout higher occurrence regions across the country.

Moderate occurrence densities (4 to 10 fires per $2,590 km^2$ per year) are found throughout Canada. In general, there is a pronounced band of moderate occurrence density starting in the Maritimes and crossing southern Québec and Ontario. The band becomes discontinuous across central Manitoba and Saskatchewan and all but ends in eastern Alberta. Additionally, significant areas of moderate occurrence are found in central Alberta and in southern British Columbia. Finally, isolated areas of moderate occurrence primarily in the vicinity of population centres, are found throughout generally lower occurrence regions across the country.

The significant areas of high occurrence (10 to 20 fires per $2,590 km^2$ per year) are in the interior valleys British Columbia, including Vancouver Island, southeastern Ontario and southwestern Québec and the central Maritimes. Again, there are scattered high occurrence areas in the vicinity of population centres and major highways throughout the generally moderate occurrence regions.

Very high occurrence areas (in excess of 20 fires per $2,590 km^2$ per year) are found primarily in the vicinity of population centres and along roads in southern British Columbia, southern Ontario, western Québec, the Maritimes and Newfoundland. An exception to the above is a significant general area in southeastern Ontario and southwestern Québec — a region noted for a high density of recreationists and cottages.

The highest occurrence density in Canada (73 fires per $2,590 km^2$ per year) is in the vicinity of Sudbury, Ontario. This is followed by 53 fires around Halifax, Nova Scotia. With the above two exceptions occurrence densities do not exceed 40 fires per $2,590 km^2$ per year.

Average annual fire occurrence is only one attribute of a many faceted problem. Average fire seasons tend to be exceptions rather than rules. Good and bad years, which deviate significantly from the norm are important, and particularly in the latter case, critical to the fire management organization." (Simard, 1975).

The latter research indicated that: (1) fires clustered around population centres; (2) bands of fires occurred along roads; and, (3) lakeshore and river valleys had higher occurrence densities than surrounding areas.

NFB – PHOTOTHEQUE – ONF – Photo by Chris Lund.

Depending on their nature, location, and course, forest fires can jeopardize the forest/soil/water resource base, wildlife habitat, and nearby communities.

The correlation of the two maps reiterates the significance of man's presence in the distribution of forest fires. It is estimated that approximately 75 per cent of fires are caused by humans, while of the remainder, fires started by lightning account for over half the area burned.

Forest Diseases

Diseases (and insects) affect forest growth by killing trees, destroying seeds and seedlings, deforming and stunting saplings and poles, reducing wood, and destroying wood. The most important types of losses that can result are: mortality of merchantable timber; destruction of wood; reduction in growth increment; reduction in wood quality; delayed regeneration; deficiencies in stocking; composition degeneration involving a change from valuable to inferior tree species; and site degeneration. (Davidson and Buchanan, 1964).

Disease is defined as "sustained physiological and resulting structural disturbances of living tissues and organs ending sometimes in death" (Ehrlich, 1941). Diseases may be caused by the non-living environment such as unfavourable soil or atmospheric conditions. Some of the more common of these non-infectious diseases include: heat defoliation, or the premature casting of leaves which occurs when the temperature rises above the maximum to which their tissues are adjusted; winter drying or winter killing, the killing of portions of trees by sudden great decreases in temperature and often accompanied by drying winds which cause excessive moisture loss which cannot be replaced because soil moisture is too cold or frozen, is not available to the roots, or the wood of the stem is frozen and water cannot pass through it; water excess, a condition that (i) can render the development of tender tissue making it more susceptible to extremes of heat and invasion by fungus parasites, and/or (ii) saturate the soil resulting in the death of roots by asphyxiation; mechanical injuries which expose the wood and make the wood susceptible to attack from wood-destroying and other fungi; smoke injury, salt spray, wind damage, and hail wounds.

Diseases may also be caused by living organisms such as bacteria, fungi, algae, slime mould, seed plant, animals, and insects. In these unfavourable environmental conditions, two or more agencies may combine to cause disease. These diseases may be either area specific attacking the root, stem, or foliage or may be systemic and progressively infect and disease all parts of the tree. The following examples of defoliating disease infestations and insect outbreaks are a representative sample of forest insects and diseases which have been or are important on a regional basis.

Heart Rot. Rot or decay in wood is caused by fungi which decompose one or more components of wood. The first class of rots, white rot, decomposes all the components of the wood including lignin reducing the affected wood "to a spongy mass, to white pockets of various sizes separated by areas of firm strong wood, or to a stringy or fibrous condition. The decomposed wood is usually white, but it may be yellow, tan, or even light brown in colour. The second class, causing brown rots, decomposes the cellulose and its associated pentosans, leaving the lignin more or less unaffected. The wood is reduced to a carbonous mass in varying shades of brown." (Boyce, 1961). While brown rot often attacks trees after white rot, white rot is unlikely to follow brown rot. Heart rot, a stem disease, therefore refers to both brown and white rots which attack the heartwood of a tree.

Heart rot is the single most destructive disease that exists. It can take place in any tree exposed to infection by natural pruning or infection and occurs in all tree species and in all forest regions in Canada; it alone accounts for an annual loss of over 22.6 million m^3.

Root Rot. Root rot attacks the root of a tree, and is a disease most widely known in Canada for its destruction of 25- to 125-year old Douglas-fir stands in British Columbia. The annual mortality rate is estimated at over one million m^3.

Studies of root rot were carried out in northwestern Ontario on black spruce, white spruce, and balsam fir, important pulpwood species of that area. Over 90 per cent of the trees examined had root rot; the average volumes of trees (both dead standing and windfallen) diseased were 20 per cent, 15 per cent, and 7 per cent for balsam fir, black and white spruce respectively. Butt rot, the logical extention of root rot, accounted for additional wood volume losses of 2.7 per cent, 3.1 per cent, and 2.5 per cent respectively; if, however, Ontario pulpwood scaling rules are applied, these percentages increase to 11 per cent, 11 per cent, and 8 per cent for each species respectively. Growth reduction on heavily diseased trees ranged from 10 per cent in balsam fir, to 12 per cent in black spruce, and to 5 per cent in white spruce. Together then, under average site conditions in northwestern Ontario, combined dead and windfallen trees and scaled cull due to root and butt rot amount to 39 per cent of balsam fir volume, 28 per cent of black spruce volume, and 14 per cent of white spruce volume at the average ages of 75 to 79 years. Of the harvestable volume of trees in northwestern Ontario, two-fifths of all balsam fir, one-quarter of all black spruce, and one-seventh of all white spruce is dead and unusable due to root rot.

Dwarf Mistletoes. Dwarf mistletoes are seed plants whose genus (*Arceuthobium (Razoumofskya)* of the family *Loranthacene*) is restricted to conifers and confined to the northern hemisphere. These parasites may deform or kill their hosts, with the greatest mortality among seedlings and saplings. In general, they reduce "the vigor and rate of growth of their hosts, so that infected stands require a longer time to mature and even then often produce a lower quality of timber" (Boyce, 1961). In addition to reducing the quality and quantity of merchantable timber, the seed crop production of the tree can be appreciably reduced.

This stem disease attacks black spruce in eastern Canada, jack and lodgepole pine in Manitoba, Saskatchewan, and Alberta and the following commercial species in British Columbia: ponderosa pine, lodgepole pine, western larch, Douglas-fir, western hemlock, and grand fir. These parasites are responsible for an average annual loss of over .7 million m^3.

Ducth Elm Disease. The Dutch elm disease, a systemic disease, is caused by a fungus (*Ceratocystis ulmi*) transmitted by bark beetles. "The fungus lives in the sapwood, fruiting on the wood and bark of logs and dead and dying trees" (Boyce, 1961), and produces a soluble toxin that causes discolouration and death of the wood.

The infection, discovered in Richelieu County in Québec in 1944, was introduced in crates made of diseased wood brought in by ship. By 1959, between 600 and 700 thousand trees over an area of 64 232 km^2 in Québec had been killed. In Ontario, the disease entered Prescott County in 1946 as a predictable extension of the Québec outbreak; however, four years later it also entered the Windsor area via the United States and infected the Niagara Peninsula. By 1963, an area of over 165,760 m^3 in Ontario was affected by the disease. It is estimated that the annual loss of elm in Ontario and Québec between the time of its introduction in 1944 and 1964 averaged 623,040 m^3 per annum. The progressive spread of Dutch elm disease in Ontario up to the 1970s is familiar to most residents of the province.

The disease entered New Brunswick via the neighbouring state of Maine in 1957, and has continued to spread throughout the province and to its neighbouring province of Nova Scotia in 1969. The year 1975 was a well-noted year in the history of the disease, as the first sightings of it were found at three locations in southern Manitoba. This is of major significance to the province as elms are not only naturally occurring along lakes and rivers but have also been planted in concentrations in urban areas for shade and amenity purposes.

Insect Infestations

In Canada, it has been estimated that insects destroy 28 million m^3 and diseases 57 million m^3 of wood on an annual basis.

The Forest Insect and Disease Survey, the most important source of information on disease and insect outbreak which exists in Canada, is carried out by the Canadian Forestry Service in conjunction with the provinces. This monitoring program does not cover all insects and diseases every year but rather selects those which are most serious in that year and reports specifically on them as well as on the general conditions on an annual basis.

Eastern Hemlock Looper (Lambdina fiscellaria fiscellaria). The eastern hemlock looper, a defoliating insect feeds rather wastefully on the foliage of mature and over-mature forest stands where eastern hemlock or balsam fir predominate.

In Canada, there have been five severe and prolonged outbreaks since 1912 which have caused tree mortality. The latest outbreak began in 1966 in Newfoundland, and continued to subsist until 1971 when only 24,282 ha were defoliated, in comparison to 155,405 ha in 1970 and 283,290 ha in 1969. Data obtained from damage appraisal surveys indicate an estimated 303,525 ha of fir forest have been severely damaged with a projected of 16,310,520 m^3 of pulpwood.

Forest Tent Caterpillar (Malacosoma disstria). The forest tent caterpillars use the trembling aspen as a major host; hosts also include other poplar trees, sugar maple, birch, ash, oak, and many other deciduous trees. In lean times, migrating populations have also attacked conifers. The young larvae feed on the expanding buds, sometimes mining them, while the advanced larvae or the caterpillars feed voraciously on the foliage. Low populations cause thinning of tree crowns while large populations strip the trees. Outbreaks of three- to six-year periods, persisting occasionally for ten or more years, occur at irregular intervals of six to fifteen years.

In Canada, the forest tent caterpillar causes great alarm to maple syrup producers. Although the amount of reduction is not known, maple syrup yields are reduced by this defoliater. In the Prairie Provinces, there have been three major outbreaks, the 1950 to 1954, the 1957 to 1965, and the 1971 outbreak which is still in progress. The 1957 to 1965 outbreak, the most widespread, extended at its peak over 350 000 km^2 of trembling aspen in the parkland, mixed-wood, and northern coniferous forest regions of the provinces.

While low populations cause a noticeable thinning of foliage in the upper crown, high populations strip the tree's foliage completely. Studies carried out between 1951 and 1954 in Manitoba and Saskatchewan showed the increment losses due to severe defoliation in average-stocked trembling aspen stands amounted to almost 4.5 m^3/ha annually over a four-year period. A corresponding Alberta study carried out between 1957 and 1970 indicated an 80 to 90 per cent loss in radial increment after three years of severe defoliation.

Bark Beetles. Bark beetles are insects which breed in living trees and destroy the trees in the process. They bore through the bark of the tree into a core and construct egg galleries in the phloem-cambium region. The larvae mine the inner bark first then move to the outer bark where they mature and pupate. In addition to the physical alteration of the tree, the beetles also infect the tissue around the gallery with fungi, yeasts, and bacteria which also disrupt the physiological processes of the host.

The various species of bark beetles have killed over 28 million m^3 of timber in British Columbia, in the 1961 to 1965 period, compared to just under 57 thousand m^3 in the 1956 to 1960 period.

In a recent study, (Safranyik, Shrimpton, and Whitney, 1974) it has been estimated that the mountain pine beetle (*Dendroctonus ponderosae Hopk*) has killed 36,816 m^3 of lodgepole pine timber per year for the last twenty years, or approximately three per cent of the average annual cut. Areas, usually the hotter drier areas with mild winters where climate favourable for the beetle frequently occurs, have a high hazard rating whereas areas with one or more climatic conditions detrimental to the beetle have a low rating.

Spruce Budworm (Choristoneura fumiferana). The spruce budworm continues to be the most destructive forest pest in eastern Canada in 1979. Currently, some 36.4 million ha of spruce fir forests in eastern Canada are heavily defoliated and dead. During this century, 1,812 million m^3 of fir spruce have been destroyed; this is enough wood to sustain the current annual harvest for 30 years in the eastern region. Historically, this insect has severely damaged the forest, killing large areas of mature forest, and leaving the area highly susceptible to fires.

The attack upon these coniferous stands begins when the moths lay their eggs on the underside of the needles near the branch tips in the host trees. Upon hatching, the small larvae feed upon the new growth of vegetation and pollen buds. The western spruce budworm is important, not because it kills trees as does the eastern species, but because its heaviest concentrations of larvae are in the upper crown causing extensive top killing. The risk of tree mortality increases when outbreak continues for longer than a three-year period.

At one time, the forest industry was able to absorb the shock of insect invasion by relocation of their logging sites. However, forested land is currently under such pressure to produce at an optimal level that such infestations and subsequent fires cannot be allowed. The budworm is a serious economic pest for the Canadian pulp-and-paper industry. In Nova Scotia "by 1977 the spruce budworm had damaged extensive areas of timber, including areas recently silviculturally treated." (Baskerville and Weetman, 1978).

Photo by Canadian Forestry Service.

Repeated attacks by the spruce budworm have resulted in the destruction of a balsam fir stand.

In 1975, an epidemic outbreak covered 51 million ha of fir spruce forest in Ontario, Québec, the Maritimes, and Newfoundland. In the boreal forests of Alberta and the Northwest Territories, budworm outbreaks have been reported since the extension of surveys into the northern region in the mid-1950s. In British Columbia, the western black-headed budworm "is most abundant west of the Cascade Mountains and in interior wet belt areas. The preferred hosts are western hemlock and the true firs (balsam); spruce and Douglas-firs are also attacked." (Koot and Morris, 1973).

In eastern Canada, the area of moderate to severe defoliation by the spruce budworm decreased from 54 million ha in 1975, to 51 million ha in 1976, and 37 million ha in 1978 (Table 14). Preservation of the Canadian forests is a necessity not only to safeguard economic interests but also because the forest is becoming an increasingly valuable recreational and aesthetic resource.

Control of the spruce budworm may be initiated two ways, 1) naturally, using parasites, predators, or diseases, and 2) chemically, using insecticides through aerial application. (Table 15). The Canadian research program has concentrated on the biology and dynamics of the budworm, chemical and biological control measures, the impact of the budworm, and control measures on the forest and the environment. These investigations are aimed towards the development of new and safer control measures for budworm management with a minimization of the harmful (hazardous) effects on the ecosystem.

In summary, special forest resource lands may include not only lands of a high-production capability for commercial forests, but also those forest areas particularly affected by a variety of hazards such as fires, diseases, and insects. Although it is not always possible to map these areas, they are nonetheless critical. If efforts to control and reduce forest losses from these influences are not successful, forest lands will be lost to all economic, recreational, aesthetic, wildlife, soil stabilization and water supply, and other uses. Such losses will be felt not only by the forestry industries but by all Canadians.

Forest Management and Administration in Canada

Ownership

About 91 per cent of the forest land of Canada is owned by the Crown. The federal government has rights to 9 per cent of this land, and the provincial governments have rights to 82 per cent. The remaining 9 per cent is owned by corporations or private individuals. Rights to cut Crown timber under lease have been

TABLE 14.

Area of moderate to severe defoliation caused by spruce budworm

Province	1975	1976	1977	1978
	(millions of ha)			
Ontario	13.3	14.7	14.1	15.2
Québec	35.0	33.2	21.4	19.5
New Brunswick	3.5	0.9	0.5	0.7
Nova Scotia	0.9	1.0	0.8	0.6
Prince Edward Island	0.2	0.2	0.1	0.1
Newfoundland	0.7	1.2	1.5	1.3
Total	53.6	51.2	38.4	37.4

Source: Canadian Forestry Service, Environment Canada. 1979. Miscellaneous unpublished data.

TABLE 15.

Forest areas sprayed*, 1975 to 1978

Province	1975	1976	1977	1978
	(thousands of ha)			
Ontario	13	40	4	1
Québec	2,853	3,614	1,380	1,230
New Brunswick	2,713	3,837	1,663	1,536
Newfoundland	–	–	76	377
Total	5,579	7,491	3,123	3,144

* Includes operational, semi-operational, and experimental treatments.

Source: Canadian Forestry Service, Environment Canada. 1979. Miscellaneous unpublished data.

Federal and Provincial Responsibility. The provincial governments have the responsibility for the management and protection of most of the Crown forests. The federal government, however, manages and protects forests in the National Parks, Northwest Territories and Yukon, and forest experiment stations. The National Parks forests are administered by the Parks Branch of the federal Department of Indian and Northern Affairs (DINA), and the Northwest Territories and Yukon by the Forest Resources Division of DINA.

The forestry activities of the federal government are defined in the Forestry Research and Development Act. In brief, these activities include: "providing for the conduct of research relating to the protection, management and utilization of the forest resources of Canada and better utilization of forest products", and "encouragement of public cooperation in the protection and use of the forest resources of Canada." In addition, under the Act, the federal government can make surveys, advise on forest management, protection, and utilization, dispose of timber on federal lands, carry out economic studies, and establish Forest Experimental Areas (Forestry Development and Research Act, 1966-67).

The federal government's main agent in forestry matters is the Canadian Forestry Service, a directorate of the Environmental Management Service, within the Department of the Environment.

There are, however, many other federal agencies, such as the Department of Regional Economic Expansion, the Department of National Defence, and the Department of Indian and Northern Affairs which are involved in forestry matters. At present the federal rôle in forestry is under review.

Traditionally, the Canadian Forestry Service's activities have been mainly concerned with research, with provincial governments and industry mainly involved in management and utilization. Some provincial governments, such as Ontario, Québec, and British Columbia, however, are actively engaged in forestry research, and so are the universities of New Brunswick, Toronto, Lakehead, and British Columbia where there are faculties of forestry.

National Forest Policy. Each province has its own forest policy, covering management, utilization, recreation, and conservation. Provincial governments have voluminous forest legislation and regulation and the federal government has national policies dealing with taxes, trade, incentives, transporation, and research.

There is, however, no forest policy for Canada as a whole. Since 1970, however, efforts have been made to construct a formal national forest policy in an effort to deal with conflicts over land use, impending wood fibre shortages, international competition, their effects on the forest industry, and national prosperity. The federal government, provincial governments, and industry have made a concerted effort to formulate a policy in discussions of the Canadian Forestry Advisory Committee, the Forest Industries Development Committee, the Canadian Council of Resource and Environment Ministers, and other groups. So far, no concrete policy has evolved, and there is some question as to whether or not an attempt to formalize a national forest policy is realistic (Reed 1978). As the Reed Report (1978) suggests, there is still a need for each of the participants in forestry "to put his own home in order."

Management

Regional Differences in Forestry Regulation and Practices. Forestry regulation and practices vary considerably from one province to another. For example, in British Columbia, where 95 per cent of the 52 million ha of productive forest land are vested in the Crown in the right of the province, the forests are managed for sustained yield as Tree Farm Licences or Public Sustained Yield Units, with some old temporary tenures, such as special timber licences, and leases as well as Pulp Licences and Leases, still continue. Tree Farm Licences reserve for the holder the annual cut on a specified area, usually for renewable periods of 21 years. The B.C. Forest Service approves the Working Plan.

Cost of forest treatments are offset against stumpage charges. Public Sustained Yield Units are managed by the B.C. Forest Service, and cutting rights are sold to the industry. The cutting contracts often require the licensee to regenerate the cutover land and offset the costs against stumpage.

The B.C. Forest Service exercises little control in forest on private lands, except for fire protection. Some private lands are managed as Tree Farms, with associ-

MAP 8

Canadian Government Office of Tourism photo.

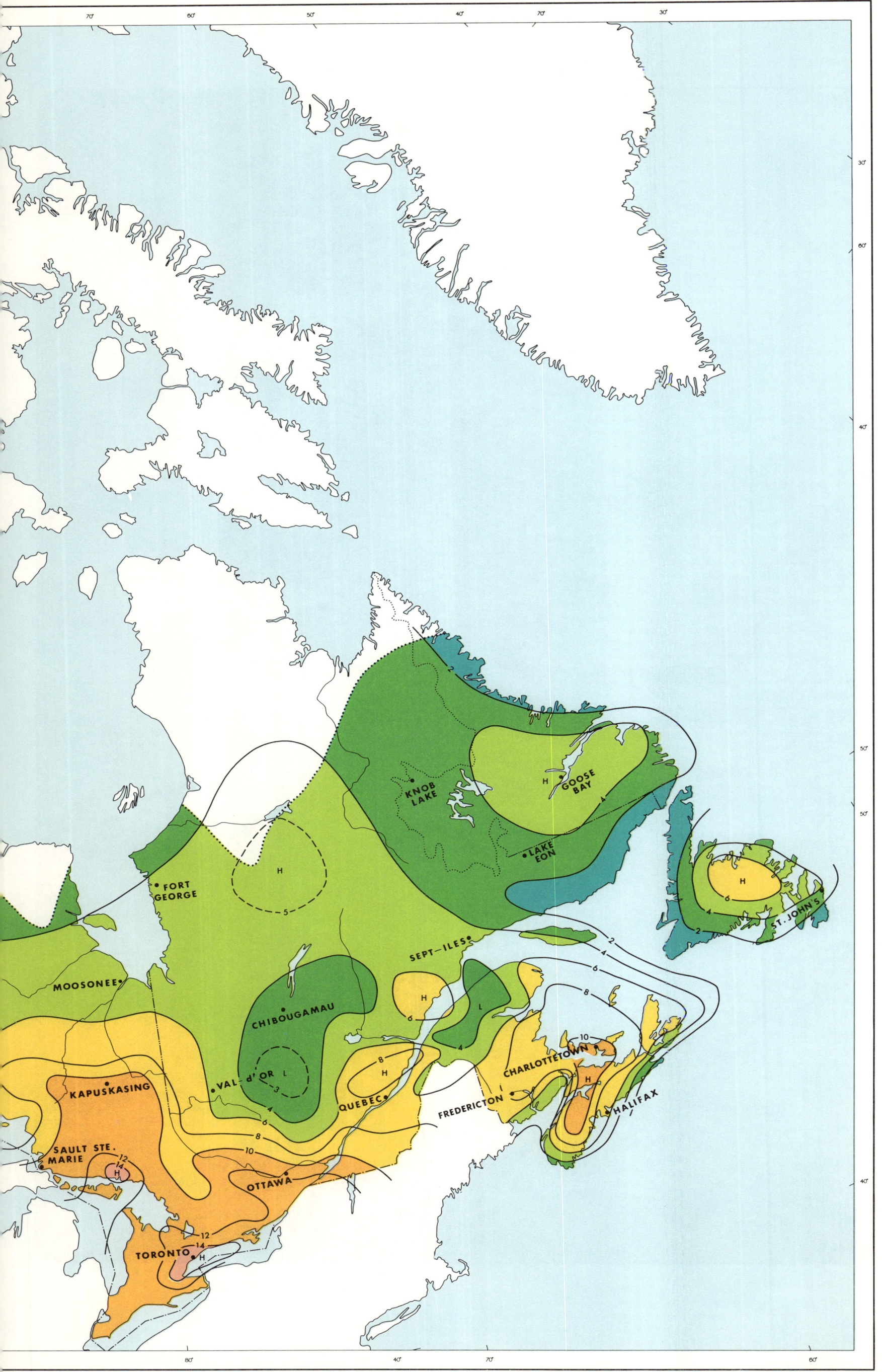

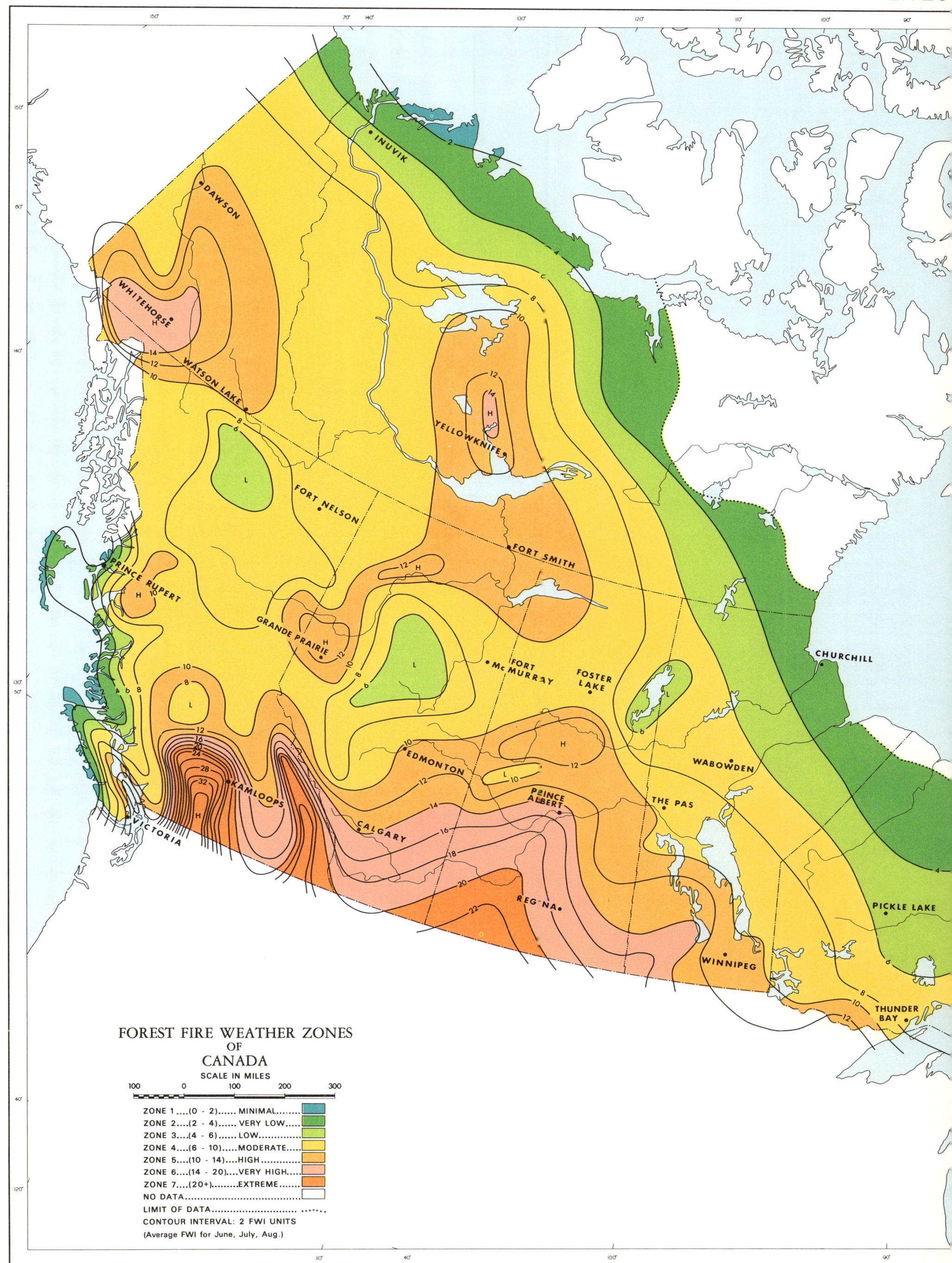

ated tax benefits and some are managed under Tree Farm Licences. In these cases, the private forests only qualify for tax concessions if they manage for sustained yield (Reed 1978). New regulations concerning the province's forest and range legislation came into effect in 1979.

In Alberta there are about 47 million ha of forest land. About 82 per cent of this area is provincial government land, about 13 per cent federal, and about 3 per cent private. Alberta's forests are managed on a sustained-yield basis, the provincial forestry service authorizing all harvesting, with general guidelines about cutting old timber, diseased trees and decadent stands first, in clearcut strips or patches. All permits to cut are issued as Forest Management agreements for large forests or as short-term permits for cutting quotas on forests managed by the provincial governments.

Licensees with Forest Management Agreements are responsible for reforestation of cutover land. Companies operating on the quota system may either regenerate the cutover land themselves or pay (on the basis of so much per unit volume of timber harvested) the Forest Service to do it for them (Reed 1978).

In contrast to British Columbia and Alberta where the organization harvesting an area bears a major part of the responsibility for regeneration, in Ontario the amended Crown Timber Act of 1962 assigned full responsibility for regeneration to the provincial government forestry service (the Ministry of Natural Resources). Industry just carries out the harvesting. This has resulted in problems in forest renewal and management, and the position is being reconsidered. The present trend in Ontario is towards assigning more responsibility for regeneration to industries.

The other provinces have different systems of land tenure and regeneration responsibility. There is a trend, however, to make the industries more responsible for forest renewal on cutover lands.

Regional Differences in Forest Management. The ways the forests of Canada are managed varies a great deal from one province to another, and even varies within a single province. For example, in coastal British Columbia the main method of site preparation of clearcut areas is burning. In interior B.C. both scarification and prescribed burning are used to prepare the sites. In Alberta, Saskatchewan, Ontario, New Brunswick, and Nova Scotia scarification is the main method of site preparation, and use of controlled burning for this purpose is not widespread, although it is used to some extent to reduce fire hazard. Manitoba uses both scarification and burning. In Québec and Newfoundland, very little site preparation was carried out in the past. In Québec, however, up to 6,000 ha per year (i.e. 1975) have been scarified in recent years, and in Newfoundland with its large areas of peat lands, methods of draining, burning, and scarifying are being considered (Reed, 1978).

In the past, most provinces have used mainly natural regeneration to renew cutover forests, but during the past decade, forest renewal by planting and seeding has greatly increased. Planting has increased in most provinces, but use of direct seeding has had varying success. In Ontario, where seeding has had some success, use of seeding has increased in recent years, while planting has declined to some extent in spite of a very active container program. In British Columbia, direct seeding is used very little and planting has been increased to meet the goals of sustained yield. Until recently, seed sources used for planting and seeding were often local or doubtful in most provinces. Even at present, very little generically improved seed is in use, but today, seed control is much more effective in most provinces. Tree improvement programs are being undertaken by the federal government and provincial governments, particularly British Columbia, Alberta, Ontario, and New Brunswick. These programs increase each year as the need to use generically superior seed becomes more generally accepted.

Efforts are being made to regenerate the huge backlog of about 28 million ha left unregenerated in Canada following logging and fires (Weetman, 1977). Even so,. of the 756,000 ha of forests cut annually only about 324,000 ha/year are currently regenerated naturally, and 239,000 ha are regenerated by planting and seeding, so the backlog on unregenerated areas is still increasing by about 193,000 ha/year (Morgenstern, 1978). Unless something is done, the backlog will have more than doubled in 14 years time. The main problem is one of money and manpower. A much greater investment in both research and operations of these unregenerated areas is required if these areas are to be brought back into production.

Forestry Statistics. Because the provinces compile their forestry data in different ways, there is a lack of comparable data across Canada, making it difficult to produce an overall picture of available resources, their potential, utilization for both consumptive and non-consumptive purposes, and regeneration. This lack of comparable data is a major obstable to planning effective resource management for Canada as a whole, and one reason that a national forest policy has been so slow to develop. There is also a lack of sound data about the quantity and type of forest products of foreign competitors, making it difficult to plan to compete successfully in the world's markets.

One step taken to standardize forestry data is the federal government's introduction of metrification. In addition, the federal Canadian Forestry Service and both provincial and industrial cooperators, are involved in a National Forestry Statistic Program. The objectives of this program are to develop common forestry definitions, standards, and procedures; co-ordinate the adoption of a standard map grid for resource data; and initiate a Canadian Forest Resource Information System that can be updated. It is expected that before long comparable forestry data will be available from all parts of Canada.

Conclusion

Impact of Forest Management. Logging, site treatment, regeneration, forest protection, and recreation in forests all affect the vegetation, fauna, soil, water and nutrient cycles, and microclimate. These man-made disturbances take place against a background of natural disturbances, such as destruction of vegetation by fire or insects which are a natural and dynamic part of the forest processes and evolution. These natural disturbances may interfere with man's need for timber on a sustained-yield basis, but the processes of natural forest are more concerned with forest survival in the long term than fibre yield.

There has been much public concern about such forestry practices as clearcutting and spraying to control budworm. Clearcutting is sometimes unsightly, affecting aesthetic and recreational values, but it is an economic way of harvesting. Also, it is the only way to harvest some trees, such as pines, that are intolerant of shade and cannot grow successfully in a selection system. If the clearcuts were large enough, they could possibly erode watesheds, diminish the local gene pool, deprive fauna of habitat, and raise the water table appreciably. However, these problems can be overcome by judicious limitation of areas of clearcuts and design of cutting patterns. In Alberta, for example, clearcuts in spruce areas are restricted to 25- to 30-ha strips or to strips 150 to 250 m in width; in pine, the cleancuts are restricted to less than 60 ha (Reed, 1978). Canadian foresters are aware of the problems and take them into account in planning.

Concern about the effects on the fauna and even public health of spraying with toxic chemicals to control spruce budworm has caused considerable public outcry. There is some doubt about the effect of the sprays, and spraying with the insecticides is still widely used. The federal government, however, is giving high priority to developing methods of biological control with bacteria or viruses pathogenic to the insect.

In recent years, the increasing use of shorter rotation and whole tree harvesting has raised questions about the effect of these practices on soil fertility. Many statements have been published that categorically state that whole tree harvesting will not affect soil fertility, and some take the opposite view. The literature shows, however, that the nutrient budget (nutrient income — nutrient outgo) associated with whole tree harvesting varies with tree species, age, and site. No general conclusion can be drawn. Each situation must be regarded on its own, and the federal government of Canada and scientists in the United States are attempting to develop predictive models to simplify assessment of effects on any site.

Man-initiated and natural fires affect the vegetation and the soil. In Canada, fire is a vital part of the forest succession, and some trees, such as jack pine and lodgepole pine, are adapted to fire and dependent on it for regeneration. Effects of fire on the soil include deposition of base rich ash and losses of volatile nitrogen. However, these effects vary with the intensity of the fire and the forest ecosystem where it occurs.

Other forest practices such as scarification, use of herbicides, road building, introduction of non-indigenous species, and draining, all have their effects. Some effects are understood and some are not, and the federal government is supporting investigations of the environmental impact of these activities.

Forestry-related Problems. Canada's forests are so huge that people have tended to assume that they are an inexhaustible supply of fibre. In recent years, however, foresters and the public, have become aware that resources are not boundless and require renewing.

In spite of the fact that forestry and forestry products are the mainstay of the nation's prosperity, investment in forest management and renewal has been inadequate. Consequently, the country is faced today with shortages of accessible timber and a huge regeneration backlog. The increasing interest in using forests as sources of cellulose for liquid fuel production will increase demands upon Canada's forests, demands that will compete with needs for conventional forest products such as pulp and lumber. Both federal and provincial governments are looking closely at this problem of escalating demands and the problems involved.

There is increasing interest in the use of intensive forestry to increase yields in accessible areas, including the use of very short rotations of less than ten years with hybrid poplars and possibly other tree species. Increased harvesting and use of shorter rotations result in more demands being made on sites, some of which already have soils of low fertility. The federal government is supporting research on the environmental, economic, and social impact of these activities upon forest ecosystems.

The present tax structure is not conducive to investment in forestry, and this problem is under review. The escalating labour costs, with wage increases exceeding increases in productivity, has put the forest industries in an unfavourable position in the world's markets. Costs of stand establishment, management, protection, and harvesting increase every year and foresters are becoming much more conscious of costs in relation to benefits. Ways to reduce labour costs are being sought by development and use of mechanical planting and harvesting equipment, and more efficient management practices.

Canadian foresters who have relied to large extent on natural forests as a source of timber have to face the problem that the yield of fibre per ha is low (about 1.4 to 5.6 m^3/ha/year) in these forests compared to natural forests of countries such as New Zealand, where fibre yield per ha is often as high as 24.5 m^3/ha/year (Thomson, 1969, and Carlisle and Teich, 1971). Consequently, harvesting costs in Canada are relatively high. The Reed Report (1978) emphasizes the need for wider adoption of intensive forestry to increase yield per ha. The federal and the provincial governments are seeking ways to increase yield by better silviculture and use of genetically superior stock.

Introduction of foreign pests and diseases has caused a great deal of damage to Canada's forests in the past, and the danger of new introductions is always present. Even as recently as 1979 the virulent European strain of Scleroderris canker (*Gremmeniella abietina*), which has caused such havoc in the pine forests of Vermont and New York State, has appeared in southern Québec. This strain kills mature trees as well as young trees. The European spruce sawfly (*Diprion hercyniae*) caused the loss of 41.3 million m^3 of timber before it was controlled by a virus. Also, the white pine blister rust (*Cronartium ribicola*), which reached North America from Europe about 1900, has caused considerable damage to five-needled pines in Canada and the United States. The balsam woolly aphid (*Adelges piceae*) is a serious pest that is not indigenous to North America (Maini and Carlisle, 1974).

Under the Seed Act there are phytosanitary regulations concerning the movement of plant propagules (plants, seeds, and cuttings) into, out of, and within Canada. The Act is administered by the federal Department of Agriculture, and the responsibility for tree seed testing has been delegated to the federal Canadian Forestry Service. At present, importation of soil or plants with soil is prohibited, and *Abies* plants cannot be moved to British Columbia. There are also constraints on movement of larch, elm, willow, spruce, Douglas-fir, and pine plants, and a range of horticultural species. Seeds, however, are not subject to such stringent restictions as plants. However, importing seeds of certain species of *Ribes, Berberis, Mahoberberis*, and *Rhamnus* is prohibited, and entry of chestnut seed is restricted. Certification requirements for small amounts of other kinds of tree seed are usually waived. It is hoped that these precautions will minimize the importation or movement within Canada of serious pests or their alternative plant hosts.

The planting and seeding of forests is increasing an annual activity throughout Canada, and there is insuffi-

CANADA'S SPECIAL RESOURCE LANDS QUESTIONNAIRE

Dear User,

Canada's Special Resource Lands is a new publication and we are interested in having your reaction. This is a necessary step to help us provide needed information in a convenient format.

Once you have had an opportunity to use this book, would you please take the time to fill out this brief questionnaire? A prepaid envelope is enclosed for your convenience. Feel free to make any further suggestions that you think may lead to better publications.

Are you interested in other maps and publications prepared by the Lands Directorate? To obtain a complimentary copy of the Lands Directorate Publications List, please indicate "yes" in Question 12.

User Profile

1. Name _____

2. Address _____

   _____ Postal Code _____

3. Occupation _____

4. Is your interest in this publication,

    (i) as a private individual ( ) yes ( ) no

    and/or

    (ii) in relation to your work ( ) yes (specify below) ( ) no

    ( ) industry ( ) elementary school
    ( ) consultant ( ) secondary school
    ( ) federal government ( ) university/community college
    ( ) provincial government ( ) other institutions (library etc.)
    ( ) municipal/regional government ( ) other (specify) _____

General Information

5. Where did you learn about Canada's Special Resource Lands? Please specify below.

    ( ) professional organization _____
    ( ) government source _____
    ( ) magazine, newspaper, periodical _____
    ( ) browsing in a bookstore _____
    ( ) from a colleague _____
    ( ) other _____

6. How have you used this publication?

    (i) as an educational tool for: elementary school ( )
    secondary school ( )
    university/community college ( )
    other _____ ( )

    (ii) as a resource reference in planning at: federal level ( )
    provincial level ( )
    municipal/regional level ( )

    (iii) as a general reference document ( )

    (iv) other _____

(PLEASE TURN OVER)

7. Do you have any comments concerning the design format (i.e. book size, map scales, foldouts, graphic illustrations, layout, size of print, colours, etc.)?

_____
_____
_____

8. Do you have any comments concerning the contents and topics of this publication (i.e. subject matter, text material, data, writing style, bibliographies, etc.)?

_____
_____
_____

9. Can you suggest how this type of publication might be improved to better suit your needs?

_____
_____
_____

Future Requirements

10. Would you be interested in seeing more of this type of land-oriented national perspective publication? ( ) yes   ( ) no

11. If yes, please suggest the topics you would like included in future publications.

_____
_____
_____

Lands Directorate Publications List

12. Are you interested in receiving a free copy of the publications list prepared by the Lands Directorate? ( ) yes   ( ) no

Thank you for taking the time to complete this questionnaire. Additional comments are welcome.

cient sound seed to meet regular demands. Both the federal and provincial governments are conscious of this problem and, in co-operation with geneticists, foresters are investigating and developing seed crop forecasting techniques, seed collection, pretreatment, storage, and testing in order to improve the availability of good seed to meet operational needs. Concern is also being expressed about gene pool depletion, particularly in heavily exploited areas near the larger cities. The southern hardwood populations are under severe pressure, and the federal government has made a range wide collection of Canadian walnuts in an effort to conserve the gene plasm.

Forestry in Canada is at a crossroads. There is a new awareness by both the public and politicians of the value of forests to the nation as well as a consciousness of a need to define the main problems, do something about them, and increase efficiency of the industry so that it can compete in the world's markets. There is also a consciousness that forests must also provide recreation and other social facilities, and that the environmental implications of forest use must be taken into account.

In many parts of Canada, forests are an important element of the landscape. If trees are to be available for commercial lumbering, soil stabilization, water supply or conservation, wildlife habitat, recreation, or other purposes, the basic forest resource must be managed with intelligence and foresight.

Acknowledgements

The author would like to acknowledge several individuals for their contributions to this chapter. Their generous assistance in the preparation of material was greatly appreciated.

Mr. F.B. Armitage (retired)
Canadian Forestry Service
Environment Canada

Dr. A. Carlisle
Petawawa Forest Experiment Station
Canadian Forestry Service
Environment Canada

Dr. L.W. Carlson
Acting Director, Forest Management and
  Conservation Branch
Canadian Forestry Service
Environment Canada

Dr. A.G. Davidson
Forest Disease Specialist, Forest Protection Branch
Canadian Forestry Service
Environment Canada

Mr. R.J. Neale
Forest Utilization Branch
Canadian Forestry Service
Environment Canada

Dr. A.J. Simard
Research Scientist, Forest Fire Research Institute
Canadian Forestry Service
Environment Canada

Mr. C. Stanton (retired)
Chief, Creative Projects
Environmental Management Service
  Information Team
Environment Canada

Mr. J.V. Stewart
Policy Analyst
Canadian Forestry Service
Environment Canada

Bibliography

Allen, Robert Thomas. 1970. The Illustrated Natural History of Canada — The Great Lakes. McClelland. Toronto.

Andresen, John W. 1975. "Urban Forestry – Trying to Meet the Needs of Urban Planners." Forum. July 1975. Canadian Institute of Planners. Ottawa.

_____. 1976a. "Urban Forestry Research Systems." Trees and Forests For Human Settlement. Proceedings of papers presented at Symposia held June 11-12, 1976 at the United Nations Habitat Forum in Vancouver, British Columbia and June 22, 1976 at the XVIth IUFRO World Congress in Oslo, Norway. Centre for Urban Forestry Studies, University of Toronto. University of Toronto Press. Toronto.

_____. 1976b. Urban Forestry in Ontario: Municipal Challenges and Opportunities. Prepared for the Forest Management Branch, Division of Forests, Ontario Ministry of Natural Resources. Toronto.

_____, and Swaigen, J. 1978. Urban Tree and Forest Legislation in Ontario. Report O-X-282. Great Lakes Forest Research Centre. Canadian Forestry Service, Environment Canada. Sault Ste. Marie.

Avery, N. 1975. Spruce Budworm Is Man's Competitor. News Release. Canadian Forestry Service, Environment Canada. Ottawa.

Bailey, R.E., and Mailman, G.E. 1972. Land Capability for Forestry in Nova Scotia. Canada Land Inventory Report No. 1. Department of Lands and Forests. Halifax.

Baird, Bonnie. 1977. "How Urban Forests Improve City Life." Canadian Geographical Journal. Vol. 92, No. 3. Royal Canadian Geographical Society. Ottawa.

Baranyay, J.A., and Smith, R.B. 1972. Dwarf Mistletoes in British Columbia and Recommendations for Their Control. Canadian Forestry Service, Environment Canada. Victoria.

Baskerville, G., and Weetman, G.F. 1978. "Forest Management at Nova Scotia Forest Industries Ltd." Forest Management in Canada. Vol. II, Case Studies. F.L.C. Reed & Associates Ltd. Forest Management Institute. Information Report FMR-X-103. Canadian Forestry Service, Environment Canada. Ottawa.

Black, William A. 1977. Case Study: National Capital Region's Greenspace. Lands Directorate, Environment Canada. Ottawa. (unpublished).

Bodsworth, Fred. 1970. The Illustrated Natural History of Canada — The Pacific Coast. McClelland. Toronto.

Bonnefoy, L., and Bonnefoy, G. 1965. Average Yields of Samples Taken in Fields with Shelterbelts. Soils and Crops Branch, Manitoba Department of Agriculture.

Boyce, John S. 1961. Forest Pathology. McGraw-Hill Book Company, Inc. Toronto.

Braithwaite, Max. 1970. The Illustrated Natural History of Canada — The Western Plains. McClelland. Toronto.

Breton, R., Villeneuve, P., et Mercier, J.-C. 1975. Étude de base relative à la politique de recherche forestière: L'importance économique et sociale de la forêt Québécoise et l'analyse de l'industrie forestière. Étude no. 2. Réalisée pour le Conseil de la recherche et du développement forestière du Québec. Ministère des Terres et Forêts. Québec.

British Columbia Department of Environment. 1976. Ecological Reserves in British Columbia. Victoria.

British Columbia Department of Forests. 1976. Annual Report 1975. Victoria.

Brown, E.A. 1970. Environmental Problems in An Urbanizing Society. Paper prepared for a Symposium at the Massachusetts Department of Natural Resources. University of Massachusetts. Amherst, Massachusetts.

Caldwell, L.K. 1973. From Talk to Action. Proceedings of the Symposium on Wildlife in an Urbanizing Environment Springfield, Massachusetts.

Camden House Publishing. 1977. Harrowsmith. Vol. II: 3, No. 9. Camden East.

Campbell, A.E., and Pratt, R.H.M. 1974. Bibliography of North American Shelterbelt Research. Northern Forest Research Centre. Information Report NOR-X-92. Canadian Forestry Service, Environment Canada. Edmonton.

Canada Land Inventory. Land Capability for Forestry. Maps at 1:1,000,000. Ontario (1974), Atlantic Provinces (1975), Saskatchewan (1976), Alberta (1976), Québec (1979), and Manitoba (1979). Lands Directorate, Environment Canada. Ottawa.

Canadian Forestry Advisory Council. 1975. The Forestry Situation in Canada - Major Concerns and Proposed Remedies. Third Report to the Minister of the Environment. Environment Canada. Ottawa.

Canadian Forestry Service. 1972. Annual Report of the Forest Insect and Disease Survey, 1971. Environment Canada. Ottawa.

_____. 1973. Canada's Eight Forest Regions. Fact Sheet. Environment Canada. Ottawa.

185

_________. 1974a. Canada: A Forest Nation. Fact Sheet. Environment Canada. Ottawa.

_________. 1974b. Canada's Forests, 1974. Fact Sheet. Environment Canada. Ottawa.

_________. 1975a. Maple Syrup Production. Fact Sheet. Environment Canada. Ottawa.

_________. 1975b. Dutch Elm Disease. Fact Sheet. Department of the Environment. Ottawa.

_________. 1975c. The Forest Tent Caterpillar. Fact Sheet. Department of the Environment. Ottawa.

_________. 1955, 1967, 1971, 1975, and 1976. Forest Insect and Disease Survey. Environment Canada. Ottawa.

_________. 1979. Miscellaneous unpublished data. Environment Canada. Ottawa.

Canadian Institute of Forestry. 1972. "Forest Land Policy Statement of the Canadian Institute of Forestry, 1971." The Forestry Chronicle. Vol. 48, No. 4. Canadian Institute of Forestry, Macdonald College. Québec.

Canadian Pulp and Paper Association. (no date). The Forest Book. Montréal.

_________. 1974a. From Watershed to Watermark. Montréal.

_________. 1974b. Reference Tables, 1974. 28th Edition. Montréal.

_________. 1974c. Pulp and Paper from Canada. Montréal.

_________. 1975a. The Pulp and Paper Industry in Canada. Fact Sheet. Montréal.

_________. 1975b. Pulp and Paper Report: A Review of the Canadian Pulp and Paper Industry in 1974. Fact Sheet. Montréal.

_________. 1975c. Recent Forest Policy Developments in Manitoba, Saskatchewan, Alberta and British Columbia. Proceedings of the National Forest Management Group Meeting held May 21-22, 1975 in Edmonton, Alberta. Montréal.

_________. 1975d. Recent Forest Policy Developments in Newfoundland, Nova Scotia, New Brunswick, Québec and Ontario. Proceedings of the National Forest Management Group Meeting held November 12-13, 1974 in Thunder Bay, Ontario. Montréal.

Carlisle, A. 1976. The Utilization of Forest Biomass and Forest Industry Wastes for the Production and Conservation of Energy. Canadian Forestry Service, Department of the Environment. Ottawa.

_________, and Teich, A.H. 1971. The Costs and Benefits of Tree Improvement Programs. Publication No. 1302. Canadian Forestry Service, Department of the Environment. Ottawa.

CCREM Task Force on Forest Policy. 1976. Forest Policies in Canada. Vol. I, II, and III. Canadian Council of Resource and Environment Ministers. Montréal.

Cliff, E.P. 1971. "Trees and Forests in the Human Environment." Trees and Forests in an Urbanizing Environment. Edited by Silas Little and John H. Noyes. University of Massachusetts. Amherst, Massachusetts.

Conservation and Utilization Committee Task Force. 1973. The Resources of the Foothills: A Choice of Land Use Alternatives. Departments of Lands and Forests, and Environment. Edmonton.

Conservation Council of Ontario. 1971. The Urban Landscape: A Study of Open Space in Urban Metropolitan Areas. Toronto.

Cook, D.I., and Van Haverbeke, D.F. 1971. "Trees and Shrubs for Noise Abatement." Trees and Forests in an Urbanizing Environment. Edited by Silas Little and John H. Noyes. University of Massachusetts. Amherst, Massachusetts.

Cranmer, Valerie. 1974a. Land Use Programs in Canada: Nova Scotia. Lands Directorate, Environment Canada. Ottawa.

_________. 1974b. Land Use Programs in Canada: Prince Edward Island. Lands Directorate, Environment Canada. Ottawa.

_________. 1974c. Land Use Programs in Canada: New Brunswick. Lands Directorate, Environment Canada. Ottawa.

_________. 1974d. Land Use Programs in Canada: Newfoundland and Labrador. Lands Directorate, Environment Canada. Ottawa.

Davidson, A.G., and Buchanan, T.S. 1964. Disease Impact on Forest Production in North America. FAO/IUFRO Symposium on Internationally Dangerous Forest Diseases and Insects held July 20-30, 1964 in Oxford. Department of Forestry. Ottawa.

_________, and Prentice, R.M. eds. 1967. Important Forest Insects and Diseases of Mutual Concern to Canada, the United States and Mexico. Department of Forestry and Rural Development. Ottawa.

Earl, D.E. 1975. Forest Energy and Economic Development. Clarendon Press. Oxford, England.

Ehrlich, J. 1941. "Etiological Terminology." Chronica Botanica. Vol. 6. Waltham, Massachusetts.

Environment Canada. 1974. Calgary–Golden Ecotour. Canadian Forestry Service. Ottawa.

Evans, R.S. 1977. Energy Self-sufficiency Prospects for the British Columbia Forest Products Industry. Information Report VP-X-166. Canadian Forestry Service, Fisheries and Environment Canada. Vancouver.

Falkner, A.C., and Carruthers, J.A. 1974. "National Parks of Canada." Conservation in Canada: A Conspectus. Edited by J.S. Maini and A. Carlisle. Publication 1340. Canadian Forestry Service, Department of the Environment. Ottawa.

Federal Interdepartmental Committee. 1973. A Working Paper Concerning the Canadian Pulp and Paper Industry with Implications for Other Forest-based Industries. Paper arising from a meeting of federal and provincial authorities held August 2, 1973 in Ottawa. Canadian Forestry Service, Department of the Environment. Ottawa.

Fillion, Jean-Louis. Consolidation of Statutes and Regulations Pertaining to Forestry. Prince Edward Island (1972), New Brunswick (1972), Saskatchewan (1972), Nova Scotia (1973), Manitoba (1973), Alberta (1974), British Columbia (1975), Canada (1975), Newfoundland (1975), Ontario — Part I and II (1975), Québec — Part I and II (1975). Canadian Forestry Service, Environment Canada. Ottawa.

Fitch, James M. 1976. "Montréal Buildings Following Poor Example of U.S." The Gazette. January 29. Montréal.

Forest Management Institute, Environment Canada. 1979. Miscellaneous unpublished data. Canadian Forestry Service. Ottawa.

Forestry Development and Research Act. 1966-67. C. 25, S. 26, R.S.C. 1970. C. 14. 2nd Supplement. Federal Statute. Ottawa.

Forrester, D.B. 1973. Forestry Proposal for Watershed Conservation Districts and Resource Conservation Districts in the Province of Manitoba. Water Resources Branch, Department of Mines, Resources and Environmental Management. Winnipeg.

Foskett, R.L. 1955. "Wind Barriers Increase Vegetable Yields." South Dakota Farm and Home Research. Vol. VI, No. 2.

Gentilcore, Louis. ed. 1972. Studies in Canadian Geography: Ontario. University of Toronto Press. Toronto.

Golding, D.L. ed. 1974. Managing Forest Lands for Water: Proceedings of Research—Management Seminar held January 13-14, 1970 in Edmonton, Alberta. Information Report NOR-X-13. Canadian Forestry Service, Department of the Environment. Edmonton.

Greater Vancouver Water District. 1972. Map of Greater Vancouver Water District with Particular Reference to Water Supply Sources and Systems. Vancouver.

_________. 1975. Greater Vancouver Water District. Victoria.

_________. 1979. Personal communication. Victoria.

Great Lakes Forest Research Centre. 1976. Forestry Research Newsletter. Symposium on Plantation Establishment held in Kirkland Lake, Ontario. Canadian Forestry Service, Environment Canada. Sault Ste. Marie.

Grenier, Fernand. ed. 1972. Études sur la géographie du Canada: Québec. University of Toronto Press. Toronto.

Halliday, W.E.D. 1937. A Forest Classification for Canada. Forest Service Bulletin 89. Lands, Parks and Forests Branch, Canada Department of Mines and Resources. Ottawa.

Hanson, W.R. (no date). Conserving a Watershed. Eastern Rockies Forest Conservation Board. Calgary.

Hare, F. Kenneth. 1950. "Climate and Zonal Divisions of the Boreal Forest Formation in Eastern Canada." The Geographical Review. Vol. XL, No. 4. The American Geographical Society. New York.

Hildahl, V., and Campbell, A.E. 1975. Forest Tent Caterpillar in the Prairie Provinces. Canadian Forestry Service, Environment Canada. Edmonton.

Hills, G.A. 1952. The Classification and Evaluation of Site for Forestry. Research Report No. 24. Ontario Department of Lands and Forests. Toronto.

Hirvonen, H.E. 1977. "The Role of Urban Forestry in Regional Landscape Design." The Forestry Chronicle. Vol. 53, No. 5. Canadian Institute of Forestry, Macdonald College. Québec.

Horton, Keith W. 1976. "Of Trees, Natural Ecosystems and Community Design." Plan Canada. Vol. 16/3, 4. Canadian Institute of Planners. Ottawa.

Hosie, R.C. 1975. Native Trees of Canada. Seventh Edition. Canadian Forestry Service, Department of the Environment. Ottawa.

Hough, Stansbury & Associates Ltd. 1973. Design Guidelines for Forest Management. Ontario Ministry of Natural Resources. Toronto.

Hustich, I. 1949. "On the Forest Geography of the Labrador Peninsula: A Preliminary Synthesis." Acta Geographica. Vol. 10, No. 2. Societas Geographica Finniae. Helsinki, Finland.

Inter Group Consulting Economists Ltd. 1976. Economic Prefeasibility Study: Large-scale Methanol Fuel Production from Surplus Canadian Forest Biomass. Part I and 2. Environmental Management Service, Fisheries and Environment Canada. Ottawa.

International Union of Forestry Research Organizations. 1976. Trees and Forests for Human Settlements. Proceedings of papers presented at Symposia held June 11-12, 1976 at the United Nations Habitat Forum in Vancouver, British Columbia and June 22, 1976 at the XVIth IUFRO World Congress in Olso, Norway. Centre for Urban Forestry Studies, University of Toronto Press. Toronto.

Jeffery, W.W. 1967. "Forest Hydrology Research in Canada." International Symposium on Forest Hydrology. Edited by W.E. Sopper and H.W. Lull. Pergamon Press. New York.

Jenkins, G.C. 1974. Whitemud River Watershed Resource Study. Manitoba Department of Mines, Resources and Environmental Management. Winnipeg.

Jones, A.R.C., and MacArthur, J.D. 1976. An Urban Forestry Model for Canada. Prepared for the International Union of Forestry Research Organizations Symposia held June 11-12, 1976 at the United Nations Habitat Forum in Vancouver, British Columbia and June 22, 1976 at the XVIth IUFRO World Congress in Oslo, Norway. University of Toronto Press. Toronto.

_________, and Thompson, E.R. 1976. "An Urban Forest Concept." Milieu. No. 12. Laurentian Forest Research Centre. Environment Canada.

_________, and MacArthur, J.D. 1977. "Morgan Arboretum — A Model Urban Forest." The Forestry Chronicle. Vol. 53, No. 5. Canadian Institute of Forestry, Macdonald College. Québec.

Jorgensen, Erik. 1970. Urban Forestry in Canada. The Shade Tree Research Laboratory, Faculty of Forestry, University of Toronto. Toronto.

_________. 1974. Towards an Urban Forest Concept. Prepared for the Tenth Commonwealth Forestry Conference in Oxford and Aberdeen, Britain. Canadian Forestry Service, Environment Canada. Ottawa.

_________. 1977. "Vegetation Needs and Concerns in Urban Areas." Ecological (Biophysical) Land Classification in Urban Areas. Ecological Land Classification Series No. 3. Edited by E.B. Wiken and G.R. Ironside. Lands Directorate, Environment Canada. Ottawa.

Jurdant, M. 1975. Les stations écologiques de référence: classification par Type Écologique (5e approximation) et par Type Physionomique de Végétation (1ère approximation). Rapport E.T.B.J. no. 24. Environnement Canada — Société de Développement de la Baie James. Ottawa.

Kabzems, A., *et al.* 1972. Land Capability Classification for Forestry in Saskatchewan. Technical Bulletin No. 6. Department of Natural Resources. Regina.

Karau, John. 1975. Water Transport of Wood: The Current Situation. EPS Report 3-WP-75-3. Water Pollution Control Directorate, Environment Canada. Ottawa.

Kelly, F. 1975. Population Growth and Urban Problems. Perceptions 1, Study on Population, Technology and Resources. Science Council of Canada. Ottawa.

Keser, N. 1970. A Mapping and Interpretation System for the Forested Lands of British Columbia — First Approximation. Research Notes No. 54. British Columbia Forest Service, Department of Lands, Forests and Water Resources. Victoria.

Koot, H.P., and Morris, E.V. 1973. Western Blackheaded Budworm in British Columbia. Pest Leaflet No. 24. Forest Insect and Disease Survey. Pacific Forest Research Centre. Canadian Forestry Service, Department of the Environment. Victoria.

Krajina, V.C. 1965. Ecology of Western North America. Department of Botony, University of British Columbia. Vancouver.

Kumar, P. 1974. "In Defence of Canada Land Inventory." The Forestry Chronicle. Vol. 50, No. 4. Canadian Institute of Forestry, Macdonald College. Québec.

Land Use Task Force. 1975. H.W. Thiessen, Chairman. Land Use Issues Facing Canadians. A discussion paper for The Canadian Council of Resource and Environment Ministers. Edmonton.

L'Anglais, Odette. 1976. Land Use Programs in Canada: Québec. Lands Directorate, Environment Canada. Ottawa.

La Roi, George H., Babb, Thomas A., and Perley, Cheryl E. 1976. Canadian Directory of IBP Areas 1968-1975. A contribution of The Conservation of Terrestrial Biological Communities Subcommittee, Canadian Committee for the International Biological Programme CCIBP/CT and The Associate Committee on Ecological Reserves, National Research Council of Canada NRCC/ACER. University of Alberta Printing Services. Edmonton.

Laurie, I.C. 1975. "Aesthetic Factors in Visual Evaluation." Landscape Assessment: Values, Perceptions, and Resources. Edited by E.H. Zube, R.O. Brush, and J.G. Fabas. John Wiley and Sons. Pennsylvania.

Lefolii, Ken. 1970. The Illustrated Natural History of Canada — The St. Lawrence Valley. McClelland. Toronto.

Lehane, J.J., and Nielsen, K.F. 1961. The Influence of Field Shelterbelts on Climatic Factors, Soil Drifting, Snow Accumulation, Soil Moisture and Grain Yields. (Mimeo.) Experimental Farm. Canada Department of Agriculture. Swift Current, Saskatchewan.

Little, S., and Noyes, J.H. 1971. Trees and Forests in an Urbanizing Environment. United States Department of Agriculture.

Loucks, O.L. 1962. A Forest Classification for the Maritime Provinces. Reprinted from the Proceedings of the Nova Scotian Institute of Science. Vol. 25, Part 2, 1959-60. Forest Research Branch, Canada Department of Forestry. Ottawa.

MacNeill, J.W. 1971. Environmental Management. Constitutional Study prepared for the Government of Canada. Queen's Printer. Ottawa.

Macpherson, Alan G. ed. 1972. Studies in Canadian Geography: The Atlantic Provinces. University of Toronto Press. Toronto.

Macquarrie, G.P. 1974. Laws Relating to Forest Resources in Nova Scotia. Department of Lands and Forests. Halifax.

Maini, J.S., and Carlisle, A. 1974. Conservation in Canada, A Conspectus. Publication No. 1340. Canadian Forestry Service, Environment Canada. Ottawa.

Manitoba Department of Mines, Resources and Environmental Management. 1975. The Forests of Manitoba (1974). Winnipeg.

Manning, G.H. 1976. The British Columbia Pulp Industry: Present Importance and Future Growth. Report No. BC-X-150. Canadian Forestry Service, Environment Canada. Victoria.

Mayost, Ruth. 1974. The Impact of the Forestry Industry on the Canadian Economy. Science Policy Branch, Planning and Finance Service, Environment Canada. Ottawa.

McCormack, R.J. 1972. Land Capability Classification for Forestry. Canada Land Inventory Report No. 4. Lands Directorate, Environment Canada. Ottawa.

McHarg, Ian L. 1971. Design with Nature. Doubleday & Co. Garden City, New York.

McLaren, Ian A., and Peterson, Everett B. 1975. "Ecological Reserves in Canada: The Work of IBP-CT." Nature Canada. Vol. 4, No. 2. Canadian Nature Federation. Ottawa.

Moon, Barbara. 1970. The Illustrated Natural History of Canada — The Canadian Shield. McClelland. Toronto.

Morgenstern, E.K. 1978. Tree Seed Production and Improvement in Canada — Research and Development Needs for 1977-87 — The National Scene. Proceedings of the Canadian Forestry Workshop on Tree Seed Production in Canada held April, 1978 at the Petawawa Forest Experiment Station. Canadian Forestry Service, Environment Canada. Ottawa.

Morris, W.V. 1969. Water. Inland Waters Branch, Department of Energy, Mines and Resources. Queen's Printer. Ottawa.

Murtha, Peter A., and Greco, M.E. 1975. Appraisal of Forest Aesthetic Values: An Annotated Bibliography. FMR-X-79. Forest Management Institute, Canadian Forestry Service, Department of the Environment. Ottawa.

Nagle, G.S. 1978. The Forest Resources of Canada: Status and Trends in 1978. Prepared for the Canadian Council of Resource and Environment Ministers. Victoria.

National Capital Act. 1958. Act Respecting the Development and Improvement of the National Capital Region. Canada. Laws and Statutes. Ottawa.

National Parks Canada. 1971. National Parks System Planning Manual. National and Historic Parks Branch. Ottawa.

Natural Areas Committee. 1973. "The CIF Scene: Forested Natural Areas of Canada." The Forestry Chronicle. Vol. 49, No. 2. Canadian Institute of Forestry, Macdonald College. Québec.

Newfoundland Department of Forestry and Agriculture. Report of the Newfoundland Federal–Provincial Task Force on Forestry. St. John's.

Newfoundland. 1973. Report of the Land Use Study Group of the Provincial Planning Task Force. St. John's.

Nicholson, E.M. 1968. Handbook to the Conservation Section of the International Biological Programme. IBP Handbook No. 5. Blackwell Scientific Publications. Oxford, England.

Northern Forest Research Centre. 1974. Poplars in the Prairie Provinces. Forestry Report. Vol. 4, No. 1. Canadian Forestry Service, Environment Canada. Edmonton.

Oke, T.R. 1972. "Evapotranspiration in Urban Areas and Its Implications for Urban Climate Planning." Teaching the Teacher on Building Climatology. Vol. 3. Swedish National Institute for Building Research. Stockholm.

_____. 1977. "The Significance of the Atmosphere in Planning Human Settlements." Ecological (Biophysical) Land Classification in Urban Areas. Ecological (Biophysical) Classification Series No. 3. Edited by E.B. Wiken and G.R. Ironside. Lands Directorate, Environment Canada. Ottawa.

Oliver, R.W. 1957a. Culture of Ornamental Trees for Canadian Gardens. Publication No. 994. Canada Department of Agriculture. Ottawa.

_____. 1957b. Trees for Ornamental Planting. Publication No. 995. Canada Department of Agriculture. Ottawa.

Ontario. 1975. Report of the Timber Revenue Task Force. Presented to the Treasurer of Ontario and the Minister of Natural Resources. Toronto.

Ouellet, C.E., and Sherk, L.C. 1973. Map of Plant Hardiness Zones in Canada. Agriculture Canada. Ottawa.

Pearse, Peter H. 1976. Timber Rights and Forest Policy in British Columbia. Report of the Royal Commission on Forest Resources. Vol. I and II. Victoria.

Pelton, W.L. 1967. "The Effect of a Windbreak on Wind Travel, Evaporation and Wheat Yield." Canadian Journal of Plant Science. Vol. 47. Agricultural Institute of Canada. Ottawa.

Peterson, Lloyd O.T. 1971. Some Effects of Shelterbelts: A Review of Literature. Prepared for the Canada Department of Regional Economic Expansion. (unpublished).

Piirvee, R. 1975. Feasibility of Canada Geographic Information System for the Purpose of Forest Management. Report No. 142. Forest Management Institute. Canadian Forestry Service, Environment Canada. Ottawa.

Plantown Consultants. 1974. North Pickering Project: Environmental Assessment; Interim Report. Ontario Ministry of Housing. Toronto.

Price Waterhouse Associates and Price Waterhouse & Co. 1973. A Study of Taxation Practices Related to the Pulp and Paper Industry. Parts I, II and III.

Project Planning Associates Ltd. 1973. Urban Open Space Study for Canadian Communities. Canadian Parks and Recreation Association. Toronto.

Prokopchuk, J.R., and Archibald, J.H. 1976. Canada Land Inventory: Land Capability Classification for Forestry in Alberta. ENR Report No. 6. Alberta Forest Service, Department of Energy and Natural Resources. Edmonton.

Read, R.A. 1964. Tree Windbreaks for the Central Great Plains. Agriculture Handbook No. 250. Forestry Service, United States Department of Agriculture.

Reed, F.L.C. & Associates Ltd. 1973. The British Columbia Forest Industry: Its Direct and Indirect Impact on the Economy. Prepared for the British Columbia Forest Service. Vancouver.

_____. 1978. Forest Management in Canada. Vol. I. Forest Management Institute. Information Report FMR-X-102, Environment Canada. Ottawa.

Rey-Lescure, Eric. 1974. Les Forêts Urbaines de Montréal. Forêt-Conservation. Vol. 40, No. 10. Association Forestière Québécoise Inc. Québec.

Robinson, J. Lewis. ed. 1972. Studies in Canadian Geography: British Columbia. University of Toronto Press. Toronto.

Rowe, J.S. 1959. Forest Regions of Canada. Bulletin 123. Forestry Branch, Department of Northern Affairs and National Resources. Ottawa.

_____. 1971. "Why Classify Forest Lands?" The Forestry Chronicle. Vol. 47, No. 3. Canadian Institute of Forestry, Macdonald College. Québec.

_____. 1972. Forest Regions of Canada. Publication No. 1300. Canadian Forestry Service, Department of the Environment. Ottawa.

Rump, P.C., and Harper, Kent. 1977. Land Use in Saskatchewan. Policy, Planning and Research Branch, Department of the Environment. Regina.

Russell, Franklin. 1970. The Illustrated Natural History of Canada — The Atlantic Coast. McClelland. Toronto.

Safranyik, L., Shrimpton, D.M., and Whitney, H.S. 1974. Management of Lodgepole Pine to Reduce Losses from the Mountain Pine Beetle. Forest Technical Report No. 1. Canadian Forestry Service, Environment Canada. Victoria.

Saskatchewan Department of Natural Resources. (no date). Forest Conservation in Saskatchewan. Regina.

Saskatchewan Department of the Environment. 1976. Designated Land Areas in Saskatchewan. Policy, Planning and Research Branch. Regina.

Schultz International Limited. 1974. Design for a Study of the Environmental Effects of Forest Harvesting Practices in Saskatchewan. Prepared for the Saskatchewan Department of the Environment. Regina.

Shafer, E.L. 1970. Forest Aesthetics. Presented at a Seminar on Silviculture and Harvesting Techniques for Recreational Use of Forests. University of Toronto. Toronto.

Sherk, L.C. 1968. A Checklist of Ornamental Trees for Canada. Publication No. 1343. Canada Department of Agriculture. Ottawa.

Silverstone, Samuel. 1974. "Open Space Values and the Urban Community." Living Places. Vol. 10, No. 2. Central Mortgage and Housing Corporation. Ottawa.

Simard, A.J. 1973. Forest Fire Weather Zones of Canada. Map. Canadian Forestry Service, Environment Canada. Ottawa.

_____. 1975. Wildland Fire Occurrence in Canada. Map. Canadian Forestry Service, Environment Canada. Ottawa.

Smirnoff, Wladimir. 1974. "The Forest Must Remain Green." Milieu. No. 8. Laurentian Forest Research Centre. Environment Canada. Ste-Foy.

Smith, P.J. ed. 1972. Studies in Canadian Geography: The Prairie Provinces. University of Toronto Press. Toronto.

Sopper, William E. 1971. Watershed Management: Water Supply Augmented by Watershed Management in Wildland Areas. Report No. NWC-EES-72-028. Prepared for the United States National Water Commission. Arlington, Virginia.

Stanton, Chas. R. 1976. Canadian Forestry: The View Beyond the Trees. Forestry Service, Environment Canada. Macmillan of Canada. Ottawa.

Staple, W.J., and Lehane, J.J. 1955. "The Influence of Field Shelterbelts on Wind Velocity, Evaporation, Soil Moisture and Crop Yield." Canadian Journal of Agricultural Science. Vol. 35, No. 5. Agricultural Institute of Canada. Ottawa.

Statistics Canada. 1978. Canadian Forestry Statistics, 1976. Catalogue 25-202. Annual. Ottawa.

Stewart, J.V., et al. 1972. The Forest Resource of Nova Scotia: Its Utilization and Potential. Information Report E-X-16. Forest Economics Research Institute. Environment Canada. Ottawa.

Swanson, R.H. 1972. Forest Hydrology in Canada: More Water Probably Not Wanted. File Report NOR-Y-44. Canadian Forestry Service, Environment Canada. Edmonton.

_____. 1973. Land Use and Resource Development in the East Slopes of Alberta. Background papers to a brief presented by the Department of the Environment of Canada to public hearings held July, 1973 by the Alberta Environment Conservation Authority. Ottawa.

Teskey, A.G., and Smyth, J.H. 1974. A Directory of Primary Wood-using Industries in West-central Canada, 1973. Information Report NOR-X-83. Canadian Forestry Service, Environment Canada. Edmonton.

_____. 1975a. Employment, Income, Products and Costs in Manitoba's Primary Wood-using Industry, 1972. Information Report NOR-X-138. Canadian Forestry Service, Environment Canada. Edmonton.

_____. 1975b. Saskatchewan's Forest Industry and Its Economic Importance, 1972. Information Report NOR-X-140. Canadian Forestry Service, Environment Canada. Edmonton.

_____. 1975c. The Economic Importance of Sawmilling and Other Primary Wood-using Industries in Alberta, 1972. Information Report NOR-X-145. Canadian Forestry Service, Environment Canada. Edmonton.

The Forestry Chronicle. 1977. Vol. 53, No. 5. Canadian Institute of Forestry. Macdonald College. Québec.

Thie, J., and Ironside, G. eds. 1976. Ecological (Biophysical) Land Classification in Canada. Ecological Land Classification Series No. 1. Proceedings of the first meeting of the Canada Committee on Ecological (Biophysical) Land Classification held May 25-28, 1976 in Petawawa, Ontario. Lands Directorate, Environment Canada. Ottawa.

Thomson, A.P. 1969. "New Zealand's Expanding Forest Resources." Commonwealth Forestry Review. Vol. 48. The Commonwealth Forestry Association. London, England.

Tweeddale, R.E. 1974. Report of the New Brunswick Forest Resources Study. Department of Natural Resources. Fredericton.

Urquhart, M.C., and Buckley, K.A.H. eds. 1965. Historical Statistics of Canada. Macmillan Company of Canada Limited. Toronto.

Van Wagner, C.E. 1974. Structure of the Canadian Forest Fire Weather Index. Publication No. 1333. Canadian Forestry Service, Environment Canada. Ottawa.

Waldron, R.M., and Hildahl, V.T. 1974. Deterioration of Shelterbelts in Southwestern Saskatchewan. Information Report NOR-X-127. Canadian Forestry Service, Environment Canada. Edmonton.

_____, and Dyck, J.R. 1975. Trees and Shrubs on Residential Lots in Edmonton, 1973. Information Report NOR-X-143. Canadian Forestry Service, Environment Canada. Edmonton.

Wallis, G.W. 1976. *Phellinus (Poria) Weirii*: Root Rot Detection and Management Proposals in Douglas-fir Stands. Forest Technical Report No. 12. Pacific Forest Research Centre. Canadian Forestry Service, Environment Canada. Victoria.

Ward, E. Neville. 1975. Land Use Programs in Canada: Alberta. Lands Directorate, Environment Canada. Ottawa.

_____. 1976. Land Use Programs in Canada: British Columbia. Lands Directorate, Environment Canada. Ottawa.

_____. 1977*a*. Land Use Programs in Canada: Manitoba. Lands Directorate, Environment Canada. Ottawa

_____. 1977*b*. Land Use Programs in Canada: Ontario. Lands Directorate, Environment Canada. Ottawa.

_____. 1978. Land Use Programs in Canada: Saskatchewan. Lands Directorate, Environment Canada. Ottawa.

Weetman, G.F. 1970. "The Need to Establish a National System of Natural Forested Areas." The Forestry Chronicle. Vol. 46, No. 1. Canadian Institute of Forestry, Macdonald College. Québec.

_____. 1977. Forest Regeneration in Canada. Proceedings of a Conference on Adequate Forest Renewal in Canada held October, 1977 in Québec City.

_____, and Cayford, J.H. 1972. "Canadian Institute of Forestry Policy for Selection, Protection and Management of Natural Areas." The Forestry Chronicle. Vol. 48, No. 1. Canadian Institute of Forestry, Macdonald College. Québec.

Whittick, Arnold. ed. 1974. Encyclopedia of Urban Planning. McGraw-Hill. New York.

Wilkinson, Douglas. 1970. The Illustrated Natural History of Canada — The Arctic Coast. McClelland. Toronto.

Urban Development

National Photography Collection.
Public Archives Canada.
C-6985

Contents

	Page
Evolution of the Canadian settlement pattern	191
1497 to 1763	191
1763 to 1867	191
1867 to 1918	191
1918 to the present	192
Physical characteristics associated with urban land	194
Soil and surficial geology	194
Water	194
Atmosphere and climate	195
Areas of demand for urban land	196
Location and accessibility	196
Spatial pattern of demand	197
Supply of land for conversion to urban uses	199
Changes in urban land use	199
Land conversion	200
Land prices	204
Factors affecting change	204
Demographic processes	204
Economic factors	204
Technological developments	205
Land, environmental quality, and the quality of life	206
Land use practices: effect on environment	206
Public attitudes to land-related matters	207
Land use conflicts	207
Conclusion	207
Acknowledgement	208
Bibliography	208
Appendix I	209

Tables

		Page
1.	Canada's urban and rural population, 1871 to 1976	192
2.	Population growth, by province, 1966 to 1971 and 1971 to 1976	193
3.	Regional population, 1976	193
4.	The most important climatic elements having an impact upon the built environment	195
5.	Average weather changes resulting from urbanization expressed as percentage, or magnitude, of rural conditions	196
6.	Land use devoted to road vehicles in a generalized large city	197
7.	Population growth in Census Metropolitan Areas with a population increase of 10,000 or more between 1971 and 1976	197
8.	Population growth and estimated residential land consumption in Census Metropolitan Areas with a population increase of 10,000 or more between 1971 and 1976	198
9.	Housing starts, 1972 to 1976, in Census Metropolitan Areas with a population increase of 10,000 or more between 1971 and 1976	198
10.	Population growth, density of new development, and house prices in Census Metropolitan Areas with a population increase of 10,000 or more between 1971 and 1976	198
11.	Housing projections from 1971 until 1986	199
12.	Land supply estimates in selected Census Metropolitan Areas	200
13.	Land conversion from rural to urban uses in and around Census Metropolitan Areas, 1966 to 1971	203
14.	Occupation structure of the labour force, 1951	204
15.	Percentage distribution of employment within regions, by industry, 1977	205
16.	Average family income for metropolitan and non-metropolitan areas, by region, 1975	205

Maps

		Page
1.	Population distribution by census divisions, Canada, 1976	192
2.	Isodemographic map of Canada	193
3.	Flood risk map	195
4.	Land for agriculture and urban development: Halifax	201
5.	Land for agriculture and urban development: Ottawa–Hull	201
6.	Land for agriculture and urban development: Toronto	202
7.	Land for agriculture and urban development: Edmonton	202

Evolution of the Canadian Settlement Pattern

Why is any city, town, or village in Canada exactly where it is; why are some settlements larger than others; why are some regions more densely populated than others? All settlements are physical manifestations of decisions made by man in the past. All settlements have functions either social, economic, political, or strategic; functions which may have changed several times since the settlement was founded.

The reason for the foundation of a settlement, its subsequent changes in fortune and functions, and the shape as well as density of settlement in a region are closely related to some particular feature of its location. To discuss land of vital importance to human settlements may seem inconsistent with the discussion of land of special importance for agriculture, wildlife, recreation, or forestry in other chapters, in which a recurring theme is the problem of the irreversible conversion to urban uses of land with high capability for other uses, and the consequent loss of a resource which yields economic, aesthetic, or environmental benefits.

In many ways, land important for urban uses *is* different from special lands for other uses. Human settlement can develop almost anywhere in Canada. Communities such as Resolute, Fort McMurray, Faro, or Thompson evolved because of their location relative to a specific resource required by a larger urban population. However, the majority of Canadians choose to live in the highly urbanized, narrow belt along the southern border. The seeds of this urban pattern were sown by early explorers and settlers. Then, land that possessed qualities that favoured construction of early settlements often favoured other uses. The same is true today.

The urban influence is so pervasive that it is felt virtually throughout the country. Land required to meet the energy, food, defence, and recreation needs of the largely urban population means direct repercussions to the land resource base. In the United States, this situation has been an important consideration in the study of critical areas. In some states, the list of critical areas has been expanded to include:

"... areas of major development potential such as a proposed site for a power generation plant, an area identified as containing a major mineral deposit, a major industrial development, a new community, an airport, or a major highway system." (Mandelker, 1975).

Large parks, oil and gas pipelines, commercial forest operations, coal mines, and other phenomena are responses to demands that originate mainly in cities. Perhaps the most significant aspect of urban land is its impact on other land uses.

This chapter discusses the characteristics which give certain lands and specific regions of Canada special importance for urban uses. The special lands being examined in this book have characteristics (soil quality, location, site, aesthetic quality, vegetation cover, mineral deposit, topography, or climate) which make them specially valuable for one or more uses. Such characteristics are as relevant to the location of human settlements as they are to other uses of land.

NFB – PHOTOTHEQUE – ONF – Photo by André Le Coz.

Site was the prime consideration in the selection of location for Québec City. The steep cliffs offered an excellent view of the St. Lawrence River at a narrow point, a distinct advantage for defence purposes.

Having said that settlements result from decisions made by man in the past, a brief look at the history of settlement in Canada will help to explain today's settlement pattern. Five key concepts are essential to an understanding of the history of settlement in Canada that has culminated in the present patterns.

Land as a Natural Resource. Any parcel of land possesses the characteristics mentioned above as part of its initial endowment that may be modified, exploited, or traded by man.

Location. The importance of location is determined by the interaction of the natural endowment of the land and its proximity or accessibility to other human settlements and the resources needed to sustain the population.

Scarcity. Since not all lands are similarly endowed or located, some are more valued than others. At one time in Canada, land in certain locations was available and anyone, subject to government regulations, could obtain a parcel for a nominal charge. Now, demand exceeds supply by varying degrees according to location and endowment.

Conflict. In certain areas, location and inherent physical characteristics make land important for more than one use. At present, a combination of government regulation and the ability of competing users to bid in the open market determines land use.

Perception. A phenomenon in nature, whether it be a mineral deposit, fertile land, or human intelligence, only becomes a resource when perceived as such by man. This concept is of particular importance to an understanding of the development of the pattern of settlement in Canada.

There are four important periods in Canadian history, which, although divided by political events, have significance for settlement patterns. These political events changed either the reasons for founding new settlements or the functions of existing ones. Parallel to the political events were changes in population, technology, and the economic system.

1497 to 1763

From the time Newfoundland was claimed as a British Colony until France ceased to be a colonial power in Canada, settlements existed as bases for fishermen and trappers. The French concentrated on the St. Lawrence River and the Great Lakes while the British used Hudson Bay as their gateway to the northern part of the continent. Hence, Churchill and Moose Factory are the oldest European settlements in Manitoba and Ontario respectively. Their locations were determined by the dominant economic activity at the time, trapping, and the strategic and political reasons against Britain's use of the St. Lawrence as a trade route.

The French utilized the St. Lawrence—Great Lakes—Mississippi trade route to avoid the British–American colonies. Montréal was founded in 1642 at the head of navigation of the St. Lawrence, where the Lachine Rapids were a natural barrier. By 1763, the French had colonized the St. Lawrence Lowlands between Montréal and Québec under a feudal system to provide food for the trading centres of Montréal and Québec.

1763 to 1867

From the Treaty of Paris until Confederation and Dominion status, the country experienced a profound change in its economic base and settlement pattern. Hardly had Britain consolidated its position in North America, when the American Revolution started in 1776. The recognition of American independence in 1783 caused a migration of Loyalists across the border to southern parts of Upper and Lower Canada. These settlers included farmers, woodsmen, craftsmen, carpenters, millers, and blacksmiths. Thus, a pattern of agricultural and lumber service centres and farms developed, whose location was determined by proximity to the international border, cultivable land and, for the towns, water power for mills.

This was the first period of industrial development in Canada. At first, water power and navigable waterways were the prime determinant of location for sawmills and textile mills. The iron industry, still dependent on wood, located on iron-ore deposits near Kingston and Trois-Rivières but, when coke superseded charcoal, a coal-field location became preferable. This gave an advantage to Cape Breton in this period, but by 1910 Ontario was producing more iron and steel than Nova Scotia. Both coal and iron were brought to Hamilton by water, and steel was manufactured near its major markets.

Montréal consolidated its early lead as a trading centre and, as Canada's largest city, became its financial centre. Upper Canada was opened up by settlers and the capital was moved from Niagara-on-the-Lake to Toronto which has a natural harbour and is the nearest point on Lake Ontario to Lake Huron. Transhipment at Toronto shortened the distance from Lake Ontario to Lake Huron and avoided the international border at Niagara and Windsor. Because of anticipated hostility between Britain and the United States, the international part of the St. Lawrence River was by-passed by the Rideau Canal whose construction provided one reason for the growth of Ottawa and an economic boost to Kingston.

1867 to 1918

During the period from Confederation until the end of World War I, Canada received large numbers of immigrants to open up the new country. The most important single factor in developing the nation from Atlantic to Pacific was the completion of the railway from coast to coast in 1885. Railways tend to follow the line of least topographical resistance, and thus a new determinant of location was introduced. In eastern and central Canada, railways linked established communities as they did in Europe. They changed many of the functions of those places and caused the rise of many others along their routes, especially at junctions. Conversely, they ruined many towns that were not served. Penetanguishene at the northern end of the military road from Toronto, declined at the expense of Collingwood, the first port on Lake Huron to be connected by railway to Toronto. In the west, the railway preceded, and was an active agent

NFB – PHOTOTHEQUE – ONF – Photo by W. Vollmann.

The railway was a powerful agent of settlement and growth, particularly in the west.

of, settlement. Here the interaction of topography, politics, and economics can be seen as a determinant of settlement location. Politics, in the form of Macdonald's National Policy, determined the all-Canadian route north of Lake Superior, spawning a series of railway towns in otherwise inhospitable country. Politics and money determined that the railway should cross the Red River at Winnipeg instead of the topographically more convenient Selkirk. Lastly, the same considerations caused the line to be built as close to the American border as feasible. This defied topographic and resource considerations making the railway cross the "Palliser Triangle" whose capabilities and limitations for agriculture were not fully appreciated at that time, taking the Kicking Horse and Rogers passes rather than the easier Yellowhead Pass. The location of the Pacific terminal was determined by topography when it was located on Burrard Inlet. This site provided easy access from the east, a suitable townsite for Vancouver, and a natural harbour.

The railway made the Prairies accessible, but it was improved farm machinery that made them cultivable. Before the introduction of the traction engine and the tractor, it was difficult for a family to cultivate enough of the Prairie soil to make a decent living. The standard

191

land grant was 260 ha, a sufficient size to support a family if the farmer could afford the machinery to cultivate all of it.

While colonization continued in the west, central Canada consolidated its economic power as a supplier of manufactured goods to the whole country under the protection of tariffs on imports from Europe and the United States. Proximity to the industrial American mid-west also favoured southern Ontario as an industrial location. As a result, Toronto emerged as a financial centre rivalling Montréal. Ottawa became the national capital, chosen originally for its central location in 1857. This period saw the development of the settlement pattern that evolved into the present regional distribution of population and economic activity.

The pattern of population growth developed faster in urban areas than in the country. Between 1871 and 1921, urban population grew from 20 per cent to 50 per cent of total population and multiplied six-fold from 0.7 million to 4.4 million (Table 1).

TABLE 1.

Canada's urban and rural population, 1871 to 1976

Year	Urban	Population	Rural
		(percentage of total population)	
1976	17,366,965	75.5 24.5	5,625,635
1971	16,410,785	76.1 23.9	5,157,525
1966	14,726,759	73.6 26.4	5,288,121
1961	12,700,390	69.6 30.4	5,537,857
1956	10,714,855	66.6 33.4	5,365,936
1951	8,628,253	61.6 38.4	5,381,176
1941	6,252,416	54.3 45.7	5,254,239
1931	5,572,058	53.7 46.3	4,804,728
1921	4,352,122	49.5 50.5	4,435,827
1911	3,272,947	45.5 54.5	3,933,696
1901	2,014,222	37.6 62.4	3,357,093
1891	1,537,098	31.8 68.2	3,296,141
1881	1,109,507	25.7 74.3	3,215,303
1871	722,343	19.6 80.4	2,966,914

Sources: Dominion Bureau of Statistics, 1963. Population: Rural and Urban Distribution. Catalogue 92-536. Urquhart and Buckley, 1965. Historical Statistics of Canada.

1918 to the Present

During the last sixty years Canada has become a predominantly urban nation. Between 1921 and 1977, the urban population rose from half to three-quarters of the total population. This trend is associated with the decline of employment in agriculture relative to manufacturing and tertiary industry, and the rise in standards of living, including widespread car ownership.

Since 1945, the automobile rather than the railway has influenced the growth of settlements and their suburban and exurban development. Also, the growth of tertiary industry, which develops more highly in the more populated areas, has increased not only the urban vis-à-vis the rural population but also the regional population disparity between central Canada and southwest British Columbia on one hand, and the Prairies and the Atlantic Provinces on the other.

The outstanding feature of the settlement pattern of Canada is the high concentration of population and economic activity in a narrow belt between Windsor and Québec City as compared to the rest of the country (Map 1). In 1976, this belt contained 55 per cent of Canada's total population and approximately 72 per cent of total manufacturing employment. Its agriculture was also very productive, receiving about 39 per cent of total farm cash receipts from 13 per cent of Canada's farmland. This heartland of Canada has benefited not only from its soil and climate, the Great Lakes transport route, and the existence of a developed settlement pattern and infrastructure during the industrial revolution, but also, particularly, from greater proximity to the American industrial belt and its coal deposits than the Maritime Provinces. The latter, in spite of an early start and deposits of coal, suffered from their distant location from major markets.

The Prairies were opened too late to overcome the industrial momentum already generated in the heartland. Railway freight rates also favoured the location of manufacturing along the Windsor–Québec axis. The present tendency on the Prairies is for rural centres to decline as agriculture requires less labour, and for economic activity and population to concentrate in a few large cities devoted overwhelmingly to tertiary industry which includes distribution of eastern-manufactured goods. Calgary has become an administrative centre for the oil business, which has developed only in the last thirty years.

British Columbia's settlement pattern is a result of the expansion of tertiary industry in an economy based on forestry and mineral exploitation and associated primary processing. The population is nucleated and is predominantly in the Lower Mainland, in Vancouver and Victoria. The interior does not have the rural settlement pattern seen in other provinces since only three per cent of the province has ever been opened up for agriculture.

In the north, non-native settlements have always been based on mineral extraction, forestry, defence, trade, or transportation while native settlements are subsistence oriented and tend to be isolated. The growth of service industries has influenced only the larger centres such as Whitehorse, Yellowknife, and Thompson.

NFB – PHOTOTHEQUE – ONF – Photo by George Hunter.

Toronto is located on a "main street" which extends from Windsor to Québec City. The city's excellent physical setting, central location, proximity to the United States, and varied resource base have all contributed to its recent emergence as Canada's largest urban centre.

In 1976, a population of almost 23 million was distributed over 1.1 million km² and occupied 11 per cent of Canada's total area. This inhabited area is adjacent to the southern border from Atlantic to Pacific and is about 200 km wide by 6,500 km long. The growth and distribution of population between provinces is by no means even (Tables 2 and 3; see also Map 1).

The largest concentration of population is along the Windsor–Québec axis, 1,167 km long and 175,000 km² in area. In 1976, this region contained 12.74 million people, nearly 55 per cent of the population in two per cent of the country's area. Another major concentration of population is in the Vancouver–Victoria region of British Columbia which contained about 1.39 million people or six per cent of the national population in 1976.

Canada is an urban country. In 1976, 75.5 per cent of the population (17.4 million) lived in 1,732 urban places of 1,000 or more people. The most urbanized provinces were Ontario, Québec, British Columbia, and Alberta (see Map 2). Together they contained 1,287 of the 1,732 urban places, 17 of the 23 Census Metropolitan Areas (CMAs), and 14.9 million of Canada's 17.4 million urban population. At the other end of the scale, Prince Edward Island had only 37 per cent of its population in urban places.

The density of population in cities varies widely. Usually it is greater in the centres of large cities, while small towns and newer suburbs contain fewer people per ha. In the 1970s, the population density of all urban areas was 23.0 persons per ha. Densities for individual communities ranged from 8.3 per ha in Nanaimo to 39.3 per ha in Montréal. Within the Windsor–Québec

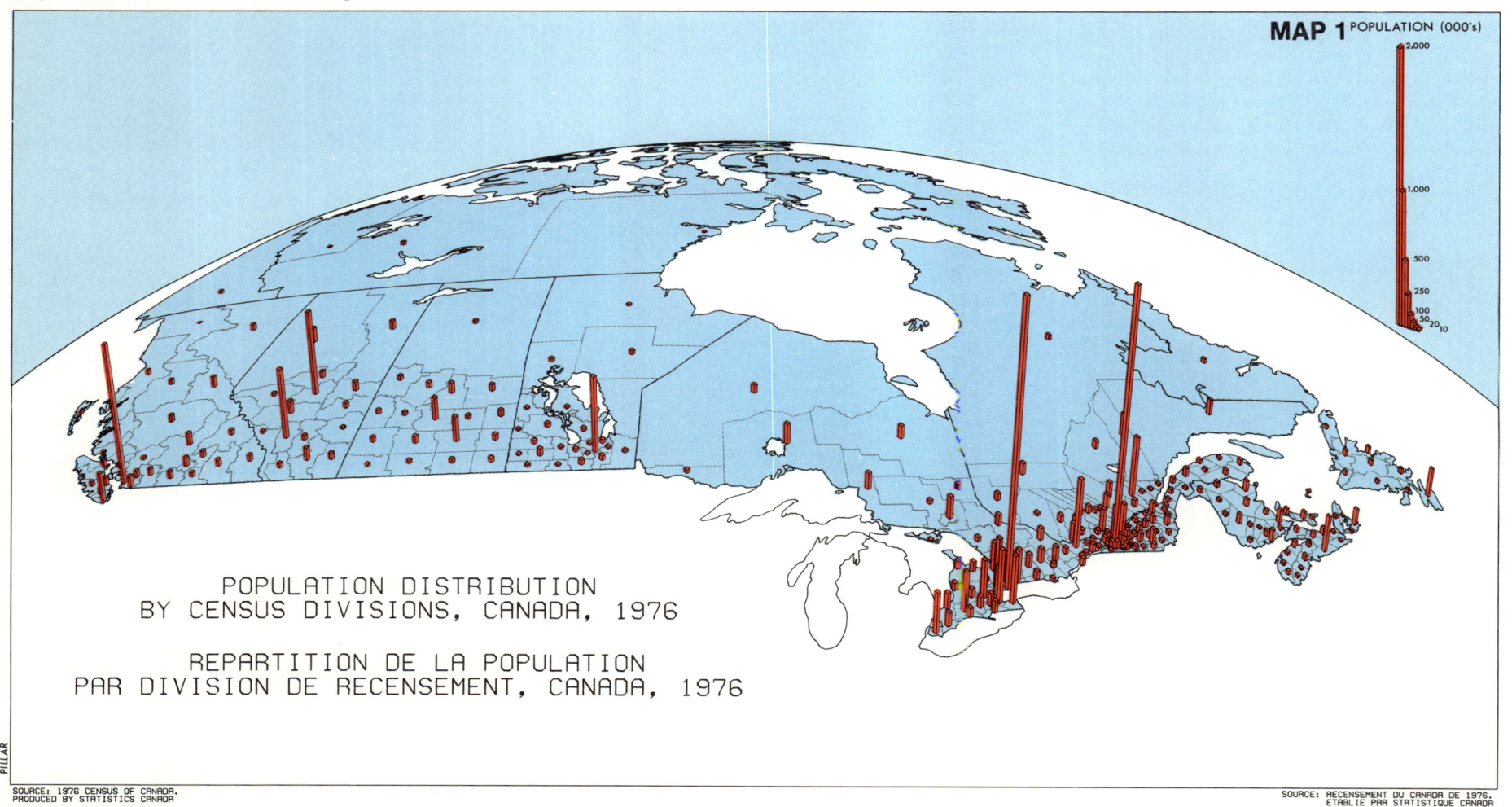

POPULATION DISTRIBUTION BY CENSUS DIVISIONS, CANADA, 1976

REPARTITION DE LA POPULATION PAR DIVISION DE RECENSEMENT, CANADA, 1976

MAP 1 POPULATION (000's)

SOURCE: 1976 CENSUS OF CANADA. PRODUCED BY STATISTICS CANADA.
SOURCE: RECENSEMENT DU CANADA DE 1976. ETABLIE PAR STATISTIQUE CANADA.

TABLE 2.

Population growth, by province, 1966 to 1971 and 1971 to 1976

Province	Population 1966	Population 1971	Population 1976	Population growth 1966 to 1971	Population growth 1971 to 1976
				(per cent)	
Newfoundland	493,396	522,104	557,725	5.81	6.82
Prince Edward Island	108,535	111,641	118,229	2.86	5.90
Nova Scotia	756,039	788,960	828,571	4.35	5.02
New Brunswick	616,788	634,557	677,250	2.88	6.73
Québec	5,780,845	6,027,764	6,234,445	4.27	3.43
Ontario	6,960,870	7,703,106	8,264,465	10.66	7.29
Manitoba	963,066	988,247	1,021,506	2.61	3.37
Saskatchewan	955,344	926,242	921,323	− 3.05	− 0.53
Alberta	1,463,203	1,627,874	1,838,037	11.25	12.91
British Columbia	1,873,674	2,184,621	2,466,608	16.60	12.90
Yukon and Northwest Territories	43,120	53,195	64,445	23.37	21.15
CANADA	20,014,880	21,568,311	22,992,604	7.76	6.60

Sources: Statistics Canada, 1972. *Advance Bulletin: Population of Census Divisions.* Catalogue 92-753.

———, 1977*a*. *Population: Geographic Distributions: Federal Electoral Districts.* Catalogue 92-801.

TABLE 3.

Regional population, 1976

Region	Population	Percentage of total
		(per cent)
Atlantic	2,181,775	9.5
Central	14,498,910	63.1
Prairies	3,780,866	16.4
British Columbia	2,466,608	10.7
Yukon and Northwest Territories	64,445	0.3
CANADA	22,992,604	100.0

Source: Statistics Canada, 1977*a*. *Population: Geographic Distributions: Federal Electoral Districts.* Catalogue 92-801.

axis, population density in the urban areas was 25.4 persons per ha.

The process of development of this country, from the early hunting and trapping years to a modern industrial nation, has been the determinant of the Canadian settlement pattern. This pattern results from the present system which operates most effectively when manufacturing, finance, administration, and distribution are located in a system of large cities, linked by efficient transport routes. There are several important elements of our economic and social system that have led to the location of settlements: elements of the present system, the expansion of the population of Canada's regions at different rates, and the growth of major cities. The first of these is the advance in technology, especially in the manner in which it has affected means of transport, agriculture, industrial production, and standards of living. Second is the increase in population due to immigrants, some attracted by the possibility of owning farmland, others by employment in the cities. Third is the growth in the national economy which is closely linked to technological advance and population growth. These subjects are discussed more fully later in this chapter.

ISODEMOGRAPHIC MAP OF CANADA

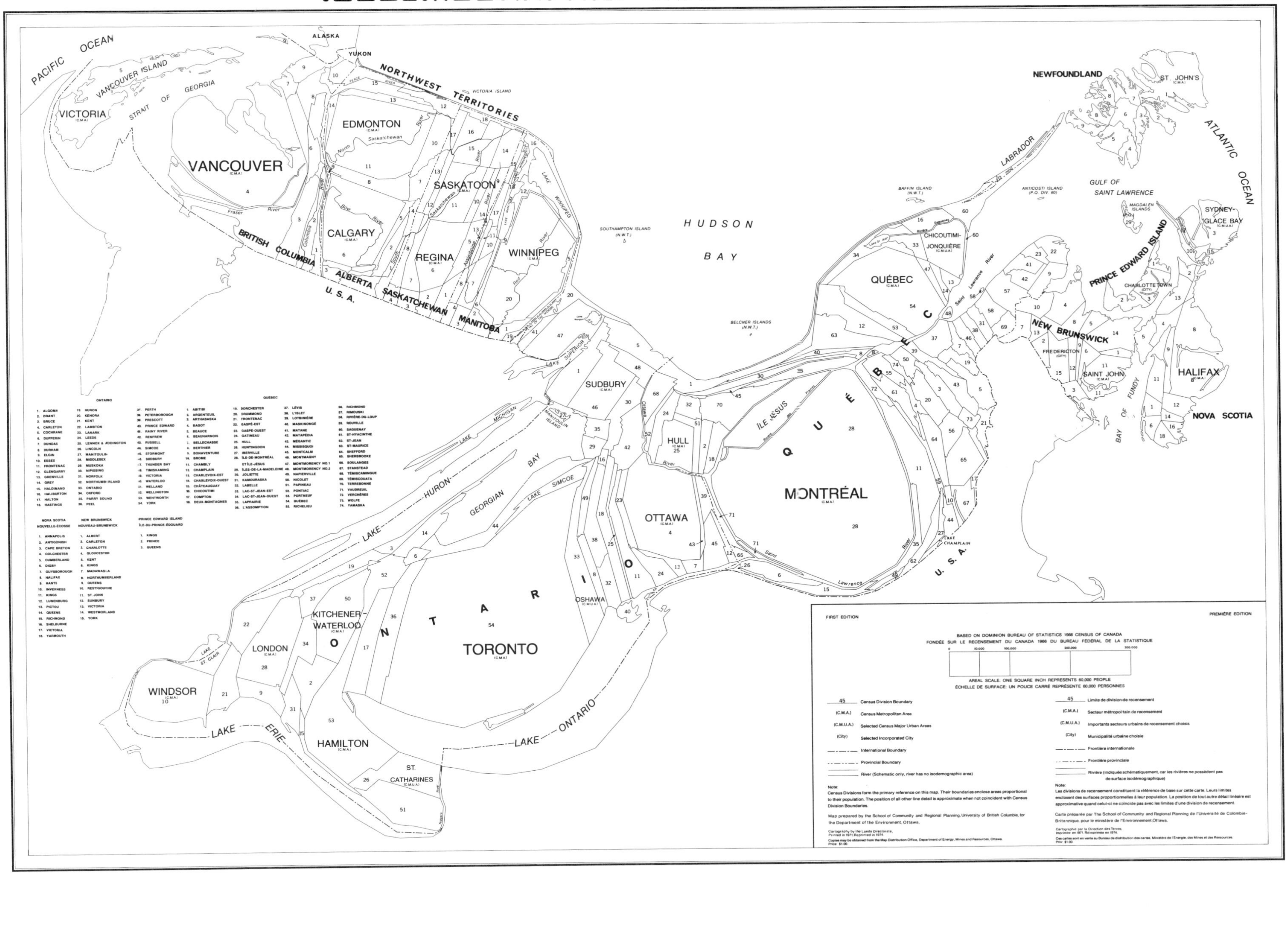

Physical Characteristics Associated with Urban Land

Human settlements are not self-contained, self-supporting systems; they depend on the natural environment for their continued existence. In the previous section, a broad picture was given of the physical attributes across Canada that first attracted settlement; furbearing animals, the navigable waterways, fertile land, strategic town sites, and mineral deposits. In this section, the physical considerations that determine the location of contemporary urban development or expansion within the existing national settlement pattern are discussed.

Man's intention throughout history has been to modify the environment for his benefit. However, the cumulative effect of many such private decisions may not always benefit the community at large. The relationship between settlements and soil, water, and the atmosphere will be examined in the light of man's need for life support, health, safety, and quality of life on one hand and the maintenance of the balance of the environment on the other. However, the mass of information on land capabilities, which is available for agriculture, forestry, recreation, and wildlife has been applied to settlements only for specific studies related to new town locations or major expansions. It is not feasible in this study to apply these principles to Canada's land and produce maps of prime urban land, based on these physical criteria. However, some of the physical factors that make a given tract of land either suitable for certain types of urban uses or unsuitable for any urbanization are discussed in this section.

Soil and Surficial Geology

Land factors such as soil wetness, rockiness, stoniness, steep slopes, drainage variability, and natural soil drainage are fundamental to many non-biological uses of land for housing sites, playgrounds, effluent disposal, septic tanks, highways, and pipelines. Such uses are affected only slightly, or not at all, by soil-specific factors such as poor structure or permeability, low fertility, and droughtiness important to non-urban uses. All these factors along with others can play major rôles in biologically-oriented uses such as reforestation, landscape architecture, playground maintenance, and recreation development.

Soil Wetness. This condition affects most land uses, and costs of improvement are often very high. However, large-scale community-sponsored drainage schemes, whereby costs of individual projects are amortized against the project as a whole, have proven successful in the past and may offer a possible solution. Such projects generally provide efficient control of soil moisture and water tables, particularly where outlets are available and where tile rather than surface drainage is feasible. Extreme wetness due to inundation generally does not lend itself to amelioration.

Rockiness. Rocky areas interfere strongly with many uses but can be an asset to some. Because of their shallowness, soils in these areas are almost impossible to work mechanically and they tend to be droughty. These areas are unsuitable for agricultural uses but might be suitable for forestry, conservation, and some restricted recreation activities. Certain large-scale urban-related projects such as high-rise apartments, industrial park and estate developments are feasible, and the extra cost of excavating foundations and drains or developing such lands may be partly offset by the lower costs of acquisition. Rocky areas are often of prime importance for industrial quarries.

Stoniness. Stones interfere least in forested lands and lands retained for conservation or watershed management. An abundance of large stones could impose special design problems and higher costs on lands for urban development, but these have generally been surmountable in the past.

Steep Slopes. Ravines and scarps formed by erosion in clay or sand-over-clay soils are dangerous for urbanization as they are subject to flow slides. Permanent structures and roads should not be built on such areas. Bedrock escarpments, on the other hand, are generally stable and provide some of the best aesthetic sites. Moderate slopes associated primarily with till and sandy aeolian soils may be subject to water erosion if left unprotected or poorly managed. In some cases, this could contribute significantly to river pollution, particularly during construction. More sandy soils are susceptible to wind erosion.

Droughtiness. Soils susceptible to droughtiness are characterized by deep sand or gravel-derived soils on well-drained ridge tops. These soils are often used as sources of sand and gravel, but in many cases they are ideal sites for residential and industrial buildings. However, they are highly susceptible to wind and water erosion and should be continuously protected, particularly during construction.

These factors are significant in the degree to which they affect urban development. They can be used to identify uses incompatible with the character of the land, or those conditions which need correction before a use is instituted. They do not indicate directly the uses for which the land is best suited. It is only through a process of careful elimination of certain uses from certain areas, or by designing to overcome limitations, that the latter aspect can be defined. (*Drawn extensively from Dumanski et al., 1976*).

Water

Another physical consideration of major importance for settlement location or urban growth is water. Water is essential for human survival, for crops, manufacturing processes, navigation, power, disposal of wastes, and as a habitat for the production of fish. Water also presents a hazard in the form of flooding and destabilization of soils. Man's activities affect the water cycle by altering either its supply, runoff, or quality.

The opportunities and constraints presented by water in the location of settlements are closely related to topography and geology. The influence of harbours, navigable waterways, and water power on urban location has already been mentioned as has the presence of excessive groundwater and its incompatibility with urban development. Since lakes, rivers, and groundwater are abundant in most of Canada, there are few areas of the country where settlement has been impossible because there has been no water. However, the urban growth that has been concentrated in a relatively small area of the country has overtaxed several local water supplies. For example, water is now piped from Lake Huron to London, Ontario. Water also becomes a determinant of unsuitability of land for urban expansion in two important ways; areas susceptible to flooding, and contamination of the water resource by human activities.

taken in the location of the various urban land uses. No permanent structures should be built in the floodway, whereas such uses as parks, gardening, wildlife habitat, or car parks are suitable. On the other hand, the uses susceptible to flood damage such as residential, commercial, and some manufacturing are more suitably located in areas of lower flood risk.

Photo by Allan R. Leishman.

Residential developments are particularly susceptible to flood damage. In most areas, flood insurance is not available.

to be considered. First, a flood plain consists of 1) an area that may be flooded, resulting in water damage to property, and 2) a floodway in which a current of moving water may have sufficient force to damage or destroy structures. Secondly, some uses are more susceptible to flood damage than others; residential, commercial, and high-technology manufacturing are especially susceptible, while railway yards or open spaces are not. Uses such as waste disposal or oil storage present a problem since they may contaminate flood waters when inundated.

Maritime Resource Management Service photo.

Fredericton is only one of many Canadian cities that experience serious flooding. Extensive damage is often caused to permanent structures built on a flood plain.

People have always been attracted to flood plains which offer flat fertile land and access to navigable waters. Railways also followed this easy terrain. However, building on a flood plain is a calculated risk. Experience shows that while the entire flood plain may be inundated only once in a century, the river may reach some intermediate level every decade. Where records exist, it is possible to map the cyclical flood levels (Map 3). When building in an otherwise favoured location, the risk of being flooded every so many years must be weighed. To prohibit all development on land that may be flooded only once in a century is too restrictive since many buildings do not last that long. Two factors have

In view of the fact that flood plains are often attractive locations for urban development, care has to be Areas that have not previously been subject to flooding can be put at risk by subsequent urban development which may modify natural water runoff characteristics. Precipitation, falling on built-over surfaces with artificial drainage, flows into streams and rivers far more quickly than by the natural process of percolation through the soil. Such artificial conditions are conducive to flash floods in some areas downstream. Consideration in siting of new development must be given to the possibility of exposing existing built-up areas to the risk of flash floods. Consideration must also be given to

194

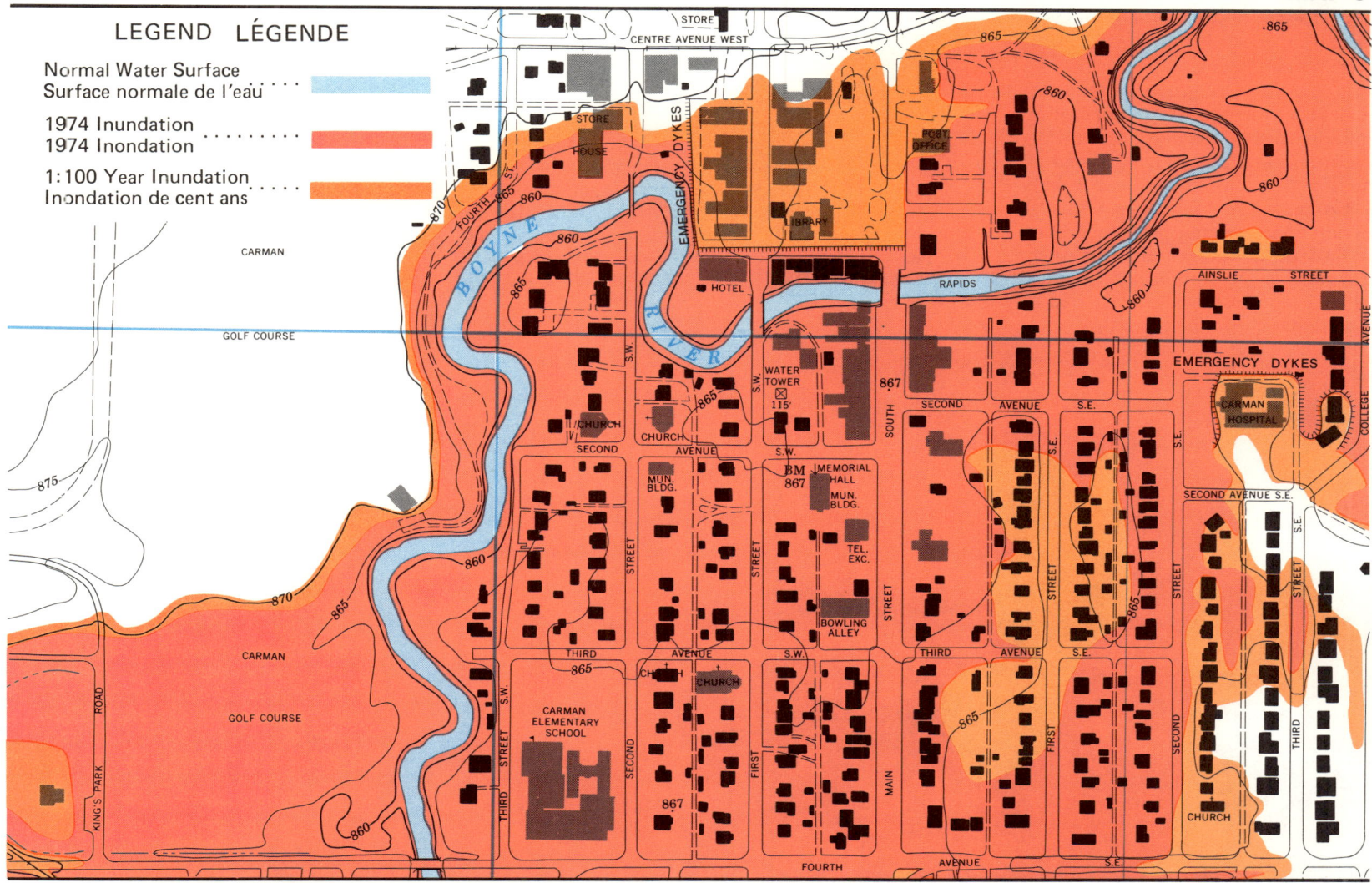

Part of a typical flood risk map prepared under the national Flood Damage Reduction Program

Source: Environment Canada. Cutting Our Flood Losses. Inland Waters Directorate. 1978.

This particular map of Carman, Manitoba is the result of a pilot project by the Inland Waters Directorate of Environment Canada and the Manitoba Department of Mines, Resources and Environmental Management.

Similar maps will be prepared jointly by the federal and provincial governments for other urban areas in Canada as part of the national program and will be available from the Inland Waters Directorate and the appropriate provincial department. On the basis of these maps, the senior levels of government will be applying policies aimed at discouraging future flood vulnerable developments in the identified risk areas.

the design of storm drains and the amount of paved area in new developments in view of the effect it has on the runoff of surface water.

It is not only the rate at which water runs off developed land, but also the contaminants that are picked up by surface water that are affected by urbanization. The nature and location of urban development which will allow the maintenance of water quality are increasingly important considerations because of urban concentration and industrialization. The demand for water is growing, as is the volume of contaminants which enters groundwater and water bodies. There is a balance between the ability of the water body or aquifer to absorb pollutants and its ability to remain capable of supplying water to human settlements. Land in certain locations is unsuitable for development for some or all urban uses, because the soil or bedrock structure or its proximity to a water body is such that pollutants will find their way directly into the water supply. Special problems of seepage or runoff of pollutants are caused by roads, waste disposal, and heavy industry. In other instances, some natural but undesirable water characteristics such as salinity or hardness must be rectified.

Water in its frozen forms, ice and snow, is a significant element in the Canadian environment. Its main impact has always been on transport facilities and more recently on recreational facilities. In our industrial society we think of snow and ice as an impediment to be cleared from roads, railways, and airports. In earlier times, it was an aid to movement especially in the forest industry when horses dragged logs over frozen ground to the banks of frozen rivers ready for floating downstream in the spring. This practice was the determinant of the location of sawmills and paper mills in locations such as Hull or Espanola. Coastal areas in which ice is absent have been favoured as ports. Halifax is ice-free all year while the ports of Québec, Montréal, and Toronto freeze in winter. Thus, water, both liquid and frozen, is an element that both contributes to man's activities in human settlements and creates difficulties and hazards.

Atmosphere and Climate

The third natural element influencing human settlements is the atmosphere and climate.

"*Impact of Climate Upon Settlements.* The 'built' environment satisfies the basic, and almost forgotten, need for shelter. This is required to protect the inhabitants from undesirable weather elements such as high winds and precipitation, and also to provide a comfortable interior climate that imposes the least thermal stress. These primary needs relate to the safety, health and comfort of the occupants, but increasingly we are also aware of the value of optimizing conditions in terms of economic operations, transportation, water resources, recreation, etc.

To a large extent, the primary needs are well understood and are reflected in the traditional building forms which have evolved in different climates on a world-wide basis. In Canada, the essential components are also embodied in the recommendations and requirements of the National Building Code.

The most important climatic elements which enter into building considerations are listed ... in conjunction with the practical features upon which they have the greatest bearing. Any inventory of climatic characteristics for urban planning should therefore include at least these parameters." (Oke, 1977). (*See* Table 4).

What are the effects of these climatic elements on settlement pattern and the internal structure of Canadian cities? Some of these effects have been implicit in the discussion of the history of settlement in the previous section. The major natural regions of Canada are distinguishable mainly by landform and vegetation, the latter being dependent largely on climate. Early settlers and traders were attracted by the furbearing animals and the soft woods of the boreal forest. Immigrant farmers from Europe went first to the mixed forests of the Maritimes and St. Lawrence Lowlands, not only because the St. Lawrence provided a natural route to the interior of the continent but because the vegetation and climate, other than the extreme cold of winter in Québec, were familiar to them. The present settlement pattern indicates a preference for the warmer damper climates of southern Ontario, southern Québec, and the lower Fraser Valley. This preference is shown by urban dwellers who are not concerned about climatic conditions for agriculture.

The impact of climate on contemporary towns and cities is less noticeable than it was in the days before central heating, air conditioning, and the automobile. The glass-walled office tower, in spite of its inefficiency in either retaining heat in winter or keeping it out in the summer, is as evident in Canada as in any other country. The low-density subdivision of detached houses is ubiquitous, regardless of climate or terrain. Large increases in heating and ventilating costs have prompted the construction of several energy-conserving buildings which use heat from sunlight, artificial lighting, and from the human occupants themselves. The most notable example is the Ontario Hydro building in Toronto. A glance at today's Canadian building codes will show that, compared to warmer climates, insulation standards are higher, the strength of roofs capable of bear-

TABLE 4.

The most important climatic elements having an impact upon the built environment

Element	Application/Impact
Solar radiation	Daylighting, temperature solar-energy potential.
Temperature	Heating/cooling demand (heating or cooling degree-days, frost-free days), heat stress on structures and people, permafrost alteration, inversion and retention of pollutants.
Wind	Wind loads on structures and people, building ventilation, air-pollution dispersal, heat loss from structures and people (including wind chill), snow drifting, dust transport, driving rain.
Precipitation	Flooding, storm-sewer design, snow loading, icing of structures, dampness, water-logging, urban hydrology.
Humidity	Fog, interior damp and condensation, comfort, pollutant transformation.

Source: *Adapted from* Oke, 1977.

ing snow is greater, and foundations are deeper in order to reach below the frost level. Servicing standards also reflect climatic factors. Streets are wide enough to leave room for snow that has been cleared from the roadway, and piped services are deep enough to be below the frost level. In northern communities, urban design is influenced to a large extent by the necessity of operating the water supply in a loop, so that the water can always be kept moving by a pump. Sometimes it is heated as well to avoid freezing. For that reason, dead-end streets have to be avoided. Communities built on permafrost have special construction and servicing problems. Heat from buildings must not be conducted through their foundations into the ground or the permafrost will melt, causing subsidence. Piped services have to be carried in heated and insulated utilidors above the ground.

NFB – PHOTOTHEQUE – ONF – Photo by Crombie McNeill.

Heated and insulated above-ground utilidors, such as this one in an Inuvik housing development, are one adaptation required by special climatic conditions in the north.

There are many other features of Canadian towns and cities that are influenced by a climate that is taken for granted. It may take a visit to another country to draw attention to them.

"Impact of Settlements Upon Climate. The process of urbanization affects to some extent every climatic element listed . . . (i.e. the construction of a settlement leads to inadvertent modification of the atmosphere). Alteration of the surface and atmospheric properties leads to a disruption of the natural solar energy and hydrologic cycles which determine the nature of local climates. Urbanization is inevitably associated with changes in the atmospheric pollutant loading (leading to effects upon radiation transfer and cloud droplet growth), the surface fabric (leading to the surface becoming a better heat store and a poorer water store), the surface geometry (making it aerodynamically rougher, and a radiative trap), and the availability of anthropogenic heat and water due to combustion. The average annual magnitude of the climatic changes for a large city are given. . . . Although some of these modifications may not appear to be very significant on an annual basis (e.g. only a 1°C increase in air temperature), they can be quite startlingly expressed under certain conditions for shorter periods. . . ." (Oke, 1977). (*See* Table 5).

Climatic Information and Urban Planning. "Sensible use of a proper data base should ensure that the most favourable aspects of the atmospheric environment are used and that negative features are avoided. Unfortunately, these features are not always mutually exclusive. For example although a valley location may be favoured on the basis of shelter from winds and a generally warmer thermal climate, in fine (often anticyclonic) weather the valley location is prone to frost and fog, and the air pollution potential is unacceptably high. Coastal locations are plagued by similar dichotomies. The climatic influence of a large water body is usually favourable because it imparts a conservative thermal influence and it maintains a supply of fresh air when flow is from the water to the city. When flow is in the opposite direction, the water acts as an uninhabited zone with potential as a pollution sink. With weak synoptic winds, however, coasts are characterized by the development of land and sea breeze systems, with essentially enclosed circulation and poor dispersion conditions (Lyons, 1975).

Settlement location should also consider adjacency to other urban centres (or those projected). Failure to do so may lead to harmful interactions. If the spacing between cities is insufficient, their alignment with the wind may give a cumulative pollution build-up. This is already evident in the megalopitan [*sic*] area of the northeastern United States where the combined emissions from many cities can be traced well out over the North Atlantic Ocean as a giant 'plume'. The plume from one city can also become fumigated into the atmosphere of a second one downstream. . . .

There are a few Canadian examples of new town plans which incorporate some climatic considerations. These include the resource towns of Kitimat, B. C. . . . and Fermont, Quebec (Clunie, 1976; Schoenauer, 1976) and the projected city of Townsend, Ontario (Munn *et al.*, 1972). The Fermont plan identified winds as the most unfavourable aspect of the subarctic climate at this location and designed the settlement to provide shelter for the inhabitants." (Oke, 1977).

TABLE 5.

Average weather changes resulting from urbanization expressed as percentage, or magnitude, of rural conditions

Parameter	Time Period		
	Annual	Cold season	Warm season
	(per cent)		
Solar radiation	− 22	− 34	− 20
Air temperature (°C)	+ 1	+ 2	+ 0.5
Relative humidity	− 6	− 2	− 8
Visibility (frequency)	− 25	− 34	− 17
Fog (frequency)	+ 60	+ 100	+ 30
Wind speed	− 25	− 20	− 30
Cloudiness (frequency)	+ 8	+ 5	+ 10
Rainfall (amount)	+ 14	+ 13	+ 15
Snowfall (amount)	± 10	± 10	
Thunderstorms (frequency)	+ 16	+ 5	+ 30
Pollution (volume)	+ 1,000	+ 2,000	+ 500

Source: *Modified after* Changnon, 1974.

In contrast to the historical review of the positive determinants of settlement location across the country, the discussions of soils, water, and atmosphere suggest elements to guard against if the natural environment is not to be degraded or life and property endangered. Physical limitations are important, however, since contemporary urban development is taking place largely adjacent to the two per cent of Canada's land that is already urbanized, and there is intense pressure to develop any land that has good accessibility to a major city, although not all of it may be physically suitable for development.

Areas of Demand for Urban Land

In this section two key concepts are introduced; the importance of location and accessibility, and the nature of demand for land. All individuals or firms must first have accessibility to the means by which they make a living. Secondly, they must be near the goods and services that are needed to maintain the style of life to which they are accustomed. The relationship between these two needs is strong, since most individuals and businesses receive their income from producing goods or supplying services needed by others. The spatial pattern of demand for urban land across the country and at the level of the city is examined, and finally some estimates of the supply of land suitable for development near major cities are made.

Location and Accessibility

In the National Perspective. "The existence of varying sized population clusters in the landscape is an inevitable feature in the spatial organization of human activity. Settlements exist because certain activities can be carried on most efficiently if they are clustered together rather than dispersed. No matter what the particular activities are, they can be generally viewed as services which are provided not just for settlements themselves, but for people living in surrounding tributary areas. Since settlements are spatially separated one from another, linkages between them are essential, and one framework for study is to view them as nodes or focal points in a transport network...

All locations are endowed with a degree of accessibility but some locations are more accessible than others. Accessibility is difficult to define explicitly, but the term generally implies 'ease of getting to a place' (Forbes, 1964). As such it is a variable quality of location. In a technical sense, accessibility is a relative quality accruing to a piece of land by virtue of its relationship to a system of transport (Wingo, 1961). In an operational sense, it is the variable quality of centrality or nearness to other functions and locations. Clearly the notion of accessibility is closely related to the concept of movement-minimization, especially when this is measured by the costs involved in overcoming distance. In this context, it is also generally accepted as the basis of the rent paid for and the value attached to sites in urban land use models.

There is a tendency for human activities to agglomerate to take advantage of scale economies. Scale economies mean the savings in costs of operation made possible by concentrating activities at common locations. In the organization of an industrial firm it is exemplified in mass production techniques. . . . The concentration of activities to form settlements themselves can be viewed as a reflection of scale economies but more important perhaps are the various agglomerations within urban areas such as shopping centres and industrial districts. Residential zones can also be viewed as agglomerations for scale economies in household costs of utilities and public services." (Chorley and Haggett, 1967).

It is the location of a community, and the accessibility of that community to other centres, upon which its economic viability rests. A community whose major industry is the manufacture of paper will only prosper if it has better access to raw materials, skilled labour, and markets than other communities, either because it is near its supplies and its markets, or has a cheap means of transport at its disposal. The same applies within a community. Different urban uses have different needs for accessibility. Manufacturers receiving supplies from, and shipping goods to, other cities need access to railways, arterial roads, or ports. A newspaper stall must be on a busy street downtown, accessible to a large number of pedestrians. An employee in an office or factory must live within a reasonable travelling distance of work. Because of these various demands for space in which to work or live, different parcels of land acquire development value according to their location. Value is a reflection of how important land is for urban development.

The importance of accessibility to transportation, communication facilities, and skilled labour, and the need to keep in touch with technological innovation has led to the concentration of industry in cities, while certain specialized activities have concentrated in a few centres. Toronto and Montréal are major financial centres; Oshawa, Oakville, and Windsor are automobile manufacturing cities, while Ottawa is the seat of the federal government.

Earlier in the chapter, the importance of the railway as a means of access during the last century was described. The towns which it served, and to which it gave accessibility, grew while those which were less accessible by railway did not. A very short distance, four or five km, would make a difference. The town of Battleford in Saskatchewan was founded on the south side of the North Saskatchewan River, but the railway was built on the north bank, and now North Battleford is the bigger centre. In the twentieth century, the road became a major determinant of location and accessibility, displacing the railway. Many Prairie towns on both the Trans-Canada Highway and the Canadian Pacific Railway have two centres; an old one opposite the railway station with a hotel, a few stores, and a grain elevator, while less than two km away is a new centre with gas stations, hamburger stands, and a supermarket on the Trans-Canada Highway.

Historically, settlements were located as a result of physical factors such as the head of navigation of a river, a waterfall, the junction of two valleys, a bridge point, or a mineral deposit. As a city grows, however, it acquires a momentum of its own until it reaches a stage where its activities bear little relationship to its physical location. London and New York have reached this stage, and in Canada, Montréal and Toronto are approaching it, while other major centres are becoming increasingly divorced from their physical setting. The city itself becomes the equivalent of a resource, and accessibility to its employment opportunities and the services it provides are important.

Within Urban Centres. We find here that "Land-use patterns result from a multitude of decisions made by individuals about location. It is not at all clear how these decisions are reached. . . . But no matter what the underlying considerations are, it appears that decisions are regulated in varying ways by the economic processes operating in society. The locational patterns of land use in urban areas result from basic economic forces, and the arrangement of activities at strategic points on the web of transportation is a part of the economic mechanism of society.

The pertinent aspects of this mechanism as it relates to the generation of land-use patterns can be briefly summarized as follows. Each activity has an ability to derive utility from every site in the urban area; the utility of a site is measured by the rent the activity is willing to pay for the use of the site. The greater the derivable utility, the greater the rent an activity is willing to pay. In the long run, competition in the urban land market for the use of available sites results in the occupation of each site by the 'highest and best' use, which is the use able to derive the greatest utility from the site and which is, therefore, willing to pay most to occupy it. As an outgrowth of the occupation of sites by 'highest and best' uses, an orderly pattern of land uses results in which rents throughout the systems are maximized and all activities are optimally located.

The rent paid for the use of a site is affected by many factors, but most importantly by the location of the site relative to other uses. The logic of this relationship is founded on the assumption that site rents represent a saving in transport costs in overcoming the 'friction' of distance. From this it is argued that competition for the use of land results in the minimization of the 'friction' of distance in the entire urban area and since accessibility increases inversely with distance, the resulting pattern of urban rents is essentially a function of transport. Savings in transport costs can be traded off for extra rent payments to ensure the use of a particular site. Therefore those activities which enjoy the greatest benefits from occupying accessible locations will have greater surpluses available with which to bid for land. Consequently, sites in the urban area are not merely occupied by activities which can pay most for their use, but more specifically, by those activities which are able to derive the greatest positive transport advantages from the use of a given piece of land. When rents are viewed in this framework they will be represented by land values, which in turn can be considered as a direct reflection of differences in intra-urban accessibility. Thus, high land values will be associated with highly accessible locations and *vice versa*." (Chorley and Haggett, 1967).

NFB – PHOTOTHEQUE – ONF – Photo by Normand Grégoire.

In Montréal, as in most cities, high land values are associated with a central location in the CBD. In the suburbs, where lower land rents result in less dense development, many areas exhibit characteristics of urban sprawl.

In Canada, the typical city has a central business district characterized by high-density office and retail development. This is surrounded by an area of decaying houses, warehouses, parking lots, and factories. Further out are residential areas of decreasing density, and industry which is usually concentrated in one sector along a railway or arterial road. On the urban fringe, commercial strips and shopping centres line arterial routes, while the rest of the land is either idle or used for waste disposal or recreation. There are also scattered residences and hobby farms.

NFB – PHOTOTHEQUE – ONF – Photo by Normand Grégoire.

Streets and highways have become a major user of urban land. In some city areas, there often seems to be a maze of roads too complex to describe.

Residential uses account for about 65 per cent of the developed area of a city. Industry uses 18 per cent, commerce eight per cent; the rest is used for institutions and recreation. These figures exclude roads which occupy about 12 per cent of the total area of large- and medium-sized cities and up to 16 per cent of smaller cities. In the core areas of large cities, however, roads are a major user of land. The total amount of urban land devoted to road vehicles changes with a number of variables including city size. When the land area utilized for parking lots, garages, and service centres is added to the road surface area, the total may constitute up to 42 per cent of a large city's core area (Table 6).

TABLE 6.

Land use devoted to road vehicles in a generalized large city*

Land use	Percentage of total developable land: Core	Frame	Fringe	Metro area
	(per cent)			
Roadway surface for transport	11	3	2	2
Expressway R.O.W.	0	1	2	2
Parking	16	3	3	3
Driveways garages	0	3	2	2
Auto sales and services	2	1	1	1
Sub total land use for road transport	29	11	10	10
Minimum roadway surface required for access	13	8	7	8
Total land use devoted to road transport and access	42	19	17	18

* Developable area about 40,470 ha.
Population about 1.5 million.

Source: Lea, 1975. Land Use Consumption by Urban Passenger Transportation.

Spatial Pattern of Demand

The demand for urban land for uses such as commerce, industry, and housing is concentrated in a limited number of areas across the country. The various uses also have different location preferences within urban areas. In the light of this, some estimates of the demand for land in the next quarter century can be made on the basis of estimates of population growth and the rate of household formation. These figures can be used as a basis for calculating the amount of land required for housing, and, knowing the proportion of the area of the average city used for housing, an estimate of the amount of land needed for urban growth up to the year 2000 can be made.

Population Growth. The population growth rate of Canada has been declining since 1961. Between 1951 and 1961, the average annual growth was 422,900 (3.0 per cent); between 1961 and 1966, 355,300 (1.9 per cent); between 1966 and 1971, 310,700 (1.6 per cent); and from 1971 to 1976, 284,859 (1.3 per cent). However, between 1971 and 1976, 56 per cent of population growth took place in 21 of the 23 Census Metropolitan Areas (CMAs) with populations of 100,000 or more. (Windsor and Sudbury CMAs had small net losses of population between 1971 and 1976). Seventeen of the CMAs grew by more than 10,000, nine of which are in the Windsor–Québec axis (Table 7, *see also* Table 3).

Housing. In 1976, Canada had an estimated 6,949,000 housing units of which 4,242,472 were in CMAs. In 1976, 59 per cent of all new housing units were built in CMAs. In Canada, the average household size is 3.25 persons while in the CMAs it is 3.02. Both figures have been declining over the last few years due to the trend to smaller families and the increase in the number of non-family households (two or more unrelated persons sharing a dwelling).

TABLE 7.

Population growth in Census Metropolitan Areas with a population increase of 10,000 or more between 1971 and 1976

CMA	1971	1976	Population growth (1971 to 1976)	
				(per cent)
Calgary	403,343	469,917	66,574	16.5
Edmonton	496,014	554,228	58,214	11.7
Halifax	250,581	267,991	17,410	6.9
Hamilton	503,122	529,371	26,249	5.2
Kitchener	238,574	272,158	33,584	14.1
London	252,981	270,383	17,402	6.9
Montréal	2,729,211	2,802,485	73,274	2.7
Oshawa	120,318	135,196	14,878	12.4
Ottawa-Hull	619,861	693,288	73,427	11.8
Québec	501,365	542,158	40,793	8.1
Regina	140,734	151,191	10,457	7.4
St. Catharines-Niagara	285,802	301,921	16,119	5.6
St. John's	131,814	143,390	11,576	8.8
Toronto	2,602,098	2,803,101	201,003	7.7
Vancouver	1,082,352	1,166,348	83,996	7.8
Victoria	195,800	218,250	22,450	11.5
Winnipeg	549,808	578,217	28,409	5.2
CANADA	21,568,311	22,992,604	1,424,293	6.6

Source: Statistics Canada, 1977*c*. Population: Geographic Distributions: Municipalities, Census Metropolitan Areas and Census Agglomerations. Catalogue 92-806.

Table 8, the estimates of land consumption for ing assume 10 detached houses, 25 row or duplex units, and 124 apartments per ha. Since residential uses occupy about one-half to two-thirds of the urban land area, between one and one-half and twice the residential land consumption approximates urban expansion. From Table 9 which indicates housing starts from 1972 to 1976 inclusive, it appears that size of population, amount of population increase, housing starts, and estimated land consumption are not directly proportional, but are related. In terms of quantity of land consumed, the most important centres are Montréal, Toronto, Vancouver, Edmonton, Calgary, and Ottawa–Hull, in that order. Compare this with the centres with the largest absolute population growth; Toronto, Vancouver, Ottawa–Hull, Montréal, Calgary, and Edmonton. Compare this again with average house prices in these cities. The highest relative prices in 1977 were found in Calgary, Toronto, Vancouver, Edmonton, Victoria, and Ottawa–Hull, in descending order (Table 10). In addition, there is a group of large centres that merits attention because their land consumption is relatively higher than their increase in population between 1971 and 1976. They are Montréal, Winnipeg, Hamilton, and St. Catharines–Niagara, which all experienced growth rates of less than the national average of 6.6 per cent over five years. The other 13 CMAs were all in excess of 6.6 per cent. This lower rate of growth is reflected in the index of house prices in which these four cities had average house prices below the national average of $53,750 in 1977.

Some apparent anomalies are evident from this. It is not surprising that Canada's largest cities experience the highest absolute increases in population, use the most land, and have the highest housing prices. The exceptions seem to be Montréal and Winnipeg, both of which have lower growth rates, lower housing prices, and higher rates of land consumption per capita than one would expect from cities of that size. At the other end of the scale, a low rate of population growth seems to

TABLE 8.

Population growth and estimated residential land consumption in Census Metropolitan Areas with a population increase of 10,000 or more between 1971 and 1976

CMAs in order of population size	Population growth 1971 to 1976		Estimated residential land consumption 1971 to 1976	
	(rank)	(number)	(rank)	(ha)
Toronto	1	201,003	2	6,084
Montréal	4	73,274	1	6,582
Vancouver	2	83,996	3	4,329
Ottawa-Hull	3	73,427	6	1,983
Winnipeg	9	28,409	7	1,703
Edmonton	6	58,214	4	2,726
Québec	7	40,793	8	1,604
Hamilton	10	26,249	9	1,568
Calgary	5	66,574	5	2,715
St. Catharines–Niagara	14	16,119	10	1,163
Kitchener	8	33,584	11	1,111
London	13	17,402	12	1,021
Halifax	12	17,410	15	757
Victoria	11	22,450	13	803
Regina	17	10,457	14	794
St. John's	16	11,576	16	585
Oshawa	15	14,878	17	557
CANADA		1,424,293		73,285

Sources: LePage, A.E. (Ontario) Ltd., 1976. Real Estate Market Surveys.
Statistics Canada, 1977c. Population: Geographic Distributions: Municipalities, Census Metropolitan Areas and Census Agglomerations. Catalogue 92-806.

bring lower housing prices, from which are derived lower land prices which encourage less economic use of land.

There is a definite correlation between city size, amount of land consumed by housing, amount of population growth, and house prices (see Tables 8 and 10). The exception seems to be Montréal, with a low rate of population growth and low house prices combined with high land consumption, large size, and a large numerical increase in population. For large cities, there is also a correlation between low amounts and low rates of population growth, low density (ratios of population increase to area (ha) of land consumed), and low house

TABLE 10.

Population growth, density of new development, and house prices in Census Metropolitan Areas with a population increase of 10,000 or more between 1971 and 1976

CMAs in order of population growth rate	Population growth 1971 to 1976	Density of new development 1971 to 1976		Estimated house price 1977	
	(per cent)	(rank)	(persons per ha)	(rank)	($)
Calgary	16.5	7	24.5	1	66,721
Kitchener	14.1	3	30.2	8	53,000
Oshawa	12.4	5	26.7		N.A.
Ottawa-Hull	11.8	1	37.0	6	56,966
Edmonton	11.7	9	21.4	4	62,038
Victoria	11.5	4	28.0	5	60,000
St. John's	8.8	10	19.8		N.A.
Québec	8.1	6	25.4	15	34,000
Vancouver	7.8	11	19.4	3	64,382
Toronto	7.7	2	33.0	2	64,391
Regina	7.4	16	13.2	13	40,000
Halifax	6.9	8	23.0	11	42,000
London	6.9	12	17.0	9	47,000
St. Catharines–Niagara	5.6	15	13.9	10	42,000
Hamilton	5.2	13	16.8	7	53,000
Winnipeg	5.2	14	16.7	14	39,000
Montréal	2.7	17	11.3	12	41,000
CANADA	6.6		19.4		53,750

N.A. means data not available

Sources: LePage, A.E. (Ontario) Ltd., 1976. Real Estate Market Surveys. Multiple Listing Service. 1977.

TABLE 9.

Housing starts, 1972 to 1976, in Census Metropolitan Areas with a population increase of 10,000 or more between 1971 and 1976

CMAs with population growth of 10,000 or more	Single detached houses	Row houses and duplexes	Multiple apartments	Total dwelling units	Estimated residential land consumption	Density of development
					(ha)	(persons per ha)
Calgary	23,262	7,898	8,587	39,747	2,715	24.5
Edmonton	22,336	9,810	11,117	43,263	2,726	21.4
Halifax	6,186	1,847	7,990	16,023	757	23.0
Hamilton	11,198	7,971	16,038	35,207	1,568	16.8
Kitchener	8,367	5,164	8,263	21,794	1,111	30.2
London	7,778	4,612	7,338	19,728	1,021	17.0
Montréal	55,750	9,144	79,528	144,422	6,582	11.3
Oshawa	3,552	4,396	3,170	11,118	557	26.7
Ottawa-Hull	12,538	12,285	29,499	54,322	1,983	37.0
Québec	14,792	930	10,866	26,588	1,604	25.4
Regina	7,301	1,067	2,635	11,003	794	13.2
St. Catharines–Niagara	9,491	4,383	4,877	18,751	1,163	13.9
St. John's	4,867	2,169	1,389	8,425	585	19.8
Toronto	36,804	44,437	77,743	158,984	6,084	33.0
Vancouver	36,908	9,596	31,509	78,013	4,329	19.4
Victoria	6,597	1,287	11,370	19,254	803	28.0
Winnipeg	13,959	4,420	16,093	34,472	1,703	16.7
CANADA	627,507	173,842	443,876	1,245,225	73,285	19.4

Sources: Central Mortgage and Housing Corporation, 1976. Canadian Housing Statistics 1975.
_____, 1978. Canadian Housing Statistics 1977.

prices (see Tables 8 and 10). Tastes for apartments or detached houses vary across the country, and the steep increase in housing and land costs that occurred in the period between 1971 and 1976, may not yet have had its full impact on land use practices. Detached housing starts in Calgary and Edmonton are twice those of apartments (see Table 9), while in Toronto and Ottawa–Hull the proportion is reversed. Row houses are of minor importance in Québec, while in Toronto and Ottawa–Hull they constitute nearly one-quarter of the total starts.

If this analysis is applied to critical land and demand for land for urbanization, the cities to watch are the large centres which are experiencing large increases in population: Toronto, Vancouver, Ottawa–Hull, Montréal, Calgary, and Edmonton. Others to watch are the large centres which, although they are experiencing important absolute population increases, have low growth rates, low land prices, and extravagant land use practices. These are Montréal, Winnipeg, Hamilton, and St. Catharines–Niagara.

Future Housing Demand. In 1971, housing completions in Canada topped 200 thousand (210,232) for the first time, and in 1972, completions of detached houses topped 100 thousand (106,508) for the first time. The year with the most completions was 1974 with 257,243 units but, in 1976, the total was 236,249 of which 30 per cent were apartments, 54 per cent were detached houses, and 16 per cent were row houses and duplexes.

Average numbers of persons per household have fallen from 3.9 in 1961 to 3.25 in 1976. The projection for 1986 of 9 million households and a population of 25.5 million indicates an average of 2.77 persons per household. By 2001, the figure is estimated at 2.26 persons per household in 12.6 million households.

Projections of household numbers, by age of head of household and the distribution between dwelling types of the respective age groups, have been proposed by Statistics Canada and the Ministry of State for Urban

NFB – PHOTOTHEQUE – ONF – Photo by Ted Grant.

It is estimated that 80 per cent of Canadians wish to own a detached house. Single-family homes are always in demand, especially in Calgary and Edmonton where detached housing starts are twice those of apartments.

Central Mortgage and Housing Corporation photo.

Row housing is a popular choice of families with young children. In urban centres, such as Ottawa-Hull and Toronto, where young families form a significant portion of the total population, new row house developments constitute nearly 25 per cent of total housing starts.

Affairs. A forecast of the number of each type of housing unit needed up to 1986 is made in Table 11. Between 1971 and 1986, a total of three million extra households will be formed, about 200 thousand per annum, totalling approximately nine million in 1986. It is projected that the housing stock will contain 5.1 million detached houses, 1.2 million row houses and duplexes, and 2.5 million apartments. To house the extra 200 thousand new households each year will require more than 200 thousand dwellings to be produced each year, to allow for replacement of obsolete housing.

NFB – PHOTOTHEQUE – ONF – Photo by Karl Sliva.

High-density housing developments, in the form of high-rise apartment buildings, are a common sight. Many such residential developments offer shopping facilities and other services for the convenience of apartment dwellers.

The useful life of a building is estimated to be 50 years. Between 1922 and 1936, 624,300 units were completed, an average of 41,620 per annum. This implies that about 240 thousand units will have to be built every year for 15 years to serve new households and replace 40 thousand or more demolitions of existing houses. On the basis of the projections for 1986, new construction each year should comprise 130 thousand detached houses, 45 thousand row houses and duplexes, and 65 thousand apartments. The 1976 figures show an excess of apartments (71,294), and a deficiency of row houses and duplexes (36,332), while single detached houses

TABLE 11.

Housing projections from 1971 until 1986

	Single detached houses	Row houses and duplexes	Multiple apartments	Total
Housing stock				
1971	3,591,770	679,590	1,699,045	5,970,405
(per cent)	60	11	29	100
1986	5,131,055	1,260,605	2,505,020	8,896,680
(per cent)	58	14	28	100
Difference	1,539,285	581,015	805,975	2,926,275
Demolitions	374,580	68,673	181,047	624,300
Total	1,913,865	649,688	987,022	3,550,575
÷ 15 years	127,591	43,312	65,801	236,704
Projected annual construction (round figures)	130,000	45,000	65,000	240,000
(per cent)	54	19	27	100
Land requirement (ha)	14,165	1,821	526	16,512
1976 completions	128,623	36,332	71,294	236,249

Sources: Canadian Habitat Secretariat, 1976a. Human Settlement in Canada.
Central Mortgage and Housing Corporation, 1976. Canadian Housing Statistics 1975.

(128,623) were nearly on target. Whether the trend over the next nine years will be an increase in detached houses, row houses and duplex units at the expense of apartments remains to be seen. Row houses and duplexes seem to be steady at around 14 per cent of total completions over the last few years, while detached houses have increased from 44 per cent to 52 per cent between 1971 and 1975.

At this rate of construction, the land consumption needs are about 16,188 ha per annum for housing alone, or about 24,282 to 32,376 ha per annum for all urban uses. This compares with a rate of 17,219 ha per annum between 1966 and 1971 in 72 communities with populations of 25 thousand or more. These 72 communities contained about 70 per cent of Canada's population, so a total land conversion figure of 24,687 ha per annum for all of Canada can be inferred. These figures, which were obtained by Gierman (1977) from airphoto interpretation, provide a useful independent check for the method of extrapolating from housing figures.

Supply of Land for Conversion to Urban Uses

The nature of demand for developable land has been discussed; basically that it should be physically suited to urbanization and that it should be in an accessible location. This research has also identified the major centres in Canada where population growth and urban expansion have taken place. The next step is to examine the physical capability of the land that has locational value, with two objectives in mind: the first is to eliminate land that is unsuitable by reason of steepness, rockiness, wetness, or risk of flood. The second is to avoid the unnecessary conversion of prime agricultural land to urban uses if it can be demonstrated that a suitably located alternative supply of land exists.

The nearest approximation that is possible to the attainment of those objectives is to consider the area that lies between circles of 8- and 24-km radii from 13 cities which had a population growth of more than 10 thousand between 1971 and 1976.

The agricultural capability for land between these circles is available from the Canada Land Inventory. Land available for urbanization was defined as class 4 to 7 agricultural land free of certain limitations (see Appendix I). Other considerations, such as climate or cost of servicing, have been ignored, and this method can only be described as approximate. Why choose 8 and 24 km? The CLI is based on a survey made several years ago and considerable urban expansion has occurred subsequently. Within eight km of the city centre, figures for available land based on the CLI would be meaningless. Twenty-four km was chosen as the outer limit because it is the largest circle one can draw round each of Oshawa, Toronto, Hamilton, Kitchener, and St. Catharines without any overlap occurring. Since 24 km is unrealistically small for these "Golden Horseshoe" cities, another set

of figures has been prepared for land beyond 24 km and within 80 km of those five cities and also London, which is closely related to them.

Table 12 shows the land available for development, according to the definition given above, around 13 selected CMAs, compared with their estimated land consumption between 1972 and 1976 inclusive. The last column gives a crude indication of how many years the available supply would last at 1972 to 1976 rates of expansion. The "Golden Horseshoe" taken as a unit, in the area between 24 and 80 km from its six centres appears to have an ample supply (36 years), but it represents only 5.6 per cent of 3.8 million ha within 80 km of the six centres. This land may be in small parcels in inaccessible locations, or it may also be of special importance for some other use such as recreation.

To illustrate the distribution of both land available for development, as well as high-capability agricultural land, in relation to existing built-up areas within a 24-km radius of city centres, Maps 4 to 7 represent the situation in four major Canadian cities.

The indicators of demand for urban land are its relative location and accessibility on the one hand, and the demographic and economic characteristics of the population on the other. Since not only the size and distribution of Canada's population are changing, but also its standard of living and pattern of economic activity, changes in patterns of urban land use are inevitable. The next section examines some of these changes and their causes, thus helping to determine which are the important lands for urban use.

Changes in Urban Land Use

In the typical urban area there are two distinct types of change taking place. The central business district and the neighbourhoods adjacent to it are becoming more densely developed with high-rise office buildings and apartment blocks replacing smaller commercial, industrial, and residential structures. On the edge of the built-up area is the urban fringe, characterized by low-density urban development and uses associated with urbanization such as solid waste disposal, sand and gravel extraction, land held idle in anticipation of urban development, golf courses, and hobby farms. Land in the fringe is in the process of being brought piecemeal into one of these uses, usually from agriculture or horticulture. As a result, the landscape consists of a mixture of subdivisions, isolated houses, farms, gravel pits, and idle land crossed by arterial roads radiating from the city which attract ribbon development of gas stations, drive-in restaurants, used-car lots, and houses.

The urban fringe is a dynamic element: it is always present at the periphery of a town or city and moves outward as the community grows. The attraction of the

NFB – PHOTOTHEQUE – ONF – Photo by Tom Bochsler.

Strip development is such a common element of the urban fringe, across Canada, that it is difficult to tell where this 1975 photo was taken. Gas stations, drive-in restaurants, and large retail outlets, located along main roads radiating from the city, contribute to the ribbon development in St. Catharines and most other Canadian cities.

TABLE 12.

Land supply estimates in selected Census Metropolitan Areas

Census Metropolitan Area	Land supply between 8 and 24 km				Land supply between 24 and 80 km			
	Total area	Class 1, 2, and 3 agricultural land	Developable area	Supply estimate	Total area	Class 1, 2, and 3 agricultural land	Developable area	Supply estimate
	(ha)			(years)	(ha)			(years)
Calgary	159,403	106,791	18,991	17				
Edmonton	159,463	119,200	18,057	16				
Halifax	111,453	6,386	1,750	5				
Montréal	143,139	106,418	5,022	0	1,558,286	751,401	192,683	145
Ottawa-Hull	153,705	69,727	17,276	21				
Québec	148,970	43,918	25,745	40				
Winnipeg	160,655	147,534	5,362	8				
Hamilton	128,377	112,275	4,136	7				
Kitchener	161,156	132,558	8,326	19				
London	161,665	154,861	2,629	6	2,750,731	2,218,864	168,294	36
Oshawa	97,121	74,866	10,593	47				
St. Catharines-Niagara	105,764	92,284	525	1				
Toronto	85,945	58,836	0	0				

Source: Neimanis, 1979. *Canada's Cities and Their Surrounding Land Resource*.

Central Mortgage and Housing Corporation photo.

Operations such as sand and gravel extraction locate near urban areas in order to minimize the cost of transporting high-bulk low-value construction material.

fringe for certain uses is the seed of many of its problems. The main attractions for all users are that land is cheaper and planning regulations are often less stringent in suburban or rural municipalities than in the city. Residents are attracted by cheaper housing and the prospect of more space and fresh air. Commercial users, especially those who need large areas to display wares such as automobiles and furniture, are attracted by cheaper land with good highway access. They substitute lower prices and higher advertising costs in city newspapers and radio stations for a highly visible and accessible, but more expensive, location downtown. An automobile dealer 40 km outside Ottawa has been saturating the local airwaves with the phrase "just beyond the fringe" for so long that it has passed into the local vocabulary, and his location is now part of the fringe. His success has undoubtedly caused agglomeration effects and a furniture warehouse and a flea market have opened nearby.

Other activities, such as sand and gravel extraction and solid waste disposal, must locate near a city because transport costs are a major factor affecting operations. Horticulture or truck farming has traditionally been an activity conducted as near to its market as possible, although the advent of refrigerated trucks has made it possible to transport perishable fruit, vegetables, and flowers from regions where climate and soils favour them.

What are the problems created by cheaper land and less municipal control over planning? As the density of development increases, problems are created for residents, commercial operations, farmers, and municipalities. Residents who move from the city to what they think of as the country may soon be disappointed to find the level of services such as water supply, sewers, street lighting, and bus service is lower. The neighbouring farm is a source of smells and drifting crop spray, and they may be unable to stop the construction of a new subdivision or the opening of a gravel pit in the neighbouring field. Retailers, farmers, and other commercial firms find that either their costs are increasing in the form of increased property tax, or, in cases where residents have enough influence to stop activities they oppose, certain activities such as scrap yards or feed lots are prohibited. Municipalities are faced with demands for higher levels of services than had been normal in their hitherto rural community. After approving, almost indiscriminately, all applications for severances for new houses or commercial operations because of the prospect of increased tax revenue, they find that they have to provide piped water and sewers, street lights, paving, and snow ploughing on most roads. The costs of these services are often more than the tax revenue from the taxpayers who are served. Scattered development means uneconomically long runs of pipe and paving per house or per user.

As the fringe becomes more densely developed, conflicts between users may become more intense. If there is no sewage and water system, there is the problem of contamination of wells by septic tanks. New subdivisions occupied by middle-class families co-exist with tarpaper structures occupied by lower-income people, which results in social problems until the latter are effectively forced out by increased property taxes. Eventually an area passes through the stage of being part of the urban fringe and becomes urban, often as a sprawling low-density suburb with no sense of community, no defined centre for shopping, schools, or employment, and inadequate opportunities for recreation. Here and there, there are vacant lots, sand pits, scrap yards, and other left-overs from a former pattern of land use.

Land Conversion

Between 1966 and 1971, a study was made of 72 of Canada's urban areas with populations of 25 thousand or more. In total they converted 17,219 ha of undeveloped land per annum to urban uses. Of that land, 54 per cent was improved agricultural, 22 per cent was unimproved pasture and 22 per cent was forest land. However, 63 per cent of the total land converted had high capability for agriculture, in other words it was in class 1, 2, or 3 of the CLI classification of agriculture (Gierman, 1977).

Of the 86,160 ha of land converted to urban uses in 72 communities between 1966 and 1971, Toronto, Montréal, Edmonton, and Calgary accounted for nearly two-fifths of that total (Table 13). The same four cities accounted for nearly half the 46,279 ha withdrawn from agriculture in the same period. The former use of land does not always correspond to its capability. Between 1966 and 1971, 54,509 ha of land with class 1, 2, or 3 capability for agriculture were converted to urban uses. Nearly three-fifths of this conversion took place around Toronto, Montréal, Edmonton, Winnipeg, and St. Catharines. Around Toronto, 97 per cent of the 11,764 ha converted to urban uses had high capability for agriculture. For Winnipeg the proportion was 100 per cent. With the exception of St. John's, Saskatoon, and Vancouver, a large proportion of the land converted to urban uses had high capability for agriculture: it was, in fact, not used for agriculture.

This indicates that good farmland is being withdrawn from agriculture and being allowed to degenerate into unimproved pasture. There are a number of reasons for this, the principal one being that the anticipated value of the land for development is much higher than the value for agriculture. Such land is not held by farmers so much as by developers who may not be interested in leasing their land for agriculture. In other cases, farmers are discouraged from cultivating fields that adjoin residential areas because of complaints about odours, dust, and fertilizer. This, combined with increasing property taxes in the urban fringe and the possibility of receiving a high price for their land, induces many farmers to leave.

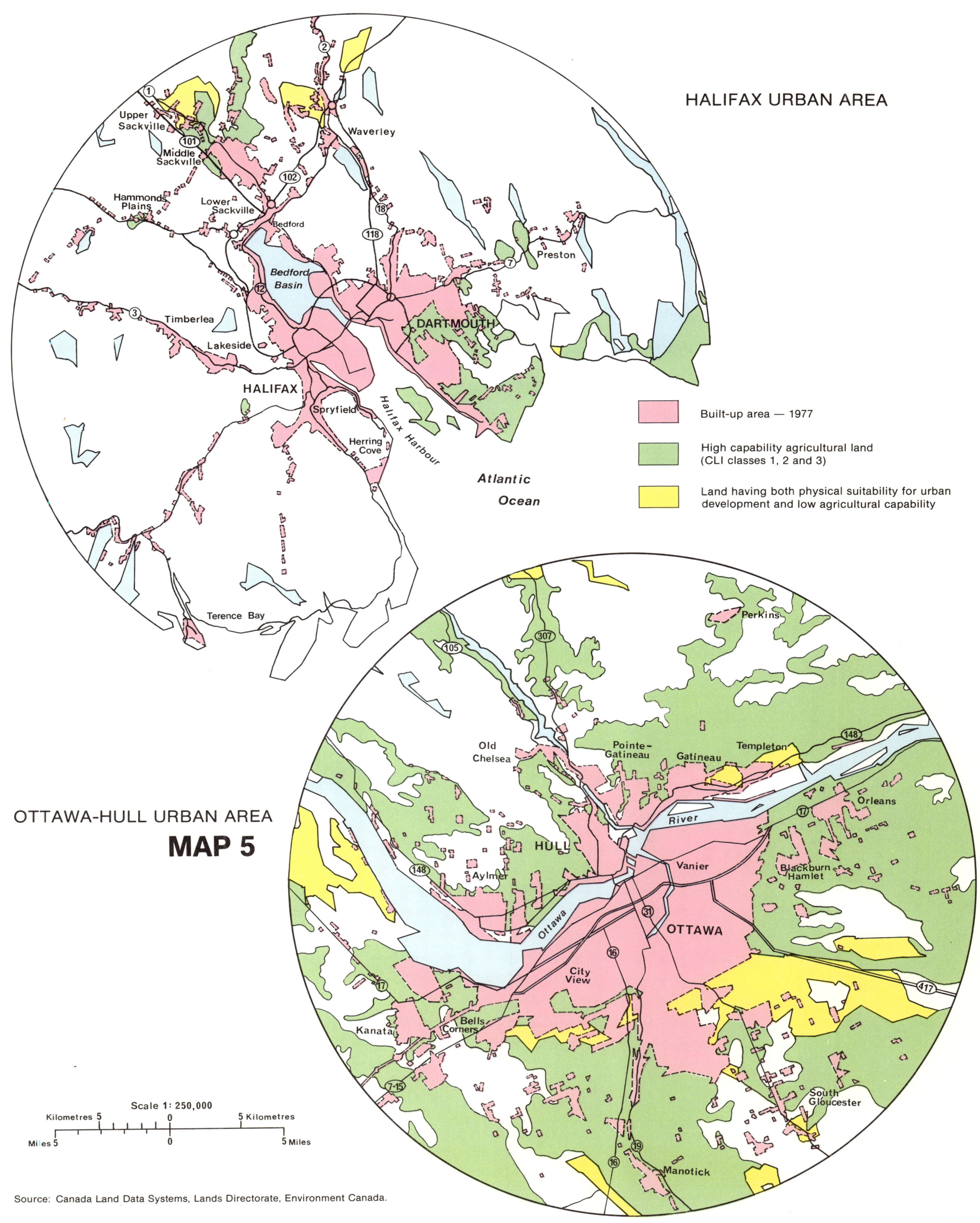

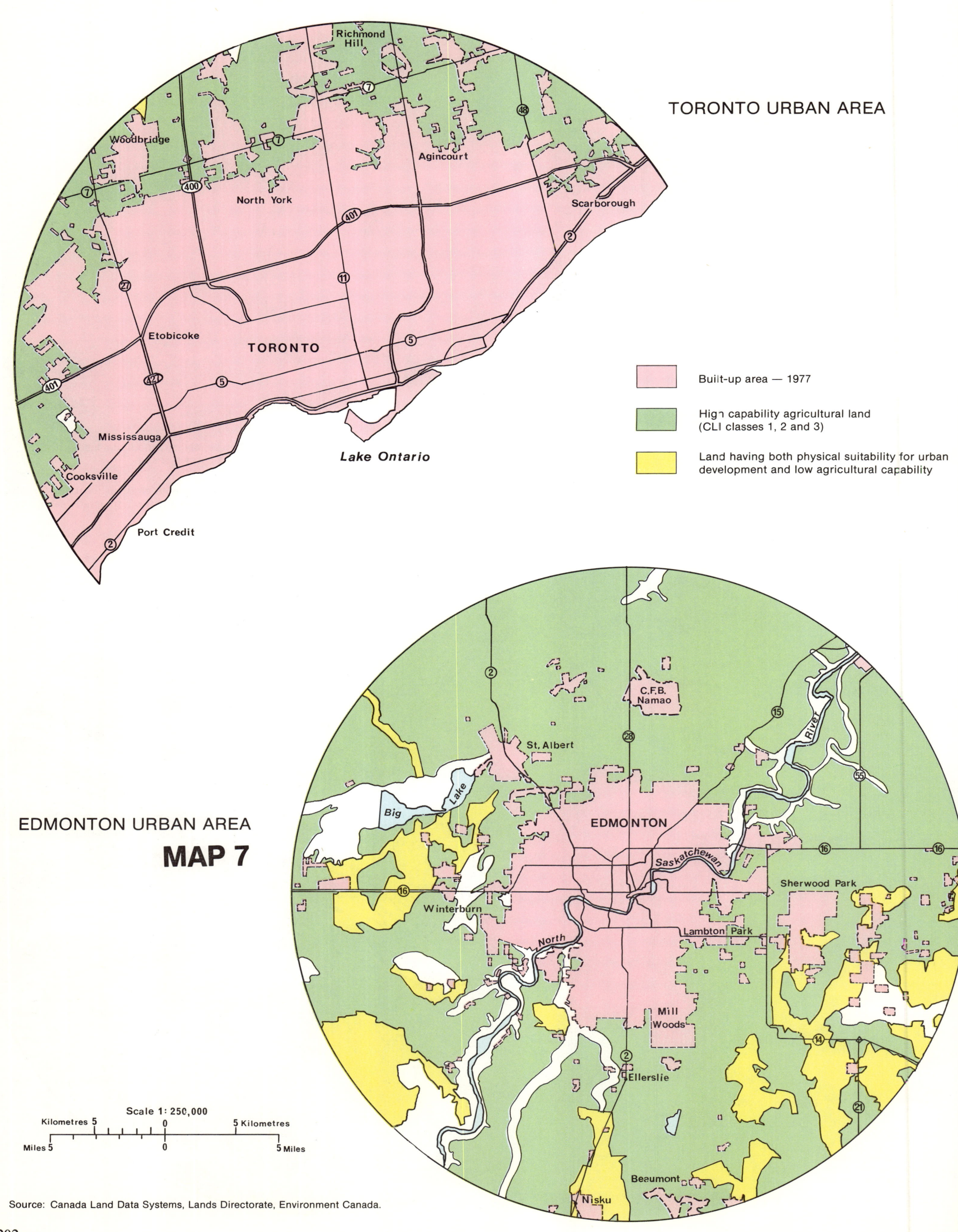

TABLE 13.

Land conversion from rural to urban uses in and around Census Metropolitan Areas, 1966 to 1971

CMA	Total area converted	Ha per 1,000 population increase	Formerly improved agriculture		Formerly unimproved pasture		Formerly forest		Formerly other non-urban		High agriculture capability	
	(ha)	(ha)	(ha)	(per cent)	(ha)	(per cent)	(ha)	(per cent)	(ha)	(per cent)	(ha)	(per cent)
Calgary	6,418	88	3,721	58	2,242	35	234	4	221	3	2,885	45
Chicoutimi-Jonquière	736	5,750	351	48	136	19	234	32	15	2	367	50
Edmonton	6,552	96	5,237	80	914	14	257	4	144	2	5,347	82
Halifax	1,425	154	52	4	6	–	1,350	95	17	1	355	25
Hamilton	2,045	53	1,377	67	403	20	159	8	106	5	1,728	85
Kitchener	2,529	75	1,534	61	603	24	363	14	29	1	1,657	66
London	1,546	49	1,006	65	371	24	151	10	18	1	1,542	100
Montréal	7,721	47	3,037	39	2,458	32	2,188	28	38	1	5,708	74
Oshawa	609	44	483	79	76	13	38	6	12	2	571	94
Ottawa-Hull	4,615	71	2,147	47	1,286	28	1,055	23	127	3	2,586	56
Québec	2,748	68	841	31	713	26	1,160	42	34	1	908	33
Regina	380	46	380	100	–	–	–	–	–	–	371	98
St. Catharines-Niagara	5,087	283	2,438	48	2,021	40	580	11	48	1	4,196	82
Saint John	1,092	717	193	18	232	21	635	58	32	3	13	1
St. John's	686	60	222	32	62	9	365	53	37	5	–	–
Saskatoon	473	45	416	88	55	12	2	–	–	–	200	42
Sudbury	1,206	88	110	9	114	9	790	66	192	16	167	14
Thunder Bay	573	148	91	16	155	27	319	56	8	2	49	9
Toronto	11,755	36	9,490	81	1,262	11	818	7	185	2	11,438	97
Vancouver	3,662	28	1,186	32	656	18	1,764	48	56	2	272	7
Victoria	473	31	55	12	212	45	204	43	2	1	–	–
Windsor	1,223	86	1,082	88	96	8	45	4	–	–	1,116	91
Winnipeg	4,386	150	2,769	63	821	19	681	16	115	3	4,385	100
URBAN AREAS IN CANADA*	86,096	69	46,244	54	19,187	22	18,812	22	1,853	2	54,469	63

* Includes all urban areas with a population of more than 25,000 in 1971.

Source: Gierman, 1977. *Rural to Urban Land Conversion*.

A14755-73 Original photo supplied by the Surveys and Mapping Branch, Department of Energy, Mines and Resources.

The 1955 photo shows the rural-urban fringe just south of Ottawa's city limits. The Rideau River is on the extreme right. New housing developments and industrial activities have intruded on farmland and forest areas. Most of the land is rated in classes 1 to 3 for agriculture.

A24625-149 Original photo supplied by the Surveys and Mapping Branch, Department of Energy, Mines and Resources.

The 1977 photo shows the extent to which the housing subdivisions have grown. Industrial expansion in the north and west has been substantial and now includes oil storage, scrap yards, car wreckers, and warehouses. At the top of the photo, additional industrial park development has begun.

The origin of many Canadian cities as market towns serving agricultural areas implies that as they expand, they do so on to agricultural land. It is not just the expansion of the built urban environment, but also the intrusion effects of cities into the neighbouring countryside that takes land out of agriculture. Land is taken for private and public recreation uses, for sand and gravel pits, for transport and utility corridors, and for waste disposal. At any given time, about ten years' supply of development land is lying idle in the urban fringe, held out of agriculture by land developers who work on the assumption that the locational value of the land will increase at a faster rate than the holding costs.

Between 1966 and 1971, for every thousand new residents entering the 72 communities studied by Gierman (1977), 70 ha of new urban development occurred. The average land utilization rate in these communities in 1966 was 41 ha per thousand population. By 1971, because of the lower density of new development, the total land utilization rate for these communities had risen to 44 ha per thousand population.

These figures for entire urban areas indicate that more space was occupied by each urban resident in 1971 than in 1966. However, a seemingly paradoxical trend is hidden in the aggregate figures; although urban population densities are decreasing, the intensity of land use is increasing. Intensity of use can be defined in physical terms as the ratio of the floor area of a building to the area of the site on which it stands. In terms of economics, intensity of use refers to the amount of value derived from a parcel of land, either as rent for private land, or some social benefit for public lands such as roads or parks. The paradox may be explained by separating two related processes. The concentration of business and commerce in the central business district has increased the intensity of land use, but has decreased the population in the downtown area. To complement the concentration of employment at the centre, residential areas expand at the periphery, usually at a lower density than older neighbourhoods. However, conversion of land in the urban fringe, from rural to low-density urban use, is an increase in intensity of use. Statistical evidence of differences in land utilization rates between centre and periphery is sparse, but some information relating to Montréal and Toronto exists. In 1970, the land utilization rate on Île-de-Montréal was 17 ha per thousand population (Yeates, 1975), while in 1971 the rate was 25 ha per thousand for the CMA of Montréal (Gierman, 1977). The CMA includes suburbs both on and around Île-de-Montréal and the higher rate for the CMA indicates lower densities of development in the outer suburbs. For Toronto, more detail is available for 1966 from the same sources. The land utilization rate for the City of Toronto was 14 ha per thousand population. For Metro Toronto the rate was 25 ha per thousand and for the CMA of Toronto it was 33 ha per thousand. These figures indicate a progressive decrease in population densities toward the periphery.

Rates of land conversion and utilization are inversely related to city size. Between 1966 and 1971, the average figure for communities of over 25 thousand population was 70 ha per thousand increase in population. However, the 48 cities with populations between 25 thousand and 100 thousand used 161 ha of land per thousand new residents, while the 18 cities of 100 thousand to 500 thousand population used 88 ha per thousand population increase. The five largest cities, all with populations of more than 500 thousand, converted the least land per new resident, 45 ha per thousand increase.

Land Prices

The demand for land is always derived, and it follows that the price of land is always a residual. The price of residential land is determined by the price of housing. In the case of detached houses, about 300,000 units change hands each year. Of this number, approximately 120,000 are new units. Thus, the price of new housing is strongly influenced by the 60 per cent of the market which consists of houses for resale. A developer has costs of materials, labour, capital, and servicing imposed. From the difference between these costs and the selling price of the house he has to buy land and take his profit. Between 1971 and 1976, land costs doubled for detached houses financed under the National Housing Act. However, these houses accounted for only 29 per cent of all detached houses built in 1976. In Toronto and Vancouver, land costs account for up to 40 per cent of the cost of a house. An Alberta Government study showed that in 1977 the cost of a 550-m^2 serviced lot in Calgary and Edmonton was 38 per cent of the price of an 110-m^2 bungalow: in Lethbridge it was 26 per cent. The effect that the increase in the price of land has had on its use is the construction of housing either at higher densities or of higher quality in urban areas, and an increase in exurban development as city dwellers moved to small towns 50 to 80 km out of large cities. These exurbanites, who work in the city, have substituted the cost of travel time and transport for housing costs.

Factors Affecting Change

The principal factors that produce change in urban land uses or create pressure to convert other land to urban uses are demographic, economic, and technological. These factors are closely connected and in some cases the distinction between them may be a little artificial.

Demographic Processes

Land use is affected by population numbers, rates of increase, local concentrations, and movements. The changes that are taking place in land used for urban development are a result of urban growth. The core is becoming more densely developed and the fringe is spreading further. Residents and commercial firms are making their choice. They can stay in the city to be near their services, amenities, and business linkages while using less space. They have the alternative of moving out to the fringe, if they are satisfied with less accessibility to the central business district, in return for cheaper land. It is notable that the response to lower land prices is to occupy more space rather than using the same amount of space and saving money. In the next section, some of the factors affecting the changes in land use are examined.

The major demographic trends in Canada are population growth, urbanization, declining birth rate, increasing life expectancy, and changing patterns of migration. Between 1971 and 1976, Canada's population grew at an annual rate of one per cent from 21.6 million to 23.0 million, mainly in Ontario, British Columbia, Alberta, and Québec.

Urban population growth between 1971 and 1976 averaged one per cent per annum, in contrast to the 1966 to 1971 period when urban population growth was twice the national average rate. Half of the national population growth between 1971 and 1976 is attributed to 15 CMAs. The crude birth rate dropped from 26.1 per thousand in 1961, to 16.0 per thousand in 1976. The three most populous provinces, Ontario, Québec, and British Columbia, have the lowest birth rates, while Newfoundland and the Territories have the highest. The crude death rate has declined from 7.7 per thousand in 1961, to 7.3 per thousand in 1976.

Internal net migration was characterized by a movement to Ontario, Alberta, and British Columbia between 1966 and 1971. From 1972 to 1975, preliminary figures indicate that the Maritime Provinces and the Yukon were also receiving migrants from other provinces, but that Ontario was not. This change may be a result of reduced employment prospects in Ontario for Maritimers who then returned home. International migrants have always favoured Ontario which receives half of the country's immigrants (about 130 thousand per annum), while Québec and British Columbia each take one-sixth in a typical year. Immigrants are attracted to the three largest cities, Montréal, Toronto, and Vancouver, and are thus reinforcing the growth of the cities and the provinces with the largest populations.

The four most populous provinces, Ontario, Québec, British Columbia, and Alberta accounted for 1.5 million of the 1.6 million population increase in Canada between 1966 and 1971, and 1.3 million of the 1.4 million increase from 1971 to 1976. The concentration of population into a few areas, principally the major cities in these provinces, is continuing, indicating where the demand for land for urban uses is the greatest.

The population characteristics and processes that will have an effect on land use are as follows:

1) An increasing proportion of the population is classed as urban. It exceeded 50 per cent for the first time shortly after 1921, and is now 76 per cent. Forty-three per cent live in 12 cities with populations of 250 thousand or more.

2) A substantial increase in the standard of living and educational attainment of the population has occurred since 1945.

3) The baby boom of 1945 to 1960 created a large group of people who are now between 18 and 33 years of age, and who will be between 41 and 55 years of age in 2001. These people are now forming households and having children, and in 2001 they will still be in the labour force.

4) Total numbers of the population and the size of the major urban communities will increase.

In Canada, between 1978 and the end of the century, Canadians will be part of the largest population the country has ever had. An exceptionally large group of people are already starting to buy or rent homes of their own, not only because of the number of people between 18 and 33 years of age, but also because young people leave their parents and live on their own at a younger age than was the case a few years ago. The effect on land consumption for new housing is already being felt, as discussed earlier in the chapter. This large group of young people will be raising families between now and the end of the century, and it is the young families that are the major consumers. They buy clothes, furniture, appliances, summer cottages, camping equipment, and other manufactured goods that imply a demand for land for industry, recreation, and transport.

Economic Factors

The economic factors that influence land use can be divided into income factors, (the location of firms and individuals where they can make a living), and expenditure factors, (the impact on land use of the amount and allocation of the disposable income of individuals).

The determinants of industrial location vary according to the type of industry. Primary industry is oriented to the natural resources it exploits; water, land, minerals, forests, or fish. Its importance as an employer has declined between 1951 and 1977, from 19.8 to 7.3 per cent of the employed labour force (Tables 14 and 15). Primary industry is most important in the Prairies, the Maritimes, and British Columbia. The implications for communities based on primary industry in these regions are clear, and a declining economic base means less demand for land for urban uses.

Secondary industry tends to be oriented to skilled labour, markets, and locations accessible to parent companies in the United States. It is concentrated in Ontario and Québec, in and around major cities. It too has been declining as an employer since 1951, from 31.3 to 26.2 per cent of the labour force in 1977. This is counter-balanced by the growth of the tertiary sector from 47.8 to 66.5 per cent of the labour force between 1951 and 1977. Tertiary industry is found in all urban settlements, and is often the major employer in small towns. However, the higher order, well-paid tertiary occupations are usually concentrated in major centres.

The growth of population and economic activity in and around major cities is the reason for some of the changes that are taking place in urban land use. Within cities, the growth of tertiary industry at the expense of the secondary sector has influenced land use patterns. Manufacturing was located traditionally in central locations near transport facilities, either railways or harbours, many of which are now under-used and ripe for redevelopment. Manufacturing has changing locational requirements which will be discussed under technological change. The rise of the tertiary sector has led to the downtown office boom, to accommodate financial institutions, commerce, and government; it has also given us downtown and suburban shopping centres and spacious college campuses. It has also maintained the construction industry as an employer of six per cent of total labour force for the last 25 years.

TABLE 14.

Occupation structure of the labour force, 1951

Occupation	Canada	British Columbia	Prairies	Ontario	Québec	Atlantic
	(per cent of total labour force)					
Primary	19.8	13.7	37.3	13.1	17.2	27.1
Manufacturing	25.1	24.0	13.6	29.8	29.4	20.1
Construction	6.2	6.8	4.8	6.4	6.8	5.9
Transportation	9.5	11.9	8.8	9.4	9.3	10.9
Trade	10.1	11.9	10.1	10.7	9.3	9.3
Service	28.2	31.7	25.1	30.6	27.9	26.1
Total	100.0	100.0	100.0	100.0	100.0	100.0

Source: Li, 1976. *Canadian Urban Trends*. Reproduced by permission of Copp Clark Publishing Limited and the Minister of Supply and Services Canada.

TABLE 15.

Percentage distribution of employment within regions, by industry, 1977

Industry category	Annual average employment					
	Canada	British Columbia	Prairies	Ontario	Québec	Atlantic
	(per cent of total)					
Primary	7.3	6.1	16.8	4.9	4.8	7.8
Manufacturing	19.6	16.3	9.2	24.5	22.6	13.3
Construction	6.6	7.6	7.8	6.1	5.8	7.3
Transportation	8.5	10.2	9.1	7.4	8.2	11.3
Trade	17.4	18.5	18.1	16.6	17.3	18.4
Service	40.6	41.4	38.9	40.5	41.3	41.9
Total	100.0	100.0	100.0	100.0	100.0	100.0

Source: Statistics Canada, 1977d. The Labour Force. Catalogue 71-001.

Real personal disposable income has been rising since 1945, which has created increased demand for housing, recreation, cultural and educational facilities, cars and the roads to drive them on. Between 1951 and 1975, personal spending on consumer goods and services increased from $1,467 to $3,052 per capita in constant dollars. The implications of this on the amount of space devoted to retail and wholesale trade are considerable, not to mention the land required for disposal of the solid waste that is the by-product of a modern consumer society. Demand for housing has increased significantly since 1946 when 60,500 units were completed, as compared with 236,249 in 1976. The increase in house-building benefits not only the construction industry but also the manufacturers of furniture and appliances.

However, the wealth is unevenly distributed. Personal disposable income per capita in the Maritimes and Saskatchewan is well below the Canadian average, in Ontario it is well above, and in the other provinces it is about average. These figures support the previous explanations of urban growth being based largely on economic growth, and show it to be strongest in Ontario. Since incomes are higher in large and growing cities than in smaller centres, and it is known that the large cities in the provinces with average personal incomes (Québec, Alberta, and British Columbia) are growing, it can be inferred that incomes outside major cities in these three provinces are below the national average (Table 16).

Technological Developments

Changing technology has affected urban land use mainly through its application to industry, transport, and construction. The first part of this chapter described how developments in sources of motive power, from water, through coal, petroleum, and electricity, have affected industrial and settlement location in the last 150 years across the country. Within urban areas, industrial location and land requirements have changed. Manufacturing industry is oriented toward facilities for the transport of raw materials and manufactured products. Heavy industry is still attracted to railway and port locations, but light industry is moving away from the railway to arterial-road locations. This usually means a migration from an inner city to a peripheral location. Modern factories tend to be single-storey buildings with ample car parks, occupying far more land than the older loft structures downtown, which are ill-suited to assembly-line production.

Changes in transportation technology have influenced the size, density of development, and internal pattern of land use in urban centres. In Canada, the first settlements were served by horse transport, but it was in the period of the street-car and the railway that major cities started to develop. Commerce and manufacturing located near the railways, while residential areas grew along street-car routes. Residential densities were high since housing located more than one-half km from the street-car route was distinctly less desirable. Then came the motor car and the truck to compete with the street-car and the train. Industry started to shift to main roads and new lower-density housing developed on the fringe of cities. In many cities, it is still possible to determine where the street-car routes ended by the marked reduction in the density of development. The increase in the

NFB – PHOTOTHEQUE – ONF – Photo by Tom Bochsler.
Manufacturing plants prefer a periphery location which offers proximity to the urban market and labour force, as well as cheap land necessary to accommodate single-storey buildings, parking lots, and storage areas.

use of private cars for journeys to the central business district, and the congestion which resulted, have caused the conversion of inner-city land to car parks and expressways. Studies have shown that the average maximum acceptable travel time for the journey to work is 45 minutes. On a bus or street-car that would be, eight km plus a 10-minute walk. By car it may be 16 km on city streets. However, an expressway makes it feasible to drive 50 km to work, causing many small towns to become dormitory communities for nearby cities. The commuting area has effectively been extended from a circle of 10-km radius to one of 50-km radius in the last 30 years.

The decline in importance of the railway in favour of the truck for transport of goods has made much inner-city railway land redundant. On the other hand, the rise of air transport has created a demand for vast tracts of flat land just outside the built-up area. The airport is also a powerful locational attraction to high-technology industry whose products have low bulk and high value, and to ancillary services such as hotels and aircraft maintenance. This effect can be seen around Toronto International Airport, and a large amount of land near Mirabel has been reserved for industrial and hotel development.

Technological change has also influenced construction methods over the last century. Such innovations as the electric elevator and the steel-framed building have enabled the central business district to be developed to a far higher density. This has affected land values and

TABLE 16.

Average family income for metropolitan and non-metropolitan areas, by region, 1975

Type of area	Canada	British Columbia	Prairies	Ontario	Québec	Atlantic
	(dollars)					
Metropolitan areas	17,607	18,703	17,572	18,484	16,202	15,234
Non-metropolitan areas						
non-metropolitan cities	15,662	15,306	17,036	16,773	15,777	13,829
small urban areas	14,511	17,057	14,262	15,197	13,950	12,056
rural areas	13,434	14,516	13,417	15,769	12,324	10,984

Source: Statistics Canada, 1977e. Family Incomes. Catalogue 13-208.

Airports, such as the Toronto International Airport, utilize large parcels of flat land that often has high capability for other uses including agriculture. In addition, airports attract high-technology and communication industries, accommodation facilities, and other services that also require land.

land use in several ways. The possibility of constructing a taller building and being able to provide more floor space for apartments or offices per unit of land, and hence derive more value from that land, increased the value of the land. Users who were unable to pay the price or rent that reflected the increased value were forced out by other users who could. As mentioned earlier, manufacturers had come to favour one-storey buildings, while financiers and administrators need central locations and are able to occupy high-rise buildings. The increased concentration of office employment in the urban core, the suburbanization of manufacturing, and the improvements in modes of transport combine to give a technological explanation to the spread of the suburbs. The urban core provides high-density accommodation for activities that rely heavily on accessibility to each other; the suburbs provide space for activities such as manufacturing, retail trade, and residential uses.

Certain land users, including financiers, administrators, and other business people, derive the greatest benefit from a central location and therefore pay high rents in the densely-developed downtown core. Toronto, one of the country's financial centres, has a concentration of tall office buildings typical of the CBD.

The changes in land use caused by population growth, economic change, and technological change have given rise to a number of issues related to land, urban growth, and the quality of life. It is not only the owner or the user of a parcel of land who is affected when the use of that land is changed, either by placing a new building on it or by renovating, extending, or demolishing an existing one. The whole community either benefits from, or suffers, a change in its environment and quality of life. In a dynamic system, such as a city, there is always some change taking place. The next section discusses some of the effects of change on the environment and quality of life, and the issues that arise.

Land, Environmental Quality, and the Quality of Life

The question now arises: How will the identification of land, either of special value or particularly unsuitable for urbanization, benefit the natural environment and the quality of life?

Briefly, the answer lies in land use practices and public attitudes toward land and housing. Attention to the environmental as well as the locational characteristics of land for development will not only improve environmental quality but will also reduce conflicts with other uses, reduce consumption of non-renewable resources, and improve the quality of life. Before the reader gains the impression that the identification of suitable land for urban uses will solve all problems, it should be noted that three-quarters of the urban structures that will exist in the year 2000 have already been built.

Land Use Practices: Effect on Environment

The land use practices that affect the environment are discussed under broad headings of settlement pattern, settlement form, and housing.

Settlement Pattern. The characteristics of settlement patterns that affect the environment are settlement size, location, and concentration, distribution of manufacturing industry, levels of personal income, and public finance.

The dense pattern of settlement and industry in southern Ontario and the lower Fraser Valley has contributed to water and air pollution and to losses of prime agricultural land. It is not only the built-up areas that cause such losses, but also electricity transmission, transport, recreation, waste disposal, and resource extraction outside urban areas. Dispersed settlement patterns are characterized by small communities with higher per-capita rates of land consumption, less sophisticated waste management, little or no public transport, and a declining share of the national population and of economic growth. This implies a declining tax base and consequently, an inability to finance environmental protection measures. A dense pattern of settlement by itself need not degrade the environment, while a dispersed pattern may not be beneficial. A dense settlement pattern characterized by high standards of living both needs, and can support, high standards of environmental protection measures such as waste treatment, land use planning, pollution abatement, public transport, and water management. In terms of quality of life, it is the dense pattern of settlement that makes possible a high standard of cultural, educational, medical, and commercial services.

Northern communities impose a special burden on the environment, and care has to be taken in construction and waste management. In cold climates, vegetation cover takes longer to regenerate and its destruction can lead to soil erosion and permafrost melting. Also the energy requirements for heating and transport are greater, which can affect air quality.

Settlement Form. The processes in the evolution of the urban structure (congestion, sprawl, suburbanization of economic activity, and associated automobile use) affect the quality of the urban environment and the natural environment in the surrounding countryside. The quality of the urban environment can be expressed in terms of factors that either affect human health or are perceived as unpleasant. These are air quality, microclimate, water quality, and urban design. All but urban design are components of the natural environment which also includes aquifers, land, sources of energy, and raw materials.

Automobiles contribute about 60 per cent of urban air pollution in Canada. They are major producers of noise and waste heat, and they ultimately become solid waste. Roads, driveways, and car parks cover about 18 per cent of the urban surface area which accelerates runoff, and causes flash flooding and aquifer depletion. The runoff is also polluted with hydrocarbons, salt, asbestos, and heavy metals.

Widespread use and ownership of the car have been the major influences in the process of urbanization and growth of suburbs. Automobiles are also an important factor in air pollution, energy consumption, and land use.

High-rise development in the urban core leads to congestion and loss of environmental quality unless a high standard of urban design is achieved. The microclimate is affected by concentrated emissions of waste heat and carbon dioxide from space heating and motor traffic. Wind funnelling and shadow effects result from poorly sited or designed high-rise buildings. Buildings and asphalt have a lower specific heat and albedo effect than vegetation and, thus, absorb more heat at a faster rate. The effects on microclimate are "heat islands", temperature inversions, fog, smog, and reduced precipitation. The fact that nearly all of the core is built or paved over affects water quality, runoff, and aquifers.

Urban sprawl, by its very nature, reduces accessibility for residents to the services they need, and to each other. It means that any trip to shop, work, or school is often too far to walk, which necessitates car travel. An American study (Real Estate Research Corporation, 1974) has shown that sprawl increases the use of energy for transport and heating, and hence increases air pollution. Sprawl also increases runoff from the greater road areas per dwelling. However, the increase in the total impact is dispersed over a larger area.

Although lower housing costs in the suburbs permit many Canadians to own their own home, low land prices encourage low-density development which means that more land is converted to urban uses.

Housing. One of the land uses that has the greatest effect on the environment and the quality of life is housing. It occupies over half of the area of most cities and is a basic need for everyone. Among economic considerations, the natural preference of most consumers, the policies of Central Mortgage and Housing Corporation (CMHC), the system of tenure, zoning by-laws, and the tax structure have all encouraged consumers to buy low-density detached houses. The system of tenure is such that not many multiple units are built for owner occupation and few of them are freehold. Zoning by-laws for detached houses often require excessively elaborate infrastructure, large lots, and road allowances. Property taxation on detached houses is often insufficient to cover the municipal costs which they incur, and the imputed income from owner-occupied houses is not taxed as income. Hence, the demand continues for owner-occupied detached houses. This has raised land and construction costs. From the social policy point of view, the rising cost of shelter is bad. From the environmental point of view, it may seem beneficial if it encourages more economic uses of land and natural resources. However, this is not entirely the case. The developer looks beyond municipal boundaries for cheaper land and lower standards of servicing in rural municipalities, where he can then construct detached houses at lower costs to satisfy the demand which he knows exists for any sort of freehold detached house.

Certain construction standards, the standard of insulation, the standard of infrastructure, and the use of raw materials, which have implications for energy use, air quality, and waste heat, have a major effect on the environment. The average detached house in Canada built before 1975 (according to a publication of the Housing and Urban Development Association of Canada, 1976) needs 3,455 L of oil or 25,000 kwh of electricity per annum to heat it. The new standards of insulation introduced in 1975 reduce these amounts by 18 per cent. In 1975, domestic and commercial sources emitted 100 Mt of carbon dioxide into the atmosphere. The publication states that fuel consumption could be reduced by 50 per cent for the expenditure of an extra $1,000 in insulation per dwelling, and that carbon dioxide emissions and waste heat could be halved.

The quadrupling of the annual rate of dwelling construction in the last 30 years has increased demand for forest products, sand, gravel, and cement. Sand and gravel, to be trucked economically, must be quarried locally, and such exploitation competes with agriculture, recreation, and housing in the urban fringe. Most provinces have legislation to enforce the reclamation of worked-out pits which previously had been left derelict. However, noise and dust from working pits create a nuisance which provincial regulations are often unable to abate.

Residential uses typically occupy about 60 per cent of the developed land in a community. Thus, good urban design at any density can show significant environmental advantages in terms of air quality through reduced automobile travel, conservation of open space, preservation of important wildlife or vegetation habitats, and reductions in noise, runoff, soil erosion, and water pollution. Although proper planning will contribute, it is well-planned higher-density developments that show the greatest environmental advantages in reduced air and water pollution, although the emissions are concentrated in a smaller area. Proper planning is essential if noise levels are to be reduced, and privacy maintained in high-density developments. An aspect of high-density living that needs examination is the demand it creates for secondary residences and outdoor recreation.

Public Attitudes to Land-Related Matters

"In terms of public policy, land is being treated as a public good, rather than as a purely private good. The total freedom of private property rights, with all their associated side effects, seems to be a thing of the past. Not only is there zoning, an instrument which is essentially a protection of private rights, but there is a whole array of new devices which limit the freedom of individuals to use land as they wish, without respect to the public good. New development controls are being introduced; regulations are being applied which limit non-resident ownership; at the provincial level, steps are being taken to preserve particularly important pieces of land, sometimes through expropriation, sometimes through open market acquisition, and sometimes through controls such as used by the B.C. Land Commission; the historic concept of rights of access is being brought back into common usage, to provide access to recreation areas and watercourses and other public facilities as long as that access right does not damage the private property across which it is exercised." (Canadian Habitat Secretariat, 1976b).

"It was enlightening, if not humourous, for the Members to hear a continuous flow of 'expert' testimony that future housing policies must be directed to the provision of multiple-unit accommodation, largely on a rental basis, while group after group of ordinary citizens voiced a deep yearning to own a single-family dwelling of their own. It became the practice of the Task Force, at its public meetings with various groups, to seek a show of hands on this question. Invariably the response indicated that at least 80 per cent of those present wanted to own their own home, the same figure incidentally which Professor Edward Michaelson of Toronto obtained in a more scientific sampling ... there does seem a definite 'philosophy of homeownership' among the Canadian people. Whether there should be such a philosophy is another issue. The Task Force, for its part, can understand why the philosophy exists under present circumstances. At the same time, it can wonder whether, in an increasingly mobile society, it would continue to exist, at least to the same degree, should more suitable alternate forms of living be developed within the Canadian marketplace". (Task Force on Housing and Urban Development, 1969).

If 80 per cent of the public want to own their own detached house and only 60 per cent actually do, then 20 per cent or 1.2 million of Canada's 6 million householders have not realized their ambition. Central Mortgage and Housing Corporation with its Assisted Home Ownership program is encouraging home ownership at the lower end of the house-buying income group, while many planners favour rental accommodation at higher densities in order to reduce housing costs, reduce urban sprawl, and to reflect the needs of an increasingly mobile population.

The foregoing quotations illustrate the public attitudes to land and housing. Many affluent members of the public, while aware of environmental matters, are unaware of the effects of their lifestyle on land and natural resources. On the other hand, less wealthy people and residents of depressed areas are far more concerned about employment than environmental and land use regulations which they often perceive as deterrents to economic growth.

Land Use Conflicts

The ability of certain users of urban land to outbid other users, particularly farmers, has focused attention on the amount and type of agricultural land that is being lost. Between 1966 and 1971, 54 per cent, or 46,244 ha, of the land converted to urban use was in agriculture (Gierman, 1977). More significantly, 63 per cent, or 54,649 ha, of the converted land had high capa-

NFB – PHOTOTHEQUE – ONF – Photo by Brian King.

Because many cities began as settlements on high-capability agricultural land, the ongoing expansion of these urban areas often occurs on good farmland. The same soils that produce high-value crops, such as fresh fruits and vegetables, are often lost to urban growth.

bility for agriculture, in other words, it was classified in the top three classes of the CLI evaluation. Compare this with the fact that 45 per cent of the land within 80 km of 19 of Canada's largest cities has high capability for agriculture. Within 80 km of Oshawa, Toronto, Hamilton, St. Catharines, Kitchener, and London, 81 per cent of the land has high capability for agriculture (see Table 12). Of the prime agricultural land converted to urban uses in Canada between 1966 and 1971, 53 per cent was in Ontario, 21 per cent of it around Toronto alone.

Compared with agriculture, the loss of productive forest land was only 12,424 ha, or 14 per cent of the total land area converted, mainly around Toronto. Losses of prime recreation land and waterfowl habitat were small in area, but the loss of ungulate habitat was considerable; 41,687 ha or 48 per cent of the total area converted, mainly around Toronto and Edmonton. Much of the area converted to urban uses had high capability for more than one use, although high capability for a particular use does not necessarily imply that the land was in that use.

The city is a dynamic process of which its buildings and infrastructure are a physical manifestation. The physical structures are constantly being redeveloped, renovated, or converted to uses other than those for which they were designed. Certain locations within the urban area either acquire or lose value as a result of public or private investment or disinvestment. For a number of reasons, sites or neighbourhoods can thus become strategic locations. The installation of the subway in Toronto was a classic example in which land was given superior accessibility by public investment. Its route can be traced by the height of the buildings which cluster around each station.

Rapid redevelopment in cities in specifically favoured locations has led to the inevitable reaction, and the questioning of values and the place of quality of environment in a community's priorities. The problem is to reconcile the need for infrastructure, improvements in business and institutional accommodation, and housing with the distinctive quality of the environment in downtown cores or residential neighbourhoods. The quality, measured in terms of air, noise, light, or architectural merit, may not be high, but it is familiar and has developed over a long time. An indicator of the importance to people of certain urban land is the volume of public reaction to proposals for redevelopment of a particular site or the amount of private investment that has been put into rehabilitation of neighbourhoods. Such actions by a community indicate that there is something valuable about the urban environment in the area that is worth maintaining and enhancing by rehabilitation and well-designed redevelopment. The quality of the urban environment can only be preserved by continual attention and careful redevelopment.

NFB – PHOTOTHEQUE – ONF – Photo by Nichaulas Walter.

Redevelopment can enhance or destroy neighbourhoods. If redevelopment involves a drastic change in land use, the former occupants may be displaced. On the other hand, private investment can help sustain existing uses in neighbourhood areas.

Private investment in residential rehabilitation, or "white-painting", has brought its own set of land use and social conflicts. White-painters favour former working-class residential areas near the urban core. These areas are of special importance for cheap housing for low-income people who cannot afford to operate a car or take public transport to work. These people are frequently displaced to the suburbs or to public housing while middle-income families move in from the suburbs to enjoy the novelty of walking to work, shopping, and cultural activities downtown.

Conflicts in land use that are resolved solely by the free market in land expose the community to the risk of having its environment and quality of life degraded as a result of private land use decisions. It is the rôle of land use planning to take the total welfare of the community and the quality of the natural environment into account. Planning at the municipal and provincial levels is intended to take the community's priorities, whether they be decent housing, clean air, preservation of good farmland, good roads, or an attractive downtown, and assess how proposed development proposals will contribute to or detract from these priorities.

Conclusion

In this discussion of land and the factors that make some land of special importance for urban uses, the intention has been to show that land is not a homogeneous commodity but a resource whose qualities are diverse. Our predecessors recognized this as they settled the country that was to become Canada. They were looking for fish, furs, lumber, farmland, trade routes, water power, and mineral deposits. They founded settlements in locations that were accessible to some or all of these resources. The siting of a settlement on a chosen location was determined by physical factors such as stable soil, a dry site, and availability of water.

The growth of a settlement has not always been the result of the same influences that caused its foundation. As the economic system changed from one of exploitation of primary resources to one of manufacturing industry and provision of services, the economic base of Canada's towns and cities has changed. Concomitant with this economic change, Canada has become an urban country, and since 1921 more people have lived in towns than in the country. Since 1945, the growth of tertiary industry and the baby boom of 1945 to 1960 have combined to create an unprecedented demand for land on which to build offices, stores, institutions, government buildings, and housing. The demand has not been distributed uniformly across the country, but has been concentrated in major cities, especially in the Windsor–Québec axis and around Vancouver.

NFB – PHOTOTHEQUE – ONF – Photo by Brian King.

The creation and maintenance of pleasant, healthy, and viable living environments is a challenge involving every Canadian.

The cities that are expanding are located in areas in which land is already being used relatively intensively for other purposes, especially agriculture, transport, or recreation. Three problems arise; one is the loss of production from land that is of high capability for a use other than urban. The second is an environmental matter; cities need water and fresh air and to obtain these, aquifers have to be protected from indiscriminate development, as do the paths of natural air movements and areas of woodland that are a source of oxygen. Thirdly, there are some lands that are unsuited to urban development on account of their exposure to flooding, their instability, or their steepness. Complementary to these constraints on urban expansion is the preservation and enhancement of the quality of the environment within existing cities where pressures for redevelopment are intense.

In view of the fact that less than two per cent of Canada's land area is covered by urban development, it is safe to say that this country will not run out of developable land in the foreseeable future. However, the more immediate issue that arises is that of the values of society. If cities are to be safe, healthy, and pleasant places in which to live, careful thought must be given to land use as well as urban design. The rôle of the aquifer, the forest, the path of the air flow, and the regime of the flood plain must be considered. On the other hand, the city is an economic unit and its form and direction of expansion influence the cost of living and conducting business there, especially at a time of increasing energy costs. Also, the benefits brought to industry and residents of a particular city may be costs to the activities displaced and to the country as a whole, the principal bearer of these costs being agriculture.

In one sense, special urban land can include specific sectors of cities. Downtown cores and central business districts, with their high daytime and low nighttime populations, present land use, energy, transportation, environmental, social, and planning problems. Here, space is at a premium for all uses. But there are concerns about the suburbs too. Demand for single-family homes was particularly strong in the 1950s, and early suburbs, while extensive in their use of land, provided housing at more moderate prices. The hidden price was the cost of sprawl . . . roads for commuter traffic, local shopping centres for suburban customers, and other uses. Industry took advantage of cheaper land and the nearby labour force and also located in the suburbs. Houses, roads, shopping centres, and industries all required land and all contributed to the expanding suburbs.

Similarly, the rural-urban fringe, a transition zone between city and country, could be termed special. The fringe is often characterized by an unplanned mixture of land uses, landscapes, and lifestyles. An increase in prices paid for farmland is a sign of anticipated urban development. Idle land of high capability for other uses awaits the next wave of urban expansion. Changes happen quickly; rural municipalities are often ill-equipped to handle land use problems; meanwhile, the dynamic fringe moves outward as the city continues to incorporate more land into its sphere of influence. Airports serve the largely urban travellers; rural township dumps receive urban wastes; and quarries and gravel pits grind out construction materials for new suburbs.

In another sense, critical urban areas could be those cities which consume the largest amounts of land. Cities such as Toronto, Montréal, and Edmonton lead urban areas in terms of the quantity of rural land converted to urban uses. Or perhaps of greater concern are the cities that, although using less land, use it less efficiently. For their relative increases in population, Chicoutimi–Jonquière, Thetford Mines, and Brandon have a much higher rate of rural land conversion than do Toronto, Montréal, or Edmonton. The haphazard conversion of land from rural to urban uses, in theory is generally condemned, but often condoned in practice, particularly in areas undergoing intense pressure from urban expansion.

In matters of urban expansion and redevelopment there are choices to be made, depending on the values of the community. It is essential that the public be aware of the environmental, economic, and social factors that are involved in land use decisions.

Acknowledgement

The author would like to acknowledge the suggestions and advice given by David Erskine of Toronto.

Bibliography

Archer, Paula, *et al.* 1977. Recent Trends in the Growth of Canadian Urban Centres. Central Mortgage and Housing Corporation. Ottawa.

Axworthy, Lloyd, and Gillies, James M. 1973. The City: Canada's Prospects Canada's Problems. Butterworth and Co. (Canada) Ltd. Toronto.

Beaubien, Charles, and Tabacnik, Ruth. 1977. People and Agricultural Land. Perceptions 4, Study on Population, Technology and Resources. Science Council of Canada. Ottawa.

Berry, Brian J.L., *et al.* 1974. Land Use, Urban Form and Environmental Quality. Research Report No. 155. Department of Geography, University of Chicago. Chicago.

Bourne, L.S., and Doucet, M.J. 1970. Dimensions of Metropolitan Physical Growth: Land Use Change, Metropolitan Toronto. Research Report No. 38. Centre for Urban and Community Studies, University of Toronto. Toronto.

Bourne, L.S., and MacKinnon, R.D. eds. 1972. Urban Systems Development in Central Canada: Selected Papers. Research Publication No. 9. Department of Geography, University of Toronto. University of Toronto Press. Toronto.

Bryant, G.W.R. 1965. "Land Speculation: Its Effects and Control." Plan Canada. Vol. V, No. 3. Canadian Institute of Planners. Ottawa.

Canada Land Data Systems. 1978. Lands Directorate, Environment Canada. Miscellaneous data.

Canadian Habitat Secretariat. 1976*a*. Human Settlement in Canada. Issued under the authority of the Minister of State for Urban Affairs. Ottawa.

__________. 1976*b*. Where Are We Headed? A Discussion Paper on Human Settlements in Canada. Ottawa.

Central Mortgage and Housing Corporation. 1976. Canadian Housing Statistics 1975. Ottawa.

__________. 1978. Canadian Housing Statistics 1977. Ottawa.

Changnon, Stanley A. Jr. 1974. "A Review of Inadvertent Mesoscale Weather and Climate Modification: An Assessment of Research Needs." Proceedings of 4th Conference on Weather Modification held November 18-21, 1974 in Fort Lauderdale, Florida. American Meteorological Society. Boston.

Chorley, Richard J., and Haggett, Peter. 1967. Socio-Economic Models in Geography. Methuen. London.

Clunie, D. 1976. "Two New Northern Communities." Contact. Vol. 8. Special Issue: New Communities in Canada: Exploring Planned Environments. Journal of Urban and Environmental Affairs. Faculty of Environmental Studies, University of Waterloo. Waterloo.

Coleman, Alice. 1976. Canadian Settlement and Environmental Planning. Urban Prospects. Ministry of State for Urban Affairs and The Macmillan Company of Canada Limited. Ottawa.

Dominion Bureau of Statistics. 1963. Population: Rural and Urban Distribution. Catalogue 92-536. Ottawa.

Dumanski, J., Marshall, I.B., and Huffman, E.C. 1978. Physical Land Characteristics, Land Capability and Land Planning in Ottawa–Hull and Its Region. Edited by R. Wesche and M. Kuglar-Gagnon. University of Ottawa Press. Ottawa.

Economic Council of Canada. 1977. Living Together: A Study of Regional Disparities. Minister of Supply and Services Canada. Ottawa.

Environment Canada. 1972. Soil Capability Classification for Agriculture. The Canada Land Inventory Report No. 2. Lands Directorate, Environment Canada. Ottawa.

__________. 1975. Fourth-Quarter Century Trends in Canada. Ottawa.

__________. 1978. Cutting our Flood Losses. Inland Waters Directorate. Ottawa.

Forbes, J. 1964. "Mapping Accessibility". Scottish Geographical Magazine. Vol. 80. Royal Scottish Geographical Society. Edinburgh.

Gertler, L.O., and Krowley, R.W. 1977. Changing Canadian Cities: The Next Twenty-Five Years. McClelland and Stewart. Toronto.

Gibson, Edward M. 1976. The Urbanization of the Strait of Georgia Region. Geographical Paper No. 57. Lands Directorate, Environment Canada. Ottawa.

Gierman, David M. 1977. Rural to Urban Land Conversion. Occasional Paper No. 16. Lands Directorate, Fisheries and Environment Canada. Ottawa.

Gottmann, Jean, and Harper, Robert A. eds. 1976. Metropolis on the Move: Geographers Look at Urban Sprawl. John Wiley & Sons, Inc. New York.

Housing and Urban Development Association of Canada. 1976. A Builders' Guide to Energy Conservation. Toronto.

Jackson, C.I. ed. 1975. Canadian Settlements–Perspectives. Ministry of State for Urban Affairs and The Macmillan Company of Canada Limited. Ottawa.

Krueger, Ralph R., and Bryfogle, R. Charles. eds. 1971. Urban Problems: A Canadian Reader. Holt, Rinehart and Winston of Canada, Limited. Toronto.

Lea, N.D. & Associates Ltd. 1975. Land Use Consumption by Urban Passenger Transportation. Report prepared for the Ministry of State for Urban Affairs. Ottawa. (unpublished).

LePage, A.E. (Ontario) Ltd. 1976. Real Estate Market Surveys. Toronto.

Li, Shiu-Yeu. 1976. "Labour Force Statistics and a Functional Classification of Canadian Cities." Canadian Urban Trends. National Perspective Volume 1. Edited by D. Michael Ray. Ministry of State for Urban Affairs. Copp Clark Limited. Toronto.

Lithwick, N.H. 1970. Urban Canada: Problems and Prospects. Central Mortgage and Housing Corporation. Ottawa.

Lyons, Walter A. 1975. "Turbulent Diffusion and Pollutant Transport in Shoreline Environments." Lectures on Air Pollution and Environmental Impact Analyses. A Workshop on Meteorology and Environmental Assessment held September 29–October 3, 1975 in Boston. Boston.

Mandelker, Daniel R. 1975. "Critical Area Controls: A New Dimension in American Land Development Regulation." Journal of the American Institute of Planners. Vol. 41, No. 1. January 1975. Washington, D.C.

Martin, Larry R.G. 1974. Problems and Policies Associated with High Land Costs on the Urban Fringe. Draft paper prepared for a conference on The Management of Land for Urban Development sponsored by the Canadian Council on Urban and Regional Research held April 5-6, 1974. Ottawa.

__________. 1975. Land Use Dynamics on the Toronto Urban Fringe. Map Folio No. 3. Lands Directorate, Environment Canada. Ottawa.

Mayer, Harold M. 1969. The Spatial Expression of Urban Growth. Resource Paper No. 7. Commission on College Geography. American Association of Geographers. Washington, D.C.

McCann, L.D. 1975. Neighbourhoods in Transition. Occasional Paper No. 2. Studies in Geography. Department of Geography, University of Alberta. Edmonton.

Multiple Listing Service. 1977. Miscellaneous data.

Munn, R.E., Hirt, M.S., and Findlay, B.F. 1972. "The Application of Meteorology to Land-use Planning in Southwestern Ontario." International Geography. Edited by W.P. Adams and F.M. Helleiner. University of Toronto Press. Toronto.

Neimanis, V.P. 1979. Canada's Cities and Their Surrounding Land Resource. Canada Land Inventory Report No. 15. Lands Directorate, Environment Canada. Ottawa.

Oke, T.R. 1977. "The Significance of the Atmosphere in Planning Human Settlements." Ecological (Biophysical) Land Classification in Urban Areas. Ecological Land Classification Series No. 3. Edited by E.B. Wiken and G.R. Ironside. Ottawa.

Ray, D. Michael, *et al.* eds. 1976. Canadian Urban Trends. National Perspective Volume 1. Ministry of State for Urban Affairs. Copp Clark Limited. Toronto.

Real Estate Research Corporation. 1974. The Costs of Sprawl. Prepared for the Council on Environmental Quality, Department of Housing and Urban Development, and the Environmental Protection Agency. Washington, D.C.

Reilly, William K. ed. 1973. The Use of Land: A Citizens' Policy Guide to Urban Growth. A Task Force Report sponsored by The Rockefeller Brothers Fund. Thomas Y. Crowell Company. New York.

Russwurm, Lorne H. 1974. The Urban Fringe in Canada: Problems, Research Needs, Policy Implications. Discussion Paper B. 74.4. Ministry of State for Urban Affairs. Ottawa.

Sargent, Frederic O. 1976. Rural Environmental Planning. University of Vermont. Vervana, Vermont.

Schoenauer, N. 1976. "Fermont: A New Version of the Company Town." Contact. Vol. 8. Special Issue: New Communities in Canada: Exploring Plannel Environments. Journal of Urban and Environmental Affairs. Faculty of Environmental Studies, University of Waterloo. Waterloo.

Simmons, James, and Simmons, Robert. 1969. Urban Canada. The Copp Clark Publishing Company. Toronto.

Spurr, Peter. 1976. Land and Urban Development: A Preliminary Study. James Lorimer & Company. Toronto.

Statistics Canada. 1972. Advance Bulletin: Population of Census Divisions. Catalogue 92-753. Ottawa.

―――――. 1974. Perspective Canada. Ottawa.

―――――. 1977a. Population: Geographic Distributions: Federal Electoral Districts. Catalogue 92-801. Ottawa.

―――――. 1977b. Perspective Canada II. Minister of Supply and Services Canada. Ottawa.

―――――. 1977c. Population: Geographic Distributions: Municipalities, Census Metropolitan Areas and Census Agglomerations. Catalogue 92-806. Ottawa.

―――――. 1977d. The Labour Force. Catalogue 71-001. Ottawa.

―――――. 1977e. Family Incomes. Catalogue 13-208. Ottawa.

Stone, Leroy O. 1976. Urban Development in Canada: An Introduction to the Demographic Aspects. Dominion Bureau of Statistics. Queen's Printer. Ottawa.

Task Force on Housing and Urban Development. 1969. Report of the Task Force on Housing and Urban Development. Chairman, P. Hellyer. Queen's Printer. Ottawa.

Urquhart, M.C., and Buckley, K.A.H. eds. 1965. Historical Statistics of Canada. Macmillan Company of Canada Limited. Toronto.

Ward, Barbara. 1976. The Home of Man. McClelland and Stewart Limited. Toronto.

Wingo, L. Jr. 1961. Transportation and Urban Land. Washington, D.C.

Yeates, Maurice. 1975. Main Street: Windsor to Quebec City. Macmillan Company of Canada Limited in association with the Ministry of State for Urban Affairs and Information Canada. Toronto and Ottawa.

Appendix I

Note on CLI Classification of Land Capability for Agriculture

Land considered both suitable for urban development and of low value for agriculture is defined as land in CLI agriculture classes 4, 5, 6, and 7, free of limitations of inundation, excess water, stoniness, depth to bedrock, and steepness. The definitions of the classes follow. (Environment Canada, 1972). For more details regarding CLI soil capability for agriculture, see the Agriculture chapter.

Classes

Class 4. Soils in this class have severe limitations that restrict the range of crops or require special conservation practices or both.

Soils in class 4 have such limitations that they are only suitable for a few crops, or the yield for a range of crops is low, or the risk of crop failure is high. The limitations may seriously affect such farm practices as the timing and ease of tillage, planting, and harvesting, and the application and maintenance of conservation practices. These soils are low to medium in productivity for a narrow range of crops, but may have higher productivity for a specially adapted crop.

The limitations include the adverse effects of a combination of two or more of those described in classes 2 and 3 or one of the following: moderately-severe climate; very low water-holding capacity; low fertility difficult or unfeasible to correct; strong slopes; severe past erosion; very intractable mass of soil or extremely slow permeability; frequent overflow with severe effects on crops; severe salinity causing some crop failures; extreme stoniness requiring considerable clearing to permit annual cultivation; very restricted rooting zone, but more than 30 cm of soil over bedrock or an impermeable layer.

Class 5. Soils in this class have very severe limitations that restrict their capability for the production of perennial forage crops, and improvement practices are feasible.

Soils in class 5 have such serious soil, climatic, or other limitations that they are not capable of use for sustained production of annual field crops. However, they may be improved by the use of farm machinery for the production of native or some species of perennial forage plants. Feasible improvement practices include clearing of bush, cultivation, seeding, fertilizing, and water control.

The limitations in class 5 include the adverse effects of one or more of the following: severe climate; low water-holding capacity; severe past erosion; steep slopes; very poor drainage; very frequent overflow; severe salinity permitting only salt-tolerant forage crops to grow; and stoniness or shallowness to bedrock that make annual cultivation impractical.

Class 6. Soils in this class are capable only of producing perennial forage crops, and improvement practices are not feasible.

Soils in class 6 have some natural sustained-grazing capacity for farm animals, but have such serious soil, climatic, or other limitations as to make impractical the application of improvement practices that can be carried out in class 5. Soils may be categorized in this class either because their physical nature prevents improvement through the use of farm machinery, or because they are not responsive to improvement practices, or because of a short grazing season, or because stock watering facilities are inadequate. Such improvement as may be effected by seeding and fertilizing, either by hand or by aerial methods, shall not change the classification of these soil areas.

The limitations in class 6 include the adverse effects of one or more of the following: very severe climate; very low water-holding capacity; very steep slopes; very severely eroded land with gullies too numerous and too deep for working with machinery; severely saline land producing only edible, salt-tolerant, native plants; very frequent overflow allowing less than ten weeks effective grazing per annum; water on the surface of the soil for most of the year; and stoniness or shallowness to bedrock that makes any cultivation impractical.

Class 7. Soils in this class have no capability for arable culture or permanent pasture.

The soils or lands in class 7 have limitations so severe that they are not capable of use for arable culture or permanent pasture. All classified areas (except organic soils) not included in classes 1 to 6 shall be placed in this class. Bodies of water too small to delineate on the map are included in this class.

Class 7 soils may, or may not, have a high capability for trees, native fruits, wildife, and recreation. Hence, no inference can be made as to the capability of the soils and land types in this class beyond the scope of their capability for agriculture.

Subclasses

The limitations mentioned in each class are expressed as subclasses. For the purpose of defining developable land the following subclasses were excluded:

Inundation by streams or lakes (I): This subclass includes soils subjected to inundation that causes crop damage or restricts agricultural use.

Excess water (W): Subclass W is made up of soils where excess water, other than that brought about by inundation, is a limitation to their use for agriculture. Excess water may result from inadequate soil drainage, a high water table, seepage, or runoff from surrounding areas.

Stoniness (P): This subclass is made up of soils sufficiently stony to significantly hinder tillage, planting, and harvesting operations. Stony soils are usually less productive than comparable non-stony soils. Stoniness is only excluded from classes 6 and 7.

Consolidated bedrock (R): This subclass includes soils where the presence of bedrock near the surface restricts their agricultural use. Consolidated bedrock at depth greater than one m from the surface is not considered as a limitation, except on irrigated lands where a greater depth of soil is desirable.

Topography (T): This subclass is made up of soils where topography is a limitation. Both the per cent of slope and the pattern or frequency of slopes in different directions are important factors in increasing the cost of farming over that of smooth land, in decreasing the uniformity of growth and maturity of crops, and in increasing the hazard of water erosion.

Bedrock and Topography are excluded from classes 5, 6, and 7 in which soils are either shallower than one m or slopes are steeper than 15 per cent.

NFB – PHOTOTHEQUE – ONF – Photo by Normand Grégoire.

NFB – PHOTOTHEQUE – ONF – Photo by Normand Grégoire.

Energy Development

National Photography Collection.
Public Archives Canada.
C-31794

Contents

	Page
Introduction	213
Physical characteristics	213
Petroleum and natural gas	214
Coal	214
Uranium	217
Hydro-electric energy	218
Economic, environmental and social considerations	218
Exploration and extraction	218
Upgrading	220
Transportation	221
End-use	222
Factors affecting change	222
Political intervention	222
Technological innovations	223
Present land use issues	223
Oil sands development	223
James Bay hydro-electric project	224
Renewable energy	226
Solar	226
Wind	227
Biomass	228
Tidal and wave	229
Geothermal	230
The future	230
Acknowledgements	230
Bibliography	231

Tables

		Page
1.	Summary of oil and natural gas resources in Canada	214
2.	Estimates of coal resources in Canada	217
3.	Estimates of recoverable uranium resources in Canada,	217
4.	Oil pipelines, 1976	222
5.	Natural gas pipelines, 1976	222
6.	Electrical transmission lines, 1976	223
7.	Balance of trade in energy commodities	223
8.	James Bay hydro-electric project	225

Figures

		Page
1.	Sources of primary energy consumption, 1958, 1968, 1976	213
2.	Energy consumption by region, 1958, 1968 and 1976	214
3.	Total coal production by mining method	220
4.	Coal production and consumption, 1940-1975	220
5.	Uranium production in Canada, 1956-1977	220
6.	Solar energy conversion processes	226
7.	Solar heating system	227

Maps

		Page
1.	Petroleum and natural gas	215
2.	Coal	216
3.	Uranium	217
4.	Major power generating stations and electric transmission systems	219
5.	Distribution of annual average radiation	227
6.	Distribution of wind energy	228
7.	Zones of "Surplus" forest biomass capacity for a methanol conversion operation	229

ENERGY DEVELOPMENT

Introduction

Canada's energy needs presently are met by a variety of sources including coal, oil, natural gas, uranium, and electricity. The use of these energy sources reflects a development pattern influenced by such factors as supply and demand considerations, available technological innovations, level of economic activity, and government policy and programs. Since Confederation, with the emergence of Canada as an industrial nation, both the growth rate of energy consumption and the composition of the energy mix have changed considerably. Although the 100-year historical energy consumption growth rate averaged 3.5 per cent per year, the rapid industrial development of the 1960s and early 1970s has witnessed the jump of this growth rate to 5.4 per cent (Steward, 1978). However, the recent economic doldrums, precipitated in part by the supply and price uncertainties of the foreign energy sources, have resulted in a temporary slowdown of the consumption growth rate. Nevertheless, Canada, when considered in the global perspective, still remains as one of the highest per capita consumers of energy. Although not an enviable position for Canadians, the intensive use of energy in Canada may be partially explained by: the heating requirements created by a northern climate, the transportation demands necessary to connect the 9,976,139 km² of the country's geographically separated regions, and the energy-intensive activities necessary for the forest products, mining, smelting, and chemical industries (see Figures 1 and 2). In addition, the energy supply industry itself is a major consumer since transformation of the raw fuel is necessary to upgrade the energy source to a usable product. Also, the production regions of domestic energy sources are often geographically separate from the primary consuming areas and have required the development of transport modes. Examples include the shipping of Alberta crude oil and natural gas to Ontario's industries, and the transmission networks which carry hydro-electricity to the end-user. In 1976, Canada consumed 6,440 trillion j of primary energy. Ontario followed by Québec and Alberta were the largest energy consumers (see Figures 1 and 2) and their demands were met by a variety of domestic and foreign sources.

Historically, the evolution of energy resources shifted from animal power to wood to coal to oil and to natural gas. Before 1870, direct water power, wind, and the combustion of wood were the primary sources of supply and were a key location determinant for towns, factories, and mills. The development of the generator in 1870 ushered in the electricity era, although distribution was limited by inadequate transmission. By 1897 the invention of the electric transformer enabled electricity to be transmitted and this was followed by a rapid development of hydro-electricity which was available in all provinces except Saskatchewan by 1900. Very quickly, industries such as pulp and paper and mineral producers accounted for the greatest share of the installed generating capacity. Coal, which has been mined in Cape Breton Island for over 300 years, displaced wood as the primary source for heating by 1900. Initially used only for heating, coal was later consumed in the production of steam, and powered the engines of the nation's railways as well as the power plants of industry until the 1950s. The ascendancy of petroleum in the 1950s was a world-wide phenomenon. Primarily based on the new technology in the automated burner market for residential and commercial heating, the cleaner burning oil fuel quickly replaced coal (Department of Energy, Mines and Resources, 1973a). In the industrial field, oil was used as a substitute for coal, and in the transportation field, the private automobile, commercial trucking and the dieselization of the railways, were all fed by domestic and foreign crude oil and oil products. Prior to the 1960s, natural gas was used only locally in Alberta where it was produced. Oftentimes, natural gas was burned off as a residual when it appeared with crude oil. With the completion of the Trans-Canada pipeline in 1958, and the development of an export-oriented market to the United States, natural gas has tripled its output during the past 15 years. Uranium, the thermal fuel used for the nuclear production of electricity, particularly in Ontario, has been developed to meet the electricity demands which apparently can no longer be satisfied by conventional thermal or hydro-electric sources.

The key link between the production of oil, gas, coal, uranium, and electricity to meet the needs of the commercial, residential, industrial, and transportation users is land. In the most general sense, Canada's land surface covers the majority of oil, natural gas, coal, and uranium resources, and underlies the fast-flowing rivers which define the hydraulic potential. At all stages of development including exploration, extraction, processing, transmission, and end-use, both the quality and the quantity of land are affected. Some activities such as surface coal mining and the creation of hydro-electric reservoirs are incompatible with other land uses. Other activities, for example, oil and gas wells, pipelines, and transmission lines are reasonably compatible with other uses, particularly agriculture in the western Prairie Region.

NFB – PHOTOTHEQUE – ONF.

The most visible impact of pipelines on the surrounding landscape occurs during construction. In forested areas, the right-of-way must be clear-cut prior to the installation of the pipe. This picture shows the laying of pipe along the Alberta foothills.

The purpose of this sector is to define Canada's special resource lands for energy development. Firstly, the resource estimates for the traditional non-renewable energy fuels of oil, natural gas, coal, and uranium are identified. These represent the regions within which past and/or present production is located, and, given the continued preference for the existing energy mix, will probably represent the locations of the near future production focal points. Secondly, the physical productivity of the energy resource base is assessed by describing the areas under intensive exploration, extraction, production, or transportation. Electricity generation is included with the fossil fuels as a primary energy source. Consumption patterns are also identified. In addition, some of the factors affecting change of supply and demand for both the sources of energy and the end-user are discussed in terms of political decisions, energy pricing, technology, and quality of life considerations. These factors may directly or indirectly relate to land. In the longer term, the application of renewable energy technologies and probable land impacts are assessed for solar, wind, biomass, tidal, and geothermal energy.

Physical Characteristics

For fossil fuels, the geologic history specifically relating to the formation of sedimentary basins defines the broadest parameters for identifying oil, natural gas, and coal. Compared to physiographic regions, the sedimen-

FIGURE 1.

Sources of primary energy consumption, 1958, 1968 and 1976

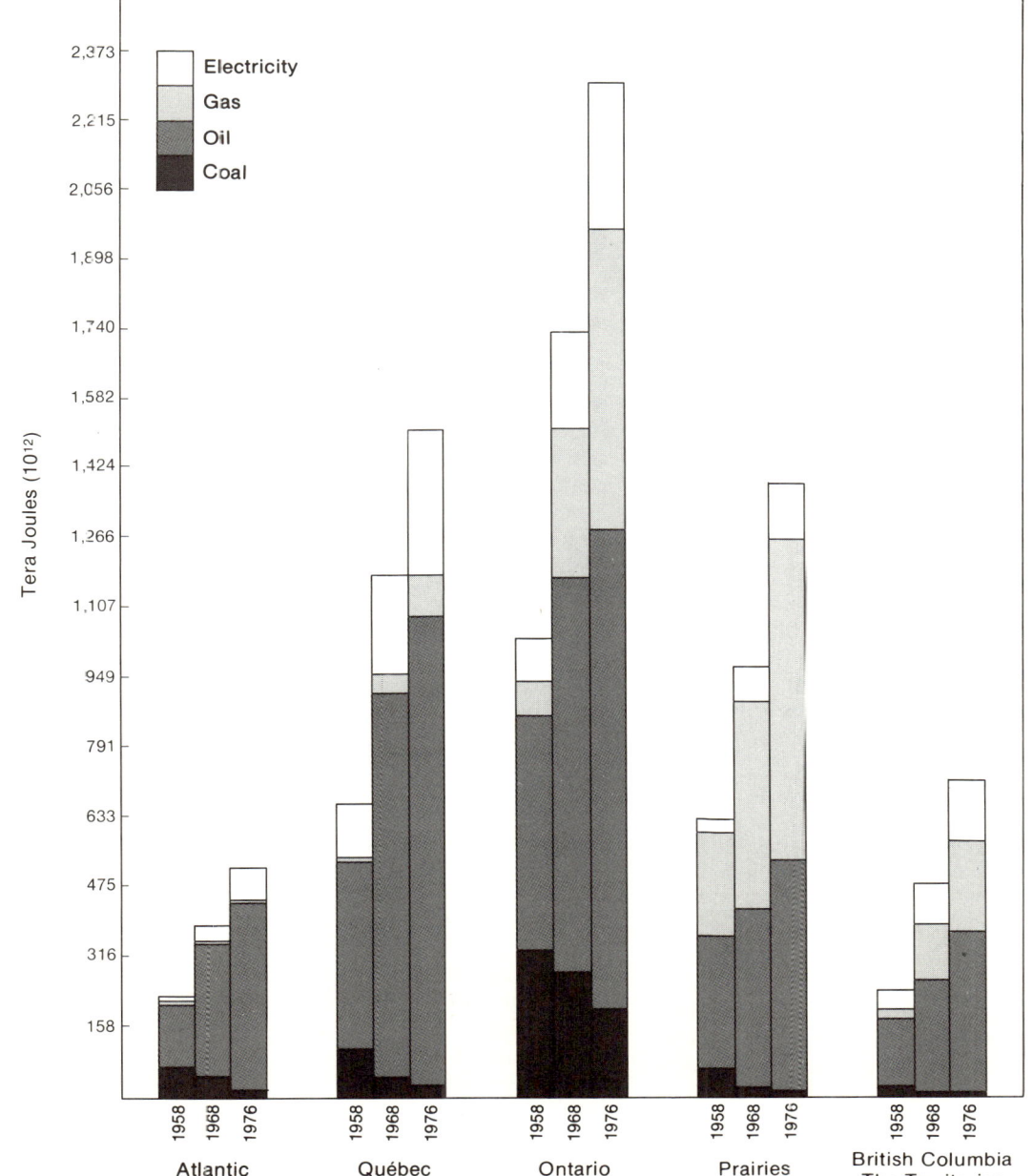

Sources: Statistics Canada. 1972. Detailed Energy Supply and Demand in Canada 1958-1969. Catalogue 57-505.
―――. 1978. Detailed Energy Supply and Demand in Canada 1976. Catalogue 57-507.

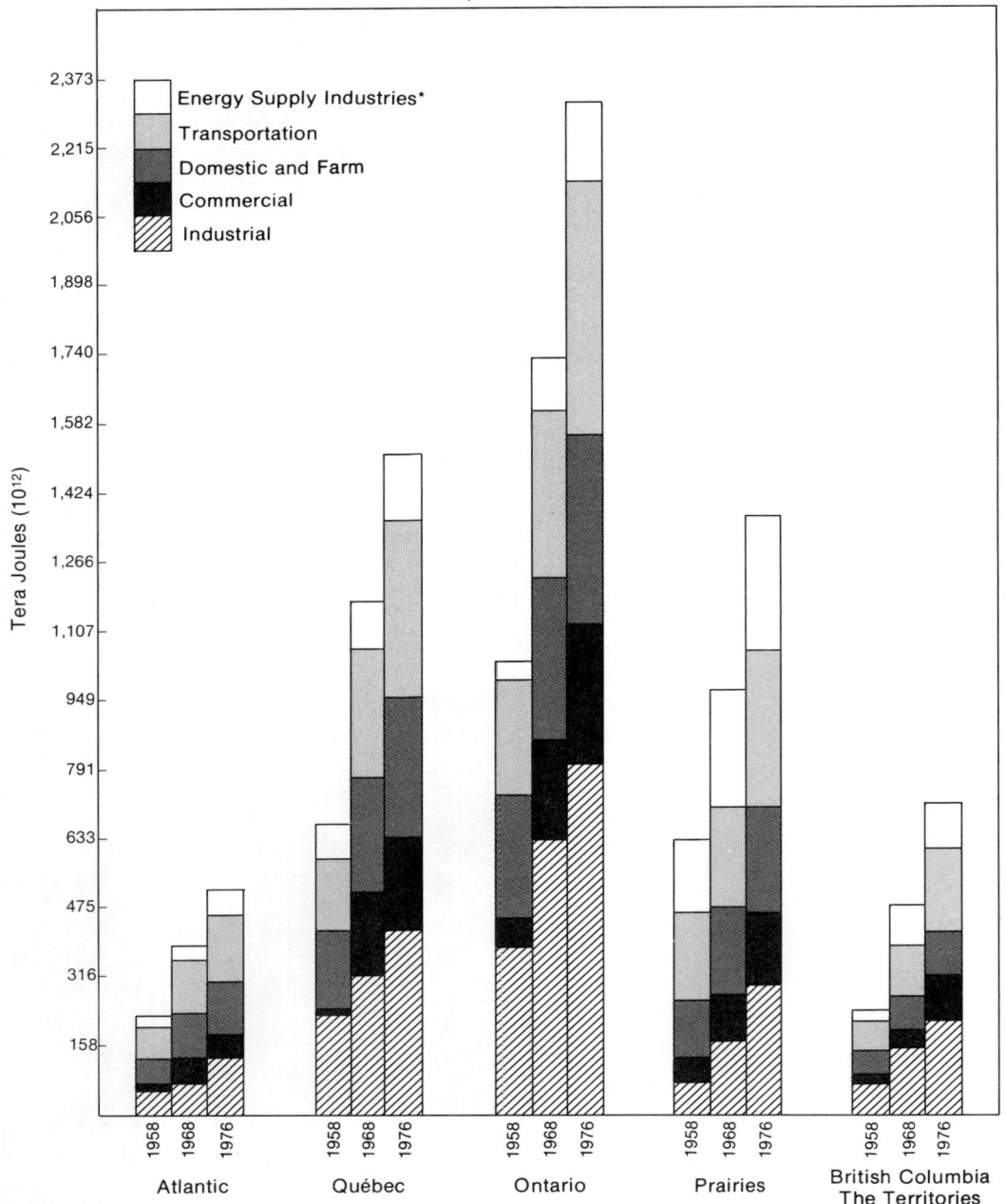

FIGURE 2.
Energy consumption by region,
1958, 1968 and 1976

*includes losses and adjustments.
Source: Statistics Canada. 1972. Detailed Energy Supply and Demand in Canada 1958-1969. Catalogue 57-505.
_____. 1978. Detailed Energy Supply and Demand in Canada 1976. Catalogue 57-507.

TABLE 1.
Summary of oil and natural gas resources in Canada, 1975

Region	High Probability 90 per cent	Medium Probability 50 per cent	Low Probability 10 per cent
		Oil Resources (billions of m³)	
East			
Atlantic Shelf South	.19	.30	.48
Labrador-East Newfoundland Shelf	.27	.41	.72
St. Lawrence Lowlands	.006	.01	.03
North-Central			
Northern Stable Platform Basins	.002	.10	.51
Mainland Territories	.05	.08	.16
Mackenzie Delta-Beaufort Sea	.68	1.10	1.91
Sverdrup Basin	.17	.32	.64
Arctic Fold Belts	.08	.29	.68
West			
Western Canada	1.7	1.86	2.15
Accessible Region of Canada	3.98	4.77	6.84
		Gas Resources (trillions of m³)	
East			
Atlantic Shelf South	.24	.37	.57
Labrador-East Newfoundland Shelf	.51	.76	1.27
St. Lawrence Lowlands	.02	.04	.09
North-Central			
Northern Stable Platform Basins	.01	.07	.34
Mainland Territories	.17	.27	.80
Mackenzie Delta-Beaufort Sea	1.10	1.7	2.80
Sverdrup Basin	.59	1.1	2.26
Arctic Fold Belts	.08	.31	.74
West			
Western Canada	2.52	2.75	3.03
Accessible Region of Canada	6.48	6.42	10.70

Source: Department of Energy, Mines and Resources, 1978d. Oil and Natural Gas Industries in Canada 1978.

Canada are found in rocks ranging in age from the beginning of the Devonian period through to the end of the Tertiary period. Older and more plentiful than oil and natural gas, coal is made up of the remains of once-living plants which were repeatedly covered by water and debris and eventually built up into layers or seams. Under pressure and high temperatures, some of the volatile gases and water were driven off, leaving a compacted mineral fuel composed primarily of carbon. The maturity of coal is related to the degree of this compaction process. Because of the diversity of coal resulting from the compaction process, a standardized classification system was devised in 1946. It ranks coal by measuring heat value, volatile matter, calorific value and the amount of fixed carbon. Anthracite, medium- and low-volatile bituminous, high-volatile bituminous, subbituminous and lignite comprise the various qualities of Canada's coal resource (Map 2).

It appears that the distribution of coal is heavily imbalanced with an estimated 99 per cent occurring under the mountains, hills, and plains of western Canada including British Columbia, Alberta and Saskatchewan (Table 2). Although no estimates have been made for the Northwest Territories or the Yukon Territory, there is every indication that the resources of northern Canada are large and upon further investigation and delineation, will eventually become a significant part of future evaluations (Department of Energy, Mines and Resources, 1977b).

As with oil and gas, the coal resource estimate identifies the known extent of coal-bearing rock, and the "measured", "indicated", and "inferred" terms outline, in decreasing probabilities, the possibility of coal occurrence and the feasibility of exploitation.

Low- and medium-volatile bituminous coal deposits, mainly of Upper Jurassic and Lower Cretaceous age, underlie the Rocky Mountains in northeastern British Columbia and transverse the Alberta boundary. Where folding has been intense, seams are thickened and are of particular interest for mining operations. Several small basins of Tertiary-era lignitic coal, with exceptionally thick seams near the surface, are found in the Tulameen, Princeton, Merritt, and Hat Creek basins of south-central British Columbia. To the north, Telkwa and Bowron River in central British Columbia support similar fields. The Groundhog field in the province's north, not yet well documented, appears to have low-volatile bituminous and anthracitic coals within the Jura-Cretaceous deposits. On Vancouver Island, high-volatile bituminous coal is found in the Upper Cretaceous coal deposits of the Nanaimo and Comox fields. Other smaller deposits have been identified on the Queen Charlotte Islands. By far, the most developed deposits of British Columbia are the low- and medium-volatile bituminous deposits of the Upper Jurassic age found in the Crowsnest field in the southeast, which ex-

tary basin includes the Rocky Mountains and Foothills, the Interior of British Columbia, the Interior Plains, the Innuitian Region, the Arctic Lowlands, the Hudson Bay Lowland, the St. Lawrence Lowlands and the Maritime Plain, a portion of the Atlantic Uplands on Cape Breton Island, and sections of the coastal lowlands on the Island of Newfoundland. Based on a variety of criteria within these regions, estimates of resource and reserve potential have been completed for each of the fossil fuels. Uranium is also identified for its resource and reserve potential. In addition, hydro-electric potential is considered as a primary energy resource.

Petroleum and Natural Gas

The vast expanse of rock within the sedimentary basin bears the complicated hydrocarbon molecules, hydrogen and large molecules of carbon from which petroleum products are derived. Representing millions of years of geologic action, these rocks contain the fossil remains of animals which once swam in the oceans defined by the known boundaries of the sedimentary basin. Estimates of oil and natural gas resources for nine hydrocarbon-bearing regions are given in Table 1 (see inset Map 1). For oil and gas the term resource is defined as:

"all conventional oil and gas accumulations known or inferred to exist..." (Department of Energy, Mines and Resources, 1978d).

and is drawn from the knowledge of actual occurrences and geologic judgement. Given the high, medium, and low levels of probability, the estimated oil resource which includes crude oil and natural gas liquids, varies from four to seven billion m³. Apart from western Canada, the areas with the greatest potential are in the Mackenzie Delta-Beaufort Sea, Labrador-East Newfoundland Shelf, and the Sverdrup Basin. Similarly, the gas resource projections indicate that between 6.5 and 10.7 trillion m³ remain in-place. Western Canada, the Mackenzie Delta-Beaufort Sea, the Sverdrup Basin in the high arctic archipelago, and the Labrador-East Newfoundland Shelf support the highest probability for future development. In addition, estimates for the heavy oil and oil sand deposits of Alberta and Saskatchewan include between 1.6 and 3.0 billion m³ at Lloydminster, 26.2 billion m³ at Cold Lake, and 125 billion m³ in the Athabasca deposit (Department of Energy, Mines and Resources, 1978d).

Although the frontiers and the potential of oil and gas are represented in resource estimates, it is the quantification of reserves which describes the present and near future development pattern. Proven reserves are defined as:

"the estimated quantity of crude oil, natural gas and natural gas liquids which analysis of geological and engineering data demonstrate with reasonable certainty to be recoverable from known oil or gas fields under existing economic conditions and using present day technology..." (Department of Energy, Mines and Resources, 1978d).

In 1976, Canada's proven reserves of recoverable conventional crude oil and natural gas liquids amounted to 1.2 billion m³. More than 85 per cent of these reserves are in Alberta. Proven reserves of marketable natural gas, of which 78 per cent lie in Alberta and 11 per cent in British Columbia, were estimated at 1.6 trillion m³ in 1976.[1]

Coal

Occurrences of coal within sedimentary basins in

---

1. Marketable natural gas is raw gas from which certain hydrocarbon and non-hydrocarbon compounds have been removed or partially removed by processing.

214

MAP 1

NFB – PHOTOTHEQUE – ONF -

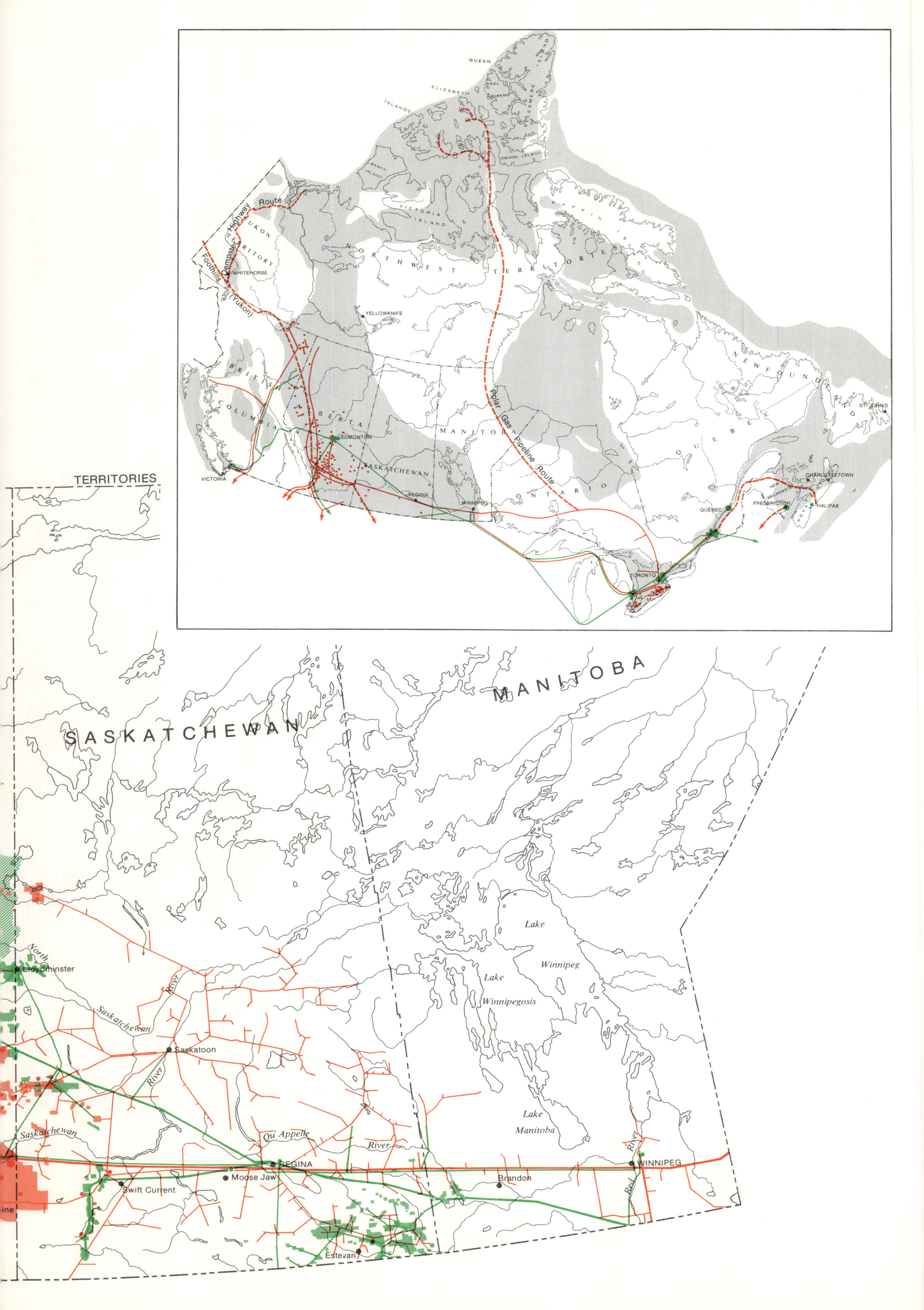

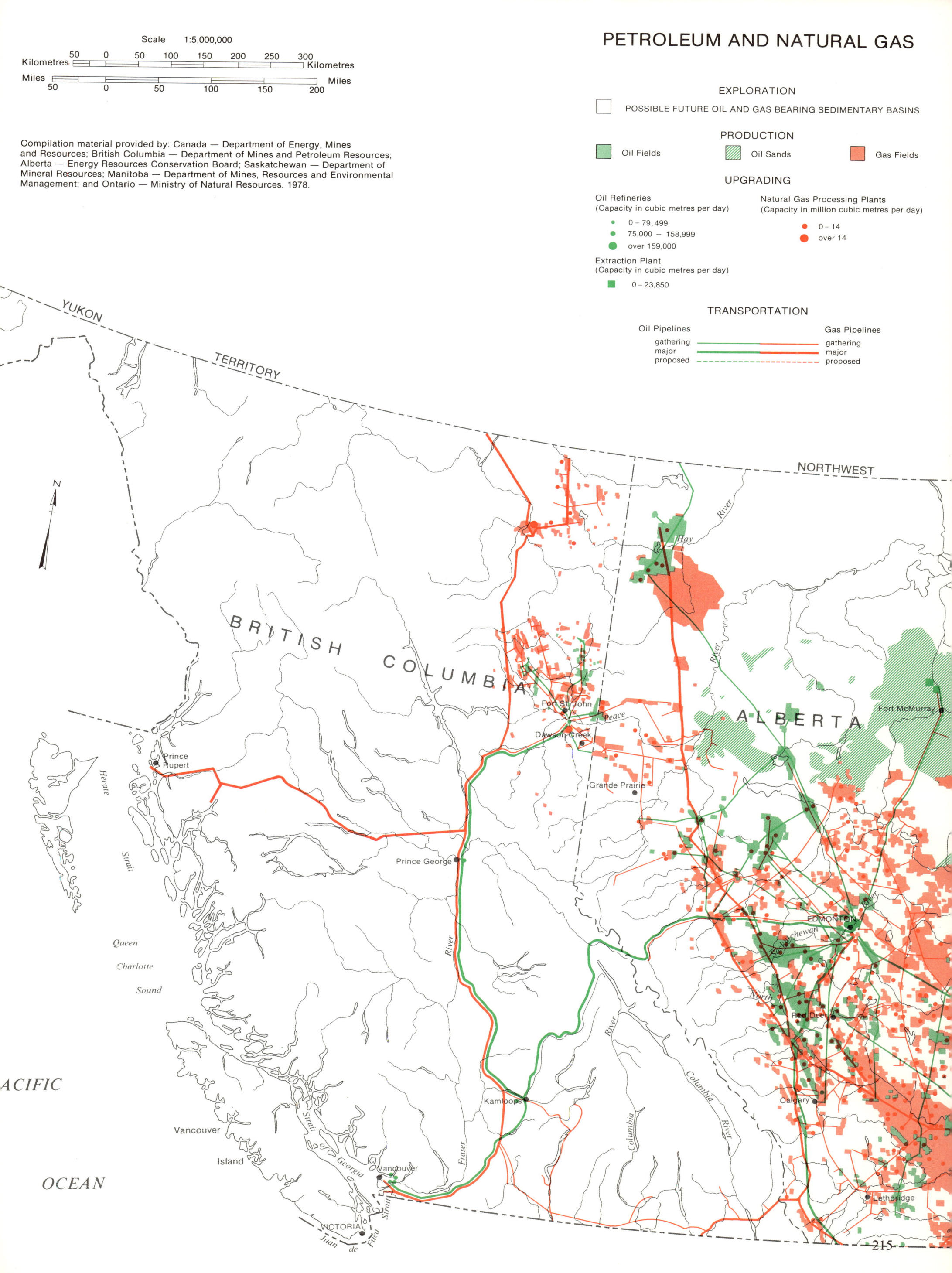

tend from the international boundary northward to the head of the Elk River. This field found within the Kootenay formation, has a length of 161 km, and a maximum width of 24 km, near Fernie and extends into Alberta.

The coal-bearing formations in Alberta are estimated to underlie some 187,200 km². Supporting most of Canada's coal resource delineated to date, the coal deposits of Alberta have been concisely described according to the physiographic regions in which they are located.

"*Mountain Region* for the most part, contains low- and medium-volatile bituminous coals suitable for metallurgical purposes. The Mountain Region covers a total area of about 25,900 km², although coal-bearing strata may be absent, as a result of faulting, from an undetermined portion of this region. Coal is associated with Upper Jurassic/Lower Cretaceous Kootenay formation and the Lower Cretaceous Luscar formation or its equivalents. Where strata are generally undisturbed, seams may be up to 13.8 m thick.

Foothills Region contains high-volatile bituminous coals, mainly usable as high grade thermal coals. The Foothills Region, which is generally bounded by about the 1,219-m contour in the east and the 1,524 to 1,829-m contour in the west, contains most of the coal-bearing Upper Cretaceous Belly River, St. Mary River and Brazeau formations, and some coal in the Upper Cretaceous/Tertiary Edmonton and Paskapoo formations. Overall, this region contains some 28,490 km² of land underlain by coal-bearing strata. In the relatively undisturbed areas, single coal seams are up to 6 m thick.

As a result of extensive thrust-faulting and folding during the Laramide orogeny, most coal-bearing strata in the Mountain and Foothills regions lie in complex tectonic environments. There is extensive repetition and much local thickening or thinning of strata, and individual coal seams are often steeply dipping.

Plains Region contains subbituminous coals suitable for heating, power plant fuel and coal conversion processes that do not necessarily require higher grade coals. Approximately 82 per cent of the total area underlain by coal-bearing strata in Alberta, some 248,640 km², lies within the Plains Region, which extends southwards from the Lesser Slave Lake and is bounded in the west by the tectonically disturbed eastern slopes of the Rocky Mountains. In the Plains Region, coal occurs in massive, laterally persistent zones associated with the Upper Cretaceous, Oldman and Foremost formations (which make up the Belly River Group) and Horseshoe Canyon formation (which is separated from the Belly River Group by the marine shales of the Bearpaw formation), and with the Upper Cretaceous/Tertiary Paskapoo formation. Northwest of Edmonton, the Horseshoe Canyon formation merges into the undifferentiated Wapiti Group" (Dames and Moore, 1977).

Seams of Paleocene lignitic coal comprise Saskatchewan's potential and are confined to mineable deposits in four major basins: Estevan, Willow Bunch, Wood Mountain, and Cypress. Within the Ravenscrag formation, the lignitic coals of the Tertiary and Lower Cretaceous era are located within a 10,000-km² area near the international boundary. In addition, there is a small deposit of lignite, with a high ash content, near Lac La Ronge. Also, thin seams of lignitic coal extend from southeastern Saskatchewan into Manitoba, in the Turtle Mountain area.

Ontario's only known coal, a thin Lower Cretaceous era rock called the Mattagami formation, underlies the lower Moose River Basin in the Hudson Bay Lowland of northern Ontario. This Onakawana coal field is a high moisture lignitic coal with a delineated extent of approximately 39 km².

The coals of the Atlantic Region are of Pennsylvanian age, and consist of bituminous coals. Approximately 25 per cent of New Brunswick is underlain by coal-bearing strata. Most of the seams are too thin to be considered for commercial production. However, the Grand Lake coal field in the Minto-Chapman area of central New Brunswick, covering 414 km², has been in production since the 17th century. Other seams which have been used for commercial output include the Beersville and Dunsinane areas. In total, there are ten known coal fields in Nova Scotia. The Sydney coal field on the east coast of Cape Breton Island extends out beneath the Atlantic Ocean. Its submarine boundaries are not yet delineated. Other smaller fields of Cape Breton Island occur on the western portion (in St. Rose-Chimney, Inverness, Mabou, and Port Hood) and in the southern section, (in Richmond County and Loch Lomond). On the mainland, deposits have been found in Pictou and Cumberland counties and in Colchester

TABLE 2.
Estimates of coal resources in Canada, 1976

Province and area	Resources of immediate interest			Resources of future interest		
	Measured	Indicated	Inferred	Measured	Indicated	Inferred
	(millions of tonnes of coal in place)					
Nova Scotia						
Sydney	216	564	451	-	-	-
Other	88	24	54	-	50	77
New Brunswick						
Minto	18	3	-	-	-	-
Other	14	14	0.9	-	-	-
Ontario						
Onakawana	218	-	-	-	-	-
Saskatchewan						
Estevan	310	497	437	41	519	6,998
Willow Bunch	748	1,044	1,420	68	1,704	10,388
Wood Mountain	278	733	1,114	44	1,447	5,665
Cypress	162	406	465	8	243	461
Alberta						
Plains	9,459	-	81,261	-	-	-
Outer Foothills	1,089	-	7,983	-	-	-
Inner Foothills	7,212	-	20,004	-	-	-
British Columbia						
Southeastern	6,288	9,437	36,318	-	-	-
Northeastern	996	463	7,719	-	-	-
Other	1,845	91	7,439	-	-	-
Canada	28,941	13,276	164,666	161	3,963	23,589

Source: Department of Energy, Mines and Resources. 1977b. *1976 Assessment of Canada's Coal Resources and Reserves*.

County near Kemptown. Various investigations on the Island of Newfoundland have shown the presence of strongly faulted Pennyslvanian coal beds with steeply dipping, high ash coal seams, rarely more than 9 cm thick.

Uranium

"The majority of the world's known and presently economic uranium resources may be found in, Lower Proterozoic quartz-pebble conglomerates (syngenetic conglomerate deposits), in veins and related deposits, in granitic-pegmatitic rock, in sandstones, and in supergene deposits..." (Ruzicka, 1977).

Using this information, Ruzicka has mapped the deposits and areas favourable for uranium in Canada (Map 3). The Lower Proterozoic uraniferous conglomerates characterize the Elliot Lake-Agnew Lake deposit in northern Ontario, the Cobalt Embayment northeast of Sudbury, and possibly in northern Québec, east of James Bay near Sakami Lake, and west of Hudson Bay. Pitchblende-bearing veins and related deposits have been identified in northern Saskatchewan near Cluff Lake, Wollaston Lake, and Rabbit Lake. Other resource possibilities are beneath the Thelon Basin and Bathurst Embayment in the Northwest Territories, and also in Ontario. Environments favourable for the formation of orthomagnetic and anatectic uranium deposits in granitic-pegmatitic rocks, are found in granitic-syenitic terranes of the Canadian Shield and in the western Cordillera. Although uranium deposits in sandstones do not yet contribute to Canada's uranium reserves, as a resource, areas favourable for the sandstone type of uranium deposits are widely dispersed throughout: the northern archipelago, the Mackenzie Delta, in the interior of British Columbia, the Interior Plains, in the Hudson Bay Lowland of northern Ontario, and in the Appalachian Region in the Atlantic Provinces. Finally, the supergene uranium deposits may exist in fossil calcrete deposits (Ruzicka, 1977). Although uranium deposits are extensive throughout the tundra, forested, and agri-

TABLE 3.
1976 Estimate of Canada's recoverable uranium resources

Mineable	Measured	Indicated	Inferred
	(tonnes U)		
Up to $40/lb	79,000	88,000	238,000
$40 to $60/lb	4,000	11,000	69,000
Total	83,000	99,000	307,000

Source: Department of Energy, Mines and Resources. 1977c. *1976 Assessment of Canada's Uranium Supply and Demand*. Report EP 77-3.

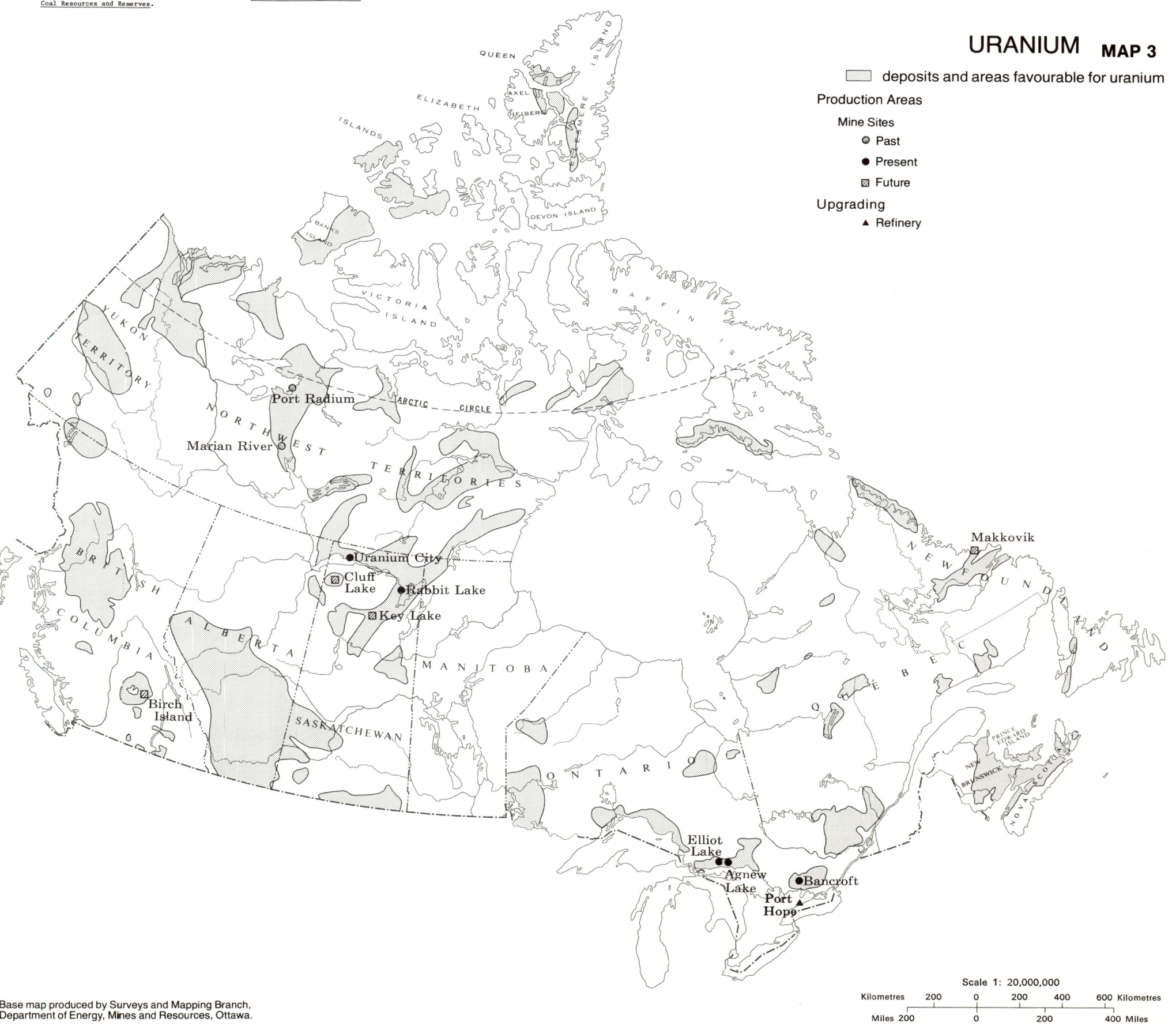

URANIUM MAP 3

Base map produced by Surveys and Mapping Branch, Department of Energy, Mines and Resources, Ottawa.

Scale 1: 20,000,000

cultural regions in Canada, in 1976 there were only five producing mines. In total, the "measured", "indicated", and "inferred" recoverable resource estimate varies between 83 thousand and 307 thousand t (Table 3) (Department of Energy, Mines and Resources, 1977c).

Hydro-electric Energy

Energy generated from falling water is a renewable resource based on natural precipitation and therefore, ultimately on the power of the sun. The energy may be extracted from river flows (run of the river) or these flows may be stored for periods in headponds or reservoirs and released through water turbines when required to meet the demand for energy. The available energy depends upon the amount of precipitation in the watershed area, which may change from year to year with variation in rainfall. It also depends on the availability of height (head) which is determined by local topography (Department of Energy, Mines and Resources, 1976d). In 1975, Québec followed by Ontario, British Columbia, Newfoundland, and Manitoba, produced 88 per cent of Canada's hydro-electric power (Map 4).

Economic, Environmental, and Social Considerations

An estimated 100 million ha of land are used either intensively or extensively for energy development in Canada (Hamilton, 1978). In 1976, this area was affected by 5,677 oil and gas wells, 31 principal coal mines including 19 surface and 12 underground mines, 473 thermal and 382 hydro-electric generating stations, 42 oil refineries, 6 uranium mines, 233 gas processing plants, 6 coking plants, 166,246 km of pipelines and 167,290 km of transmission lines (Maps 1 to 4).

Combined, this infrastructure represents the energy supply and distribution network in Canada. At the exploration and extraction stage, domestic energy sources are the input. Conversely, for the upgrading of energy forms, either by refining, processing, or coking, both domestic and imported energy are used. Transportation systems ensure the flow of energy, from site of extraction through upgrading to the end-user, from import arrival point to end-user, and from sites of extraction to export destination points. The mix of energy in the network itself, is representative of the complex interactions of economic, environmental, and social considerations.

Exploration and Extraction

The oil and gas fields (Map 1); the occurrences and deposits of coal (Map 2); and the known distributions of uranium (Map 3); identify the major regions of Canadian energy exploration and extraction. Western Canada, particularly Alberta, dominates in petroleum, natural gas, and coal (Tables 1 and 2). Although petroleum and natural gas activities are limited to the Interior Plains, coal exploration and extraction is conducted in several physiographic regions including the Rocky Mountains and foothills, and the Alberta and Saskatchewan plains. In the east, coal activities have been conducted in the plain, upland and highland areas of the Appalachian Region. Apart from the terrestrial drilling in the western provinces, the majority of northern and east coast petroleum and natural gas exploratory activities have been in the offshore areas. As indicated on Map 3, although uranium exploration is more widespread throughout the physiographic regions in Canada, the mining of uranium has been limited to northern Saskatchewan and Ontario, as well as the Northwest Territories.

Petroleum and Natural Gas. In 1976, more than one million ha were involved in the production of petroleum and natural gas (Canadian Imperial Bank of Commerce, 1977). Approximately 73 per cent of these sites were in Alberta and the remaining 27 per cent in British Columbia, Saskatchewan, and Manitoba. The Horsehead pump and the surface control valves, often considered synonymous with the Prairie wheat fields, are the visible indicators of producing oil and gas fields. Of the total area allocated for energy production, only a very small portion of land is used exclusively by the well. In 1976, these wells produced more than 200 thousand m³/d of crude oil, 7.5 thousand m³/d of synthetic crude oil, 21.3 thousand m³/d of pentanes plus and condensate, and 24.5 m³/d of butane and propane.

A significant land-related impact occurs through exploration activities conducted by oil and gas companies. About 90 per cent of the land used for energy exploration is comprised of petroleum leases. At the exploratory stage, seismic lines represent one of the more land-consuming activities.

"Seismic investigations require cleared, closely-spaced paths wide enough to permit vehicular movement. The clearing of seismic lines is a significant problem especially in Boreal forest regions. During 1971 in Alberta, more forest was cut by the petroleum industry than by the forest industries for lumbering, pulp and paper, and fuel (Department of Energy, Mines and Resources, 1973). Seismic exploration and related activities are of particular concern in northern permafrost regions where recovery, if there is to be one, from any form of disturbance to delicate ecosystems, requires many years..." (Blakeman, 1975).

A recent estimate noted that 24,816 ha have been influenced by seismic activity (Pullen, 1975) in the treed portions of British Columbia, Alberta, Saskatchewan, and the Northwest Territories. Exploration in northern areas is more ecologically sensitive than in other areas. In recent years, although government-induced exploration incentives have attempted to accelerate frontier exploration in both the Beaufort Sea and the Sverdrup Basin, northern pipeline indecision has tended to discourage activity. During 1976, more than 84 thousand m were drilled by the 27 wildcat and other exploratory wells in the Northwest and Yukon Territories. This may be compared to the drilling of five thousand development wells during the same year in Alberta.

NFB – PHOTOTHEQUE – ONF – Photo by Crombie McNeill.
Oil and agricultural production are often compatible land uses. A working well is seen in a wheat field, near Midale, Saskatchewan.

NFB – PHOTOTHEQUE – ONF – Photo by Ted Grant.
Seismic exploration is essential in delineating Canada's oil and natural gas resources. Here, an explosion, is used as a preliminary step in the exploratory process.

NFB – PHOTOTHEQUE – ONF – Photo by Ted Grant.
Seismic exploration activities must be carefully conducted in the ecologically-sensitive northern barrens. This aerial view shows vehicle tracks and a fuel cache used by geological crews.

Coal. More than 1.6 million ha of coal leases were controlled by the 12 major coal companies in 1976. In Alberta, where 80 per cent of the deposit occurs, as with mining operations, the effects of exploration in the mountains and foothills are more severe than on the surrounding plains. Slaney (1971) described exploration activities and their effects on the surrounding landscape.

"Surface trenching is carried out to expose the seams and learn more about the deposit before proceeding with the more expensive drilling operations. To determine the quality of the coal for various markets a test-pit or trench is excavated to obtain large samples from beyond the weathered or oxidized zone. This operation often leaves a substantial cut-and-fill excavation on the hillside. On steep hillsides, some excavation may also be necessary to provide level sites for drilling equipment. Roads are built on a short term basis to allow the cheapest access for exploration equipment. The road is made by running a bulldozer through the vegetation, and the surface is usually the coarse fraction of surface soils. Roadside ditches are seldom dug and crossings over minor streams are usually fords or log culverts. After exploration work has been completed, there remains a network of roads, trenches and drillsites extending for many kilometres often over very steep slopes. The disturbance of surface soils and vegetation is often severe and long-lasting. The effects are compounded by the steep gradients over many of these roads.

In the plains, the horizontal coal seams are generally covered with a mantle of glacial drift and are exposed only where major streams have cut deep channels. Thus exploration is mainly restricted to drilling operations, although test-pits must be excavated to obtain bulk samples. In forest areas these activities will also necessitate the cutting of exploration access trails" (Slaney, 1971).

Similar exploration effects are evident in the plains area of Saskatchewan and to a much lesser extent over the coal seams of eastern Canada. As with northern oil and gas exploration, the hazards posed by ecosystem instability and permafrost sensitivity must be carefully considered as increasing efforts are being directed towards quantifying the northern coal resource.

Of all the energy production techniques, coal mining has the potential for producing the most deleterious impacts on the adjacent landscapes. In the short-term, it has few compatible alternate land uses. Although only an estimated 15,339 ha of land have been disturbed by coal mining (Marshall, 1978), the impact of hydrologic and aesthetic alterations has an effect on a much larger area than the geographically concentrated mining operation. The majority of land altered is located in Alberta and may be attributed to surface mining techniques which represent 84 per cent of total coal production (Figure 3) (Department of Energy, Mines and Resources, 1976c). Longwall, and room and pillar techniques are the two underground mining methods used in British Columbia, Alberta and Nova Scotia. Surface mining techniques, used by all the producing provinces may be categorized into two types: open-pit and area-strip mining. In selecting an economic mining method, some of the important factors include:

(i) the amount and type of rock in the overburden covering the coal seam;
(ii) the characteristics of the coal seam; the quality and rank of the coal, the thickness of the seam, the dip (or pitch) of the seam, the structural strength of the coal and the presence and amount of explosive gas (methane);
(iii) the topography of the surrounding land area;
(iv) the quantity of water required for, and likely to be encountered in, the mining operations; and
(v) the quality required for the final product depending on the intended use of the coal.

Where seams are thick, uniform, and relatively continuous and where the land terrain is flat to rolling, surface mining techniques are used.

NFB – PHOTOTHEQUE – ONF – Photo by Larry Monk.
Surface coal mines, such as this one in the Alberta foothills, have been the subject of public hearings in recent years.

MAP 4

Photo by Environment Canada.

IG STATIONS and ELECTRIC TRANSMISSION SYSTEMS

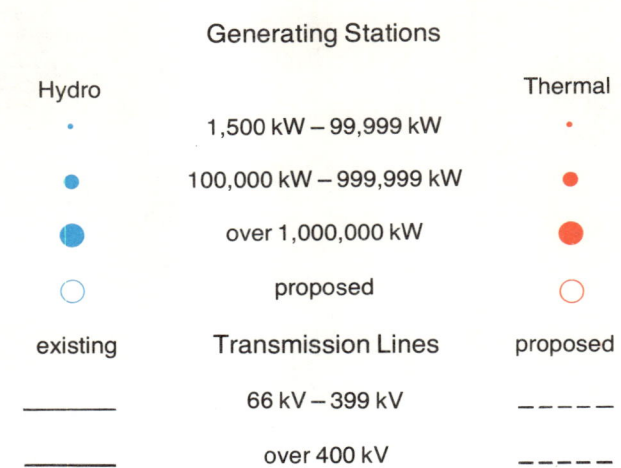

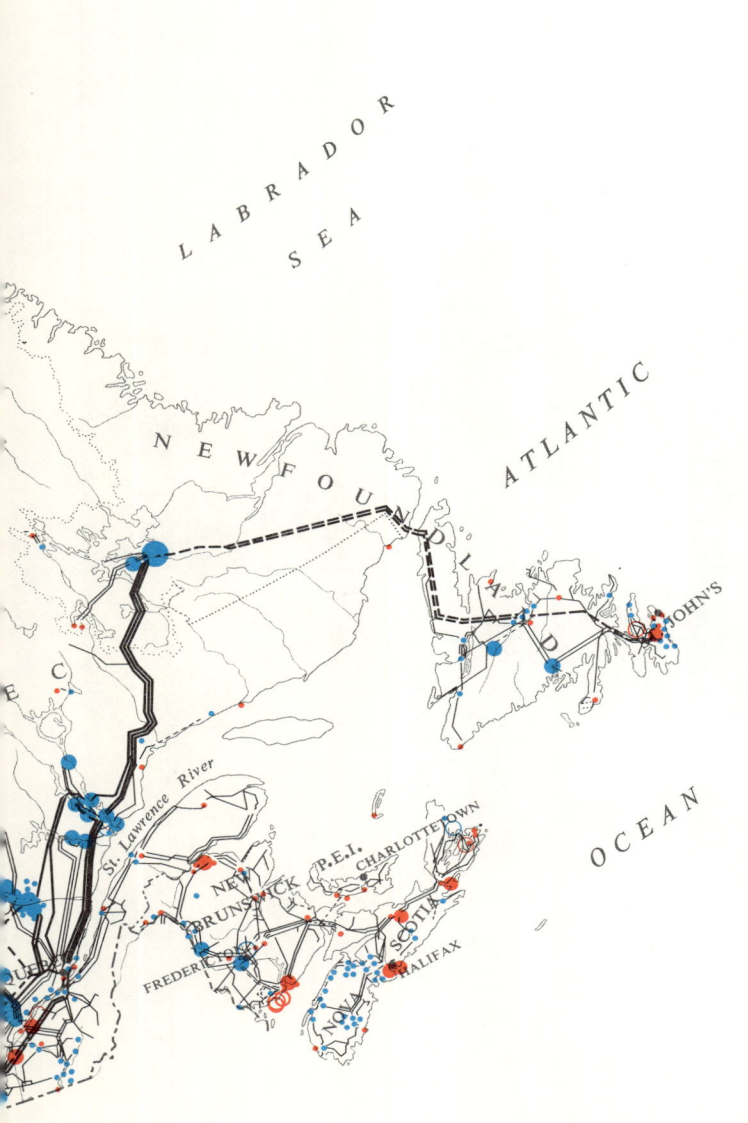

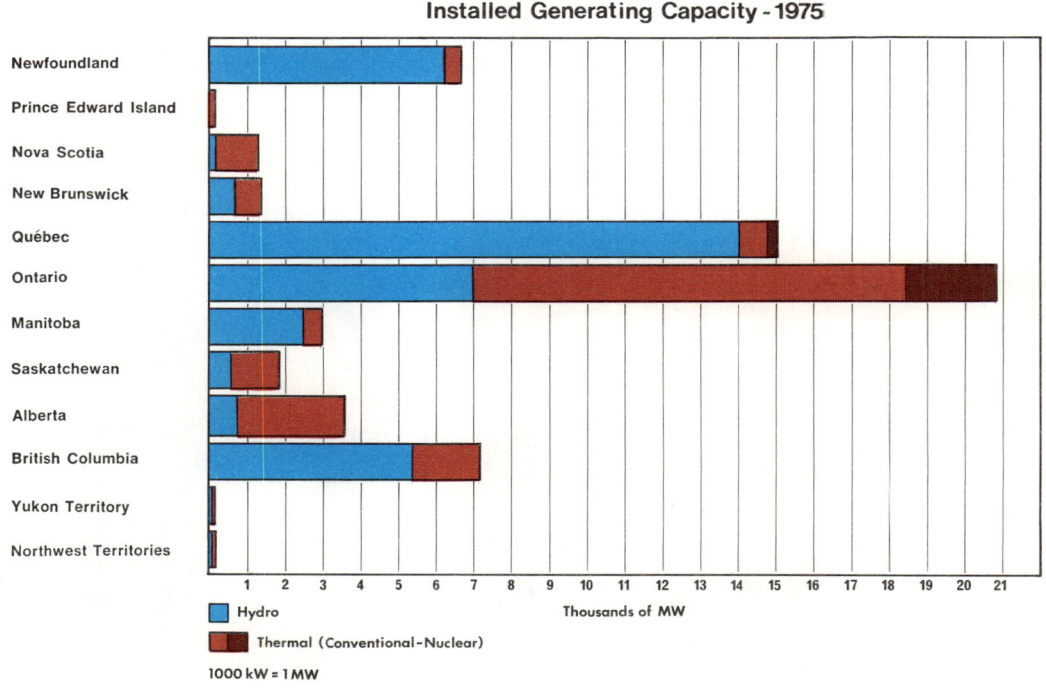

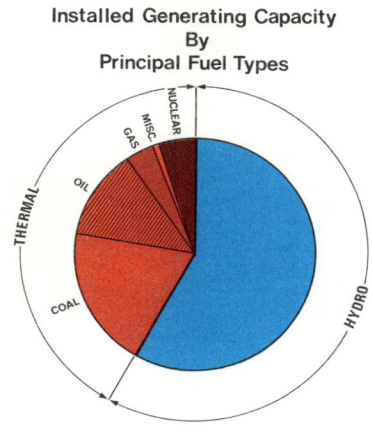

Source: Energy, Mines and Resources Energy Policy Sector, 1975. Electric Power in Canada.
Statistics Canada, 1977. Electric Power Statistics, Volume III,

MAJOR POWER GENERA

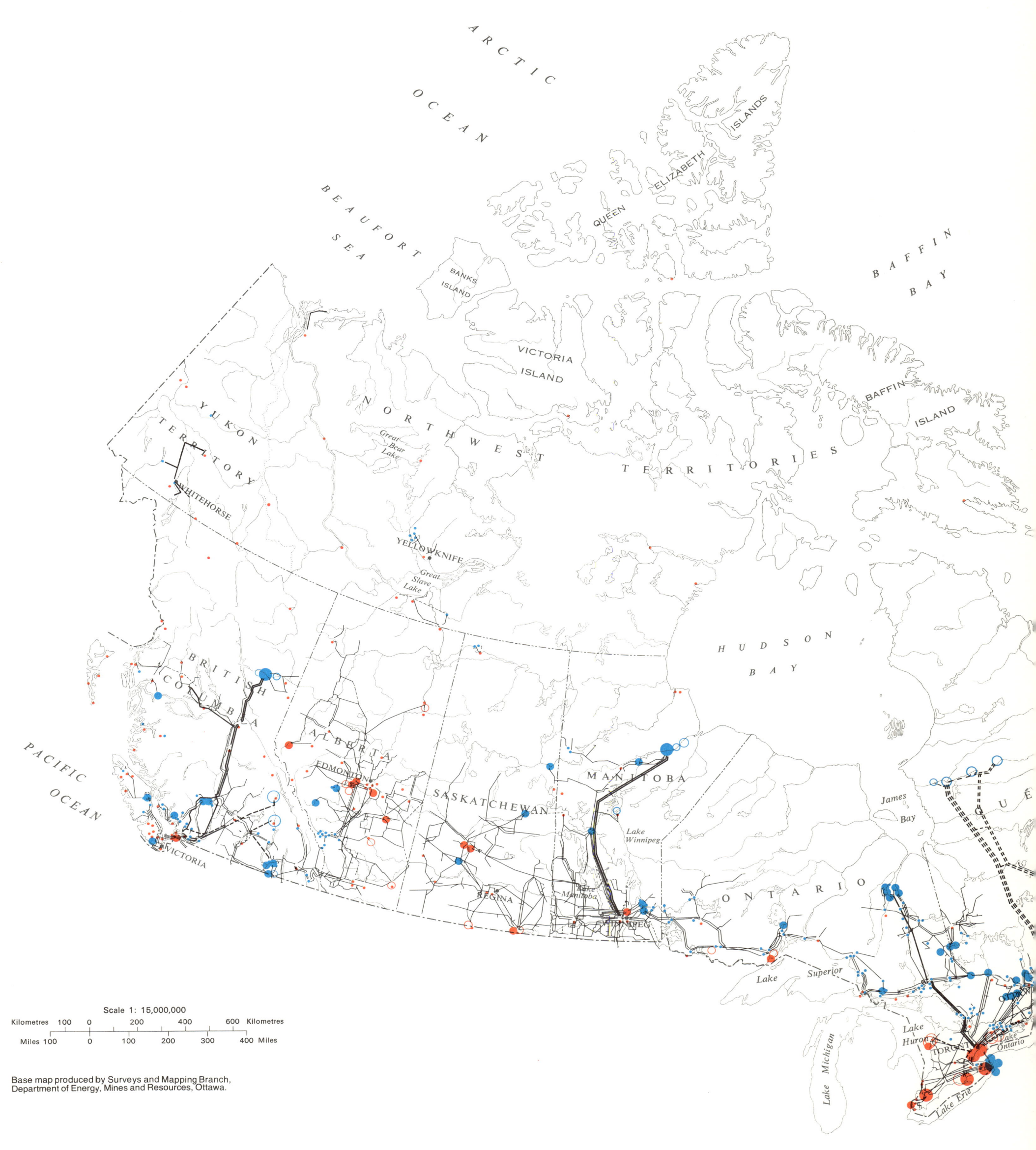

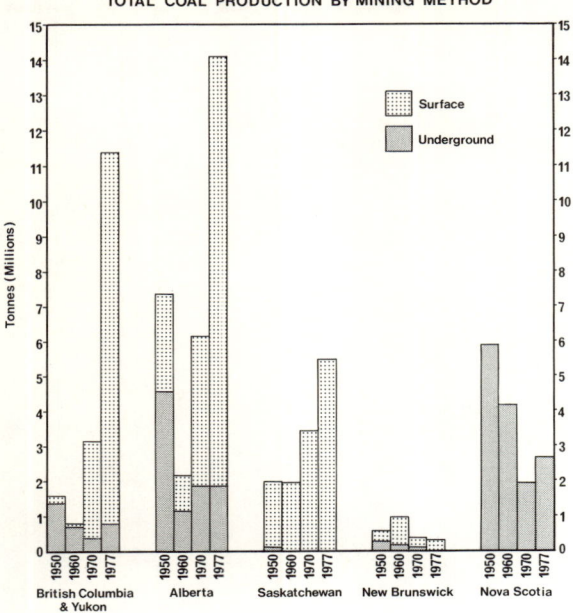

FIGURE 3.

TOTAL COAL PRODUCTION BY MINING METHOD

In 1976, the 25.5 million t of coal produced were valued at $616 million. Of this, 11.7 t of metallurgical coal were exported, primarily from the Rocky Mountains via Vancouver to Japan. An additional 14.6 million t of Pennsylvanian coal were imported via the Great Lakes to support Ontario's industrial heartland (Figure 4).

Uranium. More than 3.5 million t of ore were extracted to produce 4,850 t of uranium by the five uranium-producing mines in 1976 (Figure 5). Three underground mines in northern Ontario and one underground mine and one surface mine in northern Saskatchewan supply uranium for both export and domestic markets. Although uranium-bearing deposits appear to be extensive throughout Canada, present producing mines operate only in the boreal forest region of the Canadian Shield. Since the late 1950s, the number of producing mines has declined from 23 operations, precipitated by the saturation of the foreign military market. With few incentives, uranium exploration was essentially dormant from 1955 to 1966. However, recent demand from nuclear electric programs has renewed interest in uranium. In 1976, of the total uranium output, only about nine per cent was required for Canada's nuclear electric industry, thus substantial tonnages remain available for export.

FIGURE 4.

COAL PRODUCTION AND CONSUMPTION 1940-1975

Hydro-electric generation. In 1976, almost 40 thousand MW of hydro-electricity, representing 70 per cent of the total electricity output, were generated in Canada (Department of Energy, Mines and Resources, 1976d). Growth in the late 1960s and 1970s has been characterized by development of the mega projects, dams with capacities of more than one thousand MW (Map 4). Each of these large developments, and the other smaller hydro-electric sites, represents unique problems in terms of design and construction, and also in terms of related land impacts. Dams may be evaluated for the upstream, dam site, and downstream, physical, chemical and biological effects imposed on the surrounding landscape.

Upstream from the dam, the most visible and land-consuming entity is the reservoir or impoundment. In most cases, the primary concern is loss of land and land potential for alternative uses. The flooding of forested areas may involve the losses of wilderness, commercial timber, and recreational land. In addition, flooding of agricultural land, loss of wildlife habitat, the foregoing of mineral and metallic mine site potential, and the displacing of valuable archaeological areas are the other major uses affected by the creation of a reservoir. The huge 1,000+ MW projects, such as the W.A.C. Bennett Dam on the Peace River in northern British Columbia, the Kettle Rapids Dam on the Churchill-Nelson River in Manitoba, Manic 1, 2, and 3 dams on the Manicouagan River in Québec, and Churchill Falls on the Churchill River in Labrador, are examples of dams which require enormous headponds for hydro-electric generation. Forest clear-cutting for economic reasons, particularly with the more recent dam sites which are a further distance from consuming markets, is not always feasible. Hence, shorelines of reservoirs such as Williston Lake in British Columbia covering 1,773 km², may be delineated by stumpage. Reservoir attractiveness is also impeded by the problem of drawdown in the shoreline area which extends between low and high water levels. If a constant flow is to be maintained downstream, it is virtually impossible to maintain water levels upstream. Reservoirs normally fill during the spring, and then decrease in volume during the summer.

FIGURE 5.

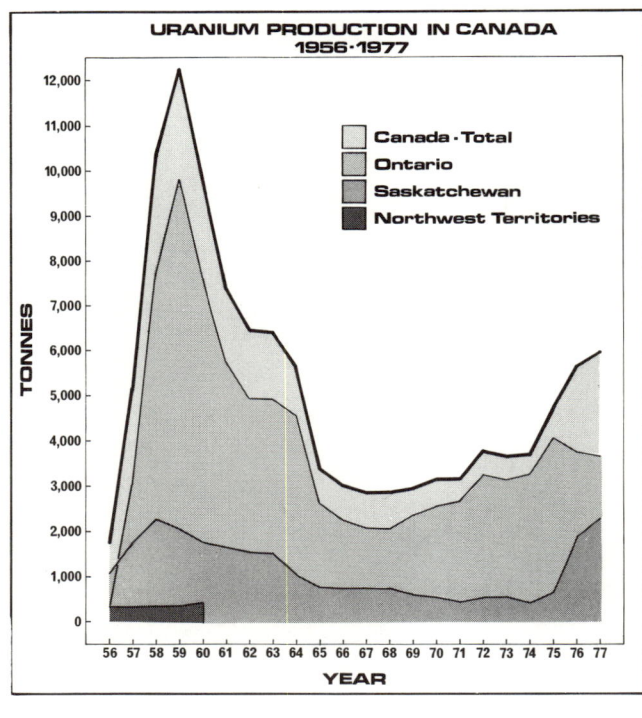

URANIUM PRODUCTION IN CANADA 1956-1977

NFB – PHOTOTHEQUE – ONF – Photo by George Hunter.

Beaverlodge, one of Canada's five producing uranium mines is located north-east of Great Slave Lake, in the Northwest Territories.

Flooding may also interfere with human settlements. Examples, such as the Kootenay lakes on the Columbia River, have involved the relocation of residents away from the flooded portions. James Bay, which will eventually affect more than 8,000 km² of northern Québec, has had a significant effect on the lifestyles of the Cree Indians in the region. Problems of sedimentation, nutrient alteration, turbidity, salinity, and temperature stratification, all factors determining water quality, may be changed by a reservoir. In addition, reservoirs have the potential to alter micro-climates and groundwater systems, as well as to transform habitat for aquatic and

NFB – PHOTOTHEQUE – ONF – Photo by George Hunter.

Hydro-electric development potential remains in the more remote northern ocations of British Columbia, Manitoba, Ontario, Québec, Labrador, and the northern territories. One of the more recent developments is a power project located on the Churchill–Nelson River system in northern Manitoba.

terrestrial flora and fauna. Thus, the impact of a reservoir extends beyond the area covered by the flooding.

The dam site itself imposes a significant impact on the surrounding landscape during the initial construction phase. A labour-intensive activity, the building of a dam requires roads, airstrips, and temporary accommodation for work crews and their families. Sometimes the infrastructure which is required for the building of a dam site encourages other economic activity in a region. For example, roads constructed in the more remote northern areas may encourage exploration for other natural resources. The removal of ground cover, the blasting, dredging, and the diversion of waters, all have a direct impact on the biogeography of the adjacent lands. One of the well-documented impacts concerns the blocking of migration routes for anadromorous fish. For example, salmon may be blocked particularly along the coastal rivers of British Columbia.

Downstream from the dam, the reduction of water flow may affect communities, water-based recreational activities, erosion, and sediment loads.

Upgrading

Raw coal extracted from the ground, crude oil or natural gas pumped to the surface, and uranium in an unprocessed state, all require upgrading to convert the natural resource into an essential end-use domestic product or to a marketable export commodity. The distribution of coal cleaning and coking plants, oil refineries, natural gas processing plants, uranium milling plants and refineries, and thermal electric plants is not necessarily dictated by the production regions of the energy fuels (*see* Maps 1, 2, and 3). Both domestic and foreign sources of energy require an upgrading process as the interim stage between production and end-use.

Petroleum and Natural Gas. At the end of 1976, oil refining capacity in Canada was approximately 340 thousand m³. The industry, which developed in the 1950s, ranked eighth highest for world crude oil-refining capacities in 1976. Of this, 57 per cent of the requirements were met by domestic supplies (Department of Energy, Mines and Resources, 1978d). Montréal, Toronto, Sarnia and Edmonton represent the four largest refining centres. Edmonton, which lies in the heart of the oil-producing region, refines Alberta's oil, which normally contains less sulphur than Venezuelan and Middle East crude oils. In addition, Alberta ships crude oil to the refining centres in Ontario and Québec. Eastern Canada also upgrades imported oil at refineries in the Atlantic Provinces, Québec, and Ontario. Although refineries in Alberta rely entirely on pipeline transport, plants in the Atlantic Provinces are located near coastal cities where crude oil is received by tanker. Québec's refineries, with one exception, are located east of Montréal, with access to crude oil either via pipeline or, during the shipping season on the St. Lawrence River, by tanker. As of 1976, the completion of the Sarnia to Montréal pipeline provided access to western Canadian crude oil for Québec's refineries. This capability supplements the Portland pipeline which carries imported crude oil via the northern United States. Toronto and Sarnia, Ontario's major refining centres, are fed primarily by western fuels.

In general, the refining industry requires industrial land which is usually located in areas favourable for

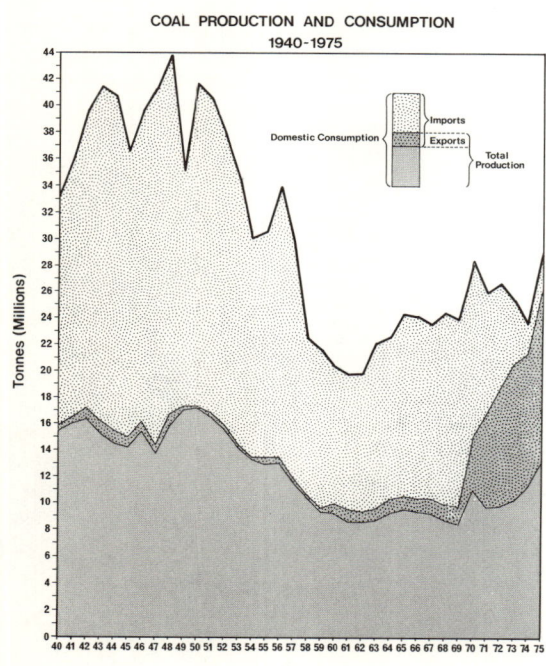

NFB – PHOTOTHEQUE – ONF – Photo by George Hunter.
The Grand Rapids dam on the Churchill–Nelson River system in northern Manitoba, is one of the recently completed 1,000 + MW projects.

growth. The key location determinants include: accessibility to pipeline or water transportation, an abundant water supply for processing, availability of a specialized labour force, suitable land for the construction of industrial equipment, and the availability of services for maintenance. Although the land use requirements of refining are not extensive, expansion may be limited by a variety of industrial zoning regulations.

The refining process involves the breakdown of crude oil into its hydrocarbon components including: light gases; light, middle, and heavy distillates; and residues. The crude oil is heated through furnaces then sent to a fractionation tower where products ranging from naphtha (gasoline) to heavy pitch (asphalt base) are extracted. Further processing (catalytic cracking and/or hydrocracking) is required to upgrade the octane levels of gasoline and to improve the efficiency of recovery for the heavy crude components including gasoline and light heating oils. Undesirable components such as sulphur are also treated. Other products include: butane, propane, and the remaining liquefied petroleum products; chemicals such as alcohols used in antifreeze; aviation fuel; specialty naphthas used in explosives, solvents, and dyes; kerosenes; light heating oils; lubricating oils; paraffin waxes; white oils and petrolatums used in salves and creams; asphalts; coke; and residual fuel oils. In addition, intermediate petrochemicals form the basis for major industries making plastics, synthetic textiles, paints, insecticides, and photographic film.

NFB – PHOTOTHEQUE – ONF – Photo by George Hunter.
Oil refineries are usually situated near urban centres and are a large industrial user of land. The refinery pictured here is located on the north side of Edmonton.

Unlike the larger oil refineries which are centralized in several locations, gas-processing plants are widely distributed, primarily throughout Alberta (Map 1). The increased demand for natural gas, which started during the 1950s, was accompanied by a steadily expanding gas-processing capacity. Gas processing may include a separator, at or near the wellhead, which separates the liquid hydrocarbon and water that condense from the reservoir gas in the well. Further upgrading is required to meet market specifications and to remove the main non-hydrocarbon constituent, hydrogen sulphide. Raw natural gas is composed of the liquid hydrocarbons (called liquified petroleum gas and includes propane and butane), and the heavier hydrocarbons, principally pentane and some hexanes, heptanes etc. (called pentanes plus), and condensate used as a petroleum refinery feedstock. Several techniques such as refrigeration, compression, and oil absorption are used to separate natural gas constituents. The majority of gas processing plants are located on or near the gas producing fields in Alberta.

Coal. Raw coal requires processing which may include washing, sorting, purifying, and drying. Ripley estimated during 1974 that about 16 per cent of the amount of raw coal produced at the mine, became the residual non-marketable surplus during the upgrading stage. This solid waste amounted to 3.8 million t in 1974, and is composed of the tailings at the mine or processing site (does not include thermal plant cleaning) (Ripley, Redmann and Maxwell, 1978).

Sulphur, ash and water occurring in raw coal in varying proportions, are the major impurities which require processing. Coal from the Appalachian Region tends to have a high sulphur content which may produce acid-mine drainage problems. Because most eastern coal is mined under the ocean, acid waters are not a land-related issue. Western coals are high in ash and water content. This residual comprises the tailings at the mine site. In addition, lignitic coals of Saskatchewan appear to be undesirably high in sodium salts.

NFB – PHOTOTHEQUE – ONF – Courtesy of B.A. Oil.
Natural gas processing plants are widely distributed throughout Alberta, usually on or near a producing gas field. The plant in this photo is located near Rimbey.

Uranium. The milling of uranium is required to reduce the raw ore to uranium oxide which may be upgraded further, by refining. Milling plants are usually juxtaposed to the mine site. Milling involves a series of chemical processes through which uranium may be recovered from the mined ore. One of the most common operations leaches the ore with a weak solution of sulphuric acid at high temperatures. Another method uses a carbonate-bicarbonate leaching system. The end-product in both systems is uranium packed in drums, which may be destined for further upgrading as a reactor fuel. Residuals which are the by-product of the milling process include water and tailings which contain varying amounts of radioactive elements.

NFB – PHOTOTHEQUE – ONF – Photo by Larry Monk.
In 1976, an estimated 15,339 ha of land had been disturbed by coal mining in Canada. Here, a truck is dumping fill in a worked-out pit as an initial step in land reclamation.

Transportation

More than 300 thousand km of oil and gas pipelines and electricity transmission lines exist throughout Canada. While the major pipelines flow in an east-west direction, the corresponding transmission line networks are oriented primarily in a north-south direction. The end-use markets are the location determinants for these transportation systems. Petroleum and natural gas are carried from Alberta either to export destination points, or to Ontario and Québec for refining. Electricity networks are generally in province, hence transmission lines transport both hydro-electricity from the northern sources to the southern consuming centres, and thermal electricity, which is usually juxtaposed to the major comsumers. Coal is transported via unit trains from Alberta to Vancouver. Recently, coal transportation eastwards has used a combination rail-water system.

NFB – PHOTOTHEQUE – ONF – Photo by George Hunter.
This aerial view of a mine-mouth operation shows a coal mine, milling plant, and thermal electric generation plant, located in the Smoky River area of Alberta.

Oil and Gas Pipelines. The distributions of oil and gas pipelines are indicated on Map 1. Although for both, the densities are concentrated in the plains of Alberta, pipelines also traverse the mountains and run west to southern British Columbia, and extend eastwards to Ontario and Québec (oil only) (*see* Tables 4 and 5). The diversity of physiographic, soil and geologic regions through which pipelines are laid, may present technical problems in design. The construction phase has the most deleterious impact on the surrounding landscape. Machinery, construction materials, and soil removal, in the short-term may affect adjacent lands uses such as agriculture, recreation, urban, industrial and other transportation activities. Certain physiographic regions, such as the Cordillera and the northern Interior Plains, are most sensitive during pipeline construction. Blasting of rock and, in some places interference with permafrost may affect delicate ecosystems. During the operation phase, leaks and spills impose the greatest threat to groundwater. Surface land use activities may resume except where road allowances and compressor stations are required for maintenance.

Transmission Lines. More than 167 thousand km of transmission lines traverse the major physiographic and vegetation regions in Canada. Ontario followed by Québec, Saskatchewan, Alberta, Manitoba and British Columbia are supported by the greatest distances of transmission lines (Table 6). Landscape alteration is most severe in forested areas where cutting of the understory is required. Sometimes controversial herbicides are used as a means of controlling re-growth. The effect of transmission lines on wildlife has been documented in many impact studies. Although some forest-dwelling species may be forced to abandon a transmission right-of-way, other species preferring edge habitat will seek the browse offered by lower growing plants. In agricultural areas, farmland is lost from production during the construction phase. However, once pylons and lines are in-place, only the area under the base of the pylon is permanently taken out of alternate production.

Rail and Water Transport. Coal uses both rail and water transport to deliver mined coal to export and consumption points. Unit trains capable of carrying 10 thousand t per trip, take coal from Alberta and British Columbia to Roberts Bank south of Vancouver, where coal is exported primarily to Japan. Coal dust is the major environmental hazard during transportation. Since 1976, coal trains have transported small amounts of coal east to Thunder Bay. Completion of the bulk-handling terminal in Thunder Bay should be followed by the arrival of increased quantities of coal. In addition, Thunder Bay will act as the transfer point for coal shipments to continue via Great Lakes tankers to southern Ontario.

Both the excavation for the pipeline and the transportation of equipment to the construction site are the primary land-consuming activities during the initial development phase.

Unit trains capable of carrying 10,000 t per trip, transport coal from Alberta and British Columbia to Roberts Bank, south of Vancouver. Since 1976, coal trains have transported small amounts of coal east to Thunder Bay.

Roberts Bank, a busy port for on-loading coal, is the export point for Canada's metallurgical coal.

Rail transport is also used to carry drums of uranium to export markets and to upgrading centres in southern Ontario.

End-use

As indicated in Figure 2, the major demands for energy are derived from the residential and farm, commercial, industrial and transportation sectors. In addition, the specific forms of energy that are used for satisfying the demand vary in the different regions of Canada and in their relative shares, which may change through time (Table 2). "The price of alternative energy forms, the existing infrastructure, convenience, tradition and other factors determine the extent to which any one form is utilized for a specific end-use" (Science Council of Canada, 1975).

Residential. More than 70 per cent of the residential sector's demand for energy is required for space heating. Fuel oils and gas supply most heating needs. Although presently consuming about 25 per cent of the total energy demand, the substitution of higher efficiency fuels (oil and gas) for lower efficiency fuels (wood and coal), the increasing use of electricity for heating, and the continuing shift toward urbanization with the associated high ratio of apartment units to single dwelling units, indicate that the share of the residential sector of the energy pie may decrease in the future.

Commercial. The expansion of this sector including building activities during the last decade has contributed to the expanding energy consumption pattern of the commercial sector. Oil and gas, followed by electricity, are the primary energy fuels required.

Transportation. Virtually all of the transportation sector's energy consumption demands are fuelled by petroleum and petroleum products. Automobiles are the largest consumer. In addition, the mechanization of agriculture has had an impact on the growth of demand for motor gasoline and diesel fuel oil (accounted for about one-tenth of total consumption in 1976).

Industrial. The industrial sector is fed by all major energy forms: coal, oil, natural gas, petroleum derivatives and electric power. For example, coal is the most important energy input to iron and steel mills; electric power for pulp and paper and chemical plants; and petroleum derivatives and natural gas for fuelling the chemical products industries. In addition, there are considerable regional variations in energy input by source. This may be attributed to regional differences in the industrial mix, (iron and steel mills are located primarily in Ontario, conversely pulp and paper mills are found mainly in British Columbia, Québec and Ontario) and the availability of energy. There are no sources of natural gas in the Atlantic Region. (*adapted from* Science Council of Canada, 1975).

Factors Affecting Change

"Through the decade from 1963-1973 the experience in Canada as in most of the world was characterized by rapid increases in the use of energy.... Spurred by the development of low-cost petroleum supplies in the Middle East and aided by Canadian government policies that provided market protection and substantial incentives to the domestic petroleum industry, the consumption of oil in Canada increased over the same period at about the same average rate as total energy, so that in 1973, petroleum products accounted for about 47 per cent of Canadian energy use... By 1973, in response to a decade of uninterrupted economic growth and continuously declining real oil prices, the degree of dependence of the industrialized countries on the Middle Eastern oil-exporting countries (OPEC), was so great, that a cartel formed in the aftermath of the October 1973 Middle East War, was able to take control over the international oil market." (Department of Energy, Mines and Resources, 1976).

The resulting price increase has had a severe economic impact on most of the industrialized oil-importing countries (Table 7). Balance-of-payments problems, continued high rates of inflation and high levels of unemployment have also plagued Canada. Since 1973, federal policy initiatives have been directed towards securing sources of energy supply, encouraging wise use of the non-renewable fossil fuels, and funding research and development in the alternative, renewable energy field.

In 1975, more than 14.6 million of Pennsylvanian coal was imported to support Ontario's heavy industries. Much of this coal is used to make coke, the primary feedstock for the steel industry.

TABLE 4.
Oil pipelines, 1976

Province and territory	Gathering	Trunk	Products	Total
		(km)		
Québec	-	452.5	247.8	700.3
Ontario	28.6	1,432.6	1,863.7	3,324.9
Manitoba	335.4	1,388.7	313.0	2,037.1
Saskatchewan	3,474.3	3,717.2	618.0	7,809.5
Alberta	7,872.7	7,831.7	567.0	16,271.4
British Columbia	824.8	1,755.6	56.3	2,636.7
Yukon			89.3	89.3
Canada	12,535.8	16,578.3	3,755.1	32,869.2

* Includes total gathering lines and total gathering pipelines of producing companies.
Source: Statistics Canada. 1978d. *Oil Pipeline Transport 1976.* Catalogue 55-201.

TABLE 5.
Natural gas pipelines, 1976

Province and territory	Gathering	Transmission	Distribution	Total
		(km)		
New Brunswick	20.8	21.6	146.1	188.5
Québec	2.1	237.7	2,890.9	3,130.7
Ontario	1,992.0	9,387.8	28,715.7	40,095.5
Manitoba	-	2,743.4	2,738.8	5,482.2
Saskatchewan	2,290.1	10,614.9	4,966.3	17,998.5
Alberta	12,848.4	15,596.0	21,554.1	49,998.5
British Columbia	2,069.8	5,087.5	9,397.6	16,554.9
Yukon and Northwest Territories	55.0	-		55.0
Canada	19,278.2	43,688.9	70,409.5	133,376.6

Source: Statistics Canada. 1978b. *Gas Utilities, Transport and Distribution Systems, 1976.* Catalogue 57-205.

Automobiles are the largest energy-consumer in the transportation sector.

Political Intervention. The development of Canada's energy resources has been influenced by a variety of government incentives and subsidization programs. The exploration and development of coal, oil and gas have each been influenced by special tax write-offs, research and development funding and regulated price agreements. The National Oil Policy introduced in 1961, divided Canada into two consuming regions. The Ottawa River Valley delineated the boundary between eastern and western Canada. The eastern consuming region was served by imported lower-priced oil than was the western consuming region which used higher-priced Canadian oil. After 1973, the balance changed. Western oil

TABLE 6.

Electrical transmission lines, 1976

Province and territory	less than 200,000 volts	200,000 to 399,999 volts	greater than 400,000 volts	Total
		(km)		
Newfoundland	3,496	1,621	608	5,725
Prince Edward Island	388	-	-	388
Nova Scotia	3,166	660	-	3,826
New Brunswick	4,541	708	-	5,249
Québec	11,366	9,555	4,271	25,192
Ontario	28,922	12,553	1,038	42,513
Manitoba	12,115	3,713	1,791	17,619
Saskatchewan	23,632	1,539	-	25,171
Alberta	21,023	2,406	-	23,429
British Columbia	10,365	3,460	2,651	16,476
Yukon	915	-	-	915
Northwest Territories	787	-	-	787
Canada	120,716	36,215	10,359	167,290

Source: Statistics Canada, 1977*b*. Electric Power Statistics Vol. II, Annual Statistics 1976. Catalogue 93-737.

prices, pegged at a lower price than on the international market, were lower than eastern oil-importing prices. In general, the cost of oil has acted as an impetus for growth of exploration, development and production of other energy sources, for example, coal and nuclear electricity, and encouraged activities in the inaccessible, more expensive areas to develop such as the Athabasca oil sands.

Technological Innovations. As costs increase for producing conventional energy resources, new thresholds for development become available. Alternative renewable energy sources, development of the more expensive hydro-carbon areas including the north and oil sand deposits, and exploring the substitutability of the more abundant coal resource have all been assessed since 1973. The implications of any of these developments on land will result in a proportionately increasing demand placed on the need for land to support the infrastructure.

Since long lead times are necessary for the development of future energy projects, a considerable priority has been given to developing conservation technologies for energy. Insulation programs, house design, reduction of car size, consumer energy-awareness projects, and industrial re-use of low grade heat are a few examples of the result of innovative technology applications which encourage conservation strategies.

TABLE 7.

Balance of trade in energy commodities

Commodity item	1965	1975
	(millions of dollars)	
Petroleum		
Export	300.8	3,673.7
Import	473.3	3,583.1
Balance	-172.5	90.6
Natural Gas		
Export	104.2	1,092.2
Import	7.5	7.5
Balance	96.7	1,084.7
Petroleum and Natural Gas		
Export	405.0	4,765.9
Import	480.8	3,590.6
Balance	-75.8	1,175.3
Coal and Coke		
Export	14.0	493.6
Import	134.8	576.3
Balance	-120.8	-82.7
Electric Energy		
Export	16.9	104.3
Import	14.3	11.8
Balance	2.6	92.5
Total		
Export	435.9	5,363.8
Import	629.9	4,178.7
Balance	-194.0	1,185.1

Source: Statistics Canada. 1977*a*. Canada Year Book 1976-77, Special Edition.

Present Land Use Issues

Paralleling the increased demand for energy to support Canada's economic development has been an increased awareness of the implications of energy use on the surrounding environment. Land, whether it is directly affected by an activity such as a surface coal mine, or indirectly affected, for example by noxious particulate emissions from a petroleum refinery, has become a focal point in the decision-making process. Public participation in inquiries such as Alberta Conservation Authority's hearings on the "Eastern Slopes" and the "Impact of Surface Mining on the Environment" has shown a strong voice in questioning previous decisions concerning the allocation of land for energy development.

A variety of environmental impact legislation exists in all provinces and, at the federal level, the Federal Environmental Assessment and Review Process has been established to monitor proposed projects affecting federal lands.

Two case studies are discussed, to illustrate the extent and type of land-related impacts which are associated with the larger energy development projects. The Athabasca oil sands and the James Bay Hydro-electric project are two examples of billion-dollar energy programs which will have a significant impact on the land resource.

Oil Sands Development

The Alberta oil sands may be a viable alternative to the conventional oil supply. Compared with other comparative sources of liquid hydrocarbons, for example, oil shales and coal liquefaction, the oil sands are closer to the major markets and have slightly more advanced technologies available for their production. From the province of Alberta's viewpoint, oil sands development will maintain the province in its traditional position as the major oil producer for Canada.

Northern Alberta is underlain by four major oil sands deposits occupying about 4.9 million ha (7.5 per cent of the surface area of the entire province). These deposits, including Athabasca, Cold Lake, Peace River and Wabasca occur at widely varying depths, usually under an overburden layer, and also differ locally in thickness and oil saturation content. Of the four major deposits, only the Athabasca area is exploitable using available oil sands surface extraction techniques which are limited to a depth of 46 m. Because the Cold Lake, Wabasca and Peace River deposits have more than 76 m of overburden, they have not yet been considered as a proven recoverable resource. Recently, these deposits have been undergoing extensive testing of new techniques by the major oil companies, in an effort to develop a commercial *in situ* production operation.

The Athabasca tar sands lie under 2.3 million ha of northeastern Alberta. They are part of a wedge of sediment that overlies Precambrian basement rock. The lower part of the wedge consists of limestone, dolomite and salt deposited from a widespread shallow sea that covered the area during the Devonian period (about 350 million years ago). These rocks were tilted and partly eroded. Then, during the Cretaceous period (about 100 million years ago) the rocks were covered by sand. At a later time, tar migrated in from some unknown source, impregnating the sand with viscous bitumen. Most of the resulting tar sand is now buried under 46 to 610 m of younger sand, shale and glacial drift. Only in the Athabasca region, where the river valley has eroded through the overlying layers, is the tar sand exposed. Unlike conventional oil deposits, the Athabasca deposits are composed of sand and some clay particles (mainly quartz) which are saturated by oil. The oil, whose chemical base and density cause it to bond to the sands, acts as a cementing material thereby giving the mixture an asphalt appearance. Water also forms a thin film around the sand grains. Because of the bonding and viscosity, the oil cannot be recovered by ordinary drilling methods and must be separated from the sands. In the Athabasca deposit, the bitumen has a gravity of six to ten per cent API, thus it is slightly heavier than water. The bitumen also has a high sulphur content of five per cent. Combined, these characteristics make the bitumen an undesirable refinery feedstock and it is impossible to ship long distances by pipeline in its natural state.

Relief and Drainage. The Athabasca tar sands deposit stretches to the western boundary of the northern Interior Plains region. Lying adjacent to the Canadian Shield, the deposit area at this point is a composite of highlands, high plains and lowlands. The area is drained by the Athabasca-Clearwater River system, whose valleys are incised into a broad muskeg-covered plain, reaching to a depth of 61 to 91 m. Relief for the area and sources for the tributary streams is provided by the Birch Mountains to the west of the Athabasca River, the Stony Mountains south of Fort McMurray and Muskeg Mountain to the east of the Athabasca River. In addition, the Thickwood Hills, a subdued highland with gentle slopes, gives rise to the northward flowing tributaries of the McKay River and several other streams flowing south to the Athabasca River. A number of shallow lakes located in the area include Eaglenest, Gardiner and Namur. These lakes are interconnected and eventually flow into the Ells River. The only other sizable water bodies are Algar and Gregoire lakes south of Fort McMurray, and McClelland Lake which is located in the lowlands, northeast of Bitumount.

Climate. The climatic patterns of the tar sands can be described as sub-arctic. The area is affected by three divergent air masses. During the summer season, the combination of Arctic continental air masses (producing hot, dry weather), the Maritime Pacific air mass (creating cloud cover and rain) and occasionally the Maritime Tropical air mass (causing high temperatures, high humidity and thunderstorms), result in unstable atmospheric conditions during the dry and limited periods of stability during the night. This instability causes vertical mixing of the atmosphere. Conversely during the winter, the dominant Arctic continental air mass (bringing clear skies, very low temperatures and light winds) and the Maritime Pacific air mass (providing occasional cloud cover, snow and higher temperatures) combine to produce stable weather conditions with frequent and intense inversions. Ice fogs occur in the river valleys, especially from December through February. They are most severe when the temperature drops to a critical level of 1.1°C or lower. The higher areas, for example, Birch Hills area, is climatically more moderate (warmer in winter, cooler in summer) and thus is not as susceptible to temperature inversions. In the vicinity of Fort McMurray, wind direction is seasonal, with the prevailing winds between October and May being east and southeast while those between June and August are more westerly.

Soils and Vegetation. At least 60 per cent of the area is covered by organic soil composed of muskeg and sphagnum moss bog. These organic soils, defined as having over 305 mm of peat at the surface, are acidic to moderately acidic in reaction and have a high water-holding capacity. Ice often occurs at depths below 406 to 762 m. The remaining soils are in the grey-wooded podzol group which have developed where there is better drainage and a continuous tree cover. Although, the oil sands area lies within the boreal forest region, the vegetation is a mixture of deciduous and coniferous trees. Where the drainage is good, the inorganic grey-wooded soils have a mixed cover of trembling aspen, white spruce and jack pine. White spruce and aspen grow in the poorly-drained areas. These inorganic soils are generally treeless but where the layer of organic matter is thin and drainage improves there is growth of black spruce and Labrador tea. Tamarack is also present, but is not common.

Resource Recovery Methods. At the end of 1973 only about one million m^3 of synthetic crude oil had been taken out of the Athabasca region. Although the political, economic and, to a lesser extent, environmental factors have impeded commercial production, by far the most important factor has been the technological limitation for bitumen extraction.

There are two different kinds of extraction which could be undertaken to produce synthetic crude oil from the oil sands. They are surface mining or *in situ* (in-place) methods. It is estimated that less than 10 per cent of the Athabasca deposit can be exploited with strip mining procedures. As previously mentioned, for oil sands which lie beneath less than 46 m of overburden, a modification of surface mining technique can be used. This operation involves four steps: (i) the removal of the overburden; (ii) the mining of the oil sands; (iii) the separation of the bitumen; and (iv) the upgrading of the bitumen to produce synthetic crude oil.

Essentially the only new technology used in this technique involves the hot water extraction process which separates the bitumen from the sand. The primary operation involves mixing the oil sands with hot water and steam. The oil in the tar sands changes its viscosity when heated and disperses in between the sand grains in flecks of various sizes.

Deposits under more than 46 m of overburden cannot be extracted by the surface mining techniques and thus a variety of *in situ* methods are being developed and

NFB – PHOTOTHEQUE – ONF – Photo by George Hunter.

The bucket-wheel excavator shown in this photo is used in the surface mining of the Athabasca oil sands. Once excavated, the sands are transported to a nearby separation plant.

tested. The major difference between these two methods is that for surface mining, a separation plant is required so that the bitumen and sand may be separated, whereas, when *in situ* methods are employed, the sand and oil are separated within the deposit. Although there are present technological inadequacies, the advantages of the *in situ* methods, (besides the much larger potentially-recoverable reserves and the minimal surface disruption), include few waste disposal problems, virtually no practical limit to the rate of extraction, and a minimum of land disturbance. The deep recovery techniques must render the oil less viscous while it is still *in situ* and then use some form of fluid injection to create enough pressure to force the dissociated oil up a standard well.

The surface mining operation begins with the clearing of trees and bush, stripping of topsoil or muskeg, and the removal of the overburden. The overburden is used either for the construction of tailings ponds or is deposited in the mined-out area. When necessary to loosen any rock in the overburden layers, blasting is used. Where the overburden consists of muskeg, the water must be drained prior to its relocation.

The removal of the oil sands follows, using bucket-wheel excavators, scrapers and electric draglines. Two unique German-designed bucket shovels have been built to scoop out the exposed tar sands. These monstrous machines sit on steel treads and use a rotating wheel of .76 m^3 buckets to rip up the sands and then deposit them on a conveyor belt or unit which carries the sands directly to the separation plant (this latter process may be supplemented by the use of large front-end loaders and trucks). An ore body of roughly 26 km^2 surface area will be mined out in operating a 15.9 thousand m^3/d plant for 30 years.

The processing of the bitumen consists of conditioning the feed, separating the bitumen from the sand, disposing of the waste and cleaning the recovered bitumen. The conditioning is carried out by slurrying oil sands with hot water, caustic soda and steam, thus forcing the oil to disintegrate, and freeing the bitumen from the sand and clay particles. In the separation of cells, sand settles to the bottom and bitumen floats to the surface. A middle layer is composed of bitumen and clay. Bitumen is recovered from the top of the cell, sand is removed from the bottom of the cell and the middle layer is tapped and put through a secondary recovery-froth flotation process. Following separation, the bitumen froth is treated with a dilutant (for example, naphtha) and finally centrifuged to remove water and the remaining mineral particles.

The tailings consist of sand, clay, water and unrecovered bitumen from the separation and centrifuging steps of the extraction process. Approximately eight to nine per cent of the bitumen in the plant feed is not recovered in the extraction process and most of this fraction goes out in the tailings stream. For example, the daily tailings from the Syncrude Limited plant are projected to contain 1,723 t of water, 146,118 t of sand, 272 t of naphtha, (based on a production level of 15.9 thousand m^3/d of synthetic crude oil).

The sand particles will settle out quickly and some of the tailings water can be recirculated through the plant. The clay material remains in suspension, forming a sludge which has to be retained and stored in the ponds indefinitely.

The residual waste products created by the hot water extraction from one t of tar sands will occupy a volume of .6 m^3 as compared with a void space of .4 m^3 created by the mining. As a consequence of this volumetric discrepancy, the final elevation of a reclaimed mining area will be more than 18.2 m higher than the original terrain.

During the initial five to ten years of plant operation, the tailings must be placed on original ground surface and retained by dikes which as previously mentioned may be constructed from overburden or tailings sands. Eventually, when a large enough pit is opened, the tailings can be deposited in the mined-out area. For a 15.9 thousand m^3/d plant, the initial tailings ponds will require an area of approximately 16 km^2 and cover potential oil sand reserves of 111 to 127 billion m^3.

Land Disturbance and Related Impacts. The amount of land surface disturbance associated with oil sands projects will be very large. The Integ report prepared for the Alberta Environment in 1973, suggests that at a level of production of 159 thousand m^3/d of synthetic oil, approximately 8,903 ha would be in a state of disturbance including 2,671 ha ahead of the mining and 3,561 ha being backfilled and revegetated. *In situ* projects will not require the huge excavations typical of surface mining operations. But, as the wells will be closely spaced, less than 121 m apart, surface clearing of comparable areas will be required. The lands will be occupied by *in situ* wells for approximately seven years. Lag times between overburden stripping and reforestation (reclamation) is estimated to take ten years.

Tailings ponds present a hazard to wildlife. Because of their toxicity and the presence of a film of tarry bitumen on the surface, the ponds pose a threat to migrating waterfowl. During the winter a persistent ice fog forms because the waste is expelled at 12.4°C. The fog reduces visibility for ground and air traffic and sometimes halts mining operations. The effects of this high humidity and low temperature are unknown. Also, caustic soda in the tailings raises the ph of the sands. Eventually, this may have a deleterious effect on potential reforestation programs because the indigenous conifers grow best on soils with a low pH content. These problems will be intensified as more plants become operational. The Syncrude Limited project required an initial tailings pond of 23 km^2 for the first years of its operation. When the mine pit is deep enough, a portion of the tailings can be deposited there. Tailings ponds associated with *in situ* operations are permanent until a method of sludge disposal is devised.

Sulphur dioxide and nitrogen oxide emissions are the main air pollutants resulting from oil sand operations. These pollutants are caused by the combustion of bituminous-based fuels or natural gas which produce the necessary steam and electrical energy required for the plants. Originally the Great Canadian Oil Sands Company was expected to be self-sufficient in electricity supply via thermal generation. But the sulphur content (six to ten per cent) of the coke was so great that natural gas had to be brought in to keep the sulphur dioxide levels in the safe range. Concern has also been expressed that with plants operating within a few km from each other, the ambient concentrations of sulphur dioxide and nitrogen oxide might become very high. In addition, diesel engines used in construction and operation of the mining site (which are kept running almost continually during the cold winter months to prevent engine seizure) could use up to 23 thousand L of fuel per day. Substantial quantities of water vapour also occur in the engine exhausts. Under inversion conditions in a mine pit, the effects of these pollutants could be aggravated.

NFB – PHOTOTHEQUE – ONF – Photo by Hans Blohm.

The Great Canadian Oil Sands Company is one of the first commercial producers in the Athabasca oil sands. Shown here are the infrastructure associated with mine-site production.

The major source of potential water pollution is from the tailings pond areas of the oil sands plants either through seepage into groundwater systems or in the case of dike failure, through massive loss of polluted water to adjacent water systems. For example, a layer of water-deposited salts called evaporites, lies above the concentrated tar sands layer. When it is exposed, surface water seeping down may dissolve the salts and eventually carry them into the Athabasca River. For each 159 thousand m^3/d surface mineable operation, the projected water demand from the Athabasca River system will represent 10 per cent of the minimum monthly flow of the river. At the same time, quantities of silt and water removed from the muskeg layer are flushed into the surface water system. The combined impact of these requirements is unknown. Experience in areas (e.g. dam construction) indicates that adverse consequences to biological ecosystems could result not only locally, but also downstream. In this case, downstream is north, throughout the entire Peace-Athabasca Delta. *In situ* recovery methods involve the injection of large quantities of water into the oil sands formation with possible impact on adjacent groundwaters. Water supply for *in situ* operations could pose serious problems, depending on plant location.

At its initial production level (15.9 thousand m^3/d), Syncrude Limited required a stockpile to dispose of some 1.8 thousand t/d of coke and 680 t of sulphur. Sulphur recovery and disposal will be necessary at these rates, or greater rates, at all oil sands plants. Coke disposal may be avoided, if technology advances permit the use of upgrading processes which do not produce coke, or if coke gasification becomes technically or economically feasible. Presently, the Great Canadian Oil Sands Company stockpiles both coke and sulphur as it is not economical to ship either of these commodities to market. The handling, storage and transportation of elemental sulphur or coke pose environmental problems relating to dusting, spontaneous combustion and water drainage.

Industrial development with its attendant population growth will affect the wildlife use of the oil sands areas. Parts of the Athabasca region are located on the Mississippi and Central flyway and are important as nesting and feeding grounds for migrating waterfowl. Large mammals of this area include the black bear, wolf, Canada lynx, white-tailed deer, mule deer, moose and caribou. Common fish species include walleye, northern pike, goldeye, lake trout and Arctic grayling.

Infrastructure requirements associated with oil sands developments such as roads, power lines, and community developments will require clearing and surface disturbance of rights-of-way, as will the construction of pipeline gathering and transmission systems.

James Bay Hydro-Electric Development Project

Lying within the coastal plain and highlands of the James Region of the Precambrian Canadian Shield, the James Bay area is traversed by boreal forest and taiga vegetation zones. The terrain, dotted with lakes, muskeg and other wetlands, rises gradually from the coastal plain to an inland height of 261 m. The majority of the power sites will occur in this coastal belt. The James Bay hydro-electric development project, will involve the drainage basins of the Nottaway, Broadback, Rupert, Eastmain, La Grande, Caniapiscau and Great Whale rivers of northwestern Québec. Together with their tributaries, these rivers comprise a drainage basin with an area of 372,960 km^2, or 25 per cent of Québec's land surface. Although four potential development projects have been designed, the La Grande River complex, is the first to be developed (Table 8).

La Grande Generating Potential. The project consists of diverting part of the waters of the Caniapiscau, Great Whale and Opinica (a tributary of the Eastmain River) rivers to the La Grande River, which has four large dams presently under construction (LG-1, LG-2, LG-3, LG-4) (*see* Map 4). More than 10 thousand MW will be in service by 1985 (Department of Energy, Mines and Resources, 1978*a*). Included in the construction will be four control dams, four large dams, 12 spillways, six regulatory works and nearly 128 km of dikes.

Dams, Dikes and Reservoirs. The La Gorge diversion and the Caniapiscau reservoir will permit the diverting of the waters of the basin north of the Caniapiscau River into those of the La Gorge River, a tributary of the La Grande River, upstream from LG-4. This reservoir will have a maximum elevation of 536 m and will be retained by a network of 32 dikes and two dams. The main dam will require about 80 per cent of the total volume of earth fill and will be located at the closing on the Caniapiscau River. The reservoir will include a spillway situated at the north end on the western arm of the

TABLE 8.
James Bay hydro-electric project, La Grande River complex

River	Reservoir	Maximum elevation before	Maximum elevation after	Area before	Area after	Area Flooded
		(m)	(m)	(km²)	(km²)	(km²)
La Grande	La Grande 1	6	32	13	78	65
La Grande	La Grande 2	38	175	207	4,015	3,807
La Grande	La Grande 3	171	256	285	1,865	1,580
La Grande	La Grande 4	262	399	52	743	692
Great Whale	Bienville	391	395	997	1,088	91
Caniapiscau	Caniapiscau	526	543	738	2,046	1,308
Caniapiscau	Delorme	492	511	259	1,295	1,036
La Grande	Puisseaux	491	504	155	324	168
			Total	2,706	11,454	8,747

Source: Report to the Joint Federal-Provincial Task Force. 1971. *A Preliminary Study of Environmental Impacts on the James Bay Development Project.*

main closure on the Caniapiscau River. This will consist of two floodgates 12 m wide and 17 m high with a capacity of 3,679 m³ which will allow surplus water to be returned to the Caniapiscau River. The discharged waters of the Caniapiscau River are directed toward a second diversion named "La Gorge," consisting of 12 dikes and several channels which then discharge into the La Gorge River, the tributary of the La Grande, upstream from LG-4.

The diversion of part of the waters of the Eastmain, Little Opinaca and Opinaca River basins achieved by constructing a dike on the Eastmain River will permit the retention of waters, thus raising the water level in the basins of the Little Opinaca and Opinaca rivers to that of the La Grande River via Lake Sakami. The main closure on the Eastmain River will consist of a rock dam with a maximum height of 34 m. The spillways which will be constructed before the dam, will divert the water from the dam construction. Located on the left bank of the Eastmain River, it will have three openings 14 m wide and 23 m high with a total capacity of 6,226 m³.

Transmission. The La Grande project will be connected to the southern consumption centres of the province by five 735-KV transmission lines which will be distributed over three corridors. Two of these three comprise lines carrying power directly from LG-2, one of which crosses Radisson where it will link up with LG-1 power station. The third corridor originates from Lemoyne Station, west of the De Pontois River.

Infrastructure. A project the size of James Bay has numerous infrastructure requirements such as roads, airports and towns. One of the most important is the main road route linking Matagami and southern Québec with Fort George by way of Radisson and LG-2. Other important routes located on the south bank of the La Grande River, provide access to the generating stations and the construction sites.

Temporary air landing facilities have been constructed near the sites of LG-2, LG-3, and LG-4. In addition, the La Grande River airport, situated several miles from LG-2, has an asphalt runway 1,981 m long and will be able to accommodate large transcontinental airplanes. A permanent town named Radisson near the site of LG-2 will be established. Also, it will be necessary to erect temporary towns at the sites of LG-3 and LG-4. Other camps are projected, as needs arise at the different construction sites.

Land-related impacts. Plans for the La Grande Complex project a flooding of some 11 thousand km². Of this area, 2,706 km² represents existing natural water bodies.

NFB – PHOTOTHEQUE – ONF – Photo by Pierre Gaudard.
A view of the temporary townsite needed to house the construction workers during the development phase of the James Bay project.

Parts of the impoundments will affect thousands of kilometres of existing shorelines. Portions of the newly-created lakes will have the appearance of drowned forests for many decades, since wood decomposition under subarctic conditions is very slow. Apart from the fact that the total environment lying within the proposed impoundment areas will be drastically altered by flooding, the adjacent water-dependent aquatic, lakeshore, riparian and marshland habitats will also be strongly influenced by fluctuating water levels. Such changes in the water table will affect wildlife which inhabit this region. Fish, beaver, moose, waterfowl, otter, mink, and muskrat will be the most severely affected species.

The creation of reservoirs with the decomposition of organic matter, changed chemical properties of the water, different water temperatures, and fluctuating water levels, will initially result in increased primary productivity but also a severe reduction in diversity of fish species. It is, however, difficult to assess the long-term physical-chemical characteristics of the reservoirs.

Downstream from the dams, the uniform flow will influence river dynamics, for example, the reduction of spring flooding, and ice scouring which have maintained riparian vegetation at early and more productive stages of biological succession. A major effect will be the deposition of sediments behind the dams, depriving downriver areas of their normal water quality. The changes in water temperature are also expected to influence fish species composition.

All rivers involved in the project, flow into salt water. Any reduction, in the rivers' flow, temporary or permanent, will be accompanied by a proportional saltwater intrusion into their estuaries. In the La Grande estuary, where the discharge is to be substantially increased, the opposite will occur. The freshwater and marine environment ratios will, therefore, be altered in all affected estuaries.

Large expanses of open black spruce forest with a thick ground cover of lichens and ericaceous shrubs, as well as sizable areas of wetlands will be inundated. Trees rarely reach merchantable size and when they do, the stands are very old, indicating that the potential for timber production is very low. This physical loss of forest habitat will cause the displacement of wildlife in all flooded areas. Apart from the fish, beaver will probably incur the heaviest loss of habitat. Most of the region is already carrying an optimal beaver population, therefore, any displaced beaver will be in competition for space already occupied. The existence of beaver during winter depends on the maintenance of precise water levels which will be upset by hydro-electric dams. In drying areas affected by headwaters, there may be some possibility for beaver population growth. Beaver play an indispensable rôle in development and maintenance of wetland habitat which could result in secondary effects to other species. Whether or not the interruption of the food chain (from terrestrial and aquatic plants and invertebrates to fish, birds, whales, seals, and polar bears) will reduce wildlife in the area, is a matter of speculation.

NFB – PHOTOTHEQUE – ONF – Photo by Pierre Gaudard.
Earth fill is transported by truck into the LG-2 dam, on the La Grande River.

The environmental effects of airports, landing strips, towns, working camps, roads, and transmission line corridors should be examined. Perhaps the greatest changes to the terrestrial environment will stem from construction activities in support of the main hydro-electric project. These activities will cause local changes in drainage patterns, soil stability, micro-climatic conditions and aesthetic quality. The improved accessibility provided by the infrastructure may attract an influx of southern tourists and recreationists which would further affect the ecological balance. However, the black fly and mosquito populations, already a deterrent to the tourist industry, are expected to increase in numbers, with flooding, and may discourage increasing tourist at-

tractivity. Although greater activity in the area will generate more forest fires, at the same time, improved access will provide better means of fire control.

The all-weather road from Matagami to Fort George is not exempt from many of the environmental effects which normally accompany road-building. For example, the road and the right-of-way have created a man-made habitat which may interfere with natural wildlife movements. The road may act as a barrier to shy animals, provide a cleared path to others, attract scavengers, and present the risk of collision with transport vehicles. Poorly-designed culverts may interfere with fish movement and spawning beds and create drainage problems. Drainage ditches can become areas of erosion. Construction debris and roadside borrow pits detract from the landscape. Application of herbicides to control roadside vegetation has varying environmental effects.

The clearing of a corridor for power transmission lines will also leave a permanent impression on the landscape. The effects of transmission lines on wildlife are not well known. The corridor may influence animal migrations. In addition, the effects of herbicides on wildlife and water quality are not predictable. Studies should be conducted to determine the impact of noise generated by the transmission lines on wildlife. The substitution of controlled clearing operations for herbicides could keep vegetation at a youthful stage, providing an essential source of food for moose, beaver and game birds.

Certain animals, particularly the polar bear, are attracted to waste foods, thus working camps and settlements could upset feeding habits and migration patterns. If poorly located, airports and landing strips alter land use, create noise, and present a possible hazard to waterfowl and birds.

Past studies and actual measurements have concluded that the climatic changes produced by hydro-electric projects and their reservoirs are restricted to local areas near the reservoirs and estuaries of the manipulated rivers in the form of slight maritime influences. Wind is indirectly the most important of the meteorological elements in exercising power over the extent of the influence of reservoir climate. The influence will extend leeward of the reservoir for a distance proportional to wind direction, wind speed and ruggedness of the terrain. An increase in local wind speeds can be expected over and in the vicinity of reservoirs. The direction of predominant winds will be slightly altered by the long axes of the reservoirs, favouring their orientation. Larger reservoirs usually experience a diurnal breeze circulation with a predominant onshore wind during the day and an offshore breeze at night. In addition, at the beginning of the warming season, the reservoir exerts a cooling influence, and in the latter part of the warm season and into the cool season until freeze-up, a warming influence is felt on air temperatures. Reservoirs also influence the diurnal range of temperatures which is one of the main indications of a lesser continentality of climate in the shore zones.

Photo by Société d'énergie de la Baie James.
Four of the sixteen turbine units at the LG-2 site are shown being assembled 137 m below the ground surface.

225

In most climates, creation of a water impoundment, although visibly increasing the amount of water, causes a loss of actual water available to man by increasing the evaporation rate. However, in the James Bay region, the amount of water loss through evapotranspiration is predicted to decrease, because precipitation will also be suppressed, resulting in a net loss of moisture. Heat storage of reservoirs will also alter monthly distribution of evapotranspiration and precipitation rates.

Renewable Energy

In the past, Canada has relied heavily on non-renewable (non-replaceable) energy resources for development. However, as suggested, shortages and escalating prices have forced a new perspective on the energy situation. The sun, wind, tides and forests, renewable energy sources which until recently were taken for granted, now are being reviewed to determine their harnessable potential.

Solar Energy. The sun drives the wind, grows the plants, warms and cycles the waters and each action can potentially be used as a renewable energy source (*see* Figure 6). Solar energy is the largest non-depletable energy source available to man. In fact, the total incoming radiant energy annually received in Canada was over seven thousand times the total energy consumed by Canadians in 1972. (Middleton, 1976). Such theoretical figures are enticing but do not evaluate the solar resource as an alternative energy form. Solar energy's magnitude, universal presence, self-renewing and non-polluting characteristics enhance its attractiveness as an alternative energy source. However, the sun does not generate a constant, concentrated quantity of energy which can be harnessed and consumed continuously, at any one location on the earth's surface, without a storage capacity. In fact, the amount of solar energy is variable upon such factors as latitude, season, time of day, and atmospheric interference from clouds, dust, or haze.

The distribution of solar energy within Canada on a national scale is indicated on Map 5. The solar energy isolines presented are based on the average amount of solar radiation received on a horizontal surface over a five-year time period and expressed in watts per m². The southern portions of the Prairie Provinces, British Columbia and Ontario reflect the highest values in Canada. The majority of Canada's land area receives 150 watts per m² whereas the sunniest parts of the world receive some 250 watts per m² (Cockshutt, 1977).

There are several limitations to the information portrayed in Map 5. The isolines are extrapolations from point observations and are therefore approximations. These isolines do not indicate the possible solar energy that may be harnessed but rather indicate the average amount of incoming radiation accumulated by a horizontal surface collector instrument.

To portray the amount of usable solar radiation, the concept of a tilted collector must be introduced and both direct and diffuse components of radiation must be considered. By tilting the recording instrument at an angle away from the horizontal toward the sun, the direct radiation component decreased while the diffuse component is increased as less sky is visible to the instrument. Reflected radiation from the ground surrounding the collector is introduced and such radiation increases with a tilted collector. The over-all net radiation is, in effect, increased by such tilting. Present solar energy applications harness both direct and diffuse radiations thereby minimizing some of the latitudinal and seasonal variations, improving the solar energy resource and its distribution in Canada. Constant supply is a basic consideration of energy systems. With solar energy, as with other alternative energy sources, a storage capacity must be available to contain energy and supply it when no source input is available. Extremes, such as the frequency of consecutive cloudy days, are important for they substantially increase the need for storage capacity. The seasonal patterns of solar supply and energy demand must also be considered. The potential energy supply in summer is some four to eight times greater than during winter when the demand is highest in terms of home heating applications. Fortunately, the cold nights of February and March are followed by short but relatively sunny days, which permits some regeneration of energy.

In Canada, 55 per cent of the total energy used is in the form of low grade heat (less than 140°C) and, in principle, solar collectors could supply this demand (Science Council of Canada, 1977). Solar energy applications in space and water heating have been pursued in Canada since 1971, with the first application for residential heating occurring in Surrey, British Columbia. To date, North America has some 800 such solar applications while Canada has about 50 such structures in existence or in a planning stage.

The basic components of a solar space heating system are: a collector, a circulating medium of water or air to which collected energy is transferred, a storage medium of rocks or water, and a space heating distribution network (Figure 7). Thermal solar panels for space heating are located on the roofs of structures or may be situated at ground level close by on the property. Energy is thus tapped and used in a non-polluting, non-grid-oriented system thereby dispensing with distribution lines. Since it has been shown that storage of solar energy is more efficient with less heat loss by using a larger storage medium, there is a possibility of creating mini-utilities which supply heating on a district or multi-unit basis as a more efficient operation.

Federal and provincial governments and academic and industrial organizations, as well as individuals, have been involved in solar projects. Six large federally-sponsored projects in this field include: Gananoque House near Kingston, Ontario; Mississauga House near Toronto, Ontario; the Ark at Cape Spry on Prince Edward Island; Manitoba Legislature Building in Winnipeg, Manitoba; Provident House near Toronto; and experimental housing for Québec Indian communities near Lac Macaza. The National Research Council sponsored some 14 single-family houses in 1976-77. Twenty-nine multi-family or senior citizen projects were to be sponsored in the 1977 fiscal year. Present direction of solar development suggests an individual unit or small grouping of units have minimal adverse consumptive land effects.

The need for collector orientation to a southerly direction and a guarantee of unobstructed solar exposure may pose siting constraints. The guarantee of no shadowing from tall trees or nearby structures can certainly be critical on a site by site basis. Such constraints may re-orient future town site developments (Nadler, 1977), but in terms of general land impact, solar energy developments in this form are indeed minimal.

The problem with solar energy implementation is its costs in construction and installation of collectors, and the large storage capacities needed to operate at 100 per cent solar power for heating. Hollands and Orgill's study (1977) showed that solar heating is economically viable in most of Canada on a combined solar/conventional heating system basis. As costs of petroleum rise, solar power becomes increasingly attractive. The initial capital outlay required poses an important restriction for solar systems. Solar systems may vary from under $2,000 for add-on collectors to over $200,000 for professionally-designed solar homes (Collins, 1977).

Applications of solar energy, other than for direct heating, must not be overlooked. The possibility of using solar energy by direct conversion to electrical power through photovoltaic cells (semi-conductor diodes of several cm²) exists. Initial applications were for spacecraft power generation. Estimated costs per unit of power are some 50 times greater than conventional power sources but costs are decreasing. Combined solar electricity/space heating systems may offer promise in the long-term.

Some futuristic large-scale applications are solar power stations which have large land areas of collectors, or solar satellites beaming power to land-based receiving stations. Both of these applications are only at a conceptual stage. Their relevance to the Canadian solar regime and energy demands remains questionable. However, it is interesting to contemplate the land requirements of such large-scale solar systems...

> "the land requirements for, say a 1000 MW power plant compare favourably with other more conventional systems. The heliostat or collector for such a plant could be 26 m². For an equivalent coal-fired plant this area would be doubled, allowing for the land demands for mining the fuel, storing it and disposing of the ash. The reservoir of a hydro plant could occupy several hundred square kilometres" (Jeffs, 1977).

The point to consider is not its actual application but rather its potential land use conflicts among a variety of feasible energy resources and supplies.

Some basic questions still require resolution in the Canadian context. These include: type of solar collectors (flat plate versus evacuated tube) and their efficiencies, whether collection should be air or water-based, the cost effectiveness of seasonal heat storage, and the need for back-up facilities in times of insufficient supply (Sasaki, 1977).

To effectively harness solar energy in space heating, some of the existing housing stock will require retrofitting and most new housing will at least have to have the facility for solar conversion. Actual large-scale imple-

Photo by Société d'énergie de la Baie James.

Construction of the LG-2 dam is scheduled to be completed by 1980. The first station will contain 16 units with a total capacity of 5,000, 328 MW.

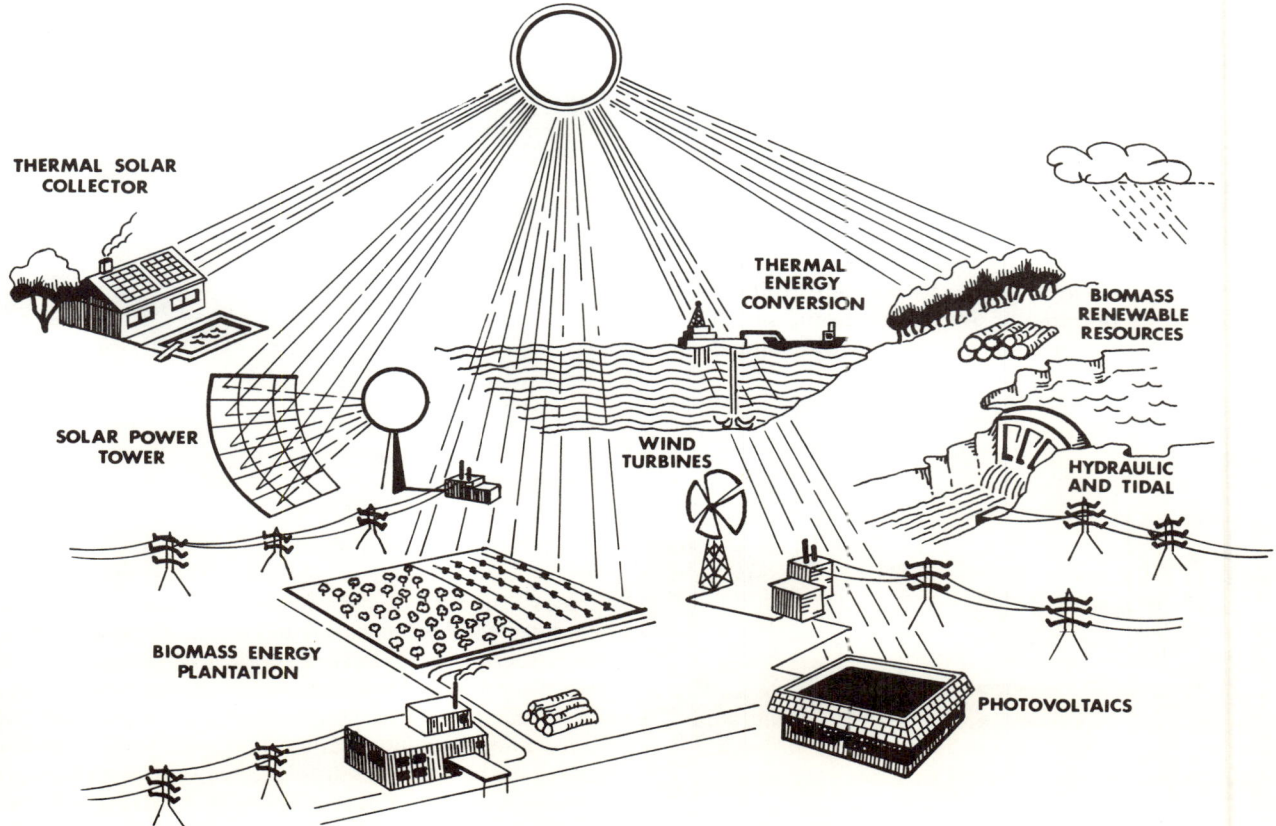

FIGURE 6.

SOLAR ENERGY CONVERSION PROCESSES

Source: J. S. Reuyl et al, <u>Solar Energy in America's Future</u>, 1977.

DISTRIBUTION OF ANNUAL AVERAGE RADIATION MAP 5

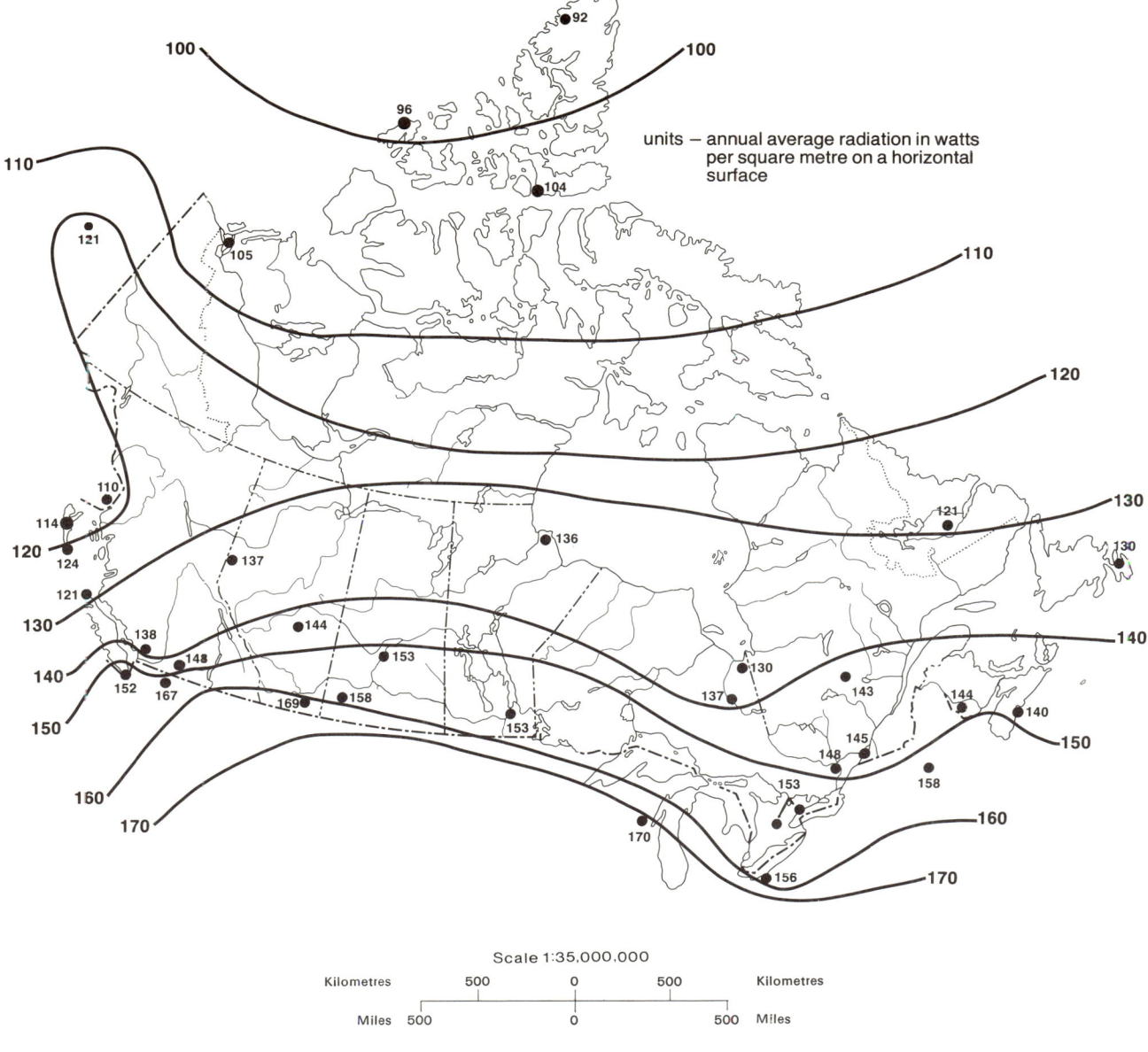

Source: E. P. Cockshutt, Solar Energy, 1977.

FIGURE 7.

SOLAR HEATING SYSTEM

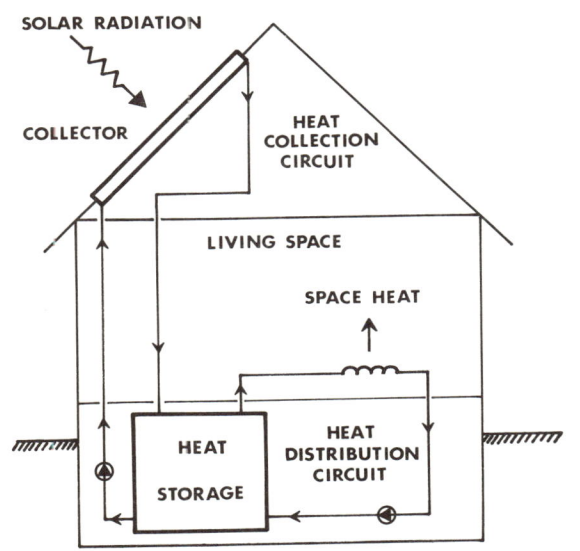

Source: E. P. Cockshutt, Solar Energy, 1977.

mentation and commercialization of solar power is yet in its infancy. Solar panels could well appear as a basic component in housing. Photovoltaic developments are yet another step away but it seems inevitable that solar power will play a significant rôle in energy supply in Canada's future.

Wind Energy. Is the answer blowing in the wind? This question is being addressed when evaluating wind as an alternative form of energy. As early as 200 BC, the Persians were using wind power to grind their grain. In Canada, windmills were first introduced in 1647 to a small settlement, Ville Marie, which now forms the city of Montréal. Wind generators were prominent in the early 20th century on farms and were used for pumping water, driving small generators, lighting, and charging batteries. Since the early 1970s, renewed interest in Canada has focused on wind as a clean, renewable energy source which can supplement Canada's future energy requirements especially in the light of escalating costs and diminishing reserves of conventional non-renewable fossil fuels.

> "Wind energy is a manifestation of solar energy and is merely air set in motion, set up and continually regenerated by a small fraction of insolation reaching the outer atmosphere" (Ramakumar, 1976).

Wind's universal presence, self-renewing and non-polluting characteristics enhance its attractiveness as an alternative energy source. However, winds are intermittent, vary seasonally, vary in intensity, and are site specific in terms of optional energy production.

Templin (1977) has mapped wind energy isolines on a national scale (Map 6). Each isoline indicates the average rate of kinetic energy flow in watts passing through one m² of vertical area located at a height of 30 m above ground level. Excessive local variation in the mountainous regions of British Columbia and Yukon precludes the plotting of wind energy isolines. Three areas in Canada clearly emerge with the highest wind energy: the southern Prairies, northern Canada especially in the vicinity of Hudson Bay, and the Atlantic coastal area.

There are several limitations to the information conveyed on the generalized map. The isolines are extrapolations based on point observations, and must be accepted as approximations. These isolines reflect potential, not actual, wind power that can be harnessed by a wind turbine power plant. Templin (1977) estimates that from 15 to 20 per cent of the indicated values may be converted to electrical power output.

Additional complications have been identified in the assessment of wind power. Precise velocities and their duration must be recorded on an annual basis for an accurate evaluation of wind potential of a site. Generally, only consistent winds above 16 km/hr can generate significant power. Local conditions may significantly alter a site's wind potential. As an example, land/water interfaces generate air movement through differential heating and cooling, favouring seacoasts and lakesides for potential development. Flat, untreed land or unobstructed areas of higher elevation have greater wind development possibilities. Wind increases significantly with height, so mountainous regions may possess high wind potential but local variations such as wind funnelling in these areas complicate accurate estimation.

A number of wind generator designs can successfully tap the wind's power (Alberta Research Council, 1976). The largest Canadian wind generator is based on a vertical axis rotor whereas the United States demonstrator near Sandusky Ohio uses a horizontal axis design. Wind energies have been tapped successfully at a number of sites throughout Canada. The largest installation is the National Research Council's experiment on the Magdalen Islands in the Gulf of St. Lawrence. The wind generator is 37 m wide and 24 m high and is located on top of a nine-m tower. Operation commenced in July, 1977 and can potentially generate 200 kW of electricity into the local power grid.[2] A successful experiment conducted by Environment Canada in the operation of a weather station in the Beaufort Sea shows yet another scale of application in a Canadian context. The station functioned on a wind-based power supply from June 1976 to February, 1977 when it drifted from satellite range. It confirms the feasibility of applications at remote locations under climatic extremes. Other applications using wind generator power are: a 40-kW installation at Frobisher Bay, N.W.T. and another at Cambridge Bay sponsored by the Northern Canada Power Commission; remote telemetry units monitoring Arctic ice movement supported by Imperial Oil; a 1,100-kW generator operated by Bell Telephone Company at Goose Bay; "The Ark", a family dwelling greenhouse aquaculture located at Cape Spry, Prince Edward Island; and an installation at Gillam, Manitoba built by Manitoba Hydro. Future applications include using wind power in powering marine beacons on the Queen Charlotte Islands, remote northern weather stations, runway lights on an airstrip near Faro, Yukon Territory, remote microwave transmitters and applications by telephone companies in British Columbia, Manitoba, northern Ontario, and the Atlantic Provinces. These lists are not exhaustive and do not include individual entrepreneurs successfully utilizing wind energies, but indicate present and potential uses for future wind development. The Science Council of Canada (1977) has estimated that by 1990, Canada may have from 1,000 to 3,000 windmills, each with a 200-kW capacity. The precise land effects of such developments are difficult to assess, since the Magdalen Islands' experiment is the only one of this size in Canada.

The only comprehensive study to date has been conducted by S.E. Rogers *et al* (1977) assessing the environmental effects of wind energy system development. In relation to the largest United States installation, the report indicates that such facilities have no major land consumption and environmental disruptions are minimal and often not measurable. In terms of climate impact, the installation of large numbers of turbines has been equated to the impact of groves of tall trees. However, the impact must be re-evaluated when arrays of over ten such machines are established. Wind turbines may pose problems to migratory bird species especially if placed on isolated hills or coastlines where flight altitudes are reduced with respect to the ground surface. Both this and ground level microclimatic influence can only be assessed in respect of individual turbine siting.

Expanded utilization of this resource must still address several complications. Naturally, the spacing and location of wind turbines is dependent upon the scale of application. Both individual unit site applications, as well as the large-scale power generation facilities, will locate only in the most favourable locations of wind regime and should approximately parallel the areas of high potential (Map 6). Assuming that generators will feed into the electrical grid, their locations must be near existing transmission lines. Naturally, alternative energy sources must serve energy demands and must then be proximal to densely populated areas. This poses a dilemma since the largest demand is along the Windsor-Québec axis but wind potential is not especially high in this area. The impact of power generation schemes may provide decentralized regional power sources for the Atlantic, southern Prairies, and selected coastal areas of British Columbia. Other siting constraints will be encountered. Although land input is minimal and analogous to the space demand for an electrical transmission tower, some lands will have to be acquired. In the case of forested regions, cleared land is required to provide unobstructed wind access. However, construction of a small tower structure may permit co-existence with vegetation below tower height; land uses in the immediate vicinity of such towers need not be disturbed. Questions

[2]Generator broke down in 1978 and production has been delayed until mid-1979.

227

DISTRIBUTION OF WIND ENERGY MAP 6

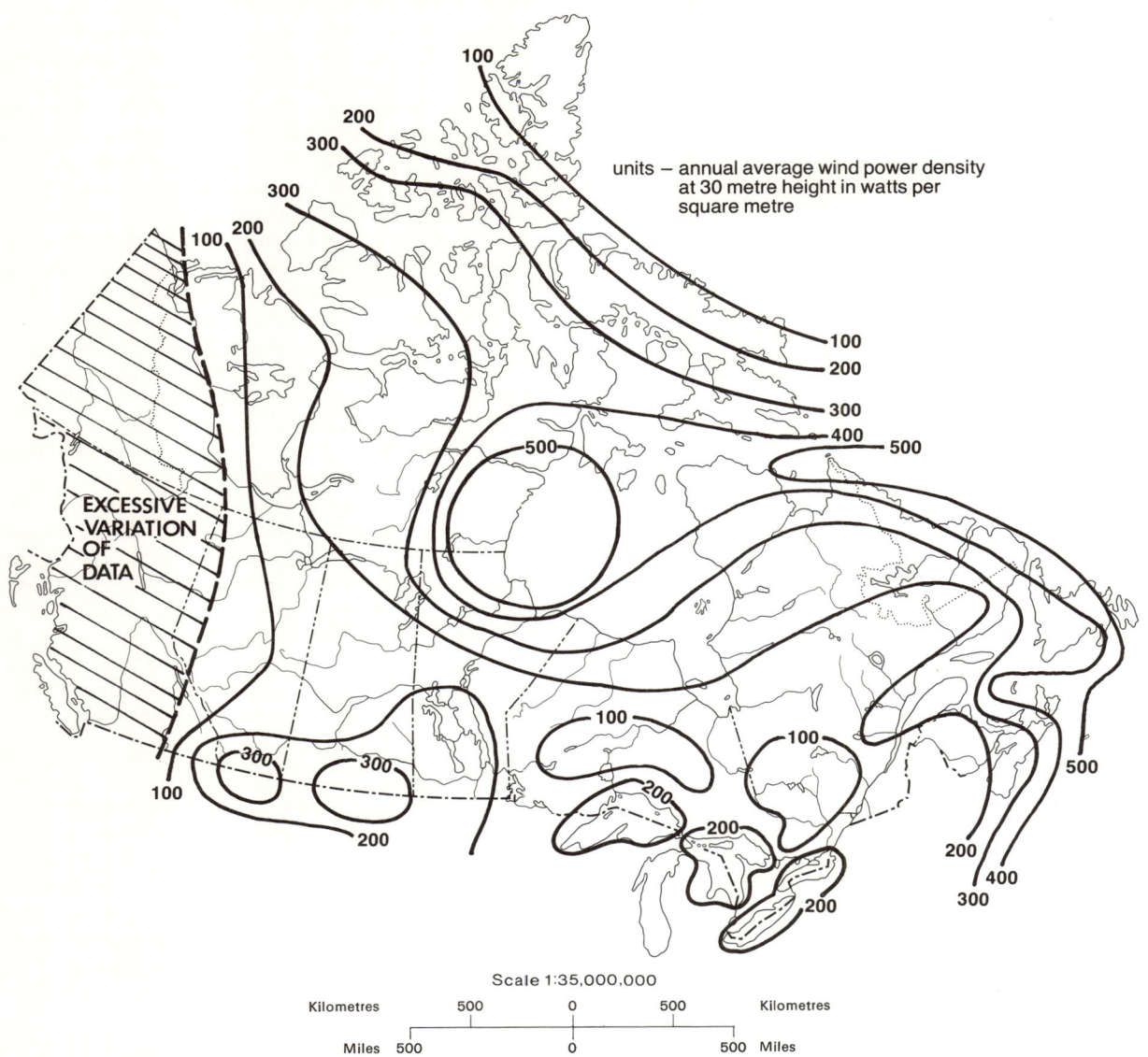

Source: R. J. Templin, "Wind Energy", 1977.

on the aesthetic and social acceptability of such towers remain unanswered. Areas of significant scenic value such as mountains and seacoasts are also suitable for wind turbine locations. Safety considerations, in case of blade throw from such installations, have to be reconciled as applications become more widespread.

Present costs of using wind energies in populated parts of Canada are excessive in relation to conventional energy sources (Science Council of Canada, 1977). As prices and transportation costs of conventional fuels increase, as in more remote areas of Canada, wind energies become more cost-feasible, presuming a sufficient wind supply. Brown and Higgin (1976) concluded that there is "... good potential for large wind generators to save diesel fuel and annual operating costs in remote communities...."

Biomass. Biomass energy is based on the retrieval of solar energy captured by the photosynthetic process in plants. This biomass energy may be directly available from plants, trees or algae or may be found in waste materials originating from urban, agricultural, animal, or industrial activities. Such energy can be released directly through conversion to heat or steam generation or through bioconversion to synthetic fuels and materials of higher energy content. The end products may be solid, liquid, or gas.

Biomass is an attractive energy source because Canada has a large reserve of potential fuels and has one of the highest biomass per capita ratios in the world (Middleton, 1976). Biomass derives from renewable resources which have relatively small amounts of polluting impurities when processed. Biomass energy may also be manufactured from waste materials thereby alleviating waste disposal problems (Science Council of Canada, 1975). There are several processes in the biomass energy conversion which may be utilized.

One common example is the direct conversion of biomass energy via combustion as illustrated in the burning of wood to release energy such as heat. Another means of biomass conversion is by pyrolysis. This involves the physical and chemical decomposition of organic matter by heat actions in the absence of oxygen (McCallum, 1977). What results is a mixture of gases, liquids, and char, each of which can serve as further energy sources. Gasification, another biomass conversion,

NFB – PHOTOTHEQUE – ONF – Photo by George Hunter

An experimental egg-beater type of windmill, designed by the National Research Council, is located in southern Saskatchewan.

is similar to pyrolysis except that the reaction is undertaken with a controlled air (or oxygen) supply. It does not necessitate additional heat input and because of its partial combustion characteristics it produces different gas mixtures than does pyrolysis. One major application has been wood gasification which produces a suitable internal combustion engine fuel.

There are also three, "wet conversion" processes. Anaerobic digestion is a result of bacterial action on organic matter (biomass) in a moist, oxygen-free environment. This process produces a versatile methane gas and a sludge with high fertilizer value. Aerobic digestion is the biological reaction on biomass in the presence of oxygen at moderate temperature. Its most lucrative product is high nutrient fertilizer and humus rather than any usable energies. Conventionally, this composting practice is found on farms and gardens. A third method is the fermentation process. Certain fungi can react with biomass containing significant sugar content, such as sugar cane, sugar beets, potatoes, or wheat, to form alcohols, primarily ethanol, which can be used as fuel for powering vehicles.

The most significant land impacts and effects in the biomass conversion process lie in the biomass supplies from which it may be possible to capture energy. There are basically three approaches: use existing resources of biomass; use present residual or waste materials as biomass; or generate renewable biomass which could then be used in the conversion process.

The forests of Canada, with 157 million ha of primary forest land (Middleton, 1976) (*see also* Forestry sector), represent an example of an existing resource for biomass conversion. Radical improvements in furnace design have raised the heat efficiency that wood provides by three times to approximately 75 per cent. Combination oil/wood-fuelled furnaces can ensure continual heat supply. Electricity generation is being tested where wood fuel is used in lieu of oil or coal at thermal electric generating plants with one such example being the 25-MW plant in Hearst, Ontario. The potential for application lies clearly in proximity to the natural distribution of the resource itself. Much of the Atlantic Region, northern Québec, Ontario, Manitoba, Saskatchewan, and British Columbia which have nearby wood reserves, are most suitable for such applications. The high bulk of wood, and the necessity for manual handling of wood restrict development. Applications in densely populated areas are constrained by the problem of fuel storage, the suitability for large applications, and the problem of potential emission problems. A large shift to more intensive forest exploitation necessitates an upgrading of forest management. Not only would the same resource have to meet existing demands by pulp and paper and lumber industries but would also have to meet wood heating applications. The environmental considerations of extensive large-scale forest use require further evaluation.

The Canadian forestry industry can also potentially be used to supply the biomass required for methanol production. Methanol is produced by a two-step conversion process first using pyrolysis to produce a gas which can be refined to methanol. Methanol is a fuel with a diversity of uses which range from a turbine and diesel fuel to home heating, and may be used as a gasoline additive. The methanol production process involves a central, large-scale facility which has to be located close to both the fuel supply and energy demand site. There are approximately 142 million m^3 of unused residues in the Canadian forestry operations (Marshall, 1975). Using only one-quarter of these materials, 8.5 billion L of methanol could be produced to serve about six per cent of projected transportation fuel requirements in 1990, assuming implementation of economically viable technology (Middleton, 1976). A pre-feasibility study by Intergroup Consulting Economists (1976) estimates that tree species not in production, plus forest wastes, could produce 22.7 billion L of methanol while the unused straw could supply another 9 billion L in a series of regionally-oriented plants located across the country. Zones that have a surplus capacity of forest biomass to be of sufficient size to support a minimal scale methanol plant and yet not deplete the natural supply in Canada are shown in Map 7 (Intergroup Consulting Economists, 1976).

There are a number of sources of organic waste materials in Canada which could be transformed into usable energies. Using pyrolysis, urban wastes can be transformed into pyrolytic fuel which, after upgrading, can be used to produce methanol and ammonia. Development work has largely focused on waste management questions rather than on energy production. This transformation process requires high temperatures (500 to 900°C) and a constant large quantity of fuel (i.e., waste) to be operationally efficient. This necessitates the siting of such plants near centres where populations are in excess of 200 thousand (Middleton, 1976). Canada presently has 15 centres of this size.

The development of such organic waste operations in Canada is at the experimental stage. The cities of Montréal, Hamilton, and Québec City have heat recovery garbage incinerators. The United States is funding six demonstration projects using pyrolysis. The impact of pursuing this type of development would be beneficial in recycling of resources. It would also offer an effective alternative waste disposal method to landfill. However, McCallum (1977) warns that the establishment of such plants should not deter other recycling and waste reduction efforts just to support the fuels of such power plants. The immediate local effects of such plants would be analogous to incinerators or thermal generating stations.

Another significant use of wastes is conversion of mixed crop and animal waste through anaerobic digestion. Animals internalize only a small portion of the energy contained in foodstuffs. Anaerobic digestion of such wastes produces methane gas and sludge which may be used as a fertilizer. Such a system is already fully operational in England at a municipal sewage fa-

ZONES OF "SURPLUS" FOREST BIOMASS CAPACITY FOR A METHANOL CONVERSION OPERATION   MAP 7

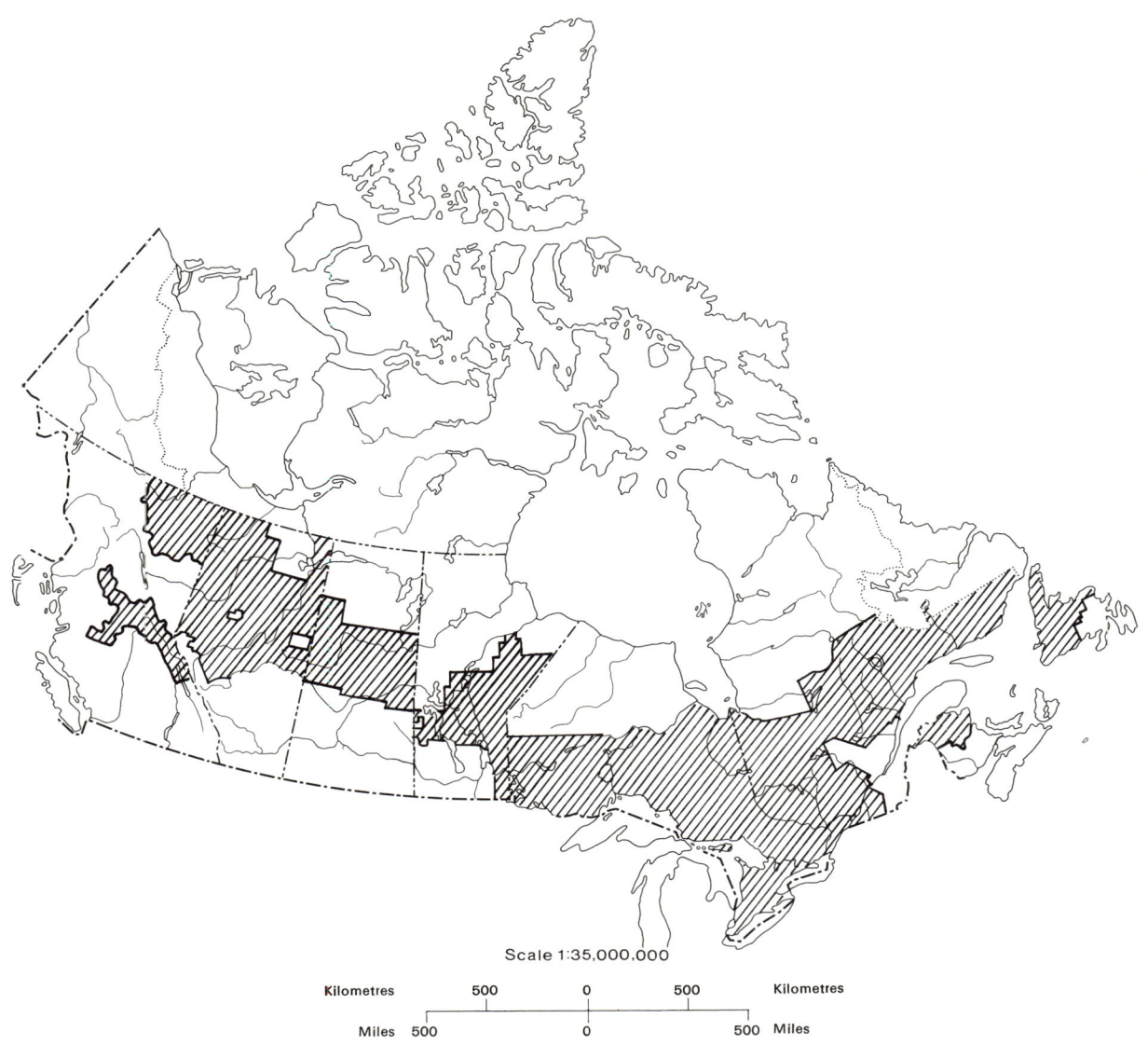

Source: Intergroup Consulting Economists Limited, Economic Pre-Feasibility Study: *Large Scale Methanol Fuel Production from Surplus Canadian Biomass*, 1977.

cility. The operational size of the process has a wide range of scales which can be applied in a diverse manner. The key to the process is microbial action which is highly sensitive to temperature (32 to 35°C range). This naturally requires external heat support in Canadian winter conditions but can produce a net energy profit (Middleton, 1976).

The value of implementation lies in the waste management, as well as a decentralization of gas production. It may also aid farmers in reducing expenses. The direct land impacts are minimal. They are no more than those that result from waste disposal but such a system could bolster the viability of agricultural operations. In the complete food cycle from growing, processing, and delivery, it should be noted that

"...for every unit of food energy consumed by Canadians and Americans, the equivalent of seven units of fossil fuel energy was required to put that food on the consumer's table" (Schute *et al.*, 1976).

Currently, the largest experimental project is a 200-swine waste digestor demonstration at the Glenlea Research Station, Manitoba. The areas of greatest potential application lie in the feedlots, stockyards, large beef, hog, and dairy operations. In Canada there are 2,400 cattle operations of more than 450 head. The basic question still to be answered is the feasibility of using annual tonnages of animal manure in an efficient anaerobic operation in the cold Canadian climate.

A third alternative for biomass is special cultivation of crops on a plantation basis specifically for conversion. Examples here include maize, red alder, kelp, algae, and cattail. The feasibility of this approach is evident from Brazil which is presently cultivating sugar cane and, by fermentation, converting it to ethanol which serves as an automotive fuel. R.S. Evans (1974) has studied this concept in Canada and his results have shown that a 168 km^2 red kelp plantation can supply sufficient fuel for powering a 150-MW thermal power plant. In Canada, emphasis has been on the hybrid poplar which can regenerate itself quickly. (Timbers, 1977).

A number of questions and problems remain to be resolved. Analysis of the optimal conversion process and the most suitable crops for energy conversion still must be evaluated in the Canadian context. The greatest problem facing plantations is land use conflict. This use would conflict with existing agricultural, forestry, recreational, and urban uses. Priorities and overall land use policies would be necessary in a total energy context. For example, compare the land demand between the wind generation system (200 MW in Magdalen Islands) and the 150-MW plant cited above. There is also a basic question of whether to use lands which could support a food supply to generate power.

The fundamental requirements of biomass production determine their optimal spatial distribution and location.

"The requirements for biomass production are sunlight, carbon dioxide, water, suitable soil nutrients and suitable air and soil temperatures. An area possessing all of these in adequate amounts will have growth potential. Limitations in one or a combination of factors will proportionately reduce yields, as will imperfect culture practices." (Biomass Energy Institute, 1974).

In the implementation of any of the biomass technologies, basic questions as to the cost competitiveness with existing energies must be considered.

"...the question of the *production* of sufficient quantities of wood biomass appears at this time to be more critical than that of having sufficient technology for its *conversion* into a useful product. The prime determining factors in the economics of production are land availability, cost and biomass yield." (Inman, 1976).

Even barring the technological barriers of production, most processes are more costly than using conventional fuels. There is, however, a basic advantage in that renewable resources are used, and that in the case of using wastes, efficient resource recycling and waste management questions are resolved. A basic re-evaluation of total energy needs in light of renewable versus non-renewable energy options and the applications of biomass is needed. Certainly the shift to biomass as an alternative energy source is a feasible approach. With Canada's land mass, the potential of biomass is significant, but poses fundamental land use questions which must be resolved in a total energy context.

Tidal Energy. Tides are caused by the earth's rotation and the changing relative positions of the earth, sun, and moon. This combination of centrifugal and gravitational forces, results in cyclic shifts of the world's oceans. When these waters are thrust upon the coasts of continents, vast amounts of energies are released. Particular physical formations concentrate these energies and accentuate the changes in water levels making specific locations more attractive for harnessing the power of the tides. The concept of using these moving water masses dates back centuries. As early as the 11th century, small mills were constructed along coastlines to harness the tides. Operations were hampered by the very nature of the tidal cycle, for the mechanical power generated had to be used immediately at the time of water movement. By the 19th century, hydro-electric facilities and fossil fuels provided more suitable and convenient energy alternatives which led to disinterest in tidal power technology and applications. Tides offer several advantages as an energy supply. Tidal energy is renewable and the generation procedure itself produces no direct pollution (Campbell, 1974). However, tides are not a continuous power source. They operate in cycles which are not always in phase with man's demands and activities, which are related to a regular diurnal solar cycle. This necessitates an expensive storage component. To harness the power of the tides, estuaries must be dammed, and turbine facilities installed which have definite environmental implications. There are only a limited number of locations throughout the world that are capable of supporting tidal development.

The principle used to harness tidal power is quite similar to hydro-electric power generation. A dam is constructed across a basin and the flow of water is directed through an opening which rotates turbines which, in turn, generate electricity. The actual implementation at a site may be more complex and may be operated from one or two basins to maximize power generation (Clarke and Walker, 1976). During the past decade, two tidal developments have been constructed. The Soviet Union installed a small tidal powered generator of 400 kW on the Kislaya Inlet on the White Sea. The major French development of a 240 thousand-kW plant at La Rance Estuary near St. Malo, France, has sparked renewed interest in the tidal potential. This project, completed in 1967, generates power from the 37-m tides.

Canada is quite fortunate with respect to potential sites for tidal development. Eastern Canada is best endowed. Ungava Bay in northern Québec, Frobisher Bay, and Cumberland Sound on Baffin Island offer potential, but attention for development has focused on the Bay of Fundy (Campbell, 1974). Since the early 1920s, the Bay of Fundy has been the subject of several investigations for tidal development. This area offers one of the world's greatest tidal ranges of 16 m. A 1969 report commissioned by the Canadian government and the provinces of Nova Scotia and New Brunswick discovered that although it was technically feasible, such development was not cost-competitive with alternative energy sources. The Atlantic Tidal Power Programming Board (1969) specifically concluded that further studies should be undertaken only when: interest rates decline; developments in construction techniques or generating equipment compensate for economic circumstances; or the relative cost of alternative energy sources increases. In light of escalating prices for fossil fuels, a re-investigation began in 1972, leading to a continued two-phase study program. The objective of this most recent program is to ascertain a firm cost of tidal energy in relation to alternative sources of power and to provide indications on whether to proceed with further detailed investigations and engineering design (Bay of Fundy Tidal Power Review Board, 1976). Studies to meet this objective are in progress.

Clearly, the feasibility of tapping tidal power exists but actual developments hinge on its feasibility in economic terms. Three scales of power developments are being examined including 1,000, 3,000, or 7,000 MW. Earliest construction of any facility appears to be 1990 but this is subject to change. In theory, by using a 20 per cent conversion of tidal energy and utilizing all available sites in the Maritimes, a Science Council of Canada estimate (1975) shows that tides are capable of meeting all projected power requirements for the three Maritime Provinces to the year 2000. Although tidal power emanates from the sea, its power extraction has land implications. The construction of impoundments and barriers alters the natural aquatic regime. Marine life may be adversely affected. Dams may disrupt tidal currents resulting in shifted silting patterns and may shorten the life of the generating facility itself.

The land requirements of a tidal energy installation may be limited to actual abutments, a dam site, and an-

229

cillary road and transmission line allotments, but its impact will be regional. Benefits could accrue in transportation, regional development, tourism, and recreation.

Clearly, tidal projects are a large-scale, highly capital intensive venture. Their siting options are limited to areas with sufficient tidal range. The power that is produced must be near to potential consumers thereby making Fundy developments superior to the other more remote sites in Canada. Although the energy being tapped is renewable, there are a number of environmental effects that are associated with development of this resource.

Wave Energy. The sun drives the wind and the wind drives the waves in the world's oceans. Waves collect and concentrate the wind's power. To place wave energy in perspective, one has only to think of the coastal erosional processes or the waves during blustery ocean storms to appreciate their power potential.

The process of extracting energy from waves is at its infancy, with Britain taking the lead rôle in development. Canadian involvement is limited. Since any power generation facilities will be offshore developments, wave energy will receive a brief overview in this report. The potential for wave energy lies on Canada's east and west coasts. Waves off the west coast are more consistent in direction and form, and are greater in height (Mosey, 1976*a*.). Generally the wave energy available to Canada is not as high as elsewhere in the world. Two systems of extracting this energy have been identified. One system is based on hinged floats which are rocked back and forth by consecutive wave fronts. A second system is based on two reservoirs which function according to the oscillating water columns. Although waves are concentrated forms of energy, their height, frequency, direction, and continuity are variable, therefore posing severe engineering problems. To place the size of any such machines in perspective, wave machines of 520 to 2,400 km in length would have to be constructed to supply British Columbia with its present total power requirement of 7,200 MW (Mosey, 1976*a*.). The implications of this scale of development should be self-evident. Further research in the wave energy extraction process is continuing at the National Research Council. At some future date, waves may supply power to Canada's coastal regions.

Geothermal Energy. Geothermal energy is one of the few alternative energy sources that is not solar supplied. Geothermal energy is based on the heat that is being continuously released from the molten core to the earth's surface. It is possible to differentiate geothermal resources according to their geological and temperature characteristics. There are five categories: steam, hot water, warm water and sedimentary reservoirs and hot dry rock (Jessop, 1977). Steam reservoirs are formed by a combination of water, heat, and geologic conditions which permit the creation of a pocket of steam whose temperature is above 235°C. A common example is a geyser. The other three reservoirs are differentiated by temperature ranges and geologic origin. Hot waters are conductive to electrical energy conversion whereas the warm waters are suitable for space heating. Sedimentary reservoirs are formed in the porous formations of sedimentary strata and are dependent more on a natural thermal gradient of the earth rather than on specific geological anomolies. Hot, dry rock reservoirs are heated areas of crust below the surface, but due to an absence of a natural heat transmission can only be tapped by an artificial introduction of a water supply. To date, the most exploitable forms of geothermal energy involve those where water serves as a medium for heat transfer. Utilizing geothermal energy, especially geysers and hot-springs, dates back to Roman days. The traditional use of such sites was simply for a bathing facility. However, with advancing technologies, such energies have been directed to space heating with the classic example of Reykjavik, Iceland where the city's heating is supplied by geothermally-heated water. Geothermal energies have also been used for certain industrial applications and for electrical generation. The largest power generation facility in New Zealand provides 1,250 MW of electrical power. Throughout the world, there are some 100 sites using geothermal power in one of the three applications mentioned above.

What is Canada's potential for effectively and economically harvesting geothermal energies? There are two geological areas in Canada which promise geothermal power. These are the sedimentary basins and the volcanic zones situated in western Canada. The sedimentary basin within the Prairie Provinces holds promise for development. The use of geothermally-heated waters in the Prairies for a heating supply has been compared favourably to reserves now being utilized in the Paris Basin in France. Although the Canadian reserves are of somewhat higher temperature, (50 versus 90°C), lower population density and colder climatic conditions pose economic hurdles to such developments (Jessop, 1976). The other large area of potential lies in the volcanic belts of the western mountains of British Columbia and the Yukon and is more of an unknown entity. The presence of reserves of geothermal energy can be estimated by extrapolation of the United States discoveries in their western coastal region. Presently, British Columbia Hydro and the Federal Department of Energy, Mines and Resources are undertaking a detailed inventory of such reserves. In Canada, applications are largely based around several hot springs at locations such as Jasper and Radium Hot Springs. The city of Whitehorse uses geothermally-heated water for heating of the city's water supply to prevent the distribution network from freezing. Savings amount to about $1 million annually when compared to the cost of heat from oil. (Jessop, 1977).

Although geothermal energy exploitation may initially appear to be without environmental hazards, some of the unique characteristics may lead to adverse consequences (Fine, 1976 and Axtmann, 1975). The waters used contain a high degree of salts, minerals, and gases which may be independent of power production and may be classed as pollutants. The number of test sites and drillings prior to actual siting of a facility add to the overall impact of a development. The waste waters from a geothermal plant may adversely affect the surrounding environment. As with oil and gas wells, blowouts are a continuing concern. Crustal subsidence may be experienced in the area where thermal fluid is drained, and many attractive sites are located in areas of geologic instability.

Some questions on the land implications of geothermal energy applications can be highlighted. This resource is highly site-specific offering no options other than proximity to a thermal reservoir. This is a fundamental locational constraint and may negate sites in rugged isolated areas. The facilities for harvesting geothermal power have similar land requirements to that of a power station or some wells and feeder pipes. For space heating applications, a distribution network must be established, but there are economic benefits to be derived from district heating. A basic population of at least ten thousand inhabitants is necessary to consider feasible district heating. Based on this prerequisite, Jessop (1975) estimates that some 11 centres in the Prairies are suitable for development. In Canada, only initial steps have been taken to evaluate geothermal energy. Space heating seems to be the most immediate course of development in the Prairies. Further developments are being investigated, the federal Department of Energy, Mines and Resources acting as a lead agency for the study of this alternative source of energy.

The Future

Recent viewpoints of the energy forecasts have ranged from predictions of the doomsday soothsayers to those of the eternal optimists. Although forecasts may vary, the necessity for change is not disputed. Canada, reeling from the shock of the quadrupling of world oil prices since 1973, has recognized the end of the era of abundant low-cost energy and is grappling with the implications for long-term sources of supply. This chapter has focused on the present supplies for Canada's energy needs and the variety of end-uses which place individual demands on the energy resource. In addition, development of the higher-cost energy production areas such as the Athabasca oil sands and the northern frontier region, are examples of future production trends. Because of the potential shortages of foreign sources of supply, the increased costs of producing domestic supplies, and the preference for cleaner forms of energy, the renewable energy sources will increase their share of energy supply, within the next 25 years.

Most future-oriented energy projections consider low, medium, and high consumption growth rates. Within these projections, the trends indicate that: there will be a shift from oil and petroleum products to increased use of electricity in most sectors and regions, there will be a higher growth rate in renewable energy sources, and, consumption of natural gas and coal will remain the same (National Energy Board, 1978). Translated into land use requirements, Smith (1978) estimated that if energy demands are to be met by the year 2000, energy-producing lands must expand to include: over 8,000 new producing oil wells, over 4,000 new gas wells, 12 Syncrude-size oil sands or heavy oil plants, 14 new coal mines, 21 new hydro plants equivalent in size to LG-1, 11 to 15 new nuclear plants similar to Bruce "A" (3,200 MW), and related mine production, the renewable energy equivalent of 6 Bruce "A" stations, and all the necessary pipeline and transmission links. In addition to the massive capital outlays needed to fund these projects, large areas of land, not yet quantified, will be essential to meet these demands.

This chapter has identified the location of Canada's special resource lands for energy development. In addition, since any social or economic activity relating to the use of land depends on the availability of energy in one form or another, the special lands identified in the five previous chapters also relate to energy. Agriculture, forestry, recreation, urban development, and other activities are all consumers of energy. The allocation of land to these and other uses is based on a complex decision-making process that includes aspects of supply, demand, user preferences, costs, accessibility, and resource availability. The ability of these uses to react to an uncertain energy future reflects the problems of energy forecasting.

If energy costs continue to escalate rapidly, how will this affect urban growth? Can urban design at the micro and macro levels respond to the situation in a manner that will help alleviate the crisis? How will rising energy costs or dwindling energy supplies affect agriculture? How much will food prices escalate? Does this have implications as to which lands will remain in farm production? Will it place a premium on the higher capability lands close to urban markets? If we are losing these most productive farmlands to other uses, what are the possible repercussions? What is likely to happen to Canadian transportation patterns with continued increases in energy costs? What are the most energy-efficient transportation modes and are they being emphasized? These and other questions remain to be answered.

Acknowledgements

The author would like to thank V. Neimanis for his contribution in the renewable energy section of this chapter.

Bibliography

Aikin, A.M., Harrison, J.M., and Hare, F.K. 1977. The Management of Canada's Nuclear Wastes. Report EP77-6. Department of Energy, Mines and Resources. Ottawa.

Alberta Conservation and Utilization Committee. 1972. Fort McMurray Athabasca Tar Sands Development Strategy. Edmonton.

Alberta Department of Energy and Natural Resources. 1976. A Coal Development Policy for Alberta. Government of Alberta. Edmonton.

Alberta Environment Conservation Authority. 1971. Environmental Impact of Surface Coal Mining Operations in Alberta. F.F. Slaney and Company Limited. Vancouver.

_____. 1972. The Impact on the Environment of Surface Mining in Alberta. Summary of the Public Hearings. December, 1971, January, 1972. Environment Conservation Authority. Edmonton.

_____. 1974. Land Use and Resource Development in the Eastern Slopes: Report and Recommendations. September, 1974. Environment Conservation Authority. Edmonton.

Alberta Research Council and Alberta Environment. 1976. Wind Power in Alberta. Alberta Research Council. Edmonton.

Anderson, B. 1975. "The Sun in a Drawer." Environment. Vol. 17, No. 17. October 1975. Scientists Institute for Public Information. St. Louis.

Argue, Robert. 1977a. Catalogue of Solar Heating Products and Services in Canada. Research Report No. 12. Office of Energy Conservation and Renewable Energy Resources Branch, Department of Energy, Mines and Resources. Ottawa.

_____. 1977b. Renewable Energy Resources: A Guide to the Literature. Report E1-77-5. Renewable Energy Resources Branch, Department of Energy, Mines and Resources. Ottawa.

Argue, Ronald. 1977. "Renewable Energy for Ontario." Alternatives. Vol. 7, No. 1. Fall 1977. Trent University. Peterborough.

Armstrong, G.T. 1976. The Canadian Energy Situation in a World Context. Report No. R10. Office of Energy Conservation, Department of Energy, Mines and Resources. Ottawa.

Atlantic Industrial Research Institute. 1970. Proceedings of an International Conference on the Utilization of Tidal Power. Held May 24-29 at Nova Scotia Technical College. Halifax.

Atlantic Tidal Power Programming Board. 1969. Feasibility of Tidal Power Development in the Bay of Fundy. Energy, Mines and Resources. Ottawa.

Axtmann, R.C. 1975. "Environmental Impact of a Geothermal Power Plant." Science. Vol. 187, No. 4179. American Association for the Advancement of Science. Washington.

Bay of Fundy Tidal Power Review Board. 1976. Preliminary Report Stage 1 of The Phase I Study Program. Prepared by the Management Committee. Ottawa.

Berger, Thomas R. 1977. Northern Frontier Northern Homeland: The Report of the Mackenzie Valley Pipeline Inquiry: Volume One. Supply and Services Canada. Ottawa.

Berkowitz, M.K. 1977. Implementing Solar Energy Technology in Canada. Report E 177-7. Renewable Energy Resources Branch, Department of Energy, Mines and Resources. Ottawa.

Bio-Energy Council. 1976. Capturing the Sun Through Bioconversion. Proceedings held in Washington, March 10-12, 1976. Council of Solar Biofuels. Washington.

Biomass Energy Institute. 1974. The Renewable Biomass Energy Guidebook. Biomass Energy Institute Inc. Winnipeg.

_____. 1976. A Preliminary Survey of Manitoba's Currently Available Renewable Biomass (carb) Fuel Potential. Prepared for Manitoba Hydro. The Biomass Energy Institute Inc. Winnipeg.

Blakeman, W.H. 1975. Land Use for Mineral and Energy Production. Prepared for Interdepartmental Task Force on Energy. Lands Directorate, Environment Canada. Unpublished. Ottawa.

Board of the Churchill River Study (Missinipe Probe). 1976. Churchill River Study: Synthesis. Saskatchewan Department of the Environment. Regina.

Böer, K.W. ed. 1976. Sharing the Sun Solar Technology in the Seventies. Proceedings of the International Solar Energy Conference, held in Winnipeg, August 15-20, 1976. Winnipeg.

British Columbia Environment and Land Use Committee. 1976. Guidelines for Coal Development. K.M. MacDonald. Victoria.

Brown, C.K., and Higgin, R. 1976. Preliminary Assessment of the Potential for Large Wind Generators as Fuel Savers in A.C. Community Diesel Power Systems in Ontario. Ontario Research Foundation. Mississauga.

Brown, D. 1977. "Something New Under the Sun." The Review. Vol. 61, No. 5. Imperial Oil Limited. Toronto.

Campbell, W. 1974. "A Formulation for Power – Mathematics of the Fundy Tides." Science Dimension. Vol. 6, No. 4. National Research Council of Canada. Ottawa.

Canadian Imperial Bank of Commerce. 1978. Canadian Oil and Natural Gas Developments. Canadian Imperial Bank of Commerce. Calgary.

Canadian Resourcecon Limited. 1974. Decision Making in the North: Oil Sands Case Study. Final Report. Prepared for Science Council of Canada. Ottawa.

Carlisle, A. 1976. The Utilization of Forest Biomass and Forestry Industry Wastes for the Production and Conservation of Energy 1976. Canadian Forestry Service, Environment Canada. Ottawa.

Carrigy, M.A. ed. 1974. Guide to the Athabasca Oil Sands Area. Information Series 65. Prepared for the Canadian Society of Petroleum Geologists. Oil Sands Symposium 1973. Alberta Research. Edmonton.

Clark, R.H. 1972. "Energy from Fundy Tides." Canadian Geographical Journal. Vol. 75, No. 5. Royal Canadian Geographical Society. Ottawa.

Clark, R.H., and Walker, R.L. 1976. Progress of Feasibility Reassessment of Exploiting Tidal Energy. Paper presented to 90th EIC Congress, held October 7, 1976. Halifax.

Classen, H.G. 1977. "Can We Use the Wind to Supply More Energy?" Canadian Geographical Journal. Vol. 94, No. 2. Royal Canadian Geographical Society. Ottawa.

Cockshutt, E.P. 1977. Solar Energy. Paper prepared for SCI-TEC briefing: Renewable Energy Resources, Energy Project. February 1977. National Research Council. Ottawa.

Collins, J. 1977. Solar Energy in Canada – 1977 and Beyond. Unpublished. National Research Council. Ottawa.

Dames and Moore. 1977. A Report on the Current Status of the Canadian Coal Mining Industry. Dames and Moore. Toronto.

Department of Energy, Mines and Resources. 1973a. An Energy Policy for Canada – Phase I, Volume 1. Analysis. Information Canada. Ottawa.

_____. 1973b. An Energy Policy for Canada – Phase I, Volume II – Appendices. Information Canada. Ottawa.

_____. 1974. Electric Power in Canada 1973. Energy Development Sector. Information Canada. Ottawa.

_____. 1976a. An Energy Strategy for Canada: Policies for Self Reliance. Energy Policy Sector. Ottawa.

_____. 1976b. Coal in Canada: Supply and Demand 1975. Energy Policy Sector. Minister of Supply and Services Canada. Ottawa.

_____. 1976c. Coal Mines in Canada. Operators List 4. January 1977. Minister of Supply and Services Canada. Ottawa.

_____. 1976d. Electric Power in Canada 1976. Publication No. E1-77-5. Energy Policy Sector. Minister of Supply and Services Canada. Ottawa.

_____. 1977a. An Inventory of Energy Research and Development Supported By The Government of Canada 1976-77. Report ER 77-3. Office of Energy Research and Development. Minister of Supply and Services Canada. Ottawa.

_____. 1977b. 1976 Assessment of Canada's Coal Resources and Reserves. Report EP 77-5. Minister of Supply and Services Canada. Ottawa.

_____. 1977c. 1976 Assessment of Canada's Uranium Supply and Demand. Report EP 77-3. Minister of Supply and Services Canada. Ottawa.

_____. 1978a. Electric Power in Canada 1977. Electrical Section, Energy Policy Sector. Minister of Supply and Services Canada. Ottawa.

_____. 1978b. Energy Update 1977. Report E1 78-2. Runge Press Ltd. Ottawa.

_____. 1978c. Energy Conservation in Canada: Programs and Perspectives. Report EP 77-7. Minister of Supply and Services Canada. Ottawa.

_____. 1978d. Oil and Natural Gas Industries in Canada 1978. Report ER 78-2. Minister of Supply and Services Canada. Ottawa.

_____. 1978e. Petroleum in Canada. Minister of Supply and Services Canada. Ottawa.

Efford, I.E. 1975. "Assessment of the Impact of Hydro-dams." Journal of the Fisheries Research Board of Canada. Vol. 32, No. 1. Fisheries and Marine Service. Environment Canada. Ottawa.

Eisenstadt, M.M., and Utton, A.E. 1976. "Solar Rights and Their Effect on Heating and Cooling." Natural Resources Journal. Vol. 16, No. 2. University of New Mexico School of Law. Albuquerque.

Environment Canada. 1975. James Bay Hydro-Electric Project, Environmental Concerns. Lands Directorate. Ottawa.

Erickson, E.W., and Waverman, L. eds. 1974. Energy Question: An International Failure of Policy, Volume 2. North America. University of Toronto Press. Toronto.

Evans, R.S. 1974. Energy Plantations Should We Grow Trees for Power-Plant Fuel? Information Report VP-X-129. Western Products Labratory, Canadian Forestry Service, Department of the Environment. Ottawa.

Federal Environmental Assessment Review Office. 1978a. Federal Environmental Assessment and Review Process: Register of Panel Projects and Bulletin. No. 5. Environment Canada and Minister of Supply and Services Canada. Ottawa.

_____. 1978b. Report of the Environmental Assessment Panel on the Eldorado Uranium Refinery Port Granby, Ontario. Fisheries and Environment Canada. Ottawa.

Fine, Richard. 1976. The Renewable Energy Handbook. Energy Probe. Toronto.

Fletcher, D., and Fletcher, R. 1977. "The Ark: habitat concept for the future?" Canadian Geographical Journal. Vol. 92, No. 3. Royal Canadian Geographical Society. Ottawa.

Foster, H.D. and Sewell, W.R.D. 1977a. Solar Heating in Canada – Why Not? Office of the Science Advisor, Department of Fisheries and the Environment. Ottawa.

_____. 1977b. Solar Home Heating in Canada: Problems and Prospects. Report No. 16. Office of the Science Advisor, Department of Fisheries and the Environment. Ottawa.

Fowler, John W. 1975. Energy – Environment Source Book. Vol. 1, Energy, Society, and the Environment. Vol. 2, Energy, Its Extraction, Conversion and Use. National Science Teachers Association. Washington.

Gaskie, M.F. 1977. "Notes From the Field: . . .approach to Solar Design." Architectural Record. Mid-August. 1977. McGraw-Hill, Inc. New York.

Glover, Michael. 1977. Renewable Energy in Remote Communities: The State of the Art Background Paper. Policy Development Division, Central Mortgage and Housing Corporation. Ottawa.

Grandt, A.F. 1978. "Mined Land Reclamation in the Interior Coal Province." Journal of Soil and Water Conservation. Vol. 33, No. 2. Soil Conservation Society of America. Ankeny.

Gray, T.J., and Gashus, O.K. 1972. Tidal Power. Plenum Press. New York.

Hamilton, S.A. 1978. Mineral Policy Sector, Department of Energy, Mines and Resources. Personal communication. Ottawa.

Hammond, A.L. 1977. "Photosynthetic Solar Energy: Rediscovering Biomass Fuels." Science. Vol. 197, No. 4305. American Association for the Advancement of Science. Washington.

Hawaeshka, O., and Stasynec, G. 1976. Alternative Energy: A Bibliography of Practical Literature. Report # 11. Agassiz Centre. Winnipeg.

Hayes, D. 1978. "The Coming of Energy Transition." The Futurist. Vol. XI, No. 5. World Future Society. Washington.

Hinrichsen, D., and Cawood, P. 1976. "Fresh Breeze For Denmark's Windmills." New Scientist. Vol. 70, No. 1004. June 10, 1976. IPC Magazine Ltd. London.

Hollands, K.E.T., and Orgill, J.F. 1977. Potential for Solar Heating in Canada. Prepared for Division of Building Research, National Research Council. Ottawa.

Inman, R.E. 1976. "Silviculture Energy Plantations." Sharing the Sun Solar Technology in the Seventies, Proceedings International Solar Energy Conference, Vol. 7. Winnipeg.

Intercontinental Engineering of Alberta Ltd. 1973. An Environmental Study of the Athabasca Tar Sands. Report and Recommendations to Alberta Department of the Environment. Alberta Environment. Edmonton.

International Energy Agency. 1978. Energy Balances of OECD Countries 1974-1976. Organisation for Economic Co-operation and Development. Paris.

Intergroup Consulting Economists Ltd. 1976. Economic Pre-Feasibility Study: Large-Scale Methanol Fuel Production from Surplus Canadian Forest Biomass. Policy and Program Development Directorate. Department of Fisheries and Environment. Ottawa.

Jackson, C.I. ed. 1978. Human Settlements and Energy. A seminar of the United Nations Economic Commission for Europe. Pergamon Press Ltd. Oxford.

Jeffs, E. 1977. "Solar Energy Prospects Grow for US Southwest." Energy International. Vol. 14, No. 6. June 1977. Miller Freeman Publications Inc. San Francisco.

Jessop, A.M. 1975. Geothermal Energy. Internal Report 75-1 Geothermal Service of Canada. Division of Seismology and Geothermal Studies, Earth Physics Branch, Department of Energy, Mines and Resources. Ottawa.

_____. 1976. Geothermal Energy From Sedimentary Basins. Geothermal Series No. 8. Department of Energy, Mines and Resources. Ottawa.

_____. 1977. Geothermal Energy. Prepared for Third Canadian National Energy Forum, Halifax, April 4-5, 1977.

Keith, R.F., and Wright, J.B. eds. 1978. Northern Transitions Volume II. Second National Workshop on People, Resources and the Environment North of 60°. Canadian Arctic Resources Committee. Ottawa.

Lewin, R. 1977. "Energy can be Green." New Scientist. Vol. 74, No. 1053. IPC Magazines Ltd. London.

Maini, J.S., and Carlisle, A. 1974. Conservation in Canada: A Conspectus. Publication No. 1340. Canadian Forestry Service, Department of the Environment. Ottawa.

Marhsall, I.B. 1978. Lands Directorate, Environment Canada. Personal communication. Ottawa.

Marshall, J.E., Petrick, G., and Chan, H. 1975. A Look at the Economic Feasibility of Converting Wood into Liquid Fuel. Report E-X-25. Forestry Service, Environment Canada. Ottawa.

McCallum, B. 1977. Environmentally Appropriate Technology. Report No. 15. Office of the Science Advisor, Fisheries and Environment Canada. Ottawa.

McCaull, J. 1973. "Windmills." Environment. January/February, 1973. Scientist's Insititute for Public Information. St. Louis.

McVeigh, J.C. 1977. Sun Power. Pergamon Press. Oxford.

MacKillop, A. 1978. "Conservation and Renewable Energy Options: Canada." Ekistics. Vol. 45, No. 269. Athens Center of Ekistics of the Athens Technological Organization. Athens.

Middleton, P. et al. 1976. Canada's Renewable Energy Resources: An Assessment of Potential. Middleton Associates. Toronto.

Mosey, D. 1976a. "Bind the Restless Wave." Science Dimension. Vol. 8, No. 5. National Research Council of Canada. Ottawa.

_____. 1976b. "Hyperion's Grandchildren." Science Dimension. Vol. 8, No. 5. National Research Council of Canada. Ottawa.

_____. 1976c. "The Unregulated Sun." Science Dimension. Vol. 8, No. 5. National Research Council of Canada. Ottawa.

Nadler, A.D. 1977. "Planning Aspects of Direct Solar Energy Generation." Journal of the American Insititute of Planners. Vol. 43, No. 4. American Institute of Planners. Washington.

National Energy Board. 1978. Canadian Oil Supply and Requirements. Minister of Supply and Services Canada. Ottawa.

National Research Council. 1978. Solar Heated Homes in Canada. Solar Information Series. No. 1. National Research Council. Ottawa.

National Swedish Board for Technical Development. 1974. Advanced Wind Energy Systems. Workshop Proceedings.

Ontario Ministry of Energy. 1977. Turn on the Sun. Ministry of Energy. Toronto.

Pearse, Charles R. 1978. "Coal Comes Back: Its Promise and Challenge." Canadian Geographical Journal. Vol. 96, No. 2. April/May 1978. The Royal Canadian Geographical Society. Ottawa.

Pharis, Richard P. 1977. "Alberta's Coal Policy." Canadian Environmental Law News. Vol. 6, No. 2. Canadian Environmental Law Association and the Canadian Environmental Law Research Foundation. Toronto.

Pullen, J.R. 1975. Canadian Society of Exploration Geophysicists. Personal communication. Calgary.

Ramakumar, R. 1976. "Wind-Electric Conversion, Utilizing Field Modulated Generator Systems." Sharing the Sun Solar Technology in the Seventies, Proceedings, International Solar Energy Conference. Vol. 7. Winnipeg.

Randall, Murray. 1977. "Energy Policy Planning: Towards A Critical Perspective." Alternatives. Winter, 1977. Trent University. Peterborough.

Rattray, D.B. 1977. Renewable Energy Resources, A Guide to the Bureaucracy. Report EI-77-18. Renewable Energy Resources Branch, Department of Energy, Mines and Resources. Ottawa.

Reuyl, J.S. et al. 1977. Solar Energy in America's Future. A Preliminary Assessment (Second Edition). Stanford Research Institute. Springfield.

Riley, M., Peters, R., and Hornby, I. 1976. The Sun Book: Heating From the Sun. Pollution Probe. Central Mortgage and Housing Corporation. Ottawa.

Ripley, E.A., Redmann, R.E., and Maxwell, J. 1978. Environmental Impact of Mining in Canada. Centre for Resource Studies, Queen's University. Kingston.

Ritchie, T. 1969. "A History of Windmills and Their Place in Canadian Life." Canadian Geographical Journal. March 1969. Royal Canadian Geographical Society. Ottawa.

Rogers, S.E. et al. 1976. Evaluation of the Potential Environmental Effects of Wind Energy System Development. Battelle Columbus Laboratories. Columbus.

Ruzicka, V. 1977. "Conceptual Models for Uranium Deposits and Areas Favourable for Uranium Mineralization in Canada." Report of Activities, Part A, Geological Survey of Canada. Paper 77-1A. Department of Energy, Mines and Resources. Ottawa.

_____. 1979. "Uranium and Thorium in Canada, 1978." Current Research, Part A, Geological Survey of Canada. Paper 79-1A. Department of Energy, Mines and Resources. Ottawa.

Sasaki, J.R. 1977. Solar Heating Systems for Canadian Buildings. Division of Building Research, National Research Council. Ottawa.

Saskatchewan Mineral Resources. 1978. Saskatchewan Coal Policy. Miscellaneous Report 78-8.

Savino, J.M. ed. 1973. Wind Energy Conversion Systems. Workshop proceedings held June 11-13, 1973 in Washington, D.C. National Aeronautics and Space Administration. Cleveland.

Schmidt, W.L. 1977. Wind Power Studies. Unpublished. Masters of Science thesis. Waterloo.

Schute, D.D. et al. 1976. "Methane Production Through Bioconversion of Agricultural Residues." Sharing the Sun Solar Technology in the Seventies. Proceedings, International Solar Energy Conference. Vol. 7. Winnipeg.

Science Council of Canada. 1975. Canada's Energy Opportunities. Report No. 23. Information Canada. Ottawa.

_____. 1976a. "Exploring Energy-Efficient Futures for Canada." Conserver Society Notes. Vol. 1, No. 4. May-June 1976. Science Council of Canada. Ottawa.

_____. 1976b. "Business Opportunities in a Conserver Society." Conserver Society Notes. Vol. 2, No. 1. Fall 1976. Science Council of Canada. Ottawa.

_____. 1976c. Population, Technology and Resources. Report No. 25. Minister of Supply and Services Canada. Ottawa.

_____. 1977. Canada as a Conserver Society. Resource Uncertainties and the Need for New Technologies. Report No. 27. Minister of Supply and Services Canada. Ottawa.

Sewell, W.R.D., and Foster, H.D. 1976. Images of Canadian Futures: The Role of Conservation and Renewable Energy. Report No. 13. Office of the Science Advisor, Environment Canada. Ottawa.

_____. 1977. Solar Home Heating and Cooling: Technology and Diffusion. Council of Planning Librarians. Exchange Bibliography 1235. Monticello.

Shaw, T. et al. 1972. "Tidal Energy From the Bay of Fundy." Civil Engineering – ASCE. American Society of Civil Engineers. New York.

Smith, Charles H. 1978. Energy Needs in Canada to the Year 2000. Presented at Energy and the Environment Needs and Constraints Conference, held November 4, 1978. Ontario Research Foundation. Mississauga.

Société de développement de la Baie James and Environment Canada. 1978. Environmental Studies James Bay Territory. Fiscal year 1976-1977. Ottawa.

Solar Energy Society of Canada. 1975. The Potential of Solar Energy for Canada. Conference held in Ottawa, June 2-3, 1975. National Research Council of Canada. Ottawa.

Statistics Canada. 1972. Detailed Energy Supply and Demand in Canada 1958-1969. Catalogue 57-505. Occasional. Ottawa.

_____. 1974. Detailed Energy Supply and Demand in Canada 1972. Catalogue 57-207. Annual. Information Canada. Ottawa.

_____. 1977a. Canada Year Book 1976-77. Special Edition. Statistics Canada and Supply and Services Canada. Ottawa.

_____. 1977b. Electric Power Statistics 1975. Vol. II. Catalogue 57-202. Annual. Ottawa.

_____. 1978a. Detailed Energy Supply and Demand in Canada 1976. Catalogue 57-207. Annual. Ottawa.

_____. 1978b. Gas Utilities Transport and Distribution Systems 1976. Catalogue 57-205. Annual. Ottawa.

_____. 1978c. Human Activity and the Environment. Catalogue 11-509E. Occasional. Ottawa.

_____. 1978d. Oil Pipe Line Transport 1976. Catalogue 55-201. Annual. Ottawa.

Steadman, P. 1975. Energy, Environment and Building. Cambridge University Press. Cambridge.

Steward, F.R. 1978. "Energy Consumption in Canada Since Confederation." Energy Policy. Vol. 6, No. 3. IPC Business Press Limited. Sussex.

Templin, R.J., and South, P. 1976. Canadian Wind Energy Program. Paper presented at Vertical-Axis Wind Turbine Technology Workshop. Albuquerque, New Mexico.

Templin, R.J. 1977. Wind Energy. Paper given at Third Canadian National Energy Forum. Halifax.

Thomas, W. 1977. "Conservation Asks How Much?" The Review. Vol. 61, No. 5. Imperial Oil Limited. Toronto.

Timbers, G.E. 1977. "Alternate Sources of Energy." Agrologist. Vol. 6, No. 4. The Agricultural Institute of Canada. Ottawa.

Williams, J.R. 1977. Solar Energy – Technology and Applications. Ann Arbor Science Publishers Inc. Ann Arbor.

Williams, R.M., and Little, H.W. 1973. Canadian Uranium Resource And Production Capability. MR 140. Mineral Development Sector, Department of Energy, Mines and Resources. Ottawa.

_____. 1972. "Windmill With No Arms." Science Dimension. Vol. 4, No. 5. National Research Council of Canada. Ottawa.

_____. 1977. "Wind Power Being Exploited." Oilweek. Vol. 28, No. 33. Maclean-Hunter Ltd. Calgary.

Wolff, B. 1975. Windworks: A Bibliography. Council of Planning Librarians. No. 730. Monticello.

A Final Thought

The current and anticipated land demands for agriculture, recreation, wildlife, forestry, wildlife, urban growth, energy development, and other activities are all placed on the same land resource base. There is a finite quantity of land in Canada, and precious little of it possesses the physical, climatic, aesthetic, economic, locational, or other characteristics required by these various land uses. It therefore stands to reason that these special resource areas warrant special attention. Their characteristics must be evaluated; they must be appreciated for their particular qualities; they must be managed for maximum benefit. How this is done, in the midst of social, aesthetic, economic, political, physical, and other influences, rests with each Canadian. The final decisions at the national level reflect all the individual decisions, preferences, and perceptions. Each and every individual must become better informed and more concerned with the country's land resources. Canada's future depends on it.